W9-CCX-140

Strategic Marketing

McGraw-Hill/Irwin Series in Marketing

Strategic Marketing

Seventh Edition

David W. Cravens
M.J. Neeley School of Business
Texas Christian University

Nigel F. Piercy
Cranfield School of Management
Cranfield University

Boston   Burr Ridge, IL   Dubuque, IA   Madison, WI   New York   San Francisco   St. Louis
Bangkok   Bogotá   Caracas   Kuala Lumpur   Lisbon   London   Madrid   Mexico City
Milan   Montreal   New Delhi   Santiago   Seoul   Singapore   Sydney   Taipei   Toronto

McGraw-Hill Higher Education

*A Division of The **McGraw-Hill** Companies*

STRATEGIC MARKETING
Published by McGraw-Hill/Irwin, a business unit of The McGraw-Hill Companies, Inc., 1221 Avenue of the Americas, New York, NY, 10020. Copyright © 2003, 2000, 1997, 1994, 1991, 1987, 1982 by The McGraw-Hill Companies, Inc. All rights reserved. No part of this publication may be reproduced or distributed in any form or by any means, or stored in a database or retrieval system, without the prior written consent of The McGraw-Hill Companies, Inc., including, but not limited to, in any network or other electronic storage or transmission, or broadcast for distance learning.

Some ancillaries, including electronic and print components, may not be available to customers outside the United States.

This book is printed on acid-free paper.

domestic   1 2 3 4 5 6 7 8 9 0 CCW/CCW 0 9 8 7 6 5 4 3 2
international 1 2 3 4 5 6 7 8 9 0 CCW/CCW 0 9 8 7 6 5 4 3 2

ISBN 0-07-246665-0

Publisher: *John E. Biernat*
Executive editor: *Linda Schreiber*
Editorial assistant: *Sarah L. Crago*
Marketing manager: *Kim Kanakes Szum*
Project manager: *Jim Labeots*
Senior production supervisor: *Michael R. McCormick*
Freelance design coordinator: *Laurie J. Entringer*
Producer, media technology: *Todd Labak*
Supplement producer: *Joyce J. Chappetto*
Photo research coordinator: *David A. Tietz*
Photo researcher: *Connie Gardner*
Cover design: *Asylum Studios*
Typeface: *10/12 Times New Roman*
Compositor: *GAC Indianapolis*
Printer: *Courier Westford*

Library of Congress Cataloging-in-Publication Data

Cravens, David W.
    Strategic marketing/ David W. Craven, Nigel Piercy.-- 7th ed.
      p.cm.
    Inludes index.
    ISBN 0-07-246665-0 (student : alk. paper) -- ISBN 0-07-115161-3 (international : alk. paper)
      1. Marketing--Decision making. 2. Marketing--Management. 3.
    Marketing--Management--Case studies. I. Piercy, Nigel. II. Title.
    HF5415.135 .C72 2003
    658. 8'02--dc21   2002016549

www.mhhe.com

To Sue and Karen

To the memory of Helena G. Piercy
(1911–2001)

DWC

NFP

Preface

The rapidly changing global business environment executives experience early in the 21st century highlights the critical role of superior customer value in achieving high levels of organizational performance. Delivering value requires understanding markets and deciding how to match the organization's distinctive capabilities with promising value opportunities. One of the more challenging executive imperatives is forming a perceptive vision about how markets will change in the future.

Strategic marketing's pivotal role in business performance is demonstrated in the market-driven strategies of successful organizations competing in a wide array of market and competitive situations. The escalating importance of superior customer value, leveraging distinctive capabilities, responding rapidly to diversity and change in the marketplace, creating new products, and recognizing global business challenges require effective marketing strategies for gaining and sustaining a competitive edge. *Strategic Marketing* examines the concepts and processes in market-driven strategies.

MARKET-DRIVEN STRATEGY

The driving force behind a market-driven strategy is the reality that the route to obtaining a competitive advantage is providing superior value to customers. Several aspects of the competitive challenge are apparent:

- Marketing strategy provides the concepts and processes that are essential in gaining a competitive advantage.

- Marketing is a major stakeholder in key organizational core processes—new product development, customer relationship management, value/supply-chain management, and business strategy implementation.

- The use of cross-functional teams to manage core business processes is altering the role and structure of the traditional hierarchical organization.

- Changes in how organizations are designed place new priorities on forging collaborative relationships with customers, suppliers, value-chain members, and competitors.

- Understanding customers, competitors, and the market environment requires the active involvement of the entire organization to manage market knowledge decisively.

- Developing processes that enable the organization to continually learn from customers, competitors, and other sources is vital to sustaining a competitive edge.

- The powerful enabling technologies provided by the Internet and the World Wide Web, corporate intranets, and advanced communication and collaboration systems for customer and supplier relationship management, underpin effective processes.

- The environmental and ethical aspects of business practice are critical concerns, requiring active involvement by the entire organization.

Customer diversity and new forms of competition create impressive growth and performance opportunities for those firms that successfully apply strategic marketing concepts and analyses in their business strategy development and implementation. The challenge to become market-driven is apparent in a variety of industries around the world. Analyzing market behavior and matching strategies to changing conditions require a hands-on approach to marketing strategy development and implementation. Penetrating financial analysis is an important skill of the marketing professional.

Strategic Marketing examines marketing strategy using a combination of text and case materials to develop relevant concepts and apply them to business situations. The book is designed for use in undergraduate capstone management marketing courses and in the MBA marketing core and advanced strategy courses.

NEW AND EXPANDED SCOPE

Competing in any market today requires a global perspective. The seventh edition accentuates this global perspective. The author team provides an extensive range of global involvement. The shrinking time-and-access boundaries of global markets establish new competitive requirements. The global dimensions of marketing strategy are integrated throughout the chapters of the book and also considered in various cases.

Internet initiatives comprise a vital part of the marketing strategies of many companies. While Web-based organizations experienced major turbulence in the 21st century, Internet strategies will expand in the future for most companies. Because of the nature and scope of the various uses of the Internet, we have integrated this important topic into several chapters rather than developing a separate chapter. Internet Features are included in all of these chapters.

Several contemporary strategy topics are discussed throughout the text. These include market orientation, strategic relationships, organizational learning, mass customization, customer relationship management, value migration, balanced scorecard metrics, competing on capabilities, and new organizational forms.

THE TEXT

Strategic Marketing uses a decision process perspective to examine the key concepts and issues involved in selecting strategies. Discussions with various instructors indicate a desire to provide a strategy perspective that extends beyond the traditional management focus on the marketing mix. An emphasis on services as well as goods is continued in the seventh edition. The length and design of the book offer flexibility in the use of the text material and cases.

The book is designed around the marketing strategy process with a clear emphasis on analysis, planning, and implementation. Part I provides an overview of market-driven strategy. Part II develops a framework for the situation analysis. Part III discusses designing market-driven strategies. Part IV considers market-focused program development. Finally, Part V examines implementing and managing market-driven strategy. Various how-to guides are provided throughout the book to assist the reader in applying the analysis and strategy development approaches discussed in the text.

THE CASES

Twenty-nine of the 43 cases are new to the seventh edition. Shorter application-focused cases are placed at the end of each part of the book. These cases are useful in applying the concepts and methods discussed in the chapters, and they can be used for class discussion, hand in assignments, and/or class presentations. The cases consider a wide variety of business environments, both domestic and international. They include goods and services; organizations at different value-chain levels; and small, medium, and large enterprises.

Several of the cases examine the strategy challenges of well-known companies. The cases are very timely, offering an interesting perspective on contemporary business practice. Many of these companies make available extensive financial and product information on the Internet, which expands analysis opportunities.

Part VI includes comprehensive cases that offer students a variety of opportunities to apply marketing strategy concepts. This section has been expanded to 25 cases. Each case considers several important strategy issues. The cases represent different competitive situations for consumer and business products as well as domestic and international markets.

CHANGES IN THE SEVENTH EDITION

The seventh edition of *Strategic Marketing* follows the basic design of previous editions. Nevertheless, the revision incorporates many significant changes, additions, and updated examples. Every chapter includes new material and expanded treatment of important topics.

The first chapter examines the characteristics of market driven strategies. Chapter 2 considers business and marketing strategy relationships and overviews the strategic marketing process. The remaining chapters follow the basic format of the sixth edition. Several chapters discuss current topics, including competing on capabilities, superior customer value, new organization forms, teamwork, mass customization, databases, activity-based costs, and market trends.

Three to four Features are included in each chapter. They follow a theme, emphasizing topics such as strategy, e-Business, cross-functional relationships, technology, and global applications.

Each chapter has been revised to incorporate new concepts and examples, improve readability and flow, and encourage reader interest and involvement. Topical coverage has been expanded (or reduced), where appropriate, to better position the book for teaching and learning in today's rapidly changing business environment. An expanded set of Internet applications is included at the end of each chapter. Financial analysis guidelines are in the Chapter 2 Appendix, and sales forecasting materials are included in the Chapter 3 Appendix.

TEACHING/LEARNING RESOURCES

A complete and expanded teaching-learning package is available on the Instructor's Resource CD-ROM. It includes an Instructor's Manual with course-planning suggestions, answers to end-of-chapter questions, Internet application guidelines, instructor's notes for cases, and a multiple-choice question bank. A PowerPoint® presentation for each chapter is also included on the CD-ROM.

This edition of the manual has been substantially revised and expanded to improve its effectiveness in supporting course planning, case discussion, and examination preparation. Detailed instructor's notes concerning the use of the cases are provided, including epilogues when available.

The text, cases, and Instructor's Manual offer considerable flexibility in course design, depending on the instructor's objectives and the course for which the book is used.

ACKNOWLEDGEMENTS

The seventh edition has benefited from the contributions and experiences of many people and organizations. Business executives and colleagues at universities in many countries have influenced the development of *Strategic Marketing*. While space does not permit thanking each person, a sincere note of appreciation is extended to all. We shall identify several individuals whose assistance was particularly important.

A special thank you is extended to the reviewers of this and prior editions and to many colleagues that have offered numerous suggestions and ideas. Throughout the development of the seventh edition, several individuals made important suggestions for improving the book.

We are also indebted to the case authors who gave us permission to use their cases. Their contributions comprise an excellent set of cases and we appreciate the opportunity to include them in the book. Each author or authors are specifically identified with each case.

A special note of thanks is due to the management and professional team of Irwin/McGraw-Hill for their support and encouragement on this and prior editions of *Strategic Marketing*. John Biernat, as publisher, has provided an important editorial leadership role. Executive Editor, Linda Schreiber, and Developmental Editor, Sarah Crago have been a constant source of valuable assistance and encouragement. Kimberly Kanakes Szum provided important marketing direction for the project. Jim Labeots and Michael McCormick guided the book through the various stages of production while Laurie Entringer polished the design.

Many students provided various kinds of support that were essential to completing the revision. In particular, we appreciate the excellent contributions to this edition made by Enrico Lange, TCU graduate assistant. We also appreciate the helpful comments and suggestions of many students in our classes.

We appreciate the support and encouragement provided by Dean Robert F. Lusch and Professor Leo Murray, Director of Cranfield School of Management. Special thanks are due to Debra Proctor at TCU and Hayley Tedder at Cranfield University for typing the manuscript and for their assistance in other aspects of the project.

David W. Cravens

Nigel F. Piercy

About the Authors

David W. Cravens

David W. Cravens holds the Eunice and James L. West Chair of American Enterprise Studies and is Professor of Marketing at Texas Christian University. Previously, he was the Alcoa Foundation Professor at the University of Tennessee, where he chaired the Department of Marketing and Transportation. Before becoming an educator, Dave held various industry and government management positions. He is internationally recognized for his research on marketing strategy and sales management and has contributed over 100 articles and books. Dave is a former editor of the *Journal of the Academy of Marketing Science.* He has held various positions in the American Marketing Association and the Academy of Marketing Science. He has been a visiting scholar at universities in Austria, Australia, Chile, Czech Republic, England, Ireland, Germany, Mexico, The Netherlands, New Zealand, Singapore, and Wales.

Nigel F. Piercy

Nigel F. Piercy is Professor of Strategic Marketing, and Director of the Strategic Sales Research Consortium at Cranfield School of Management in the United Kingdom. He has held visiting positions at Texas Christian University; the Fuqua School of Business, Duke University; the University of California, Berkeley; and, the Columbia Graduate School of Business. Nigel was, for several years, the Sir Julian Hodge Chair in Marketing and Strategy at Cardiff University. He has published approximately 200 articles and book chapters and ten books. His most recent book was *Market-Led Strategic Change: A Guide to Transforming the Process of Going To Market* (Butterworth-Heinemann, 2002). Nigel has taught management students, led in-company programs for executives, and consulted with organizations, in the United Kingdom, the U.S.A., Europe, the Far East, Africa, and Greece.

Brief Contents

Contents

Market-Driven Strategy

Chapter 1

Market-Driven
Strategy

The market and competitive challenges confronting executives around the world are complex and rapidly changing. Market and industry boundaries are often difficult to define because of the entry of new and unfamiliar forms of competition. Customers' demands for superior value from the products they purchase are unprecedented, as they become yet more knowledgeable about products (goods and services) and more sophisticated in the judgments they make. External influences from diverse pressure groups and lobbyists have escalated dramatically in country after country. Major change initiatives are under way in industries ranging from aerospace to telecommunications. Innovative business models that question the traditional roles of an industry are defining a new agenda for business and marketing strategy development. Companies are adopting market-driven strategies guided by the logic that all business strategy decisions should start with a clear understanding of markets, customers, and competitors.[1] Increasingly it is clear that enhancements in customer value provide a primary route to achieving superior shareholder value.[2]

Consider, for example, Southwest Airlines' market-driven strategy that has achieved a strong market position for the U.S. domestic carrier. The airline's growth and financial performance are impressive. Although Southwest is the fourth largest U.S. airline, its market capitalization is greater than the total capitalization of AMR (American Airlines), Delta Airlines, and UAL Corp. Southwest's revenues will approach $7.5 billion in 2002, compared with $4.2 billion in 1998. Net profits also are displaying strong records during this five-year period. Southwest uses a point-to-point route system rather than the hub-and-spoke design used by many airlines. The airline offers services to 57 cities in 29 states, with the average trip being about 500 miles. The carrier's customer value proposition consists of low fares and limited services (no meals). Nonetheless, major emphasis throughout the organization is placed on building a loyal customer base. Operating costs are kept low by using only Boeing 737 aircraft, minimizing the time span from landing to departure, and developing strong customer loyalty. The company continues to grow by expanding its point-to-point route network.

Southwest Airlines illustrates several important characteristics of market-driven organizations. The management team has built a culture and developed processes for being market oriented. Southwest's value proposition centers on offering customers on-time air travel services at prices which are so competitive that Southwest has grown the short haul air travel market by attracting passengers from road travel. Its distinctive capability is the closely linked network of activities that enable the point-to-point system to operate very efficiently, and an impressive understanding of customer needs and priorities. Management has developed a team-oriented organization with a clear focus on customer value. The airline serves business and consumer customers who want low-cost, reliable air travel services.

We begin with a discussion of market-driven strategy and its pivotal role in designing and implementing business and marketing strategies. Then we look closely at the importance and process of becoming market oriented. Next, we examine the capabilities of market-driven organizations, followed by a discussion of creating value for customers. Finally, we look at the initiatives that are necessary to become market driven.

Market-Driven Strategy

The underlying logic of market-driven strategy is that the market and the customers that form the market should be the starting point in business strategy formulation. "Considerable progress has been made in identifying market-driven businesses, understanding what they do, and measuring the bottom-line consequences of their orientation to their markets."[3] Importantly, market-driven strategy provides a company-wide perspective, which mandates more effective integration of all activities that impact on customer value. We examine the characteristics of market-driven strategy and discuss several issues associated with adopting that strategy.

Characteristics of Market-Driven Strategies

A key advantage of becoming market oriented is gaining an understanding of the market and how it is likely to change in the future. This knowledge provides the foundation for designing market-driven strategies. Developing this vision about the market requires obtaining information about customers, competitors, and markets; viewing the information from a total business perspective; deciding how to deliver superior customer value; and taking action to provide value to customers.[4] Importantly, there is support from research findings and business practice indicating that market-driven strategies enhance business performance.

The major characteristics of market-driven strategies are shown in Exhibit 1–1. The organization's market orientation helps management identify customers whose value requirements provide the best match with the organization's distinctive capabilities. Successful market-driven strategy design and implementation should lead to superior performance in an organization. Dell Computer's successful market-driven strategy is illustrative. Dell's value-chain strategy combines technologies from Intel, IBM, and Microsoft to serve customers efficiently and with state-of-the-art computer technology. Dell is able to introduce next generation products faster than its competitors can because its market-driven strategy is developed around a direct sales, built-to-order business design. This distinctive process capability is supported by effective supplier, distribution, and service partnerships with other companies. Dell's management understands its customers since company personnel are in close contact with buyers who make inquiries and place orders. Not only does Dell process some 500,000 telephone calls each week, but 65,000 corporate customers are linked to Dell through their own Dell Premier Pages on the Internet, and Dell's Internet-based sales reached $50 million a day in 2000. Indeed, in 2001, Dell became leader in global market share.

EXHIBIT 1–1
**Characteristics of
Market-Driven
Strategies**

We examine each market-driven characteristic in the remainder of the chapter. A more complete discussion of relevant strategy concepts, methods, and applications is provided throughout the book, beginning with the marketing strategy framework developed in Chapter 2.

Why Pursue a Market-Driven Strategy?

While our understanding of market-driven strategy is far from complete, the available evidence indicates a strong supporting logic for pursuing this type of strategy.[5] Importantly, the characteristics shown in Exhibit 1–1 offer guidelines for strategy development rather than advocating a particular strategy. Market-driven strategy needs to be linked to the organization's unique competitive strategy.

The achievements of companies that display market-driven characteristics are impressive. Examples include Dell Computer, Southwest Airlines, Tiffany & Company, and Wal-Mart. Many other companies are in the process of developing market-driven strategies. We examine successful and unsuccessful strategies of several companies throughout the book to illustrate the underlying strategy concepts.

The development of a market-driven strategy is not a short-term endeavor. A considerable amount of effort is necessary to build a market-driven organizational culture and processes. Also, the methods of measuring progress extend beyond short-term measures of financial performance. While this performance information is important, it may not indicate whether progress is being made in developing a successful market-driven strategy. In response to this need, "balanced scorecard" measures are being adopted by an increasing number of companies.[6] The scorecard approach includes the use of customer, learning and growth, and internal business process measures as well as financial performance measures. An underlying principle is that short-term cost savings and profit enhancements may undermine the achievement of strategic goals, and the building of superior customer value in particular.

Becoming Market Oriented

A market orientation is a business perspective that makes the customer the focal point of a company's total operations. "A business is market-oriented when its culture is systematically and entirely committed to the continuous creation of superior customer value."[7]

Switzerland's SMH Group (SMH) is an interesting example of how an executive's vision for reviving the Swiss watchmaking industry enabled it to compete with Hattori Seiko for the title of the world's number one watchmaker. The initial strategy was to launch the Swatch watch in 1983. SMH's brands now include Blancpain, Omega, Longines, Rado, Tissot, Certina, Mido, Hamilton, Balmain, Swatch, Flik Flak, and Endura.

SMH's management was not complacent in deciding how the company should compete in the watch industry. The game plan used by management included a portfolio of watch brands covering a range of prices from inexpensive to expensive. Different value offerings were targeted to different customer groups. The SMH product pyramid ranges from the Blancpain brand at the top to Swatch, Flik Flak, Endura, and Lanco at the base.

SMH's performance has been impressive. From 1983 to 1996, 200 million watches were sold. The company has a valuable portfolio of brands and sophisticated proprietary technology.

Sources: Margaret Studer, "SMH Leads a Revival of Swiss Watchmaking Industry," *The Wall Street Journal*, January 20, 1992, B4; Adrian J. Slywotzky and David J. Morrison, *The Profit Zone* (New York: Times Business, 1997), chap. 6.

Importantly, achieving a market orientation involves the use of superior organizational skills in understanding and satisfying customers.[8]

The Strategy Feature describes the SMH Group's value proposition strategy to revive the Swiss watch-making industry. At the core of the strategy is management's very perceptive understanding of customers and their value requirements.

Becoming market-oriented requires the involvement and support of the entire workforce. The organization must monitor rapidly changing customer needs and wants, determine the impact of those changes on customer satisfaction, increase the rate of product innovation, and implement strategies that build the organization's competitive advantage. We now describe the characteristics and features of market orientation and discuss several issues associated with becoming market oriented.

Characteristics of Market Orientation

A market-oriented organization continuously gathers information about customers, competitors, and markets; views that information from a total business perspective; decides how to deliver superior customer value; and takes actions to provide value to customers (Exhibit 1–2). An organization that is market oriented has both a culture committed to customer value and a process of creating superior value for buyers. Market orientation requires a customer focus, intelligence about competitors, and cross-functional cooperation and involvement. This initiative extends beyond the marketing function in an organization.

Customer Focus

The marketing concept has proposed a customer focus for half a century, yet until the 1990s that emphasis had a limited impact on managers as a basis for managing a business.[9] There are many similarities between the marketing concept and market orientation, although the marketing concept implies a functional (marketing) emphasis. The important difference is that market orientation is more than a philosophy since it consists of a process for delivering customer value. The marketing concept advocates starting with customer needs and wants, deciding which needs to meet, and involving the entire organization in the process of satisfying customers. The market-oriented organization understands customers' prefer-

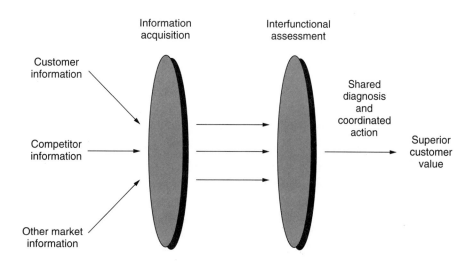

ences and requirements and effectively deploys the skills and resources of the entire organization to satisfy customers. Becoming customer oriented requires finding out what values buyers want to help them satisfy their purchasing objectives. Buyer's decisions are based on the attributes and features of the product that offer the best value for the buyer's use situation. The buyer's experience in using the product is compared to his or her expectations to determine customer satisfaction.[10]

Dell Computer's direct contact with its buyers is an important information source for guiding actions to provide superior customer value. The direct, built-to-order process used by Dell avoids the stocking of computers that may not contain state-of-the-art technology. Also, each computer contains the specific features requested by the buyer. Competitors of Dell that market their computers through distributors and retailers have higher costs because price reductions in purchased components (e.g., chips) cannot be utilized for computers in inventory.

Competitor Intelligence

A market-oriented organization recognizes the importance of understanding its competition as well as the customer:

> The key questions are which competitors, and what technologies, and whether target customers perceive them as alternate satisfiers. Superior value requires that the seller identify and understand the principal competitors' short-term strengths and weaknesses and long-term capabilities and strategies.[11]

Failure to identify and respond to competitive threats can create serious consequences for a company. For example, Western Union did not define its competitive area as telecommunications, concentrating instead on telegraph services, and eventually the 100-year-old company was outflanked by fax technology. Had Western Union been market oriented, its management might have better understood the changes taking place, recognized the competitive threat, and developed strategies to counter that threat.

Cross-Functional Coordination

Market-oriented companies are effective in getting all business functions to work together to provide superior customer value. These organizations are successful in removing the walls between business functions—marketing talks with manufacturing and finance. Cross-functional teamwork guides the entire organization toward providing superior customer value.

Performance Implications.

Companies that are market oriented begin strategic analysis with a penetrating view of the market and the competition. Moreover, an expanding body of research findings points to a strong relationship between market orientation and superior performance.[12] Companies that are market oriented display favorable organizational performance compared with companies that are not market oriented. The positive market orientation/performance relationship has been found in several U.S. and European studies.

Becoming a Market-Oriented Organization

As shown in Exhibit 1–2, becoming a market-oriented company involves several interrelated requirements. The major activities include information acquisition, interfunctional assessment, shared diagnosis, and coordinated action. The objective is to deliver superior customer value. We examine the parts of Exhibit 1–2, beginning with superior customer value.

Superior Customer Value

Customer value is the trade-off of benefits against the costs involved in acquiring a product. The bundle of benefits includes the product, the supporting services, the personnel involved in the purchase and use experience, and the perceived image of the product. The costs include the price of purchase, the time and energy involved, and the psychic costs (e.g., perceived risk).

Indeed, the search for new areas of customer value underpins many impressive success stories. Starbucks, for example, has grown from a Seattle-based coffee house into a profitable $1.3 billion business operating 2,500 outlets and many more concessions worldwide. By creating a new consumption experience for consumers, as well as very fine coffee, Starbucks can charge high prices for its coffee and snacks. The company has created and dominated a new area of customer value. On the other hand, failing to understand what drives customer value can be extremely dangerous. Wal-Mart is the world's largest retailer and has an incredible record of growth and financial performance. Nonetheless, in entering the German marketplace, Wal-Mart transferred many of its famed approaches to customer service—the "ten foot rule" (a customer coming within ten feet of an employee must be offered help), "greeters" at the store entrance, mandatory bag-packing—and to employee motivation—e.g., the Wal-Mart song. German consumers regard these approaches to customer service as invasive and highly unattractive, while employees are reportedly hiding in the bathrooms to avoid singing the company song. By 2001, Wal-Mart had come at the bottom in the annual German survey of customer satisfaction with stores, and losses were running at around $150 million. Achieving superior customer value requires superior understanding of what creates value for customers.

Information Acquisition

"A company can be market-oriented only if it completely understands its markets and the people who decide whether to buy its products or services."[13] Gaining these insights requires proactive information gathering and analysis. In many instances a wealth of information is available in company records, information systems, and employees. The challenge is to develop an effective approach to gathering relevant information that involves the participation of all business functions, not just sales and marketing personnel.

A key part of information acquisition is learning from experience. Learning organizations encourage open-minded inquiry, widespread information dissemination, and the use of mutually informed managers' visions about the current market and how it is likely to change in the future.[14] For example, Intuit's obsession with customer service gave its Quicken design team revealing insights into the problems users encounter with the Quicken personal finance software and the preferences users have concerning software features. Making the Quicken software simple to use requires sensing market needs, extensive use testing, customer feedback, and continuous product improvement.

Cross-Functional Assessment

Zara, the Spanish apparel retailer, has overcome the hurdles of getting people from different functions to share information about the market and work together to develop innovative products. Delivering superior customer value involves all business functions. Zara designs and produces some 12,000 apparel styles each year, and each style is available in stores in only 4 weeks. The short time span between new ideas and their transformation into store offerings is impressive. (See accompanying Zara photograph). Zara's shared vision about customers and competition guides the design process. Information technology plays a vital role in Zara's success. Zara's business design and operations are described in the Cross-Functional Feature.

Women shop in a Zara store in central Madrid. Zara represents a newly assertive breed of business in Spain, a country long seen as an inward-looking commercial backwater. Zara's owner Amancio Ortega, a former delivery boy, now runs one of the fastest-growing fashion clothing chains in Europe. AP Photo/Denis Doyle.

The Zara boutique is buzzing on Calle Real in the rainy northern Spanish city of La Coruña. Customers are buying out the newly designed red tank tops and black blazers, but they're pining for beige and bright purple ones, too. Most fashion companies would need months to retool and restock. Not Zara. Every Saturday the store manager pulls out a Casio handheld computer and types in orders for new clothes. They arrive on Monday.

Zara is the Dell Computer Inc. of the fashion industry. The Spanish star is using the Web to churn out sophisticated fashion at budget prices, turning the industry's traditional fashion cycle completely on its well-coiffed head. Now, a new design can go from pattern to store in two weeks, rather than six months. Founded two decades ago in a remote, impoverished area of the Iberian peninsula, Zara's privately held parent, Inditex, has become a flourishing $2 billion company with 924 stores in 31 countries.

Traditionally, fashion collections are designed only four times a year. And major retailers outsource most of their production to low-cost subcontractors in far-off developing countries such as China. Zara ignores the old logic. For quick turnaround, it makes some two-thirds of its clothes in a company-owned facility in Spain, restocks stores around the globe twice a week, and continually redesigns its clothes—an astounding 12,000 different designs a year.

Here's how Zara does it: A store manager sends in a new idea to La Coruña headquarters. The 200-plus designers decide if it's appealing, then come up with specs. The design is scanned into a computer and zapped to production computers in manufacturing, which cut the material needed to be assembled into clothes by outside workshops. The manufacturing plant is futuristic, too, stuffed with huge clothes-cutting machines that are run by a handful of technicians in a laboratory-style computer-control center.

Eventually, Zara will begin using the Web to sell clothes since finding new store sites is becoming more difficult. In America, e-tailing could boost its low profile. "Americans have less reluctance to buy online than here in Southern Europe," says Inditex CEO José María Castellano. Thanks to Zara, Americans could begin to associate Spain with Internet innovation as well as stylish tank tops.

—William Echikson

Source: "The Fashion Cycle Hits High Gear," *Business Week E.Biz,* September 18, 2000, EB66.

Shared Diagnosis and Action

The last part of becoming market oriented is deciding what actions to take to provide superior customer value. This involves shared discussions among company personnel and an analysis of trade-offs in meeting customer needs.[15] An effective cross-functional team approach to decision making facilitates diagnosis and coordinated action. Zara offers an interesting look at how these processes work in that company. The speed of new product introduction points to the importance of all business functions working together toward a common purpose.

Becoming market oriented often requires making major changes in the culture, processes, and structure of the traditional pyramid-type organization that typically is structured into functional units. Nonetheless, mounting evidence suggests that the market-oriented organization has an important competitive advantage in providing superior customer value and achieving superior performance.

Distinctive Capabilities

Leveraging the organization's distinctive capabilities (competencies) is a vital part of market-driven strategy (Exhibit 1–1). "Capabilities are complex bundles of skills and accumulated knowledge, exercised through organizational processes, that enable firms to coordinate activities and make use of their assets."[16] The major components of capabilities are shown in Exhibit 1–3, using the new product development process to illustrate each component. Note, for example, the similarities between Exhibit 1–3 and Zara's new product development process described in the Cross-Functional Feature. The new product development process applies the *skills* of the design team and benefits from the team's *accumulated knowledge*. *Coordination of activities* across business functions during new product development is facilitated by information technology. For example, Zara's product designs take into account manufacturing requirements as well as offering high-fashion products. *Assets* such as Zara's strong brand image help launch new products.

It is apparent from Exhibit 1–3 that an organization's capabilities are not a particular business function, asset, or individual but instead comprise major processes of the organization. Dell Computer's direct-to-the-customer, built-to-order process is a distinctive capability that operates using Dell's skills and accumulated knowledge in coordinating the activities that comprise the process and benefiting from Dell's strong brand image in the personal computer market. The outcome of the process is the delivery of superior customer value to the organizations that purchase Dell's computers (over 90 percent of Dell's buyers are businesses rather than consumers).

Organizational capabilities and organizational processes are closely related:

> [I]t is the capability that enables the activities in a business process to be carried out. The business will have as many processes as are necessary to carry out the natural business activities defined by the stage in the value chain and the key success factors in the market.[17]

Processes are not the same across industries or for all businesses in the same industry. For example, Dell Computer and Compaq Computer have different processes, and the processes of Dell Computer differ from those of Wal-Mart. Compared to the retailer, Dell is at an earlier stage in the value chain that links suppliers, manufacturers, distributors/retailers, and end-users of goods and services. Moreover, unlike Wal-Mart, Dell produces to order and is in direct contact with its customers.

EXHIBIT 1–3
Components of Organizational Capabilities

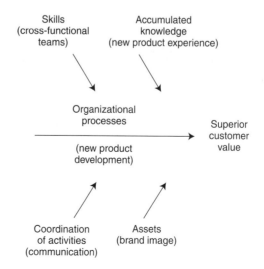

We now look more closely at the distinctive capabilities of an organization, followed by a discussion of different types of capabilities. Then we examine the relationship between capabilities and customer value.

Identifying Distinctive Capabilities

Understanding the organization's distinctive capabilities and knowing how they relate to customers' value requirements are important considerations in marketing strategy design. It is essential that management place a company's strategic focus on the company's distinctive capabilities.[18] These capabilities may enable the organization to compete in new markets, provide significant value to customers, and create market-entry barriers to potential competitors. For example, Hewlett-Packard (H-P) has a strong capability in ink jet printer technology which enabled the company to become the world leader in computer printers. H-P leveraged this capability to develop the ink jet fax through a strategic alliance with a Japanese partner which contributed a distinctive capability in fax technology.

Examples of distinctive capabilities in four companies are shown in Exhibit 1–4. Capabilities are important factors in shaping corporate and business strategies. Many companies are deciding what they do best, concentrating their strategies on their distinctive capabilities. For example, in the late 1990s Tandy Corporation, after unsuccessful ventures into computer manufacturing, computer retailing, megastore electronics, and appliance retailing, exited from those businesses and concentrated its growth initiatives on the core capabilities of the Radio Shack retail chain. The corporation's name was changed to Radio Shack to provide brand focus.

A distinctive capability (1) offers a disproportionate (higher) contribution to superior customer value or (2) enables an organization to deliver value to customers in a substantially more cost-effective manner.[19] Southwest Airlines' distinctive capability is its business design, which enables the carrier to offer travelers low fares in combination with satisfactory services.

An important issue is deciding which capability to emphasize.[20] How, for example, did Wal-Mart's management decide to invest heavily to build its information and logistics system? Why did Dell choose the direct sales, built-to-order business design? What supporting logic led Hewlett-Packard to invest heavily in ink jet technology and position its printers against dot matrix printers rather than laser printers? These choices are not always

EXHIBIT 1–4
Illustrative Distinctive Capabilities

- L. L. BEAN

  L. L. Bean's mail order products offer value to its customers, but the company is widely acknowledged for its *order fulfillment* capabilities.

- RUBBERMAID

  Rubbermaid has been successful in competing in the commodity kitchenware market with a successful *new product development* process that creates many new products each year.

- SINGAPORE AIRLINES

  Singapore Airlines performs many commercial air transportation functions well, but it is widely recognized as the industry leader in *customer service delivery*.

- WAL-MART

  Wal-Mart has value-priced products and convenient retail locations, but its efficient and responsive *distribution system* is how it mapped the path to competitiveness.

EXHIBIT 1–5
**Desirable
Capabilities**

Source: George S. Day, "The
Capabilities of Market-Driven
Organizations," *Journal of
Marketing,* October 1994, 49.

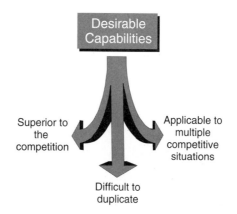

apparent and may involve developing new capabilities that offer the potential of being distinctive. In other situations the organization may pursue strategic initiatives that become distinctive over time.

The starting point in deciding which capability to pursue is identifying and evaluating the organization's existing capabilities. The three characteristics shown in Exhibit 1–5 are useful in identifying distinctive capabilities. A capability may not be applicable to multiple competitive situations (e.g., Honda's engine and drive train technology for various product applications), but to be sustainable it needs to be superior to the competition and difficult to duplicate. Multiple competitive situation applications add additional strength to the capability.

Types of Capabilities

Classifying the organization's capabilities is useful in identifying distinctive capabilities. As shown in Exhibit 1–6, one method of classification is to determine whether processes operate from outside the business to inside, operate from the inside out, or are spanning processes. The processes shown are illustrative rather than providing a complete enumeration of processes. Moreover, since a company may have unique capabilities, it is not feasible to identify a generic inventory of processes.

The process capabilities shown in Exhibit 1–6 differ in purpose and focus.[21] The outside-in processes connect the organization to the external environment, providing market feedback and forging external relationships. The inside-out processes are the activities necessary to satisfy customer requirements (e.g. manufacturing/operations). The outside-in processes play a key role in offering direction for the spanning and inside-out capabilities, which respond to the customer needs and requirements identified by the outside-in processes. Market sensing, customer linking, channel bonding (e.g., manufacturer/retailer relationships), and technology monitoring supply vital information for new product opportunities, service requirements, and competitive threats.

This process view of capabilities highlights the interrelated nature of organizational processes and points to several important issues:[22]

- The market-driven organization has a clear external focus.

- Capabilities typically span several business functions and involve teams of people.

- Processes need to be clearly defined and have identifiable owners.

- Information should be shared with all process participants.

- Processes are interconnected to other processes, and management needs to coordinate the linkages.

EXHIBIT 1–6
Classifying Capabilities

Source: George S. Day, "The Capabilities of Market-Driven Organizations," *Journal of Marketing,* October 1994, 41.

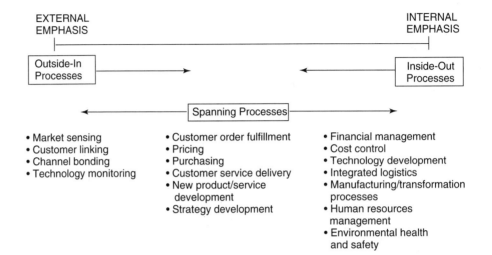

While many companies are structured according to business functions, an increasing number are placing emphasis on cross-functional processes. As companies alter their traditional organizational hierarchies, they may retain functional groupings (e.g., engineering, finance, marketing) while placing emphasis on processes like those shown in Exhibit 1–6.

Value and Capabilities

Value for buyers consists of the benefits and costs resulting from the purchase and use of products. Value is perceived by the buyer. Superior value occurs when there are positive net benefits. A company needs to identify value opportunities that match its distinctive capabilities. A market-oriented company uses its market sensing processes, shared diagnosis, and cross-functional decision making to identify and take advantage of superior value opportunities. Management must determine where and how it can offer superior value, directing those capabilities to customer groups (market segments) in a way that results in a favorable competency/value match. Dell Computer found this match by concentrating on meeting the needs of business buyers rather than trying to serve all personal computer buyers.

Creating Value for Customers

"Customer value is the outcome of a process that begins with a business strategy anchored in a deep understanding of customer needs."[23] The creation of customer value received a lot of attention from managers during the 1990s. This interest was the result of companies' experience with total quality management, intense competition, and the increasing demands of customers. Several benefits of value initiatives reported by executives in a study conducted by the Conference Board are shown in Exhibit 1–7. The purpose of the study was to determine whether companies were taking actions to improve customer value and to examine their assessment of the results (benefits) of the value initiatives. Exhibit 1–7 offers positive evidence of companies' proactive efforts to increase customer value. About half the respondents were part of the quality function, nearly one-third were from marketing, and the rest were from other business functions. About 80 percent of the participating companies were from the United States, and the remainder were from Europe.

We take a closer look at the concept of customer value and consider how value is generated. Then we look at the progress being made in the value initiatives of companies.

EXHIBIT 1–7
**A Self-Assessment:
Results of
Customer Value
Initiative**

Source: Kathryn Troy,
*Change Management:
Striving for Customer Value*
(New York: The Conference
Board, 1996), 6.

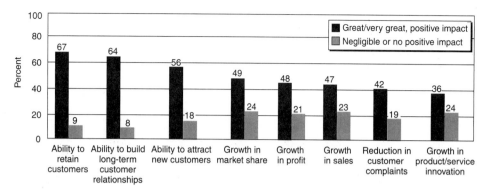

[1]Those choosing a "moderate" impact are not shown on the chart but account for the difference between the percentages shown and 100 percent.

Customer Value

Offering superior customer value is relevant to governments as well as business firms. An interesting Web initiative by the Singapore government is described in the E-Business Feature. Recognizing the opportunity to increase the customer value offered to Singapore citizens, the government invested more than $600 million to simplify the process of obtaining approvals by citizens using online contact. The government benefits through increased citizen participation and reduced operating costs.

Customers form value expectations and decide to purchase goods and services based on their perceptions of products' benefits less the total costs incurred.[24] Customer satisfaction indicates how well the product use experience compares to the buyer's value expectations. Superior customer value results from a very favorable use experience compared to expectations and the value offerings of competitors.

Providing Value to Customers

As was discussed earlier, the organization's distinctive capabilities are used to deliver value by differentiating the product offer, offering lower prices relative to competing brands, or providing a combination of lower cost and differentiation.[25] Deciding which avenue to follow requires matching capabilities to the best value opportunities.

Consider, for example, Hewlett-Packard's very successful ink jet printer strategy, which positioned the printer as an alternative to dot matrix technology. H-P's management decided not to target laser printers by offering the ink jet as a lower-cost option. The dot matrix strategy provided H-P with a much larger market opportunity. H-P's product management team's vision about the market was correct in that dot matrix users would soon become dissatisfied with the quality and capabilities of their printers.

Value Initiatives

As was shown in Exhibit 1–7 the Conference Board survey indicates that a majority of companies consider value initiatives to be producing positive results. The companies participating in the study report strong progress in the following areas:

- Analyzing customer needs and instilling customer-focused behavior in frontline employees (70 percent or more);

- Analyzing target markets and boosting service quality (60 to 70 percent);

When Agnes Tan applied for a permit to open a sandwich shop in Singapore's financial district, she had to wait in three different 90-minute lines just to get her floor plan approved. Then, surfing the Web one night, the 27-year-old accountant stumbled on Singapore's "eGovernment" Internet portals. There, she discovered, she could get the rest of the required permits—for everything from kitchen equipment to registering employees for Social Security—from her desk. "Without this," says Tan, "it's a nightmare."

Such services have put Singapore at the forefront of public-sector efforts to cut red tape using the Web. Since 1997, Singapore has invested more than $600 million to move its citizens onto the Net and out of lines. Residents can now go online to take care of dozens of tasks, such as registering births or signing up for military duty. Singapore is "ahead of the curve" in taking advantage of the Web, says Richard S. Seline, electronic-government practice manager at consultant Arthur Andersen in Washington.

The initiative is paying off in less frustration and in more dollars. Some 30% of Singapore taxpayers filed their returns online this year—saving nearly $600,000 says Yong Ying-I, chief executive of the Infocomm Development Authority, which oversees the migration to the Net. While Yong won't say how much Singapore has saved from its Web sites, residents have completed 1.5 million school registrations, trademark applications, and similar bureaucratic errands there over the past year.

Granted, it's a lot easier to be an efficient e-government in a country with just 4 million residents living in an area the size of Manhattan. But for residents such as Tan, letting a mouse do the walking keeps her out of lines and back where she wants to be—serving up sandwiches.

—*Michael Shari*

Source: "Cutting Red Tape in Singapore," *Business Week E.Biz,* September 18, 2000, EB92.

- Using cross-functional teams to develop products and services (about half);
- Achieving operational excellence (about half); and
- Innovating (about half).[26]

Twenty-five of the companies that have completed the implementation of a value initiative report major progress in instilling customer-focused behavior for employees who are not in front-line contact with customers.[27] These companies indicate stronger performance in expanding market share, innovation, and retaining customers when compared with companies which are beginning value initiatives. The companies which have value initiatives under way are becoming market oriented and leveraging their distinctive capabilities.

Nonetheless, there is an important distinction between value and innovation. An *Economist Intelligence Unit* Report in 1999 contained interviews with executives from many leading companies throughout the world: "What counts, conclude the participants, is *value innovation.* This is defined as creating new value propositions . . . that lead to increased customer satisfaction, loyalty and—ultimately—sustainable, profitable growth. Market leaders are just that—pioneers."[28]

There is growing support from such studies for the benefits of market-driven strategy.

Becoming Market Driven

The discussion so far points to the importance of becoming market oriented, leveraging distinctive capabilities, and finding a good match between customers' value requirements and the organization's capabilities. The motivation for these actions is that they should lead to superior organizational performance. Moreover, research evidence indicates that these characteristics are present in market-driven organizations, which display higher performance than do their counterparts that are not market driven.

A market-driven organization must identify which capabilities to develop and which investment commitments to make. These decisions benefit from

> a shared understanding of the industry structure, the needs of the target customer segments, the positional advantages being sought, and the trends in the environment.[29]

A major objective of this book is developing the concepts and processes for gaining a shared understanding of customers and how to satisfy their needs and preferences by favorably positioning the organization's value offer.

Market Sensing and Customer Linking Capabilities

Market orientation research, evolving business strategy paradigms, and the Conference Board study all point to the importance of market sensing and customer linking capabilities in achieving successful market-driven strategies.[30]

Market Sensing Capabilities

Market-driven companies have effective processes for learning about their markets. Sensing involves more than collecting information. It must be shared across functions and interpreted to determine what actions need to be initiated (Exhibit 1–2).

Developing an effective market sensing capability is not a simple task. However, the penalties of inferior market sensing may be substantial. Premier manufacturer of fine china dinner plates, Royal Doulton, has seen its sales declining at 20 percent a year and its market value reduced by two-thirds, as it failed to understand that the consumer trend toward informal eating has greatly reduced the size of the market for its formal dinnerware.

To be effective, various information sources must be identified, and processes must be developed to collect and analyze the information. Information technology plays a vital role in market sensing activities. Different business functions have access to useful information and need to be involved in market sensing activities.

Customer Linking Capabilities

There is substantial evidence that creating and maintaining close relationships with customers are important in market-driven strategies.[31] These relationships offer advantages to both buyer and seller through information sharing and collaboration. Customer linking also reduces the possibility of a customer shifting to another supplier. Customers are valuable assets.

Quintiles Transnational has very effective customer linking capabilities.[32] Its drug testing and sales services are available in 27 countries. The company has extensive experience in clinical trials and marketing. Quintiles' customers are drug companies in many countries around the world. Ongoing collaborative relationships are essential to Quintiles' success. It offers specialized expertise, helping drug producers reduce the time necessary to develop and test new drugs.

Aligning Structure and Processes

Becoming market driven may require changing the design of the organization. Market orientation and process capabilities require cross-functional coordination and involvement. Many of the companies in the Conference Board study discussed earlier made changes in organization structures and processes as a part of their customer value initiatives. The changes included improving existing processes as well as redesigning processes. The processes that were primary targets for reengineering included sales and marketing, customer relations, order fulfillment, and distribution.[33] This emphasis was no doubt the result of the extensive work during the last decade on quality improvement that was concentrated in operations (manufacturing and services).

The objectives of the business process changes made by the companies in the Conference Board survey were to improve the overall level of product quality, reduce costs, and improve service delivery.[34] Nine of the ten participating companies made changes in their business processes as part of their customer value efforts. Interestingly, 42 percent of the companies' change initiatives came from the top of the organizations, while nearly as many initiatives (40 percent) were grass-roots (bottom-up) approaches. This indicates the benefits of both top-down and bottom-up initiatives.

Underpinning such changes and initiatives is the importance of what has been called "implementation capabilities," or the ability of an organization to execute and sustain market-driven strategy, and to do so on a global basis.[35] In addition to formulating the strategies essential to delivering superior customer value, it is vital to adopt a thorough and detailed approach to strategy implementation.

Summary

Market-driven strategies begin with an understanding of the market and the customers that form the market. The characteristics of market-driven strategies include developing a market-orientation, leveraging distinctive capabilities, finding a match between customer value and organizational capabilities, and obtaining superior performance by providing superior customer value. The available evidence indicates a strong supporting logic for adopting market-driven strategies, recognizing that a long-term commitment is necessary to develop those strategies.

Achieving a market orientation requires a customer focus, competitor intelligence, and coordination among the business functions. Becoming market oriented involves making major changes in the culture, processes, and structure of the traditional pyramid organization that is organized into functional units. Several interrelated actions are required, including information acquisition, sharing information within the organization, interfunctional assessment, shared diagnosis, and decision making. The objective of market orientation is to provide superior customer value.

Leveraging distinctive capabilities is a key part of developing a market-driven strategy. Capabilities are organizational processes that enable firms to coordinate related activities and employ assets by using skills and accumulated knowledge. Distinctive capabilities are superior to the competition, difficult to duplicate, and applicable to multiple competitive situations. Capabilities can be classified as outside-in, inside-out, and spanning processes. The outside-in processes provide direction to the inside-out and spanning processes by identifying customer needs and superior value opportunities.

The creation of superior customer value is a continuing competitive challenge in sustaining successful market-driven strategies. Value is the trade-off of product benefits against the total costs of acquiring the product. Superior customer value occurs when the buyer has a very favorable use experience compared to his or her expectations and the value offerings of competitors. The avenues to value may be product differentiation, lower prices than competing brands, or a combination of lower cost and differentiation.

Becoming market driven is more involved than following a step-by-step sequence of actions. Capabilities need to be identified and analyzed, market sensing and customer linking capabilities developed, and necessary organizational changes implemented.

Our discussion of the major dimensions of market-driven strategy provides an essential perspective concerning the development of business and marketing strategies. In Chapter 2 we examine the major decisions necessary in developing and implementing marketing strategy.

Internet Applications

A.   Discuss how Dell Computer's website (*www.Dell.com*) supports its mission, value proposition, and brand image. What advantages (and limitations) does the website provide to business buyers?

B.   Go to *www.travelocity.com* and investigate the site. How does travelocity.com collect information about its customers, and how might this prove valuable to the company and ultimately the customer? What privacy issues could arise?

Questions for Review and Discussion

1.   Discuss some of the reasons why managing in an environment of constant change will be necessary in the future.

2.   Explain the logic of pursuing a market-driven strategy.

3.   Explain the use of market orientation as a guiding philosophy for a social service organization, paying particular attention to user needs and wants.

4.   Discuss the role of organizational capabilities in developing market-driven strategies.

5.   Describe the relationship between customer value and a company's distinctive capabilities.

6.   What role does product/service innovation play in providing superior customer value?

7.   How would you explain the concept of superior customer value to a new finance manager?

8.   Suppose you have been appointed to the top marketing post of a corporation and the president has asked you to explain market-driven strategy to the board of directors. What will you include in your presentation?

9.   Explain the importance of developing a strategic vision about the future for competing in today's business environment.

10.   Discuss the issues that are important in transforming a company into a market-driven organization.

11.   How is the Internet likely to contribute to an organization's market-driven strategy in the future?

Notes

1.   George S. Day, "The Capabilities of Market-Driven Organizations," *Journal of Marketing*, October 1994, 37–52.

2.   Peter Doyle, *Value-Based Marketing—Marketing Strategies for Corporate Growth and Shareholder Value,* Chichester: John Wiley, 2000.

3.   Day, "The Capabilities of Market-Driven Organizations," 37.

4.   Stanley F. Slater and John C. Narver, "Market Orientation, Customer Value, and Superior Performance," *Business Horizons*, March–April 1994, 22–27.

5.   Day, "The Capabilities of Market-Driven Organizations."

6. See, for example, "Robert S. Kaplan and David P. Norton, *The Balanced Scorecard* (Boston: Harvard Business School Press, 1996).

7. Slater and Narver, "Market Orientation," 22.

8. George S. Day, *Market-Driven Strategy: Processes for Creating Value* (New York: Free Press, 1990).

9. Day, "The Capabilities of Market-Driven Organizations," 37.

10. Philip Kotler, *Marketing Management*, 8th ed. (Englewood Cliffs, NJ: Prentice-Hall, 1994), chap. 2.

11. Slater and Narver, "Market Orientation," 23.

12. Day, "The Capabilities of Market-Driven Organizations," 37–52; Wolfgang Fritz, "Market Orientation and Corporate Success: Findings from Germany," *European Journal of Marketing*, 30, no. 8, 1996, 59–74.

13. Benson P. Shapiro, "What the Hell Is Market Oriented?" *Harvard Business Review*, November–December 1988, 120.

14. George Day, "Continuous Learning about Markets," *California Management Review*, Summer 1994, 9–31.

15. Shapiro, "What the Hell Is Market Oriented?" 122.

16. Day, "The Capabilities of Market-Driven Organizations," 38.

17. Ibid.

18. C. K. Prahalad and Gary Hamel, "The Core Competence of the Corporation," *Harvard Business Review*, May–June 1990, 79–91.

19. Day, "The Capabilities of Market-Driven Organizations," 38.

20. Ibid., 39–40.

21. Ibid., 40–43.

22. Ibid.

23. Kathryn Troy, *Change Management: Striving for Customer Value* (New York: The Conference Board, 1996), 5.

24. Philip Kotler, *Marketing Management*, 9th ed. (Upper Saddle River, NJ: Prentice-Hall, 1997), chap. 2.

25. George S. Day and Robin Wensley, "Assessing Advantage: A Framework for Diagnosing Competitive Superiority," *Journal of Marketing*, April 1998, 1–20.

26. Troy, *Change Management,* 6.

27. Ibid.

28. Laura Mazur, "Wrong Sort of Innovation," *Marketing Business,* June 1999, 39.

29. Day, "The Capabilities of Market-Driven Organizations," 49.

30. Ibid., 43–45.

31. Ibid.

32. David W. Cravens, Gordon Greenley, Nigel F. Piercy, and Stanley Slater, "Mapping the Path to Market Leadership: The Market-Driven Strategy Imperative," *Marketing Management*, Fall 1998, 29–39.

33. Troy, *Change Management,* 7.

34. Ibid.

35. Nigel F. Piercy, "Marketing Implementation: The Implications of Marketing Paradigm Weakness for the Strategy Execution Process," *Journal of the Academy of Marketing Science,* 13 (2/3), 1999, 113–131.

Chapter 2

Business and Marketing Strategies

The competitive and market challenges confronting businesses in a wide range of industries worldwide are unusually complex, and the propensity for failure has never been greater. The economic slowdown at the beginning of the 21st century affected a wide range of new economy and old economy companies. Developing effective strategies in this environment of constant change is a key requirement for corporate success. Market-driven organizations develop closely coordinated business and marketing strategies.

Executives in many companies are reinventing their business models with the objective of improving their competitive advantage. These changes include altering market focus, expanding product scope, partnering with other organizations, outsourcing manufacturing, and modifying internal structure. The strategic initiatives pursued by Siemens, the German electronics giant, with the objective of becoming Germany's first new economy conglomerate are illustrative.[1] The product portfolio ranges from gas-turbine generators to light bulbs. Management's product innovation, cross-functional, and cost reduction initiatives moved Siemens from the ninth to the third position in the cell phone market in Europe behind Nokia and Motorola. Production time for a mobile phone has been reduced from 13 hours to 5 minutes. Industry analysts are positive concerning Siemens' strategies, but some question whether management will be able to hold a strong competitive position. An evaluation of the company's performance is described in the Global Feature.

Corporate strategy consists of deciding on the scope and purpose of the business, its objectives, and the initiatives and resources necessary to achieve the objectives. Marketing strategy is guided by the decisions top management makes about how, when, and where to compete. Because of this close relationship, it is important to examine the major aspects of designing and implementing business strategy.

The chapter begins with a look at the nature and scope of corporate strategy. A discussion of business and marketing strategy relationships follows. Next, the marketing strategy process is described and illustrated. A discussion of Internet strategy follows. Finally, we examine the steps in preparing the strategic marketing plan.

In July, 1998, Siemens CEO Heinrich von Pierer set out a 10-point plan to rescue the company from plummeting profits. Here are some highlights:

GOAL	PERFORMANCE
• Turn around the semi-conductor division	• **EXCELLENT** Per-share earnings rose sixfold in the last quarter. The April IPO of minority stake in Infineon semiconductors unit raised $5.4 billion.
• Set clear goals for management, with consequences if benchmarks are not met	• **GOOD** Top managers must explain results to peers quarterly; some have eased out. Executive pay is now tied closely to performance. But no one talks about "Chainsaw Heinrich."
• Rigorously prune problem areas	• **FAIR** Medical Engineering unit transformed from money-loser to profit driver within two years, but power-generation and transportation units still have uncomfortably slim profit margins.
• Strengthen businesses through acquisitions to achieve world leadership	• **GOOD** April purchase of Mannesmann auto-electronics unit will create a leader in burgeoning market for onboard IT. But Siemens may have paid too much. And it still must prove it can keep pace long-term in competitive businesses such as telecommunications.
• Reorganize existing businesses	• **FAIR** Created profitable business-services arm, bundled mobile-phone businesses, and boosted market share. However, insiders complain that Siemens' internal decision-making is still too slow.
• Become more transparent by converting to U.S. GAAP accounting standard	• **VERY GOOD** Siemens on track to report results according to GAAP in the quarter ending Dec. 31, 2000.
• List shares in the U.S.	• **GOOD** Listing on track for early 2001.

Source: Jack Ewing, "Siemens Climbs Back," *Business Week*, June 5, 2000, 80.

Corporate Strategy

We describe the characteristics of corporate strategy and consider how organizations are changing. The section concludes with a discussion of the major dimensions of corporate strategy.

What Is Corporate Strategy?

It is important to reach a reasonable consensus concerning the nature and scope of corporate strategy. One authority, Michael Porter, indicates that an effective strategy should display the following characteristics:

• Unique competitive position for the company.

• Activities tailored to strategy.

- Clear trade-offs and choices vis-à-vis competitors.

- Competitive advantage arises from fit across activities.

- Sustainability comes from the activity system, not the parts.

- Operational effectiveness is a given.[2]

This view of strategy points to distinctive capabilities that are made up of business activities which form processes. An example is Wal-Mart's distribution system comprised of various activities, such as tracking each item in inventory. Other examples are Dell Computer's direct sales, built-to-order process and Southwest Airlines' city-to-city business design coupled with very efficient performance of the activities needed to transport passengers from point to point.

Corporate strategy consists of the decisions made by top management and the resulting actions taken to achieve the objectives set for the business. The major strategy components and several key issues related to each component are shown in Exhibit 2–1. The issues highlight important questions that management must answer in charting the course of the enterprise. Management's skills and vision in addressing these issues are critical to the performance of the corporation. Essential to corporate success is matching the capabilities of the organization with opportunities to achieve long-term customer satisfaction.

EXHIBIT 2–1
Corporate Strategy Components and Issues

Source: Orville C. Walker, Jr., Harper W. Boyd, Jr., and Jean-Claude Larréché, *Marketing Strategy* (Burr Ridge, IL: Richard D. Irwin, 1992), 38.

Strategy Component	Key Issues
Scope, mission, and intent	• What business(es) should the firm be in? • What customer needs, market segments, and/or technologies should be focused on? • What is the firm's enduring strategic purpose or intent?
Objectives	• What performance dimensions should the firm's business units and employees focus on? • What is the target level of performance to be achieved on each dimension? • What is the time frame in which each target should be attained?
Development strategy	• How can the firm achieve a desired level of growth over time? • Can the desired growth be attained by expanding the firm's current businesses? • Will the company have to diversify into new businesses or product-markets to achieve its future growth objectives?
Resource allocation	• How should the firm's limited financial resources be allocated across its businesses to produce the highest returns? • Of the alternative strategies that each business might pursue, which will produce the greatest returns for the dollars invested?
Sources of synergy	• What competencies, knowledge, and customer-based intangibles (e.g., brand recognition, reputation) might be developed and shared across the firm's businesses? • What operational resources, facilities, or functions (e.g., plants, R&D sales force) might the firm's businesses share to increase their efficiency?

It is apparent early in the 21st century that companies are drastically altering their business and marketing strategies to get closer to their customers, counter competitive threats, and strengthen competitive advantages. Siemens' strategic initiatives are illustrative. The challenges to management include escalating international competition, political and economic upheaval, dominance by the customer, and increasing marketing complexity.

Organizational Change

During the last decade massive changes were made in the size and structure of many business firms. These changes are described as rightsizing, reengineering, and reinventing the organization. The renewal (reforming) of the traditional organization typically moves through three phases: vertical disaggregation, internal redesign, and network formation.[3]

Vertical Disaggregation

Disaggregation reduces the *size* of the organization by eliminating jobs and layers of middle managers and leveling the hierarchy. The Conference Board, Inc., reports that 90 percent of its members downsized during the 1990s, and about two-thirds of the executives representing a broad cross-section of business say downsizing will continue.[4]

The resulting flat corporation may organize its activities into a small number of key processes (e.g., new product planning, sales generation, and customer service).[5] Alternatively, organizations may retain functional departments, overlaying them with processes. Cross-functional teams manage the processes, and providing superior customer value is a key objective and measure of performance. Employees are encouraged to make regular contact with suppliers and customers.

Internal Redesign

Organizational renewal is more than just reducing staff, eliminating layers of management, and adopting worker empowerment processes. The second phase alters the internal design of the organization. The new organization forms are lean, flexible, adaptive, and responsive to customer needs and market requirements.[6] The altered business designs involve innovation in designing products to meet customer needs, arranging supply and distribution networks, and constantly staying in touch with the marketplace. A priority of these organizations is understanding customer needs, offering value to customers, and retaining customers.

New Organization Forms

The third phase of organizational change involves the formation of relationships with other organizations and the use of processes as the basic organizing concept. Although interorganizational relationships are often present in the traditional organization, companies are expanding these relationships with suppliers, customers, and even competitors. These new organization forms are called networks since they involve several collaborative arrangements. Networks are more likely to be launched by entrepreneurs, since the traditional vertically integrated, hierarchically organized company finds it difficult to shift to the network paradigm. Transformation means fewer people on the corporate payroll, different management challenges, drastic cultural changes, and complex collaborative relationships with other organizations. Nevertheless, traditional companies such as International Business Machines are successfully transforming themselves to more flexible and adaptive network forms. The Technology Feature describes how IBM is using software alliances to compete with Oracle Corp.

- Oracle's strategy is to develop and offer corporate customers a complete and integrated package of software for managing financial operations, manufacturing, sales force, logistics, e-commerce, and suppliers.

- International Business Machines' strategy is to assemble and apply the best package of software from more than 50 software partners, leveraging the distinctive capabilities of each partner.

- The corporate software market for databases and applications (e.g., sales force automation, supply-chain management) is an estimated $50 billion.

- Oracle's management indicates that IBM's objective is to market its consulting services for applying corporate software packages.

- IBM's software is about one-fifth the price of Oracle's software, but IBM also charges consulting fees to install and integrate software packages from 59 partners such as SAP, Siebel Systems, Ariba, and PeopleSoft.

- The customer value issue is a combination of software price and software performance. Some corporate buyers are finding that IBM's total price is below Oracle's. The performance of the two firms' software packages appears to be comparable.

- Industry authorities are split concerning which software system will win the competitive battle. IBM and Oracle are expected to remain the strongest firms in the market.

Source: "IBM vs. Oracle: It Could Get Bloody," *Business Week,* May 28, 2001, 65–66.

Components of Strategy

Recognizing that there are several definitions of corporate strategy, we utilize this definition:

> Corporate strategy is the way a company creates value through the configuration and coordination of its multimarket activities.[7]

This definition emphasizes value creation, considers the multimarket scope of the corporation (product, geographic, and vertical value chain boundaries), and points to how the organization manages its activities and businesses that fall under the corporate umbrella. A key premise of this view of strategy is that the multibusiness corporation must contribute to the competitive advantage of its units.[8] Thus, there needs to be a close relationship between the corporation and the businesses that are parts of the firm.

A useful framework for examining corporate strategy which is consistent with the earlier definition consists of (1) management's long-term vision for the corporation, (2) objectives which serve as milestones toward the vision, (3) assets, skills, and capabilities, (4) businesses in which the corporation competes, (5) structure, systems, and processes, and (6) creation of value through multimarket activity.[9] Let us examine each strategy component.

Deciding Corporate Vision

Management's vision defines what the corporation is and what it does and provides important guidelines for managing and improving the corporation. The founder initially has a vision about the firm's mission, and management may alter the mission over time. Strategic choices about where the firm is going in the future—choices that take into account company capabilities, resources, opportunities, and problems—establish the vision of the enterprise. Developing strategies for sustainable competitive advantage, implementing them, and adjusting the strategies to respond to new environmental requirements is a continuing process. Managers monitor the market and the competitive environment. The corporate vision may, over time, be changed because of problems or opportunities identified by management's monitoring activities. For example, IBM's management is placing major emphasis on consulting services as a direction of future growth.

An interesting insight into the vision underpinning the Internet pioneer Amazon.com comes from Jeff Bezos' reply to a shareholder asking what she actually owned: "You own a piece of the leading e-commerce platform. . . . The Amazon.com platform is comprised of brand, customers, distribution capability, deep e-commerce expertise, and a great team with a passion for innovation and a passion for serving customers well." This vision goes far beyond simply being the biggest Internet book retailer.

Early in the strategy-development process management needs to define the vision of the corporation. It is reviewed and updated as shifts in the strategic direction of the enterprise occur over time. The vision statement sets several important guidelines for business operations:[10]

1. The reason for the company's existence and its responsibilities to stockholders, employees, society, and other stakeholders.

2. The firm's customers and the needs (benefits) that are to be met by the firm's goods or services (areas of product and market involvement).

3. The extent of specialization within each product-market area and the geographical scope of operations.

4. The amount and types of product-market diversification desired by management.

5. The stage(s) in the value-added chain where the business competes from raw materials to the end-user.

6. Management's performance expectations for the company.

7. Other general guidelines for overall business strategy, such as technologies to be used and the role of research and development in the corporation.

Objectives

Objectives need to be set so that the performance of the enterprise can be gauged. Corporate objectives may be established in the following areas: *marketing, innovation, resources, productivity, social responsibility,* and *finance.*[11] Examples include growth and market-share expectations, improvement in product quality, employee training and development, new product targets, return on invested capital, earnings growth rates, debt limits, energy reduction objectives, and pollution standards. Objectives are set at several levels in an organization, beginning with those indicating the enterprise's overall objectives.

The time frame necessary for strategic change often goes beyond short-term financial reporting requirements. Companies are using more than financial measures to evaluate longer-term strategic objectives and nonfinancial measures for short-term budgets. The "balanced scorecard" approach provides an expanded basis for tracking organizational performance.[12] It considers both long-term and short-term performance metrics. This method of keeping score includes objectives, measures, targets, and initiatives regarding financial, customer, internal business processes, and learning and growth perspectives. This concept of performance offers a promising basis for managing and evaluating market-driven strategies.

Capabilities

As we discussed in Chapter 1, it is important to place a company's strategic focus on its distinctive capabilities.[13] These capabilities may offer the organization the potential to compete in different markets, provide significant value to end-user customers, and create barriers to competitor duplication. For example, Sony has a distinctive capability in the miniaturization of electronic products, seen in the worldwide success of the Sony Walkman. However, the miniaturization capability has also led to the development of the lightweight Sony Vaio personal computers meeting customer demands for lighter machines. The Internet links the computer user to Sony's music and entertainment businesses. Interestingly, Sony has now registered as a bank, and may leverage its computer and Internet customer base for financial services.

We know that distinctive capabilities are important in shaping the organization's strategy. In contrast to the diversification wave of the 1970s, many companies are deciding what they do best and concentrating their efforts on those distinctive capabilities. A key strategy issue is matching capabilities to market opportunities. Capabilities that can be leveraged into different markets and applications are particularly valuable. For example, the GoreTex high-performance fabric is used in many applications from apparel to dental floss.

Even though capabilities, resources, opportunities, and problems create constraints, management has a lot of flexibility in selecting the mission as well as changing it in the future. Sometimes the priorities and preferences of the CEO or the board of directors may override factual evidence in selecting the business mission. For example, many of the diversifications pursued by companies in the 1980s did not work very well and resulted in the restructuring and downsizing of many companies during the last decade.

Business Composition

Defining the composition of the business provides direction for both corporate and marketing strategy design. In single-product firms that serve one market, it is easy to determine the composition of the business. In many other firms, it is necessary to separate the business into parts to facilitate strategic analyses and planning. When firms are serving multiple markets with different products, grouping similar business areas together aids decision making.

Business segment, group, or division designations are used to identify the major areas of business of a diversified corporation. Each segment, group, or division often contains a mix of related goods (or services), though a single product can be assigned such a designation. The term *segment* does not correspond to a market segment (subgroup of end-users in a product-market), which we discuss throughout the book. Most large corporations break out their financial reports into business or industry segments according to the guidelines of the Financial Accounting Standards Board. Some firms may establish subgroups of related products within a business segment that are targeted to different customer groups.

A business segment, group, or division is often too large in terms of product and market composition to use in strategic analysis and planning, and so it is divided into more specific strategic units. A popular name for these units is the *strategic business unit* (SBU). Typically, SBUs display product and customer group similarities. A strategic business unit is a single product or brand, a line of products, or a mix of related products that meets a common market need or a group of related needs, and the unit's management is responsible for all (or most) of the basic business functions. The characteristics of the ideal SBU are described in Exhibit 2–2. Typically, the SBU has a specific strategy rather than a shared

EXHIBIT 2–2
Characteristics of the Ideal Strategic Business Unit

Source: Orville C. Walker, Jr., Harper W. Boyd, Jr., and Jean-Claud Larréché, *Marketing Strategy* (Burr Ridge, IL: Richard D. Irwin, 1992), 76.

Characteristic	Rationale
• Serves a homogeneous set of markets with a limited number of related technologies	Minimizing the diversity of a business unit's product-market entries enables the unit's manager to do a better job of formulating and implementing a coherent and internally consistent business strategy.
• Serves a unique set of product-markets	No other SBU within the firm should compete for the same set of customers with similar products. This enables the firm to avoid duplication of effort and helps maximize economies of scale within its SBUs.
• Has control over the factors necessary for successful performance, such as R&D, production, marketing, and distribution	This is not to say that an SBU should never share resources, such as a manufacturing plant or a sales force, with one or more business units, but the SBU should have authority to determine how its share of the joint resource will be used to effectively carry out its strategy.
• Has responsibility for its own profitability	Because top management cannot keep an eye on every decision and action taken by all its SBUs, the success of an SBU and its managers must be judged by monitoring its performance over time. Thus, the SBU's managers should have control over the factors that affect performance and then be held accountable for the outcomes.

strategy with another business area. It is a cohesive organizational unit that is separately managed and produces sales and profit results.

Virgin Group is an interesting example of the formation of a large and diverse portfolio of business enterprises. The founder, Richard Branson, was knighted in the United Kingdom in 2000 for his entrepreneurship initiatives in launching an array of businesses under the Virgin Group corporate umbrella. The Virgin brand identifies hundreds of products from travel to financial services to entertainment.[14] Not all of the Virgin Group's initiatives have been successful, and some observers indicate that Branson may have overleveraged the brand. Nonetheless, those ventures have made him a very wealthy entrepreneur.

In a business that has two or more strategic business units, decisions must be made at two levels. Corporate management must first decide what business areas to pursue and set priorities for allocating resources to each SBU. The decision makers for each SBU must select the strategies for implementing the corporate strategy and producing the results that corporate management expects. Corporate-level management is often involved in helping SBUs achieve their objectives.

Corporate strategy and resources should help the SBU compete more effectively than it would if the unit operated on a completely independent basis. "To remain competitive, corporations must provide their business units with low-cost capital, outstanding executives, corporate R&D, centralized marketing where appropriate and other resources in the corporate arsenal."[15] Corporate resources and synergies help the SBU establish its competitive advantage. The strategic focus and priorities of corporate strategy guide SBU strategies. Finally, top management's expectations for the corporation indicate the results expected from an SBU, including both financial and nonfinancial objectives. When viewed in this context, the SBUs become the action centers of the corporation. One criticism of the SBU concept is that distinctive competencies are not leveraged across a corporation's businesses. However, the successful vertical movement of the retailer Gap into the higher quality/price apparel segment with Banana Republic and that of Old Navy into the lower quality/price segment suggest just the opposite. Both initiatives leveraged Gap's competencies in design, outsourcing, and retail operations and merchandising.

Structure, Systems, and Processes

This aspect of strategy considers how the organization controls and coordinates the activities of its various business units and staff functions.[16] Structure determines the composition of the corporation. Systems are the formal policies and procedures that enable the organization to operate. Processes consider the informal aspects of the organization's activities:

> In establishing a firm's infrastructure, corporate managers have a wide array of organizational mechanisms at their disposal, from the formal boxes in an organization chart to the more subtle elements of corporate culture and style. Because every corporate strategy is different, there is not one optimal set of structures, systems, and processes.[17]

The logic of how the business is designed is receiving considerable attention because of the threat of customers being attracted by designs that better satisfy their needs and requirements. "A business design is the totality of how a company selects its customers, defines and differentiates its offerings, defines the tasks it will perform itself and those it will outsource, configures its resources, goes to market, creates utility for customers, and captures profit."[18] The business design (or business model) provides a focus on more than the product and/or technology, instead looking at the processes and relationships that comprise the design. For example, Dell Computer's direct, built-to-order business design is viewed by many business buyers as offering superior value.

The "no-frills" business design of very successful airlines like easyJet in Europe provides very low air fares, but is based on systems and processes completely different to those of conventional airlines (and extremely difficult for them to imitate). The strength of this model is underlined by easyJet's expansion into "no-frills" automobile rental and other services.

Corporate Competitive Advantage

This part of corporate strategy looks at whether the strategy components create value through multimarket activity.[19] The strategic issues include evaluating the extent to which a business contributes positive benefits somewhere in the corporation and whether the corporation creates more value for the business than might be created by another owner.

Business and Marketing Strategy

During the 1990s many strategy guidelines were offered by consultants, executives, and academics to guide business strategy formulation. These strategy paradigms propose a range of actions, including reengineering the corporation, total quality management, building distinctive competencies, reinventing the organization, and strategic partnering. It is not feasible to review here the various strategy concepts and methods that are available in many books, seminars, and consulting services. The corporate strategy framework presented in this chapter offers a basis for incorporating relevant strategy perspectives and guidelines.

An important issue is whether selecting a successful strategy has an impact on results. Does the uncontrollable environment largely determine business performance or, instead, will the organization's strategy have a major impact on its performance? Successful businesses can be found operating in very demanding market and competitive environments. Examples include Southwest Airlines (air travel), General Electric (electronics), and Wal-Mart (discount retailing). Of course, favorable environments would further enhance the performance of these companies.

The evidence suggests that strategic choices matter.[20] While environmental factors such as market demand, intensity of competition, government, and social change influence corporate performance, the strategic choices made by specific companies also have a significant impact on their performance. Importantly, the impact may be positive or negative. For example, Kmart held the leading market position over Wal-Mart in 1980, yet Wal-Mart overtook Kmart by investing heavily in information systems and distribution to develop a powerful customer-driven, low-cost retail network. Kmart declared bankruptcy in early 2002.

Developing the Strategic Plan for Each Business

Strategic analysis is conducted to (1) diagnose business units' strengths and limitations and (2) select strategies for maintaining or improving performance. Management decides what priority to place on each business regarding resource allocation and implements a strategy to meet the objectives for the SBU. The strategic plan indicates the action agenda for the business. An example of a business plan outline is shown in Exhibit 2–3. The "major strategies" shown in Part VI of the plan include the strategic actions planned for business devel-

EXHIBIT 2–3
Plan Outline— A High-Technology Products Manufacturer

Source: Rochelle O'Connor, *Facing Strategic Issues: New Planning Guides and Practices,* Report No. 87 (New York: The Conference Board, 1985), 32.

I.	Management Summary
II.	Business Definition
	—Mission
	—Purpose
	—Role
III.	Progress Report
	—Comparison of key financial and market indicators
	—Progress made on major strategies
IV.	Market and Customer Analysis
	—Potential versus served market
	—Market segmentation
V.	Competitive Analysis
	—Description of three major competitors
	—Analysis of competitors' strategies
VI.	Objectives, Strategies, and Programs
	—Key objectives
	—Major strategies to accomplish the objectives
	—Action programs to implement strategies
	—Major assumptions and contingency programs
	—Market share matrix
VII.	Financial Projections
	—Financial projections statement
	—Personnel projections

opment, marketing, quality, product and technology, human resources, manufacturing/facilities, and finance.

The situation assessment provides a guide for establishing the SBU's mission, setting objectives, and determining the strategy to use to meet those objectives. The SBU's strategy indicates market target priorities, available resources, financial constraints, and other strategic guidelines needed to develop marketing plans. Depending on the size and diversity of the SBU, marketing plans may be included in the SBU plan or developed separately. If they are combined, the marketing portion of the business plan will represent a substantial part of the business plan. In a small business (e.g., retail store, restaurant) the marketing portion of the plan will account for most of the plan. Plans may be developed to obtain financial support for a new venture or to spell out internal business and marketing strategies.

Business Strategy and Marketing Strategy

An understanding of a business's purpose, scope, objectives, capabilities, and strategy is essential in designing and implementing marketing strategies that are consistent with the corporate and business unit plan of action.

The chief marketing executive's business strategy responsibilities include (1) participating in strategy formulation and (2) developing marketing strategies that are consistent with business strategy priorities and integrated with other functional strategies. Since these two areas are closely interrelated, it is important to examine marketing's role and functions in both areas to gain insight into marketing's responsibilities and contributions. Peter F. Drucker describes this role:

> Marketing is so basic that it cannot be considered a separate function (i.e., a separate skill or work) within the business, on a par with others such as manufacturing or personnel. Marketing requires separate work, and a distinct group of activities. But it is, first, a central dimension of the entire business. It is the whole business seen from the point of view of its final result, that is, from the customer's point of view.[21]

Frederick E. Webster describes the role of the marketing manager: "At the corporate level, marketing managers have a critical role to play as advocates for the customer and for a set of values and beliefs that put the customer first in the firm's decision making, and to communicate the value proposition as part of that culture throughout the organization, both internally and in its multiple relationships and alliances."[22] This role includes assessing market attractiveness in the markets available to the firm, providing a customer orientation, and communicating the firm's specific value advantages.

Strategic Marketing

Marketing strategy consists of the analysis, strategy development, and implementation activities in:

> Developing a vision about the market(s) of interest to the organization, selecting market target strategies, setting objectives, and developing, implementing, and managing the marketing program positioning strategies designed to meet the value requirements of the customers in each market target.

Strategic marketing is a market-driven process of strategy development that takes into account a constantly changing business environment and the need to deliver superior customer value. The focus of strategic marketing is on organizational performance rather than on increasing sales. Marketing strategy seeks to deliver superior customer value by combining the customer-influencing strategies of the business into a coordinated set of market-driven actions. Strategic marketing links the organization with the environment and views marketing as a responsibility of the entire business rather than a specialized function.

Because of marketing's boundary orientation between the organization and its customers, channel members, and competition, marketing processes are central to the business strategy planning process.[23] Strategic marketing provides the expertise for environmental monitoring, for deciding what customer groups to serve, for guiding product specifications, and for choosing which competitors to position against. Successfully integrating cross-functional strategies is critical to providing superior customer value. Customer value requirements must be transformed into product design and production guidelines. Success in achieving high-quality products and services requires finding out which attributes of product and service quality drive customer value.

Marketing Strategy Process

The marketing strategy process that we follow is described in Exhibit 2–4. The strategy stages shown are examined and applied in Parts II through V of this book. The strategic situation analysis considers market and competitor analysis, market segmentation, and continuous learning about markets. Designing marketing strategy examines customer targeting and positioning strategies, relationship strategies, and planning for new products. Marketing program development consists of product, distribution, price, and promotion strategies designed and implemented to meet the value requirements of targeted buyers. Strategy implementation and management consider organizational design and marketing strategy implementation and control. We provide an overview of each part of the strategy process in the rest of this chapter.

Strategic Situation Analysis

Marketing management uses the information provided by the situation analysis to guide the design of a new strategy or change an existing strategy. The situation analysis should be conducted on a continuing basis after the strategy is under way to guide strategy changes.

EXHIBIT 2–4
**Marketing
Strategy Process**

Strategic situation analysis

Designing marketing strategy

Marketing program development

Implementing and managing marketing strategy

Market Vision, Structure, and Analysis

Markets need to be defined so that buyers and competition can be analyzed. For a market to exist, (1) there must be people with particular needs and wants and one or more products that can satisfy buyers' needs, and (2) buyers must be willing and able to purchase a product that satisfies their needs and wants. A product-market consists of a specific product (or line of related products) that can satisfy a set of needs and wants for the people (or organizations) willing and able to purchase it. We use the term *product* to indicate either a physical good or an intangible service.

Analyzing product-markets and forecasting how they will change in the future are vital to business and marketing planning. Decisions to enter new product-markets, how to serve existing product-markets, and when to exit unattractive product-markets are critical strategic choices. The objective is to identify and describe the buyers, understand their preferences for products, estimate the size and rate of growth of the market, and find out what companies and products are competing in the market.

Evaluation of competitors' strategies, strengths, limitations, and plans is also a key aspect of the situation analysis. It is important to identify both existing and potential competitors. Competitor analysis includes evaluating each key competitor. The analyses highlight the competition's important strengths and weaknesses. A key issue is trying to figure out what each competitor is likely to do in the future.

Oracle Corporation provides an interesting example of how management has developed a vision about the Internet software market and how it is likely to change in the future. (See accompanying photograph of Oracle Corporation CEO). Oracle's 2001 sales were nearly $11 billion, double 1997 sales. Database software is the core business. As was discussed in the earlier Technology Feature, management wants to offer a suite of business applications which will allow users to run everything from accounting to customer management to Web sales. The software package is intended to provide users a simpler approach, since customers will need to purchase only one package from one company that suits all their needs. However, analysts contend that the launch might come too late and that Oracle will flounder if it really tries to create all the components of the suite itself. Oracle's proposed strategic initiatives are described in Exhibit 2–5.

Segmenting Markets

Market segmentation looks at the nature and extent of diversity of buyers' needs and wants in a market. It offers an opportunity for an organization to focus its business capabilities on the requirements of one or more groups of buyers. The objective of segmentation is to examine differences in needs and wants and identify the segments (subgroups) within the product-market of interest. Each segment contains buyers with similar needs and wants for the product category of interest to management. The segments are described using the various characteristics of people, the reasons they buy or use certain products, and their preferences for certain brands of products. Likewise, segments of industrial product-markets may be formed according to the type of industry, the uses for the product, the frequency of product purchase, and various other factors.

Each segment may vary quite a bit from the average characteristics of the entire product-market. The similarities of buyers' needs within a segment enable better targeting of the organization's value proposition to buyers with corresponding value requirements. For example, active individuals comprise an important market segment for Gatorade, the popular thirst-quenching sports drink. Teenagers are an important market segment for carbonated beverages since they have not yet developed strong brand preferences.

Chairman of the Oracle Corporation Larry Ellison speaks during a keynote presentation at the COMDEX technology convention November 13, 2000 in Las Vegas. Many corporations were in attendance at one of the largest annual computer conventions in the nation. Djamel E. Ramoul/Liaison.

Continuous Learning about Markets

One of the major realities of achieving business success today is the need to understand markets and competition. Sensing what is happening and is likely to occur in the future is complicated by competitive threats that may exist beyond traditional industry boundaries. For example, microwave dinners compete with McDonald's fast food, CD-ROMs compete with books, and fax transmission competes with overnight letter delivery.

Market-driven firms are able to sense what is happening in their markets, develop business and marketing strategies to seize opportunities and counter threats, and anticipate what the market will be like in the future.[24] Several market sensing methods are available to guide the collection and analysis of information. For example, company databases on customers offer valuable data mining opportunities.

Designing Market-Driven Strategies

The strategic situation analysis phase of the marketing strategy process identifies market opportunities, defines market segments, evaluates competition, and assesses the organization's strengths and weaknesses. Market sensing information plays a key role in designing marketing strategy, which includes market targeting and positioning strategies, building marketing relationships, and developing and introducing new products. The Strategy

EXHIBIT 2–5
**Assembling an
E-Business
Powerhouse**

Source: Steve Hamm,
"Oracle: Why It's Cool
Again," *Business Week,* May
8, 2000, 120.

Oracle Corp.'s software is the foundation for websites, e-commerce, and corporate networks. Here are its most crucial markets:

Data Storehouses	Business Applications	E-Marketplaces
Database software for storing and analyzing corporate data, inventories,	*For running everything from accounting to customer management to Web sales.*	*Website and internal software for transactions between companies, including auctions.and customer info.*
MARKET SIZE $10.5 billion in 1999 for software and maintenance; heading for $16.6 billion in 2003.	**MARKET SIZE** $26 billion in 1999; heading for $33 billion this year.	**MARKET SIZE** $3.9 billion in 1999; heading for $18.6 billion in 2003.
ORACLE'S THIRD-QUARTER SALES Software-license sales grew 32%, to $778 million.	**ORACLE'S THIRD-QUARTER SALES** Up 35%, to $199 million.	**ORACLE'S THIRD-QUARTER SALES** $26 million for supply-chain and procurement software.
MARKET SHARE 40%, compared with 18% for IBM, 5.7% for Informix, and 5.1% for Microsoft.	**MARKET POSITION** Oracle is a distant second behind SAP in the market for core corporate applications. Siebel Systems leads in customer-management software.	**MARKET POSITION** The procurement market is expanding into e-exchanges, and Oracle is an early leader along with Commerce One, Ariba, and i2.
PROSPECTS Oracle dominates the database-software realm on both Unix and Windows NT operating systems. Analysts predict it will hold off the competition indefinitely, thanks to its strong technology and new cachet with dot-coms.	**PROSPECTS** In May, Oracle plans to release the most comprehensive package of business applications available. It has a good chance to gain market share because its applications are integrated, while others offer pieces that have to be stitched together.	**PROSPECTS** Oracle has deals to power exchanges for Ford, Sears, and Chevron and is expected to have staying power, thanks to its army of 7,000 software programmers.

Feature describes the market targeting and positioning strategies employed for the successful soap brand Lever 2000.

Market Targeting and Strategic Positioning

Marketing advantage is influenced by several situational factors, including industry characteristics, type of firm (e.g., size), extent of differentiation in buyers' needs, and the specific competitive advantage(s) of the company designing the marketing strategy. The core issue is deciding how, when, and where to compete, given a firm's market and competitive environment.

The purpose of the *market targeting strategy* is to select the people (or organizations) that management wishes to serve in the product-market. When buyers' needs and wants vary, the market target is usually one or more segments of the product-market. Once the

Lever Brothers, a New York unit of the Anglo-Dutch Unilever Group, has been competing with Procter & Gamble in the soap market for 100 years. In 1991, for the first time, Lever's toilet-soap market share ($) exceeded P&G's share (see insert). The Lever 2000 brand was a major contributor to Lever's share gain. It accounted for $113 million in sales out of a market total of $1.6 billion. The targeting and positioning of Lever 2000 were major factors in the brand's successful performance.

TARGETING STRATEGY

• Entire family rather than different soaps for men, women, and children.

POSITIONING STRATEGY

• Positioned as "the mildest antibacterial soap ever created," "a soap for 2000 body parts." Heavy use of advertising ($25 million), sampling, and coupons to convince households that one soap will meet all of their needs. Premium priced compared to Ivory and Dove.

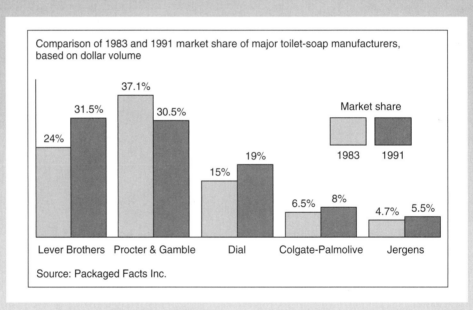

Comparison of 1983 and 1991 market share of major toilet-soap manufacturers, based on dollar volume

Source: Packaged Facts Inc.

Source: Valerie Reilman, "Buoyant Sales of Lever 2000 Soap Bring Sinking Sensation to Procter & Gamble," *The Wall Street Journal,* March 19, 1992, B1 and B8. Copyright 1992 by Dow Jones & Company, Inc. Reproduced with permission of Dow Jones & Company, Inc., in the format textbook via Copyright Clearance Center.

segments are identified and their relative importance to the firm is determined, the targeting strategy is selected. The objective is to find the best match between the value requirements of each segment and the organization's distinctive capabilities. The targeting decision is the focal point of marketing strategy since targeting guides the setting of objectives and the development of a positioning strategy. The options range from targeting most of the segments to targeting one or a few segments in a product-market. The targeting strategy may be influenced by the market's maturity, the diversity of buyers' needs and preferences, the firm's size compared to the competition, corporate resources and priorities, and the volume of sales required to achieve favorable financial results. Deciding the objectives for each market target spells out the results expected by management. Examples of market target objectives are sales, market share, customer retention, profit contribution, and customer satisfaction. Marketing objectives may also be set for the entire business unit and for specific marketing activities such as advertising and personal selling.

The targeting and positioning strategies used by ConAgra Inc. for the Healthy Choice frozen food line helped the new brand successfully enter the market in the early 1990s. The low-calorie, low-cholesterol, low-sodium frozen food line quickly gained a strong market position.[25] Frozen food is a very competitive supermarket category because freezer space in stores is limited. Healthy Choice was introduced into the stagnant male-oriented frozen dinner segment of the market. It was positioned as a "health product." This positioning was successful even though it conflicts with conventional marketing guidelines: the female-oriented frozen food is the rapid growth segment, and "health" positioning had been used to describe poor-tasting, low-calorie brands. Health is an issue of great concern to men, and the taste of Healthy Choice is appealing to consumers who try the brand. The new line of frozen foods gained an impressive 25 percent market share in the $700 million frozen dinner market. Healthy Choice extended its brand in the early 1990s to include breakfast items, deli meats, and soups. By 1992 intense price competition, new products, and the promotion actions of the competition eroded Healthy Choice's share of the frozen dinner market, demonstrating the realities of competing against experienced food marketers. Nonetheless, during the 1990s Healthy Choice built a strong brand position across several food categories.

The marketing program *positioning strategy* is the combination of product, value chain, price, and promotion strategies a firm uses to position itself against its key competitors in meeting the needs and wants of the market target. The strategies and tactics used to gain a favorable position are called the marketing mix or the marketing program.

The positioning strategy seeks to position the brand in the eyes and mind of the buyer and distinguish the product from the competition. The product, distribution, price, and promotion strategy components make up a bundle of actions that are used to influence buyers' positioning of a brand. General Motors Corp.'s (GMC) positioning problems with its automobile brands illustrate the strategic importance of positioning. In 1995 GMC launched a major marketing effort to reposition its brands. The objective was to identify the market segment targeted by each brand and develop a unique positioning strategy appropriate for the target. The problem is that GM's car brands are perceived by many buyers to be very similar. The objective of GM's new strategy is to give each brand a distinct identity geared to the preferences of the brand's market target. GM's management decided to drop the Oldsmobile brand in 2000, apparently unable to sustain a competitive position for that brand.

Marketing Relationship Strategies

Marketing relationship partners may include end-user customers, marketing channel members, suppliers, competitor alliances, and internal teams. The driving force underlying these relationships is that a company may enhance its ability to satisfy customers and cope with a rapidly changing business environment through the collaboration of the parties involved. Relationship strategies gained new importance in the 1990s as customers became more demanding and competition became more intense. Building long-term relationships with customers and value-chain partners offers companies a way to provide superior customer value. Although building collaborative relationships may not always be the best course of action, this avenue for gaining a competitive edge is increasing in popularity.

Strategic partnering is an important strategic initiative for many well-known companies and brands. Many firms outsource the manufacturing of their products. Examples include Motorola cell phones, Baskin-Robbins ice cream, Calvin Klein jeans, Pepsi beverages, and Nike footwear. Strong relationships with outsourcing partners are vital to the success of these powerful brands. The trend in the 21st century is partnering rather than vertical integration.

Planning for New Products

New products are needed to replace old products because of declining sales and profits. Strategies for developing and positioning new market entries involve all the functions of the business. Closely coordinated new product planning is essential to satisfy customer requirements and produce products with high quality at competitive prices. New product decisions include finding and evaluating ideas, selecting the most promising for development, designing marketing programs, market testing the products, and introducing them to the market.

The new product planning process starts by identifying gaps in customer satisfaction. The differences between existing product attributes and those desired by customers offer opportunities for new and improved products. One of the leaders in product innovation is Minnesota Mining and Manufacturing (3M). It has a reputation for developing products faster and better than most companies can.[26] The new product success guidelines that 3M follows include (1) keeping business units small, (2) encouraging experimentation and risk taking, (3) motivating and rewarding innovators, (4) staying close to the customer, (5) sharing technology with other firms, and (6) avoiding killing the projects of staff advocates.

Market-Focused Program Development

Market targeting and positioning strategies for new and existing products guide the choice of strategies for the marketing program components. Product, distribution, price, and promotion strategies are combined to form the positioning strategy selected for each market target. The relationship of the positioning components to the market target is shown in Exhibit 2–6.

EXHIBIT 2–6
Positioning Strategy Development

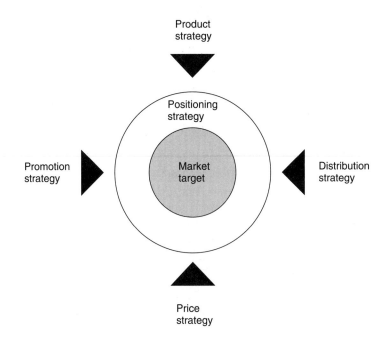

- Global brand strategy.

  Largest branded food company in Mexico, Brazil, Chile, and Thailand—building rapidly in Vietnam and China.

  Builds both a manufacturing and a political presence.

  Negotiated over a decade to get into China.

- Owns nearly 8,000 brands worldwide—but only 750 are registered in more than one country—only 80 in 10 countries.

  The ingredients or processing technology are adapted for local conditions—often using the local brand name.

- Moves into a new market with a handful of labels—from its 11 strategic brand groups.

  Nestlé is the market leader in instant coffee in Australia (71%), France (67%), Japan (74%), and Mexico (85%).·

- Nestlé's Thailand manager has worked there for 30 years.

  The 100 managers worldwide stay in only one region of the world (a key competitive advantage because they know local markets, competition, and governmental requirements).

  Coffee sales in Thailand were $25 million (1987) to $100 million (1994).

- Developed an entire milk distribution system in China from the farmer to the factory—produced 10,000 tons of powdered milk in 1994 ($700 million in sales by 2000).

- Nestlé is importing sales team and brand management techniques to supermarket chains in Thailand and other countries in the region.

Source: Carla Rapoport, "Nestlé's Brand Building Machine," *Fortune,* September 19, 1994, 147–8, 150, 154, 156.

The marketing program (mix) strategies implement the positioning strategy.[27] The objective is to achieve favorable positioning while allocating financial, human, and production resources to markets, customers, and products as effectively and efficiently as possible.

Strategic Brand Management

Products (goods and services) often are the focal point of positioning strategy, particularly when companies or business units adopt organizational approaches that emphasize product or brand management. Product strategy includes (1) developing plans for new products, (2) managing programs for successful products, and (3) deciding what to do about problem products (e.g., reduce costs or improve the product). Strategic brand management consists of building brand value (equity) and managing the organization's system of brands for overall performance.

Nestlé, the Swiss food company, has a successful product and brand management strategy for competing in world markets. As described in the Global Feature, the company's brand strategy includes responding to local preferences, providing career tracks to keep managers in the same regional areas, and applying global food processing technology to gain cost and quality advantages.

Value Chain, Price, and Promotion Strategies

One of the major issues in managing the marketing program is deciding how to integrate the components of the mix. Product, distribution, price, and promotion strategies are shaped into a coordinated plan of action. Each component helps influence buyers in their positioning of products. If the activities of these mix components are not coordinated, the actions may conflict and resources may be wasted. For example, if the advertising messages for a company's brand stress quality and performance but salespeople emphasize low price, buyers will be confused and brand damage may occur.

Market target buyers may be contacted on a direct basis using the firm's sales force or by direct marketing contact (e.g., Internet) or, instead, through a value-added chain (distribution channel) of marketing intermediaries (e.g., wholesalers, retailers, or dealers). Distribution channels are often used in linking producers with end-user household and business markets. Decisions that need to be made include the type of channel organization to use, the extent of channel management performed by the firm, and the intensity of distribution appropriate for the product or service. The choice of distribution channels influences buyers' positioning of the brand. For example, expensive watches such as the Rolex brand are available from a limited number of retailers with prestigious images. These retailers help reinforce the brand's image.

Price also plays an important role in positioning a product or service. Customer reaction to alternative prices, the cost of the product, the prices of the competition, and various legal and ethical factors establish the extent of the flexibility management has in setting prices. Price strategy involves choosing the role of price in the positioning strategy, including the desired positioning of the product or brand as well as the margins necessary to satisfy and motivate distribution channel participants. Price may be used as an active (visible) component of marketing strategy or, instead, marketing emphasis may be on other marketing mix components (e.g., product quality).

Advertising, sales promotion, the sales force, direct marketing, and public relations help the organization communicate with its customers, value-chain partners, the public, and other target audiences. These activities make up the promotion strategy, which performs an essential role in communicating the positioning strategy to buyers and other relevant parties. Promotion informs, reminds, and persuades buyers and others who influence the purchasing process. Hundreds of billions of dollars are spent annually on promotion activities. This mandates planning and executing promotion decisions as effectively and efficiently as possible.

Implementing and Managing Market-Driven Strategy

Selecting the customers to target and the positioning strategy for each target moves marketing strategy development to the action stage (Exhibit 2–4), which involves designing the marketing organization and implementing and managing the strategy.

Designing Effective Market-Driven Organizations

An effective organization design matches people and work responsibilities in a way that is best for accomplishing the firm's marketing strategy. Deciding how to assemble people into organizational units and assigning responsibility to the various mix components that make up the marketing strategy are important influences on performance. Organizational structures and processes must be matched to the business and marketing strategies that are developed and implemented. Organizational design needs to be evaluated on a regular basis to assess its adequacy and identify necessary changes. Restructuring and reengineering of many organizations in the 1990s led to many changes in the structures of marketing units. Organizational change continues to be an important initiative in the 21st century.

Strategy Implementation and Control

Marketing strategy implementation and control consists of (1) preparing the marketing plan and budget, (2) implementing the plan, and (3) using the plan in managing and controlling the strategy on an ongoing basis. The marketing plan includes details concerning targeting, positioning, and marketing mix activities. The plan spells out what is going to happen over the planning period, who is responsible, how much it will cost, and the expected results (e.g., sales forecasts). We discuss the preparation of the marketing plan in the last section of the chapter.

The marketing plan includes action guidelines for the activities to be implemented, who does what, the dates and location of implementation, and how implementation will be accomplished. Several factors contribute to implementation effectiveness, including the skills of the people involved, organizational design, incentives, and the effectiveness of communication within the organization and externally.

Marketing strategy is an ongoing process of making decisions, implementing them, and gauging their effectiveness over time. In terms of its time requirements, strategic evaluation is far more demanding than planning is. Evaluation and control are concerned with tracking performance and, when necessary, altering plans to keep performance on track. Evaluation also includes looking for new opportunities and potential threats in the future. It is the connecting link in the strategic marketing planning process shown in Exhibit 2–4. By serving as both the last stage and the first stage (evaluation before taking action) in the planning process, strategic evaluation assures that strategy is an ongoing activity.

Rubbermaid Inc. offers an interesting insight into evaluation and control. After more than a decade of superior performance, the company experienced problems in 1995.[28] Sales slowed down, and profits declined. Increases in the cost of the resin used in plastic products triggered price increases to retailers. This irritated retailers, who reduced Rubbermaid's shelf space. The already slow consumer demand for housewares was further affected by higher retail prices. Rubbermaid's management implemented cost reductions, speeded up new product introductions, and increased promotions to consumers to move results closer to expectations.

Internet Strategy

The explosive growth of Internet initiatives has resulted in a variety of Web strategies which may affect the business and marketing strategies of existing firms and lead to the formation of new business designs. We consider the reasons why the Internet is a major force for change and discuss alternative Internet strategies for existing companies and new business ventures.

Major Force for Change

The Internet era provides a new way of developing relationships between end-user customers, value-chain members, and alliance partners.[29] The Web offers a compelling opportunity to enhance one-on-one relationships. Such impressive knowledge systems enable organizations to link pricing, product, design, and promotion information with suppliers and customers. These new capabilities are not restricted to large organizations. Shirtmaker.com is a small Seoul-based tailoring business employing eleven tailors to produce bespoke shirts, where the Web page has allowed the customer to select the fabric, pocket type, cuff design, and monogram, if required. In 1999, the DaimlerChrysler Smart car (a two-seat city auto) became the first automobile that could be configured and ordered online.

Various strategic initiatives are altering the basic processes that underlie business transactions. The reverse auction is illustrative. The reverse results from prices being bid downward rather than upward. Suppliers of business-to-business companies have the opportunity via the Internet to offer competing bids to the customer. At the end of the process the low bid obtains the sale. Other Web-based initiatives are affecting buying processes. The effects can be dramatic. Major corporate buyers like Boeing and Motorola have warned that suppliers not making the transition to Web-based commerce may find themselves locked out of their businesses. The Covisint online exchange, formed by General Motors, Daimler-Chrysler and Ford and now including other auto manufacturers, already links tens of thousands of suppliers to these major customers, and is seen as a prototype for other "industry-led" online exchanges.

It is apparent that the Internet has a pervasive potential for change that is likely to affect a wide range of products and businesses. The challenge for existing businesses is to find a way to capture the advantages of the Internet without damaging important existing relationships. Avon Products Corp.'s challenge in sustaining its direct sales model while pursuing an Internet strategy is illustrative. In 2000, after 115 years of selling to the consumer at home, Avon changed strategy and took its products into department stores and shopping malls for the first time.

Strategy and the Internet

While some authorities argue that the Internet will make conventional strategies obsolete, a more compelling logic is that the Internet is a powerful complement to traditional business and marketing strategies.[30] Nonetheless, competitive boundaries are likely to be altered and competition will become more intense. Tesco, the leading British supermarket retailer, illustrates both points. Tesco has adopted a "bricks and clicks" strategy for its Tesco Direct online business, combining the strength of its chain of stores with Internet-based ordering. Groceries are selected on a Web page reflecting the customer's local store, and are picked manually from the shelves of that same store for delivery to the customer. No additional warehousing or picking facilities are required. Tesco is now leveraging its online customer base to sell a growing range of high margin nonfood products, from fresh flowers to apparel, as well as financial services. They may even sell automobiles by this route.

While there are many specific strategy initiatives regarding the Internet, they correspond to one of the following:

- Formation of a separate business model as an independent venture or an initiative by an existing company.

   Book retailer Amazon.Com Inc. is an example of the former, whereas Sabre's Travelocity.Com venture was initiated by an existing company.

- Creation of a separate value-chain channel direct from the producer to the end-user.

   Dell computer uses this Internet strategy.

- Using the Internet as an information resource.

   This initiative is used by various organizations, such as *Business Week.*

- Using the Web for advertising and sales promotion activities.

   These activities may be provided for one or more sponsors by a Web-based enterprise that offers users information at no charge. Ad revenues support the enterprise.

Despite some clear advantages—backing from such savvy financiers as Goldman Sachs and Sequoia Capital, a well-respected management team led until April by former Andersen Consulting chief George Shaheen, and more than $1 billion in cash—Webvan's business model was fundamentally untenable. It simply made little sense to pour huge amounts of capital into the grocery business—which ekes out net margins averaging barely over 1%—without evidence that enough shoppers would change their habits.

But Webvan built a huge infrastructure that could only work if droves of consumers quickly embraced buying their peaches and plenty more online. That never happened. What's more, Webvan depended too much on technology as the driver of its business while overlooking the basics of the grocery industry. "We made the assumption that capital was endless, and demand was endless," new CEO Robert Swan said in a June interview.

Bad assumptions both. In its short life, Webvan burned through more than $1 billion building automated warehouses and pricey tech gear. Never was the overspending clearer than when Webvan merged with rival HomeGrocer.com last year. Its go-for-broke approach stood in stark contrast to HomeGrocer's slower moving, more conservative strategy.

Webvan shelled out more than $25 million for each of its massive facilities vs. Home-Grocer's $5 million or so for smaller, lower-tech operations. Webvan's warehouses needed some 1,000 servers and 16 employees to run the back end, but HomeGrocer's got by with just 100 servers and two employees, insiders say. And while Webvan needed about 4,000 orders a day to break even per facility, HomeGrocer required just 1,500. . . .

So does Webvan's failure mean that online grocers' prospects are no better than that of a carton of milk past the sell-by date? Not necessarily. Some believe it can still be a solid business, though one that will likely mature more slowly than anything Webvan anticipated. A soon-to-be-released study from IBM's consulting arm predicts that by 2004, enough demand will exist in some metropolitan areas to support at least three profitable grocers in those markets. "There is demand, and there are profitable ways of servicing these markets," says IBM's Ming Tsai.

Source: Linda Himelstein, "Commentary," *Business Week,* July 23, 2001, 43.

An organization may pursue more than one of these initiatives, and the strategies may be interrelated. Also, alliances may be formed between traditional companies and Internet ventures. The strategic alliance between Toys-R-Us and Amazon.com is an example.

Independent Internet business models have experienced several failures. In more than a few cases the failures have been due to management's optimistic estimation of patronage and failure to consider basic business and marketing strategy guidelines. The analysis of Webvan's lack of success in the Internet groceries market is described in the E-Business Feature.

Internet strategy is further considered in Chapters 10 and 13. E-Business and Technology Features are included in many chapters.

Preparing the Marketing Plan

Marketing plans vary widely in scope and detail. Nevertheless, all plans need to be based on analyses of the product-market and segments, the industry and competitive structure, and the organization's value proposition. We look at several important planning considerations that provide a checklist for plan preparation.

Planning Relationships and Frequency

Marketing plans are developed, implemented, evaluated, and adjusted to keep the strategy on target. Since the marketing strategy normally extends beyond one year, it is useful to develop a three-year strategic plan and an annual plan to manage marketing activities during the year. Budgets for marketing activities (e.g., advertising) are set annually. Planning is really a series of annual plans guided by the marketing strategic plan.

The frequency of planning activities varies by company and marketing activity. Market targeting and positioning strategies are not changed significantly during the year. Tactical changes in product, distribution, price, and promotion strategies may be included in the annual plan. For example, the aggressive response of competitors to Healthy Choice's successful market entry required changes in ConAgra's pricing and promotion tactics for the frozen food line.

Planning Considerations

Suppose you need to develop a plan for a new product to be introduced into the national market next year. The plan for the introduction should include the expected results (objectives), market targets, actions, responsibilities, schedules, and dates. The plan indicates details and deadlines, product plans, a market introduction program, advertising and sales promotion actions, employee training, and other information necessary to launch the product. The plan needs to answer a series of questions—what, when, where, who, how, and why—for each action targeted for completion during the planning period.

Responsibility for Preparing Plans

A marketing executive or team is responsible for preparing the marketing plan. Some companies combine the business plan and the marketing plan into a single planning activity. Regardless of the format used, the marketing plan is developed in close coordination with the strategic plan for the business. There is also much greater emphasis today on involving all business functions in the marketing planning process. A product or marketing manager may draft the formal plan for his or her area of responsibility, coordinating and receiving inputs from advertising, marketing research, sales, and other marketing specialists. Coordination with other business functions (R&D, finance, operations) is also essential.

Planning Unit

The choice of the planning unit may vary due to the product-market portfolio of the organization. Some firms plan and manage by individual products or brands. Others work with product lines, markets, or specific customers. The planning unit may reflect how marketing activities and responsibilities are organized. The market target is a useful focus for planning regardless of how the plan is aggregated. Using the target as the basis for planning helps place the customer in the center of the planning process and keeps the positioning strategy linked to the market target.

Preparing the Marketing Plan

The Conference Board offers several examples of plan formats in its excellent reports on marketing planning.[31] Format and content depend on the size of the organization, managerial responsibility for planning, product and market scope, and other situational factors. An outline for a typical marketing plan is shown in Exhibit 2–7. We take a brief look at the

EXHIBIT 2–7
**Outline for
Preparing an
Annual
Marketing Plan**

Strategic Situation Summary
A summary of the strategic situation for the planning unit (business unit, market segment, product line, etc.).

Market Target(s) Description
Define and describe each market target, including customer profiles, customer preferences and buying habits, size and growth estimates, distribution channels, analysis of key competitors, and guidelines for positioning strategy.

Objectives for the Market Target(s)
Set objectives for the market target (such as market position, sales, and profits). Also state objectives for each component of the marketing program. Indicate how each objective will be measured.

Marketing Program Positioning Strategy
State how management wants the firm to be positioned relative to the competition in the eyes and mind of the buyer.

A. *Product Strategy*
   Set strategy for new products, product improvements, and product deletions.
B. *Distribution Strategy*
   Indicate the strategy to be used for each distribution channel, including role of middlemen, assistance and support provided, and specific activities planned.
C. *Price Strategy*
   Specify the role of price in the marketing strategy and the planned actions regarding price.
D. *Promotion Strategy*
   Indicate the planned strategy and actions for advertising, publicity, Internet, personal selling, and sales promotion.
E. *Marketing Research*
   Identify information needs and planned projects, objectives, estimated costs, and timetable.
F. *Coordination with Other Business Functions*
   Specify the responsibilities and activities of other departments that have an important influence on the planned marketing strategy.

Forecasts and Budgets
Forecast sales and profit for the marketing plan and prepare the budget for accomplishing the forecast.

major parts of the planning outline to illustrate the nature and scope of the planning process. In this discussion the market target serves as the planning unit.

The Situation Summary

This part of the plan describes the market and its important characteristics, size estimates, and growth projections. Market segmentation analysis indicates the segments to be targeted and their relative importance. The competitor analysis indicates the key competitors (actual and potential), their strengths and weaknesses, probable future actions, and the organization's competitive advantage(s) in each segment of interest. The summary should be very brief. Supporting information for the summary can be placed in an appendix or in a separate analysis.

Describe the Market Target

A description of each market target, size and growth rate, end-users' characteristics, positioning strategy guidelines, and other available information useful in planning and implementation are essential parts of the plan. When two or more targets are involved, it is helpful to indicate priorities for guiding resource allocation.

Objectives for the Market Target(s)

Here we spell out what the marketing strategy is expected to accomplish during the planning period. Objectives are needed for each market target, indicating financial performance, sales, market position, customer satisfaction, and other desired results. Objectives are usually included for each marketing program component.

Marketing Program Positioning Strategy

The positioning statement indicates how management wants the targeted customers and prospects to perceive the brand. Specific strategies and tactics for product, distribution, price, and promotion are explained in this part of the plan. Actions to be taken, responsibilities, time schedules, and other implementation information are included at this point in the plan.

Planning and implementation responsibilities often involve more than one person or department. One approach is to assign a planning team the responsibility for each market target and marketing mix component. Product and geographical responsibilities are sometimes allocated to individuals or teams. The responsibilities and coordination requirements need to be indicated for marketing units and other business functions. Importantly, the planning process should encourage participation from all the areas responsible for implementing the plan. Contingency plans may be included in the plan. The contingencies consider possible actions if the anticipated planning environment is different from what actually occurs.

Forecasting and Budgeting

Financial planning includes forecasting revenues and profits and estimating the costs necessary to carry out the marketing plan (see the Appendix to Chapter 2 for financial analysis details). The people responsible for market target, product, geographical area, or other units should prepare the forecasts and budgets. Comparative data on sales, profits, and expenses for prior years are useful to link the plan to previous results.

International Planning Process

The major phases of planning for a multinational firm operating in several countries are shown in Exhibit 2–8. The first step in the planning process is the market opportunity analysis. This may represent a major activity for a company that is entering a foreign market for the first time. Several applications are discussed in subsequent chapters. Because of the risks and uncertainties in international markets, the market assessment is very important for both new market entrants and experienced firms.

Phase 1 determines which targets to pursue and establishes relative priorities for resource allocation. Phase 2 fits the positioning strategy to each target market. The objective is to match the mix requirements to the needs identified and the positioning concept management selects. Phase 3 consists of the preparation of the marketing plan. Included are the situation assessment, objectives, strategy and tactics, budgets and forecasts, and action programs. Finally, in Phase 4, the plan is implemented and managed. Results are evaluated and strategies are adjusted when necessary to improve results. Although the international marketing planning process is similar to planning domestic marketing strategies, the environment is far more complex and uncertain in international markets.

EXHIBIT 2–8
**International
Planning Process**

Source: Philip R. Cateora, *International Marketing,* 9th ed. (Burr Ridge, IL: Richard D. Irwin, 1996), 335.

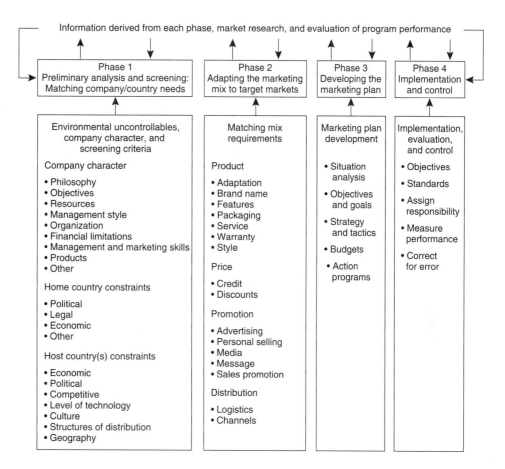

Information derived from each phase, market research, and evaluation of program performance

Phase 1	Phase 2	Phase 3	Phase 4
Preliminary analysis and screening: Matching company/country needs	Adapting the marketing mix to target markets	Developing the marketing plan	Implementation and control

Environmental uncontrollables, company character, and screening criteria	Matching mix requirements	Marketing plan development	Implementation, evaluation, and control
Company character • Philosophy • Objectives • Resources • Management style • Organization • Financial limitations • Management and marketing skills • Products • Other **Home country constraints** • Political • Legal • Economic • Other **Host country(s) constraints** • Economic • Political • Competitive • Level of technology • Culture • Structures of distribution • Geography	**Product** • Adaptation • Brand name • Features • Packaging • Service • Warranty • Style **Price** • Credit • Discounts **Promotion** • Advertising • Personal selling • Media • Message • Sales promotion **Distribution** • Logistics • Channels	• Situation analysis • Objectives and goals • Strategy and tactics • Budgets • Action programs	• Objectives • Standards • Assign responsibility • Measure performance • Correct for error

Summary

Strategy formulation for the corporation includes (1) defining the corporate mission and setting objectives, (2) determining strategic business units, and (3) establishing strategy guidelines for long-term strategic planning of the corporation and its business units. Top management must select the corporate strategy to move the firm toward its objectives. After implementing the strategy, management considers how the strategy is progressing and what adjustments are needed. Successfully executing these steps requires penetrating and insightful analyses.

The corporate vision or mission statement spells out the nature and scope of the business and provides strategic direction for the corporation. The firm's objectives indicate the performance desired by management. If management decides to move away from the core business, several paths of corporate development are possible, including expansion into new products and/or markets as well as diversification.

The available evidence indicates that well-formulated and well-executed business strategies lead to superior performance. While there are several approaches to strategy development, they have common features, including the objective of superior customer value, achieving a market orientation, and competing with distinctive capabilities.

Business unit strategies are guided by corporate strategy guidelines. The process begins by considering each business unit's market opportunity, position against the competition, financial situation and projections, and strengths and weaknesses. The situation analysis spells out the strategy alternatives for the business unit. Management selects a strategy and develops a strategic plan which is then implemented and managed.

Marketing strategy is an analysis, planning, implementation, and control process designed to satisfy customer needs and wants by providing superior customer value. The first part of the process includes product-market analysis, market segmentation, competition analysis, and continuous learning about markets. These analyses guide the choice of marketing strategy. Market definition establishes the overall competitive arena. Market segmentation describes possible customer groups for targeting by businesses. Competitor analysis looks at the strengths, weaknesses, and strategies of key competitors. Continuous learning about markets supplies information for analysis and decision making.

Designing the marketing strategy is the second stage in strategy development. The selection of the people (or organizations) to be targeted is guided by the situation analysis. The market target decision indicates the buyer groups whose needs are to be satisfied by the marketing program positioning strategy. The positioning strategy indicates how the firm will position itself against its key competitors in meeting the needs of the buyers in the market target. The relationship strategy spells out the extent of collaboration with consumers, other organizations, and company personnel. New product strategies are essential to generate a continuing stream of new entries to replace mature products that are eliminated.

The third phase of the strategy process consists of market-focused program development. Specific marketing mix strategies for products, distribution, price, and promotion must be developed to implement the positioning strategy management has selected. The objective is to combine the marketing mix components to accomplish market target objectives in a cost-effective manner.

The last phase of the process consists of marketing strategy implementation and management. These activities focus on the marketing organizational design and marketing strategy implementation and control. This is the action phase of marketing strategy.

The marketing plan indicates the actions to be taken, who is responsible, deadlines to be met, and the sales forecast and budget. The plan describes the marketing decisions and guides the implementation of the decisions and the evaluation and management of the marketing strategy.

Internet Applications

A.   Examine the websites of Borders (*www.borders.com*) and Amazon (*www.amazon.com*). Discuss the joint venture's approach to using a website as part of each company's competitive strategy.

B.   Examine the websites of ebay.com (*www.ebay.com*) and uBid.com (*www.uBid.com*). Compare and contrast the two approaches to using a website as part of each company's competitive strategy. Analyze the differences and similarities and suggest improvements as well as a marketing strategy for the two companies (i.e., solely Internet-based).

Questions for Review and Discussion

1.   Top management of companies probably devoted more time to reviewing (and sometimes changing) the corporate vision (mission) in the last decade than in any other period. Discuss the major reasons for this increased concern with the vision for the corporation.

2.   Discuss the role of organizational capabilities in corporate strategy.

3.   What is the relationship between the corporate strategy and the strategies for the businesses that comprise the corporate portfolio?

4.   Discuss the major issues that top management should consider when deciding whether to expand business operations into new business areas.

5. Discuss the environmental factors that should be assessed on a regular basis by a large retail corporation such as Target Corp.

6. Discuss what you consider to be the major issues in trying to divide a corporation into strategic business units, indicating for each problem suggestions for overcoming it.

7. Develop an outline of how you would explain the marketing strategy process to an inventor who is forming a new business to develop, produce, and market a new product.

8. Discuss the role of market targeting and positioning in an organization's marketing strategy.

9. What is the relationship between the strategic plan for a business in the corporate portfolio and the marketing plan for the business?

10. You have been asked to develop a marketing plan for a metropolitan bank that has six branch offices. How would you approach this assignment?

Notes

1. Jack Ewing, "Siemens Climbs Back," *Business Week*, June 5, 2000, 79, 80, 82.
2. Michael E. Porter, "What Is Strategy?," *Harvard Business Review*, November–December 1996, 74.
3. Raymond Miles and Charles Snow, "Fit, Failure, and the Hall of Fame," *California Management Review*, Spring 1984, 10–28; and James Brian Quinn, *Intelligent Enterprise* (New York: Free Press, 1992), chap. 5.
4. Preston Townley, Comments made by the Conference Board CEO during an address at Texas Christian University in Fort Worth, Texas, February 15, 1994.
5. David W. Cravens, Shannon H. Shipp, and Karen S. Cravens, "Reforming the Traditional Organization: The Mandate for Developing Networks," *Business Horizons*, July–August 1994, 19–28.
6. "The Virtual Corporation," *Business Week*, February 8, 1993, 98–102.
7. David J. Collis and Cynthia A. Montgomery, *Corporate Strategy* (Chicago: Irwin, 1997), 5.
8. Ibid., 7–8.
9. Ibid., 7–12.
10. Based in part on George S. Day, *Strategic Market Planning* (St. Paul, MN: West Publishing, 1984), 18–22.
11. Peter F. Drucker, *Management: Tasks, Responsibility, Practices* (New York: Harper & Row, 1974), 100.
12. Robert S. Kaplan and David P. Norton, *The Balanced Scorecard* (Boston: Harvard Business School Press, 1996).
13. C. K. Prahalad and Gary Hamel, "The Core Competence of the Corporation," *Harvard Business Review*, May–June 1990, 79–91; George S. Day, "The Capabilities of Market-Driven Organizations," *Journal of Marketing*, October 1994, 37–52.
14. Melanie Wells, "Red Baron," *Forbes*, July 3, 2000, 151–60.
15. This discussion is based on Boris Yavitz and William H. Newman, "What the Corporation Should Provide Its Business Units," *Journal of Business Strategy,* 3, no. 1, Summer 1982, 14.
16. Collis and Montgomery, *Corporate Strategy*, 10–11.
17. Ibid., 11.
18. Adrian J. Slywotzky, *Value Migration* (Boston: Harvard Business School Press, 1996), 4.
19. Collis and Montgomery, *Corporate Strategy*, 11–12.
20. Shelby D. Hunt and Robert M. Morgan, "The Comparative Advantage Theory of Competition," *Journal of Marketing*, April 1995, 1–15.
21. Peter F. Drucker, *Management: Tasks, Responsibilities, Practices* (New York: Harper & Row, 1974), 63.

22. Frederick E. Webster, "The Changing Role of Marketing in the Organization," *Journal of Marketing*, October 1992, 11.
23. Day, *Strategic Market Planning*, 3.
24. George S. Day, "Continuous Learning about Markets," *California Management Review*, Summer 1994, 9–31.
25. This example is based on D. John Loden, *Megabrands* (Homewood, IL: Business One Irwin, 1992), 184–5.
26. "Masters of Innovation," *Business Week*, April 10, 1989, 58–63.
27. Webster, "The Changing Role of Marketing," 13.
28. Paulette Thomas, "Rubbermaid Stock Plunges Over 12% on Projected Weak 2nd-Quarter Profit," *The Wall Street Journal*, June 12, 1995, B6.
29. The following discussion is based on material developed by Dr. John R. Nevin, Granger Wisconsin Distinguished Professor, University of Wisconsin.
30. Michael E. Porter, "Strategy and the Internet," *Harvard Business Review,* March 2001, 63–78.
31. David S. Hopkins, *The Marketing Plan* (New York: The Conference Board, 1981). See also Howard Sutton, *The Marketing Plan in the 1990s* (New York: The Conference Board, 1990).

Appendix 2A

Financial Analysis for Marketing Planning and Control

Several kinds of financial analyses are needed for marketing analysis, planning, and control activities. Such analyses represent an important part of case preparation activities. In some instances it will be necessary to review and interpret the financial information provided in the cases. In other instances, analyses may be prepared to support specific recommendations. The methods covered in this appendix represent a group of tools and techniques for use in marketing financial analysis. Throughout the discussion, it is assumed that accounting and finance fundamentals are understood.

Unit of Financial Analysis

Various units of analysis that can be used in marketing financial analysis are shown in Exhibit 2A–1. Two factors often influence the choice of a unit of analysis: (1) the purpose of the analysis and (2) the costs and availability of the information needed to perform the analysis.

EXHIBIT 2A–1   **Alternative Units for Financial Analysis**

Market	Product/Service	Organization
Market	Industry	Company
Market niche(s)	Product mix	Segment/division/unit
Geographic area(s)	Product line	Marketing department
Customer groups	Specific product	Sales unit:
Individual customers	Brand	Region
	Model	District branch
		Office/store

Financial Situation Analysis

Financial measures can be used to help assess the present situation. One of the most common and best ways to quantify the financial situation of a firm is through ratio analysis. These ratios should be analyzed over a period of at least three years to discern trends.

Key Financial Ratios

Financial information will be more useful to management if it is prepared so that comparisons can be made. James Van Horne comments upon this need.

> To evaluate a firm's financial condition and performance, the financial analyst needs certain yardsticks. The yardstick frequently used is a ratio or index, relating two pieces of financial data to each other. Analysis and interpretation of various ratios should give an experienced and skilled analyst a better understanding of the financial condition and performance of the firm than he would obtain from analysis of the financial data alone.[1]

As we examine the financial analysis model in the next section, note how the ratio or index provides a useful frame of reference. Typically, ratios are used to compare historical and/or future trends within the firm or to compare a firm or business unit with an industry or other firms.

Several financial ratios often used to measure business performance are shown in Exhibit 2A–2. Note that these ratios are primarily useful as a means of comparing:

1. Ratio values for several time periods for a particular business.

2. A firm to its key competitors.

3. A firm to an industry or business standard.

There are several sources of ratio data.[2] These include data services such as Dun & Bradstreet, Robert Morris Associates' *Annual Statement Studies,* industry and trade associations, government agencies, and investment advisory services.

Other ways to gauge the productivity of marketing activities include sales per square feet of retail floor space, occupancy rates of hotels and office buildings, and sales per salesperson.

Contribution Analysis

When the performance of products, market segments, and other marketing units is being analyzed, management should examine the unit's profit contribution. Contribution margin is equal to sales (revenue) less variable costs. Thus, contribution margin represents the amount of money available to cover fixed costs, and contribution margin less fixed costs is net income. An illustration of contribution margin analysis is given in Exhibit 2A–3. In this example, product X is generating a positive contribution margin. If product X were eliminated, $50,000 of product net income would be lost, and the remaining products would have to cover fixed costs not directly traceable to them. If the product is retained, the $50,000 can be used to contribute to other fixed costs and/or net income.

[1]James C. Van Horne, *Fundamentals of Financial Management*, 4th ed. (Englewood Cliffs, NJ: Prentice-Hall, 1980), 103–4.

[2]A useful guide to ratio analysis is provided in Richard Sanzo, *Ratio Analysis for Small Business* (Washington, DC: Small Business Administration, 1977).

EXHIBIT 2A–2   Summary of Key Financial Ratios

Ratio	How Calculated	What It Shows
Profitability ratios:		
1. Gross profit margin	$\dfrac{\text{Sales} - \text{Cost of goods sold}}{\text{Sales}}$	An indication of the total margin available to cover operating expenses and yield a profit.
2. Operating profit margin	$\dfrac{\text{Profits before taxes and before interest}}{\text{Sales}}$	An indication of the firm's profitability from current operations without regard to the interest charges accruing from the capital structure.
3. Net profit margin (or return on sales)	$\dfrac{\text{Profits after taxes}}{\text{Sales}}$	Shows after-tax profits per dollar of sales. Subpar profit margins indicate that the firm's sales prices are relatively low, its costs are relatively high, or both.
4. Return on total assets	$\dfrac{\text{Profits after taxes}}{\text{Total assets}}$ or $\dfrac{\text{Profits after taxes} + \text{Interest}}{\text{Total assets}}$	A measure of the return on total investment in the enterprise. It is sometimes desirable to add interest to after-tax profits to form the numerator of the ratio, since total assets are financed by creditors as well as by stockholders; hence, it is accurate to measure the productivity of assets by the returns provided to both classes of investors.
5. Return on stockholders' equity (or return on net worth)	$\dfrac{\text{Profits after taxes}}{\text{Total stockholders' equity}}$	A measure of the rate on stockholders' investment in the enterprise.
6. Return on common equity	$\dfrac{\text{Profits after taxes} - \text{Preferred stock dividends}}{\text{Total stockholders' equity} - \text{Par value of preferred stock}}$	A measure of the rate of return on the investment which the owners of common stock have made in the enterprise.
7. Earnings per share	$\dfrac{\text{Profits after taxes} - \text{Preferred stock dividends}}{\text{Number of shares of common stock outstanding}}$	Shows the earnings available to the owners of common stock.
Liquidity ratios:		
1. Current ratio	$\dfrac{\text{Current assets}}{\text{Current liabilities}}$	Indicates the extent to which the claims of short-term creditors are covered by assets that are expected to be converted to cash in a period roughly corresponding to the maturity of the liabilities.
2. Quick ratio (or acid-test ratio)	$\dfrac{\text{Current assets} - \text{Inventory}}{\text{Current liabilities}}$	A measure of the firm's ability to pay off short-term obligations without relying on the sale of its inventories.
3. Cash ratio	$\dfrac{\text{Cash \& Marketable securities}}{\text{Current liabilities}}$	An indicator of how long the company can go without further inflow of funds.

Ratio	Formula	What it shows
4. Inventory to net working capital	$\dfrac{\text{Inventory}}{\text{Current assets} - \text{Current liabilities}}$	A measure of the extent to which the firm's working capital is tied up in inventory.

Leverage ratios:

Ratio	Formula	What it shows
1. Debt to assets ratio	$\dfrac{\text{Total debt}}{\text{Total assets}}$	Measures the extent to which borrowed funds have been used to finance the firm's operations.
2. Debt to equity ratio	$\dfrac{\text{Total debt}}{\text{Total stockholders' equity}}$	Provides another measure of the funds provided the creditors versus the funds provided by owners.
3. Long-term debt to equity ratio	$\dfrac{\text{Long-term debt}}{\text{Total stockholders' equity}}$	A widely used measure of the balance between debt and equity in the firm's overall capital structure.
4. Times-interest-earned (or coverage ratios)	$\dfrac{\text{Profits before interest and taxes}}{\text{Total interest charges}}$	Measures the extent to which earnings can decline without the firm's becoming unable to meet its annual interest costs.
5. Fixed-charge coverage	$\dfrac{\text{Profits before taxes and interest} + \text{Lease obligations}}{\text{Total interest charges} + \text{Lease obligations}}$	A more inclusive indication of the firm's ability to meet all of its fixed-charge obligations.

Activity ratios:

Ratio	Formula	What it shows
1. Inventory turnover	$\dfrac{\text{Cost of goods sold}}{\text{Inventory}}$	When compared to industry averages, it provides an indication of whether a company has excessive inventory or perhaps inadequate inventory.
2. Fixed-assets turnover*	$\dfrac{\text{Sales}}{\text{Fixed assets}}$	A measure of the sales productivity and utilization of plant and equipment.
3. Total-assets turnover	$\dfrac{\text{Sales}}{\text{Total assets}}$	A measure of the utilization of all the firm's assets; a ratio below the industry average indicates the company is not generating a sufficient volume of business given the size of its asset investment.
4. Accounts receivable turnover	$\dfrac{\text{Annual credit sales}}{\text{Accounts receivable}}$	A measure of the average length of time it takes the firm to collect on the sales made on credit.
5. Average collection period	$\dfrac{\text{Accounts receivable}}{\text{Total sales} \div 365}$ or $\dfrac{\text{Accounts receivable}}{\text{Average daily sales}}$	Indicates the average length of time the firm must wait after making a sale before it receives payment.

*The manager should also keep in mind the fixed charges associated with noncapitalized lease obligations.

Source: Adapted from Arthur A. Thompson, Jr., and A. J. Strickland III, *Strategy and Policy*, 4th ed. (Burr Ridge, IL: Richard D. Irwin, 1987), 270–1.

EXHIBIT 2A–3   **Illustrative Contribution Margin Analysis for Product X ($000)**

Sales	$300
Less: Variable manufacturing costs	100
Other variable costs traceable to product X	50
Equals: Contribution margin	150
Less: Fixed costs directly traceable to product X	100
Equals: Product net income	$ 50

Financial Analysis Model

The model shown in Exhibit 2A–4 provides a useful guide for examining financial performance and identifying possible problem areas. The model combines several important financial ratios into one equation. Let's examine the model, moving from left to right. Profit margin multiplied by asset turnover yields return on assets. Moreover, assuming that the performance target is return on net worth (or return on equity), the product of return on assets and financial leverage determines performance. Increasing either ratio will increase net worth. The values of these ratios will vary considerably from one industry to another. For example, in grocery wholesaling, profit margins are typically very low, whereas asset turnover is very high. Through efficient management and high turnover, a wholesaler can stack up impressive returns on net worth. Furthermore, space productivity measures are obtained for individual departments in retail stores that offer more than one line, such as department stores. The measures selected depend on the particular characteristics of the business.

EXHIBIT 2A–4   **Financial Analysis Model**

Profit margin ↓		Asset turnover ↓		Return on assets ↓		Financial leverage ↓		Return on net worth ↓
$\dfrac{\text{Net profits (after taxes)}}{\text{Net sales}}$	×	$\dfrac{\text{Net sales}}{\text{Total assets}}$	→	$\dfrac{\text{Net profits (after taxes)}}{\text{Total assets}}$	×	$\dfrac{\text{Net Total assets}}{\text{Net worth}}$	=	$\dfrac{\text{Net profits (after taxes)}}{\text{Net worth}}$

Evaluating Alternatives

As we move through the discussion of financial analysis, it is important to recognize the type of costs being used in the analysis. Using accounting terminology, costs can be designated as fixed or variable. A cost is *fixed* if it remains constant over the observation period, even though the volume of activity varies. In contrast, a *variable* cost is an expense that varies with sales over the observation period. Costs are designated as mixed or semivariable in instances when they contain both fixed and variable components.

Break-Even Analysis

This technique is used to examine the relationship between sales and costs. An illustration is given in Exhibit 2A–5. Using sales and costs information, it is easy to determine from a break-even analysis how many units of a product must be sold in order to break even, or cover total costs. In this example 65,000 units at sales of $120,000 are equal to total costs of $120,000. Any additional units sold will produce a profit. The break-even point can be calculated in this manner:

$$\text{Break-even units} = \frac{\text{Fixed costs}}{\text{Price per unit} - \text{Variable cost per unit}}$$

Price in the illustration shown in Exhibit 2A–5 is $1.846 per unit, and variable cost is $0.769 per unit. With fixed costs of $70,000, this results in the break-even calculation:

$$\text{BE units} = \frac{\$70,000}{\$1,846 - \$0.769} = 65,000 \text{ units}$$

To determine how many units must be sold to achieve a target profit (expressed in before-tax dollars), the formula is amended as follows:

$$\text{Target profit units} = \frac{\text{Fixed costs} + \text{Target profit (before tax)}}{\text{Price per unit} - \text{Variable cost per unit}}$$

Using the same illustration as above and including a target before-tax profit of $37,700, the target profit calculation becomes:

$$\text{Target profit units} = \frac{\$70,000 + \$37,700}{\$1.846 - \$0.769} = 100,000 \text{ units}$$

EXHIBIT 2A–5   **Illustrative Break-Even Analysis**

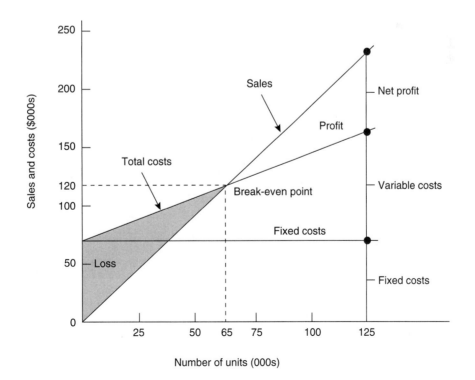

Number of units (000s)

EXHIBIT 2A–6 **Cash Flow Comparison ($000s)**

	Project X	Project Y
Start-Up Costs	<1,000>	<1,000>
Year 1	500	300
Year 2	500	400
Year 3	200	600

EXHIBIT 2A–7 **Present Value of Cash Flows**

	Time	Cash Flow	PV Factor	NPV of Cash Flow
Project X				
	0	<1,000>	$1 / (1 + .12)^0 = 1$	<1,000>
	1	500	$1 / (1 + .12)^1 = 0.8929$	= 446.45
	2	500	$1 / (1 + .12)^2 = 0.7972$	= 398.60
	3	300	$1 / (1 + .12)^3 = 0.7118$	= 213.54
			Present value	+ 58.59
Project Y				
	0	<1,000>	$1 / (1 + .12)^0 = 1$	<1,000>
	1	300	$1 / (1 + .12)^1 = 0.8929$	= 267.87
	2	400	$1 / (1 + .12)^2 = 0.7972$	= 318.88
	3	600	$1 / (1 + .12)^3 = 0.7118$	= 427.08
			Net present value	+ 13.83

This analysis is not a forecast. Rather, it indicates how many units of a product at a given price and cost must be sold in order to break even or achieve a target profit. Some important assumptions that underlie the above break-even analysis include the use of constant fixed and variable costs, a constant price, and a single product.

In addition to break-even analysis, several other financial tools are used to evaluate alternatives. Net present value of cash flow analysis and return on investment are among the most useful. For example, assume there are two projects with the cash flows shown in Exhibit 2A–6.

Though return on investment is widely used, it is limited by its inability to consider the time value of money. This is pointed out in Exhibit 2A–7. Return on investment for *both* projects X and Y is 10 percent. However, a dollar today is worth more than a dollar given in three years. Therefore, in assessing cash flows of a project or investment, future cash flows must be discounted back to the present at a rate comparable to the risk of the project.

Discounting cash flows is a simple process. Assume that the firm is considering projects X and Y and that its cost of capital is 12 percent. Additionally, assume that both projects carry risk comparable to the normal business risk. Under these circumstances, the analyst should discount the cash flows back to the present at the cost of capital, 12 percent. Present value factors can be looked up or computed using the formula $1/(1 + i)n$, where i equals our discounting rate per time period and n equals the number of compounding periods. In this example, the present value of cash flows would be as shown in Exhibit 2A–7.

Because both projects have a positive net present value, both are good. However, if they are mutually exclusive, the project with the highest net present value should be selected.

Financial Planning

Financial planning involves two major activities: (1) forecasting revenues and (2) budgeting (estimating future expenses). The actual financial analyses and forecasts included in the strategic marketing plan vary considerably from firm to firm. In addition, internal financial reporting and budgeting procedures vary widely among companies. Therefore, consider this approach as one example rather than the norm.

The choice of the financial information to be used for marketing planning and control will depend on its relationship with the corporate or business unit strategic plan. Another important consideration is the selection of performance measures to be used in gauging marketing performance. The objective is to indicate the range of possibilities and suggest some of the more frequently used financial analysis.

Pro forma income statements can be very useful when one is projecting performance and budgeting. Usually, this is done on a spreadsheet so that assumptions can be altered rapidly. Usually, only a few assumptions need be made. For example, sales growth rates can be projected from past trends and adjusted for new information. From this starting point, cost of goods can be determined as a percentage of sales. Operating expenses can also be determined as a percentage of sales based on past relationships, and the effective tax rate as a percentage of earnings before taxes. However, past relationships may not hold in the future. It may be necessary to analyze possible divergence from past relationships.

In addition, pro forma income statements can be used to generate pro forma cash flow statements. It is then possible to compare alternative courses of action by employing a uniformly comparable standard cash flow.

Supplemental Financial Analyses

The preceding sections of this appendix detailed the various forms of traditional financial analysis useful in marketing decision making. There are supplemental forms of analysis that can also be helpful in different types of marketing decisions. These supplemental techniques draw mainly from the management accounting discipline and rely on data that are available only to internal decision makers. Many of the financial analyses in the earlier sections employed data from published financial statements.

Only recently have marketing decision makers been able to look to management accounting to provide an additional set of quantitative tools to aid in the decision process.[3] These tools may be referred to collectively as strategic management accounting practices. Simmonds is generally credited with originating the term *strategic management accounting*, which he defines as "the provision and analysis of management accounting data about a business and its competitors for use in developing and monitoring the business strategy."[4] Although academic researchers may disagree about the specific techniques which constitute strategic management accounting, there are a wide selection of management accounting practices available for use in marketing decision making. These practices are described in Exhibit 2A–8 and include activity-based costing, attribute costing, benchmarking, brand valuation budgeting and monitoring, competitor cost assessment, competitive position monitoring, competitor performance appraisal, integrated performance measurement, life cycle costing, quality costing, strategic costing, strategic pricing, target costing, and value-chain costing.[5]

Exhibit 2A–8 also provides a description of the various marketing applications of strategic management accounting practices in terms of specific decision making situations. Most of these practices require the marketing decision maker to gather information additional to that normally used for the preparation of external financial statements. In most cases, this information is already available in the accounting information system of the firm. However, it may be necessary to compile data from outside the firm in a more formalized manner to perform analysis using some of these strategic management accounting practices.

[3]George Foster and Mahendra Gupta, "Marketing, Cost Management and Management Accounting," *Journal of Management Accounting Research*, vol. 6 (1994), 43–77.

[4]K. Simmonds, "Strategic Management Accounting," *Management Accounting* (UK), 59 no. 4 (1981), 26–29.

[5]For a comprehensive description of strategic management accounting techniques and differences in attitudes toward the use of these techniques between accounting and marketing managers, see Karen S. Cravens and Chris Guilding, "An Empirical Study of the Application of Strategic Management Accounting Techniques," *Advances in Management Accounting*, 10 (2001), 95–124.

EXHIBIT 2A–8 Supplemental Financial Analyses Using Management Accounting Practices

Strategic Management Accounting Practice	Description of the Practice	Description of Marketing Application
Activity-based costing	Indirect costs are assigned to a product or service in relation to the activities used to produce the product or provide the service. Decision making focuses on the collection of activities necessary to product the product or service rather than the costs in a specific category.	This technique is particularly useful in determining the costs of customization or the provision of additional services to customers. Since the activities are the central focus for costing, decision makers can evaluate customers and markets in terms of the activities required to serve their needs.
Attribute costing	Products or services are costed in terms of attributes that appeal to customers. Thus, the cost object is not the entire product but a collection of features that respond to customer needs.	The nature of the cost object can be modified to support different strategic decision-making situations. As customers modify their preferences, decision makers can consider how particular product attributes satisfy their needs relative to marketing positioning strategies.
Benchmarking	Benchmarking is improving existing processes by looking to an ideal standard. The standard may be established from an external source such as a competitor, a partner, or an unrelated industry or company or by another area of the same firm.	Benchmarking provides an opportunity to assess processes for improvement and strategic advantage in terms of operational effectiveness. Critical lapses in customer service or customer contact situations can be remedied.
Brand valuation—budgeting and monitoring	Brand valuation assesses the current and future potential of a brand in quantitative terms. A "capitalized" value for internally developed brands can be created even though in the United States this value may not be included on a balance sheet.	Current spending on brand promotion activities can be evaluated in terms of future benefits. This can assist with budgeting decisions relative to a portfolio of brands or products and in monitoring the mix and potential of existing products.
Competitive position monitoring	This type of analysis is used in evaluating the market strategy of a competitor. Overall competitor positions in the market and industry are assessed, including sales and trend information, along with market share and cost estimates.	Since this technique requires an external focus, it allows decision makers to assess the position of a product in terms of existing and future strategy relative to competitors. Situations allowing a firm to improve competitive position can be identified and acted upon.
Competitor performance appraisal	This form of analysis is a detailed part of competitive position monitoring and focuses on preparing a quantitative analysis of the competitor's external financial statements.	Decision makers can identify the key areas of a competitor's market advantage and relate areas of advantage to strategic decisions.

Term	Description	Strategic Implication
Integrated performance measurement	This form of analysis uses performance appraisal based on measures that are developed in terms of a customer focus. Integrated measures may be linked to customer satisfaction and may include nonfinancial measures monitored at the individual and departmental levels.	Measures focusing on the customer can be linked to overall strategic objectives throughout the organization. Decision makers can get a clear picture of how their decisions (and performance) affect overall corporate performance.
Life cycle costing	A product or service is costed based on stages in the life of a product rather than financial reporting periods.	Decision makers can adopt a longer-term perspective to evaluate the performance of a product without the constraints of annual reporting periods.
Quality costing	Accounting measures support determining the cost of quality and the cost of a quality failure.	Decision makers can evaluate the impact on customers and market position when choices are made regarding quality issues.
Strategic costing	Strategic costing involves recognizing that the ultimate objective of expenditures related to a product or service may be more long-term in perspective. Thus, cost minimization is not the prime objective. Choices involving costs are evaluated in terms of long-term issues and the future potential of strategies.	Long-term strategy and strategic objectives considering product positioning and market penetration can be evaluated more completely. The long-term implications of a decision receive precedence over the short-term effect.
Strategic pricing	Strategic pricing adopts a more long-term and demand-focused approach to pricing rather than considering a cost-based and historical foundation.	Pricing decisions can be evaluated more in terms of competitive and market choices.
Target costing	A market-based approach is used to determine the target cost for a future product. The target cost is the remainder after a desired profit margin is subtracted from the estimated market price of a new product.	Since the product is designed to meet the target cost, decision makers know that the product will be able to enter the market at a price that allows an adequate level of profits. External rather than internal factors determine the price.
Value-chain costing	The cost of a product is evaluated over the entire value chain of production from research and development to customer service. This value chain may include multiple functional areas within the organization and cover different financial accounting reporting periods.	Operational efficiencies and competitive positioning can be evaluated at all stages of the value chain, not merely from the costs incurred during production. Links to suppliers, customers, and competitors can be considered at all points of the value chain.

Cases for Part 1

Case 1–1

Nokia Corp.

It's fast becoming the Helsinki conundrum. When cell-phone king Nokia is thrashing Ericsson and Motorola, and those two announce dreadful earnings, what's to stop jittery tech investors from punishing the whole sector, including Nokia? In markets like today's, where fear rules supreme, absolutely nothing. So Nokia Chairman Jorma Ollila is taking preemptive steps. A day or two before his rivals release their numbers, Ollila often puts out some good news of his own. It's a nod and a wink to investors.

And sometimes it backfires. On Jan. 9, Nokia Corp. proudly previewed 2000 numbers. They showed Nokia extending its lead in handsets, rising to one-third of the 405 million unit global market—and double its closest competitor, Motorola Inc. In total, the Finns sold 128 million handsets, up an impressive 64% from 1999.

Yet as soon as the Nokia release hit the wires, all hell broke loose. Investors brushed past Nokia's competitive gains and zeroed in on the size of the market: 405 million seemed puny, some 20 million smaller than earlier analysts' projections! Suddenly fearful that the world's love affair with cell phones could be topping out, investors ditched Nokia stock, dropping the share price 9% and axing $17 billion from its market value. The current worry is that Nokia could announce disappointing results when it unveils its fourth quarter, on Jan. 30. "In this environment, any negative surprise will take the stock down," says Edward F. Snyder, analyst at J.P. Morgan H&Q in San Francisco. And a long-term bear market in telecom could dry up the pool of desperately needed capital for next-generation wireless systems.

Killer Brand

Setting aside jumpy markets, the story in cell phones is one of growing dominance. The Finnish giant, neck-and-neck with its top two rivals barely two years ago, is now lapping the field. The $27 billion company boosts its share simply by nudging down margins to a still-hefty 19%, this while the rest of the industry is struggling to make money (Exhibit 1). Nokia sits, debt-free, with $2.5 billion in cash, the biggest research-and-development budget in the industry, a killer brand, and unrivaled leverage not only over suppliers but also over customers. Those are the world's biggest phone companies, from AT&T to Deutsche Telekom, who supply millions of cell phones to the public. They pay top dollar to have the snazziest Nokias on hand. Few can afford to pass. "Nokia's the gorilla," says Joris de Beul, equity strategist at Fortis Investment Management in Brussels.

Sure, cell-phone growth will slow down from this year's 45%, especially in near-saturated Western Europe. But even pessimists project an additional 140 million units next year, many of them in developing markets such as China, India, and the United States. Within three years, the cell-phone market should reach 1 billion units per year, says International Data Corp. No one's better positioned to cash in on this monster market than Nokia. The Finns predict 25% to 35% sales growth through the next three years.

Yet in this sluttish climate, even a slight stumble on Nokia's part could jeopardize more than the Finnish giant's stock price. At risk is the company's whole ambitious gamble on the mobile Internet, which barely exists today. More than any other outfit, Nokia is spurring the global phone industry ahead on this trillion-dollar push. If the strategy pans

EXHIBIT 1
Nokia Isn't the Biggest . . .

Data: J.P. Morgan H&Q

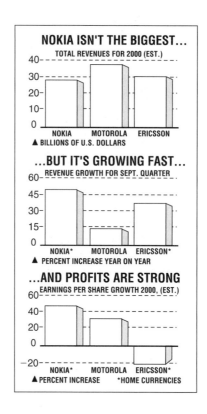

NOKIA ISN'T THE BIGGEST...
TOTAL REVENUES FOR 2000 (EST.)

▲ BILLIONS OF U.S. DOLLARS

...BUT IT'S GROWING FAST...
REVENUE GROWTH FOR SEPT. QUARTER

▲ PERCENT INCREASE YEAR ON YEAR

...AND PROFITS ARE STRONG
EARNINGS PER SHARE GROWTH 2000, (EST.)

▲ PERCENT INCREASE   *HOME CURRENCIES

out, the Finns could well sit atop the next stage of the Web, kings not just of Web-surfing machines, but also a power in software and networks.

Deep Debt

This is a dicey situation, however, because Nokia can never go back to just selling phones. Also, it needs huge commitments from its partners, the phone companies, to forge the wireless Web. But all the telcos have plunged deeply into debt. And in this new ball game Nokia faces fierce competition from the world's leading tech companies, from Silicon Valley to Tokyo.

Only a year ago, the wireless Web seemed to be falling neatly into place. The phone companies dutifully accepted Nokia's thesis that this high-speed mobile Net, known as Third Generation, was the next big thing: To miss it meant death, no matter how much it cost. With that, the telcos went on one of the biggest spending binges in history, throwing billions of dollars at spectrum licenses like so much cab fare. When Britain's Vodafone Group PLC launched a $183 billion takeover of Germany's Mannesmann, the markets barely quivered. They were too busy applauding.

It was back in those cheery times, one evening at Nokia headquarters, that Chairman Ollila mentioned his company's market value and broke into laughter. "$250 billion," he said, shaking his head. Suddenly, it didn't seem like much money.

Today, it does. In a manic market, the noise surrounding 3G is every bit as grisly as the soundtrack of *Scream 3.* Phone companies are spending a spine-tingling $125 billion just for spectrum licenses in Europe, plus another $100 billion for the networks—this before any of them have figured out how to make a business from data on mobile phones. In a

**EXHIBIT 2
Nokia's New
Firmament**

The Bright Side . . .	. . . And the Dark
• Nokia is the world's fifth-most valuable brand, ahead of Sony, Nike, and Mercedes-Benz.	• The European market for the current generation of handset is nearly saturated.
• It makes nearly one-third of all cell phones sold, enjoying huge economies of scale.	• The cellular market is struggling with the failure of early global-Internet software, called WAP.
• Its handset operating margins are 20%, compared with 5% for Motorola and −30% for Ericcson.	• Nokia's key customers, Europe's telcos, are $125 billion in debt, incurred to pay for 3G licenses.
• Nokia's strong management team has come through many crises unscathed.	• Investors are running from 3G and telcos are seeing credit ratings fall.
• It has global relationships with all the major phone companies.	• Nokia will likely be late in 3G phones and in an earlier Net-enabled format called GPRS.
• It has world-class research, design, and engineering teams.	• In handsets, Nokia faces well-capitalized Japanese rivals.

switch from cockeyed optimism to paranoia, investors have punished phone stocks, driving down giants like Deutsche Telekom and British Telecommunications PLC by 60% since last summer (Exhibit 2).

Such stampedes throw plenty of dust on Nokia. For now, though, the Finns' drive to build and dominate the mobile Web is not even off schedule. And the telcos, battered as they are, remain committed to 3G. Most of them are locked in, by the terms of their spectrum licenses, and ready to plow ahead.

Hazards lurk up ahead, though. The drive to 3G is pushing Nokia from the simple radio-based handsets it knows so well into the dizzying world of computers and consumer goodies, from digital cameras to tiny video machines—all of which will soon communicate with one another over the wireless Net. This process is known as digital convergence. And it's leading Nokia away from its home-telephone counter at Best Buy into different sections of the electronics store. It's here the Finns run smack into Microsoft Corp. and Sony Corp., which are busy making similar machines.

For Niklas Savander, Nokia's mission is like that of a surfer looking for the next wave. Savander, Nokia's vice-president for software applications, says that with mobile voice, Nokia caught a tsunami in the '90s. The first company to design colorful phones and build a consumer brand, Nokia left competitors such as Motorola and Ericsson floundering in its wake. Those engineering companies viewed mobile phones for far too long as boring and expensive business tools. And Motorola made a disastrous bet on analog phones, just as Nokia was pushing digital (Exhibit 3). But those triumphs are in the past. "The next wave," says Savander, looking out the window at the lapping Baltic, "is the mobile Net. The question is whether we can catch two in a row."

"Close-Knit"

Five floors up from Savander at the Nokia House, Jorma Ollila scowls at the wave analogy. "It's a bit too simple," the 50-year-old Nokia chairman says in his clipped British accent, a product of a stint in London at Citibank. Ollila insists that his close-knit team of managers, the same five Finns who mapped out Nokia's course in current cell phones, have been preparing the company for the mobile Web for years. He notes that Nokia produced the first

EXHIBIT 3
Motorola Can't Seem to Get Out of Its Own Way

On the frozen plains of Schaumburg, Ill., executives at Motorola Inc. might happily trade their snow boots for Nokia's shoes. Sure, Nokia's hiccup in handset sales sent its shares tumbling. But that pain pales next to Motorola's chronic performance woes.

Since last March, the one-time high-tech bellwether has lost two-thirds of its value as its shares have collapsed to $20 from $60 a share. And on Jan. 10, Motorola reported fourth-quarter earnings of $335 million—down from last summer's expectations of $615 million—on sales of $10.1 billion. Motorola, says Jane A. Snorek, vice-president at Firmco, a Milwaukee investment house that owns shares in the company, "is in a lot of trouble."

What's bugging Motorola? Certainly the $37.6 billion company—which depends on semiconductor sales for about 20% of revenues—suffers from the cyclical swings of the chip industry. But its biggest problems stem from its $13.3 billion wireless business. In the past two years, Motorola's market share in cell-phone handsets has fallen to 13% from 17%, says researcher Dataquest Inc., while Nokia today controls a third of the market, up from 27% in 1999.

Simply put, Motorola can't quickly and profitably produce the phones consumers want. The company missed the transition to digital in the mid-'90s and today grapples with a product line that's too complex and hard to manage.

Compare Motorola's product line to Nokia's. The Finnish company uses just a handful of basic designs that share components such as screens, batteries, and some chips. Motorola, by contrast, juggles many different model platforms with little overlap among parts—making it nearly impossible to get the economies of scale Nokia enjoys.

And Motorola phones haven't clicked with consumers. U.S. cellular operator Cingular Wireless, for example, says Nokia phones dominate. At Sprint PCS Group outlets, Samsung Co. usually wins. The reason: customers say Motorola designs are clunky, and too many top $200—higher than most people will pay.

The greatest challenge for CEO Christopher B. Galvin is to develop a production process matching Nokia's. To that end, Motorola is whittling its model platforms to fewer than a half-dozen, sharing many basic components such as keypads. By mid-year, Motorola should churn out handsets far more quickly—and at far lower prices, says Leif G. Soderberg, head of strategy for Motorola's phone unit. "We're going to have fewer products and make the ones we've got killers," Soderberg says.

Better hurry. Even if sleek new phones are ready as soon as promised, Motorola can't afford more lost ground. It "could fall so far behind it'll never catch up," says Edward F. Snyder, analyst at J.P. Morgan H&Q. With so much at stake, Motorola execs must be shaking in their snow boots.

By Roger O. Crockett in Chicago

Web-surfing mobile phone—a brick known as the Communicator—way back in 1996, the Jurassic era of the wireless Web. From his glass-walled office, Ollila has been reassigning radio engineers into software and Internet technologies for the past three years. And he's been preparing his managers. More than smart software, Nokia's debt-free balance sheet, or its heavyweight brand, it's Ollila's inner circle of managers that promises to power Nokia in the coming wireless Web wars.

All Finns, these top execs took over Nokia as thirty-something managers when the national icon was wavering on the brink of bankruptcy. They jettisoned much of the company to focus on wireless. There they pushed design and branding, and set up a low-cost industrial scheme that gave Nokia a head start when the cell phone became a mass-consumer good.

But while winning the cellular wars, Ollila was busy training his team for the challenges ahead. He shifted their jobs every two or three years. He dispatched his chief financial officer, Olli-Pekka Kallasvuo, to run the U.S. division in Dallas. There, the money man learned not just about manufacturing, but the all-important U.S. capital markets. Ollila sent his networks chief, Sari Baldauf, to run Asia—giving her a good look at the jumping-off markets for 3G.

Perhaps most important, Ollila pulled his No. 2 and heir apparent, Pekka Ala-Pietila, away from handsets in 1998 and sent him to Silicon Valley. Ollila says he has always counted on the 44-year-old Ala-Pietila as a visionary, and he makes a point of talking to him every day. Ala-Pietila's mandate is nothing less than to divine the future of the wireless Web—and put Nokia on track to get rich there.

From Nokia's leafy campus in Mountain View, Calif., Ala-Pietila is piecing together an entire Internet division. The idea is a bold one for a hardware company: Nokia can make all the fancy phones it wants, from almond-size units that nestle in the ear to combo phone-organizers with color touch screens and the zippiest games. But all of these phones are going to flounder—and Nokia will, too—if the network they depend on falls flat. This is driving Nokia to funnel much of its $2.5 billion R&D budget into 3G projects extending far beyond the mere handset.

Some 20,000 engineers from California to Nokia's labs in Oulu, just south of the Polar Circle, are venturing far from their radio roots, reaching into nearly every technology that touches the Web. They're developing tiny Web-browsers and firewalls, e-commerce security *sys*tems, and vast programs known as "middleware" that will allow phone companies to manage the expected blizzard of 3G traffic. Nokia's risk? In an industry where companies zero in on specialties—Ericsson on transmission towers, Qualcomm Inc. on chip design—Nokia's covering the wireless waterfront. "Nokia is clinging to a vertical industrial model," says Hjalmar Widbladh, general manager of Microsoft's Stockholm-based mobility division. "That goes against the times."

And the complexity of 3G systems is daunting. Consider a phone-toting German businesswoman in Malaysia. The network must locate her, offer a full load of German-language-services, from a list of vegetarian restaurants in Kuala-Lumpur to travel sites that permit her to postpone her Lufthansa flight by a day—and pay the $50 penalty, by phone of course. For the system to work, phone companies the world over must trace the steps of hundreds of millions of customers, adjust services to billions of different Web-surfing machines, and figure out the right billing for each customer's subscription. Building these systems "may be the most complex job humanity has ever faced," says Greg Papadopoulos, chief technology officer at Sun Microsystems Inc.

Redmond Rival

One of the few companies with resources to tackle it is Microsoft. The software giant is pulling out all the stops to extend its dominance from the desktop to the wireless Web. Three years ago, Nokia and Ericsson headed up an effort to block Microsoft from mobile-Net operating systems. Joined later by Motorola, they created a London-based joint venture called Symbian to produce a competing system.

But in the past year, Microsoft has flexed its mobile muscles. Last winter, it forged a joint venture with Ericsson to develop mini-Web browsers for handsets. "We can't do everything on our own," says Ericsson President Kurt Hellstrom. Months later, Microsoft hired away a key Symbian executive. In November, the Redmond giant unveiled prototypes of its first Internet phone, a joint venture with French phonemaker Sagem. The product is a slick palmtop device with a color screen, games, and a speaker phone—similar to Symbian-based products still in the lab. It's designed for generation 2.5, the next step in

Europe's mobile Net, which should roll out this year. The worst part? Microsoft's product, due out within months, could beat Nokia to the marketplace.

The Japanese promise to arrive early, as well. While Europeans thrash about to finance their next-generation systems and the U.S. debates which part of the airwaves to devote to it, the Japanese are forging ahead. Generation Three should debut by May in Tokyo. Already, Japanese powerhouses Sony and Matsushita Communication Industrial Co. are unveiling zippy new phones, some connected to MP3 players, others to cameras and mini-game consoles. What's more, when the first 3G systems open in Europe, early next year, the Japanese will likely be ready first with handsets. "Panasonic is going to be a good six months ahead of Nokia," says Lloyd Carney, president of wireless Internet solutions at Nortel Networks.

One question is what the machines will look like. Nokia developers predict a broad and wacky wireless world. They see wireless Barbie Dolls and Yankee caps, phones equipped with global positioning hitched to dog collars and planted in school lunch boxes. They see people eventually accumulating gobs of wireless machines, just the way we pile up clocks and radios today. "The market will be big enough for everyone," predicts Ollila. But amid the tumult, Nokia's betting that users will continue to buy phone-like devices—albeit with a camera or game console or electronic organizer attached. Those multifeatured phones will remain Nokia's core market.

WAP Woes

But don't expect the market to take off like a rocket. When 3G rolls out, the service is likely to be spotty and pricey for months, perhaps longer. Nokia is betting, with the confidence of a powerhouse, that the market won't truly develop until the Finnish giant thunders onto the stage, complete with its phones, software, and a host of service providers in tow—and a massive P.R. campaign.

Chances are the market will continue to be iffy long after Nokia arrives. That was certainly the case with Europe's first generation of the mobile Internet, a disaster known as WAP, or wireless access protocol. Launched amid great fanfare 16 months ago, WAP has limped from the beginning, hobbled by slow connections, high prices, lackluster services and, most embarrassingly, undependable phones. "Nokia's first [WAP] phones were buggy as hell," says Nigel Deighton, Gartner Group analyst.

The next phase promises to be rocky too. The market is likely to swoon every time Ericsson beats Nokia to a 3G contract, every time a Net phone appears with bugs. But from the very start, Nokia's managers have thrived precisely when they're working through crises. Every tumble Nokia takes hardens it for the wild ride ahead. It's bound to be bruising. But these Nordics are proving they have the patience, the riches, and the smarts to withstand the heat.

By Stephen Baker in Helsinki, with John Shinal in Mountain View, Calif., and Irene M. Kunii in Tokyo

Source: "Is Nokia's Star Dimming?" *Business Week,* January 22, 2001, 66–72.

Epilogue

Funny it took them so long. Years after the auto and computer industries shipped out much of their factory work, mobile-phone makers stuck to piecing together handsets in company-owned plants from Stockholm to Harvard, Ill. Now their old-fashioned ways are rapidly ending.

Battered by Finland's Nokia, Sweden's Ericsson threw in the towel, announcing on Jan. 26 that it was abandoning manufacturing. It turned the works—including six factories and 4,200 workers—over to contract manufacturer Flextronics International Ltd. Ericsson's retreat came only a month after Motorola Inc. said it would outsource much of its production. Nokia says it, too, will boost its use of low-cost outsiders to 15% of its handset production. In fact, 80% of this work will be done by contract labor in a few years, predicts Flextronics CEO Michael E. Marks.

The cost-cutting couldn't come a moment too soon. An abrupt slowdown is on the way. Nokia Chairman Jorma Ollila predicted on Jan. 30 that phone sales, projected earlier to grow 30% in 2001, to 560 million units, may come in closer to 500 million.

Leverage

But is shipping out manufacturing the best way to gird for rough times? Nokia insists it will keep most of its factory work in-house. Ollila maintains that producing its own phones constitutes one of Nokia's key advantages over its rivals. In fact, he's counting on Nokia's manufacturing edge to produce at the lowest costs in the industry, enabling the company to drive down prices. "We'll add to our share," he says, which now tops 30% of the global market.

So who's right, the outsourcing Swedes and Americans, or the do-it-yourself Finns? The answer may be both. To date, size has been Nokia's strength. With its explosive growth in the past two years, the company now towers over its rivals, producing more phones than No. 2 Motorola and No. 3 Ericsson combined. This gives Nokia a crucial edge in scale, along with leverage over suppliers, especially makers of computer chips that power these handsets (Exhibit 4).

Indeed, it is to take on this behemoth that Ericsson is in effect creating another manufacturing giant by allying with Flextronics. The $13 billion company, run from San Jose, Calif., may well become the other caller that chipmakers can't put on hold. "When it comes to scale, our partner is very, very big," points out Jan Ahrenbring, Ericsson's vice-president for marketing. Outsourcing should also go a long way in helping the laggards cut costs. Motorola's margins on phones have shrunk to a measly 3%. Ericsson's are even worse, posting a punishing yearend loss of $1.7 billion in its cell-phone unit. With the outsourcing deal, the Swedes "are looking for hundreds of millions of savings per year," says Marks.

Ugly Phones

But outsourcing alone won't save the day. What's required in this market is snazzy design, powerful marketing and, above all, teams that can anticipate consumer tastes—skills that are glaringly absent at Motorola and Ericsson. And ominously, while they're handing off more assembly work, they're both continuing to do design, engineering, and marketing

EXHIBIT 4
Nokia Pulls Ahead

Source: Company reports, Bank of America Securities

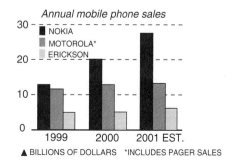

Annual mobile phone sales

▲ BILLIONS OF DOLLARS   *INCLUDES PAGER SALES

internally. "If they make ugly phones that no one wants, lower costs won't help much," asserts Tim Sheedy, a wireless analyst at International Data Corp.

Still, nimble manufacturing has been a key to Nokia's success. The company, which was nearly bankrupt nine years ago, restructured for the global economy in the early '90s. "We didn't have factories in every country, like our competitors," says Ollila. Benefiting from streamlined design and manufacturing, Nokia produces two dozen new phones each year, a regimen rivals can't match.

But Nokia can't rest. Boutique manufacturers in Europe and America now envision disposable mobile phones with an hour of talk time to be sold for $10 in vending machines. When the cell phone, once a symbol of wealth and privilege, descends into the throwaway bin, even giants can't cut costs fast enough.

Source: Stephen Baker, "Commentary," *Business Week,* February 12, 2001, 38.

Case 1–2
Polaroid Corp.

Cambridge, Mass.—"Have we lost our minds?"

When Samuel H. Liggero, an esteemed scientist at Polaroid Corp., put that question to his fellow technologists on a winter morning in 1997, they all readily agreed.

The object of their scorn: an audacious idea from the other side of the company—the "marketeers"—to create a small, clunky instant camera. It would have a cheap lens that produced fuzzy, thumbnail-size photographs.

A Reputation to Protect

Dr. Liggero sat at the head of the long wooden table and vented. This isn't a camera, he said, it's a toy. And the presumed customers, teenagers, are faddish, right? Yes, he recognized that Polaroid's fortunes had been fading for years. But he worried that such a lowbrow product would tarnish Polaroid's reputation, built by founder Edwin H. Land, for creating elegant products based on high technology.

"Dr. Land is rolling over in his grave," he said. "High-revolution rotation is going on right now." The engineers doubled over in guffaws.

As it turned out, though, this camera was no joke.

Over the next three years, the project would polarize Polaroid, pitting its old-line scientists and engineers against the insurgent marketing people in a struggle for the corporate soul. Early on, some executives were so concerned that they devised a strategy to play down the Polaroid brand name in case the camera failed. Yelling matches erupted from time to time.

"I was sort of the referee," says Chief Executive Gary T. DiCamillo.

Ads on "Buffy"

But with Mr. DiCamillo's support, the marketeers eventually prevailed, and transformed the company in the process. So Polaroid, which used to pitch its cameras in ads on "60 Minutes," now hawks its wares on "Buffy the Vampire Slayer." One commercial features a young man who sticks instant pictures on his nipples and then wiggles his chest.

Polaroid's I-Zone Instant Pocket camera became America's No. 1 selling camera in December, less than three months after it became available here. Half of the buyers are girls between 13 and 17. The camera costs about $25, and a 12-exposure roll of film runs around $7.

So how long has it been since Polaroid had this kind of hit? The most recent one, the OneStep Land Camera, was introduced the year Jimmy Carter became president.

The Pocket camera has been a huge boost in large part because its pictures can be peeled off and stuck to another surface. Polaroid's new-product revenue amounted to $270 million last year, the most in at least a decade. More than 25% of that revenue came from Pocket film and camera sales, though those products were on the U.S. market for only the last quarter. And for 1999, Polaroid reported its first annual profit (of $9 million) since 1994.

Maddie Katz is one of the reasons why. One day, Ms. Katz, a 14-year-old from Glen Mills, Pa., uses her Pocket to snap a shot of some pals dozing off at the school library. Another day, a friend takes pictures as she poses while wrapped in a feathery boa, or clad in a bikini. The sticky photos look great on her assignment book, she says: "We like to dress them up."

The Glory Days

The company's early engineers surely never imagined that their fortunes would rest on such a low-tech product. Polaroid's culture was set by Mr. Land, a Harvard University dropout who eventually became one of the most prolific inventors in American history.

There was more than a hint of manifest destiny when Mr. Land would urge his engineers to act heroically, to think big. "He used to say, 'We don't have to do our own market surveys, we make our markets.'" recalls Elkan R. Blout, vice president of research during Polaroid's heyday in the 1950s and 1960s.

At the time, the bravado made sense because Polaroid's technology was such a novelty. That changed with the rise of one-hour photo labs and digital photography in the 1980s and 1990s. Polaroid's thunder was stolen.

By late 1995, when Mr. DiCamillo arrived from Black & Decker Corp. as Polaroid's new CEO, the picture was bleak. Mr. DiCamillo, a chemical engineer by training, set off a series of painful restructurings and layoffs.

The cuts couldn't come fast enough. In 1998, turmoil in Russia and Asia caused Polaroid's significant sales there to collapse. Debt rose, its credit ranking sank, and several executives jumped ship. The mood was somber and seemed to improve only in the event of a natural disaster. The reason: Hurricanes and tornadoes prompted insurance adjusters to take more instant pictures out in the field.

By last year, analysts were speculating that Mr. DiCamillo was running out of time. Talk of a takeover mounted. But the same dismissive answer always came back: Who'd want to buy Polaroid?

On a winter day in 1997, Clifford P. Hall, then Polaroid's general manager of new-product development, was strolling through Tokyo when he noticed teenage girls cramming into photo booths that take instant minipictures. He mentioned it to a Polaroid customer, Tomy Co., a Japanese toy manufacturer. Tomy executives promptly came back to Polaroid with a small instant-camera model. Their plan: Polaroid would design it, Tomy would sell it.

Sandra B. Lawrence, then Polaroid's vice president of new products and product planning, immediately took to the idea. A mother of three, she knew from her own dinner-table conversations that kids didn't use her company's cameras. Tomy's version, she thought, would be "a cool idea."

Philip R. Norris, a veteran Polaroid inventor, went to work right away. Within weeks, he had fashioned several models, which they took to Tomy officials in their offices outside of Tokyo. The meeting started badly. Just as Mr. Norris was about to present his first camera, one with a long lens, a Tomy official immediately waved him off. "Too big," the executive said. "I don't want to see that."

Mr. Norris, actually, was quite proud of that model. But he moved on, taking out a smaller version and placing it inches from the executive's face. The inventor explained, a bit sheepishly, that this cruder Prototype worked only from short distances. The executive smiled broadly and said, "Japan's a small country. We don't mind getting close."

The Pocket camera was set in motion, and Polaroid learned an important lesson: "Quality is not the first priority," says Tadaaki Masuda, then president of Polaroid's Japanese unit. "Convenience, small size, price, compactness—these are important."

The technologists at Polaroid were another matter.

Low Expectations

In a meeting back in Cambridge, Fawwaz Habbal, then vice president of technology, listened with grave doubts as Ms. Lawrence and Mr. Hall explained the Pocket concept. "Can you see the person in the picture?" Dr. Habbal asked them. He wondered about the impact of a product with "very marginal" image quality. "If Polaroid puts its name on something like this," he asked, "can this be satisfactory in the marketplace?"

The marketing staff told him the camera was being launched in Japan, which would limit the potential damage. And they made another concession: The camera would prominently display the Tomy name and play down Polaroid's. If it did well overseas, the company would introduce a different version in the U.S. with better optics. Dr. Habbal was satisfied.

When the camera hit, Japan in May 1998, the Tomy name was emblazoned in red letters on the face of the product. The Polaroid name, in the lower left corner, blended into the black molding.

If expectations were low, there was ample reason. A lot of old-timers remembered the brief, unsuccessful life of the Swinger, a small camera aimed at youngsters in the 1960s. And executives of more recent vintage were still smarting from the failure of the Captiva, a small camera that had targeted upscale customers. Polaroid invested hundreds of millions before abandoning it in 1996, just three years after its vaunted introduction.

From John R. Jenkins, Polaroid's vice president of manufacturing, came another concern: It would cost millions to build machines to manufacture film for such small pictures. Until the camera proved it could sell, he concluded, it was more sensible to assemble the film by hand.

So Polaroid hired about 100 workers at its factory in Queretaro, Mexico, to work in the dark, using night-vision goggles to assemble the film. That cut costs but presented an unexpected diplomatic problem when film sales surged in Japan.

The U.S. State Department refused to allow the company to ship additional goggles into Mexico for its expanded work force. Such gear is restricted because it can be used in warfare.

The goggles sat in a U.S. warehouse, despite pleas from Polaroid officials in Tokyo who ran out of film for their eager teenage customers.

Polaroid tried to keep up with demand by having some Mexican workers assemble the film "in the dark, literally," without wearing goggles, Mr. Jenkins says. Finally, last summer, Polaroid persuaded the State Department that the goggles were in the best interests of the company, and the North American Free Trade Agreement.

Anonymous Gripes

Things weren't much smoother back at headquarters in Cambridge.

As word of the project spread, anonymous postings lambasting company executives cropped up on bulletin boards on the Yahoo! Web site. Mr. Hall, general manager of new-product development, was accused of turning Polaroid "into a toy company."

Others were less shy. Ed Coughlan, for one, says he thought the camera was "crazy." "I'm an old engineer. I couldn't for the life of me figure out who'd buy it."

But Mr. Coughlan was a Polaroid loyalist, and once he was tapped to oversee the film's development, there were few better advocates. Whenever he needed a "couple million bucks" for the project—and it was not infrequently—he knew there would be "hell to pay." Serafino Posa, then executive vice president in charge of marketing, would shout, "You're out of your mind," Mr. Coughlan recalls. During one of these episodes, Mr. Coughlan yelled back at him, "You don't understand the damn program!" (Mr. Posa, who resigned from Polaroid in late 1998, denies that he opposed the camera but declines to elaborate due to a nondisclosure agreement.)

The internal debate fizzled, though, as skyrocketing sales figures came in from Japan. Encouraged, Polaroid hit the U.S. with an aggressive marketing campaign. The company advertised heavily on teenage TV shows. Polaroid also advertised on popular teen Web sites, including chickclick.com. And it proudly put the Polaroid name on the camera's front, in clear white lettering.

Between November 1999 and last January, the company sold more than a half-million Pocket cameras in Wal-Mart, Target and other mass-merchandise and drugstores. Before the Pocket's introduction, the average age of a Polaroid camera owner had been 42. Now, the company says it's in the early- to mid-30s.

Much of the old guard has come around, including Dr. Liggero, now vice president of film research and development. The Pocket camera is "not elegant, it's toyish, it doesn't involve the great inventions," he says. "But what I failed to appreciate was, it was good enough."

There has been a noticeable lift in Mr. DiCamillo's mood of late. The CEO, who had cut a grim figure a year ago, now carries around a contract extension. "Our instant business has seen a remarkable turnaround," he crowed at a recent industry meeting.

Investors aren't convinced. Polaroid's' stock price has languished for months in the $20 to $25 range. And analysts aren't likely to declare a full recovery until Polaroid shows it can sustain its momentum.

To that end, the company has been expanding into new retail channels, including music outlets and toy stores. Polaroid is ramping up its U.S. advertising by 30% to $55.3 million this year and continuing to convey the message in its youth marketing that "being a little bit bad is good," according to strategists.

Meanwhile, Pocket cameras are being introduced in a variety of new colors, from wasabi green to radical red. And the company recently signed a sponsorship deal with teenage pop star Britney Spears, whose contract specifies that she use the camera during her concert tour.

During her shows, she plucks a young man from the audience, serenades him and poses with him for a Pocketsnapshot. "That was my idea," says the 18-year-old diva in her dressing room before a recent gig in Charleston, W.Va. The star effect seems to be working for some customers. Says 10-year-old Megan Price: "If Britney Spears uses it, then I'd want to use it."

Source: Alec Klein, "On a Roll," *The Wall Street Journal* May 2, 2000, A1, A10. Copyright 2000 by Dow Jones & Company, Inc. Reproduced with permission of Dow Jones & Company, Inc., in the format textbook via Copyright Clearance Center.

Epilogue

Last year, Polaroid Corp. finally broke out of its long stupor. In a brilliant stroke, it developed the $25 I-Zone instant camera that produces stamp-size sticker prints and became a runaway hit with the teeny-bopper crowd. Kids used the tiny pictures to decorate everything from their lockers to their clothes, and adults discovered uses for the sticky pics that Polaroid never imagined, such as affixing photos of their shoes to shoeboxes. The I-Zone quickly became the world's best-selling camera, in terms of units, and helped Polaroid finish in the black for the first time in five years.

But it's now clear that Polaroid is going to need a lot more than the I-Zone to deliver on its long-promised turnaround. With the U.S. economy slowing, the Cambridge (Mass.)-based company announced in October that big retailers did not place their usual flood of holiday orders in September. As a result, Polaroid earned $18 million on sales of $458 million in the third quarter, or 26% lower profits than the Street had expected. Investors hammered the stock, which has plunged to a 15-year low of less than $9 a share.

Staggering

Even more critical, however, is the question of Polaroid's next act. The company is moving aggressively to meet the exploding demand for digital cameras, but the returns there are uncertain—no one has yet figured out how to make much money in this intensely competitive market. At the same time, Polaroid is carrying a staggering debt load of $830 million, partly a vestige of the company's struggle to avoid a takeover by Shamrock Holdings Inc. in the late 1980s. Interest payments of $63 million ate up 58% of operating profits through the first nine months of the year. With $61 million in cash on hand as of Sept. 30, the company has little margin for error. "The question is whether they'll be able to carry through with their turnaround, or whether they're dead on the vine," says Brett Barner, manager of the STI Small Cap Growth Fund, one of Polaroid's largest investors.

While readily conceding these are tough days for Polaroid, Chief Executive Gary T. DiCamillo insists that his recovery plan is on track. "Turnarounds take a long time," he says. Having given Polaroid fresh momentum with the I-Zone, he is rolling out cameras that combine digital technology with instant film. That will be followed in a year or two by an all-new print technology he says will be higher quality and cheaper than traditional 35mm prints. "We have as good a chance as anyone" to make it in the digital world, DiCamillo says.

It has been slow going so far. In 1999, Polaroid eked out $9 million in earnings on $1.9 billion in sales. The consensus among analysts is for 2000 earnings to climb 17%, to about $10.5 million, says First Call Corp. Sales are expected to grow slightly, possibly rising to about $2 billion. The company has been considered takeover bait for several years for companies such as Agfa-Gevaert Group or Sony Corp. But even as its market cap has shriveled to a mere $375 million—down from $2.4 billion in August, 1997—hopes for a takeover have faded. The disappointing third quarter didn't help. Sales in that period fell 1%, on accelerated erosion of one of its core businesses—peel-apart instant film. Sales of the film fell by about 30%, to roughly $60 million, because the professional photographers who use it are rapidly switching to digital technology, says Ulysses A. Yannas, an analyst at Buckman, Buckman & Reid, a New York brokerage firm.

But DiCamillo insists that the worries about the fall results are misplaced. He says the previously delayed Christmas orders have started to roll in, and digital camera sales are now running ahead of expectations. But he acknowledges that the company's debt load is about $200 million too high. On Nov. 16, he announced the first step in reducing that debt: Polaroid said it plans to vacate and sell an I.M. Pei-designed factory near Boston that analysts estimate is worth more than $100 million.

Jump-Start

DiCamillo knows a tough turnaround when he sees one. He took the helm in 1995 after a highly successful stint as CEO of Black & Decker Corp., where he is credited with revitalizing the company's consumer power-tool business by introducing lots of new products. The first outside CEO at Polaroid, DiCamillo says he quickly discovered that the company's problems were worse than he expected. They included a lack of any R&D aimed at improving the company's core product, instant film. He responded with a three-pronged strategy. To cut costs, he slashed the workforce by 27%, from 12,300 to 9,000 workers, and sold unprofitable commercial businesses for more than $50 million. Then he jump-started the effort to find new products in the company's billion-dollar, instant-film operation, which provides more than 90% of the company's profits. Finally, he began moving Polaroid into the digital age. "Not only do we have to rejuvenate our core business," he says, "we also have to adapt to technological change."

Instant photography had been languishing for so long that it was unfamiliar to two generations of customers. The company had been concentrating on developing specialty products such as an imaging film designed to replace X-rays, which turned into a costly bomb. DiCamillo abruptly shifted direction to focus more on the consumer market. He hired a new design team, introduced loads of new products, and revitalized marketing.

The company now introduces about 20 to 25 products a year. Another big hit last year besides the I-Zone was the JoyCam, which produces bigger prints. This Christmas, the company is introducing about a dozen products, including more variations on the I-Zone, digital picture frames that display images downloaded from the Internet, and the Webster, a tiny scanner that makes digital images of I-Zone photos. Retailers are enthusiastic. "This brings the fun back into photography and introduces it to the younger shutterbug," says Shawn Haynes, director of photography sales at Amazon.com Inc.'s Web site, where eight of his recent top 10 sellers were I-Zone or JoyCam products.

Polaroid's prospects in digital photography are less certain. It's a market leader in low-end digital cameras, with its best-seller costing $175. And it is one of the few companies making a profit on them. But its 5% to 10% margins on digital cameras are tiny compared with the 60%-plus margins it makes on instant film. And the field is only growing more crowded, with more than 100 companies fighting it out.

Moreover, as digital cameras proliferate, they suck the life out of Polaroid's older instant-film products. It's only a question of how rapidly these products will fall. Already, instant-camera users are making the transition. Tom Alexander, an agent with DeWolfe Real Estate in Boston, says he now rarely uses his Polaroid: "If you want to advertise on the Internet, it's useful to have a digital camera."

Polaroid's best hope next year is for the I-Zone to stay hot and for new hybrid digital/instant cameras to kick in. That's the reasoning behind Wall Street's projections of further profit growth for the company in 2001. Still, investors have pushed the stock to new lows because of the long-term doubts. "The consumer market for hybrid products is not big," says Edward Y. Lee, a consultant at Lyra Research in Cambridge, Mass.

Count the Polaroid board among the optimists: Last December, 10 months before DiCamillo's contract was set to expire, the board extended his term to the end of 2002. But if he's going to make it that far, he'll have to start mastering a digital transition that has already claimed such CEOs as Eastman Kodak Co.'s George Fisher. The picture at Polaroid is anything but clear.

By Rochelle Sharpe in Boston, with Geoffrey Smith

Source: "Hazy Picture at Polaroid," *Business Week,* December 4, 2000, 95–96.

Case 1–3
EuroDisney*

In April 1992, EuroDisney SCA opened its doors to European visitors. Located by the river Marne some 20 miles east of Paris, it was designed to be the biggest and most lavish theme

*This case was prepared by Professor Lyn S. Amine and graduate student Carolyn A. Tochtrop, Saint Louis University, St. Louis, MO, as a basis for class discussion rather than to illustrate either effective or ineffective handling of a situation.

park that Walt Disney Company (Disney) has built to date—bigger than Disneyland in Anaheim, California, Disneyworld in Orlando, Florida, and Tokyo Disneyland in Japan. In 1989, "EuroDisney" was expected to be a surefire moneymaker for its parent Disney, led by Chairman Michael Eisner and President Frank Wells. Since then, sadly, Wells was killed in an air accident in spring of 1994, and EuroDisney lost nearly $1 billion during the 1992–93 fiscal year.

Much to Disney management's surprise, Europeans failed to "go wacky" over Mickey, unlike their Japanese counterparts. Between 1990 and early 1992, some 14 million people had visited Tokyo Disneyland, with three quarters being repeat visitors. A family of four staying overnight at a nearby hotel would easily spend $600 on a visit to the park. In contrast, at EuroDisney families were reluctant to spend the $280 a day needed to enjoy the attractions of the park, including *les hamburgers* and *les milkshakes.* Staying overnight was out of the question for many because hotel rooms were so high priced. For example, prices ranged from $110 to $380 a night at the Newport Bay Club, the largest of EuroDisney's six new hotels and one of the biggest in Europe. In comparison, a room in a top hotel in Paris costs between $340 and $380 a night.

In 1994, financial losses were becoming so massive at EuroDisney that Michael Eisner had to step in personally in order to structure a rescue package. EuroDisney was put back on firm ground. A two-year window of financial peace was introduced, but not until after some acrimonious dealings with French banks had been settled and an unexpected investment by a Saudi prince had been accepted. Disney management rapidly introduced a range of strategic and tactical changes in the hope of "doing it right" this time. Analysts are presently trying to diagnose what went wrong and what the future might hold for EuroDisney.

Expansion into Europe was supposed to be Disney's major source of growth in the 1990s, bolstering slowing prospects back home in the United States. "Europe is our big project for the rest of this century," boasted Robert J. Fitzpatrick, chairman of EuroDisney in spring 1990. The Paris location was chosen over 200 other potential sites stretching from Portugal through Spain, France, Italy, and into Greece. Spain thought it had the strongest bid based on its year-long temperate-and-sunny Mediterranean climate, but insufficient acreage of land was available for development around Barcelona.

In the end, the French government's generous incentives, together with impressive data on regional demographics, swayed Eisner to choose the Paris location. It was calculated that some 310 million people in Europe live within two hours' air travel of EuroDisney, and 17 million could reach the park within two hours by car—better demographics than at any other Disney site. Pessimistic talk about the dismal winter weather of northern France was countered with references to the success of Tokyo Disneyland, where resolute visitors brave cold winds and snow to enjoy their piece of Americana. Furthermore, it was argued, Paris is Europe's most-popular city destination among tourists of all nationalities.

According to the master agreement signed by the French government in March 1987, 51 percent of EuroDisney would be offered to European investors, with about half of the new shares being sold to the French. At that time, the project was valued at about FFr 12 billion ($1.8 billion). Disney's initial equity stake in EuroDisney was acquired for FFr 850 million (about $127.5 million). After the public offering, the value of Disney's stake zoomed to $1 billion on the magic of the Disney name.

Inducements by the French government were varied and generous:

- Loans of up to FFr 4.8 billion at a lower-than-market fixed rate of interest.

- Tax advantages for writing off construction costs.

- Construction by the French government, free of charge, of rail and road links from Paris out to the park. The TGV (*tré grande vitesse*) fast train was scheduled to serve the park by 1994, along with road traffic coming from Britain through the Channel Tunnel or "Chunnel."

- Land (4,800 acres) sold to Disney at 1971 agricultural prices. Resort and property development going beyond the park itself was projected to bring in about a third of the scheme's total revenues between 1992 and 1995.

As one analyst commented, "EuroDisney could probably make money without Mickey, as a property development alone." These words would come back to haunt Disney in 1994 as real estate development plans were halted and hotel rooms remained empty, some even being closed during the first winter.

Disney had projected that the new theme park would attract 11 million visitors and generate over $100 million in operating earnings during the first year of operation. EuroDisney was expected to make a small pre-tax profit of FFr 227 million ($34 million) in 1994, rising to nearly FFr 3 billion ($450 million) in 2001. By summer 1994, EuroDisney had lost more than $900 million since opening. Attendance reached only 9.2 million in 1992, and visitors spent 12 percent less on purchases than the estimated $33 per head. European tour operators were unable to rally sufficient interest among vacationers to meet earlier commitments to fill the park's hotels, and demanded that EuroDisney renegotiate their deals. In August 1992, Karen Gee, marketing manager of Airtours PLC, a British travel agency, worried about troubles yet to come: "On a foggy February day, how appealing will this park be?" Her winter bookings at that time were dismal.

If tourists were not flocking to taste the thrills of the new EuroDisney, where were they going for their summer vacations in 1992? Ironically enough, an unforeseen combination of transatlantic airfare wars and currency movements resulted in a trip to Disneyworld in Orlando being cheaper than a trip to Paris, with guaranteed good weather and beautiful Floridian beaches within easy reach.

EuroDisney management took steps to rectify immediate problems in 1992 by cutting rates at two hotels up to 25 percent, introducing some cheaper meals at restaurants, and launching a Paris ad blitz that proclaimed "California is only 20 miles from Paris."

One of the most worrying aspects of EuroDisney's first year was that French visitors stayed away. They had been expected to make up 50 percent of the attendance figures. Two years later, Dennis Spiegel, president of the International Theme Park Services consulting firm, based in Cincinnati, framed the problem in these words: "the French see EuroDisney as American imperialism—plastics at its worst." The well-known, sentimental Japanese attachment to Disney characters contrasted starkly with the unexpected and widespread French scorn for American fairy-tale characters. French culture has its own lovable cartoon characters such as Astérix, the helmeted, pint-sized Gaelic warrior who has a theme park located near EuroDisney. Parc Astérix went through a major renovation and expansion in anticipation of competition from EuroDisney.

Hostility among the French people to the whole "Disney idea" had surfaced early in the planning of the new project. Paris theater director Ariane Mnouchkine became famous for her description of EuroDisney as "a cultural Chernobyl." A 1988 book, *Mickey: The Sting,* by French journalist Giles Smadja, denounced the $350 million that the government had committed at that time to building park-related infrastructure. In fall 1989, during a visit to Paris, Michael Eisner was pelted with eggs by French communists. Finally, many farmers took to the streets to protest against the preferential sales price of local land.

Early advertising by EuroDisney seemed to aggravate local French sentiment by emphasizing glitz and size, rather than the variety of rides and attractions. Committed to maintaining Disney's reputation for quality in everything, Chairman Eisner insisted that more and more detail be built into EuroDisney.

For example, the centerpiece castle in the Magic Kingdom had to be bigger and fancier than in the other parks. He ordered the removal of two steel staircases in Discoveryland, at a cost of $200,000 to $300,000, because they blocked a view of the Star Tours ride. Expensive trams were built along a lake to take guests from the hotels to the park, but visitors preferred walking. An 18-hole golf course, built to adjoin 600 new vacation homes, was constructed and then enlarged to add another 9 holes. Built before the homes, the course cost $15 to $20 million and remains underused. Total park construction costs were estimated at FFr 14 billion ($2.37 billion) in 1989 but rose by $340 million to FFr 16 billion as a result of all these add-ons. Hotel construction costs rose from an estimated FFr 3.4 billion to FFr 5.7 billion.

EuroDisney and Disney managers unhappily succeeded in alienating many of their counterparts in the government, the banks, the ad agencies, and other concerned organizations. A barnstorming, kick-the-door-down attitude seemed to reign among the U.S. decision makers. Beatrice Descoffre, a French construction industry official, complained that "they were always sure it would work because they were Disney." A top French banker involved in setting up the master agreement felt that Disney executives had tried to steamroller their ideas. "They had a formidable image and convinced everyone that if we let them do it their way, we would all have a marvelous adventure."

Disney executives consistently decline to comment on their handling of management decisions during the early days, but point out that many of the same people complaining about Disney's aggressiveness were only too happy to sign on with Disney before conditions deteriorated. One former Disney executive voiced the opinion, "We were arrogant—it was like 'We're building the Taj Mahal and people will come—on our terms.'"

Disney and its advisors failed to see signs at the end of the 1980s of the approaching European recession. As one former executive said, "We were just trying to keep our heads above water. Between the glamour and the pressure of opening and the intensity of the project itself, we didn't realize a major recession was coming." Other dramatic events included the Gulf War in 1991, which put a heavy brake on vacation travel for the rest of that year. The fall of communism in 1989 after the destruction of the Berlin Wall provoked far-reaching effects on the world economy. National defense industries were drastically reduced among western nations. Foreign aid was requested from the West by newly emerging democracies in Eastern Europe. Other external factors that Disney executives have cited in the past as contributing to their financial difficulties at EuroDisney were high interest rates and the devaluation of several currencies against the franc.

Difficulties were also encountered by EuroDisney with regard to competition. Landmark events took place in Spain in 1992. The World's Fair in Seville and the 1992 Olympics in Barcelona were huge attractions for European tourists. In the future, new theme parks are planned for Spain by Anheuser-Busch with their $300-million Busch Gardens near Barcelona, as well as Six Flags Corporation's Magic Mountain park to be located in Marbella.

Disney management's conviction that it knew best was demonstrated by their much-trumpeted ban on alcohol in the park. This proved insensitive to the local culture because the French are the world's biggest consumers of wine. To them a meal without *un verre de rouge* [a glass of red wine] is unthinkable. Disney relented. It also had to relax its rules on personal grooming of the projected 12,000 cast members, the park employees. Women were allowed to wear redder nail polish than in the U.S., but the taboo on men's facial hair was maintained. "We want the clean-shaven, neat and tidy look," commented David Kannally, director of Disney University's Paris branch. The "university" trains prospective employees in Disney values and culture by means of a one-and-a-half-day seminar. EuroDisney's management did, however, compromise on the question of pets. Special kennels were built to house visitors' animals. The thought of leaving a pet at home during vacation is considered irrational by many French people.

Plans for further development of EuroDisney after 1992 were ambitious. The initial number of hotel rooms was planned to be 5,200, more than in the entire city of Cannes on the Côte d'Azur. This number was supposed to triple in a few years as Disney opened a second theme park to keep visitors at the EuroDisney resort for a longer stay. There would also be a huge amount of office space, 700,000 square meters, just slightly smaller than France's largest office complex, La Défense in Paris. Also planned were shopping malls, apartments, golf courses, and vacation homes. EuroDisney would design and build everything itself, with a view to selling at a profit. As a Disney executive commented with hindsight, "Disney at various points could have had partners to share the risk, or buy the hotels outright. But it didn't want to give up the upside."

Disney management wanted to avoid two costly mistakes it had learned from the past: letting others build the money-making hotels surrounding a park (as happened at Disneyland in Anaheim); and letting another company own a Disney park (as in Tokyo where Disney just collects royalties). This time, along with 49 percent ownership of EuroDisney, Disney would receive both a park management fee and royalties on merchandise sales.

The outstanding success record of Chairman Eisner and President Wells in reviving Disney during the 1980s led people to believe that the duo could do nothing wrong. "From the time they came on, they had never made a single misstep, never a mistake, never a failure," said a former Disney executive, "There was a tendency to believe that everything they touched would be perfect." This belief was fostered by the incredible growth record achieved by Eisner and Wells. In the seven years before EuroDisney opened, they took Disney from being a company with $1 billion in revenues to one with $8.5 billion, mainly through internal growth.

Dozens of banks, led by France's Banque Nationale de Paris, Banque Indosuez, and Caisse des Depôts & Consignations, eagerly signed on to provide construction loans. One banker who saw the figures for the deal expressed concern. "The company was overleveraged. The structure was dangerous." Other critics charged that the proposed financing was risky because it relied on capital gains from future real estate transactions.

The Disney response to this criticism was that those views reflected the cautious, Old World thinking of Europeans who didn't understand U.S.-style free-market financing. Supporters of Disney point out that for more than two years after the initial public offering of shares, the stock price continued to do well, and that initial loans were at a low rate. It was the later cost overruns and the necessity for a bail-out at the end of the first year that undermined the initial forecasts.

Optimistic assumptions that the 1980s boom in real estate in Europe would continue through the 1990s and that interest rates and currencies would remain stable led Disney to rely heavily on debt financing. The real estate developments outside EuroDisney were supposed to draw income to help pay down the $3.4 billion in debt. That in turn was intended to help Disney finance a second park close by—an MGM Studios film tour site—which would draw visitors to help fill existing hotel rooms. None of this happened. As a senior French banker commented later in 1994, EuroDisney is a "good theme park married to a bankrupt real estate company—and the two can't be divorced."

Mistaken assumptions by the Disney management team affected construction design, marketing and pricing policies, and park management, as well as initial financing. For example, parking space for buses proved much too small. Restroom facilities for drivers could accommodate 50 people; on peak days there were 200 drivers. With regard to demand for meal service, Disney executives had been erroneously informed that Europeans don't eat breakfast. Restaurant breakfast service was downsized accordingly, and guess what? "Everybody showed up for breakfast. We were trying to serve 2,500 breakfasts in a 350-seat restaurant (at some of the hotels). The lines were horrendous. And they didn't just want croissants and coffee. They wanted bacon and eggs," lamented one Disney executive. Disney reacted quickly, delivering prepackaged breakfasts to rooms and other satellite locations.

In contrast to Disney's American parks where visitors, typically, stay at least three days, EuroDisney is at most a two-day visit. Energetic visitors need even less time. Jeff Summers, an analyst at debt broker Klesch & Co. in London, claims to have "done" every EuroDisney ride in just five hours. "There aren't enough attractions to get people to spend the night," he commented in summer of 1994. Typically, many guests arrive early in the morning, rush to the park, come back to their hotel late at night, then check out the next morning before heading back to the park. The amount of check-in and check-out traffic was vastly underestimated when the park opened: extra computer terminals were installed rapidly in the hotels.

In promoting the new park to visitors. Disney did not stress the entertainment value of a visit to the new theme park. The emphasis on the size of the park "ruined the magic," said a Paris-based ad agency executive. But in early 1993, ads were changed to feature Zorro, a French favorite; Mary Poppins; and Aladdin, star of the huge money-making movie success. A print ad campaign at that time featured Aladdin, Cinderella's castle, and a little girl being invited to enjoy a "magic vacation." A promotional package was offered—two days, one night, and one breakfast at an unnamed EuroDisney hotel—for $95 per adult and free for kids. The tagline said. "The kingdom where all dreams come true."

Early in 1994 the decision was taken to add six new attractions. In March the Temple of Peril ride opened; Storybook Land followed in May; and the Nautilus attraction was planned for June. Donald Duck's birthday was celebrated on June 9. A secret new thrill ride was promised in 1995. "We are positioning EuroDisney as the No. 1 European destination of short duration, one to three days," said a park spokesperson. Previously no effort had been made to hold visitors for a specific length of stay. Moreover, added the spokesperson, "One of our primary messages is, after all, that EuroDisney is affordable to everyone." Although new package deals and special low-season rates substantially offset costs to visitors, the overall entrance fee has not been changed and is higher than in the U.S.

With regard to park management, seasonal disparities in attendance have caused losses in projected revenues. Even on a day-to-day basis, EuroDisney management has had difficulty forecasting numbers of visitors. Early expectations were that Monday would be a light day for visitors, and Friday a heavy one. Staff allocations were made accordingly. The opposite was true. EuroDisney management still struggles to find the right level of staffing at a park where high-season attendance can be 10 times the number in the low season. The American tradition of "hiring and firing" employees at will is difficult, if not impossible, in France where workers' rights are stringently protected by law.

Disney executives had optimistically expected that the arrival of their new theme park would cause French parents to take their children out of school in midsession for a short break. It did not happen, unless a public holiday occurred over a weekend. Similarly, Disney expected that the American-style short but more frequent family trips would displace the European tradition of a one-month family vacation, usually taken in August. However, French office and factory schedules remain the same, with their emphasis on an August shutdown.

Faced with falling share prices and crisis talk among shareholders, Disney was forced to step forward in late 1993 to rescue the new park. Disney announced that it would fund EuroDisney until a financial restructuring could be worked out with lenders. However, it was made clear by the parent company, Disney, that it "was not writing a blank check."

In November 1993, it was announced that an allocation of $350 million to deal with EuroDisney's problems had resulted in the first quarterly loss for Disney in nine years. Reporting on fourth-quarter results for 1993, Disney announced its share of EuroDisney losses as $517 million for fiscal 1993. The overall performance of Disney was not, however, affected. It reported a profit of nearly $300 million for the fiscal year ending September 30, 1993, thanks to strong performance by its U.S. theme parks and movies produced by its entertainment division. This compared to a profit of $817 million for the year before.

The rescue plan developed in fall 1993 was rejected by the French banks. Disney fought back by imposing a deadline for agreement of March 31, 1994, and even hinted at possible closure of EuroDisney. By mid-March, Disney's commitment to support EuroDisney had risen to $750 million. A new preliminary deal struck with EuroDisney's lead banks required the banks to contribute some $500 million. The aim was to cut the park's high-cost debt in half and make EuroDisney profitable by 1996, a date considered unrealistic by many analysts.

The plan called for a rights offering of FFr 6 billion (about $1.02 billion at current rates) to existing shareholders at below-market prices. Disney would spend about $508 million to buy 49 percent of the offering. Disney also agreed to buy certain EuroDisney park assets for $240 million and lease them back to EuroDisney on favorable terms. Banks agreed to forgive 18 months of interest payments on outstanding debt and would defer all principal payments for three years. Banks would also underwrite the remaining 51 percent of the rights offering. For its part, Disney agreed to eliminate for five years its lucrative management fees and royalties on the sale of tickets and merchandise. Royalties would gradually be reintroduced at a lower level.

Analysts commented that approval by EuroDisney's 63 creditor banks and its shareholders was not a foregone conclusion. Also, the future was clouded by the need to resume payment of debt interest and royalties after the two-year respite.

In June 1994, EuroDisney received a new lifeline when a member of the Saudi royal family agreed to invest up to $500 million for a 24 percent stake in the park. Prince Al-Walid bin Talal bin Abdul-Aziz Al-Saud is a well-known figure in the world of high finance. Years ago he expressed the desire to be worth $5 billion by 1998. Western-educated, His Royal Highness Prince Al-Walid holds stock in Citicorp worth $1.6 billion and is its biggest shareholder. The prince has an established reputation in world markets as a "bottom-fisher," buying into potentially viable operations during crises when share prices are low. He also holds 11 percent of Saks Fifth Avenue, and owns a chain of hotels and supermarkets, his own United Saudi Commercial Bank in Riyadh, a Saudi construction company, and part of the new Arab Radio and Television Network in the Middle East. The prince plans to build a $100-million convention center at EuroDisney. One of the few pieces of good news about EuroDisney is that its convention business exceeded expectations from the beginning.

The prince's investment could reduce Disney's stake in EuroDisney to as little as 36 percent. The prince has agreed not to increase the size of his holding for 10 years. He also agreed that if his EuroDisney stake ever exceeds 50 percent of Disney's, he must liquidate that portion.

The prince loves Disney culture. He has visited both EuroDisney and Disneyworld. He believes in the EuroDisney management team. Positive factors supporting his investment include the continuing European economic recovery, increased parity between European currencies, the opening of the Chunnel, and what is seen as a certain humbling in the attitude of Disney executives. Jeff Summers, analyst for Klesch & Co. in London, commented on the deal, saying that Disney now has a fresh chance "to show that Europe really needs an amusement park that will have cost $5 billion."

Sources:
"An American in Paris." *Business Week,* March 12, 1990, pp. 60–61, 64.
"A Charming Prince to the Rescue?" *Newsweek,* June 13, 1994, p. 43.
"EuroDisney Rescue Package Wins Approval." *The Wall Street Journal,* March 15, 1994, pp. A3, A13.
"EuroDisney Tries to End Evil Spell." *Advertising Age,* February 7, 1994, p. 39.
"EuroDisney's Prince Charming?" *Business Week,* June 13, 1994, p. 42.
"Disney Posts Loss: Troubles in Europe Blamed." *Los Angeles Times,* November 11, 1993, pp. A1, A34.
"How Disney Snared a Princely Sum." *Business Week,* June 20, 1994, pp. 61–62.
"Mickey Goes to the Bank." *The Economist,* September 16, 1989, p. 38.
"The Mouse Isn't Roaring." *Business Week,* August 24, 1992, p. 38.
"Mouse Trap: Fans Like EuroDisney but Its Parent's Goofs Weigh the Park Down." *The Wall Street Journal,* March 10, 1994, p. A12.
"Saudi to Buy as Much as 24% of EuroDisney." *The Wall Street Journal,* June 2, 1994, p. A4.

Situation Analysis

Part

2

Chapter 3

Market Vision, Structure, and Analysis

Markets are becoming increasingly complex and interrelated, creating challenges for managers in regard to understanding market structure and identifying opportunities for growth. Consider, for example, the pervasive impact of digital technology on the computer, telecommunications, photography, and office equipment markets. Rapid technological change, Internet access, global competition, and the diversity of buyers' preferences in many markets require continuous monitoring to identify promising business opportunities, assess the shifting requirements of buyers, evaluate changes in competitive positioning, and guide managers' decisions about which buyers to target and how to position brands to appeal to targeted buyers. A broad view of the market is important even when management's interest centers on one or a few market segments within a particular market. Mapping the entire market is necessary in the attempt to understand and anticipate market changes and competitive threats. Understanding markets and knowing how they are likely to change in the future are vital inputs to market-driven strategies.

The importance of forming a vision about the future is highlighted by the changes occurring in the photography market. A key strategic challenge for Eastman Kodak and the other companies competing in that market is anticipating the nature and scope of the impact of electronic imaging on the conventional film and camera markets.[1] Industry authorities believe digital photography will own the market no later than 2010 and possibly by 2005. Digital cameras were expected to exceed the resolution provided by film in 2002. The digital photography market is growing at a 60 percent annual rate.

Kodak's management must compete aggressively in the conventional film market while also rapidly developing capabilities to compete in digital imaging. Kodak must battle its Japanese film competitor, Fuji, around the world while moving forward with digital imaging products. The new competitive arena positions Kodak against Sony, Hewlett-Packard, Sanyo, Olympus, and other firms with electronic imaging capabilities. (See accompanying Sony advertisement). Importantly, Kodak has a huge stake in its film, photographic paper, and developing services businesses, which are critical to the company's financial performance. In 2001 Kodak's $13.2 billion sales were 6 percent below 2000 sales. Some industry observers believe that Kodak is not using enough of its resources to build the digital business. Its

digital cameras receive very positive ratings by photographers. Kodak partnered with Intel to produce sensor chips for digital cameras.

The Eastman Kodak example highlights several relevant issues concerning markets. Electronic imaging illustrates how different markets may become interrelated, as in the case of computers and imaging, and shows how competitive threats may develop from new business designs (electronic imaging versus conventional photography). Finally, the potential of electronic imaging points to the importance of market vision in determining the nature and scope of new competitive threats and developing strategies to counter those threats.

The chapter begins with a discussion of how markets and strategies are interrelated, followed by the presentation of an approach for mapping product-markets. Next we look at how buyers can be described and analyzed, and then we discuss competitor analysis. Guidelines for developing a strategic vision about the scope and composition of markets in the future follows. Finally, we consider market size estimation. Additional market forecasting guidelines are discussed in Appendix 3A.

Markets and Strategies

Market knowledge is essential in guiding business and marketing strategies. First, we look at how markets have an impact on strategy. Next, we examine the concept of value migration and how it affects market opportunities. The section concludes with a discussion of developing a shared vision about how the market is expected to change in the future.

Strategies and Markets Are Interlinked

Market changes often require altering business and marketing strategies. Managers who do not understand their markets and how they will change in the future may find the strategies they are using for competing inadequate as buyers' needs and wants change and alternative products become available to meet buyers' requirements. Many forces are causing the transformation of industries and are changing the nature of competition. The drivers of change include deregulation, global excess capacity, global competition, mergers and acquisitions, changing customer expectations, technological discontinuities, disintermediation, demographic shifts, and changing life and work styles.[2] These influences create both market opportunities and threats by changing the nature and scope of markets and the competitive space.

The dangers of faulty market sensing are illustrated by the experience of Encyclopedia Britannica, Inc. (EBI), a 200-year-old publishing company. CD-ROM technology rapidly impacted the traditional encyclopedia market in the early 1990s, and EBI's management did not respond to the competitive challenge even though the technology was available for its lower-priced Compton's brand.[3] By the end of 1994 some 16 million U.S. households had computer CD drives. EBI experienced sales drops and financial losses. By 1994 EBI's 2,300-person door-to-door sales force had declined to less than 1,100. Buyers were purchasing competitors' CD-ROM encyclopedia packages instead of reference books. Since the selling prices for CD-ROMs range from $100 to $400, compared with $1,500 or more for books, retail and direct mail sales were used to contact the customers. Management's vision about the market and how it might change was faulty. The financial losses through the mid-1990s forced the sale of the company. EBI eventually launched a new strategy for the electronic era and eliminated its direct sales force in 1996.

Value Migration

Value migration is the process of customers shifting their purchases away from products generated by outmoded business designs to new ones that offer superior value.[4] Examples include value migration from conventional typewriters to word processing and computers, from reference books to the CD-ROM format, and from camera and film to electronic imaging. Anticipating value migration threats is an essential aspect of market-driven strategy. Importantly, these threats may emerge from disruptive technologies that managers of existing products do not consider relevant competitive threats.

Value migration may affect a product category, a company, or an entire industry. Forecasting the exact nature, scope, and timing of migration may be difficult but is nonetheless essential. Market knowledge is a key input to assessing migration trends. Value migration points to the close relationship between strategies and markets and the need to define and understand the market and the competitive arena. The value migration concept also highlights the need for constant organizational learning and implementation of strategy changes to proactively respond to value migration situations.

Shared Vision about the Market

An important aspect of becoming market-oriented is developing a vision about the organization's markets and the possible future directions of change. As was discussed in Chapter 1, market orientation views the vision issue as a multifunctional responsibility. The process is too complex and too essential for reliance on a single decision maker. A knowledgeable management team is likely to be much more successful than an individual in forming an accurate vision about the market and the competitive arena.

Developing a strategic vision about the future requires (1) identifying and analyzing the forces of change that are expected to transform industry boundaries and create new competitive space and (2) forming a vision about the future.[5] Such market knowledge gives an organization the opportunity to lead the direction of industry development and compete for market position and market share. We continue the discussion of developing a strategic vision later in the chapter, after we consider how to define and analyze existing markets.

Mapping Product-Markets

The process of gaining an understanding of markets is shown in Exhibit 3–1. The first step is to define the market's boundaries and describe its structure. The result is a map of the product-market. Markets can be defined in many different ways, and they are constantly

EXHIBIT 3–1
The Process of Gaining an Understanding of Markets

Mapping the product-market

⇩

Market structure analysis

⇩

Market forecasts

⇩

Future vision about the market

Vivometrics, a Southern California startup, wants to put a shirt on your back. But the company's lightweight, stretchy garment is not your average muscle-T. Embedded in the fabric are four black bands equipped with electrodes and physiological sensors designed to record more than 40 vital signs, including fluid in the heart, breathing rate, and oxygen consumption.

The gigabytes of data stream from the sensors to a handheld computer discreetly located in a hip pocket of the shirt. Standard issue, one supposes, for Captain Kirk and the rest of the Enterprise crew. But Vivometrics says you will be able to order its Life Shirt within a year or two.

Vivometrics is blazing trails on a potentially vast frontier of e-health known as electronic care management. The first examples were fairly crude devices such as smart bathroom scales that could help heart failure patients keep accurate records of their weight. But like everything in the world of silicon, fiber optics, and radio communications, patient-care devices have shrunk in size, soared in IQ, diversified in application, and become so cheap that the most parsimonious HMO will soon consider them a bargain. As a result, gadget makers are zeroing in on a wide range of diseases, monitoring the blood sugar of diabetics, the EKGs of heart-attack survivors, and the breathing rates of asthmatics. "This is the future of medicine," says William W. George, chief executive of Medtronic Inc.

Ultimately, electronic care will save money and lives. The Institute for the Future reckons that some 120 million Americans, about 40% of the total population, will be living with a chronic disease by 2010. These patients will incur $600 billion in medical costs that year—a 16% increase from today. But Net-capable devices could help curb that escalation. Cost-effective "virtual office" exams could ease the burden on beleaguered hospitals, while improving the quality of care.

Source: Ellen Licking, "This Is the Future of Medicine," *Business Week E.Biz*, December 11, 2000, EB77.

changing, as illustrated by the Strategy Feature, which describes an emerging market called electronic care management. We look at how buyers' needs coupled with product benefits help map product-markets, and we discuss several considerations in forming product-markets.

Matching Needs with Product Benefits

The term *product-market* indicates that markets exist only when there are buyers with needs who have the ability to purchase products and products (goods or services) are available to satisfy those needs. Intuitively, it is easy to grasp the concept of a product-market, although there are differences in how managers define the term. Markets are groups of people who have the *ability* and *willingness* to buy something because they have a need for it.[6] Ability to buy and willingness to buy indicate that there is a demand for a particular product or service. People with needs and wants buy the benefits provided by a good or service to meet either a household or an organizational requirement. A product-market matches people with needs—needs that lead to a demand for a good or service—to the product benefits that satisfy those needs. Unless the product benefits are available, there is no market—only people with needs. Likewise, there must be people who have a use situation which can be satisfied by the product. Thus, a product-market combines the benefits of a product with the needs that cause people to express a demand for that product. Therefore, markets are defined in terms of needs substitutability among different products and brands and by the different ways in which people choose to satisfy their needs. "A product-market is the set of products judged to be substitutes within those usage situations in which similar patterns of benefits are sought by groups of customers."[7] The influence of competing brands becomes stronger as the substitutability becomes closer and the competition becomes more direct. The Ford Taurus competes directly with the Toyota Camry, whereas in a less direct yet relevant way, other major purchases (e.g., vacation travel) compete with automobile expenditures due to consumers' budget constraints.

As an example, a financial services product-market for short-term investments may include money market accounts of banks and brokers, U.S. Treasury bills, bank certificates of deposit, and other short-term investment alternatives. If one type of product is a substitute for another, both products should be included in the product-market.

By understanding how a firm's specific product or brand is positioned within the product-market, management can monitor and evaluate changes in the product-market to determine whether alternative targeting and positioning strategies and product offerings are needed. In mapping the product-market, it is essential to establish boundaries that contain all relevant product categories that are competing for the same buyer needs.

Mapping Product-Market Boundaries and Structure

Understanding product-market boundaries and structure provides managers with important information for developing business and marketing strategies and alerts management to new competition. Considering only a company's brands and its direct competitors may mask potential competitive threats or opportunities.

Product-Market Structure

A company's brands compete with other companies' brands in generic, product-type, and product-variant product-markets. The *generic product-market* includes a broad group of products that satisfy a general, yet similar, need. For example, several classes or types of products can be combined to form a generic product-market for kitchen appliances. The starting point in product-market definition is to determine the particular need or want that a group of products satisfies, such as kitchen functions. Since people with a similar need may not satisfy it in the same manner, generic product-markets are often heterogeneous, containing different end-user groups and several types of related products (e.g., kitchen appliances).

The *product-type product-market* includes all brands of a particular product type or class, such as ovens. The product type is a product category or product classification that offers a specific set of benefits intended to satisfy a customer's need or want in a specific way. Differences in the products within a product-type (class) product-market may exist, creating *product-variants*.[8] For example, there are electric, gas, and microwave ovens that provide heating functions but employ different technologies.

Guidelines for Definition

In mapping the product-market, it is helpful to determine (1) the basis for identifying buyers in the product-market of interest (geographical area and buyer characteristics such as age group), (2) the market size and characteristics, and (3) the brand and/or product categories competing for the needs and wants of the buyers included in the product-market. Suppose the top management of a kitchen appliance firm wants to expand its mix of products. The company's present line of laundry and dishwashing products meets a generic need

EXHIBIT 3–2
**Determining the
Structure of a
Product-Market**

Start with the generic need satisfied by
the product category of interest to
management

Identify the product categories (types)
that can satisfy the generic need

Form the specific product-markets within
the generic product-market.

for the kitchen functions of cleaning. Other kitchen use situations include the heating and cooling of foods. A logical expansion for the appliance firm would be to move into a closely related product type to gain the advantages of common distribution channels, manufacturing, advertising, and research and development. For example, in the 1980s Maytag's management acquired several companies, expanding from a specialty producer of laundry and dishwashing products into a full line of kitchen appliances, including refrigerators, stoves, and microwave ovens.

The structure (composition) of a product-market can be defined by following the steps shown in Exhibit 3–2. We consider how this process can be used to define the structure in the kitchen appliance product-market. In this example the generic need is performing various kitchen functions. The products that provide kitchen functions are ways of satisfying the generic need. The breakout of products into specific product-markets (e.g., A, B, C, and D) would include equipment for washing and drying clothing, appliances for cooling food, cooking appliances, and dishwashers. The buyers in various specific product-markets and the different brands competing in those product-markets can be analyzed. The process of mapping the product-market structure begins by identifying the generic need (function) satisfied by the product of interest to management. Need identification is the basis for selecting the products that fit into the product market.

A simplified example of the product-market structure which includes the fast-food market is shown in Exhibit 3–3. A fast-food restaurant chain such as McDonald's should consider more than its regular customers and direct competitors in its market opportunity analysis. For example, microwave oven preparation of foods affects fast-food patronage. The consumption need being satisfied is fast and convenient preparation of food. The buyer has several ways to meet that need, including purchasing fast foods, doing microwave preparation in the home, patronizing supermarket delis, buying prepared foods in convenience stores, and ordering takeouts from traditional restaurants. Thus, it is essential to analyze market behavior and trends in all the product-markets shown in Exhibit 3–3. Competition may come from any of the alternative services.

EXHIBIT 3–3
Illustrative Fast-Food Product-Market Structure

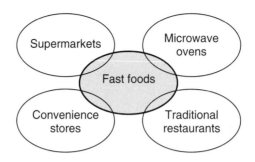

Forming Product-Markets

The factors that influence how product-market boundaries are determined include the purpose for analyzing the product-market, the rate of change in market composition over time, and the extent of market complexity.

Purpose of Analysis

If management is deciding whether to exit from a business, the primary emphasis may be on financial performance and competitive position. Detailed analysis of the product-market may not be necessary. In contrast, if the objective is to find an attractive market segment to target in the product-market, a much more penetrating analysis is necessary. When different products satisfy the same need, the product-market boundaries should contain all the relevant products and brands. For example, the photography product-market should include digital cameras and services and conventional cameras and film. Product-market boundaries should be determined in a manner that will be of strategic value, allowing management to capitalize on existing and potential opportunities and avoid possible threats.

Changing Composition of Markets

Product-market composition may change as new technologies become available and new competition emerges. New technologies offer buyers different ways to meet their needs. For example, fax technology gave people who needed overnight letter delivery an alternative way to transmit information. Entry into the market by new competitors also alters market composition. The Technology Feature describes the uncertainties of market acceptance of the third-generation (3G) wireless phone technology being developed in Europe. 3G will provide video images and broadband access to the Web.

The evolving 3G wireless phone market is an example of market volatility and evolving market structures. Increasingly, competition is more than gaining share in existing businesses; market boundaries are not well defined, customers and competitors are not clearly identified, and competitiveness extends beyond the level of the business to the entire firm or family of firms.[9] Importantly, a focus by management on existing markets may provide an incomplete strategic perspective.

Industry classifications often do not properly define product-market boundaries. For example, people may meet their needs for food with products from several industries, as shown in Exhibit 3–3. Industry-based definitions do not include alternative ways to meet needs. Industry classifications typically have a product-supply rather than a customer-demand orientation. Of course, since industry associations, trade publications, and government agencies generate a lot of information about products and markets, information from those sources should be included in a market analysis. The point is that market analysis activities should extend beyond industry boundaries.

- The potential capabilities of high-speed data transmission (3G) telecommunications include wireless purchases, video images, and broadband access to the Web.

- European telecoms paid over $100 billion in government auctions for 3G licenses, and building the wireless networks may require $100 billion.

- The uncertain issue is whether consumers will be attracted to the new services in sufficient numbers to make 3G a financial success.

- Current 2.5G networks (2.0G digital networks upgraded to handle data, although slower than 3.0G) may meet users' requirements.

- Phones in Europe will be designed to handle 2.5G and 3.0G, enabling service providers to first develop networks in highly populated urban areas.

- 3.0G services in Europe are not expected to be widely available until 2003 to 2007.

- The United States plans auctions for licenses in 2004 so that there will be an opportunity to observe users' responsiveness to 3.0G in Europe.

Sources: "Think Thin and Crispy," *The Economist,* June 9, 2001, 64; and Almar Latour, "Disconnected," *The Wall Street Journal,* June 5, 2001, A1, A8.

Extent of Market Complexity.

Three characteristics of markets capture a large proportion of the variation in their complexity: (1) the *functions* or uses of the product required by the customer, (2) the *technology* contained in the product to provide the desired function, and (3) the different *customer segments* using the product to perform a particular function.[10]

Customer function considers what the product or service does. It is the benefit provided to the customer. Thus, the function provides the capability which satisfies the needs of the customers. Functions consider the types of use situations each user encounters.[11] In the case of the personal computer, the function performed may be entertainment for the household, fax transmission, Internet purchasing, or various business functions.

Different *technologies* may satisfy the use situation of the customer. Steel and aluminum materials meet a similar need in various use situations. The technology consists of the materials and designs incorporated into products. In the case of a service, technology relates to how the service is rendered. Fax technology delivers a letter via electronic transmission. Federal Express transports a letter by air. A courier hand carries a document from the sender's location to the recipient.

Customer segment recognizes the diversity of the needs of customers for a particular product, such as automobiles. A specific brand and model won't satisfy all buyers' needs and wants. Two broad market segments for automobile use are households and organizations. These classifications can be divided further into more specific customer segments, such as preferences for European-style luxury sedans, four-wheel-drive vehicles, and sports cars.

It is helpful to focus on the consumer (or organizational) end-user of the product when defining the market, since the end-user drives demand for the product. When the end-users' needs and wants change, the market changes. Even though a manufacturer considers the

EXHIBIT 3–4
**Illustrative
Product-Market
Structure**

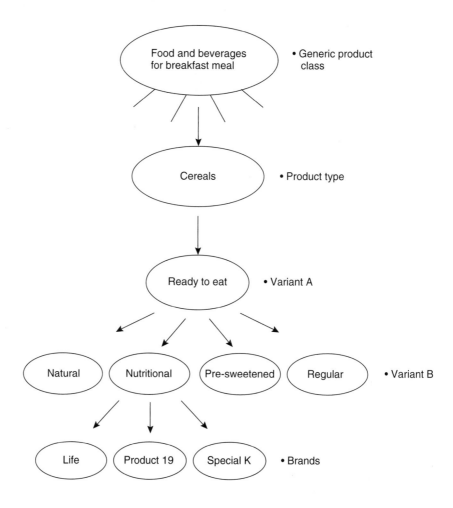

distributor to which its products are sold to be the customer, the market is really defined by the consumer and organizational end-users that purchase the product for consumption.

Illustrative Product-Market Structure

Suppose you are a brand manager for a cereal producer. You know that brands such as Life, Product 19, and Special K compete for sales to people who want nutritional benefits from a cereal. Nonetheless, our earlier discussion highlights the value of looking at a more complete picture of how competing brands such as Life, Product 19, and Special K also may experience competition from other ways of meeting needs. For example, a person may decide to eat a Kellogg's Nutri-Grain cereal bar instead of a bowl of cereal, and a consumer may want to vary the type of cereal, eating a natural or regular type of cereal. Because of the different product types and variants competing for the same needs and wants, the cereal brand manager will find it useful to develop a map of the product-market structure within which her or his brand is positioned. Exhibit 3–4 provides an illustrative product-market structure for cereals. The map can be expanded to portray other relevant product types (e.g., breakfast bars) in the generic product-market for food and beverages.

Describing and Analyzing End-Users

It is useful to develop profiles of end-user buyers for the generic, product-type, and product-variant levels of the product-market. Buyers are identified and described, purchase choice criteria are indicated, and environmental influences (e.g., interest rate trends) on buyers are evaluated. Analysis of the buyers in the market segments within a product-market is discussed in Chapter 4.

Identifying and Describing Buyers

Characteristics such as family size, age, income, geographical location, sex, and occupation are often useful in identifying buyers in consumer markets. Illustrative factors used to identify end-users in organizational markets include type of industry, company size, location, and types of products. Many published sources of information are available for use in identifying and describing customers. Examples include U.S. Census data, trade association publications, and studies by advertising media (TV, radio, magazines). When experience and existing information are not adequate in determining buyers, research studies may be necessary to locate and describe customers and prospects.

An interesting profile of the Russian middle class, along with illustrative product preferences, is shown below, divided into three income categories:[12]

Class		Lower Middle	Middle Middle	Upper Middle
Monthly Income	Moscow	$800 to $1,500	$1,500 to $3,500	$3,500 to $7,000
	Provinces	$300 to $550	$550 to $1,500	$1,500 to $3,500
Job		Receptionist, driver, security guard	Computer programmer, junior manager, accountant	Senior manager, small-business owner, investment banker
Car		Late-model Russian-made Lada	New Toyota Corolla	New Opel Cadet or used BMW
Dacha		Homemade wooden cottage, outdoor sauna	Contractor-constructed, indoor plumbing and heating	Stone and brick walls, terrace, indoor garage
Summer vacation		Resort town on Black Sea, in Soviet-style hotel	Turkish seashore resort of Antalia	Majorca on Spanish Riviera

The estimates above assume a family of two parents and one child. The size of the Russian middle class may range from 8 to 20 percent of that country's 145 million people. This population group emerged from the economic crisis in 1998, making size estimation difficult. Russian population information is useful in identifying and describing buyers in a market where income is a good predictor of purchases of goods and services such as automobiles and vacation services.

How Buyers Make Choices

Often, simply describing buyers does not provide enough information to guide targeting and positioning decisions: We also need to try to find out *why* people buy products and brands. In considering how customers decide what to buy, it is useful to analyze how they move through the sequence of steps leading to a decision to purchase a particular brand. Buyers normally follow a decision process. They begin by recognizing a need (problem

EXHIBIT 3–5
Comparing the Stages in Consumer and Organizational Purchases

Source: Eric N. Berkowitz, Roger A. Kerin, Steven W. Hartley, and William Rudelius, *Marketing,* 5th ed. (Chicago: Richard D. Irwin, 1997), 192.

Stage in the Buying Decision Process	Consumer Purchase: CD Player for a Student	Organizational Purchase: Headphones for a CD Player
Problem recognition	Student doesn't like the sound of the stereo system now owned and desires a CD player.	Marketing research and sales departments observe that competitors are including headphones on their models. The firm decides to include headphones on its own new models, which will be purchased from an outside supplier.
Information search	Student uses past experience, that of friends, ads, and *Consumer Reports* to collect information and uncover alternatives.	Design and production engineers draft specifications for headphones. The purchasing department identifies suppliers of CD player headphones.
Alternative evaluation	Alternative CD players are evaluated on the basis of important attributes desired in a CD player.	Purchasing and engineering personnel visit suppliers and assess (1) facilities, (2) capacity, (3) quality control, and (4) financial status. They drop any suppliers not satisfactory on these factors.
Purchase decision	A specific brand of CD player is selected, the price is paid, and it is installed in the student's room.	They use (1) quality, (2) price, (3) delivery, and (4) technical capability as key buying criteria to select a supplier. Then they negotiate terms and award a contract.
Postpurchase behavior	Student reevaluates the purchase decision, may return the CD player to the store if it is unsatisfactory, and looks for supportive information to justify the purchase.	They evaluate suppliers by using a formal vendor rating system and notify supplier if phones do not meet its quality standard. If problem is not corrected, they drop the firm as a future supplier.

recognition); next, they seek information; then, they identify and evaluate alternative products; and finally, they choose a brand. Of course, the length and complexity of this process vary by product and purchasing situation. Decisions that are repetitive and for which a buyer has past experience tend to be routine. One part of studying buyers' decision processes is finding out what criteria people use in making decisions. For example, how important is the brand name of a product in the purchase decision?

Illustrations of the buying decision process stages for a consumer purchase and an organizational purchase are shown in Exhibit 3–5. The consumer purchase involves a CD player, whereas the organizational purchase is a CD player component from an outside supplier. Both processes move through the major stages, but the issues and activities are quite different.

Environmental Influences

The final step in building customer profiles is to identify the external factors that influence buyers and thus affect the size and composition of the market over time. These influences include the government, social change, economic shifts, technology, and other factors that alter buyers' needs and wants. Typically, these factors are not controlled by the buyer or the firms that market the product, and substantial changes in environmental influences can have a major impact on customers' purchasing activities. Therefore, it is important to identify the relevant external influences on a product-market and estimate their future impact. During the past decade various changes in market opportunities occurred as a result of uncontrollable environmental factors. Illustrations include shifts in age-group composition, changes in tax laws affecting investments, the Asian economic crisis in the late 1990s, and variations in interest rates. Consider, for example, the population trends for the 50 states in the United States from 1995 to 2025. Note that some states (Exhibit 3–6) have high growth rates while others are declining in size.

Building Customer Profiles

The profiling process starts with the generic product-market. At this level customer profiles are likely to specify the size and general composition of the customer base. For example, the commercial air travel customer profile would include market size, growth rates, mix of business and pleasure travelers, and other general characteristics. The product-type and variant profiles are more specific about customer characteristics (needs and wants, use situations, activities and interests, opinions, purchase processes and choice criteria, and environmental influences on buying decisions). Normally, product-type analysis considers the organization's product and closely related product types.

In developing marketing strategy, management is concerned with deciding which buyers to target within generic, product-type, and product-variant markets and determining

EXHIBIT 3–6
Projected Percent Change in State Populations: 1995 to 2025

Source: U.S. Bureau of the Census, Population Division, PPL-47.

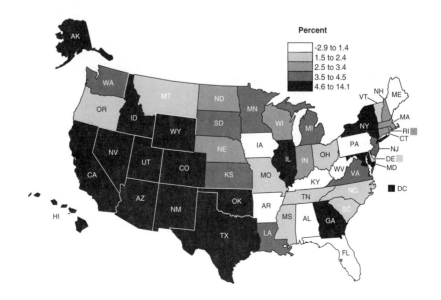

how to position to each target. The customer profiles help decision makers (or teams) make these decisions. The profiles are also useful in guiding market segmentation decisions. More comprehensive customer analyses often are undertaken in market segmentation analysis, which we discuss in Chapter 4.

Analyzing Competition

Competitor analysis considers the companies and brands that compete in the product-market of interest. Analyzing the competition follows the five steps shown in Exhibit 3–7. We begin by considering the competitive arena in which an organization competes and describing the characteristics of the competitive space. Steps 2 and 3 identify, describe, and evaluate the organization's key competitors. Steps 4 and 5 anticipate competitors' future actions and identify potential competitors that may enter the market.

Defining the Competitive Arena

We know that competition often includes more than firms that are direct competitors, such as Coke and Pepsi. For example, the different levels of competition for diet colas are shown in Exhibit 3–8. The product variant is the most direct type of competition. Nevertheless, other product categories of soft drinks also compete for buyers, as do other beverages. A complete understanding of the competitive arena helps guide strategy design and implementation. Since competition often occurs within specific industries, an examination of industry structure is useful in defining the competitive arena; here one must be aware that more than one industry may serve the same product-market, depending on the complexity of the product-market structure. For example, Microsoft and Intel may compete with firms that produce and market Internet wireless appliances.

Industry Analysis

Competitor analysis is conducted from the point of view of a particular firm. For example, a soft drink firm such as Coca-Cola should include other beverage brands in its industry analysis. This analysis looks at two kinds of information: (1) a descriptive profile of the industry and (2) an analysis of the value-chain (distribution) channels that link the various organizations in the value-added network from suppliers to end-users. Thus, the industry analysis is horizontal and covers similar types of firms (e.g., soft drink producers), whereas the value-chain analysis considers the vertical value-added group of firms that supply materials and/or parts, produce products (and services), and distribute the products to end-users.

EXHIBIT 3–7
**Analyzing
Competition**

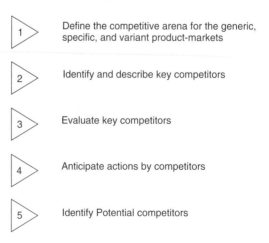

1 Define the competitive arena for the generic, specific, and variant product-markets

2 Identify and describe key competitors

3 Evaluate key competitors

4 Anticipate actions by competitors

5 Identify Potential competitors

EXHIBIT 3–8
**Example of Levels
of Competition**

Source: Donald R. Lehmann
and Russell S. Winer, *Analysis
for Marketing Planning,* 2nd ed.
(Burr Ridge, IL: Richard D.
Irwin, 1991), 22.

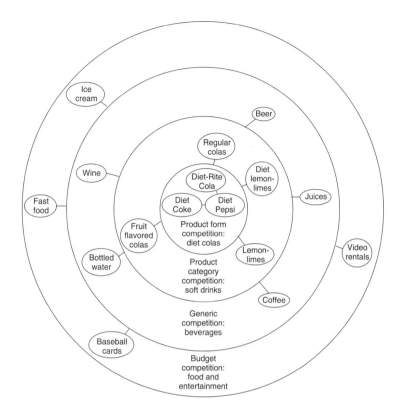

The industry analysis includes (1) industry characteristics and trends such as sales, number of firms, and growth rates and (2) operating practices of the firms in the industry, including product mix, service provided, barriers to entry, and geographical scope. An illustrative analysis of business magazine competitors is included in the Capital case (6–7), Exhibits 6 through 11. That case describes the launch of a new business magazine in France.

First, we need to identify the companies that make up the industry and develop descriptive information on the industry and its members. We should examine industry structure beyond domestic market boundaries, since international industry developments often affect regional, national, and international markets. For example, a comparison of U.S. market shares from 1994 to 1999 for personal computer (PC) manufacturers is shown in Exhibit 3–9. Included are the home, business, and education markets.[13] U.S. and global PC producers are shown, and other global producers are included in the "Others" category. In 2001, global industry sales growth of PCs began to slow down, whereas handheld devices were experiencing rapid growth.

The industry definition is based on the organization conducting the market analysis. The industry identification is based on product similarity, location at the same level in the value chain (e.g., manufacturer, distributor, retailer), and geographical scope. The industry analysis includes:

• Industry size, growth, and composition.

• Typical marketing practices.

• Industry changes that are anticipated (e.g., consolidation trends).

• Industry strengths and weaknesses.

• Strategic alliances among competitors.

EXHIBIT 3–9
Personal Computer Market Shares in the United States for 1984, 1987, and 1999 (based on unit sales)

Source: Peter Burrows, "Apple," *Business Week,* July 31, 2000, 108.

Home Market					
Maker	**1984**	**Maker**	**1987**	**Maker**	**1999**
Packard Bell	32.4%	Packard Bell NEC	23.3%	Compaq	19.0%
Apple	14.7	Compaq	18.8	H-P	16.1
Compaq	11.5	Gateway	11.1	Gateway	15.3
IBM	6.1	IBM	7.0	Emachines	11.0
Gateway	5.5	Acer	5.9	Packard Bell NEC	7.3
		Apple	5.0	Apple	7.1
Others	29.8	Others	28.9	Others	24.2

Business Market					
Maker	**1984**	**Maker**	**1987**	**Maker**	**1999**
Compaq	14.2%	Compaq	15.7%	Dell	22.4%
IBM	10.1	Dell	12.8	Compaq	15.0
Apple	6.4	IBM	9.5	IBM	9.2
Dell	5.9	H-P	8.0	H-P	6.0
Gateway	5.3	Toshiba	5.6	Toshiba	4.7
		Apple	1.4	Apple	1.3
Others	58.1	Others	47.0	Others	41.4

Education Market					
Maker	**1984**	**Maker**	**1987**	**Maker**	**1999**
Apple	47.0%	Apple	27.2%	Dell	21.4%
IBM	8.5	Compaq	13.2	Apple	16.5
Dell	4.3	Dell	10.7	Gateway	13.6
Gateway	3.3	Gateway	7.8	Compaq	9.2
Compaq	3.2	IBM	6.9	IBM	3.8
Others	33.0	Others	34.2	Others	35.5

Analysis of the Value-Added Chain

A study of supplier and distribution channels is important in understanding and serving product-markets. While producers may go directly to their end-users, many work with other organizations through distribution channels. The extent of vertical integration by competitors backward (supply) and forward toward end-users is also useful information. The types of relationships (collaborative or transactional) in the distribution channel should be identified and evaluated. The extent of outsourcing activities in the value chain is also of interest. Different channels that access end-user customers should be included in the channel analysis. For example, the distribution channel initiatives taken by Charles Schwab & Co. to become the number one online broker are described in the Strategy Feature. By looking at the distribution approaches of industry members, we can identify important patterns and trends in serving end-users. Value-chain analysis may also uncover new market opportunities that are not served by present channels of distribution. Finally, information from various value-chain levels can help in forecasting end-user demand.

Strategy Feature

It's a no brainer. We all know that Charles Schwab & Co. gets the Web. It's the No. 1 online broker and a leader in developing products and services for wired investors. With 4.1 million online accounts and a 21% share of all Web trades, the game is Schwab's to lose.

So how does it intend to stay ahead? By ensuring that customers get what they want, when they want, and how they want it. In recent months, Schwab has launched a wireless trading service and new online research tools that let customers take investment courses and hear live audio feeds of lectures. It's also building more branch offices and phone centers to complement its online services. By integrating the online and offline worlds, says e-commerce expert David K. Pecaut, president of the business development firm iFormation Group, "Schwab has become the benchmark for others going online."

And how. Some 81% of its trades are now done online, *vs.* 36% three years ago. That's great for Schwab, since processing online trades costs 80% less than offline ones. But the savings go further than that. With customers doing their own trades and research, branch employees are freer to promote higher-margin services. In June, Schwab introduced Portfolio Consultation, which lets customers meet with a Schwab adviser for $400. And a new wireless trading service went live in July.

Schwab has given offline investors more choices, too. It has added 23 branches this year, bringing the total to 363. And it's opening a fifth phone center to add 3,500 operators. That will help Schwab boost service even more, letting it process more phone trades when the still-too-frequent Web site crashes occur. All these offerings are aimed at folks like James Getzoff, a retiree in Marina del Rey, Calif., who frequently visits Schwab's site but just as often phones up the company. When a stock moves, says Getzoff, "I get right onto the site and research that company. If there's not enough there, I call one of the brokers to read me reports."

One hitch: Getzoff could do that now with rivals E*Trade Group or Merrill, Lynch & Co., which are mirroring Schwab's multi-channel strategy. Imitation may be the sincerest form of flattery, but it also means that Schwab will have to keep mining the Web to hang on to the top spot.   —*Louise Lee*

Source: Louise Lee, "When You're No. 1, You Try Harder," *Business Week E.Biz*, September 18, 2000, EB88.

The use of outsourcing of manufacturing and other business functions has grown significantly in the United States and Europe during the last decade. For example, in 1997 Sara Lee began outsourcing all manufacturing of its large portfolio of food and beverage, intimate apparel, and household product brands. Sara Lee's 2002 global revenues were expected to exceed $18 billion (43 percent international). The logic of outsourcing is that an organization may gain strategic advantage by focusing on its core competencies while outsourcing other necessary business functions to independent partners. Thus, analysis of outsourcing activities may be an important aspect of competitor analysis.

Competitive Forces

Different competitive forces are present in the value-added chain. The traditional view of competition is expanded by recognizing five competitive forces that affect industry performance:

1. Rivalry among existing firms.

2. Threat of new entrants.

3. Threat of substitute products.

4. Bargaining power of suppliers.

5. Bargaining power of buyers.[14]

The first force recognizes that active competition among industry members helps determine industry performance, and this is the most direct and intense form of competition. The aggressive competition between Coke and Pepsi is illustrative. Rivalry may occur within a market segment or across an entire product-market. The nature and scope of competition may vary according to the type of industry structure. For example, competition in an emerging industry consists of the market pioneer and a few other early entrants. A mature industry such as personal computers includes several firms (Exhibit 3–9).

The second force highlights the possibility of new competitors entering the market. Existing firms may try to discourage new competition through aggressive expansion and other types of market entry barriers. The entry of new competitors in the photography market due to digital photography has substantially expanded the competitive arena.

The third force considers the potential impact of substitutes. New technologies that satisfy the same customer need are important sources of competition. Including alternative technologies in the definition of product-market structure identifies substitute forms of competition. Encyclopedia Britannica's failure to recognize the competitive threat posed by CD-ROM technology is an example of the dangers of defining competitive boundaries too narrowly.

The fourth force is the influence that suppliers may be able to exert on the producers in an industry. For example, the high costs of labor and aircraft exert major pressures on the commercial airline industry. Companies may pursue vertical integration strategies to reduce the bargaining power of suppliers. Alternatively, collaborative relationships are useful to respond to the needs of both partners. The emphasis on quality improvement by many producers is encouraging cooperation with their suppliers.

Finally, buyers may use their purchasing power to influence their suppliers. Wal-Mart, for example, has a strong influence on the suppliers of its many products. Understanding which organizations have power and influence in the value chain provides important insights into the structure of competition. Power may be centered at any level in the channel, though producers and retailers often display strong buying power. However, major suppliers such as Intel are able to exert substantial influence on value-chain members.

A major consequence of Michael Porter's view of competition is that the competitive arena may be altered as a result of the impact of the five forces on the industry. The five competitive forces also highlight the existence of vertical and horizontal types of competition. The intensity of vertical competition is related in part to the bargaining power of suppliers and buyers. The location (level) of an organization in its value chain and the extent of its control over the channel may have a major influence on that organization's marketing strategy.

The intense competition between Reebok and Nike in the sneaker market offers interesting insights about channel of distribution power.[15] Foot Locker's 2,800 stores account for nearly one-fourth of U.S. sneaker sales. Nike has worked aggressively in building a collaborative relationship with Foot Locker, while Reebok has been less responsive to this key sneaker customer. Customers with the buying power that Foot Locker has want favorable terms, advance information on new products, exclusive lines, and fast response to orders. Nike's sales in 1995 to Foot Locker were $750 million compared to less than $200 million for Reebok. Only two years earlier Nike's sales to Foot Locker were $300 million compared to Reebok's $228 million.

Key Competitor Analysis

Competitor analysis is conducted for firms that compete directly with each other (e.g., Nike and Reebok) and other companies that management may consider important in strategy analysis (for example, potential market entrants). The rapid expansion of competitor intelligence activities by many companies in the last decade highlights the high priority executives place on monitoring competitors' activities.[16] Many companies around the world have developed very effective intelligence units. The Futures Group (business intelligence consultants) rates Microsoft as having the most effective corporate intelligence capabilities. Motorola, IBM, Procter & Gamble, and General Electric also receive high ratings. Technology intelligence initiatives are top priorities for international business spies. Corporate intelligence units collect and analyze information from competitors' consultants, suppliers, customers, and employees.

We look at two major aspects of competitor analysis: (1) preparing the descriptive profile for each competitor and (2) evaluating the competitor's strengths and weaknesses (steps 2 and 3 in Exhibit 3–7).

Describing the Competitor.

A *key competitor* is any organization going after the same market target as the firm conducting the analysis. American, Delta, and United Airlines are key competitors on many U.S. routes and certain international routes. Key competitors are often brands that compete in the same product-market or in segment(s) within the market. Different product types that satisfy the same need or want may also actively compete against each other. Thus, microwave foods may compete with fast-food operators.

A checklist of information which is typically included in the competitor profile is shown in Exhibit 3–10. Sources of information include annual reports, industry studies by government and private organizations, business magazines and newspapers, trade publications, reports by financial analysts (e.g., *Value Line Investment Survey*), government reports, standardized data services (e.g., Information Resources, Inc., and Nielsen), databases, suppliers, customers, company personnel, and salespeople. Industry trade publications (e.g., *Aviation Week & Space Technology*) are useful in tracking industry trends and examining current issues; they often publish special research studies. Direct contact with the research directors of trade publications is an important source of information about the industry and key competitors.

It is important to gain as much knowledge as possible about the background, experience, qualifications, and tenure of key executives at each major competitor. This information includes the executives' performance records, their particular areas of expertise, and the firms where they were previously employed. These analyses may suggest the future strategic initiatives of a key competitor.

The competitor profile should include a historical picture of management's marketing decisions. Past decisions show the pattern of changes in marketing strategy and tactics as management responded to changing market conditions. Matching these decisions with specific changes taking place in markets or with competitors may offer valuable insights into

EXHIBIT 3–10
Information Needed to Describe Key Competitors

- Business scope and objectives
- Management experience, capabilities, and weaknesses
- Market position and trends
- Market target(s) and customer base
- Marketing program positioning strategy
- Financial, technical, and operating capabilities
- Key competitive advantages (e.g., access to resources, patents)

EXHIBIT 3–11
**Competitor
Evaluation**

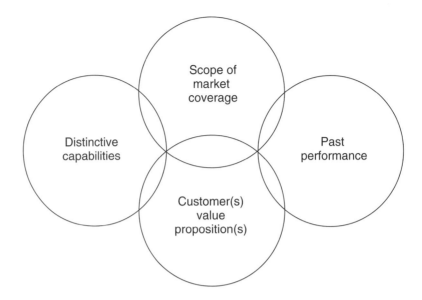

competitors' future actions. An experienced executive can then develop a feel for the management style of the key competitor by looking for patterns or consistencies in those decisions. Of course, shifts in priorities and direction also occur, and so it is important not to assume that the past is a good predictor of future strategies.

Evaluating the Competitor

Although competitor description and evaluation are interrelated, it is useful to separate the two activities. Evaluation considers the strengths and weaknesses of each competitor in the four areas shown in Exhibit 3–11.

Market coverage analysis centers on the market segments targeted by the competitor and the competitor's actual and relative market-share position. Relative market position is measured by comparing the share of the firm against that of the competitor with the highest market share in the segment. All segments in the product-market that could be targeted by the firm should be included in the competitor evaluation.

The competitor's past performance offers a useful basis for comparing competitors. The customer value proposition offered by the competitor for each segment is important information. This may indicate competitive opportunities as well as a possible threat. Finally, the competitor's distinctive capabilities need to be identified and evaluated.

Perceptual maps are useful in analyzing the competitive positioning of competing brands. A perceptual map for the brands competing in the analgesics product-market is shown in Exhibit 3–12. Note the area of vulnerability in the upper-right quadrant. Tylenol dominates the market, but there may be opportunities for new competitor brands. The map indicates how competitors are positioned relative to each other and alerts management to potential competitive threats.

An analysis of each competitor's past sales and financial performance indicates how well the competitor has performed on a historical basis. A typical period of analysis is three to five years or longer, depending on the rate of change in the market. Performance information may include sales, market share, net profit, net profit margin, cash flow, and debt. Additionally, for specific types of businesses other performance information may be useful. For example, sales per square foot often is used to compare the performance of retail stores. Operating cost per passenger mile is a popular measure in airline comparisons.

EXHIBIT 3–12
**Perceptual Map of
Analgesics Brands**

Source: William R. Dillon,
Thomas J. Madden, and Neil H.
Firtle, *Marketing Research in a
Marketing Environment*, 3rd ed.
(Chicago: Richard D. Irwin,
1994), 36.

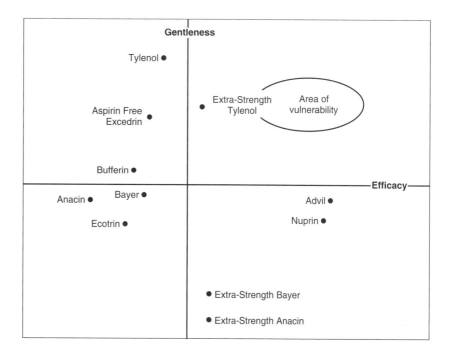

Assessing how well competitors meet customer value requirements necessitates finding out what criteria buyers use to rate each supplier. Customer-focused assessments are more useful than relying only on management judgments of value delivery. Measurement methods include customer comparisons of the value attributes of the firm versus its competitors, customer surveys, loyalty measures, and the relative market share of end-use segments.[17] Preference maps like the one shown in Exhibit 3–12 are useful in comparing the competing brands on attributes that are important determinants of customer satisfaction.

Using the competitor information, we can develop an overall evaluation of the key competitor's current strengths and weaknesses. Additionally, the summary assessment of distinctive capabilities includes information on the competitor's management capabilities and limitations, technical and operating advantages and weaknesses, marketing strategy, and other key strengths and limitations. Since competitors often have different capabilities, it is important to highlight these differences. A checklist for evaluating competitor strengths and weaknesses is shown in Exhibit 3–13.

Anticipating Competitors' Actions

Steps 4 and 5 in competitor analysis (Exhibit 3–7) consider what each key competitor may do in the future and identify potential competitors. The information obtained in the previous steps of the analysis should be helpful in estimating future trends, although strategy shifts may occur.

Estimating Competitors' Future Strategies

Competitors' future strategies may continue in the directions that they established in the past, particularly if no major external influences require them to change their strategies. Nevertheless, assuming that an existing strategy will continue is not wise. Competitors' current actions may signal probable future threats.

Consider, for example, SMW's Swatch line of watches. Swatch's strong market position was threatened by new competitors. By 1995 it was clear that Timex would continue its

EXHIBIT 3–13
Areas of Evaluation of Competitor Strengths and Weaknesses

- Sales and market position in segments served
- Level of customer satisfaction
- Business approach (price, quality, service, aggressiveness)
- Financial performance (current and historical)
  —Net profit/sales ratio
  —Return on investment
  —Number of employees
  —Facilities
- Financial resources and leverage
- Cost position relative to key competitors
- Relative product quality
- Innovativeness
- Product portfolio
- Management capabilities
- Marketing strategy and effectiveness
- Methods of distribution
- Summary of key strengths and weaknesses

aggressive new product and promotion strategy aimed at expanding its market position at the expense of Swatch.[18] Timex launched an array of new brands, including licensing the Nautica, Joe Boxer, and Timberland brand names, and offered the new $40 Expedition line. Failure to anticipate Timex's response to Swatch's market success created serious problems for Swatch in the U.S. market. The number of retailers carrying Swatch had declined while consumer tastes shifted from plastic to metal watches. Swatch's market sensing was faulty. To counter the competition, Swatch's 1995 advertising budget was over 12 times larger than in previous years, and new metal watch designs were introduced.

Identifying New Competitors

New competitors may come from four major sources: (1) companies competing in a related product-market, (2) companies with related technologies, (3) companies already targeting similar customer groups with other products, and/or (4) companies competing in other geographical regions with similar products. Market entry by a new competitor is more likely under the following conditions:

- High profit margins are being achieved by market incumbents.

- Future growth opportunities in the market are attractive.

- No major market-entry barriers are present.

- Competition is limited to one or a few competitors.

- Gaining an equivalent (or better) competitive advantage over the existing firm(s) serving the market is feasible.

If one or more of these conditions are present in a competitive situation, new competition will probably appear.

Developing a Strategic Vision about the Future

Market development and competitive activities do not always follow clearly defined and predictable paths. Nonetheless, signals can be identified that are useful in pointing to possible market changes. Answers to the following questions may indicate the possibility of a market changing significantly in the future:

1. Are industry boundaries clear and static? Are customers and competitors identifiable? Or are industry boundaries blurring and evolving?

2. Do firms compete as "distinct entities" or as families of suppliers and end-product firms?

3. Is there competition for managing migration paths?

4. Is competition taking place at product line, business, and corporate levels? Do these levels of competition influence each other?

5. Can there be competition between clusters of firms to influence standards and industry evolution?[19]

Phases of Competition

It is useful to distinguish between different phases in the development of competition. In the initial stage, companies compete in identifying product concepts, making technology choices, and building competencies.[20] This phase involves experimentation with ideas, and the path to market leadership is not clearly defined. Phase 2 involves partnering of companies with the objective of controlling industry standards, though these firms eventually become competitors, as in the case of the camera manufacturers involved in establishing the Advanced Photo System (APS) in the 1990s. Finally, as the market becomes clearly defined and the competitors become established, the competitive process concentrates on market share for end products and profits. The APS market is currently in this stage.

Anticipating the Future

Increasingly, we find that change and turbulence, rather than stability, characterize many product-markets. Moreover, as was discussed in regard to the three phases of competition, it is often possible to identify the forces under way that will alter industry structure. Though these influences are not easy to identify and analyze, organizations that choose to invest substantial time and effort in anticipating the future create an opportunity to gain competitive advantage. Executives in market-driven companies recognize the importance of developing these capabilities.

Hamel and Prahalad offer a compelling blueprint for analyzing the forces of change. While the details of their process cannot be captured in a few pages of discussion, the following questions are illustrative of the information needed to anticipate the future: [21]

1. What are the influences (discontinuities) present in the product-market that have the potential to profoundly transform market/competitor structure?
2. Investigate each discontinuity in substantial depth.
   a. How the trend will affect customers.
   b. Economic impact.
   c. How fast it is developing.
   d. Who is exploiting this trend.
   e. Who has the most to gain or lose.
   f. The new product opportunities that will be created by this discontinuity.
   g. How we can learn more about this trend.

Following the blueprint requires looking in depth at the relevant forces of change in a product-market and other markets that are interrelated. Anticipating the future requires searching beyond the existing competitive arena for influences that promise to affect product-market boundaries. The process requires the involvement of the entire organization and demands a substantial amount of time. A company with market-oriented and multifunctional processes should be able to utilize those processes for anticipating the future. Also, it is apparent that developing a vision about the future needs to be an ongoing process.

The forces of change span many markets, industries, and products. Illustrative situations that call for developing a process for anticipating the future include understanding the interlinkages of telecommunications with personal computers, home entertainment, cable television, and the Internet; the nature and scope of digital technology in regard to conventional photography; and remote electronic education programs in regard to conventional university degree programs. The following observation is illustrative of these challenges:

> It is well accepted that the traditional television and PC will, in the not too distant future, be one product, capable of multiple functions—entertainment, education, or work. Sony, Phillips, and Matsushita would like to influence this migration from the consumer electronics perspective. Silicon Graphics, Compaq, and Apple would like this migration to be influenced by the PC industry. Microsoft would like the software producers to be in the driver's seat. Groups of firms starting from different vantage points have different preferred routes toward the same goal; thus, there is competition to influence the migration paths.[22]

Market Size Estimation

An important part of market opportunity analysis is estimating the present and potential size of the market. Market size usually is measured by dollar sales and/or unit sales for a defined product-market and a specified time period. Other size measures include the number of buyers, average purchase quantity, and frequency of purchase. Three key measures of market size are *market potential, sales forecast,* and *market share.*

Market Potential

Market potential is the maximum amount of product sales that can be obtained from a defined product-market during a specified time period. It includes the total opportunity for sales by all the firms serving the product-market. Market potential is the upper limit of sales that can be achieved by all firms for a generic, product-type, or product-variant product-market. Often, actual industry sales fall somewhat below market potential because the production and distribution systems are unable to completely meet the needs of all buyers who are both *willing* and *able* to purchase the product during the period of interest.

Sales Forecast

The sales forecast indicates the expected sales for a defined product-market during a specified time period. The industry sales forecast is the total volume of sales expected by all firms serving the product market. The sales forecast can be no greater than market potential and typically falls short of that potential, as was discussed above. A forecast can be made for total sales at any product-market level (generic, product type, variant) and for specific subsets of the product-market (e.g., market segments). A sales forecast can also be made for sales expected by a particular firm.

An interesting forecasting situation is to estimate the market for commercial aircraft. The lead time in developing and producing these expensive products requires forecasts several years into the future. Moreover, passenger travel forecasts are needed to guide the aircraft forecasts. The Boeing Commercial Airplanes Group prepares an annual world forecast which includes 20-year air travel and aircraft sales projections. Boeing's 20-year aircraft forecast is shown in Exhibit 3–14. The *Current Market Outlook* is a very complete analysis

EXHIBIT 3–14
Commercial Aircraft 20-Year Forecast

Source: *Current Market Outlook 2000* (Seattle: Boeing Commercial Airplanes Group, August 2000), 32.

The market for airplanes is $1.5 trillion over 20 years. World air travel is projected to grow annually at 4.8% and air cargo at approximately 6.4% during the long-run forecast period. The world fleet is expected to more than double, with total fleet size growing to 31,755 by 2019. Two-thirds of the fleet operating today is projected to still be in operation 20 years from now. In the two decades, 22,315 commercial jets—21,512 passenger airplanes and 803 new freighters—are forecast to enter service to accommodate traffic growth and replace capacity lost as airplanes are removed from commercial airline service.

Type of Aircraft	2000–2019*
☐ Smaller Regional Jets	19%
☐ Single-Aisle	55%
☐ Twin-Aisle	21%
☐ 747 and Larger	5%
Total Deliveries 2000–2019	**22,315 Aircraft**

*Percent of total.

of demand for commercial airplanes and aviation support services. It is a useful basic forecasting guide for the various companies involved in that market.

Market Share

Company sales divided by the total sales of all firms for a specified product-market determine the market share of a particular firm. Market share may be calculated on the basis of actual sales or forecasted sales. Market share can be used to forecast future company sales and to compare actual market position among competing brands of a product. Market share may vary depending on the use of dollar sales or unit sales due to price differences across competitors.

It is essential in preparing forecasts to specify exactly what is being forecasted (defined product-market), the time period involved, and the geographical area. Otherwise, comparisons of sales and market share with those of competing firms will not be meaningful. Several operational problems may occur in forecasting as a result of differences in measures of sales (e.g., dollars versus units), problems in defining the relevant market, leads and lags in product movement through distribution channels, promotional pricing practices, and the handling of intracompany transfers.[23] Additional forecasting guidelines are provided in the Appendix to Chapter 3.

Evaluating Market Opportunity

Since a company's sales depend in part on its marketing plans, forecasts and marketing strategy are closely interrelated. Forecasting involves what-if analyses. Alternative positioning strategies (product, distribution, price, and promotion) must be evaluated for their estimated effects on sales. Because of the marketing effort/sales relationship, it is important to consider both market potential (opportunity) and planned marketing expenditures in determining the forecast. The impact of different sales forecasts must be evaluated from a total business perspective, since these forecasts affect production planning, human resource needs, and financial requirements.

The global market for personal computers (PC) in households is an interesting application of market potential and forecasting. Rapidly declining prices and software availability are stimulating sales around the world. The escalating popularity of the Internet is also contributing to PC sales growth.[24] Internet users have grown from 50 million in 1996 to an estimated 315 million in 2002. By 2001, PC sales were beginning to slow. One company's response to this market trend is discussed in Case 6–5 (Intel Corp.).

Sales forecasts of target markets are needed so that management can estimate the financial attractiveness of both new and existing market opportunities. The market potential and growth estimates gauge the overall attractiveness of the market. The sales forecast for the company's brand in combination with cost estimates provides a basis for profit projections. The decision to enter a new market or exit from an existing market depends heavily on financial analyses and projections. Alternative market targets under consideration can be compared by using sales and profit projections. Similar projections for key competitors are also useful in evaluating market opportunities.

Summary

Analyzing markets and competition is essential to making sound business and marketing decisions. The uses of product-market analyses are many and varied. An important aspect of market definition and analysis is moving beyond a product focus by incorporating market needs into the analysts' viewpoint.

Business strategies and markets are interrelated, and companies which do not understand their markets and how those markets are likely to change in the future are at a competitive disadvantage. Effective market sensing is essential in guiding business and marketing strategies. Value migration—the process of customers shifting their purchases to new business designs—needs to be anticipated, and counterstrategies must be developed. An essential part of becoming market oriented is anticipating future directions of market change.

This chapter has examined the nature and scope of mapping product-market structure. When different levels of aggregation (generic, product-type, and product-variant) are used, products and brands are positioned within more aggregate categories, providing a better understanding of customers, product interrelationships, industry structure, distribution approaches, and key competitors. This approach to product-market analysis offers a consistent guide to needed information regardless of the type of product-market being analyzed. Analyzing market opportunity includes (1) defining (mapping) product-markets, (2) describing and analyzing end-users, (3) conducting industry and value-added chain analyses, (4) evaluating key competitors, and (5) estimating market size and growth rates.

After the product-market boundaries and structure have been determined, information on various aspects of the market is collected and examined. First, it is useful to study the people or organizations that are the end-users in the product-market at each level (generic, product type, and variant). These market profiles of customers make it easier to evaluate opportunities and guide market targeting and positioning strategies. Next, we identify and analyze the firms that market products and services at each product-market level to aid in strategy development. Industry and key competitor analysis considers the firms that compete with the company performing the market opportunity analysis. Thus, industry analysis for a personal computer producer would include the producers that make up the industry. The analysis should also include firms operating at all stages (levels) in the value-added system, such as suppliers, manufacturers, distributors, and retailers.

The next step is a comprehensive assessment of the major competitors. The key competitor analysis should include both actual and potential competitors that management considers important. Competitor analysis includes (1) describing the company, (2) evaluating the competitors, and (3) anticipating the future actions of competitors. It is also important to identify possible new competitors. Competitor analysis is an ongoing activity and requires coordinated information collection and analysis.

The mounting evidence about markets points to the critical importance of understanding and anticipating changes in markets. In gaining these insights, it is useful to view competition as a three-stage process of experimenting, partnering to set industry standards, and then pursuing market share and profits. Analyzing the forces of change provides a basis for anticipating the future.

An important part of product-market analysis is estimating potential and forecasting sales. The forecasts often used in product-market analysis include estimates of market potential, sales forecasts of total sales by firms competing in the product-market, and sales forecast for the firm of interest. This information is needed for various purposes and is prepared for different units of analysis, such as product category, brands, and geographical areas. The forecasting approach and techniques should be matched to the organization's needs. Forecasting methods are discussed in the Appendix.

Internet Applications

A. Airbus and Boeing are the primary competitors in the large commercial aircraft market. Discuss how the information available at their websites (*www.boeing.com* and *www.airbus.com*) may be useful in competitor analysis. Market size information is available at *www.boeing.com/commercial/cmo*.

B. Visit Hoover's website (*www.hoovers.com*). Investigate the different options for competitive and market analysis provided there. How can these online tools best be utilized? What limitations apply?

C. Go to the website of Six Continents Hotels & Resorts and investigate the different hotel property brands. Examine the customers targeted by each brand. Define and describe the product-market and structure within which the hotel's brands are included. (See Exhibit 4–7 on page 129).

Questions for Review and Discussion

1. Discuss the important issues that should be considered in defining the product-market for a totally new product.

2. Under what product and market conditions is the end-user customer more likely to make an important contribution to product-market definition?

3. What recommendations can you make to the management of a company competing in a rapid growth market to help it identify new competitive threats early enough that counterstrategies can be developed?

4. There are some dangers in concentrating product-market analysis only on a firm's specific brand and the brands that compete directly with a firm's brand. Discuss.

5. Using the approach to product-market definition and analysis discussed in this chapter, select a brand and describe the generic, product type, and brand product-markets of which the brand is a part.

6. For the brand you selected in question 5, indicate the kinds of information needed to conduct a complete product-market analysis. Also suggest sources for obtaining each type of information.

7. Select an industry and describe its characteristics, participants, and structure.

8. A competitor analysis of the 7UP soft drink brand is being conducted. Management plans to position the brand against its key competitors. Should the competitors consist only of other noncola drinks?

9. Outline an approach to competitor evaluation, assuming you are preparing the analysis for a regional bank holding company.

10. Discuss how a small company (less than $1 million in sales) should analyze its competition.

11. Many popular forecasting techniques draw from past experience and historical data. Discuss some of the more important problems that may occur in using these methods.

12. What are the relevant issues a cross-functional team should consider in developing a strategic vision about the future for the organization's product-market(s)?

Notes

1. For additional discussion of Kodak's competitive challenges, see Benjamin Fulford, "Photo Finish," *Forbes*, March 20, 2000, 78, 80; Geoffrey Smith, "Will Kodak's Carp Miss His Photo Op?" *Business Week*, October 9, 2000, 52; Subrata N. Chakravarta and Joan Gordon, "Vindication," *Forbes*, September 7, 1998, 62, 64, 65; and Edward W. Desmond, "What's Ailing Kodak?" *Fortune*, October 20, 1997, 185, 186, 188, 192.
2. C. K. Prahalad and Gary Hamel, "Strategy as a Field of Study and Why Search for a New Paradigm?" *Strategic Management Journal*, Summer 1994, 5–16.
3. This illustration is based in part on Gary Samuels, "CD-ROM's first "Big Victim," *Forbes*, February 28, 1994, 42–44.
4. Adrian J. Slywotzky, *Value Migration* (Boston: Harvard Business School Press, 1996).
5. Gary Hamel and C. K. Prahalad, *Competing for the Future* (Boston: Harvard Business School Press, 1994), 50–52.
6. This discussion is based on suggestions provided by Professor Robert B. Woodruff of the University of Tennessee, Knoxville.
7. Rajendra K. Srivastava, Mark I. Alpert, and Allan D. Shocker, "A Customer-Oriented Approach for Determining Market Structures," *Journal of Marketing*, Spring 1984, 32.
8. George S. Day, Strategic Marketing Planning: The Pursuit of Competitive Advantage (St. Paul, MN: West Publishing, 1984), 72.
9. C. K. Prahalad, "Weak Signals versus Strong Paradigms," *Journal of Marketing Research*, August 1995, iii–vi.
10. Derek F. Abell, Defining the Business: The Starting Point of Strategic Planning (Englewood Cliffs, NJ: Prentice-Hall, 1980).
11. George S. Day, "Strategic Market Analysis: A Contingency Perspective," Working Paper, University of Toronto, July 1979.
12. "Russia's Middle Class," *Business Week*, October 16, 2000, 79.
13. Peter Burrows, "Apple," *Business Week*, July 31, 2000, 108.
14. Michael E. Porter, *Competitive Advantage* (New York: Free Press, 1985), 5.
15. Joseph Pereira, "Sneaker Attacks," *The Wall Street Journal*, September 22, 1995, A1, A5.
16. William Green, "I Spy," *Forbes*, April 20, 1998, 91, 94, 96, 100.
17. George S. Day and Robin Wensley, "Assessing Advantage: A Framework for Diagnosing Competitive Superiority," *Journal of Marketing*, April 1988, 12–16.
18. Fara Warner, "Timex, Swatch Get Set for Battle with Expensive Ad Campaigns," *The Wall Street Journal*, May 31, 1995, B7.
19. The following discussion is based on Prahalad, "Weak Signals," vi.
20. Hamel and Prahalad, *Competing for the Future*, 101.
21. Ibid., 101–102.
22. Prahalad, "Weak Signals," v.
23. Bernard Catry and Michel Chevalier, "Market Share Strategy and the ProductLife Cycle," *Journal of Marketing*, October 1974, 29.
24. "Trends to Watch," *Investor's Business Daily*, August 24, 1998, A31.

Appendix 3A

Forecasting Guidelines

The steps in developing sales forecasts consist of (1) defining the forecasting problem, (2) identifying appropriate forecasting techniques, (3) evaluating and choosing a technique, and (4) implementing the forecasting system. A brief review of each step indicates important issues and considerations.[1]

Defining the Forecasting Problem

The requirements the forecasting method should satisfy, and the output required must be decided. Illustrative requirements include the time horizon, the level of accuracy desired, the uses to be made of the forecast results, and the degree of disaggregation (nation, state, local), including product/market detail, units of measurement, and time increments to be covered.

Identify, Evaluate, and Select Forecasting Technique(s)

Since several forecasting methods are available, each with certain features and limitations, the user's needs, resources, and available data should be matched with the appropriate techniques. Companies may incorporate two or more techniques into the forecasting process. Typically, one technique is used as the primary basis of forecasting, whereas the other technique is used to check the validity of the primary forecasting method. Also, techniques offer different outputs. Some are effective in obtaining aggregate forecasts, and others are used to estimate sales for disaggregated units of analysis (e.g., products). An overview of the major forecasting techniques is provided below in "Forecasting Techniques."

Implementation

Many firms begin with very informal forecasting approaches based on projections of past experience coupled with a subjective assessment of the future market environment. As the forecasting needs increase, more formalized methods are developed. Factors that often affect the choice of a forecasting system include the type of corporate planning process used, the volatility and complexity of markets, the number of products and markets, and the organizational units that have forecasting needs.

Forecasting Techniques

The major approaches used to prepare forecasts are described briefly. Forecasting techniques generally follow two basic avenues. The first involves making direct estimates of brand sales. The second forecasts brand sales as a product of several components (e.g., industry sales and market share).[2] Several methods used for forecasting sales are described below:

Judgmental Forecasting. A common approach relies on a jury of executive opinion to obtain sounder forecasts than might be made by a single estimator. To put the results in better perspective, the jury members are usually given background information on past sales, and their estimates are sometimes weighted in proportion to their convictions about the likelihood of specific sales levels being realized.

Sales Force Estimates. The sales personnel of some firms—field representatives, managers, or distributors—are considered better positioned than anyone else to estimate the short-term outlook for sales in their assigned areas.

Users' Expectations. Although the dispersion of product users in many markets (or the cost of reaching them) would make such an approach impractical, some manufacturers serving industrial markets find it possible to poll product users about their future plans and then use that information in developing their own forecasts.

Traditional Time-Series Analysis. In a familiar approach, the historical sales series may be broken down into its components—trends and cyclical and seasonal variations, including irregular variations—which are then projected. Time-series analysis has the advantage of being easy to understand and apply. However, there is a danger in relying on strictly mechanized projections of previously identified patterns.

---

[1]The following discussion is based on Lawrence R. Small, *Sales Forecasting in Canada* (Ottawa: The Conference Board of Canada, 1980), 3–7.

[2]Vithala R. Rao and James E. Cox, Jr., *Sales Forecasting Methods: A Survey of Recent Developments* (Cambridge, MA: Marketing Science Institute, 1978), 17.

Advanced Time-Series Analysis. For short-term forecasting purposes, several advanced time-series methods have been generating new interest and acceptance. Most rely on a moving average of the data series as their starting point, and requisite computer software facilitates their use. The methods include variants of exponential smoothing, adaptive filtering, Box Jenkins models, and the state-space technique. All assume that future movements of a sales series can be determined solely from the study of its past movements. However, certain of these methods have the alternative advantage of being able to take into account external variables as well.

Econometric Methods. The econometric approach provides a mathematical simplification, or "model," of measurable relationships between changes in the series being forecast and changes in other related factors. Such models are employed most often in the prediction of overall market demand, thus requiring a separate estimate of a company's own share. Increased interest in this approach reflects a growing concern with macroeconomic events as well as a preference for spelling out assumptions that underlie forecasts.

Input-Output Analysis. When developing forecasts for intermediate or commodity products, some firms are finding it advantageous to employ input-output measures within comprehensive forecasting systems that begin with macroeconomic considerations and end with estimates of industry sales. Still other methodologies must be employed in such systems, and specialists are required for the correct application and interpretation of input-output analysis.

New-Product Forecasting. New products pose special problems that are hard for the forecaster to circumvent.

A sales forecast for a new product may rest upon any of several bases, including results of marketing research investigations, assumptions about analogous situations in the past, or assumptions about the rate at which users of such products or services will substitute the new item for ones they are currently buying.[3]

Several advantages and limitations of the various forecasting techniques are highlighted in Exhibit 3A–1. A more comprehensive discussion of forecasting techniques is provided by David M. Georgoff and Robert Murdick, "Managers' Guide to Forecasting," *Harvard Business Review,* January–February 1986, 110–20.

Sales Forecast Illustration

The annual forecast of world market demand and airplane supply requirements prepared by the Boeing Commercial Airplane Group is an interesting example of the use of forecasting methods. Copies of the *Current Market Outlook* report can be obtained from the company. The forecasting approach and how the forecasts are used are described in Exhibit 3A–2.

Portions of Boeing's product delivery forecast are shown in Exhibit 3A–3. It is one of many passenger demand and aircraft supply forecasts included in the Boeing report. The report is a penetrating analysis of the commercial aircraft industry. It highlights the importance of forecasting in this industry, where new aircraft designs require several years.

[3]David L. Hurwood, Elliott S. Grossman, and Earl L. Bailey, *Sales Forecasting* (New York: The Conference Board, 1978), i–ii.

EXHIBIT 3A–1 **Summary of Advantages and Disadvantages of Various Forecasting Techniques**

Sales Forecasting Method	Advantages	Disadvantages
User expectations	1. Forecast estimates obtained directly from buyers 2. Projected product usage information can be highly detailed 3. Insightful method aids planning marketing strategy 4. Useful for new product forecasting	1. Potential customers must be few and well defined 2. Does not work well for consumer goods 3. Depends on the accuracy of user's estimates 4. Expensive, time-consuming, labor-intensive
Sales force composite	1. Involves the people (sales personnel) who will be held responsible for the results 2. Is fairly accurate 3. Aids in controlling and directing sales effort 4. Forecast is available for individual sales territories	1. Estimators (sales personnel) have a vested interest and therefore may be biased 2. Elaborate schemes sometimes are necessary to counteract bias 3. If estimates are biased, process to correct the data can be expensive
Jury of executive opinion	1. Easily done, very quick 2. Does not require elaborate statistics 3. Utilizes "collected wisdom" of the top people 4. Useful for new or innovative products	1. Produces aggregate forecasts 2. Expensive 3. Disperses responsibility for the forecast 4. Group dynamics operate
Delphi technique	1. Minimizes effects of group dynamics	1. Can be expensive and time-consuming
Market test	1. Provides ultimate test of consumers' reactions to the product 2. Allows assessment of the effectiveness of the total marketing program 3. Useful for new and innovative products	1. Lets competitors know what firm is doing 2. Invites competitive reaction 3. Expensive and time-consuming to set up 4. Often takes a long time to accurately assess level of initial and repeat demand
Time-series analysis	1. Utilizes historical data 2. Objective, inexpensive	1. Not useful for new or innovative products 2. Factors for trend, cyclical, seasonal, or product life-cycle phase must be accurately assessed and included 3. Technical skill and good judgment required
Statistical demand analysis	1. Great intuitive appeal 2. Requires quantification of assumptions underlying the estimates 3. Allows management to check results 4. Uncovers hidden factors affecting sales 5. Method is objective	1. Factors affecting sales must remain constant and be identified accurately to produce an accurate estimate 2. Requires technical skill and expertise 3. Some managers reluctant to use method due to the sophistication

Source: Adapted from Gilbert A. Churchill, Jr., Neil M. Ford, and Orville C. Walker, *Sales Force Management,* 4th ed. (Burr Ridge, IL: Richard D. Irwin, 1993), 204–5.

EXHIBIT 3A–2   **How Boeing Forecasts Aircraft Demand**

A long-range forecast is developed annually at Boeing to determine the outlook for world air travel and cargo growth and the consequent commercial jet airplane requirements to meet this demand plus replacement of retired airplanes. It consists of the following:

- Air travel market forecasts (by econometric model)* based on:
  Changes in the cost of air travel.
  Changes in the income of the travel population.
- Airplane retirement assumptions.
- Forecasts for commercial jet airplanes.
  Airplane deliveries in dollars.
  Airplane deliveries in units.
  Categorization by range and size.

The forecasts are used within the Boeing business planning process to develop:

- Financial and production planning.
- Competitor analyses.
- Workforce and inventory requirements.
- Resource allocations.
- New product evaluations.

The market forecasts reflect the Boeing goal of producing a reasonable outlook for the future of the commercial jet aviation industry. The "balanced" single-line forecast is provided with the expectation that future results will have an equal chance of being higher or lower and will fluctuate around this forecast. There are no "cycles"† in the forecast. Internal planning is driven by this forecast, tempered by other forecasts involving risk and opportunities (i.e., evaluation of upside and downside potential), and melded with the near-term order base and sales forecasts. This document provides a summary of the baseline market forecast prepared by Boeing. It is separated into three major sections.

- The world market demand involving growth in air travel and cargo plus replacement of retired airplanes.
- The airplane supply requirement.
- The manufacturer's position in the industry.

*Boeing models are based on the interrelationships between variables that represent the forces believed to drive the commercial jet aviation industry. Airplane deliveries predicted by the forecast process are based on judgments about reasonable future values for variables in the models and are constrained to match industry requirements.
†Cycles, by definition, mean regularly sequenced phenomena. The Boeing view is that unique circumstances caused the major adverse changes in the historical market and that such events are random and therefore not predictable (e.g., energy crises, wars). Even economic growth is hardly cyclical. Good monetary and fiscal policies can prevent major economic disruptions. Only two major world recessions have occurred in the jet era, and they were begun by energy crises.

Source: *Current Market Outlook,* Boeing Commercial Airplane Group, February 1992, 1.1.

EXHIBIT 3A–3   **Product Delivery Forecast**

World Commercial Jet Airplane Deliveries

- Total commercial jet airplane delivery requirements are forecast to amount to $380 billion through the year 2000 (1992 dollars) and $857 billion through the year 2010. This is nearly the same level as forecast in last year's *Current Market Outlook.*
- Non-U.S. airlines' future share of the market is 64%, up from 62%, from 1970 through 1990.
- 65% of demand through the year 2000 will come from growth, and 35% from replacement. Through 2010, 73% of the demand is for growth and 27% for replacement because two-thirds of the fleet retirements are assumed to occur through the year 2000.
- Delivery dollars will average $45 billion per year through the year 2010, 150% higher than the 1970 to 1991 average of $18 billion.
- The Asia/Pacific area will show the greatest percentage gain.
- The U.S. market will maintain its position as the largest market.
- The total backlog of orders and firm options is expected to surpass the ASM capacity required in the mid-1990s. This reflects airline and leasing company strategy to protect upside potential requirements.

World Annual Commercial Airplane Deliveries

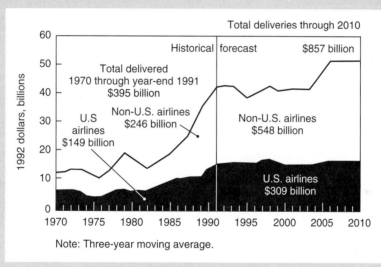

Note: Three-year moving average.

Chapter 4

Segmenting Markets

Segmenting markets is a foundation for superior business performance. Understanding how buyers' needs and wants vary is essential in designing effective marketing strategies. The Strategy Feature describing IBM's segmentation strategy underlines the fact that segmenting markets may be critical to implementing market-driven strategy.

The need to improve an organization's understanding of buyers is escalating because of buyers' demands for uniqueness and the array of technology available to generate products to satisfy those demands. Companies are responding to opportunities to provide unique customer value with products ranging from customized phone pagers for business users to self-designed greeting cards for consumers and even postage stamps that incorporate their own photographs.

Buyers vary according to how they use products, the needs and preferences that the products satisfy, and their consumption patterns. These differences in buyers' responsiveness create market segments. Market segmentation is the process of identifying and analyzing subgroups of buyers in a product-market with similar response characteristics (e.g., frequency of purchase). Recognizing differences between market segments and how they change better and faster than competitors can is an increasingly important source of competitive advantage.

The most specific form of market segmentation entails considering each buyer as a market segment. This is the basis of "one-to-one marketing."[1] Such fine-tuned segmentation is possible for an expanding array of goods and services due to mass-customization techniques. This is an exciting new approach to serving the unique needs and wants of individual buyers. Custom-designed products satisfy the individual buyer's needs and wants at prices comparable to those of mass-produced products. The growing adoption of customer relationship management (CRM) systems that integrate all information about each individual customer into a single location provides unprecedented opportunities to learn about customer's needs from their actual behavior. When information technology and production efficiencies are coupled, products are designed to meet a customer's needs at prices that are competitive with those of mass-produced products.

For example, a woman can walk into an Original Levi Store in New York, be measured by a salesperson, and try on a few pairs of jeans selected by computer from over 400 pairs to match her specific measurements. If one does not provide a perfect fit, the information is put into the computer to refine the specifications. The final match is a perfect fit at a price only $10 more than that of the mass-produced jeans. Since stocking a supply of each of the 400 jeans in every store would be very costly, the buyer's pair of jeans is shipped to the store or the buyer from the distribution center. Similarly, the Japanese bicycle manufacturer Panasonic pioneered "made to measure" bicycles, where the retail customer is measured as if for a suit of clothes and the custom-made bicycle is delivered to the store within a few days.

In the early 1990s, in an era of personal computer expansion, the traditional mainframe computer manufacturer IBM faced sluggish sales and profits. Traditionally, IBM organized around product groups and powerful geographically organized sales divisions.

In 1991 the company restructured, driven by its new segmentation approach. IBM abandoned geographic sales regions as market segments because they did not provide a way to group customers with similar needs and thus were a poor basis for target marketing. The focus for marketing strategy and efforts to stimulate market demand became Industry Solution Units (ISUs) focusing on major industrial sectors such as banking, insurance, retail, government, and utilities.

Although facing internal resistance and substantial restructuring costs, the ISU organization at IBM helped improve that company's revenue performance by sharpening its market focus and providing clearer sales targets and positioning messages. By 1994, with the new CEO's refusal to tolerate "push-back" from executives in the company, IBM moved back into profitability. Much of the market-driven culture change at IBM has been linked to its move from a sales-led structure to one based on customer segments.

By 2001 IBM was almost the only large U.S. technology company that was not issuing revenue or profit warning's to investors.

Sources: Adapted from case material compiled by Neil A Morgan and Garry Veale originally published in Nigel F Piercy, *Market-Led Strategic Change: Transforming the Process of Going to Market* (Oxford: Butterworth-Heinemann, 1997), 303–11.

We begin the chapter with a discussion of the role of market segmentation in marketing strategy, followed by a discussion of the variables used to identify segments. Next, we look at the methods for forming segments, followed by a review of high-variety strategies. Finally, we consider the issues and guidelines involved in selecting the segmentation strategy and its implementation.

Segmentation and Market-Driven Strategy

Market segmentation needs to be considered early in the development of market-driven strategy. Segments are determined, customer value opportunities explored in each segment, organizational capabilities matched to promising segment opportunities, market target(s) selected from the segment(s) of interest, and a positioning strategy developed and implemented for each market target (Exhibit 4–1). We examine each of these activities to indicate the role of segmentation in the marketing strategy process.

Market Segmentation and Value Opportunities

Market segmentation is the process of placing the buyers in a product-market into subgroups so that the members of each segment display similar responsiveness to a particular positioning strategy. Buyer similarities are indicated by the amount and frequency of purchase, loyalty to a particular brand, how the product is used, and other measures of responsiveness. Thus, segmentation is an identification process aimed at finding subgroups of buyers within a total market. The opportunity for segmentation occurs when differences in buyers' demand (response) functions allow market demand to be divided into segments,

EXHIBIT 4–1
Segmentation and the Market-Driven Strategy Process

Segments

Value opportunities

Capabilities/segment match

Targets

Positioning

each with a distinct demand function.[2] The term *market niche* sometimes is used to refer to a market segment that represents a relatively small proportion of the buyers in the total market. We consider a niche and a segment to be the same.

Segmentation identifies customer groups within a product-market, each containing buyers with similar value requirements concerning specific product/brand attributes. A segment is a possible market target for an organization competing in the market. Segmentation offers a company an opportunity to better match its products and capabilities to buyers' value requirements. Customer satisfaction can be improved by providing a value offering that matches the value proposition considered important by the buyers in a segment.

Creating New Market Space

Importantly, market analysis may identify segments not recognized or served effectively by competitors. There may be opportunities to tap into new areas of value and create a unique space in the market. For example, in France Accor has established the highly successful Formula 1 hotel chain by building a new market segment in between the traditional strategic groups in the hotel market. Traditional one-star hotels offer low prices, while two-star hotels offer more amenities and charge higher prices. Accor's analysis of customer needs found that customers choose a one-star hotel because it is cheap but trade up from a one-star hotel to a two-star hotel for the "sleeping environment"—clean, quiet rooms with more comfortable beds—not all the other amenities that are offered. Formula 1 provides the superior "sleeping environment" of a two-star hotel but not the other facilities, which allows it to offer that environment at the price of a one-star hotel. By 1999 Formula 1 had built a market share larger than the sum of those of the next five largest competitors.[3]

Matching Value Opportunities and Capabilities

While broad competitive comparisons can be made for an entire product-market, more penetrating insights about competitive advantage and market opportunity result from market segment analyses. Examining specific market segments helps identify how to (1) attain a closer match between buyers' value preferences and the organization's capabilities and (2) compare the organization's strengths (and weaknesses) to those of the key competitors in each segment.

Customer value requirements can often be better satisfied within a segment, compared to the total market. Consider, for example, Atlas Air Inc., a transportation company that offers outsourcing freight services for global air carriers. When it was launched in 1992, the founder identified an emerging customer need because carriers were replacing older aircraft with fuel-efficient planes that had half the cargo space of those being replaced.[4] Atlas customers include British Airways, China Airlines, KLM, Lufthansa, Swissair, and SAS, all attracted by low cost and reliable services. Atlas carries flowers and shoes from Amsterdam to Singapore for KLM and fish, cattle, and horses from Taipei to Europe for China Air.

Market Targeting and Strategic Positioning

Market targeting consists of evaluating and selecting one or more segments whose value requirements provide a good match with the organization's capabilities. Companies typically appeal to only a portion of the people or organizations in a product-market, regardless of how many segments are targeted. Management may decide to target one, a few, or several segments to gain the strength and advantage of specialization. Alternatively, while a specific segment strategy is not used, the marketing program selected by management is likely to appeal to a particular subgroup of buyers within the market. Segment identification and targeting are obviously preferred. Finding a segment by chance does not give management the opportunity to evaluate different segments in terms of the financial and competitive advantage implications of each segment. When segmentation is employed, it should be by design, and the underlying analyses should lead to the selection of one or more promising segments to target.

Recall from Chapter 2 the description of positioning strategy as the combination of organizational actions management takes to meet the needs and wants of each market target. The strategy consists of product(s) and supporting services, distribution, pricing, and promotion components. Management's choices about how to influence target buyers to favorably position the product in their eyes and minds help in designing the positioning strategy.

Market segmentation lays the groundwork for market targeting and positioning strategies. The skills and insights used in segmenting a product-market may give a company important competitive advantages by identifying buyer groups that will respond favorably to the firm's marketing efforts. The Atlas Air example is illustrative.

Of course, faulty segmentation reduces the effectiveness of targeting and positioning decisions. For example, in 2000 General Motors made the decision to axe the Oldsmobile brand, the oldest auto brand in the United States. Although sometimes a symbol of innovation and style, Oldsmobile failed to establish a strong position in a long-term market niche or segment—it did not deliver the "class" of Cadillac and Buick or the wider market appeal of Chevrolet.[5]

Selecting the Market to Be Segmented

Market segmentation may occur at any of the product-market levels shown in Exhibit 4–2. Generic-level segmentation is illustrated by different shopper segments (e.g., aggressive shoppers, occassional shoppers) that purchase health and beauty aids. Product-type segmentation is shown by the differences in price, quality, and features of shaving equipment. Product variant segmentation considers the segments within a category such as electric razors.

An important consideration in defining the market to be segmented is estimating the variation in buyers' needs and requirements at the different product-market levels and identifying the types of buyers included in the market. In the Atlas Air example, management defined the product-market to be segmented as air freight services between major global

EXHIBIT 4–2
Identifying the Health and Beauty Supplies Product-Market to Be Segmented

Level of Competition	Product Definition	Illustrative Competitors	Need/Want Satisfied
Generic	Health and beauty aids	Consumer products companies	Enhancement of health and beauty
Product type	Shaving equipment	Gillette, Remington, Bic	Shaving
Product variant	Electric razors	Braun, Norelco, Remington, Panasonic	Electric shaving

airports for business organizations. Segmenting the generic product-market for air freight services was too broad in scope. The market definition selected by Atlas Air excluded buyers (e.g., consumers) that were not of primary interest to management while including companies with different freight service needs.

In contemporary markets, boundaries and definitions can change rapidly, underlining the strategic importance of market definition and selection and the need for frequent reevaluation.

Market Segmentation Activities and Decisions

The process of segmenting a market involves several interrelated activities and decisions that begin with defining the market to be segmented (Exhibit 4–3). It is necessary to decide how to segment the market, which involves selecting the variable(s) to use as the basis for identifying segments. For example, frequency of use of a product (e.g., frequent, moderate, and occasional) may be a basis for segmentation. Next, the method of forming segments is decided on. This may consist of managers using judgment and experience to divide the market into segments, as illustrated by the Atlas Air example. Alternatively, segments may be formed using statistical analysis. The availability of customer purchase behavior in CRM systems, for example, provides a base for this analysis. Part of forming segments is deciding whether finer (smaller) segments should be used. Finally, strategic analysis is conducted on each segment to assist management in deciding which segment(s) to target.

Identifying Market Segments

After the market to be segmented is defined, one or more variables are selected to identify segments. For example, the United States Automobile Association (USAA) segments by type of employment. Although unknown to many people, USAA has built a successful business serving the automobile insurance needs of U.S. military personnel throughout the world. USAA maintains close relationships with its 2.6 million members using powerful information technology. The USAA service representative has immediate access to the client's consolidated file, the one-to-one service encounter is highly personalized, and USAA achieves a 98 percent retention rate in its chosen market segment.[6]

We discuss the purpose of segmentation variables, followed by a review of the variables that are used in segmentation analyses.

Purpose of Segmentation Variables

One or more variables (e.g., frequency of use) may be used to divide the product-market into segments. *Demographic* and *psychographic* (lifestyle and personality) characteristics of buyers are of interest, since this information is available from U.S. Census reports and

EXHIBIT 4–3
**Market
Segmentation
Activities and
Decisions**

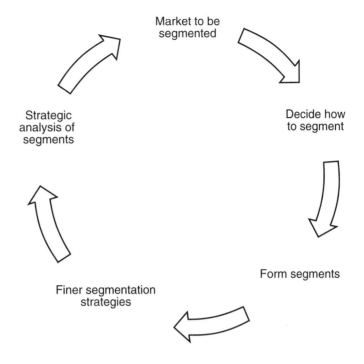

many other sources, including electronic databases. The *use situation* variables consider how the buyer uses the product, such as purchasing a meal away from home for the purpose of entertainment. Variables measuring buyers' *needs* and *preferences* include attitudes, brand awareness, and brand preference. *Purchase-behavior* variables describe brand use and consumption (e.g., size and frequency of purchase). We examine these variables to highlight their uses, features, and other considerations important in segmenting markets.

Characteristics of People and Organizations

Consumer Markets

The characteristics of people fall into two major categories: (1) geographic and demographic and (2) psychographic (lifestyle and personality). Demographics are often useful to describe consumer segments after they have been formed rather than to identify them. Nonetheless, these variables are popular because available data often relate demographics to the other segmentation variables. Geographic location may be useful for segmenting product-markets. For example, there are regional differences in the popularity of transportation vehicles. In several states the most popular vehicle is a pickup truck. The "truck belt" runs from the upper Midwest south through Texas and the Gulf Coast states. The Ford brand is dominant in the northern half of the truck belt, while Chevrolet leads in the southern half.

Demographic variables describe buyers according to their age, income, education, occupation, and many other characteristics. Demographic information helps describe groups of buyers such as heavy users of a product or brand. Demographics used in combination with buyer behavior information are useful in segmenting markets, selecting distribution channels, designing promotion strategies, and making other decisions on marketing strategy.

Lifestyle variables indicate what people do (activities), their interests, their opinions, and their buying behavior. Lifestyle characteristics extend beyond demographics and offer a more penetrating description of the consumer.[7] Profiles can be developed using lifestyle characteristics. This information is used to segment markets, help position products, and guide the design of advertising messages.

An array of specialty magazines enables companies to identify and access very specific lifestyle segments. For example, Peterson Publishing Co. publishes 23 monthlies, 9 bi-monthlies, and 45 annuals.[8] The company's magazine portfolio includes *Motor Trend, MTB* (mountain bikes), *Circle Track,* and *Teen* magazine. Specialty magazines match buyers' lifestyle interests with articles that correspond to those interests. Subscriber profiles help companies match their market target profiles with the right magazines. Many specialty magazines conduct subscriber research studies that are useful to companies targeting lifestyle segments.

Organizational Markets

Several characteristics help in segmenting business markets. The type of industry (some-times called a vertical market) is related to purchase behavior for certain types of products. For example, automobile producers purchase steel, paint, and other raw materials. Since au-tomobile firms' needs may differ from those of companies in other industries, this form of segmentation enables suppliers to specialize their efforts and satisfy customer needs. Other variables for segmenting organizational markets include the size of the company, the stage of industry development, and the stage of the value-added system (e.g., producer, distribu-tor, retailer). Dell Computer, for example, targets the following organizational segments: global enterprises, large companies, midsize companies, government agencies, education, and small companies. Organizational segmentation is aided by first examining (1) the ex-tent of market concentration and (2) the degree of product customization.[9] Concentration considers the number of customers and their relative buying power. Product customization determines the extent to which the supplier must tailor the product to each organizational buyer. If one or both of these factors indicate quite a bit of diversity, segmentation oppor-tunities may exist.

Boeing caters to the specific needs of each air carrier purchasing commercial aircraft. For example, an airline ordering a 747 has a choice of four configurations for the interior wall at the front of the rear cargo compartment.[10] This decision affects how 2,550 parts are installed. While Boeing's efforts to provide customized designs are preferred by its cus-tomers, the costs are high and Boeing is evaluating the value/cost relationships of its at-tempts to satisfy the needs of single airline segments.

Product Use Situation Segmentation

Markets can be segmented on the basis of how the product is used. As an illustration, Nikon, the Japanese camera company, offers a line of high-performance sunglasses de-signed for activities and light conditions encountered while skiing, driving, hiking, flying, shooting, and participating in water sports. Nikon competes in the premium portion of the market with prices somewhat higher than those of Ray-Ban, the market leader. Timex uses a similar basis of segmentation for its watches.

Needs and preferences vary according to different use situations. Consider, for example, segmenting the market for prescription drugs. Astra/Merck identifies the following seg-ments based on the type of physician/patient drug use situation:

• Health care as a business—customers such as managed care administrators who con-sider economic factors of drug use foremost.

• Traditional—physicians with standard patient needs centered on the treatment of disease.

- Cost sensitive—physicians for whom cost is paramount, such as those with a sizable number of indigent patients.

- Medical thought leaders—people on the leading edge, often at teaching hospitals, who champion the newest therapies.[11]

A sales representative provides the medical thought leader with cutting-edge clinical studies, whereas the cost-sensitive doctor is provided information related to the costs of treatments.

Mass customization offers a promising means of responding to different use situations at competitive prices. For example, Lutron Electronics gives its buyers customized light dimmer switches by programming desired features using computer chips built into the switches. The company holds 80 percent of all dimmer patents and has a 75 percent market share, with a product catalog including several thousand product variations in dozens of colors.[12]

Buyers' Needs and Preferences

Needs and preferences that are specific to products and brands can be used as segmentation bases and segment descriptors. Examples include brand loyalty status, benefits sought, and proneness to make a deal. Buyers may be attracted to different brands because of the benefits they offer. For example, seeking to generate additional revenues in the mid-1990s, Credit Lyonnaise, France's largest commercial bank, segmented and began targeting customers with annual incomes in excess of 500,000 francs ($100,000 in late 1995) who wanted quality service, financial advice, and upscale facilities.[13] Several new branch offices were designed to appeal to Credit Lyonnaise's wealthy clients. One office in Bordeaux, called Club Tourney, had an elegant townhouse with salons where clients met with advisors to discuss financial needs. The branch served 100 wealthy clients.

Consumer Needs

Needs motivate people to act. Understanding how buyers satisfy their needs provides guidelines for marketing actions. Consumers attempt to match their needs with the products that satisfy those needs. People have a variety of needs, including basic physiological needs (food, rest, and sex), the need for safety, the need for relationships with other people (friendship), and personal satisfaction needs.[14] Understanding the nature and intensity of these needs is important in (1) determining how well a particular brand may satisfy the need and/or (2) indicating what change(s) in the brand may be necessary to provide a better solution to the buyer's needs.

Attitudes

Buyers' attitudes toward brands are important because experience and research findings indicate that attitudes influence behavior. Attitudes are enduring systems of favorable or unfavorable evaluations about brands.[15] They reflect the buyer's overall liking of or preference for a brand. Attitudes may develop from personal experience, interactions with other buyers, or marketing efforts such as advertising and personal selling.

Attitude information is useful in marketing strategy development. A strategy may be designed either to respond to established attitudes or, instead, to attempt to change an attitude. In a given situation, relevant attitudes should be identified and measured to indicate how brands compare. If important attitude influences on buyer behavior are identified and a firm's brand is measured against these attitudes, management may be able to improve the brand's position by using this information. Attitudes are often difficult to change, but firms may be able to do this if buyers' perceptions about the brand are incorrect. For example, if the trade-in value of an automobile is important to buyers in a targeted segment and a company learns through market research that its brand (which actually has a high trade-in value) is perceived as having a low trade-in value, advertising can communicate this information to buyers.

Perceptions

Perception is defined as "the process by which an individual selects, organizes, and interprets information inputs to create a meaningful picture of the world."[16] Perceptions are how buyers select, organize, and interpret marketing stimuli, such as advertising, personal selling, price, and the product. Perceptions form attitudes. Buyers are selective in the information they process. As an illustration of selective perception, some advertising messages may not be received by viewers because of the large number of messages vying for their attention. Or a salesperson's conversation may be misunderstood or not understood because the buyer is trying to decide if the purchase is necessary while the salesperson is talking.

People often perceive things differently. Business executives are interested in how their products, salespeople, stores, and companies are perceived. Perception is important strategically in helping management evaluate the current positioning strategy and in making changes in that strategy. Perception mapping is a useful research technique for showing how brands are perceived by buyers according to various criteria. We discuss how preference mapping is used to form segments later in the chapter.

Purchase Behavior

Consumption variables such as the size and frequency of a purchase are useful in segmenting consumer and business markets. Marketers of industrial products often classify customers and prospects into categories on the basis of the volume of the purchase. For example, a specialty chemical producer concentrates its marketing efforts on chemical users that purchase at least $100,000 of chemicals each year. The firm further segments the market on the basis of how the customer uses the chemical.

The development of CRM systems offers fast access to records of actual customer purchase behavior and characteristics. The Technology Feature describes how CRM and loyalty programs are generating insights into customer behavior and segment differences and providing the ability to respond more precisely to the needs of customers in different segments.

Since buying decisions vary in importance and complexity, it is useful to classify them to better understand their characteristics, the products to which they apply, and the marketing strategy implications of each type of purchase behavior. Buyer decisions can be classified according to the extent to which the buyer is involved in the decision.[17] A high-involvement decision may be an expensive purchase, have important personal consequences, and affect the consumer's ego and social needs. The decision situation may consist of extended problem solving (high involvement), limited problem solving, or routine problem solving (low involvement). The characteristics of these situations are illustrated in Exhibit 4–4.

These categories are very broad since the range of involvement covers various buying situations. Even so, the classifications provide a useful way to compare and contrast buying situations. Also, involvement may vary from individual to individual. For example, a high-involvement purchase for one person may not be so for another person, since perceptions of expense, personal consequences, and social impact may vary across individuals.

Exhibit 4–5 summarizes the various segmentation variables and shows examples of segmentation bases and descriptors for consumer and organizational markets. As we examine the methods used to form segments, the role of these variables in segment determination and analysis is illustrated.

Technology Feature

While retailers have huge volumes of purchase data available to them from electronic point-of-sales scanning systems and their own customer loyalty programs (potentially linking consumer data precisely to purchase behavior), manufacturers are also making advances in exploiting this new data richness.

Consodata is a CRM company working for the Jigsaw consortium of some of the largest fast-moving comsumer goods companies in the world. Unilever, Kimberley-Clark, and Cadbury Schweppes are sharing the costs of a giant database that can divide countries into any size segment and determine exactly who lives there, where they shop, what they buy, their lifestyles, and attitude data. Initial applications are in the precise merchandising of supermarket shelves to reflect local segment characteristics.

Accor, the French-based hotel group, has adopted Pegasus Business Intelligence systems for its Sifitel and Novotel hotels in the United States. Bob Macket, Accor's vice president for sales and marketing in North America, says that the group will be able to "market with a microscope rather than a telescope." The potential is to identify different customers' preferences, differentiate, and customize. Using survey data, records of guests' visits, and guests' preferences or problems, the data are mined to draw up "golden nugget maps" to identify which customer segments have major potential, which already been heavily exploited, and which have limited potential.

Sources: Christopher Field, "Loyalty Cards Are Unlikely to Carry All the Answers," *Financial Times*, May 3, 2000, IV, Marian Edwards, "Your Wish Is on My Database," *Financial Times*, February 28, 2000, 20.

Forming Segments

The credit card division of American Express (AMEX) identifies market segments based on purchase behavior. One group of cardholders pays the annual fee for the card but rarely (or never) uses it.[18] This group of zero spenders is made up of (1) those who cannot afford much discretionary spending and (2) those who use cash or competitors' cards. AMEX's objective is to identify the second group of potential buyers because they offer card usage opportunities and may potentially give up their cards. AMEX uses self-selecting incentive offers (e.g.,

EXHIBIT 4–4
Characteristics of Consumer Involvement Situations

Source: Eric N. Berkowitz, Roger A. Kerin, Steven W. Hartley, and William Rudelius, *Marketing*, 5th ed. (Chicago: Richard D. Irwin, 1997), 156.

Characteristics of Purchase Decision Process	Consumer Involvement		
	High		Low
	Extended Problem Solving	Limited Problem Solving	Routine Problem Solving
Number of brands examined	Many	Several	One
Number of sellers considered	Many	Several	Few
Number of product attributes evaluated	Many	Moderate	One
Number of external information sources used	Many	Few	None
Time spent searching	Considerable	Little	Minimal

125

EXHIBIT 4–5
**Illustrative
Segmentation
Variables**

	Consumer Markets	Industrial/Organizational Markets
Characteristics of people/organizations	Age, gender, race Income Family size Lifecycle stage Geographic location Lifestyle	Type of industry Size Geographic location Corporate culture Stage of development Producer/intermediary
Use situation	Occasion Importance of purchase Prior experience with product User status	Application Purchasing procedure New task, modified rebuy, straight rebuy
Buyers' needs/preferences	Brand loyalty status Brand preference Benefits sought Quality Proneness to make a deal	Performance requirements Brand preferences Desired features Service requirements
Purchase behavior	Size of purchase Frequency of purchase	Volume Frequency of purchase

two free airline tickets for heavy card use over six months) to identify the valuable nonuser cardholders. While this segmentation approach is expensive, it costs less than obtaining a new customer to replace one who leaves AMEX. It also does not require using expensive marketing research to identify cardholders with the ability (financial) to use their cards.

The requirements for segmentation are discussed first, and then we describe and illustrate the methods of segment formation.

Requirements for Segmentation

An important question is deciding if it is worthwhile to segment a product-market. While in many instances segmentation is a sound strategy, its feasibility and value need to be evaluated. Five criteria are useful for this purpose.

Response Differences

Determining differences in the responsiveness of the buyers in the product-market to positioning strategies is a key segment identification requirement. Suppose the customers in a product-market are placed into four groups, each a potential segment, using a variable such as income (affluent, high, medium, and low). If each group responds (e.g., amount of purchase) in the same way as all the other groups to a marketing mix strategy, the four groups are not market segments. If segments actually exist in this illustration, there must be differences in the responsiveness of the groups to marketing actions, such as pricing, product features, and promotion. The presence of real segments requires actual response differences. Simply finding differences in buyers' characteristics such as income is not enough.

For example, income is useful in finding response differences in India. A study conducted by a New Delhi think tank identifies a premium segment in the Indian consumer market.[19] Families with an annual income in excess of 1 million rupees ($29,200 in late 1995) have as much buying power as a U.S. family with three times that income. Living costs for the Indian family are very low (e.g., a two-bedroom apartment for $130 a month).

The premium segment is a promising target for luxury goods brands like Mercedes-Benz, Cartier, and Christian Dior. There are 600,000 Indian households in the premium segment, including 200,000 in Bombay (now Mumbai). BMW has a joint venture with Hero Motors Ltd. to produce luxury cars in India.

Identifiable Segments

It must be possible to identify the customer groups that exhibit response differences, and sometimes finding the correct groups may be difficult. For example, even though variations in the amount of purchase by customers occur in a market, it may not be possible to identify which people correspond to the different response groups in the market. While it is usually feasible to find descriptive differences among the buyers in a product-market, these variations must be matched to response differences. Recall AMEX's approach to identifying cardholders with buying power who use the card infrequently. Incentives are used to attract nonuser cardholders with buying power.

Actionable Segments

A business must be able to aim a marketing program strategy at each segment selected as a market target. As was discussed earlier, specialty magazines offer one means of selective targeting. Ideally, the marketing effort should focus on the segment of interest and not be wasted on nonsegment buyers. Cable television, magazine, and radio media are able to provide coverage of narrowly defined market segments. The Internet offers great potential for direct marketing channels to reach specialized segments. Similarly, databases offer very focused access to buyers.

Cost/Benefits of Segmentation

Segmentation must be financially attractive in terms of revenues generated and costs incurred. It is important to evaluate the benefits of segmentation. While segmentation may cost more in terms of research and added marketing expenses, it should generate more sales and higher margins. The objective is to use a segmentation approach that offers a favorable revenue and cost combination.

For example, British-based ICI Fertilisers experienced substantial losses in the late 1980s, but rebuilt its business around an innovative market segmentation strategy. Research showed that farmers' priorities in fertilizer purchasing were dominated by price only in 10 percent of cases; other farmers were more influenced by advanced technology, loyalty to traditional merchants, and loyalty to brands. ICI created new product ranges around these needs, restructured the business around these ranges, and built impressive profitability.[20]

Stability over Time

Finally, the segments must show adequate stability over time so that the firm's marketing efforts will have enough time to produce favorable results. If buyers' needs change too fast, a group with similar response patterns at one point may display quite different patterns several months later. The time period may be too short to justify using a segmentation strategy.

The distinction between product differentiation and market segmentation is not always clear. *Product differentiation* occurs when a product offering is perceived by the buyer as different from the competition on any physical or nonphysical product characteristic, including price.[21] Using a product differentiation strategy, a firm may target an entire market or one (or more) segments. Competing firms may differentiate their product offerings in trying to gain competitive advantage with the same group of targeted buyers. Market targeting using a differentiation strategy is considered further in Chapter 6.

Approaches to Segment Identification

Segments are formed by two approaches: (A) grouping customers using descriptive characteristics and then comparing response differences across the groups or (B) forming groups based on response differences (e.g., frequency of purchase) and determining if the groups can be identified based on differences in their characteristics.[22] Exhibit 4–6 illustrates the two approaches. Approach A uses one or more characteristics such as income or family size believed to be related to buyer response. After the groups are formed, they are examined to see if response varies across groups. Approach B places buyers with similar response patterns into groups and then develops buyer profiles using buyer characteristics. We describe each approach to show how it is used to identify segments.

Customer Group Identification

After the product-market of interest is defined, promising segments may be identified, using management judgment in combination with analysis of available information and/ or marketing research studies. Consider, for example, hotel lodging services. Exhibit 4–7 illustrates ways to segment the hotel lodging product-market. An additional breakdown can be made according to business and household travelers. These categories may be further distinguished by individual customer and group customer segments. Groups may include conventions, corporate meetings, and tour groups. Several possible segments can be distinguished. Consider, for example, Marriott's Courtyard hotel chain. These hotels fall into the midpriced category and are targeted primarily to frequent business travelers who fly to destinations, are in the 40-plus age range, and have relatively high incomes.

When using the customer group identification approach, it is necessary to select one or more of the characteristics of people or organizations as the basis of segmentation. Using these variables, segments are formed by (1) management judgment and experience or (2) supporting statistical analyses. The objective is to find differences in responsiveness among the customer groups. We look at some of the customer grouping methods to show how segments are formed.

EXHIBIT 4–6
**Approaches to
Segment
Identification**

A. Start with
identifiers of
customer groups

B. Start with
customer response
profile

Characteristics
of people and
organizations

Use situation

Buyers needs
and preferences

Purchase
behavior and
loyalty

EXHIBIT 4–7
**Product-Market
Segment
Dimensions for
Hotel Lodging
Services**

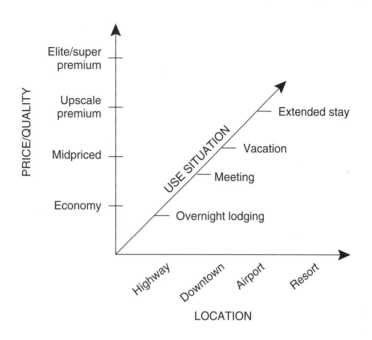

Experience and Available Information

Management's knowledge of customer needs is often a useful guide to segmentation. For example, both experience and analysis of published information are often helpful in segmenting business markets. Business segment variables include type of industry, size of purchase, and product application. Company records often contain information for analyzing the existing customer base. Published data such as industry mailing lists can be used to identify potential market segments. These groups are then analyzed to determine if they display different levels of response.

Segmenting using management judgment and experience, the Italian fashion designer and retailer Prada markets an expensive array of dresses, handbags, hats, shoes, and other women's apparel.[23] The best-selling $450 backpacks are designed to appeal to affluent women who do not want to flaunt their status. Each knapsack has a small triangular logo. Prada's products offer an antistatus (lifestyle) appeal to a segment of affluent women. The luxury retailer has 47 stores, including 20 in Japan and two in the United States. Prada's goods are also sold in department stores.

Cross-Classification Analyses

Another method of forming segments is to identify customer groups by using descriptive characteristics and compare response rates (e.g., sales) by placing the information in a table. Customer groups form the rows, and response categories form the columns. Review of industry publications and other published information may identify ways to break up a product-market into segments. Standardized information services such as Information Resources Inc. collect and publish consumer panel data on a regular basis (see Chapter 5). These data provide a wide range of consumer characteristics, advertising media usage, and other information which are analyzed by product and brand sales and market share. The data are obtained from a large sample of households through the United States. Similar statistical data are available in many countries.

Information is available for use in forming population subgroups within product-markets. The analyst can use many sources as well as management's insights and hunches regarding the market. The essential concern is whether a segmentation scheme identifies customer groups that display different product and brand responsiveness. The more evidence of meaningful differences, the better chance that useful segments exist. Cross-classification has some real advantages in terms of cost and ease of use. There may be a strong basis for choosing a segmenting scheme that uses this approach. This occurs more often in business and organizational markets where management has a good knowledge of user needs because there are fewer users than there are in consumer product-markets. Alternatively, this approach may be a first step leading to a more comprehensive type of analysis.

Database Segmentation

The availability of computerized databases offers a wide range of segmentation analysis capabilities. This type of analysis is particularly useful in consumer market segmentation. Databases are organized by geography and buyers' descriptive characteristics. They may also contain customer response information, as shown in the AMEX cardholder illustration. Databases can be used to identify customer groups, design effective marketing programs, and improve the effectiveness of existing programs. The number of available databases is rapidly expanding, the costs are declining, and the information systems are becoming user-friendly. Several marketing research and direct mail firms offer database services.

Segmentation Illustrations

Mobil Corporation studies buyers in the gasoline market to identify segments. The findings, including information obtained from over 2,000 motorists, are summarized in Exhibit 4–8. The research identified five primary purchasing groups.[24] Interestingly, Mobil found that Price Shoppers spend an average of $700 annually, compared to $1,200 for Road Warriors and True Blues. Mobil's marketing strategy is to offer gasoline buyers a quality buying experience, including upgraded facilities, more lighting for safety, responsive attendants, and quality convenience products. The target segments are Road Warriors and Generation F3, involving a major effort in convenience stores and reduced time at the gas pump based on the Mobil Speed Pass. The test results from the new strategy raised revenues by 25 percent over previous sales for the same retail sites.

As shown by the profiles described in Exhibit 4–8, needs and preferences vary quite a bit within a market. Trying to satisfy all the buyers in the market with the same marketing approach is difficult. There are too many differences across buyers. Analyzing both the customer and the competition is important. Specific competitors may be better (or worse) at meeting the needs of specific customer groups (e.g., Mobil's Road Warriors). Finding gaps between buyers' needs and competitors' offerings provides opportunities for improving customer satisfaction. Also, companies study competitors' products to identify ways to improve their own.

By identifying customer groups using descriptive characteristics and comparing them to a measure of customer responsiveness to a marketing mix such as product usage rate (e.g., number of fax ink cartridges per year), potential segments can be identified. If the response rates are similar within a segment and differences in response exist between segments, promising segments are identified. Segments do not always emerge from these analyses, because in some product-markets distinct segments may not exist or the segment interrelationships may be so complex that an analysis of these predetermined groupings will not identify useful segments. Product differentiation strategies may be used in these situations.

In an era of increased globalization, it is also important to recognize that segmentation has an international dimension in many markets. This is not simply a matter of country

EXHIBIT 4–8   **Diversity of Gasoline Buyers**

Road Warriors:	True Blues:	Generation F3:	Homebodies:	Price Shoppers:
Generally higher-income, middle-aged men, who drive 25,000 to 50,000 miles a year . . . buy premium with a credit card . . . purchase sandwiches and drinks from the convenience store . . . will sometimes wash their cars at the carwash.	Usually men and women with moderate to high incomes who are loyal to a brand and sometimes to a particular station . . . frequently buy premium gasoline and pay in cash.	(for fuel, food, and fast): Upwardly mobile men and women—half under 25 years of age—who are constantly on the go . . . drive a lot and snack heavily from the convenience store.	Usually housewives who shuttle their children around during the day and use whatever gasoline station is based in town or along their route of travel.	Generally aren't loyal to either brand or a particular station; and rarely buy the premium line . . . frequently on tight budgets . . . efforts to woo them have been the basis of marketing strategies for years.
16% of buyers	**16% of buyers**	**27% of buyers**	**21% of buyers**	**20% of buyers**

Source: Alanna Sullivan, "Mobil Bets Drivers Pick Cappuccino over Low Prices," *The Wall Street Journal*, January 30, 1995, B1. Reprinted by permission of *The Wall Street Journal*, © 1995 Dow Jones & Company, Inc. All Rights Reserved Worldwide.

differences, such as, differences in sizes of products for apparel and household furniture based on ethnic identity in overseas countries. Roper Starch Worldwide, based on interviews about core values with 1,000 people in 35 countries, identified six global consumer segments that exist to varying degrees in each country:

- *Strivers*—place more emphasis on material and professional goals than do the other groups.
- *Devouts*—tradition and duty are very important.
- *Altruists*—interested in social issues and social welfare.
- *Intimates*—value close personal and family relationships.
- *Fun seekers*—high consumption of restaurants, bars, movies.
- *Creatives*—strong interest in education, knowledge, and technology.

The global study found that people in different segments generally pursued different activities, purchased different products, and used different media.[25]

Forming Groups Based on Response Differences

The alternative to selecting customer groups based on descriptive characteristics is to identify groups of buyers by using response differences to form the segments. A look at a segmentation analysis for the packaging division of Signode Corporation illustrates how this method is used.[26] The products consist of steel strappings for various packaging applications. An analysis of the customer base identified the following segments: programmed buyers (limited service needs), relationship buyers, transaction buyers, and bargain hunters (low price, high service). Statistical (cluster) analysis formed the segments by using 12 variables concerning price and service trade-offs and buying power. The study included 161 of Signode's national accounts. Measures of the variables were obtained from sales records, sales managers, and sales representatives. The segments vary in responsiveness based on relative price and relative service.

The widespread adoption of CRM systems offers a greater opportunity for timely and detailed analysis of response differences between customers. The "data warehouse," by integrating transactional data around customer types, makes possible complex analyses to understand differences in the behavior of different customer groups, observe customer lifecycles, and predict behavior.[27]

Response difference approaches draw more extensively from buyer behavior information than do the customer group identification methods discussed earlier. Note, for example, the information on Signode's customer responsiveness to price and service. We now look at additional applications to more fully explore the potential of the customer response approaches.

Cluster Analysis

Cluster analysis, a statistical technique, groups people according to the similarity of their answers to questions such as brand preferences on product attributes. This method was useful in forming segments for Signode Corporation. The objective of cluster analysis is to identify groupings in which the similarity within a group is high and the variation among groups is as great as possible. Each cluster is a potential segment.

Perceptual Maps

Another promising segmentation method uses consumer research data to construct perceptual maps of buyers' perceptions of products and brands. The information helps select market target strategies and determine how to position a product for a market target.

While the end result of perceptual mapping is simple to understand, its execution is demanding in terms of research skills. Although there are variations in approach, the following steps are illustrative:

1. Select the product-market area to be segmented.

2. Decide which brands compete in the product-market.

3. Collect buyers' perceptions about attributes for the available brands (and an ideal brand) obtained from a sample of people.

4. Analyze the data to form one, two, or more composite attribute dimensions, each independent of the others.

5. Prepare a map (two-dimensional X and Y grid) of attributes on which are positioned consumer perceptions of competing brands.

6. Plot consumers with similar ideal preferences to see if subgroups (potential segments) will form.

7. Evaluate how well the solution corresponds to the data that are analyzed.

8. Interpret the results as to market target and product positioning strategies.

An example of a perception map is shown in Exhibit 4–9. Each Group (I–V) contains people from a survey sample with similar preferences concerning expensiveness and quality for the product category. The brands (A–E) are positioned using the preference data obtained from the survey participants. Assuming you are the product manager for Brand C, what does the information indicate concerning possible targeting? Group V is a logical market target, and Group III may represent a secondary market target. To appeal most effectively to Group V, we will probably need to change somewhat Group V consumers' price

EXHIBIT 4–9
**An Illustrative
Consumer
Perception Map**

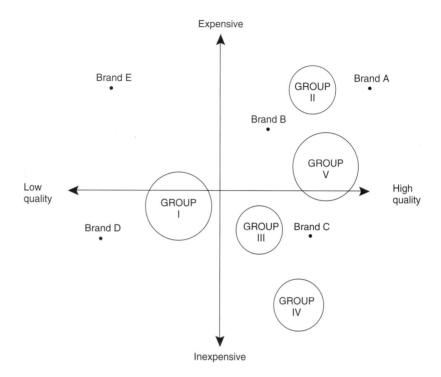

perceptions of Brand C. Offering a second brand less expensive than C to appeal to Group IV is another possible action. Of course, it is necessary to study the research results in much greater depth than this brief examination of Exhibit 4–9. Our intent is to illustrate the method of segmenting and show how the results might be used.

Perceptual mapping, like many of the research methods used for segment identification, is expensive and represents a technical challenge. When used and interpreted properly, these methods are useful tools for analyzing product-market structure to identify possible market targets and positioning strategies. Of course, there are many issues to be considered in specific applications, such as choosing the attributes, identifying relevant products and brands, sample design, and evaluation of the strength of results.

It may be useful for managers to use their market knowledge and experience to create a perception map for their brand and its competitors. While this approach is not a substitute for a map created from a set of data obtained from a sample of buyers, the managers' map may help them better understand the market. When used in combination with other market and competitor information, the managers' map should help guide targeting and positioning analysis. Caution should be exercised since managers' perceptions may not be good indicators of buyers' perceptions of brands.

Finer Segmentation Strategies

A combination of factors may help a company utilize finer segmentation strategies. Technology may be available to produce customized product offerings. Furthermore, highly sophisticated databases for accessing buyers can be used, and buyers' escalating preferences for unique products encourage consideration of increasingly smaller segments. In some situations, an individual buyer may constitute a market segment. Thus, an important segmentation issue is deciding how small segments should be.

We consider the logic of finer segments, followed by a discussion of the available finer segmentation strategies.

Logic of Finer Segments

Several factors working together point to the benefits of considering very small segments—in some cases, segments of one. These factors include (1) the capabilities of companies to offer cost-effective, customized offerings, (2) the desires of buyers for highly customized products, and (3) the organizational advantages of close customer relationships.

Customized Offerings

The capabilities of organizations to offer customized products are feasible because of extensive information flow and comprehensive databases, computerized design and manufacturing systems, and integrated value chains.[28] At the center of these capabilities to provide buyers with customized offerings is information technology. Database knowledge, computer-aided product design and manufacturing, and distribution technology (e.g., just-in-time inventory) offer promising opportunities for serving the needs and preferences of very small market segments. This technology combined with the Internet has led to the emergence of "sliver" companies or "micro-multinationals"—small, flexible organizations selling highly specialized products across the world.

Diverse Customer Base

The requirements of an increasingly diverse customer base for many products are apparent. Buyers seek uniqueness, and companies such as Lutron Electronics try to respond to unique preferences. Global competitors seek to offer more attractive value in their goods and services.

Close Customer Relationships

Companies recognize the benefits of close relationships with their customers. By identifying customer value opportunities and developing cost-effective customized offerings, companies can form relationships that are profitable and effective in creating competitive barriers.

Finer Segmentation Strategies

We examine three approaches for finer segmentation opportunities: microsegmentation, mass customization, and variety seeking.[29]

Microsegmentation

This form of segmentation seeks to identify narrowly defined segments by using one or more of the previously discussed segmentation variables (Exhibit 4–5). It differs from more aggregate segment formation in that microsegmentation results in a large number of very small segments. Each segment of interest to the organization receives a marketing mix designed to meet the value requirements of that segment.

Mass Customization

Providing customized products at prices not much higher than those of mass-produced items is feasible by using mass-customization concepts and methods. Achieving mass-customization objectives is possible through computer-aided design and manufacturing software, flexible manufacturing techniques, and flexible supply systems.

There are two forms of mass customization. One employs standardized components but configures the components to achieve customized product offerings.[30] For example, using standardized paint components, retail stores are able to create customized color shades by mixing the components. The other mass-customization approach employs a flexible process. Through effective system design, variety can be created at very low costs. For example, Casio's customization approach enables the company to offer 5,000 different watches.

Variety-Seeking Strategy

This product strategy is intended to offer buyers opportunities to vary their choices in contrast to making unique choices.[31] The logic is that buyers who are offered alternatives may increase their total purchases of a brand. Mass customization methods also enable companies to offer extensive variety at relatively low prices, thus gaining the advantages of customized and variety offerings.

Finer Segmentation Issues

While the benefits of customization are apparent, there are several issues that need to be examined when considering finer segmentation strategies:[32]

1. How much variety should be offered to buyers? What attributes are important in buyers' choices, and to what extent do they need to be varied?

2. Will too much variety have negative effects on buyers? Is it possible that buyers will become confused and frustrated when offered too many choices?

3. Is it possible to increase buyers' desire for variety, creating a competitive advantage?

4. What processes should be used to learn about customer preferences? This may involve indirect methods (e.g., database analysis) or involving buyers in the process.

High-variety strategies, properly conceived and executed, offer powerful opportunities for competitive advantage by providing superior value to customers. As highlighted by the issues discussed above, pursuing these finer segmentation strategies involves major decisions, including which strategy to pursue and how to implement the strategy. Important in deciding how fine the segmentation should be is estimating the value and cost trade-offs of the relevant alternatives.

Selecting the Segmentation Strategy

We have considered several approaches to market segmentation, ranging from forming segments via experience and judgment to finer segmentation strategies. We now discuss deciding how to segment the market and analyze the segments that have been identified.

Deciding How to Segment

The choice of a segmentation method depends on such factors as the maturity of market, the competitive structure, and the organization's experience in the market. The more comprehensive the segmentation process is, the higher the costs of segment identification will be, reaching the highest level when field research studies are involved and finer segmentation strategies are considered. It is important to maximize the available knowledge about the product-market. An essential first step in segmentation is analyzing the existing customer base to identify groups of buyers with different response behavior (e.g., frequent purchase versus occasional purchase). Developing a view of how to segment the market by managers may be helpful. In some instances this information will provide a sufficient basis for segment formation. If that does not occur, experience and existing information are often helpful in guiding the design of customer research studies.

The five segmentation criteria discussed earlier help to evaluate potential segments. Deciding if the criteria are satisfied rests with management after examining response differences among the segments. The segmentation plan should satisfy the responsiveness criterion plus the other criteria (end-users are identifiable, they are accessible through a marketing program, the segment(s) is economically viable, and the segment is stable over time). The latter criterion may be less of an issue with mass customization since changes can be accommodated.

It is useful to consider the trade-off between the costs of developing a better segmentation scheme and the benefits gained. For example, instead of using one variable to segment, a combination of two or three variables might be used. The costs of a more insightful segmentation scheme include the analysis time and the complexity of strategy development. The potential benefits include a better determination of response differences, which enable the design of more effective marketing mix strategies. Importantly, segmentation should not be viewed as static but as dynamic: As Dell Computers learned more about the PC market, the segmentation approach evolved and developed.

The competitive advantage gained by finding (or developing) a new market segment can be very important. Segment strategies are used by a wide range of small companies with excellent performance records. Consider, for example, segmenting the market for paper. One way to segment is according to the use situation. The uses of paper include newspapers, magazines, books, announcements, letters, and other applications. Crane & Company, a firm competing in this market, is the primary supplier of paper for printing money.[33] This segment of the high-quality paper market consists of a single customer: the U.S. Treasury. The company's commitment to making quality products has sustained its competitive advantage in this segment since 1879. In the early 1990s Crane introduced a new currency paper designed to identify counterfeit bills by placing a polyester thread in the paper. The other three-quarters of Crane's sales includes fine writing papers and high-quality paper products.

Strategic Analysis of Market Segments

Each market segment of interest needs to be studied to determine its potential attractiveness as a market target. The major areas of analysis include customers, competitors, positioning strategy, and financial and market attractiveness.

Customer Analysis

When forming segments, it is useful to find out as much as possible about the customers in each segment. Variables such as those used in dividing product-markets into segments are also helpful in describing the people in the same segments. The discussion of customer profiles in Chapter 3 includes information needed to profile a product-market. Similar information is needed for the segment profile, although the segment-level analysis is more comprehensive than the product-market profile.

The objective is to find descriptive characteristics that are highly correlated to the variables used to form the segments. Standardized information services are available for some product-markets, including foods, health and beauty aids, and pharmaceuticals. Large markets involving many competitors make it profitable for research firms to collect and analyze data that are useful to the firms serving the market.

Information Resources, Inc. (IRI), a Chicago-based research supplier, has combined computerized information processing with customer research methods to generate information for market segmentation. Its Behavior Scan system electronically tracks total grocery store sales and individual household purchase behavior through complete universal product code (UPC) scanner coverage. People in the 2,500 household samples in each of several metropolitan markets covered by the service carry special identification cards and are individually tracked via scanner in grocery stores and drugstores. IRI publishes *The Marketing Fact Book*, which has consumer purchase data on all product categories. An example is shown in Exhibit 4–10. The database can be used for follow-up, in-depth analyses to meet the needs of specific companies.

An essential aspect of customer analysis is determining how well the buyers in the segment are satisfied. We know that customer satisfaction is measured by comparing customer *expectations* about the product and supporting services with the *performance* of the product and supporting services.[34] Some research indicates that *prior experience* may be a better basis of comparison than are *expectations*.[35]

Customer satisfaction depends on the perceived performance of a product and supporting services and the standards that customers use to evaluate that performance.[36] The customer's standards complicate the relationship between organizational product specifications (e.g., product attribute tolerances) and satisfaction. Standards may involve something other than prepurchase expectations, such as the perceived performance of competing products. Importantly, the standards are likely to vary across market segments.

Competitor Analysis

Market segment analysis considers the set of key competitors currently active in the market in which the segment is located plus any potential segment entrants. In complex market structures, mapping the competitive arena requires detailed analysis. The competing firms are described and evaluated to highlight their strengths and weaknesses. Information useful in competitor analysis includes business scope and objectives; market position; market target(s) and customer base; positioning strategy; financial, technical, and operating strengths; management experience and capabilities; and special competitive advantages (e.g., patents). It is also important to anticipate the future strategies of key competitors.

Value-chain analysis can be used to examine competitive advantage at the segment level. A complete assessment of the nature and intensity of competition in the segment is important in determining whether to enter (or exit from) the segment and how to compete in the segment. Examining the five forces suggested by Porter (Chapter 3) is useful to determine segment attractiveness.

Positioning Analysis

We consider positioning strategy in Chapter 6. Segment analysis involves some preliminary choices about positioning strategy. One objective of segment analysis is to obtain guidelines for developing a positioning strategy. Flexibility exists in selecting how to position the firm (or brand) with its customers and against its competition in a segment. Positioning analysis guides how to combine product, distribution, pricing, and promotion strategies to favorably position the brand with buyers in the segment. Information from perception maps such as Exhibit 4–9 is useful in guiding positioning strategy. The positioning strategy should meet the needs and requirements of the targeted buyers at a cost that yields a profitable margin for the organization.

Estimating Segment Attractiveness

The financial and market attractiveness of each segment needs to be evaluated. Included are specific estimates of revenue, cost, and segment profit contribution over the planning horizon. Market attractiveness can be measured by market growth rate projections and attractiveness assessments made by management.

EXHIBIT 4–10
**Analysis of Age of
Soap Purchasers**

Source: The Marketing Fact
Book® (Chicago: Information
Resources, 1986), p.10.

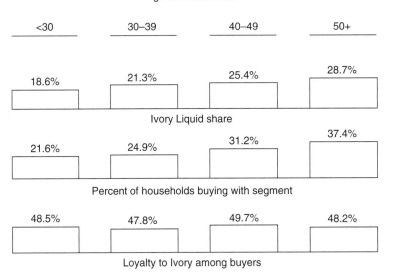

Demographics
Q. Within which demographic segments is Ivory Liquid share strongest? Weakest? How do I go about building the weaker segments?

A. With respect to age of female household head, Ivory Liquid performance differs dramatically.

Age of female head

<30	30–39	40–49	50+

18.6%   21.3%   25.4%   28.7%

Ivory Liquid share

21.6%   24.9%   31.2%   37.4%

Percent of households buying with segment

48.5%   47.8%   49.7%   48.2%

Loyalty to Ivory among buyers

The relatively weaker performance among younger households traces to fewer buyers. Among those who *did* buy, loyalty was similar in all segments.

To build a share, promotions (perhaps high-value coupons) and/or advertising aimed at trial generation among younger female household heads should be considered.

This analysis can, of course, include a fill range of additional demographic variables.

Note: The above data are entirely fictional. Brand names are used only to add an element of reality. Any similarity to actual brand data is entirely coincidental.

Financial analysis obtains sales, cost, and profit contribution estimates for each segment of interest. Since accurate forecasting is difficult if the projections are too far into the future, detailed projections typically extend two to five years ahead. Both the segment's competitive position evaluation and the financial forecasts are used in comparing segments. In all instances the risks and returns associated with serving a particular segment need to be considered. Flows of revenues and costs can be weighted to take into account risks and the time value of revenues and expenditures.

It should be recognized that as information availability grows, for example, through the data warehouses associated with CRM systems, the evaluation of segment attractiveness also has the potential for identifying unattractive market segments and even individual customers who may be candidates for deletion.

Segmentation "Fit" and Implementation

One important aspect of evaluating segment attractiveness is how well the segments match a company's capabilities and ability to implement marketing strategies around those segments.[37] There are many organizational barriers to the effective use of segmentation strategies. New segment targets which do not fit into conventional information reporting, planning processes, and budget systems in the company may be ignored or not adequately resourced. Innovative models of customer segments and market opportunities may be rejected by managers or the culture of the organization.

There are dangers that managers may prefer to retain traditional views of the market and structure information in that way or that segmentation strategy will be driven by existing organizational structures and competitive norms.[38] Recall the "push-back" issue discussed in the Strategy Feature.

It is important to be realistic in balancing the attractiveness of segments against the ability of the organization to implement appropriate marketing strategies to take advantage of the opportunities identified. Building an effective marketing strategy around market segmentation mandates an emphasis on actionability as well as technique and analysis.[39]

Many of the issues we consider in later chapters affect the operational capabilities of a company to implement segmentation strategies. For example, strength in cross-functional working may be a prerequisite to delivering value to new segments, and the ability to work with partners may be needed to develop new products and services to build a strong position in a key market segment. The existence of these capabilities or the ability to develop them should be considered in making segmentation decisions.

Segment Analysis Illustration

An illustrative market segment analysis is shown in Exhibit 4–11. A two-year period is used for estimating sales, costs, contribution margin, and market share. Depending on the forecasting difficulty, estimates for a longer time period can be used. When appropriate, estimates can be expressed as present values of future revenues and costs. Business strength in Exhibit 4–11 refers to the present position of the firm relative to the competition in the segment. Alternatively, it can be expressed as the present position and an estimated future position, based upon plans for increasing business strength. Attractiveness typically is evaluated for some future time period. In the illustration a five-year projection is used.

EXHIBIT 4–11
Segment Financial and Market Attractiveness Analysis

Estimated ($ millions)	Segment		
	X	Y	Z
Sales*	10	16	5
Variable costs*	4	9	3
Contribution margin*	6	7	2
Market share†	60%	30%	10%
Total segment sales	17	53	50
Segment position:			
Business strength	High	Medium	Low
Attractiveness‡	Medium	Low	High

*For a two-year period.
‡Percent of total sales in the segment.
‡Based on a five-year projection.

The example shows how segment opportunities are ranked according to their overall attractiveness. The analysis can be expanded to include additional information such as profiles of key competitors. The rankings are admittedly subjective since decision makers will vary in their weighing of estimated financial position, business strength, and segment attractiveness. Place yourself in the role of a manager evaluating the segments. Using the information in Exhibit 4–11, rank segments X, Y, and Z as to their overall importance as market targets. Unless management is ready to allocate a major portion of resources to segment Z to build business strength, that segment is a candidate for the last-place position. Yet Z has some attractive characteristics. That segment has the most favorable market attractiveness of the three, and its estimated total sales are nearly equal to Y's for the next two years. The big problem with Z is its business strength. The key question is whether Z's market share can be increased. If it cannot, X looks like a good prospect for top rating, followed by Y and then by Z. Of course, management may decide to go after all three segments.

Summary

Market segmentation is often a requirement for competing in many product-markets because buyers differ in their preferences for products and services. Finding out what these preferences are and grouping buyers with similar needs is an essential part of business and marketing strategy development. Market segmentation provides an opportunity for a small firm to focus on buyers where its competitive advantages are most favorable. Large firms seeking to establish or protect a dominant market position can often do so by targeting multiple segments.

Segmentation of a product-market requires that response differences exist between segments and that the segments be identifiable and stable over time. Also, the benefits of segmentation should exceed the costs. Segmenting a market involves identifying the basis of segmentation, forming segments, describing each segment, and analyzing and evaluating the segment(s) of interest. The variables useful as bases for forming and describing segments include the characteristics of people and organizations, the use situation, buyers' needs and preferences, and purchase behavior.

Segments can be formed by identifying customer groups using the characteristics of people or organizations. The groups are analyzed to determine if the response profiles are different across the candidate segments. Alternatively, customer response information can be used to form customer groupings, and then the descriptive characteristics of the groups can be analyzed to find out if segments can be identified. Several examples of segment formation are discussed to illustrate the methods that are available for this purpose.

Finer segmentation strategies present attractive options for moving toward small segments and responding to buyers' unique value requirements. Technology, buyer diversity, and relationship opportunities are the drivers of finer segmentation strategies. These strategies include microsegmentation, mass customization, and variety seeking. While potentially attractive, finer segmentation strategies are more complex than other forms of segmentation and require comprehensive benefit and cost evaluations.

Segment analysis and evaluation consider the strengths and limitations of each segment as a potential market target for the organization. Segment analysis includes customer descriptions and satisfaction analysis, evaluating existing and potential competitors and competitive advantage, marketing program positioning analysis, and financial and market attractiveness. Segment analysis is important in evaluating customer satisfaction, finding new product opportunities, selecting market targets, and designing positioning strategies. Nonetheless, it is also important to understand the organizational barriers to implementing segmentation strategy which may exist in a company and to evaluate the "fit" of segmentation with company capabilities. Effectively implemented, a good segmentation strategy creates an important competitive edge for an organization.

Internet Applications

A. Explore several of the following websites:

www.adquest.com
www.americanet.com
www.autosite.com
www.mlm2000.com
www.sidewalk.com
www.monster.com
www.realtor.com

How does the information from these sites affect our traditional concept of market segmentation? How is the segmentation process altered by such Internet providers?

B. Evaluate the following website for additional ideas and material concerning market segmentation and the types of support that can be provided for companies:
www.marketsegmentation.co.uk

Questions for Review and Discussion

1. Competing in the unified European market raises some interesting market segment questions. Discuss the segmentation issues regarding this multiple-country market.

2. Why are there marketing strategy advantages in using demographic characteristics to break out product-markets into segments?

3. The real test of a segment formation scheme occurs after it has been tried and the results have been evaluated. Are there ways to evaluate alternative segmenting schemes without actually trying them?

4. Suggest ways of obtaining the information needed to conduct a market segment analysis.

5. Why may it become necessary for companies to change their market segmentation identification over time?

6. Is considering segments of one buyer a reality or a myth? Discuss.

7. Is it necessary to use a unique positioning strategy for each market segment targeted by an organization?

8. Under what circumstances may it not be possible to break up a product-market into segments? What are the dangers of using an incorrect segment formation scheme?

9. What are some of the advantages in using mass-customization technology to satisfy the needs of buyers?

10. Does the use of mass customization eliminate the need to segment a market?

Notes

1. Don Peppers and Martha Rogers, *Enterprise One-to-One* (New York: Doubleday, 1997).
2. Peter R. Dickson and James L. Ginter, "Market Segmentation, Product Differentiation, and Marketing Strategy," *Journal of Marketing*, April 1987, 1–10.
3. W. Chan Kim and Renee Mauborgne, "Finding Rooms for Manoevre," *Financial Times*, May 27, 1999.
4. James Samuelson, "Flying High," *Forbes*, August 12, 1996, 84–85.
5. Nikki Tait, "Mixed Emotions as Olds Guard Bows Out," *Financial Times*, December 20, 2000, 27.

6. Leonard L. Berry, "Relationship Marketing of Services—Growing Interest, Emerging Perspectives," *Journal of the Academy of Marketing Science*, Fall 1995, 238–40.
7. Henry Assael, *Consumer Behavior and Marketing Action*, 2nd ed. (Boston: PWS-Kent Publishing, 1984), 225.
8. Jerry Flint, "The Magazine Factory," *Forbes*, May 22, 1995, 160–62.
9. Jay L. Laughlin and Charles R. Taylor, "An Approach to Industrial Market Segmentation," *Industrial Marketing Management*, 20 (1991), 127–36.
10. Ronald Henkoff, "Boeing's Big Problem," *Fortune*, January 12, 1998, 96–99, 102–03.
11. Daniel S. Levine, "Justice Served," *Sales & Marketing Management*, May 1995, 53–61.
12. Michael Malone, "Pennsylvania Guys Mass Customize," *Forbes ASAP*, April 10, 1995, 82–85.
13. Nicholas Bray, "Credit Lyonnaise Targets Wealthy Clients," *The Wall Street Journal*, July 24, 1994.
14. A. H. Maslow, "Theory of Human Motivation," *Psychology Review*, July 1943, 43–45.
15. Assael, *Consumer Behavior and Marketing Action*, 650.
16. Bernard Berelson and Gary A. Steiner, *Human Behavior: An Inventory of Scientific Findings* (New York: Harcourt Brace Jovanovich, 1964), 88.
17. Eric N. Berkowitz, Roger A. Kerin, Steven W. Hartley, and William Rudelius, *Marketing*, 5th ed. (Chicago: Richard D. Irwin, 1997), 155–56.
18. Louise O'Brien and Charles Jones, "Do Rewards Really Create Loyalty?" *Harvard Business Review*, May–June 1995, 78.
19. Miriam Jordan, "In India, Luxury Is within Reach of Many," *The Wall Street Journal*, October 17, 1995, A15.
20. Malcolm McDonald, "A Slice of the Action," *Marketing Business*, July–August 1998, 47.
21. Dickson and Ginter, "Market Segmentation," 4.
22. George S. Day, *Market Driven Strategy* (New York: Free Press), 1990, 101–04.
23. Nancy Rotenier, "Antistatus Backpacks, $450 a Copy," *Forbes*, June 19, 1995, 118–20.
24. Allanna Sullivan, "Mobil Bets Drivers Pick Cappuccino over Low Prices," *The Wall Street Journal*, January 30, 1995, B1, B4.
25. *Marketing News*, July 20, 1998.
26. V. Kasturi Ranga, Rowland T. Moriarity, and Gordon S. Swartz, "Segmenting Customers in Mature Industrial Markets," *Journal of Marketing*, October 1992, 72–82.
27. *Understanding Customer Relationship Management*, London: Financial Times, Spring 2000.
28. Ali Kara and Erdener Kaynak, "Markets of a Single Customer: Exploiting Conceptual Developments in Market Segmentation," *European Journal of Marketing* no. 11/12 (1997), 873–95.
29. Barbara E. Kahn, "Dynamic Relationships with Customers: High-Variety Strategies," *Journal of the Academy of Marketing Science*, Winter 1998, 45–53.
30. Kahn, "Dynamic Relationships"; Joseph B. Pine II, *Mass Customization: The New Frontier in Business Competition* (Boston: Harvard Business School Press, 1993).
31. Kahn, "Dynamic Relationships." 48.
32. Ibid.
33. Linda Killian, "Crane's Progress," *Forbes*, August 19, 1991, 44.
34. A. Parasuraman, Valarie A. Zeithami, and Leonard L. Berry, "A Conceptual Model of Service Quality and Its Implications for Future Research," *Journal of Marketing*, Fall 1985, 41–50.

35. Robert B. Woodruff, Ernest R. Cadotte, and Roger L. Jenkins, "Modeling Consumer Satisfaction Processes Using Experienced-Based Norms," *Journal of Marketing Research*, August 1983, 296–304.

36. The following discussion of customer satisfaction is based on discussions with Robert B. Woodruff, the University of Tennessee, Knoxville.

37. Nigel F. Piercy and Neil A. Morgan, "Strategic and Operational Segmentation," *Journal of Strategic Marketing*, 1., no. 2 (1993), 123–40.

38. Noel Capon and James M. Hulbert, *Marketing Management in the 21st Century* Englewood Cliffs, (New Jersey: Prentice-Hall, 2001), 185–86.

39. D. Young, "The Politics behind Marketing Segmentation," *Marketing News*, October 21, 1996, 17.

Chapter 5

Continuous Learning about Markets

Understanding markets and competition is critical to achieving market orientation. "Every discussion of market orientation emphasizes the ability of the firm to learn about customers, competitors, and channel members in order to continually sense and act on events and trends in present and prospective markets."[1] Market-driven companies display superior skills in gathering, interpreting, and using information to guide their business and marketing strategies.

Increasingly, learning about markets is more about interpreting information than about finding it. Manco, a distributor of duct tape, mailer envelopes, shelf liners, and related products, has developed an effective market sensing and analysis system. With annual sales in the range of $160 million, Manco is not a huge corporation, but the company employs cross-functional shared information collection, analysis, and decision making where the information focus is the customer. It uses focus groups, advisory panels, consumer hotlines, and employee feedback to sense what is happening in the marketplace. A key market sensing and learning objective is encouraging the employee to enter the mind of the customer. One of Manco's key sensing processes is its three-hour weekly meetings of 80 white-collar employees who discuss what is happening in the industry (globally) and what salespeople have learned in the field. Learning is a continuous process at Manco, and shared information analysis and decision making help the company achieve strong performance in very competitive markets.[2]

The challenge is increasingly one of knowledge management to build company-wide understanding of the marketplace and responsiveness rather than simply collecting information. Consider, for example, the superior market sensing and learning characteristics that underpin the global success of Dell Computers, as described in the Strategy Feature.

In this chapter we examine how continuous learning about markets improves competitive advantage. First, we look at the relationship between market orientation and organizational learning. Next, we discuss several sources of information. Then we provide an overview of information methods and capabilities, including marketing research, standardized information services, management information systems, database systems, and decision support systems. Finally, several important issues are highlighted concerning the collection and use of information in the organization and the growing importance of knowledge management to effective market-driven strategy.

Michael Dell founded his company in 1984 and from a zero base has built a Fortune 500 company that is now the leading supplier of personal computers, with annual sales of over $30 billion. From the outset, Dell's business model exploited the advantages of selling direct to customers and building products to order instead of estimating demand and building to stock. The direct business model was ideally placed to use the Internet to full advantage.

Underpinning the success of Dell's direct business model are processes of learning and responsiveness to customers, utilizing the company's technology and the Internet but also the human processes of listening to customers and learning from them.

Dell describes the unique advantage of the direct business model as the opportunity to build different types of relationships with suppliers and customers, which he calls "virtual integration." While maintaining the ability to shop around for something better, Dell and suppliers share information and plans freely—external suppliers are treated as if they were internal to Dell's organization. Internet and direct selling relationships with customers also provide Dell with unique insights into their needs, preferences, and changing requirements.

Dell is almost the information technology (IT) department for its major corporate customers. Sales account managers work with customers to develop plans to meet future IT needs. Dell works with customers to save them money by standardizing their global PC purchasing (providing the company with information about its own global PC purchasing patterns). Major customers have their own Dell Premier Pages on the Internet, providing an interactive product catalog, and also have access to Dell support tools and technical resources.

Close customer relationships uncover new opportunities for enhancing customer value—Dell now routinely preloads customers' own software onto PCs before they leave the Dell factory. But virtual integration also includes Dell's "listening philosophy." Dell's Platinum Councils are regional meetings of large customers every six to nine months to review technology advances and Dell's performance in serving customers. Dell is liable to overrule his own technical experts when their views are inconsistent with those of customers.

Dell's market sensing and learning capabilities have created a new competitive advantage which is uniquely difficult for competitors to equal. In the harsh PC marketplace in 2001, Dell was able to leverage its competitive advantage in aggressive price cutting to increase market share. Dell comments: "We like to think we are taking over our competitors one customer at a time." In 2001, Dell's direct competitor Gateway moved into loss and cutback, and Dell overtook Compaq as the PC market leader.

Sources: Adapted from Nigel F Piercy, *Tales from the Marketplace: Stories of Revolution, Reinvention and Renewal* (Oxford: Butterworth-Heinemann, 1999 Chapter 4); Nigel F Piercy, *Market-Led Strategic Change: A Guide to Transforming the Process of Going to Market* (Oxford: Butterworth-Heinemann, 2001), 202–204.

Market Orientation and Organizational Learning

Information plays a vital role in management's decision making at Frito-Lay, a subsidiary of PepsiCo Inc.[3] Responding to the diversity of buyers' preferences, the leading chip maker sells 85 varieties of potato chips. Frito-Lay relentlessly studies what consumers like—and don't like—about snack foods, conducting nearly 500,000 interviews a year. Quality control closely monitors chip thickness, since marketing research indicates that consumers complain if their chips are 8/1,000ths of an inch too thick or thin. Over 6,000 taste tests are conducted each year to gain feedback from consumers on new flavors that are being evaluated. Package colors are tested to make sure consumer reactions are favorable. Frito-Lay's 10,000-person sales force is part of the market sensing process, sending headquarters inventory data and information about competitors' new products with their handheld computers. Frito-Lay's commitment to customer satisfaction has helped the company gain an awesome market leadership position.

Companies like Frito-Lay, Dell, and Manco illustrate the close relationship between a market-oriented culture and organizational learning. We review the characteristics of market orientation and look at the role of organizational learning in creating superior customer value. Next, the process of learning about markets is described, followed by a discussion of how learning helps create superior customer value. Finally, we examine and illustrate the available methods of obtaining information.

Market Orientation

Market orientation is both a culture and a process committed to achieving superior customer value (Chapter 1). The process consists of information acquisition, broad information dissemination, and shared diagnosis and coordinated action.[4] Market orientation provides the foundation for organizational learning, although some cautions need to be considered in achieving the potential of learning:[5]

1. Market intelligence may be so focused that opportunities or threats outside the current product-market are ignored.

2. Prevailing views of market orientation consider current customers and competitors, whereas other learning sources, including suppliers, noncompeting businesses, consultants, and government, may provide important information.

The market orientation perspective needs to extend beyond traditional market boundaries to include all the relevant sources of knowledge and ideas. A key issue is deciding how broad this orientation should be. The section on learning about markets offers several guidelines concerning this issue.

Characteristics of the Learning Organization

Our understanding of the learning organization continues to unfold as the processes used by successful organizations are studied and interpreted. These organizations share several characteristics:

> Learning organizations are guided by a shared vision that focuses the energies of organizational members on creating superior value for customers. These organizations continuously acquire, process, and disseminate throughout the organization knowledge about markets, products, technologies, and business processes. They do not hesitate to question long held assumptions and beliefs regarding their business. Their knowledge is based on experience, experimentation, and information from customers, suppliers, competitors, and other sources. Through complex communication, coordination, and conflict resolution processes, these organizations reach a shared interpretation of the information, which enables them to act swiftly and decisively to exploit opportunities and defuse problems. Learning organizations are exceptional in their ability to anticipate and act on opportunities in turbulent and fragmenting markets.[6]

Additional research promises to further expand our knowledge about these complex organizational processes.

Learning and Competitive Advantage

The advantage gained from learning is that the organization is able to quickly and effectively respond to opportunities and threats and satisfy customers' needs with new products and improved services.[7] Learning reduces the time necessary to accomplish projects such as new product development. For example, after listening to a customer, Manco developed its nonadhesive shelf liner, which is similar to rubber mesh and can be easily cut and fitted in and out of shelves.[8] In 1997 the product had sales of $30 million, accounting for nearly one-fifth of Manco's annual sales. Superior learning capabilities create a new competitive advantage which may be extremely difficult for competitors to imitate or equal. Recall the characteristics of Dell's approach in the Strategy Feature.

Learning about Markets

Learning about markets requires developing processes throughout the organization for obtaining, interpreting, and acting on information from sensing activities. The learning processes of market-oriented companies include a sequence of activities that begins with open-minded inquiry.[9]

Open-Minded Inquiry

One danger to be avoided is failing to explore new views about markets and competition. The search for information is of little value if management already has a view on which new information will have no influence.

As discussed in Chapter 1, the members of market-oriented organizations recognize the importance of market sensing and coordinated interpretation of market intelligence to guide strategies. Nonetheless, not all companies see the value in continuous learning about markets. Managers who are not part of market-driven cultures may be unwilling to invest in information to improve their decision-making results. The same companies often encounter problems because of faulty or incomplete market sensing.

A framework of the type shown in Exhibit 5–1 can be used as a participative, cross-functional structure for market sensing. This challenges managers to identify the most significant events affecting their business and its markets over a three- to five-year horizon and to position the events in the matrix according to estimated probability of occurrence and the effect of an event on the business. Importantly, by including external views, such as suppliers, technology experts, distributors, and customers, it is possible to build a view of the world that breaks free of traditional company beliefs, challenges management assumptions, and identifies the highest priorities for information collection and use in making strategic decisions.[10]

Developing processes for continuous learning allows firms to capture more information about customers, suppliers, and competitors. This capability provides the potential for growth based on informed decisions and a more complete mapping and analysis of the competitive environment. Also, firms can respond much more quickly to competitors' actions and take advantage of situations in the marketplace. Open-minded inquiry also helps anticipate value migration threats, which are frequently initiated by competitors from outside the traditional market or industry.[11] For example, monitoring potential competitors such as electronic imaging companies by conventional film producers is essential in designing strategies for coping with the competitive threats from electronic technology.

EXHIBIT 5–1
A Framework for Market Sensing

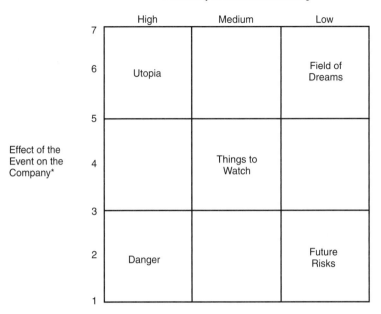

*1 = disaster, 2 = very bad, 3 = bad, 4 = neutral, 5 = good, 6 = very good, 7 = ideal.

Synergistic Information Distribution

This step encourages the widespread distribution of information in the organization. The objective is to leverage the value of the information by cutting across business functions to share information on customers, channels of distribution, suppliers, and competitors. Traditional information processing in organizations allocates relevant information to each business function, and information possession becomes a source of internal power. Synergistic distribution works to remove functional hurdles and practices. Cross-functional teams are useful to encourage the transfer of information across functions.

The explosion in information connectivity (access) resulting from electronic communication facilitates widespread information distribution.[12] Unbundling information from its physical carrier, such as salespeople, will provide access as well as speed in organizations. This will help cross-functional teams and alter hierarchical structures and proprietary information systems. Expanded information connectivity promises to encourage cooperation among functions, reduce the power of information possession, and enhance organizational learning.

Mutually Informed Interpretations

The mental model of the market guides managers' interpretation of information. The intent is to reach a shared vision about the market and about the impact that new information has on this vision. The market-oriented culture encourages market sensing, but the process requires more than gathering and studying information. "This interpretation is facilitated by the mental models of managers, which contain decision rules for deciding how to act on the information in light of anticipated outcomes."[13] The model reflects the executives' vision about the forces influencing the market and likely future directors of change. Learning occurs as members of the organization evaluate the results of their decisions based on their vision at the time the decisions were made. The market sensing framework in Exhibit 5–1 may support addressing these issues.

Deciding to take the high risk of cutting-edge ventures requires managers to reach a shared vision about uncertain future market opportunities. For example, the British supermarket company Tesco operates an outstanding and successful Internet grocery channel alongside its store network. The planning for this venture started in the mid-1990s, long before the much-publicized "dot-com revolution" was under way, leading to a national rollout in 2000, a time when other Internet ventures were crashing in ruins. The five-year gestation period involved close study of what consumers wanted from Internet grocery shopping and a developing understanding that shoppers wanted the Internet channel to provide a complement to store-based shopping, not a substitute for it. The management team has sustained its vision that an Internet channel would become a profitable part of the core business over a seven-year period before reaching operating profitability.

Accessible Memory

This part of the learning process emphasizes the importance of keeping and gaining access to prior learning. The objective is not to lose valuable information that can continue to be used. Doing this involves integrating the information into the organizational memory and not losing information when people leave the organization. Hewlett-Packard's (H-P) vision about computer printer technology was that inkjet technology would replace dot matrix printers, providing an excellent growth opportunity. H-P beat Japanese companies to the market even though Canon had the technology. Hewlett-Packard's InkJet product design team continued to learn how to improve the product and develop strategies based on monitoring competitors' actions. For example, prices were lowered when the team sensed that Japanese competitors were about to enter the market.

Urban Outfitters, Inc., is a successful specialty retailer that is guided by management's shared vision about the market based on an effective learning process. The company targets style-conscious young adults. Fiscal 2001 sales were $295 million from 45 stores, providing a 7 percent annual growth rate. The retailer's products include fashion apparel, accessories, household items, and gifts. Urban Outfitters' unique value proposition is the shopping environment it provides to the 18–30 targeted age group. To stay ahead of unpredictable buyers with whimsical tastes, management employs over 75 fashion spies who sense what is happening in fashion in neighborhoods in New York, California, London, and Paris.[14] The salaries and expenses of this market sensing team total several million dollars annually. Market feedback guides new product decisions and signals when buyer interest is slowing down. Stores are located near colleges and places where youths gather. Management is testing new retail concepts in its Anthropologie stores to appeal to its buyers when they move to an older age group in the life cycle.

Information, Analysis, and Action

Deciding what information is needed is the starting point in planning for and acquiring information. Because of the costs of acquiring, processing, and analyzing information, the potential benefits of needed information have to be compared to costs. Normally, information falls into two categories: (1) information regularly supplied from internal and external sources and (2) information obtained as needed for a particular problem or situation. Examples of the former are sales costs analyses, information from 800 number calls, market share measurements, and customer satisfaction surveys. Information from the latter category includes new product concept tests, brand preference studies, and studies of advertising effectiveness.

Several types of marketing information are available. A description of each type of information follows:

Marketing Research Studies

These studies consist of customized information collected and analyzed for a particular research problem. A study of customers' reactions to a new product concept is an example. The information may be obtained through field surveys and/or published sources.

Standardized Information Services

This information is available from outside vendors on a subscription or single-purchase basis. The services collect and analyze information that is sold to several customers, such as prescription sales for drugs marketed by pharmaceutical firms.

Management Information Systems (MIS)

Computerized systems supply information for a variety of purposes, such as order processing, invoicing, customer analysis, and product performance. The information in these systems may include both internal and external data.

Database Systems

This special form of MIS includes information from internal and external sources that is computerized and used for customer and product analyses, mailing lists, identification of sales prospects, and other marketing applications.

Decision Support Systems

These computerized systems provide decision-making assistance to managers and staff. Their capabilities are more advanced than those of an MIS. American Airlines' revenue (pricing and yield) management system for aircraft seat utilization includes effective decision support techniques to assist analysts in obtaining maximum revenue for each flight.

Customer Relationship Management (CRM) Systems

Designed to manage the relationship with a customer more effectively by integrating all needed information sources and systems to provide seamlessness at the point of contact with the customer, CRM systems also provide rich information sources relating to customers' actual purchase behavior. Frequently associated are "data warehouses," which are capable of being "mined" for customer information. CRM systems provide a formidable new type of marketing information.

Competitor Intelligence Systems

Companies are using competitor intelligence systems to help monitor existing and potential competitors. Intelligence activities include searching databases, conducting customer surveys, interviewing suppliers and other channel members, forming strategic alliances with competitors, hiring competitors' employees, and evaluating competitors' products.

The organization's complete information needs should be considered before deciding what types of information to use. Most firms benefit from a routine and complete evaluation of their information situation. Cooperation among departments can save the firm countless employee-hours and dollars. Far too often a department launches an expensive information-gathering project only to discover later that another department already had the type of information sought. Synergistic information distribution encourages sharing.

In the remainder of the chapter we examine the various methods of acquiring and processing information for use in marketing decision making. The objective is to show how the various information capabilities assist decision makers in making strategic and operating decisions. A good marketing information management strategy takes into account the interrelationship of these capabilities.

Marketing Research Information

The starting point in obtaining marketing research information is defining the problem to be studied, indicating specific objectives, and determining what information is needed to help solve the problem. Problem definition examples for a new candy product and the quality of fast-food services are shown in Parts A and B of Exhibit 5–2.

Marketing research information is obtained from internal records, trade contacts, published information, surveys, and many other sources. An example of a research study is shown in Exhibit 5–3. The objective is to test the effectiveness of an advertising commercial. Marketing research studies range in cost from less than $10,000 to over $100,000.

Marketing research is "the systematic gathering, recording, processing, and analyzing of marketing data, which—when interpreted—will help the marketing executive to uncover opportunities and to reduce risks in decision making."[15] Strategies for obtaining marketing research information include collecting existing information, using standardized research services, and conducting special research studies.

Collecting Existing Information

The internal information system of the firm affects the extent and ease of the collection of existing information. The nature and scope of the information and the information system network vary greatly from firm to firm and among industries. Many firms have extensive internal information systems, or at least the capability to implement such systems. Recall the new customer information resources being created by CRM systems.

There is considerable value and potential in using the information in the organization's current system. This is essential for the strategic mission of the firm as well as for efficient utilization of assets. Information is a resource that needs to be consciously managed.[16] Management should structure the information system to capture this resource and control its use. Information is not a by-product of activities of the firm. It is a scarce, valuable resource that affects the future success or failure of the firm. Management may not have control over the actions of competitors or consumers, but an effective information system provides a way to anticipate and react.

The product mix and the nature of business operations influence what type of internal marketing information system is appropriate in a particular firm. Nonetheless, electronic information systems are necessary in all kinds of companies. The system must be designed to meet the information needs of the organization. Manufacturers have information requirements that differ from those of retailers or wholesalers. The size and complexity of the firm also influence the composition of the information system.

The costs and benefits of the information must be evaluated for both short-term and long-term planning. Incremental efforts and expenditures in the early stages of creating an internal information system may help the firm avoid future costly modifications. Achieving long-term performance may require temporary losses to finance a system. It is critical to consider a long-term perspective in evaluating information system decisions.

AT&T's competitor monitoring system draws from a variety of sources. The company has an electronic directory that is a collection of databases designed to assist with competitive intelligence.[17] Employees at all levels in the organization input information into the system. Newspaper and periodical items are also collected from print and electronic

EXHIBIT 5–2
**Illustrative
Marketing
Research Problem
Definitions**

Source: William R. Dillon,
Thomas J. Madden, and Neil H.
Firtle, *Marketing Research in a
Marketing Environment,* 3rd ed.
(Burr Ridge, IL: Richard D.
Irwin, 1994), 34.

Problem Setting A: A Consumer Package Goods Firm	
Project:	A major package goods firm is deciding on whether to continue development of a new "hard candy" product. The new product is a line extension offering a distinctive new ingredient that should be attractive to at least some category users. Brand managers want to collect information on the likely success of the new product.
Research Objective:	To determine the likely market success of a new "hard candy" product containing ingredient X and its relation to existing products.
Possible Research Questions:	1. What volume and market share will the new product achieve when it is rolled out nationally? 2. What trial rate can be expected? 3. Will the new product cannibalize existing products in our line? 4. Which existing products does the new product draw its share from? 5. Are there segments of consumers who have a greater likelihood of trying the new product? 6. Are there segments of consumers who are particularly attracted to the new ingredient?
Problem Setting B: A Fast-Food Chain	
Project:	The corporate management of a national fast-food chain wants to determine whether customer perceptions of service are uniform across their franchises. The parent corporation has followed a policy of minimizing variation in services provided. The intent of management is to assess whether customer perceptions of services are consistent with corporate standards.
Research Objective:	To evaluate customers' perceptions of the services provided by franchise operators and to identify areas that need attention.
Possible Research Questions:	1. What is the relevant set of service features on which franchises should be evaluated? 2. What is the perceived value of each service feature? 3. Do perceptions of services vary by meal? 4. Does the value of a service feature vary by meal? 5. Are there regional differences across franchises in terms of services provided? 6. What factors contribute to any differences that are observed?

sources. A competitive digest is issued to top management daily, and the system is always available for inquiry or special requests. This is an integrated system combining knowledge from a multitude of sources in an organized and standardized manner. It provides a complete analysis of the competitors for AT&T's various product lines. Competitors can be analyzed, highlighting growth opportunities or strategies for maintaining market position.

Standardized Information Services

A wide variety of marketing information is available for purchase in special publications and on a subscription basis. In some instances the information may be free. Sources include

EXHIBIT 5–3
Off-Air Test Marketing Research Project Proposal

Source: William R. Dillon, Thomas J. Madden, and Neil H. Firtle, *Marketing Research in a Marketing Environment*, 3rd ed. (Burr Ridge, IL: Richard D. Irwin, 1994), 611.

Brand:	Colgate.
Project:	Copy Test: "Midnight Delight."
Background and purpose:	A new commercial has been developed—"Midnight Delight." Brand Group is interested in determining its effectiveness. The objectives of this study will be to determine

- Brand recall.
- Copy recall.
- Purchase intent shifts.
- Comparison with previous copy testing results.

Research method: This research will be conducted using central location mall facilities in Boston, Atlanta, Milwaukee, and San Francisco. Each commercial will be viewed by 200 past-30-week toothpaste users as follows:

			Age Group	Number of Respondents
Males	50%		8–11	30
Females	50%		12–17	50
			18–24	25
			25–34	25
			34–49	10
			50+	10
				150

Information to be obtained:
- Brand recall.
- Copy recall.
- Pre- and postpurchase intentions.

Action standard: This study, which is being done for information purposes, will be used in conjunction with previous copy testing results.

Cost and timing: The cost for one commercial will be $6,500 ± 10%. The following schedule will be established:

Field work	3 weeks
Top-line reports	1 week
Final report	3 weeks
Total	7 weeks

Supplier: Legget Lustig Firtle, Inc.

government agencies, universities, private research firms, industry and trade organizations, and consultants. A key advantage to standardized information is that the costs of collection and analysis are shared by many users. The major limitation is that the information may not correspond well with the user's needs. These services offer substantial cost advantages, and many are quite inexpensive (for example, data distributed from the U.S. Census of Population and most governmental statistical services in developed countries). Many services allow on-line access to data, enabling subscribers to automatically input external information into their own information systems.

Many standardized information services are available to meet a wide range of decision-making needs. Some examples follow:[18]

Nielsen Media Research collects information on television audience measurement. Decisions to continue or drop shows often depend on these ratings.

The Petroleum Information Corporation unit supplies information on drilling and production for firms interested in oil and gas exploration activities around the world.

Information Resources Inc.'s InfoScan market tracking service provides weekly sales, price, and store condition information for a sample of food, drug, and mass merchandise stores.

A. C. Nielsen Corp. offers product movement data for food, drug, and other retail stores in more than 65 countries. Its ScanTrack service provides weekly data on packaged goods in the United States.

IMS International provides information such as pharmaceutical audits of sales to the pharmaceutical and health care industries worldwide. Audits are available in over 65 countries.

Using the large data banks collected and organized by these services, many different analyses can be made, depending on a company's information needs. The cost of the information for use by one company would be prohibitive. When the database is shared, a wide range of company information needs can be met.

Information Resources Inc. (IRI) uses electronic retail store scanning systems to record purchases by people participating on consumer panels (see the accompanying IRI advertisement). Scanning systems in stores automatically record consumers' purchases, eliminating the need for diaries and providing accurate data. The InfoScan panel data are obtained from a sample of 60,000 households. IRI installs a complete electronic monitoring system in each city where it has a consumer panel. IRI can also monitor the television programs watched by participants and insert test commercials into programming. Commercials can be targeted to households with specific demographic characteristics since these data are recorded for all participants. Subsequent purchases measure the effect of a commercial. The use of coupons can be monitored to test products and the strength of competitors. With this network, IRI can respond to various queries from clients such as Campbell Soup Company, Procter & Gamble, Johnson & Johnson, and General Foods Corporation. IRI monitors consumers' reactions and preferences without alerting them to which products are being tested. Firms can introduce advertising campaigns and determine optimal marketing strategies.

Special Research Studies

Research studies are initiated in response to problems or special information needs. Examples include market segmentation, new product concept tests, product use tests, brand-name research, and advertising recall tests. Studies may range in scope from exploratory research based primarily on analysis of published information to field surveys involving personal, phone, or mail interviews with respondents who represent target populations.

Recent developments include online market research services that offer less expensive and more rapidly available market research surveys. For example, launched in 1999, InsightExpress provides clients with a survey template to build an online questionnaire, allowing them to sample from a panel of 700,000 respondents, pay by credit card, and download the results within a few days. A research project costing perhaps $25,000 using traditional services is estimated to cost only $1,000 online.[19] Reservations exist regarding the quality of the data produced by online services, but they provide an inexpensive route to sensing the market quickly.

Research studies follow a step-by-step process that begins with defining the problem to be investigated and the objectives of the research. An example of a project proposal for a study of customers' usage of low-salt/unsalted crackers is shown in Exhibit 5–4. The proposal indicates the objectives, research method, sampling plan, method of analysis, and cost. The project illustrates the steps involved in the research process (problem definition, information required, research method, sampling plan, questionnaire design, data collection, analysis, and research report).

In deciding whether to employ marketing research and when interpreting the results, several considerations are important.

Courtesy Information Resources, Inc.

Defining the Problem

Care must be exercised in formulating the research problem. It is essential to spell out exactly what information is needed to solve the problem. If this cannot be done, exploratory research should be conducted to help define the research problem and determine the objectives of the project. Caution should be exercised to avoid defining a symptom rather than the underlying problem.

It is useful to prepare a written statement of the research problem, specific objectives, the information that is needed, information sources, and when the information is needed. Many companies contract with research firms to do the research. It is important that the supplier be as familiar as possible with the problem to be studied. Management needs to

EXHIBIT 5–4
Illustrative Marketing Research Proposal

Source: William R. Dillon, Thomas J. Madden, and Neil H. Firtle, *Marketing Research in a Marketing Environment,* 3rd ed. (Burr Ridge, IL: Richard D. Irwin, 1994), 49.

Category:	Low-salt crackers
Project:	Market study
Objectives:	To continue to build low-salt/unsalted cracker business and to effectively defend these brands against new competitive entries, a better understanding of consumers' use of low-salt/unsalted crackers and their attitudes toward low-salt/unsalted crackers is needed.
Research method:	A two-phase research study (screening and follow-up) will be conducted among households who are members of the supplier's mail panel.
Screening phase:	To address the marketing questions outlined above, it will be necessary to obtain a basic sample of low-salt/unsalted cracker users and readable samples (N = 150 in follow-up phase) for each of the brands of interest.
Sampling frame:	Screening questionnaires will be mailed to a nationally balanced sample of 36,000 panel member households. Within each household, men and women, age 18 or older, will complete the questionnaire. Returns are expected from 25,200 individuals, a response rate of 70 percent. A random sample of 2,000 of these respondents will be fully processed in the second phase of the study.
Follow-up phase:	In the follow-up phase, an extensive self-administered survey will be mailed to individuals having certain characteristics (i.e., category/specific brand usage) as identified in the screening phase.
Analysis:	Analysis will include standard cross-tabular analyses plus a number of multivariate statistical techniques (specifically a segmentation analysis) to help answer key research questions. For example: 1. What is the underlying need structure within the low-salt cracker market? 2. How is the market segmented in terms of usage dynamics? 3. What are the (particular brand's) strengths and weaknesses among its franchise?
Action standard:	Not applicable.
Cost:	The cost for conducting the study as specified within this proposal will be $121,500 ± 10% ($28,500 for screener and $93,000 for follow-up). This cost includes sample selection, questionnaire production, first-class postage (out and back), reminder postcards (follow-up study only), respondent incentives (follow-up study only), data processing (up to 12 cards and 6 open ends), four banners of tabulations at the follow-up phase, all necessary multivariate statistical analyses, and one presentation or report.
Timing:	Scheduling for the study will be as follows:

	Weeks Elapsed (from start of field, August 3)
Screeners returned	4
Phase I data available	7
Phase II commences	8
Phase II data collection ends	12
Phase II data available	16
Draft presentation available	20

clearly define the intended project and may choose to involve the research supplier in defining the problem.

Understanding the Limitations of the Research

Most studies are unable to do everything that the user wishes to accomplish while staying within the available budget. Priorities for the information that is needed should be indicated. Also, obtaining certain information may not be feasible. For example, measuring the impact of advertising on profits may not be possible due to the influence of many other factors on profits.

Research suppliers should be able to indicate the limitations that may exist for a particular project. Discussions with a potential supplier are advisable before making a final commitment to the project. This will be useful in finalizing information need priorities.

Quality of the Research

There are many challenges to obtaining sound research results. The available evidence indicates that some studies are not well designed and implemented and may contain misleading results. Factors that affect the quality of study results include the experience of the research personnel, the size of the sample, the wording of questions, and how the data are analyzed. This example highlights the difficulties in achieving reliable results:[20]

> A Gallup poll sponsored by the disposable diaper industry asked: "It is estimated that disposable diapers account for less than 2 percent of the trash in today's landfills. In contrast, beverage containers, third-class mail, and yard waste are estimated to account for about 21 percent of trash in landfills. Given this, in your opinion, would it be fair to ban disposable diapers?"

Not surprisingly, because of the wording of the question, 84 percent of the respondents answered no to the question.

Evaluating and Selecting Suppliers

Typically, research studies are not conducted by the user. When selecting a supplier, it is important to talk with two or three prior clients to determine their satisfaction with the research firm. It is also important to identify consultants who are experienced in conducting the particular type of research needed by the user. Familiarity with the industry may also be important.

Spending some time in evaluating a potential research supplier is very worthwhile. Experience and qualifications are important in selecting the supplier. Several useful screening questions are shown in Exhibit 5–5. These questions could be used to evaluate possible suppliers before asking for a detailed research proposal from a supplier.

Costs

Customized research studies are expensive. The factors that affect study costs include the sample size, the length of the questionnaire, and how the information will be obtained. The complexity of the study objectives and the analysis methods also increase the required professional capabilities of research personnel. Study costs may range from less than $10,000 (Exhibit 5–3) to over $100,000 (Exhibit 5–4).

Standardized subscription services (e.g., IRI's InfoScan) are also expensive, but for companies with various product types the annual cost is very reasonable and considerably below the cost of a company collecting and analyzing its own data. The top 25 marketing research firms had revenues of $8.8 billion in 2000, representing 56 percent of total world spending for research services and an increase of 9 percent above 1999.[21] The consumer nondurables industry (packaged goods) accounted for 28 percent of research revenues,

EXHIBIT 5–5
Ten Questions for Screening a New Supplier

Source: Seymour Sudman and Edward Blair, *Marketing Research: A Problem-Solving Approach* (Burr Ridge, IL: Irwin/McGraw-Hill, 1998), 67.

1. Ask the supplier's recent clients: *Would you recommend this supplier?* The biggest mistake research buyers make is not checking references. Do not let the supplier give you just any three references; ask for references from the five most recent jobs, and check dates as well as evaluations.

2. Ask the supplier: *Do you have sufficient funds for this job?* Get a bank reference, and check it. Underfinanced suppliers are tempted to cut corners. If the supplier is well qualified but not well financed, make arrangements such as a fieldwork drawing fund to ensure that the supplier has enough cash to do all work properly.

3. Ask the supplier: *What parts of the project will be subcontracted, and how do you control subcontractors?* Many suppliers subcontract parts of the research, and you should know how they manage their subcontractors. A ready answer indicates that the supplier understands the issue and has procedures in place.

4. If the research involves survey interviews, ask the supplier: *May I see your interviewer's manual and data entry manual?* You don't have to read these manuals, but they should be readily available and should appear well used. The use of manuals suggests that formal management procedures are in place.

5. Also ask: *How do you train and supervise interviewers?* Supervision and training cost money and are not visible to clients, so some suppliers cut corners in these areas. The best suppliers do a good job of supervision and training as a matter of professional standards and welcome the chance to show off these standards.

6. Also ask: *What percentage of interviews are validated? How many invalid questionnaires are needed for you to do a 100 percent check on an interviewer's work?* If the answer is "What numbers do you want?" ask "What are your usual standards?" Interviewer cheating is most likely to occur in operations that do not have standards for finding and correcting it. You are looking for those standards, and you want them to be as high or higher than your own.

7. If the research involves survey interviews, ask the supplier: *May I see a typical questionnaire?* If the supplier shows you a questionnaire written for one of your competitors, leave immediately, because this is a violation of confidentiality and is unacceptable. Check whether the questionnaire will be easy for the respondent, the interviewer, and data entry people to use.

8. If the research involves any type of sampling, ask the supplier: *Who draws your samples?* Sampling is a technical aspect of research in which novices can easily make mistakes.

9. If the research involves any data being entered into the computer, ask the supplier: *What percentage of your data is verified?* Again, you are looking for standards, and the standard for data entry is 100 percent verification.

10. Ask your managers: *What do you think about this supplier?* Don't limit the value of research by using a supplier that your managers have doubts about. Also, the most useful research is research that produces new, even counterintuitive information, and managers often resist new information by raising the possibility that the supplier "did it wrong" or "didn't understand the issues." Make them raise any doubts at the start of the project, and save credibility questions for other problems.

followed by 21 percent for media and advertising and 17 percent for pharmaceutical and health care companies. Agency research consists predominantly of market measurement studies, media audience research, and customer satisfaction measurement. Research into the impact of the Internet on markets is growing rapidly.

Information Systems

There are many types of information systems within the organization. Manual systems are also used and may provide crucial information. Yet for the purposes of this chapter, attention is focused on computer-based information systems. "Strategic systems are those that change the goals, products, services, or environmental relationships of organizations."[22] These information systems alter how a firm does business with competitors, suppliers, and customers. Since the scope of strategic planning is so broad, information generated by the system is invaluable in strategic marketing planning. The system may provide information to assist decision makers with strategic planning or may actually prepare a plan and formulate decisions. We describe management information systems, database systems, and decision support systems.

Management Information Systems

Management information systems provide raw data to decision makers within a firm. The system collects data on the transactions of the firm and may include competitor and environmental information. Decision makers (and systems analysts) are responsible for extracting the data relevant for a decision and in the appropriate format to facilitate the process. The system can provide information for decisions at all levels of the organization. Lower- and middle-level managers are likely to use the system most often for operating decisions. The system may generate routine reports for frequent operating decisions, such as weekly sales by product, or may be queried for special analyses on an as-needed basis. Nonroutine decisions may consist of tracking the sales performance of a sales district over several months, determining the number of customer returns for a particular good, or listing all customers or suppliers within a given geographic area. The basic MIS collects data and allows for the retrieval and manipulation of format in an organized manner. Typically, the MIS does not interact in the decision-making process. More advanced MIS capabilities provide important decision analysis capabilities.

Consider this MIS application. A sophisticated marketing information system enables a major airline to focus on the needs of specific market segments.[23] The system determines mileage awards for frequent fliers and provides a reservation support database organized by market segments. The company's top 3 percent of customers account for 50 percent of sales. These key accounts are highlighted on all service screens and reports. Reservations agents are alerted that a person is an important customer. The frequent fliers receive a variety of special services, including boarding priority and first-class upgrades.

Database Systems

Database systems are an important information resource in many companies. Target uses an effective database system to respond to customer diversity in its stores. Management's model of the market takes into account differences in product needs and preferences by store location. The Technology Feature describes how Target uses micromarketing to satisfy customers. Interestingly, it also indicates how internal personnel initially resisted the learning process.

Databases are a form of MIS. Some database systems offer capabilities similar to those of decision support systems. Computerized databases are indispensable for companies pursuing direct marketing strategies. Discussion of database marketing as a form of promotional strategy is included in Chapter 13.

The components of database systems include relational databases, personal computers, electronic publishing media, and voice systems.[24] The intent of database marketing is to

The purpose of micromarketing is to tailor retail store offerings to customers' needs and preferences.

Rather than offer the same merchandise at all of Target's 600-plus retail stores, the discount chain uses computer technology to offer specialized merchandise in various stores.

The objective is to have the right merchandise in the location where and when buyers want it.

Target's internal buyers resisted micromarketing because they were accustomed to using buyer power to get the best prices from suppliers. This required shifting from a vendor to an end-user focus.

Target's sophisticated computerized buying, planning, and store operations systems help create merchandise mixes that cater to racial, ethnic, and age characteristics of different customer segments.

Store managers further refine the merchandise offering based on local tastes and practices. Individual stores can add merchandise without headquarters' approval.

Interestingly, the merchandise variations that respond to specific customer groups is only 15 to 20 percent. The plan is to raise this to 30 percent.

Source: Gregory A. Patterson, "Different Strokes: Target 'Micromarkets' Its Way to Success; No Two Stores Are Alike," *The Wall Street Journal*, May 31, 1995, A1, A9. Republished by permission of Dow Jones, Inc. via Copyright Clearance Center, Inc. © 2000 Dow Jones and Company, Inc. All rights reserved worldwide.

effectively use a computerized customer database to facilitate a significant and profitable communication with customers.

One of the challenges in the use of databases is identifying what patterns are present in the huge accumulations of information. Data mining software technology is available to assist in diagnosing patterns in databases.[25] Computer power enables analysis of as many as 10,000 customer attributes to help identify key patterns such as how to keep the best customers. For example, MCI Communications Corp. has developed through data mining software a highly secret set of 22 statistical profiles to monitor on a regular basis.

Recall earlier comments regarding the growing role of customer relationship management (CRM) technology in building new databases—or data warehouses—from the company's own customer contacts. These new data sources are likely to be the focus of many data mining exercises and create new insights into customer behavior. For example, Wal-Mart's discovery of a correlation between Friday evening purchases of disposable diapers and those of beer is associated with the identification of a new product category comprising leisure and family products for families with small children.

Decision-Support Systems

A decision-support system (DSS) assists in the decision-making process by using the information captured by the MIS. A marketing decision support system (MDSS) integrates data that are not easily found, assimilated, formatted, or manipulated with software and hardware into a decision-making process that provides a marketing decision maker with assistance when needed.[26] The MDSS gives the user flexibility in applications and format. A MDSS can be used for various levels of decision making, ranging from determining reorder points for inventory to launching a new product.

The components of the MDSS consist of the database, the display, the models, and the analysis capabilities.[27]

Database

Various kinds of information are included in the database, such as standardized marketing information produced by Nielsen and other research suppliers, sales and cost data, and internal information such as product sales, advertising data, and price information. The design and updating of the database are vital to the effectiveness of an MDSS. The information should be relevant and organized to correspond to the units of analysis used in the system.

Display

This component of the MDSS enables the user to communicate with the database. Mangers and staff professionals need to interact with the database:

> They must be able to extract, manipulate, and display data easily and quickly. Required capabilities range from simple ad hoc retrieval to more formal reports that track market status and product performance. Also needed are exception reports that flag problem areas. Many presentations should have graphics integrated with other materials.[28]

Models

This component of the MDSS provides mathematical and computational representations of variables and their interrelationships. For example, a sales force deployment model would include an effort-to-sales response function model and a deployment algorithm for use in analyzing selling effort allocation alternatives. The decision support models are useful in analysis, planning, and control.

Analysis

This capability consists of various analysis methods, such as regression analysis, factor analysis, time series, and preference mapping. Software capabilities may be included in the system. Analysis may be performed on a data set to study relationships, identify trends, prepare forecasts, and examine the impact of alternative decision rules.

MDSSs may operate autonomously or instead may require interaction with the decision maker during the process. There may be several stages before a recommendation is formed where the decision maker responds to queries to refine the scenario. Thus, an interactive MDSS requires more assistance from the decision maker and has more room for variation than does an autonomous MDSS. The system is dependent on the quality and accuracy of the information and assumptions that are used in designing the system. The process should be viewed as a tool to assist in decision making and is not a final product in itself.

Ideally, the experience and shared vision of management are built into the model. But often information is missing, and the decision maker has the best grasp of the entire situation. The most complete decisions incorporate the recommendation of the MDSS but do not solely rely upon them. However, a DSS often serves to create or support a consensus, and evidence exists that a DSS does yield favorable decision-making performance when it is properly designed and applied to appropriate decision situations. Evaluations of DSS effectiveness show some positive results.[29] Using controlled laboratory tests of senior undergraduate students enrolled in a business policy course, researchers found that groups using the DSS made significantly better decisions than did their non-DSS counterparts. Nevertheless, further evaluation is needed to better define the conditions and applications where success is likely to occur.

The concept of the MDSS as a tool is most apparent in considering strategic decisions rather than operating decisions. Clear, concise answers may not always be possible, yet the system is a very valuable tool in the process. Consider the following:

> A DSS developed by William Luther analyzes key success factors in the marketplace and makes comparisons with competitors. This system is called a Strategic Planning Model, and is most useful for smaller companies. Managers input their definition of key success factors by means of a standardized questionnaire format. Comparisons are made between the firm and competitors for these factors. The factors can be weighted for importance, and multiple situations can be considered. The model makes projections and recommendations of strategies.[30]

In using this system, it is important that managers identify key success factors; otherwise the model will lose a great deal of credibility. When properly applied, it offers a useful framework for decision makers, recognizing that it is not a complete replica of the decision-making situation.

Marketing Intelligence Systems and Knowledge Management

Importantly, the emphasis on market sensing in market-driven companies does not rely on hard data alone. Many companies are investing in in-company intelligence units to coordinate and disseminate "soft" or qualitative data and improve shared corporate knowledge.[31] Intelligence may come from published materials in trade and scientific journals, salesperson call reports, programs of customer visits by executives, social contacts, feedback from trade exhibitions and personal contacts, or even rumor in the marketplace.

For example, when Southwestern Bell Telephone Co. heard rumors about new competitors entering the market with special packages for home renters, it was able to counter this rapidly by appointing apartment complex managers as Southwestern Bell sales agents. Similarly, market feedback suggesting that new "micro" phone companies appealed particularly to younger telephone renters led Southwestern to move resources into product offers and promotions based in colleges.[32] This shows a market sensing capability based on market intelligence.

Conversely, there is widespread evidence that while it may take a substantial period of time for information about a company's shortcomings to reach senior executives, they are well known to customers and employees much earlier.[33] For example, the performance of the British retailer Marks & Spencer collapsed during the late 1990s, with its share value falling from 650p to 150p between 1997 and 2000. Customer surveys in 1997 and 1998 showed rapidly declining customer satisfaction and increasing defection. The retiring CEO, Sir Richard Greenbury, said in 2000 that he simply did not know that there were customer problems and that the decline in sales was a "surprise."[34] Market information which is ignored by management or poorly communicated to management cannot impact effectively on decision making.

Knowledge Management

There is increasing recognition that knowledge about customers should be managed as a strategic asset, because competitive advantage can be created by not merely possessing current market information but knowing how to use it. Market knowledge is inextricably linked to organizational learning and market orientation in the market-driven company.[35]

Peter Drucker argues, for example, that often 90 percent of the information that companies collect is internal—market research and management reports that only tell executives only about their own company—while the real challenge is to build knowledge about new markets they do not yet serve and new technologies they do not yet possess.[36] Knowledge that builds competitive advantage involves a major emphasis on rigorous customer perspectives and competitor comparisons.[37]

Role of the Chief Knowledge Officer

To meet the knowledge management challenge, some companies have established positions with titles such as chief knowledge officer. While the titles and the job responsibilities vary, all appear linked to improving an organization's knowledge management and learning processes. This may be a staff position with only a few people involved or, instead, with responsibility for databases, a technical infrastructure, and related knowledge functions.[38] The position may report to the chief executive officer, the information officer, or another high-level executive. Companies that have these positions include Ernst & Young, International Business Machines, and the World Bank.

While there appear to be differences between the role and functions of knowledge and learning officers, both positions do not exist in the same company.[39] Knowledge management is concerned with knowledge (information) collection and linking information within the organization. While the future of the position is not clear, as it develops, there is likely to be a relationship between knowledge management and the discussion in this chapter of continuous learning about markets.

For example, Xerox claims a saving of $200 million from a single project that uncovered and shared expertise across the group. Internal benchmarking revealed that its Austrian subsidiary was unusually successful at persuading customers to renew contracts. Sharing the Austrian approach with other groups brought 70 percent up to the Austrian standard in three months.[40] The E-Business Feature illustrates the potential power of Internet-based technology in enhancing this form of knowledge sharing to solve customer problems in market-driven companies.

Leveraging Customer Knowledge

Several methods are being employed by companies to improve the availability and use of customer knowledge in affecting strategic decisions.[41]

Creating "Customer Knowledge Development Dialogues"

For example, DaimlerChrysler's Jeep division runs customer events called "Jeep Jamborees," attracting enthusiasts for the vehicle. Jeep employees connect with customers through informal conversations and semiformal roundtables. Engineers and ethnographic researchers focus on the Jeep owner's relationship with the vehicle, driving changes to existing models and plans for new models.

Operating Enterprisewide "Customer Knowledge Communities"

IBM uses collaborative Internet workspace called the CustomerRoom with major accounts, where individuals throughout its divisions and functions can exchange knowledge with each other and with the customer.

Capturing Customer Knowledge at the Point of Customer Contact

Customer relationship management systems capture customer behavior and response information which offers rich potential for better insights into issues like customer defection and competitors' strengths as well as emerging customer needs and perceptions.

Management Commitment to Customer Knowledge

Management's responsibility includes investing resources, time, and attention in maintaining customer dialogs and communities as a commitment to enhanced organizational

The president of Manistique Papers Inc., Leif Christensen, was concerned with the effectiveness of the peroxide used in his new recycling plant to remove ink from old magazines—the paper produced was just not white enough.

Christensen told Buckman Labs sales representatives about his whiteness problem. They immediately posted a message on Buckman's Internet discussion group.

Buckman has 54 Internet discussion groups focused on its main products. Typically, employees post 50 to 100 messages a day. The company has amassed an easily searchable database of in-house expertise and past lessons learned—all accessible to employees and customers via a Web browser.

Within hours of Christensen's white paper problem being posted, other Buckman personnel in Finland and Belgium helped explain the problem—a rare bacteria that breaks down the peroxide.

Christensen was notified immediately with the information and the antidote. The total time elapsed between Buckman learning about the problem and delivering the solution to the customer was around 48 hours. In the past this kind of problem solving would have taken weeks, if it happened at all.

Harnessing the brainpower of an entire global specialty chemicals company to assess and solve one customer's problem fast underlines the power of knowledge sharing and the Internet.

The customer's comment: "I don't think Buckman's competitors can pool the whole brainpower of the organization like Buckman can. . . ."

Source: Marcia Stepanek, "Spread the Knowhow," *Business Week E.Biz,* October 23, 2000, EB52.

understanding of the customer. For example, the vice president of marketing at Ford's LincolnMercury division actively participates in customer-related chatrooms on the Internet and encourages other employees to follow his lead. Other approaches include planned programs of customer visits for cross-functional teams of executives as a systematic way of acquiring customer information, but also building superior understanding and responsiveness to customer perspectives.[42]

Issues in Collecting and Using Information

Lastly, important privacy and ethical issues concerning the role of information in the organization need to be assessed by managers and professionals.

Invasion of Customer Privacy

The escalation in the use of databases has generated concern about invasion of the privacy of individuals. Companies have responded to the issue by asking customers to indicate their preferences concerning mailing lists and other uses of the information. Nonetheless, concern about this issue will undoubtedly continue as communications technology and software develop in the future.

Consider, for example, the use of patent information in the drug industry. Database marketing by pharmaceutical companies is guided by information obtained from toll-free number calls, subscriptions to magazines, and pharmacy questionnaires.[43] This information can be used to guide database marketing programs, targeting people with specific health concerns such as depression, arthritis, and other problems. Some patients are objecting to the use of their prescription data to guide direct mail and other promotional efforts.

Information and Ethics

Related to the issue of invasion of privacy is the issue of how companies and research suppliers should respond to ethical issues. For example, should a prospective client share a supplier's detailed project proposal with a competing supplier? A central issue concerns which organization pays for the cost of preparing the proposal. If the proposal is prepared at the expense of the supplier, then the proposal is the property of the supplier.[44] Sharing the proposal with its competition would be ethically questionable.

Information sharing with research suppliers, other external contractors, strategic alliance partners, and acquisition/merger prospects often involves highly confidential information. There are many possible situations that present ethical questions and concerns. Companies normally sign confidentiality agreements.[45] Nonetheless, revealing trade secrets is a risk that relies primarily on the ethical behavior of the participants. Moreover, these situations offer excellent opportunities for learning.

Summary

Information performs a vital strategic role in an organization. Information capability creates a sustainable competitive advantage by improving the speed of decision making, reducing the costs of repetitive operations, and improving decision-making results. Market sensing is vital to the effectiveness of the market-oriented company. Managers' models of their markets guide the interpretation of information and the resulting strategies designed to keep the firm ahead of its competition. Learning about markets necessitates open-minded inquiry, widespread distribution of information within the organization, mutually informed interpretation, and developing a memory to provide access to prior learning.

Marketing information capabilities include marketing research, marketing information systems, database systems, decision support systems, and expert systems. Research information supports marketing analysis and decision making. This information may be obtained from internal sources, standardized information services, and special research studies. The information may be used to solve existing problems, to evaluate potential actions such as new product introductions, and as inputs to computerized data banks.

Computerized information systems include management information systems, database systems, CRM technology, and decision support systems. These systems include capabilities for information processing, analysis of routine decision making, and decision recommendations for complex decision situations. The vast array of information processing and telecommunications technology that is available offers many opportunities to enhance the competitive advantage of companies.

The development of useful information systems is a key success requirement for competing in the rapidly changing and shrinking global business environment. Marketing decision-making results are improved by the use of effective information systems. Gaining an information advantage requires more than technology. The systems demand creative (and cost-effective) design that focuses on decision-making information needs.

Importantly, we recognize the growing importance of knowledge management in strategic marketing as a vital source of competitive advantage, the role of the chief knowledge officer, and several approaches to enhancing the development of customer knowledge.

Finally, we consider some important issues in collecting and using information. These include invasion of customer privacy and information and ethics.

Internet Applications

A. Visit the website of Project 2000 (*www.2000.ogsm.Vanderbilt.edu*), founded at the Owen Graduate School of Vanderbilt University. Discuss how this website can assist a company in its market sensing activities.

B. Select a well-known company or brand and use a search engine to find Web pages that include its name. Review the content of Web pages from different sources. Discuss the impact of Internet-based information on traditional ideas about confidentiality and privacy.

Questions for Review and Discussion

1. Discuss how an organization's marketing information skills and resources contribute to its distinctive capabilities.

2. How would you explain to a group of top-level executives the relationship between market orientation and continuous learning about markets?

3. Outline an approach to developing an effective market sensing capability for a regional full-service bank.

4. Compare and contrast the use of standardized information services as an alternative to special research studies for tracking the performance of a new packaged food product.

5. Discuss the probable impact of cable television on marketing research methods during the next decade as this medium penetrates an increasing number of U.S. households and closer relationships are developed with telecommunications companies.

6. Comment on the usefulness and limitations of test-market data as a source of marketing information.

7. Suppose the management of a retail floor covering (carpet, tile, wood) chain is considering a research study to measure household awareness of the retail chain, reactions to various aspects of wallpaper purchase and use, and identification of competing firms. How could management estimate the benefits of such a study to determine if the study should be conducted?

8. Are there similarities between marketing strategic intelligence and the operations of the U.S. Central Intelligence Agency? Do companies employ business spies?

9. Discuss how manufacturers of U.S. and Swiss watches could have used market sensing to help avoid the problems that several firms in the industry encountered as Seiko and other Japanese companies entered the watch market.

10. Examine the strategic implications for small independent retailers and regional chains of the expanding strategic use of information technology by large retailers like Wal-Mart.

11. Data mining from databases is receiving increased attention in many companies. Discuss the underlying logic of data mining.

12. What are the relevant issues that need to be considered when obtaining the services of an outside supplier for a marketing research project?

Notes

1. George S. Day, "The Capabilities of Market-Driven Organizations," *Journal of Marketing,* October 1994, 43.
2. This illustration is drawn from Roger D. Blackwell, *From Mind to Market* (New York: HarperBusiness, 1997), 5–11.
3. Robert Johnson, "In the Chips," *The Wall Street Journal,* March 22, 1992, B1, B2.
4. Stanley F. Slater and John C. Narver, "Market Orientation, Customer Value, and Superior Performance," *Business Horizons,* March–April 1994, 22–27.
5. Stanley F. Slater and John C. Narver, "Market Orientation and the Learning Organization," *Journal of Marketing,* July 1995, 63–74, at p. 71.
6. Ibid.

7. Ibid.
8. Blackwell, *From Mind to Market,* 9.
9. The following discussion is based on Day, "The Capabilities of Market-Driven Organizations." See also Stanley F. Slater and John C. Narver, "Market-Oriented Isn't Enough: Build a Learning Organization," Report No. 94-103 (Cambridge, MA: Marketing Science Institute, 1994).
10. Nigel F. Piercy and Nikala Lane, "Marketing Implementation: Building and Sustaining a Real Market Understanding," *Journal of Marketing Practice: Applied Marketing Science* 2, no. 3 (1996), 15–28.
11. Adrian J. Slywotzky, *Value Migration* (Boston: Harvard Business School Press, 1996).
12. Philip B. Evans and Thomas S. Wuster, "Strategy and the New Economics of Information," *Harvard Business Review,* September–October 1997, 70–82. See also Philip Evans and Thomas S. Wurster, *Blown to Bits: How the New Economics of Information Transforms Strategy* (Boston: Harvard Business School Press, 2000).
13. Day, "The Capabilities of Market-Driven Organizations," 43.
14. Robert La Franco, "It's All about Visuals," *Forbes,* May 22, 1995, 108, 110, 112.
15. William R. Dillon, Thomas J. Madden, and Neil H. Firtle, *Marketing Research in a Marketing Environment,* 3rd ed. (Homewood, IL: Richard D. Irwin, 1994), 737.
16. Kenneth C. Laudon and Jane Price Laudon, *Management Information Systems* (New York: Macmillan, 1988), 235.
17. Blaine E. Davis and Martin Stark, "American Telephone & Telegraph Co.: A Network of Experts," in Howard Sutton, *Competitive Intelligence,* Report No. 913 (New York: The Conference Board, 1988), 22–24.
18. A description of the top 50 companies in the marketing research industry can be found in the "Honomichl 50" special section of *Marketing News,* June 5, 2001.
19. Valerie Marchant, "First E-Marketing, Now E-Research," *Time.com,* January 24, 2000.
20. Cynthia Crossen, "Margin of Error," *The Wall Street Journal,* November 11, 1991, A1.
21. Jack Honomichl, "Colossal Changes," *Marketing News,* August 13, 2001, H1–H23.
22. Laudon and Laudon, *Management Information Systems,* 62.
23. Michael Miron, John Cecil, Kevin Bradicich, and Gene Hall, "The Myths and Realities of Competitive Advantage," *DATAMATION,* October 1, 1988, 76.
24. Bob Shaw and Merlin Stone, "Competitive Superiority through Database Marketing," *Long Range Planning,* October 1988, 24–40.
25. "Coaxing the Meaning Out of Raw Data," *Business Week,* February 3, 1997, 134, 136–38.
26. John D. C. Little and Michael Cassettari, *Decision Support Systems for Marketing Managers* (New York: AMA, 1984), 7.
27. Ibid., 12–15.
28. Ibid., 14.
29. A discussion of DSS effectiveness is provided in Ramesh Sharda, Steve H. Barr, and James C. McDonnell, "Decision Support System Effectiveness: A Review and an Empirical Test," *Management Science* 34, no. 2 (February 1988), 139–59.
30. Illustration from Robert J. Mockler, "Computer Information Systems and Strategic Corporate Planning," *Business Horizons,* May–June 1987, 35.
31. Thomas A. Stewart, "Getting Real about Brainpower", *Fortune,* November 27, 1995, 154–55.
32. Pat Long, "Turning Intelligence into Smart Marketing," *Marketing News,* March 27, 1995, 11.
33. Michael Skapinker, "How to Bow Out without Egg on Your Face," *Financial Times,* March 8, 2000, 21.

34. Kate Rankine, "Marks Ignored Shoppers' Fall in Faith," *Daily Telegraph,* October 30, 2000, 21.
35. Rohit Deshpande, "From Market Research Use to Market Knowledge Management," in Rohit Deshpande (ed.), *Using Market Knowledge* (Thousand Oaks, CA: Sage, 2001), 1–8.
36. Peter Drucker, *Peter Drucker on the Profession of Management* (Boston: Harvard Business School Press, 1998).
37. George S Day, "Learning about Markets," in Deshpande, *Using Market Knowledge,* 9–30.
38. Thomas A. Stewart, "Is This Job Really Necessary?" *Fortune,* January 12, 1998, 154–55.
39. Ibid.
40. Vanessa Houlder, "Xerox Makes Copies," *Financial Times,* July 14, 1997, 10.
41. Eric Lesser, David Mundel, and Charles Wiecha, "Managing Customer Knowledge," *Journal of Business Strategy,* November–December 2000, 35–37.
42. Edward F. McQuarrie and Shelby H. McIntyre, "Implementing the Marketing Concept through a Program of Customer Visits," in Deshpande, *Using Market Knowledge,* 163–90.
43. William M. Bulkeley, "Prescriptions, Toll-Free Numbers Yield a Gold Mine for Marketers," *The Wall Street Journal,* April 17, 1998, B1, B3.
44. Dillon, Madden, and Firtle, *Marketing Research in a Marketing Environment,* 48.
45. Elizabeth MacDonald and Joann S. Lublin, "In the Debris of a Failed Merger: Trade Secrets," *The Wall Street Journal,* March 10, 1998, B1, B10.

Cases for Part 2

Case 2–1

Gatorade

BARRINGTON, Ill.—One of the most studied athletes in the world is a 55-year-old concrete salesman named Al Train.

As he runs on a treadmill, researchers hover nearby to jab him with needles and probe him with tubes. Every gauge of his performance, from heart rate to fluid loss, is recorded from workout to workout.

After studying Mr. Train for 12 years, scientists here at the Gatorade Sports Science Institute have reached two firm conclusions: Running makes him sweat. And the ideal medium for replenishing his lost fluids is a blend of water with 6% carbohydrates and electrolytes.

As it happens, that's the formula for Gatorade.

It may come as no surprise that the primary accomplishment of the 15-year-old Gatorade Sports Science Institute has been to document the benefits of Gatorade. What is surprising is the commercial effectiveness of its research, which Gatorade has used to turn its brand into one of the food-and-beverage industry's stars.

Gatorade is the Michael Jordan of the industry. Its dominance of the sports-drink category appears to be unassailable, and its status as the market's pioneer doesn't fully account for its success. Coca-Cola and Kellogg pioneered markets, too, but their market shares tumbled when rivals came along.

A Standout at Quaker

Gatorade, by contrast, lost only a few points of market share even after competitors PepsiCo Inc. and Coca-Cola Co. entered the sports-drink business in the 1990s. Gatorade's share still stands at 81% in what has become the hottest-selling segment of the beverage industry. Its sales reached $1.5 billion last year and have grown at double-digit rates for five years, making Gatorade a standout at parent Quaker Oats Co., whose overall sales growth is in the low single digits.

How did Gatorade do it? The answer can be traced to the place where Mr. Train's sweat has been siphoned, analyzed and stored. The Gatorade Sports Science Institute has made Gatorade one of the most researched foods or beverages in history. Though the studies' findings may not be scientifically ironclad, their marketing value is phenomenal.

"Other products in the category don't back it up with the science we've come to expect from Gatorade," says Dean Kleinschmidt, until recently a trainer for football's New Orleans Saints. They drank about 60,000 gallons of the stuff last year.

At Gatorade, science was supposed to play the role it traditionally played in corporate America: product development. In 1985, two years after Quaker Oats acquired Gatorade from Stokely Van-Camp Inc., it recruited Robert Murray from Idaho's Boise State University to create the Gatorade Sports Science Institute. His assignment: improve the Gatorade formula. That shouldn't be so tough, the thinking went, since Gatorade wasn't invented in a food-science laboratory, but by football trainers at the University of Florida in Gainesville, who developed it in 1965 and named it for their team, the Gators.

Today, new flavors have been added to the original options of orange and lemon-lime, but the Gatorade formula is substantially unchanged. Improving it, says Dr. Murray, 50, turned out to be a very "hard nut to crack."

But early on, the institute found a new mission: substantiating the need for any kind of sports drink. Many athletes and trainers then believed liquids impaired athletic performance. Athletes, fearing cramps or bloating, would swish water in their mouths to cool off, then spit it out.

But in 1987, the American College of Sports Medicine, an Indianapolis organization for health professionals, recommended for the first time that fluid stations be included along long-distance race courses and that runners be encouraged to drink at every station to prevent dehydration. At about the same time, an independent study showed that runners who lost as little as 2% of their body weight to dehydration in 5,000- and 10,000-meter events saw their speeds decline by 6% to 7%. Those who lost 3% of their body weight often needed days to fully recover.

While it didn't initiate this field of research, the Gatorade Institute seized control of it and has never let go. At the institute, Dr. Murray established a pool of about 100 volunteers such as Mr. Train, the concrete salesman. For $20 an hour, they agreed to let Dr. Murray and his 12-person staff monitor them as they ran on a treadmill or pedaled an exercise bike in rooms heated to 80 degrees.

Their blood was drawn, tubes were inserted in their stomachs to monitor their fluid flows, and their sweat was sampled. Before and after their workouts, they stepped on a scale so sensitive that if they spit, it would detect the weight loss.

Gatorade also underwrote studies at many of the nation's top universities. The Gatorade Institute is a top source of funding for sports science, or kinesiology; a budding program at many institutions. The institute financed graduate-level research and invited dozens of exercise scientists to serve on its advisory boards. The company won't disclose how much it spends on science, except to say it amounts to at least a million dollars a year.

Before long, the institute was armed with dozens of studies that made a medical and athletic argument for substantial fluid intake during exercise, particularly of sports drinks. The results were published in peer-reviewed academic journals then reprinted in Gatorade's own newsletters. One of the reprinted studies, published 12 years ago in the British journal Science and Football, showed that soccer players covered 25% more distance during a game when they consumed a sports drink at halftime; that study wasn't funded by Gatorade.

The research indicated that sports drinks were superior to water because they contained carbohydrates and electrolytes—basically, sugar and salt—that are lost during vigorous exercise. But flavor was also a factor. For an endurance athlete, the cup after cup of water he needs to replenish severe fluid loss can gradually become undrinkable. But with flavored sports drinks, athletes in competitions managed to drink 25% more.

Back then, there was only one major sports drink: Gatorade, which controlled about 90% of the market. Using its studies and a fat marketing budget, Gatorade managed to place big orange coolers with its logo on the benches of nearly every pro sports team and 60 big colleges, as well as on the roadsides of about 5,000 races, including the nation's biggest marathons.

As soon as the athletes had access to the drink, Gatorade's scientists flooded them with information. They invited coaches and trainers to visit the Barrington laboratory and sent them home with big piles of published studies, as well as pamphlets and videos designed to explain how the product worked. Before long, Gatorade became the drink of choice not only for pro athletes and their young fans but also for weekend warriors and people who only watched sports on television.

"It's not just that we're paying to be on the sidelines—we deserve to be," says P. J. Sinopoli, Gatorade's communications director. "It's a lot more than image."

Consumption skyrocketed. Gatorade's double-digit sales growth attracted some serious competitors. With sports-drink sales growing faster than those of carbonated soft drinks, Coke and Pepsi entered the market in the early 1990s with their PowerAde and AllSport brands. Beverage experts predicted that the two powerhouses would clobber Quaker, whose officials acknowledged that they expected market-share erosion.

But Coke and Pepsi's superior distribution systems proved no match for the Gatorade Sports Science Institute. It started a bimonthly research review called Sports Science Exchange, which it sent to 25,000 coaches, educators, dieticians and scientists. It sponsored conferences, published textbooks for sports scientists, produced videos for young athletes and established a 100-person speakers bureau. Topics ranged from motivating athletes to maintaining the proper balance between fats and proteins, but the overriding message never varied: Athletes need to drink a lot, and no drink is better than Gatorade.

Career Boost

Many of the sports world's supporting players were exposed to Gatorade's blitz early in their careers. Trainer Julie Burns, who designs diet and exercise regimes for members of the Chicago Bulls and Chicago Bears, as well as for many amateur athletes, first heard a lecture on Gatorade's benefits about 12 years ago at a workshop run by the Chicago-based American Dietetic Association. "They're really top scientists there," Ms. Burns says of the Gatorade Institute, for whom she has since become a paid speaker. "And they're very objective, too."

Ms. Burns says she began recommending Gatorade because it was the only brand backed by reliable research. She continues to do so because Dr. Murray and the institute aid her in her work. Last month, for example, she told Dr. Murray that a couple of her Chicago Bears clients were getting benched by severe muscle cramps late in some games. He invited her to bring the players in for testing. Now, Gatorade is helping to design special diets for them. Those diets include plenty of Gatorade.

Mr. Kleinschmidt, who was dismissed by the Saints last month in a broad personnel shake-up, says he called the institute in 1996 when the team's owner, Tom Benson, was considering going on a trendy diet to lose weight. Gatorade's scientists analyzed the diet plan and recommended some revisions. "I don't care whether they're doing this for marketing reasons," says Mr. Kleinschmidt. "My job is to keep the athletes healthy, and I feel I'm doing a better job if I have their scientific information behind me."

Today, about 10 years after their introduction, Coke's PowerAde has a 12% share, while Pepsi's AllSport has a 4% share.

A Positive Perception

Even athletes who have never heard of the institute, such as pro mountain-bike racer Audrey Augustin, associate Gatorade with an aura of scientific credibility. "I'm skeptical of some of the imitations," Ms. Augustin says. "You don't know how much they've really been researched."

Now, Gatorade is trying to cement that conviction among golfers, tennis players and other weekend athletes. Its television and print ads, which feature athletes dripping orange and green sweat, make subtle references to science without going into the physiological details.

Coke and Pepsi, meanwhile, play down the science and don't put much research behind their sports drinks. "I think you can overcomplicate the issue of what a sports drink really is," says Coke spokesman Scott Jacobson.

In the marketplace, it hardly matters that not a single independent study has shown Gatorade to be superior to, say, Coke's PowerAde. "Look, we respect what they do with their research, but there's not such a huge difference among the brands," says Mr. Jacobson. Indeed, though Gatorade officials insist there are many subtle differences, the only obvious one is that PowerAde boasts 8% carbohydrates, two percentage points more than Gatorade.

PowerAde is the official sports drink of the 2000 Olympics and the National Hockey League, but such victories are so rare that Gatorade officials say they don't worry much about them. "We're not in a share game with Coke and Pepsi," says Ms. Sinopoli, Gatorade's communication director.

Overcoming Data

Instead, Gatorade is trying to expand the sports-drink market. Its first challenge is to overcome data suggesting that sports drinks offer no benefit over water during brief workouts. Until recently, even Gatorade's studies showed that athletes performed just as well with water as they did with sports drinks so long as their exercise period didn't exceed 50 minutes—the length of an average aerobics class. But last year, a new Gatorade-funded study, published in the peer-reviewed International Journal of Sports Nutrition, refuted that finding, showing some performance enhancement among cyclists in as little as 30 minutes of exercise. The article disclosed Gatorade's support for the research.

To Larry Armstrong, professor of environment and exercise physiology at the University of Connecticut and one of the few sports scientists not on the payroll of Gatorade, the new research is highly suspect. "I believe the vast majority of people do not exceed 50 minutes, so I would think the vast majority of people who use Gatorade don't need it," he says.

But Dr. Armstrong adds that he is reluctant to press the point for fear of offending his academic peers. "I have too many friends that deal with them," he says. "It's not necessarily a bad thing, but it does affect objectivity."

Gatorade's newest strategy is to reach consumers who are thirsty from light workouts—or from cutting the lawn. The amount of Gatorade the institute recommends drinking for an hourlong workout contains 500 calories, more than are burned in the average exercise session. To counter that problem, Gatorade is rolling out a new product. Called Propel, it is a fitness water containing some of the carbohydrates and electrolytes of Gatorade, but only a fifth the calories.

Epilogue

Jessica Goldin, an Illinois high school swimming champion, is the kind of consumer companies pay good money for. She's devoted to a brand—the 16-year-old drinks only Gatorade when she's practicing or competing. And she has absorbed the marketing message: The salty sweet liquid is "the thirst-quencher," Goldin says. She won't even touch plain water.

Millions of other athletes are right there with her. Gatorade commands a stunning 83% share of the sports-drink market. In the food and beverage industry, that kind of market share is "almost illegal," says William Leach, a food analyst at Banc of America Securities. Coca-Cola Co.'s Powerade has captured no more than 11% of the market; PepsiCo's All

Sport has just 3%. Gatorade is so dominant that Quaker Oats Co. executives smugly say its main competitor is tap water. "When we're done, tap water will be relegated to showers and washing dishes," Susan D. Wellington, president of Quaker's U.S. beverages division, said to analysts earlier this year. Quaker executives declined to comment for this article.

It's no wonder that rivals are thirsting after the brand. Pepsi's $14 billion stock offer for Quaker was rebuffed by Chief Executive Robert S. Morrison on Nov. 2. Pepsi may well try again. But if it doesn't, Coke, Danone Group, and Nestlé are all possible buyers.

Why so much interest in Gatorade now? After all, its sales have been growing by about 10% a year for the past decade. First, the global food and beverage industry is consolidating. Second, U.S. consumers are taking to what's known as nutraceuticals, those drinks with nutrients, vitamins, herbs—anything that seems healthy. It's a market that could grow as much as 20% annually over the next several years, according to Patrick Schumann, an analyst at St. Louis brokerage Edward Jones. And, although Gatorade is only a borderline nutraceutical (providing sodium, potassium, and chloride), it could bill itself as one. Sales are already up 15%, to $1.82 billion, for the first nine months of 2000. Morrison has said he expects a double-digit profit increase this year, following last year's 18% rise.

Precious Fluids

If there were ever a testament to the power of marketing, Gatorade is it. The company sells consumers on the idea that the drink is the best way to replenish minerals and fluid lost during exercise. Truth is, a blend of water, sugar, and salt would work just as well. But what fun is that?

Last year, Quaker spent $81 million on advertising; that was about five times as much as Coke gave to Powerade and 275 times as much as Pepsi devoted to All Sport. Gatorade is now the official drink of almost every major sports league, except the National Hockey League (that went to Powerade). The company sponsors some 1,000 athletic events a year, including the New York City and Boston marathons.

Gatorade's most prominent spokesman has long been superathlete Michael Jordan. Quaker signed him to a 10-year endorsement contract back in 1991. Two years later, Gatorade hit the $1 billion mark in sales. "The promotions they built around Jordan, particularly the 'Be Like Mike' campaign, are some of the best known among their target audience," says Christie Nordhielm, a marketing professor at Northwestern University's Kellogg Graduate School of Management. More recently, the company has signed on soccer star Mia Hamm and the New York Yankees shortstop Derek Jeter.

Having sewn up the sports-drink market, Gatorade is trying to broaden its base from the serious competitor to the weekend athlete. Its ads now ask: "Is it in you?" The idea is to "drive up the emotional equity in the brand," says John Fraser, senior vice-president at FCR Worldwide, the Chicago advertising company that holds the Gatorade account.

Quaker is also working to expand distribution beyond grocery and convenience stores. It's putting Gatorade in vending machines and kiosks near golf courses, parks, and schools. The company expects to increase such distribution from a January level of some 50% of the country to 70% by yearend. That will mean adding about 15,000 "alternative sites" to the existing 40,000.

Gatorade won cult status in the late 1960s. University of Florida researchers had developed the concoction in 1965 to prevent dehydration, testing it on the school football team. It seemed to work: The Gators often outplayed their opponents in the second half of games. In 1967, Stokely-Van Camp Inc., of baked beans fame, bought the rights to distribute the drink nationally.

But Gatorade really took off when Quaker acquired it in 1983. The company's former chief executive, William D. Smithburg, had been drinking Gatorade on the tennis court for years. When he took over the brand, Gatorade was still largely a southern drink with modest sales of $90 million. It was available only in glass bottles and in only two flavors—lemon-lime and orange. Smithburg gets most of the credit for improving the taste and the packaging, and for broadening the distribution. Gatorade now is available in 19 flavors; there are two other versions (one that's crisper and one that's sweeter); and it sells energy bars in a few cities.

Over the years, some 100 rival drinks have come and gone. Even Coke and Pepsi have failed to pose a serious threat to Gatorade. In part, that's because of Gatorade's dominance. But in Coke's case, it was also because former CEO M. Douglas Ivester resisted making a big commitment to sports drinks and other noncarbonated products—figuring it was more profitable to churn out more Cokes and Sprites than to take on entrenched brands such as Gatorade. "Coke and Pepsi had distribution, but we had brand equity," says Smithburg.

Parts Unknown

All Sport, Pepsi's sports drink, remains only a small piece of its business. The brand was launched nationally in 1994. Recently, though, Pepsi has targeted states such as Washington, West Virginia, and Oregon, where outdoor sports are particularly popular. "Even for marketing powerhouses like Coke and Pepsi, competing against a brand which is well-established, strong, and continuously well-marketed is very difficult," says John Sicher, editor of *Beverage Digest.* He's impressed that Coke has won as much as 11% of the market.

Quaker's real challenge lies in international markets, where it is easily overtaken by rivals such as Coke, Danone, and Nestlé. "Quaker isn't big, so they don't have the wherewithal to get better distribution," says Leach of Banc of America Securities. In 1999, international sales were $333 million, down 10% from the previous year. The company was hurt by currency devaluations in Latin America, its largest international market. It's struggling to make an impact in Europe, where Gatorade's gung-ho, All-American message doesn't always play well, and in China, where it's still a relatively unknown brand.

Under such circumstances, Quaker might be expected to form a joint venture for international distribution. But Quaker is likely to go it alone overseas. That will make it easier to sell the company, Quaker's ultimate endgame.

By Julie Foster in Chicago, with Diane Brady in New York and Dean Foust in Atlanta

Source: "Gotta Get That Gator," *Business Week,* November 27, 2000, 91, 94.

Case 2–2

Nike Inc.

It's hard to say exactly when Nike Inc., one-time corporate brat, began to transform itself into a pillar of the community. But it may have been during a meeting in 1998, at a time when the company was under attack for allegedly exploiting overseas factory workers. Nike, in its usual maverick style, had initially tried to slough off the issue. But now, as managers argued over whether to raise the minimum age of workers in those factories from 14 to 18, Nike Chairman and co-founder Philip H. Knight ended the debate with a surprising call: Just do it.

The issue became a galvanizing force for both him and Nike. One of Corporate America's true free spirits, the brash Knight had long cultivated an aloof, even arrogant, style. When the outcry over working conditions in Nike's overseas factories started in the late '90s, he glossed over the complaints, claiming he had little control over suppliers. But as

EXHIBIT 1

Data: Footwear Market Insights,
Nike, Inc., Black & Co.,
Bloomberg Financial Markets.

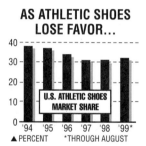

AS ATHLETIC SHOES LOSE FAVOR...

U.S. ATHLETIC SHOES MARKET SHARE

▲ PERCENT   *THROUGH AUGUST

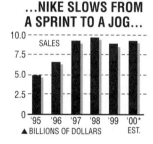

...NIKE SLOWS FROM A SPRINT TO A JOG...

SALES

▲ BILLIONS OF DOLLARS   EST.

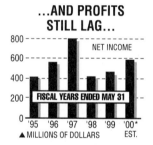

...AND PROFITS STILL LAG...

NET INCOME

FISCAL YEARS ENDED MAY 31

▲ MILLIONS OF DOLLARS   EST.

protests mounted on college campuses, Knight seemed to snap to attention. Suddenly, he was scouring the negative press coverage for errors; writing college presidents about the issue, and bringing in Maria S. Eitel from Microsoft Corp. as vice-president for corporate responsibility. "Phil made clear from the day I started that this is a huge priority," says Eitel.

These days, Knight is plugged into Nike's operations like never before. He has little choice. The backlash against Nike's labor practices isn't the only crisis the company faces. Two years ago, jolted by shifting teen fashions and the Asian economic downturn, sales of its sneakers and sports apparel hit a brick wall, and the hard times aren't over. On February 8, Nike told analysts that earnings this year and next would fall short of estimates because important retail chains are closing stores and the strong dollar is resulting in unfavorable currency translations (Exhibit 1). Immediately, the stock swooned 18%, to 37, lopping a stunning $2.4 billion off Nike's stock market valuation. "Investors feel that the turnaround they've been waiting for is being pushed off again," says Dana Eisman Cohen, an analyst with Donaldson, Lufkin & Jenrette. "People are losing patience."

With that kind of pressure, Knight, the ultracompetitive former college miler who co-founded Nike 28 years ago by selling running shoes out of his car trunk, is struggling to re-build the company from top to bottom. That's required a huge attitude adjustment at Nike's headquarters in Beaverton, Ore. Knight quadrupled sales in the '90s with a buccaneer style that had Nike thumbing its nose at the sports Establishment. This, for example, was the company that in 1994 paid $25,000 to help defend skating outcast Tonya Harding. But two years ago, Knight, 61, woke up to discover that Nike was so big that it had become the Es-tablishment. And like a middle-aged rock-and-roller who finds himself raising a family in the 'burbs, he has had to learn to accept the responsibility that comes with age. "There are some things you can do as a $100 million company that you can't get away with as a $9 bil-lion company," Knight explains to BUSINESS WEEK in his first major interview about Nike's new strategy. "We're not as rebellious as we were five years ago."

No wonder—many of the rebels are gone. Over the past two years, Knight and his No. 2, President Thomas E. Clarke, have trimmed Nike's payroll by 1,600, or 8%. At the same time, several executives identified with Nike's go-go years left, replaced by outsiders schooled at some of the nation's biggest corporations. Nine of Nike's 41 vice-presidents have worked at the company for fewer than two years, compared with just one of 27 four years ago. Three months ago, Nike hired a chief financial officer from PepsiCo Inc. Other newly minted vice-presidents have come from Disney, General Motors, and SBC Commu-nications. Competitors say Nike needed to upgrade and deepen its management ranks. "I'm sure Nike's looking for fresh perspective, and newcomers bring a fresh perspective," says Paul Heffernan, vice-president for global marketing at Boston-based New Balance Athletic Shoe Inc.

The new team is immersed in the effort to reinvent Nike. Newcomers are heading ini-tiatives that include a unit charged with reaching nontraditional markets, particularly extreme-sports enthusiasts such as skateboarders and snowboarders. Others are revamping Nike's manufacturing and logistics systems. Even the swoosh is no longer sacred. The logo is shrinking on some items and may disappear entirely from others.

The biggest change around the Beaverton campus, though, is that for the first time in years, Nike executives are taking a hard look at costs. Years of breakneck growth encouraged free spending. In the past, managers had plenty of big-picture goals but no hard budget numbers to rein them in. "Cost controls were a far second to boosting sales," recalls former marketing executive Elizabeth G. Dolan, who worked at Nike for a decade before leaving in 1997 to start her own consulting firm. Now, managers have to hold expense increases to about 3% below revenue increases. Nike also recently launched an effort to streamline manufacturing and logistics. "We grew really fast from 1994 to 1997, but I don't think anybody would suggest we were efficient," says Knight. "We couldn't be. We were just chasing the growth."

That chase was breathtaking while it lasted. In the mid-'90s, Nike blew away competitors such as Reebok and Adidas, its sales exploding from $3.8 billion in 1994 to $9.2 billion in 1997. Investors reaped a 320% increase in the stock price from Jan. 1, 1995, to a high of 75 in early 1997. But in 1998, the sprinter pulled up lame. Sales plummeted in Asia and stalled in the U.S. For the fiscal year ended May 31, sales slipped 8%. Even after overseas markets recovered late last year, Nike's domestic sales rose a paltry 2%. Now, the company has lowered sales projections for this year to an increase of just 3% to 4% from last year's $8.8 billion.

Nike's new lean focus helped it eke out a 13% increase in net income last year. But hopes for a 31% gain in 2000 were dashed when Clarke told analysts that earnings would come in slightly below estimates for this year and next. He said earnings-per-share growth would be held to "at least 20%" in fiscal year 2000 and to the mid-teens in 2001. Jennifer Black, an analyst at Black & Co. in Portland, Ore., believes Nike can generate a net earnings increase of 28% this year, still far below the glory days in 1996 and 1997 when Nike racked up gains of 38% and 44%, respectively.

Nike's news was especially troubling because, like other mature consumer-products companies, it was counting on overseas markets to speed growth. But with a weak euro, big gains in Europe are unlikely. Meanwhile, Knight expects only single-digit sales gains in the U.S. for the next few years. "Back in the mid-1990s, it was nirvana in the U.S. That's over," says Susan Zeeb, an analyst at Northern Trust Corp., which manages about 1 million Nike shares for wealthy individuals.

The result is a more measured, but hardly humbled, Phil Knight. He still tools around Beaverton in a black '92 Acura with NIKEMN (Nike Man) license plates and may be the only major American CEO to have his corporate logo tattooed on his ankle. And he's just as visible back at headquarters, where he still runs five miles a day. When top Nike-sponsored athletes drop by—golfer Tiger Woods, for instance, whom the company will pay an estimated $60 million to $80 million over five years—Knight is right by their side.

Knight may not have lost his ebullience, but his company is still in recovery from a downturn that hit it like a body blow. Starting in 1997, thousands of fickle teens suddenly switched from Nike Air Jordans to hiking boots and casual leather shoes. In 1994, athletic shoes accounted for 38% of all shoes sold in the U.S.; four years later, that had slipped to 31%, according to industry researcher Footwear Market Insights. Of course, that's still a healthy slice of the overall market, and Nike dominates the category with a 40% share. Nike's own sales slide was accelerated by its lingering association with arrogant millionaire athletes and overseas sweatshops.

Knight was blindsided by the ferocity of the anti-Nike sentiment about its overseas workers. The damage to the brand was real—and not just on college campuses. "They exploit people with what they pay as minimum wage in Third World countries," said Peter George, a runner from Melbourne, Australia, just after he finished competing in last November's New York City Marathon. He was wearing Asics shoes.

Once Knight figured out that the critics weren't going away, he abruptly changed tactics. "As part of our evolution, we've chosen to engage our critics rather than saying that they're wrong, which is my natural instinct," he says. Since Eitel came on board in 1998, her staff has doubled, to 95, one of the company's few areas of expansion. Nike maintains that it has made real progress on the issue, citing for example a literacy program it started for workers in Indonesia. Even activists acknowledge some basic improvements in working conditions. For instance, Nike has replaced the solvent toluene, which can produce harmful fumes, with a water-based cement on most production lines. Still, critics say they haven't done enough. "You get the sense they're flailing around, trying to make enough changes to satisfy critics without making changes that cost lots of money," says Medea Benjamin, executive director of Global Exchange, a San Francisco-based activist group.

Getting Nike back on the fast track will require a broad effort. Knight must wean it away from the Old Nike, sometimes literally. Last year, he carved off the part of the business that makes products for extreme sports into a separate unit called ACG—short for "all-conditions gear." The ACG group moved into its own floor in a building away from the main footwear business and built its own staff, budget, and marketing plan.

Why the separation? Nike has failed to build credibility among fans of nontraditional sports, a small but important demographic that tends to originate fashion trends among teens. "To certain kids who are still excited about the NFL, Nike might still be cool. But to the portion of Generation Y that's individual-oriented and identifies with these newer sports it isn't relevant," says Gary H. Schoenfeld, CEO of Vans Inc., maker of shoes and clothing for skateboarders, snowboarders, and surfers.

Even at the Magdalena Ecke Family YMCA Skate Park in Encinitas, Calif., which Nike helped to rebuild a few years ago with a $100,000 donation, many kids don't know that Nike makes a skateboard shoe. Some of those who do aren't impressed. "Nikes aren't good at all," says 10-year-old Jesse Satterfield, who wears Osiris shoes. "They wear down easily, and they're not comfortable."

ACG is supposed to change that. Knight put the business under the charge of Gordon O. McFadden, a 17-year veteran of Norwegian outdoor-apparel maker Helly Hansen. Four of the five top ACG executives are outsiders, hired from places like Dr Pepper/Seven Up Inc. and Fila Holding. A skier, snowboarder, and mountain biker himself, McFadden, 49, is developing new products, such as a $175 snowboarding jacket with a dozen pockets designed to hold such essentials as gloves, goggles, and headphones. To learn these markets, he's putting 15 or 20 designers in a studio close to the action in Southern California, the epicenter of the skateboarding and surfing worlds. And ACG will soon take the wraps off a clog-like shoe, the Rufus, that it hopes will slow the onslaught of "brown shoes," the hiking boots and other casual footwear that many young customers prefer over athletic shoes.

But ACG knows that cool new products alone won't solve Nike's problems: The company needs a new image to go with them. ACG plans to start its first big marketing push in June, with new print ads and in-store promotions. And starting this September, McFadden intends to open dozens of ACG stores at ski lodges and outdoor resorts. The new stores and products will bear ACG's logo: an inverted triangle with the letters ACG underscored by a swoosh. McFadden expects ACG's sales of action-sports products to grow by about 20% annually, compared with an 8% rate before the unit was given its independence. "We've got a startup mentality," says McFadden. "They want us to break rules, be the kind of renegade Nike was when Phil started."

But this isn't the '70s. To project that kind of attitude in the new millennium, a strong Internet presence is a must. Until recently, however, Nike was clueless when it came to cyberspace. But last summer, Knight invited a star-studded cast of Net-industry executives to educate Nike employees about the Web. One speaker, Novell Inc. CEO Eric E. Schmidt, recalls: "Phil got up at the beginning and said: 'I don't understand all this stuff, but it's incredibly important, and we're going to get ahead of it.'"

Now, Knight meets with his Internet team daily. Topics include ways to drive traffic to Nike.com and partnerships, such as the one with Ask Jeeves Inc., which recently added an automated customer-service feature to the site. Nike's electronic commerce site, which has been selling shoes for almost a year, was jazzed up recently to let customers choose colors and personalize them with a name or jersey number.

Nike is pushing the envelope in other key areas, too. It now takes Nike, and much of the industry, about 18 months to design and produce a shoe. Roland Wolfram, hired from SBC's Pacific Telesis unit in 1998, is trying to cut that to 12 months, and even shorter on some products. "Traditionally, Nike has relied on its product excellence and brand moxie, but we also want to have this other leg of the stool to stand on," says Wolfram.

Shortening the design and manufacturing cycle has implications up and down the sales chain. Right now, Nike has to place its bets far in advance of actual demand, leaving it vulnerable to swift changes in fashion. Last year, for instance, it ordered 400,000 pairs of one of its sports sandals from its contract factories. But when the actual retail orders came in months later, they totaled more than a million pairs, leaving Nike scrambling to fill the demand.

Nike is also putting in place an automatic replenishment system that ships out basic, high-volume merchandise without waiting for retailers to place orders. In the past, retailers often ran out of simple polo-style tops or shorts. That hurt sales of higher-priced items like halter tops, since consumers frequently purchase basic and fashion items together. Nike is now selling $100 million of merchandise a year through auto-replenishment. Retailers say the improvements have smoothed out many of the supply problems that dogged the company in 1998. "They're delivering on time, something that was a real challenge," says John Douglas Morton, CEO of Denver-based Gart Sports Co., which operates 130 apparel and equipment stores.

If this sounds like a more disciplined and calculated approach to doing business, it is. A good part of the enforcement has fallen to Clarke, a 20-year Nike veteran who became president in 1994. He has spent much of the past two years increasing financial accountability around the company to make employees more conscious of sales performance and expenses. In 1998, Nike gave managers in each region—the U.S., Europe, Asia, and Latin America—their own profit-and-loss statements and now ties compensation more closely to performance.

As part of the new emphasis on financial responsibility, Knight and Clarke are pounding home the need to cut costs. Layoffs and cutbacks have hit every area of the company. Nike last year held its annual executive retreat in Beaverton—a far cheaper alternative to the seaside resort in the Netherlands where managers gathered a few years back. Little things count, too, these days: In the past, Nike paid its advertising agency to assemble videos highlighting new products for the retreat. Last year, it did that work itself.

Knight admits that his unconventional style—he was known to disappear from day-to-day operations for weeks at a time—contributed to his company's current predicament. In April, 1998, Knight summoned the headquarters staff to "the Bo," Nike's gymnasium named for former football/baseball star Bo Jackson. There, Knight apologized for taking his eye off the ball during Nike's boom years and failing to prepare it for the rough times that followed (Exhibit 2).

EXHIBIT 2
Take Our Swoosh.
Please

In the old days, Nike Inc. didn't have to do a lot of research to figure out what kids thought was cool. The answer was "Nike." For years, the brand was a mainstay of Young & Rubicam's annual survey of preferred labels among teens. But three years ago, it fell off the list and has yet to climb back on. Even sales of its once hot Air Jordan sneakers are down. Business at its glitzy NikeTown stores has dropped off, too. Says Marian Salzman, who heads the Brand Futures Group at Young & Rubicam Inc.: "Nike just ain't cool."

What went wrong? Nike was hurt by accusations that it fosters sweatshop factory conditions overseas. But there were basic marketing mishaps, too. Lackluster ads, a series of fashion miscues, and overexposure of the swoosh all damaged Nike's image. To fight back, the company is listening hard these days to what kids say they're interested in—instead of assuming it already knows.

Gen Bending

Take its latest TV ads, launched in January. They're a complex blend of celebrity athletes, teenspeak, and the Internet. In one, champion sprinter Marion Jones challenges viewers to a race. The camera weaves through a maze of streets and houses and winds up crashing into a man juggling chainsaws. It ends with a shot of airborne, whirring saws, a scream—and a Web address, whatever.nike.com. There, visitors can choose from among several possible conclusions, including one in which Jones punches the viewer in the nose. In another, the viewer is decapitated by a chainsaw. It's more than just an attention-getting ad: The company says the campaign has boosted online orders for sneakers. Another recent campaign features famous athletes displaying the physical costs of competition: scars, missing fingers, and knocked-out teeth.

But Nike has also figured out that national ad campaigns only go so far with younger consumers. "Generation Y wants a sense of having discovered it themselves," says Wendy Liebmann, president of New York-based marketing consultant WSL Strategic Retail. That means getting the message out through narrowly targeted sponsorships or events, like the stickball game that Nike staged last year between the Yankees and the Mets.

Nike is still doing plenty of big-ticket endorsements and sponsorships. But it is targeting some of those dollars differently. Nike's push into women's and girl's athletic gear got a huge boost from the company's support of the Women's World Cup soccer tournament last summer. The company followed up the famous image of a victorious Brandi Chastain ripping off her jersey by rolling out products such as its line of $47 "Inner Actives" sports bras. "Athletic bras that work without smashing you down," says one ad.

To combat a sense among kids that Nike is simply ubiquitous, the company is starting to use its powerful swoosh symbol more selectively. One former Nike executive recalls a meeting in early '98 where product designers and marketers scrutinized a running shoe and discovered it had at least nine swooshes. "No one had ever really counted," he says. Now, Nike CEO Philip H. Knight is looking for less obvious ways to use the logo. "If you blast it on every T shirt, every sign in the soccer match, you dilute it," says Knight. "There's more thought given to how we use it."

The biggest blow to Brand Nike has been the controversy surrounding its overseas labor practices. Top execs now take the issue seriously and have made efforts, from contests to ads in college papers, to keep kids informed of the changes they've made. Knight thinks Nike is making headway. "You're seeing a bit of resurgence with the younger consumer," he says hopefully. Now, if he can't just translate that momentum into store traffic, he just might score a come-from-behind victory with kids.

By Louise Lee in Beaverton, Ore.

Despite that mea culpa, Knight shrugs off any suggestions that the struggles of the past two years have transformed him personally. But he acknowledges that he has had to swallow some pride. "Where's a fine line between being a certain size and being a bully. And we don't want to be a bully," he says. He acknowledges that creating a big-company culture "is not as much fun, but I think it's part of the evolution you've got to go through."

Knight hasn't given up hope that his company can regain its old stride. "I don't think we're middle-aged, I think we're in our twenties. I think there is great opportunity for growth," he says gamely. But putting Nike back on track will require a delicate balancing act—taming the company's brash, in-your-face style while injecting a new sense of vigor. Nike's CEO likes to point out that he has weathered other rough patches. "This is the fourth downturn in 18 years as a public company. I said going into the 1990s that if we can get through it with only two downturns, we'll have a great decade. And I'll look forward to 2000 through 2010 coming up with the same statement." That may be the only good thing about slowing down as you get older—it gives you a chance to put things in perspective.

Source: Louise Lee, "Can Nike Still Do It?" *Business Week,* February 21, 2000, 120–22, 124, 126, 128.

Case 2–3

Campbell Soup Co.

CAMDEN, N.J.—When R. David C. Macnair, Campbell Soup Co.'s chief technical officer, summoned doctors and nutritionists for a preview of the company's promising new product, he wasn't prepared for the gasps as he unveiled a helping of mashed potatoes.

Unexpectedly, they were glowing bright green.

The fluorescent spuds might have been a harbinger for Campbell back in 1992, as the soup company pursued its most ambitious and secretive product in a century: a regimen of nutrient-fortified meals promising therapeutic benefits and called Intelligent Quisine.

IQ would go beyond the increasingly popular low-fat products of the time, and Campbell backed its therapeutic claims with clinical trials at eight universities. Several medical experts and groups heralded the IQ line as a breakthrough: the first foods scientifically proven to lower high levels of cholesterol, blood sugar and blood pressure.

The testimonials were one reward for the seven years and $55 million Campbell would eventually invest in developing IQ, but a bigger payoff was expected in the marketplace. As the company began selling 41 breakfasts, lunches, dinners and snacks in a market test in Ohio in January 1997, then-Chief Executive David W. Johnson told analysts that Campbell foresaw $200 million in annual sales when the brand went nationwide.

But after 15 months in Ohio, Campbell yanked the line last March, surrendering to problems outside and within the company. While many test subjects enjoyed the meals and added their testimonials to those of the experts, others found the IQ line too expensive or lacking in variety. In the end, sales fell far short of expectations. Inside Campbell, Mr. Johnson's enthusiasm collided with the skepticism of his eventual successor, Dale Morrison. And in hindsight, some observers suggest that Campbell may have pulled out too soon, noting that IQ's therapeutic side made it analogous to a new drug, which can take more than two years to garner the support it needs from the medical establishment.

Campbell's own postmortem suggests the company may have bitten off more than it could chew. Spokesman Michael Kilpatric says, "Business results in Ohio didn't meet expectations and would have required more health-care resources, and that is not a core competency of Campbell." After its bold plunge into innovation, the big conservative company, built on one main product, went back to its breadwinner. Mr. Kilpatric says Campbell made a decision to exit the frozen-food business and "put our resources behind soup."

Did Campbell quit too soon? Other companies continue to regard so-called functional foods—snacks and meals with medical benefits—as the next blockbuster to snap stagnant sales in the $650 billion food industry, which has been suffering from a shortage of innovative hits. Kellogg Co., which spent $75 million to open a functional-food lab, is expected to launch new products early next year. ConAgra Inc. and Nestle SA are also developing what the industry has dubbed "nutraceuticals." By some estimates, sales of functional foods could reach $24 billion a year by 2001, as the huge baby-boomer population enters old age.

Campbell began casting about for a cutting-edge health food in 1990. At the time, the company was still king of soup, with more than three-quarters of the American market. But soup consumption had stalled, leaving the company worried about where future growth would come from just as rivals were digging into a hot new market. ConAgra's Healthy Choice and H. J. Heinz & Co.'s Weight Watchers frozen meals were taking off as Americans became more aware of the link between diet and disease.

So Campbell researchers began working to push the envelope, with foods that could help people manage or prevent ailments such as diabetes and cardiovascular disease. Campbell saw a demographic gold mine. About 58 million Americans have high-blood pressure and other forms of cardiovascular disease, America's No. 1 killer. An additional 16 million Americans have diabetes, the seventh leading cause of death.

In 1991, Dr. Macnair. who has a Ph.D. in biochemistry, assembled a medical advisory board comprising specialists in nutrition, heart disease and diabetes to help Campbell run its foods through the scientific gauntlet. It would be an expensive undertaking, but it had a lot of support at the top from Mr. Johnson, IQ's biggest champion.

Plucked from the chief executive's job at Novartis AG's Gerber Products, Mr. Johnson arrived at Campbell in 1990 with orders to boost sagging earnings and soup sales. He soon resurrected an early version of the healthful food product, which had been referred to internally as Project Apple. He was drawn to the "explosive potential," as he now puts it, of "something that tastes great, is good for you, and is therapeutically as effective as a drug."

Soon he was dropping in on the medical advisory board, sitting through technical discussions on systolic and diastolic blood pressures. "Wouldn't you be dumbfounded by the opportunity to take a quantum leap and develop a product that could help improve the health and nutrition of the world?" asks Mr. Johnson, now 66 years old and Campbell's chairman.

Few inside Campbell knew anything about the development work, which was initially code-named Project Nightingale (as in Florence). Campbell kept IQ researchers away from the rest of the company, and organized some of them into small, segregated groups that focused on snacks or desserts. Mr. Johnson and Dr. Macnair were so fearful of a leak that many top Campbell executives were kept in the dark. Marketing tasks were farmed out with demands for total confidentiality.

Developing a menu of meals packed with vitamins and minerals pushed Campbell's food-technology skills to the limit, and not just on mashed potatoes. (Dr. Macnair says he never figured what caused the green glow; he suspects it had something do with oxidation or heating of the nutrients added.) Of the early entrees, Mary Winston, a retired science consultant at the American Heart Association, says, "The best analogy would be airline meals." An early fiber-enriched dinner roll "could have been marketed as a hockey puck," Dr. Macnair recalls.

By late 1994, Campbell had developed what it considered 24 palatable meals, or about a week's worth, and the medical advisory board began conducting clinical trials at the eight universities where the board members worked. Of the 560 subjects who ate the meals for a 10-week period, 73% lowered their blood cholesterol from what were considered high levels, 75% reduced their blood pressure and 62% reduced their blood sugar. None of the testers experienced any side effects that can accompany medications, Campbell says, though some reported having a little gas.

"I've never had so much blood drawn before in my life," says Mary Ann Haisch, 57, a trial participant from Vancouver, Wash. She was provided with free chow for 10 weeks. In return, she had to check into a clinic regularly, have four samples of blood taken and answer questions about her well-being, including her sex life. Her cholesterol dropped to 200 milligrams a deciliter from 240, and she lost 13 pounds. And the food? "Best raisin bran I ate in my life," she says. But the dinner roll, speckled with nutrients, she says, tasted like a grainy "energy bar."

With the clinical trials going well, Campbell turned to marketing issues, preparing for a yearlong market test. Up to this point, trial subjects had gotten their meals in plain, white boxes. But Campbell's marketing department and consultants began conjuring up a name for the food and flashy packaging. It chose "Intelligent Quisine" and designed medicinal-looking blue boxes and cans for dishes such as French toast with sausage, New England clam chowder and sirloin beef tips. Each week, 21 meals, most of them frozen, would be delivered to a buyer's door by United Parcel Service.

By early 1995, at Dr. Macnair's suggestion, Mr. Johnson created a new division called the Center for Nutrition and Wellness, with the nutritionists' "food pyramid" as its logo. It employed more than 30 nutrition scientists, dietitians and others, and was based at the Camden, N.J., headquarters in Building 81, known for its wide open offices and occasional squirrel infestations.

Two years later, in January 1997, IQ was ready to stride into Ohio with fanfare. "Introducing the first and only meal program clinically proven to help people reduce high cholesterol, blood pressure and blood sugar," blared a print ad in Ladies' Home Journal. A 10-minute infomercial showed men and women in lab coats, inspecting tomatoes, cauliflower and spices.

All the ads featured trial participants. "When I was first diagnosed with high cholesterol, I got scared. . . . Now I get the food I love and my cholesterol went down 36 points," one testified. Another proclaimed: "I ate cheesecake on the meal program and my cholesterol went down 15 points."

At Campbell's phone bank in Salt Lake City, the toll-free switchboard lit up, but when the callers were told that IQ's one-week "sample pack" cost $80 and that the recommended 10-week plans went for $700, many hung up. The price was just too high for many older people who live on Social Security and other sources of fixed income. Etta Saltos, a nutritionist at the U.S. Department of Agriculture, ordered a week's worth of meals for her father, a diabetic who lived alone in Ohio. "When he found out what they cost," she says, he "put them in the freezer for a rainy day."

Campbell also tapped the medical community for marketing help. The company sought what it called the "implied endorsement" of hospitals, health-maintenance organizations and insurers, which could then target their thousands of members in direct mailings. The IQ team quickly persuaded the Cleveland Clinic, for one, to distribute meals and promotional material to its heart patients.

In addition, Campbell hired 24 part-time pharmaceuticals salespeople to storm doctors offices around Ohio. May Ann DiStasi of Cincinnati met with 25 physicians a week, zapping IQ meals in their office microwaves, and serving them for lunch or a snack. After her pitch, she left behind IQ "scratch pads" resembling prescription pads.

IQ wasn't always warmly received. In January 1997, at a lunch at the American Heart Association's Columbus, Ohio, office, about 40 dietitians and other professionals noshed on salad with IQ dressing, and chicken divan with rice, as Campbell touted IQ's clinical-trial results. But in the back of the room, some dietitians groused that IQ offered nothing more than a motivated person could whip up on his own, recalls Yvonne Sebastian, a program manager with the American Diabetes Association who attended the meeting.

Meanwhile, Mr. Johnson was working the Wall Street crowd, bragging to analysts at a food-industry convention in Florida of the healing power of IQ. Most had paid little attention to the embryonic product. The headline for one analyst's report in late 1996 reflected the skepticism: "UPS T.V. Dinners Drive Top Line?"

By March 1997, the doubts had surfaced in-house: Several division presidents at Campbell had begun questioning the costly project they knew so little about. To appease them, Mr. Johnson called for a review, and a team of consultants from the Boston Consulting Group swept into Building 81 to size up the business prospects for IQ. Mr. Morrison, Campbell's new head of international and specialty foods and a leading contender to succeed Mr. Johnson, thought IQ's $20 million budget was excessive, slashed it to $13 million, and poured the savings into Campbell's overseas expansion.

Two months later, with the consultants still hovering, sales results in Ohio were looking bad. Fewer than 2,500 people had ordered slightly more than six weeks' worth of food on average—far short of the yearlong target of 40,000 orders. Desperate to rev up sales, Campbell had its salespeople cold-call those who had previously ordered IQ meals, offering discounts.

Some IQ diners did notice dramatic changes in their health and lifestyle. Yvonne Holsinger, 72, saw her blood sugar dip to between 110 and 135 milligrams a deciliter from more than 300 after 10 weeks. So dedicated was she that she was able to quit taking the medication Glyburide for her adult-onset diabetes.

Others, however, found the IQ meal program tedious. Patricia Bowers, a 68-year-old diabetic, got tired of the same eight or nine dinners over about 40 weeks. She called the IQ 800 number to complain and was happy to hear there was a pizza on the drawing board.

In June, the consultants recommended to Mr. Morrison that Campbell quit trying to drum up grass-roots support from consumers and individual doctors and instead set up storefronts near medical clinics where the infirm could pick up their meals and receive dietary counseling.

But by July 1997, the tide was turning against IQ within Campbell. Mr. Johnson relinquished his position as chief executive officer, and Mr. Morrison, as expected, became president and CEO. The former executive of PepsiCo Inc.'s Frito-Lay unit had a specific game plan: to focus on key brands and expand overseas. He spun off Campbell's huge Swanson and Vlasic businesses and smaller lines, representing $1.4 billion of Campbell's $7.9 billion in sales for the fiscal year ended July 1997.

And he began the death watch for IQ by putting it on the corporate back burner. With no marketing budget for the project, Campbell stopped promoting IQ, although it continued funding new clinical trials and working with the Cleveland Clinic. Researchers at the Center for Nutrition and Wellness were reassigned to other Campbell divisions. Finally, last fall, Campbell made plans to sell IQ, at a price tag that has varied from as much as $15 million to as little as $3 million.

Campbell certainly had gathered some important market intelligence on functional foods. IQ showed that many Americans resist a long-term eating plan; they want a quick fix, a magic bullet. The project's fate also may reflect the impatience of food companies.

Dr. Macnair and some marketing people began making IQ presentations at companies including Bristol-Myers Squibb Co. and Monsanto Co. And the team prepared for IQ's sale by creating a "due-diligence room" at Building 81, with all of the marketing material, clinical-trial results and packaging on display. No prospects showed, and today that room in Building 81 is empty and dark.

Source: Vanessa O'Connell, "Food for Thought: How Campbell Saw a Breakthrough Menu Turn into Leftovers," *The Wall Street Journal,* October 6, 1998, A1, A12. Copyright 1998 by Dow Jones & Co. Inc. Reproduced with permission of Dow Jones & Co. Inc. in the format textbook via Copyright Clearance Center.

Case 2–4

Pfizer, Inc., Animal Health Products (A)*

Kipp Kreutzberg was putting the finishing touches on his marketing plan for the coming year. As the senior marketing manager of Pfizer's Cow/Calf Division, he was responsible for a full range of animal health products that Pfizer marketed to cattle ranchers, including vaccines for newborn calves and their mothers, medications (dewormers, antidiarrheals, etc.), and antibiotics (for pneumonia and other diseases). Pfizer positioned its products on the combination of superior science (resulting from its significant R&D efforts) and high-quality production/quality control techniques. Pfizer's pride in its sophisticated research and development was based on its new and useful products for the market. The company invests more in research and development than any other animal health company does.

Pfizer historically had segmented ranchers in the cow/calf business on the basis of herd size, as shown in Exhibit 1.

"Hobbyists" are so called because in many cases these ranchers run their cattle as a sideline to another job. For example, a schoolteacher may keep a herd of cattle simply because he grew up on a ranch and couldn't imagine not doing so. In many cases hobbyists' ranch income accounts for a minor percentage of their overall income. The average age of hobbyists is 50 years, and 15 percent have a college degree. They have been in the cattle business for an average of 26 years and spend 51 percent of their time with their cattle businesses.

The main livelihood of "traditionalists" is their cattle operation. The average age of traditionalists is 51 years, and 26 percent have a college degree. They have been in the cattle business for 30 years and spend 70 percent of their time with their cattle operations.

The "business" segment operations are headed by ranchers who average 53 years of age, 22 percent of whom have a college degree, and who average 33 years in the business. They spend 80 percent of their time with their cattle. These large ranch businesses are owned either by a family or by a corporation.

Pfizer had an extensive network of field sales representatives who visited ranchers to inform them of products, offer seminars on herd health, and sponsor industry activities such as stock shows and 4-H. Time spent with accounts typically is allocated on the basis of volume of product purchased. Ranchers then buy the animal health products they need from either a veterinarian or a distributor/dealer (typically, animal feed stores and similar establishments). The field sales reps also call on the vets and distributors/dealers to help them manage inventory and inform them of new products and merchandising programs.

EXHIBIT 1
Pfizer Market Segmentation, 1998

Segment	No. Cattle	No. Operations	Percent of National Cattle Inventory
Hobbyist	<100	808,000	50%
Traditionalist	100–499	69,000	36
Business	500+	5,900	14

*This case was written by Jakki Mohr and Sara Streeter, University of Montana. © Copyright by Jakki J. Mohr, 1999. All rights reserved. Support from the Institute for the Study of Business Markets, Pennsylvania State University, is greatly appreciated.
Some of the information in this case has been modified to protect the proprietary nature of firms' marketing strategies. The case is intended to be used as a basis for class discussion rather than to illustrate either effective or ineffective marketing strategies.

The Problem: Industry Challenges and Change and a Need to Evaluate Segmentation Practice

As the leader of the marketing team, Kipp recognized that his customers were facing some daunting challenges that would result in significant changes in the industry, changes that probably would affect Pfizer's animal health business. For example, the market share of beef products had declined from 44 percent in 1970 to 32 percent in 1997, while pork and poultry had gained share. The decline in beef consumption was due in part to well-known concerns about cholesterol and fat. In addition, preparation issues affected the demand for beef, as they did for poultry and pork demand as well. For example, two-thirds of all dinner decisions are made by a consumer on the same day. In these same-day decisions, three-fourths of the consumers still don't know what they are going to make as late as 4:30 P.M. Obviously, many beef products require cooking and preparation time, and this limits consumer selection.

Of course, other types of meat products also require cooking and preparation time. A key difference, however, is that consumers were being bombarded with new products from the poultry and pork industries. For example, in 1997 Tyson Foods introduced stuffed chicken entrees, roasted chicken dinners, Southwest-style blackened fajitas, and a host of other creative products. The names Tyson and Purdue are well recognized by the public, unlike the names of most beef products.

Some of the changes that had occurred in the poultry and pork industries were expected to diffuse into the cattle industry. Industry analysts believed that the beef industry would need to develop products that could be more easily prepared and develop branded products that consumers could recognize and rely on for quality and convenience.

In addition, industry analysts believed that the beef industry would have to improve the quality of its products in terms of more consistent taste and tenderness. Beef quality is assessed on the basis of U.S. production targets for tenderness, juiciness, flavoring, and marbling (fat) of cuts of beef. The targets are based on two dimensions. The first dimension is based on taste quality (tenderness and juiciness) and specifies that 70 percent of beef production should be rated high quality (choice or prime). The second dimension is based on yield and specifies that 70 percent of beef cattle should be rated grade 1 or grade 2 (implying a good amount of beef for the carcass size), with 0 percent poor yield (meaning that the carcass did not yield much meat). Currently, only 25 percent of beef cattle meet these criteria.

One way to improve the percentage of cattle meeting these criteria is participation in the Beef Quality Assurance program run through the federal government. This is a voluntary quality control program that is based on the education, awareness, and training of cattle producers to influence the safety, quality, and wholesomeness of beef products. It specifies injection sites (neck versus rump) for shots, a seven-step quality check for cows, a method and location for branding, and so forth. Forty percent of ranchers say they have participated in this program in the last two years, among whom 67 percent have changed the way they manage their cattle.

In summary, consumer demand for beef products had declined over the years, resulting in a situation of overcapacity, which depressed prices. A flood of imports resulting from NAFTA regulations further worsened the situation, as did high prices for feed. Most industry analysts were predicting a period of consolidation and alliances. Furthermore, many industry experts expected that beef would have to improve in quality and be better marketed and packaged to fit consumers' changing lifestyles.

Kipp wondered how the ranchers, who were the lifeblood of his division's sales, would handle the changes. From reports by the sales representatives in the field, he knew that the situation was dire for many ranchers. He wondered whether Pfizer's approach to marketing took account of the complicated situation. In particular, the Cow/Calf Division had been segmenting the market of ranchers on the basis of herd size for at least 15 years. In light of the significant challenges posed by industry changes, Kipp wondered whether his team's approach to the marketplace was still a useful one. Perhaps a different approach to segmenting the market might allow his division to develop more effective marketing strategies in light of the changes looming on the horizon.

Research Method

To provide some insight into the continued viability of segmenting the market on the basis of herd size, Kipp asked Joan Kuzmack, the manager of marketing research for the Livestock Division, to conduct a series of depth interviews with cattle ranchers in the Rocky Mountain/Midwest region. These interviews offer qualitative insights into behavioral and attitudinal differences among cow/calf ranchers. More specifically, the objectives of the research were to do the following:

- Identify the inputs driving ranchers' success as cow/calf producers.

- Identify whether ranchers' values and beliefs about herd management differed by herd size.

- Determine what motivates cow/calf producers in selecting products.

- Examine ranchers' views about the future.

A stratified random sample was used to select ranchers for interviews. Rocky Mountain and Upper Midwest ranchers in each of the three groups (hobbyist, traditionalist, and business) were identified and randomly selected from within those strata. Exhibit 2 provides descriptive statistics on the types and numbers of ranchers interviewed.

Ranchers were asked a variety of questions, using a semistructured questionnaire. The questionnaire focused on their herd management activities; attitudes, values, and beliefs about herd management; and views of the future trends in their industry.

Research Findings

Inputs Driving Ranchers' Success as Cow/Calf Producers

The results from the interviews suggested that commercial producers across all three herd-size categories look for maximum output (weight gain, number of calves) with the minimum inputs. They attempt to improve the quality of their calves through *health and nutrition programs, genetics, and herd culling.* Activities used to manage the herd include vaccinations, nutrition, and breeding programs. Ranchers also strive for uniformity in the calves, typically on the basis of size. These goals in managing the herd are traded off against the cost of achieving them. As one respondent stated:

> We strive for the largest amount of production with the least amount of input going in. That's really the only thing we can control at this point with the economy the way it is. We can't control the price that we get for our product, so the only way we can make ends meet is to control the input cost.—Traditionalist

Some ranchers also focused on range management of their grasslands as another objective in managing their operations:

EXHIBIT 2
**Summary of Types
of Ranchers
Interviewed**

	Hobbyist	Traditionalist	Business
Number of Interviews	3	6	3
Size of Herd			
<100	3		
100–250		2	
251–500		4	
501–1,000			2
>1,000			1
Percent of Time Spent with Cattle			
<80%	2		1
81–90%			
91–99%		1	
100%	1	5	2
Percent of Income from Cattle			
<80%	3	2	1
81–90%		2	1
91–99%		1	1
100%		1	
Type of Operation*			
Seed stock	2	2	
Commercial	1	4	3

Seed-stock operators focus on breeding high-quality bulls for use by commercial producers. The bulls are measured by the quality of their offspring. Desirable characteristics include low birth weight, rapid growth, high carcass yield, and grading of choice or better-quality meat. *Commercial producers* raise calves to sell to feedlots. The feedlots fatten the calves, are sold to packing houses, and move on to the retail distribution channel for consumers. In some cases, commercial producers retain ownership of their calves, in which case the rancher pays the feedlot to feed out the calves but the rancher still owns them. Then the rancher sells the calves to the packing houses.

Basically I think of us as ranchers; we're in the business of grass managers. We grow grass, and if we don't manage our lands to grow a lot of grass, the right kind of grass, we can't run the cows properly. All the genetics in the world won't be of use without the right grass.—Traditionalist

The degree to which ranchers felt that *health management* was critical to their herds' success varied greatly. Some valued herd health as one of the most important concerns:

You start off with the best breeding that you think you can do through bull selection. From there, it goes on with nutrition and herd health. You're expecting more from the cows. You have to put more into them with nutrition and herd health. You can't cut corners on either one of those. Some feeds will be cheaper some years than others, but we stay with the same drugs.—Traditionalist

Others tended to put in the bare minimum into herd health, sometimes because they were uncertain what results the health management programs yielded:

We only do the bare minimum on health care. We do more of a preventative maintenance than anything else. We don't do any more than we have to because you can vaccinate for so many things. Our philosophy has been, if you don't need it, don't do it. You can get an awful lot of money in your cows giving them shots of stuff I don't know if you need.—Traditionalist

> I try to keep them healthy with shots and nutrition. I don't want to skimp on the health of a cow, but if I can save some money by supplementing different things in the ration or with vaccinations. . . . —Hobbyist

Seed-stock producers were seeking "best genetics," a loosely defined goal that commonly focused on breeding bulls that would maximize weight gain in commercial calves. Seed-stock producers consistently used artificial insemination in their cows and kept computer records to track information on their herds. They used software programs provided through the breed association to record animal registry and performance information.

Use of Information in Herd Management

To aid in herd management, most of the ranchers in the hobbyist and traditionalist categories collected information on their cows and calves. The information collected on calves included birth date, birth weight, sex, and weaning weight. The information collected on the cows included calving history, mothering ability (temperament and/or milk production), calving ease, and which cows birthed the replacement heifers. This information typically was handwritten in a book of some type. The ranchers maintained an intimate familiarity with their cattle and saw them as individuals.

> We knew everything there was to know about our cattle. . . . We knew more about our cattle than we did about our family. We could tell you every calf a cow had, pretty much the exact minute she had it every year. I've got little books here that I wrote everything down exactly.—Traditionalist

In the business category, ranchers collected some information on their cows and calves. That information might be collected on an exception basis because of the number of head with which the ranchers were working. The ranchers were familiar with their cattle, but not to the degree demonstrated by the owners of smaller herds.

Some ranchers used a very sophisticated approach to gathering information in order to refine their herd management practices. For example, one purebred operation sent some of its calves to a test station where all the calves from various ranches were fed and cared for similarly. This allowed the rancher to show how well his bulls stacked up to bulls from other ranches in a controlled experiment. Another rancher stated:

> We've performed quite a few experiments of our own over the years, and still do. I have a fair sense of what a true experiment is with controls and so forth. We get a lot of cooperation from the pharmaceutical industry. We've tested new products such as ear tags. We get a lot of things free as long as we're willing to put in some controls and report on the results. I enjoy that sort of thing. We've had some experiments going for a couple of years on range management. The opportunities are out there if you're co-operative. I think I probably have an advantage because I know how to conduct an experiment. We can get information firsthand from experiments we conduct ourselves. . . . We've changed our method of supplementing cattle in the winter. We're using more expensive supplements that don't rely on salt. We seem to distribute cattle better. I think it worked. It's cheaper in the long run because you have more grass.—Business

The changes made on the basis of the information ranchers collected varied in their sophistication. Some made changes that were based primarily on judgment and intuition.

> It's done by eye and is not as scientific as it could be.—Business

> A lot of times you know in the back of your mind what you want to do with a cow. It's sure nice to have the records, because you go back and refer to it.—Hobbyist

Many of the ranchers attempted to get information back from the feedlot on their calves in order to assess how well they did after leaving the ranch. In some cases they also received carcass data, which allowed them to assess weight gain, quality of the meat, and other types of information.

There were isolated but notable exceptions to gathering and using information about the herd. One rancher kept no information on his herd, did not attempt to get new information on herd management practices, and relied strictly on the information "in his head" based on his cumulative years of experience. Another said:

> It was just a matter of whatever the good Lord gives them when they come out; that's what they are. I can't change that very much.—Hobbyist

The information ranchers gathered was used primarily as a tool in culling the herd. Culling of open (not pregnant) cows or those that were "unsatisfactory producers" usually occurred in the fall. In general, it seemed that changes in herd management were highly judgment-based. Cause-and-effect links for possible problems were hard to establish. For the larger herds, information was not collected on a detailed enough level to analyze and draw specific conclusions.

> Where I've got a thousand head, and we've got one full-time employee, we don't track detailed information on a cow-by-cow basis. I've always got a book with me, so when we're working them, I put things down in the book. That information will be put on the computer. After a while you kind of know your cows. It's visual, when you see things you don't like.—Business

Motivations in Selecting Products

Ranchers as a whole were interested in getting additional information about how to manage their operations better. They read industry trade publications, attended seminars, and talked to neighbors. They were most likely to view information as credible if it came from a local source that was familiar with specific local conditions. As a whole, it was clear that the person the ranchers trusted most was the veterinarian. The ranchers also found the animal health product firm reps to be a good source of information, but not as credible as the veterinarian.

> On a drug situation, I wouldn't necessarily trust one person over another, but I would certainly pay attention to my veterinarian. He knows my area and my situation better than the drug rep from the company does. Even though I know the drug rep from that company is going to represent the drugs he sells, I don't necessarily not trust what he says. I just like to have more information about what works in my environment. —Traditionalist

Ranchers bought their animal health products from both veterinarians and supply houses. Price was an important consideration but not an overwhelming concern.

Ranchers' Views about the Future

The ranchers all expressed concern about the future. The number one concern among the commercial hobbyists and traditionalists was the low prices for their calves. While business producers also were concerned about price for their "outputs" (cattle), they were concerned about the input side of the equation (expenses) as well. All the ranchers noted that with the low prices they were getting for their calves, they couldn't afford to maintain and replace the old, dilapidated equipment they were using.

It takes a lot of calves to buy a new pickup, when they want about $30K or something.—Hobbyist

[My number one concern is] pricing, and not just the price of the product but the price of what it costs to produce that product. Compare the price of beef with the price of machinery. Calves are bringing what they brought in the 60s, but a tractor costs three times as much.—Traditionalist

In addition, they noted the high price of land. One rancher stated, "The land around here grows houses better than cattle."

Ranchers spoke vehemently against NAFTA and the influx of cheaper imports.

Well, the biggest issue we have right now is NAFTA. NAFTA is probably the worst thing they've come up with. It has lowered our cattle market so bad, it's put a lot of people out of business, driving the prices down so low. It is not fair trade from the standpoint of shipping Australian cattle into Mexico; they become Mexican cattle and come right into the U.S. They can get our top dollar (whatever we're getting here—say, 60 cents) but were brought in through Mexico at 30 cents. They flooded the market. They didn't have to make as much; they don't have as much in their cattle. With this R-Calf thing, they're investigating Canada. Let's face it: They're overrunning our market. It takes away the supply and demand. It's not just affecting us, it's affecting everybody—for example, the beef business, the car business, the timber industry.—Traditionalist

Tightening environmental regulations (the Endangered Species Act, pesticides, water quality, etc.) also had an impact on the economics of ranching operations.

The increasing market strength of the packers was viewed with fear and trepidation and also with a sense of increasing helplessness. Ranchers sold their calves to the feedlots, which in turn sold them to the meatpackers. Packer concentration (four packers controlled 80 percent of the market) and the packers' perceived ability to set prices (the implication is "collusively") for the industry was a recurring theme. Moreover, fears of vertical integration by the packers, or packers that own their own cattle and feedlots, further worried the ranchers.

We have no market for our agriculture products. To back that up, when you've got packers controlling 80 percent of the cattle and they'll buy cattle for a half hour in the middle of the week, you either take the offer or you leave it. If you turn them down, pretty soon they won't come back and look at your cattle or price your cattle. This is where we're going to have to have more players in our market or we're going to have to become one of the major players against the packer in supplying food to the consumer. We cannot compete with packers that own their own cattle and slaughter their own cattle instead of paying the market value for cattle they don't own. So that's why I say we have no market. The grain is the same way, because basically, the same companies that control the grain control the cattle: Cargill, ConAgra, ADM. You just look through the hall of mergers. One of these days, if things don't change, we will know the true value of our food when the corporations get it and we're all working for those people. The consumer will find out what the value of it is.—Business

In general, the view among the commercial producers was one of extreme pessimism. They saw a lot of other ranchers going broke (but usually not themselves).

I think it's all offset by the good things, but sometimes you wonder. You have to wonder about your mentality. You work and you work and you work and you work and you work and then you sell your cows at a loss, and you think, "Why am I doing this?" Either I'm really stupid or really stubborn.—Traditionalist

I think the day that the old rancher who gets on his horse at daybreak and gets off his horse at sunset and never sees another human being, and everybody is knocking on his door to buy his calves—those days are through. I hate to admit it, but everywhere you turn, somebody is trying to put you out of business. If it isn't the Bambi-huggers, then it's the prices, and if it isn't that, then somebody's coming along with those brainy ideas. The small producer is really going to have to work at it to stay in business.—Traditionalist

Solutions: Value-Added Marketing, Branded Beef, and Quality

Ranchers were asked about possible solutions to the depressed prices they were facing. The solutions discussed in industry publications included value-added marketing, or marketing strategies designed to increase the value and quality customers receive from beef purchases, and a branded beef model. The development of branded beef would require a tracking system from "birth to beef" in the supply chain. Such tracking would allow standardized health, quality, and management protocols as well as improved feedback through the entire production model.

Branded beef production would move the industry from a cost-based (production) model to a value-added model. This change also would require the producers to be more closely linked to the feedlots to improve the quality of the beef. Better coordination along the supply chain would ensure an increased flow of information from the consumer to the producer. Alliances between the cow/calf producers and the feedlots would allow ranchers to better track the success of their calves (based on health and weight gain). Those data could allow the ranchers to further improve the genetics of their herds by tracking which cow-bull combinations had delivered the higher-yield calves. As part of these trends, some degree of integration or vertical coordination would occur in the beef industry. Ranchers would have to participate to ensure market access for their product. Ranchers would have to think beyond the boundaries of their own ranches.

Most ranchers were familiar with the concepts of value-added marketing and a branded beef model. However, most were dubious about their viability and impact on ranchers' independence.

I don't know if any kind of marketing at this point is going to get us where we need to be without a change in the price structure of cattle.—Traditionalist

If there is a demand for high-quality beef, then the market should show it, and the packers will start bidding more for a piece of that quality. There may be some niches somewhere that people can fall into, but it's not going to be the salvation of many ranches. What we need is a mass market. Whatever niche there is, is going to be saturated very quickly, and the price will come down. I think the solution is cutting costs. People are eating a tremendous amount of beef, but the production is enormous as well. Numbers are down, but tons are up. The amount of beef being eaten is still quite high. I just think that some people have got to quit producing beef.—Business

We are concerned about the vertical marketing approach big companies are introducing into the system. Ranchers are very independent-minded people. We are fearful about the control that companies will be able to exert on us.—Traditionalist

Skepticism about value-added marketing is also derived from history: Other programs used in the past to provide a more consistent product to the feedlots, with supporting documentation, did not result in noticeable price differences. Of all the information ranchers collected on their herds, only vaccination records seemed to be valued by cattle buyers. Ranchers with complete histories of their cattle were selling their calves at the same price as ranchers without that information. Hence, the information was not viewed as a way to command a premium for the calves.

> For many years, it seemed like having good health records on the calves didn't matter. One herd would keep excellent records and be real progressive, and the next-door neighbor was the exact opposite, and it was the exact same price for both. The local cattle buyers didn't give a premium to keep the records, give the vaccines. . . . There were green tag programs in the 1980s (we followed one) where the vet certified you used them [preconditioning records]. But the cattle buyers didn't pay a premium for them. They as much as said, "We don't care." Today, 10 years later, cattle buyers are starting to ask, Will you precondition your calves? Will they be "bunkbroke" (so when they get to the feedlot, the calves will be trained to go to a feedbunk to eat)? Will they be weaned? There's a stress period associated with weaning. So there's more of a focus on those questions now than there has been. But there's still no rule; it's not a given. It's still ambiguous when it comes to marketing the cattle whether the information matters or not [results in a better price for the cattle].—Traditionalist

The feeling was that price premiums, if any, would accrue to others in the supply chain (the packers, retailers, and others). Despite that, some with more progressive views noted the need to have more of a consumer focus in their efforts:

> We need better beef quality if we're going to increase consumption. A lot of the breed associations are concentrating on carcass quality right now. There's measurement; there's selection for marbling and yield on cattle. I think as long as there is a possibility there might be some added value, a person should start working on it a little bit, along with the other production traits. I think it's something to pay attention to.— Traditionalist

> I think in the future, all ranchers are going to have to retain ownership of their cattle more and follow them closer to the consumer. I think that's part of our problem right now with our packer concentration. The producer's going to have to be a meat producer and not just sell calves. I think some of our long-range goals are going to have to be to get closer to the consumer with our product and know what he wants instead of listening to the packer tell us what he wants.—Business

> The money in agriculture is not in producing it. It's in processing it. This is where more ranchers and farmers have to realize that you can't produce the raw product anymore; you've got to follow it on through.—Business

Ranchers also noted that the idea of consistent quality beef was important.

> I'm expecting to see a change to where quality is more important. I think, down the road, that it's going to be mandatory that you know exactly what your cattle are doing. Those that aren't producing well at the kill floors are going to come back to haunt you.—Business

Interestingly, each of the respondents who was interviewed felt that the quality of his or her beef was above average. However, there was some doubt about whether consistent quality could be achieved easily with range cattle.

> That's going to be pretty tough with cattle. With chickens and hogs, you can throw up a confinement building. One person can control *x* amount of hogs and turkeys and

chickens. But how do you do that with cattle? You can only have so many cattle in one spot because they're bigger and they need more feed. You're going to have to have pasture. It's going to be pretty tough to get everything uniform. There are a lot of small producers with just a few cows around.—Hobbyist

I'm not convinced that branded products are going to magically save the beef industry. I think we're in competition on a world scale, and we're going to have to cut our costs of production. I think we could get our costs down to about 45 cents per pound of critter sold if we had to. Our total production would go down, but I think our costs would go down more.—Business

Because of the doubts about the viability of moving to a branded beef model, ranchers tended to focus more on controlling the cost of inputs and weathering the current downturn in the production cycle. One respondent cited earlier summed this up as "striving for the largest amount of production with the least amount of input."

Rancher's Concluding Thoughts

Despite these hardships and concerns, the ranchers were passionate about their love for their lifestyle, feeling that the benefits of living a life on the land outweighed the drawbacks.

You get up in the morning and go out there, and everything's bright and fresh. We're fortunate in this part of the world that we don't have a lot of noise from cars and trains. It's gratifying to see what happens when spring turns around, new things start to grow, new animals come into the world. It's pretty special, something that you can't explain to a lot of people because they don't understand what you're talking about. . . . It isn't the highest-paying job in the world, but it's got a lot of happiness that money can't buy.—Traditionalist

They expressed pride in their work and a sense of ownership for feeding the country's people.

Back to the Segmentation Decision

As Joan perused the findings from the qualitative interviews, she wondered what she would report to Kipp about possible changes in their approach to market segmentation. Joan wondered whether their historical approach to segmenting the market on the basis of herd size was consistent with the changes in the industry and the changing needs of ranchers.

Despite the insights gathered, there was a lack of understanding of the various segments of beef consumers and their needs, how brand marketing could affect consumer demand, and how alliances within the supply chain could affect the ranchers' situation. Unfortunately, the fragmented nature of the cow/calf producers, combined with their focus on production rather than marketing, meant that the beef industry was not very consumer-focused.

As she pondered how all these pieces fit together, Joan began to brainstorm new ways to look at the market. She wanted to work with Kipp in developing a plan to maintain Pfizer's market position in light of the changes in the industry.

Designing Market-Driven Strategies

Chapter 6

Market Targeting and Strategic Positioning

Deciding which buyers to target and how to position the firm's products for each market target are the core dimensions of market-driven strategy, guiding the entire organization in its efforts to provide superior customer value. Effective targeting and positioning strategies are essential in gaining and sustaining superior organizational performance. Faulty decisions negatively affect performance.

Through effective targeting and positioning, Colgate-Palmolive achieved a major turnaround in the U.S. consumer goods market during the late 1990s with its toothpaste products.[1] Procter & Gamble's (P&G) Crest brand held a commanding market position for decades, yet by the end of 1997 Colgate's toothpaste market share had moved ahead of P&G's share. Colgate continues to hold the leadership position in this market. The two brands account for over half of total sales in this mature and highly competitive market. In an aggressive move to dominate toothpaste sales, Colgate introduced its Total brand in the United States, positioning the brand as a gum-disease fighter and toothpaste for bad breath. Total's broad-spectrum antibiotic, Trichosan, is used in several bacteria-fighting products. Total was the first oral pharmaceutical dentifrice approved by the U.S. Food and Drug Administration (FDA). Colgate's launch effort for Total included a 1998 promotion budget of $100 million. Colgate had already gained strong market positions for Total in over 100 other countries. The tests required by the FDA would take a few years, and so Colgate had some time to build market position before competitors could introduce a similar product.

In analyzing the successful strategies of companies like Colgate-Palmolive, one feature stands out. Each has a market target and positioning strategy that is a major factor in gaining a strong market position for the firm, although the specific strategies of companies are often quite different. Examples of effective targeting and positioning strategies are found in all kinds and sizes of businesses, including companies that market industrial and consumer goods and services.

We begin the chapter by examining market targeting strategy and discussing how targets are selected. Next, we consider strategic positioning and look at what is involved in developing the positioning strategy. We conclude with a discussion of how positioning effectiveness is determined.

Market Targeting Strategy

The market targeting decision identifies the people or organizations in a product-market toward which an organization directs its positioning strategy. Selecting good market targets is one of management's most demanding challenges. For example, should the organization attempt to serve all the people who are willing and able to buy a particular good or service or, instead, selectively focus on one or more subgroups? Study of the product-market, its buyers, the organization's capabilities and resources, and the structure of competition is necessary in order to make this decision. The situation analysis chapters in Part II provide important guidelines for the targeting decision.

Consider, for example, Dell Computer's decision to target business users of personal computers. This targeting focus is an important factor in Dell's competitive edge. Using an integrated direct selling approach (Internet, catalogs, and teams of inside and field salespeople), Dell's primary market targets are (1) Fortune 500 companies, (2) multinational companies in the Fortune 501 to 2,000 range, and (3) medium-size businesses with 200 to 2,000 employees.[2] These targets account for 70 percent of total sales and are serviced via direct salesperson contact, though Dell is perceived by many people as a mail order company. The medium-size business target is Dell's fastest-growing customer group.

Targeting Strategies

Targeting and positioning strategies consist of (1) identifying and analyzing the segments in a product-market, (2) deciding which segment(s) to target, and (3) designing and implementing a positioning strategy for each target.

Many companies use some form of market segmentation, since buyers have become increasingly differentiated in regard to their needs and wants. Microsegmentation (finer segmentation) is becoming popular, aided by effective segmentation and targeting methods such as database marketing and mass customization. The Internet offers an opportunity for direct access to individual customers. In the following discussion we assume that the product-market is segmented on some basis. Emerging markets may require rather broad macrosegmentation, resulting in a few segments, whereas more mature markets can be divided into several microsegments. A new market may need to advance to the growth stage before meaningful segmentation is feasible.

Targeting Alternatives

The targeting decision determines how many customer groups the organization will serve. Management may select one or a few segments or go after intensive coverage of the product-market by targeting most of the segments. A specific marketing effort (positioning strategy) is directed toward each target that management decides to serve. For example, PepsiCo, Inc., with its portfolio of beverage brands, targets major population groups within the total product-market. Several of the targets are quite large, and people may buy more than one of the Pepsi brands. The firm's market target strategy is guided by market segmentation since different brands, prices, distribution, and promotional programs are involved. Teens are a prime target for Mountain Dew. Segmentation is based on needs and motivations as well as demographics.

In certain product-markets organizations may select strategies that offer buyers a variety of products. While there is diversity in needs and wants, buyers' preferences are diffused, making it difficult to define segments.[3] Sometimes we may be unable to distinguish whether a firm is using a segmentation strategy or a variety strategy, and there may be some elements of both strategies present. For example, a firm may offer variety to buyers in a particular

EXHIBIT 6–1
**Market Targeting
Approaches**

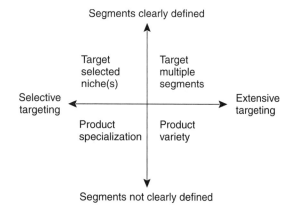

market segment. Providing customers different flavors or varieties of food and beverage products, such as Kellogg breakfast cereals, is an illustration of variety strategies.

Market targeting approaches tend to fall into two major categories: segment targeting and targeting through product differentiation. As shown by Exhibit 6–1, segment targeting ranges from a single segment to targeting all or most of the segments in the market. American Airlines uses extensive targeting in air travel services, as does General Motors with its different brands and styles of automobiles. An example of selective targeting is Autodesk's targeting of architects with its line of computer-aided design software. When segments are difficult to identify even though diversity in preferences exists, companies may appeal to buyers through product specialization or product variety. Product specialization involves offering buyers a product differentiated from competitors' products and designed to appeal to customer needs and wants not satisfied by a competitor's product. In contrast, the Vanguard Group offers a wide variety of mutual funds to investors that are not targeted to particular investor segments. Vanguard's variety-based positioning is intended to appeal to a wide array of customers, but in most cases it meets a subset of their investment needs.[4]

Factors Influencing Targeting Decisions

Market segment analysis, discussed in Chapter 4, helps to evaluate and rank the overall attractiveness of the segments under consideration as market targets. These evaluations include analysis of customers, competitor positioning, and the financial and market attractiveness of the segments under consideration. An important factor in targeting is determining the value requirements which are important to the buyers in the segment. Market segment analysis information is used to evaluate both existing and potential market targets. An interesting example of how Southwest Airlines uses the Internet to sell tickets is described in the E-Business Feature. The Web helps the airline simplify ticketing for the customers it targets.

Management needs to decide if the organization will target a single segment, selectively target a few segments, or target all or most of the segments in the product-market. The factors that influence the choice of the targeting strategy include:

- Stage of product-market maturity.

- Extent of diversity in preferences.

- Industry structure.

- Capabilities and resources.

- Opportunities for competitive advantage.

Can a Web site be too simple? A lot of Southwest Airlines Co. passengers thought so. After it became the first major carrier to sell tickets online in 1996, the airline says, its reservations center kept getting calls from customers who had just booked tickets on the site. The transactions happened so fast and so easily that they feared they had been scammed.

Not at all. For the scrappy low-fare king, simplicity—including one aircraft type, no meals, and a straightforward fare structure—has always been the key to satisfying customers and improving profits. Southwest's Spartan Web site, built on the same customer-service philosophy, is also winning passengers in droves. "Simple is better," says Ron E. Stewart, global managing partner for transportation and travel services at Andersen Consulting. "Bells and whistles don't sell tickets."

And therein lies the innovation: Southwest has shown that when it comes to the Web, less can be more. The airline now gets about 30% of its revenue from online bookings, almost all from its own site—compared with an estimated 6% to 7% for other big carriers, says Forrester Research Inc. That means big savings on commissions and reservation-system fees: Southwest expects the Web to save it $80 million this year, says Chief Financial Officer Gary C. Kelly.

Another big benefit is that this no-nonsense focus attracts more customers. "Southwest seems to be doing a much better job [than other airlines of] driving people to the Web," says Bear, Stearns & Co. analyst Robert A. LaFleur. In five years, he figures, Southwest could book 50% to 75% of its sales online.

With bigger rivals such as American Airlines Inc. furiously adding new features, such as wireless access to flight information, Southwest is trying to make sure the site stays as smart as it is simple, says Kevin Krone, Southwest's senior director of marketing automation. Since last fall, customers have been able to check the status of their frequent-flier credits online. And later this year, the company expects to add the ability to rent a car and check a flight's arrival or departure status.

Don't expect big changes, though. Southwest CEO Herbert D. Kelleher isn't likely to be swept up in Web mania: On the computer in his office is a Post-It note telling him how to turn it on. At Southwest, keeping it simple starts at the top.

Source: Wendy Zellner, "The Trick to Selling Airline Tickets Online? Minimalism," *Business Week E-Biz,* September 18, 2000, EB90.

We look at each factor to assess its influence on the market target decision. The relative importance of these factors often varies by company situation. The objective is to consider how each factor affects the market target strategy. Since several of the factors often vary according to the stage of product-market maturity, we use maturity as the basis for describing different targeting situations.

Targeting in Different Market Environments

The industry environment is influenced by the extent of concentration of its firms, the stage of its maturity, and its exposure to international competition. Five generic environments portray the range of industry structures:[5]

Emerging

Industries newly formed or re-formed are categorized as emerging, created by factors such as a new technology, the changing needs of buyers, and the identification of unmet needs by suppliers. The digital camera industry is illustrative.

Fragmented

Typically, a large number of relatively small firms make up the fragmented industry. No company has a strong position regarding market share or influence in this industry structure. Services like lawn care and industrial chemical distribution are examples of fragmented industries.

Transitional

These industries are shifting from rapid growth to maturity, as represented by the product life cycles of the products in the industry. Growing rapidly until reaching high levels of household penetration, microwave ovens are now in the maturity stage.

Declining

This industry structure is not cyclical, where sales rise and fall over time. Rather, a declining industry is actually fading away instead of experiencing a temporary decline. Word processing led to the decline of traditional typewriter producers.

Global

Firms in this category compete on a global basis. Examples include automobiles, consumer electronics, steel, and telecommunications. This classification may involve traditional or declining industry market situations.

These five industry categories are neither exhaustive nor mutually exclusive. Moreover, changing environmental and industry conditions may alter an industry classification. Also, rapid industry growth may occur in some countries while it is declining in other countries.

The stages of the life cycles of the products in the industry offer useful insights about the industry environment. The generic environments discussed above are closely related to the product life cycle (PLC) stages. Looking at competition during the product life cycle and at different product-market levels provides insights into different types and intensities of competition. We know that products, like people, move through life cycles.

The life cycle of a typical product is shown in Exhibit 6–2. Sales begin at the time of introduction and increase over the pattern shown. Profits initially lag sales, since expenses

EXHIBIT 6–2
Life Cycle of a Typical Product

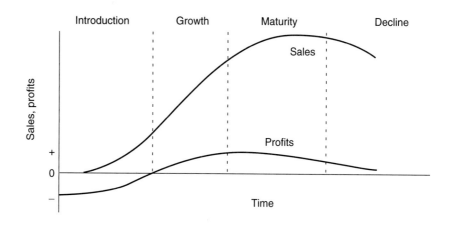

often exceed sales during the initial stage of the product life cycle as a result of heavy introductory expenses. Industry sales and profits decline after the product reaches the maturity stage. Often profits fall off before sales do.

Since an industry may contain more than one product-market and different industries may compete in a given market, it is useful to consider the market environment as the basis of discussion. Emerging, growth, mature, declining, and global market environments are described to illustrate different targeting situations.

Emerging Markets

"The most pervasive feature of emerging markets is uncertainty about customer acceptance and the eventual size of the market, which process and product technology will be dominant, whether cost declines will be realized, and the identity, structure, and actions of competitors."[6] Digital photography, which began to develop in the 1990s, is an example of an emerging market. Today digital photography is in the growth stage. Market definition and analysis are rather general in the early stages of product-market development. Buyers' needs and wants are not highly differentiated because buyers do not have experience with the product. Determining the future scope and direction of growth of product-market development may be difficult, as is forecasting the size of market growth.

Buyer Diversity

The similarity of buyers' preferences in the new product-market often limits segmentation efforts. It may be possible to identify a few broad segments. For example, heavy, medium, and low product usage can be used to segment a new product-market where usage varies across buyers. If segmentation is not feasible, an alternative is to define and describe an average or typical user, directing marketing efforts toward these potential users.

Industry Structure

Study of the characteristics of market pioneers indicates that new enterprises are more likely to enter a new product-market than are large, well-established companies. The exception is a major innovation in a large company coupled with strong entry barriers. The pioneers developing a new product-market "are typically small new organizations set up specifically to exploit first-mover advantages in the new resource space."[7] These entrepreneurs often have limited access to resources and must pursue product-market opportunities that require low levels of investment.

Industry development is influenced by the rate of acceptance of the product by buyers, entry barriers, the performance of firms serving the market, and future expectations. The pioneer's proprietary technology may make entry by others impossible until they can gain access to the technology. Xerox with its copying process and Polaroid with its instant film held monopoly positions for several years. Major change during the initial years is a common feature of emerging industries.

Capabilities and Resources

A firm entering a new product-market is more likely to achieve a competitive edge by offering buyers unique benefits rather than by offering lower prices for equivalent benefits, though cost may be the basis of superior value when the new product is a lower-cost alternative technology to an existing product. For example, fax transmission of letters and brief reports is both faster and less expensive than overnight delivery services. The development of e-mail capabilities gave this form of transmission an advantage over fax transmissions.

Research concerning the order of market entry indicates that the pioneer has a distinct advantage over firms subsequently entering the market. These studies estimate that the

EXHIBIT 6–3
**Illustrative
Market-Entry
Situations for New
Products**

Targeting Strategy	New Market	Existing Market
Single target	A. Targeting a new product-market (new drug for incurable disease)	B. Targeting existing product-market (digital photography)
Multiple targets	D. Targeting a few broad segments	C. Targeting several substitute markets (fax machines for overnight delivery and other substitutes)

second firm entering the market will obtain 60 to 70 percent of the share of the pioneer.[8] The pioneer can develop entry barriers, making it more difficult and costly for others to enter. The advantage of an early follower is the opportunity to evaluate the pioneer's performance and thus reduce the risk of entry failure. Entry timing may also depend on the firm's resources and skills.

Targeting Strategy

Despite the uncertainties in an emerging industry, some evidence indicates "that more successful or longer-living firms engage in less change than firms which fail."[9] Instead, these experienced firms select and follow a consistent strategy on a continuing basis. If this behavior is characteristic of a broad range of successful new ventures, then choosing the entry strategy is very important.

Several new product-market entry situations are shown in Exhibit 6–3. In situation A, the customer target is the potential user of a product that meets a need not previously satisfied. A cure for the AIDS virus is an example. The market target for this type of entry should include a substantial portion of potential buyers who are willing and able to buy the product. The price of the product, how well it satisfies buyers' needs and wants, and other factors may restrict the size of the potential market.

Entry situation B requires a more focused strategy than does A. Digital photography at the market entry stage was expensive and relatively complex in use. Initial potential users were professional photographers for newspapers. Ease of transmission and other digital features offered benefits greater than the high prices charged for the equipment.

Situation C involves targeting two or more segments in the product-markets where a new product offers a promising substitute solution to buyers' needs and wants. As mentioned earlier, fax communication technology is a substitute for other communications alternatives (and e-mail is a substitute for fax). For example, one segment for fax machines is made up of large and medium-size businesses that have been using overnight delivery services for letters and short reports.

Situation D may occur when there is an opportunity for buyer need differentiation and the entering firm wants to establish a dominant position in the new market by targeting a few broad segments. If the initial targeting is too narrow, the firm may fail to develop its capabilities in meeting customer needs for more than one group of users. Apple Computer's 2001 introduction of its iPod is an example of this targeting situation. The $399 pocket size personal digital music player has the capacity to store the equivalent of 100 CDs.

Growth Market

Segments are likely to be found in the growth stage of the market. Identifying customer groups with similar needs improves targeting, and "experience with the product, process, and materials technologies leads to greater efficiency and increased standardization."[10]

During the growth stage the market environment moves from highly uncertain to moderately uncertain. Further change in the market is likely, but information is available about the forces that influence the size and composition of the product-market.

Patterns of use can be identified, and the characteristics of buyers and their use patterns can be determined. Segmentation by type of industry may be feasible in industrial markets. Demographic characteristics such as age, income, and family size may identify broad macrosegments for consumer products such as food and drugs. Analysis of the characteristics and preferences of existing buyers yields useful guidelines for estimating market potential.

Industry Structure

We often assume that high-growth markets are very attractive and that early entry offers important competitive advantages. Nevertheless, there are some warnings for industry participants:

> First, a visible growth market can attract too many competitors—the market and its distribution channel cannot support them. The intensity of competition is accentuated when growth fails to match expectations or eventually slows. Second, the early entrant is unable to cope when key success factors or technologies change, in part because it lacks the financial skills or organizational skills.[11]

The fiber-optic cable network market in the United States attracted far too many competitors (some 1,500). Most of the networks were not being used in 2001 due to significant overbuilding. Industry structure generalizations in growth markets are difficult. There is some evidence that large, established firms are more likely to enter growth markets than to enter emerging markets. This is the case because these companies may not be able to move as quickly as small specialist firms in exploiting the opportunities in the emerging product-market.[12] The established companies have skills and resource advantages for achieving maket leadership. These powerful firms can overcome the timing advantage of the market pioneers. Later entrants also have the advantage of evaluating the attractiveness of the product-market during its initial development.

Capabilities and Resources

Survival analysis of firms in the minicomputer industry highlights two performance characteristics in the rapid growth stage of the product-market: (1) Survival rates are much higher for aggressive firms competing on a broad market scope compared to conservative firms competing on the same basis, and (2) survival rates are high (about three-quarters) for both aggressive and conservative specialists.[13] This research suggests that survival requires aggressive action by firms that seek large market positions in the total market. These firms must possess the capabilities and resources necessary to achieve market position. Other competitors are likely to be more successful by selectively targeting one or a few market segments.

Targeting Strategy

Targeting decisions in growth market situations are influenced by several factors: (1) the capabilities and resources of the organization, (2) the competitive environment, (3) the extent to which the product-market can be segmented, (4) the future potential of the market, and (5) the market-entry barriers confronting potential competitors. There are at least three possible targeting strategies: extensive market coverage by firms with established businesses in related markets, selective targeting by firms with diversified product portfolios, and very focused targeting strategies by small organizations serving one or a few market segments.[14]

A selective targeting strategy is feasible when buyers' needs are differentiated or when products are differentiated. The segments that are not served by large competitors provide an opportunity for the small firm to gain competitive advantage. The market leader(s) may not find small segments attractive enough to seek a position in one of those segments. If the buyers in the market have similar needs, a small organization may gain advantage through product specialization. This strategy would concentrate on a specific product or component. Dell Computer is an interesting example of a successful market entry in the growth stage of the personal computer market. The company used standard components to assemble made-to-order computers marketed through direct order channels and targeted to business buyers.

The objective of the targeting strategy is to match the organization's distinctive capabilities to value opportunities in the product-market. The number of specific targets to pursue depends on management's objectives and the available segments in the market. During the growth stage of the business market for personal computers, the three major segments were small, medium-size, and large companies. There are likely to be relatively few segments in the growth stage, identified by one or a few general characteristics (e.g., size of business, household size).

Strategies for Mature and Declining Markets

Not all firms that enter the emerging and growth stages of the market survive in the maturity stage. The needs and characteristics of buyers also change over time. Market entry at the maturity stage is less likely than it is in previous life cycle stages.

Buyer Diversity

Segmentation is often essential at the maturity stage of the life cycle. At this stage, the product-market is clearly defined, indicating buyers' preferences and the competitive structure. The factors that drive market growth are often apparent. The market is not likely to expand or decline rapidly. Nonetheless, eventual decline may occur unless actions are taken to extend the product life cycle through product innovation and the development of new product applications.

Identification and evaluation of market segments are necessary to select targets that offer each firm a competitive advantage. Since the mature market has a history, experience should be available concerning how buyers respond to the marketing efforts of the firms competing in the product-market. Knowledge of the competitive and environmental influences on the segments in the market helps to obtain accurate forecasts and select positioning strategies.

The maturity of the product-market may reduce its attractiveness to the companies serving the market, and so the market-driven organization may benefit from (1) scanning the external environment for new opportunities that are consistent with the organization's skills and resources (core competencies), (2) identifying potential disruptive technology threats to the current technologies for meeting customer needs, and (3) identifying opportunities within specific segments for new and improved products.

Buyers in mature markets are experienced and often demanding. They are familiar with competing brands and often display preferences for particular brands. The key marketing issue is developing and sustaining brand preference, since buyers are aware of the product type and its features. Many top brands, such as Coca-Cola, Gillette, and Wrigley's, have held their leading positions for more than half a century. This highlights the importance of obtaining and protecting a lead position at an early stage in the development of a market.

Industry Structure

The characteristics of mature industries include intense competition for market share, emphasis on cost and service, slowdown in new product flows, international competition, pressures on profits, and increases in the power of channel of distribution organizations that link manufacturers with end-users.[15] Deciding how to compete successfully in the mature product-market is a demanding challenge. Recall how Colgate was successful in gaining market share leadership from P&G in the toothpaste market.

The typical mature industry structure consists of a few companies that dominate the industry and several other firms that pursue market selectivity strategies. The larger firms may include a market leader and two or three competitors with relatively large market positions compared to the remaining competitors. Entry into the mature product-market is often difficult because of major barriers and intense competition for sales and profits. Those that enter follow market or product selectivity strategies. Acquisition may be the method for market entry rather than trying to develop products and marketing capabilities. Acquisitions were used by the companies creating mega-automobile dealerships in the late 1990s in the United States. Mature industries are increasingly experiencing pressures for global consolidation. Examples include automobiles, foods, household appliances, prescription drugs, and consumer electronics.

Capabilities and Resources

Depending on the firm's position in the mature market, management's objective may be cost reduction, selective targeting, or product differentiation. Poor performance may lead to restructuring the corporation to try to improve financial performance. If improvement is not feasible, the decision may be to exit from the business.

Audi AG implemented a major turnaround strategy in the mid-1990s designed to appeal to more automobile buyers with an exciting image. The midrange Audi A4 introduced in 1995 attracted new buyers and was part of a major new product strategy to increase sales and profits. Leveraging Audi's capabilities and resources, the A4's initial entry was very successful. Supported by a major advertising campaign, the new model attracted younger buyers. Appealing to this target was a major objective of the new marketing strategy. Audi followed with the A6 and A8 models, which were targeted to additional market segments.

Targeting

Both targeting and positioning strategies may change in moving from the growth stage to the maturity stage of the product-market. Targeting may be altered to reflect changes in priorities among market targets. Positioning within a targeted market may be adjusted to improve customer satisfaction and operating performance. When the product-market reaches maturity, management is likely to place heavy emphasis on efficiency.

Targeting segments is appropriate for all firms competing in the mature product-market. The strategic issue is deciding which segments to serve. Market maturity may create new opportunities and threats in a company's market target(s). Firms pursuing extensive targeting strategies may decide to exit from certain segments. The targets that are retained in the portfolio can be prioritized to help guide product research and development, channel management, pricing strategy, advertising expenditures, and selling effort allocations. Exits from some targets and shifts in targeting priorities by large competitors may create new opportunities for smaller competitors that use selective targeting strategies.

Global Markets

Understanding global markets is important regardless of where an organization decides to compete, since domestic markets often attract international competitors. The increasingly smaller world linked by instant communications, global supply networks, and international finance markets mandates evaluating global opportunities and threats. In selecting strategies for global markets, there are two primary options for consideration: (1) the advantages of global reach and standardization and (2) the advantages of local adaptation.[16]

Global Reach and Standardization

This strategy considers the extent to which standardized products and other standardized strategy elements can be designed to compete on a global basis. The world is the market arena, and buyers are targeted without regard to national boundaries and regional preferences. Global standardized products are not commodities. Instead, they are differentiated but standardized across nations. The objective is to identify market segments that span global markets and to serve these needs with global positioning strategies.

Nestlé is the world's largest food producer. The company's management recognizes the potential value of Internet initiatives in managing Nestlé's global portfolio of brands in operations located throughout the world. The Global Feature describes how the company is using the Web in producing and marketing its chocolate bars.

Local Adaption

In some international markets, domestic customers are targeted and positioning strategies are designed to consider the requirements of domestic buyers. A wide variety of social, political, cultural, economic, and language differences among countries affect buyers' needs and preferences. These variations need to be accounted for in targeting and positioning strategies. For example, food and beverage preferences vary across national and regional boundaries. Instant coffee is popular in Britain but not in France. Nestlé employs domestic and regional strategies for several of its food products.

Industry Structure

Industry structure and competition are changing throughout the world as companies seek to improve their competitive advantage in the rapidly shrinking global marketplace. Corporate actions include restructuring, acquisitions, mergers, and strategic alliances. For example, General Mills has a strategic alliance with Nestlé to market General Mills' products in Europe, offering a major opportunity for General Mills to increase sales of cereal products. Nestlé has the experience and distribution network needed to tap the cereal market.

Targeting

Strategies for competing in international markets range from targeting a single country, to regional (multinational) targeting, to targeting on a global basis. The strategic issue is deciding whether to compete internationally and, if so, how to compete. Also, the choice of a domestic focus requires an understanding of relevant global influences on the domestic strategy.

Selecting strategies for global markets requires examining the trade-offs between global reach/standardization and local adaptation.[17] If there are no advantages to either standardization or local adaptation, there may be advantages in applying a domestic strategy that has been successful in one country to other countries with similar needs and market conditions. When both standardization and local adaptation are important, a composite strategy can be followed using decentralized marketing and a standard product with selected options.

Three strategic options are available for a multinational threatened by global competition.[18] One possibility is to convert to a global strategy. The strategies used by Boeing for commercial aircraft and IBM for computers are examples of global strategies. A second option is establishing a strategic alliance with one or more companies that provide market access and other global benefits (see Chapter 7). A third option is to target a market segment that the organization can dominate and build entry barriers against global competitors. The segment strategy may be domestic or international in scope. Producers of expensive Swiss watches follow this strategy. Millipore in water treatment equipment also follows this strategy.

Here's how Nestlé is harnessing the Web to more efficiently make and sell chocolate bars, from KitKats to Butterfingers:

TAKING ORDERS

How It Works

Since July, U.S. storeowners have had the option of ordering Nestlé chocolates and other products via a new Web site, NestléEZOrder.

The Benefit

Nestlé hopes to eliminate most of the 100,000 phoned or faxed orders a year from mom-and-pop shops. That would reduce manual data entry and cut processing costs by 90%, to 21 cents per order.

GETTING INGREDIENTS

How It Works

Nestlé buyers have purchased cocoa beans and other raw ingredients on a country-by-country basis, with little info about how colleagues were buying the same products. Now they share price info via the Net and pick suppliers that offer the best deals.

The Benefit

Nestlé has reduced the number of suppliers by as much as two-thirds and cut procurement costs by up to 20%.

MAKING THE CHOCOLATE

How It Works

Nestlé has traditionally processed its own cocoa butter and powder and manufactured most of its own chocolate. The Web lets Nestlé better communicate with suppliers, making outsourcing a more viable option.

Positioning Strategy

Positioning strategy is discussed in the rest of the chapter. First, we provide an overview of what is involved in strategic positioning and discuss the selection of the positioning concept. Next, we examine the composition of the positioning strategy and how the positioing components are combined into an integrated strategy. Finally, we look at how positioning effectiveness is evaluated.

Positioning may focus on an entire company, a mix of products, a specific line of products, or a particular brand, although positioning is often centered on the brand. Nonetheless, positioning is closely linked to business strategy. The major initiatives necessary in strate-

The Benefit

Last, year, outside contractors in Italy and Malaysia won orders to produce raw chocolate. Expect more such deals: Nestlé plans to sell or close a third of its 86 chocolate plants in coming years.

CUTTING INVENTORIES

How It Works

In the past, Nestlé guessed at how many KitKat or Crunch bars it might be able to sell in a promotion. Today, electronic links with supermarkets and other retail partners give Nestlé accurate and timely information on buying trends.

The Benefit

That lets Nestlé trim inventories by 15% as it adjusts production and deliveries to meet demand.

MARKETING THE CANDY BARS

How It Works

Nestlé spends $1.2 billion on advertising through traditional print and TV ads. Within two years, more than 20% of that will go online.

The Benefit

New marketing approaches include a chocolate-lover's Web site with advice, recipes, and paeans to the pleasures of chocolate. Nestlé has similar sites for coffee, Italian food, and infant nutrition.

Source: William Echikson, "Nestlé: An Elephant Dances," *Business Week E-Biz,* December 11, 2000, EB44.

gic positioning are described in Exhibit 6–4. The buyers in the market target are the focus of the positioning strategy. The *positioning concept* indicates the desired positioning of product (brand) in the eyes and minds of the targeted buyers. It is a statement of the product (brand) meaning derived from the value requirements of the buyers in the market target.[19] Positioning is intended to deliver the value proposition appropriate for each market target segment pursued by the organization. Gatorade is targeted to active people experiencing hot and thirsty situations. It is positioned as the best thirst quencher and replenisher, backed by scientific tests. Selecting the desired positioning requires an understanding of buyers' needs, wants, and perceptions of competing brands. The *positioning strategy* is the combination of marketing program (mix) strategies used to portray the positioning concept

EXHIBIT 6–4
**Strategic
Positioning**

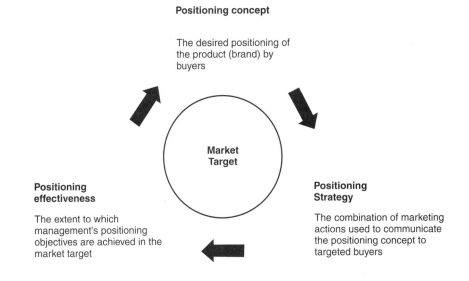

Positioning concept

The desired positioning of
the product (brand) by
buyers

**Market
Target**

**Positioning
effectiveness**

The extent to which
management's positioning
objectives are achieved in the
market target

**Positioning
Strategy**

The combination of marketing
actions used to communicate
the positioning concept to
targeted buyers

to targeted buyers. The positioning strategy includes the product, supporting services, distribution channels, price, and promotion.

As shown in Exhibit 6–5 the positioning objective is to have each targeted customer perceive the brand distinctly from other competing brands and favorably compared to the other brands. Of course, the actual positioning of the brand is determined by the buyers' perceptions of the firm's positioning strategy (and buyers' perceptions of competitors' strategies). Positioning is in the eyes and mind of the buyer. A company's positioning strategy (marketing program) works to persuade buyers to favorably position the brand. *Positioning effectiveness* considers how well management's positioning objectives are being achieved in the market target.

Positioning strategy is a pivotal initiative in Hyundai's plan to gain market position in the U.S. automobile market. The Korean carmaker is using new models, price, and a generous warranty to attract American buyers of automobiles, as described in Exhibit 6–6. A key component of the plan is the new 2001 XG 300, which offers full-size luxury at prices substantially below those of Japanese brands. Hyundai's market position has shown major growth since 1998. The competitive threat is likely to affect U.S. car brands rather than European or Japanese companies.

The close relationship between market targeting and positioning is illustrated by Johnson & Johnson's marketing strategy for Tylenol, the leading brand in the pain relief market. Johnson & Johnson's strategy for positioning its successful Tylenol brand is described in the accompanying Strategy Feature.

EXHIBIT 6–5
**Positioning in
Perspective**

Objective:	Match the organization's distinctive capabilities with the customer value requirements in each market target. (How do we want to be perceived by target market buyers?)
Desired result:	Gain a relevant, distinct, and enduring position that is considered important by the buyers in the target market.
Actions taken by the organization:	Design and implement the positioning strategy (marketing program) for the market target.

Tylenol's success in gaining and keeping its dominant brand position in the pain relief market is due to a brilliantly executed marketing strategy that simultaneously targets doctors, hospitals, and consumers with effective, complementary positioning programs. Tylenol's sustained competitive advantage is particularly impressive in view of the devastating product tampering problems in the early 1980s and strong competitive challenges by several competitors going after Tylenol's $600 million in sales.

- A core element in Tylenol's strategy is its strong association with doctors and hospitals.

- Using a micromarketing strategy for the Tylenol line, Johnson & Johnson targets its professional and consumer segments using different product mixes, separate sales organizations, and specific communications programs.

- Tylenol with codeine is a prescription product that is available from physicians, enabling the brand to sustain a strong loyalty with physicians.

- Consumer advertising positions the Tylenol brand featuring its doctor and hospital heritage.

- All of the Tylenol advertising is focused on Extra-Strength Tylenol which supports the regular-strength product and creates name awareness for other advertised line extensions in related categories.

- Competitors describe Tylenol's powerful brand image as being "in a class by itself."

Source: D. John Loden, *Megabrands* (Burr Ridge, IL: Irwin Professional Publishing, 1992), 141–42.

EXHIBIT 6–6
Hyundai, the Korean Carmaker, Positions Its New Luxury Model

Source: "And Now, a Luxury Hyundai," *Business Week,* February 26, 2001, 33.

- The 2001 XG 300 full-size sedan is priced $10,000 above the previous high-end entry, the Sonata.

- The new entry is attracting a lot of buyers, even though Hyundai experienced quality problems during the 1990s.

- The XG is priced $10,000 below the Toyota Avalon and Infiniti I30.

- Hyundai sold 90,000 cars in 1998 in the United States but received very low quality rankings.

- Hyundai offers a generous 10-year warranty on engines and transmissions.

- Management's 2001 sales estimates exceed 300,000 cars.

- Central to Hyundai's plan is its customer value–driven positioning strategy.

- Current buyers of U.S. automobile brands are the primary targets for Hyundai's cars.

Selecting the Positioning Concept

The positioning concept indicates the perception or association that management wants buyers to have concerning the company's brand. David Aaker and J. Gary Shansby comment on the importance of this decision:

The position can be central to customers' perception and choice decisions. Further, since all elements of the marketing program can potentially affect the position, it is usually necessary to use a positioning strategy as a focus for the development of the marketing program. A clear positioning strategy can insure that the elements of the marketing program are consistent and supportive.[20]

Choosing the positioning concept is an important first step in developing the positioning strategy. The positioning concept of the product (brand) is "the general meaning that is understood by customers in terms of its relevance to their needs and preferences."[21] The positioning strategy is the combination of marketing mix actions that implement the product (brand) concept into a specific position with targeted buyers.

Positioning Concepts[22]

The positioning concept should be linked to buyers' value preferences. The concept may be *functional, symbolic,* or *experiential.* The *functional* concept applies to products that solve consumption-related problems for externally generated consumption needs. Examples of brands using this basis of positioning include Crest toothpaste (cavity prevention), Clorox liquid cleaner (effective cleaning), and a checking account with ABC Bank (convenient services). *Symbolic positioning* relates to the buyer's internally generated need for self-enhancement, role position, group membership, or ego identification. Examples of symbolic positioning are Rolex watches and Hermès luxury goods. Finally, the *experiential* concept is used to position products that provide sensory pleasure, variety, and/or cognitive stimulation. BMW's automobile brands are positioned using an experiential concept that emphasizes the driving experience.

Three aspects of positioning concept selection are important.[23] First, the positioning concept applies to a specific brand rather than all the competing brands that compose a product classification such as toothpaste. Second, the concept is used to guide positioning decisions over the life of the brand, recognizing that the brand's specific position may change over time. However, consistency is important. Third, if two or more concepts—for example, functional and experiential—are used to guide the positioning strategy, the multiple concepts are likely to confuse buyers and perhaps weaken the effectiveness of positioning actions. Of course, the specific concept selected may not fall clearly into one of the three classifications.

The Positioning Decision

In deciding how to position, it is useful to study the positioning of competing brands using attributes that are important to existing and potential buyers of the competing brands. The objective is to find the preferred position of the buyers in each market segment of interest and to compare this preferred position with the actual positions of competing brands. Management then seeks a distinct position that corresponds with the buyers' preferred position in the target of interest.

Determining the existing positioning of a brand by targeted buyers and deciding whether the position satisfies management's objectives are considered later in the chapter. First we discuss developing the positioning strategy, and then we examine several resource allocation guidelines for combining the positioning components.

Developing the Positioning Strategy

The positioning strategy places the marketing program (mix) components into a coordinated set of actions designed to achieve the positioning objective(s). Developing the positioning strategy includes determining the activities and results for which each marketing program component (product, distribution, price, promotion) will be responsible, choosing the amount to spend on each program component, and deciding how much to spend on the entire program.

Selecting the positioning strategy may involve a combination of management judgment and experience, trial and error, some experimentation (e.g., test marketing), and sometimes field research. First we will look at several considerations regarding targeting and supporting activities, followed by deciding how to develop the positioning strategy.

Considerations about Targeting/Supporting Activities

The positioning strategy is usually centered on a single brand (Total toothpaste) or a line of related products (kitchen appliances) for a specific market target. Whether the strategy is brand-specific or greater in scope depends on such factors as the size of the product-market, the characteristics of the good or service, the number of products involved, and the product interrelationships in the consumer's use situation. For example, the marketing programs of Johnson & Johnson, Procter & Gamble, and Sara Lee position their various brands, whereas firms such as General Electric Company, Caterpillar, IBM, and Nike use the corporate name to position the product line or product portfolio. In serving several market targets, an umbrella strategy covering multiple targets may be used for some of the marketing program components. For example, advertising may be designed to appeal to more than a single target, or the same product (coach airline seats) may be targeted to different buyers through different distribution channels.

Marketing Program Decisions

A look at Pier 1 Imports' positioning strategy illustrates how the specialty retailer combines marketing mix components into a coordinated strategy.[24] The company competes in the United States, Canada, England, Puerto Rico, and Mexico. Pier 1's 2001 sales should exceed $1.5 billion, nearly a 60 percent increase since 1996. Profits have shown similar growth. Pier 1's positioning strategy includes unique merchandise, national advertising, strategically located stores, attractive store environments, outstanding customer service, and modern retail systems.

Product Strategy

Pier 1's array of merchandise includes decorative home furnishings, furniture, housewares, and bed and bath products. The merchandise is unique and ever-changing, imported from 1,500 suppliers in 60 countries around the world. Management's objective is to create a casual, sensory store environment. The merchandise offers customers an opportunity to satisfy their desire for diversity.

Value-Chain Strategy

The retailer manages the value chain from supplier to end-user, integrating its global supply network with its retail stores. Pier 1 has over 800 stores in 48 states. It uses freestanding and strip retail sites that can be accessed quickly and conveniently by customers. Extensive use is made of windows. Store layouts and exteriors are attractively designed. Information systems are installed throughout company operations to provide real-time information to manage the business. Seven regional distribution centers supply merchandise to the retail store networks.

Pricing Strategy

Pier 1's global supply network and purchasing know-how result in merchandise costs that enable the company to offer quality merchandise at attractive prices. China, Indonesia, and

India account for the majority of Pier 1's products. Information systems target slow-moving merchandise for possible pricing actions. The pricing strategy emphasizes the value and uniqueness of the merchandise.

Promotion Strategy

The retailer uses an effective combination of advertising, sales promotion, personal selling, and public relations to communicate with customers. Its aggressive national television advertising strategy positions Pier 1 as "a fun, affordable place to shop." Television advertising and store enhancements have helped generate impressive sales growth. Attractive color print ads encourage people to visit the stores by supporting monthly sale events. (See accompanying example of Pier 1's advertising.) Experienced store managers and sales associates convey the corporate culture of a customer-driven company. The customer service policy states, "The customer is always right."

Competitive Advantage

Pier 1 Imports' advantage is a combination of value and uniqueness of merchandise that is competitively priced. The specialty retailer has been very effective in building brand image and customer loyalty. The slowdown in household relocation during the 1990s encouraged spending on accent pieces and decorative home furnishings. These pressures forced many small retailers to close, strengthening Pier 1's market position. Management's continual investment in market research studies keeps the retailer's strategy focused on customer needs and wants.

An overview of the various decisions that are made in developing a positioning strategy is shown in Exhibit 6–7. Several of these actions are included in the Pier 1 illustration. We examine each positioning strategy component in detail in Chapters 9–13. The present

EXHIBIT 6–7
Positioning Strategy Overview

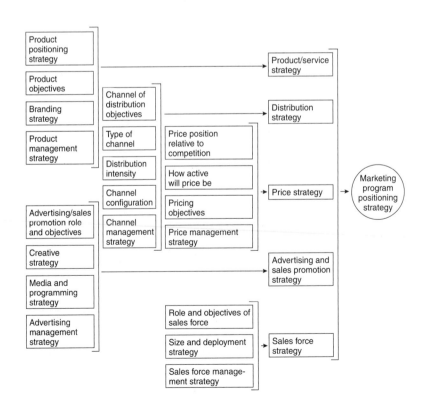

Courtesy Pier 1 Imports.

objective is to show how the components fit into the positioning strategy. The positioning concept is the core focus for designing the integrated strategy. The positioning strategy indicates how (and why) the product mix, line, or brand is to be positioned for each market target. This strategy includes:

- The product strategy, including how the product(s) will be positioned against the competition in the product-market.

- The value-chain (distribution) strategy to be used.

- The pricing strategy, including the role and positioning of price relative to competition.

- The advertising and sales promotion strategy and the objectives these promotion components are expected to achieve.

- The sales force strategy and direct marketing strategy, indicating how they are used in the positioning strategy.

Designing the Positioning Strategy

First, it is necessary to establish the major strategy guidelines for each marketing program component. For example, will more than one channel of distribution be utilized? Second, management strategies for each of the program components are implemented. For example, Pier 1's retail management strategy involves informing store managers about new merchandise, providing logistical support to the stores, and making necessary changes in the strategy over time.

Functional Relationships

Responsibilities for the positioning strategy components (product, distribution, price, and promotion) are often assigned to various functional units within a company or business unit. This separation of responsibilities (and budgets) highlights the importance of coordinating the positioning strategy. Responsibility should be assigned for coordinating and managing all aspects of the positioning strategy. Some companies use strategy teams for this purpose. Product and brand managers may be given responsibility for coordinating the positioning strategy across functional units.

Determining Positioning Effectiveness

Estimating how the market target will respond to a proposed marketing program or determining how the target is responding to a program that has been implemented is essential in selecting and managing positioning strategies. Positioning analysis is concerned with identifying the competitors serving a target market; determining how they are perceived, evaluated, and positioned by buyers; and analyzing customer needs and preferences.[25] "Positioning helps customers know the real differences among competing products so that they can choose the one that is of most value to them."[26] Positioning shows how a company or brand is distinguished from its competitors. Buyers position companies or brands using specific attributes or dimensions of products or corporate values. Management's objective is to gain (or sustain) a distinct position that corresponds to target customers' preferences for the brand or company being positioned.

Several methods are available for analyzing positioning alternatives and determining positioning effectiveness. They include customer and competitor research, market testing of proposed strategies, and the use of analytical models (Exhibit 6–8).

EXHIBIT 6–8
**Determining
Positioning
Effectiveness**

Determining Positioning Effectiveness

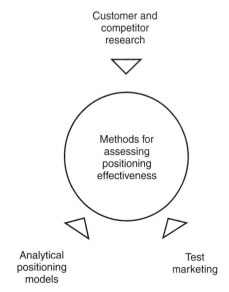

Customer and Competitor Research

Research studies provide useful buyer and competitor information for designing positioning strategies. Several of the research methods discussed in Part II help determine the position of a brand. For example, preference maps can be helpful in formulating a marketing program strategy by mapping customer preferences for various competing brands.

Methods are available for considering the effects on sales responses of several marketing program components. For example, using applied multivariate testing (MVT), a screening experiment can be conducted to identify important causal factors affecting market response.[27] The advantage of MVT is testing the effects of several factors at the same time. A medical equipment firm identified seven factors as possible influences on the sales of a new product for use by surgeons in the operating room. The factors are (1) special training of salespeople, (2) monetary incentives for salespeople, (3) vacation incentives for salespeople, (4) mailing product information to physicians, (5) mailing product information to operating room supervisors, (6) a letter from the president of the firm describing the product, and (7) a customized surgical product (in contrast to a standardized product). The effect of each factor is measured using field tests to vary the amount of the factor exposed to targeted buyers. For example, the high level of factor 1 consisted of training, whereas the low-level treatment was no training. A fractional factorial experimental design was used to evaluate the effects of the seven factors. Different factor combinations were tested. One factor combination included no training, a monetary incentive, no vacation incentive, no mailing to physicians, mailing to operating room supervisors, letter from the president, and the standard product. A sample of 64 salespeople was randomly selected, and groups of 8 were randomly assigned to each of the eight treatment combinations. The eight treatment combinations were designed to allow testing of the effects of each factor plus the influence of various combinations of factors.

One useful finding of the screening experiment was that several of the factors had no impact on sales. For example, the customized product did not sell as well as the standard product. This information saved the firm an estimated $1 million in expenses by eliminating the need to offer customized product designs. Before conducting the experiment, management had planned to customize the product for surgeons' use. The other results of the screening experiment were useful in designing the positioning strategy for the product. Interestingly, the vacation incentive had the largest effect on sales of all the factors, surpassing even the money incentive.

Test Marketing

Test marketing generates information about the commercial feasibility of a promising new product or about new positioning strategies for new products. The research method can also be used to test possible changes in the marketing program components (e.g., different amounts of advertising expenditures). The decision to test market is influenced by the following factors:

1. How much risk and investment are associated with the venture? When both are low, launching the product without a test market may be appropriate.

2. How much of a difference is there between the manufacturing investment required for the test versus the national launch? A large difference would favor a test market.

3. What are the likelihood and speed of the competitive response to the product offering?

4. How do the marketing costs and risks vary with the scale of the launch?[28]

While usually costing less than a national introduction, test marketing is expensive. Market tests of packaged consumer products often cost $2 million or more, depending on the scope of the tests and locations involved.[29] The competitive risks of revealing one's plans must also be weighed against the value of test market information. The major benefits of testing are risk reduction through better demand forecasts and the opportunity to fine-tune a marketing program strategy.

Test marketing provides market (sales) forecasts and information on the effectiveness of alternative marketing program strategies. Forecasts and other information are highly dependent on how well results from one or a few test markets provide accurate projections of the national market or regional market. Model-based analysis helps overcome problems associated with idiosyncrasies of test cities.[30] A detailed behavioral model of the consumer is used to analyze test market information and develop forecasts that can be made for the effect of modified marketing strategies. We continue the discussion of test marketing of new products in Chapter 8.

Virtual shopping is a potentially powerful computer-simulated environment for testing buyers' reactions to new products and developing positioning strategies.[31] A virtual retail store can be created as a marketing laboratory for testing new product concepts before commercial introduction. In addition to evaluating new product concepts, the virtual shopping laboratory can test different retail display formats and other marketing program components, such as product styles and sizes.

Positioning Models

Obtaining information about customers and prospects, analyzing it, and then developing strategies based on the information coupled with management judgment is the crux of positioning analysis. Some promising results have been achieved by incorporating research data into formal models of decision analysis. For example, ADVISOR is a comprehensive marketing mix budgeting model developed for industrial products.[32] It sets a marketing budget and then splits it into budgets for personal and impersonal (e.g., advertising) communications. ADVISOR is a type of multiple regression model that has several predictor variables, including the number of users, customer concentration, fraction of sales made to order, attitude differences, proportion of direct sales, life cycle stage, product plans, and product complexity. ADVISOR concentrates on the marketing budget and its components rather than on offering complete strategies for business units or products. Comprehensive discussion of marketing modeling is available from other sources.[33]

Positioning Effectiveness

How do we know if we have a good positioning strategy? The company's marketing offer and image should be both distinct and valued in the minds of the customers in the market target.[34] Does the strategy yield the results that are expected concerning sales, market share, profit contribution, growth rates, customer satisfaction, and other competitive advantage outcomes? Gauging the effectiveness of a marketing program strategy using specific criteria such as market share and profitability is more straightforward than evaluating competitive advantage. Yet developing a positioning strategy that cannot be easily copied is an essential consideration. For example, a competitor would need considerable resources—not to mention a long time period—to duplicate the powerful Revenue Management decision support system developed by American Airlines. In contrast, an airline can respond immediately with a price cut to meet the price offered by a competitor.

Companies do not alter their positioning strategies on a frequent basis, although adjustments are made at different stages of product-market maturity and in response to environmental, market, and competitive forces. For example, Pier 1 began national television advertising in 1995, and the expenditures generated a very favorable sales response. Even though frequent changes are not made, a successful positioning strategy should be evaluated on a regular basis to identify shifting buyer preferences and changes in competitors' strategies.

The importance of clear, strong positioning is undermined by faulty positioning, which can undermine a company's marketing strategy. Positioning errors include:

- *Underpositioning*—when customers have only vague ideas about the company and its products and do not perceive anything distinctive about them.

- *Overpositioning*—when customers have too narrow an understanding of the company, product, or brand. For example, Mont Blanc sells pens for several thousand dollars, but it is important to the company that the consumer is aware that Mont Blanc pens are available in much cheaper models.

- *Confused positioning*—when frequent changes and contradictory messages confuse customers regarding the positioning of the brand.

- *Doubtful positioning*—when the claims made for the product or brand are not regarded as credible by the customer.[35]

Positioning and Targeting Strategies

Recognizing the interrelationship between market target and positioning strategies is important:

> Positioning usually means that an overt decision is being made to concentrate only on certain segments. Such an approach requires commitment and discipline because it's not easy to turn your back on potential buyers. Yet, the effect of generating a distinct, meaningful position is to focus on the target segments and not be constrained by the reaction of other segments.[36]

Positioning becomes particularly challenging when management decides to target several segments. The objective is to develop an effective positioning strategy for each segment. The use of a different brand for each targeted segment is one way to focus a positioning strategy. The Gap employs this strategy with its Gap, Banana Republic, and Old Navy brands.

Determining Positioning Feasibility

"It is tempting but naive—and usually fatal—to decide on a positioning strategy that exploits a market need or opportunity but assumes that your product is something it is not."[37] In selecting a positioning strategy, management must realistically evaluate the feasibility of the strategy, taking into consideration the product's strengths, the positions of competing brands, and the probable reactions of buyers to the strategy.

Cherry Coke, which was introduced nationally in 1985, surprised many industry observers with its strong sales performance at the same time that New Coke and Classic Coke were in the limelight.[38] Network TV and radio spots positioned Cherry Coke as an "out and outrageous" alternative to the other cokes. The new brand was launched with a $50 million budget, which generated a strong and fast payback. Positioning was in terms of the flavor of the soft drink, thus using an experiential positioning concept.

Summary

Choosing the right market target strategy can affect the performance of the enterprise. The targeting decision is critical to guiding the positioning of a brand or company in the marketplace. Sometimes a single target cannot be selected because the business competes in several markets. Moreover, locating the firm's best match between its distinctive capabilities and a market segment's value requirements may first require a detailed analysis of several segments. Targeting decisions establish key guidelines for strategic planning.

The market targeting options include a single segment, selective segments, or extensive segments. Choosing among these options involves consideration of the stage of product-market maturity, buyer diversity, industry structure, and the organization's competitive advantage. When segments cannot be clearly defined, product specialization or product variety strategies may be used.

Market targeting decisions need to take into account the product-market life cycle stage. Risk and uncertainty are high in the emerging market stage because of the lack of experience in the new market. Targeting in the growth stage benefits from prior experience, although competition is likely to be more intense than it is in the emerging market stage. Targeting approaches may be narrow or broad in scope based on the firm's resources and competitive advantage. Targeting in mature and declining markets often involves multiple targeting (or product variety) strategies by a few major competitors and single/selective (or product specialization) strategies by firms with small market shares. Global targeting ranges from local adaptation to global reach.

The positioning concept describes how management wants buyers to position the brand. The concept used to position the brand may be based on the functions provided by the product, the experience it offers, or the symbol it conveys. Importantly, buyers position brands whereas companies seek to influence how buyers position brands.

Developing the positioning strategy requires integrating the product, value-chain, price, and promotion strategies to focus them on a market target. The result is an integrated strategy designed to achieve management's positioning objectives while gaining the largest possible competitive advantage. Shaping this bundle of strategies is a major challenge to marketing decision makers. Since the strategies span different functional areas and responsibilities, close coordination is essential.

Building on an understanding of the market target and the objectives to be accomplished by the marketing program, positioning strategy matches the firm's capabilities to buyers' value preferences. These programming decisions include selecting the amount of expenditure, deciding how to allocate these resources to the marketing program components, and making the most effective use of resources within each mix component. The factors that affect program strategy include the market target, the competition, resource constraints, management's priorities, and the product life cycle. The positioning strategy describes the desired positioning relative to the competition.

Central to the positioning decision is examining the relationship between the marketing effort and the market response. Positioning analysis is useful in estimating the market response as well as in evaluating competition and buyer preferences. The analysis methods include customer/competitor research, market testing, and positioning models. Analysis information, combined with management judgment and experience, is the basis for selecting a positioning strategy.

Internet Applications

A. Procter & Gamble (P&G) competes in the United States and many other countries. Consider how P&G may utilize maps in analyzing and selecting market targets (see *tiger.census.gov* and *www.nationalgeographic.com*).

B. Go to *www.jnj.com* and click on "Background" and then on "Fast Facts." Describe the different business segments of Johnson & Johnson.

C. Go to *www.ual.com/site/primary/0,10017,1314,00.html* (Economy Plus United Airlines). Discuss how this site impacts United Airlines' market targeting strategies. How is positioning considered by the website?

Questions for Review and Discussion

1. Discuss why it may be necessary for an organization to alter its targeting strategy over time.

2. What factors are important in selecting a market target?

3. Discuss the considerations that should be evaluated in targeting a macromarket segment whose buyers' needs vary versus targeting three microsegments within the macrosegment.

4. How might a medium-size bank determine the major market targets served by the bank?

5. Select a product and discuss how the size and composition of the marketing program may require adjustment as the product moves through its life cycle.

6. Suggest an approach that can be used by a regional family restaurant chain to determine the firm's strengths over those of its competitors.

7. Select and discuss a strategy that corresponds to each of these positioning approaches: attribute, price/quality, competition, application, product users, and product class.

8. Discuss some of the more important reasons why test market results may *not* be a good gauge of how well a new product will perform when it is launched in the national market.

9. "Evaluating marketing performance by using return-on-investment (ROI) measures is not appropriate because marketing is only one of several influences on ROI." Develop an argument against this statement.

10. Two factors complicate the problem of making future projections about the financial performance of marketing programs. First, the flow of revenues and costs is likely to be uneven over the planning horizon. Second, sales may not develop as forecasted. How should we handle these factors in financial projections?

11. Discuss the relationship between the positioning concept and the positioning strategy.

12. Select a product-type product-market (e.g., ice cream). Discuss the use of functional, symbolic, and experiential positioning concepts in this product category.

13. Discuss the conditions that might enable a new competitor to enter a mature product-market.

14. Competing in the mature market for air travel promises to be a demanding challenge in the 21st century. Discuss the marketing strategy issues facing Delta Airlines during the next decade.

Notes

1. Based in part on Tara Parker-Pope, "Colgate Places a Huge Bet on a Germ-Fighter," *The Wall Street Journal,* December 29, 1997, B1, B2; and Linda Grant, "Outmarketing P&G," *Fortune,* January 12, 1998, 150–51.

2. Michele Marchetti, "The Dell Way," *Sales & Marketing Management,* October 1997, 48–53.

3. Ravi S. Achrol, "Evolution of the Marketing Organization: New Forms for Turbulent Environments," *Journal of Marketing,* October 1991, 82–83.

4. Michael E. Porter, "What Is Strategy?" *Harvard Business Review,* November–December 1996, 66.

5. Michael E. Porter, *Competitive Strategy* (New York: Free Press, 1980), chap. 9.

6. Mary Lambkin and George S. Day, "Evolutionary Processes in Competitive Markets: Beyond the Product Life Cycle," *Journal of Marketing,* July 1989, 4.

7. Ibid., 13.

8. See, for example, William T. Robinson and Claes Fornell, "Sources of Market Pioneer Advantages in Consumer Goods Industries," *Journal of Marketing Research,* August 1985, 305–15; and Glen L. Urban, Theresa Carter, Steven Gaskin, and Zofia Mucha, "Market Share Rewards to Pioneering Brands: An Empirical Analysis and Strategic Implications," *Management Science,* June 1986, 645–59.

9. Elaine Romanelli, "New Venture Strategies in the Minicomputer Industry," *California Management Review,* Fall 1987, 161.

10. Lambkin and Day, "Evolutionary Processes in Competitive Markets," 14.

11. Romanelli, "New Venture Strategies," 161.

12. Lambkin and Day, "Evolutionary Processes in Competitive Markets," 11.

13. Romanelli, "New Venture Strategies," 170–72.

14. Lambkin and Day, "Evolutionary Processes in Competitive Markets," 12.

15. Porter, *Competitive Strategy,* 238–40.

16. George S. Day, *Market-Driven Strategy* (New York: The Free Press, 1990), 266–70.

17. Ibid.

18. Robert D. Buzzell and John A. Quelch, *Multinational Marketing Management* (Reading, MA: Addison-Wesley, 1988), 7–8.

19. C. Whan Park, Bernard J. Jaworski, and Deborah J. Macinnis, "Strategic Brand Concept-Image Management," *Journal of Marketing,* October 1986, 135–45.

20. David A. Aaker and J. Gary Shansby, "Positioning Your Product," *Business Horizons,* May–June 1982, 56–62.

21. C. W. Park and Gerald Zaltman, *Marketing Management* (Chicago: Dryden Press, 1987), 248.

22. This discussion is based on Park, Jaworski, and Macinnis, "Strategic Brand Concept" 136–37.

23. Ibid., 135–45.

24. This illustration is drawn from discussions with management, annual reports, and published information.
25. Aaker and Shansby, "Positioning Your Product," 60.
26. Edward D. Mingo, "The Fine Art of Positioning," *Journal of Business Strategy,* March–April 1988, 34.
27. Rita Koselka, "The New Mantra: MVT," *Forbes,* March 11, 1996, 114–16; David W. Cravens, Charles H. Holland, Charles W. Lamb, Jr., and William C. Moncrief III, "Marketing's Role in Product and Service Quality," *Industrial Marketing Management,* November 1988, 301.
28. N. D. Cadbury, "When, Where, and How to Test Market," *Harvard Business Review,* May–June 1975, 97–98.
29. Glen L. Urban and John R. Hauser, *Design and Marketing of New Products,* 2nd ed. (Englewood Cliffs, NJ: Prentice-Hall, 1993), 495.
30. Ibid.; see Chapter 17 for a discussion of alternative methods for analyzing test markets.
31. Raymond R. Burke, "Virtual Shopping: Breakthrough in Marketing Research," *Harvard Business Review,* March– April 1996, 120–31.
32. Gary L. Lilien, "Advisor Z: Modeling the Marketing Mix Decision for Industrial Products," *Management Science,* February 1979, 191–204.
33. See, for example, Gary L. Lilien, Philip Kotler, and K. Sridhar Moorthy, *Marketing Models* (Englewood Cliffs, NJ: Prentice-Hall, 1992).
34. Philip Kotler, *Marketing Management,* 8th ed. (Englewood Cliffs, NJ: Prentice-Hall, 1994), 307.
35. Graham J. Hooley, John A. Saunders, and Nigel F. Piercy, *Marketing Strategy and Competitive Positioning,* 2nd ed. (London: Prentice-Hall Europe, 1998), 205.
36. Aaker and Shansby, "Positioning Your Products," 61.
37. Ibid., 62.
38. Julie Franz, "Cherry Coke Takes the Fizz Out of Sister Brands," *Advertising Age,* October 28, 1985, 4.

Chapter 7

Relationship Strategies

Strategic relationships among suppliers, producers, distribution channel organizations, and customers (end-users of goods and services) occur for several reasons. The objective may be to gain access to markets, enhance value offerings, reduce the risks generated by rapid environmental change, share complementary skills, or obtain resources beyond those available to a single enterprise. These relationships are not recent innovations, but they are escalating in importance because of the environmental complexity and risks of a global economy and the skill and resource limitations of a single organization.[1] Strategic alliances, joint ventures, and supplier-producer collaborations are examples of cooperative relationships between independent firms.

Gaining competitive advantage increasingly demands cooperative relationships to access technology, expand resources, improve productivity and quality, and penetrate new markets. A clear and effective relationship strategy is a characteristic of the market-driven company, and traditional buyer-seller and competitor relationships may increasingly be replaced by collaboration to deliver superior value.

An interesting example of an evolving relationship strategy is the distinctive "store-within-a-store" format developed by Radio Shack with several strategic partners, as described in the Strategy Feature. It illustrates powerful cobranding in which two well-known brands decide to collaborate to enhance the brand strengths of both.

Marketing relationships are important avenues to building strong bonds with customers. The Radio Shack illustration indicates how important it is to consider all the participating organizations involved in linking buyers with sellers in the relationship strategy. The objective is to offer end-user customers superior value through collaboration of the organizations involved in the process.

However, it is important to recognize that collaborative relationship strategies may radically transform traditional buyer-seller and competitor structures in unexpected ways. For example, consider the following actual situation. Company X produces specialty chemicals for the pharmaceutical industry. A customer requests a supply of a new material for a clinical diagnostic product formulated by the customer's own research and development (R&D) department. Company X has the production facilities and expertise to make the new material, which the customer does not, but does not have access to the raw materials needed or to a packaging plant. The customer sources the raw materials from another source for X and arranges for X to lease packaging line time at Company Y (Y is X's major competitor). Company X supplies the new material to the customer in bulk for use in clinical diagnosis kits. The customer also supplies the new material in bulk to others, as well as marketing its test kits. Company X also sells the bulk material under license to its

Radio Shack (formerly known as Tandy Corporation) is the largest consumer electronics retailer in the United States, with 7,200 retail outlets. The company estimates that a million customers visit Radio Shack every day, and one in three U.S. households buy from Radio Shack every year. Radio Shack sales revenue in 2000 reached $4.8 billion.

Radio Shack has formed a series of strategic alliances with leading brands in the electronics and computer industry to pursue a "stores-within-a-store" strategy in which strategic partners fund their own "stores" within Radio Shack. Spanning the years 1997 to 2001, these alliances include:

- *Sprint* (the Sprint Store at Radio Shack).

- *Compaq* (Compaq Creative Learning Center at Radio Shack).

- *RCA/Thomson Electronics* (the RCA Digital Entertainment Store at Radio Shack).

- *Microsoft* (the Microsoft Internet Center at Radio Shack, providing high-speed Internet access).

- *Verizon Wireless* (the Verizon Wireless Store at Radio Shack, providing cellular phone services).

- *Blockbuster* (the "Radio Shack Cool Things" Store at Blockbuster), extending the concept to Radio Shack stores within Blockbuster, spanning the home entertainment and consumer electronics sectors.

The Sprint alliance, offering wireless phones and other telephone services in Radio Shack outlets, has been successful for both partners. Compaq successfully won over IBM for the exclusive relationship with Radio Shack, under which Radio Shack sells and services computers. The servicing arrangement, which has attractive margins, also includes Compaq's commercial computers. The retailer had previously sold only IBM's Aptiva personal computers. Radio Shack's computer sales total about $420 million, accounting for 9 percent of total annual revenue. The strategic relationship between Compaq and Radio Shack combines a strong product brand with a leading retail electronics brand. The cobranding strategy will nearly double Compaq's retail distribution of its Presario brand of consumer personal computers.

Sources: Mark P. Couch, "Tandy, Compaq Agree to PC Deal," *Fort Worth Star Telegram,* January 29, 1998, C1, C3; Evan Ramstad, "Compaq Beats IBM to Supply PCs to Tandy," *The Wall Street Journal,* January 29, 1998, A3–A4; Gail Gaboda, "Sprint Retail Stores Aim to Demystify Phone Technology for Consumers," *Marketing News,* November 10, 1997, 2; *www.radioshackcorporation.com.*

customer's competitors and to Company Y, its own major competitor in its traditional lines of business. Such situations are increasingly common in high-technology and process industries. In many market situations traditional clarity about buyer and seller roles and competitive relationships no longer exists.

Increasingly often, business and marketing strategies involve more than a single organization. In this chapter we examine the nature and scope of the strategic relationships among various partners. First, we consider the rationale for interorganizational relationships and discuss the logic underlying collaborative relationships. Next, we look at different kinds of relationships among organizations, followed by a discussion of several considerations that are important in developing effective interorganizational relationships. We emphasize the risks and strategic vulnerabilities that new types of business relationship strategies may create. Finally, we examine several issues that are important for global relationships.

The Rationale for Interorganizational Relationships

In the past companies frequently established relationships to achieve tactical objectives such as selling in minor overseas markets.[2] Today strategic relationships among organizations consider the elements of overall competitive strength: technology, costs, and marketing. Unlike tactical relationships, the effectiveness of these strategic agreements among companies can affect their long-term performance and even survival.

Several factors create a need to establish cooperative strategic relationships with other organizations. These influences include the opportunities to enhance value offerings to customers; the diversity, turbulence, and riskiness of the global business environment; the escalating complexity of technology; the existence of large resource requirements; the need to gain access to global markets; and the availability of an impressive array of information technology for coordinating intercompany operations. As shown in Exhibit 7–1, the various drivers of relationships fall into three broad categories: (1) value-enhancing opportunities by combining the competencies of two or more organizations, (2) environmental turbulence and diversity, and (3) skills and resource gaps.

Value-Enhancing Opportunities

The opportunity present in many markets today is that organizations can couple their competencies to offer superior customer value. Even when partnering is not required, a relationship strategy may result in a much more attractive value offering. Radio Shack's "store-within-a-store" concept gives customers the combined advantages of strong producer/service supplier and retail brands. Customers work with experienced electronics retailers and also gain access to strong product brands. Similar logic underpins the alliance between Amazon.com and Toys'R'Us formed in 2000 to market toys through a cobranded website, combining the Toys'R'Us's purchasing and stockholding capabilities with Amazon's superior Internet business model and fulfillment expertise.

Modularity in product and process design offers a promising basis for leveraging interorganizational capabilities to create superior customer value. It consists of "building a complex product or process from smaller subsystems that can be designed independently yet function together as a whole."[3] A key feature of modularity is the flexibility gained by designers, producers, and product users. Companies are able to partner with others in the design and production of modules or subsystems. The computer industry has performed a

EXHIBIT 7–1
Drivers of Interorganizational Relationships

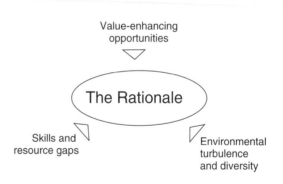

leadership role in advancing the use of modularity. Chip designers, computer manufacturers, component specialists, and software firms are able to make unique contributions to product design, manufacture, and use by working within the framework of an integrated architecture which indicates how the modules fit together and how each of the functions will perform.[4]

Environmental Turbulence and Diversity

Since the changing and turbulent global business environment is examined in several chapters, the present discussion is brief. Diversity refers to differences between the elements in the environment, including people, organizations, and social forces that affect resources.[5] Interlinked global markets create important challenges for companies.

Coping with diversity involves both the internal organization and its relationships with other organizations. Environmental diversity reduces the capacity of an organization to respond quickly to customer needs and new product development.[6] Organizations meet this challenge by (1) altering their internal organization structures and (2) establishing strategic relationships with other organizations.

Environmental diversity makes it difficult to link buyers and the goods and services that meet buyers' needs and wants in the marketplace. Because of this, companies are teaming up to meet the requirements of fragmented markets and complex technologies. These strategies may involve supplier and producer collaboration, strategic alliances between competitors, joint ventures between industry members, and network organizations that coordinate partnerships and alliances with many other organizations.[7] Examples of these organization forms are discussed later in the chapter.

The business environment creates risks for organizations that are unable to make changes rapidly. One response to turbulence and risk is to establish relationships with other organizations, thus avoiding ownership investments in sources of supply, production, and distribution. Ownership of the entire value-added system may be less effective and more risky in a turbulent environment. Exhibit 7–2 illustrates growth trends in strategic relationships.

Companies may coordinate an independent network of suppliers, producers, and distributors. For example, Benetton, the global casual wear company, contracts much of its

EXHIBIT 7–2
Growth in Strategic Relationships

Sources: Laura Mazur, "The Only Way to Compete Now Is with Alliance," *Marketing,* February 15, 2001, 20; Matthew Schifrin, "Partner or Perish," *Forbes,* May 21, 2001, 26–28; Maria Gonzalez, "Strategic Alliances," *Ivey Business Journal,* September–October 2001, 47–51.

- ❏ It was estimated in 2001 that the top 500 global businesses have an average of 60 major strategic alliances each.
- ❏ The consulting firm Accenture estimates that U.S. companies with at least $2 billion in sales formed an average of 138 alliances each from 1996 to 1999.
- ❏ In 1993, when Lou Gerstner took over as CEO, only 5 percent of IBM's sales outside personal computers were derived from alliances. By 2001, IBM was managing almost 100,000 alliances which contributed over one-third of its income. The company expects these partnerships to boost sales by $10 billion by 2003.
- ❏ A survey of global alliances by Accenture Consulting in 1999 found that:
  - • Eighty-two percent of the executives surveyed believed that alliances will be the prime vehicle for growth.
  - • Alliances account for an average of 26 percent of Fortune 500 companies' revenues, up from 11 percent five years earlier.
  - • Alliances account for 6 to 15 percent of the market value of the companies surveyed, and this is expected to increase to 16 to 25 percent of the average company's market value within five years.
  - • Senior management at 25 percent of the companies surveyed expects alliances to contribute more than 40 percent of the company's value within five years.

production to producers throughout the world. All of Benetton's retailers are independent dealers. The Benetton core organization coordinates and directs the global production and distribution system, using its powerful information capabilities. The computer network monitors sales and sends incoming orders to the factories. Similar strategies involving networks of participating organizations are employed by Casio in electronics, Nike in athletic shoes, and Dell in personal computers.

Skill and Resource Gaps

During the last two decades expenditures for research and development have grown three times faster than has spending on capital assets.[8] The skills and resource requirements of technologies in many industries often surpass the capabilities of a single organization. Even companies that can develop the capabilities may do so faster via partnering. Thus, the sharing of complementary technologies and risks is an important driver for strategic partnerships. In addition to technology, financial constraints, access to markets, and the availability of information systems encourage the establishment of relationships among independent organizations. For example, the airframe manufacturer Boeing, seeking to provide airline passengers with live television and Internet access, joined forces with units of Loral Space and Communications Ltd., Italy's Finmeccanica SpA, and Japan's Mitsubishi group to create an in-flight communications venture which also includes CNN and CNBC to provide news content.[9]

An interesting and unusual illustration is provided by the Anglo-German alliance between Warren Kade, a small British clothing company, and Siemens, the German engineering and electronics conglomerate. The alliance helps position Siemens' mobile phones as fashion accessories associated with designer clothing on the Paris catwalk, but with the potential for new design concepts to be incorporated in the phones and for advanced electronics to be designed into high-fashion clothing. The alliance brings fashion and technology closer together.[10]

Increasing Complexity of Technology

Technology constraints affect industry giants as well as smaller firms. Small companies with specialized competitive strengths are able to achieve impressive bargaining power with larger firms because of their high levels of competence in specialized technology areas and their ability to substantially compress development time. The partnerships between large and small pharmaceutical companies are illustrative. The small firm gains financial support, while the large firm gets access to specialized technology. Similarly, in 2001 IBM managed 59 strategic software alliances to bring "the hot, the cool, the fast, where IBM needs it."[11]

Access to technology and other skills, specialization advantages, and the opportunity to enhance product value are important motivations for establishing relationships among organizations. These relationships may be vertical between suppliers and producers or horizontal across industry members.

Financial Constraints

The financial needs for competing in global markets are often beyond the capacity of a single organization. As a result, many companies must seek partners in order to obtain the resources essential for competing in many industries or to spread the risks of financial loss with another firm.

The development of large commercial aircraft illustrates the limitations of a single company trying to compete in this global market. Boeing and Airbus Industrie, the industry leaders, are confronting the challenge of developing strategies for competing effectively in the 21st century. One option is a supersonic long-range aircraft, and the other is a substantially larger and longer-range successor to the Boeing 747. Much of the growth in passenger miles was expected to be in Asia, requiring longer-range aircraft. Development costs were estimated to be as high as $15 billion. This size of the expenditure represents a huge risk for Boeing. Airbus could share the costs with its consortium members (four companies from England, France, Germany, and Spain form Airbus). Another alternative is a joint development effort between the competing companies Airbus and Boeing. The Asian economic crisis, which began in 1997, created new market uncertainties for the aircraft producers, and the escalation of international conflicts and the threat of economic recession underline the risks to which they are exposed. While March 2000 saw Boeing planning two new long-range aircraft for the Boeing 777 family, by late 2001 a decline in demand from airlines was leading to layoffs and factory closures.

Access to Markets

Organizational relationships are also important in gaining access to markets. Products traditionally have been distributed through marketing intermediaries such as wholesalers and retailers in order to access end-user markets. These vertical channels of distribution are important in linking supply and demand. During the 1990s several horizontal relationships were established between competing firms to access global markets and domestic market segments not served by the cooperating firms. These cooperative marketing agreements expand the traditional channel of distribution coverage and gain the advantage of market knowledge in international markets.

International strategic alliances are used by many companies competing throughout the world. Commercial air travel is one of the more active industries involving overseas partners and competing through strategic alliances.[12]

Information Technology

Information technology makes establishing organizational relationships feasible in terms of time, cost, and effectiveness. Advances in information technology provide an important resource for improving the effectiveness of both internal and interorganizational communications:

> Advances in information technology and telecommunications have removed many of the communications barriers that prevented companies from drawing on overseas technical resources. Indeed, the ability to transmit documents and even complex design drawings instantaneously from one part of the globe to another by electronic mail means that it is often more efficient to collaborate globally in product development.[13]

Information systems enable organizations to communicate effectively even though the collaborating firms are widely dispersed geographically. In particular, the Internet provides a powerful means to reduce product development times by sharing designs for components and subassemblies with suppliers, customers, and collaborators throughout the world.[14] Electronic mail, file-sharing, Web-based conferencing, and collaboration tools do much to support working across traditional corporate boundaries.

An interesting example of a new business model based on the Internet that is reshaping relationships between buyers and sellers is described in the E-Business Feature.

Examining the Potential for Collaborative Relationships

Collaborative relations include shared activities such as product and process design, cooperative marketing programs, applications assistance, long-term supply contracts, and

The Swiss-Swedish-owned ABB group, with sales of $20 billion, is one of the three largest electrical engineering companies in the world. Recent events underline the link between the Internet and relationship strategy:

- In 2000, CEO Gran Lindahl resigned because he was convinced that ABB's leadership required an information technology background, not traditional engineering skills.

- Instead of using the Web just to support buying and selling of goods and services, ABB's e-business model tries to use the Web as a communications pathway to feed its technology expertise and knowledge of industry trends to customers.

- Moreover, the Internet relationship provides the means for customers to share ideas and problems with each other as well as with ABB.

- By linking customers to ABB's "brainpower"—the knowledge of its employees—the Internet provides the basis for knowledge sharing within the company and with customers.

- Information sharing is between customers as well—Lindt, the Swiss chocolate company, can use its ABB Web page to see how other customers are using "preventative maintenance" to operate factories efficiently.

- The model brings ABB's R&D closer to customers and to business decisions, speeding up the commercialization of technology and reducing overlap between research projects, with savings estimated at tens of millions of dollars.

Source: Peter Marsh, "Welding Metal to the Internet," *Financial Times,* October 30, 2000, 22.

just-in-time inventory programs.[15] The amount of collaboration may vary substantially across industries and individual companies. Moreover, in a given competitive situation a firm may pursue different degrees of collaboration across its customer base. For example, some supplier-customer relationships are transactional, but the same supplier may seek collaborative relationships with other customers.

There are several criteria that need to be evaluated in considering possible collaborative relationships with other organizations. We examine each factor, indicating important issues concerning how a factor may have an impact on a strategic relationship.

What Is the Strategic Logic?

Partnering is the result of two organizations working together toward a common objective such as sharing technologies, market access, or compressing new product development time. For example, a supplier may benefit from a customer's leading-edge application of the supplier's product.[16]

When Wal-Mart wanted to expand in Mexico in anticipation of NAFTA, it established a joint venture with Mexico's Cifra, providing Wal-Mart with a firm base and greatly reducing its learning time in a new market. Cifra/Wal-Mart is now Mexico's leading retailer under the name Wal-Mart de Mexico. Interestingly, Wal-Mart has taken that experience and applied it to Brazil and other parts of Latin America.[17]

The key issue is that there should be a strong underlying logic for collaboration.

Is Partnering a Promising Strategy?

It is important to consider the costs as well as the benefits of partnering with customers, suppliers, and competitors. Strategic relationships are demanding in terms of both time and resources. The relationship may require substantial investments by the partners and often cannot be transferred to other business relationships.[18] Because of this, the benefits need to be candidly assessed and compared to the costs. This requires careful planning of the relationship to spell out activities, participants, and costs.

How Essential Is the Relationship Strategy?

Normally, relationships are formed because the partners believe that combining their efforts is essential and that pursuing the project alone is not feasible. However, experience indicates that strategic relationships are more likely to succeed when dependence is important and equivalent between the collaborating organizations.

Are Good Candidates Available?

Promising partners may be unwilling to collaborate or already may be involved with other organizations. For example, many of the desirable global airline alliance partners have established relationships, and partnering with weaker companies is increasingly undesirable in this sector.

Do Relationships Fit Our Culture?

The corporate cultures of the partners should be adaptable to the partnership.[19] This issue is particularly important for partners from countries with substantial cultural differences. The partners' approaches to business activities and priorities should be compatible.

We will discuss shortly the related question of partnering capabilities. It is becoming clear that the ability to operate effective relationship strategies between organizations relies on skills and capabilities which vary between organizations.

Types of Organizational Relationships

The types of relationships that may be formed by a firm are shown in Exhibit 7–3. Included are supplier and buyer (vertical), lateral (horizontal), and internal relationships. A useful way to examine organizational relationships is to consider whether the tie between firms is vertical or horizontal. The focal firm may participate in both vertical and horizontal relationships. We look first at vertical relationships among organizations and then at strategic alliances and joint ventures, followed by internal relationships. Evolving global relationships among organizations are examined in a subsequent section.

Customer–Supplier Relationships

Moving products through various stages in the value-added process often involves linking suppliers, manufacturers, distributors, and consumer and business end-users of goods and services into vertical channels. Functional specialization and efficiency create the need for different types of organizations. For example, wholesalers stock products in inventory and deploy them when needed to retailers, thus reducing the delays inherent in ordering direct from manufacturers.

During the 1990s the use of supplier/manufacturer collaborative relationships expanded in many industries. While problems such as industrial secrets, labor objections, and loss of control occurred, the benefits of leveraging the distinctive capabilities of partners are substantial in developing new products and manufacturing processes. These relationships are

EXHIBIT 7–3
**Types of
Organizational
Relationships**

Source: Robert M. Morgan and
Shelby D. Hunt, "The
Commitment–Trust Theory of
Relationship Marketing,"
Journal of Marketing, July
1994, 21.

used extensively in the automotive and computer industries. A related development is the outsourcing of activities such as transportation, repair and maintenance services, information systems, and human resources.

The suppliers and buyers of a vast array of raw materials, parts and components, equipment, and services (e.g., consulting, maintenance) are linked together in vertical channels of distribution. The relationships between the supplier and the customer range from transactional to collaborative. Exhibit 7–4 describes Eastman Chemical Company's collaborative relationships with the customers to which it supplies industrial chemicals.

Distribution Channel Relationships

Vertical relationships also occur between producers and marketing intermediaries (e.g., wholesalers and retailers). These value-chain relationships give the producer access to consumer and organizational end-users. Interorganizational relationships vary from highly collaborative to transactional ties. A strong collaborative relationship exists in a vertical marketing system (VMS).[20] These systems are managed by one of the channel members, such as a retailer, distributor, or producer. The VMS may be owned by a channel firm, linked together contractually (e.g., a franchise system), or held together by the power and influence of the firm administering the channel relationships.

American Family Life Assurance Company (AFLAC) is the world's largest marketer of cancer insurance.[21] The U.S. company has a very successful strategy for selling its insurance policies in Japan, which account for 75 percent of AFLAC's revenues. The company sells its cancer insurance to consumers through partnerships with over 90 percent of Japanese companies. Those companies encourage their employees to buy the insurance, and the premiums are deducted from employees' paychecks. AFLAC insures 28 million people in Japan. The relationship strategy eliminates the high costs of selling direct to consumers, and the cooperative relationship with employers helps build AFLAC's brand image with consumers. If the employer cooperates with the insurance provider, this endorsement should have a positive effect on employees' perceptions about AFLAC.

There is some evidence that the organizations in distribution channels are becoming involved to a greater extent in collaborative relationships compared to traditional power and dependence ties. Examples include the previously mentioned Radio Shack store-within-a-store relationships with other companies (see the Strategy Feature), AFLAC's ties with

EXHIBIT 7–4
Eastman Chemical Company

Source: William Keenan, Jr., "What's Sales Got to Do with It?" *Sales and Marketing Management,* March 1994, 66–73.

In 1982 Eastman Chemical started the quality management program (QMP) called Customers and Us. These are the major QMP activities:

- Review and assessment of customer relationships (including suppliers).
- Identify opportunities for improvements.
- Initiate projects to make those improvements.
- Report these improvements back to the customer.

Eastman has a flattened structure comprising 10 major business units (e.g., packaging plastics, coatings, fine chemicals).

- $4 billion in worldwide sales.
- 7,000 customers served by a 500-person sales organization.
- Some 250 quality improvement teams following a problem-solving approach called Make Eastman the Preferred Supplier (MEPS).

MEPS projects focus on process improvement (e.g., delivery, product improvement, order processing).

Cross-functional teams are assembled depending on the nature and scope of the MEPS project:

- A team may include representatives from supply and distribution, manufacturing, product support services, sales, and the customer.
- The project may be ongoing or targeted to solve a particular problem.

The two most valuable inputs to Eastman's market sensing are the:

- Complaint process.
- Customer satisfaction survey.

Complaint Process

Salespeople are encouraged to ask customers about problems:

- A 24-hour 800 number is available for reporting problems and complaints.
- Customer service advocates are assigned by the complaint hotline (they must call the customer back within 24 hours).

Customer Satisfaction Survey

Managed by the sales organization:

- There are eight variations for major customer groups (printed in nine languages).
- The survey comprises about 25 performance factors (order processing/delivery, product quality, pricing practice, introduction of new products, management contacts, and sharing market information).

Customers rate Eastman on each performance factor—this is also done for the customer's "best" other supplier (18-month cycle).

Internal responsibility is assigned for the different factors reported in the survey (factor stewardship program).

- On-time and correct delivery is the responsibility of supply and distribution.
- Pricing policy is the responsibility of the individual business unit.
- Follow-up is the responsibility of the sales organization.

Survey results show composite rankings of all Eastman customers in that product group.

The salesperson focuses discussion on the customer ratings that differ significantly from the composite.

The salesperson highlights improvement efforts completed or under way that may affect the customer's satisfaction rating.

Japanese companies, and Tommy Hilfiger apparel shops in department stores. We discuss value-chain relationships in Chapter 10.

End-User Customer Relationships

The driving force underlying strategic relationships is that a company may enhance its ability to satisfy customers and cope with a rapidly changing business environment through partnering. Several customer relationship examples are shown in Exhibit 7–5. Although building collaborative relationships may not always be the best course of action, this avenue for gaining a competitive edge is increasing in popularity. We examine developing a customer focus and assessing customer value.

Customer Focus

Relationship marketing starts with the customer—understanding needs and wants and how to satisfy requirements and preferences:

> Customers think about products and companies in relation to other products and companies. What really matters is how existing and potential customers think about a company in relation to its competitors. Customers set up a hierarchy of values, wants, and needs based on empirical data, opinions, word-of-mouth references, and previous experiences with products and services. They use that information to make purchasing decisions.[22]

The importance of understanding customers' needs and wants encourages the development of long-term collaborative relationships. Driving the necessity of staying in close contact with buyers is the reality that customers often have several suppliers of the products they wish to purchase. Customer diversity complicates the competitive challenge. Consistent with being market-oriented, developing a customer-oriented organization includes:

- Instilling customer-oriented values and beliefs supported by top management.

- Integrating a market and customer focus into the strategic planning process.

- Developing strong marketing managers and programs.

- Creating market-based measures of performance.

- Developing customer commitment throughout the organization.[23]

The development of customer relationship management (CRM) systems has led to an extension of relationship marketing to customers. CRM provides a structure for managing the

EXHIBIT 7–5
Illustrative Partnering with Customers

Company/Brand	Customer Partner
• Boeing (commercial aircraft)	Involving airlines in the design of the Boeing *777*
• Harley-Davidson (motorcycles)	Harley Owners Group with over 100,000 members
• Marriott (hotels)	Partnering with corporate customers
• Dell Computer	Partnering with large corporate customers

point of customer contact by integrating information technology and data around the customer. CRM provides competitive advantage if it:

- Delivers superior customer value by personalizing the interaction between the company and the customer.

- Demonstrates trustworthiness.

- Tightens connections with customers.

- Achieves the coordination of complex capabilities within the company (functions, resources) around the customer relationship.[24]

Similarly, in the management of relationships with large corporate customers, many organizations have moved to the adoption of key account management structures and global account management approaches as ways to build teams dedicated to managing the relationship with the most valuable customers.[25]

Assessing Customer Value

An important issue is selecting the customers with which to develop relationships, since some may not want to partner and others may not offer enough potential to justify partnering with them. A look at Marriott's partnering strategy is illustrative.

> Building customer relationships is the core sales strategy of Marriott International, Inc.'s Business Travel Sales Organization. The travel manager is the target for the selling activities of the 2,500 person sales organization. The key features of the major account sales strategy are: (1) choose customers wisely (Marriott follows a comprehensive customer evaluation process); (2) build customer research into the value proposition (understanding what drives customer value and satisfaction); (3) lead with learning by following a step-by-step sales process; (4) invest in the customer's goal setting process, rather than Marriott's; and (5) develop a relationship strategy with a sense of purpose, trust, open access, shared leadership, and continuous learning. Marriott's management recognizes that customers who regularly purchase the company's services are valuable assets who demand continuous attention by high-performance teams. Rapidly changing markets and customer diversity add to the importance of developing strong ties with valuable customers to stay in touch with their changing requirements.[26]

Relationship strategies need to recognize differences in the value of customers to the seller as well as the specific requirements of customers.[27] Marriott's emphasis on carefully selecting customers with which to partner illustrates the importance of prioritizing sales strategies by segmenting accounts for corporate influence and profit. Relationship building is appropriate when large differences exist in the value of customers. Valuable customers may want close collaboration from their suppliers concerning product design, inventory planning, and order processing, and they may proactively pursue collaboration. The objective is to develop buyer and seller relationships so that both partners benefit from the relationship.

The frequent flier programs have been very successful in building long-term relationships with customers. The Advantage program pioneered by American Airlines attracted other airlines as well as hotel chains, credit card companies, and rental car companies. In many different business situations, a small percentage of customers account for a very large percentage of purchases. The 80/20 rule is illustrative; it states that 20 percent of customers are the source of 80 percent of sales.

The introduction of CRM systems has provided new mechanisms for managing the transactional relationship with the customer but, significantly, also for evaluating and predicting the value of the customer.

Strategic Alliances

A strategic alliance between two organizations is an agreement to cooperate to achieve one or more common strategic objectives. The relationship is horizontal in scope, between companies at the same level in the value chain. While the term *alliance* is sometimes used to designate supplier-producer partnerships, it is used here to identify collaborative relationships between companies that are competitors or are in related industries. The alliance relationship is intended to be long-term and strategically important to both parties. Several reasons for forming strategic alliances are shown in Exhibit 7–6. The following discussion assumes an alliance between two parties, recognizing that a company may have several alliance partners.

Each organization's contribution to the alliance is intended to complement the partner's contribution. The alliance requires each participant to yield some of its independence: "Alliances mean sharing control."[28] The rationale for the relationship may be to gain access to markets, utilize existing distribution channels, share technology development costs, or obtain specific skills or resources.

The alliance is not a merger between two independent organizations, although the termination of an alliance may eventually lead to an acquisition of one partner by the other partner. It is different from a joint venture launched by two firms or a formal contractual relationship between organizations. Moreover, the alliance involves more than purchasing stock in another company. Instead, it is a commitment to actively participate in a common project or program that is strategic in scope.

General Electric's (GE) jet engine partnership with SNECMA, a French government-controlled aerospace company, is an example of a successful long-term strategic alliance.[29] Formed in 1974 to help GE sell aircraft engines in Europe, the alliance was successful for both partners. The relationship illustrates several of the challenges and success requirements of strategic partnerships:

- GE's personnel must resolve cultural, linguistic, logistical, and foreign exchange problems.

- Investment and revenue are shared on equal basis by GE and SNECMA.

- The two partners delegate broad responsibilities to their senior engine executives.

- GE is responsible for system design and most of the complex engine technology.

- SNECMA concentrates on fans, boosters, low-pressure turbines, and related work.

- SNECMA's marketing role is expanding, although until the early 1990s GE was responsible for most of the marketing activities.

The GE-SNECMA partnership is a model of a well-structured alliance. First, we discuss the success record of alliances. Next, we describe different uses of alliances. Finally, we examine several alliance success requirements.

Success of Alliances

The competitive realities of surviving and prospering in the complex and rapidly changing business environment encourage companies to form strategic alliances in many different industries. Nonetheless, the record of success of alliances is not favorable, although there have been some notable successes, such as the GE-SNECMA jet engine alliance. While the alliance is a promising strategy for enhancing the competitive advantage of the partners, several failures have occurred due to the complexity of managing these relationships.

The Conference Board, Inc., surveyed the chief executive officers (CEOs) of 350 companies in the United States, Europe, Canada, and Mexico concerning their experiences with strategic alliances. The CEOs considered about half of their recent alliances to be successful.

EXHIBIT 7–6
Motives Underlying Entry of Firms into Strategic Alliances

Source: P. Rajan Varadarajan and Margaret H. Cunningham, "Strategic Alliances: A Synthesis of Conceptual Foundations," *Journal of the Academy of Marketing Science,* Fall 1995, 285.

Market entry and market position-related motives

Gain access to new international markets.

Circumvent barriers to entering international markets posed by legal, regulatory, and/or political factors.

Defend market position in present markets.

Enhance market position in present markets.

Product-related motives

Fill gaps in present product line.

Broaden present product line.

Differentiate or add value to the product.

Product/market-related motives

Enter new product-market domains.

Enter or maintain the option to enter evolving industries whose product offerings may emerge as either substitutes for, or complements to, the firm's product offerings.

Market structure modification-related motives

Reduce potential threat of future competition.

Raise entry barriers/erect entry barriers.

Alter the technological base of competition.

Market entry timing-related motives

Accelerate pace of entry into new product-market domains by accelerating pace of R&D, product development, and/or market entry.

Resource use efficiency-related motives

Lower manufacturing costs.

Lower marketing costs.

Resource extension- and risk-reduction-related motives

Pool resources in light of large outlays required.

Lower risk in the face of large resource outlays required, technological uncertainties, market uncertainties, and/or other uncertainties.

Skills enhancement-related motives

Learning new skills from alliance partners.

Enhancement of present skills by working with alliance partners.

Several reasons are cited for those that were not successful, which are summarized in Exhibit 7–7. The alliance failures are divided into logic and process failures.

Kinds of Alliances

An alliance typically involves a marketing, research and development, operations (manufacturing), and/or financial relationship between the partners (Exhibit 7–6). Capabilities may be exchanged or shared. In addition to functions performed by the partners, other aspects of alliances may include market coverage and effectively matching the specific characteristics of the partners.

EXHIBIT 7–7
**Why Strategic
Alliances Fail**

Source: Margaret Hart and
Stephen J. Garone, *Making
International Strategic
Alliances Work,* R-1086 (New
York: The Conference Board,
1994), 19.

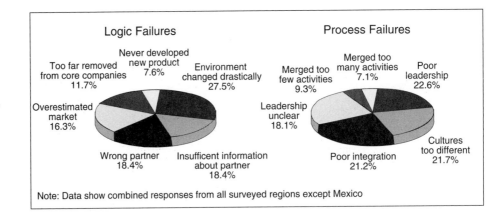

Logic Failures

Too far removed
from core companies
11.7%

Never developed
new product
7.6%

Environment
changed drastically
27.5%

Overestimated
market
16.3%

Wrong partner
18.4%

Insufficent information
about partner
18.4%

Process Failures

Merged too
few activities
9.3%

Merged too
many activities
7.1%

Poor
leadership
22.6%

Leadership
unclear
18.1%

Poor integration
21.2%

Cultures
too different
21.7%

Note: Data show combined responses from all surveyed regions except Mexico

The alliance helps each partner obtain business and technical skills and experience that are not available internally. One partner contributes unique capabilities to the other organization in return for needed skills and experience. The intent of the alliance is for both parties to benefit from sharing complementary functional responsibilities rather than independently performing them.

Alliance Success Requirements

The success of the alliance may depend heavily on effectively matching the capabilities of the participating organizations and achieving the full commitment of each partner to the alliance. The benefits and the trade-offs in the alliance must be favorable for each of the partners. The contribution of one partner should fill a gap in the other partner's capabilities. In the GE-SNECMA alliance, GE gained market access and knowledge of Airbus operations while SNECMA obtained technical skills and experience in engine design and production. Both benefited from the financial success of the venture.

One important concern in the alliance relationship is that the partner may gain access to confidential technology and other proprietary information. While this issue is important, the essential consideration is assessing the relationship's risks and rewards and the integrity of the alliance partner. A strong bond of trust between the partners exists in most successful relationships. The purpose of the alliance is for each partner to contribute something distinctive rather than to transfer core skills to the other partner.[30] It is important for the managers in each organization to evaluate the advisability and risks of transferring skills and technologies to the partner.

Alliance Vulnerabilities

Relatedly, it is important to recognize that alliance relationships may be fragile and difficult to sustain effectively, particularly if there is a lack of trust or mutuality of interest between partners.[31] Moreover, careful analysis is required of the impact of a failed alliance on a company's ability to compete and survive afterward. For example, in 2001, when Motorola withdrew from a joint project with Psion to develop a product to rival the Palm Pilot, Psion's shares fell 19 percent on the day, and that company was left without sufficient resources to complete the project alone.[32]

The higher the level of dependence on a partner organization, the greater the strategic vulnerability created if the alliance fails. An interesting illustration of the potential impact of alliance failure is provided in the Technology Feature, which describes the collapse of the global telecommunications alliance between AT&T and British Telecom. BT was left with

In October 2001 the global alliance between AT&T and British Telecom (BT)—Concert—came to an end after only two years. Concert aimed to provide multinational corporations with a single, global telecoms source based on "virtual private networks," with target sales of $10 billion. Concert had failed to meet targets and had been plagued by collapsing telecom prices and persistent squabbling between the partners.

- BT had a history of failed partnerships in its globalization strategy going back over a number of years—in 1997 an attempt to merge with MCI collapsed acrimoniously at the last moment.

- AT&T lacked experience in collaborative situations, and its earlier global alliance—Unisource—had foundered over AT&T's reluctance to cooperate with foreign partners or commit to common investment.

- Both companies faced major problems in their domestic markets, which in both cases led to major restructuring and management turnover. BT investments (primarily in third-generation mobile telephony in Europe) created a $50 billion debt burden by 2001, leading to a desperate rights issue and major asset sales.

- After starting operations in November 1999, by January 2000 Convert warned that sales were $3 billion below original estimates.

- By July 2000, Concert management complained that BT and AT&T were neglecting it and complained about "bureaucracy."

- In September 2000, BT and AT&T admitted Concert was failing, and having looked at combining their other business services divisions with Concert to resolve the competitive conflicts, started talks about a full merger between BT and AT&T.

- In February 2001, AT&T threatened to withdraw if problems were not solved.

- In April 2001, Concert revealed half-year losses of around $500 million, leading to discussions about its closure, with final terms agreed on in October 2001 and each company taking back the networks, major customers, and assets it contributed to the venture.

BT estimates that ending the venture will cost it around $2.1 billion in restructuring costs, redundancy payments, and unwinding costs, with its businesses reclaimed from the venture running at annual losses of around $200 million. AT&T estimates charges of $5.5 billion from Concert's demise and BT walking away from increasing its stake in AT&T Canada. In October 2001, BT CEO Sir Peter Bonfield left the company, and City investors marked BT's value up by almost $1.5 billion.

Sources: Richard Inder, "Three Year Slide From £7bn Giant to Oblivion," *Daily Mail,* October 17, 2001, 65; Richard Inder, "End of Concert 'Will Help BT to Break Even in 2003,'" *Daily Mail,* October 17, 2001, 56; "Concertina'd," *Financial Times,* October 17, 2001, 28.

a major gap in its global technology strategy and no obvious alternative in place. Given that estimates suggest that as many as 70 percent of alliances fail, implying that every alliance agreement should include an exit strategy, recognizing that alliances are impermanent may maximize their useful life.[33]

Joint Ventures

Joint ventures are agreements between two or more firms to establish a separate entity. These relationships may be used to develop a new market opportunity, access an international market, share costs and financial risks, gain a share of local manufacturing profits, or acquire knowledge or technology for the core business.[34] Joint ventures can grow valuable assets: In 2001 Xerox was able to sell half its stake in Fuji Xerox Co. to Fuji for $1.3 billion to counter liquidity problems.[35]

While joint ventures are similar to strategic alliances, a venture results in the creation of a new organization. Environmental turbulence and risk set the rationale for the venture more than does a major skill/resource gap, although both pressures may be present.

Honeywell, Inc., has several joint ventures worldwide. The manufacturer and marketer of control systems and components for homes and businesses has been operating outside the United States for nearly 60 years. The company's CEO, Michael R. Bonsignore, describes one venture:

> *Sinopec-Honeywell* involves one of Honeywell's customers, the Chinese National Petroleum Company—Sinopec. In January 1993, Honeywell entered into a joint equity company with Sinopec for a number of reasons: geographic expansion, market share, and risk diversification. Orders from Sinopec doubled in the first year and Honeywell has since attained the central government's acceptance. However, says Bonsignore, "we do have a number of concerns that we monitor constantly, such as MFN, the potential for Sinopec to become a competitor, and ongoing decentralization of the decision authority in the Chinese government."[36]

A study of cooperative research joint ventures among competitors in Japan provides some interesting findings concerning power and dependence in organizational relationships:[37]

1. Cooperative research is likely to be more successful for projects involving applied rather than basic research.

2. Research and development costs are reduced and the chances of project success are increased when the partners provide complementary skills and resources.

3. Large firms have a greater incentive to cooperate, although they favor small partners (thus limiting the loss of revenues from the venture's results).

4. Small firms, if they possess the necessary skills and resources, prefer to conduct their own R&D efforts.

Because of the hesitancy of small firms to cooperate with large companies, relationships may be more likely to occur among large competitors. Not surprisingly, this research indicates that competitive relationships offer the potential for conflict among the participants.

Internal Partnering

Internal partnerships may occur between business units, functional departments, and individual employees (Exhibit 7–3). The intent is to encourage and facilitate cross-functional cooperation rather than specialization. Key internal processes such as new product development benefit from cross-functional cooperation in areas such as research and development, marketing, purchasing, finance, and operations working together to identify, evaluate, develop, and commercialize new product concepts.

For example, Procter & Gamble (P&G) uses a corporate collaboration network—*My Idea*—to allow employees throughout the company to send ideas to an innovation panel. The projects selected can tap into P&G's entire global resource base. P&G's Corporate New Ventures Group was established in 1997, and by the end of 1998, 58 new products had been launched. The *Swiffer* cleaning product reached market in 10 months, half the normal P&G time.[38]

The success of internal relationship strategies requires the development of strong internal collaboration that cuts across functional boundaries. As noted in earlier chapters, many companies are using teams of people from various functions to manage processes such as new product development, customer relationships, order processing, and delivery of products. As noted in Exhibit 7–4, Eastman Chemical includes customer representatives on some of its teams.

As we discussed in Chapter 1, a market-oriented organization is committed to delivering superior customer value through market sensing, interfunctional cooperation, and shared decision making. Several guidelines for developing effective internal relationships follow:[39]

1. Demonstrate management support.

2. Start with a pilot team.

3. Keep the teams small—and together.

4. Link the teams to the strategy.

5. Seek complementary skills for the team—and look for potential.

6. Educate and train.

7. Address the issue of team leadership.

8. Motivate and reward team performance, not just individual performance.

The relationship strategy requires attention to the internal structure. The starting point is building a collaborative customer-driven internal culture.

Developing Effective Relationships between Organizations

We know that forming and managing effective collaborative partnerships between independent organizations is complex, and so we need to look further into the process of developing effective relationships. The objective of the relationship is considered first, followed by a discussion of several relationship management guidelines.

Objective of the Relationship

We look at possible strategic objectives of relationships.[40] In some situations collaborative action may be an option rather than a requirement.

Identifying and Obtaining New Technologies and Competencies

This objective is a continuing challenge for many companies because of the increasing complexity of technology and the short time span between identifying and commercializing new technologies. For example, failure to identify and monitor important telecommunications technologies was a key factor in the serious competitive problems of Western Union Corporation during the 1980s.

There are several ways to locate and exploit external sources of research and development:

- Collaboration with university departments and other research institutions.

- Precompetitive collaborative R&D to spread research resources more widely.

- Corporate venturing—making systematic investments in emerging companies to gain a window on the technologies and market applications of the future.

- Joint ventures and other forms of strategic partnership that enable a company to acquire new competencies by "borrowing" from a company with a leadership position.[41]

Japanese companies aggressively pursue all these strategies, whereas U.S. companies rely more heavily on internal R&D. However, the future trend is toward expanded use of external R&D collaboration by U.S. and other companies throughout the world. For example, collaboration is extensive among component manufacturers, personal computer producers, and software firms.

The role of the Internet in encouraging and facilitating technology sharing is becoming significant. The Italian company Olivetti has pioneered multinational collaboration between companies and research institutions in its multimedia product development project.[42]

Developing New Markets and Building Market Position

Alliances and other collaborative relationships may be promising alternatives for a single company interested in developing a market or entering a global market. This strategy requires finding potential partners that have strong marketing capabilities and/or market position. Collaboration may be used to enter a new product market or to geographically expand a position in a market already served.

Increasingly, major corporations are pursuing collaborative strategies in research and development and in gaining market access. General Electric has a corporate objective of globalization, which requires participation in each major market in the world:

> This requires several different forms of participation: trading technology for market access; trading market access for technology; and trading market access for market access. This "share to gain" becomes a way of life.[43]

GE's globalization objective has led to the forming of over 100 collaborative relationships.[44]

Market Selectivity Strategies

Competing in mature markets often involves either market domination or market selectivity strategies. Competition in these markets is characterized by a small core of major firms and several smaller competitors that concentrate their efforts in market segments. Firms with a small market position need to adopt strategies that enable them to compete in market segments where they have unique strengths and/or the segments are not of interest to large competitors. Cooperative relationships may be appropriate for these firms. The possible avenues for relationships include purchasing components to be processed and marketed to one or a few market segments, subcontracting to industry leaders, and providing distribution services to industry leaders.

The high entry barriers in producing semiconductors encourage the formation of strategic alliances.[45] Partnerships are essential in developing niche markets in this industry. Alliances exist between small U.S. firms that have specialized design expertise and Japanese, Korean, Taiwanese, and European companies with large-scale electronics manufacturing capabilities. The alliances make possible market entry for the design specialists. The cost of moving a complex new chip design to commercialization is in excess of $1 billion.

Restructuring and Cost-Reduction Strategies

Competing in international markets often requires companies to restructure and/or reduce product costs. Restructuring may result in forming cooperative relationships with other organizations. Cost-reduction requirements may encourage the firm to locate low-cost sources of supply. Many producers in Europe, Japan, and the United States establish relationships with companies in newly industrialized countries such as Korea, Taiwan, and Singapore. These collaborative relationships enable companies to reduce plant investment and product costs.

Relationship Management Guidelines

While collaborative relationships are increasingly necessary, the available concepts and methods for managing these partnerships are limited. Contemporary business management skills and experience apply primarily to a single organization rather than offering guidelines for managing interorganizational relationships. However, the experience that companies have gained in managing distribution-channel relationships provides a useful, although incomplete, set of guidelines. To expand the existing base of management knowledge, Collins and Doorley conducted a major global study of strategic partnerships.[46] Companies in North America, Europe, Japan, and Korea participated in the study. The research identified the eight key guidelines for strategic partnership management shown in Exhibit 7–8. A brief discussion of each guideline follows.

Planning

Comprehensive planning is critical in combining the skills and resources of two independent organizations to achieve one or more strategic objectives. The objectives must be specified, alternative strategies for achieving the objectives evaluated, and decisions made concerning how the relationship will be structured and managed. To determine the feasibility and attractiveness of the proposed relationship, the initiating partner may want to evaluate several potential partners before selecting one.

Trust and Self-Interest

Successful partnerships involve trust and respect between the partners and a willingness to share with each other on various self-interest issues. Confrontational relationships are not likely to be successful. Prior informal experience may be useful in showing whether the participants can cooperate on a more formalized strategic project.

Trust is enhanced by meaningful communication between the partners.[47] The process of building trust leads to better communication. Thus, building and sustaining partnership relationships require both communication and the accumulation of trust between the organizations. Trust, in turn, leads to better cooperation between the partners.

EXHIBIT 7–8
Relationship Management Guidelines

- Planning
- Trust/self-interest
- Conflicts
- Leadership
- Flexibility
- Technology transfer
- Learning

Conflicts

Realizing that conflicts will occur is an important aspect of the relationship. The partners must respond when conflicts occur and work proactively to resolve the issues:

> Even firms in successful partnerships would readily acknowledge that disagreements are inevitable. Rather than allowing these conflicts to run their course capriciously, however, adroit partner firms develop mediating mechanisms to diffuse and settle their differences rapidly.[48]

Mechanisms for conflict resolution include training the personnel who are involved in relationships, establishing a council or interorganizational committee, and appointing a mutually acceptable ombudsman to resolve problems.

Leadership Structure

"Failure to create an effective leadership structure can be fatal; it makes coordination difficult and expensive, slows down development, and can seriously erode the decision-making process."[49] Strategic leadership of the partnership can be achieved by (1) developing an independent leadership structure or (2) assigning the responsibility to one of the partners. The former may involve recruiting a project director from outside. The latter option is probably the more feasible of the two in many instances.

Flexibility

Recognizing the interdependence of the partners is essential in building successful relationships. Each organization has different objectives and priorities. "Management must be predominantly by persuasion and influence, with a willingness to adapt as circumstances change."[50] Relationships change over time. The partnership must be flexible in order to adjust to changing conditions and partnership requirements.

Cultural Differences

Strategic relationships between companies from different nations are influenced by cultural differences. Both partners must accept these realities. If the partners fail to respond to the cultural variations, the relationship may be adversely affected. These differences may be related to stage of industrial development, political system, religion, economic issues, and corporate culture.

Technology Transfer

When the partnership involves both developing technology and transferring the technology to commercial applications, special attention must be given to implementation. Important issues include organizational problems, identifying a commercial sponsor, appointing a team to achieve the transfer, and building transfer mechanisms into the plan. Planners, marketers, and production people are important participants in the transfer process.

Learning from Partner's Strengths

Finally, the opportunity for an organization to expand its skills and experience should be exploited. Japanese companies are particularly effective in taking advantage of this opportunity. One objective of the partnership should be to learn the skills of the cooperating firm as well as completing a specific project or program.[51] Surprisingly, U.S. companies often fail to capitalize on this opportunity in their interorganizational relationships. Japanese companies view cooperative ventures as another form of competition where they can transfer acquired skills to other parts of the business.

Partnership Capabilities

In addition to establishing a sound process for designing and managing alliances, it is important to consider what is necessary to build organizational competence in a strategic alliance. The capability to manage effectively through partnerships does not exist in all organizations. Recall the collapse of the BT and AT&T strategic alliance for global telecommunications described in the Technology Feature. Partnering effectively with other organizations is a key core competence which may need to be developed. Eli Lilly is recognized as a company that generates value from its alliances, and this company addresses the skills gap by running partnership training classes for its managers and partners. Other successful alliance strategies are operated by companies like Hewlett-Packard and Oracle by establishing a dedicated strategic alliance function in the company.[52]

Control and Evaluation[53]

Many conventional approaches to control and evaluation are inappropriate and ineffective in managing interorganizational collaborations. Alliance performance evaluation is a critical success factor which requires the development and implementation of a formal evaluation process that reflects the unique differences between alliances and more traditional organizational forms. A "balanced scorecard" approach allows evaluation criteria to be specified in the financial, customer focus, internal business process, and learning and growth dimensions. The goal is to have measurement metrics with both short- and long-term importance and to incorporate both quantitative measures (e.g., sales, growth, costs) and also important qualitative measures which speak to the strength and sustainability of the alliance (e.g., trust, communications flows, conflicts, culture gaps). Importantly, in the early stages of an alliance relationship, qualitative metrics may be the most important predictors of success.

Global Relationships Among Organizations

Types of Global Organizations

Several kinds of organizations compete in global markets. One form is the multinational corporation that may operate in several countries, using a separate organization in each country. The present discussion considers organizational forms that involve relationships with other organizations.

Examples of joint ventures and strategic alliances competing in international markets are discussed throughout the chapter. The use of cooperative agreements by companies in the United States, Japan, and the European Community expanded during the 1990s. Global relationships offer significant advantages in gaining market access and leveraging the capabilities of individual firms.

The need to develop more flexible organizational forms to compete in rapidly changing global markets is illustrated by two types of organizations: (1) the network corporation and (2) the Japanese form of trading company.[54] We also discuss the strategic role of government in global relationships among organizations.

The Network Corporation

This kind of organization consists of a core corporation that coordinates activities and functions between sources of supply and end-users of the product. The network, or hollow corporation, has a relatively small workforce, relying instead on independent organizations for manufacturing and distribution, often located at several places throughout the world. The organizations are linked by a sophisticated information system. The core company may be vertically integrated at the retail level or, instead, may utilize an independent distribution system.

One organization of the network manages the various partnerships and alliances. This network organization coordinates R&D, finance, global strategy, manufacturing, information systems, marketing, and the management of relationships.[55] The primary organizing concept is a small network control center that uses independent specialists to perform various functions. Thus, priority is placed on "buying" rather than "producing" and on "partnership" rather than "ownership." The network organization must define the skills and resources that it will use to develop new knowledge and skills. For example, a core competency of the network organization may be designing, managing, and controlling partnerships with customers, suppliers, distributors, and other specialists.

Trading Companies

The use of trading companies dates far back into history in Asia. Since trading companies share some of the characteristics of network organizations, a look at this organization form provides additional insights into interorganizational relationships. Japanese companies have been very successful in developing and coordinating extensive global operations and information management.[56] These *sogo shosha* concentrated primarily on commodity products, worked most directly with suppliers, and maintained a strong national (rather than global) perspective. An example of a trading company's network of relationships is shown in Exhibit 7–9. This trading company functions as an intermediary organization for the steel industry by developing sources of supply and demand.

The skills and experience developed by Japanese companies through the *sogo shosha* provide these companies with an important competitive advantage in forming other kinds of flexible organizations, such as the network company discussed above. Japan's needs for natural resources were important influences on the development of trading companies. Today these giant organizations are active in helping emerging countries develop their markets, such as China and Vietnam.

The Strategic Role of Government

While the role of the government in the United States is largely one of facilitating and regulating free enterprise, governments in several other countries play a proactive role with business organizations. For example, the Japanese government encouraged the development of the *sogo shosha*. In considering the role of government, we look at three types of relationships between government and private industry: (1) the single-nation partnership, (2) the multiple-nation partnership, and (3) the government corporation.

Single-Nation Partnership

A country's government may form a partnership with one company or a group of companies to develop an industry or achieve another national objective. Japan has successfully used this method of creating a national competitive advantage in a targeted industry in several instances.[57] For example, the Japanese Ministry of International Trade and Industry (MITI) performs a coordinating role in industry development. MITI resources and personnel establish alliances among companies, provide planning and technical assistance, and sponsor research. Government policy helped Japan build its competitive advantage by encouraging demand in new industries, fostering intraindustry competition, and identifying and encouraging the development of emerging technologies.

EXHIBIT 7–9
How Japanese Trading Companies Contribute to Trade Development

Source: *The Role of Trading Companies in International Commerce* (Toyko: Japan External Trade Organization, 1983), 15–16. Courtesy of JETRO (Japan External Trade Organization).

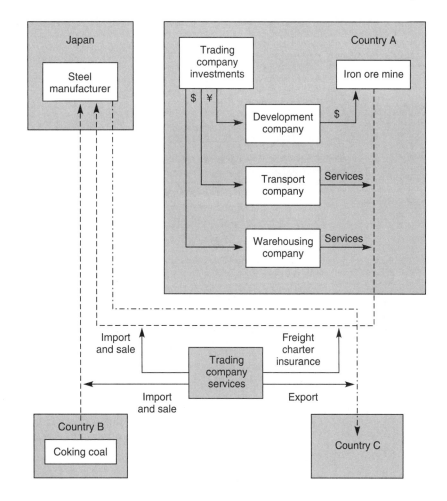

Multiple-Nation Partnerships

Regional cooperation among nations may encourage companies to form consortium relationships in selected industries. The Airbus Industrie consortium is an example. Airbus Industrie members have received more than $12 billion in loans from the governments of the participating companies.[58] Boeing dominated the industry until government subsidies and multinational sharing of skills and resources enabled Airbus to gain second place in the worldwide market for large commercial aircraft in the early 1990s. Government subsidies for Airbus have continued into the 21st century.

Negotiations for landing rights by international airlines is an interesting multiple-nation issue. For example, the proposed strategic alliance between American Airlines (AA) and British Air (BA) created negative reactions from U.S. and European airlines. The airlines asked their respective governments to require the partners to release gates to them. The United States and the European Union eventually approved the alliance, but BA and AA considered the cost too great to proceed. The Global Feature describes the major global airline alliances, illustrating how essential these relationships have become to competing in this industry (see the accompanying advertisement describing the OneWorld alliance).

Global Feature

The accompanying table shows the major global airline alliances operating at the end of 2000. The alliances also involve varying degrees of immunity from antitrust prosecution and some code-sharing deals outside the alliances. For example, Germany's Lufthansa and United Airlines cooperated closely since the mid-1990s in an immunized alliance, which led to the Star grouping. American Airlines and British Airways have yet to achieve immunity status. KLM and Northwest have cooperated with antitrust immunity since the early 1990s, and Delta and Air France are applying for immunity to cover the members of the SkyTeam alliance.

The volatility of the sector is underlined by the bankruptcy of Swissair announced late in 2001 and major losses at its subsidiary in Belgium, Sabena. In the meantime, KLM was seeking code-sharing arrangements with BA and American, cutting across the existing alliance relationships.

Nonetheless, of the 10 largest airlines in the world, only 3 operate outside global alliances, and they are expected to become alliance members in the future.

Major International Airline Alliances

Alliance	Slogan	Founded	No. of Aircraft	Founding Members	Additional Members	Former Members
Oneworld	"Oneworld revolves around you"	February 1999	1,975	American Airlines, British Airways, Cathay Pacific, Qantas	Finnair, Iberia, Aer Lingus, LAN Chile	Canadian (merged into Air Canada in 2000)
Star Alliance	"The airline network for Earth"	May 1997	2,711	Air Canada, Lufthansa, Scandinavian, Thai, United	Air New Zealand, All Nippon Airways, Ansett Australia, Austrian Airlines, British Midland, Lauda Air, Mexicana, Singapore Airlines, Tyrolean, VARIG	
The Qualiflyer Group	"Flying European Style"	March 1998	496	Swissair, Austrian Airlines, TAP Air Portugal, AOM French Airlines, Crossair, Sabena, Turkish Airlines	Air Europe, Air, Lottoral LOT, Portugalia, Volare Airlines, Air Liberte	Austrian Airlines joined Star in 1999
SkyTeam	"Caring more about you"	June 2000	1,283	Air France, AeroMexico, Delta Airlines, Korean Air	Alitalia	
Wings	"Worldwide reliability" (KLM/Northwest slogan)	Plan announced in 1989, approval of KLM/NW cooperation since 1993	824	KLM, Northwest	Alitalia	

Source: Airline Alliance, September 2000.

Sources: Mark Odell, "AA and BA Plan to File Again for US Anti-Trust Immunity," Financial Times, August 4, 2001, 19; "Wings over the Atlantic," Financial Times, August 4, 2001, 31; www.airlinealliance.tripod.com.

Government Corporations

Nations may operate government-owned corporations, though in recent years a trend toward privatization of these corporations has occurred in the United Kingdom, Australia, Mexico, and other countries. Nevertheless, government-supported corporations continue to compete in various global industries, including air transportation, chemicals, computers, and consumer electronics. Not surprisingly, competitors often are critical of government organizations because of their unfair advantage resulting from government financial support. Interestingly, in the European airline industry, the privatized carriers show substantially stronger profit performance compared to state-owned carriers.[59]

Government Legislation

Antitrust laws in the United States prohibit certain kinds of cooperation among direct competitors in an industry. The intense global competition and loss of competitiveness in many industries seem to be changing the traditional view of lone-wolf competition among companies. While the antitrust laws continue to be in place, there may be more flexibility by government agencies in interpreting whether collaboration among firms in an industry is an antitrust issue. For example, the granting of antitrust immunity is essential in certain aspects of the airline alliances described in the Global Feature.

Summary

The competitive realities of surviving and prospering in the complex and rapidly changing business environment encourage teaming up with other companies, and so cooperative strategic relationships among independent companies are escalating in importance. The major drivers of interorganizational relationships are value opportunities, environmental turbulence and diversity, and skill and resource gaps. The increasing complexity of technology, financial constraints, the need to access markets, and the availability of information technology all contribute to skill and resource gaps.

In examining the potential for collaborative relationships, several criteria need to be evaluated. Important criteria include determining the underlying logic of the proposed relationship, deciding whether partnering is the best way to achieve the strategic objective, assessing how essential the relationship is, determining if good candidates are available, and considering whether collaborative relationships are compatible with the corporate culture.

Relationships between organizations range from transactional exchange to collaborative partnerships. These relationships may be vertical in the value-added chain or horizontal within or across industries. Vertical relationships involve collaboration between suppliers and producers and distribution-channel linkages among firms. Horizontal partnerships may include competitors and other industry members. The horizontal or lateral relationships include strategic alliances and joint ventures.

Collaborative relationships are complex and, not surprisingly, generate conflicts. Many horizontal relationships have not been particularly successful even though the number of these partnerships is escalating throughout the world. Trust and commitment between the partners are critical to building a successful relationship. Planning helps improve the chances of success. The capability to manage effectively through partnerships requires distinct skills and new approaches that are not available in all organizations.

Several objectives may be achieved through strategic relationships, including gaining access to new technologies, developing new markets, building market position, implementing market segmentation strategies, and pursuing restructuring and cost-reduction strategies. The requirements for successfully managing interorganizational relationships include planning, balancing trust and self-interest, recognizing conflicts, defining leadership structure, achieving flexibility, adjusting to cultural differences, facilitating technology transfers, and learning from partners' strengths. The development of appropriate control and evaluation approaches for these new business forms has become a priority.

Global relationships among organizations may include conventional organizational forms, alliances, joint ventures, network corporations, and trading companies. Governments in several countries play a proactive role in organizational relationships through coordination, financial support, and government corporations.

Internet Applications

A. Visit the website of Streamline (*www.streamline.com*), a consumer direct shopping firm. Describe how Streamline uses the Internet to run its business. Also, identify Streamline's strategic partners and describe how these partners relate to Streamline's strategies.

B. Review the airline alliance lists, statistics, and news on *www.airlinealliance.tripod.com* in comparison to the Global Feature in this chapter. Examine the changes happening and predicted in airline alliances. What conclusions can be drawn about the strategic vulnerabilities of alliances?

C. Go to the investor information and company history information on *www.amazon.com*. Identify the evolving network of strategic relationships with customers, suppliers, and collaborators both on the Web and with conventional organizations. Which of these relationships are the most important to Amazon?

Questions for Review and Discussion

1. Discuss the major factors that encourage the formation of strategic partnerships between companies.

2. Compare and contrast vertical and horizontal strategic relationships between independent companies.

3. Discuss the similarities and differences between strategic alliances and joint ventures.

4. A German electronics company and a Japanese electronics company are discussing the formation of a strategic alliance to market the other firm's products in their respective countries. What are the important issues in making this relationship successful for both partners?

5. Establishing successful interorganizational relationships is difficult, according to authorities. Will the success record improve in the future as more companies pursue this strategy?

6. Are vertical relationships more likely to be successful than horizontal relationships? Discuss.

7. Suppose you are seeking a Japanese strategic alliance partner to market your French pharmaceutical products in Asia. What characteristics are important in selecting a good partner?

8. Discuss how alliances may enable foreign companies to reduce the negative reaction that is anticipated if they try to purchase companies in other countries.

9. Discuss how government may participate in helping domestic companies develop their competitive advantages in an industry such as aerospace products.

10. Identify and discuss important issues in deciding whether to create internal cross-functional relationships.

Notes

1. David W. Cravens, Shannon H. Shipp, and Karen S. Cravens, "Analysis of Cooperative Interorganizational Relationships, Strategic Alliance Formation, and Strategic Alliance Effectiveness," *Journal of Strategic Marketing,* March 1993, 55–70.

2. Timothy M. Collins and Thomas L. Doorley, *Teaming Up for the 90s* (Homewood, IL: Business One Irwin, 1991), 5.

3. Carliss Y. Baldwin and Kim B. Clark, "Managing in an Age of Modularity," *Harvard Business Review,* September–October 1997, 84–93, at 84.

4. Ibid.

5. Ravi S. Achrol, "Evolution of the Marketing Organization: New Forms for the Turbulent Environments," *Journal of Marketing,* October 1991, 78–79.

6. Ibid.

7. Frederick E. Webster, Jr., "The Changing Role of Marketing in the Organization," *Journal of Marketing,* October 1992, 1–17.

8. Collins and Doorley, *Teaming Up for the 90s,* 5.

9. Andy Pasztor and Jeff Cole, "Boeing Plans TV, Web Alliance for Inflight Access," *Wall Street Journal,* April 28, 2000, 5.

10. Gill South, "Upwardly Mobile," *The Business,* September 2, 2000, 26–29.

11. Matthew Schifrin, "Partner or Perish," *Forbes,* May 21, 2001, 26–28.

12. Terril Yue Jones, "Musical Chairs," *Forbes,* January 12, 1998, 60, 63.

13. Collins and Doorley, *Teaming Up for the 90s,* 8.

14. Andrew Baxter, "Internet Heralds New Era of Collaboration," *Financial Times,* November 1, 2000, V.

15. The following discussion is based on James C. Anderson and James A. Narus, "Partnering as a Focused Market Strategy," *California Management Review,* Spring 1991, 96–97.

16. Ibid., 100–03.

17. Schifrin, "Partner or Perish."

18. Lars Hallen, Jan Johanson, and Nazeem Seyed-Mohamed, "Interfirm Adaptation in Business Relationships," *Journal of Marketing,* April 1991, 30.

19. Anderson and Narus, "Partnering as a Focused Market Strategy."

20. Bert C. McCammon, Jr., "Perspectives for Distribution Programming," in *Vertical Marketing Systems,* ed. Louis P. Bucklin (Glenview, IL: Scott, Foresman, 1970), 43.

21. Peter Lynch, "A Company after My Own Heart," *Worth,* March 1994, 31, 32, 34.

22. Regis McKenna, *Relationship Marketing* (Reading, MA: Addison-Wesley, 1991), 43.

23. Frederick E. Webster, Jr., "The Rediscovery of the Marketing Concept," *Business Horizons,* May–June 1988, 37.

24. George S. Day, "Tying In an Asset," in *Understanding CRM* (London: Financial Times, 2000), 10–13.

25. Noel Capon, *Key Account Management and Planning* (New York: Free Press, 2001).

26. David W. Cravens, "The Changing Role of the Salesforce in the Corporation," *Marketing Management,* Fall 1995, 50.

27. Ibid.

28. Kenichi Ohmae, *The Borderless World* (New York: HarperBusiness, 1990), 114.

29. This illustration is based on Bernard Wysocki, Jr., "Global Reach: Cross-Border Alliances Become Favorite Way to Crack New Markets," *The Wall Street Journal,* March 26, 1990, A1, A5.

30. Gary Hamel, Yves L. Doz, and C. K. Prahalad, "Collaborate with Your Competitor—and Win," *Harvard Business Review,* January–February 1989, 135–36.

31. Douglas M. Lambert, Margaret A. Emmelhainz, and John T Gardner, "So You Think You Want a Partner?" *Marketing Management,* Summer 1996, 25–41.

32. Caroline Daniel, "Psion Falls 19% After Motorola Pulls Out of Project," *Financial Times,* January 30, 2001, 38.

33. Maria Gonzalez, "Strategic Alliances," *Ivey Business Journal,* September–October 2001, 47–51.

34. Collins and Doorley, *Teaming Up for the 90s,* 205–209.

35. Schifrin, "Partner or Perish."

36. Margaret Hart and Stephen J. Garone, *Making International Strategic Alliances Work,* R-1086 (New York: The Conference Board, 1994), 19.

37. Deepak K. Sinha and Michael A. Cusumano, "Complementary Resources and Cooperative Research: A Model of Research Joint Ventures among Competitors," *Management Science,* September 1991, 1091–1106.

38. "A Swiffer Path to Market," *Business Week E.Biz,* September 18, 2000, online.

39. Leonard L. Berry, *On Great Service* (New York: Free Press, 1995), 139–42.

40. The following discussion is based on Collins and Doorley, *Teaming Up for the 90s,* chap. 3.

41. Ibid., 30.

42. P. Zagnoli and C. Cardini, "Patterns of International R&D Cooperation for New Product Development: The Olivetti Multimedia Product," *R&D Management* 24, no. 1 (1994), 3–15.

43. General Electric Company, *Operating Objectives to Meet the Challenges of the 90s* (Fairfield, CT: General Electric Company), March 14, 1988.

44. George S. Day, *Market Driven Strategy* (New York: Free Press, 1990), 275–76.

45. William B. Scott, "Global Alliances Spur Development of Niche Market Semiconductors," *Aviation Week and Space Technology,* September 9, 1991, 70–71.

46. The following discussion is drawn from Collins and Doorley, *Teaming Up for the 90s,* chap. 5.

47. James C. Anderson and James A. Narus, "A Model of Distributor Firm and Manufacturer Firm Working Partnerships," *Journal of Marketing,* January 1990, 45.

48. Ibid., 56.

49. Collins and Doorley, *Teaming Up for the 90s,* 108.

50. Ibid., 110.

51. Wysocki, "Global Reach," A1, A5.

52. Jeffrey H. Dyer, Prashant Kale, and Harbir Singh, "How To Make Strategic Alliances Work," *Sloan Management Review,* Summer 2001, 37–43.

53. This discussion is based on Karen Cravens, Nigel Piercy, and David Cravens, "Assessing the Performance of Strategic Alliances," *European Management Journal* 18, no. 5 (2000), 529–41.

54. Achrol, "Evolution of the Marketing Organization," 84–85; and Webster, "The Changing Role of Marketing," 8–9.

55. Webster, "The Changing Role of Marketing," 8–9.

56. Achrol, "Evolution of the Marketing Organization," 84.

57. Michael E. Porter, *The Competitive Advantage of Nations* (New York: Free Press, 1990), 414–16.

58. David W. Cravens, H. Kirk Downey, and Paul Lauritano, "Global Competition in the Commercial Aircraft Industry: Positioning for Advantage by the Triad Nations," *Columbia Journal of World Business,* Winter 1992, 46–58.

59. Brian Coleman, "Among European Airlines, the Privatized Soar to the Top," *The Wall Street Journal,* July 19, 1995, B4.

Chapter 8

Planning for New Products

Many executives are likely to rank customer satisfaction and the use of technology ahead of innovation in priority. However, a major research study sponsored by *Forbes ASAP* and Ernst and Young placed innovation at the top of eight potential value drivers, whereas the use of technology (number 7) and customer satisfaction (number 8) were not ranked as statistically significant drivers of market values.[1] The researchers analyzed the primary nonfinancial factors which create market value (above that explained by traditional accounting metrics) for the modern corporation. These findings emphasize the importance of innovation for competing in today's complex and rapidly changing marketplace.

Broad-based innovation is a pivotal requirement for survival in the global marketplace.[2] Innovation initiatives extend beyond new goods and services to include ideas, processes, and business practices. Importantly, even when the critical role of innovation is recognized by managers, the choice of the best strategy for pursuing innovation opportunities is a demanding challenge. Organizations must develop a culture of innovation and build effective processes to identify innovation opportunities and transform ideas into new product successes.

New products provide vital avenues for company growth. For example, Whirlpool Corporation is developing Net-Savvy kitchen appliances because of management's belief that Net features will enable 20 percent annual industry growth in the future compared to the current single-digit growth.[3] Consider the following illustration:

> Mike Charles is tight with his appliances. When the Stanford University history lecturer runs out of milk, he tells his refrigerator by tapping the keys on its door. . . .
>
> Then there's his washing machine. Charles recently sent it an e-mail because he had spilled part of an Italian dinner on his tie. For $2, the washer downloaded a special pesto-on-silk cleaning program from Whirlpool's smart-products Web site. The result? The washer knew what cycle time, agitation level, water temperature, and type of soap were needed to get rid of the spot. That saved Charles a trip to the dry cleaner and a bill that would have run $7 or so.
>
> Sound weird? Get used to it. Whirlpool is planning to make Net-Savvy appliances commonplace over the next few years. The world's biggest appliance maker has 1,500 people testing its new Web products and is set to deliver some of them to stores before Christmas. If all goes as planned, the Benton Harbor (Mich.)-based company will lead the appliance industry into the Digital Age.[4]

The Whirlpool new products group estimates that in the future, households will replace appliances on a three-year cycle rather than every nine years. The company is forming alliances with technology firms like Cisco Systems, IBM, Sun Microsystems, and Nokia to develop new services.

In this chapter we consider the planning of new products, beginning with a discussion of customer needs analysis. Next, we discuss the steps in new product planning, including generating ideas, screening and evaluating those ideas, business analysis, product development and testing, designing the market entry strategy, market testing, and new product introduction. The chapter concludes with a discussion of several new product planning issues.

Product Planning as a Customer-Driven Process

New product introductions can be classified according to (1) newness to the market and (2) newness to the company, resulting in the following types of new products:

- *Discontinuous innovations:* new products that create an entirely new market.

- *New product category*: new product lines that enable a company to enter an existing market with an existing product.

- *Product line extensions*: new products that expand a company's product offering within a product line.

- *Incremental improvements to existing products*: new products that provide improved performance or greater perceived value (or lower cost), and replace existing products.

A company's new product portfolio may include items in one or more of these four categories. The reality is that many new products are extensions of existing product lines and are incremental improvements rather than totally new products. The planning process we discuss in this chapter applies to any of the four categories and is used in planning new services as well as tangible products. The Strategy Feature describes interesting innovation initiatives by Intel Corp. and Microsoft Corp. that extend outside their core business focus but leverage their brand recognition and proprietary technologies.

New product planning is guided by customer needs analysis. Even new-to-the-world product ideas should have some relationship to needs that are not being met by existing products. However, as we discuss shortly, potential customers may not always be good sounding boards for discontinuous innovations. Importantly, these innovations may have a disruptive impact on existing products.

Corporate and Business Strategies

The corporate mission, objectives, and business strategies identify the product-market areas that are of interest to management. Corporate purpose and scope set important guidelines for new product planning. Top management often defines the scope of new product ideas to be considered by a company. The objective is to establish priorities to guide new product planning. Intel's Corp.'s development and marketing of devices indicate an expansion in product and market scope by top management. This change in mission scope is influenced by the expected slowdown in personal computer (PC) sales and Intel's heavy dependence on microprocessor sales (Strategy Feature).

Customer needs yield important information for determining where value opportunities exist for developing new products. Market segment identification and evaluation help identify which segments offer new product opportunities to the organization. Extensive analysis of existing and potential customers and the competition are vital in guiding effective new product planning.

For years, personal computer makers have cheered whenever their biggest suppliers, Intel Corp. and Microsoft Corp., have hawked new processors or software at industry trade shows. But they aren't likely to coo about what those companies will introduce at this year's Consumer Electronics Show on Jan. 5 and Jan. 6.

Rather than unveil new goodies for PCs, the two will preview computer-like appliances that could siphon consumer dollars spent on PCs. The moves could also cut off promising new markets for PC makers. Intel will reveal a digital music player, while Microsoft will show off its much anticipated Xbox game console.

The introductions could kick off a more troubled era between PC makers and the chip and software kingpins. Although the Wintel duo has dabbled in selling hardware such as mice and home-networking gear to consumers, this is the first time it will go head-to-head with PC makers in markets with sizable potential. "You're going to step on a lot of toes when you start competing for the same consumer dollars as your customers," observes IDC analyst Bob O'Donnell. The assault couldn't come at a worse time for PC makers. Partly because of market saturation, computer sales are expected to slow dramatically in 2001. Furthermore, electronic appliance makers such as Palm Inc. and Nintendo have been busy picking off niche PC functions like personal organizers, photography, music players, and games. Analysts now expect sales of non-PC devices to grow at least 40% through 2004, versus mid-teen growth for PCs....

Of course, it's far from certain whether Microsoft and Intel will be successful. Neither has much experience competing against long-established electronics suppliers such as Sony and Panasonic, much less Compaq and Gateway. But both have spent billions on brand recognition, and analysts say their new offerings are technologically superior.

Source: "Microsoft and Intel Moving in on PC Makers Turf," *Business Week,* January 15, 2001, 41.

Finding Customer Value Opportunities

We know that customer value is the combination of benefits provided by a product or brand minus the costs incurred by the buyer (Chapter 1). Customer satisfaction indicates how well the product use experience compares to the value expected by the buyer. The closer the match between expectations and the use experience, the better the resulting value.

Customer Value

The objective of customer value analysis is to identify needs for (1) new products (2) improvements in existing products, (3) improvements in production processes, and (4) improvements in supporting services. Analysis seeks to find gaps between buyers' expectations and the extent to which they are being met (Exhibit 8–1). The entire organization needs to be involved in this process. This market-driven approach to product planning helps avoid a mismatch between technologies and customer needs. Market segment analyses are often necessary to identify specific customer needs and competitive opportunities.

A difference between expectations and use experience may provide a new product or improvement opportunity. For example, an alert U.S. Surgical Corporation (USS) salesperson saw an opportunity to satisfy a surgical need that was not being met with existing products. USS's products include staplers for skin closure and other surgical applications. The close working relationship of USS sales representatives with surgeons in operating rooms gives

EXHIBIT 8–1
Finding New Product Opportunities

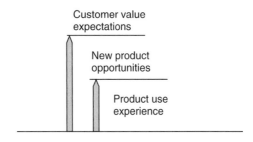

USS a critical competitive advantage.[5] The salesperson identified a new product opportunity by observing surgeons' early experiments in laparoscopy. Using this procedure, the surgeon inserts a tiny television camera into the body with very thin surgical instruments. USS responded quickly to this need by designing and introducing a laparoscopic stapler. The product is used in gallbladder removal and other internal surgical applications.

Buyers' satisfaction with existing products and brands is evaluated by considering various product/service attributes that identify buyers' preferences and comparisons of competing brands. The comparisons may include preference mapping and other analyses that we discussed in earlier chapters. The USS surgical product idea is an example of "lead" customer analysis. Lead customers are those that are the first to anticipate new product trends. The objective of the various preference analysis techniques is to identify the important preferences of the buyers in specific market segments.

Matching Capabilities to Value Opportunities

The value opportunity should be considered in terms of the organization's capabilities for delivering superior customer value. Organizational capabilities should correspond well to product line extensions and incremental improvements. Developing products for a new category requires an objective assessment of the organization's capabilities concerning the new category. Partnering with a company that has the required capabilities is an option concerning the addition of a new product category. For example, Healthy Choice (ConAgra) Foods, Inc., partnered with Kellogg to offer a new line of breakfast cereals.

Discontinuous Innovations

Customers are not always good guides to totally new product ideas which are called discontinuous or radical innovations since they create new families of products and businesses.[6] When "new-to-the-world" ideas are under consideration, potential customers may be unable to anticipate how a new product will replace an existing product. The problem is that customers may not anticipate a preference for a revolutionary new product.[7] For example, the initial response from potential users of optical fibers, VCRs, Federal Express, and CNN was not encouraging. In these situations, the initiating firm must form a vision about an innovation and be willing to make the commitment to develop the technology as Corning Inc. did with optical fiber technology. The risk, of course, is that management's vision may be faulty.

A study of successful U.S. firms competing against Japanese companies in electronics-related markets points to the critical role of both discontinuous innovations and incremental product improvements:

> These businesses built and renewed, and continue to build and renew, their competitive advantage through radical and generational innovations. They sustained that advantage over time through incremental product line improvements and extensions—but it is on the basis of the riskier, failure-laden, expensive and time-consuming efforts to pioneer new businesses and new generations of technology that their competitive advantage was and still is established.[8]

Incremental product improvements are guided by analyzing customer value opportunities (Exhibit 8–1), whereas conventional approaches to finding new product opportunities are not very useful in evaluating potential discontinuous innovations:

> The familiar admonition to be customer-driven is of little value when it is not at all clear who the customer is—when the market has never experienced the features created by the new technology. Likewise, analytic methods for evaluating new product opportunities (e.g., discounted cash flow and market diffusion analyses) appear to be much more appropriate for incremental than for discontinuous innovation.[9]

Discontinuous innovations have the potential to disrupt existing (sustaining) technologies and create negative impacts on the leading firms that pursue innovation strategies using existing technologies.[10] Examples of disruptive innovations include digital photography, CD-ROM encyclopedias, and steel minimills. These disruptive technologies are often not considered to be threats by firms pursuing sustaining technologies. Identifying and developing viable strategies for disruptive technologies represent a major management challenge. Christensen offers a compelling analysis of these threats and provides important guidelines for managing disruptive technological change.[11] A key initiative is positioning the disruptive technology in a separate organization independent from the core organization. For example, for fear of missing out on new technologies, IBM has changed the way it identifies and pursues promising new ideas. Because new ideas fall between organizational boundaries and may conflict with existing business units, they are managed separately and differently:

- *Horizon One Businesses* are traditional, mature businesses such as mainframe computers.

- *Horizon Two Businesses* are the current growth businesses.

- *Horizon Three Businesses* are new, young businesses which are put in separate organizational units, are insulated from traditional management methods and performance yardsticks, and receive personal sponsorship from senior managers to protect them from other interests in the company.[12]

If this is not done, the sustaining technology is likely to dominate innovation initiatives. A good market/technology match is important in being successful with discontinuous technologies. Priority should be given to market niches that the traditional technology does not serve well. Christensen also proposes that products from discontinuous technologies that are not currently valued by customers may match future value requirements very well.

The new product planning process discussed in this chapter is appropriate for planning incremental product improvements. It can also be used in planning discontinuous innovation as a separate organizational initiative. We discuss variations of the generic new product planning process at the end of the chapter.

Drivers of Successful Innovations

Certain companies seem to consistently perform better than others in developing successful new products. Moreover, successful innovators often display similar characteristics. The factors shown in Exhibit 8–2 have proved to be good predictors of successful innovation based on research studies, management judgment and experience, and analysis of specific companies' innovation experience. These initiatives refer to the organization rather than to specific new product projects, which may be affected by situation-specific factors.

Creating an innovative culture is an essential initiative in generating successful new products. Research findings point to the importance of an innovative climate and culture.[13] Deciding on the right innovation strategy involves spelling out the product, market, and

EXHIBIT 8–2
**Characteristics of
Successful
Innovators**

technology scope of interest for the organization. However, a high-quality new product process is essential to implement the organization's innovation strategy. Importantly, achieving successful new product outcomes requires allocating adequate resources to new product initiatives. Finally, the extent to which the organization can leverage its capabilities into promising new product and market opportunities enhances innovation performance (if the leveraging efforts are successful). Our earlier discussion of Intel and Microsoft consumer products provided examples of leveraging. Brand leveraging is discussed in Chapter 9.

Steps in New Product Planning

A new product does not have to be a high-technology breakthrough to be successful, but it must deliver customer value. Post-it Notes has been a big winner for Minnesota Mining & Manufacturing Co.[14] We know that the notepaper pads come in various sizes and that each page has a thin strip of adhesive on the back which can be attached to reports, telephones, walls, and other places. The idea came from a 3M researcher. He had used slips of paper to mark songs in his hymnbook, but the paper kept falling out. To eliminate the problem, the employee applied an adhesive that had been developed in 3M's research laboratory but had failed to provide the adhesive strength needed in the original use situation. It worked fine for marking songs in the book. Interestingly, office supply vendors initially saw no market for the sticky-backed notepaper. The 3M Company employed extensive sampling to demonstrate the value of the product. Over the signature of the CEO's administrative assistant, samples were sent to executive assistants at all Fortune 500 companies. After using the supply of samples, the assistants wanted more. Today Post-it-Notes are indispensable in both offices and homes.

Creating an innovative culture is an important foundation for innovation. It is also useful to set some boundaries concerning the types of new products to be considered for possible development. First, we examine these issues. Next, the steps in the new product planning process are described. The section concludes with a look at how responsibility may be assigned for new product planning.

Developing a Culture and Strategy for Innovation

Open communications throughout the organization and high levels of employee involvement and interest are characteristic of innovative cultures. Intel's chief executive officer (CEO) implemented a series of seminars in 1997 for the firm's top 400 managers (in groups of 50) intended to encourage innovation beyond the core chip business.[15] Management also changed the structure of the organization to make it more flexible so that new ideas could thrive. Evidence of innovative cultures may be found in corporate mission statements, advertising messages, presentations by top executives, and case studies in business publications.

The organization's innovation strategy delineates the most promising opportunities for new products. This strategy needs to be formulated by taking into account the organization's distinctive capabilities, relevant technologies, and the market opportunities that provide a good customer value match with capabilities. A major benchmarking study of 161 business units from a broad range of industries in the United States, Germany, Denmark, and Canada indicates that a carefully formulated and communicated new product innovation strategy is one of three cornerstones of superior new product performance.[16] A successful new product strategy includes:

1. Setting specific, written new product objectives (sales, profit contribution, market, share, etc.).

2. Communicating across the organization the role of new products in contributing to the goals of the business.

3. Defining the areas of strategic focus for the corporation in terms of product scope, markets, and technologies.

4. Including longer-term, discontinuous projects in the portfolio along with incremental projects.

Building Effective Development Processes

Creating the right culture and selecting the right innovation strategy are essential but not sufficient initiatives in successful innovation. Innovation is achieved through the organization's processes. The benchmarking study found that having a high-quality new product process in place is the most important cornerstone of performance, ahead of selecting the right innovation strategy and committing the necessary resources to new product development.

Developing successful new products requires systematic planning to coordinate the many decisions, activities, and functions necessary to move a new product idea to commercial success. A generic planning process can be used in planning a wide range of new products, although there may be necessary modifications in the process in certain situations, and they are discussed in the last section of the chapter. The major stages in the new product planning process are shown in Exhibit 8–3. We examine each stage to see what is involved, how the stages depend on each other, and the importance of interfunctional coordination of new product planning.

Successful new product planning requires (1) generating a continuing stream of new product ideas that will satisfy management's requirements for new products and (2) putting in place procedures and methods for evaluating new product ideas as they move through the planning stages.

The following initiatives are important in effectively applying the planning process to develop and introduce new products. First, the process involves different business functions, and so it is necessary to develop ways of coordinating and integrating cross-functional activities in the planning process. Second, compressing the time frame of product development creates an important competitive advantage. For example, U.S. Surgical's quick response to laparoscopy equipment enabled that company to establish first position in the market. Third, the product planning activities consume resources and must be managed so that the results deliver high levels of customer satisfaction at acceptable costs. Finally, the planning process is used for the

EXHIBIT 8-3
**New Product
Planning Process**

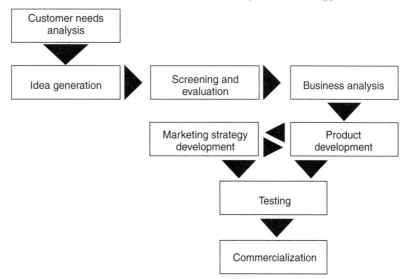

development of new services as well as physical products. Certain differences in new service planning are highlighted as we discuss the planning stages.

Lucent Technologies, the giant telecommunications equipment producer, encountered several operating problems in 2000, including a large drop in market value. A key concern of investors and industry authorities was the targeting of Lucent's research and development activities. One concern was the lack of attention given to optical networking. Lucent's new product planning challenges are described in Exhibit 8–4.

Responsibility for New Product Planning

Since new product development involves different business functions, such as marketing, finance, operations, and research and development (R&D), ways of encouraging cross-functional interaction and coordination are essential. Various organizational initiatives may be employed to coordinate interfunctional interactions that are necessary in developing successful new products, including:[17]

- Coordination of new product activities by a high-level general manager.

- Interfunctional coordination by a team of new product planning representatives.

- Creation of a project task force responsible for new product planning.

- Designation of a new products manager to coordinate planning between departments.

- Formation of a matrix organizational structure for integrating new product planning with business functions.

- Creation of a design center which is similar in concept to a new product team except that the center is a permanent part of the organization.

The design team and the design center are recent new product coordination mechanisms. Though cross-functional teams are widely cited as promising new product planning mechanisms, research findings suggest that they may be most appropriate for planning truly new and innovative products.[18] The more traditional bureaucratic structures (e.g., new products manager) may be better in planning line extensions and product improvements.

EXHIBIT 8–4
Why Lucent Is Struggling

Source: "Can Rich McGinn Revive Lucent?" *Business Week*, June 26, 2000, 183.

Lucent Technologies is the largest player in the $200 billion global communications-equipment business. It has strong positions in existing sectors but faces challenges in the markets of the future.

Optical Systems Lucent is No. 2 with about 25% of the $16.1 billion market. Now it's in danger of losing ground. Earlier this year, it stumbled badly by not having a product in the fast-growing segment for high-speed switches. So Lucent is paying big bucks to get the latest in optical technology, including $4.5 billion for Chromatis in May. It's also doubling optical production capacity each quarter.

Data Networking Lucent has the largest slice of the $25 billion market for data equipment for communications carriers. That's because it sells a lot of old data technology. It has virtually no presence in high-speed Internet routers, the most important market of the future. So Lucent is reselling a Net router from a small company called Spring Tide.

Wireless Infrastructure Lucent has been well positioned, with 22% of the $21 billion global market, second only to Ericsson's 28% share. Competition is heating up, though, to supply phone companies with the next generation of wireless equipment that will let mobile phone users tap the Net. Ericsson, in particular, has a broader portfolio of cutting-edge wireless technology.

The nature and scope of new product projects may influence how the responsibilities are allocated. Several characteristics of different new product development efforts are described in Exhibit 8–5. Consider, for example, the enormous team of people involved in developing the Boeing 777 commercial aircraft. The organizational design for such a large-scale project is likely to be more formal than that for a small-scale project like the Stanley screwdriver. Interestingly, the complete design and production for the 777 aircraft were accomplished by computers which linked together the various people and functions involved. We discuss organizational designs further in Chapter 14.

EXHIBIT 8–5
Attributes of Five Products and Their Associated Development Efforts (all figures are approximate, based on publicly available information and company sources)

Source: Karl T. Ulrich and Stephen D. Eppinger, *Product Design and Development,* 2nd ed. (Burr Ridge, IL: Irwin/McGraw-Hill, 2000), 6.

	Stanley Tools Jobmaster Screwdriver	Rollerblade In-Line Skate	Hewlett-Packard DeskJet Printer	Volkswagen New Beetle Automobile	Boeing 777 Airplane
Annual production volume	100,000 units/year	100,000 units/year	4 million units/year	100,000 units/year	50 units/year
Sales lifetime	40 years	3 years	2 years	6 years	30 years
Sales price	$3	$200	$300	$17,000	$130 million
Number of unique parts (part numbers)	3 parts	35 parts	200 parts	10,000 parts	130,000 parts
Development time	1 year	2 years	1.5 years	3.5 years	4.5 years
Internal development team (peak size)	3 people	5 people	100 people	800 people	6,800 people
External development team (peak size)	3 people	10 people	75 people	800 people	10,000 people
Development cost	$150,000	$750,000	$50 million	$400 million	$3 billion
Production investment	$150,000	$1 million	$25 million	$500 million	$3 billion

Idea Generation

Guided by the new product innovation strategy, finding promising new ideas is the starting point in the new product development process. Idea generation ranges from incremental improvements of existing products to new-to-the-world products. An example of an incremental improvement is Frito Lay's 1998 introduction of its line of WOW chips, made with Olean fat-free cooking oil. An example of a totally new product is a drug that will cure AIDS.

Idea Generation

New product ideas come from many sources. Limiting the search for new product ideas to those generated by internal research and development activities is far too narrow an approach for most firms. Sources of new product ideas include company personnel, customers, competitors, outside inventors, acquisitions, and channel members. Both solicited and spontaneous ideas may emerge from these sources, and some even occur by accident. Procter & Gamble's Ivory soap, for example, was the result of an accident that occurred over 100 years ago. Overmixing in the manufacturing process created air bubbles in the soap, causing it to float. The soap was packaged and sold, and buyers returned to retail stores to repurchase the soap bars that floated.

The objective is to establish a proactive idea generation and evaluation process that meets the needs of the enterprise. Answering several questions is helpful in developing the idea generation program:

- Should idea search activities be targeted or open-ended? Should the search for new product ideas be restricted to ideas that correspond to corporate mission, business segment, and business unit strategies?

- How extensive and aggressive should new product idea search activities be?

- What specific sources are best for generating a regular flow of new product ideas?

- How can new ideas be obtained from customers?

- Where will responsibility for the new product idea search be placed? How will new product planning activities be directed and coordinated?

- What are potential value migration threats from alternative products that may satisfy customers better than our products do?

An important issue is deciding how far to expand beyond the organization's core technology in generating new product ideas. For example, Microsoft Corp. spends large amounts of money on basic computer science research which may not result in new products.[19] Management established a quasi-academic pure-research division—Microsoft Research—to aggressively pursue pioneering research opportunities. While this division spends only about $250 million of Microsoft's $4 billion R&D budget, it nonetheless indicates management's commitment to pursuing new technologies. Microsoft's total R&D budget is over 16 percent of sales, which is much higher than that of other major technology firms.

For most companies, the idea search process should be targeted within a range of product and market involvement that is consistent with corporate mission and objectives and business unit strategy. While some far-out new product idea may occasionally change the future of a company, more often an open-ended idea search dissipates resources and misdirects efforts. However, management should be proactive in monitoring potential disruptive technologies.

Want to send your sweetie a box of chocolates? In Helsinki, you can do it from the back of a taxicab. With a push of a few buttons on a mobile phone, you can tap into an Internet site called Zed, zip an electronic order to a local warehouse, and have the chocolates sent to an address anyplace in Finland. Paying for it is a snap: The $3 for the gift is simply added to your next wireless phone bill.

The company behind the buttons? It's Sonera Corp., the leading Finnish wireless carrier. Because of Sonera, which controls over 60% of the national mobile phone market, the wireless Web is becoming an important part of Finnish life. Customers download the latest pop jingles from the Net to use as their mobile phone ring. Executives make airline reservations on Zed. Sonera even developed a mobile matchmaking service so that customers can use their phones to find mates with similar interests—say, skiing or ABBA. "We try to understand how people live their lives on a day-to-day basis," says Antti Viitanen, who develops products for Zed, Sonera's consumer wireless portal.

The services are bringing in the bacon. Revenues from Zed's mobile commerce and information services are expected to generate $248 million by 2003, up from $126 million in 1999, according to Merrill Lynch. And that's just the start. Sonera is so cutting-edge that it's able to sell its homegrown software and services to other mobile phone companies around the world. Count Powetel Inc. in the U.S. and KPN in the Netherlands among Sonera's software customers. That has helped propel the company's market cap to $27 billion.

Why is little-known Sonera leading the way to the mobile Web? It helps that a world-leading 66% of Finns use mobile phones, vs. 36% in the U.S. More than that, Sonera keeps pushing the envelope. It was, for example, one of the first to let customers pay for a Pepsi by dialing a phone number on a vending machine.

Source: Dennis K. Berman, "Killer Apps for a Wireless World," *Business Week E.Biz,* September 18, 2000, EB43.

The favorable performance of several companies argues strongly for pursuing an aggressive and continuing effort to find and develop new product ideas. Consider, for example, Sonera Corp., the leading wireless carrier in Finland. The company obtains new product ideas by distributing cameras in Europe and asking people to use photos to describe their daily routines. The photos help the company identify new product ideas like those described in the Global Feature.

Identifying the best idea sources depends on many factors, including the size and type of firm, the technologies involved, new product needs, resources, management's preferences, and corporate capabilities. Management needs to consider these issues and develop a proactive strategy for idea generation that will satisfy the firm's requirements. Market-oriented cultures and processes should be useful in generating new product ideas.

Many new product ideas originate from the users of products and services. Lead user analyses offer promising potential for the development of new products.[20] The objective is to try to identify the companies that pioneer new applications and study their requirements to improve the productivity of new product development in product-markets that change rapidly. The intent is to satisfy the lead users' needs, thus accelerating new product adoption by other companies.

Methods of Generating Ideas

We look at several ways to obtain ideas for new products. Typically, a company considers several of these options in generating product ideas.

Search

Tapping several information sources may be helpful in identifying new product ideas. Publications on new product ideas are available from companies that wish to sell or license ideas they do not want to commercialize. New technology information is available through commercial and government computerized search services. News sources may also yield information about the new product activities of competitors. Many trade publications contain new product announcements. Companies need to identify the relevant search areas and assign responsibility for an idea search to an individual or group.

Marketing Research

Surveys of product users help identify needs that can be satisfied by new products. The focus group is a useful technique to identify and evaluate new product concepts, and the research method can be used for both consumer and industrial products. A focus group consists of 8 to 12 people invited to meet with an experienced moderator to discuss a product use situation. Idea generation may occur in the focus group discussion of product requirements for a particular product use situation. Group members are asked to suggest new product ideas. Later, focus group sessions may be used to evaluate product concepts intended to satisfy the needs identified in the initial session. More than one focus group can be used at each stage in the process. Focus groups can be conducted using distribution-channel members and company personnel as well as customers. Several applications of focus groups are described in Exhibit 8–6.

Another research technique that is used to generate new product ideas is the advisory panel. The panel members are selected to represent the firm's target market. For example, a panel for a producer of mechanics' hand tools would include mechanics. Companies in various industries, including telecommunications and pharmaceuticals, use customer advisory groups. These groups provide insights and evaluations for new and existing products.

Internal and External Development

Companies' research and development laboratories generate many new product ideas. The United States is the leading spender in research and development, although Germany and Japan allocate a larger percentage of gross domestic product to R&D. Industry expenditures for U.S. R&D in 2001 were $191 billion, up 6 percent from the previous year. Federal government R&D is about one-third the size of industry expenditures. U.S. R&D allocations for services are increasing, particularly with respect to computers, software, and communications technology. Escalating R&D costs encourage the formation of strategic alliances as well as mergers.

New product ideas may originate from development efforts outside the firm. Sources include inventors, government and private laboratories, and small high-technology firms. Strategic alliances between companies may result in identifying new product ideas as well as sharing responsibility for other activities in new product planning.

Other Idea Generation Methods

Incentives may be useful in getting new product ideas from employees, value chain members, and customers. The amount of the incentive should be high enough to encourage

EXHIBIT 8–6
Uses of Focus Groups

Source: William R. Dillon, Thomas J. Madden, and Neil H. Firtle, *Marketing Research in a Marketing Environment,* 2nd ed. (Burr Ridge, IL: Richard D. Irwin, 1990), 160.

Generating New Creative Ideas

Listening to consumers talk about how they use a product or what they like or dislike about a product can provide input for creative teams in developing advertising copy. Advertising agencies often use focus group interviews for this reason.

Uncovering Basic Consumer Needs and Attitudes

In talking about a product or product category, consumers often express basic needs and attitudes that can be useful in generating hypotheses about what may or may not be accepted and about the factors responsible for the perceived similarity or dissimilarity among a set of brands.

Establishing New Product Concepts

Focus group interviews are particularly useful in providing information on the major strengths and weaknesses of a new product idea. In addition, the focus group interview can be effective in judging whether strategy-supporting promises of end-benefits have been communicated clearly.

Generating New Ideas about Established Markets

Listening to consumers talk about how they discovered ways to put a product to alternative use can stimulate marketing executives to recognize new uses for old products.

Interpreting Previously Obtained Quantitative Data

In some instances focus group interviews are used as the last step in the research process to probe for detailed reasons behind quantitative test results obtained in earlier marketing research studies.

submission. Management should also guard against employees leaving the company and developing a promising idea elsewhere. For this reason many firms require employees to sign secrecy agreements.

Finally, acquiring another firm offers a way to obtain new product ideas. This strategy may be more cost-effective than internal development and can substantially reduce the lead time required for developing new products. IBM's 1995 acquisition of Lotus Development is an example.

Idea generation identifies one or more new product opportunities which are screened and evaluated. Before comprehensive evaluation, an idea for a new product must be transformed into a defined concept which states what the product will do (anticipated attributes) and the benefits that are superior to those of available products.[21] The product concept expresses the idea in operational terms so that it can be evaluated as a potential candidate for development into a new product.

Screening, Evaluation, and Business Analysis

Moving too many ideas through too many stages in the new product planning process is expensive. Management needs a screening and evaluation procedure that will eliminate unpromising ideas as soon as possible while keeping the risks of rejecting good ideas at acceptable levels. Expenditures build up from the idea stage to the commercialization stage, whereas the risks of developing a bad new product fall as more and more information is obtained about product performance and market acceptance. The objective is to eliminate the least promising ideas before too much time and money are invested in them. However, the tighter the screening procedure, the higher the risk of rejecting a good idea. Based on the specific factors involved, a company needs to establish a level of risk that is acceptable.

Evaluation occurs regularly as an idea moves through the new product planning stages. While the objective is to eliminate the poor risks as early as possible in the planning process, evaluation is necessary at each stage in that process. We examine several evaluation techniques as the stages in new product planning are discussed. Typically, evaluation begins by screening new product ideas to identify those that are considered the most promising. These ideas are subjected to concept evaluation. Business analysis is the final assessment before deciding whether to develop the concept into a new product.

Screening

A new product idea receives an initial screening to determine its strategic fit in the company or business unit. Two questions need to be answered: (1) Is the idea compatible with the organization's mission and objectives? (2) Is the product initiative commercially feasible? The compatibility of the idea considers factors such as internal capabilities (e.g., development, production, marketing), financial needs, and competitive factors. Commercial feasibility considers market attractiveness, technical feasibility, and social and environmental concerns. The number of ideas generated by an organization is likely to influence the approach utilized in screening the ideas. A large number of ideas call for a formal screening process.

Screening eliminates ideas that are not compatible or feasible for the business. Management must establish how narrow or wide the screening boundaries should be. For example, managers from two similar firms may have very different missions and objectives as well as different propensities for risk. An idea could be strategically compatible in one firm and not in another. Also, new product strategies and priorities may change when top management changes. The Intel Corp and Avon Products Inc. cases (6–5 and 6–9) describe how those companies made major changes in the scope of new product ideas after the appointment of new CEOs.

After identifying relevant screening criteria, some firms use scoring and importance weighting techniques for the factors considered in the screening process. When the weighted scores are summed, a score is obtained for each idea being screened. Management can set ranges for passing and rejecting. The effectiveness of these methods is highly dependent on including relevant criteria and gaining agreement on the relative importance of the screening factors from the managers involved.

Concept Evaluation

The boundaries between idea screening, evaluation, and business analysis are often not clearly drawn. Some firms combine these evaluation stages, particularly when only a few ideas are involved. After the initial screening has been completed, each idea that survives becomes a new product concept and receives a more comprehensive evaluation. Several of the same factors used in screening may be evaluated in greater depth, including buyers' reactions to the proposed concept. A team representing different business functions is often responsible for concept evaluation.

Extensive research on companies' new product planning activities highlights the critical role of extensive market and technical assessments *before* beginning the development of a new product concept.[22] These "up-front" evaluations should result in a clearly defined new product concept indicating its market target(s), customer value offering, and positioning strategy. Research and analysis of product failures strongly suggest that companies do not devote enough attention to the up-front evaluation of product concepts.

The failure of the handheld CueCat scanner offers compelling evidence of the value of concept evaluation. CueCat reads a bar code and, when attached to a personal computer, provides a direct access Web page for the product. The founder of Digital Convergence Corp. raised $185 million from investors to commercially launch CueCat.[23] Large investors included Belo Corp. (37.5 million), Radio Shack ($30 million), and Young & Rubicam ($28 million). The business plan was to give away 50 million CueCats ($ 6.50 cost) and obtain revenues from advertisers and licensing fees. Four million CueCats were given away, but few were used. People did not want to carry the scanner around and could quickly access Web sites by typing the address. CueCat did not fill a consumer need. Importantly, this weakness could have been identified at the concept stage before large expenditures were made to produce and distribute the product.

Concept tests are useful in the evaluation and refinement of proposed new products. The purpose of concept testing is to obtain a reaction to the new product concept from a sample of potential buyers before the product is developed. More than one concept test can be used during the evaluation process. The technique supplies important information for reshaping, redefining, and coalescing new product ideas.[24] Concept tests help evaluate the relative appeal of ideas or alternative product positionings, supply information for developing the product and marketing strategy, and identify potential market segments. A proposal to conduct a concept test for evaluating alternative investment products is described in Exhibit 8–7. The estimated cost of the test is $15,000. Concept tests may be used to evaluate both physical product concepts and services.

The concept test is a useful way to evaluate a product idea very early in the development process. The costs of these tests are reasonable, given the information that can be obtained. Nonetheless, there are some important cautions. The test is not a definitive gauge of commercial success. Since the actual product and a commercial setting are not present, the test is somewhat artificial.

The concept test is probably most useful in signaling very favorable or unfavorable product concepts. It also offers a basis for comparing two or more concepts. An important requirement of concept testing is that the product can be described in words and visually and that the participant has the experience and capability to evaluate the concept. The respondent must be able to visualize the proposed product and its features based on a verbal or written description and/or picture. Computer technology offers promising capabilities for visual testing of concepts.

Several concept evaluation issues are highlighted in Exhibit 8–8. Evaluation includes more than concept tests. For example, the new product team may perform competitor analyses, market forecasts, and technical feasibility evaluations. The questions in Exhibit 8–8 are helpful in deciding how to evaluate the new product concept.

Business Analysis

Before the decision is made to move the concept into the product development stage, an assessment needs to be made of the estimated revenues and costs for developing and commercializing the new product. Business analysis evaluates the commercial performance of the new product concept. Obtaining an accurate financial projection depends on the quality of the revenue and cost forecasts. Business analysis is normally accomplished at several stages in the new product planning process, beginning before the product concept moves into the development stage. Financial projections are refined at later stages.

Revenue Forecasting

The newness of the product, the size of the market, and the competing products all influence the accuracy of revenue projections. In the case of an established market such as

EXHIBIT 8–7
**Project Proposal:
New Product
Concept Screening
Test**

Source: Adapted from William
R. Dillon, Thomas J. Madden,
and Neil H. Firtle, *Marketing
Research in a Marketing
Environment,* 3rd ed. (Burr
Ridge, IL: Richard D. Irwin,
1994), 562.

Brand:	New products.
Project:	Concept screening.
Background and objectives:	The New York banking group has developed 12 new product ideas for investment products (services). The objectives of this research are to assess consumer interest in the concepts and to establish priorities for further development.
Research method:	Concept testing will be conducted in four geographically dispersed, central location facilities within the New York metropolitan area.
	Each of the 12 concepts plus 1 retest control concept will be evaluated by a total of 100 men and 100 women with household incomes of $25,000. The following age quotas will be used for both male and female groups within the sample:
	18–34 = 50 percent
	35–49 = 25 percent
	50 and over = 25 percent
	Each respondent will evaluate a maximum of eight concepts. Order of presentation will be rotated throughout to avoid position bias.
	Because some of the concepts are in low-incidence product categories, user groups will be defined both broadly and narrowly in an attempt to assess potential among target audiences.
Information to be obtained:	This study will provide the following information to assist in concept evaluation:
	Investment ownership.
	Purchase interest (likelihood of subscription).
	Uniqueness of new service.
	Believability.
	Importance of main point.
	Demographics.
Action standard:	To identify concepts warranting further development, top-box purchase intent scores will be compared to the top-box purchase intent scores achieved by the top 10 percent of the concepts tested in earlier concept screening studies. Rank order of purchase intent scores on the *uniqueness, believability,* and *importance* ratings will also be considered In the evaluation and prioritization of concepts for further development.
Material requirements:	Fifty copies of each concept.
Cost and timing:	The cost of this research will be $15,000 ± 10%
	This research will adhere to the following schedule:
	Field work 1 week
	Top-line 2 weeks
	Final report 3 weeks
Supplier:	Burke Marketing Research.

EXHIBIT 8–8
**Concept
Evaluation Issues**

- What is the objective (purpose) of concept evaluation?
- How much time/resources should be allocated to evaluation?
- What are the risks?
- Who will perform the evaluation?
- Who decides the outcomes?
- What evaluation techniques are most useful?

breakfast cereals, potato chips, or toothpaste, estimates of total market size are usually available from industry information. Industry associations often publish industry forecasts, and government agencies such as the U.S. Commerce Department forecast sales for various industries. The more difficult task is estimating the market share that is feasible for a new product entry. For example, the size of the ready-to-eat (RTE) cereal market can be projected accurately, but estimating the market share of a new cereal brand is far more difficult. A range of feasible share positions can be indicated at the concept stage and used as a basis for preliminary financial projections. Established markets also may have success norms. Experience indicates that a 1 percent market share is considered a successful entry for a new RTE cereal. When available, the success norm provides a basis for estimating the possibility of reaching a successful level of sales.

Preliminary Marketing Plan

An initial marketing strategy is developed as a part of the business analysis. Included are market target(s), positioning concepts, and marketing mix plans. While this plan is preliminary, it encourages strategy development and coordination among marketing, design, production, and other business functions early in the planning process. The choice of the marketing strategy is necessary in developing the revenue forecast.

Cost Estimation

Several different costs occur in the planning and commercialization of new products. One way to categorize the costs is to estimate them for each stage in the new product planning process (Exhibit 8–3). The costs increase rapidly as the product concept moves through the development process. Expenditures for each planning stage can be further divided into functional categories (e.g., marketing, research and development, and manufacturing).

Profit Projections

Several types of profit projections can be used to gauge a new product's financial performance. Illustrative financial analysis techniques are discussed in the Appendix to Chapter 2. Analyses appropriate for new product evaluation include breakeven, cash flow, return on investment, and profit contribution. Breakeven analysis is particularly useful to show how many units of the new product must be sold before it begins to make a profit. Management can use the breakeven level as a basis for assessing the feasibility of the project. The issue is whether management considers reaching and exceeding breakeven to be feasible.

The appropriate length of time for projecting sales, costs, and profits should be determined. For example, the product may be required to recoup all costs within a certain time period. Business analysis estimates should take into consideration the probable flow of revenues and costs over the time span used in the analysis. Typically, new products incur heavy costs before they start to generate revenues.

Other Considerations

Several other issues are considered in the business analysis of a new product concept. First, management often has guidelines for the financial performance of new products.

These guidelines can be used to accept, reject, or further analyze the product concept. Another issue is assessing the amount of risk associated with the venture. This factor should be included either in the financial projections or as an additional consideration beyond the financial estimates. Finally, possible cannibalization of sales by the new product from existing products needs to be considered. This is not necessarily a negative factor since management's intent may be to cannibalize its brand and competitors' brands with the new product.

Product and Process Development

After completing the business analysis stage, management must decide either to begin product design or to abort the project. In order to continue our look at the new product planning process, we assume a favorable outcome even though deciding not to proceed with product and process development may be the best option based on the business analyses. During the development stage the concept is transformed into one or more prototypes. The prototype is the actual product, but it is produced by research and development rather than by an established manufacturing process. Use testing of the product may occur during the development stage.

Our earlier discussion of customer-guided new product planning emphasized the importance of incorporating customer preferences into guidelines for internal product design. Product design decisions need to be guided by customer preferences and analysis of competitors' advantages and weaknesses. Product development should involve the entire new product planning team. We examine the product development process, followed by a discussion of collaborative development.

Product Development Process

The development of the new product concept includes product design, industrial design (ease of use and style), process (manufacturing) design, packaging design, and decisions to make or purchase various product components. Development typically consists of various technical activities but also requires continuing interaction among R&D, marketing, manufacturing, finance, and legal functions. The relative importance of development activities differs according to the product involved. For example, product and process design are extensive for complex products like large commercial aircraft (see Exhibit 8–5). In contrast, line extensions (e.g., new flavors and package sizes) of food products or bank services do not require extensive design activities.

Product Specifications

The R&D technical team needs guidelines in order to develop the product. Product specifications describe what the product will do rather than how it should be designed and indicate the product planners' expectations regarding the product benefit based on customer analysis, including essential physical and operating characteristics.[25] This information allows the technical team to determine the best design strategy for delivering the benefits.

Recall the earlier discussion of U.S. Surgical's development of laparoscopy equipment. Illustrative specifications for developing this type of product include equipment size, features (e.g., ease of operation), functions to performed (visual view of the inside of the patient's body via a TV camera), types of material, and cleaning requirements. The more complete the specifications for the product are, the better the designers can incorporate the requirements into the design. The specifications also provide a basis for assessing design feasibility. In some situations benefit/cost assessments may lead to changing the specifications.

Prototype

R&D uses the product specifications to guide the design of one or more physical products. Similar information is needed to guide software design and the design of new services. At this stage the product is called a prototype since it is not ready for commercial production and marketing. It is a custom version. Many of the parts may be custom built, and materials, packaging, and other details may differ from the commercial version. Nevertheless, the prototype needs to be capable of delivering the benefits spelled out in the specifications. Scale models are used in some kinds of products, such as commercial aircraft, which can be tested in wind tunnels to evaluate their performance characteristics. Computer technology is also used in the testing and evaluation of new products such as automobiles and aircraft.

Expanded use is being made of three-dimensional computer modeling of new product designs. The computer design of the Boeing 777 aircraft is illustrative. Computer-aided design is used in new automobile development. Information technology is playing an expanding role in product design in the 21st century.

Use Tests

When use testing of the prototype is feasible, designers can obtain important feedback from users concerning how well the product meets the needs that are spelled out in the product specifications. A standard approach to use testing is to distribute the product to a sample of users and ask them to try the product. Follow-up occurs after a test participant has had sufficient time to evaluate the product. The design of new industrial products may include the active involvement of users in testing and evaluating the product at various stages in the process. The relatively small number of users in industrial markets compared to consumer markets makes use testing very feasible. Use tests are also popular for gaining reactions to new consumer products such as foods, drinks, and health and beauty aids.

An example of a proposed use test for a new soup flavor is described in Exhibit 8–9. Unlike a market test, a use test normally does not identify the brand name of the product or the company name. While the use test is less accurate in gauging market success than is the market test, the use test yields important information such as preferences, ratings, likes/dislikes, advantages/limitations, unique features, usage and users, and comparisons with competing products.[26]

Manufacturing Development

A company must also develop a process for producing the product in commercial quantities. Manufacturing the product at the desired quality level and cost is a critical determinant of profitability. The new product may be feasible to produce in the laboratory but not in a manufacturing plant because of costs, production rates, and other considerations. Initial production delays can also jeopardize the success of a new product.

The concepts of *mass customization* and *modularity* may have a major impact on product and process design.[27] As we discussed in Chapter 4, mass customization enables customizing product offerings at relatively low costs. Modularity involves developing and producing a product using interrelated modules, thus facilitating mass customization. The system architecture links the modules together, but each can be designed and produced independently within the organization or by suppliers. Modularity was pioneered by the computer industry but is applicable to many other products.

Japanese new product designers have modified the new product planning process (Exhibit 8–3) by determining a target cost based on the price the market is likely to accept for a new product *before* design is initiated.[28] The target cost becomes an integral part of the planning process. Cost engineers with experience in purchasing, design, and other functions such

EXHIBIT 8–9
Project Proposal:
Product Test

Source: William R. Dillon,
Thomas J. Madden, and Neil H.
Firtle, *Marketing Research in a
Marketing Environment,* 3rd ed.
(Burr Ridge, IL: Richard D.
Irwin, 1994), 583.

Brand:	New product: Hardy Soup.
Project:	Campbell's versus new Hardy Soup blind product test.
Background and objectives:	R&D has developed a new Hardy Soup in two different flavors (chicken noodle and mushroom). Additionally, each flavor has been developed at two different flavor strengths. The brand groups have requested that research be conducted to determine (1) whether this product should be considered for introduction, (2) If so, if one or both flavors should be introduced, and (3) which flavor variation(s) would be preferred most by the consumer.
	The objective of this research will be to determine consumers' preferences for each flavor variation of the new product relative to Campbell's Chunky products.
Method:	There will be four cells. In each cell, a blind paired-product test will be conducted between a different flavor variation of the new product and the currently marketed Campbell's product, as follows:

- Campbell's Chunky Chicken Noodle versus Hardy's Chicken Noodle 1.
- Campbell's Chunky Chicken Noodle versus Hardy's Chicken Noodle 2.
- Campbell's Chunky Mushroom versus Hardy's Mushroom 1.
- Campbell's Chunky Mushroom versus Hardy's Mushroom 2.

	In each cell, there will be 200 past-30-day ready-to-serve soup user/purchasers.
	Respondents will be interviewed in a shopping mall and given both products to take home and try. Additionally, to be used in the test, respondents must be positively disposed toward chicken noodle or mushroom flavors. Order of product trial will be rotated to minimize position bias. Telephone callbacks will be made after a one-week period.
Action standard:	Each new soup flavor will be considered for introduction if one or more of its flavor variations achieves at least absolute parity with its Campbell's Chunky control.
	If for either flavor alternative more than one flavor level variation meets the action standard, the one that is preferred over Campbell's at the highest level of confidence will be recommended to be considered for introduction.
	A single-sample t-test for paired comparison data (two-tail) will be used to test for significance.
Cost and timing:	The cost of this study will be $32,000 \pm 10\%$.
	The following schedule will be established:

Field work	2 weeks
Top-line	2 weeks
Final report	4 weeks

Research firm:	Burke Marketing Research.

as sales participate in the planning process to assure that the product meets the desired target cost. This eliminates the need to redesign products whose costs are too high, and the planning approach also helps compress product development time.

Collaborative Development

Collaborative research and development partnerships are used to increase the competitive advantage of a single company and reduce the time required to develop and market new products. These relationships may be strategic alliances or supplier-producer collaborations (Chapter 7). The development of Hewlett-Packard's (H-P) HP FAX-300 is the result of an alliance between H-P and Matsushita, a leading Japanese producer of fax machines.[29] H-P applied the technology from its very successful DeskJet printer. Matsushita contributed the fax technology. H-P gained important copier cost savings by producing the fax in the same plant as the DeskJet. The result was a plain paper fax at a price competitive with the prices of thermal fax machines and far below those of laser machines.

Outsourcing of the manufacturing of new products to other firms became very popular in the 1990s. For example, Sara Lee Corp., the $18 billion (2002) producer of an array of consumer brands from foods to apparel, announced a strategy in the late 1990s of shifting production of its products to independent producers. Previously, Sara Lee had produced many of its brands in-house. Tommy Hilfiger has only 4,100 employees (and $2 billion in sales in 2002) because of outsourcing and licensing of its clothing and accessories. Coke and Pepsi outsource the bottling and distribution of their beverage brands. Outsourcing reduces the investment required by the product designer but requires close coordination with the producer firm.

Developing Marketing Strategy and Market Testing

Guidelines for marketing strategy depend largely on the new product being developed. A totally new product requires complete targeting and positioning strategies (Chapter 6). An incremental product improvement may need only a revised promotion strategy to convey to target buyers information about the benefits the improved product offers. It is also important to consider how the new product will affect the sales of existing products. Regardless of the newness of the product, reviewing the proposed marketing strategy helps avoid problems and identify opportunities.

Marketing Decisions

Product evaluation efforts (e.g., use tests) conducted during product development supply information that may be helpful in designing the marketing strategy. Examples of useful planning guidelines include user characteristics, product features, advantages over competing products, use situations, feasible price range, and potential buyer profiles. The design of the marketing strategy begins as soon as possible in new product planning, since several activities need to be completed and reducing the time to market introduction provides an important competitive advantage. Marketing strategy planning begins at the concept evaluation stage and continues during product development. Activities such as packaging, name selection, environmental considerations, product information, colors, materials, and product safety must also be decided on between engineering, manufacturing, and marketing.

Market Targeting

Selection of the market target(s) for the new product ranges from offering a new product to an existing target to identifying an entirely new group of potential users. Examining the prior marketing research (concept tests and use tests) for the new product may yield useful insights into targeting opportunities. It may also be necessary to conduct additional research before finalizing the market targeting strategy.

Positioning Strategy

Several positioning decisions are resolved during the marketing strategy development stage. Product strategy regarding packaging, name selection, sizes, and other aspects of the product must be decided on. A channel strategy is needed to access new channels of distribution. It is also necessary to formulate a price strategy and develop an advertising and sales promotion strategy. Testing of advertisements may occur at this stage. Finally, sales management must design a personal selling strategy, including deciding about sales force training and allocation of selling effort to the new product.

Market Testing Options

Market testing can be considered after the product is fully developed, assuming the product is suitable for market testing. Market tests gauge buyer response to the new product and evaluate one or more positioning strategies. Test marketing is used for consumer products such as foods, beverages, and health and beauty aids. In addition to conventional test marketing, less expensive alternatives are available, such as simulated test marketing and scanner-based test marketing.

A description of the different new product evaluation tools is shown in Exhibit 8–10. The stages where each testing tool is used are indicated. Note also how market testing fits into the planning process. The exhibit provides an overview of the entire new product planning process.

Simulated Test Marketing

One way to implement simulated testing is recruiting potential buyers while they are shopping. The simulation technique:

> involves intercepting shoppers at a high-traffic location, sometimes prescreening them for category use, exposing the selected individuals to a commercial (or concept) for a proposed

EXHIBIT 8–10
How Market Testing Relates to the Other Testing Steps

Source: C. Merle Crawford and C. Anthony Di Benedetto, *New Products Management,* 6th ed. (Burr Ridge, IL: Irwin/ McGraw-Hill, 2000), 411.

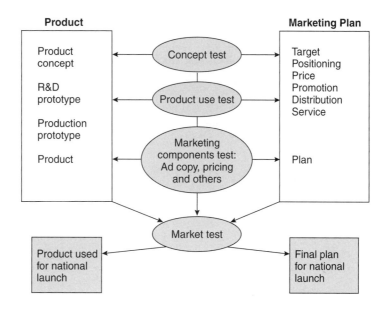

new product, giving them an opportunity to buy the new product in a real life or laboratory setting, and interviewing those who purchased the new product at a later date to ascertain their reaction and repeat-purchase intentions.[30]

Simulated tests offer several advantages, including speed (12 to 16 weeks), low cost (less than $100,000 compared to more than $2 million for full-scale market tests), and relatively accurate forecasts of market response.[31] The tests also eliminate the risk in conventional testing that competitors will jam the test. The use of simulated test marketing is described in the Technology Feature.

Scanner-Based Test Marketing

This method employs an actual market environment in contrast to simulated testing and is less expensive than a conventional market test. Information Resources Inc.'s BehaviorScan system pioneered the use of cable television and a computerized database to track new products. The system uses information and responses from 2,500 panel members in each test city. Each member has an identification card to show to participating store cashiers. Purchases are recorded electronically and transmitted to a central data bank. Cable television enables BehaviorScan to use controlled advertisement testing. Some viewers can be exposed to ads that are withheld from other viewers.

Conventional Test Marketing

Market testing puts the product under actual market conditions in one or more test cities.[32] It is used for frequently purchased consumer products. Test marketing employs a complete marketing program, including advertising and personal selling. Product sampling is often an important factor in launching the new product in the test market. The product is marketed on a commercial basis in each city, and test results are then projected to the national or regional target market. Because of its high cost, conventional test marketing represents the final evaluation before full-scale market introduction. New product managers may decide not to test market in order to avoid competitor awareness, to avoid high testing costs, and to accelerate introduction.

Testing Industrial Products

Market testing can be used for various industrial products. Selection of test sites may need to extend beyond one or two cities to include sufficient market coverage. For example, a region of a country might be used for testing. The test firm has substantial control of an industrial products test since it can use direct mail and personal selling. The relatively small number of customers also aids targeting of marketing efforts. The product should have the characteristics necessary for testing: It should be producible in test quantities, relatively inexpensive, and not subject to extensive buying center influences throughout the buyer's organization.

Selecting Test Sites

Test sites should exhibit the buyer and environmental characteristics of the intended market target. Since no site is perfect, the objective is to find a reasonable match between the test and the market target for the new product. The following criteria are often used to evaluate potential test sites for consumer products:

1. Representation as to population size.
2. Typical per capita income.
3. Typical purchasing habits.

- STM consists of analyzing detailed marketing plan information, estimated costs, and responses from a sample of target market prospects.

- Potential buyers of the good or service are exposed to the new product and the competitors' products in a simulated store environment.

- Participants are asked questions about possible purchase of the product and reactions to variations in features (e.g., different prices).

- As prospects move through different scenarios about features and price, estimates can be made about how the alternative offerings will perform during market introduction.

- The marketing plan details, costs, and participant response information are analyzed using an STM computer model developed to fit the specific market environment.

- STM generates sales and profit forecasts and valuable insights about improving the effectiveness of marketing mix components.

- STM helps answer important questions, such as describing the target market, positioning preferences, and responsiveness to pricing.

Source: Kevin J. Clancy and Robert S. Shulman, "Test for Success," *Sales and Marketing Management,* October 1995, 111–14.

4. Stability of year-round sales.

5. Relative isolation from other cities.

6. Not easily jammed by competitors.

7. Typical of planned distribution outlets.

8. Availability of retailers that will cooperate.

9. Availability of media that will cooperate.

10. Availability of research and audit service companies.[33]

Some of the best metropolitan test markets in the United States are Detroit; St. Louis; Charlotte–Gastonia–Rock Hill, NC–SC; Fort Worth–Arlington, TX; and Kansas City.[34] Cities can be ranked according to an "index of dissimilarity." The index takes into account age, race, and housing value (a proxy for income). Detroit has the lowest cumulative index value of the 20 best metropolitan areas. An index of zero is a perfect match to overall U.S. demographics. Detroit's 23 is a very good score. The top 20 cities' cumulative index values range from 23 to 29.

Length of the Test

The length of the test affects the test results. A. C. Nielsen's analyses of more than 100 market tests of new-brand introductions indicate that the predictability of national results from test market data increases significantly with time.[35] After 4 months of testing, 37 percent of the predictions were correct; after 18 months, the figure was 100 percent. The testing firm needs 10 months to be reasonably sure that market share data are representative. Market tests of more than a year are not unusual.

External Influences

Probably the most troublesome external factor that may affect test market results is competition that does not compete on a normal basis. Competitors may attempt to drive test market results awry by increasing or decreasing their marketing efforts and making other changes in their marketing actions. It is also important to monitor the test market environment to identify other unusual influences, such as major shifts in economic conditions.

New Product Models

New product analytical models are useful in analyzing test market data and predicting commercial market success. They fall into two categories: (1) first-purchase models designed to predict the cumulative number of new product tries over time and (2) models designed to predict the repeat purchase rate of those buyers who have tried the product.[36] The latter model combines a first-purchase model with a repeat-purchase model. A brief overview of the consumer adoption process for new products sets the stage for our look at the two types of models.

Consumer Adoption Process

Extensive research concerning the adoption of innovations indicates that (1) new product adopters follow a sequence of stages in their adoption process, (2) adopters' characteristics vary according to how soon they adopt the product after introduction, and (3) adoption findings may be of value in new product planning. The adoption stages are awareness, interest, evaluation, trial, and adoption.[37] By finding and targeting the "early adopters," firms may be able to accelerate a new product's adoption. Early adopters tend to be younger, of generally higher socioeconomic status, and more in contact with impersonal and cosmopolitan sources of information than are later adopters.[38] The early adopter also uses a variety of information sources.

First-Purchase Models

These models are based on the diffusion of the new product into the market. The models generate a life-cycle sales curve using a mathematical model that contains a small number of parameters.[39] The parameters are estimated based on analysis of adoption patterns for similar products, consumer pretests, or early sales results. The models range from simple exponential curve fitting using market potential and rate of penetration as parameters to more complex multistage models. Mahajan and Peterson provide a comprehensive critique and comparative assessment of first-purchase diffusion models of new product acceptance.[40]

Repeat-Purchase Models

Many consumer and industrial new products are nondurables that are repurchased on a regular basis. Models are available for projecting the sales of these products and for evaluating marketing program positioning strategy. The ASSESSOR model illustrates this group of models.[41] It evaluates the new product before test marketing but after decisions have been made regarding marketing program positioning strategy. Management can use this information, in combination with direct behavior and attitude data obtained from laboratory and usage tests, to make market-share predictions and obtain diagnostic information. Trial/repeat and attitude models are built into the structure of ASSESSOR. The model uses two parallel approaches (trial/repeat and preference models) to estimate the brand's market share. A laboratory facility and a simulated shopping experiment are included in the modeling process. Applications typically use samples of 300 people.

New product models such as ASSESSOR are very data-dependent and complex. Their validity has not been fully tested, although for certain kinds of applications the results have been promising. The strengths of such models include their capacity to analyze interrelationships among several variables and to generate outputs based on input data. Applications appear most appropriate for frequently purchased nondurable products that are not totally new (e.g., incremental improvements), so that purchasers have some experience with the product category. Model applications like ASSESSOR are expensive, but they cost a small fraction of a market test or full-scale commercialization.[42]

Commercialization

Introducing new products into the market requires finalizing the marketing plan, coordinating introduction activities with business functions, implementing the marketing strategy, and monitoring and controlling the product launch. Procter & Gamble's entry into Japan's dish soap market in 1995 was an interesting new product venture.[43] P&G's Joy brand had gained a leading 20 percent share of the $400 million dish soap market by 1997. The successful strategy included offering new technology, packaging that retailers liked, attractive margins for retailers, and heavy spending on innovative commercials that got consumers' attention. At the time of market entry, Kao and Lion (Japanese companies) together had nearly 40 percent of the market. P&G developed a highly concentrated formula for Joy to eliminate consumers' concerns about Joy's strengths compared to those of other brands. Encouraged by commercials to try the new product, Japanese homemakers were pleased with Joy's performance.

The Marketing Plan

Market introduction requires a complete marketing strategy which is spelled out in the marketing plan. The plan should be coordinated with the people responsible for the introduction, including salespeople, sales and marketing managers, and managers in other functional areas, such as production, distribution, finance, and human resources. Responsibility for the new product launch normally is assigned to the marketing manager or product manager. Companies may assign responsibility to product planning and market introduction teams.

The timing and geographic scope of the launch are important decisions. The options range from a national market introduction to an area-by-area rollout. In some instances the scope of the introduction may extend to international markets. The national introduction is a major endeavor, requiring a comprehensive implementation effort. A rollout reduces the scope of the introduction and enables management to adjust marketing strategy based on the experience gained in the early stages of the launch. Of course, the rollout approach, like market testing, gives the competition more time to react.

Monitoring and Control

Real-time tracking of new product performance at the commercialization stage is extremely important. Standardized information services are available for monitoring sales of products such as foods, health and beauty aids, and prescription drugs. Information is collected through store audits, consumer diary panels, and scanner services. Special tracking studies may be necessary for products that are not included in standardized information services.

The Internet is rapidly becoming an essential new product information gathering and monitoring capability. These activities include private online communities and research panels which provide companies with shoppers' feedback. The E-Business Feature

HALLMARK CARDS

Research:

The company hosts an online bulletin board for 200 consumers who chat about everything from holiday decorating ideas to prayers for ill loved ones. Hallmark breaks in to steer the conversation or conduct surveys.

Payoff:

New ideas for cards such as less sentimental ones for mothers-in-law or sympathy cards for the anniversary of a death, and an entire new product line that Hallmark has yet to disclose.

STONYFIELD FARM

Research:

Stonyield's higher-priced yogurt appeals to a niche audience that can't easily be found in phone surveys or mail interviews. So it went online to ask 105 yogurt eaters for feedback on new products.

Payoff:

The survey was done in two days, down from a month, for 20% less cost than a phone survey. The company ditched the name YoFemme after consumers panned it, in favor of YoSelf.

COCA-COLA

Research:

Coke created an online panel of 100 teenagers and asked how to remake its flagging Powerade sports drink. Coke wanted to move fast, and by going deep with the same panelists, it could count on quality results.

Payoff:

Powerade relaunched in June with. B vitamins, thanks to input from the panel. Coke cut the time and cost of product-development research by 50%.

KRAFT FOODS

Research:

The company surveyed 160 panelists about frozen vegetables, then chose 24 to do a taste-test for a new product. Consumers sent responses via e-mail that were more detailed than traditional surveys.

Payoff:

Research was 30% faster and 25% cheaper than a typical focus group. And Kraft reached consumers nationwide rather than in just a few major cities.

Source: Faith Keenan, "Friendly Spies on the Net," *Business Week E.Biz,* July 9, 2001, EB27.

describes how Coca-Cola, Kraft Foods, Hallmark Cards, and Stonyfield Farm are using the Web to generate new product ideas from consumers and spot problems with new products.

It is important to include product performance metrics with performance targets in the new product plan to evaluate how well the product is performing. Often included are profit contribution, sales, market share, and return on investment objectives—including the time horizon for reaching objectives. It is also important to establish benchmarks for objectives that indicate minimum acceptable performance. For example, market share threshold levels sometimes are used to gauge new product performance. Repeat purchase data are essential for tracking frequently purchased products. Regular measures of customer satisfaction are also relevant measures of market performance. Management needs to be prepared to drop a new product if it is apparent that poor performance will continue.

Variations in the Generic New Product Planning Process

The new product planning process (Exhibit 8–3) is based on the logic of being market-driven and focused on customer needs. While a market-oriented focus is always important, some variations in the generic perspective discussed so far may occur due to the new product strategy of a particular company. The variants from the generic process fall into four categories: technology push, platform, process-intensive, and customized products.[44] Several characteristics of each variant of the generic process are shown in Exhibit 8–11. We examine each variant, highlighting situations where it may be applicable and how it differs from the generic process. The chapter concludes with a discussion of proactive cannibalization.

Technology Push Processes

Technology push product planning starts with a new technology, and then the planning team looks for a market need that can be satisfied by the technology. The technology is the primary driver of the new product planning process. Nonetheless, the various stages of the generic process are applicable. The technology provides the focus for generating new product ideas.

The development of inkjet technology by Hewlett-Packard followed the technology push process. The printing capability was developed first, and then a product team pursued applications of the technology. The technology could have been used to develop printers to compete against laser printers, since the inkjet technology offered distinct advantages. Instead, the team decided to develop a line of printers to compete against dot matrix printers. This proved to be a much more attractive option because users were becoming dissatisfied with dot matrix printers, and this market was much larger than the laser market.

Platform Products

The platform product is the result of an organization developing a capability that provides a foundation for generating other products. The planning process starts with an existing platform. The platform is an existing design that can be adapted to other product extensions. The objective is to leverage the platform to develop new products. Platform strategies are used for automobile designs, computers, appliances, and many other products.

Process-Intensive Products

Planning for process-intensive products centers on the production process that an organization already has in place. The objective is to generate products that utilize the organization's process capabilities. New product ideas are those that can be produced by the existing

EXHIBIT 8–11   **Summary of Variants of the Generic Development Process**

	Generic (Market Pull)	Technology Push	Platform Products	Process Intensive	Customized
Description	The firm begins with a market opportunity, then finds appropriate technologies to meet customer needs.	The firm begins with a new technology, then finds an appropriate market.	The firm assumes that the new product will be built around an established technological subsystem.	Characteristics of the product are highly constrained by the production process.	New products are slight variations of existing configurations.
Distinctions with respect to generic process		Planning phase involves matching technology and market. Concept development assumes a given technology.	Concept development assumes a technology platform.	Both process and product must be developed together from the very beginning, or an existing production process must be specified from the beginning.	Similarity of projects allows for a highly structured development process.
Examples	Most sporting goods, furniture, tools.	Gore-Tex rainwear, Tyvek envelopes.	Consumer electronics, computers, printers.	Snack foods, cereal, chemicals, semiconductors.	Switches, motors, batteries, containers.

Source: Karl T. Ulrich and Stephen D. Eppinger, *Product Design and Development,* 2nd ed. (Burr Ridge, IL: Irwin/McGraw-Hill, 2000), 21.

process. Examples of process-intensive products include foods, beverages, chemicals, and semiconductors. Pepsi's development of the Sierra Mist carbonated beverage is an example of a process-intensive product.

Customized Products

Customized products are incremental variations of existing products and may be developed to meet the specific needs of customers. The organization pursues a very structured and detailed development process. The intent is to customize the product to meet the customer's specific specifications. For example, large commercial aircraft orders are often customized to meet the specific preferences of airline carriers. This category of new products is also related to mass customization, where the design and production process is designed to respond to customized requirements.

Proactive Cannibalization

Proactive cannibalization consists of the pursuit of a deliberate ongoing strategy of developing and introducing new products that attract the buyers of a company's existing products. The strategic logic of this concept is offering buyers a better solution to a need currently being satisfied. Executive resistance to cannibalization is driven by the belief that it is unproductive for a company to compete with its own products and services rather than targeting those of competitors. However, the reality is that changes in market requirements and customer value opportunities result in threats to existing products and technologies. Nonetheless, managers often avoid actions that cannibalize established products.

There are various examples of the negative consequences of avoiding cannibalization initiatives in the communications, financial services, retailing, and other sectors. Encyclopedia Britannica's failure to recognize the threat of CD-ROM technology is illustrative. Proactive cannibalization may be essential to many firms to sustain a competitive advantage and achieve financial performance and growth objectives. In support of the logic of proactive cannibalization, research sponsored by the Marketing Science Institute indicates that managers of successful firms proactively resist the instinct to retain the value of past investments in product development.[45] They pursue proactive cannibalization initiatives.

Summary

New product planning is a vital activity in every company and applies to services as well as physical products. Companies that are successful in new product planning follow a step-by-step process of new product planning combined with effective organization designs for managing new products. Experience helps these firms improve product planning over time. The corporate cultures of companies like Microsoft encourage innovation.

Top management often defines the product, market, and technology scope of new product ideas to be considered by an organization. The steps in new product planning include customer needs analysis, idea generation and screening, concept evaluation, business analysis, product development and testing, marketing strategy development, market testing, and commercialization (Exhibit 8–3).

Idea generation starts the process of planning for a new product. There are various internal and external sources of new product ideas. Ideas are generated by information search, marketing research, research and development, incentives, and acquisition. Screening, evaluation, and business analysis help determine if the new product concept is sufficiently attractive to justify proceeding with development.

Design of the product and use testing transform the product from a concept into a prototype. Product development creates one or more prototypes. Product testing obtains users' reaction to the new product. Manufacturing development determines how to produce the product in commercial quantities at costs that will enable the firm to price the product at a level attractive to buyers. Marketing strategy development begins early in the product-planning process. A complete marketing strategy is needed for a totally new product. Product-line additions, modifications, and other changes require a less extensive development of marketing strategy.

Completion of the product design and marketing strategy moves the process to the market testing stage. At this point management may decide to obtain some form of market reaction to the new product. Testing options include simulated test marketing, scanner-based test marketing, and conventional test marketing. Industrial products are not market tested as much as consumer products are, although frequently purchased nondurables can be tested. Instead, use tests of product prototypes are more typical for industrial products. Commercialization completes the planning process, moving the product into the marketplace to pursue sales and profit performance objectives.

The market-driven, customer-focused generic planning process provides the basic guide to developing new products. Nonetheless, some variations exist in the process when technology plays a lead role, platforms influence new product development, manufacturing processes constrain product scope, or incremental variations are used to customize products. Finally, the consideration of proactive cannibalization initiatives should be considered in the innovation strategies of all companies.

Internet Applications

A. Visit the website of the Gap (*www.gap.com*). Discuss how the Web can be used in new product planning for a bricks-and-mortar retailer such as the Gap.

B. Virgin Group Ltd. is an interesting corporate conglomerate headed by the British tycoon Sir Richard C. N. Branson. Visit *virgin.com* and develop a critical analysis of Virgin's new product strategy of launching a portfolio of online businesses.

C. Visit Bank One's website (*www.bankone.com*) and familiarize yourself with the bank's on-line branch and the product mix offered online. How do the product offerings compare to your home bank? Can you identify ways to improve www.bankone.com's product mix?

Questions for Review and Discussion

1. Discuss the relationship between customer satisfaction and customer value.

2. In many consumer products companies marketing executives seem to play the lead role in new product planning, whereas research and development executives occupy this position in firms with very complex products such as electronics. Why do these differences exist? Do you agree that such differences should occur?

3. Discuss the features and limitations of focus group interviews for use in new product planning.

4. Identify and discuss the important issues in deciding how to organize for new product planning.

5. Discuss the issues and trade-offs of using tight evaluation versus loose evaluation procedures as a product concept moves through the planning process to the commercialization stage.

6. What factors may affect the length of the new product planning process?

7. Compare and contrast the use of scanner tests and conventional market tests.

8. Is the use of a single-city test market appropriate? Discuss.

9. Examine the new product planning process (Exhibit 8–3), assuming a platform strategy is being used by the organization. How does the platform strategy alter the planning process?

10. Analyze the potential role of the Internet in the new product planning process.

Notes

1. Geoff Baum, Chris Ittner, David Larcker, Jonathan Low, Tony Siesfeld, and Michael S. Malone, "Introducing the New Value Creation Index," *Forbes ASAP,* April 3, 2000, 140–143.
2. Tasaddura Shervani and Philip C. Zerrillo, "The Albatross of Product Innovation," *Business Horizons,* January–February 1997, 57–62.
3. Marcia Stepanek, "As I Was Saying to My Refrigerator . . ." *Business Week E.Biz,* September 18, 2000, EB4–41.
4. Ibid.
5. "Getting Hot Ideas from Customers," *Fortune,* May 18, 1992, 86–87.
6. Gary S. Lynn, Joseph G. Morone, and Albert S. Paulson, "Marketing and Discontinuous Innovation: The Probe and Learn Process," *California Management Review,* Spring 1996, 8–37.
7. Ibid.
8. Joseph Morone, *Winning in High-Tech Markets* (Boston: Harvard Business School Press, 1993), 217.
9. Lynn et al., "Marketing and Discontinuous Innovation," 11.
10. Clayton M. Christensen, *The Innovator's Dilemma* (Boston: Harvard Business School Press, 1997).

11. Ibid.
12. Richard Walters, "Never Forget to Nurture the Next Big Idea," *Financial Times,* May 15, 2001, 21.
13. "Producer Power," *The Economist,* March 4, 1995, 70; Robert Cooper, "Benchmarking New Product Performance: Results of the Best Practices Study," *European Management Journal,* February 1998, 1–17.
14. Lawrence Ingrassia, "By Improving Scratch Paper, 3M Gets New-Product Winner," *The Wall Street Journal,* March 31, 1983, 27.
15. Andy Reinhardt, "The New INTEL," *Business Week,* March 13, 2000, 110–24.
16. Cooper, "Benchmarking New Product Performance."
17. Eric M. Olsen, Orville C. Walker, Jr., and Robert W. Ruekert, "Organizing for Effective New-Product Development: The Moderating Role of Product Innovativeness, *Journal of Marketing,* January 1995, 48–62.
18. Ibid.
19. Rebecca Buckman, "Window into the Future," *The Wall Street Journal,* June 25, 2001, R19.
20. Glen L. Urban and Eric von Hippel, "Lead User Analyses for the Development of New Industrial Products," *Management Science,* May 1988, 569–82.
21. C. Merle Crawford and C. Anthony Di Benedetto, *New Products Management,* 6th ed. (Burr Ridge, IL: Irwin/McGraw-Hill, 2000), chap. 4.
22. Cooper, "Benchmarking New Product Performance."
23. Elliot Spagat, "A Web Gadget Fizzles Despite a Salesman's Dazzle," *The Wall Street Journal,* June 27, 2001, B1, B4.
24. William R. Dillon, Thomas J. Madden, and Neil H. Firtle, *Marketing Research in a Marketing Environment,* 3rd ed. (Burr Ridge, IL: Richard D. Irwin, 1994), 558–60.
25. Crawford and Di Benedetto, *New Products Management,* chap. 12.
26. Dillon, Madden, and Firtle, *Marketing Research,* 582–84.
27. See, for example, James H. Gilmore and B. Joseph Pine II, "The Four Faces of Mass Customization," *Harvard Business Review,* January–February 1997, 91–101; and Kathleen M. Eisenhardt and Shona L. Brown, "Time Pacing: Competing in Markets That Won't Stand Still," *Harvard Business Review,* March–April 1998, 67.
28. Ford S. Worthy, "Japan's Smart Secret Weapon," *Fortune,* August 12, 1991, 72–75.
29. "Hewlett-Packard's Generation Gap," *Ad Week's Marketing Week,* November 4, 1991, 34–35.
30. Dillon, Madden, and Firtle, *Marketing Research,* 639.
31. Ibid.
32. Ibid.
33. Ibid.
34. Judith Waldrop, "All-American Markets," *American Demographics,* January 1992, 24–28.
35. "The True Test of Test Marketing Is Time," *Sales & Marketing Management,* March 15, 1982, 76.
36. Gary L. Lillien and Philip Kotler, *Marketing Decision Making* (New York: Harper & Row, 1983), chap. 19.
37. Everett M. Rogers, *Diffusion of Innovations* (New York: Free Press, 1962).
38. Ibid.
39. Lilien and Kotler, *Marketing Decision Making,* 706.
40. Vijay Mahajan and Robert A. Peterson, "First-Purchase Diffusion Models of New-Product Acceptance," *Technological Forecasting and Social Change* 15 (1979), 127–46.

41. Glen L. Urban and John R. Hauser, *Design and Marketing of New Products,* 2nd ed. (Englewood Cliffs, NJ: Prentice-Hall, 1993), 463–67.

42. Ibid.

43. Norihiko Shirouzu, "P&G's Joy Makes an Unlikely Splash in Japan," *The Wall Street Journal,* December 19, 1997, B1, B8.

44. The following discussion is based on Karl T. Ulrich and Steven D. Eppinger, *Product Design and Development,* 2nd ed. (Burr Ridge, IL: Irwin/McGraw-Hill, 2000), 20–23.

45. Rajesh K. Chandy and Gerald J. Tellis, "Organizing for Radical Product Innovation," *MSI Report No. 98-102* (Cambridge, MA: Marketing Science Institute, 1998).

Cases for Part 3

Case 3–1

Samsung Electronics

To managers of Samsung Electronics' sprawling television plant in Suwon, South Korea, it seemed like a no-brainer. During the depth of the country's economic crisis in early 1998, the Korean won was wallowing at 1,800 to the dollar—less than half its value of a year earlier. That provided a golden opportunity to throw production lines into overdrive and flood export markets with TVs while the currency was still cheap.

But rather than giving the green light, Samsung Electronics President Yun Jong Yong rebuked his eager managers. Just a few months earlier, he had shut down the Suwon plant for two months because so many unsold TVs and other appliances had piled up in Samsung warehouses. The costs of carrying that inventory had been devastating to the company's balance sheets. Samsung wouldn't repeat the mistake. Declaring war on unsold inventory, Yun said Samsung factories would only produce goods after orders were in hand and profitability assured.

Putting profitability before gross sales is basic business common sense in the West. But it was a radical concept at Samsung and other Korean conglomerates, which for decades had been obsessed with exports and record production runs. Now, Samsung Electronics managers hail Yun's profits-first decree as pivotal in a remarkable corporate comeback. "Shutting, the TV plant sent a very strong signal to the staff," says Park Sung Chil, Samsung's director of supply chain management. The just-in-time approach to production has enabled Samsung to shave $3 billion in inventory costs and accounts receivable (Exhibit 1).

High-End Focus

Yun is spearheading what may well be a revolution in Korean industry. Since he took the helm of the sprawling Samsung Group's electronics businesses in January, 1997, Yun, a 30-year company veteran, has been reversing many practices that have long characterized Korea's *chaebol*. Samsung Electronics has dramatically reduced its debts, sold or spun off dozens of assets unrelated to its core businesses, set up financial and managerial fire walls between itself and other Samsung companies, and cut a third of its workforce. And it is striving to abandon its dependence on cheap commodity products to focus instead on high-end goods employing innovative designs.

The ultimate aim is to guide the company into the global electronics elite. With core strengths in microelectronics, telecom equipment, PCs, and consumer appliances, Samsung is positioned in each major segment of the so-called "digital convergence" and aims to rank alongside the likes of Sony Corp. and Philips Electronics. In the coming years, Samsung plans to spin out a full range of Next Age products, from affordable digital televisions and "smart cards" loaded with movies and data to sleek wireless phones enabling users to access the Web, watch TV, and listen to music.

The management transformation is hardly complete. And many *chaebol* critics warn that the lack of accountability to outside shareholders means the founding families behind groups such as Samsung could resort to business as usual once they are safely out of crisis. "Sure, Samsung has built up competence in its core businesses," says Korea University finance professor Jang Ha Sung. "The problem is that changes in its financial and business structures could be temporary without a change in corporate governance."

EXHIBIT 1
**Anatomy of a
Turnaround**

Source: *Business Week.*

ANATOMY OF A TURNAROUND

FINANCIAL RESTRUCTURING Some $10 billion in debt has been wiped out since 1997. Dozens of companies have been sold off or spun off. Stakes in money-losing Samsung Motor and computer maker AST have been written off.

PROFITS FIRST The old obsession with market share and setting production and export records is giving way to a focus on making money with high-end products based on innovative designs.

STREAMLINING Managers now strive to produce goods only after orders are placed and get them to customers within days, eliminating billions of dollars in inventory costs and accounts receivable.

DIVERSIFICATION Once dependent on commodity memory chips for half of sales and 90% of profits, Samsung Electronics has greatly broadened its base to become a global giant in telecom devices, flat-planel displays, and digital appliances. Is investing in nonmemory semiconductors.

▲ Billions of Dollars

Source: Samsung Electronics.
Projections by Salomon Smith Barney.

"Exemplary Student"

But there's little doubt the improvement has been dramatic. After weathering a harrowing free fall in profits and sales that started with the 1996 slump in memory chips, Samsung Electronics is stronger than ever. This year, Salomon Smith Barney figures the company should post a net profit of at least $2.7 billion on a 24% increase in sales, to $22 billion. The results even reflect a $700 million write-off of Samsung Electronics' investments in cars and failed U.S. computer maker AST Research Inc. "Samsung has been an exemplary student," says Lee Hun Jai, chairman of the Financial Supervisory Commission, which is overseeing Korea's corporate and financial overhaul.

Of course, a strong rebound in demand for Samsung's bread-and-butter product, dynamic random access memory (DRAM) chips, accounts for a good chunk of this turnaround. Since June, prices for 64-megabit DRAMs have surged from around $4 to $10. Samsung, one of the few big memory chip producers that kept investing in capacity through the down cycle, benefited the most, blowing past Japanese rivals.

But memory chips are not the whole story. Although DRAMs probably will account for 45% of 1999 profits, other sectors also are coming on strong. Samsung Electronics has emerged as the world's leader in thin-film transistor flat-panel displays for computers, another sector where prices have leapt. Samsung's telecom division, bolstered by soaring demand at home for its $380 voice-activated SCH-A100 cell phone and a rising share of the U.S. cellular market, now ranks among the world's top six producers of wireless handsets. It also is the world's leading producer of computer monitors. All 15 of Samsung Electronics' main product groups, including the consumer-appliance unit that had lost money for five years, are now in the black. That's a claim Samsung couldn't make even in the fat mid-'90s.

Samsung Electronics' diversification means its business is much better balanced than before the crisis. In 1995, memory chips accounted for 90% of corporate profits and half of all sales. They now account for about 20% of sales, with the rest spread more evenly among computer and telecom products. Samsung also is making gains in nonmemory chips, where it badly lags U.S. and Japanese producers. The focus is now on chips used in Samsung's array of digital phones, TVs, cameras, and smart cards.

Samsung Electronics executives concede none of these vital changes would have occurred were it not for two disasters—the crash in memory-chip prices, followed in 1997 by Korea's financial collapse. A $3.2 billion profit in 1995, when 16-Mb DRAMs fetched $40 apiece, offset steady losses in many of the company's other businesses. When DRAM prices plunged, Samsung Electronics realized that its reliance on a volatile commodity product "was a very, very risky strategy," says Yun. The company long knew it had to improve efficiency, restructure, and pare back its workforce.

Public Pressure

Nor did Samsung Electronics seriously tackle its wasteful manufacturing practices. In TVs, the company was carrying up to three months of excess inventory by 1997. Not only was Samsung paying to finance the inventory, but also prices for its electronics products were often 30% lower by the time they were sold. "In the past, we were evaluated by unit manufacturing cost alone," explains supply-chain director Park. "So we produced and produced and produced, not caring whether or not it was sold." At the same time, Samsung Group Chairman Lee Kun Hee was under intense public pressure for allowing the group's debts to pile up so high and for forcing affiliates such as Samsung Electronics to subsidize such ill-considered investments as a $3.5 billion plunge into cars.

Since 1997, Yun has sold or spun off 57 businesses, from refrigerators and pagers to satellite receivers. Such asset sales have helped Samsung Electronics to slash debt by $10.8 billion. It also has cut the number of employees from 84,000 to 54,000.

The restructuring helped persuade bankers to keep Samsung's credit lines open at a critical time in the semiconductor cycle. Betting the DRAM market would rebound, Yun kept adding cutting-edge capacity while the Japanese held back. The move paid off when the cycle turned to boom again. Just as important was better supply-chain management, which has halved inventory from an average of $3.6 billion in 1997.

Samsung's next goal is to rank alongside the consumer-electronics giants of Japan and Europe. It has made the biggest strides in cellular phones (Exhibit 2). In Korea, the company expects to sell around 7 million wireless handsets this year. It already is marketing a new phone with a flip-up touch screen that allows users to send e-mails and access English/Korean dictionaries, the Bible, Buddhist songbooks, and games. Another phone has a built-in TV receiver; still another is small enough to wear as a wristwatch.

Samsung also is surging in the U.S. A team-up with Sprint PCS has helped it grab 19% of the CDMA phone market. One big hit is the SCH-3500, a $149 set that dials numbers on voice command. By test-marketing innovative products in Korea, "when they hit here, they have a product that's absolutely ready to go to market," says Andrew Sukawaty, president of Sprint's PCS unit. "We don't go through the teething problems we go through with some other vendors."

Samsung is making a similarly bold bet on digital TVs, hoping to grab 10% of the market when prices fall within reach of middle-class families. Because digital home appliances are evolving so rapidly, it's too early to tell whether Samsung Electronics will emerge a winner. Kimihide Takano, a Tokyo-based electronics analyst with Dresdner Kleinwort Benson Asia, warns that the consumer electronics sector is poised for a shakeout. To survive, he says, a company "won't be able to just churn out commodity products." That is a major reason why Samsung Electronics is now plowing much of its profits from DRAMs into nonmemory chips. By producing cutting-edge chips with telecom, graphics, and processing capability in-house, Samsung hopes to have an edge over rivals who depend on outsiders for key components.

EXHIBIT 2
**Growth Is Now
Better Balanced**

Source: Samsung Electronics.
Projections by Salomon
Smith Barney.

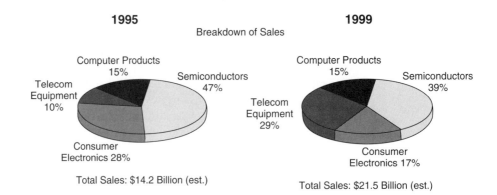

1995

Breakdown of Sales

Computer Products
15%
Telecom
Equipment
10%
Semiconductors
47%
Consumer
Electronics 28%

Total Sales: $14.2 Billion (est.)

1999

Computer Products
15%
Telecom
Equipment
29%
Semiconductors
39%
Consumer
Electronics 17%

Total Sales: $21.5 Billion (est.)

While its manufacturing prowess is clear, Samsung Electronics has its work cut out showing it can also succeed as an innovator in specialty-chip design. But this year, the non-memory unit hopes to earn up to $200 million on sales of $1 billion, with 50% sales growth expected in 2000. By next year, it hopes to supply half of Samsung's internal needs for telecom chips. Samsung also is making chip sets for digital TVs. And soon it will market Alpha microprocessors under license from Compaq Computer Corp. Rivals aren't counting Samsung out. "This is a company that is investing in technology and new equipment to stay ahead," says Kenji Tokuyama, who will head NEC's new DRAM venture with Hitachi. "We regard it as a formidable competitor."

A bigger question may be whether Samsung Electronics will maintain its financial discipline long enough to fulfill Yun's vision, especially if the government's *chaebol* watchdogs let down their guard. Insider practices and an obsession with expansion are deeply ingrained in Korea's industrial psyche. But the memories of Korea's economic catastrophe will be impossible to erase. If Samsung Electronics continues to win applause for profits and innovation—rather than size—it could have plenty of motivation to finish the job of reshaping a sprawling conglomerate into a focused, truly global enterprise.

By Moon Ihlwan and Pete Engardio in Seoul, with Irene Kunii in Toyko and Roger Crockett in Chicago

Source: "Samsung: The Making of a Superstar," *Business Week,* December 20, 1999, 137, 138, 140.

Case 3–2

McDonald's

"I don't know what we'll be serving in the year 2000, but we'll be serving more of it than anybody"
—Ray L. Kroc, founder of McDonald's Corp.
The McDonald brothers' first restaurant, founded in 1937 in a parking lot just east of Pasadena, Calif., didn't serve hamburgers. It had no playground and no Happy Meals. The most popular item on the menu was the hot dog, and most people ate it sitting on an outdoor stool or in their cherished new autos while being served by teenage carhops.

That model was a smashing success—for about a decade. Then America's tastes began to change, and the Golden Arches changed with them. As cars lost some of their romance, indoor restaurants took over. When adults became bored with the menu in the 1960s, a new sandwich called the Big Mac wooed them back. As consumers grew weary of beef,

EXHIBIT 1
Where's the Sizzle?

Source: Interbrand, Bloomberg
Financial Markets

Stock Performance of the World's Top Six Brands	
Brand	**2-Year Total Return**
Coca-Cola	71%
Eastman Kodak	−8
Gillette	101
McDonald's	3
Sony	49
Walt Disney	78
S&P 500	63

McDonald's introduced bite-size chunks of chicken in the early '80s and within four years was the nation's second-largest poultry seller.

The changes were vital, but never radical. McDonald's gave us what we wanted before we even knew we wanted it, whether it was movie tie-ins or Egg McMuffins. Along the way, it built one of the world's best-known corporate icons and its most ubiquitous store. The philosophy was neatly summarized by Ray Kroc's brash vow: whatever people ate, McDonald's would be the ones to sell it.

But now, two years shy of Kroc's benchmark for the far-off future, that goal seems less assured than ever. Forget for a moment all the recent talk about Burger King Corp. and Wendy's International Inc. stealing customers from McDonald's. With a 42% share of the U.S. fast-food burger market, McDonald's easily outpaces its rivals. Nonetheless, the problems under the famous Golden Arches are far more serious than a failed Arch Deluxe here or a french-fry war there. Quite simply, McDonald's has lost some of its relevance to American culture—a culture that it, as much as any modern corporation, helped to shape. Not even a still booming international division, responsible for half of sales and 60% of profits, can mask the troubles (Exhibit 1).

The company that once seemed a half-step ahead of pop culture today is unable to construct even an appealing new lunch sandwich. Its last successful new product was the Chicken McNugget, which launched in 1983. In the '90s, the company has careened from tests with pizza and veggie burgers to confusing discount promotions such as last year's Campaign 55. Earnings in 1997 inched up 4%, to $1.6 billion, on sales of $11.4 billion, up 7%. That's well below projections McDonald's itself made just a few years ago (Exhibit 2).

For a company that enjoyed sizzling growth for five decades based on its ability to read and shape popular trends, the breadth of its problems is astonishing. Since 1987, McDonald's share of fast-food sales in the U.S. has slipped almost two percentage points, to 16.2%. The drop has come even as the company has increased its number of restaurants by 50%, far outpacing the industry's expansion rate. The result: Domestic sales have climbed only 18% since 1989, while operating profits haven't even kept pace with inflation. They've risen just 2% a year in that period. That trend has slashed U.S. per-store profits by 20% since 1989—or a huge 40% after inflation. Meanwhile, nearly every other top consumer brand, from Disney to Marlboro, has prospered.

Menu Tweaking

McDonald's has chalked up that dismal record despite the fact that it owns one of the best known brands on the globe. The company has been unable to harness the strength of its

EXHIBIT 2
Market Share and
Store Profit Trends

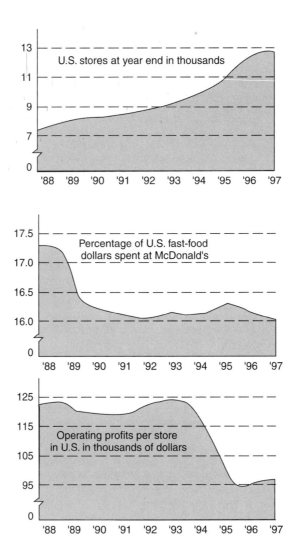

brand to grow beyond its basic formula of burgers and fries. During a period when Americans have abandoned their kitchens in droves for food cooked elsewhere, the Golden Arches—easily the world's largest provider of prepared food—has failed to profit. It's as if hundreds of thousands of people started drinking soda for breakfast and Coca-Cola Co. wasn't benefiting. "McDonald's has totally failed to adapt its original concept," says Simon C. Williams, chairman of the Sterling Group, a New York-based brand consultancy that works with food companies.

Now, McDonald's is embarking on an effort at reform. Last year, Chief Executive Michael R. Quinlan shuffled his U.S. management team. He says the decentralized structure will rekindle the company's entrepreneurial flair. A new cooking system set for 2000 should make it easier to customize sandwiches, improve quality, and expand the menu. Fundamentally, however, tomorrow's McDonald's won't be much different. "Do we have to change?" asks Quinlan. "No, we don't have to change. We have the most successful brand in the world."

McDonald's, though, is doing some tinkering. The new head of the domestic division—Jack M. Greenberg, a pleasant 54-year-old lawyer who has been with the company 16 years—has brought in a handful of new managers, including executives from Burger King, Boston Market, and General Electric Co. "We are not afraid to do things differently," Greenberg says. In a first for the burger giant, McDonald's in February bought another restaurant, a 14-outlet chain in Denver called Chipotle Mexican Grill.

But execs emphasized that the heart of the company's menu will remain the same—and that it believes it can squeeze new profits from the U.S. burger business, even though McDonald's already dominates the crowded segment. "We will extend our line, rather than going in more radical, different directions," says Quinlan, 53, who started in the company mailroom at age 19. "I'm a fan of menu tweaking."

Compare the McDonald's strategy with that at other companies that have prospered despite wrenching changes in their industries. When GE realized that manufacturing had become less profitable, it moved into financing. When Walt Disney Co. found it hard to lure more people to its theme parks, it built hotels and captured more dollars from the tourists already there. And Coca-Cola spun off its bottling business and focused instead on becoming a marketing powerhouse. The difference is profound: If McDonald's had added shareholder value at the same rate as Coca-Cola over the past ten years, its shares today would be worth $170 each. Instead, they bring less than $55.

Family Values

By contrast, McDonald's core recipe has changed little since the early '80s. "McDonald's needs to move the question from 'How can we sell more hamburgers?' to 'What does our brand allow us to consider selling to our customers?'" says Adrian J. Slywotzky, a partner at Corporate Decisions Inc., a consulting firm in Cambridge, Mass.

Such sweeping vision will not come easily. McDonald's is one of the nation's most insular large companies, with a management team more typical of a private company than a global powerhouse. The average top executive started working at the company when Richard Nixon was President. The 15-member board of directors has sat out the corporate-governance revolution and is more than two-thirds filled with current and former executives, vendors, and service providers.

As the company's performance has deteriorated, top execs have tended to blame others. They have publicly blasted dissident franchisees, whom they dismiss as a small faction. Negative news accounts are chalked up to misperceptions by reporters. And one persistently critical Wall Street analyst—Damon Brundage, now at J.P Morgan & Co.—was barred from the company's latest biennial briefing.

And while some companies, such as IBM and AT&T, have brought in outside leaders—albeit reluctantly—to help guide management as the business changed, McDonald's has largely clung to the "McFamily" philosophy of the 1950s and 1960s, which rewards managers who start young and stay for life. Headhunters, noting that virtually no alumni from the McDonald's Oak Brook (Ill.) headquarters can be found running other companies, say it isn't where they look for talent. "They are no longer the beacon of great success they used to be," says a Chicago-area recruiter.

Wall Street seems to share that sentiment. Over the past two years, while the Standard & Poor's 500-stock index grew by 63%, McDonald's shareholders could have made more money in an insured savings account. Had you invested $100 in the company two years ago, you'd be holding $103 today. Of the world's 10 most powerful brands, as ranked by Interbrand, a New York consultant, only beleaguered Eastman Kodak Co. has had a worse run over that period (Exhibit 1). Shareholders of Gillette Co., meanwhile, have more than doubled their money.

"Not Holding the Past Sacred"

Even some investors who still believe in the brand are concerned. Davis Selected Advisers, with $500 million in McDonald's stock, has been a shareholder since 1994 on the strength of the company's international operations, but the big investor believes there needs to be changes in management and in the business. "It means not holding the past sacred," says Chris Davis, a portfolio manager. "There needs to be a sense of urgency."

Even McDonald's formidable international business faces some serious challenges. On the plus side, operating earnings have more than doubled in the past five years, and some emerging markets will soon see economies of scale. Says James R. Cantalupo, who runs the division: "We're nowhere near any kind of penetration that I think is possible."

But the easy markets have been tapped. Now McDonald's is expanding beyond the bustling Londons and Moscows. As it does, margins are dropping—from 20.5% in '94 to 19.1% last year in overseas company-owned outlets. In each of the past two years, McDonald's has badly missed its projection of 18% to 20% international earnings growth, falling short of 10% per year after accounting for currency fluctuations. In the fourth quarter, key markets such as Germany and Japan underperformed, largely because of local economic climates and a strong dollar. Overall, says analyst Dean T. Haskell of EVEREN Securities Inc., "the international story is not quite as good as McDonald's would have you believe."

And the Arches' domestic woes raise a troubling question for the overseas operations: If McDonald's cannot respond to changing market forces at home, how will it adapt over time as its most important overseas markets mature? "It's hugely problematic," Slywotzky says. "If the same set of conditions duplicate themselves abroad, then you have a dead end waiting to happen."

Of course, the strength of the McDonald's brand gives it opportunities to avoid that dead end. Thanks to the movie tie-in trinkets that it gives away, for example, McDonald's is hugely popular with kids. Imagine, says Slywotzky, if it used low-margin burgers to sell a line of high-margin toys—instead of vice-versa. McDonald's says that's not its core business. But the point, says Slywotzky, is that it needs to worry less about market share and more about new profit vehicles.

First, though, McDonald's needs to address an even more fundamental problem: the quality of its food. While the burger giant focused on building more stores, consumers have decided they want better food and more variety. Consumers who eat fast food at least once a month say that both Wendy's and Burger King offer better-tasting fare, according to a recent BUSINESS WEEK/Harris Poll. And in a soon-to-be-released survey for *Restaurants & Institutions* magazine in which 2,800 consumers graded chains based on the taste of their food, McDonald's ranked 87th out of 91—just behind Hooters. "We clearly think we have to do some things with our menu," says Greenberg, who believes the new cooking system will be a turning point.

The fact is, convenience is no longer enough. In the Harris Poll, more than 90% of consumers listed both taste and quality as "very important" factors in their choice of a restaurant, while location and speed were selected by barely half. Why? With an abundance of choices, consumers no longer choose McDonald's just because there's one around the corner. And with new entrants offering ethnic fare, vegetarian menus, and fully stocked salad bars, fast food no longer has to mean fried food.

Kids' Pleas

Take Stephen J. Char, a 31-year-old government scientist in Denver. He has cut his trips to McDonald's in half over the past few years. "A cheeseburger and fries will kill me for the day," he says. He's found tastier options near his office for about the same price: a taco restaurant, a German deli, and even Haji Babba's—a food counter at a Texaco station that serves stuffed grape leaves.

Even some regulars say it's not the food that keeps them coming back. Julie Lake is the Austin (Tex.) mother of 3-year-old Chloe and 5-year-old Evan. "After preschool, when they are whiny and hungry, we go there," she says, adding that she rarely eats the food herself. That's bad news for McDonald's, which has had little luck creating dishes that appeal to grown-ups. Last year's Arch Deluxe, though still on the menu, is hardly a blockbuster. As their kids move beyond the Ronald McDonald years, baby boomers like Lake will need a new reason to visit the Arches.

All the while, McDonald's has concentrated on adding restaurants, angering store owners and cutting into margins. It began a major U.S. expansion in the early '90s, even as business was slowing. "They built a whole bunch of new stores in the wrong places," says Dick Adams, who heads up a group of concerned franchisees.

That single-minded focus left a huge opportunity for new competitors eager to take advantage of changing eating habits. In the same nine years that McDonald's U.S. profits have stagnated, Starbucks Corp. has become a $1 billion company. Supermarket sales of prepared food have doubled, and the "casual dining" segment has emerged. In fact, Americans now spend more on prepared meals sold at delis, supermarkets, and casual dining restaurants such as Applebee's International Inc. than they do at burger chains, according to Technomic Inc., a market-research firm based in Chicago.

Even among burger chains, McDonald's is no longer the shrewdest innovator. Burger King has nibbled at McDonald's market share with better-tasting burgers. Wendy's has used its new stuffed pitas and spicy chicken sandwich to drive it toward 21 months of sales gains in existing outlets. Carl's Jr., a 708-restaurant chain based in Anaheim, Calif., has opened a Mexican eatery called Green Burrito within 120 of its stores. That has helped boost the typically slow dinner business and led to a $250,000 revenue jump in some stores.

It's not that McDonald's hasn't made a stab at new products. The past decade has seen an array of test products, such as pasta, fried chicken, and fajitas. But customers have been unimpressed, and McDonald's invariably has returned to its core menu. It pulled the plug in 1995 on one of its most interesting ideas, a one-store test of a Boston Market-like chain called Hearth Express, saying it wanted to focus on building more hamburger restaurants. "The brand expectation, at least until now, hasn't been as broad [as it could be], and that's been an issue for us in the U.S.," Greenberg says. "When you try to sell something that doesn't necessarily fit people's expectations for the Golden Arches, you have a very difficult time." Analysts, however, say that too often the new products just didn't taste good.

The company's recent stake in Chipotle could be a sign that McDonald's is considering new ways to leverage its brand. Chipotle's fresh, inexpensive burrito wraps are precisely the type of food that has drawn consumers away from the Arches in recent years. Executives have said that they would like to eventually expand and franchise Chipotle, though they caution that the investment, estimated to be less than $15 million, is far too small to have any impact soon.

Whitewash?

More significant than the Chipotle venture is McDonald's management reorganization of last summer. Quinlan nudged Edward H. Rensi, who formerly was head of the domestic division, into early retirement and replaced him with Greenberg, who franchisees say is easier to talk to. Five new regional division chiefs, whose territories divvy up the country, now report to Greenberg. The idea: create smaller companies within the larger McDonald's that will recapture its earlier entrepreneurial zeal.

But even the shuffling shows signs of McDonald's discomfort with change. Of the five new division heads, none has set up shop outside the Chicago area, and only one has immediate plans to do so. The majority of franchisees still report to the same person. The reorganization, charges EVEREN analyst Haskell, "is an effort to whitewash the public by trying to convince Wall Street things have changed when they really haven't." Says one investor who manages more than $30 million in McDonald's stock: "The changes were an improvement, but I don't think it's a dramatic improvement."

One of the most troubling signs of McDonald's unwillingness to grapple with underlying problems is its reaction to outside critics. Greenberg has dismissed the Consortium, a San Diego-based group of franchisees unhappy with the company's direction, as "eight people and a guy with a fax machine."

Adams, a former McDonald's owner who runs the Consortium, claims membership of 300 but refuses to release a list, saying franchisees fear reprisals. But other evidence indicates that unhappiness is more widespread than Greenberg's comment suggests. In a 1997 internal survey, only 28% of franchisees said they thought McDonald's was on the right track. The controversial push to put up more stores remains a flashpoint for many. Says one former operator who claims new stores helped to put him out of business: "Ray Kroc once told me, 'If you work hard, you get treated fairly.' But these guys don't care about the operators."

The media also get blamed for McDonald's bad news. During a guest lecture at Northwestern University's Medill School of Journalism last year, chief McDonald's spokesman Charles Ebeling lashed out at reporters. Ebeling dismissed as "bullshit" a story in *The Wall Street Journal* that prophetically detailed the problems with Campaign 55, a complicated discount promotion. Then he called *Crain's Chicago Business,* a respected weekly that had run critical stories on the company, "a scandal sheet" with a "corrupt" editor. Ebeling says the remarks, reported in *Rolling Stone* magazine, were taken out of context.

"Absolutely Baffling"

Indeed, after eight years in which real domestic operating profits have actually fallen, the head of marketing for McDonald's USA says the biggest problem with the brand is the media's view of it. "If there were one thing I would want to change about McDonald's," says Senior Vice-President Brad A. Ball, "it would be to correct the misconceptions and perceptions that have become so pervasive in the last few years."

Wall Street analysts struggling to evaluate the company's prospects say they, too, have largely been frozen out. They say McDonald's is the only big company they follow in which top executives, including Quinlan, refuse to meet with them. "It's absolutely baffling," says Howard Penney of Morgan Stanley Dean Witter, Discover & Co, one of four analysts McDonald's identifies as knowing the most about the corporation. "Here we are trying to educate people about what we think about the company, and the top management guy won't speak to us." Quinlan says he's in touch with Wall Street.

Through it all, he and other executives maintain that the company remains strong. Quinlan has cut his projections for future growth but still predicts a doubling or near-doubling of earnings per share over the next five years—which analysts call feasible, if optimistic. "In the U.S., we've made some mistakes," Quinlan acknowledges, but he says: "Our greatest days lie ahead."

So what's the problem? Simply put, it's hard to dismiss a lagging stock price, the end of growth in domestic profits, missed international projections, and a decade's worth of failed initiatives. This much is clear: The world's most successful restaurant company is far from achieving its potential—and may be sowing the seeds for further disappointment down the road.

It doesn't have to be that way. Imagine the possibilities: The company uses its powerful brand to figure out a way to grow in its own backyard. The new kitchen production system allows executives to think more broadly about high-quality menu additions. Domestic earnings no longer drag down international growth but add to it. And overseas markets, upon saturation, have a model for future growth.

Of course, doing all that requires thinking about the business in fundamentally new ways and refusing to be tied to the past. It wouldn't be the first time for McDonald's. After all, consider where the Golden Arches would be now if its first owners had insisted on keeping hot dogs as the centerpiece of the menu.

Coca-Cola Co.'s largest customer is McDonald's Corp. Sonnenschein Nath & Rosenthal has been the hamburger chain's lead law firm for decades. DDB Needham Worldwide Inc. and Leo Burnett Co. are two of its longtime ad agencies. And Dean Foods Co. supplies the Arches with pickles.

What else do these firms have in common? Each has an executive, retired executive, or director on the McDonald's board. In fact, by current standards of corporate governance, only 4 of McDonald's 15 directors can be called independent—meaning they don't work for the company, do outside business with it, or have a McDonald's exec sitting on their own board.

"Not Even Close"

That's not all: Cross-directorships, in which directors serve on each other's boards, are common, too. Gordon C. Gray, for example, chairman of a Canadian mining company and an independent director, also sits on the board of a subsidiary of Stone Container Corp., a McDonald's packaging supplier whose CEO, Roger W. Stone, is a fellow McDonald's director.

Thanks to pressure from shareholders and regulators, Corporate America over the past decade has raised the quality of its boards and increased its directors' accountability. But that trend has passed McDonald's by. "They are not even close to keeping up with corporate-governance standards that most other companies their size meet," says Anne Hansen, deputy director of the Council of Institutional Investors in Washington. Adds Warren Bennis, a University of Southern California professor who studies leadership: "For a company that size, it's stunning." The National Association of Corporate Directors recommends "a substantial majority" of a company's directors be independent. And many shareholder groups discourage cross-directorships; governance experts say they can lead directors to look out for each others' interests, rather than those of shareholders.

McDonald's denies that the many relationships between its board members and the company are a problem. "We have always had a board that was fairly heavily peopled by inside directors. I am not troubled by that at all," says CEO and Chairman Michael R. Quinlan. He argues that insiders bring detailed knowledge of McDonald's to the board. And director Robert N. Thurston, a former Quaker Oats Co. executive, calls it an active board that "can stick our noses anywhere we want to." To suggest that directors are hampered by company ties "discounts the independence and the pride and the intelligence and the fortitude of the people on the board," he adds.

The proper question, though, may not be whether the directors have integrity—there is no evidence they don't—but whether, as a group, they bring the type of broad experience and objectivity that a company facing a watershed requires. Despite the hamburger chain's lackluster performance in the past few years, its board has done little to agitate for change, say people who follow the company. "This board is so stale, it's hard to imagine it asking the right questions," Bennis says. Or, as one major shareholder puts it: "If McDonald's is one of your largest customers, I don't think you're going to challenge the CEO too much."

Compare the McDonald's board with those at another globally branded company. Nine of Coca-Cola's 13 directors are independent. The board includes former Senator Sam Nunn, former baseball Commissioner Peter V. Ueberroth, former Delta Air Lines CEO Ronald W. Allen, and superinvestor Warren Buffett.

In fact, inspect almost any company with a brand similar in strength to McDonald's, and you will find more outside directors, a shorter average term, a younger board, and greater diversity of experience. Inspect McDonald's, on the other hand, and you will find a disproportionate number of directors who rely on the company for one kind of paycheck or another.

Source: David Leonhardt, "McDonald's: Can It Regain Its Golden Touch?" *Business Week,* March 9, 1998, 70–77.

Case 3–3
Apex Chemical Company

The Executive Committee of Apex Chemical Company—a medium-sized chemical manufacturer with annual sales of $60 million—is trying to determine which of two new compounds the company should market. The two products were expected to have the same gross margin percentage. The following conversation takes place between the vice president for research, Ralph Rogovin, the vice president for marketing, Miles Mumford, and the president, Paul Prendigast.

VP-Research:	Compound A-115, a new electrolysis agent, is the one; there just isn't any doubt about it. Why, for precipitating a synergistic reaction in silver electrolysis, it has a distinct advantage over anything now on the market.
President:	That makes sense, Ralph. Apex has always tried to avoid "me too" products, and if this one is that much better . . . what do you think, Miles?
VP-Marketing:	Well, I favor the idea of Compound B-227, the plastic oxidizer. We have some reputation in that field; we're already known for our plastic oxidizers.
VP-Research:	Yes, Miles, but this one isn't really better than the ones we already have. It belongs to the beta-prednigone group, and they just aren't as good as the stigones are. We *do* have the best stigone in the field.
President:	Just the same, Ralph, the beta-prednigones are cutting into our stigone sales. The board of directors has been giving me a going-over on that one.
VP-Marketing:	Yes, Ralph, maybe they're not as good scientists as we are—or think we are—but the buyers in the market seem to insist on buying

beta-prednigones. How do you explain that? The betas have 60 percent of the market now.

VP-Research: That's your job, not mine, Miles. If we can't sell the best product—and I can prove it *is* the best, as you've seen from my data and computations—then there's something wrong with Apex's marketing effort.

President: What do you say to that, Miles? What *is* the explanation?

VP-Marketing: Well, it's a very tricky field—the process in which these compounds are used is always touch-and-go; everyone is always trying something new.

VP-Research: All the more reason to put our effort behind Compound A-115, in the electrolysis field. Here we know that we have a real technical breakthrough. I agree with Paul that that's our strength.

President: What about that, Miles? Why not stay out of the dogfight represented by Compound B-227, if the plastic oxidizer market is as tricky as you say?

VP-Marketing: I don't feel just right about it, Paul. I understand that the electrolysis market is pretty satisfied with the present products. We did a survey and 95 percent said they were satisfied with the Hamfield Company's product.

President: It's a big market, too, isn't it, Miles?

VP-Marketing: Yes, about $10 million a year total.

President: And only one strongly entrenched company—Hamfield?

VP-Marketing: Yes, I must admit it's not like the plastic oxidizer situation—where there are three strong competitors and about a half-dozen who are selling off-brands. On the other hand, oxidizers are a $40 million market—four times as big.

President: That's true, Ralph. Furthermore our oxidizer sales represent 25 percent of our total sales.

VP-Research: But we've been losing ground the past year. Our oxidizer sales dropped 10 percent, didn't they, Ralph? While the total oxidizer market was growing, didn't you say?

VP-Marketing: Well, the electrolysis field is certainly more stable. Total sales are holding level, and as I said before, Hamfield's share is pretty constant, too.

President: What about the technical requirements in the electrolysis field? With a really improved product we ought to be able . . .

VP-Marketing: Well, to tell you the truth, I don't know very much about the kind of people who use it and how they . . . you see, it's really a different industry.

President: What about it, Ralph?

VP-Research: It's almost a different branch of chemistry, too. But I have plenty of confidence in our laboratory men. I can't see any reason why we

	should run into trouble . . . It really does have a plus-three-point superiority on a scale of 100—here, the chart shows it crystal clear, Miles.
VP-Marketing:	But aren't we spreading ourselves pretty thin—instead of concentrating where our greatest know-how . . . You've always said, Paul, that …
President:	Yes, I know, but maybe we ought to diversify, too. You know, all our eggs in one basket.
VP-Marketing:	But if it's a good basket . . .
VP-Research:	Nonsense, Miles, it's the kind of eggs you've got in the basket that counts—and Compound A-115, the electrolysis agent, is scientifically the better one.
VP-Marketing:	Yes, but what about taking eggs to the market? Maybe people don't want to buy that particular egg from us, but they would buy Compound B-227—the plastic oxidizer.
President:	Eggs, eggs, eggs—I'm saying to both of you, let's just be sure we don't lay any!

Source: Edward C. Bursk and Stephen A. Greyser, *Cases in Marketing Management,* 2nd ed. (Englewood Cliffs, NJ: Prentice-Hall, 1975), 204–10. Reprinted by permission of Prentice-Hall, Englewood Cliffs, NJ.

Case 3–4

Dunkin' Donuts*

It was a hot Massachusetts day in late August 1996, and Chris Booras, the Dunkin' Donuts purchasing director responsible for coordinating supply, was feeling the heat. It was a trying time for Dunkin' Donuts as it tried to leverage its image from quality donut seller to bagel expert. The bagel introduction was the largest initiative ever for Dunkin' Donuts, and a host of problems had erupted, mostly in supply and distribution. With two weeks left before the largest advertising campaign the bagel industry had ever experienced, the supply chain had dried up.

Chris Booras stared forlornly out the window. A lot was at stake here. The pressure was definitely on. Jack Shafer, the COO overseeing Dunkin' Donuts, had recently commented,

> The combination of the new Dunkin' Donuts freshly baked bagels and our legendary coffee is the key to our future growth. We have invested a year and a half developing the perfect bagel. When paired with the magic of the Dunkin' Donuts name, the equity in our coffee business, our advertising strength and our far reaching network of shops, we become uniquely positioned to lead the bagel category.[1]

Dunkin' always moved fast to stay ahead. Chris hoped he could get the supplier problems straightened out and keep pace with the expectations of the company's top management.

*This case was prepared by Eric Nyman, Boston College, under the supervision of Victoria L. Crittenden, associate professor of marketing, Boston College, as the basis for class discussion rather than to illustrate either effective or ineffective handling of a managerial situation.

1. Editor, *Milling and Baking News* (June 25, 1996): 1.

The Background

Dunkin' Donuts will strive to be the dominant retailer of high quality donuts, bakery products and beverages in each metropolitan market in which we choose to compete.

company mission statement

In 1948 Bill Rosenberg had a dream. He envisioned a morning destination shop centered on quality donuts and the freshest coffee. He opened his first donut shop, the Open Kettle, on the Southern Artery in Quincy, Massachusetts. The popularity of this shop convinced Rosenberg of his concept's potential, and for the next five years he opened one shop per year. In 1950, with a six-store operation, Rosenberg opened the first Dunkin' Donuts.

Rosenberg quickly realized that to maximize his organization's growth potential, he would have to franchise. In 1955 he signed the company's first franchise agreement, and he went to work aligning himself with business partners willing to take on the risks of the franchise system. Those risks included paying Rosenberg a percentage of sales, paying a fee for the franchise name, and paying large up-front costs for land and construction. This strategy allowed Rosenberg to grow Dunkin' Donuts to a 24-shop chain in New England with annual sales of US$3 million by 1960.[2]

Astronomical growth continued into the next decade. In 1963, the 100th shop opened and the company attained revenues of US$10 million. In 1968, with Rosenberg at the helm as president and CEO, Dunkin' Donuts went public. Operating with the pledge to make donuts fresh every four hours and to brew fresh coffee every 14 minutes, Dunkin' Donuts reached US$44 million in sales by 1969.

The 1970s was a big decade for the company. During this period, the company expanded internationally and developed new products. In 1974 the Dunkin' Munchkin was released and became one of the food service industry's most successful product spin-offs ever. The Munchkin, a donut hole, was offered in a variety of flavors and was considered to "truly be a bite-sized treat." Sales were strong, with the Munchkin remaining a mainstream product into the 1990s.

As the chain entered the 1980s, sales reached US$300 million in 1,000 shops. Plans were formulated to accelerate expansion. The strategy for growth and profits centered on distribution, advertising, new products, remodeling, and standards improvement. To implement the strategy, Dunkin' Donuts developed what would become known as the gold standard in franchise distribution when it created the first of six regional distribution centers. These regional distribution centers allowed for quick delivery to individual stores along with good pricing for all outlets in a given region. This period also marked the national advertising debut of "Fred the Baker." Fred was a hero to working-class America as he rose at all hours of the night as a franchise owner to ensure that his customers were always given fresh products and a smile. Fred popularized the saying "It's time to make the donuts." Dunkin' began to remodel stores during this period as well. Brightly lit, colorful nonsmoking stores were created to replace the dimly lit, smoky coffee shops consumers had been accustomed to. Standards were improved to ensure freshness across all product lines.

In 1990 Dunkin' Donuts, with a firm balance sheet and strong brand equity in the morning food retail business, became an attractive takeover target. After trying unsuccessfully to ward off a hostile takeover, Dunkin' Donuts was acquired under friendly terms by Allied Domecq, a world leader in spirits and retailing. Its international spirits brands included Ballantines, Beefeater, and Kahlua. Allied was the world's leading brandy company and the

---

2. The New England states include Connecticut, Maine, Massachusetts, New Hampshire, Rhode Island, and Vermont.

second largest distributor of Scotch whiskey, tequila, and liqueurs. The company had over 13,800 retail outlets that included 4,100 pubs and 8,200 franchised stores, including the popular California-based Baskin-Robbins ice cream chain. After the takeover, Dunkin' Donuts, acting as a wholly owned subsidiary of Allied Domecq, operated over 3,200 shops with total sales in excess of US$1 billion.[3]

By the mid-1990s, Dunkin' Donuts franchise stores were seeing sales between US$20,000 and US$50,000 a month. Dunkin' Donuts reported sales of US$1.4 billion around the globe in 1995. Entering the mid-1990s, however, Dunkin' Donuts was experiencing organizational turbulence. Both of Allied Domecq's American concerns, Baskin-Robbins (based in California) and Dunkin' Donuts (headquartered in Massachusetts), were attempting to merge cultures, which was causing some discomfort on both sides. Baskin-Robbins had been experiencing flat growth for several years, and it was thought that the merger with Dunkin' Donuts would instill some life into the brand. Initial problems included simple logistics, resentment from the Baskin-Robbins organization over placement of Dunkin' Donuts people in high-level Baskin positions, and general fear among all parties about whether their jobs would continue to exist. To further complicate matters, Dunkin' Donuts was restructuring along the lines of category management. That meant that individuals in a given department (e.g., marketing, purchasing, quality assurance) would be given a product category to manage. These categories included bakery, beverages, and the product expected to redefine Dunkin' donuts—bagels.

The Bagel Market

Once an ethnic specialty food, bagels had gained acceptance as an American breakfast and lunch item. Bagels were a low-fat, boiled bread product. A study of national eating trends conducted by the NPD Group Inc., a Chicago-area research firm, found that per capita bagel consumption soared 65 percent between 1990 and 1995. Market reports revealed that the bagel business was a US$2.5 billion industry by the mid-1990s.[4]

By 1995, there were over 700 bagel retail outlets and wholesale bakeries in the United States, with annual sales of over US$1 billion. The market's growth rate was estimated at over 30 percent.[5] Analysts projected that growth would remain steady throughout the decade. The major players in this primarily breakfast food segment were Bruegger's, Manhattan Bagel, and Einstein Brothers. The rest of the market was dominated by small chains and mom-and-pop operations. No dominant national market presence by any single company had been established.

Most retailers agreed that the popularity of bagels was a long-term trend. However, food retail analysts expected a shakeout as the marketplace became increasingly crowded. Nancy Krause, vice-president of Technomic, Inc., thought that success in this industry was related to the rate of increase of bagel shops and the extent to which they cluster in the same markets.[6]

The bagel marketplace was divided among various types of outlets. Approximately 44 percent of all bagels were sold in retail shops and bakeries, 26 percent at in-store bakeries, 20 percent by food services, and 10 percent frozen by wholesale bakeries. At the beginning

3. Twenty-seven hundred of these shops were owned by Dunkin' Donuts; the rest were acquired when Dunkin' bought Mister Donuts.
4. Jennifer Brown, *Bagel Boom,* July 1996, 62.
5. Dan Malovany, *Bakery Production and Marketing,* May 24, 1995, 12.
6. Jennifer Brown, "Bagel Boom," *Baking & Snack* (Kansas City, MO: Sosland Publishing Company, July 1996).

of 1995 only 15 percent of these sales were by multiunit chains. Furthermore, 70 percent of the bagel stores were concentrated in New York, New Jersey, Florida, and California. This alluded to a positive growth situation as bagel stores spread across America.[7]

The chains competed on quality of product, physical appearance of their facilities, flavor variety of both bagels and cream cheese, and the bagel "experience" (a hard-to-quantify atmosphere that bespoke freshness and a homemade feel). These bagel shops were beginning to grab market share from the dominant player in the breakfast food category, Dunkin' Donuts, as more and more health-minded Americans jumped on the bagel bandwagon. The product fit the perfect nutrition profile, as a plain 2.5-ounce bagel had approximately one gram of fat. As a spokesperson from Lender's Bagels said, "Bagels are the food of the nineties."[8]

The outlook for the bagel chains' future appeared to include rapid expansion through franchising and acquisition. Consolidation was predicted, and so speed to market was essential. Already, Einstein Bros. had acquired Noah's Bagel, and Manhattan Bagel had joined forces with Specialty Bakeries, a franchiser of the Bagel Builders chain. The top two or three dominant players in this industry were expected to be the last ones standing. As stated by Krause, "Only those who really have established their brand image and dominance within their trade areas will survive."[9]

Dunkin' Donuts' Market Entry

In 1995 it was becoming quite clear to Dunkin' Donuts President Will Kussell and many members of senior management that the bagel industry, while hurting Dunkin' sales at that point, held a great deal of potential for the company. The Dunkin' Donuts sales mix at that time was as follows:

Coffee	65%
Donuts	25
Muffins and cookies	10

Kussell envisioned the company's sales mix changing dramatically and foresaw Dunkin' Donuts becoming the biggest and most dominant player in the bagel industry. Simple math revealed that if Dunkin' Donuts jumped into the bagel business with its 2,700 North American outlets, it would more than triple the entire retail industry's 700 outlets. Furthermore, the sales opportunity that bagels could inspire in this growing billion-dollar U.S. retail market was staggering. After some initial research of the industry and a search for a high-quality supplier, Dunkin' Donuts made the decision to compete in the bagel business.

The company's goal was to have the best product in the market and to be the largest bagel retailer in the United States. Several research and development tests were conducted to discover the attributes that customers found most appealing in a bagel. The results of those tests showed that consumers desired a large bagel in a variety of flavors and insisted on the complementary product of cream cheese. Dunkin' Donuts then designed a bagel around these considerations and created a new cream cheese line to go with it.

7. Ibid.
8. Dan Malovany, "Don't Change That Dial; Wholesale Bakery Industry Trends," *Bakery Production and Marketing* (Chicago: Delta Communications, May 24, 1995).
9. Brown, *Bagel Boom,* 62.

The Search for Supply

Dunkin' Donuts felt that it had developed the perfect bagel. Consistent with its outsourcing strategies for muffins and cookies, it needed someone to produce the bagel in large enough quantities to supply its geographically dispersed retail outlets.

Many suppliers wanted to get into the bagel business with Dunkin' Donuts. Manufacturing giants such as Harold's Bakery Products,[10] Sara Lee, and Brooklyn Bagel Boys bid on the business. Criteria for supplier selection included a proven track record, a sizable cash flow to enter into a new business, and, most important, the speed to act quickly in building new lines for bagel production. No company had the existing capacity for a project of this scope. Therefore, when Harold's promised a nine-month delivery time on new bagel production lines with the ability to sign copacker relationships in the interim, a deal was consummated. Harold's was chosen as the vendor that would supply Dunkin' Donuts with its fresh bagels.

Harold's gave Dunkin' Donuts a standard volume guarantee, including a nine-month construction promise for new lines. The $8 million cost of the new lines would be paid for by Harold's. However, the costs were to be amortized on those lines—meaning that the finished cost to Dunkin' Donuts for the bagels would be lower over the long term. Dunkin' provided Harold's with a volume guarantee along with the promise that outside vendors would not be looked at unless Harold's violated the supply guarantee. The supply guarantee centered on production numbers at Harold's and at copackers' plants. (Copackers were short-term outside vendors that would assist Harold's in supplying the Dunkin' system with bagels while the Harold's lines were being built.)

Dunkin' Donuts' Planned Rollout

Using Harold's theoretical capacity numbers on lines that had not yet been built, along with the projected capacity of copackers, the Dunkin' Donuts marketing team went to work. A national rollout plan was developed that called for 2,700 stores to be supplied with bagels in one year. Some objections were raised by both purchasing and quality assurance, as both departments pointed out the risks of creating such an aggressive schedule. However, these concerns were overshadowed by senior management's drive to get fiscal year 1997 (which started in September 1996) off to a great start. The new budget was built around the expectation that the bagel program would be a rousing success, with franchisees targeted to achieve a 10 percent growth in sales with the $0.55 bagel, up from an average of 2 to 4 percent.[11] Cream cheese would sell for US$1.29 to US$1.99. Expected bagel-related sales per store were projected at over US$1,000 a week for many stores.

There were several steps to follow for a Dunkin' franchisee to get into the bagel program. The cost of construction (to the franchisee) was expected to be around $25,000, as all enrolling shops were required to remodel with new signs, bagel cases, and cream cheese merchandisers to give the look and feel of a bagel enterprise. The marketing department expected that 80 percent of all shops in a given market would enroll and used that number as a goal for franchisee sell-in. Importantly, all shops did not have to sign up as bagel carriers. However, a franchisee that did not sign up initially would go to end of the line on the rollout schedule. This could mean that a shop in Boston that did not sign up on the first rollout opportunity could have to wait up to nine months while the rest of the country's 2,700

10. A pseudonym is used to protect the Dunkin' Donuts supplier relationship.
11. This would mean greater profits for Dunkin' Donuts, which received a percentage of sales from the franchisees both for marketing support and for the brand equity the Dunkin' Donuts name provided.

stores were remodeled before being allowed to sell bagels. Furthermore, all participating shops had to agree to carry all of Dunkin' Donuts' proprietary bagel products (including all flavor varieties of bagels and all cream cheese types created by the company).

Before attempting to sell the product to franchisees, Dunkin' Donuts selected 20 of the best stores (termed fast-track stores—traditionally high performers) in various markets to serve as model stores. Dunkin' Donuts then used the fast-track stores' impressive sales results with the new bagels to entice other franchisees to join the bagel program. The average fast-track store had a sales boost of 15 percent with the new bagel program.

The U.S. rollout was to start in the New England states, the company's strongest sales region. From there, the rollout would go on to the Mid-Atlantic (which included New York, Baltimore, and Washington D.C.), continue to the Midwest (where markets such as South Bend, Indiana, existed), and finish off in the Southeast (which included Atlanta, Georgia, and Orlando, Florida). Once this phase of the rollout was complete, Dunkin' Donuts planned to head westward, where its presence was much smaller, and then into Canada. The plan was to supply 65 stores a week with bagels starting the second week of May 1996 and continue until all interested Dunkin' Donuts stores were selling bagels.

Sales Projections

Taking an aggressive approach, the bagel marketing team used past and present data to determine how many bagels the average shop would use. A case contained 96 bagels. The highest-performing fast-track store (in South Weymouth, Massachusetts) had sold 60 cases a week of the new bagels—amazingly, without any advertising support!

Bagel usage projections therefore built in this preadvertising sales jump. The marketing department projected that the average store would sell 18 cases of the new bagels each week before advertising. Once advertising began, historical Dunkin' figures showed that a 100 percent sales jump usually occurred. With this prediction, a US$25 million advertising campaign was planned.

The Crisis

Dunkin' Donuts' bagel team projected that with advertising, it would be selling almost 40 cases of bagels a week per store. Through the month of July 1996, with no advertising, the current system supply of 14,500 cases per week was being used up on a weekly basis. This presented both short- and long-term problems.

In the short term, volume promises from the supplier were not being met, and that was hurting the rollout plan. The rollout already had been delayed for three weeks in July, as demand had exceeded capacity. It was costly to delay the rollout, as lost sales could never be recaptured.

Supplying the system in the long term presented challenges as well. Harold's was already experiencing several problems with regard to constructing the new lines. Harold's was having difficulty locating the proper equipment and suffering product-related problems with one of its copackers.

The Decision

At a supplier meeting, Kussell had stated,

Bagels are a tremendous opportunity for our company. It is once in a lifetime that an opportunity comes along in the food service industry with this kind of growth. The speed at which the bagel market is growing is the kind of growth that high technology companies in the

Internet are seeing. We cannot afford not to be in this game. Another point, however, is a business decision. I want to be out ahead of the competition. I don't want to send the message that we are pulling back, only that we are plowing ahead.

Chris Booras had several decisions to make. Should the rollout be slowed? Could the shops delayed in July be added back into the rollout schedule? Should advertising be pushed back and, if so, to what date? Should the contract with Harold's be reevaluated? Should Dunkin' Donuts begin looking for a new supplier?

These decisions were the basis for three options under consideration by Booras and the Dunkin' Donuts bagel team:

1. They could continue the rollout at the current pace with a partial product line.

2. They could slow the rollout by limiting advertising or limiting the pace of store expansion.

3. They could stop the rollout until there was some certainty of supply.

If the Dunkin' team decided to stop the rollout until supply was guaranteed, it would have to do one of two things: (1) work with Harold's to find more copackers in the short term or (2) terminate the contract with Harold's, since Harold's had been unable to keep its short-term supply commitments, and begin the process of finding a new supplier. Before dissolving the contract with Harold's, however, the Dunkin' team had to keep in mind the rumor that all U.S. production facilities capable of making bagels were signing long-term supplier contracts with different firms, leaving very few opportunities for additional capacity to be obtained.

Chris Booras knew that his and his team's reputations were on the line with Allied Domecq and the franchise community. And a recommendation had to be made immediately!

Market-Focused Program Development

Part 4

Chapter 9

Strategic Brand Management

The pivotal contribution of new products to a company's success is widely recognized, as we discussed in Chapter 8. However, in many situations new products alone do not generate the sales and profits required to maintain the vitality of the business. The effective management of products at various stages of maturity is also a key contributor to success. Strategic management of the company's system of brands is frequently critical to the organization's performance in the marketplace. Major companies such as Coca-Cola and Intel develop market-driven product strategies.[1] For many businesses, this is a key link between marketing processes and the technical functions of the company: production, operations, research and development (R&D), and sourcing. Strategic brand management is a critical part of the value offering to customers. Product management and brand strategy are closely related. The relationship between product and brand may be complex and may evolve over time, as illustrated by product and brand initiatives at Church & Dwight.[2]

Church & Dwight (C&D) is not a well-known household name even though it is the world's largest producer of sodium bicarbonate. Its popular baking soda (bicarbonate of soda) in the distinctive little yellow box can be found in most U.S. kitchens. The company is best known for its Arm & Hammer brand and logo. Baking soda can be used in several applications other than as a baking ingredient. Examples of uses include cleaning teeth and as a freshener in refrigerators. C&D's product strategy has focused on diverse applications of the basic chemical material.

In the 1980s Church and Dwight's management decided to launch a broad multiproduct line strategy intended to take advantage of the market potential for industrial cleaners, baking soda toothpaste, laundry detergent, cat litter, carpet deodorizer, air freshener, and antiperspirant. During the decade ending in 1992 the company's sales and profits more than tripled, and it had 60 percent of the world market for bicarbonate of soda. In 1994 C&D's profit declined to one-third of 1993's $31 million. Arm & Hammer toothpaste initially held over a 40 percent share of the $300 million baking soda toothpaste market, but problems began to develop. Management tried to enter too many markets too fast. Faulty decisions such as pricing toothpaste too high created problems in competing against aggressive and experienced companies like Procter & Gamble, Colgate, and Unilever. Sales declined to $486 million, and low profit continued into 1995, though with a profit recovery in 1996 and 1997. C&D introduced a new cat litter product and baking soda dental care gum. In 2001, C&D's sales were expected to exceed $1 billion (partly leveraged by the acquisition of new brands).

The company has specialized in sodium bicarbonate–based products primarily sold under the familiar Arm & Hammer (A&H) brand name but has increasingly leveraged the market access gained by its A&H branded products to add other product categories sold in the same markets through the same channels, for example, household cleaning products such as Brillo and Cameo (purchased in 1997 from Dial Corp). In 2001, C&D agreed to purchase USA Detergents, with the prospect of becoming the third largest player in the laundry detergent market behind Procter & Gamble and Lever Brothers, following the earlier acquisition of Carter-Wallace's consumer products business (antiperspirants and pet care).

Developing a market-driven product strategy requires effective decision making on a variety of strategic brand management issues like those confronting Church & Dwight. First, we discuss several important product management issues. Next, we consider analyzing product performance and strategies for existing products. We follow this with a discussion of strategic brand management.

Product Management Issues

"A product is anything that is potentially valued by a target market for the benefits or satisfactions it provides, including objects, services, organizations, places, people, and ideas."[3] This view of the product covers a wide range of situations, including tangible goods and intangible services. Thus, political candidates are products, as are travel services, medical services, refrigerators, gas turbines, and computers.

We know that services differ from physical products in several ways. A service is intangible.[4] It cannot be placed in inventory; a service is consumed at the time it is produced. There is often variability in the consistency of services rendered. Services are often linked to the people who produce them. Establishing a brand position for a service requires association with the tangible components, such as the people who produce the service or are somehow related to the service. The use of well-known personalities in advertisements for the American Express Card is illustrative. Internet-based brands are particularly illustrative of the problems faced in establishing effective brands for intangibles like services.

First, we look at new and existing product interrelationships, followed by a discussion of responsibility for managing products. Next, we consider why product success requires more than a promising product. Finally, we examine marketing's role in product strategy.

New and Existing Product Interrelationships

As shown in Exhibit 9–1, successful new products become part of the organization's product portfolio. Increasingly, companies are adopting team approaches for managing new and existing products. These approaches involve both internal and external relationships (Chapter 7). Market-driven product planning has considerable merit, as is discussed in previous chapters. This involves developing a market orientation and focusing on product strategies that offer superior customer value. Continuous learning about markets guides managers in making new product and product portfolio decisions.

Responsibility for Managing Products

Responsibility for product strategy extends to several organizational levels. Three product management levels often are present in companies that have strategic business units, different product lines, and specific brands within lines.

Product/Brand Management

This responsibility consists of planning, managing, and coordinating the strategy for a specific product or brand. These activities include market analysis, market targeting,

EXHIBIT 9–1
Interrelationships between New Product Planning and Managing the Product Portfolio

positioning strategy, performance analysis and strategy adjustment, identification of new product needs, and management and coordination of product/brand marketing activities. Marketing plans for specific products or brands are often prepared at this level. Product or brand managers typically do not have authority over all product management activities. Nevertheless, they have product responsibility. These managers are sponsors or advocates of their products, negotiating on behalf of their products with the sales force, research and development, operations, marketing research, and advertising support managers.

Product Group/Marketing Management

A business with several products or brands may assign responsibility for managing its product (or brand) managers to a product director, group manager, or marketing manager. This person coordinates the activities and approves the recommendations of a group of product or brand managers. The nature and scope of the group responsibilities are similar to those of product/brand managers. Additionally, the product group manager coordinates product management activities and decisions with the strategic business unit (SBU) management.

Product Mix Management

This responsibility is normally assigned to the chief executive at the SBU or corporate level of an organization or to a team of top executives. Illustrative decisions include product acquisitions, research and development priorities, new product decisions, and resource allocation. Evaluation of product portfolio performance is also centered at this level. In a corporation with two or more SBUs, top management may coordinate and establish product management guidelines for the SBU management. We look at the organization of marketing activities in Chapter 14.

By the mid-1990s many companies were reevaluating the traditional approaches to managing products. The changes were particularly apparent in fast-moving consumer goods, as described below:[5]

- Unilever's British soap unit and Elida Gibbs personal products division eliminated their marketing director positions.

- Marketing and sales groups were combined and focused on consumer research and product development.

- Customer development teams were formed to work with retailers across all of the companies' brands.

Similar changes are being made by other companies to integrate sales, marketing, and other business functions into cross-functional teams. A study by the Boston Consulting Group indicated that 90 percent of the responding companies have restructured their marketing departments. It is possible that traditional product- and brand-based organizations will increasingly adopt customer- and market-based approaches to implement more effectively the mandate for customer focus.[6]

Product Success Depends on Several Factors

It is apparent that products are essential to execute a business strategy, but they alone do not guarantee successful performance. It is necessary to match the firm's products with market needs. Consider, for example, the difference in the sales performance of the Plymouth Laser and the Mitsubishi Eclipse sports coupes. These cars were identical in design. Both were produced by Diamondstar Motors (equal partnership between Chrysler and Mitsubishi).[7] In 1990 Laser sales averaged 13 cars per dealer compared to 100 cars per Eclipse dealer. The Japanese quality image may help explain Eclipse's high sales, but Mitsubishi also used a better marketing strategy. Both brands targeted women, but different positioning strategies were employed. Mitsubishi launched an earlier and more focused advertising program. The Eclipse was positioned as a woman's car, using a symbolic positioning concept—the "in" car to own. Contests encouraged aerobics students to take test drives. This experience suggests that a high-quality product alone cannot achieve management's performance goals and must be matched with other key business and marketing strategies.

Competitive pressures and the changing needs and wants of buyers help explain why many companies devote a lot of attention to managing their products. Product strategies are often a key component in top management's plans for improving the performance of a business. Actions may include modifying products, introducing new products, and eliminating products. Several examples of product decisions are shown in Exhibit 9–2.

Marketing's Role in Product Strategy

Marketing executives have three major responsibilities in the organization's product strategy. First, market sensing is needed at all stages of product planning, providing information for matching new product ideas with customer needs and wants. The knowledge,

EXHIBIT 9–2
Illustrative Product Decisions and the Strategic Implications

Decision	Strategic Implications of the Decision
Coca-Cola's withdrawal of Classic (old) Coke from the market	Coca-Cola's market share was threatened by Pepsi. On the basis of extensive favorable taste tests of a new, sweeter formula, old Coke was replaced by new Coke. Loyal old Coke consumers revolted, and management reintroduced old Coke as Classic Coke. The old formulation was outselling new Coke by a substantial margin.
Hewlett-Packard's introduction of the DeskJet printer in the early 1990s	H-P relentlessly pursues a product strategy that offers both value and cost advantages to customers.
Gillette's introduction of the Sensor razor in 1988	The new razor was an awesome market success and was followed by the Sensor for Women.
The Beef Industry Council's marketing strategy to promote beef consumption	Responding to declining per capita consumption of beef, advertising, public relations, and product development activities were launched to increase the demand for beef.

experience, and marketing research methods of marketing professionals are essential in product strategy development. Customer and competitor information is needed in finding and describing unmet needs, evaluating products as they are developed and introduced, and monitoring the performance of existing products.

Marketing's second responsibility in product strategy concerns product specifications. Increasingly, top management is looking to marketing executives to identify the characteristics and performance features of products. Information about customers' needs and wants is translated into specifications for the product. Matching customer value requirements with product capabilities is essential in designing and implementing successful product strategies.

The third responsibility of marketing in product strategy is guiding target market and program-positioning strategies. These decisions are often critical to the success of both new and existing products. Since the choice of product specifications and positioning are very much interrelated, product positioning should be considered at an early stage in the product-planning process. Positioning decisions may include a single product or brand, a line of products, or a mix of product lines within a business unit.

Product decisions affect all businesses, including suppliers, producers, wholesalers, distributors, and retailers. While many of these decisions involve the evaluation, selection, and dropping of products by manufacturers, value chain members may also develop new products and services.

Analyzing Product Performance

A company may have a single product, a product line, or a mix of product lines. In our discussion of managing existing products, we assume that product/brand strategy decisions are being made for an SBU. The product composition of the SBU consists of one or more product lines and the specific product(s) that make up each line. The SBU may have a single product or a single line or various lines and specific products within each line.

Evaluating the performance of the product portfolio helps guide strategies for new products, modified products, and the elimination of products. Consider, for example, Apple's decision to drop the Newton handheld computer.[8] Apple invested an estimated $500 million in the product since development began in 1987. The core concept was a computer that could convert the user's handwriting into an electronic format. Introduced in 1993 at around $1,000, Newton was too expensive for many users and there were problems with the handwriting recognition feature. Competition eventually developed from the very successful Palm Pilot, which was introduced in 1996. Over 1 million units were sold in a two-year period. The designers created a handheld unit that could do a few things well. Apple's Message Pad was never profitable, although some industry observers suggest that Apple could have been the market leader though continuing product improvement. The handheld units were a disruptive technology that required time to develop a position in the mainstream market (see Chapter 8).

Tracking Product Performance

Evaluating existing products requires tracking the performance of the products in the portfolio, as shown in Exhibit 9–3. Management needs to establish the performance objectives and acceptable levels of performance for gauging product performance. The objectives may include both financial and nonfinancial factors. For example, in evaluating the performance of commercial airline routes, seat utilization, revenues generated, and operating costs are important. Because of the demand and cost interrelationships among products, it is

EXHIBIT 9–3
Tracking Product Performance

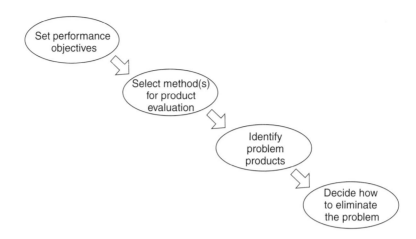

necessary to sort out the sales and costs attributable to each product to show how well it is doing. The concepts and methods of activity-based cost analysis are useful for this purpose.[9]

The next step in tracking performance is selecting one or more methods to evaluate product performance. The results of the analyses should identify problem products and those performing at or above management's expectations. The information from the analyses also helps management consider how to eliminate a problem with a product.

An interesting application of performance analysis for a service is the revenue management system used by American Airlines (AA) to evaluate and management route performance. Each route (e.g., Los Angeles–Dallas/Fort Worth) is a unit in the route system or network. Based on performance, forecasts of demand, competition, and other strategic and tactical considerations, the airline makes decisions to expand, reduce, or terminate service throughout the route network. Analysts are responsible for a group of routes, and based on management guidelines, they determine seats on each flight which will be allocated to AA advantage miles and those assigned to the other fare classifications. American Airlines pioneered this system and is recognized throughout the industry for its distinctive revenue management capabilities. Assisting the analysts are complex computer models developed using experience data and management science techniques.

We look at product life cycle analysis, product grid analysis, and positioning analysis to illustrate methods for diagnosing product performance and identifying product strategy alternatives (Exhibit 9–4). Standardized information services, research studies, and financial analysis are discussed in previous chapters.

Product Life Cycle Analysis

In Chapter 6 we described the major stages of the product life cycle (PLC): introduction, growth, maturity, and decline. Relevant issues in PLC analysis include:

- Determining the length and rate of change of the PLC.

- Identifying the current PLC stage and selecting the product strategy that corresponds to that stage.

- Anticipating threats and finding opportunities for altering and extending the PLC.

Rate of Change

Product life cycles are becoming shorter for many products due to new technology, rapidly changing preferences of buyers, and intense competition. Cycles also vary for different

EXHIBIT 9–4
**Methods for
Analyzing Product
Portfolio
Performance**

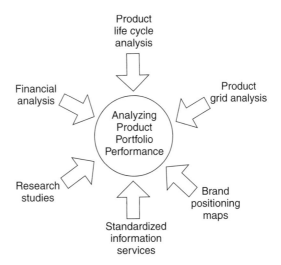

products. A clothing style may last only one season, whereas a new commercial aircraft may be produced for many years after its introduction. Determining the rate of change of the PLC is important because of the need to adjust the marketing strategy to correspond to the changing conditions.

Failure to respond to life cycle changes eventually led to bankruptcy for Smith Corona Corporation in the mid-1990s. It was one of the last American typewriter makers.[10] The threat of personal computers might have been anticipated by management, considering the rapid growth of the computer market in the 1980s. Perceptive market sensing would have alerted Smith Corona's management to the need to develop a product strategy to counter that threat.

Produce Life Cycle Strategies

The PLC stage of the product has important implications regarding all aspects of targeting and positioning (see Chapter 6). Different strategy phases are encountered in moving through the PLC. This calls for changing the focus of marketing strategy over the PLC. In the first stage the objective is to establish the brand in the market through brand development activities such as advertising. In the growth stage the brand is reinforced through marketing efforts. During the maturity stage product repositioning efforts may occur by adjusting size, color, and packaging to appeal to different market segments. Finally, during the decline stage the features of the product may be modified.

Analysis of the growth rate, sales trends, time since introduction, intensity of competition, pricing practices, and competitor entry/exit information is useful in PLC position analysis. Identifying when the product has moved from growth to maturity is more difficult than is determining other stage positions. Analysis of industry structure and competition helps in estimating when the product has reached maturity.

Dole Food Co. provides an interesting example of product life cycle analysis. Many of its foods (fruits, vegetables, etc.) are in mature PLC stages. Dole acquired two fresh-cut flower suppliers in 1998 and planned to use its powerful brand name to expand into a market offering higher profit margins than fruits and vegetables.[11]

Product Grid Analysis

Product grid analysis considers whether each product is measuring up to management's minimum performance criteria and assesses the strengths and weaknesses of the product relative to other products in the portfolio. The comparative analysis of products can be performed by incorporating market attractiveness and competitive strength assessments using two-way (horizontal and vertical) grids. These grids highlight differences among products. For example, Dole Food's management responded to the attractive potential of the $7 billion flower market coupled with Dole's distribution power in supermarkets.[12] After the relative market attractiveness and competitive strength of the products in the portfolio are identified, more comprehensive analysis of specific performance factors may also be useful, including profit contribution; barriers to entry; sales fluctuations; extent of capacity utilization; responsiveness of sales to prices, promotional activities, and service levels; technology (maturity, volatility, and complexity); alternative production and process opportunities; and environmental considerations.[13]

Brand Positioning Analysis

Perceptual maps are useful in comparing brands.[14] Recall our discussion of these methods in earlier chapters. The map is developed by obtaining preference information about a set of competing brands or firms from a sample of buyers. Various product attributes are used, and the results are summarized by the preference map.

Competitive mapping analysis offers useful guidelines for strategic product positioning. The analyses can relate buyer preferences to different brands and indicate possible brand repositioning options. New product opportunities may also be identified in the analysis of preference maps. Potential opportunities are shown by preferences that are not satisfied by the existing brands. Positioning studies over time can measure the impact of repositioning strategies.

Virtual shopping technology is another promising method for studying product positioning. This kind of research enabled Goodyear to assess its brand equity and pricing strategy for automobile tires and examine potential competitor actions. The Technology Feature describes the research technique.

Other Product Analysis Methods

The financial analysis tools in the Appendix to Chapter 2 are used to evaluate product financial performance. Other product analysis methods include research studies that show the relative importance of product attributes to buyers and rate brands against these attributes. This information indicates brand strengths and weaknesses. Many of the standardized information services provided by marketing research firms such as Information Resources, Inc., and A. C. Nielsen Company are useful in monitoring the market performance of competing brands of food and drug products. Industry trade publications also publish market share and other brand performance data.

Product Cannibalization[15]

A major consideration when introducing new products that meet needs similar to those met by a firm's existing brands is estimating how much sales volume the new product will attract from one or more existing brands. Such cannibalization may reduce the overall performance of the product portfolio. For example, Gillette's Sensor razor offered a possible cannibalization threat to the company's Atra and Trac II sales.[16] Gillette's plan was to target users of disposable razors, recognizing that some cannibalization would occur. Also, the Sensor blades were priced about 25 percent higher than Atra. Since both Atra and Trac II were in the mature stages of their life cycles, the new brand was needed to strengthen Gillette's position in the market. The Sensor performed even better than the sales and profit forecasts made by Gillette's management.

Decision makers with successful products may be reluctant to innovate because of the cannibalization threat. For example, British Airways' (BA) defensive launch of Go as a

Virtual shopping technology offers a powerful research approach for studying shoppers' reactions to new and existing products.

The approach employs a computer-simulated shopping environment in three dimensions. The imaging technology provides a way to study what attracts the customer's attention and how to motivate buyers to select particular brands in retail stores.

Virtual store shoppers can move their carts down the aisle to examine many products and brands. A particular brand can be imaged to the center of the computer screen and rotated for inspection. It can be purchased by touching the shopping cart.

The computer records all the details of the shopping process (e.g., quantity purchased, prices, sequence of purchase, and time used in the purchase). While virtual shopping is a simulated experience, validation studies indicate that it is a valuable research method for the kinds of products that can be displayed in this format.

Similar to other forms of simulated shopping, participants must be recruited. This may result in some differences compared to actual shopping behavior, but the technique offers very favorable cost/benefit trade-offs. The technology also can be used to study and develop strategies for Internet shopping.

Ray Burke in the Graduate School of Business at Indiana University is a virtual shopping research pioneer. His three-dimensional grocery shopping simulation is called iShop. He has an array of studies under way in the school's Customer Interface Lab.

Sources: Margaret Garrison, "Marketing Magic Is Created in IU's 3-D World of Virtual Shopping," *IU Business,* Spring 1997, 3; Raymond R. Burke, "Virtual Shopping," *OR/MS TODAY,* August 1995, 28–37.

no-frills airline failed to hold back the advances of no-frills rivals easyJet and Ryanair in Europe but did cannibalize BA's own sales. In 2001 BA sold Go. Nonetheless, proactive cannibalization can yield positive benefits, and the willingness to risk cannibalization may be important to innovation success.[17] Intel's continuous improvement of computer processors is illustrative of proactive cannibalization with positive effects. Similarly, Volkswagen (VW) has achieved domestic market leadership in the European car market with its multibrand strategy. In the mass market, VW sells vehicles under the VW, Audi, Seat, and Skoda brands that share the same production platform and compete directly with each other.

Strategies for Products/Brands

Analyzing performance shows how well existing product strategies are performing. This information helps management identify new product needs and points to where existing product strategies need to be altered.

Brands that have been successful over a long time period offer useful insights about product strategies. Established brands like Budweiser, Hershey, IBM, and Intel continue to build strong market positions. The performance records of powerful brands are the result of (1) marketing skills, (2) product quality, and (3) strong brand preference developed through years of successful advertising.[18] The value (brand equity) of top brands like RJR Nabisco, Kraft, and Pillsbury made these firms very attractive takeover candidates in the 1980s. Kohlberg Kravis Roberts & Co. paid $25 billion in 1989 to acquire RJR Nabisco Inc. The brand equity that has been developed for the company's many famous brands is a valuable asset. A common characteristic of many enduring brands is that the targeting and positioning strategy initially selected has generally been followed during the life of each brand. "These brands haven't strayed much from the basic marketing strategies that made them stars."[19] We discuss brand equity in the next section.

The evidence suggests that selecting and implementing good product strategies pays off. Research findings indicate that the leading brands are as much as 50 percent more profitable than their nearest competitors.[20]

Strategies for Improving Product Performance

Product improvement strategies include decisions for each product, each product line, and the product mix, as shown in Exhibit 9–5. Product line actions may consist of adding a new product, reducing costs, improving the existing product, altering the marketing strategy, or dropping the product. Product mix strategy may involve adding a product line, deleting a line, or changing the priority of a line (e.g., increasing the marketing budget for one line and cutting the budget for another line).

Once the need to change the strategy for an existing product is identified, there are several options for responding to the situation (Exhibit 9–5). We discuss each strategy to indicate the issues and scope of the action.

Add a New Product

Management may decide to add a new product to the line to counter the low performance of a product or product line. Alternatively, a strongly performing brand may provide an opportunity to leverage its strengths by adding a new related line or product category. For example, in 1998 the lingerie retailer Victoria's Secret launched a new line of cosmetics to be sold in its stores and subsequently through its successful Web page direct marketing channel.[21] By the end of 2000, the growing line of prestige beauty products was contributing 16 percent of Victoria's Secret sales, and the $150 million sales of the Dream Angels line made it the leading prestige fragrance in the United States. This has led Victoria's Secret into a joint venture with Shisheido for a 2002 launch of new cosmetics lines. We discuss line and brand extension options later in the chapter.

EXHIBIT 9–5
Strategies for Improving Product Performance

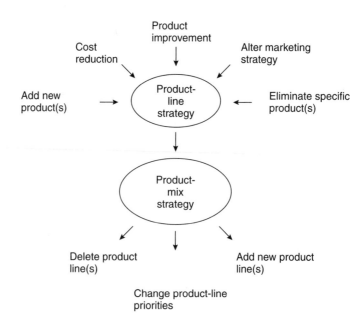

Cost Reduction

We know that low costs give a company a major advantage over the competition. As an illustration, Nabisco's Ritz Cracker was introduced in 1934 and is the best-selling cracker in the world.[22] In 2000, Nabisco's Ritz had U.S. sales of $475 million and a market share almost twice that of its nearest competitor.[23] In addition to a flavor that has wide appeal, the low price compared to other types of crackers gives Ritz a major competitive advantage. Ritz's high-volume production helps keep costs low. A product's cost may be reduced by changes in its design, manufacturing improvements, reduction of the cost of supplies, and improvements in marketing productivity.

Product Improvement

Products are often improved by changing their features, quality, and styling. Automobile features and styles are modified on a continuing basis. Many companies allocate substantial resources to the regular improvement of their products. Compared to a decade ago, today's products, such as disposable diapers, cameras, computers, and consumer electronics, show vast improvements in performance and features. For example, the Skoda automobile brand was associated with low mechanical standards and reliability until it was acquired by Volkswagen, whose engineering and production expertise has transformed the Skoda product into one of the leading European brands.

One way to differentiate a brand from the competition is with unique *features*. Another option is to let the buyer customize the features desired in a product. Recall, for example, the discussion of mass customization in earlier chapters. Optional features offer the buyer more flexibility in selecting a brand. The capability to produce products with varied features that appeal to market diversity is an important competitive advantage.

Style may offer an important competitive edge for certain product categories. Moreover, style may serve as a proxy for quality in some product categories. Seiko has very effectively used style (and other features) to make its watches attractive to buyers. The many different styles offered by Seiko give consumers a wide range of choice.

Marketing Strategy Alteration

Changes in market targeting and positioning may be necessary as a product moves through its life cycle. Problems or opportunities may point to adjusting the marketing strategy during a PLC stage.

For example, Grand Metropolitan PLC (subsequently the Diageo Group) faced a major challenge in turning around the Green Giant Company, which had been acquired in the late 1990s with the purchase of the Pillsbury Company.[24] Management moved out of manufacturing, using strategic alliances to reduce inventories and manufacturing expenses. These changes provided money for product development and marketing. The results of the strategy change were favorable. Green Giant's 1994 sales were an estimated $900 million worldwide. By 1995 Green Giant had a 21 percent market share for frozen vegetables compared to Bird's Eye's 14 percent. In 1988 both brands held nearly equal 16 percent shares. By 1998 Green Giant had 28 percent of the U.S. frozen mixed vegetables market. New product development was directed to value-added frozen items such as the Create a Meal! line of meal starters, consisting of mixed vegetables and sauce, and complete frozen skillet meals.

Product Elimination

Dropping a problem product may be necessary when cost reduction, product improvement, or marketing strategies are not feasible. In deciding to drop a product, management may consider a variety of performance criteria in addition to the product's sales and profit contribution. Elimination may occur at any PLC stage, although it is more likely to be considered in either the introduction or the decline stage. Risks are involved in eliminating products that have loyal buyers. For example, when the cosmetics retailer The Body Shop attempted to rationalize its products by eliminating some product variants, hostile reactions by consumers forced the rapid reinstatement of several of those variants.

Environmental Effects of Products

Environmental issues concerning product labeling, packaging, use, and disposal need to be considered in the product strategies of companies whose products have potential environmental impact. Protection of the environment involves a complex set of trade-offs among social, economic, political, and technology factors. Companies like McDonald's, Procter & Gamble, and Rubbermaid, among many others, incorporate environmental considerations into their product strategies. Moreover, these environmental issues are global in scope.

Environmental issues and concerns may be very complex and require consumers to change their use and disposal behavior. Even technical authorities do not always agree on the extent to which environmental problems exist or how to solve those problems. Nevertheless, many companies, governments, and special-interest groups are proactively working toward reducing environmental contamination.

In some cases stringent legislative controls have been developed. The European Union's end-of-life vehicles directive comes into force in 2007 and mandates that car manufacturers cover the costs of recycling old vehicles as well as ensure that recyclable components make up 85 percent of the weight of new vehicles. Manufacturers are already setting aside funds to meet compliance costs. Some expect similar legislation to be developed in other countries and across other sectors, such as white goods.[25]

Product Mix Modifications

Adding a new line of products to the product mix is a major product strategy change (Exhibit 9–5). The motivation for changing the product mix may be to:

- Increase the growth rate of the business.
- Offer a more complete range of products to wholesalers and retailers.
- Gain marketing strength and economies in distribution, advertising, and personal selling.
- Leverage an existing brand position.
- Avoid dependence on one product line or category.

The product mix may be expanded through internal development or by purchasing an entire company or a line of products. Purchase was a popular option in the 1990s as a result of favorable stock market prices compared to the costs of internal development. Acquisition is also a faster means of expanding the product mix. Strategic alliances among competitors are also used to expand product lines. As discussed in Chapter 7, these collaborative relationships have escalated greatly in importance as a way of doing business in the 21st century.

Strategic Brand Management

The discussion so far has centered on actions that may be taken for specific products in the portfolio. Managers in a company or business unit are also concerned with managing the portfolio or brand system for optimal performance. The importance of a strategic brand management perspective is described as follows:

> Many organizations offer a number of brands across a variety of markets. If these brands are managed separately and independently or on an ad hoc basis, overall resource allocation

among the brands may be less than optimal. For example, if Grand Metropolitan, which owns a host of worldwide brands, including J&B, Bailey's, Smirnoff, Pillsbury, Green Giant, Haägen-Dazs, and Burger King, does not treat its brands and their markets as a cohesive portfolio, then strategic decisions made for the benefit of individual brands might in the end hurt the company's overall performance.[26]

Managing the product (brand) portfolio requires decisions on whether to increase or decrease resource allocations to particular brands. The measures discussed earlier are useful in portfolio management. In addition, the use of brand equity measures for guiding portfolio management is receiving increased attention from managers. Brand equity considers the strength of a brand and how it may change over time. This measure provides a longer-term focus compared to short-term financial measures:

> Also needed are brand equity measures that can be used to evaluate the brand-building activities of managers in different product markets. Which managers have been successful at strengthening their brand and which have presided over a decline in brand health?[27]

There are many powerful forces mandating a critical strategic management focus on brands. These forces include overcapacity and intense price competition in many sectors, the proliferation of similar competing products, and powerful retailers with their own category management and private branding interests.[28]

We turn now to a discussion of strategic brand management. First, the role and value of brands are discussed and the importance and measurement of brand equity are considered, followed by an assessment of brand identification strategy. Next, possible brand leveraging strategies are examined. Finally, we look at the issues and processes for managing systems of brands (Exhibit 9–6).

The Role of Brands

Strategic branding has become a key issue in many major organizations and is not the domain only of packaged consumer goods companies. In 1999 the new head of Boeing Co.'s marketing and public relations department was told that the company did not have and did not need a brand. Nonetheless, by 2000 the company's first brand strategy was formalized as part of an overall strategy to extend the company's reach beyond the commercial airplane business. The newly appointed vice-president in charge of brand management comments, "It goes hand in hand with your reputation. We see having a strong brand as a competitive advantage." Boeing now measures its brand awareness through brand tracking, employee surveys, and comparative studies against 17 major companies, including General Electric, Microsoft, and IBM. In 2002 Boeing's sponsorship of the National Symphony concerts in Europe will take its "Forever New Frontiers" message into the European marketplace of its rival Airbus.[29]

A strategic brand perspective requires managers to be clear about what role brands play for the company in creating customer value and shareholder value. This understanding should be the basis for directing and sustaining brand investments in the most productive areas. One approach distinguishes between the functions of brands for buyers and sellers.[30]

For buyers, brands can serve a function of reduction. Brands can:

- Reduce customer search costs by identifying products quickly and accurately.

- Reduce a buyer's perceived risk by providing an assurance of quality and consistency (which may then be transferred to new products).

- Reduce the social and psychological risks associated with owning and using the "wrong" product by providing psychological rewards for purchasing brands that symbolize status and prestige.

EXHIBIT 9-6
**Strategic Brand
Management**

For sellers, brands can serve a function of facilitation by making easier some of the tasks the seller has to perform. Brands can:

- Facilitate repeat purchases that enhance the company's financial performance, because the brand enables the customer to identify and reidentify the product compared to alternatives.

- Facilitate the introduction of new products, because the customer is familiar with the brand from previous buying experience.

- Facilitate promotional effectiveness by providing a point of focus.

- Facilitate premium pricing by creating a basic level of differentiation compared to competitors.

- Facilitate market segmentation by communicating a coherent message to the target audience, telling it for whom the brand is intended and for whom it is not.

- Facilitate brand loyalty; this is of particular importance in product categories where loyal buying is an important feature of buying behavior.

The potential contribution of brand strength to building customer value and competitive advantage has encouraged managers to focus attention on global estimates of the value of brands and the concept of brand equity.

The Value of Major Brands

A strong brand offers an organization several important advantages. The brand name distinguishes the product and helps position it relative to competitors' products. A powerful brand identity creates a major distinctive capability. A brand that is recognized by buyers encourages repeat purchases. "A brand is a distinguishing name and/or symbol (such as a logo, trademark, or package design) intended to identify the goods or services of either one seller or group of sellers, and to differentiate those goods or services from those of competitors."[31]

The financial value of brands receives major attention from investors, particularly in regard to changes in the estimated value of a company's brand. Exhibit 9–7 shows some key

**EXHIBIT 9–7
Interbrand Brand
Valuation
Illustrations**

Source: Joint
Interbrand/Citigroup survey
published in "The Best Global
Brands," *Business Week,* August
6, 2001, 50–57.

The World's 10 Most Valuable Brands in 2001

Rank	Brand	2001 Brand Value ($billion)	Brand Value as % of Market Capitalization
1	Coca-Cola	68.9	61%
2	Microsoft	65.1	17
3	IBM	52.8	27
4	GE	42.4	9
5	Nokia	35.0	34
6	Intel	34.7	17
7	Disney	32.6	54
8	Ford	30.1	66
9	McDonald's	25.3	—
10	AT&T	22.8	15

The World's Most Valuable Brand Portfolios

Rank	Brand Portfolio	2001 Brand Value ($billion)	Brand Value as % of Market Capitalization
1	Johnson & Johnson	68.2	48%
2	Procter & Gamble	45.4	54
3	Nestlè	41.7	50
4	Unilever	37.9	67
5	L'Oreal	17.8	40
6	Diageo	15.0	40
7	Colgate-Palmolive	14.4	42
8	Danone	13.6	73

Fastest Growth in Brand Value

Rank	Brand	2001 Brand Value ($billion)	2000 Brand Value ($billion)	% Change
88	Starbucks	1.8	1.3	+32%
42	Samsung	6.4	5.2	+22
95	Financial Times	1.3	1.1	+14
4	GE	42.4	38.1	+11
94	Guinness	1.4	1.2	+11

Biggest Falls in Brand Value

Rank	Brand	2001 Brand Value ($billion)	2000 Brand Value ($billion)	% Change
45	Xerox	6.0	9.7	−38%
76	Amazon.com	3.1	4.5	−31
59	Yahoo!	4.4	6.3	−31
62	Duracell	4.1	5.9	−30
8	Ford	30.1	36.4	−17

illustrations from the Interbrand brand valuations of global brands and brand portfolios with a value greater than $1 billion. Interbrand calculates brand value as the net present value of the earnings the brand is expected to generate in the future. The Interbrand model bases brand earnings on forecasts of brand revenues that allow for risk and the role of the brand in stimulating customer demand. The Interbrand measure of brand strength includes leadership (ability to influence the market), stability (survival ability based on customer loyalty), market (security from change of technology and fashion), geography (ability to cross geographic borders), support (consistency and effectiveness of brand support), and protection (legal title).

Brand Equity

Brand equity is frequently a difficult concept for managers to accept, but a strategic brand management perspective requires that we understand brand equity and allow for its impact in making decisions of several kinds.

> Brand equity is a set of brand assets and liabilities linked to a brand, its name, and symbol, that add to or subtract from the value provided by a product or service to a firm and/or to that firm's customers.[32]

The assets and liabilities that affect brand equity include name awareness, brand loyalty, perceived quality, brand associations (e.g., Nike's association with athletes), and proprietary brand assets (e.g., patents).

The possible inclusion of brand equity values on balance sheets is the subject of considerable debate in the United States. Note from Exhibit 9–7 that brand value may be a very large percent of market capitalization; for example, in Interbrand's listing of brand values (Exhibit 9–7), for one in five of the top 100, brand value represents more than 40 percent of market capitalization. The option to include brand value on the balance sheet is available in countries like the United Kingdom and Australia. Starting in 2002, U.S. companies will no longer be required to "write off" goodwill in recording assets after a merger. The intent is to show a brand's financial worth. Correspondingly, it may also be necessary to show the damage to an intangible asset like a brand, for example, if a major product recall undermines customer confidence in that brand. However, the measurement of brand equity lies at the center of this question.

Measuring Brand Equity

Aaker proposes several measures to capture all relevant aspects of brand equity:[33]

- Loyalty (price premium, satisfaction/loyalty).

- Perceived quality/leadership measures (perceived quality, leadership/popularity).

- Associations/differentiation (perceived value, brand personality, organizational associations.

- Awareness (brand awareness).

- Market behavior (market share, price and distribution indices).

These components provide the basis for developing operational measures of brand equity for several purposes.

Several methods for brand valuation have been proposed. Interbrand's approach was discussed earlier. One promising method is momentum accounting, which considers how the earning power of the brand changes over its life cycle because of the revenues and expenses associated with the brand:

> Momentum accounting uses functions similar to depreciation curves in conventional accounting to monitor the sources of change in brand value over time. Momentum accounting tries to capture managers' intuition about the reasons for momentum change in terms of "impulses"—the marketing, competitive, and environmental events that affect a brand's value.[34]

Young & Rubicam (Y&R) has developed a brand evaluation tool, Brand Asset Valuator (BAV).[35] The technique uses a brand's vitality (relevance and differentiation) and brand stature (esteem and familiarity) to gauge the health of the brand. Y&R conducted studies with 30,000 consumers and 6,000 brands in 19 countries in 1993–1994. Brands with high differentiation include Disney, Jaguar, and Victoria's Secret. AT&T and Kodak fall into the high relevance category. Brands with high esteem include Band-Aid and Rubbermaid, while Coca-Cola and Kellogg's fall into the high familiarity category.

How to measure brand equity and whether to include its value on the balance sheet continue to be discussed. Nevertheless, the attention given to brand equity has increased executives' recognition of the power and value of brands and the importance of managing brand equity over the life cycle of the brand. The measurement of brand equity is important in guiding strategic brand management and indicating brand performance over time.

Brand Health Reports

The need to focus not simply on absolute brand values and investments but also on the change in brand value over time indicates the necessity for regular evaluation of brand health. Several major companies have adopted brand health report cards, including health indicators to assess the direction of change in brand equity and key issues to be addressed. Brand health reports can be compiled for individual brands or for the whole brand portfolio.[36] The brand report card can assess the brand against the characteristics of the strongest brands by scoring against key criteria of brand strength:

- The brand excels at delivering the benefits customers truly desire.
- The brand stays relevant.
- The pricing strategy is based on consumers' perceptions of value.
- The brand is properly positioned.
- The brand is consistent.
- The brand portfolio and hierarchy make sense.
- The brand makes use of and coordinates a full repertoire of marketing activities to build brand equity.
- The brand's managers understand what the brand means to consumers.
- The brand is given proper support, and that support is sustained over the long run.
- The company monitors sources of brand equity.[37]

Others suggest that brand health check measures should include market position (e.g., market share and repeat purchase behavior), perception (e.g., awareness, differentiation), marketing support (e.g., share of advertising spending in the sector compared to market share), and profitability.[38] Brand health reports need to be produced on a regular and systematic basis to alert managers to necessary changes in strategy and new market opportunities.

Brand Identification Strategy and Implementation

One of several brand identification options may be appropriate for a company. We look at the features of each one. The major identification alternatives are shown in Exhibit 9–8. Branding applies to services as well as physical products. For example, Lucent Technologies' spin-off from AT&T required the creation of a new name for the telecommunications company. The Strategy Feature describes how this was done.

EXHIBIT 9–8
**Brand
Identification
Strategies**

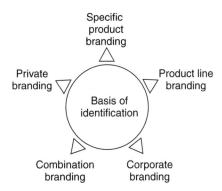

Specific Product Branding

The strategy of assigning a brand name to a specific product is used by various producers of frequently purchased items such as Procter & Gamble's Crest toothpaste, Pampers diapers, and Ivory soap. The brand name on the product gives it a unique identification in the marketplace. A successful brand develops strong customer loyalty over time. Products that are low-involvement purchases benefit from a popular brand name. The major limitation of using brand names on individual products is the expense of building and supporting each brand through advertising and sales promotion. One danger is that the brand name may be so popular that it becomes a generic term for the product type. Companies work aggressively to avoid this consequence and other misuses of their popular brand names. Building a new brand name through advertising initially can cost over $50 million, plus the expense of maintaining the brand identity in the marketplace.

Product-Line Branding

This strategy places a brand name on a line of related products. Palm Inc.'s popular line of personal digital assistants is an example of product-line branding. It provides focus and offers cost advantages by promoting the entire line rather than each product. This strategy is effective when a firm has one or more lines, each of which contains an interrelated offering of product items. One advantage of product-line branding is that additional items (line extensions) can be introduced utilizing the established brand name.

Corporate Branding

This strategy builds brand identity by using the corporate name to identify the entire product offering. Examples include IBM in computers, Lucent Technologies in telecommunications, Victoria's Secret in intimate apparel, and Detroit Diesel in truck engines. Corporate branding has the advantage of using one advertising and sales promotion program to support all of the firm's products. It also facilitates the promotion of new products. The shortcomings of corporate branding include a lack of focus on specific products and possible adverse effects on the product portfolio if the company encounters negative publicity for one of its products. Using corporate branding as a primary approach to branding may be necessary when it is not feasible to establish specific brand identity and when the product offering is relatively narrow.

Combination Branding

A company may use a combination of the branding strategies shown in Exhibit 9–8. Sears, for example, employs both product-line and corporate branding (e.g., the Kenmore appliance and Craftsman tool lines). Combination branding benefits from the buyer's

- Lucent's spin-off from AT&T required selecting a new name for the $36 billion telecommunications designer, developer, and manufacturer.

- The name selection was unusually successful, though the rapid building of a brand name was costly.

- Lucent spent an estimated $100 million in communicating the new corporate name, but the impressive brand visibility was achieved in one year.

- The success was the result of an effective name selection process, followed by a consistent message and look that spanned everything from annual reports to TV ads.

- The selection process, guided by a brand identity consultant, involved many information sources, including executives and focus groups.

- At one point in the process the name team had over 700 name candidates.

- The name Lucent was selected, in part, because it did not have a prior meaning attached to it other than "marked by clarity" or "glowing with light."

- The color red was selected for the Lucent logo to distinguish it from the popular blue color used by other firms in the industry.

- In 1997 there were 1,625 corporate name changes, the highest number in the past decade, stimulated by mergers, acquisitions, and spin-offs.

Based on Maricris G. Briones, "When a Rose Is No Longer a Rose," *Marketing News,* April 13, 1998, 1–2.

association of the corporate name with the product or line brand name. However, corporate advertising may not be cost-effective for inexpensive, frequently purchased consumer brands. For example, companies like Procter & Gamble and Cheesebrough-Ponds (Vaseline, Q-tips) do not actively promote the corporate identity.

Private Branding

In another form of corporate branding, retailers with established brand names, such as Kroger, Target, and Wal-Mart Stores, Inc., contract with producers to manufacture and place the retailer's brand name on products sold by the retailer. This is called private branding, and the major advantage to the producer is eliminating the costs of marketing to end-users, although a private-label arrangement may make the manufacturer dependent on the firm using the private brand. Producing private-label merchandise for a single company is risky since the arrangement may be terminated by the buyer. Nevertheless, the arrangement can yield benefits to both the producer and the middleman. The sales volume of the producer is expanded rapidly. The retailer uses its private brand to build store loyalty, since the private brand is associated with the retailer's stores. Private brands are often profitable for retailers. Over the last two decades private labels have accounted for about 14 percent of total sales in supermarkets.[39]

Extending the Brand Identification Concept

In addition to the brand as product or the brand as organization, David Aaker extends brand identification to the brand as person and the brand as symbol.[40] The brand as person, or brand personality, perspective recognizes that strong brands may have an identity beyond the product or the company that has a positive impact on the customer relationship and the perception of value. For example, the Saturn car established a personality of a reliable, down-to-earth friend with which consumers identified. The brand as symbol underlines the role in brand building of visual imagery, metaphors, and brand heritage. For example, consider Nike's "swoosh" visual symbolism, the Energizer bunny metaphor for long battery life, and Starbuck's Seattle coffeehouse tradition. Relatedly, Don Schultz refers to this as "getting to the heart of the brand" to understand the promise that the brand makes to the customer and its value proposition.[41] A clear and effective brand identification strategy is a foundation for building brand strength.

Strategies for Brand Strength

Strategies for building brand strength and sustaining that strength for the brand system require attention to the implementation of brand identification in brand-building strategies, revitalizing brands in the later stages of their life cycles, and the strategic vulnerabilities of core brands, since it is important to understand that like any asset, brands may be vulnerable to competitive attack or changing market conditions.

Brand-Building Strategies

The essence of strategies for brand strength is that management should actively "build, maintain, and manage the four assets that underlie brand equity—awareness, perceived quality, brand loyalty, and brand association."[42] Critical to this process is developing the brand identification strategy and implementing that identity throughout the company and the marketplace. The goal is to enhance brand equity. The successful approach to global brand building of Colgate Palmolive is described in the Global Feature.

In addition to creating brand identification, attention is frequently also needed to coordinating that identity across the organization, the different media it uses, and the different markets it serves.[43] For example, IBM's corporate brand is used by a great number of products and company divisions in diverse end-user markets. The challenge is to implement the brand identification consistently across these different situations. The risk of failing to do so is customer confusion and reduced brand equity. Particular challenges are faced in managing brand identification consistently across a brand's Internet and offline applications.

Brand Revitalization

In increasingly competitive markets, weaker brands may cease to be viable and may be withdrawn or sold to other companies. However, mature brands which still fit the company's overall strategy and direction may require rejuvenation. The challenge may be to find new uses. For example, Eagle Brand Sweetened Condensed Milk was created in the pre–Civil War, prerefrigeration era to prevent food poisoning and was used for 100 years as a constituent of Thanksgiving pumpkin pies. The product has been repositioned as a sweet whitener for fashionable mocha coffees and fondues, and the company is exploring further new uses for the product.

Other revitalization approaches may rely on the brand's heritage. Procter & Gamble's Oil of Olay has a 53-year-old brand history and retains a strong position in the skin care market by adding products that are linked to the brand heritage.[44] Similarly, when Procter & Gamble acquired the mature Old Spice men's fragrance brand, that brand was underperforming in its target market of older consumers. P&G successfully repositioned the brand for younger consumers and rebuilt market share. Apple Computers transformed the company's position with the launch of the iMac and its 1997 "Think Different" campaign directed at the loyal core of Macintosh users.[45]

Colgate is synonymous with toothpaste in many emerging global markets, sometimes commanding a market share of 80 percent or more. Success in the United States came when Colgate overtook Procter & Gamble's Crest toothpaste late in 1997, and Colgate holds around one-third of the U.S. market.

Colgate's constant innovation and marketing power involve several initiatives:

- Every year Colgate sends its people around the world to preach the message of oral hygiene.

- The goal is to convert the world to Colgate—whether squeezing toothpaste onto neem sticks in India or pushing free toothbrushes into the hands of 50 million schoolchildren worldwide.

- Colgate has changed the product offer for different overseas markets—it is a cheap tooth powder in India, a chalky flavored paste in China, and elsewhere a trendy gel aimed at high-growth youth markets.

- Colgate is promoted at rock concerts, rural road shows, mobile dental clinics, schools—anywhere people bare their teeth.

- Colgate was first to market with a plaque-fighting product and the first to target gum disease with its products (important with an aging U.S. population), as well as products for sensitive teeth, and a "2-in-1" product for children.

- Colgate's brand strategy involves "touching consumers wherever they are"—from conventional advertising to sponsoring a contest with Blockbuster Video to pick which stars have the brightest smiles.

Source: "How Colgate Chomps on the Competition," *Business Week Online,* August 6, 2001.

The size of investments in building brand identification may mandate brand rejuvenation to rebuild earnings.

Strategic Brand Vulnerabilities

A strategic perspective on brands also requires that decision makers be aware of the vulnerability of brands. For example, brand equity can be negative. When Skoda cars were first launched in the United Kingdom, with a heritage of low-quality vehicles assembled in part by convict labor in a then-communist country, consumer tests revealed that perceived value was lower when the brand was known than it was when the brand badges were removed from the cars. In the early 1990s Encyclopedia Britannica rebuffed an approach from Microsoft to produce a digital version of its encyclopedia. In less than two years Microsoft's Encarta dominated the market. When Encyclopedia Britannica approached Microsoft to reopen negotiations, Microsoft management told it that its research showed that Britannica had negative brand equity and would have to pay Microsoft to have its name on a joint product.[46]

Manufacturer brands may be increasingly susceptible to competition from retailer private brands as well as brand copying and brand counterfeiting. Category management structures operated by major retailers may also substitute the issue of "position in category" for traditional brand leadership.

In addition, brand strength may not protect a company from major shifts in consumer tastes or market preferences. For example, while Coca-Cola is recognized as the most valuable brand in the world (Exhibit 9–7), falling world demand for carbonated cola drinks has led to job cuts and heavy costs in withdrawing cola concentrate from the supply chain in the early 2000s. The company has launched new products to meet market preferences for flavored waters and fruit juice–based drinks and in 2001 had an extensive portfolio of brands. Several new products do not carry the Coke brand name. A fragmented market demands local brands: Coke's best-selling cola in India is Thums Up, not Coke.

Competitive actions may also undermine the position of an established brand. Gillette has an outstanding reputation for innovation and brand strength in the razor and blade market, with a stream of innovations in higher-priced, higher-margin shaving products. Nonetheless, in 2001 Gillette faced major setbacks, with operating profits dropping 14 percent in the first half year. While Gillette spent more than $1 billion on the innovative Mach3 razor for men and the Venus for women, it neglected its low-price razors and disposables, allowing competitors to gain market share in that part of the market. The company now faces the challenge of reestablishing its brand dominance in the shaving market.[47]

Unexpected events may also attack a brand's position. In the 1980s Perrier mineral water was associated with benzene contamination, and the brand has never recovered its previously preeminent position in the market. Interestingly, at a similar time Tylenol was faced with a cyanide poisoning scare, and the product was withdrawn from the market. However, the brand recovered its position quickly when distribution and promotion were restarted. It seems that Tylenol was a more resilient brand than Perrier and was better able to recover.

Brand health checks will assist in making decision makers more aware of the critical strategic vulnerabilities that brands may face, their resilience when things go wrong, and the development of appropriate strategies.

Brand Leveraging Strategy

Established brand names may be useful in introducing other products by linking the new product to an existing brand name. The primary advantage is immediate name recognition for the new product. Methods of capitalizing on an existing brand name include line extension, stretching the brand vertically, brand extension, cobranding, and licensing.

Line Extension

This leveraging strategy consists of offering additional items in the same product class or category as the core brand. Extensions may include new flavors, forms, colors, and package sizes. The same name may be used (e.g., BMW 300, 500, 700), or the brand name may be linked less directly (Courtyard by Marriott). Most new products are line extensions.

Stretching the Brand Vertically[48]

This strategy may include moving up or down in price/quality from the core brand. It may involve subbrands that vary in price and features. The core name may be linked to the extension (e.g., different types of Kodak film and Mercedes automobiles). The advantages of this strategy include expanded market opportunities, shared costs, and leveraging distinctive capabilities. The primary limitation is damage to the core brand (e.g., lower price/quality versions of a premium brand).

Brand Extension

This approach benefits from buyers' familiarity with an existing brand name in a product class to launch a new product line in another product class.[49] The new line may or may not be closely related to the brand from which it is being extended. Examples of related extensions include Ivory shampoo and conditioner, Nike apparel, and Swiss Army watches. Critics of both brand and line extensions indicate that they often do not succeed and may damage the core brand.[50] Critics argue that a brand name is weakened when it stands for two things. For example, some observers have questioned Procter & Gamble's use of the Duncan Hines brand image to launch its bagged cookies because some ads encourage using bake mixes while others promote the purchase of ready-made cookies. P&G sold the Duncan Hines brand in 1997. One of the more successful brand extensions of the 1990s consisted of the various lines of Healthy Choice foods.

Regardless of the possible dangers of brand extension, it continues to be popular. Two considerations are important. First, there should be a logical tie between the core brand and the extension. It may be a different product type while having some relationship to the core brand. For example, the Victoria's Secret brand was used to introduce a new cosmetics line. Similarly, in the United kingdom, the successful fashion retailer French Connection is extending its famous "fcuk" branding from clothes to eye-glasses, cosmetics, underwear, and watches alongside its clothes, as well as homewares such as towels and bed linen. Second, the extension needs to be carefully evaluated as to any negative impact on the brand equity of the core brand. An interesting example of how the Virgin Group in the United Kingdom is extending the brand into new industries is described in Exhibit 9–9 (see the accompanying photograph of Sir Richard Branson and the Virgin Atlantic air crew).

Cobranding

This strategy consists of two well-known brands working together in promoting their products. The brand names are used in various promotional efforts. Examples include airlines cobranding with credit card companies. Delta Airlines' cobranding alliance with American Express via the Sky Miles credit card is illustrative. The advantage is leveraging the customer bases of the two brands. Joint products may be involved, or instead, a composite product such as the Healthy Choice–Kellogg line of cereals may be cobranded.

EXHIBIT 9–9
Brand Extension in Action

Source: Stephen J. Garone, *Managing Reputation with Image and Brands* (New York: The Conference Board, 1998), 11.

An Experienced Virgin

Virgin Group is one of the greatest examples of extending a brand into new industries without diverging from its core values—irreverent, unconventional, creative, entertaining, active. "Each time Virgin entered a new business," explains John Mathers, director, Sampson Tyrrell Enterprise, "all the commercial pundits suggested it was stretching the brand too far. They reasoned that few people would want to buy financial services, for example, from a youth brand with a rock and roll image." But ever since its inception in the early 1970s, Virgin has been racking up an impressive number of notches on its corporate bedpost.

Virgin's businesses now include book publishing, radio and television broadcasting, hotel management, entertainment retail, trading and investments, and an airline—"a highly successful migration of core values that are very much the product of an ideology," says Interbrand's Tom Blackett.

Andrew Welch of Landor cites an example of how the Virgin megastore in Paris has been able to transcend its boundaries of being purely a retailer: "It has become a temple for young consumers and youth culture. Paris youth place their trust in Virgin for guidance on what is contemporary culture. As such, Virgin is considered the consummate specialist in all things for youth fashion and fashionability."

"Virgin has succeeded in many markets in creating a new reality that its competitors have been compelled to follow because it touches the consumer in a fundamental way," summarizes Blackett, "which may actually be the key to shaking up mature environments in the future."

Flight attendants surround Sir Richard Branson, center right, and Ontario Tourism, Culture, and Recreation Minister Tim Hudak, center left, following the inaugural flight of Virgin Atlantic that touched down at Pearson International Airport in Toronto June 12, 2001. Virgin Atlantic's daily nonstop scheduled service between Toronto and London began on this day.

AP Photo/Canadian Press, Aaron Harris.

Cobranding may involve business-to-business channels. In 2001, Dell Computers signed an agreement with EMC to cobrand its Clarion line of data storage systems.[51] More commonly cobranding is used to link consumer brands. Disney, for example, is cobranding breakfast cereals, toaster pastries, and waffles with Kellogg, as well as Disney Xtreme! Coolers with Minute Maid.[52]

Cobranding can be very effective in providing synergy to the two brands.[53] Promotional budgets can be shared, and new product introductions facilitated. The important challenge is selecting the right brand combination and coordinating the implementation between two independent companies. An effective cobranding arrangement is a strong competitive strategy.

Licensing

Another popular method of using the core brand name is licensing. The sale of a firm's brand name to another company for use on a noncompeting product is a major business activity. Total U.S. retail sales of licensed products were estimated at more than $100 billion in 2000.[54] The firm granting the license obtains additional revenue with only limited costs. It also gains free publicity for the core brand name.

For example, Land Rover has taken its name into a range of product categories, including outdoor clothing, an "adventure kit" for children, wristwatches, and an "all-terrain pushchair" for infants designed for off-road use like Land Rover vehicles. The company sees the advantages as additional revenue for the brand but also reinforcing the rugged lifestyle identification of the brand. Similarly, PepsiCo Inc. employs licensing as a strategic tool to enhance and build the identification of the brand and generate an additional revenue stream; the use of the Pepsi logo on young men's and women's apparel is intended to reflect the lifestyles of drinkers of Pepsi and Mountain Dew.[55]

The main limitation is that the licensee may create an unfavorable image for the brand. Licensing may be used for corporate, product-line, or specific brands. Anheuser-Busch Companies, Inc. (Budweiser beer), is one of the largest corporate licensors.

Overleveraging

Decision makers may be under great pressure to leverage their brands over a larger number of products to justify investments in brand building and to increase profitability. There may be significant risks in stretching brands too far. The brand extension may not succeed if it is not compatible with the established brand identification and may even dilute or damage the brand equity for established products.[56] Recall, for example, earlier comments about the leveraging of Richard Branson's Virgin brand on diverse products from airlines, music, mobile telephones, and food and drink products to financial services (Exhibit 9–9). There are fears that the continued failure of Virgin Trains to provide a high standard of railroad service (difficult with out-of-date rolling stock and the United Kingdom's ailing railroad system) may undermine consumer appeal for other Virgin branded products and services and reduce the value of the brand. Regular brand health checks and a strategic brand system perspective are important in identifying and managing these risks.

Global Branding

Companies operating in international markets face various strategic branding challenges. For example, the European multinational Unilever is reducing its brand portfolio from 1,600 to 400 to focus on its strong global brands like Lipton while acquiring more global brands for its portfolio: SlimFast, Ben & Jerry's Homemade, and Bestfoods (Knorr, Hellmans). The company's global brand strategy aims to put it on an equal footing with international retailers.[57]

The development of global brands like Coca-Cola, Colgate, and Ford is supported by increasingly cosmopolitan consumers in many countries with similar tastes drawn from exposure to similar media as well as the economies of scale of global brand identification and communications. However, global brand identity may also create barriers to building strong identification with local markets, and for some companies the mantra has become "think global, act local."

Aaker and Joachimsthaler argue that global brand strategy is often misguided and that the priority should not be building global brands (although they may result) but instead working for global brand leadership—strong brands in all markets supported by effective, strategic global brand management.[58] Nonetheless, this may involve approaches different from those successful in the domestic market. For example, Procter & Gamble has traditionally emphasized individual product brands, not its corporate identity. However, in some overseas markets, like Japan, Russia, and India, the company uses the corporate umbrella identification of P&G to create value. Japanese consumers want to know about the company behind the brands they buy.[59]

Multinational operations increasingly face the challenge of managing brand systems containing global, regional, and local brands. For example, Nestlé manages a four-level brand portfolio: 10 worldwide corporate brands (e.g., Nestlé, Carnation, Buitoni); 45 worldwide strategic brands (e.g., KitKat, Polo, Coffee-Mate), the responsibility of general management at the strategic business unit level; 140 regional strategic brands (e.g., Stouffers, Contadina, Findus), the responsibility of strategic business units and regional management; and 7,500 local brands (e.g., Texicana, Brigadeiro, Rocky), the responsibility of local markets. Individual brands may shift between these levels over time.[60]

Internet Brands

Some controversy surrounds the issue of branding on the Internet. That controversy relates mainly to the sustainability of brands that exist only on the Internet but extends to how the Web can have an impact on the brand equity of conventional brands. It is all but impossible for the decision maker to ignore the linkage between the brand and the Internet. The E-Business Feature describes the struggle of LastMinute.com to establish its brand and value proposition as an Internet company.

The Interbrand estimates in Exhibit 9–10 illustrate the high expenditures required to establish Internet brands compared to conventional brands in 1999 (before the collapse of the market values of many Internet companies). However, research suggests that even large expenditures to create Internet brand awareness have been ineffective in many cases in building consumer trust or other brand strengths.[61] Failures in Internet companies' product offers and order fulfillment and a lack of strategic perspective have undermined Internet brand building.[62]

The Internet can play a pivotal role in enhancing brand relationships and corporate reputation by offering customers a new degree of interactivity with the brand and creating speed and adaptability in the relationship-building process.[63] For established brands seeking to reinforce brand identification strategy and enhance brand equity through the Web, the website should:

- Create a positive experience by being easy to use, delivering value, and being interactive, personalized, and timely.

- Reflect and support the brand.

- Look for synergy with other communications programs.

- Provide a home for loyalists and extend the relationship with those customers.

- Differentiate with strong subbranded content.[64]

While much remains to be learned about the requirements for effective brand building on the Internet, the issues should be incorporated in strategic brand management.

EXHIBIT 9–10
Brand-Building Costs on the Internet

Source: "The Cost of Building a Brand," *Business Week Online,* November 15, 1999.

Established Brands

Rank	Brand	1999 Brand Value ($billion)	1999 Marketing Budget ($million)	Marketing as a % of Revenue
1	Coca-Cola	83.8	4,000	20.5%
2	Microsoft	56.7	3,752	16.7
3	IBM	43.8	1,000	1.1

Internet Brands

Rank	Brand	1999 Brand Value ($billion)	1999 Marketing Budget ($million)	Marketing as a % of Revenue
35	AOL	4.3	807	16.9%
53	Yahoo!	1.8	206	35.9
57	Amazon.com	1.4	402	25.9

Founded by Martha Lane Fox and Brent Hoberman in November 1998, LastMinute.com uses the reach of the Internet to offer reduced prices direct to consumers—theater tickets, airline tickets, hotel reservations, gifts, and "lifestyle services" for the cash-rich, time-poor urban consumer who has not planned ahead. Started in the United Kingdom, Last-Minute.com has websites in that country, France, Italy, Spain, and Holland.

- The LastMinute.com business model could not operate without the Internet; it has created a "last minute marketplace" said to have been conceived by Hoberman because of his inability to plan anything in advance.

- The business is a "Web brand" that provides only information and customer service, taking a commission from suppliers; it links buyers and sellers without getting involved in fulfillment.

- Nonetheless, launch advertising was almost totally offline—London Underground posters, print and billboard advertising, promotional tie-ins with other companies, and a much-hyped "Blonde Ambition" PR tour by Martha Lane Fox.

- In 2000 LastMinute.com went public in a badly handled launch; it was grossly overvalued, and between March 2000 and December 2000 share values fell from 560p to 120p.

- Late in 2000, Allan Leighton joined the company as nonexecutive chairman, bringing outstanding retailing skills; he is credited with the turnaround of Asda (the number three British supermarket chain) and headed Wal-Mart's European operations for a time.

- At Christmas 2000 LastMinute.com ventured successfully into offline trading with a Christmas gifts catalog and telephone ordering of gifts.

- In 2001 LastMinute.com formed a Web-based alliance with the travel company Thomas Cook.

- Under Leighton's influence, LastMinute.com is increasing its focus on the core markets of the United Kingdom, France, and Germany; reducing staff levels; reducing advertising expenditures; and focusing on revenue growth instead of customer acquisition.

- With growing revenues and falling costs, predictions are for breakeven by 2002 and full profitability after that.

Source: Adapted from Nigel F. Piercy, "LastMinute.com—Myth and Reality," in *Market-Led Strategic Change: A Guide to Transforming the Process of Going to Market* (Oxford: Butterworth-Heinemann, 2001), 188–90.

Managing Brand Systems

Companies that have several different brands and products should manage them as a system rather than pursuing independent brand strategies. The objectives should be to:[65]

- Leverage commonalities to generate synergy. Even though sharing brand names and brand identities may be different because different products or markets are involved, the challenge is to generate synergy in the form of enhanced brand impact.

- Reduce damage to brand identity. Differences between brand identities in different contexts have the potential to undermine brand identity.

- Obtain clarity of product offerings. The goal is to reduce confusion and achieve clarity among different the product offerings.

- Enable change and adaptation. As brands adapt and change, a systems perspective should help manage the process effectively.

- Guide resource allocations among brands. Resource allocations should consider the impact of each brand on others in the system and the future roles that each may play.

The importance of a brand system perspective is illustrated by the response of Daimler-Benz to new product test failure. In the late-1990s DaimlerBenz's management targeted the small car market with the new A-Class Baby Benz, alongside the prestigious Mercedez-Benz C-Class and E-Class lines. In 1997, wholly unexpectedly, in a test drive a Swedish journalist rolled the A-Class Benz when simulating a swerve around an imaginary elk (the "Elk Test"). The company responded with expensive changes to the vehicle—new tires, electronic stabilizing as a standard feature—but after 3,000 canceled orders it was forced to take the car off the market for three months to undertake chassis modifications. Rumors spread that the company had stretched itself too far, too quickly to get into the mass car market and were fueled by the subsequent delay of the launch of the Smart car because of similar safety concerns. Nonetheless, the company survived the crisis, and its measured and careful approach has protected the brands from long-term damage. The A-Class Benz is now a highly successful product line.[66]

A brand system perspective encourages the use of brands to support the brand system as well as to support each brand:

> A key to managing brands in an environment of complexity is to consider them as not only individual performers but members of a system of brands that must work to support one another. A brand system can serve as a launching platform for new products or brands and as a foundation for all brands in the system.[67]

A key concept that guides the management of the brand system is that specific brands play different roles in the system. For example, one brand may play a lead or driver role whereas other brands in the system may play supportive roles.

An important issue in managing brand systems is deciding how many brands should comprise the system. Four questions are relevant in deciding whether to introduce a new brand name:

1. Is the brand sufficiently different to merit a new name?

2. Will a new name really add value?

3. Will the existing brand be placed at risk if it is used on a new product?

4. Will the business support a new brand name?[68]

As an illustration, Levi's successful Dockers brand has a strong positive score on all four questions.

Summary

Strategic brand management provides the foundation for selecting strategies for each of the remaining components of the positioning strategy. It forms the leading edge of efforts to influence buyers' positioning of the company's brands. Product strategy needs to be matched to the right distribution, pricing, and promotion strategies. Product decisions shape both corporate and marketing strategies and are made within the guidelines of the corporate mission and objectives. The major product decisions for a strategic business unit include selecting the mix of products to be offered, deciding how to position an SBU's product offering, developing and implementing strategies for the products in the portfolio, selecting the branding strategy for each product, and managing the brand system.

Most successful corporations assign an individual or organizational unit the responsibility for strategic brand management. Product managers for planning and coordinating product activities are used by many companies, although new customer-based and market-based structures are emerging.

Evaluating a company's existing products and brands helps establish priorities and guidelines for managing the product portfolio. The methods include portfolio screening, analysis of the product life cycle, product grid analysis, positioning analysis, and financial analysis. Product cannibalization is an important issue in this analysis. It is necessary to decide for each product if (1) a new product should be developed to replace or complement the product, (2) the product should be improved (and, if so, how), or (3) the product should be eliminated. Product strategy alternatives for existing products include cost reduction, product alteration, marketing strategy changes, and product elimination. Product mix modification may also occur.

The role of branding in positioning products is pivotal for many companies. Brand equity is a valuable asset that requires continuous attention to build and protect the brand's value. The equity of a brand includes both its assets and its liabilities, including brand loyalty, name awareness, perceived quality, brand associations, and proprietary brand assets. Increasingly, companies are measuring brand equity to help guide product portfolio strategies and adopting regular brand health checks. Mature brands may require specific revitalization approaches. Managers also must be aware of existing and emerging strategic brand vulnerabilities.

Brand identification strategy involves deciding among private branding, corporate branding, product-line branding, specific product branding, and combination branding. Brand identification in the marketplace offers a firm an opportunity to gain a strategic advantage through brand equity and brand leveraging.

Opportunities for leveraging brands include line extensions in the existing product class, extending the line vertically, extending the brand to different product classes, cobranding with other brands, and licensing the brand name. Line extensions are widely used alongside the other forms of leveraging. For companies with international operations, additional concerns relate to global branding issues. Increasingly, attention also must be paid to the role of the Internet in implementing brand identification.

Finally, management is concerned with the system of brands in the portfolio. Each brand should contribute to the system as well as benefiting from it. The objective should be to coordinate strategies across the system rather than manage each brand on an independent basis.

Internet Applications

A. Examine the Fortune Brands website (*www.fortunebrands.com*). Analyze and evaluate the strategic initiatives used by Fortune Brands in its strategic brand management.

B. Visit the website of LastMinute.com (*www.LastMinute.com*). Map the business model used by this Web brand. Review the strengths and weaknesses of the model and consider how the brand has been established and how it may be extended.

C. Go to *www.e4m.biz*, operated by the United Kingdom's Marketing Council. Register at the site and choose the Business-to-Consumer area and the Brand Consistency option under the Strategy Area. Review several of the short cases describing how major companies are striving for consistency in their brand identification while using multiple channels, including the Internet. What conclusions can you draw regarding the requirements for brand consistency across multiple channels?

Questions for Review and Discussion

1. Eli Lilly & Company manufactures a broad line of pharmaceuticals with strong brand positions in the marketplace. Lilly is also a manufacturer of generic drug products. Is this combination branding strategy a logical one? If so, why?

2. Discuss the advantages and limitations of following a branding strategy of using brand names for specific products.

3. In 1985 Philip Morris Incorporated acquired General Foods Company. Discuss the advantages and limitations of acquiring a company in order to obtain its established brand names.

4. To what extent are the SBU strategy and the product strategy interrelated?

5. Suppose that a top administrator of a university wants to establish a product-management function covering both new and existing services. Develop a plan for establishing a product planning program.

6. Many products like Jell-O reach maturity. Discuss several ways to give mature products new vigor. How can management determine whether it is worthwhile to attempt to salvage products that are performing poorly?

7. How does improving product quality lower the cost of producing a product?

8. Why do some products experience long, successful lives while others have very short life cycles?

9. How can a company combine the strengths of global brands with the need to adapt to local market requirements in a multinational operation?

10. Discuss the underlying logic of managing brand systems.

Notes

1. David W. Cravens, Nigel F. Piercy, and Ashley Prentice, "Developing Market-Driven Product Strategies," *Journal of Product and Brand Management* 9, no. 6 (2000), 369–88.

2. This illustration is based on Meera Somasundram, "Missteps Mar Church & Dwight's Plans," *The Wall Street Journal,* April 28, 1995, B5A; Gabriella Stern, "Baking-Soda Toothpaste Gains Popularity," *The Wall Street Journal,* December 28, 1993, B6; Peter Nulty, "No Product Is Too Dull to Shine," *Fortune,* July 27, 1992, 95–96; Noreen O'Leary, "Return of the Shadow," *Chief Executive,* May 1999, 26–27; and Bill Schmitt, "Church & Dwight Buys Consumer Units from Carter-Wallace," *Chemical Week,* May 16, 2001, 9.

3. David W. Cravens, Gerald E. Hills, and Robert B. Woodruff, *Marketing Management* (Homewood, IL: Richard D Irwin, 1987), 375.

4. Leonard Berry, "Services Marketing Is Different," *Business,* May–June 1980, 24–30.

5. "Death of the Brand Manager," *The Economist,* April 9, 1994, 67–68.

6. Pierre Berthon, James M. Hulbert, and Leyland F. Pitt, *Brands, Brand Managers, and the Management of Brands: Where to Next?* (Boston: Marketing Science Institute, 1997), Report No. 97-122.

7. John Harris, "Advantage Mitsubishi," *Forbes,* March 18, 1991, 100, 104.

8. Jim Carlton, "Apple Drops Newton, an Idea Ahead of Its Time," *The Wall Street Journal,* March 2, 1998, B1, B8.

9. Robert Cooper and Robert S. Kaplan, "Measure Costs Right: Make the Right Decisions," *Harvard Business Review,* September–October 1998, 96–103.

10. Jonathan Auerbach, "Smith Corona Files Under Chapter 11; Typewriter Maker Loses Ground to PCs," *The Wall Street Journal,* July 6, 1995, C11.

11. Stacey Kravetz, "King of Pineapples Tiptoes to Tulips for Faster Growth," *The Wall Street Journal,* July 6, 1998, A17, A20.

12. Ibid.

13. George S. Day, "Diagnosing the Product Portfolio," *Journal of Marketing,* April 1977, 37.

14. The development of these maps is discussed in William R. Dillon, Thomas J. Madden, and Neil H. Firtle, *Marketing Research in a Marketing Environment,* 3rd ed. (Burr Ridge, IL: Richard D. Irwin), appendix to chap. 17.

15. This section is based on David W. Cravens, Nigel F. Piercy, and Georgie S. Low, "The Innovation Challenges of Proactive Cannibalization and Discontinuous Technology," *European Business Review,* forthcoming, 2002.

16. Lawrence Ingrassia, "Face-Off: A Recovering Gillette Hopes for Vindication in a High-Tech Razor," *The Wall Street Journal,* September 29, 1989, A1, A4.

17. Rajesh K. Chandry and Gerald J. Tellis, "Organizing for Radical Product Innovation: The Overlooked Role of the Willingness to Cannibalize," *Journal of Marketing Research,* November 1998, 474–87; Rajesh K. Chandry and Gerald J. Tellis, *Organizing for Radical Product Innovation* (Boston: Marketing Science Institute, 1998), Report 98-102.

18. Ronald Alsop, "Enduring Brands Hold Their Allure by Sticking Close to Their Roots," *The Wall Street Journal,* Centennial Edition, B4, B5.

19. Ibid.

20. Ibid.

21. Yumiko Ono, "Victoria's Secret to Launch Makeup with Sexy Names," *The Wall Street Journal,* September 14, 1998, B8.

22. "If It's Not Broken, Don't Fix It," *Forbes,* May 7, 1984, 132.

23. Kelly Beamon, "The Great Bake Off," *Supermarket Business,* August 15, 2000, 41.

24. Richard Gibson, "How Grand Met Made Ailing Green Giant Jolly Again," *The Wall Street Journal,* June 6, 1995, B4.

25. Jonathan Guthrie, "Industry Left to Bear the Burden," *Financial Times,* March 19, 2001, 15.

26. David A. Aaker, "Measuring Brand Equity across Products and Markets," *California Management Review,* Spring 1996, 102.

27. Ibid., 103.

28. David A. Aaker and Erich Joachimsthaler, *Brand Leadership* (New York: Free Press, 2000), ix.

29. "The Best Global Brands," *Business Week,* August 6, 2001, 50–57.

30. The discussion in this section is based on Berthon, Hulbert, and Pitt, *Brands, Brand Managers, and the Management of Brands.*

31. David A. Aaker, *Managing Brand Equity* (New York: Free Press, 1991), 7.

32. Ibid., 15.

33. Aaker, "Measuring Brand Equity," 102–20.

34. Peter H. Farquhar, Julie Y. Han, and Yuji Iiri, "Brands on the Balance Sheet," *Marketing Management,* Winter 1992, 19.

35. Chip Walker, "How Strong Is Your Brand," *Marketing Tools,* January–February 1995, 46–53.

36. Kevin Lane Keller, "The Brand Report Card," *Harvard Business Review,* January–February 2000, 147–57.

37. Ibid., 148–49.

38. Noel Capon and James M. Hulbert, *Marketing Management in the 21st Century* (Upper Saddle River, NJ: Prentice-Hall, 2001).

39. John A. Quelch and David Harding, "Brands versus Private Labels: Fighting to Win," *Harvard Business Review,* January–February 1996, 99–100.

40. This discussion is based on David A. Aaker, *Building Strong Brands* (New York: Free Press, 1996).

41. Don E. Schultz, "Getting to the Heart of the Brand," *Marketing Management,* September–October 2000, 8–9.

42. Aaker, *Building Strong Brands,* 35.

43. Ibid., 340.

44. Dana James, "Rejuvenating Mature Brands Can Be a Stimulating Exercise," *Marketing News,* August 16, 1999, 16–17.

45. James Heckman, "Don't Let the Fat Lady Sing: Smart Strategies Revive Dead Brands," *Marketing News,* January 4, 1999, 1.

46. L. Downes and C. Mui, *Unleashing the Killer App: Digital Strategies for Market Dominance* (Boston: Harvard Business School Press, 1998).

47. Any Feldman, "Recharging Gillette," *Money,* September 2001, 41–43.

48. Aaker, *Building Strong Brands,* 278–91.

49. Aaker, *Managing Brand Equity,* 208.

50. Ronald Alsop, "Firms Unveil More Products Associated with Brand Names," *The Wall Street Journal,* December 13, 1984, 31.

51. Joseph F. Kovar, "EMC-Dell Blockbuster," *Crn,* October 29, 2001, 3.

52. Stephanie Thompson, "The Mouse in the Food Aisle," *Advertising Age,* September 10, 2001, 73.

53. Aaker, "Measuring Brand Equity," 208.

54. Robert Gray, "Brands Profit from Loaning Out Kudos," *Marketing,* October 4, 2000, 29.

55. Gerry Khermouch, "'Whoa, Cool Shirt.' 'Yeah, It's a Pepsi,'" *Business Week,* September 10, 2001, 84.

56. D. R. John, B. Loken, and C. Joiner, "The Negative Impact of Extensions: Can Flagship Products Be Diluted?" *Journal of Marketing* 62 (January 1998), 19–32.

57. Richard Tomkins, "Manufacturers Strike Back," *Financial Times,* June 16, 2000, 14.

58. Aaker and Joachimsthaler, *Brand Leadership,* 309.

59. Alison Smith, "Moving Out of the Shadows," *Financial Times,* June 5, 1998, 22.

60. A. J. Parsons, "Nestlé: The Visions of Local Managers," *The McKinsey Quarterly* 2 (1996), 5–29.

61. Sarah Ellison, "Knowing Often Isn't Believing, Net Brand-Building Study Says," *Wall Street Journal,* June 5, 2000, 32.

62. Jennifer Pellet, "When E-Brands Fail: Building New Brand Value with Old Brand Tricks," *Chief Executive,* May 2000, 54–66.

63. Larry Chiagouris and Brant Wansley, "Branding on the Internet," *Marketing Management,* Summer 2000, 34–38.

64. Aaker and Joachimsthaler, *Brand Leadership,* 242.

65. Aaker, *Building Strong Brands,* 241–42.

66. David Woodruff, "A-Class Damage Control at DaimlerBenz," *Business Week,* November 24, 1997, 62; Rufus Olins and Matthew Lynn, "A-Class Disaster," *Sunday Times,* November 16, 1997, 54.

67. Aaker, *Building Strong Brands,* 241.

68. Ibid., 264–66.

10

Managing Value-Chain Relationships

The value chain is a group of vertically aligned organizations that add value to a good or service in moving from basic supplies to finished products to consumer and organizational end-users. We use the term *value chain* in preference to other terms describing distribution activities from other perspectives (such as that of manufacturing or operations functions), in order to underline the central purpose of superior customer value. Terms such as *physical distribution management, logistics, distribution,* and *supply chain management* are all used to identify certain aspects of the value chain and its management as well as the new organizational units found in many companies. We use the term *value chain* to focus on the processes, activities, organizations, and structures that combine to create value for customers as products move from their point of origin to the end-user.

We consider the value chain from two perspectives. First, we examine the decisions faced by a company in developing a channel of distribution strategy. Channels of distribution are a central issue in managing the value chain. An effective and efficient distribution channel provides the member organizations with an important strategic edge over competing channels. Distribution strategy concerns how a firm reaches its market targets. While some producers market their products directly to the end-users of goods and services, many others make their products available through one or more channels of distribution. Various independent channel intermediaries (e.g., wholesalers, retailers) perform necessary value-added functions.

Second, we examine the broader perspective of strategic value-chain management to emphasize the need for decision makers to incorporate into their thinking the impact of supply chain strategy, Internet-based business models, and escalating distributor power. These initiatives may be relevant in maintaining the ability of the market-driven company to realign its value chain when necessary to meet the changing needs of its customers and markets.

Consider, for example, Hewlett-Packard's strategy for distributing information technology products to companies with fewer than 500 employees. Hewlett-Packard's (H-P) management recognized the market opportunity offered by these companies. The issue was how to make contact with small businesses since the costs of direct contact via H-P salespeople would exceed the margins available from sales to these customers. Distribution strategy analyses led to H-P's use of multiple channels: value-added resellers (VARs), mail order, and the Web.[1] H-P's strategy to serve small business end-users included developing products specifically for these firms and deploying a staff of 1,000 people to manage and serve this customer base. H-P partnered with 3,000 VARs, which provide value-added solutions to small and medium-size businesses. The objective of the multiple channels is to support the VARs rather than compete with them.

H-P's channel of distribution strategy included several key success features.[2] Management first studied H-P's customers, distribution channels, and competition. Channels that small firms prefer were identified. H-P partnered with its channels rather than competing with them. Customer value requirement solutions were the focus of the channel strategy. Communications (website, brochures, advertising, and newsletters) were designed for specific customers and channels.

While some manufacturers and service providers distribute direct to consumer or organizational end-users by using a company sales force, many producers use value-added partners to perform all or part of the distribution functions. As shown in the H-P illustration, a good distribution strategy requires a penetrating analysis of the available alternatives in order to select the most appropriate channel network. Significantly, H-P's strategy combines the Internet with more conventional channels. Channel of distribution decisions are important to organizations in a wide range of industries. A company's channel strategy may involve (1) developing and managing the channel or (2) gaining entry into a particular channel by a supplier, producer, wholesaler, or retailer.

We first look at the role of distribution channels in marketing strategy and discuss several channel strategy issues. Next, we examine the process of selecting the type of channel, determining the intensity of distribution, and choosing the channel configuration of organizations. A discussion of managing the distribution channel follows. We then look at distributing through international channels. Finally, we emphasize the need for a strategic value-chain management perspective.

Strategic Role of Distribution

A good distribution network creates a strong competitive advantage for an organization. For example, as we saw in Chapter 7, international airlines are adopting collaborative distribution strategies by forming strategic partnerships to gain market access, share reservation codes, coordinate marketing activities, and utilize partners' travel routes. The benefits include seamless routing between international locations, better equipment utilization, airport access, reduced capital expenditures, and expanded market coverage. Airline alliances highlight the importance of distribution strategy in business performance and also show that value-chain relationships are relevant to companies distributing services as well as goods. The airlines example also underlines the impact of the Internet on distribution channels. For example, for a growing number of airlines, an e-mailed reservation number has replaced the multipart ticket that the traveler had to collect from a travel agent or receive through the mail. Significantly, European no-frills airlines like easyJet and Ryanair are working to achieve 100 percent direct Internet booking and ticketing, replacing the traditional functions of the travel agent. Channels are a major element in how airlines compete.

We describe the distribution functions in the channel and then look at the distribution of services. Then we examine several factors affecting the choice of whether to use distribution intermediaries or go direct to end-users.

Distribution Functions

The *channel of distribution* is a network of value-chain organizations performing functions that connect goods and services with end-users. The distribution channel consists of *interdependent* and *interrelated* institutions and agencies, functioning as a system or network, that cooperate in their efforts to produce and distribute a product to end-users. Thus,

EXHIBIT 10–1
**Common
Channels of
Distribution**

Source: Gilbert A. Churchill,
Jr., and J. Paul Peter,
Marketing, 2nd ed. (New
York: Irwin/McGraw-Hill,
1998), 369, 371.

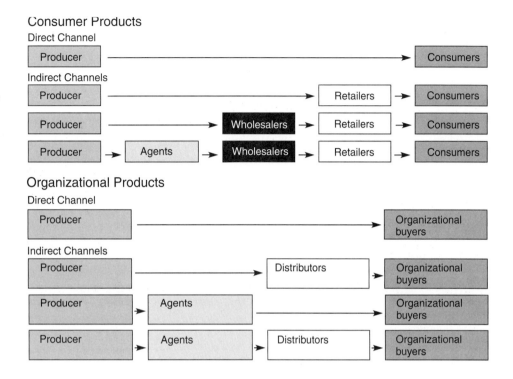

hospitals, ambulance services, physicians, test laboratories, insurance companies, and drugstores make up a channel of distribution for health care services.[3] Managed health care organizations are increasingly coordinating the activities of these channel members. Examples of channels of distribution for consumer and industrial products are shown in Exhibit 10–1. In addition to the intermediaries that are shown, many facilitating organizations perform services, such as financial institutions, transportation firms, advertising agencies, and insurance firms. The Internet has been responsible for many changes in the array of distributive organizations in many markets. The E-Business Feature describes, for example, the development and potential of the Internet café.

Several value-added activities are necessary in moving products from producers to end-users. *Buying and selling* activities by marketing intermediaries reduce the number of transactions for producers and end-users. *Assembly* of products into inventory helps meet buyers' time-of-purchase and variety preferences. *Transportation* eliminates the locational gap between buyers and sellers, thus accomplishing the physical distribution function. *Financing* facilitates the exchange function. *Processing and storage* of goods involves breaking large quantities into individual orders, maintaining inventory, and assembling orders for shipment. *Advertising and sales promotion* communicate product availability, location, and features. *Pricing* sets the basis of exchange between buyer and seller. *Reduction of risk* is accomplished through mechanisms such as insurance, return policies, and futures trading. *Personal selling* provides sales, information, and supporting services. *Communications* between buyers and sellers include personal selling contacts, written orders and confirmations, and other information flows. Finally, *servicing and repairs* are essential for many types of products. Increasingly, the Internet provides an enabling and information-sharing technology, changing the ways in which these value-adding functions are carried out.

Major factors in channel strategy are deciding which functions are needed and deciding which organizations will be responsible for each function. Middlemen offer important cost and time advantages in the distribution of a wide range of products. Steel service centers

Many countries around the world have seen the development of chains of Internet cafés that combine food and drink with access to Internet-linked computers. By the end of 2001 a visit to *www.cybercafe.com* provided details about more than 4,200 cafés in 148 countries (and this certainly undercounts the true total).

- Stelios Haji-Ioannou, the Greek founder of the European no-frills airline easyJet, has established easyEverything, the world's largest Internet café. Occupying a 10,000-square-foot area, it has a Nescafé concession, a team of Internet tutors in bright orange uniforms, and a Net nanny to prowl the workstations to ensure that no one has found any cyber-porn. Stelios sees this as the start of a $200 million empire of 24-hour Internet cafés, stimulated by his goal of 100 percent Internet booking for tickets on his airline. Advertising revenues and home-page links to online shops underline his goal of making his Internet cafés into centers for e-commerce—cyber-supermarkets for music, entertainment, or travel.

- The British supermarket leader Tesco is establishing Internet cafés in existing in-store restaurants. Several coffee shop chains, including Starbucks, run Internet cafés, as do booksellers like Waterstones in the United Kingdom. Realtors are also combining coffee shops with online access to house sales websites in Internet cafés. Richard Branson has incorporated Internet cafés into his V-Shops, alongside mobile phones and hi-tech gadgets.

- Estimates by Forrester Research suggest that "homeless surfers" make up around 30 percent of the Internet population (people who have no Internet access at home or at work or who are traveling away from home or work).

Sources: Rob Griffith, "Cyber Cafés Assured of Success," *Sunday Business,* July 23, 2000, 17; Wayne Asher, "E-Mails on the Menu," *Daily Mail,* March 10, 1999, 65.

---

illustrate functional specialization.[4] These centers buy steel coil or bar in bulk from steel producers. They cut and shape the steel at lower costs than the producers can, and the value-added resellers can react more quickly than steel mills can to customer needs. This responsiveness helps reduce the buyer's inventory.

In first selecting a channel of distribution for a new product, the pricing strategy and desired positioning of the product may influence the choice of the channel. For example, a decision to use a premium price and a symbolic positioning concept calls for retail stores that buyers will associate with this image. While the consumer can view and configure alternative models on the company's Web page, it is not possible to buy a new Rolex watch on the Internet. The market entry of Escada A.G. into the U.S. high-fashion women's apparel market was enhanced by selecting department stores and specialty retailers with prestigious images. The German company is vertically integrated from manufacturing to retailing, with automated factories located in Bavaria. Over 40 Escada stores were opened in the United States in the early 1990s. Interestingly, Escada's vertical integration runs counter to outsourcing manufacturing by brand name apparel designers like Nike and The Limited, underlining the competitive differentiation potential in channel choices.

Once the channel of distribution design is complete and responsibilities for performing the various marketing functions are assigned, these decisions establish guidelines for pricing, advertising, and personal selling strategies. For example, the manufacturers' prices must take into account the requirements and functions of middlemen as well as pricing practices in the channel. Likewise, promotional efforts must be matched to the various channel participants' requirements and capabilities. Consumer-products manufacturers often direct advertising to consumers to help *pull* products through distribution channels. Alternatively, promotion may be concentrated on middlemen to help *push* the product through the channel. Intermediaries may also need help in planning their marketing efforts and other supporting activities.

Channels for Services

Services such as air travel, banking, entertainment, health care, and insurance often involve distribution channels. The service provider renders the service to the end-users rather than the service being produced like a good and moved through marketing intermediaries to the end-user. Because of this, distribution networks for services differ somewhat from those used for goods. While channels for services may not require as many levels (e.g., producer, distributor, retailer), the network may actually be more complex.

A look at the distribution channels for commercial air travel services highlights several of the characteristics of channels for services. While the airline produces the services, it works with several distribution partners. Tickets may be obtained from independent travel agencies, from airline ticket offices, by telephone, direct from the airline's Internet site, or from an Internet travel agent and include special group arrangements. Airlines have cooperative arrangements with hotel chains, car rental companies, and tour groups. Airline sales forces call on large corporate customers, travel agencies, and other partners. Credit card companies offer charge services and may participate in the airlines' frequent flier programs. Strategic alliances with other airlines may extend a carrier's geographic coverage.

The objectives of channels for services are similar to those of channels for goods, although the functions performed differ somewhat from those for goods. Services are normally rendered when needed rather than placed into inventory. Similarly, services may not be transported, although the service provider may go to the user's location to render the service. Processing and storage are normally not involved with services. Servicing and repair functions may not apply to many services. The other functions previously discussed apply to both goods and services, such as buying and selling, financing, advertising and sales promotion, pricing, reduction of risk (e.g., lost baggage insurance), and communications.

Direct Distribution by Manufacturers

We consider channel of distribution strategy from a manufacturer's point of view, although many of the strategic issues apply to firms at any level in the distribution channel—wholesale or retail. Manufacturers are unique because they may have the option of going directly to end-users through a company sales force or serving end-users through marketing intermediaries. Manufacturers have three distribution alternatives: (1) direct distribution, (2) use of intermediaries, and (3) situations in which both (1) and (2) are feasible. The Internet direct channel makes alternative (1) open to many more companies. The factors that influence the distribution decision include buyer considerations, product characteristics, and financial and control considerations.

Buyer Considerations

Manufacturers look at the amount and frequency of purchases by buyers as well as the margins over manufacturing costs that are available to pay for direct selling costs. Customers' needs for product information and applications assistance may determine whether a company sales force or independent marketing intermediaries can best satisfy buyers' needs.

Dell Computer's direct sales, built-to-order business design has proved to be a major competitive edge, reinforced by the Internet. However, Dell's targets are business buyers and relatively sophisticated consumers, and this greatly influences the type and level of service required. The customer's "techno-readiness," or preparedness to deal over the Internet, is an important consideration in evaluating the direct Internet channel possibility.[5]

Product Characteristics

Companies often consider product characteristics in deciding whether to use a direct or a distribution-channel strategy. Complex products and services often require close contact between customers and the producer, who may have to provide application assistance, service, and other supporting activities. For example, chemical-processing equipment, mainframe computer systems, pollution-control equipment, and engineering-design services are often marketed directly to end-users via company sales forces. Another factor is the range of products offered by the manufacturer. A complete line may make distribution by the manufacturer economically feasible, whereas the cost of direct sales for a single product may be prohibitive. High-volume purchases may make direct distribution feasible for a single product. Companies whose product designs change because of rapidly changing technology often adopt direct sales approaches. Also, qualified marketing intermediaries may not be available because of the complexity of the product and the requirements of the customer. Direct contact with the end-user provides feedback to the manufacturer about new product needs, problem areas, and other concerns. Many supporting services may be Web-based. In the Dell example, while the products are complex, customer service is provided to major corporate buyers through Dell's Premier Pages websites, while e-service links the user computer to Dell support (for simple problems, the computers may resolve the issue without troubling the user).

Financial and Control Considerations

It is necessary to decide if resources are available for direct distribution and, if they are, whether selling direct to end-users is the best use of the resources. Both the costs and the benefits need to be evaluated. Direct distribution gives the manufacturer control over distribution, since independent organizations cannot be managed in the same manner as company employees. This may be an important factor for the manufacturer.

Exhibit 10–2 highlights several factors favoring distribution by the manufacturer. A firm's financial resources and capabilities are also important considerations. The producers

EXHIBIT 10–2
Factors Favoring Distribution by the Manufacturer

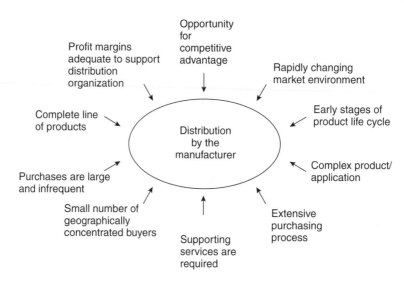

of business and industrial products are more likely than are producers of consumer products to utilize company distribution to end-users. This is achieved by a direct to the end-user network of company sales offices and a field sales force or by a vertically integrated distribution system (distribution centers and retail outlets) owned by the manufacturer. Companies with superior Internet capabilities may also favor the direct channel more than others.

A producer may decide to work through middlemen to avoid investing to provide direct contact and to utilize the competencies of experienced value-added organizations. For example, most steel producers utilize independent service centers.[6]

Channel of Distribution Strategy

We now consider the decisions that are necessary in developing a channel of distribution strategy. The steps in channel strategy selection are shown in Exhibit 10–3. They include (1) determining the type of channel arrangement, (2) deciding on the intensity of distribution, and (3) selecting the channel configuration.

Management may seek to achieve one or more objectives by using the channel of distribution strategy. While the primary objective is gaining access to end-user buyers, other related objectives may also be important, as shown in Exhibit 10–4. These objectives include providing promotional and personal selling support, offering customer service, obtaining market information, and gaining favorable revenue/cost performance.

Types of Distribution Channels

The major types of channels are conventional channels and vertical marketing systems. The conventional channel of distribution is a group of vertically linked independent organizations, each trying to look out for itself, with limited concern for the total performance of the channel. The relationships between the conventional channel participants are rather informal, and the members are not closely coordinated. The focus of the channel organizations is on buyer-seller transactions rather than close collaboration throughout the distribution channel.

EXHIBIT 10–3
Steps in Channel Strategy Selection

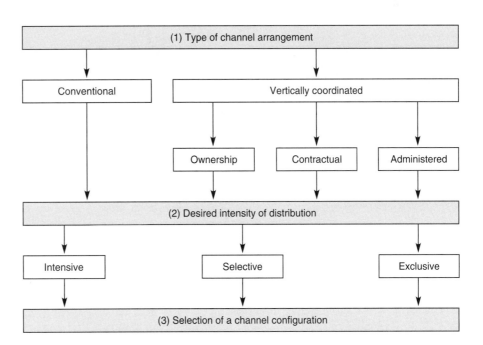

EXHIBIT 10–4
Distribution Channel Objectives and Measurement Criteria

Source: Harper W. Boyd, Jr., Orville C. Walker, Jr., and Jean-Claude Larréché, *Marketing Management*, 3rd ed. (Burr Ridge, IL: Richard D. Irwin, 1998), 317.

Performance Objective	Possible Measures	Applicable Product and Channel Level
Product Availability		
• Coverage of relevant retailers	• Percent of effective distribution	• Consumer products (particularly convenience goods) at retail level
• In-store positioning	• Percent of shelf-facings or display space gained by product, weighted by importance of store	• Consumer products at retail level
• Coverage of geographic markets	• Frequency of sales calls by customer type; average delivery time	• Industrial products; consumer goods at wholesale level
Promotional Effort		
• Effective point-of-purchase (POP) promotion	• Percent of stores using special displays and POP materials, weighted by importance of store	• Consumer products at retail level
• Effective personal selling support	• Percent of salespeople's time devoted to product; number of salespeople receiving training on product's characteristics and applications	• Industrial products; consumer durables at all channel levels; consumer convenience goods at wholesale level
Customer Service		
• Installation, training, repair	• Number of service technicians receiving technical training; monitoring of customer complaints	• Industrial products, particularly those involving high technology; consumer durables at retail level
Market Information		
• Monitoring sales trends, inventory levels, competitors' actions	• Quality and timeliness of information obtained	• All levels of distribution
Cost-Effectiveness		
• Cost of channel functions relative to sales volume	• Middlemen margins and marketing costs as percent of sales	• All levels of distribution

The second type of distribution channel is the vertical marketing system (VMS). Marketing executives in an increasing number of firms realize the advantages to be gained by managing the channel as a coordinated or programmed system of participating organizations. We consider later the influence of supply chain management approaches and the Internet on the operations of channels. These vertical marketing systems dominate the retailing sector and are significant factors in the business and industrial products and services sectors.

EXHIBIT 10–5
Illustrative Vertical Marketing Systems*

Product/Service		
	Consumer	**Industrial**
Ownership	The Bombay Company (furniture) The Gap (apparel)	Vallen Corporation (industrial safety equipment)
Contractual	Ethan Allen, Inc. (furniture) Wendy's International, Inc. (fast foods)	Snap-On Tools, Inc. (mechanics' tools) Deere & Company (farm equipment)
Administered	Procter & Gamble (health and beauty aids) Wal-Mart (discount goods)	Johnson & Johnson (health care products) Loctite Corp. (industrial adhesives)

*Several of the companies fall into more than one category.

A primary feature of a VMS is the management (or coordination) of the distribution channel by one organization. Programming and coordination of channel activities and functions are directed by the firm that is the channel manager. Operating rules and guidelines indicate the functions and responsibilities of each participant. Management assistance and services are supplied to the participating organizations by the firm that is the channel leader.

Three types of vertical marketing systems may be used: *ownership, contractual,* and *administered.* During recent years, a fourth form of VMS has developed in which the channel organizations form collaborative relationships rather than being controlled by one organization. We consider this as a *relationship* VMS.

Examples of companies using the three vertical marketing systems managed or coordinated by one channel member are shown in Exhibit 10–5. The firm managing the channel is not always the manufacturer. Through its buying power, The Limited (retailer) exerts considerable influence on its suppliers. A company may also use a combination arrangement (e.g., ownership and contractual).

Ownership VMS

Ownership of distribution channels from source of supply to end-user involves a substantial capital investment by the channel coordinator. This kind of VMS is also less adaptable to change than are the other VMS forms. For these reasons a more popular alternative may be to develop collaborative relationships with channel members (e.g., supplier/manufacture alliances). Such arrangements tend to reduce the coordinator's control over the channel but overcome the disadvantages of control through ownership. The relationship VMS is discussed below. Nonetheless, in highly competitive markets, the need for control of distribution may make channel ownership more attractive. Globally, many auto manufacturers are establishing their own retail outlets and buying out independent franchisees and distributors to regain channel control.

Contractual VMS

The contractual form of the VMS may include various formal arrangements between channel participants, including franchising and voluntary chains of independent retailers. Franchising is popular in fast foods, lodging, and many other retail lines. Traditional automobile dealerships are another example of a contractual VMS. Wholesaler-sponsored retail chains are used by food and drug wholesalers to establish networks of independent retailers. Contractual programs may be initiated by manufacturers, wholesalers, and retailers.

Administered VMS

The administered VMS exists because one of the channel members has the capacity to influence the channel members. This influence may be the result of financial strengths, brand image, specialized skills (e.g., marketing, product innovation), and assistance and support to channel members. The Strategy Feature describes how DeBeers managed the worldwide distribution of rough diamonds through its marketing cartel before shifting strategy in 2000.

Relationship VMS

This channel form shares certain characteristics with the administered VMS but differs in that a single firm does not exert substantial control over other channel members. Instead, the relationship involves close collaboration and sharing of information. The relationship VMS may be more logical in channels with only two or three levels. An example is the relationship between Radio Shack and Compaq (computers) and Sprint (telephone services).

The economic performance of vertical marketing systems is likely to be higher than that in conventional channels if the channel network is properly designed and managed. However, the participating firms in the channel must make certain concessions and be willing to work toward overall channel performance. There are rules to be followed, control is exercised in various ways, and generally there is less flexibility for the channel members. Also, some of the requirements of the total VMS may not be in the best interests of a particular participant. Nonetheless, competing in a conventional distribution channel against a VMS is a major competitive challenge, and so a channel member may find membership in a VMS beneficial.

Distribution Intensity

Step 2 in channel strategy is selecting distribution intensity (Exhibit 10–3). Industrie Natuzzi SpA's management made an important distribution intensity decision in 1982 when it rejected an R. H. Macy & Company proposal to serve as the leather furniture producer's exclusive retailer in the New York area.[7] Instead, the Italian manufacturer decided to distribute its products in a wide range of retail outlets, though only to one in each price and quality category. In 2000 it had 220 retail customers in New York, including Macy & Company. Natuzzi has 10,000 stores carrying its products and holds an estimated 20 percent of the U.S. market compared to 4 percent in Europe and 10 percent worldwide. Sales and profits have increased rapidly. Using a form of mass customization, Natuzzi offers 540,000 different leather furniture combinations at competitive prices. Standardized components (modules) can be combined to provide the design combinations. Production is provided by 20 efficient plants in Italy.

Distribution intensity is best examined in reference to how many retail stores (or industrial product dealers) carry a particular brand in a geographic area. If a company like Natuzzi decides to distribute its products in many of the retail outlets in a trading area that might normally carry such a product, it is using an *intensive* distribution approach. A trading area may be a portion of a city, the entire metropolitan area, or a larger geographic area. If one retailer or dealer in the trading area distributes the product, management is following an *exclusive* distribution strategy. Examples include Lexus automobiles and Caterpillar industrial equipment. Different degrees of distribution intensity can be implemented. *Selective* distribution falls between the two extremes. Rolex watches and Coach leather goods are distributed on a selective basis.

DeBeers Consolidated Mines Ltd. controls two-thirds of the world supply of rough diamonds (producing around 40 percent of the world supply from its own mines). For over a century DeBeers has maintained strong control over diamond distribution and prices. This position was threatened in the late 1990s by pressures created by the market dumping of Russian and Australian diamonds and the collapse of the Asian market. DeBeers' strategy has evolved.

- Its London-based Central Selling Organization (CSO) coordinates the sales of uncut diamonds. Some 125 dealers and cutters attend "sightings" every five weeks where each has the opportunity to purchase a box of assorted rough stones. DeBeers controls the quantity of the stones sold.

- DeBeers' role was to achieve market stability and steady price appreciation of polished diamonds.

- Huge investments in rough diamond inventory were necessary to keep supply and demand in balance so that prices would not experience large decreases or increases. DeBeers acted as the industry's "buyer of last resort" for all diamonds on the market, and by 1998 its diamond stockpile peaked at $5 billion.

- Despite market pressures, DeBeers continued to exert a powerful influence on the worldwide distribution of diamonds throughout the twentieth century.

- In 2000, DeBeers shifted strategy toward no longer acting as the buyer of last resort for excess supply and selling its diamond stockpile. To prevent prices from crashing, this was accompanied by aggressive advertising to the consumer to boost demand. The goal was to be the market leader and no longer a monopolist dictating market prices.

- DeBeers advertises to consumers to encourage diamond purchases for various occasions. In a largely unbranded market, DeBeers' positioning concept, "A Diamond is Forever," highlights eternal love and value retention. In fact, DeBeers has successfully piloted a system for etching its brand name microscopically on its diamonds, and its brand is associated with "conflict-free" diamonds (i.e., not the illegally mined stones that fund wars in Africa and other parts of the world).

- Recognizing that while the rough diamond market is worth $8 billion, the finished jewelry market is worth $60 billion, DeBeers is moving emphasis down the value chain. Although excluded from the U.S. market because of antitrust and price-fixing charges, DeBeers has entered a joint venture with LVMH, the French luxury goods company. The goal is to open U.S. outlets under DeBeers' brand name (notwithstanding the fact that DeBeers' directors cannot visit the country for fear of arrest).

- DeBeers' strategic realignment puts it in competition with its rough diamond customers but may resolve the antitrust problems in the United States.

Sources: "Cracks in the Diamond Trade," *Business Week,* March 2, 1998, 106; "The Diamond Business: Glass with Attitude," *The Economist,* December 20, 1997, 113–115; Matthew Curtin, "DeBeers Faces Challenge to Its Power," *The Wall Street Journal,* August 22, 1994, A58; Gillian O'Connor and Emma Muller, "DeBeers' New Deal Loses a Little Sparkle," *Financial Times,* January 17, 2001, 29; Gillian O'Connor and Richard Wolffe, "The King of Diamonds Attempts to Polish Its Rough Edges," *Financial Times,* June 2, 2000, 34; Francesco Guerrera and Andrew Parker, "DeBeers: All That Glitters Is Not Sold," *Financial Times,* July 11, 2000, 38.

Choosing the right distribution intensity depends on management's targeting and positioning strategies and product and market characteristics. The major issues in deciding distribution intensity are:

- Identifying which distribution intensities are feasible, taking into account the size and characteristics of the market target, the product, and the requirements likely to be imposed by prospective intermediaries (e.g., they may want exclusive sales territories).

- Selecting the alternatives that are compatible with the proposed market target and marketing program positioning strategy. For example, exclusive distribution was not consistent with Natuzzi's U.S. targeting strategy.

- Choosing the alternative that (1) offers the best strategic fit, (2) meets management's financial performance expectations, and (3) is attractive enough to intermediaries that they will be motivated to perform their assigned functions.

The characteristics of the product and the market target to be served often suggest a particular distribution intensity. For example, an expensive product such as a Toyota Lexus luxury automobile does not require intensive distribution to make contact with potential buyers. Moreover, several dealers in a trading area could not generate enough sales and profits due to the luxury car's limited sales potential. Similarly, Escada's management, in choosing to serve the middle to upper price-quality segment of the apparel market, essentially preempted consideration of an intensive distribution strategy. In contrast, Kodak film needs to be widely available in the marketplace.

The distribution intensity should correspond to the marketing strategy management selects. For example, Estée Lauder distributes cosmetics through selected department stores that carry quality products. Management decided not to meet Revlon head-on in the marketplace and instead concentrates its efforts on a small number of retail outlets. By doing this Estée Lauder avoids huge national advertising expenditures and uses promotional pricing to help attract its customers to retail outlets. Buyers are offered free items when they purchase other specified items.

Strategic requirements, management's preferences, and other constraints help determine the distribution intensity that offers the best strategic fit and performance potential. The requirements of intermediaries are considered, along with management's desire to coordinate and motivate them. For example, exclusive distribution is a powerful incentive to intermediaries and also simplifies management activities for the channel leader. But if the company that is granted exclusive distribution rights is unable (or unwilling) to fully serve the needs of target customers, the manufacturer will not take advantage of the sales and profit opportunities that could be obtained by using more intermediaries.

Channel Configuration

The third step in selecting the distribution strategy is deciding how many levels of organizations to include in the vertical channel and the specific kinds of intermediaries to be selected at each level (Exhibit 10–3). The type (conventional or VMS) of channel and the distribution intensity selected help in deciding how many channel levels to use and what types of intermediaries to select. Different channel levels are shown in Exhibit 10–1. As an example, an industrial products producer might choose between distributors and sales agents (independent organizations that receive commissions on sales) to contact industrial buyers. We discuss several factors that may influence the choice of one of the channel configurations shown in Exhibit 10–1.

End-User Considerations

It is important to know *where* the targeted end-users might expect to purchase the products of interest. The intermediaries that are selected should provide an avenue to the market segment(s) targeted by the producer. Analysis of buyer characteristics and preferences provides important information for selecting firms patronized by end-users. This in turn guides decisions concerning additional channel levels, such as the middlemen selling to the retailers that contact the market target customers.

Product Characteristics

The complexity of the product, special application requirements, and servicing needs are useful in guiding the choice of intermediaries. Looking at how competing products are distributed may suggest possible types of intermediaries. The breadth and depth of the products to be distributed are also important considerations since intermediaries may want full lines of products.

Manufacturer's Capabilities and Resources

Large producers with extensive capabilities and resources have a lot of flexibility in choosing intermediaries. These producers also have a great deal of bargaining power with the middlemen, and a producer may be able (and willing) to perform some of the distribution functions. Such options are more limited for small producers with capability and resource constraints.

Required Functions

The functions that need to be performed in moving products from producer to end-user include various channel activities, such as storage, servicing, and transportation. Studying these functions is useful in choosing the types of intermediaries that are appropriate for a particular product or service. For example, if the producer needs only the direct-selling function, independent manufacturers' agents may be the right middlemen to use. Alternatively, if inventory stocking and after-sales service are needed, a full-service wholesaler may be essential.

Availability and Skills of Intermediaries

Evaluation of the experience, capabilities, and motivation of the intermediaries which are under consideration for channel membership is also important. Firms within the same industry often vary in skills and experience. Also, qualified channel members may not be available. For example, some types of middlemen will not distribute competing products.

A channel with only one level between the producer and the end-user simplifies the coordination and management of the channel. The more complex the channel network is, the more challenging it is to complete various distribution functions. Nevertheless, using specialists at two (or more) levels (e.g., brokers, wholesalers, dealers) may offer substantial economies of scale through the specialization of functions. The channel configuration that is selected typically takes into account several important trade-offs. As an example, manufacturer's agents (independent sales representatives) may provide the producer with greater channel control compared to full-service wholesalers. However, the agents make it necessary for the manufacturer to perform several functions, such as inventory stocking, invoicing, and service.

Selecting the Channel Strategy

The major channel-strategy decisions we have examined are summarized in Exhibit 10–3. Management (1) chooses the types of channel to be used, (2) determines the desired intensity of distribution, and (3) selects the channel configuration. One of the first issues to be resolved is deciding whether to manage the channel, partner with other members, or be a participant. This choice often rests on the bargaining power a company can exert in negotiating with other organizations in the channel system and the value (and costs) of performing the channel management role. The options include deciding to manage or coordinate operations in the channel of distribution, becoming a member of a vertically coordinated channel, and becoming a member of a conventional channel system. The following factors need to be assessed in choosing channel strategy.

Market Access

As emphasized throughout the chapter, the market target decision needs to be closely coordinated with channel strategy, since the channel connects products and end-users. The market target decision is not finalized until the channel strategy is selected. Information about the customers in the market target can help eliminate unsuitable channel-strategy alternatives. Multiple market targets may require more than a single channel of distribution. One advantage of middlemen is that they have an established customer base. When this customer base matches the producer's choice of market target(s), market access is achieved very rapidly.

Value-Added Competencies

The channel selected should offer the most favorable combination of value-added competencies. Making this assessment requires looking at the competencies of each participant and the trade-offs concerning financial and flexibility and control considerations.

Financial Considerations

Two financial issues affect the channel strategy. First, are the resources available for launching the proposed strategy? For example, a small producer may not have the money to build a distribution network. Second, the revenue-cost impact of alternative channel strategies needs to be evaluated. These analyses include cash flow, income, return on investment, and operating capital requirements (see the Appendix to Chapter 2).

Flexibility and Control Considerations

Management should decide how much flexibility it wants in the channel network and how much control it would like to have over other channel participants. An example of flexibility is how easily channel members can be added (or eliminated). A conventional channel offers little opportunity for control by a member firm, yet there is a lot of flexibility in entering and exiting from the channel. The VMS offers more control than does the conventional channel. Legal and regulatory constraints also affect channel strategies in such areas as pricing, exclusive dealing, and allocation of market coverage.

Channel Strategy Illustration

Suppose a producer of industrial controls for fluid processing (e.g., valves, regulators) is considering two channel strategy alternatives: using independent manufacturer's representatives (agents) versus recruiting a company sales force to sell its products to industrial customers. The representatives receive a commission of 8 percent on their dollar sales volume. Salespeople will be paid an estimated $100,000 in annual salary and expenses. Salespeople must be recruited, trained, and supervised.

An illustrative channel strategy evaluation is shown in Exhibit 10–6. The company sales force alternative is more expensive (using a two-year time frame) than the use of independent sales agents. Assuming both options generate contributions to profit, the trade-off of

EXHIBIT 10–6
Illustrative Channel Strategy Evaluation

Evaluation Criteria	Manufacturer's Representatives	Company Sales Force
Market access	Rapid	One- to three-year development
Sales forecast (two years)	$10 million	$20 million
Forecast accuracy	High	Medium to low
Estimated costs	$1 million*	$2.4 million†
Selling expense (costs/sales)	10%	12%
Flexibility	Good	Fair
Control	Limited	Good

*Includes 8% commission plus management time for recruiting and training representatives.
†Includes $100,000 for 10 salespeople, plus management time.

higher expenses needs to be evaluated against flexibility and control considerations. One possibility that is often used by manufacturers seeking access to a new market is to initially utilize manufacturer's representatives, with a longer-term strategy of converting to a company sales force. This offers an opportunity to gain market knowledge while keeping selling expenses in line with actual sales.

Strategies at Different Channel Levels

We have looked at distribution largely from the producer's viewpoint. Wholesalers and retailers are also concerned with channel strategies, and some of them may exercise primary control over channel operations. For example, The Limited is a powerful force in its channels, as is Wal-Mart. Large food wholesalers and retailers are major factors in their channels of distribution. Moreover, decisions by wholesalers, distributors, brokers, and retailers about which manufacturers' products to carry often affect the performance of all channel participants.

Channel strategy can be examined from any level in the distribution network. The major distinction lies in the point of view (retailer, wholesaler, producer) used to develop the strategy. Intermediaries may have fewer alternatives to consider than producers do and thus less flexibility in channel strategy. Nevertheless, their approach to channel strategy is often active rather than passive.

Managing the Channel

After the channel design has been decided on, the actual channel participants are identified, evaluated, and recruited. Finding competent and motivated intermediaries is critical to successfully implementing the channel strategy. Channel management activities include choosing how to assist and support intermediaries, developing operating policies, providing incentives, selecting promotional programs, and evaluating channel results. These activities consume much of management's time, since once it is established, the channel design may be difficult to modify. Importantly, changes in channel design may have serious consequences for the members. Consider, for example, Goodyear Tire & Rubber Company's decision in 1992 to include Sears, Roebuck & Company in its distribution network. The decision was very unpopular with Goodyear's 2,500 independent dealers.[8] Hundreds of the dealers took on competing tire brands. Goodyear's motivation for the change was the rapid growth in tire sales in the previous five years by less expensive chain stores, department stores, and warehouse clubs compared to a 4 percent share decline by tire dealerships. Not surprisingly, the dealers were concerned that Goodyear would make further additions to its distribution network by adding Kmart and possibly the warehouse clubs.

To gain a better insight into channel management, we discuss channel leadership, management structure and systems, physical distribution management, channel relationships, conflict resolution, channel performance, and legal and ethical considerations.

Channel Leadership

Some form of interorganization management is needed to assure that the channel has satisfactory performance as a competitive entity.[9] One firm may gain power over the other channel organizations because of its specific characteristics (e.g., size), experience, and environmental factors and its ability to capitalize on such factors. Gaining this advantage is more feasible in a VMS than in a conventional channel.

Performing the leadership role may also lead to conflicts arising from differences in the objectives and priorities of channel members. The conflicts with retailers created by the channel strategy changes of Goodyear are illustrative. The organization with the most power may make decisions that are not considered favorable by other channel members.

Management Structure and Systems

Channel coordination and management are often the responsibility of the sales organization (Chapter 13). For example, a manufacturer's salespeople develop buyer-seller relationships with wholesalers and/or retailers. The management structure and systems may vary from informal arrangements to highly structured operating systems. Conventional channel management is more informal, whereas the management of a VMS is more structured and programmed. The VMS management systems may include operating policies and procedures, information system linkages, various supporting services to channel participants, and the setting of performance targets.

Physical Distribution Management

Physical distribution (logistics) management has received considerable attention from distribution, marketing, manufacturing, and transportation professionals. The objective is to improve the distribution of supplies, goods in process, and finished products. The decision to integrate physical distribution with other channel functions or to manage it separately is a question that must be resolved by a particular organization. There are instances when either approach may be appropriate. Physical distribution is a key channel function and thus an important part of channel strategy and management. Management needs to first select the appropriate channel strategy, considering the physical distribution function and other essential channel activities. Once a strategy is selected, physical distribution management alternatives can be examined for the channel network. Recent moves to extend physical distribution management in the form of supply chain strategy are considered in the assessment of strategic value-chain management later in the chapter.

Channel Relationships

Chapter 7 considered various forms of relationships between organizations, examining the degree of collaboration between companies, the extent of commitment of the participating organizations, and the power and dependence ties between the organizations. We now look at how these issues relate to channel relationships.

Degree of Collaboration

Channel relationships are often transactional in conventional channels but may become more collaborative in VMSs. The extent of collaboration is influenced by the complexity of the product, the potential benefits of collaboration, and the willingness of channel members to work together as partners. Just-in-time inventory programs, total quality management activities, and supply chain models encourage collaboration and information sharing between suppliers and producers.

Commitment and Trust among the Channel Members

The commitment and trust of channel organizations are likely to be higher in VMSs than in conventional channels. For example, a contractual arrangement (e.g., a franchise agreement) is a commitment to work together. Yet the strength of the commitment may vary depending on the contract terms. For example, contracts between manufacturers and their independent representatives or agents typically allow either party to terminate the relationship with a 30-day notification.

Highly collaborative relationships among channel members call for a considerable degree of commitment and trust between the partners. The cooperating organizations provide access to confidential product plans, market data, and other trade secrets. Trust normally develops as the partners learn to work with each other and find the relationship to be favorable to each partner's objectives.

Power and Dependence

In VMSs, power is concentrated with one organization and the other channel members are dependent on the channel manager. This concentration of power does not exist with the relationship VMS. Power in conventional channels is less concentrated than it is in VMSs, and channel members are less dependent on each other. Conventional channel relationships may nevertheless result in some channel members possessing more bargaining power than others.

Hallmark Cards is the market leader in the greeting card industry. Changing patterns of distribution present Hallmark with a difficult power and dependence situation. For decades Hallmark relied on independent specialty shops to sell its cards. Yet mass merchandisers like Target stores now account for a rapidly growing share of the market. If Hallmark expanded into this distribution channel, its shop owners would be very unhappy. Nonetheless, Hallmark had to make this change or continue to lose market share. By the late 1990s many mass merchandise retailers carried Hallmark cards. The company also partnered with Microsoft to offer personalized cards via personal computer.

Conflict Resolution

Conflicts are certain to occur between the channel members because of differences in objectives, priorities, and corporate cultures. Examination of a proposed channel relationship by each participating organization may identify areas (e.g., incompatible objectives) that are likely to lead to major conflicts. In such situations, management may decide to seek another channel partner. Effective communications before and after establishing the channel relationships can also help eliminate or reduce conflicts.

Several methods are used to resolve actual and potential conflicts.[10] One useful approach is to involve channel members in the decisions that will affect their organizations. Another helpful method of resolving or reducing conflict is developing effective communications channels between channel members. Pursuing objectives that are important to all channel members also helps reduce conflict. Finally, it may be necessary to establish methods for mediation and arbitration.

Conflicts between channel members may require resolution in court if the stakes merit such extreme action. In 2001 Levi Strauss won a decision in the European Court of Justice against the powerful British retailer Tesco. In Europe Levi jeans are a premier brand sold at a premium price (the British recommended price for Levi 501s is around $75, more than twice the U.S. price). Levi refused to supply its jeans to the discounter supermarket Tesco. Tesco used its global sourcing to buy 501s outside Europe, imported them, and sold them in British supermarkets for around $40. Levi's view was that the supermarket distribution channel was undermining its brand and that it had the right to determine where its products were sold. While the European Court supported Levi Strauss, there is some question whether Tesco will adhere to the European ruling in its British stores. Levi's actions in upholding its rights to control the distribution channels for its brand have attracted considerable adverse consumer and media comment.[11]

Channel Performance

The performance of the channel is important from two points of view. First, each member is interested in how well the channel is meeting the members' objectives. Second, the organization that is managing or coordinating the channel is concerned with its performance and the overall performance of the channel. Tracking performance for the individual channel members includes financial and market measures such as profit contribution, revenues, costs, market share, customer satisfaction, and rate of growth. Several criteria for evaluating the overall performance of the channel are shown in Exhibit 10–4.

Companies gain a strategic advantage by improving distribution productivity. Reducing distribution costs and the time to move products to end-users is a high-priority action area in many companies. The opportunity to lower costs may be substantial. These costs may account for as much as one-third or more of total product costs. Consider these examples:[12]

- Helene Curtis reduced distribution costs 40 percent by replacing six older warehouses with a new distribution center that uses computer-controlled forklifts and automated order processing and shipment.

- Mervyn's has reduced the average time merchandise is in the pipeline from vendor to retail store from 14 days to fewer than 9.

- Sun MicroSystems' distribution is handled by Federal Express Business Logistics Services Unit, which moves Sun's machines from the factory floor to customers.

Further examples are considered when we examine supply chain management.

Monitoring the changes that are taking place in distribution and incorporating distribution strategy considerations into the strategic planning process are essential strategic marketing activities. Market turbulence, global competition, and information technology create a rapidly changing distribution environment.

Legal and Ethical Considerations

Various legal and ethical considerations may affect channel relationships. Legal concerns of the federal government include arrangements between channel members that substantially lessen competition, restrictive contracts concerning products and/or geographic coverage, promotional allowances and incentives, and pricing practices.[13] State and local laws and regulations may also have an impact on channel members. Recall the pressures on DeBeers discussed in the Strategy Feature.

The importance of ethics is shown by a research survey of Fortune 1000 companies indicating that 98 percent of the responding companies have formal ethics policy statements or documents and that more than one-half have an executive specifically assigned to deal with ethics and conduct issues.[14] Ethical issues are heavily influenced by corporate policies and practices. Corporate pressures on performance may create ethical situations. Deciding whether a practice is ethical is sometimes complex. Complexity increases in international channels that cross different cultures. Channel decisions that affect other channel members may create ethical situations. Many companies have established internal standards on how business should be conducted. Written statements of working relationships among channel members may also include such statements. For example, the Target Corporation publishes a statement of Standards of Vendor Engagement, specifying the ethical and environmental standards to be maintained by its suppliers, backed by a compliance inspection program.

International Channels

The distribution channels that are available in international markets are not totally different from the channels in a particular country such as the United States. Uniqueness is less a function of structural alternatives and more related to the vast range of operational and market variables that influence channel strategy.[15] Several channel of distribution alternatives are shown in Exhibit 10–7. The arrows show many possible channel networks linking producers, middlemen, and end-users.

Examining International Distribution Patterns

While the basic channel structure (e.g., agents, wholesalers, retailer) is similar across countries, there are many important differences in distribution patterns among countries. "Only when the varied intricacies of actual distribution patterns are understood can the complexity of the distribution task be appreciated."[16] Generalization about distribution practices throughout the world is obviously not possible.

Studying the distribution patterns in the nation(s) of interest is important in obtaining guidelines for distribution strategy. Various global trends such as satellite communications, the Internet, regional cooperative arrangements (e.g., European Union), and transportation networks (e.g., intermodal services) affect distribution systems in various ways, reflecting globalization. Global market turbulence and corporate restructuring create additional influences on distribution strategies and practices.

EXHIBIT 10–7
International Channel of Distribution Alternatives

Source: Phillip R. Cateora, *International Marketing,* 9th ed. (Homewood, IL: Richard D. Irwin, 1996), 455.

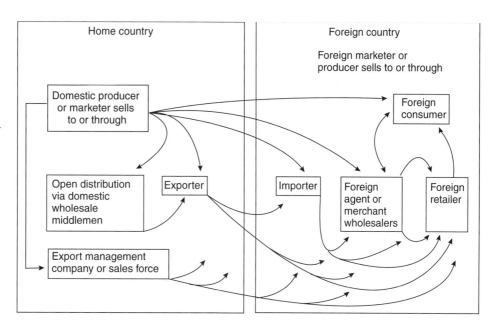

The Dutch multinational's subsidiary, Unilever Tanzania, was established in 1998 to make inroads with a basic range of goods, but in an economy where distribution had been dominated by traditional wholesalers.

Traditional distribution channels were unpromising. Local wholesaling produced patchy product availability, brands lost their franchise, and pricing was difficult to manage.

Unilever chose to go direct to retail outlets, facing the immense challenge that Tanzania has 100,000 retail outlets spread across the country in 9,000 villages. With half the population living below the poverty line, many consumers buy rice, maize, and flour in tiny quantities every day from minikiosks in lanes too narrow for vehicles.

- In the Tanzanian towns, Unilever delivers its goods by vans to larger shops.

- But to reach outlets in inaccessible rural areas, they have formed a "bicycle brigade."

- Wearing Unilever's "battle dress" of an "Omo" shirt (Omo is the leading detergent brand) and a yellow "Key" baseball cap (Key is a local soap brand), acting almost as mobile advertisements, salespeople on bicycles take Unilever products to the country's villages.

- Each salesperson has a company bicycle with large boxes welded on the back to transport small packages of detergent powder, margarine, soap, and oil and visits 20 to 30 shops a day on a fixed itinerary. When the goods are delivered, the bicycle stocks are replenished at a central distribution point.

- A typical transaction sees salesman Sospeter Jackson cycling to a tiny outlet at the side of a dusty road near Kiwalani to sell two bars of Key soap (conveniently marked on both sides so the shopkeeper can cut and sell chunks of soap for a few cents) and a dozen 50-gram sachets of Omo detergent.

- In the first five months of operations, the bicycle brigade grew Unilever's sales fivefold—making tiny packs of Omo detergent and Blue Band margarine into market leaders.

Source: Mark Turner, "Bicycle Brigade's Mission," *Financial Times,* August 16, 2000, 14.

The globalization of distribution channels is underlined by the launch of Internet-based online exchanges. For example, in 2000 a group of large retailers announced an Internet-based alliance to create the Worldwide Retail Exchange. Participants included Target, Albertsons, CVS, K-Mart, and Safeway Inc. in the United States; Tesco, Marks & Spencers, Woolworth, and Kingfisher in the United Kingdom; Auchan and Casino in France; and Royal Holland in the Netherlands. The 12 companies had some 30,000 outlets and sales approaching $300 billion. By the end of 2001 the Exchange had 59 retailer members internationally, with combined revenues of $845 billion. In full operation, the Exchange will link them with more than 100,000 suppliers of food, general merchandise, and health care products. The goal is to have suppliers around the world compete with each other through a single website with complete price transparency. Though in their infancy, such schemes are likely to be a prototype for the globalization of channels of distribution.[17]

However, even in the Internet era designing channels to reach overseas customers, particularly in the developing countries, may require some adaptability. The Global Feature describes how Unilever has adapted its distribution strategy in Tanzania.

Factors Affecting Channel Selection

The channel strategy analysis and selection process presented in the chapter can be used to develop or evaluate international channel strategy, recognizing that many situational factors affect channel decisions in specific countries. Several of the factors influencing channel decisions are also similar between nations. The factors affecting the choice of international channels include cost, capital requirements, control, coverage, strategic product-market fit, and the likelihood that the middlemen will remain in business over a reasonable time horizon.[18] The political and economic stability of the country is, of course, very important. Stability needs to be evaluated early in the decision to enter a country.

Strategic Alliances

A strategic alliance between an organization that wants to enter an international market and a firm already serving the market may offer the advantage of existing distribution channels for the foreign firm and a new product for the domestic firm. For example, several American companies are seeking cooperative arrangements with firms serving the European marketplace. Such an agreement between General Mills, Inc., and Nestlé S.A. provided entry into Nestlé's vast sales and distribution network and its factories in Europe.[19] General Mills contributes the cereals to stock the shelves of food stores. Many of the cereal eaters around the world are located in English-speaking countries. The development of cereal preference in other countries could provide a huge growth market. Europe had the potential by the year 2000 of being equal in size to the current U.S. cereal market. By 2001, this alliance had grown into a joint venture between the companies—Cereal Partners Worldwide, the world's number two cereals company—operating in more than 80 countries. General Mills has repeated the alliance and joint venture strategy with PepsiCo in Europe, leading to Snack Ventures Europe, the leading snack company in continental Europe.

A comparison of different ways to gain distribution in Europe is shown in Exhibit 10–8. Each offers certain advantages and disadvantages. As the exporter makes a greater commitment in terms of resources to market entry, the risks are higher if the venture does not prove to be successful. Of course, greater commitment will enable the exporter to have more influence on performance.

Strategic Value-Chain Management

In addition to the design and management of channel systems, a strategic perspective for value-chain management requires consideration of several emerging ways of doing business that have major impacts on channel strategy. We consider supply chain management, electronic-business models and the Internet, the market power of branded retailers and distributors, and pressures for flexibility and change in channel strategy.

Supply Chain Management[20]

Many organizations have adopted supply chain management structures which have developed out of physical distribution and operations management. However, the impact of supply chain strategies has extended beyond transportation, storage, and stockholding issues to influence relationships between channel members and customer value. Consider for example, the Efficient Consumer Response (ECR) program described in the Technology Feature. The results of ECR approaches have been impressive cost savings:

> In a detergent project in Sweden involving Lever Brothers, 20 percent of the category's stock-keeping units (SKUs) was delisted as surplus to consumer requirements, but the result of better focus was a 9 percent sales increase.

EXHIBIT 10–8
Advantages and Disadvantages of Routes into Europe

Source: Richard Lynch, *European Marketing* (Burr Ridge, IL: Irwin Professional Publishing, 1994), 155.

Advantages	Disadvantages
Exporting	
Cheaper	Slow
Lower risk; less commitment	May miss opportunities through lack of knowledge
Good route for unique product	Allows home competitors to assess and build response
Allows slow buildup and learning about market conditions	Building scale economies may be high-risk and expensive
More control	
Keeps economies of scale at home base	
No need to share technology	
Strategic Alliance	
More permanent than mere exporting	Slow and plodding approach
Close contact	Needs constant work to keep relationship sound
Uses joint expertise and commitment perhaps not available to exporter	Partners have only a limited joint commitment to success
Allows potential partners to learn about each other	Unlikely to build economies of scale
Locks out other competitors	
Joint Venture	
Build scale quickly	Control lost to some extent
Obtain local knowledge and distribution	Works best where both parties contribute something to the mix
Cheaper than takeover	Difficult to manage
Local entry where takeover not possible	Share profits with partner
Can be used where outright takeover not feasible	
Can be used where similar product available	
Takeover	
Can be relatively fast	Premium paid: expensive
Useful for national expertise acquired	High risk if wrong
Buys presence	Best targets may have already gone in some markets
Buys size and market share	Not always easy to dispose of unwanted parts of company

In the dental care market, a Colgate Palmolive project involved a 25 percent reduction in SKUs, but retailer market share increased 11 percent and profit margins increased 9 percent.[21]

As a result of ECR, retailer and supplier companies are collaborating in such areas as forecasting, category management, and electronic commerce.[22]

Collaboration and information sharing have become central to supply chain design. Integrating processes across organizational boundaries is essential to building a seamless supply chain where "all players think and act as one."[23] The competitive impact of supply chain strength is emphasized: "It is supply chains that compete, not companies."[24]

The development of Internet software for use in supply chain management offers significant opportunities for improving the performance of supply chains. The supply chain can be seamlessly interlinked with suppliers, other supply chain organizations, and customers. SAP is one of several software firms offering the technology (see the accompanying SAP advertisement).

Technology Feature

Efficient Consumer Response (ECR) is based on "cooperative partnerships" between retailers and manufacturers to reduce costs in the supply chain and enhance value for consumers. ECR started in the United States in the early 1990s, when the leading participants were Krogers and Procter & Gamble, and by 1995, 90 percent of firms in the U.S. grocery business were applying ECR. The goal was to reduce costs by 10 percent, or around $30 billion a year. ECR was designed to address traditional channel problems:

- *Forward buying and diverting.* Retailers were buying products at low prices and not passing price cuts on to consumers or buying in regions where prices were lower and shipping goods elsewhere to show an internal profit.

- *Excessive inventories.* Retailers on average were holding more than three months of supplies.

- *Damaged and unsalable goods.* Such goods were at unacceptably high levels.

- *Complex deals and deductions.* Negotiated deals were so complicated, as many as 80 percent of invoices were processed manually.

- *Promotions and coupons.* In 1996 estimates suggested that 261 billion coupons were issued in the United States, with less than 2 percent redeemed.

- *New products.* In 1996, 22,400 new products were launched in the U.S. grocery business, dominated by imitative "me-too" brands, with expectations that 90 percent would survive less than two years, while the bottom 25 percent of brands stocked in supermarkets gave retailers less than 1 percent of their sales.

The ECR response to these problems focused on increased efficiency in retail assortments, sales promotions, product replenishment systems, and product launches. The central issue is improved management of flows of products, information, and cash. The key elements of ECR are:

- *Category management*—collaborative planning by retailers and manufacturers around groups of products in the store as perceived by customers (e.g., "ready meal solutions"), not brands as perceived by producers, which has removed around 20 percent of products from supermarket shelves.

- *Promotions*—drastic reductions in coupons and special offers in favor of "value pricing."

- *Continuous replenishment and cross-docking*—managing a continuous flow of products from manufacturers for direct store delivery, with no stock held at retail or wholesale levels, resulting in 20 percent less stock held in the channel.

- *Electronic data interchange*—automation of ordering and payment systems in a paperless information flow through the channel (e.g., point-of-sales scanning data trigger new orders automatically).

- *Performance measures*—new ways of evaluating performance.

- *Organizational change*—reorganizing around ECR processes.

- The next stage of ECR in the United States involves a standardized, Internet-based network for supplier-buyer trading. The UCCnet network will allow trading partners to share product data by using an open extranet format.

The success of ECR in reducing supply chain costs in the U.S. grocery business has led to the program's spread to Canada, Europe, Australia, and other parts of the world.

Sources: Ginger Koloszyc, "Grocery Industry Develops Standardized, Internet-Based Trading Network," *Stores,* June 1999, 26–28; Nigel F. Piercy, *Market-Led Strategic Change: A Guide to Transforming the Process of Going to Market* (Oxford: Butterworth-Heinemann, 2002).

Courtesy of SAP.

EXHIBIT 10–9
The Elements of the Lean Supply Chain

Source: James P. Womack and Daniel T. Jones, *Lean Thinking: Banish Waste and Create Wealth in Your Corporation* (New York: Simon & Schuster, 1996).

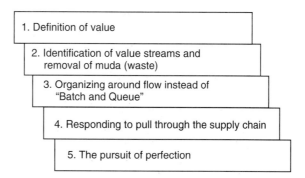

1. Definition of value
2. Identification of value streams and removal of muda (waste)
3. Organizing around flow instead of "Batch and Queue"
4. Responding to pull through the supply chain
5. The pursuit of perfection

Lean Supply Chains[25]

A major initiative in supply chain management has developed from Japanese management approaches and the example of Toyota in the automotive field in particular. This development focuses on the application of lean thinking to supply chains.[26] The elements of the lean supply chain are shown in Exhibit 10–9.

The foundation of the lean supply chain is defining value from the perspective of the end-customer to identify the value stream of activities in the supply chain that are needed to place the correctly specified product with the customer. All non-value-creating activities are "muda," or waste, and should be eliminated. Attention is given to the continuous flow of products in the supply chain instead of traditional "batch and queue" approaches to eliminate time wasting, storage, and scrap. Products are not produced upstream in the supply chain until ordered by the downstream customer, that is, pulled through the supply chain, removing the need for large inventories and customer waiting time. An example is Toyota's Daily Ordering System for auto parts in Japan. The lean philosophy also advances the need for a constant search for improvement and perfection. The goal is to remove demand instability through collaboration between suppliers and distributors and ultimately to allow customers to order direct from the production system.[27]

Examples of lean supply chains are provided by Dell Computers and the industrywide ECR program in the U.S. grocery sector (Technology Feature).

While the arguments for a lean supply chain are compelling, some critics suggest that the lean approach creates supply chains which are vulnerable to unexpected market change and do not have the capacity to be responsive to customers.

Agile Supply Chains

In response to the impact of turbulent volatile markets which are difficult to predict, emphasis has been placed on creating supply chains which are not lengthy and slow-moving "pipelines" but instead are agile and responsive to market change.[28] Supply chain agility means using market knowledge and a virtual corporation to respond to marketplace volatility, as opposed to the lean approach, which seeks to remove waste and manage volatility out of the supply chain by leveling demand.[29] The agile supply chain reserves capacity to cope with unpredictable demand.[30] While lean supply chains require a long-term partnership with suppliers, the agile model mandates fluid and market-based relationships to enhance responsiveness to the market and the capacity for rapid change.[31] Agile supply chain models emphasize customer satisfaction rather than meeting a more limited set of value criteria based on reduced costs.

Internet-Based Supply Chains

It is important to note that in several approaches to designing modern supply chains, the Internet and customized intranets and extranets are essential enabling technologies that support interfirm collaboration, the integration of ordering and fulfillment processes, and the sharing of information. The role of the Internet in reshaping channels is expanded on below.

Limitations and Risks in Supply Chain Strategies

In spite of the advances made in recent years, there remain substantial barriers to effective supply chain collaborations. Research suggests that those barriers include complexity in technology integration and the costs of integration, lack of trading partners with technology sophistication, lack of clear benefits, cultural resistance to new trading partner paradigms, few Web-based applications available, and lack of shared technical standards.[32] Importantly, consideration should also be given to recovery from the collapse of supply chain collaborations and the impact on a company's competitive position.

The Impact of Supply Chain Management on Marketing

Already in many sectors, corporate purchasers are reducing their supplier numbers to improve their companies' supply chain efficiency, providing another competitive pressure on suppliers. However, in addition to this marketplace pressure, supply chain strategies have an impact on several critical issues for marketing strategy and the value chain: product availability in the market, speed to market with innovations, the range of product choices offered to customers, product deletion decisions, prices, and competitive positioning.

In the market-driven company, a strategic value-chain perspective requires collaboration and integration between marketing and supply chain management. Chapter 14 considers this critical interface between managers from different functions. Important issues to consider are:

1. Supply chain decisions are made with an understanding of the real drivers of customer value in different market segments and the forces for value migration, not simply on the basis of measurable quality and technical product specification.

2. Supply chain decisions do not create inflexibility and inability to respond to marketplace change.

3. Supply chain decisions should be made in the light of strategic marketing questions such as brand identification, product choice for customers, product promotion, and building sustainable competitive advantage, not only short-term cost savings.

4. Supply chain strategy may not be a source of competitive advantage if all the players in the market have similar technology and designs.

5. Supply chain collaborations may be vulnerable to failure, and recovery strategies may be required.

Electronic-Business Models

It is clear that the Internet has provided access to a direct marketing channel for domestic and international markets for a large number of companies and is also an information source for customers to make price and product comparisons on a global basis. For example, the U.S. online consumer market was estimated to be worth $10 billion, or 3 percent of total retail sales, at Christmas 2000.[33] The share of markets like music, videos, books, and software was much higher than this average. The business-to-business impact of Internet trading is expected to be much larger. Estimates suggest a market worth $1,500 billion in the United States by 2005 and online transactions accounting for 44 percent of all business-to-business revenues worldwide by 2004.[34]

Many suppliers are using the Internet channel to bypass traditional distributors. For example, Lego and Mattell offer their entire product ranges online, automobile manufacturers sell direct to consumers over the Web, and business customers can buy electric motors from ABB.[35]

The direct Internet channel may also display new capabilities for creating customer value that are not otherwise available. For example, the build-to-order automobile built in three days after the customer's order is placed, potentially saving suppliers more than $3,000 a vehicle, is a major project for car manufacturers.[36] In December 1999 Daimler-Chrysler's Smart car (a two-seat town car) became the first car that could be configured and purchased online.[37]

However, beyond providing another channel of distribution, the Internet has the potential to change the competitive structure of an industry by allowing more efficient and effective networking between customers, suppliers, intermediaries, employees, and partners. Recall the impact of the Internet in Dell Computer's "virtual integration" with suppliers and customers.

Recall that industrywide forms include online exchanges on the Internet. General Motors, DaimlerChrysler, and Ford established the online exchange Covisint, linking tens of thousands of suppliers in their $200 billion a year components business. Renault and Nissan have also joined. In retail, Sears Roebuck in the United States, and Sainsbury in the United Kingdom, along with Germany's Metro and France's Carrefour, have established GlobalNet Exchange. Some major organizations, like Wal-Mart and Sun Microsystems, are instead developing "private exchanges" on the Internet, linking them with their suppliers but not with their competitors.[38]

Despite problems of technology integration as well as antitrust questions, it is estimated that Internet-based procurement systems may cut costs 30 percent.[39] It is telling that in 1999 major purchasers like Boeing and Motorola were warning that suppliers unable or unwilling to make the transition to Web-based commerce would be locked out of their businesses.[40]

A further impact of the Internet on channel organization relates to the form of intermediaries. Direct channels and e-business models threaten the existence of some intermediaries. For example, the survival of many travel agents is threatened by online flight and vacation sales. Nonetheless, perhaps more remarkable is the emergence of new types of intermediaries operating new types of business models. Recall that Amazon.com has evolved into a new type of Internet trader and market maker through collaborations way beyond any concept of selling books. Reverse auctions also have created a new type of intermediary.

Retailer and Distributor Power

In many sectors suppliers face unprecedented pressure from powerful channel members. New merchandising strategies with this effect include house branding and category killers.[41] House branding includes retailers that have established the retail outlet as the brand, such as Gap, Banana Republic, and Victoria's Secret. They rely on contract manufacturers to produce their brands. Category killers are companies, such as Toys'R'Us, Home Depot, Staples, and Linens'n Things, that attempt to dominate one segment of the market, often with very low prices. Suppliers may have substantially less control over channels than they did in the past. Responses may include suppliers reclaiming important value-added services from distributors to build stronger relationships with end-users, eliminating layers in the conventional channel, or creating new channels.

Significantly, major retail chains have expanded internationally. In the period 1995–1999 retailer global acquisitions amounted to more than $65 billion, as opposed to $26 billion in the period 1990–1994.[42] With the ability to source and merchandise globally, efficient supply chains, and powerful information technology, major retailers have more bargaining power than do most of their suppliers.

Importantly, collaborative supply chain relationships rest on information sharing, which may ultimately create strategic vulnerability. Supply chains may create new competitors. For example, a farming products distributor for Monsanto planned to undertake packaging fertilizer instead of buying it packaged from Monsanto and requested bulk supplies from Monsanto. When Monsanto refused, the distributor bought bulk supplies from another manufacturer. The distributor was able to leverage its strong relationships with farmers to deny Monsanto access to the end-user.[43]

Flexibility and Change

One important marketing task is the regular review and evaluation of the adequacy of existing distribution systems. Changes in distribution may improve both customer satisfaction and organizational effectiveness. Companies with direct sales forces may consider using indirect channels (wholesalers, distributors, dealers, and retailers) to serve part of the customer base. The Hewlett-Packard distribution strategy discussed earlier in the chapter is illustrative. Manufacturers are also using other customer contact methods, such as telephone sales, Internet ordering, and catalog sales.

An important trend in distribution is the use of multiple channels to gain greater access to end-user customers. For example, Dayton-Hudson (renamed Target Corporation in 2000) markets through its traditional department stores (Marshall Field's), through its discount retailers (Target and Mervyn's), and through several specialty stores, as well as through Target Direct, operating several websites. The unifying component of Dayton-Hudson's strategy is merchandising and the merchant orientation of top management.[44] In the mid-1960s, Dayton-Hudson recognized the mass-merchandising trend and moved into discount retailing through Target and more recently Mervyn's to promote the latest fashion and the best deal. Thirty years later Target stores represented 75 percent of the company's revenue, and the company name was changed to reflect this.

The explosive growth of direct marketing in the 1990s represents an important trend in distribution. Customer contact is made by mail or phone. These channels include catalog retailers such as Lands' End and L. L. Bean, phone and media retailers, and electronic shopping. Direct marketing companies take business away from conventional retailers. Convenience buying is stimulated by today's lifestyles (two-income families, limited leisure time, high incomes), the ease of shopping via catalogs, toll-free phone numbers, and effective marketing by the firms involved. Using an existing customer list facilitates entry into direct marketing. American Express has been very successful in using its credit card membership list. Database marketing provides access to buyers for direct marketing programs. An existing customer base must be willing to purchase by mail. Direct marketing is discussed further in Chapter 13.

Importantly, a strategic value-chain perspective mandates that channel systems and surrounding issues be realigned and restructured as an important source of competitive differentiation. For example, L'eggs hosiery built a strong and differentiated competitive position by developing the capability to market its products through supermarkets.

While the supply chain manager's focus is on cost efficiency, the strategic value-chain issue is positioning in the market to build and sustain competitive advantage. Issues of cost efficiency in supply should not be allowed to obscure the importance of marketing strategy. In addition, value-chain strategy and channel decisions should be regarded as variable, not fixed. Recall that notwithstanding 115 years of selling its cosmetics in the home, Avon is taking its products into department stores and kiosks in malls because its target consumers are increasingly working away from the home during the day.[45] Consider also the dramatic shift in DeBeers' value-chain positioning described in the Strategy Feature.

As market situations change, market-driven companies will respond with value-chain strategy adjustments. The speed and magnitude of change in many markets mandate that the value-chain and channel structures be reviewed regularly as a source of competitive advantage in building superior value for customers.

For example, the Italian apparel company Benetton built an extremely successful international fashion business through outsourced production and distribution, utilizing a form of franchising with agents responsible for particular markets. For many years Benetton's approach of direct retailing operated by third parties was one of the company's most distinctive and successful strategies. However, by 1999 Benetton was concerned that its retail locations were being suffocated by the aggressive competition of its international competitors, typically with significantly larger stores. Benetton's strategy to reshape its channels involves enlarging existing outlets to carry its whole product range; where this is not possible, focusing smaller stores on a single market segment or product (e.g., only women's products or only knitwear); and opening large outlets on the main shopping streets of major cities. The aim is to develop a network of larger shops directly owned and managed by Benetton itself. The company plans to have 100 megastores open by the end of 2002.[46]

Summary

The value chain consists of the organizations, systems, and processes that add to customer value in moving products to end-users. A strategic value-chain perspective aims to align a company's value chain with changing customer and competitive requirements. The core of the value chain is the channel of distribution. A strong channel network is an important way to gain competitive advantage. Distribution channels provide access to market targets. The choice between company distribution to end-users and the use of intermediaries is guided by end-user needs and characteristics, product characteristics, and financial and control considerations.

Manufacturers select the type of channel to be used, determine distribution intensity, design the channel configuration, and manage various aspects of channel operations. These channels are either conventional or vertical marketing systems (VMSs). The VMS, the dominant channel for consumer products, is increasing in importance for business and industrial products. In a VMS, one firm owns all the organizations in the channel, a contractual arrangement exists between the organizations, one channel member is in charge of channel administration, or members develop collaborative relationships. Channel decisions also include deciding on the intensity of distribution and the channel configuration. Channel management includes implementing the channel strategy, coordinating channel operations, and tracking the performance of the channel.

The choice of a channel strategy begins when management decides whether to manage the channel or assume a participant role. Strategic analysis identifies and evaluates the channel alternatives. Several factors are evaluated, including access to the market target, channel functions to be performed, financial considerations, and legal and control constraints. The channel strategy adopted establishes guidelines for price and promotion strategies.

International channels of distribution may be similar in structure to those found in the United States and other developed countries. Nevertheless, important variations exist in the channels of different countries because of the stage of economic development, government influence, and industry practices. Strategic alliances offer one means of gaining market access to the existing channels of a company operating in a country of interest to the firm. The Internet has had a dramatic impact on the globalization of channels of distribution.

A strategic value-chain perspective requires that managers in the market-driven company regularly review the adequacy of their channels strategy and consider the impact of major market and technology changes. This perspective emphasizes the entire value chain and the company's strategic positioning in its markets rather than short-term cost savings. It also requires that managers incorporate new distribution and communications concepts into their channel design where this provides competitive advantage.

Internet Applications

A. Examine the websites of Aveda (*www.aveda.com*) and The Body Shop (*www.bodyshop.com*). Compare and contrast the distribution networks of these two retailers.

B. Go to the website of the Worldwide Retail Exchange (*www.worldwideretailexchange.org*) and review the public pages describing the history, membership, and operation of this international online exchange for retailers. Identify and list the ways in which the exchange alters distribution strategy for suppliers and the impact on consumers.

Questions for Review and Discussion

1. In the late 1990s several airlines started selling tickets by using the Internet. Discuss the implications of this method of distribution for travel agencies.

2. Distribution analysts indicate that costs for supermarkets equal about 98 percent of sales. What influence does this high breakeven level have on supermarkets' diversification into delis, cheese shops, seafood shops, and flowers?

3. Why do some large, financially strong manufacturers choose not to own their dealers but instead establish contractual relationships with them?

4. What are the advantages and limitations of the use of multiple channels of distribution by a manufacturer?

5. Discuss some likely trends in the distribution of automobiles in the 21st century, including the shift away from exclusive distribution arrangements.

6. In the late 1990s Radio Shack initiated cobranding strategies with Compaq Computer and Sprint. Discuss the logic of this strategy, pointing out its strengths and shortcomings.

7. Identify and discuss some of the factors that should increase the trend toward collaborative relationships in vertical marketing systems.

8. Why might a manufacturer choose to enter a conventional channel of distribution?

9. Suppose the management of a raw materials supplier is interested in performing a financial analysis of a distribution channel consisting of manufacturers, distributors, and retailers. Outline an approach for doing the analysis.

10. Discuss some of the important strategic issues facing a drug manufacturer in deciding whether to distribute veterinary prescriptions and over-the-counter products through veterinarians or distributors.

Notes

1. Erika Rasmusson, "The Channels to Watch," *Sales & Marketing Management,* March 1998, 54–56.
2. Ibid., 56.
3. Louis W. Stern, Adel I. El-Ansary, and James R. Brown, *Management in Marketing Channels,* (Englewood Cliffs, NJ: Prentice-Hall, 1989), 4.
4. Chris Adams, "Steel Middlemen Are Finding Fatter Profits in the Metal," *The Wall Street Journal,* August 8, 1997, B4.
5. A. Parasuraman and Charles L. Colby, *Techno-Ready Marketing: How and Why Your Customers Adopt Technology* (New York: Free Press, 2001).

6. Adams, "Steel Middlemen."

7. Lisa Bannon, "Natuzzi's Huge Selection of Leather Furniture Pays Off," *The Wall Street Journal,* November 17, 1994, B4.

8. Dana Milbank, "Independent Goodyear Dealers Rebel," *The Wall Street Journal,* July 8, 1992, B2.

9. For a complete discussion of channel management, see Louis W. Stern and Adel I. El-Ansary, *Marketing Channels,* 4th ed. (Englewood Cliffs, NJ: Prentice-Hall, 1992).

10. James A. Narus and James C. Anderson, "Turn Your Industrial Distributors into Partners," *Harvard Business Review,* March–April 1986, 66–71.

11. Sally Pook, "Tesco Loses Fight to Sell Levi's at American Prices," *Daily Telegraph,* November 21, 2001, 7.

12. Rita Koselka, "Distribution Revolution," *Forbes,* May 25, 1992, 54, 58, 60, 62.

13. An expanded discussion of these issues is available in Lou E. Pelson, David Strutton, and James R. Lumpkin, *Marketing Channels* (Chicago: Richard D. Irwin, 1997), chap. 6 and 7.

14. Gary R. Weaver, Linda Klebe Trevino, and Philip L. Cochran, "Corporate Ethics Practices in the Mid-1990s: An Empirical Study of the Fortune 1000," *Journal of Business Ethics* 18, no. 3 (1999), 283–94.

15. Philip R. Cateora, *International Marketing,* 9th ed. (Homewood, IL: Richard D. Irwin, 1996), chap. 15.

16. Ibid., 449.

17. Peter Cunliffe, "Worldwide Superstore for Retailers," *Daily Mail,* April 1, 2000, 31; Dan Roberts, "Tesco Joins Online Consortium," *Daily Telegraph,* April 1, 2000, 44.

18. Cateora, *International Marketing,* chap. 15.

19. Richard Gibson, "General Mills Would Like to Be Champion of Breakfasts in Europe," *The Wall Street Journal,* December 1, 1989, B5.

20. This section of the chapter benefited from the advice and insightful contributions of Niall C. Piercy, Lean Enterprise Research Centre, Cardiff University, United Kingdom.

21. Alan Mitchell, "ECR's Big Idea Requires Sharing of Information," *Marketing Week,* April 16, 1998, 22–23.

22. Mark Tosh, "ECR—A Concept with Legs, Heart and Soul," *Progressive Grocer,* December 1998, 4–5; Richard J. Sherman, "Collaborative Planning, Forecasting and Replenishment: Realizing the Promise of Efficient Consumer Response through Collaborative Technology," *Journal of Marketing Theory and Practice* 6, no. 4 (1998), 6–9.

23. Denis R. Towill, "The Seamless Supply Chain: The Predator's Strategic Advantage," *International Journal of Technology Management* 13, no. 1 (1997), 37–56.

24. Martin Christopher, *Marketing Logistics* (Oxford: Butterworth-Heinemann, 1997).

25. This section is based on Nigel F. Piercy, "Marketing Implementation: The Implications of Marketing Paradigm Weakness for the Strategy Execution Process," *Journal of the Academy of Marketing Science* 26, no. 3 (1998), 222–36.

26. James P. Womack and Daniel T. Jones, *Lean Thinking: Banish Waste and Create Wealth in Your Corporation* (New York: Simon & Schuster, 1996); James P. Womack and Daniel T. Jones, "Beyond Toyota: How To Root Out Waste and Pursue Perfection," *Harvard Business Review,* September–October 1996, 140–58; James P. Womack and Daniel T. Jones, "From Lean Thinking to the Lean Enterprise," *Harvard Business Review,* March–April 1994, 93–103.

27. Daniel T. Jones, "The Route to the Future," *Manufacturing Engineer,* February 2001, 33–37.

28. Martin Christopher, "The Agile Supply Chain," *Industrial Marketing Management* 29, no. 1 (2000), 37–44.

29. J. B. Naylor, M. M. Naim, and D. Berry, "Legality: Interfacing the Lean and Agile Manufacturing Paradigm in the Total Supply Chain," *International Journal of Production Economics* 62 (1999), 107–18.

30. Martin Christopher and Denis R. Towill, "Supply Chain Migration from Lean to Functional to Agile and Customized," *Supply Chain Management* 5, no. 4 (2000), 206–21.

31. B. Evans and M. Powell, "Synergistic Thinking: A Pragmatic View of 'Lean' and 'Agile,'" *Logistics and Transport Focus* 2, no. 10 (December 2000), 26–32; Mark Whitehead, "Flexible: Friend or Foe," *Supply Management,* January 6, 2000, 24–27.

32. Steve Jarvis, "Up The Down Supply Chain," *Marketing News,* September 10 2001, 3.

33. Garth Alexander, "Christmas Brings Little Cheer for American E-Tailers," *Daily Telegraph,* December 24, 2000, 38.

34. Annie Counsell, "To B2B or Not to B2B?" *Connectis,* May 2001, 22–24.

35. David Bowen, "How to Use the Web as a Recession-Busting Tool," *Financial Times,* January 18, 2001, 26.

36. "A Long March: Mass Customization," *The Economist,* July 14, 2001, 63–65.

37. Christiane Schilzki-Haddouti, "Up Close and Personal," *Connectis,* May 2001, 25–26.

38. Simon London, "Keeping It in the Family," *Financial Times,* Understanding SCM Supplement, Autumn 2001, 10.

39. Jonahan Fenby, "B2B, or Not to Be?" *Sunday Business,* March 26, 2000, 14.

40. Weld Royal, "Death of a Salesman," *www.industryweek.com,* May 17, 1999, 59–60.

41. Robert Meehan, "Create, Revise Channels for Customers," *Marketing News,* October 23, 2000, 48.

42. "Shopping All Over the World," *The Economist,* June 19, 1999, 59–61.

43. Noel Capon and James M. Hulbert, *Marketing Management in the 21st Century* (Upper Saddle River, NJ: Prentice-Hall, 2000), 124.

44. M. Howard Gelfand, "Dayton-Hudson Keeps Its Vision," *Advertising Age,* July 9, 1984, 4, 46–47.

45. Andrew Cave, "Avon Calls on Big Stores in Makeover Plan," *Daily Telegraph,* September 19, 2000, 1.

46. Arnaldo Camuffo, Pietro Romano and Andrea Vinelli, "Back to the Future: Benetton Transforms Its Global Network," *Sloan Management Review,* Fall 2001, 46–52.

Chapter 11

Pricing Strategy

The pricing of goods and services performs a key strategic role in many firms because of deregulation, informed buyers, intense global competition, slow growth in many markets, and the opportunity for firms to strengthen market position. Price affects financial performance and is an important influence on buyers' value positioning of brands. Price may become a proxy measure for product quality when buyers have difficulty evaluating complex products.

The $2.7 billion U.S. paper towel market provides an interesting look at the strategic role of price in the competitive marketplace.[1] Procter & Gamble (P&G) began losing market position in this and 15 other consumer products markets in the late 1990s. In 2000 Kimberly-Clark's Scott brand cut into P&G's Bounty market share by using effective pricing in combination with other marketing strategy initiatives. P&G had made no product improvements in Bounty since 1994. Kimberly utilized product innovation, cost control, pricing, promotion, advertising, and customer relationship strategies, resulting in Bounty losing more market share than any of P&G's top nine U.S. brands. Because of increased paper supply prices, P&G raised Bounty prices by 9 percent, while Kimberly responded with only a 6 percent increase. Surprisingly, P&G reduced advertising spending on Bounty by 31 percent, while Kimberly increased advertising spending for Scott by 16 percent. P&G also experienced brand manager turnover for Bounty (four managers in 18 months). Kimberly discounted Scott to stores more frequently than P&G did. During the 1990s P&G had reduced its supermarket coverage by salespeople. P&G reduced its price increase by one-half in late 2000 and began to make aggressive promotion expenditures; Bounty experienced strong sales increases.

Pricing decisions may have substantial consequences, as illustrated by the effects of prices in the paper towel industry. Once it is implemented, it may be difficult to alter a price strategy, particularly if the change calls for a significant increase. Pricing actions that violate laws can land executives in jail. Price has many possible uses as a strategic instrument in business strategy. Changes in pricing practices have led to more flexible strategies and tactics by both producers and retailers.

The realities of the pricing environment are apparent.[2] Airline electronic revenue management pricing methods, which were pioneered by American Airlines in 1985, previewed the expanding role of technology in pricing today. E-commerce is extending flexible pricing initiatives to other product categories. Aggressive price competition occurs frequently in a wide range of markets for both goods and services. The motivation for these actions includes attempts to use production capacity, survival actions by companies in financial trouble, and competitive pressures on market-share position. Producers and service providers have money invested in fixed assets that management is unable or unwilling to liquidate.

We first examine the strategic role of price in the organization's marketing positioning strategy and then consider several pricing situations. Following a step-by-step approach to pricing strategy, we describe and illustrate the steps. We then outline an approach to situation analysis for pricing decisions, using several application situations to highlight the nature and scope of pricing analysis activities. Next, we consider the selection of a pricing strategy. Finally, we discuss the determination of pricing policies and look at several special pricing issues.

Strategic Role Of Price

Several factors influence management's decisions about how price will be used in marketing strategy. An important concern is estimating how buyers will respond to alternative prices for a product or service. The cost of producing and distributing a product sets lower boundaries on the pricing decision. Costs affect an organization's ability to compete. The existing and potential competition in the market segments targeted by a company constrains management's flexibility in selecting prices. Finally, legal and ethical constraints create pressures on decision makers.

The Internet promises to have an increasingly important impact on the role of price in many organizations. The Internet Feature considers several aspects of the impact of the Internet on pricing.

A strategic perspective on price may provide new opportunities and open new market space. For example, there may be advantages in pricing across the substitutes for a product rather than just against the immediate competition. Consider the advantage secured by Southwest Airlines by setting fares that were close to the road travel costs for short-haul journeys, not just against the established airlines' fares.

Another illustration of the competitive advantage that may be achieved in some situations by strategic pricing decisions that focus on the costs of alternatives and substitutes is provided by Berkshire Hathaway's Executive Jet company. The company sells expensive small jet aircraft for corporate travel. However, while executives may prefer a private jet, those jets are extremely expensive. The bulk of executive travel involves first-class and business-class tickets for conventional airlines. Berkshire Hathaway's pricing strategy was to compete with conventional airlines for a greater share of the corporate travel budget by selling companies shares of time in a corporate jet. Companies obtain the cachet and convenience of private air travel at a cost comparable to the annual business-class travel budget for many companies. Berkshire took business from premium-ticket airline customers, but also from companies preferring a time share to the full costs of owning a corporate jet that would spend much of its time sitting on the ground.[3]

A strategic perspective also mandates understanding how price is perceived and understood by customers instead of accepting the conventional view of the target buyer. For example, in the industrial lighting market, traditional strategies focus on corporate purchasing managers, who buy on the basis of how much lightbulbs cost and how long they last. All competitors compete head to head on these aspects of value. The Dutch company Philips reasoned that basic price and bulblife do not account for the full cost of lighting. This type of bulb contains toxic materials that force customers to pay high disposal costs. Typically, corporate purchasing officers are not accountable for disposal costs. Philips launched Alto, an expensive but environmentally friendly bulb, to appeal to chief financial officers (on lower total costs if disposal is included) and to marketing departments (on environmental image issues). The Alto replaced more that 25 percent of the total market for traditional industrial fluorescent lamps in the United States.[4]

- *Price Information.* The Web makes it simple for buyers to visit suppliers' sites or those of distributors to check and compare prices quickly and easily. In many product-markets, such as computers and software, books and CDs, and automobiles, price comparison services exist on the Web specifically to identify lower-priced outlets, such as pricewatch.com and bottomdollar.com. The impact of growing price transparency is likely to have a substantial impact on pricing. In some business-to-business markets companies are already finding that they no longer compete against the prices of conventional competitors but against the lowest price that the customer can find anywhere on the Web. Online exchanges are designed to achieve exactly this.

- *Auctions.* In many markets there are online auctions in which customers bid in a conventional way for products (e.g., eBay.com and uBid.com), but there are also reverse auctions like Priceline.com where customers declare the price they are willing to pay (for example, for an air ticket) and Priceline.com searches for a supplier at that price.

- *Group Buying.* Services have been established where the prices of products drop according to how many purchasers there are, encouraging customers to form groups and buy at the lower price, such as MobShop.com.

- *Price Differences.* The Web undermines the ability of a company to leverage differences in demand to charge different prices in different parts of the market. For example, The Gap sells blue jeans for around $30 in its U.S. stores and from its website. British customers can see those prices on the Web but then find they are paying £30 for the same blue jeans in British stores. The Gap's problem is that selling to British consumers from the U.S. website will undermine its store prices. Its current strategy is to refuse to supply British customers from the Web. Opportunities to charge price premiums in certain segments of the market will be increasingly rare.

- *Real-Time Pricing.* Puget Sound Energy has pioneered real-time pricing for customers for electricity. Smart meters and Internet-based technologies give customers nearly real-time information on the variable, time-sensitive cost of providing energy. Providing fast price signals in advance allows customers to reduce costs by choosing to consume power off-peak at lower prices. The effect is that consumers have the ability to react to and drive down wholesale market prices by reducing peak-hour energy use.

Source: Gary B. Swofford, "The Imperative for Real-Time Pricing," *Utility Business,* September 2001, 36–38; Robert J. Kauffman and Bin Wang, "New Buyers' Arrival under Dynamic Pricing Market Microstructure," *Journal of Management Information Systems* 18, no. 2 (Fall 2001), 157–88.

Price in the Positioning Strategy

Strategic choices about market targets, products, and distribution set guidelines for both price and promotion strategies. Product quality and features, type of distribution channel, the end-users served, and the functions performed by value-chain members all help establish a feasible price range. When an organization forms a new distribution network, selection of the channel and intermediaries may be driven by price strategy. The influence of price on other marketing-mix components may vary in different strategy situations. In some cases, price plays a dominant role in the marketing strategy, whereas in other situations, price may perform a more passive role.

Responsibility for pricing decisions varies among organizations. Marketing executives are responsible for price strategy in many companies. Pricing decisions may be made by the chief executive officer in some firms, such as aircraft producers and construction firms. Manufacturing and engineering executives may be assigned price responsibility in companies that produce customer-designed industrial equipment. The vital importance of pricing decisions argues strongly for cross-functional participation. Pricing affects all business functions. Operations, engineering, and finance executives should participate in strategic pricing decisions regardless of where responsibility is assigned. Coordination of strategic and tactical pricing decisions with other aspects of marketing strategy is also critical because of the interrelationships involved.

Product Strategy

When only one product is involved, the price decision is simplified, yet in many instances a line or mix of products must be priced. Consider a situation involving a product and consumable supplies for that product. One popular strategy is to price the product at competitive levels and set higher margins for supplies. Examples include parts for automobiles and cartridge refills for computer printers. Also, the prices for the products in a line do not necessarily correspond to the cost of each item. For example, prices in supermarkets are based on a total mix strategy rather than on individual item pricing. Understanding the composition of the mix and the interrelationships among products is important in determining pricing strategy, particularly when the brand identity is built around a line or mix of products rather than having a brand-by-brand basis. Product quality and features affect price strategy. A high-quality product may require a high price to help establish a prestige position in the marketplace and satisfy management's profit performance requirements. Alternatively, a manufacturer supplying private-branded products to a retailer like Wal-Mart or Kmart must price competitively in order to obtain sales. Pricing decisions require analysis of the product mix, branding strategy, and product quality and features to determine the effects of these factors on price strategy.

Distribution Strategy

Type of channel, distribution intensity, and channel configuration also influence price strategy. The needs and motivation of intermediaries must be considered in setting prices. Value-added resellers require price margins to pay for their activities and give them incentives for cooperation. Pricing is equally important when distribution is performed by the manufacturer. Pricing in vertically coordinated channels reflects total channel considerations more than it does in conventional channels. Intensive distribution is likely to call for more competitive pricing than does selective or exclusive distribution.

An important consideration in pricing strategy is the role and influence of various channel members. A particular firm may be very active or passive, depending on its role and power in the channel network. A firm that manages the channel usually plays a key role in pricing for the entire channel, subject to legal constraints and restrictions.

Pricing Situations

Pricing strategy requires continuous monitoring because of changing external conditions, the actions of competitors, and the opportunities to gain a competitive edge through pricing actions. Our look at the competitive battle for paper towel market position is illustrative. Situations requiring pricing actions include:

- Deciding how to price a new product or line of products.

- Evaluating the need to adjust price as the product moves through the product life cycle.

- Changing a positioning strategy that requires modifying the current price strategy.

- Deciding how to respond to the pressures of competitive threats.

Decisions about price for existing products may include price increases or decreases, or holding prices at current levels. Understanding the competitive situation and possible actions by competitors is important in deciding if and when to alter prices. Demand and cost estimates are strong influences on new product pricing. Deciding how to price a new product also requires considering competing substitutes since few new products occupy a unique position.

Gillette's Sensor razor was an outstanding success in the early 1990s, strengthening the company's market position and attracting shavers away from disposable razors. Gillette introduced a new razor in 1998. The MACH3 was priced 35 percent higher than the SensorExcel, which was substantially more expensive than its predecessor, Atra.[5] Gillette's pricing strategy for MACH3 is value-driven, positioning the razor as offering a superior shaving experience. The triple-bladed shaving system cost $750 million to bring to the commercialization stage plus an estimated $300 million for marketing the new product in the first year. The key issue is whether shavers will perceive MACH3 to be worth a 35 percent premium over the cost of SensorExcel blades. The new razor was available in 100 countries by the end of 1999. Gillette's consumer use tests of MACH3 compared to SensorExcel and competing brands gave the razor a 2:1 preference, strongly supporting the premium pricing strategy. MACH3 is the world's best-selling razor, and in 2002 Gillette is launching the MACH3 Turbo with new features and a 15 percent higher price.

Uses of Price in Positioning Strategy

Price is used in various ways in the marketing program positioning strategy—as a signal to the buyer, an instrument of competition, a means to improve financial performance, and a substitute for other marketing-mix functions (e.g., promotional pricing).

Signal to the Buyer

Price offers an immediate means of communicating with the buyer. The price is visible to the buyer and provides a basis of comparison between brands. Price may be used to position the brand as a high-quality product or to pursue head-on competition with another brand.

Instrument of Competition

Price offers a way to quickly attack competitors or, alternatively, to position a firm away from direct competition. For example, off-price retailers use a low-price strategy against department stores and other retailers. Price strategy is always related to the competition whether firms use a higher, lower, or equal price.

Improving Financial Performance

Since price and costs determine financial performance, price strategies are assessed as to their estimated impact on the firm's financial statements both in the short run and in the long run. Gillette's huge investment in the MACH3 razor will be recovered and profits will be generated if the venture is successful. Global competition has forced many firms to adopt pricing approaches that will generate revenues in line with forecasts. Yet both revenues and costs need to be taken into account in selecting pricing strategies.

EXHIBIT 11–1
**Pricing Strategy
for New and
Existing Products**

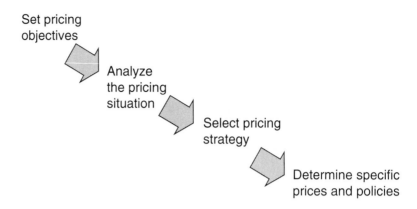

Set pricing
objectives

Analyze
the pricing
situation

Select pricing
strategy

Determine specific
prices and policies

Marketing Program Considerations

Price may serve as a substitute for selling effort, advertising, and sales promotion. Alternatively, price may be used to reinforce these activities in the marketing program. The role of price often depends on how other components in the marketing mix are used. For example, price can be used as an incentive to channel members, as the focus of promotional strategy, and as a signal of value. In deciding on the role of price in marketing strategy, management evaluates the importance of price to competitive positioning, probable buyers' reactions, financial requirements, and interrelationships in the marketing program.

Pricing Strategy

The major steps in selecting a pricing strategy for a new product or altering an existing strategy are shown in Exhibit 11–1. The pricing objectives provide a frame of reference for strategy development. Next, it is essential to analyze the pricing situation, taking into account demand, cost, competition, and legal and ethical forces. These analyses show how much flexibility there is in setting the price for a new product or changing the price for an existing product. Interestingly, Gillette's consumer tests of MACH3 indicated that there was little resistance to a price 45 percent above that of SensorExcel.[6] This information indicated that management had a lot of flexibility in deciding how to price MACH3. Based on the situation analysis and the price objectives, the pricing strategy is selected. Finally, specific prices and policies are determined to implement the strategy.

Pricing Objectives

Managers use their price strategies to achieve one or more of several objectives. More than one pricing objective is usually involved, and sometimes the objectives may conflict. If so, adjustments may be needed on one of the conflicting objectives. For example, if one objective is to increase market share by 30 percent and the second objective is to obtain a high profit margin, management should decide if both objectives are feasible. If not, one must be adjusted. Objectives set essential guidelines for pricing strategy.

Pricing objectives vary according to the situational factors present and management's preferences. A high price may be set to recover investment in a new product. A low price may be intended to gain market position, discourage new competition, or attract new buyers. Several examples of pricing objectives follow:

Gain Market Position

The use of low prices to gain sales and market share is an illustrative objective. Limitations include encouraging price wars and reduction (or elimination) of profit contributions. Even though buyers may have been responsive to a price for MACH3 that was 45 percent above that of SensorExcel, Gillette's management used a 35 percent price increase that was more likely to gain market position.

Achieve Financial Performance

Prices may be selected to contribute to financial objectives such as profit contribution and cash flow. Prices that are too high may not be acceptable to buyers. A key objective for Gillette's MACH3 pricing strategy was to achieve financial performance.

Product Positioning

Prices may be used to enhance product image, promote the use of the product, create awareness, and other positioning objectives. The visibility of price (high or low) may reduce the effectiveness of other positioning components, such as advertising.

Stimulate Demand

Price is used to encourage buyers to try a new product or to purchase existing brands during periods when sales slow down (e.g., recessions). A potential problem is that buyers may balk at purchasing when prices return to normal levels. Discount coupons for new products like Colgate's Total toothpaste help stimulate demand without actually lowering prices.

Influence Competition

The objective of pricing actions may be to influence existing or potential competitors. Management may want to discourage market entry or price cutting by current competitors. A price leader may want to encourage industry members to raise prices. One problem is that competitors may not respond as predicted.

A pricing objective for Eastman Kodak has been to gain market share for its film sales in Japan. Its efforts accelerated in late 1995 through a cobranding arrangement with retailers.[7] The new film was sold by 800 sales outlets at about half the price charged by Fuji. Cobranding uses both the Japanese retailer's name and the Kodak name. Kodak was already producing a private-label film for the 2,500-store Japanese Consumer Cooperative Union. Fuji was not expected to substantially reduce its film prices. Nonetheless, competitors do not always react as predicted to price changes. Also, the cobranding strategy could steal sales away from other higher-priced Kodak brands. Fuji hit back by reducing prices as much as 50 percent on some packs but did that in the U.S. market and not in Japan.

Analyzing the Pricing Situation

Pricing analysis is used in evaluating new product ideas, developing test marketing strategy, and selecting a new product introduction strategy. This information is also relevant for existing products because of changes in the market and the competitive environment, unsatisfactory performance of products, and modifications in marketing strategy over the product's life cycle. The factors influencing the pricing situation include (1) customer price sensitivity, (2) product costs, (3) current and potential competitive actions, and (4) legal and ethical constraints (Exhibit 11–2). We examine each factor and illustrate what is involved in the analyses.

Customer Price Sensitivity

One of the challenges in pricing analysis is estimating how buyers will respond to alternative prices. The pricing of Procter & Gamble Company's analgesic brand Aleve illustrates

EXHIBIT 11–2
**Factors Affecting
the Pricing
Situation**

Customer price
sensitivity

Legal and
ethical
constraints

Analyzing the
pricing
situation

Competitors'
likely
responses

Product
costs

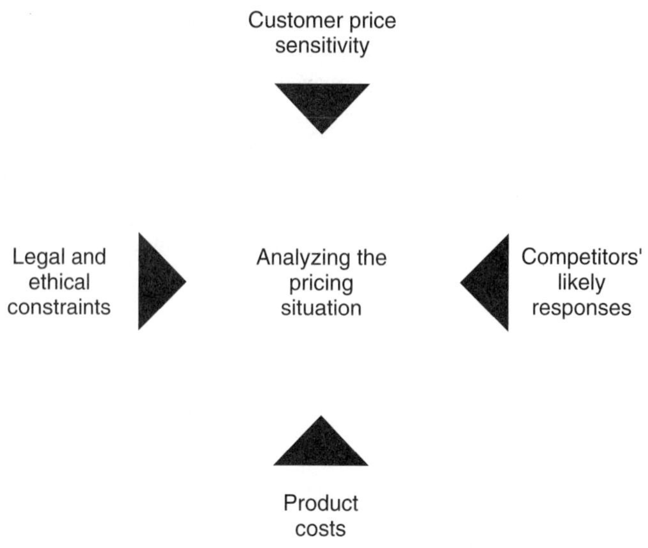

this situation. The product was introduced in the highly competitive $2.38 billion market in 1994.[8] Aleve is the over-the-counter version of Naprosyn (developed by Syntex Corporation). P&G estimated first year sales of $200 million. A $100 million marketing effort spearheaded Aleve's market entry. The pricing was the same as that of Advil, though Aleve lasts 8 to 12 hours compared to Advil's 8 hours. Aggressive promotional pricing (coupons) was anticipated from the market leaders, Tylenol ($700 million in sales) and Advil ($330 million). Some industry authorities believe Aleve poses a greater threat to the weaker brands (Bayer, Bufferin, and Nuprin).

Analysis of buyers' responsiveness to price should answer the following questions:

1. How large is the product-market in terms of buying potential?

2. What are the market segments, and what market target strategy is to be used?

3. How sensitive is demand in each segment to changes in price?

4. How important are nonprice factors such as features and performance?

5. What are the estimated sales at different price levels?

Let's examine these questions for Aleve. The analgesic market was growing at about a 3 percent annual rate. Aleve offers extended relief benefits to arthritis sufferers and people with sore muscles. P&G apparently wanted to stress the brand's performance (value proposition) rather than encourage price competition. Management's $200 million sales estimate would position Aleve in third place behind Tylenol and private-label brands. Since forecasting product-market size, segmentation, and targeting are discussed in Chapters 5, 6, and 9, the last three questions are now considered.

The core issue in pricing is finding out what value (benefits-costs) the buyer places on the product or brand.[9] Pricing decision makers need this information in order to determine price. Basing price only on cost may lead to pricing too high or too low compared to the value perceived by the buyer. Buyers see different values depending on their use situation, and so market segment analysis is essential. For example, people who want an analgesic that lasts longer will place a high value on Aleve.

Price Elasticity

Price elasticity is the percentage change in the quantity sold of a product when the price changes divided by the percentage change in price. Elasticity is measured for changes in price from some specific price level, and so elasticity is not necessarily constant over the range of prices under consideration. Surprisingly, research indicates that in some situations people will buy more of certain products at *higher* prices, thus establishing a price-quantity relationship that slopes upward to the right. In these instances buyers seem to be using price as a measure of quality because they are unable to evaluate the product. Estimating the exact shape of the demand curve (price-quantity relationship) is probably impossible in most instances. Even so, there are ways to estimate the sensitivity of customers to alternative prices. Test marketing can be used for this purpose. A study of historical price and quantity data may be helpful. End-user research studies such as consumer evaluations of price are also used. Recall the earlier discussion of Gillette's consumer tests of the MACH3 razor. These approaches, coupled with management judgment, help indicate the sensitivity of sales to price in the range of prices under consideration.

Nonprice Factors

Factors other than price may be important in analyzing buying situations. Buyers may be willing to pay a premium price to gain other advantages or, instead, be willing to forgo certain advantages for lower prices. Factors other than price that may be important are quality, uniqueness, availability, convenience, service, and warranty. In an attempt to recover from intense price competition, fast-food chains are marketing value menus of higher-priced items. These value strategies include the quality of the food, user-friendly service, and attractive dining facilities. For example, McDonald's advertising message "What you want is what you get" emphasizes the concept of value.

Value mapping is a useful technique for analyzing how buyers perceive the offerings of different brands.[10] One approach is to first develop the map based on managers' opinions, followed by obtaining value perceptions from a sample of consumers. The results of the two maps can then be compared and analyzed. An illustrative value map is shown in Exhibit 11–3 for brands A–E. Brands A and D offer better than fair value (the diagonal line).

In some instances the buying situation may reduce the importance of price in the buyer's choice process. The price of the product may be a minor factor when the cost is low compared to the importance of the use situation. Examples include infrequently purchased electric parts for home entertainment equipment, batteries for appliances, and health and beauty aids bought during a vacation. The need for important but relatively inexpensive parts for

EXHIBIT 11–3
Buyers' Perceptions of Value Offerings of Brands A–E

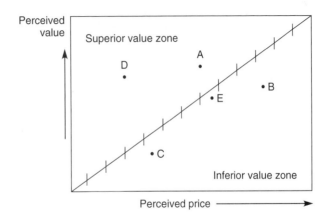

industrial equipment is another situation that reduces the role of price in the buyer's purchase decision. Quick Metal, an adhesive produced by Loctite Corporation, is used by maintenance personnel to repair production equipment. At less than $20 a tube, the price is not a major concern since one tube will keep an expensive production line operating until a new part is installed.

Other examples of nonprice factors that affect the buying situation include (1) purchases of products that are essential to physical health, such as pain relief, (2) choice between brands of complex products that are difficult to evaluate, such as stereo equipment (a high price may be used as a gauge of quality), and (3) image-enhancement situations such as serving prestige brands of drinks to socially important guests.

Forecasts

Forecasts of sales are needed for the price alternatives that management is considering. In planning the introduction of Aleve, P&G's management could look at alternative sales forecasts based on different prices and other marketing program variations. These forecasts, when combined with cost estimates, indicate the financial impact of different price strategies. The objective is to estimate sales in units for each product (or brand) at the prices under consideration.

Controlled tests can be used to forecast the effects of price changes. For example, a fast-food chain can evaluate the effects of different prices on demand by conducting tests in a sample of stores. Experimental designs can be used to measure or control the effects of factors other than price. We discussed methods for analyzing the effects of positioning strategy components and positioning results in Chapter 6.

Cost Analysis

Cost information is also needed in making pricing decisions. A guide to cost analysis is shown in Exhibit 11–4.

Composition of Product Cost

First, it is necessary to analyze the costs involved in producing and distributing the product. This includes determining the fixed and variable components of cost. Also, it is important to estimate the amount of the product cost accounted for by purchases from suppliers. For example, a large proportion of the costs of a personal computer is accounted for by the components purchased from suppliers. It is useful to separate the costs into labor, materials, and capital categories when studying cost structure.

Activity-based costing (ABC) is a promising technique which also yields applications for pricing strategy. Many firms have adopted ABC as a costing mechanism to more appropriately assign indirect costs to products and services. The key component of ABC is assigning costs to goods and services based on the activities that are performed to create the good or provide the service. With ABC, decision makers are provided with a much more accurate representation of product costs. This information allows for pricing decisions and comparisons across product lines and customer groups. Since ABC estimates the cost of the product in terms of a collection of activities, it is much easier to evaluate pricing for particular product attributes or service levels. Similarly, it is possible to make comparisons with competitors by evaluating the costs of activities necessary to produce product or service enhancements.

Firms that successfully implement ABC do so initially as an accounting technique, yet the ultimate objective is to facilitate activity-based management (ABM). In this manner, the cost data become an integral part of the product strategy in terms of considering the entire

EXHIBIT 11–4
Cost Analysis for Pricing Decisions

- Determine the composition of product cost.
- Estimate how volume of sales affects cost.
- Analyze the competitive advantage of the product.
- Decide how experience in producing the product affects costs.
- Estimate how much control the organization has over costs.

value chain, encompassing suppliers, customers, and competitors. For example, products that may require packaging or delivery modifications incur additional costs. With ABM, decision makers have a better understanding of these additional costs, can price accordingly, and can consider these costs in conjunction with the offerings of competitors.

Volume Effect on Cost

The next step in cost analysis examines cost and volume relationships. How do costs vary at different levels of production or quantities purchased? Can economies of scale be gained over the volume range that is under consideration, given the target market and program positioning strategy? At what volumes are significant cost reductions possible? The main task in this part of the analysis is to determine the extent to which the volume produced or distributed should be taken into account in selecting the pricing strategy.

Competitive Advantage

In analyzing competitive advantage, comparing key competitors' costs is often valuable. Are their costs higher, lower, or about the same? Although such information is sometimes difficult to obtain, experienced managers can often make accurate estimates. It is useful to place key competitors into relative product cost categories (e.g., higher, lower, same). In some situations analysts can estimate competitive cost information from a knowledge of wage rates, material costs, production facilities, and related information.

Experience Effect

It is important to consider the effect of experience on costs. Experience or learning-curve analysis (using historical data) indicates that costs and prices for various products decline by a given amount each time the number of units produced doubles. Price declines may be uneven because of competitive influences. When unit costs (vertical axis) are plotted against total accumulated volume (horizontal axis), costs decline with volume. This effect occurs when experience increases the efficiency of production operations. The experience-curve effect needs to be examined on an industry and company basis since the effect is not the same across all product categories.

There are several issues to be evaluated in experience-curve estimation, including the effect of aggregation of product data, errors in variables, the functional form of the relationship, and measurement.[11] The experience curve can be estimated using the total direct costs required to produce the first unit (or a later unit) and the improvement rate due to experience.[12] The cumulative total direct cost at any point will be equal to cost of the first unit times the number of units raised to the power equal to 1 minus the improvement rate. The improvement rate ranges from 0 to 1, and the equation for cumulative cost is:

$$(\text{Unit 1 cost}) \times (\text{Number of units})^{1 - \text{Improvement rate}}$$

Power retailers like Carrefour and Wal-Mart are targeting Latin America to help sustain growth and profits. Carrefour had 11 discount centers in Argentina and over 30 in Brazil when Wal-Mart entered the Argentine market in 1995.

Wal-Mart alleges that the French competitor is pressuring its local suppliers to stop supplying Wal-Mart with personal care products, paper products, and other goods. Carrefour denies the charge. Wal-Mart's concern is that without strong support from local manufacturers, the retailer will be unable to purchase 85 percent of its goods in Argentina. Importing will substantially increase Wal-Mart's costs.

The battle for market position by the two giant discounters promises to be interesting. Carrefour has a head start with sales of $1.5 billion in Argentina. Both are matching prices. Wal-Mart is stressing customer service and trying to build collaborative relationships with suppliers. Carrefour does not have a strong reputation for service. The number of supermarkets, hypermarkets, and self-service outlets in Argentina nearly doubled from 1984 to 1994.

By 1997 Wal-Mart had strengthened its market position in Argentina. Store managers were responding to local preferences by selling smokehouses because of the local taste for smoked meats. Worldwide, Carrefour competed in 13 international markets compared to 7 for Wal-Mart. Carrefour's sales were $12 billion compared to Wal-Mart's $5 billion.

Sources: Jonathan Friedland, "Big Discounters Duel over Hot Market," *The Wall Street Journal,* August 23, 1995, A6; "Wal-Mart Spoken Here," *Business Week,* June 23, 1997, 138–44.

Control over Costs

Finally, it is useful to consider how much influence the company may have over its product costs in the future. To what extent can research and development, bargaining power with suppliers, process innovation, and other factors help reduce costs over the planning horizon? These considerations are interrelated with experience-curve analysis yet may operate over a shorter time range. The bargaining power of an organization in its channels of distribution, for example, can have a major effect on costs, and the effects can be immediate. An example of bargaining power with suppliers by the French retailer Carrefour in the fast-growing retail market in Argentina is described in the Global Feature.

Competitor Analysis

Each competitor's pricing strategy needs to be evaluated to determine (1) which firms represent the most direct competition (actual and potential) for buyers in the market targets that are under consideration, (2) how competing firms are positioned on a relative price basis and the extent to which price is used as an active part of their marketing strategies, (3) how successful each firm's price strategy has been, and (4) the key competitors' probable responses to alternative price strategies.

The discussion in Chapter 3 considered methods for competitor identification. It is important to determine both potential and current competitors. The fiber-optic cable network industry presents an interesting competitor analysis situation. In 2001, an estimated 39 million miles of fiber networks covered the United States, while only 2.6 percent of this

EXHIBIT 11–5
Pricing Consequences of Intense Competition in Consumer Electronics in 2001

Source: Cliff Edwards, "Attention Shoppers: Enjoy the High-Tech Price War," *Business Week,* April 23, 2001, 46.

A slowing economy, weaker demand, and large inventories resulted in major price declines

	November 2000–February 2001
▶ Flat-screen TVs	−33.0%
▶ Laptops	−11.7%
▶ Inkjet printers	−16.0%
▶ Digital still cameras	−16.0%
▶ Cell phones	−16.0%
▶ Home CD recorders	−12.0%
▶ DVD players	− 7.6%
▶ PDAs	− 5.2%

capacity was actually in use.[13] The anticipated escalating demand for telecommunications bandwidth encouraged many firms like the industry pioneers Quest Communications International Inc. and Level 3 Communications Inc. to rapidly build underground fiber-optic networks. Barriers to entry were low. Nearly 1,500 firms had developed cable networks by 2001. Global Crossing Ltd., losing money on over $1 billion in revenues, spent $20 billion to build a 100,000-mile global network. The excess capacity was expected to cause prices for network space to fall more than 60 percent in 2001. An industry shakeout is likely since there is not enough demand to support the large number of competitors.

The success of a competitor's price strategy is usually gauged by financial performance. Quest appears to be one of the few firms in fiber-optic systems that is performing well. This apparently is due to its expansion into local phone services. One problem with using performance to gauge pricing success is accounting for influences other than price on profits. Quest's other products contribute to its profitability.

The most difficult of the four questions about competition is predicting what competitors will do in response to alternative price actions. No changes are likely unless one firm's price is viewed as threatening (low) or greedy (high). Competitive pressures, actual and potential, often narrow the range of feasible prices and rule out the use of extremely high or low prices relative to the competition. In new product markets, competitive factors may be insignificant except for the fact that very high prices may attract potential competitors.

The consumer electronics market offers an interesting look at the effects of intense and overcrowded competition. There were major price declines in 2001 for various electronics products, as shown in Exhibit 11–5. Some 80 companies were selling digital music players at the end of 2000, compared to only 5 a year earlier. Industry observers predicted a wave of consolidations and bankrupties. Companies like Dell Computer were using the market slowdown to gain market share though aggressive pricing.

Game theory is a promising method for analyzing competitors' pricing strategies. It can be used to analyze competitive pricing situations. The technique became very popular in the 1990s. An interesting application of this type of analysis is discussed in the Strategy Feature.

A popular exercise in seminars and executive briefings we hold is to ask executives to participate in a prisoner's dilemma pricing game. Each team must decide whether to price its products high or low compared to those of another team in 10 rounds of competition. The objective is to earn the most money; results are determined by the decision that two competitors make in comparison with each other.

The game fairly accurately simulates a typical profit/loss scenario for price competition in mature markets. The objective is to impart several lessons in pricing competition, the first being that pricing is more like playing poker than solitaire. Success depends not just on a combination of luck and how the hand is played but also on how well competitors play their hands. In real markets, outcomes depend not only on how customers respond but, perhaps more important, on how competitors respond to changes in price.

If a competitor matches a price decrease, neither the initiator nor the follower will achieve a significant increase in sales and both are likely to have a significant decrease in profits. In developing pricing strategy, managers need to anticipate the moves of their competitors and attempt to influence those moves by selectively communicating information to influence competitive behavior.

The second lesson is that managers must adopt a very long time horizon when considering changes in price. Once started, price wars are difficult to stop. A simple decision to drop price often becomes the first shot in a war that no competitor wins. Before initiating a price decrease, managers must consider how it will affect the competitive stability of markets.

Philip Morris discovered this when it initiated a price war in the cigarette business by cutting the prices of its top brands. Competitors followed, and the net result was a $2.3 billion drop in operating profits for Philip Morris, even as the Marlboro brand increased its market share seven points to 29%. The manufacturer of Camels experienced a $1.3 billion drop in profits.

The third lesson from the prisoner's dilemma is that careful use of a value-based marketing approach can reverse a trend toward price-based marketing. This is accomplished through signaling, a nonprice competitive tactic that involves selectively disclosing information to competitors to influence their behavior. The steel and airline industries provide prominent examples of the signaling strategy's use. They often rely on announcements that conveniently appear on the front pages of the *Wall Street Journal* to signal competitors of pending price moves and provide them with opportunities to follow. The strategy takes time to implement, but it provides a far better long-term competitive position for marketers who employ it.

Source: Reed Holden and Thomas T. Nagle, "Kamikaze Pricing," *Marketing Management,* Summer 1998, 34.

Game theory was used to design the auction process for the simultaneous sale of several third-generation (3G) wireless phone licenses in Great Britain.[14] The process was very successful for the government. After 150 rounds of bidding, the final bidders for five licenses paid a total of $34 billion, more than seven times the amount anticipated by the government.

Legal and Ethical Considerations

The last step in analyzing the pricing situation is identifying possible legal and ethical factors that may affect the choice of a price strategy. A wide variety of laws and regulations affect pricing actions. Legal constraints are important influences on the pricing of goods and services in many different national and cooperative regional trade environments. Pricing practices in the United States that have received the most attention from government include:[15]

Horizontal price fixing

Price collusion between competitors. Products with narrow profit margins are more likely to lead to price fixing. The Sherman Antitrust Act prohibits price fixing between companies at the same level in the channel.

Price discrimination

Charging different customers different prices without an underlying cost basis for discrimination. The Robinson-Patman Act prohibits price discrimination if it lessens or damages competition.

Deceptive pricing

This pricing practice involves misleading the buyer with a high price that is subsequently reduced to the normal price. This practice is prohibited by the Federal Trade Commission Act.

Price fixing in channels of distribution

The Consumer Goods Pricing Act places vertical price fixing under the jurisdiction of the antitrust laws.

Price information

This practice involves violating requirements concerning the form and availability of price information for consumers. Unit pricing and consumer credit requirements are examples. For example, the Consumer Credit Protection Act requires full disclosure of annual interest rates and other financial charges.

Ethical issues in pricing are more subjective and difficult to evaluate than are legal factors. Companies may include ethical guidelines in their pricing policies. Deciding what is or is not ethical is often difficult. The important consideration is to include an evaluation of possible ethical issues when developing a pricing strategy.

The prescription drug industry is under continuing pressure from consumers, politicians, and business concerning high drug prices. Drug pricing raises possible ethical issues, although the suppliers indicate that their prices are necessary due to large research and development expenses. Nonetheless, one study reported that the average price of the 50 drugs most used by the elderly increased 3.9 percent in 1999 compared to a 2.2 percent inflation rate.[16] Price controls have been proposed by consumer groups. The pharmaceutical industry was criticized for spending $14 billion in 1999 on promotion, public relations, and advertising as well as drug samples to doctors.

Selecting the Pricing Strategy

Analysis of the pricing situation provides essential information for selecting the pricing strategy. Based on the analysis, management needs to (1) determine the extent of pricing flexibility and (2) decide how to position price relative to costs and decide how visible to make the price of the product. The pricing strategy needs to be developed in the context of the entire marketing program since in most, if not all, instances there are other important influences on buyers' purchasing behavior.

How Much Flexibility Exists?

Demand and cost factors determine the extent of pricing flexibility. Within these upper and lower boundaries, competition and legal and ethical considerations also influence the choice of a specific pricing strategy. Exhibit 11–6 illustrates how these factors determine flexibility. The price gap between demand and cost may be narrow or wide. A narrow gap simplifies the decision; a wide gap suggests a greater range of feasible strategies. The choice of the pricing strategy is influenced by competitors' strategies, present and future, and by legal and ethical considerations. Management must determine where to price within the gap (flexibility band) shown in Exhibit 11-6. In competitive markets the feasibility range may be very narrow. Recall, for example, P&G's pricing of Aleve, which was priced the same as a key competitor's brand. New markets or emerging market segments in established markets may give management more flexibility in strategy selection.

A pricing decision situation is described in the Cross-Functional Feature, which highlights several important pricing issues. Before reading the next paragraph, identify the issues that you believe need to be considered in deciding what action to take concerning the pricing of Novaton. Also decide whether you agree or disagree with the decision made by the pricing team as described in the Cross-Functional Feature.

A central issue is determining why Novaton is not selling well in the market.[17] The problem may be price, but it could also be low awareness (25 percent). Surprisingly, the team's analyses did not consider customers' perceptions of Novaton. Depending on how customers position the brand, a price cut may not be effective. The information about Holycon's plans may be correct, but the team is basing a very important pricing decision on very limited intelligence. Similarly, the competitor's manufacturing capacity information came from only one person. Finally, the competitor's costs were estimated, assuming Holycon to have similar operations. This premise may be faulty.

The issues point to serious questions about Fritz's pricing strategy.[18] It was later determined that the underlying problem was low awareness. Customers actually considered Novaton to be better than Holycon. Holycon's costs were 60 percent lower than Novet's. Novet came into the market at prices 40 percent below Novaton's original price. After two

EXHIBIT 11–6
**Determinants of
Pricing Flexibility**

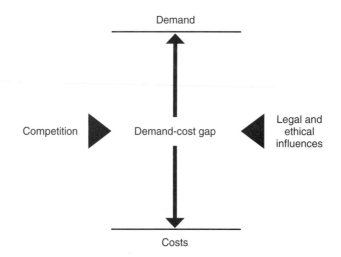

Cross-Functional Feature

Can You Identify the Pricing Issues in This Decision Situation?

The meeting was held on a snowy day in January. Novet's corporate offices, located in a large midwestern city, were quiet as people arrived late because of the new snowstorm. Mary Fritz, a marketing manager, started the discussion: "Let me review our progress on Novaton. We introduced it 18 months ago to a marketplace containing no competitive products, and we knew this product would be really valuable to our customers. We set our initial price at $250 per unit, expecting to sell 5,000 units in our first year, an additional 20,000 units this year, and 40,000 units next year. We just knew that as customers started to use the product, they would tell others. And word of mouth would be our best advertisement.

"We know this new product is really great," Fritz said, "and the customers who bought it like it a lot. But we've only sold 492 units so far. Now we're hearing Holycon Inc. is about to introduce a competing unit called the H-200. Some of our distributors have seen the H-200 and say it's just as good. Holycon has told the distributors they will price at 15 percent below us. In other markets where we've faced Holycon, we've had to be really aggressive in cutting prices in order to keep share. This time, we would like to get ahead of them, and use a preemptive strategy."

Fritz's group manager, Nina Pacofsky, responded: "OK, what do you suggest? And don't forget, we've committed to some very hefty profit goals this year. I'm not ready to tell Division we're not going to make it—especially this early in the year."

"Well, here's what we propose," said Fritz. "Since Holycon has always cut prices in the past, we're going to cut prices first this time and make it hard for them to compete. We propose to cut prices by 30 percent. In order to keep our profitability level, we're going to cut back on advertising. And, we figure that the lower price will not only discourage Holycon, but be so attractive when combined with our features that volume will go way up. We'll actually exceed our projected profit level for the year."

John Fine, the product manager, asked what the awareness level was for Novaton. Fritz didn't know, but Sally Olson found a note in a market research report indicating that awareness was about 25 percent.

Pacofsky hesitated. "Does anyone know if Holycon has actually built manufacturing facilities for their product?"

James Busky, the manufacturing manager, responded: "I heard from an extruder salesman that he had sold two extruders to Holycon. The salesman told me what the extruders were and said they were for a secret project. But, based on the type of extruders, they could only be used to compete with us. And, given the size of the extruders, Holycon's capacity will probably be about 40,000 units per year, almost 60 percent of our capacity."

Pacofsky wanted to know what Holycon's costs were likely to be and also wondered whether Holycon would be able to make any money if Novaton's prices were 30 percent lower.

"Based on our costs, and the fact that Holycon invested two years after us, we believe Holycon will have a margin of 3 percent on sales," said Tom Jeffries, the group competitive intelligence and market research specialist. "Because we were first to market, and customers know us better, we think Holycon will not get enough share to justify its entry. We think they'll drop out of the market if we cut our prices."

(continued)

"OK," Pacofsky said. "Go ahead with the price cut. We know Holycon always cuts prices, and it's clear we're not getting customers to buy because our prices are too high. Keep me up-to-date on sales. And we've got to keep our profits up."

The meeting adjourned. Mary Fritz headed off to draft new price lists and announcements to the sales force. Heading to her office, she dropped into the advertising manager's office, and asked him to stop all advertising on Novaton.

Source: George E. Cressman Jr., "Snatching Defeat from the Jaws of Victory," *Marketing Management,* Summer 1997, 10.

years of tough price competition Novet dropped out of the market. This might have been avoided if the pricing team had recognized that a better strategy would have been to position Novaton as offering superior value that was worth its original price and aggressively communicated the value proposition to build awareness with potential buyers.

Price Positioning and Visibility

A key decision is how far above cost to price a new product within the flexibility band (Exhibit 11-6). Assuming that management wishes to price above the cost of the product, a relatively low market entry price may be used with the objective of building volume and market position, or, alternatively, a high price may be selected to generate large margins. The former is a "penetration" strategy, whereas the latter is a "skimming" strategy. Analysis of the results of low price strategies in highly competitive markets indicates that while the strategies are sometimes necessary, they should be used with considerable caution.[19]

Lack of knowledge about probable market response to the new product complicates the pricing decision. Several factors may affect the choice of a pricing approach for a new product, including the cost and life span of the product, the estimated responsiveness of buyers to alternative prices, and assessment of competitive reaction.

A decision should also be made about how visible price will be in the promotion of the new product. The use of a low entry price requires active promotion of the price to gain market position. When firms use a high price relative to cost, price often assumes a passive role in the marketing mix. The performance and other attributes of the product are stressed in the marketing program positioning strategy.

Illustrative Pricing Strategies

The pricing strategy selected by an organization depends on how management decides to position the product relative to the competition and whether price performs an active or passive role in the marketing program. The use of price as an active (or passive) factor refers to whether price is highlighted in advertising, personal selling, and other promotional efforts. Exhibit 11–7 illustrates a range of price strategies which companies may pursue. Many firms choose neutral pricing strategies (at or near the prices of key competitors), emphasizing nonpricing factors in their marketing strategies.[20] The neutral pricing strategy seeks to remove price as a basis of choosing among competing brands. We examine each of the strategies shown in Exhibit 11–7, describing their characteristics and features.

High-Active Strategy

The underlying logic of emphasizing the high price in promotional activities is to convey to the buyer that because the brand is expensive, it offers superior value. While not widely

EXHIBIT 11–7
**Illustrative Pricing
Strategies**

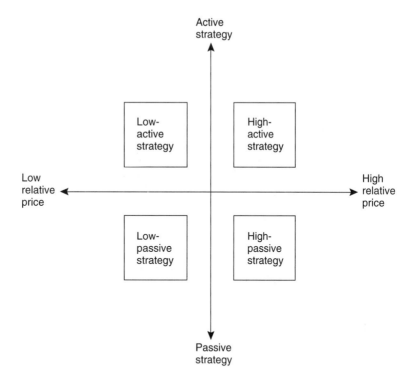

used, this pricing strategy has been employed to symbolically position products such as high-end alcoholic beverages. When the buyer cannot easily evaluate the quality of a product, price can serve as a signal of value. Also, high prices may be essential to gain the margins necessary to serve small target markets, produce high-quality products, or pay for the development of new products. Making price visible and active can appeal to the buyer's perceptions of the quality, image, and dependability of products and services. A firm using a high-price strategy is also less subject to retaliation by competitors, particularly if its products are differentiated from other brands.

High-Passive Strategy

Relatively high-priced brands are often marketed by featuring nonprice factors rather than using high-active strategies. Product features and performance can be stressed when the people in the target market are concerned with product quality and performance. BMW and Mercedes have successfully followed this strategy for many years. Nonetheless, the realities of competing against Japanese luxury automobiles required improving the value offerings of European brands in the late 1990s. Rubbermaid in kitchen aids (e.g., plastic containers) competes effectively against commodity-type competition through innovation and product differentiation.

Low-Active Strategy

Several retailers use this pricing strategy, including Home Depot (home improvement), Dollar General Stores (apparel), Office Depot (office supplies), Toys "R" Us (toys), and Pic 'N Pay Shoe Stores (family shoes). The low-active strategy is also popular with discount stockbrokers. When price is an important factor for a large segment of buyers, a low-active price strategy is very effective, as indicated by the rapid growth of these retailers. However, this strategy may encourage competitors to offer comparable prices. It is a more attractive option when the competition for the market target is not heavy or when a company has cost advantages and a strong position in the product-market. Southwest Airlines has performed very well using the low-active pricing strategy for its city-to-city route network.

Low-Passive Strategy

This strategy may be used by small manufacturers whose products have lower-cost features than those of other suppliers. By not emphasizing a low price, the firm runs less risk that potential buyers will assume the product quality is inferior to that of other brands. Some firms participating in conventional distribution channels may not spend much on marketing their products and thus can offer low prices because of lower costs. Other firms that have actual cost advantages for comparable competing products may decide to stress value rather than price even though they are offering prices lower than those of competing brands.

Determining Specific Prices and Policies

The last step in determining the pricing strategy (Exhibit 11–1) is selecting specific prices and formulating policies to help manage the pricing strategy. Pricing methods are examined, followed by a discussion of pricing policy. The chapter concludes with a discussion of several special pricing issues.

Determining Specific Prices

It is necessary either to assign a specific price to each product item or to provide a method for computing price for a particular buyer-seller transaction. Many methods and techniques are available for calculating price.

Price determination is normally based on cost, demand, competition, or a combination of these factors. Cost-oriented methods use the cost of producing and marketing the product as the basis for determining price. Demand-oriented pricing methods consider estimated market response to alternative prices. The most profitable price and market response level is selected. Competition-oriented methods use competitors' prices as a reference point in setting prices. The price selected may be above, below, or equal to competitors' prices. Typically, one method (cost, demand, or competition) provides the basis for pricing, although the other factors may have some influence on the decision.

Cost-Oriented Approaches

Break-even pricing is a cost-oriented approach to determining prices. The computation is as follows:

$$\text{Break-even (units)} = \frac{\text{Total fixed costs}}{\text{Unit price} - \text{Unit variable cost}}$$

When using this method, we select a price and calculate the number of units that must be sold at that price to cover all fixed and variable costs. Next, we assess the feasibility of exceeding the break-even value and thus generating a profit. One or more possible prices may be evaluated in the analysis. Break-even analysis is not a complete basis for determining price, since both demand and competition are important considerations in the pricing decision. With break-even price as a frame of reference, demand and competition can be evaluated. The price selected is typically at some level higher than the break-even price.

Another popular cost-oriented pricing method is cost-plus pricing. This technique uses cost as the basis for calculating the selling price. A percentage amount of the cost is added to cost to determine price. A similar method that is popular in retailing, markup pricing, calculates markups as a percentage of the selling price. In using markup pricing, this formula determines the selling price:

$$\text{Price} = \frac{\text{Average unit cost}}{1 - \text{markup percent*}}$$

Competition-Oriented Approache.

Pricing decisions are always affected by the actions of competitors. Pricing methods that use competitors' prices in calculating actual prices include setting prices equal to or at some specified percentage above or below the competition's. In industries such as air travel, one of the firms may be viewed by others as the price leader. When the leader changes its prices, other firms follow with similar prices. American Airlines has attempted to perform such a leadership role in the United States, although its pricing changes are not always adopted by competing airlines. Another form of competition-oriented pricing is competitive bidding, where firms submit sealed bids to the purchaser. This method is used in the purchase of various industrial products and suppliers.

Reverse auction pricing is an interesting competitive form of Internet pricing. This method of determining price involves sellers bidding for organizational buyers' purchases:

> In many cases, suppliers (sellers) must be prequalified before their bids are considered. These sites generally will have links to prospective sellers. Many times, supplier performance is rated, and these ratings are presented by the site as a benefit to current and prospective buyers. Freemarkets.com conducts online auctions of industrial parts, raw materials, commodities, and services. Suppliers bid lower prices in real time until the auction is closed to fill the purchase orders of large buying organizations. In 1999 this site auctioned off more than $1 billion worth of purchases and saved buyers between 2 and 25 percent.[21]

Demand-Oriented Approaches

The buyer is the frame of reference for these methods. One popular method is estimating the value of the product to the buyer. The objective is to determine how much the buyer is willing to pay for the product based on its contribution to the buyer's needs or wants. This approach is used for both consumer and business products. Information on demand and price relationships is needed in guiding demand-oriented pricing decisions. Internet auction pricing is a demand-oriented method of pricing.

Many pricing methods are in use, and so it is important to select specific prices within the guidelines provided by price strategy and to incorporate demand, cost, and competition considerations. Other sources provide extensive coverage of pricing decisions.[22]

Establishing Pricing Policy and Structure

Determining price flexibility, positioning price against the competition, and deciding how active a component it will be in the marketing program do not spell out the operating guidelines necessary for implementing the pricing strategy. It is helpful to also determine policy guidelines for use in deciding on pricing decisions and pricing structure.

Pricing Policy

An illustration shows how pricing decisions are guided by policies. Mervyn's, the 276-store retail chain, experienced poor performance in the early 1990s due to faulty merchandise

---

*Percent expressed in decimal form

selection and pricing policy.[23] The retailer's pricing policy was to offer large price reductions on many items that were advertised one week each month. For example, a blanket was sale-priced at $17.99, compared to the regular $25 price. Since many buyers were aware of Mervyn's pricing policy, they waited until the week the item of interest was sale-priced. The faulty policy reduced sales and profits.

A pricing policy may include consideration of discounts, allowances, returns, and other operating guidelines. The policy serves as the basis for implementing and managing the pricing strategy. The policy may be in written form, although many companies operate without formal pricing policies.

Pricing Structure

Any time more than one product is involved, management must determine product mix and line-pricing interrelationships in order to establish price structure. For example, Home Depot must determine specific prices for each item the firm offers. When more than one market target is involved, is it necessary to decide what relationship exists between the products offered in each one? Assuming differences in products, should price be based on cost, demand, or competition?

Price structure concerns how individual items in the line are priced in relation to one another: The items may be aimed at the same market target or at different end-user groups. For example, department stores often offer store brands and premium brands. In the case of a single product-market, price differences among products typically reflect more than variations in costs. Large supermarket chains price for total profitability of the product offering rather than for the performance of individual items. These retailers have developed computer analysis and pricing procedures to achieve sales, market-share, and profit objectives. Similarly, commercial airlines must work with an array of fares in the pricing structure.

The pricing of the Toyota Camry and the Lexus ES 300 is an interesting example of pricing products in relation to each other. The ES 300 is targeted to the semiluxury market.[24] The ES 300 has essentially the same body as the Camry, but the Lexus sells for substantially more than the Camry. Of course, the Lexus has certain unique features (e.g., leather seats), but some of the price difference has to be image rather than substance. Interestingly, both cars display good sales records.

Once product relationships are established, some basis for determining the price structure must be selected. Many firms base price structure on market and competitive factors as well as differences in the costs of producing each item. Some use multiple criteria for determining price structure and have sophisticated computer models to examine alternative pricing schemes. Others use rules of thumb developed from experience.

Most product line pricing approaches include not only cost considerations but also demand and competitive concerns. For example, industrial equipment manufacturers sometimes price new products at or close to cost and depend on sales of high-margin items such as supplies, parts, and replacement items to generate profits. The important consideration is to price the entire mix and line of products to achieve pricing objectives.

Special Pricing Considerations

Special pricing situations may occur in particular industries, markets, and competitive environments. Some examples follow.

Price Segmentation

Price is used in several markets to appeal to different market segments. For example, airline prices vary depending on the conditions of purchase. Different versions of the same basic product may be offered at different prices to reflect differences in materials and product features. Industrial products firms may use quantity discounts to respond to differences in the quantities purchased by customers. Price elasticity differences make it feasible to appeal to different segments.

Distribution Channel Pricing

The pricing strategies of producers that use marketing middlemen need to include consideration of the pricing needs of channel members. The strategy adopted by the producer should allow the flexibility and incentives necessary to achieve sales objectives. These decisions require analysis of cost and pricing at all channel levels. If producer prices to intermediaries are too high, inadequate margins may discourage intermediaries from actively promoting the producer's brand. Margins vary with the nature and importance of the value-added activities that intermediaries in the channel are expected to perform. For example, margins between costs and selling prices must be large enough to compensate a wholesaler for carrying a complete stock of replacement parts.

Price Flexibility

Another special consideration is deciding how flexible prices will be. Will prices be firm, or will they be negotiated between buyer and seller? Perhaps most important, firms should make price flexibility a policy decision rather than a tactical response. Some companies' price lists are very rigid, while other companies have list prices that give no indication of actual selling prices. It is also important to recognize the legal issues in pricing products when using flexible pricing policies.

In considering reducing prices, it is important to estimate how operating profits will be affected. Estimates of how operating profits will be reduced for a 1 percent price cut provided by McKinsey & Co. are 24 percent for food stores and drugstores, 13 percent for airlines, and 11 percent for computers and office equipment.[25] Smaller operating profit decreases are estimated for tobacco (5 percent), semiconductors (4 percent), and diversified financials (2.4 percent). Thus, the impact of price cuts (and price wars) can be substantial.

Product Life Cycle Pricing

Some companies have policies to guide pricing decisions over the life cycle of the product. Depending on its stage in the product life cycle, the price of a particular product or an entire line may be based on market share, profitability, cash flow, or other objectives. In many product-markets, price declines (in constant dollars) as the product moves through its life cycle. Because of life cycle considerations, different objectives and policies may apply to particular products within a mix or line. Price becomes a more active element of strategy as products move through the life cycle and competitive pressures build, costs decline, and volume increases. Life cycle pricing strategy should correspond to the overall marketing program positioning strategy used.

Counterfeit Products

The production and sales of counterfeit brands costs companies like Philip Morris, Nike, Gillette, and Microsoft billions of dollars each year.[26] The competitive challenge is not to meet prices that are a small fraction of the prices for the actual brands. Instead, companies whose brands are copied work toward gaining support from nations like China to prohibit and police the counterfeiting. Poor copies not only reduce the sales of the real brands, they also cause brand damage. Exhibit 11–8 provides several examples of brand pirating in China.

EXHIBIT 11–8
**Brand
Counterfeiting
in China**

Source: Dexter Roberts,
Frederick Balfour, Paul
Magnusson, Pete Engardio, and
Jennifer Lee, "China's Piracy
Plague," *Business Week*, June 5,
2000, 48.

Procter & Gamble The company estimates that 15% of the soaps and detergents bearing its Head & Shoulders, Vidal Sassoon, Safeguard, and Tide brands in China are fake, costing $150 million in lost sales.

Gillette As many as one-quarter of its Duracell batteries, Parker pens, and Gillette razors sold in China are believed to be pirated.

Bestfoods Bogus versions of Skippy Peanut Butter and Knorr boullion result in tens of millions of dollars in lost sales.

Yamaha The company estimates that five of every six JYM150-A motorcycles and ZY125 scooters bearing its name in China are fake. Some state-owned factories produce copies four months after a new model is launched.

Nike Replicas of its sport shoes and T-shirts are a growing problem in China.

Microsoft Counterfeiters are moving beyond crude knockoffs to high-quality versions of Windows and Windows NT—with packaging virtually indistinguishable from the real product—and sold in authorized outlets.

Anheuser-Busch Bogus Budweiser is sold in 640 ml bottles in China.

DaimlerChrysler Fake brake disks, windshields, oil filters, and shock absorbers for Mercedes cars are being made and sold in China.

Epson Copying machines as well as ink cartridges are counterfeited.

Summary

Pricing strategy gains considerable direction from the decisions management makes about the product mix, branding strategy, and product quality. Distribution strategy also influences the choice of how price will work in combination with advertising and sales force strategies. Pricing strategy may also influence distribution strategy and other marketing mix decisions. Price, like other marketing program components, is a means of generating market response, though price can be deployed much faster than can other mix components.

Two important trends are apparent in the use of price as a strategic variable. First, companies are designing far more flexibility into their strategies in order to cope with the rapid changes and uncertainties in the turbulent business environment. Second, price is more often used as an active rather than a passive element of corporate and marketing strategies. This trend is particularly apparent in the retail sector, where aggressive low-price strategies are used by firms such as Wal-Mart, Office Depot, and Home Depot. Assigning an active role to price does not necessarily lead to low prices relative to those of the competition—companies may use relatively high prices.

Product, distribution, price, and promotion strategies must fit together into an integrated positioning strategy. Pricing strategy for new and existing products includes (1) setting pricing objectives, (2) analyzing the pricing situation, (3) selecting (or revising) the pricing strategy, and (4) determining specific prices and policies. Companies use their pricing strategies to achieve one or more of several possible objectives. These include gaining market position, achieving financial performance, positioning the product, stimulating demand, and influencing the competition.

Analyzing the pricing situation is necessary in developing a pricing strategy for a mix or line of products or selecting a pricing strategy for a new product or brand. Underlying strategy formulation are several important activities, including analyses of customer price sensitivity, cost, competition, and legal and ethical considerations. These analyses indicate the extent of pricing flexibility by determining the pricing zone between cost and probable demand for the good or service being analyzed.

Pricing may be relatively high (skimming), neutral, or relatively low (penetration) compared with the competition. The choice of a pricing strategy includes consideration of price positioning and visibility. Alternative price strategies can be examined according to the firm's price relative to the competition and how active the promotion of price will be in the marketing program. Pricing approaches include high-active, high-passive, low-active, and low-passive strategies. Variations within the four categories occur. In many industries market leaders establish prices that are followed by other firms in the industry.

The determination of specific prices may be based on costs, competition, and/or demand influences. Implementing and managing the pricing strategy also includes establishing pricing policy and structure. Finally, several special pricing considerations include price segmentation, distribution channel pricing, price flexibility, product life cycle pricing, and counterfeit products.

Internet Applications

A. Explore the website of American Airlines (www.aa.com). Consider how the Web can facilitate price discrimination.

B. Visit the website of Amazon.com. Evaluate Amazon's pricing strategy. How do its prices compare to those of "bricks and mortar" retailers? Critically evaluate the company's product offering and determine potential market segments.

Questions for Review and Discussion

1. Discuss the role of price in the marketing strategy for Rolex watches. Contrast Timex's price strategy with Rolex's strategy.

2. In 1992 Toyota introduced two new automobiles. The redesigned Camry and the Lexus ES 300 were very similar, but the ES 300 was priced substantially higher than the Camry. Discuss the features and limitations of this pricing strategy.

3. Indicate how a fast-food chain can estimate the price elasticity of a proposed new product such as a chicken sandwich.

4. Real estate brokers typically charge a fixed percentage of a home's sale price. Advertising agencies follow a similar price strategy. Discuss why this may be a sound price strategy. What are the arguments against it from the buyer's point of view?

5. Cite examples of businesses to which the experience-curve effect is not applicable. What influence may this have on price determination?

6. In some industries prices are set low, subsidies are provided, and other price-reducing mechanisms are used to establish a long-term relationship with the buyer. Utilities, for example, sometimes use incentives to encourage contractors to install electric- or gas-powered appliances. Manufacturers may price equipment low and then depend on service and parts for profit contribution. What are the advantages and limitations of this pricing strategy?

7. Some private clubs exclude prices from their menus. Analyze and evaluate this price strategy.

8. Discuss some of the ways in which estimates of the costs of competitors' products can be determined.

9. Discuss how a pricing strategy should be developed by a new firm to price its business analysis software line.

10. Suppose a firm is considering changing from a low-active price strategy to a high-active strategy. Discuss the implications of this proposed change.

11. Describe and evaluate the price strategy used for the Toyota Lexus 400 European-style luxury sedan.

Notes

1. This illustration is based on "Can Procter & Gamble Clean Up its Act?" *Business Week,* March 12, 2001, 80, 82–83.

2. "CAPITAL: How Technology Tailors Price Tags," *The Wall Street Journal,* June 21, 2001, A1; Bill Saporito, "Why the Price Wars Never End," *Fortune,* March 23, 1992, 68–71, 74, 78.

3. W. Chan Kim and Renee Mauborgne, "Now Name a Price That's Hard to Refuse," *Financial Times,* January 24, 2001.

4. W. Chan Kim and Renee Mauborgne, "Creating New Market Space," *Harvard Business Review,* January–February 1999, 83–93.

5. See "Taking it on the Chin," *The Economist,* April 18, 1998, 60–61; Mark Maremont, "How Gillette Brought Its MACH3 to Market," *The Wall Street Journal,* April 15, 1998, B1, B8; Mark Maremont, "A Cut Above?" *The Wall Street Journal,* April 14, 1998, A1; A10.

6. Maremont, "How Gillette Brought Its MACH3 to Market," B1.

7. Erle Norton, "Kodak to Slash Prices for Film It Sells in Japan," *The Wall Street Journal,* August 24, 1995, A2.

8. Laura Bird, "P&G's New Analgesic Promises Pain for Over-the-Counter Rivals," *The Wall Street Journal,* June 16, 1994, B9.

9. Robert J. Dolan, "How Do You Know When the Price Is Right," *Harvard Business Review,* September–October 1995, 174–83.

10. Guidelines for constructing value maps are discussed in George E. Cressman, Jr., "Snatching Defeat from the Jaws of Victory," *Marketing Management,* Summer 1997, 14.

11. David B. Montgomery and George S. Day, "Experience Curves: Evidence, Empirical Issues, and Applications," in *Strategic Marketing and Management,* ed. H. Thomas and D. Gardner (Chichester, UK: John Wiley & Sons, 1985), 213–38.

12. A guide to determining experience curves is provided in Kent B. Monroe, *Pricing: Making Profitable Decisions,* 2nd ed. (New York: McGraw-Hill, 1990), chap. 11.

13. Rebecca Blumenstein, "Overbuilt Web," *The Wall Street Journal,* June 16, 2001, A1, A8; Deborah Solomon, "Global Crossing Finds That the Race Has Just Begun," *The Wall Street Journal,* June 22, 2001, B4.

14. Almar Latour, "Disconnected," *The Wall Street Journal,* June 5, 2001, A1, A8.

15. These and other aspects of marketing and the law are discussed in Gilbert A. Churchill, Jr., and J. Paul Peter, *Marketing,* 2nd ed. (Chicago: Irwin/McGraw-Hill, 1998), 325–27.

16. Shailagh Murry and Lucette Lagnado, "Drug Companies Face Assault on Prices," *The Wall Street Journal,* May 11, 2000, B1, B4.

17. The following issues are based on Cressman, "Snatching Defeat from the Jaws of Victory," 10–11.

18. Ibid.

19. Reed K. Holden and Thomas T. Nagle, "Kamikaze Pricing," *Marketing Management,* Summer 1998, 31–39.

20. Ibid.

21. Jeffrey F. Rayport and Bernard J. Jaworski, *E-Commerce* (New York: McGraw-Hill/Irwin), 2001, 157.

22. See, for example, Monroe, *Pricing;* Thomas T. Nagle and Reed K. Holden, *The Strategy and Tactics of Pricing,* 2nd ed. (Englewood Cliffs, NJ: Prentice-Hall, 1995).

23. Gregory A. Patterson, "Mervyn's Efforts to Revamp Result in Disappointment," *The Wall Street Journal,* March 29, 1994, B4.

24. Jerry Flint, "Alfred Sloan Spoken Here," *Forbes,* November 1991, 96, 101.

25. Janice Revell, "The Price Is Not Always Right," *Fortune,* May 14, 2001, 240.

26. Dexter Roberts, Frederick Balfour, Paul Magnusson, Pete Engardio, and Jennifer Lee, "China's Piracy Plague," *Business Week,* June 5, 2000, 44–48.

Chapter 12

Promotion, Advertising, and Sales Promotion Strategies

Promotion strategy consists of a group of interrelated communications activities. It combines advertising, personal selling, sales promotion, direct marketing, and public relations into an integrated program for communicating with buyers and others who influence purchasing decisions. The Internet offers a fast-growing avenue for one-to-one marketing for business and consumer buyers. Billions are spent every week in the United States and around the world on promotion. Effective management of these expensive resources is essential to gain the optimum return from the promotion expenditures.

Promotion plays an important role in Ford's growth strategy for Jaguar. The automaker is spending an estimated $500 million a year as part of management's strategy to transform Jaguar into a high-volume luxury global brand.[1] The new Jaguar X-Type, introduced in 2001, is targeted to minority group members and younger buyers at a $30,000 price. The design echoes the styling of the top-of-the-line Jaguar XJ. The communications strategy positions the X-Type as luxury styling at an affordable price (see the accompanying Jaguar X-Type website advertisement). Management's sales objectives for the Jaguar brand portfolio are to double unit global sales to nearly 200,000 units in 2002, compared to about 90,000 units in 2000. The X-Type is expected to be a major contributor to the growth strategy. Some potential risks are involved. Reaching the X-Type sales target of 100,000 units by 2002 will require persuading as many as 40,000 or more Europeans to switch to the brand. There is also potential brand damage resulting from the downward brand extension of the X-Type.

The communications activities that make up promotion strategy inform people about products and persuade the company's buyers, channel organizations, and the public at large to purchase brands. The objective is to combine the promotion components into an integrated strategy for communicating with buyers and others who influence purchasing decisions. Since each form of promotion has certain strengths and shortcomings, an integrated strategy incorporates the advantages of each component into a cost-effective promotion mix.

We begin the chapter with an overview of promotion strategy and examine the decisions that are involved in designing the strategy. The intent is to develop an integrated view of

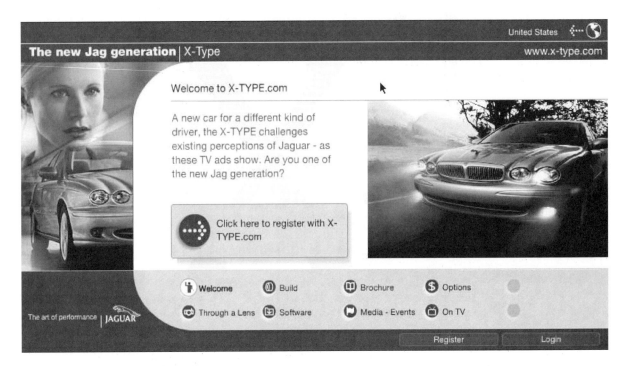

communications strategy to which each of the promotion components (advertising, sales promotion, public relations, personal selling, and direct marketing) contributes. Next, we discuss each component, beginning with the major decisions that constitute advertising strategy and the factors affecting advertising decisions. The final section considers the design and implementation of sales promotion strategies. Personal selling, direct marketing, and Internet strategies are discussed in Chapter 13.

Promotion Strategy

Promotion strategy consists of planning, implementing, and controlling an organization's communications to its customers and other target audiences. The purpose of promotion in the marketing program is to achieve management's desired communications objectives with each audience. An important marketing responsibility is planning and coordinating the integrated promotion strategy and selecting the specific strategies for the promotion components. It is important to recognize that word-of-mouth communications among buyers and the communications activities of other organizations may influence the firm's target audience(s).

The Components of Promotion Strategy

Advertising

Advertising consists of any form of nonpersonal communication concerning an organization, product, or idea that is paid for by a specific sponsor. The sponsor makes the payment for the communication via one or more forms of media (e.g., television, radio, magazines, newspapers). Advertising expenditures in the United States were up 8 percent in 2000 to $205 billion.[2] A decline was expected in 2001. The United States accounts for about 45 percent of worldwide advertising. Large advertising expenditures are often necessary to introduce new consumer products and build the brand equity of existing products. For example, during the first year Procter & Gamble (P&G) spent an estimated $100 million in advertising to introduce the Aleve pain relief over-the-counter drug.[3] The Tagamet HB heartburn drug advertising campaign cost Smith Kline Beecham $100 million, and Johnson & Johnson spent an equal amount on the Pepcid AC heartburn drug.

Among the advantages of using advertising to communicate with buyers are the low cost per exposure, the variety of media (newspapers, magazines, television, radio, Internet, direct mail, and outdoor advertising), control of exposure, consistent message content, and the opportunity for creative message design. In addition, the appeal and message can be adjusted when communications objectives change. Cable television enables advertisers to target their communications to specific buyers with more focus than is possible with the large networks. Advertising also has some disadvantages. It cannot interact with the buyer and may not be able to hold the viewer's attention. Moreover, the message is limited to the duration of an exposure.

Personal Selling

Personal selling consists of verbal communication between a salesperson (or selling team) and one or more prospective purchasers with the objective of making or influencing a sale. Annual expenditures on personal selling are much larger than those for advertising, perhaps twice as high. However, both promotion components share some common features, including creating awareness of the product, transmitting information, and persuading people to buy. Personal selling is expensive. For example, in the U.S. pharmaceuticals sector, the industry spends more on salespeople than on scientists. Some 70,000 U.S. salespeople cost the pharmaceuticals industry roughly $7 billion a year.[4] The cost of a sales call is estimated to average over $500 for industrial goods and services, and typically multiple calls are necessary to sell the product.[5] Personal selling has several unique strengths: Salespeople can interact with buyers to answer questions and overcome objections, can target buyers, and have the capacity to accumulate market knowledge and provide feedback. Top management may participate in selling by making calls on major customers. For example, the chief executive officer of Coca-Cola makes a presentation to the employees attending McDonald's annual meeting.

Sales Promotion

Sales promotion consists of various promotional activities, including trade shows, contests, samples, point-of-purchase displays, trade incentives, and coupons. Sales promotion expenditures are substantially greater than the amount spent on advertising. This array of special communications techniques and incentives offers several advantages: Promotion can be used to target buyers, respond to special occasions, and create an incentive for purchase. One of the more successful sales promotion initiatives is the frequent flier incentive program. American Airlines launched the innovative AAdvantage program in 1981. It was first developed with a core customer group of 250,000 frequent fliers.[6] AAdvantage has over 15 million members, and 200,000 people join each month. American's reservation system enables the company to track mileage and efficiently manage the program. American's costs per member per year for communications and administration are very low.

Direct Marketing

Direct marketing includes the various communications channels that enable companies to make direct contact with individual buyers. Examples are catalogs, direct mail, telemarketing, television selling, radio/magazine/newspaper selling, electronic shopping, and kiosk shopping (e.g., purchase of flight insurance in airports). The distinguishing feature of direct marketing is the opportunity for the marketer to gain direct access to the buyer. Direct marketing expenditures account for a large proportion of promotion expenditures.

Interactive/Internet Marketing

Included in this promotion component are the Internet, CD-ROMs, and interactive television. Interactive media enable buyers and sellers to interact. The Internet performs an important and rapidly escalating role in promotion strategy. In addition to providing a direct sales channel, the Internet may be used to identify sales leads, conduct Web-based surveys, provide product information, and display advertisements. The Internet provides the platform for a complete business strategy in the case of Internet business models. Marketing strategies are increasingly linked to Internet initiatives. The Internet has become an important component of many communications programs.

Public Relations

Public relations for a company and its products consists of communications placed in the commercial media but not paid for directly by the sponsor. For example, a news release on a new product may be published in a trade magazine, but the company does not pay for the communication. The objective of the public relations unit is to encourage relevant media to include company-released information in media communications. Public relations activities can make an important contribution to promotion strategy if the activity is planned and implemented to achieve specific promotion objectives. (Public relations is also used for publicity purposes such as communicating with financial analysts.) Publicity in the media can be negative as well as positive and cannot be controlled by the organization to the same extent that other promotion components can. Since a company does not purchase the media coverage, publicity is a cost-effective method of communication. The media are usually willing to cover topics of public interest. Many companies retain public relations consultants who proactively pursue publicity opportunities.

Technology plays an important role in companies' promotion strategies. For example, the Internet provides car buyers with access to important information in making purchase decisions. One estimate is that half of all new car buyers used the Internet in making purchase decisions in 2000.[7] An interesting use of the Internet to promote new movies and gather viewer information is described in the E-Business Feature.

Developing Promotion Strategy

Market targets and positioning strategy guide promotion decisions. Several decisions are involved in designing the promotion strategy, including (1) setting communications objectives, (2) deciding on the role of each of the components that make up the promotion mix, (3) determining the promotion budget, and (4) selecting a strategy for each mix component (Exhibit 12–1). Specific strategies are determined for advertising, personal selling, sales promotion, direct marketing, the Internet, and public relations.

Market targets and product, distribution, and price decisions provide a frame of reference for (1) deciding on the role of promotion strategy in the total marketing program and (2) identifying the specific communications tasks of the promotion activities. One important question is deciding on the role that promotion will play in marketing strategy. Advertising and personal selling are often a major part of a firm's marketing strategy. In consumer package goods firms, sales promotion and advertising are a major part of the promotional mix. In industrial firms, personal selling often dominates the promotion mix, with advertising and sales promotion playing a supporting role. The use of sales promotion and public relations varies considerably among companies. The use of direct marketing

It's all part of the most elaborate Internet marketing blitz ever to hit Hollywood. In post-*Blair Witch* Internet marketing, Fox has few peers in mastering the interactive power of the Web to boost interest in its films. Besides egging on mutant snitchers, Fox used online games, chat-room talks with the stars, and even a series of fake news articles of mysterious events to whip up online chatter.

The results are promising. The Web campaign capped a $50 million marketing program that helped *X-Men* gross more than $150 million. Fox exit polls showed that 28% of those who saw the film had visited the *X-Men* Web site—nearly five times the number of movie-goers who usually surf movie sites, say Hollywood marketing experts.

The potential reward, say industry marketing experts: a whole new customer base to target during later promotions—and larger-than-ever focus groups on which to test future films and plotlines. Up to six months before the movie's opening, for instance, mutant-watch.com was full of phony news accounts of freak hurricanes started by mutants and Badger Scouts in Michigan patrolling the streets in search of mutants. That's what drew those 65,000 mutant spotters—and their valuable data.

To be sure, this "viral marketing," the online equivalent of word-of-mouth advertising, can't work miracles. The apocalyptic animated film *Titan A.E.,* for example, died at the box office despite a hefty Web a campaign that included off-line events, such as a well-publicized skateboard contest on the Fox Sports Channel designed to drive folks to the *Titan* site.

But it's that kind of wasted spending that spurred Fox to develop a $1 million Web-powered data analysis program, code-named Eight Ball, that allows execs to track sales for most Fox films even before the box office closes for the night. Using its own data—plus some from box-office tracker ACNielsen EDI Inc.—Fox can decide where to boost advertising and where to yank it before financial disaster strikes. If a movie bombs in Boise, for instance, Fox can pull it—or run more ads in areas where sales are starting to build.

Source: Ronald Grover "Lights, Camera, Web Site," *Business Week E.Biz,* September 18, 2000, EB55.

varies considerably across companies and industries, although Internet initiatives are under way at a broad range of companies.

Interestingly, Singapore Airlines (SIA) performs an important promotion role in marketing that nation. SIA displays superior margins, high yields, and customer satisfaction, with top rankings in the industry's index of competitiveness, although ranking only eleventh in size among international carriers.[8] The airline's favorable image helps position the country to executives, government officials, and tourists who experience SIA's renowned services. The tiny city-state with a population of less than 5 million has a strong brand image that is enhanced by the airline's favorable reputation with customers and competitors throughout the world. The airline's advertising in business and travel magazines is designed to favorably position its distinctive bundle of values.[9]

Communications Objectives

Communications objectives help determine how the promotion strategy components are used in the marketing program. We examine illustrative communications objectives.

EXHIBIT 12–1
**Developing the
Promotion Strategy**

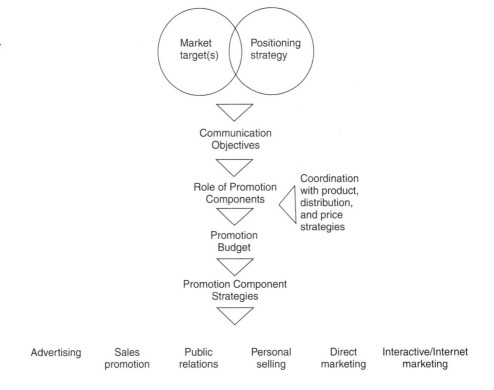

Need Recognition Finding Buyers Brand Building

Need Recognition

One communications objective that is typical for new product introductions is to trigger a need. Need recognition may also be important for existing products and services, particularly when the buyer can postpone purchasing or choose not to purchase (life insurance is a good example). For example, P&G emphasized the need to control dandruff in its advertising of Head & Shoulders shampoo in China. The ads focused attention on how dandruff is very visible on people with black hair.

Finding Buyers

Promotion activities can be used to identify buyers. When used in this way, the communication seeks to get the prospective buyer to respond. Recall, for example, the use of the Internet to attract potential movie viewers discussed in the E-Business Feature. Salespeople may be given responsibility for identifying and screening prospects. The use of toll-free phone numbers is often helpful in identifying customers as well as issues and problems of interest to callers.

Brand Building

Promotion can aid a buyer's search for information. One of the objectives of new product promotional activities is to help buyers learn about the product. Prescription drug companies advertise to the public to make people aware of diseases and the brand names of products used for their treatment. In the past, they targeted only doctors through ads in medical journals and contacts by salespeople. Advertising is often a more cost-effective way to disseminate information than personal selling, particularly when the information can be exposed to targeted buyers by electronic or printed media.

Evaluation of Alternatives

Promotion helps buyers evaluate alternative products or brands. Both comparative advertising and personal selling are effective in demonstrating a brand's strengths compared to competing brands. An example of this form of advertising is to analyze competing brands of a product, showing a comparison favorable to the brand of the firm placing the ad. Specific product attributes may be used for the comparison. For example, PepsiCo's ads in 2001 for its leading bottled water brand, Aquafina, were positioned "to strip away the elite image to make it look accessible to everyone."[10] The objective was to differentiate Aquafina from competing brands as the most mouth-watering water available.

Decision to Purchase

Several of the promotion components may be used to stimulate the purchase decision. Personal selling is often effective in obtaining a purchase commitment from the buyers of consumer durable goods and industrial products. Door-to-door selling organizations such as Cutco use highly programmed selling approaches to encourage buyers to purchase their products. Communications objectives in these firms include making a target number of contacts each day. Point-of-purchase sales promotions such as displays in retail stores are intended to influence the purchase decision, as are samples and discount coupons. One of the advantages of personal selling over advertising is its flexibility in responding to the buyer's objectives and questions at the time the decision to purchase is being made.

Customer Retention

Communicating with buyers after they purchase a product is an important promotional activity. Follow-up by salespeople, advertisements stressing a firm's service capabilities, and toll-free numbers placed on packages to encourage users to seek information or report problems are illustrations of postpurchase communications. Hotels leave questionnaires in rooms for occupants to use in evaluating hotel services.

Various communications objectives may be assigned to promotion strategy. The uses of promotion vary according to the type of purchase, the stage of the buyer's decision process, the maturity of the product-market, and the role of promotion in the marketing program. Objectives need to be developed for the entire promotion program and for each promotion component. Certain objectives, such as sales and market-share targets, are shared with other marketing program components. Examples of promotion objectives include:

- Creating or increasing buyers' awareness of a product or brand.

- Influencing buyers' attitudes toward a company, product, or brand.

- Increasing the level of brand preference of the buyers in a targeted segment.

- Achieving sales and market-share increases for specific customer or prospect targets.

- Generating repeat purchases of a brand.

- Encouraging trial of a new product.

- Attracting new customers.

- Encouraging long-term relationships.

In the following sections and the next chapter we discuss and provide examples of objectives for each promotion component.

Deciding on the Role of the Promotion Components

Promotion objectives guide the specific role of each component in the promotion mix. For example, the role of the sales force may be to obtain sales or, instead, to inform channel of distribution organizations about product features and applications. Advertising may be used to generate repeat purchases of a brand. Sales promotion (e.g., trade shows) may be used to achieve various objectives in the promotion mix. Direct marketing may play a major role in certain companies such as Avon products.

Early in the process of developing the promotion strategy, it is useful to set guidelines for the expected contribution of each of the promotion-mix components. These guidelines help determine the strategy for each promotion component. It is necessary to decide which communications objective(s) will be the responsibility of each component. For example, advertising may be responsible for creating awareness of a new product. Sales promotion (e.g., coupons and samples) may encourage trial of the new product. Personal selling may be assigned responsibility for getting retailers to stock the new product. It is also important to decide how large the contribution of each promotion component will be; this will help determine the promotion budget.

Budgeting Approaches

Selecting an optimal budget for promotion expenditures is difficult because factors other than promotion influence sales. Isolating the effects of promotion may not be feasible due to lags in the impact of promotion on sales, the effects of other marketing program components (e.g., retailers' cooperation), and the influences of uncontrollable factors (e.g., competition, economic conditions). Realistically, budgeting in practice is likely to emphasize improving promotion effectiveness compared to past results. Because of this, more practical budgeting techniques are normally used. These methods include (1) objective and task, (2) percent of sales, (3) competitive parity, and (4) all you can afford. The same approaches are used to determine advertising and sales promotion budgets. The personal-selling budget is determined by the number of people in the sales force and their qualifications. Direct marketing budgets are guided by the unit costs of customer contact, such as cost per catalog mailed.

In many companies, the promotion budget may include only planned expenditures for advertising and sales promotion. Those companies typically develop separate budgets for the sales organization, which may contain sales promotion activities such as incentives for salespeople and channel members. Public relations budgets also are likely to be separate from promotion budgeting. Even so, it is important to consider the size and allocation of total promotion expenses when formulating the promotion strategy. Unless this is done, the integration of the components is likely to be fragmented.

An example of a promotion budget (excluding sales force and public relations) for a pharmaceutical product is shown in Exhibit 12–2. Note the relative size of advertising and sales promotion expenditures. Advertising accounts for only 28 percent of the total budget. The distribution of drug samples to doctors by salespeople accounts for a substantial amount of the promotion budget. Sampling is an important promotion component in this industry.

Objective and Task

This logical and cost-effective method is probably the most widely used budgeting approach. Management sets the communications objectives, determines the tasks necessary to achieve the objectives, and adds up the costs. This method also establishes the mix of

EXHIBIT 12–2
**Illustrative
Promotion
Budget for a
Pharmaceutical
Product**

Promotional Activity	2003 Budget
Promotional material	$135,000
Samples	270,000
Direct mail	203,000
Journal advertising	236,000
Total budget	$844,000

promotion components by selecting the component(s) appropriate for attaining each objective. Marketing management must carefully evaluate how the promotion objectives are to be achieved and choose the most cost-effective promotion components. The effectiveness of the objective and task method depends on the judgment and experience of the marketing team. The budget shown in Exhibit 12–2 was determined by using the objective and task method. The executives involved in the budgeting process included product managers, the division manager, sales management, and the chief marketing executive.

Percent of Sales

Using this method, the budget is calculated as a percent of sales and is therefore quite arbitrary. The percentage figure is often based on past expenditure patterns. The method fails to recognize that promotion efforts and results are related. For example, a budget of 10 percent of sales may be too much or not enough promotion expenditures to achieve forecasted sales. Budgeting by percent of sales can lead to too much spending on promotion when sales are high and too little when sales are low. In a cyclical industry where sales follow up-and-down trends, a strategy of increasing promotion expenditures during low sales periods may be more appropriate.

Competitive Parity

Promotion expenditures for this budgeting method are guided by how much competitors spend. A major shortcoming of the method is that differences in marketing strategy between competing firms may require different promotion strategies. For example, Revlon uses an intensive distribution strategy, while Estèe Lauder targets buyers by distributing through selected department stores. A comparison of the promotional strategies of these firms is not very meaningful, since their market targets, promotion objectives, and use of promotion components are different.

All You Can Afford

Since budget limits are a reality in most companies, this method is likely to influence all budget decisions. Top management may specify how much can be spent on promotion. For example, the guideline may be to increase the budget to 110 percent of last year's actual promotion expenditures. The objective and task method can be combined with the "all-you-can-afford" method by setting task priorities and allocating the budget to the higher-priority tasks.

   Research sponsored by the Marketing Science Institute indicates that in practice, promotion budgeting in consumer products firms involves a process that is a combination of rational, political, and expedient actions. The Cross-Functional Feature summarizes the study's findings.

Cross-Functional Feature Promotion Budget Setting in Action

Researchers' in-depth interviews with managers in consumer products firms provide interesting insights into actual budget setting processes. The budget components included advertising, consumer promotion, and trade promotion.

Budgets are developed by cross-functional teams of managers from brand/category management, sales, trade marketing, manufacturing, accounting, and marketing research. The teams conduct situation analyses as the basis for marketing plan development. Out of this process, marketing objectives and the brand strategy are determined. The brand manager also forecasts sales and profits based on the strategy.

Using the strategy guidelines, the team makes a preliminary allocation of the promotion budget to advertising, consumer promotion, and trade promotion, guided by post expenditures. The budget is then modified to take into account estimated competitors' promotions and other market-driven factors. Next, the brand plan is presented to top management (e.g., president, vice presidents of marketing and sales, and group managers, including finance).

Based on top management's assessment and changes, the plan is finalized and implemented. The brand manager is responsible for managing the promotion budget during the year, making necessary tactical adjustments based on competitive and market factors.

Source: George S. Low and Jakki J. Mohn, "The Advertising Sales Promotion Trade-off: Theory and Practice," Report No. 92-127 (Cambridge, MA: Marketing Science Institute, October 1992).

Integrating the Promotion Strategy Components

Several factors may affect the promotion mix, as shown by Exhibit 12–3. Advertising, public relations, personal selling, direct marketing, Internet, and sales promotion strategies are likely to be fragmented when responsibility is assigned to more than one department. Moreover, there are differences in priorities, and evaluating the productivity of the promotion components is complex. For example, coordination between selling and advertising is difficult in firms marketing to industrial buyers, and these firms tend to follow promotion strategies driven by personal selling. The separation of selling and advertising strategies also prevails in a variety of consumer products firms. An important marketing management issue is how to integrate the promotion strategy components.

Integrated marketing communications (IMC) strategies are replacing fragmented advertising, publicity, and sales programs. These approaches differ from traditional promotion strategies in several ways, as described by the following characteristics of IMC strategies in retailing:

1. IMC programs are comprehensive. Advertising, personal selling, retail atmospherics, behavioral modification programs, public relations, investor relations programs, employee communications, and other forms are all considered in the planning of an IMC.

2. IMC programs are unified. The messages delivered by all media, including such diverse influences as employee recruiting and the atmospherics of retailers on which the marketer primarily relies, are the same as or supportive of a unified theme.

3. IMC programs are targeted. The public relations program, advertising programs and dealer/distributor programs all have the same or related target markets.

EXHIBIT 12–3
**Illustrative
Factors Affecting
Promotion Strategy**

Advertising/sales promotion-driven	Balanced	Personal selling-driven
Large	Number and dispersion of buyers	Small
Low	Buyers' information needs	High
Small	Size and importance of purchase	Large
Channel	Distribution	Direct
Low	Product complexity	High
No	Postpurchase contact required	Yes

4. IMC programs have coordinated execution of all the communications components of the organization.

5. IMC programs emphasize productivity in reaching the designated targets when selecting communication channels and allocating resources to marketing media.[11]

The Gap, the apparel retailer, has been very successful in implementing an integrated marketing communications program.[12] Management positions the promotion components into the IMC program. Advertising plays a key role at the Gap, but other components are also important. The IMC is effectively combined with the marketing strategy components.

Developing and implementing integrated communications strategies is essential for manufacturers as well as retailers and for both consumer and business products. Effective management of these strategies has a positive impact on revenues and the productivity of promotion strategy.

Advertising and sales promotion strategies are examined in the remainder of the chapter to illustrate how these strategies are developed. Public relations is also a very important promotion component. Since these activities vary widely in scope and are similar in certain ways to advertising, they are not included in the discussion.

Advertising Strategy

Management's perception of how advertising can contribute to the promotion objectives has an important influence in determining the role of advertising. Estimating the impact of advertising on buyers helps management decide on advertising's role and scope in the marketing program and choose specific objectives. The Strategy Feature describes how Gillette positions its line of women's shaving products. These products account for one-fifth of Gillette's U.S. sales. Advertising plays a key role in Gillette's marketing strategy for women's shaving products.

Identifying and describing the target audience is the first step in developing an advertising strategy. Next, it is important to set specific objectives and decide on the advertising budget. There may be an adjustment (up or down) of this initial budget as the specific advertising activities are determined. The selection of the creative strategy follows, as illustrated by Gillette's "Are You Ready?" campaign. The creative strategy determines how the objectives will be accomplished. Specific messages need to be designed for each ad. Ads may be pretested (see the example later in the chapter). Choices of the advertising media and programming schedules implement the creative strategy. The final step is getting the advertising strategy under way and evaluating its effectiveness. We examine each of these activities, highlighting important features and strategy issues. In the discussion we assume that the target audience(s) has been selected.

Setting Advertising Objectives and Budgeting

Advertising Objectives

Exhibit 12–4 shows alternative levels for setting advertising objectives. In moving from the most general level (exposure) toward the most specific level (profit contribution), the objectives are increasingly more closely linked to the purchase decision. For example, knowing that advertising causes a measurable increase in sales is much more useful to the decision maker than knowing that a specific number of people are exposed to an advertising message. The key issue is whether the objectives at the general levels in Exhibit 12–4 are related to purchase behavior. For example, how much will exposure to the advertising increase the chances that people will purchase a product? The trade-off is that achievement of very general and midlevel objectives often can be measured, whereas the sales and profit impact of advertising may be very difficult to measure due to the effects of other factors on sales and profits. Because of these measurement problems, exposure and awareness objectives are used more often than are attitude change, sales, and profit objectives.

Wendy's International Inc. uses a value-based positioning strategy that emphasizes quality food at competitive prices.[13] The objective of Wendy's advertising is to offer buyers value and product choices. Ads often feature the founder, Dave Thomas, discussing how Wendy's provides value to customers, including a money-back guarantee to any customer who is not satisfied. By following the value strategy, Wendy's has avoided the fast-food industry's price wars.

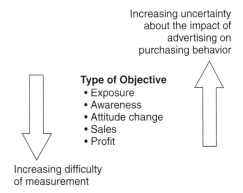

EXHIBIT 12–4
**Alternative Levels
for Setting
Advertising
Objectives**

Budget Determination

The budgeting methods for promotion discussed earlier in the chapter are also used in advertising budgeting. The objective and task method has a stronger supporting logic than do the other methods. Consider, for example, the Italian government's advertising program intended to position Italian fashion designers and craftsmen favorably as the world's finest.[14] The objectives were to increase Italy's share of U.S. imports and enhance the prestige of its brands. The Italian Trade Commission budgeted $25 million on advertising and other promotion activities in the five-year period through 1997 to achieve those objectives. The aggressive campaign generated positive results, with an increase in Italy's U.S. imported apparel share from 4.5 to 5.9 percent. Much larger increases were obtained by more expensive imports like Giorgio Armani.

Analytical models of sales response have been developed to help guide advertising budgeting decisions for frequently purchased consumer products.[15] One model uses multiple regression analysis with ad expenditures and other predictors for estimating brand sales. Data from several previous time periods are used to build the models. A key assumption is that historical relationships will hold in the future.

Budget determination, creative strategy, and media/programming strategy are closely interrelated, and so these decisions need to be coordinated. A preliminary budget may be set, subject to review after the creative and media/programming strategies are determined. Using objective and task budgeting, creative plans and media alternatives should be included in the budgeting process.

Creative Strategy

The creative strategy guides the advertising campaign, as illustrated earlier in the Gillette women's shaving products example. Two considerations may influence the strategy selection: (1) whether the campaign is intended to maintain or to change market conditions and (2) whether the campaign will communicate information or imagery and symbolism.[16] Maintenance and reinforcement strategies are used to support an established brand. A strategy to change market conditions may reposition a brand, expand the market for a brand, or launch a new product. Information messages communicate product benefits, whereas image messages seek to either reinforce or create change by using symbolism and imagery.

The creative strategy is guided by the market target and the desired positioning for the product or brand. In Chapter 6 we discussed positioning according to the *functions* performed by the brand, the *symbol* to be conveyed by the brand, or the *experience* provided by the brand. The creative theme seeks to effectively communicate the intended positioning to buyers and others influencing the purchase of the brand.

Several successful advertising campaign themes have been used for many years. Examples include Nike's "Just Do It," "You are in good hands with Allstate," "Intel inside," and Timex's "It takes a licking and keeps on ticking."[17] BMW has used "the ultimate driving machine" for more than 25 years. Interestingly, some of the highest-rated and lowest-rated ads have been created by the same advertising agency (we discuss the agency's role later in the chapter).

Creative advertising designs enhance the effectiveness of advertising by providing a unifying concept that binds together the various parts of an advertising campaign. Advertising agencies, which traditionally received 15 percent of gross billings, are experts in designing creative strategies. The agency professionals may design unique themes to position a product or firm in a particular way or use comparisons with the competition to enhance the firm's brands. Choosing the right creative theme for the marketing situation can make a major contribution to the success of a program. While tests are used to evaluate creative approaches, the task is more of an art than a science. Perhaps the best guide to creativity is an agency's track record.

The costs of developing ads can be substantial, particularly TV commercials. The average cost of making a national 30-second commercial in 1997 was $303,000, up 11 percent from 1996.[18] This cost excludes actors' fees, which averaged an additional $12,000 per ad. A 30-second commercial on the top four channels averaged $110,000 in 1997. These costs provide part of the motivation for companies to transfer resources to online advertising, such as banners and click-throughs, where production and media costs are much lower.

The creative strategy used for Murphy's Oil Soap shows the importance of a market segment focus and brand positioning through creative advertising. For nearly 100 years the soap was marketed in a single region of the United States.[19] Fourteen years after a national rollout program starting in 1976, the brand gained sixth position in its product category. Sales in 1990 increased to over $30 million, eight times more than in 1980. The brand is positioned as an effective wood cleaner. Its "Great Houses" advertising campaign portrays impressive old homes that highlight the beauty of wood and the special requirements of a wood-cleaning product. More recently, advertising and sales promotion have been positioning the soap as effective in "cleaning wood surfaces…and more."

Media/Scheduling Decisions

A company's advertising agency or media organization normally guides media selection and scheduling decisions. The agency or media organization has the experience and technical ability to match media and scheduling to the target audience specified by the firm. The media, timing, and programming for television and radio decisions are influenced largely by two factors: (1) access to the target audience(s) and (2) the costs of reaching the target group(s). A comparison of advertising rates for several media is shown below:[20]

Medium	Vehicle	Cost	Reach	CPM*
Television	30 seconds on network in prime time	$120,000	10 million households	$12
Consumer magazine	Page, four-color, in *Cosmopolitan*	$86,155	2.5 million paid readers	35
Online service	Banner on CompuServe's major-topic page	$10,000 per month	750,000 visitors	13
Website	Banner on Infoseek	$10,000 per month	500,000 page views per month	20

*CPM = cost per thousand exposures.

The audience coverage varies considerably, and so access to the target audience is also important. The various media provide extensive profile information on their viewers. *Standard Rates and Data Services* publishes advertising costs for various U.S. media. The costs are determined by circulation levels and the type of publication. In deciding which medium to use, it is important to evaluate the cost per exposure and the characteristics of the subscribers. The medium should provide coverage of the market target for the product or brand being advertised.

Media models are available to analyze allocations and decide which media mix best achieves one or more objectives.[21] These models typically use an exposure measure (Exhibit 12–4) as the basis for media allocation. For example, cost per thousand of exposure can be used to evaluate alternative media. The models also consider audience characteristics (e.g., age group composition) and other factors. The models are useful in selecting media when many advertising programs and a wide range of media are used.

Role of the Advertising Agency

Advertising agencies perform various functions for clients, including developing creative designs and selecting media. Full-service agencies offer a range of services, including marketing research, sales promotion, and marketing planning. The traditional basis of compensation is a 15 percent fee on media expenditures. For example, $1 million of advertising provides a commission of $150,000. The agency pays $850,000 for the media space and bills the client $1,000,000. Cash discounts for payment may be involved.

Agency Relationship

The normal basis of operation between a corporate client and the agency is a cooperative effort. The client briefs the agency on the marketing strategy and the role of advertising in the marketing program. In some instances agency executives may be involved in the development of the marketing strategy. The better the agency understands the company's marketing program, the more effective the agency can be in providing advertising services. The agency may assign one or more personnel full-time to a client with a large advertising budget.

Choosing an advertising agency is an important decision. It is also necessary to evaluate the relationship over time since a company's advertising requirements change. Good agency relationships are usually the result of teaming with an agency that has the capabilities and commitment needed by the client. Several factors which should be considered in evaluating an agency are shown in Exhibit 12–5.

Agency Compensation

Most agencies today operate on some type of commission or fee-based arrangement, though the arrangement may involve a commission for media placement and a separate arrangement for other services. For example, media placement would receive a 5 percent commission, whereas other services associated with the advertising would yield an additional 10 percent. These changes in the original 15 percent commission are the consequence of advertising specialists (e.g., media buying) offering reduced fees and negotiations by large advertisers in many parts of the world.

Clients may work out flexible payment arrangements with the agency. The agency may keep a record of its costs, and the client pays for the services it requires. The resulting compensation may be more or less than the traditional 15 percent commission. In some arrangements agencies may share cost savings with the client.

EXHIBIT 12–5
Checklist for Evaluating Advertising Agencies

Rate each agency on a scale from 1 (strongly negative) to 10 (strongly positive).

General Information
- ☐ Size compatible with our needs.
- ☐ Strength of management.
- ☐ Financial stability.
- ☐ Compatibility with other clients.
- ☐ Range of services.
- ☐ Cost of services; billing policies.

Marketing Information
- ☐ Ability to offer marketing counsel.
- ☐ Understanding of the markets we serve.
- ☐ Experience dealing in our market.
- ☐ Success record; case histories.

Creative Abilities
- ☐ Well-thought-out creativity; relevance to strategy.
- ☐ Art strength.
- ☐ Copy strength.
- ☐ Overall creative quality.
- ☐ Effectiveness compared to work of competitors.

Production
- ☐ Faithfulness to creative concept and execution.
- ☐ Diligence to schedules and budgets.
- ☐ Ability to control outside services.

Media
- ☐ Existence and soundness of media research.
- ☐ Effective and efficient media strategy.
- ☐ Ability to achieve objectives within budget.
- ☐ Strength at negotiating and executing schedules.

Personality
- ☐ Overall personality, philosophy, or position.
- ☐ Compatibility with client staff and management.
- ☐ Willingness to assign top people to account.

References
- ☐ Rating by current clients.
- ☐ Rating by past clients.
- ☐ Rating by media and financial sources.

Source: William F. Arens, *Contemporary Advertising,* 6th ed. (Burr Ridge, IL: Richard D. Irwin, 1996), 93.

Industry Composition

Large, full-service agencies like Dentsu in Tokyo and Young and Rubicam in New York account for the dominant proportion of billings. Nonetheless, several local and regional agencies have created pressures for change throughout the industry. Concerns of clients about arbitrary commission rates and lack of flexibility in client services have led to placing business with small specialty agencies which provide media buying, creative design, and other services. There are many local and regional agencies that serve small and medium-size clients.

Problem Areas

A company does not like an agency to serve clients competing in the same industry. The agency requires access to sensitive information (e.g., sales by product line and by geographic area) in order to effectively serve the client. The advertiser is hesitant to share confidential information when the agency has clients that are viewed as competitors. In the case of large accounts, agencies do not work with competing clients. Achieving this objective is more difficult in working with companies that have smaller advertising budgets. It is important when selecting an agency to determine who its clients are and what sort of policies the agency has concerning serving clients that are competitors.

Implementing the Advertising Strategy and Measuring Its Effectiveness

Before the advertising strategy is implemented, it is advisable to establish the criteria which will be used for measuring advertising effectiveness. Advertising expenditures are wasted if firms spend too much or allocate expenditures improperly. Measuring effectiveness provides necessary feedback for future advertising decisions. Importantly, the quality of advertising can be as critical to getting results as is the amount of advertising.

Tracking Advertising Performance

As previously discussed, the impact of advertising on sales may be difficult to measure because other factors also influence sales and profits. Most efforts to measure effectiveness consider objectives such as attitude change, awareness, and exposure (Exhibit 12–4). Comparing objectives and results helps managers decide when to stop or alter advertising campaigns. Services such as Nielsen's TV ratings are available for the major media. These ratings have a critical impact on the allocation of advertising dollars, although recent research findings question the accuracy of the ratings. Various measurement concerns have resulted in several changes in the rating process.

A TV rating service is available from Statistical Research Inc. (SRI). Its other services include radio audience measurement, use of the Yellow Pages, and people's reactions to fund-raising drives.[22] The TV measurement system uses sensors and is connected to existing wiring in the household. Household participants record their responses before and after watching TV. Viewing results are made available to business subscribers on their computers. SRI's pilot measurement program includes 29 sponsors. The plan was to roll out the service nationally in 2001 at an estimated cost of $100 million.

Methods of Measuring Effectiveness

Several methods are used to evaluate advertising results. Analysis of historical data identifies relationships between advertising expenditures and sales by using statistical techniques such as regression analysis. Recall tests measure consumers' awareness of specific ads and campaigns by asking questions to determine if a sample of people remember an ad. Longitudinal studies track advertising expenditures and sales results before, during, and after an advertising campaign. Controlled tests are a form of longitudinal study in which extraneous effects are measured and/or controlled during the test. Test marketing can be used to evaluate advertising effectiveness. Effort/results models use empirical data to build a mathematical relationship between sales and advertising effort.

Consumer panels provide a useful method for measuring advertising effectiveness for frequently purchased consumer food and drug products in cities with cable TV. The panel consists of a group of consumers who agree to provide information about their purchases on a continuing basis. Cash register scanning of the purchases of panel members provides data on brands purchased, prices, and other information. Samples of consumers can be split into groups that are exposed or not exposed to advertising on cable television. Using equivalent samples, the influence on sales of factors other than advertising can be controlled. The difference in sales between the control and the experimental (exposed) groups over the test period measures the effect of advertising.

Advertising research is used for more than just measuring the effectiveness of advertising. Research can be used for various activities in advertising strategy development, including generating and evaluating creative ideas and concepts and pretesting concepts, ideas, and specific ads.

An example of a popular test used to evaluate TV commercials is shown in Exhibit 12–6. The test commercial is shown in several test cities. After the commercial is shown, a sample of people who viewed the program is asked several questions to determine reactions to the commercial. The basis of the evaluation is the respondent's recall about the commercial. While such tests have been criticized because they do not evaluate ad quality or relevance, recall continues to be the primary way commercials are evaluated.

EXHIBIT 12–6
How TV Commercials Are Tested

Source: William R. Dillon, Thomas J. Madden, and Neil H. Firtle, *Marketing Research in a Marketing Environment,* 3rd ed. (Burr Ridge, IL: Richard D. Irwin, 1994), 612.

Brand:	Juicy Fruit.
Project:	"False Start" Burke on-air test.
Background and objectives:	The William Wrigley Company has requested a Burke on-air test for the new copy execution of "False Start." The objective of this research is to measure the communication effectiveness of the "False Start" execution.
Research method:	A sample of 150 past-30-day chewing gum users in the commercial audience will be interviewed. The air date is scheduled for the first Tuesday of the month in December, on "NYPD Blue." Interviewing will be conducted within five metro areas: Boston, Atlanta, Indianapolis, Dallas, and Phoenix.
Information to be obtained:	—Total commercial recall. —Copy recall. —Visual recall.
Action standard:	The commercial will be considered acceptable in the areas of memorability and sales message communication if: a. It generates 25 or better related recall score. b. At least 25 of the commercial audience remembers at least one sales message.
Timing and cost:	Fieldwork first Tuesday in December Top line 1 week Final report 4 weeks The cost for this research will be $15,000 ± 10%.
Research supplier:	Burke Marketing Research.

Sales Promotion Strategy

Sales promotion expenditures are increasing more rapidly than is advertising in many companies.[23] Manufacturers' expenditures for sales promotion are estimated to be as high as 75 percent of the total spent on the two promotion components. Both advertising and sales promotions are receiving major attention by companies in their attempts to boost productivity and reduce costs. With marketing expenditures accounting for one-third or more of total sales in many companies, the bottom-line impact of improving the effectiveness of promotion expenditures and/or lowering costs is substantial.

Sales promotion activities provide extra value or incentives to consumers and value-chain participants.[24] The intent is to encourage immediate sales. Managers often use the term *promotion* when referring to sales promotion activities. Sales promotion is some form of inducement (e.g., coupon, contest, rebate). It is intended to accelerate the selling process to build sales volume. Importantly, sales promotion activities can be targeted to various points of influence in the value chain.

We look at the nature and scope of sales promotion, the types of sales promotion activities, the advantages and limitations of sales promotion, and the decisions that make up sales promotion strategy.

Nature and Scope of Sales Promotion

Japanese companies employ an interesting form of promotion—showrooms that have hands-on new product displays.[25] The intent is to give people an opportunity to examine new products placed in attractive surroundings. The items displayed are not for sale in the showrooms. The sponsors want potential buyers to see the products, try them out, and become familiar with their features. For example, the Matsushita Electric Works showroom has a state-of-the-art home displaying the newest Japanese furnishings and appliances as well as many gadgets.

The responsibility for sales promotion activities often involves several marketing functions, such as advertising, merchandising, product planning, and sales. For example, a sales contest for salespeople is typically designed and administered by sales managers, and the costs of the contest are included in the sales department budget. Similarly, planning and coordinating a sampling or coupon refund program may be assigned to a product manager. Point-of-purchase promotion displays in retail stores may be handled by the field sales organization. Growth in the use of this form of sales promotion has led to the use of outsourced field marketing companies by some organizations.

Total expenditures for sales promotion by business and industry in the United States are much larger than the total spent on advertising, probably exceeding $300 billion. The complete scope of sales promotion is often difficult to identify because the activities are included in various departments and budgets.

A relevant issue is deciding how to manage the various sales promotion activities. While these programs are used to support advertising, pricing, channel of distribution, and personal selling strategies, the size and scope of sales promotion suggest that the responsibility for managing sales promotion should be assigned to one executive or a team of executives. Otherwise, sales promotion activities may not be properly integrated with other promotion components. The chief marketing executive should coordinate and evaluate sales promotion activities as part of the marketing program.

Sales Promotion Activities

Many activities may fit into the total promotion program, including trade shows, specialty advertising (e.g., imprinted calendars), contests, point-of-purchase displays, coupons, recognition programs (e.g., awards to value-chain members), and free samples. Expenditures for sales promotion may be very substantial. Companies may direct their sales-promotion activities to consumer buyers, industrial buyers, middlemen, and salespeople, as shown in Exhibit 12–7. Sales promotion programs fall into three major categories: incentives, promotional pricing, and informational activities.

Promotion to Consumer Targets

Sales promotion is used in the marketing of many consumer goods and services. It includes a wide variety of activities, as illustrated in Exhibit 12–7. A key management concern is evaluating the effectiveness of promotions such as coupons, rebates, contests, and other awards. The large expenditures necessary to support these programs require that the results and costs be objectively assessed.

Information technology offers important insights into the productivity of promotion programs.[26] For example, sophisticated checkout scanner data analyses can be used to indicate trade and consumer promotions that perform well (or poorly). This information helps in shifting promotion spending to more productive programs, customer groups, and product categories. Promotion programs can be evaluated on a financial basis by combining customer response data with cost information.

EXHIBIT 12–7
Sales Promotion Activities Targeted to Various Groups

Sales Promotion Activity	Targeted To:			
	Consumer Buyers	Industrial Buyers	Channel Members	Salespeople
Incentives				
Contests	X	X	X	X
Trips	X	X	X	X
Bonuses			X	X
Prizes	X	X	X	X
Advertising support			X	
Free items	X	X		
Recognition			X	X
Promotional Pricing				
Coupons	X			
Allowances		X	X	
Rebates	X	X	X	
Cash	X			
Informational Activities				
Displays	X			
Demonstrations	X	X	X	
Selling aids			X	X
Specialty advertising (e.g., pens)	X	X	X	
Trade shows	X	X	X	

The sponsoring of sports events and individuals is a major initiative by various companies and brands. Sales promotion results from the association of the brand with the event or person. An example is PepsiCo's sponsorship of the Pepsi 400 NASCAR race. Similarly, sports celebrities may be sponsored, such as the cyclist Lance Armstrong in the Tour de France. The strategy issue is determining the benefits versus costs of these sales promotion activities.

Promotion to Industrial Targets

Many sales promotion methods that are used for consumer products also apply to industrial products, although the role and scope of the methods may vary. For example, trade shows perform a key role in small and medium-size companies' marketing strategies. The advantage of the trade show is the heavy concentration of potential buyers at one location during a very short time period. The cost per contact is much less than that of a salesperson calling on prospects at their offices. While people attending trade shows also spend their time viewing competitors' products, an effective display and buyer/seller interactions offer a unique opportunity to hold the prospects' attention.

The Internet has many of the features of trade shows while eliminating some of their limitations. For example, the Web enables the French woolens manufacturer Carreman to provide its customers with fabric samples in one day. Carreman's interesting Internet initiatives are described in the Internet Feature.

Sales promotion programs that target industrial buyers may consume a greater portion of the marketing budget than advertising does. Many of these activities support personal

Francois Morel is the prototypical New Economy European fashion executive. The CEO of Castres-based Carreman, France's second-largest woolens manufacturer, has embraced the Web as a way to boost his company's fortunes. But, knowing that he can't thrive unless the entire European textile industry changes the way it operates, Morel signed up as an early client of Etexx. The year-old startup, based in Nice, has created an e-marketplace where buyers and sellers of fabrics get news, exchange product info, and, starting this month, will buy and sell goods.

Indeed, Carreman is the guinea pig for this grand experiment. The company posted its top 40-odd fabrics on the Etexx site for online sample ordering—cutting the time it takes to get samples into customers' hands from many weeks to one day. Morel has no illusions that this overhaul will be easy or quick. "Textile industry people are truly stuck in the age of Emile Zola," the 19th century French novelist, he quips. Yet he's optimistic: The majority of Carreman's clients are avid Internet users, so it's just a matter of time before they, too, join the grand experiment.

Source: "Streamlining," *Business Week E.Biz,* September 18, 2000, EB70.

selling strategies. They include catalogs, brochures, product information reports, samples, trade shows, application guides, and promotional items such as calendars, pens, and calculators.

Promotion to Value-Chain Members

Sales promotion is an important part of manufacturers' marketing efforts to wholesalers and retailers for such products as foods, beverages, and appliances. Catalogs and other product information are essential promotional components for many lines. The Internet offers an alternative way to make catalog information available. Promotional pricing is often used to push new products through channels of distribution. Various incentives are popular in marketing to middlemen. Specialty advertising items such as calendars and memo pads are used in maintaining buyer awareness of brands and company names.

Promotion to the Sales Force

Incentives and informational activities are the primary forms of promotion used to assist and motivate company sales forces. Sales contests and prizes are popular. Companies also make wide use of recognition programs like the "Salesperson of the Year." Promotional information is vital to salespeople. Presentation kits help salespeople describe new products and the features of existing products.

A high-tech promotion tool with exciting potential is the automated sales presentation created with the integrated use of sound, graphics, and video briefcase computers. These multimedia or interactive techniques give salespeople powerful presentation capabilities, allowing them to have access to a complete product information system in the notebook computer.

Suppose an Acme Bicycle sales representative is trying to close a sale with a major sporting goods dealership.[27] Acme produces high-quality bicycles and accessories. The salesperson's multimedia package contains videos of bikes in action, photographs of the

419

product line, information on competing models, and text describing key product features. The salesperson's presentation to three executives of the firm is described below.[28]

- A short sound video shows riders who match the profile of the dealership's target customers and discusses the features of a high-performance bicycle.

- The salesperson describes Acme's products in words, pictures, and animated graphics.

- The dealer's chief mechanic has reservations about the pedals on the bike shown in the presentation.

- The salesperson counters this objection with a display of several alternative pedal designs available on Acme Bicycles.

- The owner asks for a comparison of Acme's prices and features with those of competitors.

- At the close of the meeting, the salesperson promises a proposal for later that day.

- The salesperson uses the notebook's proposal generator to prepare a customized proposal.

- The proposal is sent to Acme headquarters for approval and returned to the dealer by fax.

Given the features and flexibility of interactive multimedia promotion, it is not surprising that it is an essential selling tool for many products.

Advantages and Limitations of Sales Promotion

Because of its wide array of incentive, pricing, and communication capabilities, sales promotion has the flexibility to contribute to various marketing objectives. A marketing manager can target buyers, intermediaries, and salespeople and can measure the sales response of the sales promotion activities to determine their effectiveness. For example, a company can track its coupon redemption or rebate success. Many incentive and price promotion techniques trigger the purchase of other products.

Sales promotion is not without disadvantages, however. In most instances, rather than substituting for advertising and personal selling, sales promotion supports other promotional efforts. Control is essential to prevent people from taking advantage of free offers, coupons, and other incentives. Value-added resellers may build inventories on products receiving manufacturers' trade discounts. Incentives and price-promotional activities need to be monitored. An effective advertisement can be run thousands of times, but promotional campaigns are usually not reusable. Thus, the costs of development must be evaluated in advance.

Sales Promotion Strategy

The steps in developing the sales promotion strategy are similar to those in the design of advertising strategy. It is necessary to first define the communications task(s) that the sales promotion program is expected to accomplish. Next, specific promotion objectives are set regarding awareness levels and purchase intentions. It is important to evaluate the relative cost-effectiveness of feasible sales promotion methods and select those that offer the best results/cost combination. Both the content of the sales promotion and its timing should be coordinated with other promotion activities. Finally, the program is implemented and is evaluated on a continuing basis. Evaluation measures the extent to which objectives are achieved. For example, trade show results can be evaluated to determine how many show contacts are converted to purchases.

Summary

Promotion strategy is a vital part of the positioning strategy. The components—advertising, sales promotion, publicity, personal selling, and direct marketing—offer an impressive array of capabilities for communicating with market targets and other relevant audiences. However, promotion activities are expensive. Management must decide on the size of the promotion budget and allocate it to the communications components. Each promotion activity offers certain unique advantages and also shares several characteristics with the other components. The major budgeting methods are objective and task, percent of sales, competitive parity, and all you can afford. Several product and market factors affect whether the promotion strategy will emphasize advertising, sales promotion, personal selling, or a balance between the forms of promotion. The effective integration of communications mixes is a major challenge for many firms today.

The steps in developing advertising strategy include identifying the target audience, deciding on the role of advertising in the promotional mix, indicating advertising objectives and budget size, selecting the creative strategy, determining the media and programming schedule, and implementing the program and measuring its effectiveness. Advertising objectives may range from audience exposure to profit contribution. Advertising agencies offer specialized services for developing creative strategies, designing messages, and selecting media and programming strategies. Measuring advertising effectiveness is essential in managing this expensive resource.

Our discussion of sales promotion highlights several methods which are available for use as incentives, advertising support, and informational activities. Typically, firms use sales promotion activities in conjunction with advertising and personal selling rather than as a primary component of promotion strategy. Promotion programs may target consumer buyers, industrial buyers, middlemen, and salespeople. Sales promotion strategy should be based on the selection of methods which provide the best results/cost combinations for achieving the communications objectives.

Internet Applications

A. Discuss how Godiva Chocolatier's website (*www.godiva.com*) corresponds to the brand image portrayed by its retail stores. What are the promotion objectives that Godiva's management seems to be pursuing on the website?

B. Go the websites of NBC and the BBC (*www.nbc.com* and *www.bbc.co.uk*). Contrast the ways NBC and the BBC promote their daily TV programs online. Which similarities and differences do you detect? Suggest ways of improvement considering the respective cultural frames of reference and target markets for NBC and the BBC.

C. Go to the website of Six Continents Hotels (*www.sixcontinentshotels.com*). Investigate the different product types (hotel brands) and examine the respective target market segments for each hotel brand. How should the promotion strategy differ for each brand? Suggest methods for co-marketing and mutual brand reinforcement.

Questions for Review and Discussion

1. Compare and contrast the role of promotion in an international public accounting firm with promotion by American Airlines.

2. Identify and discuss the factors that are important in determining the promotion mix for the following products:

    a. Videotape recorder/player.

    b. Personal computer

    c. Boeing 777 commercial aircraft.

    d. Residential homes.

3. What are the important considerations in determining a promotion budget?

4. Under what conditions is a firm's promotion strategy more likely to be advertising/sales promotion-driven rather than personal selling-driven?

5. Discuss the advantages and limitations of using awareness as an advertising objective. When might this objective be appropriate?

6. Identify and discuss the important differences between advertising and sales promotion strategies in the marketing promotion strategy.

7. Coordination of advertising and personal selling strategies is a major challenge in large companies. Outline a plan for integrating these strategies.

8. Discuss the role of sales promotion methods in the promotion strategy of a major airline.

9. How and to what extent is the Internet likely to be useful in companies' promotion strategies?

Notes

1. This illustration is based on "Jaguar May Find It's a Jungle Out There," *Business Week,* March 26, 2001, 62.

2. "Ads as Far as the Eye Can See," *Business Week,* June 12, 2000, 54; Sally Beatty and Yumiko Ono, "U.S. May Outpace World '98 Outlays," *The Wall Street Journal,* December 9, 1997, B12; Vanessa O'Connell, "Ad Slump May Be Worse Than Thought," *The Wall Street Journal,* August 14, 2001, B2.

3. Jim Fuquay, "Drugmakers Prescribe Higher Doses of Advertising to Avoid Revenue Decline," *Fort Worth Star Telegram,* September 3, 1995, B1.

4. Gardiner Harris, "Drug Makers Go Hollywood, Finding Marketing Pays," *The Wall Street Journal,* July 6, 2000, 1.

5. Gilbert A. Churchill, Jr., Neil M. Ford, Orville C. Walker, Jr., Mark W. Johnston, and John F. Tanner, *Sales Force Management,* 6th ed. (Chicago: Richard D. Irwin, 2000), 37.

6. "Exclusive Interview: Mike Gunn of American Airlines," *Colloquy* 3, no. 2 (1992), 8–10.

7. "Downloading Their Dream Cars," *Business Week,* March 9, 1998, 93–94; Brandon Michener, "Mercedes Dealers Offer New Kind of Test Drive," *The Wall Street Journal,* March 26, 1998, B8.

8. "SIA Presses for Higher Yields with New Aircraft, IFE Systems," *Aviation Week & Space Technology,* June 4, 2001, 69–70.

9. "Singapore Airlines: Flying Beauty," *The Economist,* December 14, 1991, 74.

10. Betsy McKay, "PepsiCo Bases Water Ads on 'Nothing,'" *The Wall Street Journal,* June 25, 2001, B10.

11. Roger D. Blackwell, *From Mind to Market* (New York: HarperBusiness, 1997), 182–83.

12. Ibid.

13. Marilyn Much, "How Wendy's Avoids Burger Industry Price Wars," *Investor's Business Dailey,* April 11, 1994, 4.

14. Wendy Bounds and Deborah Ball, "Italy Knits Support for Fashion Industry," *The Wall Street Journal,* December 15, 1997, B8.

15. Advertising budgeting models are discussed in Gary L. Lilien, Philip Kotler, and Sridhar Moerlhy, *Marketing Models* (Englewood Cliffs, NJ: Prentice-Hall, 1992), chap. 6.

16. Henry Assael, *Marketing Management: Strategy and Action* (Boston: PWS-Kent Publishing, 1985), 392.

17. George E. Belch and Michael A. Belch, *Advertising and Promotion,* 5th ed. (New York: Irwin/McGraw-Hill, 2001), 262.

18. Sally Beatty, "Cost of Making a TV Commercial Leaped 11% in 1997, Survey Shows," *The Wall Street Journal,* August 19, 1998, B6.

19. D. John Loden, Megabrands (Homewood, IL.: Business One Irwin, 1992), 188–90.

20. Belch and Belch, *Advertising and Promotion,* 517.

21. Roland T. Rust, *Advertising Media Models* (Lexington, MA: D. C. Heath, 1986).

22. Michelle Wirth Fellman, "A Smart Move: 'Boutique' Firm Breaks Out in TV Ratings Game," *Marketing News,* September 24, 1998, 1, 7, 43.

23. George S. Low and Jakki J. Mohr, "Advertising vs. Sales Promotion: A Brand Management Perspective," *Journal of Product & Brand Management* 9, no. 6 (2000), 389–414; Andrew J. Parsons, "Focus and Squeeze: Consumer Marketing in the '90s," *Marketing Management,* Winter 1992, 51–55.

24. Belch and Belch, *Advertising and Promotion,* chap. 16.

25. Mary Roach, "Attack of the Killer Showroom," *American Way,* November 15, 1995, 108, 110, 112.

26. Parsons, "Focus and Squeeze."

27. Jeff Anderson, "Mastering Multimedia," *Sales & Marketing Management,* January 1993, 55–58.

28. Ibid.

Chapter 13

Sales Force, Internet, and Direct Marketing Strategies

Salespeople make face-to-face contact with buyers, whereas direct marketing reaches customers by phone, mail, television, and computer. The Internet is rapidly becoming an important avenue of direct contact between customers and companies selling goods and services. While quite different in execution, these methods of customer contact enable an organization to communicate one on one with buyers. Companies may use a combination of salespeople, direct marketing, and the Internet to make customer contacts. Coordinating an organization's activities across multiple customer contact initiatives is essential to avoid conflicts and enhance the overall results.

The growth of Internet strategies is affecting the traditional role of salespeople, particularly in companies that sell business-to-business products. Sales of computers and other high-technology hardware via the Internet are expected to expand very rapidly during the next few years. Wholesaling of office supplies, electronics goods, and scientific equipment is another high-growth area. Customer interactions may vary with the product and the amount purchased. For example, large customers may be given access to customized pricing and product information. The consequences for face-to-face personal selling are that the Internet will replace salespeople in some selling situations while improving the effectiveness of face-to-face selling in many other situations (see the accompanying salesforce.com website). Companies are increasingly examining how the Internet and other technologies can provide effective ways to meet customers' requirements. Salespeople will be utilized in selling situations that require person-to-person direct contact and interaction.[1] Personal selling is likely to evolve into more of a consulting role in customer relationship management.

Office Depot Inc. is an interesting example of a company that has successfully implemented an Internet strategy while avoiding conflict with the large direct sales force of its Business Services Group that sells to medium-size to large organizational customers. The company's Internet strategy is described in the E-Business Feature.

In this chapter we first discuss developing and implementing sales force strategy. Next, we consider the issues and initiatives concerning Internet strategy. Finally, we describe and illustrate the various methods used in direct marketing.

Developing and Implementing Sales Force Strategy

The sales force strategy considers the issue of how to use personal selling to contact sales prospects and build the kinds of customer relationships that management considers necessary to accomplish the organization's marketing objectives. Personal selling activities vary considerably across companies, based on how personal selling contributes to the marketing positioning strategy and promotion strategy. For example, a drug company salesperson maintains regular contact with doctors and other professionals, but actual purchases are made at the retail outlets where the prescriptions are filled. The drug salesperson provides information on new products, distributes samples, and works toward building long-term relationships.

Developing sales force strategy includes six major steps. First, the role of the sales force in the promotion strategy is determined. This requires deciding how personal selling is expected to contribute to the marketing program. Second, the selling process is determined, indicating how selling will be accomplished with targeted customers. Third, in selecting sales channels, management decides how field selling, major account management, telemarketing, and the Internet will contribute to the selling process. Fourth, the design of a new sales organization is determined or the effectiveness of the existing organization is evaluated. Fifth, salespeople are recruited, trained, and managed. Sixth, the results of the selling strategy are evaluated and adjustments are made to narrow the gap between actual and desired results.

- Using a seamless network, Web operations are integrated into Office Depot's existing businesses.

- An easy-to-use electronic link is provided between the online store and companies' internal networks.

- Purchasing authorizations and limits are incorporated into the system.

- Ease of use rather than technology is a key priority for improving the online network.

- Bonuses are offered to salespeople to encourage corporate customers to use online ordering.

- Sales applicants are tested concerning Internet familiarity and informed of the importance of Office Depot's online initiatives.

- With nearly $1 billion in sales in 2000 (and $1.5 billion expected in 2001), Office Depot is second in online sales to Amazon.Com Inc., and the online business was profitable in its first year.

Source: Charles Haddad, "Office Depot's E-Diva," *Business Week E.Biz,* August 6, 2001, EB22–EB24.

The Role of Selling in Promotion Strategy

Salespeople's responsibilities may range from being order takers to having a major involvement as consultants to customers. While management has some flexibility in choosing the role and objectives of the sales force in the marketing program, several factors often shape the role of selling in a firm's marketing strategy. These factors are shown in Exhibit 13–1. Considerable direction for the role of personal selling is provided by the target market, product characteristics, distribution policies, and pricing policies. The selling effort needs to be integrated into the overall communications program. It is also useful to indicate how the other promotion-mix components, such as advertising, support and relate to the sales force. Sales management needs to be aware of the plans and activities of other promotion components.

The objectives assigned to salespeople frequently involve management's expected sales results. Sales quotas are used to state these expectations. Companies may give incentives to salespeople who achieve their quotas. Team selling incentives may also be used. Objectives other than sales are important in many organizations. These objectives include increasing the number of new accounts, providing services to customers and channel organizations, retaining customers, selecting and evaluating middlemen, and obtaining market information. The objectives selected need to be consistent with marketing strategy and promotion objectives and measurable so that sales performance can be evaluated.

Sales & Marketing Management uses four categories of responsibilities to define the range of personal selling roles. The categories are as follows:[2]

- *Transactional Selling:* Selling is largely based on price, and the products involved are often commodities.

- *Feature/Benefit Selling:* In these selling situations, price and features are equally important.

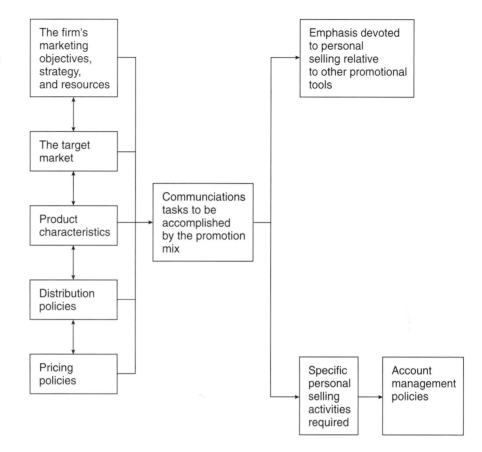

EXHIBIT 13–1
Factors Influencing the Role of Personal Selling in a Firm's Marketing Strategy

Source: Gilbert A. Churchill, Jr., Neil M. Ford, Orville C. Walker, Jr., Mark W. Johnston, and John F. Tanner, Jr., *Sales Force Management,* 6th ed. (Burr Ridge, IL: Richard D. Irwin, 2000), 38.

- *Solution Selling:* The product is matched to clients' needs, and price is secondary to obtaining a successful product application.

- *Value-Added Selling:* These situations involve consulting-type relationships using team approaches. Price is relevant but is not the driver.

Not surprisingly, compensation is highest for value-added selling ($172,000 average in 2000, compared to $87,500 for transactional selling). The Internet is replacing salespeople in transactional selling, whereas it is more likely to provide support for the other three categories.

Types of Sales Jobs

The salespeople who sell to ultimate consumers (door-to-door sales, insurance sales, real estate brokers, retail store sales, etc.) account for a major portion of the number of salespeople, but a much greater volume of sales is accounted for by industrial (organizational or business-to-business) salespeople.[3] Industrial sales may be to resellers (e.g., retail chains), business users, and institutions. Consumer and industrial sales are similar in several respects, but industrial sales may involve more complex products, larger and more complex purchasing processes, different selling skills, and more extensive management processes (e.g., training, coaching, directing, and evaluating).

Illustrative sales positions for industrial salespeople include new business selling, trade selling, missionary selling, and consultative/technical selling.[4]

New Business Selling

This selling job involves obtaining sales from new buyers. The buyers may be one-time purchasers or repeat buyers. For example, recruiting a new online business customer by an Office Depot salesperson is an illustration of a one-time selling situation. Alternatively, the selling strategy may be concerned with obtaining new buyers on a continuing basis. Commercial insurance and real estate sales firms use this strategy.

Trade Selling

This form of selling provides assistance and support to value-chain members rather than obtaining sales. A manufacturer marketing through wholesalers, retailers, or other intermediaries may provide merchandising, logistical, promotional, and product information assistance. Grocery wholesalers' salespeople assist retailers in merchandising and provide other support activities. Distribution channel selling activities in Wal-Mart and Deere & Co. channels are described in Exhibit 13–2.

Missionary Selling

A strategy similar to trade selling is missionary selling. A manufacturer's salespeople work with the customers of a channel member to encourage them to purchase the manufacturer's product from the channel member. For example, pharmaceutical sales representatives contact physicians, providing them with product information and samples and encouraging them to prescribe the producer's drugs.

Consultative/Technical Selling Strategy

Firms that use this strategy sell to an existing customer base and provide technical and application assistance. These positions may involve the sales of complex equipment or services such as management consulting. The selling of commercial aircraft to airlines is illustrative.

An organization may use more than one of these selling strategies. For example, a transportation services company might use a new business strategy to expand its customer base and a missionary selling strategy to service existing customers. The skills needed by the salesperson vary according to the selling strategy used.

Several changes are under way in many sales organizations.[5] The reforming process requires redesigning the traditional sales organization, leveraging information technology to lower costs and provide quick response, designing the sales strategy to meet different customer needs, and building long-term relationships with customers and business partners. The sales force continues to be a key contributor in many organizations, but salespeople are being asked to assume new responsibilities and the methods for keeping score are changing. An interesting analysis of the changes occurring in both consumer and business marketing is shown in the Strategy Feature. This feature highlights the emerging emphasis on customer management and the use of direct marketing methods (databases) in combination with personal selling activities (processes).

Defining the Selling Process

Several selling and sales support activities are involved in moving from identifying a buyer's needs to completing the sale and managing the postsale relationship between buyer and seller. This selling process includes (1) prospecting for customers, (2) opening the relationship, (3) qualifying the prospect, (4) presenting the sales message, (5) closing the sale, and (6) servicing the account.[6] The process may be very simple, consisting of a routine set of actions designed to close the sale. Alternatively, the process may extend over a long time

EXHIBIT 13–2
**Examples of
Distribution
Channel Selling
Activities**

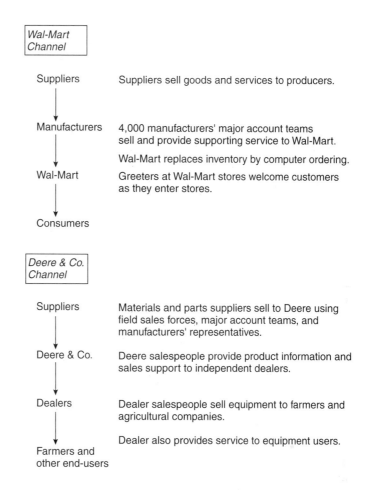

Wal-Mart Channel

Suppliers — Suppliers sell goods and services to producers.

↓

Manufacturers — 4,000 manufacturers' major account teams sell and provide supporting service to Wal-Mart.

Wal-Mart replaces inventory by computer ordering.

↓

Wal-Mart — Greeters at Wal-Mart stores welcome customers as they enter stores.

↓

Consumers

Deere & Co. Channel

Suppliers — Materials and parts suppliers sell to Deere using field sales forces, major account teams, and manufacturers' representatives.

↓

Deere & Co. — Deere salespeople provide product information and sales support to independent dealers.

↓

Dealers — Dealer salespeople sell equipment to farmers and agricultural companies.

Dealer also provides service to equipment users.

↓

Farmers and other end-users

period, with many contacts and interactions between the buyers, other people who influence the purchase, the salesperson assigned to the account, and technical specialists in the seller's organization. Recall the different selling roles discussed earlier, which range from routine actions (transactional selling) to consulting relationships (value-added selling).

The selling process changes made by i2 Technologies Inc. highlight the importance of this phase of sales force strategy. The company provides software and consulting services to corporate clients for supply chain, product life cycle, and customer relationship management. Management's selling process initiatives in responding to unfavorable economic conditions are described in the Technology Feature.

Sales management determines the selling process by indicating the customer and prospects the firm is targeting and the guidelines for developing customer relationships and obtaining sales results. This process represents management's strategy for achieving the sales force objectives in the selling environment of interest. Salespeople implement the process by following the guidelines set by management, such as the product strategy (relative emphasis on different products), customer targeting and priorities, and desired selling activities and outcomes.

The selling process normally is managed by the salesperson who has the responsibility for a customer account, although an increasing number of companies are assigning this

Decaying: **The Old Consumer Marketing Paradigm**	Emerging: **New Common Paradigm**	Decaying: **The Old Business Marketing Paradigm**
Broadcast communication, hard to customize	Conversations managed from the center	Communication in the field, hard to standardize
Segments	Markets of one	Territories
Market share	Share of customer	Account potential
Survey research	Transaction databases	Call reports
Products	Processes	Products
Brand equity	Customer equity	Account profitability
Brand managers	Customer relationship managers	Account managers

Source: John Deighton, "Commentary on Exploring the Implications of the Internet for Consumer Marketing," *Journal of the Academy of Marketing Science,* Fall 1997, 350.

responsibility to customer relationship management teams. Account management includes the planning and execution of the selling activities between the salesperson and the customer or prospect. Some organizations analyze this process and set guidelines for use by salespeople to plan their selling activities. Process analysis may result in programmed selling steps or, alternatively, may lead to highly customized selling approaches where the salesperson develops specific strategies for each account. A company may also use team selling (e.g., product specialists and salesperson), major account management, telemarketing, and Internet support systems.

Corporate restructuring in the 1990s created the need to reengineer sales processes in many companies.[7] Indications of a possible need for a change in the sales process include discontinued sales of a new product, sales declines, lost customers, drops in profit margins, and price wars. The changes made by at Kraft Foods are illustrative.[8] This former division of the Philip Morris Company includes Kraft, General Foods, Oscar Mayer Foods, and Maxwell House products. The 3,500 people from the four specialized sales forces were placed into one unit organized into 300 marketing support teams, with each one responsible for a chain of stores. The salesperson, formerly a product specialist, is responsible for Kraft's entire portfolio of grocery products. Kraft has account-service teams and other support personnel to help manage the various food categories. These changes are illustrative of the customer management strategies being implemented by several companies.

The selling process provides guidelines for sales force recruiting, training, allocation of effort, organizational design, and the use of selling support activities such as telemarketing. Understanding the selling process is essential in coordinating all the elements of the marketing program.

Sales Channels

An important part of deciding on the personal selling strategy is consideration of alternative channels to end-user customers. For example, management may decide to contact major accounts by using a field sales force while serving small accounts via telemarketing

Technology Feature

i2 Technologies has experienced impressive sales growth, with sales in 2002 estimated to exceed $800 million, up from $362 million in 1998. However, 2002 sales declined from those of the previous year due to the global economic slowdown.

i2's selling process had been concentrated on forming long-term relationships with corporate clients, involving expensive software applications for improving logistics operations. The big-ticket projects with clients like Caterpillar, Dell Computer, General Electric, and others displayed a major slowdown.

Management responded to the problem by altering i2's selling process. The new strategy is to drive growth by concentrating on less expensive and more focused projects.

Salespeople are directed to pursue multiple corporate prospects and shorten the time span for sales development to much less than the six months required for the big projects. This change in focus involves a major change in the selling approach for salespeople who were previously assigned to go after one big sale at a time. Moreover, the new selling approach will need to emphasize ease of use and rapid results.

i2's new strategy reflects the realities of a weak economy but also an apparent preference by corporate customers for more focused projects. The strategy shift has moved i2 into a different competitive environment.

Sources: Based in part on company reports and Elliot Spagat, "I2 Thinks Small Is Beautiful in Difficult Times," *The Wall Street Journal,* August 9, 2001, B6.

---

or the Internet. The reality is that direct contact by face-to-face salespeople is very expensive, and this resource should be analyzed in terms of benefits and costs.

The choice of a particular sales channel is influenced by the buying power of customers, the selling channel threshold levels, and the complexity of buyer-seller relationships.[9] We discuss customer contact requirements to illustrate the strengths and limitations of alternative sales channels.

Customer Buying Power

The purchasing potential of customers and prospects often places them into different importance categories. The "major" or "global" account represents the most important customer category. This customer (1) purchases a significant volume on an absolute dollar basis and as a percent of a supplier's total sales and (2) purchases (or influences the purchase) from a central or headquarters location for several geographically dispersed organizational units.[10] The buying power of a supplier's total customer base may range from several major accounts to a large number of very low volume purchasers. Customers and prospects can be classified into major accounts, other customers requiring face-to-face contact, and accounts whose purchases (or potential) do not justify regular contact by field salespeople.

Threshold Levels

The number of customers in each buying power category influences the selection of selling channels. The value of a multiple selling channel strategy should be determined. For example, the amount of telemarketing effort that is needed determines if establishing a telemarketing support unit should be considered. Similarly, enough major accounts should exist in order to develop and implement a major account program. If the customer base does not display substantial differences in purchasing power and servicing requirements, the use of a single selling channel may be the way to go.

Complexity of the Customer Relationship

The account management relationship is also a key factor in the type of sales channel that is appropriate. For example, a customer that (1) has several people involved in the buying process, (2) seeks a long-term cooperative relationship with the supplier, and (3) requires specialized attention and service creates a relatively complex buyer-seller relationship.[11] Such a relationship coupled with sufficient buying power suggests the use of a major (key) account management channel. In contrast, a simple, routinized buying situation suggests direct marketing or Internet buyer-seller linkages. The field selling channel corresponds best to customer relationships that fall between very complex and highly routinized.

As was noted earlier, there is an apparent trend toward greater use of customer management strategies by companies such as IBM, Kraft, and Procter & Gamble. General Motors (GM) announced in 1998 major organizational changes designed to focus marketing efforts on dealer relationships.[12] GM plans to combine five separate sales, marketing, and service staffs into one organization. The result will be 200 teams that will work with all dealers regardless of the specific GM brands they sell. End-user customer databases will also be merged into one system. The Saturn car organization will operate independently of the new umbrella organization.

Key Account Management

Many companies have adopted key account management (KAM) and global account management (GAM) structures to focus teams of executives on the complex needs of major customers. In some cases this removes major customers from the jurisdiction of the sales force. The pressures leading to this development have been increased account concentration in many sectors, the growing importance of centralized procurement, and policies among large corporate buyers to reduce their supplier numbers and partner with a smaller number of vendors. KAM and GAM may be a necessary response to these pressures.[13] KAM raises important questions of integration for companies operating with this approach alongside the conventional sales organization.

Designing the Sales Organization

Designing a sales organization includes selecting an organizational structure and deciding on the size and deployment of the sales force.

Organizational Structure

The organizational approach adopted should support the firm's sales force strategy. As companies adjust their selling strategies, organizational structure may also require changes. Kraft's shift to a single sales force for various product lines is illustrative, as is General Motors' merging of five marketing divisions into one. The general trend is toward a greater focus on customers (market-driven) rather than products or geography as the basis for the design of the organization.

Important influences on organizational design are the customer base, the product, and the geographic location of buyers. The answers to several questions are helpful in the choice of an organizational design.

1. What is the selling job? What activities are to be performed by salespeople?

EXHIBIT 13–3
**Sales Organization
Designs**

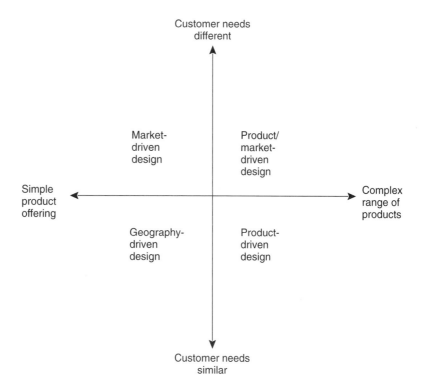

2. Is specialization of selling effort necessary according to type of customer, different products, or salesperson activities (e.g., sales and service)?

3. Are channel of distribution relationships important in the organizational design?

4. How many and what kinds of sales management levels are needed to provide the proper amount of supervision, assistance, and control?

5. Will sales teams be used, and if so, what will be their composition?

6. How and to what extent will sales channels other than the field sales force be used?

The sales force organizational design needs to be compatible with the selling strategy and other marketing program strategies. The major types of organization designs are shown in Exhibit 13–3. These designs take into account the extent of product diversity and differences in customer needs. Whenever the customer base is widely dispersed, geography is likely to be involved in the organizational design. The market driven design is heavily influenced by the customer base, although geographic location may also influence the design. The product/market design takes both factors into account in determining how the organization is structured. Similar customer needs and a complex range of products point to the product-driven design. If the product or the customer base does not dominate design considerations, a geographic organization is used. The assigned area and accounts that are the responsibility of the salesperson constitute the sales territory.

Sales Force Deployment

Sales management must decide how many salespeople are needed and how to deploy them to customers and prospects. Several factors outside the salesperson's control often affect his or her sales results, such as market potential, number and location of customers, intensity

EXHIBIT 13–4
**Sales Force
Decision Model
Output for Jones's
and Smith's
Territories**

	Trading Area[†]	Present Effort (percent)	Recommended Effort (percent)	Estimated Sales[*]	
				Present Effort	Recommended Effort
Jones:					
	1	10%	4%	$ 19	$ 13
	2	60	20	153	120
	3	15	7	57	50
	4	5	2	10	7
	5	10	**3**	21	16
	Total	100%	36%	$ 260	$ 206
Smith:					
	1	18%	81%	$ 370	$ 520
	2	7	21	100	130
	3	5	11	55	65
	4	35	35	225	225
	5	5	11	60	70
	6	30	77	400	500
	Total	100%	236%	$1,210	$1,510

[*]In $000.
[†]Each territory is made up of several trading areas.

of competition, and market position of the company. Sales force deployment analysis considers both salesperson factors and the relevant uncontrollable factors.

Several methods are available for analyzing sales force size and the deployment of selling effort, including (1) revenue/cost analysis, (2) single-factor models, (3) sales and effort response models, and (4) portfolio deployment models. Normally, sales and/or costs are the basis for determining sales force size and allocation.

Revenue/cost analysis techniques require information on each salesperson's sales and/or costs. One approach compares each salesperson to an average break-even sales level, thus helping management spot unprofitable territories. Another approach analyzes the profit performance of accounts or trading areas to estimate the profit impact of adding more salespeople or to determine how many people a new sales organization needs. These techniques are very useful in locating high- and low- performance territories.

Single-factor models assume that size and/or deployment are determined by one factor, such as market potential or workload (e.g., number of calls required), whose values can be used to determine the required selling effort. Suppose there are two territories, X and Y. Territory X has double the market potential (opportunity for business) of territory Y. If selling effort is deployed according to market potential, X should get double the selling effort of Y.

Consideration of multiple influences (e.g., market potential, intensity of competition, and workload) on market response can improve deployment decisions. Several promising *sales and effort response models* aid in size and deployment decisions.[14] Exhibit 13–4 shows an illustrative output provided by one of these models. The analysis indicates that Jones's territory requires only about 36 percent of a person whereas Smith's territory can support 2.36 people. The allocations are determined by increasing selling effort in high-response areas and reducing effort in areas where sales response is low. Note that Exhibit

EXHIBIT 13–5 **Characteristics Related to Sales Performance in Different Types of Sales Jobs**

Type of Sales Job	Characteristics That Are Relatively Important	Characteristics That Are Relatively Less Important
Trade selling	Age, maturity, empathy, knowledge of customer needs and business methods	Aggressiveness, technical ability, product knowledge, persuasiveness
Missionary selling	Youth, high energy and stamina, verbal skill, persuasiveness	Empathy, knowledge of customers, maturity, previous sales experience
Technical selling	Education, product and customer knowledge—usually gained through training, intelligence	Empathy, persuasiveness, aggressiveness, age
New business selling	Experience, age and maturity, aggressiveness, persuasiveness, persistence	Customer knowledge, product knowledge, education, empathy

Source: Gilbert A. Churchill, Jr., Neil M. Ford, and Orville C. Walker, Jr., Mark W. Johnston, and John F. Tanner, Jr., *Sales Force Management,* 6th ed. (Burr Ridge, IL: Richard D. Irwin, 2000), 348.

13–4 includes only two territories of a large sales organization. Sales response is determined from a computer analysis of the effort-to-sales relationship.

Managing the Sales Force

Salespeople differ in ability, motivation, and performance. Managers are involved in selecting, training, monitoring, directing, evaluating, and rewarding salespeople. A brief look at each activity shows the responsibilities and functions of a sales manager.

Finding and Selecting Salespeople

A major study of the chief sales executives in over 100 firms selling business-to-business products asked them to indicate on a scale of 1 to 10 how important 29 salesperson characteristics are to the success of their salespeople.[15] The executives indicated that the three most significant success characteristics are (1) being customer-driven and highly committed to the job, (2) accepting direction and cooperating as a team player, and (3) and being motivated by one's peers, financial incentives, and oneself.

Exhibit 13–5 shows several characteristics that are often important in different types of selling situations. The characteristics vary with the type of selling strategy being employed, and so we must first define the job that is to be performed. Managers use application forms, personal interviews, rating forms, reference checks, physical examinations, and various kinds of tests to assist them in making hiring decisions. The personal interview is widely cited as the most important part of the selection process for salespeople.

Training

Some firms use formal programs to train their salespeople; others use informal on-the-job training. Factors that affect the type and duration of training include size of firm, type of sales job, product complexity, experience of new salespeople, and management's commitment to training. Training topics may include selling concepts and techniques, product knowledge, territory management, and company policies and operating procedures.

In training salespeople, companies may seek to (1) increase productivity, (2) improve morale, (3) lower turnover, (4) improve customer relations, and (5) enable better management of time and territory.[16] These objectives are concerned with increasing results from the salesperson's effort and/or reducing selling costs. Sales training needs to be evaluated concerning its benefits and costs. Evaluations may include before-and-after training results, participant critiques, and comparison of salespeople receiving training to those who have not been trained. Product knowledge training is probably more widespread than any other type of training.

Supervising and Motivating Salespeople

The manager who supervises salespeople plays a key role in implementing a firm's selling strategy. He or she faces several important management issues. Coordinating the activities of a field sales force is difficult due to lack of regular contact. Compensation incentives are often used to encourage salespeople to obtain sales. However, salespeople need to be internally motivated. As was discussed earlier, sales executives want salespeople who are customer-driven and committed to the company and to team relationships.

The most widely used compensation plan is a combination of salary and incentive (80 percent salary and 20 percent incentive pay is a typical arrangement). The compensation plan should be fair to all participants and create an appropriate incentive. Salespeople also respond favorably to recognition programs and special promotions such as vacation travel awards.

Managers assist and encourage salespeople, and incentives highlight the importance of results, but the salesperson is the driving force in selling situations. Sales management must match promising selling opportunities with competent and self-motivated professional salespeople while providing the proper company environment and leadership. Although most sales management professionals consider financial compensation the most important motivating force, recent research indicates that personal characteristics, environmental conditions, and company policies and procedures are also important motivating factors.[17]

Sales Force Evaluation and Control

Sales management is continually working to improve the productivity of selling efforts. During the last decade personal selling costs increased much faster than did advertising costs, and so achieving high sales force performance is important. The evaluation of sales force performance considers sales results, costs, salesperson activities, and customer satisfaction. Several issues are important in this evaluation, including the unit(s) of analysis, measures of performance, performance standards, and factors that the sales organization and individual salespeople cannot control.

Unit of Analysis

Evaluation extends beyond the salesperson to include other organizational units, such as districts and branches. Selling teams are used in some types of selling. These companies focus evaluations on team results. Product performance evaluation by geographic area and across organization units is relevant in firms that produce more than one product. Individual account sales and cost analyses are useful for customers such as national accounts and accounts assigned to salespeople.

Performance Measures

Management needs yardsticks for measuring salesperson performance. For example, the sales force of a regional food processor that distributes through grocery wholesalers and large retail chains devotes most of its selling effort to calling on retailers. Since the firm does not have information on sales of its products by individual retail outlet, evaluations are based on the activities of salespeople rather than on sales outcomes. This type of control system focuses on "behavior" rather than "outcomes."

Sales managers may use both activity (behavior) and outcome measures of salesperson performance. Research indicates that multiple-item measures of several activities and outcomes are useful in performance evaluation.[18] Illustrative areas include sales planning, expense control, sales presentation, technical knowledge, information feedback, and sales results. Achievement of the sales quota (actual sales/quota sales) is a widely used outcome measure of sales performance. Other outcome measures include new business generated, market-share gains, new product sales, and profit contributions.

Performance evaluation is influenced by the sales management control system used by the organization. Emphasis may be placed on salesperson activities, outcomes, or a combination of activities and outcomes. The objective is to use the type of control that is most effective for the selling situation. Direct selling organizations like Mary Kay focus more on outcome control. Companies like American Airlines include both activity and outcome control. An important aspect of management control is the compensation plan. When salespeople are compensated primarily by commission earnings on sales results, pay becomes the primary management control mechanism.

Setting Performance Standards

Although internal comparisons of performance are frequently used, they are not very helpful if the performance of the entire sales force is unacceptable. A major problem in setting sales performance standards is determining how to adjust them for factors beyond the salesperson's control (i.e., market potential, intensity of competition, differences in customer needs, and quality of supervision). A competent salesperson may not appear to be performing well if he or she is assigned to a poor sales territory (e.g., salesperson Smith in Exhibit 13–4). Such differences need to be included in the evaluation process since territories often are not equal in terms of opportunity and other uncontrollable factors.

We know that evaluating performance is one of sales management's more difficult tasks. Typically, performance tracking involves assessing a combination of outcome and behavioral factors. In compensation plans other than straight commission, performance evaluation may affect the salesperson's pay, and so obtaining a fair evaluation is important.

By evaluating the organization's personal selling strategy, management may identify various problems requiring corrective action. Problems may be linked to individual salespeople or to decisions that affect the entire organization (e.g., i2 Technologies' changes in the selling process). A well-designed information system helps in the diagnosis of performance and guides corrective actions when necessary.

Internet Strategy

We now consider Internet strategy alternatives, examine integration of the Internet with marketing and promotion strategies, discuss options for measuring effectiveness, and look at the Internet's future in business and marketing strategies. Also, recall our discussion of this topic in Chapters 2, 10, and 11.

"The Internet is a worldwide means of exchanging information and communicating through a series of interconnected computers."[19] It offers a fast and versatile communications capability. Internet initiatives span a wide range of global industries and companies, and there have been successes but also many failures that have been stimulated by overly optimistic expectations. Initiatives have been pursued by both traditional enterprises and new business designs. One of the most visible new enterprises is Amazon.com Inc., which has yet to report a profit with estimated 2001 sales of more than $3 billion. Business-to-business use of the Internet has been far more extensive than consumer adoption of the Internet. The impacts of the Internet on business organizations in the future are expected to be both transformational and incremental in scope. Importantly, the Internet provides capabilities for use in marketing strategy.[20] Recall our earlier discussion on online exchanges and Internet-based supply chain collaborations.

Strategy Development

The first step in strategy development is to determine the role of the Internet in the organization's business and marketing strategies. As was discussed in Chapter 2, this role may involve a separate business model, a value-chain channel, a marketing communications tool, or a promotional medium:

> Many companies recognize the advantages of communicating via the Internet and are developing Web strategies and hiring interactive agencies specifically to develop their websites and make them part of their integrated marketing communications program. However, companies that are using the Internet effectively are integrating their Web strategies with other aspects of their IMC programs.[21]

Importantly, the integration of Internet-based channels into the value chain offers a powerful "bricks and clicks" model. Recall that the successful Internet grocery business operated by Tesco in the United Kingdom is designed to be a supplement to conventional store-based shopping, not a replacement for it. Several examples of how companies are using the Internet are described in Exhibit 13–6. The various initiatives, ranging from e-commerce to customer relationships, show how the Internet is leveraging the operating processes of many companies.

Deciding Internet Objectives

The capabilities of the Internet fall into two broad categories: a communications medium and a direct response medium enabling users to purchase and sell products. A summary of the communications features of the Internet follows.[22]

Disseminating Information

Providing product, application, and company information via the Internet is essential in the competitive marketplace. This capability offers an opportunity for direct one-on-one contact.

Creating Awareness

Advertising on the Internet offers important advantages to many companies. The opportunity for global exposure provides a useful brand-building capability.

Obtaining Research Information

The Internet offers a very cost-effective means of obtaining information such as user profiles. However, concerns have been voiced about invasion of consumer privacy.

Brand Building

Access to users provides an opportunity to build a brand that is unique compared to that built with other media. This highlights the importance of developing effective designs for websites.

Encouraging Trials by Buyers

There are several ways the Internet can be used to encourage trials through online purchase and incentives to visit retailers.

EXHIBIT 13–6
Hitting Pay Dirt in the Virtual World

Source: Michael J. Mandel and Robert D. Hof, "Rethinking the Internet: E-Biz: Down but Hardly Out," *Business Week,* March 26, 2001, 128.

Electronic Commerce

Pegged to hit $6.8 trillion in 2004, with 90% of that coming from business-to-business sales, says Forrester Research. About 80% of Cisco Systems' orders are taken online, about $5 billion last quarter—saving the networking giant $760 million in annual operating costs.

E-Marketplaces

Transactions on e-marketplaces expected to reach $2.8 trillion in 2004, says AMR Research. Defense contractor United Technologies bought $450 million worth of metals, motors, and other products from an e-marketplace in 2000 and got prices about 15% less than what it usually pays.

Procurement

Businesses will buy $2.8 trillion in supplies over the Internet in 2004, excluding e-marketplace purchases, says AMR Research. Eastman Chemical is buying 19% of its supplies online now, up from almost nothing two years ago. That has helped boost productivity 9% per year.

Knowledge Management

Companies will spend $10.2 billion to store and share their employees' knowledge over the Net by 2004, says IDC. Electronics manufacturer Siemens has spent $7.8 million to create a Web site for employees to share expertise to help win contracts. The result: new sales of $122 million.

Customer Relationships

Corporations will invest $12.2 billion by 2004 on linking customers, sales, and marketing over the Web, says the META Group. Lands' End converts more than 10% of its Web visitors to buyers—compared with the average 4.9%—in part because it offers live chat and other customer-service extras. Even with the crash in Internet stocks, companies are investing heavily in online initiatives. Here's a look at where they're putting their money—and the payoff.

Improving Customer Service

The Internet offers an important avenue of after-the-sale customer contact. Dell Computer offers a wide range of services to its corporate customers via the Internet.

Expanding Distribution

The opportunity to link websites of different companies is a useful initiative for expanding distribution. This is a form of cobranding that offers advantages to the cooperating firms.

We now consider what is involved in developing an e-commerce capability. This initiative may be pursued by an existing company such as Avon Products Corp. or a new Web-based business model.

E-Commerce Strategy

Designing and launching a new e-commerce business that enables buyers to purchase products is a major initiative. Moreover, faulty evaluation of market opportunities and inadequate planning have resulted in the failure of many Web-based businesses. Several interrelated decisions must be made:

1. Which customer groups should I serve?

2. How do I provide a compelling set of benefits to my targeted customer? How do I differentiate my "value proposition" from those of online and offline competitors?

3. How do I communicate with customers?

4. What are the content, "look and feel," level of community, and degree of personalization of the website?

5. How should I structure my organization? What business services and applications software choices do I need to consider?

6. Who are my potential partners? Whose capabilities complement ours?

7. How will this business provide value to shareholders?

8. What metrics should I use to judge the progress of the business? How do I value the business?[23]

The intent of the present discussion is to describe what is involved in an e-business initiative; extensive coverage of this topic is provided by several other sources.[24]

Value Opportunities and Risks

The earlier discussion highlighted several unique features of the Internet as a communications medium. Properly designed and managed Web-based initiatives provide important opportunities for offering superior customer value. These opportunities include the following:[25]

1. Very focused targeting is possible via the Web.

2. Messages can be designed to address the needs and preferences of the target audience.

3. The Web offers a compelling opportunity for interaction and feedback.

4. A core value offering of the Internet is access to a wide range of information.

5. The sales potential offered by the Internet is substantial (see Exhibit 13–6).

6. The Internet provides an exciting opportunity for communications innovation.

7. The exposure opportunities provided by the World Wide Web are significant, enabling many small companies and professionals to attain cost-effective access to customers and prospects.

8. The speed of response via the Internet is impressive. Recall, for example, the Feature about the French woolens manufacturer in Chapter 12.

The extensive value opportunities offered by the Web explain the pervasive initiatives pursued by companies. Nonetheless, there are some risks associated with the use of the Internet as a communications medium. They include difficulties in measuring effectiveness, changes in audience characteristics, access and response delays, multiple-ad exposure, potential for deception, and costs that may be higher than those of traditional media.[26]

The market-driven company will need to focus on the readiness of customers in its markets to adopt the new technology. Research suggests that customers differ in their predisposition to adopt new technology. It suggests that they may be grouped as *explorers,* who are highly optimistic and innovative; *pioneers,* who are innovative but cautious; *skeptics,* who need to have the benefits of the technology proved to them; *paranoids,* who are insecure about the technology; and *laggards,* who resist the technology.[27] Relatedly, research also suggests that there have been substantial problems for many Internet operations in meeting consumers' expectations and in the levels of service quality achieved. Major efforts may be needed to achieve e-service superiority.[28]

Measuring Internet Effectiveness

Measurement problems associated with the Internet are particularly challenging. This is not surprising given the explosive growth of Web-based initiatives and limited experience with the medium. Nonetheless, measurement capabilities are rapidly developing. Evaluating the quality and relevance of alternative measurement sources requires careful assessment by an organization pursuing Internet strategies.

The more popular measures of Internet effectiveness track exposure, recall, and retention of Web users. Several sources of measurement data are offered. The following are illustrative, but many other Internet measurement services are available:[29]

- Arbitron supplies demographic, media usage, and lifestyle data on Internet users.

- Marketing Resources Inc. supplies viewership profiles. This service is also offered by Nielsen.

- Audit Bureau of Circulation is developing a Web count certification product.

- Internet Advertising Bureau offers information on statistics, usage, and Internet strategies.

This is only a sampling of services, and new entries are likely as the Internet expands and acceptable measurement criteria are developed.

The Future of the Internet

The widespread optimism concerning the potential of the Internet has suffered major setbacks. Perhaps the shakeout was inevitable because of the race to develop Internet capabilities and business designs. Despite the setbacks, there is little doubt that Internet initiatives will expand in the future. Importantly, the early years of the Internet are best characterized as an essential learning process.[30] Learning at the early stages of a new technology involves risks, and mistakes are expected to occur.

The reality is that the Internet will not result in a massive transformation of business practices.[31] Its impact is expected to be much greater for companies and organizations that are very dependent on the flow of information. As indicated in Exhibit 13–7, the impact of the Internet in the future promises to be revolutionary for certain industries and incremental for others.

Direct Marketing Strategies

The underlying logic of direct marketing is making direct contact with end-user customers through alternative media (e.g., telephone, mail, kiosk). Many direct marketing methods are available, each offering certain advantages and limitations. The rapid growth of direct marketing during the last decade indicates the importance to many companies of these direct avenues to customers. For example, Williams-Sonoma, the kitchenware retailer, generates 40 percent of its $255 million annual revenues from catalog sales.[32] Using a two-stage strategy, the company first builds a catalog customer base in a metropolitan area. At the second stage, Williams-Sonoma opens a retail store when sufficient catalog shoppers are identified, targeting catalog buyers with store promotion mailings.

First, we look at several considerations in the use of direct marketing. Next, we discuss the major direct marketing methods. Finally, we consider how direct marketing strategies are developed and implemented.

EXHIBIT 13–7
The Impact of the Internet on Different Industries

Source: Michael J. Mandel and Robert D. Hof, "Rethinking the Internet: E-Biz: Down but Hardly Out," *Business Week,* March 26, 2001, 118.

These information-intensive industries are good candidates to be transformed by the Web

Financial Services

Most financial services can potentially be handled electronically. But so far, banks can't even figure out a good way of letting people pay bills online.

Entertainment

Much of entertainment can easily be digitized. But no one knows how to make money yet, and the technology is lagging.

Health Care

The benefits of shifting health-care transactions to the Web could be enormous. But so are the institutional barriers.

Education

E-learning could cut the costs of education, but only at the price of making education more impersonal.

Government

Delivering information to citizens electronically has enormous appeal, but requires massive investments.

Industries where information plays a relatively small role

Retailing

The glitzy Web sites got all the attention. But dot-com success turned more on who had the best logistics.

Manufacturing

Web-enabled supply chains and intranets are important, but ultimately a manufacturer lives or dies on the quality of its goods.

Travel

Online travel sites are popular, but the ultimate constraint on travel is the physical capacity of the air and road systems.

Power

Online energy exchanges get the publicity, but power generation and transmission capabilities will have the bigger economic impact.

Considerations in the Use of Direct Marketing

The expanding popularity of direct marketing methods is driven by a combination of factors such as socio economic trends, low costs, databases, and buyers' demands for value. We examine how these influences affect companies' use of mail, phone, media, and computers to access individual buyers.

Socioeconomic Trends

Several trends make the availability of direct marketing purchases attractive to many buyers. When both spouses work this imposes major time constraints on households, and so direct purchase by phone and mail is a useful way of saving time as well as making contact at the convenience of the customer. Many single-person households also favor direct marketing purchases. Buyers can shop at home, save time, and avoid shopping congestion. Rapid response to order processing and fast shipping enable buyers to obtain their purchases in a few days. Liberal exchange policies reduce the risks of direct purchases.

Low Access Costs

While the cost per contact varies with the method of direct contact, costs are much lower than they are in face-to-face sales contact. Telephone contact ranges from $10 to $20, compared to much lower costs per contact by mail and advertising media. The availability of databases that can target specific customer groups enables companies to target buyers selectively. Companies like American Express can market products to their credit card users. Similarly, airline frequent flier mailing lists provide cost-effective access to buyers.

Database Management

The use of computerized databases escalated during the last decade, driven by advances in hardware and software technology. The availability of computerized databases is an important determinant of successful direct marketing.[33] The information in the systems includes internal data on customers and purchased data on customers and prospects. The customer and prospect information contained in databases can be used to generate mailing lists and prospect lists and to identify market segments. These segments offer a direct communications channel with customers and prospects.

Database information enables companies to identify and target individuals or small microsegments of people. The systems are very useful in sales and sales management support and for direct marketing programs. Database marketing has three main benefits: (1) strategic advantage through the more effective use of marketing information internally, (2) improvement in the use of customer and market information, and (3) a basis for developing long-term customer relationships.[34] Databases can be used in mail-order marketing, telemarketing, and support of personal selling activities. A major objective of database marketing is to find and develop strong relationships with the customers who account for a large proportion of a firm's annual sales.

Value

The shopping information provided via direct marketing, convenience, reduced shopping time, rapid response, and competitive prices give buyers an attractive bundle of value in many buying situations. Effective database management enables direct marketing to identify buyers who purchase on a continuing basis.

The differentiated needs and wants of buyers can be addressed through direct marketing, thus enhancing the value offered by the direct marketer. Offerings may be mass customized when the direct marketer has the capability to modulize the product offering. For example, kiosks can be linked to information networks that transmit customized customer orders.

Direct Marketing Methods

Various direct marketing methods are shown in Exhibit 13–8. We briefly examine each method to highlight its features and limitations.

Catalogs and Direct Mail

Contact by mail with potential buyers may be intended to generate orders by phone or mail or, instead, to encourage buyers to visit retail outlets to view goods and make purchases. Examples of companies using catalogs and other printed matter to encourage direct response include Lands' End (clothing), L. L. Bean (outdoor apparel and equipment), Calyx & Corolla (flowers), and Conference Board Inc. (management conferences).

EXHIBIT 13–8
Direct Marketing Methods

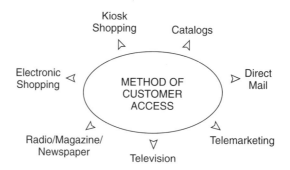

Telemarketing

This form of direct marketing consists of the use of telephone contact between the buyer and the seller to achieve all or some of the selling function. Telemarketing offers two key advantages—low contact cost and quick access by both buyer and seller. It may be used as the primary method of customer contact or as a way to support the field sales force. Telemarketing escalated in importance during the last decade and is a vital part of the selling activities of many companies. Telemarketing, like the Internet, is a potential avenue of conflict with an organization's face-to-face sales force.

Direct Response Media

Many companies use television, radio, magazines, and newspapers to obtain sales from buyers. Direct response from the advertising is obtained by mail, telephone, and fax. People see the ads, decide to buy, and order the item from the organization promoting the product.

The TV Home Shopping Network markets a wide range of products for many companies. The products are displayed, and their features described. Prices are discounted below list prices. The buyer places an order by using a toll-free number. Individual companies may also market their products by using commercials for specific products such as housewares, magazines, and music recordings.

Magazines, newspapers, and radio offer a wide range of direct marketing advertisements. The intent of direct response communications is to persuade the person reading or hearing the ad to order the product. The advantage of using these media is the very low cost of exposure. While the percent of response is also low, the returns can be substantial for products that buyers are willing to purchase through these media.

Electronic Shopping

The computer age has created two major methods of direct marketing: computer ordering by companies from their suppliers and consumer and business shopping via the Internet, as was discussed earlier in the chapter. Electronic shopping by business buyers is appropriate when the customer's requirements involve the routine repurchase of standard items and direct access to the buyer is not necessary. Electronic capabilities may be used to support a field sales force rather than as the sole method of customer contact. Computer ordering helps the seller establish a close link to customers and reduces order cycles (time from order placement to receipt) and inventory stocks. Computer ordering enables the buyer to reduce inventory levels, cut costs, and monitor customer preferences. For example, Wal-Mart's computerized scanning equipment in its stores informs the retailer about what (and where) customers are buying and enables the company to meet their needs via the computerized ordering system. While some customers may resist becoming dependent on suppliers through electronic linkages, there is a strong trend toward closer ties between suppliers and organizational buyers.

As was discussed earlier in the chapter, virtual shopping on the Internet has received much publicity during the last few years. Many companies are considering the potential opportunities of direct marketing to computer users. The business-to-business sector accounts for the largest proportion of total Internet sales. There are three types of networks: (1) The Internet is a global interlink of computer networks that have a common software standard, (2) an intranet is a company internal capability using Internet software standards, and (3) an extranet provides external partners with access to the Intranet.[35] For example, a retail chain may serve customers via the Internet, coordinate store operations via an intranet, and utilize an extranet to interact with freelance product designers and other external partners.

Kiosk Shopping

Similar in concept to vending machines, kiosks offer buyers the opportunity to purchase from a facility (stand) located in a retail complex or another public area (e.g., an airport). Kiosks may have Internet linkages. Airline tickets and flight insurance are examples of products sold using kiosks. In some instances the order may be placed at the kiosk but delivered to the customer's address. The advantage to the seller is exposure to many people, and the buyer benefits from the shopping convenience. Kiosks are best suited for selling products that buyers can easily evaluate due to prior experience.

Direct Marketing Strategy

As highlighted in our discussion, direct marketing promotion has the primary objective of obtaining a purchase response from individual buyers. While the methods differ in nature and scope, all require the development of a strategy. The market target(s) must be identified, the objectives set, the positioning strategy developed, the communications strategy formulated, the program implemented and managed, and the results evaluated against performance expectations.

The direct marketing strategy should be guided by the organization's marketing strategy. Direct marketing provides a way to reach the customer on a one-to-one basis. Product strategy must be determined, prices set, and distribution arranged. Direct marketing may be the primary avenue to the customer, as in the case of L. L. Bean, Inc., in its targeting of the outdoor apparel niche by using catalog marketing. Other companies may use direct marketing as one of several ways of communicating with their market targets. Dell Computer employs direct sales contact with business customers, telephone sales, and Internet sales. The Internet may also be used by Dell's customers to obtain information before placing an order by phone.

Summary

Management analyzes the firm's marketing strategy, the target market, product characteristics, distribution strategy, and pricing strategy to identify the role of personal selling in the promotion mix. New business, trade selling, missionary selling, and consultative/technical selling strategies illustrate the possible roles that may be assigned to selling in various firms. The selling process indicates the selling activities necessary to move the buyer from need awareness to a purchase decision. Various sales channels are used in conjunction with the field sales force to accomplish selling process activities.

Sales force organizational design decisions include the type of organizational structure to be used, the size of the sales force, and the allocation of selling effort. Deployment involves decisions regarding sales force size and effort allocation. Managing the sales force includes recruiting, training, supervising, and motivating salespeople. Evaluation and control determine the extent to which objectives are achieved and determine where adjustments are needed in selling strategy and tactics.

The Internet provides a unique and compelling means of electronic contact between buyers and sellers. The core capability of the Internet is communicating with buyers and prospects via an interactive process. The Internet is a new medium, and companies are learning how to obtain its advantages and avoid its risks. The key organizational decision is determining what role the Internet will play in the business and marketing strategies. The options range from a separate business model to a promotional medium.

The Internet offers several communications features, including disseminating information, creating awareness, obtaining research information, brand building, encouraging trials, improving customer service, and expanding distribution. Developing an e-commerce business model is a major initiative that involves the design of a new business. Faulty evaluation of market opportunities and inadequate planning have resulted in many Web-based failures.

The Internet's unique features provide important opportunities for offering superior customer value. It also has some potential risks in its use as a communications medium. A major challenge is measuring the effectiveness of Internet initiatives.

The purpose of direct marketing is to obtain a sales response from buyers by making direct contact using mail, telephone, advertising media, or computer. The rapidly expanding adoption of direct marketing methods that has occurred in the last decade is the consequence of several influences, including socioeconomic trends, low costs of exposure, computer technology, and buyers' demands for value. Direct marketing is used by many companies to contact organizational and consumer buyers.

Companies have many options available for direct marketing to buyers. The methods include catalogs, direct mail, telemarketing, television, radio, magazines/newspapers, electronic shopping, and kiosk shopping. Developing a strategy for using each method includes selecting the market target(s), setting objectives, selecting the positioning strategy, developing the communications strategy, implementing and managing the strategy, and evaluating the results.

Internet Applications

A. Examine the website of K&L Wine Merchants (*www.klwines.com*). Describe how its direct marketing strategy is enhanced by a Web-based approach.

B. Visit Nokia's U.S. website (*www.nokiausa.com*). Evaluate Nokia's sales approach online. How does Nokia enhance its direct marketing strategy through Web-based offerings?

C. Review the website of Merrill Lynch (*www.ml.com*). How does Merrill Lynch leverage its global position to adjust to local markets through the Internet? Why is the Internet particularly relevant for firms in the financial services industry?

Questions for Review and Discussion

1. What information does management require to analyze the selling situation?

2. Suppose an analysis of sales force size and selling effort deployment indicates that a company has a sales force that is the right size but that the allocation of selling effort requires substantial adjustment in several territories. How should such deployment changes be implemented?

3. What questions would you want answered if you were trying to evaluate the effectiveness of a business unit's sales force strategy?

4. Discuss some of the advantages and limitations of recruiting salespeople by hiring the employees of companies with excellent training programs.

5. Is incentive compensation more important for salespeople than for product managers? Why?

6. Select a company and discuss how sales management should define the selling process.

7. What are the unique capabilities offered by the Internet to business users of the communications medium?

8. Discuss whether the Internet may replace conventional catalogs and direct mail methods of promotion.

9. Direct marketing is similar in many ways to advertising. Why is it important to view direct marketing as a specific group of promotion methods?

10. Discuss the reasons why many companies are interested in the marketing potential of the Internet.

11. Select one of the direct marketing methods and discuss the decisions that are necessary in developing a strategy for using the method.

12. Suppose you have been asked to evaluate whether a regional camera and consumer electronics retailer should obtain Internet space. What criteria should be used in the evaluation?

Notes

1. This illustration is based in part on "The 'Click Here' Economy," *Business Week,* June 22, 1998, 122–28; and Melanie Berger, "It's Your Move," *Sales & Marketing Management,* March 1998, 45–56.

2. "What a Sales Call Costs," *Sales & Marketing Management,* September 2000, 79–81.

3. The following discussion is based on Gilbert A. Churchill, Jr., Neil M. Ford, Orville C. Walker, Jr., Mark W. Johnston, and John F. Tanner, Jr., *Sales Force Management,* 6th ed. (Homewood, IL: Richard D. Irwin, 2000), 58–60.

4. Ibid.

5. David W. Cravens, "The Changing Role of the Sales Force," *Marketing Management,* Fall 1995, 48–57.

6. Churchill, Ford, Walker, Johnston, and Tanner, *Sales Force Management,* chap. 3..

7. Andy Cohen, "Starting Over," *Sales and Marketing Management,* September 1995, 40–45.

8. Greg Burns, "Will So Many Ingredients Work Together?" *Business Week,* March 27, 1995, 40–44, 188, 191.

9. The following discussion is drawn from Raymond W. LaForge, David W. Cravens, and Thomas N. Ingram, "Evaluating Multiple Sales Channel Strategies," *Journal of Business and Industrial Marketing,* Summer–Fall 1991, 37–48.

10. Jerome A. Colletti and Gary S. Tubridy, "Effective Major Account Management," *Journal of Personal Selling and Sales Management,* August 1987, 1–10.

11. Ibid.

12. Gregory L. White, "GM to Crunch Five Marketing Divisions into One," *The Wall Street Journal,* August 5, 1998, A3, A6.

13. Noel Capon, *Key Account Management and Planning* (New York: Free Press, 2001).

14. Churchill, Ford, Walker, Johnston, and Tanner, *Sales Force Management,* chap. 7.

15. David W. Cravens, Thomas M. Ingram, Raymond W. LaForge, and Clifford E. Young, "Hallmarks of Effective Sales Organizations," *Marketing Management,* Winter 1992, 56–67.

16. Churchill, Ford, Walker, Johnston, and Tanner, *Sales Force Management*, 382–84.

17. Ibid, chap. 9.

18. David W. Cravens, Thomas M. Ingram, Raymond W. LaForge, and Clifford E. Young, "Behavior-Based and Outcome-Based Sales Force Control Systems," *Journal of Marketing*, October 1993, 47–59.

19. George E. Belch and Michael A. Belch, *Advertising and Promotion*, 5th ed. (New York: McGraw-Hill Irwin, 2001), 495.

20. Michel E. Porter, "Strategy and the Internet." *Harvard Business Review*, March 2001, 63–78.

21. Belch and Belch, *Advertising and Promotion*, 190.

22. The following is based on ibid. 502–04.

23. Jeffrey F. Rayport and Bernard J. Jaworski, *E-Commerce* (New York: McGraw-Hill/Irwin, 2001), 12.

24. See, for example, ibid.

25. Belch and Belch, *Advertising and Promotion*, 516–17.

26. Ibid.

27. A. Parasuraman and Charles L. Colby, *Techno-Ready Marketing: How and Why Your Customers Adopt Technology* (New York: Free Press, 2001).

28. Valerie A. Zeithaml, A. Parasuraman, and Arvind Malhotra, *A Conceptual Framework for Understanding E-Service Quality: Implications for Future Research and Managerial Practice* (Boston: Marketing Science Institute), Report No. 00-115, 2000.

29. Belch and Belch, *Advertising and Promotion*, 515.

30. Michael J. Mandel and Robert D. Hof, "Rethinking the Internet," *Business Week*, March 26, 2001, 117–22.

31. Ibid.

32. Sandra Baker, "Mail Bonding," *Fort Worth Star Telegram*, December 16, 1996, B1, B3.

33. William J. McDonald, *Direct Marketing* (Burr Ridge, IL: Irwin/McGraw-Hill, 1998), 93.

34. Keith Fletcher, Colin Wheeter, and Julia Wright, "The Role and Status of U.K. Database Marketing," *Quarterly Review of Marketing*, Autumn 1990, 7–14.

35. Andy Reinhardt, "Log On, Link Up, Save Big," *Business Week*, June 22, 1998, 136.

Cases for Part IV

Case 4–1

Amazon.com Inc.

Since the beginning of the year (2000), it has been evident that Wall Street has become disenchanted with its former Internet darling, Amazon.com Inc. Sure, Amazon still had its impressive customer base, over $1 billion in cash, and expanding sales. But as with the smaller dot-coms, Amazon seemed a long way from profitability and was boasting an increasingly unjustifiable valuation. Top tech-fund managers began to reduce and even eliminate Amazon from their portfolios. It was the end of Amazon's fairy-tale existence as the one e-tailer with seemingly unlimited prospects. After hitting a peak of $106\frac{11}{16}$ on Dec. 10 and trending downward until mid-June, Amazon's stock price appeared to settle into a trading range between the mid-40s and mid-50s.

Holy War

Nonetheless, Amazon still had plenty of true believers among investors and the equity analysts. For them, it was the world according to Amazon CEO Jeffrey P. Bezos: The dot-com's balance-sheet negatives could be easily overlooked. Why? Because the company went into the red to build up a dominant position in e-commerce, and as triple-digit growth rates and expansion into new product lines led to far heftier sales, Amazon would eventually cross over into profitability.

Then, on June 22, Lehman Brothers Inc. debt analyst Ravi Suria released a scathing report about Amazon's deteriorating credit situation. And the Holy War began in earnest.

Suria painted the picture of a company hemorrhaging money. The only triple-digit growth that mattered, he argued, was in Amazon's cash-flow losses. The report shook many remaining stalwarts, and the stock dropped 19% in one day. Suria addressed Wall Street's darkest fears: that the business model on which Amazon—and for that matter, most e-tailers—is based may be flawed. Arguing that excessive debt and poor inventory management will make Amazon's operating cash-flow situation worse the more it sells, Suria suggested that cash was being devoured at such a rate that the company might eventually find it difficult to meet its obligations by the end of the first quarter next year.

This is scary stuff. After all, if Amazon can't make money in e-retailing, who can? Amazon was quick to scoff at the notion that its model is flawed, although it concedes execution could be improved as it ramps up from selling books and CDs to offering up everything from lawn chairs to power saws. Dismissing Suria's concerns as "baloney," Bezos claims the company will have positive operating cash flow over the next three quarters. And even though the company acknowledges that it may be forced to dip into its cash stash again in the first quarter of 2001, Bezos insists that Amazon is on the road to profitability (Exhibit 1).

EXHIBIT 1
**A Look at
Amazon's
Performance**

Source: Lehman Brothers Inc.;
Goldman, Sachs & Co.;
Bloomberg Financial Markets

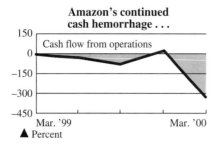

**Amazon's continued
cash hemorrhage . . .**

Cash flow from operations

▲ Percent

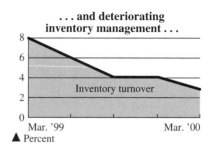

**. . . and deteriorating
inventory management . . .**

Inventory turnover

▲ Percent

**. . . have investors
spooked . . .**

Stock price

▲ Dollars

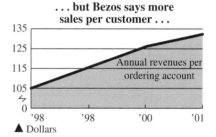

**. . . but Bezos says more
sales per customer . . .**

Annual revenues per
ordering account

▲ Dollars

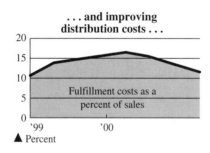

**. . . and improving
distribution costs . . .**

Fulfillment costs as a
percent of sales

▲ Percent

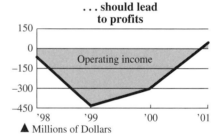

**. . . should lead
to profits**

Operating income

▲ Millions of Dollars

Ticking Clock

On the surface, the debate appears to focus on arcane accounting issues. But underlying them is a fundamental question: Can Amazon deliver profits—and how soon? The timing is crucial, because until now, Amazon hasn't had to generate cash or profits. Its growth, critics contend, has been almost entirely funded by investors and the debt market.

But the dot-com implosion means that Amazon's access to new capital will likely be cut off now, so the clock is ticking. It must begin to replenish its cash through its operations rather than constantly depleting it. Although many analysts think Suria is overly pessimistic and give Amazon closer to six quarters before its bankroll runs out, that is still not far off.

Suria's report got Wall Street's attention because it had the audacity to evaluate this icon of the New Economy as a traditional retailer. Up until Suria, Amazon was usually viewed under a rose-colored microscope that overlooked divergence by dot-coms from standard business measures. Suria's reasoning was simple: Because Amazon has built up a vast infrastructure of warehouse and distribution centers to house burgeoning inventories of product lines, relies on brand-name identification, and needs to spend relentlessly to attract each dollar of sales, it faces many of the same difficulties managing its business as old-line retailers do.

So Suria used the standard yardstick of retail success—the ability to generate a positive cash flow. And for retailers, traditional or otherwise, this often boils down to an ability to properly estimate the right amount of inventories needed to meet demand, at the right price, without overstocking. Simply put, stock up too much, and the costs of holding that inventory far outweigh the thin margins you make on whatever you sell.

This is hardly the most becoming angle from which to view Amazon—and that classic retail error, Suria argued, is exactly the mistake Amazon made in last year's Christmas season. That's why he focused on the results of the first quarter of this year, when gross operating cash flow nose-dived from a positive $31.5 million to a negative $320.5 million. This performance was far worse than any in the previous nine quarters, only four of which were in the black. "As has been said before, cash is a fact, profit is an accounting opinion. And the company's inability to make hard cash per unit sold is clearly manifested in its weak balance sheet, poor working-capital management, and massive negative operating cash flow—the financial characteristics that have driven innumerable retailers to disaster throughout history," Suria wrote in the report.

Debt Trouble

Ironically, a key contributor to this first-quarter debacle was Amazon's efforts to implement its strategy for growth. By adding product lines such as electronics and toys, and building distribution centers all over the country, the job of policing its inventories became much more difficult, particularly for a retailer that concedes it is lacking in retail experience. On $676 million in sales in the fourth quarter, Amazon was forced to take a $39 million write-down on inventory. The question now is whether Amazon will manage the process any better this year, with far higher sales and an evermore complex product mix. "They may have to settle for a little lower growth," says Bob Grandhi, manager of Monument Fund Group's Internet Fund, who sold all its e-tailing stocks including Amazon when he joined in April. "We can't ask them to be profitable and also grow as fast as they have."

Suria and other critics also point out that Amazon's ability to turn over its inventory rapidly enough has declined since the end of 1998; that, too, is a classic measure of poor retail management. Amazon's rate of inventory turnover plummeted from 8.5 times in the first quarter of 1998 to 2.9 times for the first quarter of this year. In 1999, when Amazon's sales grew 170% from the previous year, its inventories ballooned by 650%, Suria pointed out. "When a company manages inventory properly, it should grow along with its sales-growth rate," he noted. When inventory grows faster than sales, "it means simply that they're not selling as much as they're buying."

Amazon's fast-growing debt load, which has risen to a staggering $2.1 billion, is also a source of concern. From 1997 through the latest quarter, the company may have reported as much as $2.9 billion in revenues, but it raised $2.8 billion to meet its cash needs—amounting to 95¢ for every $1 of merchandise sold, Suria noted. In the future, Amazon will be under far greater pressure to meet its obligations by generating its own cash. "Bondholders are in effect being paid cash from money they lent the company," says Marie Menendez, Moody's senior corporate finance analyst of the interest payments of about $150 million a year.

Not surprisingly, Amazon vehemently disagrees with Suria's portrayal. Bezos insists that the company is getting a handle on its costs and generating new sources of revenue to take the place of market support. Bezos promises that Amazon will show positive operating cash flow for the last three quarters of this year, an assessment that equity analysts accept. He's not predicting what will happen in 2001's first quarter, however, when Amazon will have to pay suppliers for an expected $1 billion in holiday sales. But until then, he expects rising

EXHIBIT 2
Big Jobs for Bezos

Will Amazon ever be in the black? To get there, it needs to bolster revenues and improve operations—fast. Here's what it must do:

Increase efficiencies in distribution and customer-service centers by reducing headcount and installing new computer systems and automation gear

Open more new stores on its site to provide greater selection and draw more customers

Persuade customers to turn to Amazon to buy more than books and music

Demonstrate savvier merchandising, from anticipating product demand to personalizing offers to individual customers

Sign up more e-merchant partners to bring in high-profit revenue

sales and greater efficiencies handling the company's vast, relatively new network of distribution centers to not only end the cash drain but also to produce cash flow (Exhibit 2).

Indeed, many analysts believe the Amazon of year 2000 is actually in better position than ever. Operating losses fell from 26% of sales in the fourth quarter to 17% in the first quarter. As a result, analysts expect operating losses to drop to a single-digit percentage of sales by yearend—when books, music, and video are expected to be profitable on their own—and they predict a companywide operating profit by the end of 2001. Says Merrill Lynch & Co. Internet analyst Henry Blodget: "I'm not at all concerned about the cash side."

Where Bezos and his band of Wall Street believers think Lehman's report went astray was in focusing on the one year of Amazon's greatest expansion and projecting those costs forward into the future. The costs came up front, but now, they argue, Amazon will exploit its ability to handle far higher volumes. "For a company that's changing at this velocity, looking only back at finances can lead to misleading conclusions," says Amazon.com Treasurer Russ Grandinetti.

One controversy seems to be over the vast network of distribution centers that Amazon built over the past couple of years. While largely empty and unused, the centers gave Amazon a leg up on online and traditional rivals last Christmas: It could ship on time over the holidays, creating an intensely loyal customer base. In the first quarter, repeat orders constituted 76% of sales.

Suria's critics claim he was looking at these one-time capital costs and assuming that Amazon would have to keep spending at those levels. Now that the centers are built, Bezos says Amazon can work on making them more efficient. In fact, the costs of the construction are not in the operating cash-flow calculations upon which Suria bases his criticism.

There is early evidence that Amazon is beginning to manage its unwieldy portfolio of products better, moving customers more quickly to new products. For instance, it became the largest CD seller after only four months. And sales of children's products, mostly toys, hit $95 million in the fourth quarter, less than five months after Amazon's "toy store" opened. Customers are also ordering more every quarter: Annual sales per customer rose to $121 in March from $107 a year before.

Amazon is also developing new sources of revenues other than direct sales. It is trying to line up partners, particularly ones that can handle highly regulated or difficult-to-ship products such as sofas and drugs. In return for cash payments of up to $150 million apiece over three to five years, Amazon allows other e-merchants, such as Living.com and Drugstore.com, to host stores on its site. While this on the whole is a strategic plus, the plan also leaves Amazon's revenue base vulnerable to the travails of its dot-com partners—some of which are already facing layoffs and difficulties raising capital.

Bezos and supporters also object to Amazon being lumped in with Old Economy giants like Wal-Mart, claiming that there are more differences than similarities. The argument: Amazon will not be forced to build new stores, stock shelves, or hire new people to generate sales. As Amazon's sales grow, analysts say it will require no more than a third of the investment of a brick-and-mortar retailer for the same amount of sales. Goldman, Sachs & Co., the company's original underwriter, estimates for the next year, Amazon's operating expenses will rise only 8% and marketing only 7% while driving a 59% jump in sales, to $4.5 billion. The ultimate result, says J. P. Morgan & Co. analyst Tom Wyman: "Their operating margin will be twice that of brick-and-mortar retailers."

Brand Power

Ultimately, Bezos contends, Amazon should be more profitable than conventional retailers, though he won't hazard by how much. Indeed, he implies that Amazon aims to produce not necessarily higher profit margins but higher profits overall—which he contends is more important to investors. His take: a company with $10 billion in sales and a 5% profit margin—that is, $500 million in profits—is much more valuable than a $1 billion company with 10% margins, which has $100 million in profits.

But whether Amazon is more or less like retailers, it certainly must contend with many of the same forces. Just like retailers, Amazon is highly dependent on brand recognition and identity to bring customers back to its site. And just like retailers that overextend themselves, some critics believe that Amazon's one-stop shopping mentality is a threat. Expanding beyond its signature items—books, CDs, and videos—could muddy the Amazon brand at a time in consumer history when success demands a clear image. "The most powerful brands in the world stand for something simple," says Al Ries, brand management consultant and author of *The 11 Immutable Laws of Internet Branding.* "Volvo stands for safety. Dell is a personal computer. Even Microsoft is software. Now Amazon is going to stand for books and charcoal grills. This makes no sense to me."

Bezos argues Amazon stands for high-quality customer service over the Web—and that customers looking for that will return again and again. But the debate is far from academic. The power of the retail brand has been demonstrated repeatedly over the past decade. The most successful retail chains, from Gap to Target Stores to the mighty Wal-Mart, have unadulterated images that stick with consumers and keep them coming back. Retailers that have stumbled, from Tandy Corp. to Kmart Corp., shared a common misstep: They failed to build a coherent theme for consumers by selling unrelated merchandise or not providing a consistent level of service.

Amazon and other e-tailers were fortunate in having been launched in a boom economy (Exhibit 3). But a consumer spending slowdown would endanger revenues at Amazon as much as at any other retailer.

Worse, Bezos is finding it necessary to cut prices on one of its newest lines: consumer electronics. True, low prices are what drew customers to the Web in the first place. But from the start, Amazon has tried to depend on a wide selection to be its strongest drawing card.

Ultimately, Amazon and those on Wall Street who still back it have made a giant bet that none of these factors will be enough to keep it from boosting sales enough to get to profitability. At base, it is a bet on Amazon's ability to outrace the financial squeeze that all money-losing e-businesses now face. But as the difficulties of beating the debt clock increase—and the questions multiply about how the numbers will ever add up—a growing number of investors and analysts are bailing out, no longer liking the odds. Who is right? Coming down on either side ultimately requires something of a leap of faith. The only

Exhibit 3   Commentary *By Heather Green and Norm Alster*

Guess What—Venture Capitalists Aren't Geniuses

Wasn't it only a matter of months ago that venture capitalists were the smartest people on Wall Street? Investors were beating down their doors to throw billions of dollars at every high-tech prodigy they could bring public.

But as the Nasdaq has continued to stumble, and even the prospects of erstwhile high-tech superstars such as Amazon.com Inc. are being widely questioned, VCs are no longer undoubted financial gurus. Today, they are increasingly finding themselves forced back into the market to prop up flagging startups.

On April 25, Benchmark Capital Partners LP, one of Silicon Valley's hottest venture-capital firms, bought 1.3 million shares in a private placement for its once celebrated E-LOAN, an online provider of consumer loans whose stock has fallen to less than 5 from a high of 74⅜ last July. Around the same time, Benchmark was also buying shares of luxury-goods Web site Ashford.com, which has seen its shares tumble to less than 10% of its November high of $35. Nor is Benchmark alone in lending a financial helping hand. On June 20, Internet holding company CMGI teamed up with Compaq Computer Corp. to provide $75 million to Engage Inc., the Web ad-delivery outfit whose stock has slid from a high of 94½ in March to 13⅜.

Resource Shift. Propping up failing stocks isn't exactly normal VC behavior. Typically, they don't look back after the entrepreneurial offspring leave the fold. But some VCs are eager to prop up the valuations of their lagging investments. So instead of putting money into new consumer startups, they're supporting old ones. "It's a defensive strategy," says C. Kevin Landry, CEO of venture firm TA Associates in Boston. "They're conserving capital to protect existing investments."

But don't shed too many tears: By and large, venture capitalists are responsible for their current predicament. The industry threw too much money at too many companies that were following the same business model. Last year, some $5.5 billion was invested in consumer e-commerce companies, up from $607 million in 1998, according to Venture Economics, a researcher that tracks venture funding. Nobody, but nobody, really believed the world needed that many new Net stores.

Then, in many cases, VCs took these clones to market way too soon. Instead of the four to five years it used to take before a company could get public investors to pony up, companies are now being pushed out after less than two years on average, estimates PricewaterhouseCoopers. Snowball.com Inc. beat even that: The teen-information and e-commerce site filed for its IPO a mere 10 months after its online debut. The problem with that kind of strategy is that neither the company nor its management has enough experience to prove consistent performance.

Indiscriminate Investing. Every VC was, instead, eager to have the next America Online Inc. or Amazon.com Inc. So they tossed huge amounts of money at redundant companies in an attempt to outspend and underprice rivals. As a result, heavily funded startups became locked into price-cutting strategies that turned into death struggles. Last Christmas, eToys duked it out with venture-funded companies KBkids.com, Toysmart.com, ToyTime, and Toysrus.com. Now, ToyTime and Toysmart.com are out of business, and KBkids pulled its initial public offering. And when the consumer market seemed to be played out, VCs engaged in some of the same type of indiscriminate investing in business-to-business Web sites, infrastructure, wireless, and optical networking. The same trends could eventually play out in those sectors. VCs could have handled this differently. Instead of pushing everything out the door, everyone would have been better served if the VCs had used their considerable business acumen to decide which companies were worth investing in for the long haul. And they could have done so with later rounds of private financing, not IPOs. Now, investors are disillusioned with the very model that promising e-tailers depend on for growth. And without further capital, many green e-tailers are getting a savage business lesson that may well spell their demise.

Green, in New York, and Alster, in Boston, track venture capital. Timothy J. Mullaney contributed reporting.

certainty: In its short life as a public company, Amazon's experience has often set the rules under which e-commerce companies operate. Survive or stumble, that will continue to be the case.

Source: Robert Hof, Debra Sparks, Ellen Neuborne, and Wendy Zellner, "Can Amazon Make It?" *Business Week*, July 10, 2000, 38–43

Case 4–2

Pier 1 Imports

Recent earnings growth and robust sales gains at Pier 1 Imports are worthy of the cheery, colorful displays that fill the company's home furnishings stores.

Spirits are high, too, at the company's Fort Worth headquarters, where executives are crafting a strategy to expand by at least one-third and working to develop or acquire a second retail concept to ensure long-term growth.

The picture wasn't so bright 11 months ago. Last August, Pier 1 announced that earnings wouldn't meet expectations because of slumping sales, that the company's chief financial officer had resigned, and that it was abandoning plans to acquire another retail chain—all in one day.

Marvin Girouard, the company's chief executive, was called on to explain the stumble.

"We recognized a year ago that we had a problem with our pricing," Girouard says.

Essentially, Pier 1 was losing customers to sticker stock. The company that built its reputation selling eclectic imports at reasonable prices had lost its focus by trying to compete with more upscale retailers. Pier 1 was out of sync with customer expectations.

At the same time, the company was encountering the increased competition from discounters such as Wal-Mart and especially Target, which has earned customer kudos for its lines of low-price, trendy home furnishings and accessories.

On top of that, rising freight costs were cutting into profits.

As the story unfolded, investors retreated. Pier 1's stock price dropped 33 percent in one day to a then 52-week low of $5.875. Over the next few weeks it dropped to $5.25 a share.

The situation compelled a swift response.

Management dropped expansion plans to focus on the core business. Pier 1 executives were already aware of the pricing problems, but a return to "value pricing" became even more imperative. That meant reducing regular prices on key items—primarily in the tabletop and decorative accessories categories—and refining the overall merchandise mix so price variations within a product category could be justified by clear distinctions in quality.

For example, in the past, the company might have stocked two similar wine glasses priced at $6 and $8. Under the revised strategy, the company would stock two wine glasses with visible differences in craftsmanship and price them accordingly, say, at $2 and $9.

Improvement was slow at first. Growth of same-store sales—which measure sales growth at stores open more than one year and are considered a good performance indicator among retailers—hovered in the low single digits through fall (Exhibit 1).

Momentum picked up in December, and sales took off in the new year. Since January, Pier 1 has reported double-digit same-store sales and beat the national chair store average growth rate—as calculated by Bank of Tokyo-Mitsubishi in New York—in every month but May.

New long-term shipping contracts have also helped stabilize costs.

Pier 1's first-quarter earnings were up 33.5 percent to $16.9 million, or 17 cents a share, for the quarter ended May 27, compared with $12.6 million, or 13 cents a share, for the same quarter a year ago. Gradually, investors have responded. On Friday, Pier 1 stock rose 37½ cents to close at $11.43¾ on the New York Stock Exchange.

In retrospect, analysts commend Girouard on the recovery.

"I think he responded very quickly to the slowdown of the business last summer," says Lynn Detrick, an analyst with Sanders Morris Harris in Houston.

EXHIBIT 1
Pier 1 Imports

Founded: 1962
Headquarters: Fort Worth
CEO: Marvin Girouard, 60
Stores: more than 830 in the United States, Canada, Mexico, Puerto Rico, the United Kingdom, and Japan
Number of employees: more than 13,600

	Fiscal year sales in millions	Earnings in millions
1996	$810.7	$10.1
1997	$947.1	$44.1
1998	$1,075.4	$78.0
1999	$1,138.6	$80.4
2000	$1,231.1	$74.4

Same-store sales growth

July '99	−9.9 percent
Aug. '99	.4 percent
Sept. '99	3.6 percent
Oct. '99	2.4 percent
Nov. '99	2.4 percent
Dec. '99	6.1 percent
Jan. '00	10.8 percent
Feb. '00	15.1 percent
Mar. '00	12.4 percent
Apr. '00	12.1 percent
May '00	4.8 percent
June '00	13.5 percent

Ozarslan Tangun, senior vice president and director of research for Southwest Securities in Dallas, says the company is on the right track but will have to make some more moves to capture significant investor interest.

"First of all, it's going to depend on same-store sales," he says. "Really in order to get the stock to the next level, we need to see some good growth potential."

So far, the company has expressed plans to expand from its current 830-store base to between 1,300 and 1,500 stores. That means opening 65 to 75 new stores a year for the next seven years, in new markets as well as in established metropolitan markets.

For example, Pier 1 has seven stores in Tarrant County.

"Now, we're looking very carefully, watching the west side and to the north," Chief Financial Officer Cary Turner says.

With the core business back on track, Girouard says the company will return to the task of finding a second vehicle to promote earnings growth.

"The reason we believe investing in our stores is our best bet is because they become profitable in three years," Girouard says.

"The limitation is, I can't open 500 a year. We've got to come up with something to give us additional growth."

Since late 1998, Girouard has discussed either developing or buying a second chain that would feature home furnishings products at a price point either a notch above or a notch below Pier 1's core stores. The acquisition abandoned last summer was reported to have been with California-based Z Gallerie, an upscale home furnishings chain similar to a Pottery Barn but with more vibrant colors and an extensive selection of framed wall decor.

Dennis Telzrow, an analyst at the Hoak Breedlove Wesneski investment firm in Dallas, says Pier 1 has good cash flow and is well-positioned financially to support both core store expansion and a new acquisition.

"The capital spending is pretty set going forward," he says.

The only apparent financial limitation is finding a company at the right stage of development.

"They won't go after a company three times their size," he says. "They're looking for a smaller-type company that can grow rapidly."

In the past few months, the range of acquisition possibilities has broadened to include nonfurnishings options, Girouard says.

"What would be a logical thing is to do something relative to our core competencies," which include retailing, merchandising, and general store operations, as well as familiarity with a certain market segment, he says.

"The best thing for us to do is what we know best," he says.

Kurt Barnard, president of Barnard's Retail Trend Report, a retail consulting firm in Upper Montclair, N.J., says the product itself is less important than "to have a clear notion in mind of what kind of customer you want to attract."

Barnard lauds Pier 1 for building a brand identity and customer loyalty "by bringing to the customer unusual, decorative items that make the house stand out with a sense of taste and sophistication."

Since opening its first store in San Mateo, Calif., in 1962, the company has earned a reputation for offering eclectic fashions at a value price.

"In the 1960s, we were a funky little import company," Girouard says.

The mix has changed over the year. In the early days, stores were often stocked with impractical "spice items" like a full suite of body armor and a regimental rice cooker. There was also a brief foray into the tropical fish market. About four years ago, the company stopped selling apparel.

Today, furniture accounts for about 38 percent of annual sales. The stores' most notable categories are wicker, candles, and tabletop items.

"In the areas where they are strongest they have particularly differentiated their product," Detrick says.

Jay Jacobs, senior vice president of merchandising, says Pier 1's merchandising strengths and overall strategy are fundamentally built on the foundation established 38 years ago.

Today's Pier 1 works with about 1,500 vendors in 60 countries. About 90 percent of those relationships go back several years.

"It's a hard thing to get your first order at Pier 1," Jacobs says.

The company regularly gets offers from manufacturers who say they can make "whatever you want," Jacobs says.

But that's not good enough.

"If they come in, they've got to understand Pier 1 and the style of Pier 1," he says.

And today, as trends breed imitations, "you've got to be moving and changing your product more quickly," he says.

That also means being on the alert for new ideas.

For example, Jacobs was traveling through Italy recently with another Pier 1 buyer. While driving through the countryside, they stopped by the side of the road to buy some fruit. The vendor produced a rare variety of highly fragrant vanilla-scented oranges that he had gathered from a small carefully cultivated grove.

"We were just blown away by this vanilla orange," Jacobs says.

Remember that story: Pier 1 is working to perfect a candle to mimic that aroma.

Not all product notions are so inspired, but the company is constantly looking for ways to stretch the ones that are. For example, a design from a piece of flat art could be incorporated into a fabric pattern, a plate motif or a beaded design on a pillow.

In furniture, Pier 1 is known for its cautious approach of introducing only a few or even one piece in a particular style and expanding the line depending on how well the first item is received.

"Their initial buys in products aren't that deep," Detrick says. "Pier 1 doesn't make big bets on products. I think that's smart."

To balance that, the company tries to develop collections of stylistically similar products that customers can match and coordinate, Jacobs says.

And often, all the customers want is one piece or a few accent accessories.

"It's not as fast as apparel," he says. "You can't afford to totally redecorate your house" every season.

Before a product makes it into a Pier 1 store, it has gone through at least one, if not several, reviews during which buyers evaluate products and then make alteration requests to the vendors.

"Sometimes, we'll see it and say, 'I love it,'" Jacobs says. "Other times, we struggle and struggle and will never buy it."

The small group of buyers travels frequently but stays in close touch, which helps the company develop themes across product lines.

There's also the final filter: Jacobs signs every purchase order.

"Some things I know I'm never going to sign," he says looking quizzically at a pair of monkey candlestick holders on review in the company's Fort Worth sample room. "I'm never going to sign those monkeys."

About 65 percent to 70 percent of the merchandise in Pier 1 stores changes annually. Most stores carry about 4,500 regularly priced items, with 3,000 to 4,000 on clearance depending on timing.

About 95 percent of Pier 1 stores carry the company's full product line, although a few smaller stores carry an abbreviated assortment.

But variations in store size and design mean that every Pier 1 store is laid out differently, with general guidelines from the home office.

"Pier 1 being a national chain, we want to have consistent mixes throughout the country," Jacobs says. "But all the stores feel different to the customers."

Pier 1's core customer base—women in their 20s, 30s, and 40s—has remained fairly consistent over the years. The company is working to broaden its appeal across gender lines and to make connections with its younger customers.

The company relaunched its Web site last month with online shopping capabilities and connections to its gift registry. The site offers about 1,400 items, which can be returned or exchanged in local stores. Fingerhut handles logistics and distribution.

Pier 1 spent about $2 million last fiscal year to develop the site and expects to invest an additional $2 million to $4 million this year to enhance it.

The company is also developing an ad campaign with actress Kirstie Alley as celebrity spokeswoman.

The company expects to unveil the first elements of the campaign—which will eventually include print and TV components—in late summer or early fall.

When asked to consider his competitors in the home furnishings arena, Girouard is particularly optimistic about Pier 1's prospects.

"Nobody has the presence we have with stores all over the country," he says.

As for the company's balance of product image and perceived value, there's not much he would change.

"We like being right here," Girouard says.

"Typically, we do well during strong economic times, but we also do well in a downturn because people see us as having economic value."

Analysts say that is a fair assessment.

"They are doing well and will continue to do well as long as housing sales continue," Barnard says. "Even once the growth begins to contract, their price range is such that they won't feel it as much."

Detrick says there will be some effect.

"To the extent that consumer spending slows, it does make the environment a little more competitive," she says.

But underlying trends in the home furnishings market show increased spending among the core demographic—aging baby boomers—who are spending more on their homes, and buying second homes.

Also, Detrick says, the home furnishings industry remains a fairly fragmented market, which means that during slowdowns, "there are opportunities for the better-positioned players to take share."

Source: Lyla LaHood, "Back in Its Niche," *Tarrant Business,* July 17, 2000, 14–16.

Case 4–3
Virgin Group Ltd.

Richard C. N. Branson has made a career of confounding his critics. His Virgin Group Ltd. spans 170 businesses, from airlines and railroads to music stores and condoms. So when the British tycoon moves online, one shouldn't expect just digital music and virtual airline reservations. Try some 5,500 London households paying gas and electric bills online through Virgin's Web site since July. An additional 2,000 Brits tooling around in cars they bought on the Net, thanks to a new Virgin service launched a month earlier. Then there are the nearly 2 million people in the country booking train tickets through Virgin—and 1 million using the Web to tap Virgin's help in managing $4 billion in assets, including insurance, mortgage, and investment funds. And don't forget the $58,000 worth of wine they're buying online from Branson each week (Exhibit 1).

The irony here is that Britain's most colorful and controversial entrepreneur is no big fan of technology. "I'm not that interested in the Net, personally," says the 50-year-old founder and chairman, who doesn't use a computer and instead keeps copious notes in leatherbound notebooks. What Branson does like is the ability to use the Net to bring order to his unwieldy conglomerate. "A lot of people never thought Virgin was very logical because we didn't specialize in any one area," says Branson, comfortably seated in the London townhouse that doubles as his office. "But then the Internet comes along, and I'm able to pretend that it was all a carefully crafted plan," he jokes.

Carefully crafted or not, virgin.com is a digital giant in the making. Still in its first year, the Web site is attracting 1.9 million visitors a month and ranks as the 12th most popular Web destination in Britain, according to market researcher MMXI Europe. Now, Branson is trying to build virgin-com into one of the world's top portals. He has spent more than $225 million to develop Net businesses and services, ranging from a global mobile-phone company to radiofreevirgin.com, a sister site offering software to turn a PC into a digital radio. Branson believes the Virgin name, known for its hip, consumer-friendly image and exceptional service, will translate well across a rash of Web businesses. "Virgin.com isn't a company, it's a brand," says Will Whitehorn, a Virgin director who oversees the company's e-commerce activities.

The stellar red-and-white Virgin logo is a big draw for partners, too. They like the fact that Branson splashes the Virgin logo and its Web address across everything from shopping bags in the Virgin Megastores to the sides of trains and the tails of planes, saving a fortune in advertising. "Virgin's approach to the Net has been very clever," says Simon Knox, professor of brand marketing at the Cranfield University School of Management in Bedford. "Each launch of a new business builds upon the one before, rather than developing isolated branded businesses."

And then there's the way Branson is using the Web to streamline operations inside his empire. His Virgin Atlantic Airways Ltd. and record stores now order inventory online as needed, instead of having to keep huge stashes of CDs and parts close by. The privately held

EXHIBIT 1
**Behind Branson's
E-Empire**

Source: Company Reports.

British entrepreneur Richard Branson is turning his Virgin Group empire—170 or so businesses—virtual. He has set up virgin.com as the Web portal for his online businesses, everything from booking airline tickets to buying wine. Here's a sampling:

Virgin Atlantic Airways
This is Virgin's biggest online moneymaker. The airline uses the Net to sell tickets and to cut inventory costs by ordering spare parts as needed over the Web instead of stocking them in a warehouse.

Virgintravelstore.com
The online travel agency launched in December. Netizens can book everything from airline flights to hotel rooms to guided tours from a wide selection of travel companies, including Virgin.

Virgin Mobile
The joint venture with Deutsche Telekom's cellular company, One 2 One, was launched in November, 1999. Virgin Mobile has 548,000 customers in Britain and is expanding to Australia and Southeast Asia. Customers get mobile-phone service, e-mail, and online services such as dining tips.

Virgin Money
The financial service, launched in June, is similar to Charles Schwab. Besides online trading, users get financial info and can compare every financial product available on the market—not just Virgin's.

Radiofreevirgin.com
The free digital radio tuner, when downloaded to a PC, gives listeners CD-quality music from 50 Net channels. Launched in the U.S. in February, the site boasts 500,000 users and hopes to go global.

Virgin Energy
The Internet-based gas and electricity supplier went live in July. The venture, 25% owned by London Electricity, has attracted 5,500 consumers and plans to roll out across Europe. Customers who haven't saved money after switching will receive a refund of the difference plus 20%.

Virginwines.com
The site for British wine connoisseurs was launched this summer. It uses software to analyze buyers' purchase patterns to help guide them through a list of 17,500 wines. Sales are averaging $58,000 per week.

Virgin Direct
Along with partners, Virgin sells insurance, mortgages, and investment funds. It has more than 1 million customers and $4 billion in assets. Losses in 1999 were around $35 million, with a goal to break even in 2000.

Thetrainline.com
It was started in February, 1999, as a joint venture with British transport company Stagecoach. The site sells tickets for Britain's 23 train operators, has 1.8 million users, and is adding 55,000 new ones each week. It expects to break even by next October.

Virgin Cars
A virtual showroom where consumers can compare models before buying online at prices 17% cheaper than traditional dealerships. Buyers get maintenance thrown in and can arrange financing, as well as sell their existing car on the site. Since its June launch, 1,950 cars have been sold.

company estimates that the Internet will boost efficiencies and shave 15% off its overall costs this year, although it declines to provide specific figures.

Branson is betting the efficiencies will grow as virgin.com becomes a cyberconglomerate. By putting all of Virgin's businesses on one easily accessibly site, he can cross-promote the company's seemingly limitless offerings. For instance, users might log on to the Web site to buy an airline ticket on Virgin Atlantic and then check out a mortgage or order a case of wine. "I normally use Virgin's Web site for entertainment listings, but I was surprised by the amount of stuff they offer," says London Web designer Steven Scott, who logged on recently to check our airfares and ended up buying CDs.

Now, Brits can find another online service on Virgin. On Dec. 8, Branson launched an auction business available through virgin.com. To kick off the service, nine Virgin companies will auction flights, cars, wine, and mobile phones. For the first two weeks, consumers were able to name their price—since all bidding began at $1.50. Beginning Jan. 31, the range of goods and services will change weekly. "Considering the brand recognition that Virgin has wherever it operates, they've got the right strategy in place: an online marketplace for offline products," says Jamie Wood, head of European equity research at J. P. Morgan & Co. "The Web works best when a brand aggregates a variety of services into one place with a guaranteed level of service."

Despite all its nifty Net services, Virgin is late to the Web. So far, most of the ventures behind virgin.com are available only in Britain. The company's online sales total a puny $216 million. That's just a fraction of Virgin's overall sales of $5.2 billion. And it's way behind the $500 million in e-commerce and advertising revenues that rival America Online Inc. generated for the fiscal year 2000 ended June 30. Critics also question whether plastering Virgin's logo over such a disparate range of businesses undermines the clarity or integrity of the brand.

The Virgin brand hasn't gained much traction among Net shoppers in the U.S. In December, Virgin announced it was temporarily pulling back from online music sales in the U.S. through its Virgin Megastore site. Virgin says the level of U.S. sales has not been sufficient to justify maintaining a full-service e-commerce operation. Virgin Megastore now plans to focus its online efforts on providing music-related content while expanding the number of stores in the U.S. from 19 to about 40 by 2005. Because the U.S. is still a small share of Virgin Megastore's overall sales, the company hopes that increasing its presence in America will eventually strengthen its position online.

Brand leverage

Branson also faces tough competition from such global Net players as AOL and Yahoo! Inc., which already have well-established portals offering almost the same fare. "Everyone wants to be a leading portal these days," says analyst Mikael Arnbjerg of market researcher IDC in Copenhagen. "Virgin can leverage its brand in certain market sectors, but that's not enough to become a major player."

Branson doesn't deny any of these challenges. But he insists that Virgin's strength is that the brand isn't inextricably linked to just one business or product. Unlike other cell-phone operators, Virgin can cross-sell a variety of products and services to its mobile phone customers. And because brick-and-mortar retailers tend to specialize in one area of the market, Virgin believes its diverse offerings will be a major advantage. Virgin is betting that selling its own merchandise, something neither AOL nor Yahoo! does, will give it an edge over the big online players. "Being complete virtual and simply selling other people's products is a zero-sum game," says Whitehorn.

Where Branson's strategy has the potential to pay off handsomely is on the wireless Web. Virgin already sells mobile phones and offers Virgin Mobile, a wireless network that is a joint venture with Deutsche Telekom's cellular company, One 2 One. By 2005, mobile phones are expected to account for more than 40% of the estimated $20 billion in European e-commerce transactions, according to London-based market research company Mintel. "Branson realizes the considerable potential for mobile phones as a distribution channel, and any of his businesses can benefit from this," says Peter Richardson, principal analyst at The Gartner Group, a consultancy in Egham, Surrey.

How? Virgin Mobile gives Branson a direct line to customers without incurring extra marketing costs. Using short text messages, Virgin can offer targeted promotions for any of its products and services. Today, some 20% of Virgin Mobile's revenue is e-mail and other data communications, but Branson estimates that nearly 50% of the wireless network's revenues will come from non-voice traffic by 2005. By then, Branson believes most of the transactions on virgin.com will be made through cell phones instead of PCs. Branson envisions a day when Virgin Mobile users will be able to reserve a seat on Virgin Trains while waiting on the platform, simply by pressing a button on their phones. Once aboard, Virgin Mobile users can check their investments through the Virgin Direct financial services site, book a vacation through Virgin Holidays Ltd., or listen to the top-selling tracks at the Virgin Megastores.

The day when people use their phones to buy tickets for the train is coming soon—thanks to Branson. Skeptics doubted he would be able to make a business out of booking tickets online. After all, buying via the Web requires planning—something people who purchase their tickets at the station are not used to doing. But TheTrainLine.com, a joint venture with British transportation company Stagecoach Holdings PLC, is doing a brisk trade. The site sells tickets for Britain's 23 train operators, including Virgin's train line. Some 2 million people use the service, and 55,000 new customers visit the site each week. By yearend, revenue for the operation is expected to hit $144 million, and Virgin expects to break even by next October.

What could give Branson a bigger boost on the Web is Virgin's reputation for super service. In June, the company launched Virgin Cars, an online site where British consumers can buy a broad range of makes and models at an average discount of 17% from those sold in dealerships. Virgin can offer lower prices by buying cars from European dealerships, where the vehicles are far cheaper than in Britain due to the strength of the pound. That advantage won't last forever. So Branson is building a reputation for quality and white-glove treatment by offering a service package that includes warranty, roadside assistance, and pickup-and-delivery maintenance, including a clean car when it's returned.

Branson doesn't view the Web as a tool simply to boost the top line. Virgin is using the Internet to streamline its far-flung operations. Virgin Atlantic Airways, for instance, is tapping into the Net to improve the efficiency of its supply chain. The airline now buys most of its new and used parts online. Whenever mechanics need a part, they log on and place their order—instead of Virgin having to stock a complete array of plane parts. This just-in-time approach, says Whitehorn, has helped the carrier achieve great savings by reducing the amount of inventory it needs to warehouse. If a plane is stranded on the tarmac or in the hangar because of a faulty part, Virgin Atlantic can check the Web for a local supplier that stocks that part and have it sent to the runway in a matter of hours, something that would have been impossible three years ago.

Using the Net, Branson has even resuscitated his money-losing V Shop retail chains. The British chain, known until recently as Our Price, is a miniature version of the Virgin Megastore, where customers can buy music, videos, entertainment gear, software, and mobile phones. In September, the stores were renamed V Shops. Instead of stocking massive amounts of CDs, videos, and games, V Shops now keep only the most popular products on its shelves. The rest are held at a fulfillment house contracted by Virgin. Customers who want to buy something other than what the store has in stock can choose from an additional 110,000 products available via in-store kiosks hooked to the Net. Currently, 10% of all sales are through the in-store kiosks.

The impact on the bottom line is considerable. By slashing its in-store inventory in half, Virgin is saving around $300,000 a year at each of the 150 V Shops. Monthly sales are up an average of 40%, and Virgin anticipates all of the retooled V Shops will be profitable in their first year. "Technology has enabled us to put a dying business back on its feet and make a small store big," says Virgin Entertainment Group CEO Simon Wright.

For Branson, a self-confessed techno-illiterate, the Internet may be just another means of building the Virgin brand and bringing order to his vast empire. Yet, if his efforts pay off, the Virgin name might one day stand for techno-savvy.

Source: Kerry Capell, "Virgin Takes E-wing," *Business Week E.Biz,* January 22, 2001, 30, 33–34.

Case 4–4
Sun Microsystems Inc.

Late last June, Sun Microsystems Inc. President Edward Zander got the kind of call every tech executive dreads. After eBay Inc. suffered a 22-hour outage of its Web site and a spate of smaller crashes, CEO Margaret Whitman called to tell Zander that the problem was a bug in Sun's top-of-the-line server. Sun would learn something just as startling over the next few days of round-the-clock meetings with eBay: The Internet upstart didn't have a clue about running a $1 million-plus computer. The company hadn't provided sufficient air conditioning to keep the machine cool. And even though there had been a software problem with the machine for which Sun had issued a patch many months before, eBay had simply neglected to install it. The list went on—fueling the sentiment, as one Sun manager put it, that "selling computers to some of these dot-coms is like giving a gun to a 5-year-old."

That's when Zander realized things could get much worse. For most dot-coms, starting their business on a Sun server is almost a given. Already, more than 40% of the servers found in the computing centers that house most Web sites are Sun's, and that market is expected to boom as everyone from new Net companies to the click-and-mortar crowd set up shop online. "It suddenly hit me," says Zander. "How many future eBays are buying their first computer from us this very minute?" Adds Sun CEO Scott G. McNealy: "It was our Pentium moment," comparing the eBay incident to the lesson Intel Corp. learned in 1994 after the chip giant angered customers by initially trying to downplay a bug in its new Pentium chip. "That's when we realized it wasn't eBay's fault," says McNealy. "It was our fault."

McNealy and Zander didn't need another wake-up call. Since then, the two have been tearing apart Sun and rebuilding it in an effort to make the Net as reliable as the telephone system. Just as AT&T became Ma Bell, providing that always available dial tone, Sun is shooting for no less than Ma Web, the supplier of super-reliable Web tone. To do that, Sun is moving far beyond Web servers to providing many of the technologies required to make this possible: storage products, a vast array of e-business software, and consultants that not only supply all the gear but also hold customers' hands every step of the way (Exhibit 1).

EXHIBIT 1
The Net Effect

Almost from its founding in 1982, Sun has pursued a vision in which computing power resides on huge servers, whisking data and other services to PCs, handheld gadgets, and other devices. Thanks to the Web, Sun's vision is becoming reality. So Sun is honing its strategy, management techniques, and technology to become the dominant computer company in the Internet Age.

STRATEGY

Redefine Net Software: Today, hundreds of niche software outfits hawk a mind-numbing patchwork of applications. Sun wants to create a new category of software that combines many Net programs into one super-reliable whole that's included with its server.

As Reliable as the Phone Network: Sun is moving beyond just hardware to offer pretested configurations that include storage, Net software, and popular applications. That's how telco switchmakers like Lucent and Nortel managed to make the phone network fail-safe.

Lock Up the Service Providers: Having guessed right that software would be delivered over the Net rather than as CDs to be installed on PCs, Sun has the early lead with companies that will deliver the software—from Net newbies to huge telcos.

MANAGEMENT

Central Authority: On July 1, Sun created into one uber-sales operation, rather than fiercely independent server, software, chip, and services units. That way, customers can deal with one salesman. More important, engineers are working together to design resilient systems by making sure, for example, that Net software can detect chip or disk-drive failures.

No More Cowboys: Sun has been known as the freewheeling cowboy of the computer business. Now it's adding big-company processes—such as extensive audits of a customer's tech operations before taking the order.

TECHNOLOGY

The Grand Design: Sun is the architect of some of the sexier elements of the Web, such as its Java Net software. Now engineers are focusing on keeping the Net running all the time—like how to build backup systems to avoid failures in chips, servers, software, and networks.

Pay-as-You-Grow: Sun is working on hardware and software components that allow fast-growing customers to add what they need without ever having to scrap old equipment.

The Storage Is the Network: New VCR-sized storage devices that can be located anywhere on the Net—instead of just in central data centers—putting information closer to users.

LEADERSHIP

Forging Industry Standards: With Java a Net standard, Sun continues to push its Jini technology, which promises to let any digital device talk to any other. That way, your browser-equipped cell phone could print on any nearby Jini-ready printer.

Setting Ground Rules: Not all Net companies know how to operate around the clock. So Sun has a program to lay out best practices, from how to ensure backup to how to prevent data centers from becoming overheated. Some 300 companies have qualified for this stamp of approval of the Net Age.

Safe Bet

If the duo can pull it off, Sun could emerge as the King of the Net—every bit as dominant as Big Blue in its mainframe heyday or Microsoft Corp. in the PC era. Just as high-tech managers used to say, "No one gets fired for choosing IBM," Zander aims to have the same said of Sun. "I want to be the safe bet for companies that need the most innovative technology," he says.

Sun hopes to go down in the history books as that rare company with the vision to change an industry and the ability to cash in on that vision. Since it was founded in 1982, Sun has promoted the notion that "the network is the computer," a view of computing where the action isn't on desktop PCs but on big central servers where computing can be doled out in easy-to-use chunks, wherever and whenever desired. With the explosion of the Internet and rapid deployment of high-bandwidth networks, Sun's vision finally is becoming a reality. "McNealy held out for the pot of gold," says Bill Raduchel, a former Sun executive who is now chief technologist at America Online Inc. "It took a decade to play out, but now the pot of gold is here."

That's why Sun has been on a tear. In the most recent quarter, revenue climbed 35%—more than any other computer company, including PC darling Dell Computer Corp., which grew 30%. Sun is growing faster than at any time since 1991, when it was one-fifth the size it is today. And with gross profit margins of 52%, it is the most profitable computer maker in all of techdom.

McNealy vows this is just the beginning. Known for having the strategic vision, slickest sales reps, and hottest new products—but not the best service—Sun has made reliability the top priority. That means pumping up the services business and overhauling the way the company designs and sells its products. In the past year, Sun has reduced the number of configurations it sells from thousands by pushing customers to choose from under 200 models. And now, managers and sales reps are compensated largely on customer satisfaction. What's more, McNealy, a sometime golfing buddy of General Electric Co. Chairman John F. Welch, has become a convert of GE's Six Sigma quality program that builds in checks to make sure customers' operations stay up and running. By far, the boldest element of McNealy's plan is software. Sun is trying to define and dominate a new category of software that combines many of today's e-business software segments, including e-mail, e-commerce portals, and programs for serving up Web pages and wireless applications. The idea: Wrap a suite of applications into one fail-safe whole available on any Sun server. On July 17, iPlanet, Sun's Net software joint venture formed with AOL last year, unveiled the new suite, along with an audacious goal: Within 18 months, the company expects to hit the $1 billion mark in e-commerce software sales, according to Margaret Breya, iPlanet's vice-president of marketing. By 2005, she says Sun could have a $5 billion to $10 billion software business. Other executives, however, say it may take a buying binge to get there.

Put it all together, and Sun is designing its own take on an old trend: vertical integration, in which it sells software, hardware, and services as one—just like telecom equipment makers Lucent Technologies or Nortel Networks Corp. do with their phone switches. "The computing model of tomorrow is the telecom model of today," says Masood Jabbar, Sun's senior vice-president of sales. How does Sun fit in? It plans to make the "big frigging Webtone switches," as McNealy calls them—the powerful servers that can whisk billions of bits around the Net, along with the software that manages Web pages, dishes up data, and executes transactions. "The world's moving in our direction at 8 gazillion miles per hour. Our biggest problem is just trying to keep up," says McNealy.

That's why he has lit a bonfire under Sun. After the eBay incident, Zander called a meeting of all managers and read them the riot act. Late last summer, his staff identified 14 key initiatives, such as new processes for conducting customer audits, with one of Zander's top vice-presidents in charge of each. And on July 1, McNealy reorganized Sun, combining fiercely independent sales operations within product units into one single sales organization. Now, customers see one sales rep for their entire business, instead of being bombarded by reps from different divisions. And McNealy has created a Customer Advocacy Organization to make sure all divisions are putting reliability and customer satisfaction first. Division president Mel Friedman, for instance, has authority to request the redesign of any Sun product for suspected glitches. Says Breya: "It's about Sun growing up."

As we all know, though, growing up is hard to do. For Sun to shake off its upstart ways, it will have to make the shift from an engineering-driven company to a full-service company. That means mastering software sales, a historic weakness, and building up consulting to help companies design their e-business around Sun gear. And it must do all this while holding off heavyweights such as IBM and Hewlett-Packard. The stalwarts may have been slow to grok the Net, but they have a legacy of ultra-dependable products that could be a major advantage. "Sun rode the wave of dot-coms, but those companies have different needs now. And taking care of those needs is IBM's and HP's forte, not Sun's," says Bruce L. Chovnick, senior vice-president at Network Solutions, a Web registry company that recently ditched a Sun high-end server for a mainframe from IBM.

McNealy will have to stare down other challengers, as well. At a time when servers based on Sun's new UltraSparc3 chip are a few months late, longtime PC industry rivals are massing for yet another assault on the server market. Using Microsoft's four-month-old Windows 2000 program or the free Linux operating system, PC makers will continue to chip away at the market for less powerful servers—especially after Intel brings out its new IA-64 chips, due by year end. "Customers are willing to pay high prices and go with the safe bet [Sun] in these early days of the Net. But ultimately, we'll be able to redefine the economics of the Internet," says Compaq Computer Corp. CEO Michael D. Capellas. Adds International Data Corp. analyst Jean S. Bozman: "Everyone is shooting at Sun, there's no question about it."

The company with the most ammunition is Microsoft. On June 22, Microsoft announced its version of Sun's Webtone scheme—an initiative dubbed .net that is designed to make the Web much easier to use. In it, unrelated Web sites, Net services, and traditional Windows software programs can be linked together to do useful things—say, to get your bank's Web site to transfer money to your e-broker, who buys a stock and then records the trade to your Microsoft Money program on your PC. Such complexity requires software expertise, snorts Microsoft CEO Steve A. Ballmer, "and Sun's not really a software company." Counters Sun chief scientist Bill Joy: "I've been writing about network-based computing for 20 years. Microsoft embraced it last week."

Sniping aside, Sun faces even more software challenges. Throw into the mix programs such as Napster that make it easy to link files directly from PC to PC, altogether bypassing huge servers, and some analysts think McNealy & Co. could face a resurgence of powerful PCs that can store and move data around the Net. That could put a squeeze on server profits. Sanford C. Bernstein & Co. analyst Toni Sacconaghi thinks profit margins for Sun's servers could fall from the mid-50s to the low-30s within three years. So it's crucial that Sun crank up sales of hugely profitable software and storage products, with gross profit margins of 80% and 60%, respectively.

Only then can Sun continue to fund its $2 billion research-and-development effort and keep spending at an industry-leading rate of 10% of revenue. If it can't, Sun may find itself boxed into a high-end corner of the computer industry, adding to the list of once proud computer companies such as Digital Equipment Corp. that have been whittled away by PC makers.

EXHIBIT 2

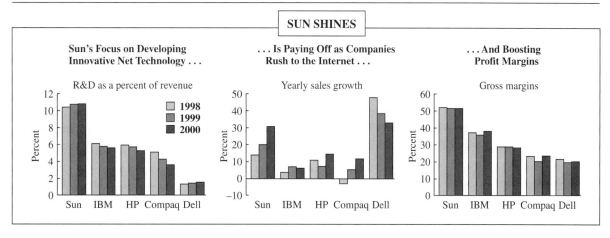

SUN SHINES

Sun's Focus on Developing Innovative Net Technology . . . . . . Is Paying Off as Companies Rush to the Internet . . . . . . And Boosting Profit Margins

Source: Data; Sanford C. Bernstein & Co.

Sun has managed to outfox the doomsayers before. In the early 1990s, when profits collapsed for the technical workstations that brought in 90% of the company's revenue, McNealy bet the next big opportunity would be servers. He poured billions into developing technologies such as the Solaris operating system. Now, servers and related gear bring roughly 80% of Sun's $11.7 billion in sales. Even more remarkable is Sun's assault on the high-end server market once dominated by IBM mainframes. While the market for $1 million-plus servers shrank 17.8% last year, to $11.4 billion, Sun's revenue has rocketed 28% because of runaway sales of its e10,000 Starfire machines, according to IDC (Exhibit 2).

Unlike high-tech dynasties such as IBM or Microsoft, Sun's grand plan is not based on locking customers into its own proprietary technology. IBM and Microsoft modulated the flow of new technology in the mainframe and PC eras largely by maintaining control of technical interfaces that others would need to create compatible programs and peripherals. But Sun wants to dominate Internet-style—that is, by doing as much innovation as possible, licensing leading-edge work as the standard for others, and then racing to stay ahead.

That puts the pressure on Sun's big thinkers, like Joy (Exhibit 3). For starters, Joy and Sun's other technologists have coined the term "Net Effects" to describe the challenge of keeping up with spiraling demand as a billion people use the Net more often, from more devices, and in different ways over the next few years. To keep pace, Sun's servers will have to accelerate in power at a rate at least 100 times faster than Moore's Law, which holds that chips double in speed every 18 months, says Sun chief technologist Greg Popadopolous. Sun is working on two tracks—massive single machines with millions of microprocessors, as well as distributed computing schemes so the computing load can be divvied up between smaller machines linked by high-speed networks.

Sun also is betting it can leapfrog the competition by giving customers the essential software they need to run their e-businesses in one neat, foolproof package. Today, companies face a blizzard of offerings—application servers to host and handle e-mail, Web servers to manage and send out Web pages, and portal programs on which to give the sites a unique look and feel. While these stand-alone software products may deliver the latest bells and whistles, it costs a fortune in consulting fees to make them work together.

Sun's approach is different. iPlanet packs snazzy programs into a suite known as the Internet Service Deployment Platform. Don't be fooled by the clunky name. Using this

**EXHIBIT 3
The Joy of
Questioning**

It was a bona fide mood killer. On May 15, the 100 or so chief technology officers at San Francisco's Palace Hotel were flying high. They spent the morning at a high-tech conference getting jazzed about how they could help their companies cash in on the limitless wealth-making potential of the Internet. Then Bill Joy took the stage. The Sun Microsystems Inc. chief scientist used his lunchtime keynote to lay out his view of technology: He fears that rapid high-tech advances could lead to man-made electronic and biological scourges—and the possible extinction of the human race by mid-century. For most of the speech, the audience sat in respectful silence. Then Joy gave a sense of what the future could hold by reading a long description of a horrific plague that wiped out much of medieval Greece. Nervous chuckles began to break the uncomfortable silence.

Joy is a surprising candidate to be making such dire warnings. After all, he has helped shape Sun's vision of superfast computers zipping all manner of digital transactions along the Net. And, he admits, it's computers from Sun and others that will make possible the scientific advances he fears. Still, no one at Sun is trying to talk Joy down from his high-tech bully pulpit. "The concept took me by surprise," admits Sun CEO Scott G. McNealy. "A lot of people think Bill is shooting the golden goose. But hey, I've got kids, too, and Bill's [discussing his views] in a very prudent, responsible way. He's not some lunatic. He's not a prophet of doom." Adds Melvin Schwartz, a Nobel prize winner for physics in 1988: "He's thinking about the things that should be thought about. What sounds wild today won't be in 20 to 30 years."

Indeed, Joy says he's out to shake the mindset that technology offers boundless good. Since publishing an article in *Wired* magazine last April entitled "Why the Future Doesn't Need Us," the 45-year-old Joy has been spending a third of his time on his latest concern. Discoveries in genetic engineering, robotics, and molecular-level engineering (nanotechnology) will soon make it possible for terrorists to unleash mayhem far more dangerous than the nuclear threat, he says. "These technologies are going to create a quadrillion dollars of wealth in the next century," says Joy. "But we do have to deal with the risks. The future is rushing at us at incredible speed, and people just haven't thought it through."

There have been plenty of doomsayers in the past, but few have Joy's credentials. In 1976, as a graduate student, Joy created a version of the Unix operating system that is the standard for most Web sites. In 1982, he co-founded Sun, and was a driving force behind its Java software. These days, Joy is working on new technology to make computers resistant to software bugs.

Joy is by no means turning his back on the Information Society that has made him rich. He says he's simply trying to start a debate. He suggests that companies exploring planet-threatening technologies pay high insurance premiums to discourage them from simply dabbling in such technology. Joy fears the only answer could be one that appalls scientists—including himself: put an end to the spirit of unfettered freedom of scientific inquiry. Lewis M. Branscomb, IBM's former chief scientist and a professor emeritus at Harvard University, credits Joy with raising important issues, but cautions that "once the politicians are allowed to start censoring 'dangerous knowledge,' we will lose both our democracy and our ability to understand how to manage our future." For Joy, the debate is just beginning.—*Peter Burrows*

suite, customers can get up and running quickly because Sun has made sure the software works in sync. With the price starting at $500,000, Sun isn't looking to undercut the competition. Instead, customers will save on installation. "This could cut my development time by 30%," says Norbert Nowicki, a senior partner with Computer Sciences Corp., an El Segundo (Calif.) computer services consultancy.

Sun isn't the only company offering such a suite. Oracle, IBM, and Microsoft do, as well. But none of those companies is the dominant provider of the computers on which the software must run. "Sun isn't just dragging the software along anymore," says Goldman, Sachs &Co. analyst Laura Conigliaro. "It can be a serious driver of new business." Especially with partner AOL using the software suite internally and promoting it to its Net customers. "AOL is customer No. 1 for iPlanet," says David Gang, an AOL executive who recently became iPlanet's executive vice-president. "If we can build products that satisfy AOL, it should work for everyone else."

The irony of McNealy's software approach is that he's stealing a page from the Microsoft playbook—a twist on Microsoft's "embrace and extend" strategy of absorbing fresh technologies into its Windows software. Instead, Sun wants to either bundle or weave Net software into its Solaris operating system. The process already has begun. While competition used to be fierce in the market for arcane directory software, where companies store their databases of employees, customers, and suppliers, now Sun dominates because it has embedded directory software into the latest version of Solaris. "This could be every bit as big as Oracle's [$7.4 billion database] business," says Mark Tolliver, general manager of iPlanet.

In recent months, the company has made a push into hot new areas, such as a wireless server that will go head-to-head with IBM and others, and e-commerce and e-marketplace applications that will compete with offerings from Commerce One, Oracle, and others. And while iPlanet doesn't have a product to rival red-hot programs like Vignette's software for managing Web pages, Sun may develop offerings in this niche or buy the pieces necessary to offer it. "With our stock where it is, we'd be remiss if we didn't look at this," says Jonathan Schwartz, recently named Sun vice-president for corporate strategy.

Storage Breakthrough

One area where Sun hasn't been able to get off the ground is storage. The company has made two failed attempts to introduce new products in the last three years. "This business takes focus, but storage was an afterthought for Sun," says Raduchel. No more. Sun claims it has made a breakthrough and has created a specialized sales and support organization to push it. Never mind lining up big cabinet-size storage racks tethered to servers—the way most storage farms operate. Instead, customers put Sun's new T3 storage boxes wherever makes the most sense—without having to be within close proximity to a server. An Internet service provider, for example, could put one in a Boston office to speed Red Sox scores to the locals—regardless of whether that site uses servers from Sun or a rival. "The upside for Sun in storage is immense," says Goldman's Conigliaro, who thinks Sun's $2 billion business will grow 25% a year for the next three years. Still, in that time frame, rival EMC Corp. is expected to shoot past the $15 billion mark.

When did Sun get so serious about growing up? Rumblings began in 1998, when Sun's brain trust began to sense that customers' needs for keeping their Web sites up and running were far outstripping Sun's know-how. But for McNealy and Zander, the eBay incidents in mid-1999 underscored how fast those requirements were rising—and how far behind Sun really was.

Sun sprang into action to solve eBay's problem, and within weeks, it worked out a plan with software partners Oracle and Veritas Software Corp. to stabilize eBay's server—even devising back-up systems that have kept eBay out of the news despite six or so crashes in recent months. "We were pushing Sun's products to places they'd never had to go," says eBay Chief Technology Officer Maynard Webb, who last fall nearly switched to IBM. "For Sun to still have our business is a testament to their ability to solve those issues."

Zander was worried it was more like dumb luck. He knew last-minute heroics would not be possible should eBay-like debacles become commonplace. So in early July, Zander assigned Vice-President John C. Shoemaker to come up with a set of initiatives to meet customer demand for rock-solid gear. By the end of August, after key areas for improvement were identified, Zander decided it was time to turn up the pressure inside Sun, calling for daily 8 A.M. meetings with the management team to discuss any problems at customer sites. "Scott and I decided to ruin everyone's morning," he says.

Now, all high-end systems must be pretested with the customer's software before they ship. Another team is making sure that all new products can be monitored remotely from one of Sun's data centers, finally bringing it up to speed with rivals such as EMC and IBM. Sun has also done two-day, lengthy audits of 75 top customers, sometimes issuing 100-page reports that recommend making changes such as adding a humidity sensor to ensure that atmospheric conditions are optimal for Sun equipment.

And McNealy has become a crusader for the new quality program, dubbed Sun Sigma. Now, Sun's top execs will get four days of training and will then lead teams that will get four weeks of training in Six Sigma-style practices. Any manager who doesn't lead such a team over the next 18 months, says Zander, can forget getting promoted to vice-president.

Why the hardball tactic? With 35,000 employees, Sun will have to start behaving less like a mob of high-tech freedom fighters and more like an icon of big management control. If McNealy can pull that off, then Sun might one day truly be worthy of the nickname Ma Web.

Source: Peter Burrows, "Sun's Bid to Rule the Web," *Business Week E.Biz,* July 24, 2000, EB 31–EB 42.

Implementing and Managing Market-Driven Strategy

Part 5

14

Designing Market-Driven Organizations

An expanding base of evidence from a wide range of companies points to the critical importance of aligning the strategy and capabilities of the organization with the market in order to provide superior customer value.[1] Organizational change is essential in many companies to achieve this objective. The market-driven organization must alter its design, roles, and activities in line with customer requirements.

The 1990s and the early 2000s have been a period of unprecedented organizational change. Companies have realigned their organizations to establish closer contact with customers, improve customer service, bring the Internet into operations and marketing, reduce unnecessary layers of management, decrease the time interval between decisions and results, and improve organizational effectiveness in other ways. Organizational changes include the use of information systems to reduce organizational layers and response time, the use of multifunctional teams to design and produce new products, and the creation of flexible networks of organizations to compete in turbulent business environments.

Since 1999, the Procter & Gamble Company (P&G) has been implementing major global organizational changes as part of its "Organization 2005" plan, at a total cost estimated to approach $2 billion.[2] P&G is widely recognized for its powerful marketing capabilities but faces intense competition throughout the world and loss of position in several key product markets. By 1999 only half its brands were building market share, and the company has struggled to maintain sales and earnings growth.

P&G previously was organized into four business units covering the regions of the world; in 1998 seven new executives reporting to the chief executive officer (CEO) were given profit responsibility for global product units such as baby care, beauty, and fabric and home care (Global Business Units). Several of the Global Business Units are headquartered overseas. The new design concept also includes eight Market Development Units intended to tackle local market issues (e.g., supermarket retailing in South America), as well as Global Business Services and corporate functions. Key objectives were to increase the speed of decision making and move new products into commercialization faster and to manage the business on a global basis.

"Change agents" have been appointed to work across the Global Business Units to lead cultural and business change by helping teams work together more effectively through the use of real-time collaboration tools. Virtual innovation teams are linked by intranets, which can be accessed by senior executives to keep up with developments. The program has involved considerable downsizing in personnel numbers and substantial change—25 percent of P&G brand managers left the company in 18 months. The sales organization is being revised to focus salespersons' attention more specifically on individual brands.

P&G's "Organization 2005" program underlines the nature of the fundamental changes facing many companies in realigning their structures and processes with the requirements of a turbulent and intensely competitive environment.

First we look at several organization design issues and consider alternative designs and the features and limitations of each one in different situational settings. Next, we discuss selecting an organization design. Finally, we look at several global aspects of organizations.

Considerations in Organization Design

Several factors influence the design of marketing organizations. They include (1) matching structure to the strategic goals and direction of change of the company, (2) deciding on the extent of process-type organizational design, (3) confronting the need to design value-creating activities around customers, (4) partnering with independent organizations to perform marketing activities, and (5) understanding the impact of the Internet on the organization's processes.

Strategy and Organization

As strategies change and evolve in a company, it may be necessary to reconsider organizational issues in the implementation of market strategy. Exhibit 14–1 describes several recent realignments of marketing structures in companies making major strategic changes and responding to new customer requirements. Building new strategies in the market-driven company underlines the need to manage organizational change effectively.

Organizational change is a continuing process in many companies. The trend is away from vertical structures and toward flat horizontal structures with a greater emphasis on processes (for example, new product development) and less emphasis on functional specialization.

EXHIBIT 14–1
Strategic Change and Organizational Change

Sources: Jean Halliday, "Chrysler Refits Brand Team," *Advertising Age,* May 14, 2001, 35; Theresa Howard, "Organization Next," *Brandweek,* July 31, 2000, 5; "Hershey Consolidates Marketing Group," *Candy Industry,* January 2000, 13–14.

- In 2001, the troubled Chrysler Group restructured its marketing organization, with marketing communications directors and managers at Chrysler, Jeep, and Dodge taking responsibility for total brand plans, including pricing and incentives. Previously their focus had been mainly on advertising strategy. The goal is greater product and brand focus and cultural change at Chrysler.

- PepsiCo's market strategy shows a greater emphasis on increasing sales of noncarbonated beverages and focusing on ethnic markets. In 2000, the company split its marketing department into carbonated and noncarbonated beverages and appointed a vice-president-level post dedicated to ethnic marketing. The company is also bringing the sales force closer to key retail customers with reorganization into five separate groups: field sales, national accounts sales, strategy and customer development, fountain beverage, and "Power of One" teams.

- Previously organized into business units focused on chocolate, nonchocolate, grocery, and special markets, Hershey Foods has replaced this structure with a consolidated U.S marketing organization to align marketing more closely with sales and to emphasize brand equity and new products. The new Vice President U.S. Marketing manages six marketing units: seasons, new products, special channels, brand equity, pack types, and event marketing.

EXHIBIT 14–2
Alternative Organizational Structures

Source: George S. Day, "Aligning the Organization to the Market," in *Reflections on the Future of Marketing,* Donald R. Lehmann and Katherine E. Jocz, eds. (Cambridge, MA: Marketing Science Institute, 1997), 69–73.

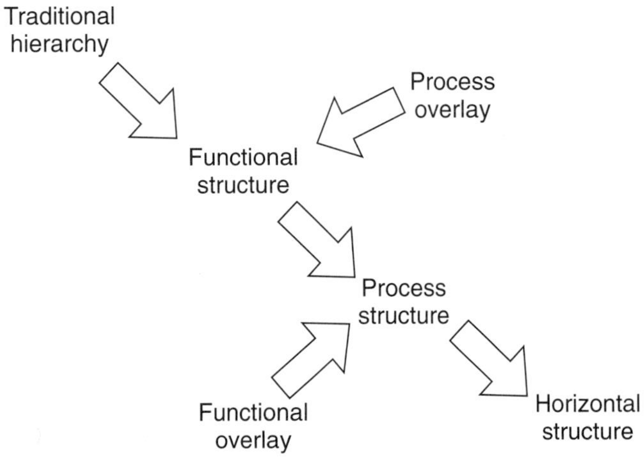

Traditional hierarchy

Process overlay

Functional structure

Process structure

Functional overlay

Horizontal structure

The vertical organization structure concerns the number of management levels and reporting relationships. Vertical design issues include determining reporting relationships, establishing departmental groupings, and creating vertical information linkages.[3] Reporting relationships indicate who reports to whom in the organizational hierarchy. Departmental grouping considers how sets of employees are assigned responsibilities. Groupings may be according to function, geography, product, market, or combinations of these factors. Vertical information linkages are necessary to aid communications among organizational participants. Various techniques help move information through the organization, including approval of proposed actions, rules and procedures, plans and schedules, creation of additional levels or positions, and information systems.

Organizations today have fewer levels than traditional organizations did and are beginning to organize around processes such as order processing, new product planning, customer services, and value/supply chain management. These flat organizations have fewer managers and are information-based. Information storage, processing, and decision-support technology move information up and down and across the organization. Recall the use of virtual teams linked by intranet at Procter & Gamble. Levels of management usually are eliminated, since people at those levels function primarily as information relays rather than as decision makers and leaders. In many organizations, management is under pressure to reduce operating costs, and so eliminating organizational levels and increasing the number of people supervised reduce staff size.

Exhibit 14–2 shows possible new structures as companies move away from traditional hierarchical structures.[4] A study of 73 companies by the Boston Consulting Group placed 32 percent in the hierarchy, 38 percent in the process overlay, and 30 percent in the functional overlay forms. No horizontal structures were reported. The prevailing organizational forms appear to be the hybrid overlay structures.

Hybrid, Process-Type Structures

The structures of large established companies are moving toward horizontal business processes while retaining integrating functions (marketing, human resources) and specialist functions (research and development, marketing).[5] The processes are major clusters of strategically important activities such as new product development and order generation and fulfillment. As companies adopt process structures, various organizational changes occur, including fewer levels and managers, a greater emphasis on building distinctive

- Managing and participating in process-driven organizations present new skill requirements and challenges.

- Functional organizations require individual skills in information gathering, data analysis, and (external) persuasion.

- The process-driven organization emphasizes skills in negotiation, conflict resolution, relationship management, internal communication and persuasion, managing interfaces, team building, teaching, information interpretation, and strategic reasoning.

- Central to the process orientation is defining the organization in terms of the capabilities and processes necessary to provide superior customer value.

- The market-driven enterprise will be customer focused rather than product or technology focused.

- This mandates positioning the organization in the value chain, market sensing, customer linking, and supply-chain management.

Source: Frederick E. Webster, Jr., "The Future Role of Marketing in the Organization," in *Reflections on the Futures of Marketing,* Donald R. Lehmann and Katherine E. Jocz, eds. (Cambridge, MA: Marketing Science Institute, 1997), 39–66.

capabilities by using multifunctional teams, customer value-driven processes and capabilities, and continuously changing organizations that reflect changes in the market and the competitive environment.[6] The Cross-Functional Feature highlights several initiatives in moving an organization from a functional to a process orientation.

Consumer packaged goods companies such as Kraft Foods are moving toward hybrid structures and away from traditional product and brand management approaches in order to place emphasis on customer relationship management:

> Teams are organized around three core processes: the consumer management team, replacing the brand management function, is responsible for customer segments; customer process teams, replacing the sales function, serve the retail accounts; and the supply management team, absorbing the logistics function, ensures on-time delivery to retailers. There is also a strategic integration team, to develop effective overall strategies and coordinate the teams. Although this team relies on deep understanding of the market, it might not be in the marketing function. While functions remain, their roles are to coordinate activities across teams to ensure that shared learning takes place, to acquire and nurture specialized skills, to deploy specialists to the cross-functional process teams, and to achieve scale economies.[7]

The design of an organization affects its ability (and willingness) to respond quickly. The advantage of doing things faster than the competition is clearly established in various kinds of businesses. Recall that Zara's skills in moving women's apparel from design to the store in weeks instead of months enable the retailer to market new designs ahead of its competition. Organizations that can do things faster have a competitive advantage. General Electric reduced the time between order receipt and delivery for custom-made industrial circuit breaker boxes from three weeks to three days.[8] The company formed a team of manufacturing, design, and marketing experts with the responsibility for changing the manufacturing process.

The Challenge of Integration

The development of new organizational forms with new specializations and internal relationships and processes underlines the importance of effective integration around the drivers of customer value. There have been several problems related to integration between marketing and other activities in companies. Effectiveness depends on developing strong linkages between marketing and other functional units. This may involve a variety of approaches.

Integration Problems

Many traditional approaches to organization have hindered the ability of companies to coordinate and integrate activities around customer needs.[9] In some organizations there are major barriers to effective communication between marketing and other units, leading to misunderstanding and conflict, for example, in poor use of market information by research and development (R&D) departments as a result of rivalry and political behavior.[10] In other cases, the integration problem is exacerbated by "ownership" of key activities by other functions: customer relationship management systems span departments and systems to integrate customer knowledge; critical new product "pipelines" may place priority on leveraging R&D capabilities faster than the competition; the implementation of electronic commerce may leave traditional marketing behind; many of the people and processes that affect customer value are outside the control of the marketing area.[11] Accordingly, the imperative for integration becomes more urgent: "An organization can no longer consist of a group of unrelated activities and work groups because customers won't accept it."[12]

Marketing's Links to Other Functional Units

Increasingly, marketing professionals must display superior skills in coordinating and integrating their activities with other functional areas of the business. The move toward process-based organizations underlines this requirement. Examples include new product planning, distribution-channel coordination, pricing analysis, and strategic marketing alliances. Research by Ruekert and Walker offers guidelines regarding these interactions:[13]

> Effectiveness is improved by developing organizational structures and processes to move resources faster across departments with strong resource dependencies.

> Promising coordination mechanisms are formalized operating rules and procedures and horizontal resolution of conflicts. However, resolving conflicts may decrease efficiency.

> Communications between functions appear to be enhanced by similarity in departmental tasks and objectives and when formal operating rules and procedures are used.

> There is mixed support for the proposition that higher conflict occurs when higher levels of interaction or resource flows exist between marketing and other functional areas.

These research findings offer useful insights into marketing's horizontal organizational relationships. Additional research is needed to determine how applicable these preliminary findings are in different internal and external organizational environments.

Additional Approaches to Achieving Effective Integration

Several additional approaches to building effective integration may be considered parts of organization design. Formal mechanisms for integration include:

- Relocation and design of facilities to encourage communication and exchange of information.

- Personnel movement using joint training and job rotation to facilitate managers' understanding of other functions.

- Reward systems that prioritize higher-level goals (e.g., company profits from a cross-functional project), not just functional objectives.

- Formal procedures, for example requiring coordinated input from marketing, finance, operations, and information technology (IT) to project documentation.

- Social orientation facilitating nonwork interaction between personnel from different functions.

- Project budgeting to centralize control over financial resources so that they are channeled, for example, to a project or process team, not to a functional department.[14]

Evidence relating to the effectiveness of these approaches is mixed. Nonetheless, they emphasize the need to examine more than simple structural choices in designing the effective market-driven organization. Interestingly, several routes to enhanced integration: (e.g., increased personal communication, spatial proximity, social interaction) will become progressively more difficult in the intranet-based hollow organization. In such cases, integration issues may become a high priority for management attention.

The impact of effective integration between key functions is illustrated in the Strategy Feature describing the teamwork between marketing and sales and other functions at Johnson Controls Inc. Importantly, the feature underlines the importance of considering information, process, and culture issues alongside structural choices in designing the market-driven organization for the future.

The management philosophy at GE summarizes several of these themes:

> One clear message in our approach is the value of the borderless culture which breaks down the horizontal barriers between functions and the vertical barriers between organizational levels. This means that employees are encouraged to collaborate with others and given considerable freedom to turn their creativity into productivity.[15]

Partnering with Other Organizations

Marketing organization design includes consideration of the trade-offs between performing marketing functions within the organization and having external organizations perform those functions. The discussion of relationship strategies in Chapter 7 examined the use of partnering to perform various business functions. Contractual arrangements are often made for advertising and sales promotion services, marketing research, and telemarketing. Services are also available to perform marketing functions in international markets. Strategic alliances are popular market entry and product development strategies.

The importance of outsourcing various business functions expanded rapidly in the 1990s. This trend has continued into the 21st century due to pressures for cost reduction, the availability of competent services, increased flexibility, and shared risk. There are various marketing functions that may be provided by independent suppliers. Examples include telemarketing, database marketing, field marketing, logistics, website design and management, and information services. Dell Computer's outsourcing of computer services is illustrative.

Internal units provide more control of activities, easier access to other departments, and greater familiarity with company operations. The commitment of the people to the organization is often higher since they are part of the corporate culture. Nonetheless, internal units display difficulty in quickly expanding or contracting size, lack of experience in other

Johnson Controls is a market leader in automotive seating, interiors, and batteries, with interests in automated control systems for buildings. Late in 2001, in the middle of a slump in high-technology markets, Johnson marked its 27th consecutive year of enhanced dividends. That year was the company's 55th year of uninterrupted sales gains and the 11th straight year of record earnings. The company's culture of teamwork underpins this remarkable performance:

- Executives from marketing and sales have frequent meetings, collaborate on marketing promotions, take training courses together, make sales calls together, and share information freely, with a shared focus on making sure customers get what they want.

- Making a sales call at Ford to win seat business in Ford's F Series trucks, Johnson fields five employees—three from sales and two from marketing—with the goal of demonstrating such deep understanding of the consumer that Ford will not think of going to another supplier.

- Customer visits often involve sales, marketing, engineering, and design personnel together.

- Salespeople are paid an end-of-year performance bonus, not a commission on sales, while marketing employees, engineers, and product designers receive bonuses based on company performance.

- Auto manufacturers have shifted from buying parts from suppliers like Johnson to assemble vehicles toward buying systems of parts that basically just snap into the car.

- Johnson positioned itself to take advantage of this shift in customer needs by creating partnerships with its customers, undertaking exhaustive market research, and actively fostering an internal environment based on cooperation.

- Johnson's teamwork philosophy extends to its alliances, such as that with Philips for in-car DVD entertainment systems. Each alliance has an executive to oversee it and a Web page for alliance partners to share critical information.

Sources: Andy Cohen, "In Control," *Sales and Marketing Management,* June 1999, 32–38; Harlan S. Byrne, "Johnson Controls: Back In Gear," *Barron's,* June 5, 2000, 21–22; Shirley A. Lazo, "Speaking of Dividends: Just Like Clockwork," *Barron's,* November 19, 2001, 37.

business environments, and limited skills in specialized areas such as advertising, marketing research, Web design, and database management.

External organizations offer specialized skills, experience, and flexibility in adapting to changing conditions. These firms may have lower costs than an organization that performs the function(s) internally. Obtaining services outside the firm also has limitations, including loss of control, longer execution time, greater coordination requirements, and lack of familiarity with the organization's products and markets. Identifying core competencies, coordinating relationships, defining operating responsibilities, establishing good communications, and monitoring and evaluating performance are essential to achieving effective use of external organizations.

The office supply company Staples Inc. shows the combination of the Internet's impact on customers and the organization itself.

- Staples Inc.'s Web sales reached $512 million in 2000, growing 400 percent from the previous year.

- Internal business reports are distributed through an intranet—replacing the expensive process of printing hard copies in central data centers and mailing them to managers.

- Sales associates in stores use Web kiosks on the shop floor to access the intranet and customize reports to get the information most useful to their store, without leaving the floor to go to a back office. The company estimates saving $600,000 a year in paper and distribution costs.

- Staples also uses its intranet to distribute "Plan-O-Grams" providing schematics of how products and promotions should be displayed, customized to the store's location and size. This saves $250,000 annually in printing costs.

- Executives at headquarters buy material, furniture, and other supplies through a Web procurement application, which routes orders through the Internet to preapproved vendors. The saving is $500,000, mostly in reduced administration costs and better control over the payment process.

- Previously, store managers completed employment forms for new hires and submitted them to corporate for approval through the mail. Now they do it through the intranet. What previously took four days now takes one. Savings from reduced labor are estimated at $1.2 million a year.

Source: Ted Kemp, "Web Helps Merchants Save in Down Market," *Internetweek,* October 15, 2001, 42–43.

The Impact of the Internet on Organizational Design Decisions

In addition to its impact on buyer-seller relationships by providing a direct marketing channel, the Internet affects the internal processes and management of organizations. The Internet Feature illustrates the widespread impact not only of the Internet direct marketing channel but also of the company's intranet on internal processes.

It is suggested that the Internet mandates attention to revision of the whole of the organization's structure, systems, and processes and that new managerial roles and practices are required by the Web.[16] However, Forrester Inc. research in 2001 suggested that companies have made little progress toward building the organizational structures needed to manage Internet-based business.[17] It is likely that organizational issues reflecting the impact of the Internet on company processes will include:

- Fast access to information from any location in the organization and remote access from distributed locations.

- Accelerated trends toward flatter organizations.

- Virtual teams working on projects across geographic and traditional organizational boundaries.

- New approaches to supplier relationship management (SRM) as well as customer relationship management (CRM).

- Managing and controlling the outsourcing of more business processes and activities to specialist third-party suppliers.

Organizational Design Options

Functional specialization is often one consideration in selecting an organizational design. Specialist functions are attractive because they develop expertise, resources, and skills in a particular activity. An emphasis on functions may be less appropriate in trying to direct activities toward market targets, products, and customers. Market targets and product scope also influence organizational design. When two or more targets and/or a mix of products are involved, companies often depart from functional organizational designs that place advertising, selling, research, and other supporting services into functional units (e.g., sales department). Similarly, distribution channels and sales force considerations may influence the organizational structure adopted by a firm. For example, the marketing of home entertainment products targeted to business buyers of employee incentives and promotional gifts might be placed in a unit separate from a unit marketing to consumer end-users. Geographic factors have a strong influence on organization design because of the need to make the field supervisory structure correspond to how the sales force is assigned to customers.

Mary Kay Cosmetics, Inc., found an interesting opportunity when launching its direct sales organization in Russia in 1993.[18] Management followed a sales geographic design similar to that used in the United States. Starting with 30 salespeople, the sales organization expanded to 17,000 people at the end of 1995 and estimated sales of over $30 million. Recruiting is not difficult due to the shortage of jobs for women in Russia and the earning opportunities. A really top sales representative earns $1,500 a month compared to the $112 average monthly pay in Russia. Unlike the United States, job turnover is low in Mary Kay's Russian organization. The lessons learned led to entry into the China market in 1995, with sales reaching $12 million by the end of 1997 with a 12,000 strong sales force. In China the Mary Kay business model has been modified to conform with local law and culture—sales are not made in consumers' homes, for example, but at classes in beauty centers and offices. The Mary Kay China operation is focused on cities where consumers have higher than average incomes.[19]

In our discussion of organizational design options we assume that the marketing organization is part of a strategic business unit. Companies with two or more business units may have corporate marketing organizations as well as business unit marketing organizations. Corporate involvement may range from a coordinating role to one in which the corporate staff has considerable influence on business unit marketing operations. Also, the chief marketing executive and staff may participate to varying degrees in strategic planning for the enterprise and the business unit.

We first look at several traditional approaches to organizing marketing activities and assigning responsibilities and then examine the role of corporate marketing. This is followed by a discussion of some new approaches in marketing organization design.

Traditional Designs

The major forms of marketing organizational designs are *functional, product, market,* and *matrix* designs.

Functional Organizational Design

This design assigns departments, groups, or individuals responsibility for specific activities such as advertising and sales promotion, pricing, sales, marketing research, and marketing planning and services. Depending on the size and scope of its operations, the marketing organization may include some or all of these activities. The functional approach often is used when a single product or a closely related line is marketed to one market target.

Product-Focused Design

The product mix may require special attention in the organizational design. New products often do not receive the attention they need unless specific responsibility is assigned to the planning and coordination of the new product activities. This problem may also occur with existing products when a business unit has several products and technical and/or application differences. We examine several approaches to organizing by using a product focus.

The *product/brand manager,* sometimes assisted by one or a few additional people, is responsible for planning and coordinating various business functions for the assigned products. Typically, the product manager does not have authority over all product-planning activities but may coordinate various product-related activities. The manager usually has a background and experience in research and development, engineering, or marketing and normally is assigned to one of those departments. Product managers' titles and responsibilities vary widely across companies.

Product management structures continue to be used in many organizations even though there is a trend toward process designs.[20] The product management system assigns clear responsibility for product performance, and the system also encourages coordination across business functions. These positions are also excellent training grounds for higher-level jobs. Nonetheless, the product focus may take emphasis away from the market. Also, there may be a short-term focus on financial performance. An example of a product-focused structure is shown in Exhibit 14–3.

One interesting forecast is that traditional product management structure will evolve into customer-based structures where several customer portfolios replace products as the

EXHIBIT 14–3
Product-Focused Structure

Source: Donald R. Lehmann and Russell S. Winer, *Product Management,* 2nd ed. (Chicago: Richard D. Irwin, 1997), 4.

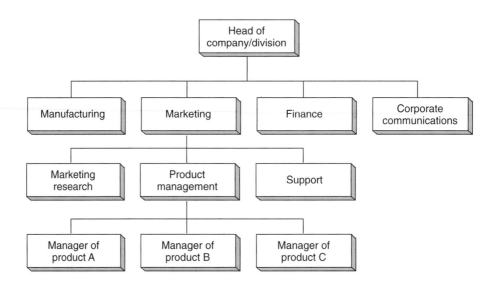

"pillars" of the organization and that product managers will provide services to each customer portfolio group (as will functional specialists).[21]

Associated with the efficient consumer response approach to supply chain management (Chapter 10), one development in a product-focused organization is the adoption of *category management* structures. Categories are groups of products defined by consumer purchase behavior patterns. For example, Nestlé and Interbrew are working with retailers to develop category structures within which their brands can be developed and are restructuring their organizations around the categories.[22]

The *venture team* requires the creation of an organizational unit to perform some or all of the new product planning functions. This unit may be a separate division or company created specifically for new product or new business ideas and initiatives.[23] Examples of successful products planned by venture units include Boeing 757 aircraft, the IBM personal computer line, and Xerox products other than photocopiers. Venture teams offer several advantages, including flexibility and quick response. They provide functional involvement and full-time commitment, and they can be disbanded when appropriate. Team members may be motivated to participate in a project that offers possible job advancement opportunities. The traditional venture team approach has been extended into a new organizational model—the venture marketing organization—that is considered in the next section.

The *new product team* is similar to a venture team in that it consists of functional specialists working on a specific new product development project.[24] The product team has a high degree of autonomy, with the authority to select leaders, establish operating procedures, and resolve conflicts. The team is formed for a specific project, although it may be assigned subsequent projects.

Factors that often influence the choice of a product organization design include the kinds and scope of products offered, the amount of new product development, the extent of coordination necessary among functional areas, and the management and technical problems previously encountered with new products and existing products. For example, a firm with an existing functional organizational structure may create a temporary team to manage and coordinate the development of a major new product. Before or soon after commercial introduction, the firm will shift responsibility for the product to the functional organization. The team's purpose is to allocate initial direction and effort to the new product so that it is properly launched.

Market-Focused Design

This approach is used when a business unit serves more than one market target (e.g., multiple market segments) and customer considerations are an important factor in the design of the marketing organization. For example, the customer base often affects the structuring of the field sales organization. A key advantage of this design is its customer focus.[25] Greater use of organization designs that focus on customer groups is predicted.[26] A potential conflict may exist if a company also has in place a product management system. Some firms appoint market managers and have a field sales force that is specialized by type of customer. The market manager operates much as a product manager does, with responsibility for market planning, research, advertising, and sales force coordination. Market-oriented field organizations may be deployed according to industry, customer size, type of product application, or in other ways to achieve specialization by end-user groups. Conditions that suggest a market-oriented design are (1) multiple market targets being served within a strategic business unit, (2) substantial differences in the customer requirements in a given target market, and/or (3) each customer or prospect purchasing the product in large volume or dollar amounts.

EXHIBIT 14–4
A Marketing Organization Based on a Combination of Functions and Products

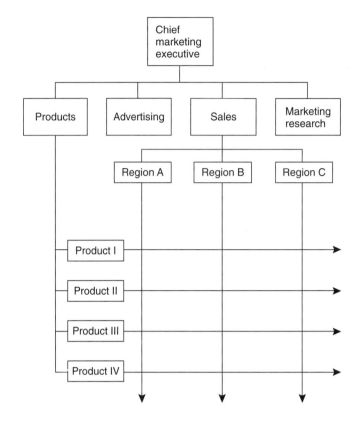

Matrix Design

This design utilizes a cross-classification approach to emphasize two different factors, such as products and marketing functions (Exhibit 14–4). Field sales coverage is determined by geography, whereas product emphasis is obtained by using product managers. In addition to working with salespeople, product managers coordinate other marketing functions, such as advertising and marketing research. Of course, other matrix schemes are possible. For example, within the sales regions shown in Exhibit 14–4, salespeople may be organized by product type or customer group. Also, marketing functions may be broken down by product category, such as appointing an advertising supervisor for Product II.

The combination approaches are effective in that they respond to different influences on the organization and offer more flexibility than do the other traditional approaches. A major difficulty with these designs is establishing lines of responsibility and authority. Product and market managers frequently complain that they lack control over all marketing functions even though they are held accountable for results. Nevertheless, the matrix approaches are popular, and so their operational advantages must exceed their limitations.

Marketing's Corporate Role

An important organizational issue in firms with two or more operating units is deciding whether a corporate marketing function should be established, and if so, what its role and scope should be. The Conference Board identifies three possible roles of corporate marketing:

1. Performing services for the company and/or its operating units.

2. Controlling or monitoring the performance of operating unit marketing activities.

3. Providing an advisory or consulting service to corporate management and/or operating units.[27]

Services may include media purchases, marketing research, planning assistance, and other supporting activities. Control may cover pricing policies, new product planning, sales force compensation, and other monitoring/control actions. Advisory or consulting services provide professional marketing expertise such as market segmentation analyses, new product planning, and marketing strategy.

Influenced by the trend toward decentralized management, corporations are moving marketing functions away from the corporate level and to the business unit level. Decentralized marketing activities are more likely to occur when:

Senior management is moving the company toward further diversification into areas having little or no relation to its present array of businesses.

New growth leads to added organizational complexities and a further proliferation of the company's operating components.

Senior management makes no attempt to integrate newly acquired businesses into the company's existing corporate structure.

Senior management tends to focus on financial results and asset management.

Areas other than marketing are the principal sources of a company's strength, efficiency, and momentum.

Senior management strongly prefers decentralizing as much responsibility as possible to the company's operating units.

A company has to cut corporate staff to reduce costs.[28]

Thus, the corporate role of marketing is influenced by top management's approach to organizing the corporation as well as the nature and complexity of business operations. Marketing strategy decisions typically are centered at the business-unit and product-market levels. Nevertheless, it is very important for the top management team to include strategic marketing professionals. The market-driven nature of business strategy requires the active participation of marketing professionals.

New Forms of Marketing Organizations

As we discussed early in the chapter, the use of self-managing employee teams, an emphasis on business processes rather than activities, and the application of information technology are creating major changes in organization design. However, the adoption of these organization designs is more likely to occur in newly formed companies or units than in established companies. First, we explore how these influences are altering the traditional vertical organization. Then, we look at some new marketing organization designs.

New Marketing Roles

One issue confronting managers is the emergence of new roles in marketing processes and how to locate them in the structure of the organization. Recall that we have described the potential for the chief knowledge or information officer in marketing (Chapter 5) and the possible role of the chief relationship officer (Chapter 7). The introduction of such roles requires attention to their organizational positioning.

One major issue faced by companies is where and how to position Internet-based channels in the marketing organization and the business unit. Early approaches isolated Internet channels from the rest of the business, while the real challenge for most companies is how to integrate the Internet into the core business.[29] Major "bricks and clicks" companies like Staples are rethinking the policy of separating their dot-com operations from the rest of the business and bringing them back into the main operation.[30] The Web operations of successful retailers like Walgreens in the United States and Tesco in the United Kingdom are closely integrated with the retail stores of those companies. Several important organizational issues are involved in achieving that integration.

Considerable attention is also being given to the impact of customer relationship management systems on marketing organizations. Some companies have, for example, appointed a chief customer officer whose job focuses only on customer interactions and the customer experience. Investment in CRM and its utilization in building relationship marketing strategy may lead to the division of marketing into activities associated with customer acquisition processes and activities focused on customer retention, since these are often very distinct and different processes.[31]

Transforming Vertical Organizations

Corporate restructuring is changing how organizations are configured. This transformation involves defining the business as a group of interrelated processes rather than as functions of research and development, manufacturing, marketing, and finance. Since most business processes involve several business functions, the basis of organization becomes the process rather than the function. Consider, for example, the process of "order generation and fulfillment"[32] The process owners are manufacturing and marketing. The process team responsible for defining, analyzing, and continually improving the process includes the workers who perform the various activities necessary to create the process outputs (completed orders delivered to customers).

The process concept of managing a business is a dramatic departure from traditional, functional organizational designs. The use of matrix and team-oriented designs provides experience in coordinating the activities of multifunctional teams. For example, a large industrial products company uses teams to develop and implement its marketing plans. Team members include product managers, research and development managers, manufacturing managers, sales management, finance executives, and top management. Nonetheless, making the transition to the true process-driven organization requires a major alteration in how the organization is designed and how it functions.

It is clear from the organizational changes which occurred during the last decade that structures are changing, and market-driven companies are seeking to more closely align the organization to the market. One strategy and structure authority anticipates the following changes in structure:[33]

1. Companies will migrate toward hybrid organization forms by coupling the strengths of horizontal processes and vertical functional forms.

2. Organizational designs will differ significantly based on the organization's value strategy and core capabilities.

3. Data network advances will play a pivotal role in linking internal teams and obtaining information from the customer.

4. Greater dispersion of information and shared decision making throughout the organization will be essential to interactive strategies.

EXHIBIT 14–5
**The Marketing
Coalition Company**

Source: Ravi S. Achrol,
"Evolution of the Marketing
Organization: New Forms for
Turbulent Environments,"
Journal of Marketing, October
1991, 88.

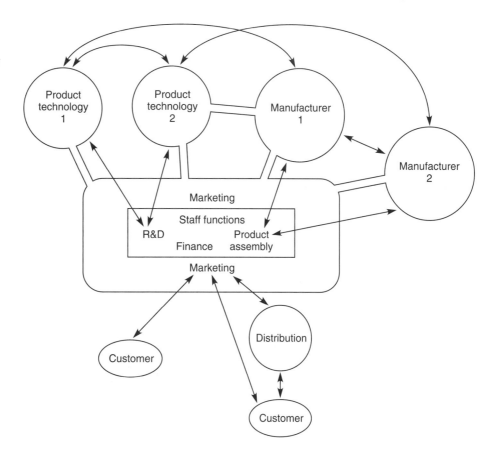

New Organization Forms

An example of one new organization form is the marketing coalition company shown in Exhibit 14–5.[34] This horizontally aligned organization is the control center for organizing a network of specialist firms. The core of this organization is a functionally specialized marketing capability that coordinates a network of independent functional units. Those units perform such functions as product technology, engineering, and manufacturing.

No pure forms of the marketing coalition company are known to exist. Several Japanese companies have certain characteristics of the coalition company. One U.S. retail chain, the Bombay Company, is organized in a similar form to the coalition design in its supplier network. Bombay has a global network of specialized suppliers of its home furnishings. Specific components (e.g., legs, top) of a table are produced by different manufacturers, shipped to Bombay's product-assembly faculty, and deployed through a national distribution system to Bombay's company-owned retail stores. While the Bombay design is not identical to the one in Exhibit 14–5, there are several similarities.

The marketing coalition design is an example of a network organization. Networks are groups of independent organizations that are linked together to achieve a common objective.[35] They consist of a network coordinator and several network members who typically are specialists. Network organizations occur in new ventures and reformed traditional organizations. The underlying rationale for network formation is leveraging the skills and resources of the participating organizations.

Venture Marketing Organizations

An interesting new approach adopted by some companies extends the idea of venture teams as a way of responding to high-priority opportunities faster than conventional organizational approaches allow. The venture marketing organization (VMO) adopts the principles of venture capitalism: These organizations aggressively seek new opportunities and allocate resources to the best but cut their losses as they go. The VMO has a number of defining characteristics:

- Fluidity. To keep pace with the market, the VMO continually reconfigures, with little formal structure or fixed membership.

- People are allocated roles, not jobs.

- Fast decision making is done from the top.

- Opportunity identification is everyone's job.

- Resources are focused on the highest payback opportunities, and losers are quickly pruned.[36]

The impact of a VMO-style approach to new market opportunities at Starbucks is described in the Innovation Feature.

Selecting an Organization Design

The design of the marketing organization is influenced by market and environmental factors, the characteristics and capabilities of the organization, and the marketing strategy followed by the firm. A good organizational scheme displays several characteristics:

The organization should correspond to the strategic marketing plan. For example, if the plan is structured around markets or products, the marketing organizational structure should reflect that emphasis.

Coordination of activities is essential to successful implementation of plans both within the marketing function and with other company and business unit functions. The more highly specialized marketing functions become, the more likely it is that coordination and communications will be hampered.

Specialization of marketing activities leads to greater efficiency in performing the functions. As an illustration, a central advertising department may be more cost-efficient than an advertising unit for each product category. Specialization can also provide technical depth. For example, product or application specialization in a field sales force will enable salespeople to provide consultative-type assistance to customers.

The organization should be structured so that responsibility for results will correspond to a manager's influence on results. While this objective is often difficult to achieve fully, it is an important consideration in designing the marketing organization.

Finally, one of the real dangers in a highly structured and complex organization is the loss of flexibility. The organization should be adaptable to changing conditions. Recall the rationale for the venture marketing organization described earlier in the chapter.

Since some of these characteristics conflict with others, organizational design requires looking at priorities and balancing conflicting consequences.

First we look at several organizing concepts, followed by a discussion of organizing the sales force.

The venture marketing organization (VMO) is a fluid approach to identifying new opportunities and concentrating resources on the best ones. Starbucks has a VMO-style approach to innovation.

- Starbucks approaches new opportunities by assembling teams whose leaders often come from the functional marketing areas most critical to success. The originator of the idea may take the lead role only if qualified.

- If teams need skills that are not available internally, they look outside. To lead the "Store of the Future" project Starbucks hired a top executive with retail experience from Universal Studios, and to develop its lunch service concept it chose a manager from Marriott.

- After the new product is launched, some team members may stay to manage the venture, while others are redeployed to new opportunity teams or return to line management. Success on a team is vital for promotion or a bigger role in another project.

- Teamwork extends to partner organizations. When pursuing a new ice cream project, Starbucks quickly realized it lacked the in-house packaging and channel management skills to move quickly. Teaming up with Dreyer's Grand Ice Cream got the product to market in half the normal time, and within four months it was the top-selling brand of coffee ice cream.

- Starbucks emphasizes the importance of identifying new opportunities throughout its organization. Anyone in the company with a new idea for an opportunity uses a one-page form to pass it to a senior executive team. If the company pursues the idea, the originator, regardless of tenure or title, usually is invited onto the launch team as a full-time member.

- In its first year Starbucks' Frappuccino, a cold coffee drink, contributed 11 percent of company sales. The idea originated with a front-line manager in May 1994 and gained high-priority status from a five-person senior executive team in June. The new team developed marketing, packaging, and channel approaches in July. A joint venture arrangement with PepsiCo was in place by August. The first wave of rollout was in October 1994, with the national launch in May 1995.

- A high-level steering committee meets every two weeks to rate new opportunities against two simple criteria: impact on company revenue growth and effects on the complexity of the retail store. The committee uses a one-page template to assess each idea, relying on a full-time process manager to ensure that the information is presented consistently.

Sources: Nora A. Aufreiter, Teri L. Lawver, and Candance D. Lun, "A New Way to Market," *The McKinsey Quarterly* (2), 2000, 52–61; Nora Aufreiter and Teri Lawver, "Winning the Race for New Market Opportunities," *Ivey Business Journal*, September–October 2000, 14–16.

Organizing Concepts

How marketing activities are organized affects strategy implementation. Consider, for example, the four organizing concepts shown in Exhibit 14–6. Note the usage context and performance characteristics of each structure. Since implementation may involve a usage context

EXHIBIT 14–6   **Four Archetypical Organizational Forms**

	Market versus Hierarchical Organization	
	Internal Organization of Activity	**External Organization of Activity**
Structural Characteristics	**Bureaucratic Form**	**Transactional Form**
Centralized Formalized Nonspecialized	*Appropriate usage context* • Conditions of market failure • Low environmental uncertainty • Tasks which are repetitive, easily assessed, requiring specialized assets *Performance characteristics* • Highly effective and efficient • Less adaptive *Examples in marketing* • Functional organization • Company or division sales force • Corporate research staffs	*Appropriate usage context* • Under competitive market conditions • Low environmental uncertainty • Tasks which are repetitive, easily assessed, with no specialized investment *Performance characteristics* • Most efficient form • Highly effective for appropriate tasks • Less adaptive *Examples in marketing* • Contract purchase of advertising space • Contract purchase of transportation of product • Contract purchase of research field work
	Organic Form	**Relational Form**
Decentralized Nonformalized Specialized	*Appropriate usage context* • Conditions of market failure • High environmental uncertainty • Tasks which are infrequent, difficult to assess, requiring highly specialized investment *Performance characteristics* • Highly adaptive • Less efficient *Examples in marketing* • Product management organization • Specialized sales force organization • Research staffs organized by product groups	*Appropriate usage context* • Under competitive market conditions • High environmental uncertainty • Tasks which are nonroutine, difficult to assess, requiring little specialized investment *Performance characteristics* • Highly adaptive • Highly effective for nonroutine, specialized tasks • Less efficient *Examples in marketing* • Long-term retainer contract with advertising agency • Ongoing relationship with consulting firm

Source: Robert W. Ruekert, Orville C. Walker, Jr., and Kenneth J. Roering, "The Organization of Marketing Activities: A Contingency Theory of Structure and Performance," *Journal of Marketing,* Winter 1985, 20.

that combines two of the structures, trade-offs are involved. The adopted organization structure may facilitate the implementation of certain activities and tasks. For example, the bureaucratic form should facilitate the implementation of repetitive activities such as telephone processing of air travel reservations and ticketing. Once management analyzes the task(s) to be performed and the environment in which they will be done, it must determine its priorities. An example is the objective performance and short-run efficiency or adaptability and longer-term effectiveness:

Activities in different categories should be structured differently whenever feasible. Some firms appear to be moving in this direction, as shown by reports of cuts in corporate staff departments, the shifting of more planning and decision-making authority to individual business unit and product-market managers, and the increased use of ad hoc task forces to deal with specific markets or problems—all of which indicate a shift toward more decentralized and flexible structures.[37]

The corporate culture may also have an important influence on implementation. For example, implementing new strategies may be more difficult in highly structured, bureaucratic organizations. General Motors' difficulty in responding to global competitive pressures during the last decade is illustrative. Management should consider its own management style, accepted practices, specific performance of executives, and other unique characteristics in deciding how to design the organization.

The bureaucratic form shown in Exhibit 14–6 corresponds to the previously discussed traditional vertical organization forms. The relational form displays several characteristics of a network organization, though network design involves a more extensive group of independent partners. The transactional form may be used for certain repetitive, nonspecialized activities. The organic form has some similarities to process-type organizations but also displays several characteristics of traditional structures.

Organizing the Sales Force

In many companies, the sales force accounts for the largest part of the marketing organization. Therefore, organizing the sales force is often a central part of the marketing organization design. The design of the sales organization was discussed in Chapter 13, which also looked at designs that correspond to variations in product offering and customer needs. We now examine some additional aspects of organizing the sales force.

Organizing Multiple Sales Channels

Expanding the sales organization beyond the field sales force to include major-account programs, telemarketing, and/or Internet sales programs requires consideration of how to organize the channel network. A key issue is whether to establish separate organizational units or to combine two or more channels into one unit. For example, should the national account salespeople be placed in a separate organizational unit or instead be assigned to field sales units (e.g., regions or districts)? The use of multifunctional customer management processes, as discussed earlier in the chapter, may affect these decisions.

When sales channel activities are relatively independent of the field sales force, a separate channel organization is appropriate. This occurs when major-account managers or telemarketing salespeople provide all the contacts with assigned accounts. An example is the assignment of low-sales-volume accounts to telemarketing salespeople. A more likely situation is one in which contacts are made by both field personnel and other channels. These contacts require coordination between salespeople. The creation of independent sales channel organizations complicates the coordination of selling activities.

Coordinating Major-Account Relationships

A look at the alternatives for coordinating key account relationships highlights several multiple-channel issues. A major-account program requires assignment of account responsibility to account managers. When the customer has several purchasing locations, coordination of selling and service activities is necessary. Several alternatives are available, including (1) assigning key accounts to top sales executives (e.g., sales vice president), (2) creating a separate corporate division, and (3) establishing a separate major-accounts sales force.[38] Factors that influence the choice of an alternative include the number of major accounts served by the organization, the number of different geographic contacts with an account, the organizational level of contact (e.g., vice president versus maintenance supervisor), and the sales and service functions to be performed.

Global Dimensions of Organizations

Implementing the global strategies of companies creates several important organizational issues. The president of the Conference Board, Inc., comments on managing in a competitive global environment:

> Finding that critical point where regional differentiation can give way to product standardization will spell success. In many instances your core product will be essentially the same in every market, but marketing will differ widely according to local tastes.[39]

The Internet is playing a major role in the globalization of business. As more customers buy and make comparisons through the Web on an international basis, competition is becoming global for many more companies. In addition, the impact of the Internet on internal organizational processes and the development of intranets encourage teaming and projects that span geographic, cultural, and time-zone barriers. Working in international project teams through an intranet mandates dealing with international issues in the market-driven organization.[40]

Several issues in organizing global marketing strategies are examined, followed by a discussion of organizational concepts that are used to manage global marketing activities. Much of the earlier material in the chapter applies to international operations. This discussion highlights several additional considerations.

Issues in Organizing Global Marketing Strategies

The important distinction in marketing throughout the world is that buyers differ in their needs, preferences, and priorities. Since such differences exist *within* a national market, the variations between countries are likely to be greater. "What success would Swedish car makers or Italian pasta manufacturers have in the United States if they went after the same solid consumer of their home markets instead of appealing to affluent, trendy consumers of their products in this country?"[41] Similarly, brands like Budweiser beer and Levi's jeans have significantly different market positions in international markets compared to those they occupy in the United States. Global market targeting and positioning strategies create several marketing organizational issues.

Variations in Business Functions

Global decisions concerning production, finance, and research and development are often more feasible than making the marketing decisions that span these markets. Marketing strategies require sensitivity to cultural and linguistic differences. Foreign currencies, government regulations, and different product standards further complicate buyer-seller relationships. The important issue is recognizing when standardized marketing strategies can be used and when they must be modified.

Organizational Considerations

The marketing organization selected for competing in national markets is influenced by the market *scope* (e.g., single-country, multinational, or global strategy) and by the market *entry strategy* (export, licensing, joint venture, strategic alliance, or complete ownership). Recall the discussion of marketing strategies in global markets in Chapter 6. The adoption

EXHIBIT 14–7
Marketing Organization Plan Combining Product, Geographic, and Functional Features

Source: Philip R. Cateora, *International Marketing,* 9th ed. (Burr Ridge, IL: Richard D. Irwin, 1996), 346.

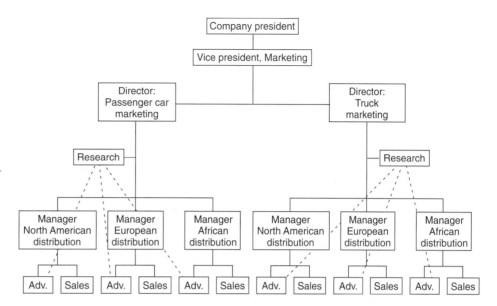

of a global strategy using joint ventures, alliances, and/or complete ownership presents the most complex organizational challenge.

The marketing organization design in international operations may take one of three possible forms: (1) a global product division, (2) geographic divisions, each with product and functional responsibilities, or (3) a matrix design incorporating (1) or (2) in combination with centralized functional support or instead a combination of area operations and global product management.[42] The global form corresponds to situations of rapid growth firms that have a broad product portfolio. The geographic form is used to obtain a close relationship with national and local governments. The matrix form is utilized by companies reorganizing for global competition. An example of a combination organization design is shown in Exhibit 14–7.

Coordination and Communication

Organizing marketing activities to serve international markets creates important coordination and communication requirements. Language and distance barriers complicate organizational relationships. Beech Aircraft Corporation uses an international team-marketing approach to respond faster to market opportunities, manage budgets more effectively, and coordinate goals and objectives.[43] The world is divided into three geographic landmasses, with a marketing team assigned to each area. Previously, Beech utilized 10 independent regional managers to cover the world. The new teams are responsible for analyzing markets, planning strategy, presenting their recommendations to top management, and executing the strategy. The three teams provide quarterly briefings for the president.

"Global teamwork approaches are now being tested by companies with vastly different organizational structures and varying levels of international involvement."[44] The Conference Board, Inc.'s, study of 30 major U.S. multinational companies indicates that global teamwork improves market and technological intelligence, contributes to more flexible business planning, leads to a stronger commitment to corporate worldwide goals, and achieves closer coordination in implementing strategic actions. Enabling technology provided by the Internet and collaboration software facilitates the operation and management of global teams.

Strategic Alliances

Recall the growth in alliance strategies among global firms described in Chapter 7. Expanded use of alliances is expected into the 21st century. IBM, for example, obtains a third of its income from a complex network of alliances throughout the world. Recall also that the alliance relationship presents major interorganizational coordination and strategy implementation requirements. Peter Drucker offers several guidelines for improving strategic alliances:

> Before the alliance is completed, all parties must think through their objectives and the objectives of the "child."
> Equally important is advance agreement on how the joint enterprise should be run.
> Next, there has to be careful thinking about who will manage the alliance.
> Each partner needs to make provisions in its own structure for the relationship to the joint enterprise and the other partners.
> Finally, there has to be prior agreement on how to resolve disagreements.[45]

The effectiveness of the alliance depends on how well operating relationships are established and managed on an ongoing basis and how well the partners can work together.

Executive Qualifications

International experience and proven capabilities will increasingly be required for executive advancement in the 21st century.[46] Managing international marketing operations requires knowledge of finance, distribution, manufacturing, and other business functions. The trend toward flat organizations with wide spans of control will make on-the-job executive development more difficult. Similarly, the qualifications for the chief executive's job will include experience in several areas. With creative financing techniques that turn financial decisions into marketing questions, manufacturing processes that are driven by computer technology, and product designs that depend on rapid market feedback, the chief executive will need a varied background.[47] Market-driven strategies will increasingly require management abilities to lead into new areas and to work in new ways that do not depend on formal authority, and the international context underlines the importance for the market-driven company of nurturing and retaining superior management talent.[48]

Summary

Differences in environmental situations create specific organization design requirements. The design and adaptation of organizations to their environments involve consideration of several important issues for marketing organization design, including decisions regarding the use of internal and external organizations, designing the vertical structure, coordinating horizontal relationships, increasing the speed of response, and analyzing environmental complexity and the forces of change. The Internet plays a major role as an enabling technology, underpinning several aspects of organizational change.

Several traditional marketing organization designs may be used to implement market strategy. The options include functional, product, market, and matrix designs. Increasingly, aligning the organization with the market is a central issue in organization designs. Building appropriate organization designs to integrate marketing with other functions, position new marketing roles and responsibilities effectively, and work with partner organizations is a priority for many companies.

The role and scope of corporate marketing are changing in many firms with multibusiness operations. The importance of corporate marketing appears to be declining in many firms, with marketing strategy emphasis instead being focused on the business level. The venture marketing organization is an interesting development being used by some companies.

New forms of marketing organizations are developing, driven by the use of cross-functional teams in organizations that manage business processes rather than functions and the use of powerful information technology. These influences are transforming vertical organizations into horizontal ones. An example is the marketing coalition company.

The choice of an organization design involves finding a good structural-environmental match. The match is influenced by the complexity of the environment and the unpredictability and interconnectedness of the environment. The design also involves selecting the best organizational form based on structural characteristics and the internal versus external orientation of marketing operations. The key role of the sales force in many organizations makes the sales force a central part of marketing organization design.

Finally, the global strategies of companies highlight several marketing organizational issues. These issues include recognizing the differences in business functions in international operations and the increased coordination and communication requirements in international markets. Strategic alliances, an expanding area of global activity, present complex management and coordination situations. Executive qualifications in marketing and other business functions increasingly include international experience.

Internet Applications

A. Visit the website of Coca-Cola Inc. (*www.cocacola.com*). Use the corporate information pages (Our Company, Our Brands, and Around the World) to identify the growth in brands marketed by the company and its geographic emphasis. Identify the challenges for this company in organizing marketing for a growing brand portfolio in a diverse global marketplace.

B. Go to the website of Calyx & Corolla (C&C) (*www.calyx-corolla.com*) and examine the company's product offering and its story (located under "About Us"). Then use your search engine to identify Web pages related to Calyx & Corolla's business. Draw a simple chart of how C&C goes to market through partnerships. Consider how marketing processes can be managed in a hollow organization of this type. Discuss how many other types of product-markets might be approached using this business model and how you would design appropriate marketing processes and structures.

Questions for Review and Discussion

1. The chief executive of a manufacturer of direct-order personal computers is interested in establishing a marketing organization in the firm. A small sales force handles sales to midsize businesses, and advertising is planned and executed by an advertising agency. Other than the CEO, no one inside the firm is responsible for the marketing function. What factors should the CEO consider in designing a marketing organization?

2. Among the various approaches to marketing organization design, which one(s) offers the most flexibility in coping with rapidly changing market and competitive situations? Discuss.

3. Discuss the conditions where a matrix-type marketing organization would be appropriate, indicating important considerations and potential problems in using this organizational form.

4. Assume that you have been asked by the president of a major transportation services firm to recommend a marketing organizational design. What important factors should you consider in selecting the design?

5. Discuss some of the important issues related to integrating marketing into an organization such as a regional women's clothing chain compared to accomplishing the same task in The Limited Inc.

6. What are possible internal and external factors that may require changing the marketing organization design?

7. Is a trend toward more organic organizational forms likely in the future?

8. Summarize and chart the current and future impact of the Internet on marketing processes and organization.

9. Discuss the important organizational design issues in establishing an effective strategic alliance between organizations.

10. What are the major approaches to organizing the marketing function for international operations? Discuss the factors that may affect the choice of a particular organization design.

11. As companies begin to replace functions with processes, what are the possible effects on organizational designs?

Notes

1. George S. Day, "Aligning the Organization to the Market," in *Reflections on the Future of Marketing,* Donald R. Lehmann and Katherine E. Jocz, eds. (Cambridge, MA: Marketing Science Institute, 1997), 67–93.

2. The following example about P&G is based on Tara Parker-Pope and Joanne S. Lublin, "P&G Will Make Jager CEO Ahead of Schedule," *The Wall Street Journal,* September 10, 1998, B1, B8; Steve Bell, "P&G Forced by Rivals to Change Old Habits," *Marketing,* June 17, 1999, 15; Patricia Van Arnum, "Procter & Gamble Moves Forward with Reorganization," *Chemical Market Reporter,* February 1, 1999, 12; John Bissell, "What Can We Learn From P&G's Troubles," *Brandweek,* July 10, 2000, 20–22; Christine Bittar, "Cosmetic Changes," *Brandweek,* June 18, 2001, 2.

3. Richard L. Daft, *Organization Theory and Design,* 3rd ed. (St. Paul, MN: West Publishing, 1989), 212–17.

4. Day, "Aligning the Organization to the Market," 69–72.

5. Ibid., 70–71.

6. Ibid.

7. Ibid., 72.

8. Brian Dumaine, "How Managers Can Succeed through Speed," *Fortune,* February 13, 1989, 54–59.

9. Don E. Schultz, "Structural Straitjackets Stifle Integrated Success," *Marketing News,* March 1, 1999, 8.

10. Elliot Maltz and Ajay Kohli quoted in Regina Fazio Maruca, "Getting Marketing's Voice Heard," *Harvard Business Review,* January–February 1999, 10–11; Elliot Maltz, William E. Souder, and Ajith Kumar, "Influencing R&D/Marketing Integration and the Use of Market Information by R&D Managers," *Journal of Business Research* 51, no. 2 (2001), 69–82.

11. Nigel F. Piercy, *Market-Led Strategic Change: A Guide to Transforming the Process of Going to Market* (Oxford: Butterworth-Heinemann, 2002), 242.

12. Don E. Schultz, "Integration Is Critical for Success In the 21st Century," *Marketing News,* September 15, 1997, 26.

13. Robert W. Ruekert and Orville C. Walker, Jr., "Marketing's Interaction with Other Functional Units: A Conceptual Framework and Empirical Evidence," *Journal of Marketing,* January 1987, 1–10.

14. Elliot Maltz and Ajay Kohli, "Reducing Marketing's Conflict with Other Functions: The Differential Effects of Integrating Mechanisms," *Journal of the Academy of Marketing Science,* Fall 2000, 479–92.

15. Robert Nardelli quoted in *Reinventing America: The 1993 Business Week Symposium of Chief Executive Officers* (New York: Business Week, 1994).

16. Jill Kickul and Lisa Gundry, "Breaking through Boundaries for Organizational Innovation: New Managerial Roles and Practices in E-Commerce Firms," *Journal of Management* 27, no. 3 (2001), 347–61.

17. Nicole Lewis, "E-Biz Goals Thwarted by Lack of Structure, Skills," *Ebn,* January 22, 2001, 64.

18. Neela Banerjee, "For Mary Kay Sales Reps in Russia, Hottest Shade Is the Color of Money," *The Wall Street Journal,* August 30, 1995, A8.

19. Virginia A. Hulme, "Mary Kay in China," *The China Business Review,* January–February 2001, 42–46.

20. Donald R. Lehmann and Russell S. Winer, *Product Management,* 2nd ed. (Chicago: Richard D. Irwin, 1997), 4–7.

21. Pierre Berthon, James M. Hulbert, and Leyland F. Pitt, *Brands, Brand Managers, and the Management of Brands* (Boston: Marketing Science Institute, 1997), Report No. 97–122.

22. "FMCG Firms Need to Focus on Category before Brand," *Marketing,* September 27, 2001, 5.

23. Erick M. Olson, Orville C. Walker, Jr., and Robert W. Ruekert, "Organizing for Effective New Product Development: The Moderating Role of Product Innovativeness," *Journal of Marketing,* January 1995, 48–62.

24. Christopher K. Bart, "New Venture Units: Use Them Wisely to Manage Innovation," *Sloan Management Review,* Summer 1988, 35.

25. Lehmann and Winer, *Product Management,* 7–9.

26. Christian Homburg, John P. Workman, and Ove Jensen, "Fundamental Changes in Marketing Organization: The Movement Toward a Customer-Focused Organizational Structure," *Journal of the Academy of Marketing Science* 28, no. 4 (2000), 459–78.

27. David S. Hopkins and Earl L. Bailey, *Organizing Corporate Marketing* (New York: the Conference Board, Inc., 1984), 23.

28. Ibid., 40.

29. Michael Porter, "Strategy and the Internet," *Harvard Business Review,* March 2001, 63–78.

30. Andrew Edgecliffe-Johnson, "Staples Brings Dotcom Back into Fold," *Financial Times,* April 4, 2001, 34.

31. Russell S. Winer, "A Framework for Customer Relationship Management," *California Management Review* 43, no. 4 (2001), 89–105.

32. Thomas A. Stewart, "The Search for the Organization of Tomorrow," *Fortune,* May 18, 1997, 94.

33. Day, "Aligning the Organization to the Market," 93.

34. Ravi S. Achrol, "Evolution of the Marketing Organization: New Forms for Turbulent Environments," *Journal of Marketing,* October 1991, 77–93.

35. David W. Cravens, Nigel F. Piercy, and Shannon H. Shipp, "New Organization Forms for Competing in Highly Dynamic Environments, the Network Paradigm," *British Journal of Management* 7 (1996), 203–18.

36. Nora A. Aufreiter, Teri L. Lawver, and Candance D. Lun, "A New Way to Market," *The McKinsey Quarterly* 2 (2000), 52–61.

37. Quote from Robert W. Ruekert, Orville C. Walker, Jr., and Kenneth J. Roering, "The Organization of Marketing Activities: A Contingency Theory of Structure and Performance," *Journal of Marketing,* Winter 1985, 23–24. See also Hopkins and Bailey, *Organizing Corporate Marketing;* and "A New Era for Management," *Business Week,* April 25, 1983, 50–67.

38. For an expanded discussion of this and other sales force organizational design issues, see Gilbert A. Churchill, Jr., Neil M. Ford, Orville C. Walker, Jr., Mark W. Johnston, and John F. Tanner, Jr., *Sales Force Management,* 6th ed. (New York: McGraw-Hill/Irwin, 2000), chap. 5.

39. *The Conference Board's Management Briefing: Marketing,* December 1989–January 1990, 5.

40. John A. Quelch and Lisa R. Klein, "The Internet and International Marketing," *Sloan Management Review,* Spring 1996, 60–68.

41. *The Conference Board's Management Briefing.* 5.

42. This discussion is based on Phillip R. Cateora, *International Marketing,* 9th ed. (Burr Ridge, IL: Richard D. Irwin, 1996), 345–48.

43. *The Conference Board's Management Briefing: Marketing,* February–March, 1989, 1–2.

44. Ibid., 2.

45. Peter F. Drucker, "From Dangerous Liaisons to Alliances for Progress," *The Wall Street Journal,* September 8, 1989, A8.

46. Morgan W. McCall and George P. Hollenbeck, *Developing Global Executives: The Lessons of International Experience* (Boston: Harvard Business School Press, 2001).

47. Amanda Bennett, "Going Global: The Chief Executives in Year 2000 Will Be Experienced," *The Wall Street Journal,* February 27, 1989, A1.

48. Stratford Sherman, "How Tomorrow's Best Leaders Are Learning Their Stuff," *Fortune,* November 27, 1995, 90–97.

Chapter

15

Marketing Strategy Implementation and Control

The ultimate performance of market targeting and positioning decisions rests on how well the marketing strategy is implemented and managed on a continuing basis. Placing the strategy into action and adjusting it to eliminate performance gaps are essential factors in success.

The importance of effective implementation and control approaches is illustrated by the rebranding strategy at Continental Savings Bank (CSB), now HomeStreet Bank.[1] Founded in Seattle in 1921, CSB had 30 branches that were under pressure in the 1990s from strong, larger competitors and online banking. The bank's strategic response was to reposition the brand and build stronger brand awareness among customers and employees. The process started with a comprehensive brand audit to identify the brand's core values and reexamine attributes of the brand that had long been taken for granted. The audit identified the bank as honest, friendly, dependable, and knowledgeable, with superior customer service but with low brand visibility and lack of awareness of the full range of products and services as well as confusion associated with the bank's name.

The strategy was to change the bank's name to HomeStreet Bank to differentiate better against the competition, build stronger links to the customer as "a bank that's like a family" and "a bank for life," design an identity system covering all contacts with customers, and systematically implement the new strategy with the public launch in May 2000. Implementation involved communications with customers but also detailed training of all employees in the new brand identity system and senior management involvement throughout. HomeStreet Bank illustrates the need for rigorous and systematic plan development allied with close attention to implementation and evaluation.

We begin with an overview of the marketing plan, followed by a discussion of implementing the plan. We examine internal marketing as an approach to effective implementation. Next, we provide an overview of developing a strategic evaluation and control program. Finally, the major evaluation activities are discussed and illustrated. These activities include conducting the strategic marketing audit, selecting performance criteria and measures, determining information needs and analysis, evaluating performance, and taking needed actions to keep performance on track.

The Marketing Plan

The marketing plan guides implementation and control, indicating marketing objectives and the strategy and tactics for accomplishing those objectives. Since Chapter 2 presented a step-by-step planning process, we briefly consider several planning issues and offer examples of marketing planning activities.

How the Marketing Plan Guides Implementation

The relationships between marketing strategy and the annual plan are shown in Exhibit 15–1. The planning cycle is continuous. Plans are developed, implemented, evaluated, and revised to keep the marketing strategy on target. Since a strategy typically extends beyond one year, the annual plan is used to guide short-term marketing activities. The planning process is a series of annual plans guided by the marketing strategy. An annual planning period is necessary, since several of the activities shown require action within 12 months or less and budgets also require annual planning.

A look at the marketing planning process used by a large pharmaceutical company illustrates how planning is done. Product managers are responsible for coordinating the preparation of plans. A planning workshop is conducted midyear for the kickoff of the next year's plans. The workshop is attended by top management and product, research, sales, and finance managers. The firm's advertising agency account manager also participates in the workshop. The current year's plans are reviewed, and each product manager presents the proposed marketing plan for the next year. The workshop members critique each plan and suggest changes. Since the requested budgets may exceed available funds, priorities are placed on major budget components. Each product manager must provide strong support for requested funds. The same group meets again in 90 days, and the revised plans are reviewed. At this meeting the plans are finalized and approved for implementation. Each product manager is responsible for coordinating and implementing the plan. Progress is reviewed throughout the plan year, and the plan is revised when necessary.

Contents of the Marketing Plan

An outline for developing the marketing plan was presented in Chapter 1. Many plans follow this general format. An executive summary provides top management and other executives not closely involved in implementation with an overview of the plan. The summary outlines the current situation, indicates marketing objectives, summarizes strategies, outlines action programs, and indicates financial expectations.[2]

EXHIBIT 15–1
Marketing Planning Relationships

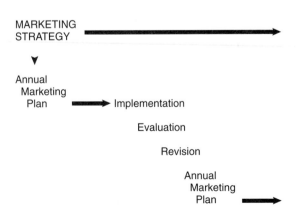

EXHIBIT 15–2 **Sonesta Hotels: Marketing Plan Outline**

Note: Please keep the plan concise—maximum of 20 pages plus summary pages. Include title page and table of contents. Number all pages.

I. *Introduction.* Set the stage for the plan. Specifically identify marketing objectives such as "increase average rate," "more group business," "greater occupancy," or "penetrate new markets." Identify particular problems.

II. *Marketing Position.* Begin with a single statement that presents a consumer benefit in a way that distinguishes us from the competition.

III. *The Product.* Identify all facility and service changes that occurred this year and are planned for next year.

IV. *Marketplace Overview.* Briefly describe what is occurring in your marketplace that might have an impact on your business or marketing strategy, such as the economy, the competitive situation, etc.

V. *The Competition.* Briefly identify your primary competition (three or fewer), specifying number of rooms, what is new in their facilities, and marketing and pricing strategy.

VI. *Marketing Data*

  A. Identify top five geographic areas for transient business, with percentages of total room nights compared to the previous year.

  B. Briefly describe the guests at your hotel, considering age, sex, occupation, what they want, why they come, etc.

  C. Identify market segments with percentage of business achieved in each segment in current year (actual and projected) and projected for next year.

VII. *Strategy by Market Segment*

  A. Group

    1. *Objectives:* Identify what you specifically wish to achieve in this segment (for example, more high-rated business, more weekend business, larger groups).

    2. *Strategy:* Identify how sales, advertising, and public relations will work together to reach the objectives.

    3. *Sales Activities:* Divide by specific market segments.

      a. Corporate

      b. Association

      c. Incentives

      d. Travel agent

      e. Tours

      f. Other

    Under each category include a narrative description of specific sales activities geared toward each market segment, including geographically targeted areas, travel plans, group site inspections, correspondence, telephone solicitation, and trade shows. Be specific on action plans and designate responsibility and target months.

    4. *Sales Materials:* Identify all items so that they will be budgeted.

    5. *Direct Mail:* Briefly describe the direct mail program planned, including objectives, message, and content. Identify whether we will use existing material or create a new piece.

    6. *Research:* Indicate any research projects you plan to conduct in 1990 identifying what you wish to learn.

  B. Transient (the format here should be the same as group throughout)

    1. *Objective*

    2. *Strategy*

(continued)

EXHIBIT 15–2   *(concluded)*

      3. *Sales Activities:* Divide by specific market segments.
         a. Consumer (rack rate)
         b. Corporate (prime and other)
         c. Travel agent: business, leisure, consortia
         d. Wholesale/airline/tour (foreign and domestic)
         e. Packages (specify names of packages)
         f. Government/military/education
         g. Special interest/other
      4. *Sales Materials*
      5. *Direct Mail*
      6. *Research*
  C. Other Sonesta Hotels
  D. Local/Food and Beverage
      1. *Objectives*
      2. *Strategy*
      3. *Sales Activities:* Divide by specific market segments.
         a. Restaurant and lounge, external promotion
         b. Restaurant and lounge, internal promotion
         c. Catering
         d. Community relation/other
      4. *Sales Materials* (e.g., banquet menus, signage)
      5. *Direct Mail*
      6. *Research*
VIII. *Advertising*
  A. Subdivide advertising by market segment and campaign, paralleling the sales activities (group, transient, F&B).
  B. Describe objectives of each advertising campaign, identifying whether it should be promotional (immediate bookings) or image (longer-term awareness).
  C. Briefly describe contents of advertising, identifying key benefit to promote.
  D. Identify target media by location and type (newspaper, magazine, radio, etc.).
  E. Indicate percent of the advertising budget to be allocated to each market segment.
 IX. *Public Relations*
  A. Describe objectives of public relations as it supports the sales and marketing priorities.
  B. Write a brief statement on overall goals by market segment paralleling the sales activities. Identify what proportion of your effort will be spent on each segment.
  X. *Summary:* Close the plan with general statement concerning the major challenges you will face in the upcoming year and how you will overcome these challenges.

Source: Adapted from Howard Sutton, *The Marketing Plan in the 1990s* (New York: The Conference Board, 1990), 34–35.

The marketing plan outline for Sonesta Hotels is shown in Exhibit 15–2. The activities include making the situation assessment, setting objectives, developing targeting and positioning strategies, deciding on action programs for the marketing-mix components, and preparing supporting financial statements (budgets and profit-and-loss projections).

Strategy Feature

Our planning process begins with a half-day meeting to discuss strategic issues. The meeting includes just three people—the president of the division (me), the chairman of the board, and the president of the corporation. I have about three sheets of paper, maybe four, that talk about these things: What are the issues? What are the market dynamics, as I see them today and what do I see in the next three years? What should we be spending in terms of protecting our market share? Where is the market going, from a demographic standpoint?

This is a high-level strategic discussion. We just sit and talk about my business—not a lot of slides, not a lot of pictures, more informal than formal—to get a frame around what I think the strategic issues in the division are. I want to get agreement from them, the chairman and the president, that, yes, those are the issues they're concerned about as well, and that we need to develop plans around those issues.

What we agree to is that there are five or six strategic imperatives. In each case, we agree that a particular objective has to be successfully achieved or the division will not succeed in its business efforts, and we have a three-year horizon. The objectives might have to do with share, or new-product technologies, or management development, or organizational issues that need to be addressed.

Then I draw up a two-page response. It says, here's what we talked about, here's what we agreed to do. Then I go back to the division with this document in my hand. I say, "OK, here's what we're headed for, here's where we got strategic agreement from the corporation." Then we start developing a plan around that direction.

There isn't an awful lot of planning that goes into that first meeting. I mean, we get bunches of numbers, and we look at the most strategic spots, such as share, such as technology. But it's really an opportunity for one time during the year for the three of us to sit down and just talk. That's much better than having a bunch of people in the room, presenting and showing what they want us to see. The next step is to come back to the division and put together a team to prepare a plan based on the strategic plan. This book, which we call a marketing strategic plan, deals with marketing and the whole focus on what we're going to do, and what we're going to do different.

The preparation is typically done by the marketing department, supervised by the manager or director of marketing services and planning. He sort of heads up the committee that puts the book together. Then, once the book is done, we have a meeting at corporate headquarters. We go over very specific areas, with a 35- to 50-page report. That's basically the way it ends up. That seems to be a basic Marketing 101 kind of process, but it's amazing how much disagreement there can be. You have one idea of what your job is, and other people in the organization may have a different idea. I think the key is to get agreement on the mission: what are we really trying to accomplish?

—*President of a division of a manufacturer of consumer products*

Source: Howard Sutton, *The Marketing Plan in the 1990s* (New York: The Conference Board, 1990), 20.

The typical planning process involves quite a bit of coordination and interaction among functional areas. Team planning approaches like the pharmaceutical company's planning workshop are illustrative. Successful implementation of the marketing plan requires a broad consensus among various functional areas.[3] For example, a consensus is essential between product managers and sales management. Product managers must obtain a commitment from the sales department to provide sales effort for their products. Multiple products require negotiation in reaching agreement on the amount of sales force time that should be devoted to various products. Recall the discussion in Chapter 14 of the importance of efforts to secure the integration of marketing with other functions and units in the organization and approaches to achieving this goal. The Strategy Feature provides a chief executive officer's (CEO's) view of how marketing plans are developed by a consumer-products manufacturer.

Managing the Planning Process

The Strategy Feature underlines the fact that planning is an organizational process in which interactions and discussions between executives shape outcomes. Planning involves more than the use of analytical techniques and computation. Research suggests that problems faced in making marketing planning effective may be addressed by considering the behavior of executives in conducting planning and the organizational context in which planning is done as well as formal training in planning techniques and procedures.[4] An effective planning process is closely linked to the successful implementation of plans. Exhibit 15–3 shows planning process as having three dimensions—analytical, behavioral, and organizational—which should be managed consistently.

The analytical dimension of the planning process consists of the tools for systematic planning—analytical techniques, formal procedures and systems—which are needed to develop robust and tested plans and strategies. However, the behavioral dimension of planning is concerned with how managers perceive planning activities and the strategic assumptions they make, as well as the degree and extent of participation in planning. Correspondingly, the organizational dimension of planning is concerned with the organizational structure in which planning is carried out, along with the associated information resources and corporate culture. One challenge to management is to manage all these aspects of the planning process in a consistent way.

The Global Feature describes how a manager addresses planning process issues at a strategic business unit (SBU) of the 3M Corporation in the United Kingdom. It illustrates the advantages of linking the planning process to implementation issues.

EXHIBIT 15–3
Dimensions of the Marketing Planning Process

Source: Adapted from Nigel F. Piercy, *Market-Led Strategic Change: A Guide to Transforming the Process of Going to Market* (Oxford: Butterworth-Heinemann, 2002), 586.

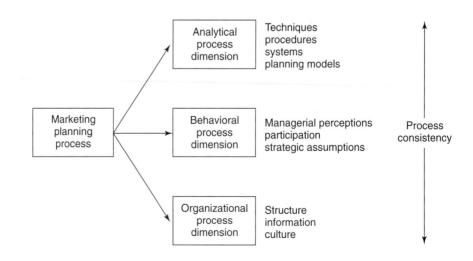

3M is a global enterprise that manufactures more than 60,000 products from a base of 112 technology platforms and consists of 28 autonomous business units, of which Abrasive Systems Division (ASD) is one. ASD is 3M's original business and operates in a mature market, supplying abrasives mainly to manufacturing companies.

- At 3M (UK), the early 1990s saw ASD's market share falling, accompanied by declining staff morale (compared to other company units and benchmark companies outside 3M).

- The appointment of Stuart Lane as ASD business unit manager in 1992 had three key goals: to restore sales growth to a minimum of 5 percent annually, to return gross margin to the levels of the 1980s, and to bring the employee satisfaction level to at least the company average.

- Lane's first observations were that people felt that they were not treated with respect or thanked for jobs well done, they lacked freedom to use initiative and make decisions, and there was little information sharing and too much bureaucracy.

- Lane's first decision was to double ASD's sales growth target from the 25 percent required by senior management (for 1992–1996) to 50 percent.

- In collaboration with 3M's Corporate Marketing business planners, he designed what he describes as a "semiformal, structured, iterative process" of planning for ASD.

- The new planning process started with a two-day planning workshop in spring 1992, followed by five workshops over the following three months. Lane sees the workshops as critical to developing a robust plan for ASD but also for the team building, ownership, enthusiasm, and commitment to make the plan happen and confidence among the team members that they were going to achieve the ambitious "stretch" goals for ASD. Lane was prepared to sacrifice some sophistication in planning in favor of simplicity and involvement to win people's support.

- The planning was linked directly to an implementation process with three key elements:
  - A written plan, presented to management but also reduced to an index card containing the essence of the plan in simple and memorable terms.
  - The launch of the new plan to the ASD organization at the annual sales conference and distribution of the index cards, to be kept at the front of people's diaries.
  - The introduction of Segment Action Teams (with a member of the management team as leader but including people from sales, marketing, customer service, and technical services from different levels in the organization) to take responsibility for segment-specific tactics and programs. The Segment Action Teams have evolved into a key and permanent part of the ASD structure.

  The results achieved by 1996 were 53 percent growth in sales, 100 percent growth in gross margin contribution, 30 percent increase in market share, and employee satisfaction 12 percent above the company average. This was achieved, you will recall, in a mature market showing little growth.

Source: Adapted from Stuart Lane and Debbie Clewes, "The Implementation of Marketing Planning: A Case Study in Gaining Commitment at 3M (UK) Abrasives," *Journal of Strategic Marketing* 8, no. 3 (2000), 225–40.

Implementing the Plan

Implementation effectiveness determines the outcome of marketing planning. The management of the planning process may enhance implementation effectiveness, by building commitment and "ownership" of the plan and its execution. For example, actively managing the participation of different functions and executives from different specializations may improve the fit between the plan and the company's real capabilities and resources and avoid implementation barriers. Marketing managers may increasingly function as boundary spanners both internally between functional areas and externally with suppliers, organizational partners, and customers.[5] Additional efforts to make the strategy implementation process more effective are a high priority in many companies. Many companies now recognize that implementation capabilities are an important corporate capability that requires detailed management attention.[6]

Implementation Process

Recent research underlines the influence of two sets of factors on marketing strategy implementation: *structural* issues, including the company's marketing functions, control systems, and policy guidelines, and *behavioral* issues, concerning marketing managers' skills in bargaining and negotiation, resource allocation, and developing informal organizational arrangements.[7] We consider several organizational and interpersonal aspects of effective implementation process.

A good implementation process spells out the activities to be implemented, who is responsible for implementation, the time and location of implementation, and how implementation will be achieved (Exhibit 15–4). Let's evaluate the following statement from a product manager's marketing plan:

> Sales representatives should target all accounts currently using a competitive product. A plan should be developed to convert 5 percent of these accounts to the company brand during the year. Account listings will be prepared and distributed by product management.

In this instance, the sales force is charged with implementation. An objective (5 percent conversion) is specified, but very little information is provided as to *how* the accounts will be converted. A strategy is needed to penetrate the competitors' customer base. The sales force plan must translate the proposed actions and objective (5 percent conversion) into assigned salesperson responsibility (quotas), a timetable, and selling strategy guidelines. Training may be necessary to show the product advantages—and the competitors' product limitations—that will be useful in convincing the buyer to purchase the firm's brand.

The marketing plan can be used to identify the organizational units and managers responsible for implementing the various activities in the plan. Deadlines indicate the time available for implementation. In the case of the plan above, the sales manager is responsible for implementation through the sales force.

Improving Implementation

Managers are important facilitators in the implementation process, and some are better implementers than others. Planners and implementers often have different strengths and weaknesses. An effective planner may not be good at implementing plans. Desirable implementation skills include:

- The ability to understand how others feel and good bargaining skills.

- The strength to be tough and fair in putting people and resources where they will be most effective.

EXHIBIT 15–4
The
Implementation
Process

- Effectiveness in focusing on the critical aspects of performance in managing marketing activities.

- The ability to create a necessary informal organization or network to match each problem with which it is confronted.[8]

Research underlines the importance of engendering a sense of role significance among those responsible for implementation.[9] In addition to skillful implementers, several factors facilitate the implementation process. They include *organizational design, incentives,* and *effective communications.* The features of each factor are highlighted.

Organizational Design

Certain types of organizational designs aid implementation. For example, product managers and multifunctional coordination teams are useful implementation methods. Management may create implementation teams consisting of representatives from the business functions and/or marketing activities involved. The flat, flexible organization designs discussed in Chapter 14 offer several advantages in implementation, since they encourage interfunctional cooperation and communication. Recall also the discussion in Chapter 14 of venture marketing organizations as fluid groupings that apply venture capitalism principles to develop and implement strategies around new opportunities. These designs are responsive to changing conditions.

As organizations shift from functional to process structures, the resulting changes promise to strengthen as well as complicate implementation strategies.[10] The use of cross-functional teams will aid implementation activities. The challenges of process definition, design, and management call for new skills and a multifunctional perspective, which will complicate implementation activities and require careful attention by management.

Incentives

Various rewards may help achieve successful implementation. For example, special incentives such as contests, recognition, and extra compensation are used to encourage salespeople to push a new product. Since implementation often involves teams of people, the creation of team incentives may be necessary. Performance standards must be fair, and incentives should encourage something more than normal performance.

Communications

Rapid and accurate movement of information through the organization is essential in implementation. Both vertical and horizontal communications are needed in linking together the people and activities involved in implementation. Meetings, status reports, and informal discussions help transmit information throughout the organization. Computerized information and decision-support systems like corporate intranets help improve the speed and effectiveness of communications.

Problems often occur during implementation and may affect how fast and how well plans are put into action. Examples include competitors' actions, internal resistance between departments, loss of key personnel, supply chain delays affecting product availability (e.g., supply, production, and distribution problems), and changes in the business environment. Corrective actions may require appointing a person or team to troubleshoot the problem, increasing or shifting resources, or changing the original plan. Consider, for example, Gillette's experience in moving the Sensor razor to market in early 1990. Production and distribution were unable to meet initial demand for the new product. Management corrected the problem by speeding up production and delaying the introduction of Sensor in Europe.

Internal Marketing

One promising approach to enhancing strategy implementation effectiveness is the adoption of internal marketing methods. Internal marketing involves developing programs to win line management support for new strategies, change the attitudes and behavior of employees working at key points of contact with customers, and gain the commitment of those whose problem-solving skills are important to superior execution of the strategy. Exhibit 15–5 shows internal marketing and external marketing programs as parallel outputs from the planning process. While external marketing positions the strategy in the customer marketplace, internal marketing is aimed at the internal customer within the company. Internal marketing goals may include promoting the external market strategy and determining how employees fit, developing better understanding between customers and employees (regardless of whether they have direct contact), and providing superior internal customer service to support external strategy.[11]

An internal marketing approach involves examining each element of the external marketing program to identify the changes that will be needed in the company's internal marketplace and how these changes can be achieved. If used as part of the planning

EXHIBIT 15–5
Internal Marketing

Source: Adapted from Nigel F. Piercy, *Market-Led Strategic Change: A Guide to Transforming the Process of Going to Market* (Oxford: Butterworth-Heinemann, 2002), 676.

Implementation Feature

- The original "no-frills airline," Southwest is rated highly for offering customers below-market prices and above-average customer service. The company has won many industry awards for fewest customer complaints, most on-time arrivals, and highest-quality baggage service.

- The company's internal marketing treats front-line employees as internal customers.

- Southwest uses high employee morale and service quality as a route to excellent and sustained profitability in a turbulent marketplace.

- At Southwest, internal marketing involves:

  - Providing employees with a clear vision that is worth pursuing.

  - Competing aggressively to attract the best people.

  - Preparing people with the right skills and knowledge to perform.

  - Emphasizing teamwork.

  - Motivating employees through measurement and rewards.

  - Providing people with the freedom to do well.

  - Ensuring that management understands the internal customer.

- Southwest's strong mission and vision shape a unique corporate culture that puts employees first—they believe that the better they treat employees, the better the employees will perform in providing excellent service to customers.

Source: Adapted from Andrew J. Czaplewski, Jeffery M. Ferguson, and John F. Milliman, "Southwest Airlines: How Internal Marketing Pilots Success," *Marketing Management,* September–October 2001, 14–17.

process, analysis of the internal marketplace can isolate organizational change requirements (e.g., new skills, processes, organizational structures), implementation barriers (e.g., lack of support and commitment in key areas of the company), and new opportunities (by uncovering organizational capabilities otherwise overlooked).[12] Internal marketing is a promising method for identifying and resolving some of the implementation issues associated with the move from functional to process-based organizational designs.

One developing aspect of internal marketing is the opportunity to actively market plans and strategies not only inside the company but also with partner organizations and their employees. The global advertising business WPP has targeted internal marketing as the fastest growth area for marketing services.[13] The Implementation Feature describes the operation of internal marketing at Southwest Airlines.

A Comprehensive Approach to Improving Implementation

One comprehensive way to deal with difficulties in the implementation of the marketing plan is to employ the balanced scorecard method.[14] This process is a formalized management control system that implements a given business unit strategy by means of activities across four areas: financial, customer, internal business process, and learning and growth (or innovation).

The balanced scorecard was created by Kaplan and Norton in reaction to the difficulties that many managers experienced when trying to implement a particular strategy. A strategy often is not defined in a manner that describes how it might be achieved. Merely communicating the strategy to employees does not provide any instruction about what actions they must take to help achieve the strategy. More importantly, managers may even take action to the detriment of other areas in an organization when attempting to implement the strategy. The balanced scorecard provides a framework to minimize such an occurrence by encouraging implementation of a common strategy which is communicated and coordinated across all major areas of the organization. The "balanced" component of the balanced scorecard reflects the need to consider how all areas of the organization function together to achieve a common goal of strategy implementation.

The major benefit of the balanced scorecard is that an often aggregate, broadly defined strategy is translated into very specific actions. Through execution and monitoring of these actions, management can assess the success of the strategy and modify and adjust the strategy if necessary. Another major benefit of the balanced scorecard methodology is that it is feasible for any business-unit level strategy and provides a means to link performance evaluation to strategy implementation.

For example, the marketing plan outline for Sonesta Hotels shown in Exhibit 15–2 can be adapted to the balanced scorecard format. The marketing plan for Sonesta Hotels is designed to achieve specific objectives through a set of strategies. In part VII, A.3., the most difficult area is determining which activities will lead to achieving market segment objectives and ensuring that activities in the sales area do not interfere with activities in another area. The balanced scorecard approach allows consideration of specific sales activities which will accomplish the objective but also formally includes an assessment of the strategy component (part A.2.) across all aspects of the business unit at the same time. This assessment is forward-focused rather than concentrating only on sales, advertising, and public relations. It also helps to include performance measures and targets that are more long-term oriented and are not solely financially based. Therefore, a consideration of sales activities to execute a strategy would also involve how these activities affect four major areas of the company: (1) the financial perspective, (2) the customer, (3) internal business processes, and (4) learning and growth. This integrated assessment would reflect on how the strategy would affect all major areas of the company and what performance indicators should be monitored in each of the four major areas. In this manner, it is much easier to integrate any marketing plan with the overall business strategy.

Internal Strategy-Structure Fit

It is important that the organization's competitive and marketing strategy be compatible with the internal structure of the business and its policies, procedures, and resources.[15] Several internal factors that may affect the implementation of marketing strategy are shown in Exhibit 15–6. These factors include higher-level corporate and business strategies, SBU and corporate relationships (e.g., extent of autonomy), the SBU's internal organization structure and coordination mechanisms, and the specific actions programmed in the marketing plan.

Coping with the influence of these factors during implementation requires close coordination of the strategies at the four levels shown in Exhibit 15–6. Marketing plans must be compatible with this internal structure. Otherwise, implementation and performance will be constrained. For example, a major objective of the marketing planning process of the pharmaceutical company discussed earlier is to communicate and respond to issues and concerns at these four levels. Similarly, the earlier Strategy Feature highlights a CEO's methods of achieving a good strategy-structure fit.

EXHIBIT 15–6
Factors Affecting the Implementation of Business and Marketing Strategies

Source: Harper W. Boyd, Jr., and Orville C. Walker, Jr., *Marketing Management* (Burr Ridge, IL: Richard D. Irwin, 1990), 826.

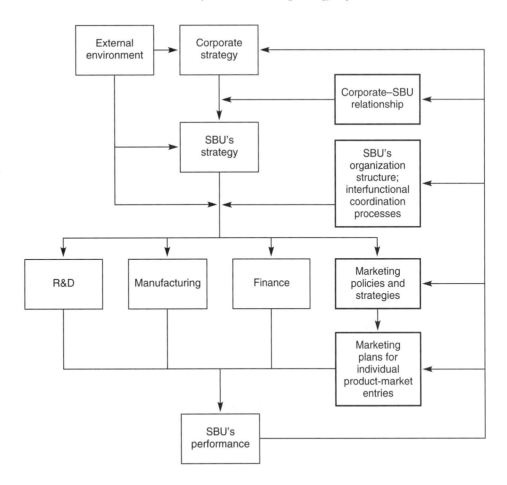

Developing a Market Orientation

Encouraging and facilitating a market orientation throughout the business is an important responsibility of marketing management. The chief executive officer of a large transportation services company states that the marketing and operations functions are the customer-service components of the firm and that the role of accounting, finance, human resources, and information systems is to support customer-service activities. He emphasizes that the supporting functions are evaluated on the basis of how effectively they meet the needs of marketing and operations. Since the entire organization is concerned with delivering customer satisfaction, this CEO's operating philosophy encourages (and rewards) a customer-driven approach throughout the organization.

The Customer Is First

A key issue in developing a market orientation throughout the organization is convincing every employee that customer satisfaction is a shared responsibility. Training programs are used to achieve this objective. The starting point is getting the entire management team to recognize its role and responsibility for market-oriented leadership. Customer advisory groups are sometimes used in developing internal awareness of the importance of the marketplace. Multifunctional (e.g., finance, marketing, operations) teams or task forces may also be helpful integrating methods.

Both the characteristics and the culture of an organization affect the development of a market orientation. Small companies achieve this integration more easily than do large, multilayered corporations. The corporate culture may aid or constrain integration. Managers of nonmarketing functions must be encouraged to recognize the importance of meeting customer needs through their activities. A strong commitment and active participation by the chief executive officer are essential to integrate marketing into the thinking and actions of everyone in the firm. The chief executive officer of Southwest Airlines has been very successful in achieving this objective (Implementation Feature). The airline is a customer-driven organization. Internal marketing may underpin building and sustaining market orientation.

The Role of External Organization

The implementation of marketing strategy is affected by external organizations such as strategic alliance partners, marketing consultants, advertising and public relations firms, channel members, and other organizations participating in the marketing effort. These outside organizations present a major coordination challenge when they actively participate in marketing activities. Their efforts should be identified in the marketing plan, and their roles and responsibilities clearly established and communicated. There is a potential danger in not informing outside groups of planned actions, deadlines, and other implementation requirements. For example, the organization's advertising agency account executive and other agency staff members need to be familiar with all aspects of promotion strategy as well as the major aspects of marketing strategy (e.g., market targets, positioning strategies, and marketing-mix component strategies). Withholding information from participating firms hampers their efforts in strategy planning and implementation.

The development of collaborative relationships between suppliers and producers improves implementation. New supply chain management strategies encourage reducing the number of suppliers and building strong relationships (see Chapter 10). We noted earlier that internal marketing is playing a growing role in sustaining alliance- and network-based organizations that rely on partnering. Companies that are effective in working with other organizations are likely to also do a good job with implementation inside the organization, since they have skills in developing effective working relationships. Total quality programs also encourage internal teamwork among functions.

Adaptation in the Balanced Scorecard

If the balanced scorecard approach is used in conjunction with a market orientation, some modification may be necessary.[16] The balanced scorecard advocates measures of performance across four main areas which should remain in balance. However, many companies seeking a market orientation do so through emphasis on a particular core competency. These competencies may range from product or brand leadership to a strong customer focus. Consequently, companies with such a strong focus on an area of primary importance will continue to need a more extensive set of performance measures in those areas even after adopting of the balanced scorecard approach. Thus, a company competing on the basis of product leadership is dependent on continual innovation to retain a strong market presence. Some advocate that in this case, the balanced scorecard should not be balanced and emphasis should be placed on the innovation perspective. Similarly, other perspectives may be emphasized according to the organization's core competency.

Even with an "unbalanced" approach the balanced scorecard methodology assists in linking business strategy to actions. With a formalized consideration of all major areas in the business, it is more likely that appropriate performance measures can be created and that important areas will not be overlooked.

Strategic Evaluation and Control

Marketing strategy has to be responsive to changing conditions. Evaluation and control keep the strategy on target and show when adjustments are needed. The relentless pursuit of cost reduction through strategy adjustments is a reality for businesses/companies competing in the 21st century.

Strategic evaluation requires analyzing information to gauge performance and taking the actions necessary to keep the results on track. Managers need to monitor performance continually and, when necessary, revise their strategies due to changing conditions. Strategic evaluation, the last stage in the marketing strategy process, is really the starting point. Strategic marketing planning requires information from ongoing monitoring and evaluation of performance. Discussion of strategic evaluation has been delayed until now in order to first consider the strategic areas that require evaluation and to identify the kinds of information needed for assessing marketing performance. Thus, the first 14 chapters establish an essential foundation for building a strategic evaluation program. We now examine the impact of customer relationship management systems, provide an overview of evaluation activities, and discuss the role of the strategic marketing audit.

Customer Relationship Management

The widespread adoption of customer relationship management (CRM) systems to integrate all customer data from different sources, in combination with electronic point-of-sale customer data capture, offers several new and powerful resources for strategic evaluation and control. For example, data mining is becoming an important tool for improving marketing strategies. Penetrating analysis of databases may reveal important purchasing patterns and the effect of marketing actions. Exhibit 15–7 illustrates this use of new data sources. Data mining applications highlight the important role of information technology in the implementation and control of marketing strategy.

The CRM database should contain information regarding *transactions*—complete purchase history for the individual customer with details of prices paid and products delivered; *customer contacts*—how the customer chooses between multiple channels and contact points; *descriptive information*—relating to customer characteristics; and *response to marketing stimuli*—whether the customer responded to a direct marketing stimuli, a sales contact, or another type of direct contact.[17]

The ability to identify profitability at the level of the individual customer by combining CRM and purchase data with other databases is becoming an especially important point of strategic appraisal for marketing management. Together with growing emphasis on customer retention rather than just acquisition, a focus on customer lifetime value is important in guiding management decisions and evaluating the effectiveness of the marketing strategy. CRM systems have the potential to greatly expand the measures of performance used and to take a more fine-grained look at marketing effectiveness related to customer acquisition and defection rates, customer tenure, customer value and worth, proportion of inactive customers, and cross-selling.[18]

EXHIBIT 15–7
Data Mining and CRM in Marketing Evaluation and Control

Sources: Roger D. Blackwell, *From Mind to Market* (New York: HarperBusiness, 1997), 188–89; Todd Wasserman, Gerry Khermouch, and Jeff Green, "Mining Everybody's Business," *Brandweek,* February 28, 2000, 32–36; Russell S. Winer, "A Framework for Customer Relationship Management," *California Management Review* 43, no. 4 (2001), 89–105.

Victoria's Secret	Data mining to improve merchandise managers' decisions concerning inventory levels.	The retailer stocked each bra style in 12 sizes, each with different colors. Restocking decisions were based on managers' judgment, and this resulted in an excess of certain items and a lack of others. A test was initiated to monitor sales and restock inventory according to decision rules applied to the database. Victoria's Secret's sales in the test stores increased by 30 percent using the new decision rules, with no increases in inventory.
Music marketing company	Data mining of purchase data revealed that a significant proportion of people over the age of 62 were buying rap music. They were not fans of Snoop Doggy Dogg but were buying presents for their grandchildren.	Senior citizen purchases had not been considered in the marketing strategy. The unexpected spending pattern produced a new profit center addressed through direct marketing emphasizing the company's low prices (for fixed-income senior citizens).
Wal-Mart	Uses data mining to allow each store to adapt its merchandise mix to local preferences.	Individual stores stock the range of colors, sizes, and price points that match spending patterns at the neighborhood level.
AT&T	Analyzes CRM data to identify the profitability of individual customers.	Service levels are adapted according to the profitability of the customer. Profitable customers receive personalized service, while less profitable customers are offered an automated, menu-driven service.

Overview of Evaluation Activities

Evaluation consumes a high proportion of marketing executives' time and energy. Evaluation may seek to (1) find new opportunities or avoid threats, (2) keep performance in line with management's expectations, and/or (3) solve specific problems that exist.

An example of a threat identified via product-market analysis is the shift away from wearing suits and more formal business attire and toward wearing sporty clothing. These changes in preferences are major threats for companies which produce men's suits. Similarly, Royal Doulton, a premier brand of formal chinaware famed for its expensive dinner plates, saw its sales falling 20 percent a year in the late 1990s because of the move by consumers towards informal dining and management's inability to reposition the brand.

The second form of evaluation is illustrated by the HomeStreet Bank example, which shows the importance of keeping performance on track. Finally, evaluating the effectiveness of alternative TV commercials is an example of solving specific problems. Areas of evaluation include environmental scanning, product-market analysis, brand equity analysis, marketing program evaluation, and gauging the effectiveness of specific marketing mix components such as advertising. Recall also the impact of CRM databases on evaluation.

EXHIBIT 15–8
Strategic Marketing Evaluation and Control

Conduct strategic
marketing audit

Select performance
criteria and measures

Obtain and
analyze information

Assess performance and
take necessary action

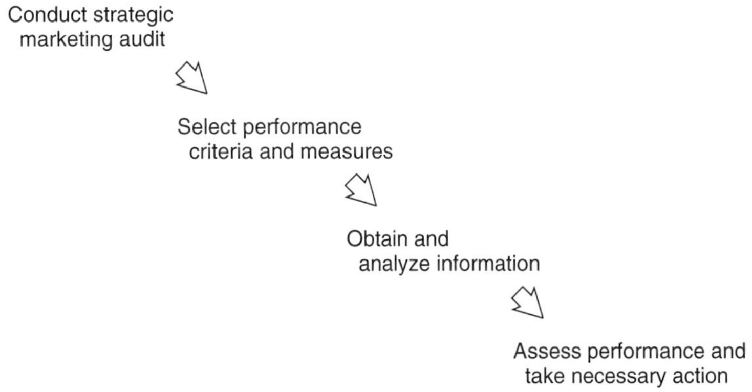

The major steps in establishing a strategic evaluation program are described in Exhibit 15–8. Strategic and annual marketing plans set the direction and guidelines for the evaluation and control process. A strategic marketing audit may be conducted when setting up an evaluation program and periodically thereafter. Next, performance standards and measures need to be determined, followed by obtaining and analyzing information for the purpose of performance-gap identification. Actions are initiated to pursue opportunities or avoid threats, keep performance on track, or solve a particular decision-making problem.

The Strategic Marketing Audit

A marketing audit is useful in initiating a strategic evaluation program. Since evaluation compares results with expectations, it is necessary to lay some groundwork before setting up a tracking program. This complete review and assessment of marketing operations is similar in some respects to the situation analysis discussed in Part II. However, the marketing audit goes beyond customer and competitive analysis to include all aspects of marketing operations. The audit is larger in scope than the situation analysis and is a more complete review of marketing strategy and performance. The audit can be used to initiate a formal strategic marketing planning program and may be repeated on a periodic basis. Normally, the situation analysis is part of the annual development of marketing plans. Audits may be conducted every three to five years.

A guide to conducting the strategic marketing audit is shown in Exhibit 15–9. This format can be adapted to meet the needs of a particular firm. For example, if a company does not use indirect channels of distribution, this section of the audit guide will require adjustment. Likewise, if the sales force is the major part of a marketing program, this section may be expanded to include other aspects of sales force strategy. The items included in the audit correspond to the strategic marketing plan because the main purpose of the audit is to appraise the effectiveness of the strategy being followed. The audit guide includes several questions about marketing performance. The answers to these questions are incorporated into the design of the strategic tracking program.

Besides starting an evaluation program, there are other reasons for conducting a strategic marketing audit. Corporate restructuring may bring about a complete review of strategic marketing operations. Major shifts in business activities such as entry into new product and market areas or acquisitions may require strategic marketing audits. The growing impact of Internet-based business models may also encourage management to undertake an audit.

EXHIBIT 15–9   **Guide to Conducting the Strategic Marketing Audit**

I. CORPORATE MISSION AND OBJECTIVES

    A. Does the mission statement offer a clear guide to the product-markets of interest to the firm?

    B. Have objectives been established for the corporation?

    C. Is information available for the review of corporate progress toward objectives, and are the reviews conducted on a regular (e.g., quarterly, monthly) basis?

    D. Has corporate strategy been successful in meeting objectives?

    E. Are opportunities or problems pending that may require altering marketing strategy?

    F. What are the responsibilities of the chief marketing executive in corporate strategic planning?

II. BUSINESS COMPOSITION AND STRATEGIES

    A. What is the composition of the business (business segments, strategic planning units, and specific product-markets)?

    B. Have business strength and product-market attractiveness analyses been conducted for each planning unit? What are the results of the analyses?

    C. What is the corporate strategy for each planning unit (e.g., develop, stabilize, turn around, or harvest)?

    D. What objectives are assigned to each planning unit?

    E. Does each unit have a strategic plan?

    F. For each unit what objectives and responsibilities have been assigned to marketing?

III. MARKETING STRATEGY (FOR EACH PLANNING UNIT)

    A. Strategic planning and marketing:

        1. Is marketing's role and responsibility in corporate strategic planning clearly specified?

        2. Are responsibility and authority for marketing strategy assigned to one executive?

        3. How well is the firm's marketing strategy working?

        4. Are changes likely to occur in the corporate/marketing environment that may affect the firm's marketing strategy?

        5. Are there major contingencies that should be included in the strategic marketing plan?

    B. Marketing planning and organizational structure:

        1. Are annual and longer-range strategic marketing plans developed, and are they being used?

        2. Are the responsibilities of the various units in the marketing organization clearly specified?

        3. What are the strengths and limitations of the key members of the marketing organization? What is being done to develop people? What gaps in experience and capabilities exist on the marketing staff?

        4. Is the organizational structure for marketing effective for implementing marketing plans?

    C. Market target strategy:

        1. Has each market target been clearly defined and its importance to the firm established?

        2. Have demand, industry, and competition in each market target been analyzed and key trends, opportunities, and threats identified?

        3. Has the proper market target strategy been adopted?

        4. Should repositioning or exit from any product-market be considered?

    D. Objectives:

        1. Are objectives established for each market target, and are these consistent with planning unit objectives and the available resources? Are the objectives realistic?

        2. Are sales, cost, and other performance information available for monitoring the progress of planned performance against actual results?

        3. Are regular appraisals made of marketing performance?

        4. Where do gaps exist between planned and actual results? What are the probable causes of the performance gaps?

EXHIBIT 15–9   *(continued)*

   E. Marketing program positioning strategy:
   1. Does the firm have an integrated positioning strategy made up of product, channel, price, advertising, and sales force strategies? Is the role selected for each mix element consistent with the overall program objectives, and does it properly complement other mix elements?
   2. Are adequate resources available to carry out the marketing program? Are resources committed to market targets according to the importance of each?
   3. Are allocations to the various marketing mix components too low, too high, or about right in terms of what each is expected to accomplish?
   4. Is the effectiveness of the marketing program appraised on a regular basis?
IV. MARKETING PROGRAM ACTIVITIES
   A. Product strategy:
   1. Is the product mix geared to the needs and preferences that the firm wants to meet in each product-market?
   2. What branding strategy is being used?
   3. Are products properly positioned against competing brands?
   4. Does the firm have a sound approach to product planning and management, and is marketing involved in product decisions?
   5. Are additions to, modifications of, or deletions from the product mix needed to make the firm more competitive in the marketplace?
   6. Is the performance of each product evaluated on a regular basis?
   B. Channel of distribution strategy:
   1. Has the firm selected the type (conventional or vertically coordinated) and intensity of distribution appropriate for each of its product-markets?
   2. How well does each channel access its market target? Is an effective channel configuration being used?
   3. Are channel organizations carrying out their assigned functions properly?
   4. How is the channel of distribution being managed? What improvements are needed?
   5. Are desired customer service levels being reached, and are the costs of doing this acceptable?
   C. Price strategy:
   1. How responsive is each market target to price variations?
   2. What role and objectives does price have in the marketing mix?
   3. Should price play an active or passive role in program positioning strategy?
   4. How do the firm's price strategy and tactics compare to those of the competition?
   5. Is a logical approach used to establish prices?
   6. Are there indications that changes may be needed in price strategy or tactics?
   D. Advertising and sales promotion strategies:
   1. Have a role and objectives been established for advertising and sales promotion in the marketing mix?
   2. Is the creative strategy consistent with the positioning strategy that is being used?
   3. Is the budget adequate to carry out the objectives assigned to advertising and sales promotion?
   4. Do the media and programming strategies represent the most cost-effective means of communicating with market targets?
   5. Do advertising copy and content effectively communicate the intended messages?
   6. How well does the advertising program measure up in meeting its objectives?

(continued)

EXHIBIT 15–9 *(concluded)*

E. Sales force strategy:
    1. Are the role and objectives of personal selling in the marketing program positioning strategy clearly specified and understood by the sales organization?
    2. Do the qualifications of salespeople correspond to their assigned roles?
    3. Is the sales force of the proper size to carry out its function, and is it efficiently deployed?
    4. Are sales force results in line with management's expectations?
    5. Is each salesperson assigned performance targets, and are incentives offered to reward performance?
    6. Are compensation levels and ranges competitive?
V. IMPLEMENTATION AND MANAGEMENT
  A. Have the causes of all performance gaps been identified?
  B. Is implementation of planned actions taking place as intended? Is implementation being hampered by marketing or other functional areas of the firm (e.g., operations, finance)?
  C. Has the strategic audit revealed areas requiring additional study before action is taken?

Performance Criteria and Information Needs

The next two stages in the evaluation and control process (Exhibit 15–8) are (1) selecting the performance criteria and the measures to be used for monitoring performance and (2) identifying the information management needs to perform various marketing control activities.

Selecting Performance Criteria and Measures

As marketing plans are developed, performance criteria need to be selected to monitor performance. Specifying the information needed for marketing decision making is important and requires management's concentrated attention. In the past, marketing executives could develop and manage successful marketing strategies by relying on intuition, judgment, and experience. Successful executives in the 21st century need to combine judgment and experience with information and decision support systems. Similarly, the balanced scorecard approach is used by many companies to help select performance measures that are linked to strategy. Information systems are increasingly important in gaining a strategic edge in industries such as airline services, direct marketing, packaged foods, wholesaling, retailing, and financial services.

The purpose of objectives is to state the results that management is seeking and provide a basis for evaluating the strategy's success. Objectives set standards of performance. Progress toward the objectives in the strategic and short-term plans is monitored on a continuing basis. In addition to information on objectives, management requires other kinds of feedback for use in performance evaluation. Some of this information is incorporated into regular tracking activities (e.g., the effectiveness of advertising expenditures). Other information is obtained as the need arises, such as a special study of consumers' preferences for different brands.

Examples of performance criteria are discussed in several chapters. They should be selected for the total plan and its important components. Illustrative criteria for total performance include sales, market share, profit, expense, and customer satisfaction targets. Brand-positioning map analyses may also be useful in tracking how a brand is positioned relative to key competitors. These assessments can be used to gauge overall performance and for specific market targets. Performance criteria are also needed for the marketing-mix components. For example, the tracking of new customers and lost customers is often included in sales force performance monitoring. Pricing performance monitoring may include comparisons of actual to list prices, extent of discounting, and profit contribution. Since many possible performance criteria can be selected, management must identify the key measures that will show how the firm's marketing strategy is performing in its competitive environment and point to where changes are needed. Recall that the growing impact of CRM systems offers management access to a larger number of performance measures, particularly those relating to customer retention and defection.[19]

Marketing Metrics

The critical issue of selecting appropriate performance criteria is also illustrated in the development of marketing metrics, or measures of the impact of marketing on the whole business, provided to senior management. The goal is to make better causal links between marketing activities and financial returns to the business.[20]

For example, Shell's large expenditure on sponsoring Ferrari in Formula One motor racing underlines the need for financial justification for this expenditure. Before signing a new five-year sponsorship contract, Shell management evaluated costs and benefits in five ways:

- Comparing attitudes toward the Shell brand among those who were aware of the Ferrari link and those who were not.

- Examining changes in purchasing behavior associated with shifts in attitudes toward the brand.

- Commissioning an independent evaluation of brand value, including branding, sales, price premium, and advertising effects.

- Making country-by-country comparisons—different Shell companies had merchandised the sponsorship locally to varying extents, and so if the sponsorship was profitable, those which promoted it more should have obtained more benefit.

- Surveying managers' opinions and their ratings of the impact of the sponsorship on return on investment.

After top management review, Shell approved the new five-year contract for the sponsorship as an important part of the company's marketing strategy.[21]

Tim Ambler of the London Business School proposes the following questions to assess if a company's marketing tracking system (or performance measures), is adequate: Are the results reported to senior management regularly? Are the results compared with the forecast levels in business plans? Are they compared with key competitors using the same indicators? Is short-term performance adjusted to allow for changes in market-based assets? Is consumer behavior (purchase, frequency, retention, usage) researched and the drivers of behavior understood and monitored (e.g., satisfaction and brand awareness)?[22]

In Ambler's research into marketing metrics, the most important marketing metrics used by companies were found to be relative perceived quality, loyalty/retention, total number of customers, customer satisfaction, relative price (market share/volume), market share (volume or value), perceived quality/esteem, complaints (level of dissatisfaction), awareness, and distribution/availability.[23]

Obtain and Analyze Information

The costs of acquiring, processing, and analyzing information are high, and so the potential benefits of needed information must be compared to costs. Normally, information falls into two categories: (1) information regularly supplied to marketing management from internal and external sources and (2) information obtained as needed for a particular problem or situation. Examples of the former are sales and cost analyses, market share measurements, and customer satisfaction surveys. Recall the growing impact of CRM systems in enhancing the availability of this type of information. Information from the latter category includes new product concept tests, brand preference studies, and studies of advertising effectiveness.

Several types of information may be needed by management. Information for strategic planning and evaluation can be obtained from these sources:

1. The *internal information system* is the backbone of any strategic evaluation program. These systems range from primarily sales and cost reports to highly sophisticated computerized marketing information systems and CRM/data mining technology.

2. *Standardized information services* are available by subscription or on a one-time basis, often at a fraction of the cost of preparing such information for a single firm. Nevertheless, these services are expensive. Standardized services are available in both printed form and data files for computer analysis. Nielsen's TV rating data service is an example.

3. Marketing managers may require *special research studies*. A study of distributor opinions concerning a manufacturer's services is an example.

4. The firm's *strategic intelligence system* is concerned with monitoring and forecasting external, uncontrollable factors that influence the firm's product-markets. These efforts range from formal information activities to informal surveillance of the marketing environment.

Sources and types of marketing information were discussed in Chapter 5.

The importance of information in building competitive advantage is underlined by the need to protect proprietary information as part of strategic evaluation and control. For example, nearly 75 percent of Fortune 1000 companies indicate that "theft or attempted theft by computers of customer information, trade secrets and new product plans has increased over the past five years."[24] The reasons cited for the increase in the theft of corporate secrets include computer technology and decline in worker loyalty. Important in supporting claims of corporate theft is showing that an organization has taken reasonable precautions to protect secret information.

Performance Assessment and Action

The last stage in the marketing evaluation and control process is determining how the actual results compare with planned results. When performance gaps are too large, corrective actions are taken.

Opportunities and Performance Gaps

Strategic evaluation activities seek to (1) identify opportunities or performance gaps and (2) initiate actions to take advantage of the opportunities or to correct existing and pending problems. Strategic intelligence, internal reporting and analysis activities, standardized information services, and research studies supply the information needed by marketing decision makers.

The real test of the value of the marketing information system is whether it helps marketing management identify problems. In monitoring, there are two critical factors to take into account:

Problem/opportunity definition. Strategic analysis should lead to a clear explanation of an opportunity or problem since this will be needed to guide whatever strategic action may be taken. Often it is easy to confuse problem symptoms with problem causes.

Interpreting information. Management must also separate normal variations in performance from significant gaps in performance, since the latter are the ones that require strategic action. For example, how much of a drop in market share is necessary to signal a performance problem? Limits need to be set on the acceptable range of strategic performance.

No matter how extensive the information system may be, it cannot interpret the strategic importance of the information. This is the responsibility of management.

An illustration of opportunity monitoring is the growth of day spas for women in the United States. There are about 900 of these beauty parlors, and they accounted for 37 percent of cosmetic sales in 1997 compared to 15 percent in 1990.[25] Interestingly, this growth in spa sales has come from department store sales, which declined from 53 percent to 31 percent during that period. These changes have important implications for both cosmetics producers and department stores. Distribution through spas is important, particularly for higher-priced brands like Estée Lauder. Department stores are creating minispas, though some observers question this strategy because of the lack of privacy.

Environmental concerns are ongoing areas of strategic evaluation. Companies must identify important areas of concern and implement strategies that take into account consumer, public policy, and organizational priorities. Surprisingly, European consumers appear to be changing their priorities about ecofriendly products,[26] while in the United States polls suggest that in 2001 only 50 percent of Americans considered themselves to be environmentalists, compared to 76 percent in 1989.[27] Buyers may not be willing to pay a premium for green products.

Several explanations are offered, including lower performance, higher prices, and environmentally responsible regular products. The British supermarket chain Iceland took the decision in 2000 to move totally to organic produce in its own-label products in order to make organic food part of mass market grocery shopping, in line with the growth in sales of this type of produce. In 2001, after a 6 percent fall in sales and the loss of one-fifth of the company's market value, the decision was reversed. Iceland's largely blue-collar consumers did not find organic products appealing and objected to having the choice taken away. Philips, the European electronics multinational, claims that its success in marketing green products is based on understanding the need to link green product attributes like energy reduction, materials reduction, and toxic substance reduction with other consumer benefits (e.g., lower costs, convenience, higher quality of life).[28]

Company experiences with the paradoxes of consumer attitudes toward the purchase of green products underline the importance of extremely careful interpretation of the available evidence before decisions are made and continuous monitoring of changes.

Determining Normal and Abnormal Variability

Operating results such as sales, market share, profits, order-processing time, and customer satisfaction display normal up-and-down fluctuations. The issue is determining whether these variations represent random variation or instead are due to special causes. For example, if a salesperson's sales over time remain within a normal band of variation, the results are acceptable under the present operating conditions. Random high and low variations do not indicate unusually high or low performance. If this range of performance is *not* acceptable to management, the system must be changed. This may require salesperson training, redesign of the territory, improvement in sales support, or other changes in the salesperson's operating system.

Statistical process-control concepts and methods are useful in determining when operating results are fluctuating normally or instead are out of control.[29] Quality-control charts can be used to analyze and improve results in marketing performance measures such as the number of orders processed, customer complaints, and territory sales. Control-chart analysis indicates when the process is experiencing normal variation and when the process is out of control.

The basic approach to control-chart analysis is to establish average and upper and lower control limits for the measure being evaluated. Examples of measures include order-processing time, district sales, customer complaints, and market share. Control boundaries are set by using historical data. Future measures are plotted on the chart to determine whether the results are under control or instead fall outside the acceptable performance band determined by the upper and lower control limits. The objective is to continually improve the process that determines the results.

Deciding What Actions to Take

Many corrective actions are possible, depending on the situation. Management's actions may include exiting from a product-market, new product planning, changing the target market strategy, adjusting marketing strategy, and improving efficiency.

An illustration shows how evaluation and control guide corrective action. Deere & Company, the giant farm equipment producer, had a strong performance record during the agriculture slump of the late 1980s.[30] Management invested in product and process research, reduced employment, and cut costs. Monitoring of performance indicated the need to take further corrective action in 1989. The industry shakeout had weakened farmers' brand loyalty and created two strong competitors. Deere was losing customers who had been buying the popular green farm equipment for three generations. The nation's 2.2 million farmers were making money and buying equipment.

Case Corporation was the number two firm in the U.S. market, strengthened by acquisitions of International Harvester and Steiger Tractor. Case had 1989 global farm equipment sales of $2.9 billion compared to Deere's $4.1 billion. The number three competitor was the Ford Motor Company with sales of $2.3 billion. Both firms were fighting Deere for top position in the $8 billion-a-year domestic market. Farmers' purchases are heavily influenced by equipment quality, price, and dealer service. Competitors were beginning to penetrate Deere's loyal customer base with high-quality equipment, aggressive selling, and dealer support.

Deere had a reputation for high-quality products. Its greatest edge was its strong U.S. dealer network. To strengthen its advantage, Deere's factory employees phoned or visited farmers who had purchased Deere products. Service teams were deployed to the field for troubleshooting during periods of heavy equipment usage such as harvesting. Continued investment in new and improved products occurred in the 1990s, but competitors challenged Deere with requests for equipment comparisons.

In 1999, Case Corporation merged with New Holland, instantly narrowing Deere's lead in the market—their combined sales of $11 billion were close to Deere's $14 billion. However, the new company, CNH Global, was unpopular with customers who feared that the merger would lead to duplicate products being discontinued. While CNH management was focused on the merger, farmers and dealers began to switch brands. In addition, Deere responded aggressively to the new competitor with discounts for Case and New Holland loyalists who switched to Deere equipment and fueled farmers' nervousness about the resale value of their Case red and New Holland blue machinery. CNH lost market share across its entire product range and started to report losses.[31]

The early 2000s saw Deere reporting losses during the slump in the U.S. farming equipment market and reducing output, but with aggressive plans for diversification and global build-to-order for new products.[32] The battle for position in the farm equipment market is a continuing marketing challenge for advantage in a highly competitive, cyclical, technologically changing global marketplace.

Managing in a changing environment is what strategic marketing is all about. Responding to and anticipating change is the essence of evaluation and control. Executives develop innovative marketing strategies and monitor their effectiveness, altering the strategies as a result of changing conditions.

Summary

Marketing strategy implementation and control are vital links in a series of strategic marketing activities. These actions emphasize the continuing process of planning, implementing, evaluating, and adjusting marketing strategies. Strategic evaluation of marketing performance is the first step in strategic marketing planning and the last step after launching a strategy. The objective is to develop an approach to strategic evaluation, building on the concepts, processes, and methods developed in Chapters 1 through 14. Strategic evaluation is one of marketing management's most demanding and time-consuming responsibilities. While the activity lacks the glamour and excitement of new strategy development, perceptive evaluation often separates the winners from the losers. The management of successful companies anticipates and responds effectively to changing conditions and pressures. Regular strategic evaluation processes guide these responses.

Marketing strategy implementation and control are guided by the marketing plan and budget (Exhibit 15–1). The plan indicates the activities to be accomplished, how this is to be done, and the costs. The planning process moves into action through the annual marketing plan. It shows the activities to be implemented, responsibilities, deadlines, and expectations. Growing attention is being given to the management of the planning process for effective strategy implementation, emphasizing not only analytical approaches but also the commitment of managers to planning and the necessary organizational support.

Implementation (Exhibit 15–4) makes the plan happen. Many companies are concerned with enhancing implementation effectiveness. Organizational design, communications, and internal marketing may affect implementation effectiveness. The balanced scorecard is a promising approach to coordinating a comprehensive approach to improving marketing implementation.

Much of the actual work of managing involves strategic and tactical evaluation of marketing options, yet performing this function depends greatly on management's understanding of the planning process and the decisions that form plans. Strategic evaluation is a continuing cycle of making plans, launching them, tracking performance, identifying performance gaps, and initiating problem-solving actions. In accomplishing strategic evaluation, management must select performance criteria and measures and then set up a tracking program to obtain the information needed to guide evaluation activities. The choice and tracking of performance measures are increasingly affected by the adoption of customer relationship management systems. As an initial step in the strategic evaluation program (and periodically thereafter), a strategic marketing audit provides a useful basis for developing the program.

It is easy for practicing managers to become preoccupied with day-to-day activities, neglecting to step back and review overall operations. The development of marketing metrics reporting the added value of marketing to the whole company to senior management supports this need for strategic review. Regular audits and continuous monitoring of the market and the competitive environment can prevent sudden shocks and alert management to new opportunities. Building on findings from the strategic marketing audit, this chapter examines the major steps in acquiring and using information for strategic analysis. While the execution of the steps varies by situation, the steps provide a useful basis for guiding a strategic evaluation program in any type of firm. An important part of this process is setting standards for gauging marketing performance. These standards help determine what information is needed to monitor performance.

Internet Applications

Visit the website for 1-800-FLOWERS (*www.1800flowers.com*). How does this company employ its website to adapt to a constantly changing environment?

Questions for Review and Discussion

1. Discuss the similarities and differences between strategic marketing *planning* and *evaluation.*
2. What is involved in managing marketing planning as a process? What issues should be addressed in managing the planning process in a company that manufactures high-technology components for the automotive sector?
3. Selecting the proper performance criteria for use in tracking results is a key part of a strategic evaluation program. Suggest performance criteria for use by a fast-food retail chain to monitor strategic marketing performance.
4. What justification is there for conducting a marketing audit in a business unit whose performance has been very good? Discuss.
5. Examination of the various areas of a strategic marketing audit shown in Exhibit 15–9 would be quite expensive and time-consuming. Are there any ways to limit the scope of the audit?
6. Several kinds of information are collected for a strategic marketing evaluation. Develop a list of information that would be useful for a strategic evaluation in a life insurance company.
7. One of the more difficult management control issues is determining whether a process is experiencing normal variation or is actually out of control. Discuss how management can resolve this issue.
8. What role can internal marketing play in enhancing the effectiveness of both planning and implementation?
9. How can the "balanced scorecard" methods assist managers in their implementation efforts?
10. Discuss how management control differs for a strategic alliance compared to internal operations.
11. What are the important factors that managers should take into account to improve the implementation of strategies?
12. Discuss the role of customer relationship management and data mining in improving marketing planning, implementation, and control activities.

Notes

1. This illustration is based on Ted Leonhardt, "A (Rebranded) Star Is Born!" *Bank Marketing,* May 2001, 20–24.
2. Donald R. Lehmann and Russell S. Winer, *Analysis for Marketing Planning*, 4th ed. (Burr Ridge, IL: Richard D. Irwin, 1997), 10–13.
3. Ibid., 5–7.

4. Nigel F. Piercy and Neil A. Morgan, "The Marketing Planning Process: Behavioral Problems Compared to Analytical Techniques in Explaining Marketing Planning Credibility," *Journal of Business Research* 29 (1994), 167–78.

5. Frederick E. Webster, "The Future Role of Marketing in the Organization," in Donald R. Lehmann and Katherine E. Jocz (eds.), *Reflections on the Future of Marketing* (Cambridge, MA: Marketing Science Institute, 1997), 39–66.

6. Nigel F. Piercy, "Marketing Implementation: The Implications of Marketing Paradigm Weakness for the Strategy Execution Process," *Journal of the Academy of Marketing Science* 26, no. 3 (1998), 222–36; Nigel F. Piercy and Frank V. Cespedes, "Implementing Marketing Strategy," *Journal of Marketing Management* 12 (1996), 135–60.

7. Charles H. Noble and Michael P. Mokwa, "Implementing Marketing Strategies: Developing and Testing a Managerial Theory," *Journal of Marketing,* October 1999, 57–73.

8. Thomas V. Bonoma, "Making Your Marketing Strategy Work," *Harvard Business Review,* March–April 1984, 75.

9. Noble and Mokwa, "Implementing Marketing Strategies," 71.

10. David W. Cravens, "Implementation Strategies in the Market-Driven Strategy Era," *Journal of the Academy of Marketing Science,* Summer 1998, 237–38.

11. Dana James, "Don't Forget Staff in Marketing Plan," *Marketing News,* March 13, 2000, 10–11.

12. Nigel F. Piercy and Neil A. Morgan, "Internal Marketing: The Missing Half of the Marketing Programme," *Long Range Planning* 24, no. 2 (1991), 82–93.

13. "…As Sorrell Starts Internal Marketing Drive," *Marketing Week,* July 12, 2001, 10.

14. Robert S. Kaplan and David P. Norton, *The Balanced Scorecard,* (Boston: Harvard Business School Press, 1996).

15. This discussion is based on Harper W. Boyd, Jr., and Orville C. Walker, Jr., *Marketing Management* (Homewood, IL: Richard D. Irwin, 1990), 824–25.

16. See Stanley F. Slater, Eric M. Olson, and Venkateshwar K. Reddy, "Strategy-Based Performance Measurement," *Business Horizons,* July–August 1997, 37–44, for a complete discussion of the modification of the balanced scorecard approach to achieving a market orientation.

17. Russell S. Winer, "A Framework for Customer Relationship Management," *California Management Review* 43, no. 4 (2001), 89–105.

18. Lawrence A. Crosby and Sheree L Johnson, "High Performance Marketing in the CRM Era," *Marketing Management,* September–October 2001, 10–11.

19. Larry Yu, "Successful Customer-Relationship Management," *Sloan Management Review,* Summer 2001, 18–29.

20. Wayne R. McCullough, "Marketing Metrics," *Marketing Management,* Spring 2000, 64.

21. "Marketers Still Lost in the Metrics," *Marketing,* August 10, 2000, 15–17.

22. Tim Ambler, *Marketing and the Bottom Line: The New Metrics of Corporate Wealth* (Hemel Hempstead, UK: Prentice-Hall, 2000).

23. Allyson L. Stewart-Allen, "Marketing Metrics for Corporate Boards," *Marketing News,* December 4, 2000, 14.

24. Milo Geyelin, "Why Many Businesses Can't Keep Their Secrets," *The Wall Street Journal,* November 20, 1995, B1, B3.

25. Anne Marie Chaker, "Makeup Brands Take Note as Day Spas Sell Cosmetics," *The Wall Street Journal,* July 8, 1998, B1, B11.

26. Tara Parker-Pope, "Europeans' Environmental Concerns Don't Make It to the Shopping Basket," *The Wall Street Journal,* August 18, 1995, B3A.

27. Vadim Liberman, "The Green Conundrum," *Across the Board,* May–June 2001, 17–18.

28. Jacquelyn A. Ottman, "Green Marketing," *In Business*, September–October 2000, 31.

29. Kaori Ishikawa, *Guide to Quality Control* (Tokyo: Asian Productivity Organization, 1982).

30. This account is based on Robert L. Rose, "Tougher Row: Deere Faces Challenge Just When Farmers Are Shopping Again," *The Wall Street Journal,* February 8, 1990, A1, A6.

31. Michael Arndt, "A Merger's Bitter Harvest," *Business Week,* February 5, 2001, 112–14.

32. "Deere Swings to Loss in 4th Quarter, Expects Market To Remain Weak," *Wall Street Journal,* November 21 2001, 4; Gene G. Marcial, "A Deere Heart for Ingersoll," *Business Week,* February 19, 2001, 107; Doug Smock, "Deere Takes A Giant Leap," *Purchasing,* September 6, 2001, 26–35.

Cases for Part V

Oracle Corp.

For the past decade, Lawrence J. Ellison has been Silicon Valley's Bad Boy. The chairman of No. 2 software maker Oracle Corp. watched with unbridled envy as the PC industry became the most powerful force in the Information Age—and William H. Gates III and his Microsoft Corp. along with it. But Oracle, after its initial success as a flashy Silicon Valley startup, seemed stuck in Dullsville. The company's database software, with its ability to organize reams of information, was a crucial but oh-so-boring adjunct to grey-flannel-suit corporate computing.

So Ellison squawked for attention. He tried to buy a Russian MiG for $20 million—but ran afoul of U.S. Customs. He riled authorities in San Jose by repeatedly landing his executive jet after the 11 P.M. curfew. He was nearly killed winning the Sydney-to-Hobart race in his 78-foot yacht, Sayonara. And he cooked up one Oracle announcement after another that seemed to be aimed at upstaging Gates. Interactive TV would merge Hollywood with Silicon Valley to create Siliwood. Oracle would build a stripped-down "network computer" that would make PCs obsolete. Neither happened. The headlines were entertaining, but few took Ellison seriously.

Database Fever

Now, as the Information Age gives way to the Internet Age, Silicon Valley's Bad Boy is having his revenge. Suddenly, databases are all the rage, as troves of information—from product catalogs on Amazon.com to the global order stats of GE Medical Systems—are being made instantly available to customers and employees over the Internet. Two-and-a-half years ago, when the Web was still in short pants, Oracle's database sales inched along at 3% and 5% growth per quarter. Last quarter, they surged 32%, to $778 million.

And that could be just a warmup. Envisioning a day when companies would shift their internal operations to the Net, Ellison began creating software programs that hooked into his database to do a host of other big corporate jobs over the Web, such as purchasing and managing inventory (Exhibit 1). Now that daunting engineering effort looks to be paying off. Since November, Oracle has landed big-name customers such as Ford Motor, Chevron, and Sears. They've signed on for technology that allows them to operate virtual marketplaces on the Web in which anybody who wants to sell them supplies or services places a bid. "I always saw Oracle as a database company," says David J. O'Reilly, CEO of Chevron. "But they've come a long way to transform themselves into an Internet software company."

And Oracle's stock shows it. After puttering along for more than five years, Oracle's shares have joined the superheated elite. Since November, the company's stock has nearly quadrupled, to about 72 a share, giving the world's No. 2 software maker a market cap of $205 billion—surpassing mighty IBM. Though the tech correction brought Oracle's price down from an all-time high of 90, it has weathered the storm far better than the Nasdaq composite, which has dropped 28% from its peak and is down 10% year-to-date. Oracle is up 29% for the year, bolstered most recently by a rave report from Lehman Bros. And Microsoft? Its stock price was hammered down 15.6% on Apr. 24 by the double-whammy

EXHIBIT 1
**Squeezing
Savings Out of
an E-Business**

Tom Scott and Tom First started off in business on Nantucket in 1989 by delivering supplies to visiting yachts. When they added fresh juice to their repertoire, Nantucket Nectars was born. Now, the company is installing Oracle software to help it keep growing at 40% a year.

1. Suppliers

In the past, Nantucket Nectars communicated with its 900 suppliers the old-fashioned way—by phone and fax. Besides being slow and costly, the system didn't keep track of inventories or demand well. Oracle software allows them to create more accurate forecasts and will enable them to forge close links with the likes of Ocean Spray.

2. Bottlers

Nantucket Nectar's six bottlers are also its warehouses. With better forecasting and Web links, the company can alert bottlers to rev up production lines. It enables bottlers to better plan so their plants aren't idle. Nantucket Nectars also can size up inventories at the warehouses and ship juices from one if stocks are low at another.

3. Headquarters

Anybody in sales, marketing, or operations can tap into the computer system via a Web browser and check on the status of orders, inventory levels, and changes in demand. Executives like the two Toms and sales managers can dice sales data by region, distributor, and salesperson. If somebody is asleep at the switch, they'll know it instantly.

4. Sales Force

Each morning, Nantucket Nectars' 85 field salespeople can log on to the Internet from their homes and tap into NectarNet, the company's business Web site. If they see that Orange Mango has to be substituted for Pineapple Orange Guava in a shipment, they'll be able to warn the customer. Plus, they can track promotions at sports events.

5. Distributors

The 150 distributors can log into NectarNet to place and check orders. If a drink is out of stock, they can avoid an unwanted substitution by specifying what they'd like instead. Nantucket's marketers can check promotional budgets to see if distributors have kept up their commitments to pass out coolers to retailers.

6. Retailers

The company uses sales-analysis software to help retailers figure out how to stock the right juices. Marketers at headquarters can review sales records for various distributors in a given region and rate which combination of drinks does best. The company alerts distributors, who pass the info on to mom-and-pop shops.

7. Website

Nantucket Nectars sells T-shirts, hats, and frisbees decorated with its logo on its website *www.Juiceguys.com.* It's planning a major overhaul that will turn the website into a real store and is sizing up Oracle's iStore software to power the site. Possible merchandise: juice blenders, herbs, nutrition items, and health aids.

of a disappointing third-quarter report and word that the Justice Department might call for a breakup of the company. The capper: To Ellison's delight, on Apr. 25 his stake in Oracle actually surpassed Gate's Microsoft holdings, by $52.1 billion to $51.5 billion.

Ellison revels in Oracle's good fortune. "We're cool again," he says. And aiming to stay that way. With his database business on cruise control. Ellison is about to launch Phase Two of his Net assault. In May, Oracle plans to unveil its most important product update in years. It's a suite of business applications that work seamlessly with one another to handle everything from customer service on one end to relationships with suppliers on the other. And it's all rejiggered to run on the Web.

Ellison's vision for what he calls the first-ever "e-business suite" is to create something as popular as Microsoft's Office desktop suite. Now, Ellison figures, everyone from giant corporations to tiny dot-coms can buy a single package from Oracle to run their e-businesses, rather than buying software from a host of competitors and trying to stitch it all together.

If it works, Ellison's dream of knocking Gates down a peg might actually come to pass. As computing moves from desktop PCs to huge Internet servers that run everything from Web sites to complex corporate networks, Oracle's skills and technologies are taking center stage. Ellison gloats that Microsoft's tangle with Netscape Communications Corp. over Web browsers, which landed it in hot water with the Justice Department, didn't get it ahead in the Net-server realm. "They robbed the wrong bank," Ellison says. Now, if Microsoft is actually broken up, the ensuing confusion would help Oracle, though long term, it might make Microsoft's database program a stronger competitor if it is adapted to run on other operating systems besides Microsoft's Windows. For now, Oracle has a shot at becoming the biggest supplier of crucial software that extends beyond the PC, out onto the Web, and into the heart of a company. "We have a chance to pass Microsoft and become the No. 1 software company," Ellison says. "If I said that two years ago, I would have been sedated and locked up. But now we're the Internet and they're not."

Such braggadocio frosts Oracle's competitors. They would all love to burst what they see as its stock-price bubble. They erupt at the mere mention of Ellison's name. When it comes to electronic marketplace software, "Oracle has nothing to offer. They have no position," says Steven A. Ballmer, Microsoft's CEO. Steven A. Mills, general manager of software strategy at IBM, charges that Oracle's hyperaggressive sales force will promise anything to make a deal. "They take the P. T. Barnum approach to business: There's a sucker born every minute," he says. And Thomas Siebel, chairman of customer-management software leader Siebel Systems Inc., calls Oracle's e-business suite "vacuous." Claims Siebel: "After all their chest-beating, they're basically failing in applications."

Behind Schedule

Clearly, the long knives are out. With Oracle's stock runup and early successes with e-business, it's a target for some of the most powerful companies in software. Oracle faces Microsoft and its allies such as corporate software kingpin SAP on one side and IBM and its cronies such as Siebel Systems on the other. IBM, for instance, has agreed that its 163,000-person consulting and sales team will hawk Siebel's customer-management software—a daunting prospect for Oracle, given the size of its 30,000-person consulting and sales force.

And it's no cinch that Oracle's e-business suite will be a runaway hit. The broad package of programs will go head to head with products by the biggies and by dozens of smaller companies that have a one- or two-year lead and are focused on doing one thing really well. Already, Oracle's e-business suite is a year late. David Yockelson, director of e-business strategies at Meta Group Inc., believes there's no way Oracle can build all of this technology itself and match the capabilities of its rivals. "Oracle has a not-invented-here philosophy," he says. "And building it all themselves is going to be too slow." Even after the suite ships, consultants such as Gartner Group Inc. warn corporate customers that it probably won't be stable enough to handle the most crucial jobs until the end of the year.

If Ellison is worried, he isn't showing it. Sitting in his four-story Pacific Heights home in front of a breathtaking panorama of the Golden Gate Bridge, he concedes that development of the e-business suite has been devilish. "It's a huge job," he says. "But it's the right strategy for Oracle." Indeed, he insists that the suite, called Oracle Release 11i, is on track for a May launch and will catapult the company to dizzying heights. It offers customers a

EXHIBIT 2   **Assembling an E-Business Powerhouse**

Oracle Corp.'s software is the foundation for websites, e-commerce, and corporate networks. Here are its most crucial markets:

Data Storehouses	Business Applications	E-Marketplaces
Database software for storing and analyzing corporate data, inventories, and customer info.	*For running everything from accounting to customer management to Web sales.*	*Web-site and internal software for transactions between companies, including auctions.*
Market Size $10.5 billion in 1999 for software and maintenance; heading for $16.6 billion in 2003.	**Market Size** $26 billion in 1999; heading for $33 billion this year.	**Market Size** $3.9 billion in 1999; heading for $18.6 billion in 2003.
Oracle's Third-Quarter Sales Software-license sales grew 32%, to $778 million.	**Oracle's Third-Quarter Sales** Up 35%, to $199 million.	**Oracle's Third-Quarter Sales** $26 million for supply-chain and procurement software.
Market Share 40%, compared with 18% for IBM, 5.7% for Informix, and 5.1% for Microsoft.	**Market Position** Oracle is a distant second behind SAP in the market for core corporate applications. Siebel Systems leads in customer-management software.	**Market Position** The procurement market is expanding into e-exchanges, and Oracle is an early leader along with Commerce One, Ariba, and i2.
Prospects Oracle dominates the database-software realm on both Unix and Windows NT operating systems. Analysts predict it will hold off the competition indefinitely, thanks to its strong technology and new cachet with dot-coms.	**Prospects** In May, Oracle plans to release the most comprehensive package of business applications available. It has a good chance to gain market share because its applications are integrated, while others offer pieces that have to be stitched together.	**Prospects** Oracle has deals to power exchanges for Ford, Sears, and Chevron and is expected to have staying power, thanks to its army of 7,000 software programmers.

Source: International Data Corp., AMR Research, Companies.

simpler approach: one software product from one company—no more lavish consulting fees for making disparate products work together. "You ain't seen nothin' yet," he vows. "If this e-business-suite plan works, we're going to be an extraordinary company."

Not that Oracle is a slouch now. The company's core business looks rock-solid (Exhibit 2). It leads in the fastest-growing piece of the database market with a 40% market share to IBM's 18%, according to International Data Corp. And with its critical application-suite upgrade on the way, Oracle seems poised for a new burst of growth. Oracle's third-quarter revenues for the period ended Feb. 29 grew 18%, to $2.4 billion. And profits? They shot up 80%, to $498 million. Oracle's application-software business also saw a healthy rise—35% growth, to $199 million. Next fiscal year looks like another winner, with applications revenue forecasted to grow 35%, according to Goldman, Sachs & Co. "They've gone from out of the game to the front of the pack," says analyst Robert Austrian of Banc of America Securities.

Samurai Warrior

Product sales don't deserve all the glory. Surprisingly, Ellison has turned Oracle into a tightly run company. Gone are the days when a "let's-make-a-deal" negotiating philosophy ruled the sales force and feudal country managers ran their businesses as they saw fit. A year ago, Ellison kicked off a massive belt-tightening blitz that has curbed the company's free-spending ways. The workforce has been pared by 2,000 in the past two quarters. Routine sales are being shifted to the Web and away from high-paid reps. And hundreds of computing systems are being consolidated into a handful.

The result: Oracle has trimmed $500 million from expenses and boosted operating margins from 19.4% to 31.4% over the past nine months. Ellison promises he can wipe out another $1.5 billion in costs and push the margin to 40% or more in the next year, which would make Oracle one of the most efficient software outfits on the planet—though still less so than Microsoft with its 50%-plus margin.

Ellison, a penny-pinching model of efficiency? Hard to believe, but true. This is the guy, after all, who spent $3 million for Sayonara, his carbon-hull sailing yacht—the fastest craft under sail in its class. He owns a Japanese-style home in tony Atherton, Calif., where his graceful gardens and koi ponds are overshadowed only by the suits of samurai armor on display inside. Along with his glass, steel, and stone home overlooking the Golden Gate Bridge, construction is under way on a $40 million estate in the Santa Cruz foothills that's modeled on a medieval Japanese palace and will be built around a man-made lake. But all this has come from his personal fortune.

When it's Oracle's money, Ellison is downright parsimonious. But he's not tightfisted just for the sake of goosing margins. The millions that Oracle has saved so far serves as a bold advertisement for what Oracle's technologies can do for its customers. Ellison had watched other companies such as Dell Computer Corp. harness the Web to make themselves more efficient, which attracted new customers. "Why not us?" he recalls asking. So Ellison, who had long kept to product development and marketing, grabbed hold of operations with a vengeance. "Larry has got Buddhas all over his house, but he's not a Buddha. He's a samurai warrior. He's the destroyer, the transformer. It's what he does best," says Marc Benioff, a former Oracle executive who is now chairman of Web startup Salesforce.com, in which Ellison has invested $2 million.

Everywhere that Ellison looked, he saw something that needed fixing. Each of Oracle's 70 country operations had its own computing systems and ways of tracking sales, revenues, and profits. Not for long. By the end of this year, the company will eliminate 2,000 server computers scattered around the world and consolidate on 158 machines at its Redwood Shores (Calif.) headquarters. All the company's data will be stored on one central database accessible via the Web. That makes it easy for executives to get a comprehensive view of operations and spot trouble before it gets out of hand. "Larry has the people in this company screwed down tight," says Chief Financial Officer Jeffrey O. Henley.

The Oracle boss has been just as aggressive about establishing new business practices. Ellison personally rewrote sales contracts and established standard pricing to cut down on dickering by field salespeople. He changed the compensation system to prevent more than one salesperson from getting a full commission on a sale. And he compensated country managers for meeting ambitious profit-margin targets—not meeting sales goals at any cost.

It's all about centralized control—with Ellison in charge. The way he sees it, he's creating a management style for the Internet Age. "When you're an e-business, everything is mediated by computers," says Ellison. "All the individuality is bled out of the system and replaced by standards. People don't run their own show anymore."

That has been tough on some of Ellison's sidekicks. Oracle President Raymond J. Lane remembers getting the phone call from Ellison in December, 1998, when the boss decided to insert himself into every corner of the company's business, including Lane's sales and consulting operations. "My mouth just hit the table," he recalls. Since then, everything has changed. "All of sudden, Larry is in your mess kit drilling down for four hours. Some days, I'll walk out of a meeting saying, 'I don't need this.' But then you look at the stock price. What Larry's doing is working. There's not a hotter company around."

To get staffers to bend to his will, Ellison uses the carrot first—and then the stick. When European country managers were slow to give up their computing systems, he offered them an option: If they kept control of their computers, they had to pay the cost out of their own budgets. Otherwise, they got their computing for free. That ended the holdout. Canada was another story. The subsidiary dragged its feet even after Ellison dispatched Gary Roberts, senior vice-president of global information technology, to Canada last August to deliver an ultimatum. "We had to send a Navy SEAL team to blow up our Canadian data center," quips Ellison. What really happened was just as effective: He shuffled management responsibilities and the problem melted away.

One of the cornerstone's of Ellison's e-engineering is the Oracle Business Online Web site. Launched last October, it targets small and midsize businesses, selling them programs for accounting and planning. What's unusual about it is that Oracle then runs the software for them as a service, charging a monthly fee. This saves small fry the cost of buying their own computers. For Pointclick.com Inc., a company in American Fork, Utah, that offers product purchase-incentive programs on the Web, Oracle Business Online provided an accounting system for $5,000 a month. And Pointclick got going in just two weeks.

Calling All Newbies

In the past, dot-coms simply couldn't afford Oracle software. They often bought Microsoft's then-less-expensive database and made do with accounting software designed for small businesses. But Oracle has made a concerted effort to turn itself into an easy choice for newbies. For starters, it gives away versions of its database software for free on its Web site to software developers. Later, when they are ready to go into business, they pay their license fees. But Oracle makes that affordable, too. Last October, it began selling a starter kit of all the basic software a "garage" startup needs to establish a Web site for just $6,750. In the first month, 150 companies signed on. And, Oracle knocked about 40% off its standard database prices in December, making them competitive with Microsoft's.

The strategy is to win over dot-coms when they're in the cradle and keep them when they grow up to be adult businesses. It's already starting to work. Pointclick.com now plans on buying several million dollars' worth of Oracle database and accounting software. "We're going to be spending so much money with Oracle, it's not even funny," says Craig Brown, the company's chief technology officer. Partly to stimulate the dot-com business, Oracle has set aside $500 million in an Oracle Venture Fund to invest in promising startups. One condition: They've got to buy Oracle software.

Thanks to these ventures—and the fact that high-flying dot-coms like eBay Inc. use its stuff—Oracle has become a favorite for Net companies. These startups often buy high-octane technology right on the starting line, figuring they won't have to switch later when they're in fast-growth mode. "You talk about the four horsemen of the Internet—it's Sun Microsystems, Cisco, EMC, and Oracle," says James Schanzenbach, chief technology officer for Drug Emporium Inc., a Columbus (Ohio) company that launched an online drugstore in September using Oracle software.

To reinforce that image, Oracle has forged tight partnerships with other horsemen. For example, Oracle and EMC Corp., the leading maker of data storage computers, tune their technologies to run together well and avoid downtime—which is death to e-commerce Web sites. "Oracle has been right on track riding the dot-com wave," says EMC CEO Michael C. Ruettgers.

That partnership is a far cry from the gut-it-out-alone approach Oracle used when it nabbed e-marketplace customers like Ford, Chevron, and Sears. Late last year, e-marketplaces—which connect buyers and sellers of products in specific industries such as chemicals or cars—were starting to explode on the Web. Stocks of B2B companies have declined of late, but the long-term software market opportunity seems strong: Online business-to-business transactions are pegged to climb to $1.4 trillion by 2004.

B2B Edge

Oracle wanted a piece of the action. Oracle's Lane learned that both Ford Motor Co. and General Motors Corp. wanted to tap the Internet to overhaul the way they buy $160 billion a year in parts and supplies and were looking for a software partner to help out. Lane hoped he could pull off a coup by making deals with each of them. So he ping-ponged between meetings in Detroit. But on Oct. 28, talks with GM broke down because Oracle wouldn't surrender a chunk of its stock to GM as part of the deal, say sources close to the discussions.

Lane was more determined than ever to win over Ford. He raced across town with a proposal to set up an independent company co-owned by Ford and Oracle that would let Ford get bids from suppliers via a Web site. Lane had no time to waste. He knew GM was negotiating a similar agreement with Oracle rival Commerce One Inc., and he didn't want to leave empty-handed. Even though Lane had to fly to a wedding in Los Angeles that Saturday, he kept up the pressure through the weekend—clinching the deal by promising to spend whatever it took to get the e-marketplace up and running quickly. He nailed down the final agreement in face-to-face talks with Ford CEO Jacques A. Nasser in Las Vegas on the following Monday, Nov. 1. A day later, both GM and Ford announced their exchanges, and Oracle's stock took off. "These were the first major exchange announcements ever," says Lane. "We had to be in the game." The two e-marketplaces later merged.

Now Ellison is hoping he can build on these early e-marketplace successes with his e-business suite. And customers are starting to buy in. Take GE Medical Systems, a $7.4 billion operation that sells in more than 100 countries and has dozens of factories in places like China, Hungary, France, and the U.S. In December, the GE subsidiary agreed to buy Oracle's entire 11i suite and install it worldwide. The plan is to operate one database accessible to both customers and employees—rather than scattering information across a handful of computing systems. "We're creating a global e-business," says Joseph F. Eckroth, the subsidiary's CIO. "With Oracle, it's integrated. I don't have to make connections between a lot of different pieces of software." Eckroth, who has dealt with Oracle for more than seven years, says the company has become much easier to work with. Because of Oracle's new sales and pricing policies, it took only two days to negotiate a deal. In the past, it might have taken weeks.

Other large organizations will be a tougher sell. Many companies choose the software that they feel is best for each task—whether it's running a Web site, managing a field sales force, or coordinating relationships with suppliers. Siebel Systems, for instance, specializes in sales-force software. Broadvision Inc. focuses on personalizing Web sites. And i2 Technologies is the leader in supply-chain software. Each is considered the best in its category. Even some major Oracle database customers, such as BellSouth Corp., prefer to mix and match so-called best-of-breed programs. BellSouth is considering other suppliers in addition to Oracle for its customer-management software. "Yes, it's important for applications to be integrated, but we can pick what we think is best and do some of the integration ourselves," says Francis A. Dramis, chief information and e-commerce officer for BellSouth.

There's another negative to selling a soup-to-nuts suite. By trying to do so much itself, Oracle misses out on benefits it could get from partnerships with other software makers

EXHIBIT 3
**How Long Will
Microsoft Play
Second Fiddle?**

By Jay Greene in Seattle.

Microsoft Corp. CEO Steven A. Ballmer could barely contain himself after announcing a deal on Mar. 13 with Andersen Consulting. Andersen would train 25,000 consultants to put together high-end computer systems using the software giant's technology. Ballmer called it a "pinch me" moment. Now Microsoft would have the consulting firepower to bid on huge contracts, especially in the lucrative market for business-to-business Internet software.

It may take more than a nip-on-the-arm moment for Microsoft to beat back archrival Oracle Corp., especially if it faces a possible breakup. When it comes to PC software, Microsoft only sees Oracle through its rearview mirror. But in the world of database and e-commerce software for building robust Web sites, Microsoft is sucking Oracle's exhaust. "Microsoft has not been a factor in the B2B market. They're not driving any business momentum—and that's the big growth area," says Morgan Stanley Dean Witter analyst Charles E. Phillips.

Beefing Up. Microsoft denies it's an also-ran. "What's so good about their performance?" Ballmer says of Oracle. "Maybe they'll pull it off. But I wouldn't trade spots with them." He's confident because Microsoft is in the midst of a massive effort to leapfrog ahead in the e-business sphere. The software giant's new Windows 2000 software is the company's first product that has enough muscle to power the biggest computer network. Combine that with SQL Server 2000, its new database that will be released later this year, and Microsoft says it will be able to handle the busiest Web sites. Moreover, the company is beefing up its software for Web-site sales and is creating technology that helps companies trade products with one another via the Web.

Still, all of Ballmer's bravado could be for naught. The federal government may push to split Microsoft's operating-system business from its software-applications operations to remedy the software giant's monopolistic abuses. If it succeeds, Windows 2000 may end up in a different company than the database program and the two products would have to compete with Oracle independently. That could make the gap between Microsoft and Oracle Grand Canyon-esque.

Even then, don't count Microsoft out. It has gained a smidgen of ground in the database business. According to Dataquest Inc. analyst Norma Schroder, Microsoft's SQL Server 7.0, launched in November, 1998, helped the company line up dot-com business and crack the corporate computer market. She hasn't completed her analysis of 1999, but preliminary data suggest that Microsoft's share of the database market may grow a couple of percentage points from the 10.2% she gave it in 1998.

Still Oracle's lead in selling databases for both the Windows 2000 and Unix operating systems will put it well ahead of Microsoft in 1999—with a market share in the high 20s. Analyst Carl Olofson of International Data Corp., who measures the database market differently, gave Microsoft just a 5.1% market share in 1998 and believes leaders Oracle and IBM will hold their own against Microsoft when the results are in for 1999.

Just the notion that Oracle is leading in e-business software gets under Microsoft's skin. Microsoft isn't used to playing second fiddle, particularly to a company run by Larry Ellison, who has made a sport of mocking it. "That will keep Microsoft alive and running like hell," says Usama Fayyad, a former senior Microsoft researcher who helped develop the soon-to-be-released SQL Server 2000 and recently left Microsoft to start his own Internet startup, digiMine.com.

With the intense Ballmer leading its charge, it's a safe bet that Microsoft won't let up until it's a serious player in e-business software.

(Exhibit 3). While it's going it alone in the exchange business, i2, procurement-software maker Ariba, and IBM announced late last month that they will pool their resources to create e-marketplaces. Former Oracle executive Barry M. Ariko, now CEO of supply-chain specialist Extricity Software Inc., believes Ellison is making a serious mistake. "The notion that you can do everything flies in the face of what the Net is all about," he says. "A lot of the new technology comes from the smallest companies. You can work with them—or you can try to do everything yourself and be 18 months behind."

Ellison admits he's playing catch-up. But he's betting that his 7,000 software programmers can deliver a package whose pieces are in some cases every bit as good as software from the specialists. He has 800 programmers focusing on customer-management software alone. Oracle still has more to do to make its e-marketplace software robust enough for the most demanding jobs. Even Oracle Business Online has run into glitches. "It was harder to get going than we expected," admits Oracle Executive Vice-President Gary L. Bloom. The service's first 50 customers had to put up with frequent service interruptions. Now, Oracle is forging alliances with telecoms to obtain more trustworthy network connections.

Oracle had better get this right. Ellison believes that over the next few years, the company will stop being a traditional software company and deliver most of its technology to customers the way its Oracle Business Online operation does—as an online service for a monthly fee. Already, about 70% of the software in the new e-business suite is designed to be dished up that way.

That means Ellison's troops are in for several more years of roiling change. "Life is like a shark," he says. "You have to continue to move forward and do things better every day, or you die." And Ellison is enjoying being cool too much to slow down now.

Source: Steve Hamm, "Oracle: Why It's Cool Again," *Business Week,* May 8, 2000, 115–126.

Case 5–2

Ford Motor Co.

Jacques A. Nasser is on a tear. Prowling in his shirtsleeves among tables ringed with young managers in a Dearborn (Mich.) conference room. Ford Motor Co.'s new chief executive is outlining his vision of the new Ford as part of a three-day training program for newly minted junior executives. The fast-changing auto business is brutally competitive, he reminds them. And nowhere is that more true these days than within the walls of Ford. If playing at this level doesn't make "the hair stand up on the back of your neck when you talk about it," he suggests, "then go somewhere else. Go to our competition. We'd love it."

But Nasser's fervor really starts boiling over when he describes the mentality he's trying to banish forever. He grabs a blue folder from a table and tells a story about the old Ford. "I knew a senior officer who used to carry a list of the 50 top officers in the company with their birth dates," he tells them, waving the folder. Why? So the officer would know when they were retiring and he would get his next promotion. Nasser is shouting now, and the managers are frozen in their seats, barely breathing. "There is nobody today carrying around a birthday list!" he thunders, slapping down the folder. "You've got to earn [a promotion]. The days of entitlement at Ford Motor Co. are gone forever."

Are they ever. Since the hard-charging 51-year-old executive took over in January, he has picked up the whole organization by the lapels and shaken it. His goal? To reinvent the 96-year-old industrial giant as a nimble, growth-oriented consumer powerhouse for the 21st century, when a handful of auto giants will battle across the globe.

That's why Nasser has declared war on Ford's stodgy, overly analytic culture. In its place, he envisions a company in which executives run independent units—cut loose from a stifling bureaucracy and held far more accountable for success and failure. And with a consumer focus at the heart of his retooled Ford, he's banking on a future in which designers, engineers, and marketers someday will do a better job of anticipating the wants and needs of car buyers.

He's hardly there yet, but Ford's new CEO is off to a jackrabbit start. In his first nine months, Nasser seems to have more initiatives in the works than a used-car dealer has negotiating ploys. Since January, he has spent $6.45 billion buying Volvo, revved up efforts to overhaul the way Ford designs its cars, and launched plans to increase Ford's luxury-car sales. And with an innovative deal Nasser struck in early September with Microsoft's MSN CarPoint service, he's moving far faster than other automakers to embrace the Net.

All Stars

That's not all. Nasser soon plans to unveil an organizational shakeup that will rock Ford's units around the world. Moving away from the centralized authority established by his predecessor, Alex J. Trotman, Nasser is creating semi-autonomous businesses out of the company's brands and regions, such as Ford of Europe and Ford of South America. And to sharpen profits, he's pushing to spin off Ford's low-margin parts operation, Visteon Automotive Systems, even as he trolls for higher-margin services. He already has taken tentative first steps toward a risky cradle-to-grave strategy in which Ford will have a hand in everything from auto repair to junkyard recycling.

To help him out, Nasser has recruited an all-star team of executives, including a key designer of Volkswagen's new Beetle and the man who revived BMW's luxury line. Indeed, with DaimlerChrysler in turmoil and General Motors still run by its old guard, Nasser's Ford is suddenly the place to be for ambitious Motown executives. "Nasser is positioning Ford to make a quantum leap," says consultant Noel M. Tichy, an adviser to General Electric Co. CEO Jack Welch, who is now working with Ford. "He wants his legacy to be that he did for Ford what Welch did for GE."

It's an ambitious strategy—and if he pulls it off, Nasser will have created not just one of the best global auto companies but one of the best global companies, period. Yet it's also full of risks, not the least of which is that he may simply be pushing too hard in too many different directions to put his stamp on the place. Within the once-hidebound corridors of Ford's headquarters, there's a sense of excitement and uncertainty about where Nasser is going. "Ford is an amazing place right now; we haven't seen a personality like Jac's in this business for so long," says David E. Cole, director of the University of Michigan's Office for the Study of Automotive Transportation. "It's either going to explode in greatness—or it's going to explode."

It's also a pretty heady place to be for a restless, Lebanese-born outsider. Since starting as a young manager in Australia 31 years ago, he has spent nearly all of his career in the far reaches of the Ford empire, bringing along Jennifer Nasser, his wife of 26 years, three daughters, and a son. Nasser early on showed the impatience with Ford's bureaucratic fiefdoms that still fuels him today. He recalls that when he left in 1977 for Ford's struggling Philippines unit, his boss warned: "If you leave, you'll never come back to Ford of Australia."

He did, though, returning to turn the troubled unit around in 1990 before moving on to do the same in Europe. By the time he finally hit headquarters in 1994 to head product development, Nasser had developed a nimble entrepreneurial style, says Robert A. Lutz, an ex-Chrysler vice-chairman who was once Nasser's boss at Ford. "Jac learned to make decisions in smaller markets where you could make fast decisions without a lot of bureaucratic oversight from Dearborn," says Lutz, now chairman of battery maker Exide Corp. Recreating that experience for a new generation of Ford managers—even those at Dearborn—drives many of the changes Nasser is pushing today.

But why such a rush to tear things up? After all, Ford is already the strongest player in the global auto industry—thanks to the trail Nasser blazed on his way to the corner office.

EXHIBIT 1 Automaker Performance Comparisons

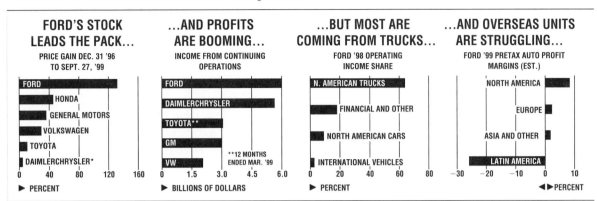

*Based on Daimler Benz shares pre-merger: DaimlerChrysler shares post-merger.

Source: Data: Bloomberg Financial Markets, Standard & Poor's Compustat, Company Reports, Merrill Lynch & Co., Wasserstein Perella Securities Inc.

Back in 1996, when Nasser was elevated to chief of global auto operations, Ford had the worst profits from total vehicle sales of any U. S. auto maker, and two-thirds of its $4.4 billion net income came from financial services. Nasser swept in like a tornado, chopping car models and jobs and squeezing suppliers for a cumulative $6.2 billion in savings.

But Nasser—who has come to despise his "Jac the Knife" sobriquet—did much more than cut costs. His push for more creative design has been instrumental in allowing Ford to seize the lead in the red-hot markets for pickups and sport-utility vehicles. The result: Ford is now the world's most profitable auto maker, with $5.9 billion in net income from continuing operations last year. Thanks to its purchase of Volvo and its increased control of Mazda, Ford looks likely to overtake GM for the global sales crown by 2001. And car buyers aren't the only ones pleased. Ford's stock price has risen 130% since the end of '96, outracing the 71% gain of the Standard & Poor's 500-stock index as well as its global auto rivals.

But now, Nasser needs to take his game up a notch. For if Ford appears to be firing on all cylinders, in fact it's hitting on just one: trucks (Exhibit 1). Torrid SUV, minivan, and pickup sales in North America controlled 64% of Ford's operating income last year, though they accounted for just 45% of vehicle revenues. Meanwhile, car sales in North America bring in barely 12% of profits. Ford makes just $489 on its average car sale, says John A. Casesa, an analyst at Merrill Lynch & Co., compared with a fat $1,785 on each truck. "Cars in North America—that's been a downer for us," Nasser admits.

Just as alarming, there are signs that Ford's truck profits are getting squeezed. Toyota, Honda, Mercedes, and BMW are rushing to cash in on the truck-profit bonanza with a flood of new pickups, SUVs, and minivans of their own. Chrysler and GM are piling on rebates unthinkable a few months ago. The heightened competition, coupled with recent tight supplies trimmed Ford's F-150 pickup sales nearly 8% in August. That's one reason Ford's stock is down 15% this year.

Global Gut

Nasser's cost-cutting also did little to patch up Ford's woeful overseas operations. Facing mounting losses in South America, Ford announced a $2 billion restructuring of its

EXHIBIT 2
**Europe: Where
Ford Needs to
Step on the Gas**

Ford Motor Co. brought an impressive stable of brands to the Frankfurt Auto Show last month: Jaguars, Volvos, Mazdas, even Aston Martins. Just one thing seemed to be missing: Fords. Cars carrying the trademark oval huddled in a corner of Ford's exhibition space, next to the espresso bar and the free food, far from center stage.

The placing was all to symbolic of the fate of Ford-brand cars in Europe. Ford's product line grew stale under a corporate structure that centralized too much power thousands of miles away at Dearborn (Mich.) headquarters. The No. 2 auto maker in Western Europe five years ago—General Motors was No. 1—Ford slipped to fourth this year. Its market share fell from 11.7% in 1994 to 9.3% in 1999. Still the best-selling brand in Britain, Ford is elsewhere in danger of become an also-ran.

If CEO Jacques A. Nasser wants to make Ford the world's biggest car company, he'll have to deal with Europe. Analysts expect Western Europeans to buy more than 15 million cars this year, right behind the U.S. To catch up, Ford will have to invest big-time, expanding its product line—even as declining real prices and overcapacity hurt margins.

Under the Ford 2000 organization set up five years ago, Ford centralized much product development and marketing. As a result, designers didn't focus enough on making cars specifically for Europe, says John R. Lawson, an auto analyst at Salomon Smith Barney.

Now, Nasser is moving to give regional managers more input. Nick Scheele, 55, who took over as Ford of Europe's president in July after heading Jaguar, now vows new designs tht will give the line more identity. Ford of Europe recently moved its headquarters to Cologne, partly to cash in on the esteem consumers have for German engineering. And Scheele is trimming capacity, converting a plant near Liverpool to produce Jaguars instead of Fords.

FORD FADES OUT

SHARE OF EUROPEAN MARKET*

▲ PERCENT

'94 '95 '96 '97 '98 '99 EST.

* FORD BRAND ONLY. EXCLUDES
VOLVO AND JAGUAR SALES.

Source: Data: Standard & Poor's DRI

The good news for Ford: Its new Focus line of small cars is a hit, selling half a million models in a year. In Germany, the Focus compact sedans, hatchbacks, and station wagons have sold 73% more this year than the Escort line they replaced. Magazines praise the Focus' combination of interior room, handling, and new-wave styling. And in a break with its recent past in Europe, Ford kept up marketing pressure after the launch. "We have to do that across the board," says Scheele.

Mindful that Scheele doubled sales during his seven years as CEO of Jaguar by making the cars' reliability match their good looks, competitors are bracing for a counteroffensive by Ford. "He understands European customers as few others do," says Robert W. Hendry, CEO of Opel. "I expect Ford to prosper."

But rivals have a big head start. Renault's Scenic microvan, launched in 1996, was a runaway hit for which Ford had no answer. Volkswagen's midsize Passat, redesigned in 1996, invaded turf occupied by Ford's Mondeo. And Mercedes' snub-nosed $28,000 A-Class brought the prestige brand into Ford's territory.

Scheele says Nasser is giving him a free hand and no stated deadline to turn things around. But, he adds with a smile, "Jac is quick, and he expects everyone else to be quick." Alas, quickness is the thing Ford of Europe has so far lacked.

By Jack Ewing in Frankfurt

Source: "Remaking Ford," *Business Week*, October 11, 1999, 132–136, 138, 140.

Brazilian unit on Sept. 22. Things aren't much better in Europe, where Ford eked out only $245 million in profits in the first half, on sales of $14.6 billion (Exhibit 2). Morgan Stanley Dean Witter's Stephen J. Girsky says he hoped strong North American results

EXHIBIT 3
Nasser's Game Plan

New Blood

In a bid to juice up Ford's stodgy executive suite, Nasser has hired a slew of highly regarded managers from auto makers around the globe. He has also tapped top consumer-goods makers for marketing and sales talent. His all-star team is now considered among the industry's best.

Customer Focus

Nasser is pushing everyone from engineers to marketing staffers to get closer to customers rather than rely on second-hand marketing research. He's also backing innovative new ventures, such as Ford's recent stake in MSN's CarPoint Web site. Nasser's goal: to mine the site's data from online purchases to understand buyers better.

More Autonomy

Ford 2000, the five-year-old plan that centralized global decision-making, brought big cost savings but hurt regional managers' ability to react to local markets. With problems brewing in Ford's international units, Nasser will launch a structural shakeup next year aimed at giving regional executives more power over car brands and marketing.

Going for Growth

Nasser wants to boost Ford stock's price-earnings ratio from 9 to the 30 range enjoyed by consumer companies. So he's moving into higher-margin service businesses, such as quick-repair stations.

would buy Nasser room "to fix the rest of the world. [But] Ford may be running out of time."

The rivalry can only get fiercer. With each megamerger—just in the past year, Daimler Benz acquired Chrysler, Ford bought Volvo, and Renault took a big stake in Nissan—the industry is moving closer to the day when a handful of companies have the scale to squeeze purchasing and manufacturing costs and plow billions into new models. In the meantime, the world is awash with capacity: The industry can make 20 million more cars and trucks than it can sell.

To keep Ford on top of that scrambling heap, Nasser has snatched up some of the hottest management talent in the world (Exhibit 3). First up, three years ago, was James C. Schroer, a former Nabisco marketing chief who was working as a Booz, Allen & Hamilton consultant when Nasser recruited him to be Ford's global marketing vice-president. He has been put in charge of building up Ford's brands, especially its weaker Mercury and Ford nameplates. Next, in October, 1997, came J Mays, the 44-year-old hotshot who sketched the first eye-catching designs for what became VW's new Beetle. And Chris Theodore, an engineer known for work that helped make Chrysler's bread and butter minivans a hit, came on board to run large- and luxury-car development in March.

The biggest coup, though, was scooping up former BMW whiz Wolfgang Reitzle to take control of Ford's four luxury brands: Jaguar, Volvo, Lincoln, and Aston Martin. Reitzle, who had been the German auto maker's No. 2 executive, won much of the credit for its resurgence in the '90s. He joined Ford in March after he lost out in a boardroom shakeup. His arrival at Ford signaled Nasser's determination to turn Dearborn into a sort of Camelot for car mavericks.

Perhaps the most daunting challenge for Nasser's new management team will be to capture the magic that Ford found in trucks and sprinkle it onto the car side. So far, the most visible changes have come in the already-profitable luxury-car unit, where Reitzle is moving quickly to expand sales and margins. Reitzle envisions saving costs by sharing parts or even whole chassis between the brands, but "only where the customer can't see or feel it." First up: the surprisingly stylish Lincoln LS and $42,500 Jaguar S-type introduced this year, both of which are selling well.

"Baby Jag"

Reitzle's toughest task, though, will be to boost Ford's luxury-car sales from 650,000 units last year to 1 million by 2004. To succeed, he'll have to broaden the market for new Jags and Volvos without tarnishing their images. The first test for Volvo comes with the more affordable S40 sedan and V40 wagon, now showing up in the U. S. starting at around $23,000. And in two years, Jaguar, too, will take a leap with its downright thrifty $30,000 "Baby Jag."

Still, it's one thing to create Jaguars with sizzle; it's another thing to bring excitement to more plebeian cars such as the Taurus. That's why one of Nasser's highest priorities has been revamping how Ford designs its vehicles. His overhaul started when, on arriving in Dearborn, he banished Ford's longtime practice of updating aging models to match those of top competitors. He has also ended the dependence on overly quantitative analysis and market research based on showing preordained options to focus groups.

The shortcomings in Ford's old design approach led to some classic missteps. Take the 1995 Windstar minivan. Ford looked at research that asked customers if they wanted an additional sliding door on the driver's side. Having never seen one, a third said yes, a third said no, and the rest said maybe. Ford stayed with three doors, while Chrysler, with a stronger gut sense of its buyers, went for the fourth. It became a smash hit, and it cost Ford $560 million to catch up.

Now Nasser is pushing designers, engineers, and marketers to develop a similar kind of customer understanding. To shake his troops out of the old mind-set, they are sent to a Consumer Insight Center for a daylong course in how to listen to consumers and engage them in dialogue. From there small teams are sent out for eight weeks of customer immersion.

So it was that Richard Parry-Jones, Ford's product development chief, found himself club-hopping in London one recent morning until 4 a.m. with about 20 teens and twenty-somethings. It made for an odd scene: Parry-Jones, 48, a Welsh-born man with thinning hair and a business suit, hanging out discussing music and fashion with a hairdresser and a clothes designer. Although Parry-Jones won't point to any specific changes that will result from his nocturnal adventures, Nasser's hope is that by getting customers in uninhibited settings, the car folks can get a better intuitive feel for what they want.

Touchy-feely? Sure. But it follows an approach Nasser championed three years ago to supercharge its truck fortunes. Then, a Ford designer and a consultant created generational "value groups" that translated the traits and tastes of consumers from different age groups into car preferences. Ford used those insights to give the '97 F-150 pickup a softly sculpted front end and more passenger room. It bucked all notions of a successful truck but became a huge hit with baby boomers.

A natty dresser given to three-button Savile Row suits and Patek Philippe watches—one of his new hobbies is collecting Swiss watches—it's no surprise Nasser has focused on design. Although trained as a financial analyst, he has long stood out: He combines financial smarts and instinctive product sense.

Those qualities brought Nasser to the fore in 1993 when he took over troubled European operations. He established that the overhaul would go far beyond head counts. Malcolm

Thomas, then chief of the Mondeo car program, recalls their first meeting. "I expected a business review," he says. "What I got was Jac crawling all over the vehicle, poking here and there." He grabbed Thomas' hand and ran it over a rough plastic strip underneath the passenger seat. "Feel how sharp that is? A customer wouldn't like that," Nasser said. It was smoothed off immediately.

That was just the beginning. The European operation was short of cash to develop the tiny new Ka. Nasser suggested shrink-wrapping the Ka's cute body around the existing Fiesta subcompact platform. Ford wound up selling 214,000 Kas in 1997. Combined with more cost slashing, Nasser lifted Europe into the black. So it made sense when Trotman tapped Nasser to head the new global product-development group in 1994. "Nasser came to Europe as an astute businessman," says Thomas. "What he demonstrated was ingenuity in creating product."

Elan

Today, Nasser remains a frequent Saturday visitor to Ford's design studios. And Mays receives a steady stream of notes, photos, and sketches from his boss, inspired by everything from MTV to the Pebble Beach classic-car show. "He might see the badges on some old cars and say, 'Gosh, why don't ours look that good?'" Mays says.

It takes three to four years for a new design to hit the showrooms, so the full force of Ford's new approach is a ways off. But Mays, who moved from Germany, brought a bevy of Europeans to the team and has made no bones about his intention to shake up the old guard. The 2001 Thunderbird will be the first major Mays-influenced Ford car. He simplified the design and made it "far more European." Volumes will be small, but Nasser is counting on the sleek coupe, which evokes the elan of the 1957 T-bird, to do for Ford what the Viper sports car did for Dodge—give sex appeal to a stodgy brand.

In the meantime, Ford is applying its customer insights to the marketing of new models already under way. Executives concluded that the offspring of baby boomers like product they can customize, for example. So when the $12,280 Focus small car arrives in showrooms this month, buyers will be encouraged to personalize it with kitschy add-ons, such as a "pet package" for a few hundred dollars.

Yet even as Nasser concentrates on improving Ford's performance with cars, he is also facing far stiffer competition in trucks. That core franchise is now under siege from Japanese and German auto makers. This summer, Toyota launched its Tundra pickup, in a class with Ford's F-150 and the Chevrolet Silverado trucks. BMW will launch its X5 SUV in December. And Toyota and Honda have jumped out ahead with car-based SUVs, the Lexus RX300, and Honda CRV. The battle is likely to put big pressure on Ford's juicy margins.

Nasser is convinced that the key to staying ahead now is providing upscale baby boomers with even more passenger-cabin versatility and macho good looks. So next spring, Ford will unveil the Explorer Sport Trac and F-150 SuperCrew, vehicles that combine SUV cabins with pickup beds. Then it will launch the Escape, a carlike SUV. The radically new vehicles show how designers are getting freer rein, says Dee Kapur, manager of Ford's pickups: "Ten years ago, this would not have happened in our rigid command-and-control environment."

Rising truck competition isn't Nasser's only problem. He must also fix Ford's troubled overseas operations for good. So he's tearing up some parts of the global structure Trotman put in place five years ago—known, ironically, as Ford 2000. Although huge cost savings have come from unifying such things as purchasing, engineering, and manufacturing globally, regional managers complain they've lost too much say over products. So next year, Nasser will give them back more power to shape local brands and marketing.

The costs of weak local management have become all too clear. In Brazil, Ford has lost a stunning four points of market share since early '98 after government moves to slow capital flight sent interest rates skyrocketing. Other big carmakers worked quickly with dealers to arrange special customer financing, but Ford dallied, and its sales plummeted. "Management was stuck and didn't act quickly enough,: says Diego Portillo, an analyst with Standard & Poor's DRI's global automotive group. Now, with a new head of its Brazilian unit in place, Ford plans to retire debt, repair its dealer network, and add a new small car.

Elsewhere, too, Nasser is pushing Ford to move aggressively. The topper came two weeks ago when Ford announced that it would invest an undisclosed amount in Microsoft's MSN CarPoint Web site. CarPoint will soon launch a "build to order" service that should let customers seek out exactly the color and features they want in a Ford. Although any orders will be filled by traditional dealers, CarPoint will sell aggregated customer data back to Ford. Nasser figures that could prove an invaluable, unfiltered view of what buyers— particularly the young ones on whom Ford's future depends—want.

Moreover, the Internet is just one part of a broader vision Nasser has of powering up Ford's sales growth and margins. To lift Ford's stock price— and boost its price-earnings ratio from 9, closer to GE's 36 or Procter & Gamble's 30—Nasser insists Ford must evolve from a car company into "a leading consumer company for automotive products and services." The difference? Nasser wants to expand beyond the initial $20,000 a passenger car sells for. Over a decade, Ford figures a car generates about $68,000 in revenues—from the sales price to maintenance, spare parts, gas, and insurance. So last spring, he tapped Ford's $24 billion cash pile and paid $1.6 billion for Kwik-Fit, a chain of nearly 2,000 auto-service centers in Britain. And in perhaps the strangest move of all, Nasser even bought a small junkyard business.

Scoffing

In theory, these deals help Ford tap into service businesses with higher returns than manufacturing. Nasser and his team also claim they will provide more of that prized consumer feedback. Running a junkyard can provide valuable information about parts durability and reliability, says Michael D. Jordan, vice-president of Ford's customer service.

Still, rivals scoff at the notion these moves will pay off. "You don't have to own a rental-car company to learn about…the maintenance experience," says James E. Press, executive vice-president for Toyota Motors Sales USA, the Japanese company's U.S. auto group. Investors, too, seem uncertain. One large shareholder says Nasser's grand plan strikes him as a rush to glory. "I told Jac, 'Become the best auto company in the world before you become the best consumer company in the world. Walk before you run.'" Nasser's response? "He chewed me out," says the investor.

Nasser discounts such critics. "They just don't get it. They're back in the nuts-and-bolts age," he huffs. For now, he has the support that counts most: that of Chairman William C. Ford Jr., who represents the Ford family, the controlling shareholder. By staying close to the core business, Ford sees a big difference between Nassers move into repair shops and the company's disastrous diversification into banking and other nonauto businesses in the '80s. And he notes that the board has "never said no to Jac because, frankly, we've bought into the strategy." Still, Ford's directors want Nasser to explain his long-term plans in greater detail. So they've made plans for a two-day board meeting in early October.

The pace of change is already upsetting some longtime Ford employees. Managers grumble about burnout in an organization that has been flooded with new initiatives and new faces the past five years. "Nasser is grabbing people by the throat and threatening their careers," says one insider. "They say, 'If I can get through boot camp, I'll survive.' But the boot camps just keep coming." Indeed, few expect Nasser to let up on the accelerator anytime soon. He has spent a career propelling himself forward at maximum speed. Now, this restless outsider is taking the entire company along on the ride.

Source: "Remaking Ford," *Business Week*, October 11, 1999, 132–136, 138, and 140.

Case 5–3
Fuji Photo Film Co.

For a frontline view of the coming digital-camera wars, head for Tokyo's teeming, neon-lit Akihabara district. In the world's largest electronics bazaar, hundreds of shops display dozens of new camera models—most of them gaudily labeled "megapixel," the latest geek-speak for "supersharp digital picture." There are plenty of choices from Sony Corp., Olympus, and 18 other manufacturers. But the best-selling brand isn't difficult to spot. Just look for the "Sold Out" tags on the display models, and you'll see that many of them bear the brand Fujifilm. That's Fuji Photo Film Co., of course. It's the world's second-largest maker of photographic film and paper, known to Americans as the company that has given Eastman Kodak Co. a harrowing run for its money. But to Japanese gadget fanatics, who snap up about 40% of all the consumer digital-cameras sold worldwide, Fujifilm's kelly-green packaging goes deep into the digital subconscious. Faster than you can smile and say "*chee-zu*," Fujifilm has been cranking out new digital cameras—averaging one every two months since March, 1998. That helped it win a leading 28% share of Japan's market, according to a Business Computer News poll of 218 top retailers.

Fresh Goodies

Fujifilm has staged a remarkable makeover on its home turf. But the world of digital photography is still new. It will be years before any company is declared victor on this virgin territory. And Japan is just one market, albeit a key one. Long term, Fujifilm's digital gamble will depend on the U. S., where Sony, Eastman Kodak, and Olympus are market leaders.

So in the next two years, as Fujifilm courts Americans with a whole new bag of digital goodies, it will confront the most confusing obstacle course in its 65-year history. The global market for photo film and paper, however cutthroat, is a tidy duopoly with clearly defined rules. The digital-camera market, by contrast, is uncharted, chaotic, and already crowded with newcomers. Profits are as uncertain in this world as they are for makers of calculators, cell phones, notebook computers, and almost all other digital gewgaws.

In this topys-turvy universe of digital imaging, all bids are up in the air. Talk to camera strategists at Hewlett-Packard Co., and you'll hear about the eternal appeal of paper: HP has built its digital strategy around its world-beating printer business. Visit Nikon, Olympus, Konica, or Canon, and the digital cameras may look surprisingly similar to today's beguiling compact models. But don't limit your sights to such players. Sony and Toshiba already sell laptops featuring digital cameras. Nokia wants to put them in cell phones: Kyocera already has. In one scenario, the biggest winners could be dot.com Web-site operators who store consumers' pictures libraries, giving access to their friends and families.

EXHIBIT 1
**How Fujifilm
Stacks Up Against
Rivals**

Source: Data: Jardine Fleming,
Warburg Dillon Reed

	Return on Equity	Operating Profit Margin
Fujifilm	4.9%	11.5%
Kodak	34.9	14.1
Olympus	4.7	10.5
Konica	-2.0	2.5
Sony	9.8	5.0

Perhaps most perplexing for Fujifilm is that, in digital cameras, it will be selling the equivalent of the razors, not the razor blades. Instead of film, most of these gizmos store images on memory chips, which Fujifilm doesn't make. "Fujifilm must cannibalize its main source of cash flow, which is film,"says longtime Asia watcher Thomas Murtha, an analyst and investment manager at Rowe Price-Fleming International Inc. in Baltimore. "Will the margins on digital come anywhere close to Fujifilm's silver-halide consumables?"

That's the crux of Fujifilm's dilemma. Some conservative managers in the company want to stick their heads in the silver-halide sand and ignore the digital hurricane. But the chairman and CEO of Fujifilm has been a convert to digital since the early 1980s and is personally forcing the company forward. Says Minoru Ohnishi, 74: "We've reached a major turning point. The new technology poses a challenge for the entire industry, and we're ready for it."

Ohnishi comes from a position of strength. Despite currency fluctuations and the Asian crisis, the company has remained a strong performer (Exhibit 1). With 1998 sales of $13.7 billion—up 4.3% from the previous year—Fujifilm is one-fifth the size of Sony or Matsushita. And yet it posted a hefty $1.6 billion in operating profits, compared with $3.2 billion for Sony and $1.8 billion for Matsushita. Its average operating profit matches Kodak's and is far above the usual margin for Japanese manufacturers (Exhibit 2).

Digital gear, to be sure, is still a tiny franchise within the company. In the year ended in March, 1999, Fujifilm's sales of digital cameras were worth about $400 million. But that's up 80% from the previous year. "Fujifilm is very aggressive," says Nicholas Smith, a senior analyst at Jardine Fleming Securities Ltd. in Tokyo. "Looking at sales, growth, or returns, it leaves the others in the dust."

Single-Minded

Driven by one overriding aim, to be No.1, Fujifilm has pounded away at its competitors. On its home turf in traditional film, Fujifilm has nearly demolished Konica and overtaken Kodak, whose yellow-and-black boxes once dominated Japanese store shelves. Fujifilm now controls 70% of Japan's $3.6 billion photo-film-and-paper market. Even in the U.S., Fujifilm expects soon to account for about 25% of photo-related sales, up from around 10% a decade ago.

It's clear, however, that Fujifilm needs a new source of profits. In Japan, declining prices have dragged the total value of film and paper shipments down 27% from a peak of $4.9 billion in 1992. So Chairman Ohnishi is applying the same single-mindedness to digital cameras that the company has brought to film. And he has just taken the wraps off some

EXHIBIT 2

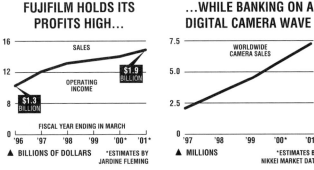

FUJIFILM HOLDS ITS PROFITS HIGH...

Data: Company Reports

...WHILE BANKING ON A DIGITAL CAMERA WAVE

Data: Japan Electronic Development Assn.

heavy-duty artillery. Its first-of-a-kind PrinCam, a $950 digital camera with a built-in printer to produce instant photos, will hit Japanese shops in November and overseas outlets next year.

On Oct. 20, Fujifilm also unveiled a groundbreaking image sensor, the Super CCD (supercharged coupled device). This honeycomb-patterned feature is the electronic "eye" of the digital camera. The new, half-inch size chip uses octagonal pixels (picture elements), instead of rectangular ones. These pixels are packed more closely together than in regular CCDs—and pixels per square inch is the measure that defines the sharpness of a digital image. Fuji says its new, 1.9 million pixel Super CCD prototype has a resolution equivalent to a conventional 3 million pixel sensor. Next year, Fujifilm will unleash a new arsenal of digital products, from supercompact digital still/video cameras to video cell phones, that incorporate its new device. Others will unveil similar chips, predicts International Data Corp. analyst Kevin Kane. "But Fujifilm is the pioneer of this movement."

Ohnishi has invested hundreds of millions of dollars in CCD research and development. But he expects returns to dwarf those sums. Certainly, it's a dazzling technology. Born in 1969, at Bell Telephone Laboratories, CCDs convert light into digital data that are then rendered into images. Sony was the first to commercialize the chips: In 1985, it built them into camcorders.

But Fujifilm caught up by poaching engineers from Toshiba Corp. and other high-tech companies and enlisting the help of semiconductor ace Junichi Nishizawa, former president of Tohoku University. In 1988, Fujifilm developed its first CCD sensor and in 1991 launched the world's first commercial digital camera, aimed at professionals.

Mystical

None of this expertise came cheap. Tally up research and manufacturing budgets reaching all the way back to the early 1980s, and Fujifilm's commitment to digital products easily tops $2 billion. Within company ranks, belief in this investment borders on the mystical. "We're not going to quit, and we're not going to lose this battle," swears the company's chief scientist and senior adviser, Hirozo Ueda.

Fujifilm's dread of depending upon larger competitors inspires its strategy in key components. In addition to CCDs, the company makes its own lenses, image processors, and signal-processing chips. Norihiko Katoh, director of Fujifilm Microdevices Co., the CCD plant in Sendai, calls this a survival strategy and draws a parallel with camcorders: "In the beginning, many companies made them," he notes. "The handful left are those whose technological edge enabled them to stay ahead with superior products."

Fujifilm's CCDs and image-processing chips aren't a cash cow for the company. But that day could come. Last year, the company earned about $10 million selling such chips to other companies, including Sony. And the chips keep getting more powerful. Soon, Fujifilm will begin producing CCD sensors with a resolution exceeding 3 million pixels per square inch. Among its rivals, only Sony has announced plans to make a half-inch CCD exceeding 3 million pixels per square inch.

Fujifilm strategists estimate that the Japanese will snap six times as many pictures this year as last, thanks to the digital craze. Users are starting to send favorite shots over the Net to digital processing centers, so they can receive high-quality prints, which use Fuji-made photographic paper. Tens of thousands of consumers print their own pictures out on home printers. Owners of the new PrinCam create instant prints directly off the camera in 35 seconds or so.

Panoply

Fujifilm hopes to expand this type of service. Today, its photo centers cater to owners of its digital cameras by preparing prints or postcards, creating photo indexes, or loading customers' images onto compact disks. In November, Fujifilm teamed up with Japan's largest Internet service provider, Nifty, to let subscribers store images online or e-mail them to friends. And in the U.S., Fujifilm has partnered with Wal-Mart Stores Inc. to store and transmit pictures. The service kicks off on Jan. 1 and will compete with a service called You've Got Mail that is offered by America Online Inc. in a partnership with Kodak.

In other words, in the digital domain, as in the world of film, Kodak is squarely in Fujifilm's sights. Kodak says that all of its digital products and services will reach $3.5 billion to $4 billion in sales by 2004, up from $400 million last year. It's adding new digital products every few months and luring customers with Picture Maker kiosks in 20,000 locations that turn digital images into quality prints.

In partnership with printer maker Lexmark, Kodak has just unveiled for the U.S. market a printer that functions as a home photo-processing unit. The device eliminates the need for digital photographers to fuss with a personal computer. You just pop out a memory card from a Kodak camera and plug it directly into the printer.

Its digital strides aren't the only thing making Kodak smile. In 1997 the company launched a $2 billion cost-cutting program, and it is now reaping the benefits. Kodak's return on equity of 35% dwarfs Fujifilm's 5%. In conventional film, Kodak claims that it has stopped the loss of market share to Fujifilm.

Kodak may even be getting a lift in Japan. A recent survey done by a competitor shows Kodak is the hip brand among Tokyo's young crowd. And Kodak executives are ready for Fuji in the digital arena. Kodak's president of digital and applied imaging, Willy C. Shih, says Kodak recently began beefing up its push into the Japanese markets with a more diverse line of cameras. And he says Kodak is battling hard to remain a leader in the U. S., where Sony and Olympus are Kodak's top competitors and Fuji is back in the pack.

In America, this focus makes sense. According to IDC, Sony accounted for 35% of all digital camera shipments in the U.S. for the most recent quarter, compared with 20% for Kodak. Sony's top-selling product, the Mavica, stores images on 3.5-inch floppy disks that are more familiar to Americans than image-storage chips used by most Japanese vendors. Even Sony expresses surprise at the success of the Mavica, which trails the flashy megapixel models in terms of image quality: "We thought consumers would shift to smaller, chip-based products by now," says Teruaki Aoki, president and COO of Sony Electronics Inc., the U. S. hardware subsidiary.

Ohnishi is determined to get into the race before Sony and Kodak build up unbeatable leads. Growth in digital-camera use in both North America and Europe is expected to follow the Japanese pattern, say U.S. analysts, shifting from low-end to top-quality devices that can produce image quality that is comparable to regular photos. But even then, conventional film won't totally disappear, analysts say. As a backup, Fujifilm still innovates in traditional film. It is improving a new thin-film coating process for use in high-density tapes that store data for most of the large corporations.

And while traditional 35mm film consists of three color-sensing layers, Fujifilm has developed a fourth-layer film, its new Superia, to control the color red and render more natural hues. Fujifilm also sparked the boom in single-use cameras—effectively shifting clout in consumer photography from camera makers to film-makers. The latest throw-aways, 70% of which are recycled in Japan, now offer panoramic shots and zoom lenses.

New Vistas

As Fujifilm's first digital advocate, Ohnishi gets credit for reacting quickly to early warning signals. First there was the "silver shock" of 1979, when sky-high silver prices forced manufacturers to curtail production of all types of silver-halide film, for X-ray, movie, and photographic use. In 1984, Sony triggered a shock wave with its first Mavica test model. "That's when I realized filmless technology was possible," recalls Ohnishi, who had taken over as president in 1980. A penny-pincher who over the years has amassed a $5.5 billion pile of cash for Fujifilm, Ohnishi nevertheless spared no expense in building up the company's electronic-imaging division.

What it has not demonstrated, however, is the ability to keep pace with digital vistas that are unfolding at Internet speed. Fujifilm's global film triumph was built on thousands of measured steps. "We never tried to grab a big chunk of the American market all at once," says James L. Chung, director of finance at Fujifilm's U. S. subsidiary. Now, the company is launching its biggest-ever U.S. ad campaign to promote awareness of its brand. And it is introducing digital cameras geared to Americans, who demand such features as a zoom lens and a PC interface and who insist on a reasonable price.

Yet Fujifilm may have to pick up the pace further: Restraint is a luxury no dot.com company can afford. In the U. S., the company inhabits a world of startups, stock options, and wacky business models. While middle-aged Japanese parents are still pasting Fujifilm photos into family albums, teenagers are shooting "GIFs" and "TIFs" (compressed image files) across the globe and loading photos with attached sound clips up onto their personal home pages on Yahoo! Inc.'s GeoCities. Fuji needs to be more aggressive in these areas says Rebecca Runkle, an imaging analyst at Morgan Stanley in New York. "There is no reason why this company cannot be leading the charge into digital photography," she says (Exhibit 3).

Onishi feels that his company's strengths in the home market will tide him over the learning curve—and keep it ticking when he steps down to make way for a new generation of senior managers. Fujifilm has already mastered lightning-speed manufacturing. At its main digital-camera assembly plant in Sendai, young men and women, some sporting locks dyed blond or orange, work side-by-side in efficient teams. On average, each person assembles a digital camera in 1½ minutes. With everyone motivated to cut costs, productivity has risen 50% since 1997.

At the same time, Fujifilm has kept to its core strengths. Says Toshihiko Ginbayashi, Morgan Stanley's director of research in Tokyo: "Many Japanese companies have gone astray by speculating in land and stocks, but not Fujifilm. It never wavered." Today, outside Japan, the name Fujifilm may not be associated with much more than those neat stacks of

EXHIBIT 3
A Whole New Bag of Digital Tricks

It would be nice for Fuji Photo Film Co. if digital cameras were as simple to make as the disposable film variety. But these complex devices pack about 200 components—from chips to software to liquid-crystal display screens and lenses—into a sleek metal box. And the dozens of manufacturers vying to survive in this cutthroat business are building digitals in almost as many flavors as ice cream. Fuji has mastered key ingredients in the recipe. But the competition is brutal, and where Fuji lags, the others excel.

So *Business Week* took one of Fuji's latest cameras, the MX-1700, out for a test drive to check how it stacks up against two of its top rivals in the U. S., Eastman Kodak Co.'s DC280 and Sony Corp.'s Cybershot DSC-F505. The verdict: They're all impressive examples of digital imaging technology, but the standout on pure image quality is the Kodak.

PC-Friendly. The Fuji and Kodak cameras most closely resemble traditional point-and-shoot models in appearance. The Sony takes a radical approach, with a big Zeiss lens attached to the camera on a hinge that rotates 120 degrees and with an LCD screen that makes an unconventional viewfinder. All three cameras store pictures on tiny memory cards, display pictures you've just taken on LCD screen on the back of the camera, and let you download pictures onto a PC where they can be edited and printed out.

As high-end digital cameras, they are all designed to produce photo-quality pictures. None captures the rich colors of traditional film—no consumer digital camera can do that yet. But all three produce attractive 5 X 7 prints off a standard Hewlett-Packard Co. 832 inkjet printer and photo-quality inkjet paper. That said, the image quality of these cameras is closely tied to the resolution of their charged coupled devices (CCDs)—the chips that are responsible for capturing images. The performance of these chips is measured in picture elements, or pixels. And while other factors affect the resolution, in general, a higher pixel count means a better picture. The Fuji camera uses a 1.5-megapixel CCD—meaning 1.5 million pixels per square inch. the others use 2.1 megapixels, and the difference is reflected in the price tags: The Sony lists for $999, the Kodak $799, and the Fuji $599. Fuji also makes a 2.3 megapixel camera, the MX-2700—but you pay for the extra quality. In short, the Fuji MX-1700 is a bargain. It is also the lightest and sleekest of the three. It's for people on the move who want a simple point-and-click design. It has a zoom lens and easy-to-use controls on the back, including an on-off switch for the LCD, to save battery power. But the Fuji has a limited bag of tricks. The Sony gives you the option of recording 15 seconds of video with sound, while the others produce only stills.

A critical piece of the digital-camera equation is getting the images onto a PC, editing them, and printing them out. On that score, Fuji and Sony both play second fiddle to Kodak, whose software proved the most flexible when it came to downloading images and printing in different sizes.

Kodak's simple software and the high image quality of its DC 280 give it an edge over the others, regardless of price. But Fuji and Sony aren't far behind, and Kodak can't count on holding on to any lead. It may last only until the next generation of digital cameras arrives. These days, that never takes more than a few months.

By Geoffrey Smith in Boston

green film boxes. But in Japan, its digital future has already come into focus. And the rest of the world is only a click away.

By Irene M. Kunii in Toyko, with Geoffrey Smith in Boston, and Neil Gross in New York

Source: "Fuji: Beyond Film," *Business Week*, November 22, 1999, 132–136, 138.

Comprehensive Cases

Cases for Part 6

Case 6–1

Microsoft Corp.

When 20,000 Microsofties streamed into Seattle's Safeco Field last September for the annual employee meeting, CEO Steven A. Ballmer knew he had to fire up the troops. It had been a stinker year for the software giant. Microsoft Corp.'s revenue growth had slowed to 8% from an average annual rate of 36% through the 1990s, a federal judge had ordered the company snapped in two for violating antitrust laws, and $250 billion had evaporated from Microsoft's market value. Worst of all, with the Internet moving to the center of computing, PC pioneer Microsoft seemed on the edge of irrelevance.

So Ballmer dipped deep into his bag of motivational tricks. On a huge video screen, he played a clip from a documentary about the epic 1974 title fight between Muhammad Ali and George Foreman. Foreman, seven years younger, was expected to win. But Ali was the people's choice, and the 60,000 fans in Zaire that night broke into spontaneous chants: "Ali, *bomaye!* Ali, *bomaye!*" meaning "Ali, kill him!" Ali leaned back against the ropes and absorbed blows from Foreman on his gloves and his forearms but gradually wore him out. Finally, Ali pounced, sending Foreman to the canvas. As the video ended, the loudspeakers resounded with a new chant. Microsoft, *bomaye!* Microsoft, *bomaye!*"

Like Ali, Microsoft had absorbed some bruising body blows in its own Rumble in the Jungle, Ballmer told the crowd. "We were getting shots from everywhere. Maybe we even had a little fear in our eyes." Then his voice suddenly rose to a shout. "You know what I say? I say we're off the ropes!" The Microsofties roared.

Back then, Ballmer's rallying cry was mostly wishful thinking. Now it's starting to look like an understatement. Not only do Microsoft's over-the-hill days seem over, but it is emerging more powerful than ever. Instead of the Internet relegating Microsoft to the sidelines, the software maker has grown stronger in its core PC business, gained ground in the lucrative enterprise corporate market, and fought its way very nearly to the top of the Internet heap.

All the while, it has been making mind-boggling amounts of money. While competitors are pinching pennies in this harsher economic environment, Microsoft is awash in cash: $30 billion, more than any other company in Corporate America. Moreover, it's adding $1 billion a month to its bank account, thanks to its Windows and Office monopolies. That gives it the luxury to invest in other companies and spend lavishly on new business ventures while stoking its product pipeline—all crucial for extending its dominance. This year, Microsoft will spend $4.2 billion on research and development, more than rivals America Online, Sun Microsystems, and Oracle combined (Exhibit 1).

EXHIBIT 1
Microsoft's Treasure Chest

Source: Data: Standard & Poor's, company reports.

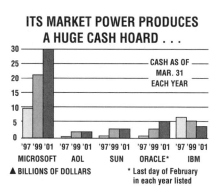

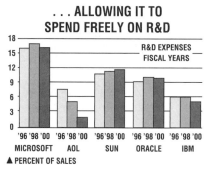

Now, Microsoft is about to unleash the biggest onslaught of new products in its 25-year history (Exhibit 2). It starts on May 31 with the launch of Office XP, the latest version of its word processing and spreadsheet program that accounts for roughly a third of the company's revenue. Next up, Stinger, a new operating system for cell phones, followed by Xbox, Microsoft's bold leap into the game-console business. And on Oct. 25 comes the big kahuna: Windows XP, a potent new version of its desktop operating system that Chairman William H. Gates III says is Microsoft's most important product since Windows 95. "We've never had a year with this many new products," he crows.

Windows XP is far more than just another spiffy rev of Windows software. With XP, Microsoft can finally harness its battery of products and Web sites, feeding customers from one product into another in a chain reaction with a potentially explosive result. Text versions of Windows XP include quick access to an easy-to-use browser that has a button that starts Microsoft's Windows Media Player. That browser zips you to Microsoft's MSN Web portal, which then offers simple ways to sign up for its instant-messaging and Internet mail service. What's more, Windows XP offers to plug you in to altogether new Internet services, such as Microsoft's alert system that e-mails or pages you when a flight is late or a stock dips low enough to buy.

Hooks Everywhere

Add it up, and Microsoft's ability to elbow aside rivals is staggering. Start with Windows. Analysts expect computer makers to sell 160 million PCs running Windows next year. On the Web, its MSN Internet-access service has 5 million subscribers. More than 50 million surfers hit its MSN portal each month. Its free e-mail service just landed its 100-millionth account. And its instant-messaging software is approaching 30 million users. Each product will feed on another. Its instant-messaging service will encourage users to sign up for Microsoft's Hotmail. Netizens who land on the MSN portal will be hawked to the access service. And Windows will push users to each piece of the empire. These hooks from one product to the next have rivals in a tizzy. "The threat that Microsoft poses is to turn the Internet into a company town—a Microsoft town," says Jonathan Schwartz, senior vice-president of corporate strategy and planning at Sun Microsystems Inc.

Nonsense, says Gates, the Web is too vast for one company to rule. He insists that the way he's handling Windows doesn't stifle innovation by others. "There's no block to people putting features on Windows," he snaps. Indeed, there are dozens of markets where Microsoft doesn't play, such as online stock trading and e-tailing. And Microsoft has had its share of busts. Remember its Sidewalk hometown portals?

Instead, he sees the intertwining of Microsoft's products as a way to make the Internet a richer experience. His latest offerings bring Microsoft closer to the grand vision he has spun since he awoke to the Web six years ago. Gates sees a day when Microsoft software will run on any device, easily connecting people to the Internet wherever they happen to be. He's convinced that the way to achieve this "anytime, anywhere" computing is by weaving Microsoft's PC, server, set-top box, cell-phone, and handheld programs in with its Internet service technologies. Once that happens, Microsoft hopes to deliver software like a steady flow of electricity, collecting monthly or annual usage fees that will give it a lush, predictable revenue stream. "This era is one where we are certainly out front," says Gates, rocking in his chair with trademark intensity.

Home Free?

If everything works as planned, Microsoft's software could be at nearly every point a consumer or corporation touches the Web. Since the Internet is now the backbone of most

EXHIBIT 2   The Money Machine

Microsoft is building on top of its huge and profitable franchises for desktop and server software by forging into such markets as game consoles, small-business software, and Web services. Its goal: To return to 20% revenue growth, up from 14% today.

The Cash Generators

WINDOWS Windows XP, the biggest update in five years, is set for Oct. 25. This version has a sleek look, is less crash-prone, and works better with the Web. The computer industry hopes the software, which has 97% of the market, could spark a PC buying wave. That could be tough in a saturated market and a slowing economy.	**BUSINESS SERVERS** Microsoft is busting out of the low end of the server market with its powerful Windows 2000, which began shipping last year. Servers running Win2000 claimed 41% of the market last year, up from 38% in 1999, says market researcher IDC.	**OFFICE** The applications suite, which has more than 90% of the market, gets a face-lift on May 31 with Office XP. It's easier to use and is better linked to the Web. With companies pinching pennies, it may not catch on until Windows XP ships. That's because the new applications will work best on the new operating system.	**MSN** MSN is now one of the most trafficked sites on the Web. The msn.com portal ranks second in the U.S., behind Yahoo! Hotmail is the world's most used free e-mail service. And MSN Internet Access trails only America Online as the most popular way for consumers to hop onto the Web.	**POCKET PC** After years of false starts, the newest version of its tiny operating software for hand-held devices is starting to eat into rival Palm's share. IDC says PocketPC should grab 19% of the handheld market by yearend, up from 10% two years ago. By 2004, that number could climb to 36%.

The New Bets

.NET SERVICES This technology lets unrelated Web sites talk with one another and with PC programs. One click can trigger a cascade of actions without the user having to open new programs or visit new Web sites. Microsoft hopes to use .Net to create Web services. First up: an alert service due next year.	**XBOX** Microsoft's leap into the $20 billion game-console business begins on Nov. 8 with Xbox. Its game box will be three times more powerful than rival consoles by Sony and Nintendo. Microsoft plans to spend $500 million in the first 18 months on advertising alone. But it may not be able to match rivals' game offerings.	**SMALL BUSINESS** This year, Microsoft will enter the $19 billion small-business software arena. It bought accounting software specialist Great Plains Software for $1.1 billion in April. And it plans to offer customer-relationship, human-resources, and supply-chain software.	**STINGER** This is the latest iteration of Microsoft's software for cell phones. Stinger trials begin later this year with Vodafone in Britain, Telefónica in Spain, and T-Mobile in Germany. It's no slam dunk, with phonemakers Nokia, Ericsson, and Motorola backing rival Symbian.	**ULTIMATE TV** Launched this spring, it's a set-top box on steroids. The $399 device not only lets people surf the Web and interact with TV shows but also record multiple programs on a hard drive for later viewing.

computing, that puts Microsoft at the center of all things digital. It's a huge turnabout for a company that was mocked for being late to the Net. "We're not playing catch-up," Gates says. "We're back in a pioneering position."

And, soon, Microsoft might not have a breakup order hanging over its head. The D.C. Circuit Court of Appeals is expected to rule any day now on the company's appeal (Exhibit 3). Based upon the questions asked at oral arguments, most legal experts believe

EXHIBIT 3   **How Microsoft Stays Two Steps Ahead of the Courts***

Presidents come and go, antitrust waxes and wanes, and the Microsoft case gets passed from judge. But one thing never changes: the company's personality. Chairman William H. Gates III is still in charge, he still uses the same controversial techniques to expand his business, and he's as aggressive as ever.

For evidence, look no further than Windows XP, the latest version of the company's PC operating system, which is scheduled for release on Oct. 25. It's a monopoly product. More than 95% of all PC buyers will get it. And it's being packaged with a raft of Microsoft's other products, including MSN Internet service, Windows Media Player 8.0 and the MSN Messenger instant-messaging service. The transparent goal: to push the vast installed base of Windows customers to use other Microsoft software as more and more aspects of their lives migrate to the Net.

This land grab raises an important question: Does Microsoft's strategy violate antitrust law? Critics say yes. By weaving into the Windows interface software that other companies sell separately, such as its media player, they believe Microsoft is guilty of illegal "tying." That's the legal term used to describe a company that leverages a monopoly in one market into an adjacent area. Opponents also contend that Windows XP, when viewed in combination with Microsoft's other aggressive actions, such as writing contracts that discourage makers from distributing rival products, could be construed as illegal monopolization. That's when a company tries to kill rivals who threaten an existing monopoly.

NO VICTIM. Sound familiar? It should. These are the charges leveled against Microsoft in the current antitrust case. And they are the legal issues that will likely hang over the company for many years to come. Microsoft is committed to pushing its operating system ever outward, adding capabilities as new technologies emerge. And that means trustbusters are likely to keep monitoring whether the Windows behemoth is getting too big.

Whether a successful legal assault could be mounted against Windows XP depends, in large part, on how the District of Columbia Circuit Court of Appeals rules on the pending Microsoft case. This will mark the first time that a major appeals court has considered the application of tying and monopolization principles to the software industry. If the court finds that the government's case was valid, then it probably wouldn't be that hard to attack Windows XP.

But if, as expected, the appeals court takes a laissez-faire approach, then bringing a successful suit against Microsoft becomes much harder. Another factor could complicate any antitrust attack on Windows XP: the lack of an obvious poster child—a struggling young company like Netscape that is an innovative pioneer of the Web and faces destruction because of Microsoft's conduct.

Bottom line: Reining in Microsoft could be an iffy proposition. Given the complexity and rapid changes in high-tech industries, most federal judges are "skeptical of [their] ability to make technological judgments," says George Washington University antitrust scholar William E. Kovacic. "They're unlikely to intervene in markets unless they are highly confident that they have a good reason for doing so."

Over the long term, if Microsoft's opponents want to defang Windows XP, their best bet could be to work on an argument that the Justice Dept. raised in the antitrust trial: that the company is retarding innovation. In several briefs filed with Judge Thomas P. Jackson last year, the government argued that Microsoft was scaring rivals out of its path, thereby chasing away new ideas that could improve computing.

This reasoning impressed Judge Jackson, but it's still not widely accepted in the antitrust community? Because Microsoft's XP operating system is clearly good for many consumers who are grateful that the company bundles so many of the services they want into one easy package. Look for this debate—between consumer convenience, on the one hand, and innovation, on the other—to grow more urgent in coming years.

While the U.S. twiddles its thumbs over antitrust policy, Europe could take the issue into its own hands. Until recently, the European Commission let Washington take the lead in policing the software maker. That's changing. European Competition Commissioner Mario Monti has become alarmed by signs that U.S. courts could turn lenient against the software maker. He announced an investigation in August. Instead of duplicating the Justice Dept. attack on Microsoft's dominance of the browser market, however, Monti has zeroed in on its attempt to corner the server market. He could expand his inquiry at any time.

DIRE CONSEQUENCES. This is no faint-hearted effort. Only one official is deployed in most EC antitrust inquiries. Against Microsoft, though, lawyers in Brussels say Monti has formed a "SWAT team" with more than half a dozen full-time investigators. Unlike the U.S., the EC isn't examining the possibility of breaking up Bill Gates's empire. But the European punishment could end up being quite severe—forcing Microsoft to reveal at least part of its Windows source code.

EXHIBIT 3   *Continued*

> So don't be surprised if the Microsoft drama drags on for a while longer—in fact, quite a while longer. If regulators are to do much more than nip at Bill Gates's heels, it will take strong action in Europe or clear support in the U.S. for some of the novel theories raised in the Netscape case.
>   *With William Echickson in Brussels*

*Mike France, "Commentary."

the court will reverse at least one of Judge Thomas P. Jackson's findings: that the company illegally "tied" a browser into its operating system, that it acted illegally to defend its Windows monopoly, and that it attempted to divide the browser market with Netscape Communications Corp. If any part is thrown out, it's unlikely the breakup order will be sustained. Instead, the appeals court would probably send the case back to a lower court to determine remedies, which could trigger settlement talks. If the lower-court ruling is overturned, Microsoft is home free, pending an appeal to the U.S. Supreme Court by the state attorneys general who brought the suit along with the Justice Dept.

To competitors, there is no worse nightmare. It's as if the appeals court is about to unleash a hungry rottweiler in a steakhouse. In an effort to keep the collar cinched, rival AOL Time Warner Inc. has launched a clandestine lobbying campaign, warning Senate staffers about new threats to competitors and consumers. A presentation prepared for the meetings that was obtained by *BusinessWeek* calls Microsoft's Internet strategy "the boldest, most aggressive move in Microsoft's history to leverage their [Windows] monopoly to create a bottleneck that will constrict the Internet." Says AOL Executive Vice-President Kenneth B. Lerer: "It appears they're doing all over again what they did when they previously went into foul territory." Sun Microsystems CEO Scott G. McNealy says letting Microsoft off the hook will stifle innovation. "We'll have to live with the consequences," he warns.

Already, many of the innovative Web software upstarts are in a mess, but of their own making. The Internet revolution promised a world where thousands of companies would flourish and the Web—not Microsoft—would be king, since it is built with industry-standard technology that everyone can use. The theory was that even while the antitrust case dragged on, market forces would keep Microsoft in restraints. But with the collapse of Net stock prices, the venture-capital well running dry, and not enough profits in the upstart's coffers, these would-be revolutionaries are hard-pressed to continue their fight. More than 400 Net companies have gone out of business in the past year. Many of those that remain have seen their stock prices sink by 90% or more.

"Their Vietnam"

Microsoft is a study in the opposite. Even with the Nasdaq off 9%, its stock price has soared 60% this year, to 70, outperforming the rest of the Dow Jones industrials. The company bested analysts' expectations for the quarter that ended Mar. 31, earning $2.45 billion on sales of $6.46 billion. That led influential Goldman, Sachs & Co. analyst Rick Sherlund to add it back to his recommended list. "Microsoft has been playing defense for the last six years," says Sherlund. Its Internet technology "is all about turning the tide and going on the offense." Sherlund expects Microsoft to post revenue growth approaching 20% within a couple of years.

You can feel the old feistiness on the sprawling campus in Redmond, Wash. During the antitrust trial, Microsoft became an industry pariah, with only its most loyal partners coming to its defense. Burnt out or lured by the Net, about 20 top managers left, including Chief Financial Officer Greg Maffei and Paul Maritz, the architect of the new Net strategy. Microsoft often lost out on recruiting the brightest college grads. "It was their Vietnam," says Roger S. Siboni, CEO of software maker E.piphany Inc. Now, the departures have slowed to a trickle. And Microsoft says that 86% of candidates offered jobs accept, vs. 79% during the dot-com craze. While industry stalwarts such as Cisco Systems, Yahoo!, and Dell Computer are laying off workers, Microsoft expects to hire 8,000 people in this fiscal year.

Still, the heavy lifting has only just begun. Much of Microsoft's success will depend on its ambitious Internet strategy dubbed .Net. This year, Microsoft will spend $2 billion on .Net technology that will make it possible for unrelated Web sites to talk with one another and to programs on a PC. One click can trigger a cascade of actions without requiring the user to open new programs or visit other sites. The strategy relies on Microsoft persuading software programmers to use the technology, yet many tech companies still harbor a deep distrust of the company. At the same time, Windows 2000, its operating system for powerful server computers, has only begun to convince corporations that it's ready to handle the most demanding jobs. And to succeed as a Web services company, Microsoft will have to get consumers to pay, while most experiences on the Web are free. Fierce competitors await: AOL in the Internet market. Sun Microsystems in servers. Oracle Corp. in heavy-duty corporate software. And IBM everywhere.

The new Microsoft is once again like the old Microsoft: undaunted. "We want to keep the pedal to the metal," says Ballmer. Indeed, Microsoft seems more aggressive than ever. Windows is where its bundling strategy notches up a level. In test versions, when consumers start up a PC equipped with Windows XP for the first time, they'll see a host of changes making Microsoft products available with one or two clicks of a mouse. Consider the Passport service. Windows XP prompts consumers to sign up the first time they log on to the Web. If they agree, they'll be asked a series of questions about where they live, their e-mail address, and their credit-card numbers. Rather than fill out a new form every time a Web surfer visits a site or submit a password on sites requiring it, Passport transmits the information directly, saving time and hassles.

Sounds pro-consumer. But Microsoft's enemies are portraying Passport as the Trojan Horse that could allow the company to dominate much of the Internet. Because of the software maker's incredible distribution power, opponents fear that Microsoft will be able to turn it into the ubiquitous payment and identity-authentication system on the Net. Microsoft already boasts 160 million Passport accounts. Although many of those are duplicates, this base of customers will only get bigger, since 160 million new Windows PCs are expected to be sold next year. As sales grow, it will be easier for the company to convince Web-site owners that they ought to accept Passport. That, in turn, will trigger more consumers to sign up—the type of powerful cycle that winds up creating monopolies. That puts Microsoft in the position, if it wants, to charge online merchants a fee for its Passport service. Although the company now denies that's the plan, its executives in the past talked about collecting fees for every e-commerce transaction.

Microsoft executives bristle at talk of Trojan Horses and the suggestion that bundling its Net services into Windows is unfair. "We have behaved consistently," says Ballmer. "We believe the law entitles us and encourages us to continue to innovate and add new capability. We thought that five years ago, two years ago, one year ago, now. We have not varied in our craft. We haven't stopped adding things to Windows."

Once you're a Passport member, you're set up to subscribe to a new set of services called Hailstorm. These include everything from notifying users of specific events to automatically updating their calendars when they purchase tickets or make an appointment online.

Already, a half-dozen corporations have signed up, including No. 1 Internet auctioneer eBay Inc., which is building a service that instantly notifies customers when their bid has been trumped.

"All the Pieces"

Other companies are expected to engineer similar technologies for linking Web sites, but Microsoft has tremendous advantages. It can mobilize the army of 5.5 million Windows developers. It has an array of now-mature server software handling everything from e-commerce to databases. And it has Windows. "Microsoft has all the pieces to make this thing go, and no one else does," says analyst Ted Schadler of Forrester Research Inc. (Exhibit 4).

Hailstorm is the next step in Microsoft's monumental switch from selling software programs to offering a vast array of services over the Web. Gates and Ballmer foresee a time when most of their revenues will come from subscriptions. In addition to Web services, Microsoft is retooling its software programs so they, too, can be rented out via the Net. Consumers will be able to buy a basic package of services: word processing, say, for a few dollars a month. Or they could shell out $20 for a package that includes word processing, scheduling, and e-mail services, along with online storage to keep music collections and photos.

There's still a lot of packaged software to be sold, especially to corporations. Microsoft is just now becoming a major player in the upper reaches of corporate computing. For much of the past decade, Microsoft unsuccessfully tried to run the technical plumbing of huge organizations—the industrial-strength servers that kept corporate networks humming and handled their most important transactions. Windows 2000 Datacenter Server, released late last year, began to change all that. Now, J. P. Morgan Chase & Co. is running its commercial-loan processing system on Windows server software, and the electronic stock-trading network, Archipelago, handles 100 trades per second using Windows and

EXHIBIT 4 **Bill Gates's Innovation Factory**

Critics say Microsoft doesn't come up with innovations that change the face of computing. Still, its engineers have hatched scores of modest advances that are in nearly every new Microsoft product. Moreover, promising projects are in the pipeline:

Tablet PC	Natural-Language Processing	Face Mapping	Information Agents
Long a favorite of Gates, the first tablet PCs will hit the market next year. Microsoft has signed up five companies to make laptops with a screen to scribble on. While the handwriting recognition is still imperfect, Microsoft believes that buyers will use the devices to store hand-written notes.	The idea is to communicate with a computer the way you talk to a person. Already, users can retrieve info from Microsoft's SQL Server database software by typing in simple questions. The next version of Windows, due out two years ago, will use even more natural-language technology.	Researchers are cooking up a way to use a digital camera to scan a PC user's head into a 3D image. Software then adds a full range of emotions. The point? Microsoft thinks that gamers will want to use their own images in role-playing games.	Researchers are creating software agents that help you sort through the deluge of electronic information. One day, an agent will study what types of messages you read first and know your schedule. Then it will sort e-mail and voice mail, interrupting you with only key messages.

Microsoft's database software. The market for Windows servers grew 32% last year, to $13.9 billion, while sales of servers running rival Unix grew only 14%, to $29 billion. The software impresses even former naysayers. "The giant is back," says Gary Bloom, the former No. 2 at Microsoft archrival Oracle who is now CEO of storage software company Veritas Inc.

The key to winning more corporate business will be .Net. Microsoft aims to provide the technology that will turn Web sites and software programs into virtual Lego pieces. If it comes together as planned, companies will be able to snap sales, accounting, and inventory software programs together so that customer orders automatically update balance sheets and set off requests to replenish supplies. Today, each of those steps is handled separately. Microsoft is betting that customers will pony up for its server software and tools to build their own creations.

One of its first converts is Matthew W. Dunn, the chief information officer at Intrawest Corp., a Vancouver (B.C.)-based skiing operator with 10 resorts, including Whistler Mountain in British Columbia and Copper Mountain in Colorado. He wanted to set up a single Web site where skiers could book vacations to any of its resorts, arranging for lodging, lift tickets, ski rentals, and classes. But Dunn also wanted to tie those orders back into Intrawest's software programs that track customer relationships and accounting.

Slippery Slope

It proved tricky. He ran into glitches with software from Oracle and e-commerce software maker BroadVision Inc. But using early versions of Microsoft's .Net technology and e-business software from Vancouver-based Pivotal Corp., he got the system running in just 90 days. Intrawest booked about $1.5 million worth of business online last winter, even though about half of its destinations weren't tied into the new system for most of the season. With those properties available next season, Dunn expects the Intrawest site to generate $10 million. Equally important, Intrawest is creating a customer database that tracks everything from the kind of lodging visitors like to resorts they have visited. With this data, it can offer customers special deals they're likely to find appealing.

With Microsoft's girth and need to grow quickly, there's hardly a sizable market it can ignore. Next up: programs for small and medium-size businesses. For years, Microsoft left that market to others, content that the accounting, human-resources, and procurement applications would run on top of Windows. Microsoft jumped in headfirst last December when it agreed to acquire Great Plains Software Inc. for $1.1 billion. The Fargo (N.D.) company is a leader in finance and accounting software for smaller businesses. But accounting is just the first step for Microsoft. "It's good but not that interesting," says Jeffrey S. Raikes, group vice-president of the productivity and business services division. "Steve [Ballmer] is telling me to build the multi-billion-dollar business."

So Microsoft is cobbling together an entire suite of business applications that handles everything from accounting to customers to procurement. What it doesn't build, it will buy, or it will partner with other software makers to fill in the gaps. This "suite" approach is how Microsoft conquered the market for desktop applications. Ultimately, Microsoft plans to plug these applications into bCentral, its small-business Web site, and offer the software as services. According to AMR Research, small and medium-size companies spent $19.3 billion on software last year. "It's quite compelling and quite frightening, I'm sure, in some quarters," says analyst Dwight Davis of Summit Strategies.

Who should be scared? London-based Sage Group, for one. The niche software maker went *mano a mano* with Great Plains, a company its size, and did quite well. Now it faces a giant with the deepest pockets in tech. "Are they a gorilla? Absolutely," says Sage CEO Paul Walker. He has confidence, though, in the ability of Sage's products to succeed. But that's what the execs at WordPerfect and Lotus thought when Microsoft set its sights on the word processing and spreadsheet markets.

Microsoft is tapping its war chest to attack new consumer markets, too. Take Xbox, the $299 game console that Microsoft plans to launch on Nov. 8. Microsoft will spend tens of millions developing the box. And it plans to spend $500 million more marketing it over the next 18 months, competing with Sony Corp.'s $299 PlayStation 2 and Nintendo Co.'s $199 Gamecube. Merrill Lynch estimates that Microsoft will lose $800 million on Xbox in the next fiscal year. But with a $20 billion market in its sights and with competing game consoles adding Web browsing and e-mail, Microsoft is running a marathon, not a sprint. "When we see a strategic need, we're very persistent, we're very committed," says Xbox boss Robert J. Bach.

They'd better be. Although Xbox will deliver more than three times the processing speed of other consoles, it has a long way to go to match the competition's hit games. Nintendo's Pokèmon and PlayStation's Crash Bandicoot drive console sales. "Microsoft is an amazing company and Bill Gates is a great leader. But the people at Microsoft are human, and that means there are things they don't know," says Nintendo President Hiroshi Yamauchi. "The game business happens to be one thing they know nothing about."

Only One Taker

Microsoft has stumbled before. Take interactive TV. In the past three years, the company has invested more than $8 billion in cable companies to secure a spot for its set-top-box software. But after nearly a decade tinkering with interactive TV, Microsoft's set-top-box software is still hard to find. Only one cable company is using it: Globo Cabo in Brazil, which will begin a trial in 250 homes in Sorocaba later this month.

When Microsoft targets a market, it often perseveres (Exhibit 5). Its MSN portal and Internet-access service languished for nearly six years. Today, it's the second-most popular portal on the Web, behind Yahoo! Inc. And its Web-access service is second only to AOL. Microsoft was able to dip into its war chest, investing $100 million in RadioShack Corp. and $200 million in Best Buy Co. in exchange for those retailers promoting access service—something smaller competitors can't afford to do. "MSN, through an incredible war of attrition, has built an incredibly powerful franchise," says Merrill Lynch analyst Henry Blodget.

EXHIBIT 5 **How Microsoft Muscles into New Markets**

| **1** Start with an existing monopoly. Microsoft controls desktop computing. When it ships its Windows XP in October, the product will be included with most personal computers sold. | **2** Bundle a new service into your monopoly product. When consumers access the Web from Windows XP, they will be asked to join Passport, a service that packages their name, address, and credit-card numbers into a digital wallet. With Passport, they don't have to type in their vital data each time, they go to a Web site. | **3** Extend into a new market. By turning most PC users into Passport users, Microsoft hopes to build large base of consumers using the service. That makes it attractive for more Web-site operators to adopt Passport for authenticating customer data. | **4** Cash in. Once a large number of consumers and Web sites are using Passport, the company could be in a position to charge transaction fees for services based on Passport—such as alerts when a traveler's airplane flight is late. |

Microsoft shows the same dogged persistence when it comes to basic research. Even while its latest products are waiting on the launchpad, it continues to pour money into R&D in search of the Next Big Thing. Gates is so jazzed about the future of software that he stepped down as CEO 18 months ago to become Chief Software Architect. That lets him spend more time with the company's 620 researchers. Walk through the warren of shoebox-size offices, and you'll find engineers working on the most vexing problems, such as getting computers to understand what you say. Gates gets wound up like a kid over stuff like creating a computer that watches your actions with a small video camera and determines if you're too busy to be interrupted with a phone call or e-mail. "The whole idea of valuing the user's time, that's the Holy Grail," he says, jumping out of his seat with excitement.

Perhaps the most ambitious research foray is Microsoft's 10-year march toward solving natural-language processing. It's a techie name, but the concept behind it is simple and quite powerful. It's the idea that computers will be able to respond to questions or commands in everyday language, not just computerese or a long series of mouse clicks. Combine that with speech recognition—another area where Microsoft researchers are plugging away—and one day you'll be able to talk to your computer the same way you do to another person. Microsoft has woven rudimentary natural language into such products as Office. The next step is delivering more advanced capabilities in the version of Windows due out in two years or so, code-named Blackcomb.

A lot of these markets remain a gleam in Gates's eyes. Time and again, though, Microsoft has shown it has the focus and the financial staying power to get it right eventually. That could mean we'll hear echoes of "Microsoft, *bomaye!*" for years to come.

With Mike France in New York, Amy Borrus in Washington, D.C., and Peter Burrows in San Mateo, Calif.

Source: Jay Greene, "Microsoft: How It Became Stronger Than Ever," *Business Week,* June 4, 2001, 75–79, 81, 84, 85.

Case 6–2

Toys 'R' Us

For now, the interior of the building at 44th Street and Broadway in the heart of New York's Times Square is a dusty demolition site. But as John H. Eyler Jr., the latest chief executive of long-troubled Toys 'R' Us Inc., strides through in his hard hat and shirtsleeves, what he sees is a retailing phoenix ready to emerge from the rubble. Or maybe it's going to be more of a peacock.

His plans for the site, which will open as the new Toys 'R' Us flagship next fall, are massive. The store's outsize attractions will include a 30-foot-tall animatronic dinosaur, a two-story Barbie townhouse with its own elevator, an indoor Ferris wheel able to take 600 people a day for a spin, and a life-size version of the Candy Land board game that doubles as a candy store. Add in personal shoppers and, for VIPs, a skybox balcony from which they can survey all this from on high. To make sure that none of it is lost on passersby, a 30-foot-tall glass wall facing Broadway will feature scrolling technology that switches it from a window into a billboard in three seconds flat.

If this doesn't sound like the Toys 'R' Us you remember—the store of unhelpful sales clerks, warehouse-length aisles done in dismal gray and blue, and Christmas-eve frustration—that's just how Eyler wants it. Recruited from upscale toy vendor FAO Schwarz last January, Eyler has gone from the Ritz to the Motel 6 of toy retailers. Part of his plan is to bring along a bit of the Schwarz magic but at a price Toys 'R' Us can afford. "All of retail has become more theatrical," says Eyler, 53. "It's about making it fun. What's fun about going to a warehouse?"

Not much. And that, in a nutshell, is what's behind a string of sales and earnings disappointments and management turmoil at the once high-flying Toys 'R' Us, based in Paramus, N.J. In his first 10 months in command, Eyler has been a whirlwind of activity, mostly focused on revamping the poor customer service and layout of the chain's 707 U.S. toy stores. Don't expect a giant *T. rex* at your local branch, but Eyler is beefing up staffing and training, greatly increasing the chain's supply of exclusive products, and striving to keep toys in stock and on shelves that people can reach. The hope is that by showing shoppers a friendlier, more helpful face and lining shelves with great toys not available elsewhere, Toys 'R' Us can break out of the low-price supermarket approach that hyperefficient Wal-Mart Stores Inc. does much better. Two years ago, the Bentonville (Ark.) giant overtook Toys 'R' Us as the No. 1 U.S. toy seller.

Eyler is the third Toys 'R' Us CEO to try to stop the onslaught of the discounters since founder Charles Lazarus retired in 1994 (Exhibit 1). And his store overhaul is the company's third since 1996. Toys 'R' Us has found that offering the widest selection 12 months a year just isn't enough to keep customers happy. The chain struggled so hard trying to figure out how to beat the latest challenge—online toy stores—that it finally joined them

EXHIBIT 1   **52 Years of Toys 'R' Us**

Started in a bike shop, Toys 'R' Us went on to define big-box toy retailing. Then came Wal-Mart.

1948 Returning from a stint in the Army, 25-year-old Charles Lazarus feels too old to start college. So he starts selling baby furniture in his father's Washington (D.C.) bike shop with $5,000. His idea is to supply families of G.I.'s returning from the war.

1952 Mr. Potato Head becomes the first toy to be nationally advertised on TV. This sparks a multibillion-dollar system of selling toys. Lazarus starts opening **toy supermarkets,** creating one of the first big-box retailers. Modeled on supermarkets, it has customers pulling goods from shelves and packing them in their own bags and boxes.

1957 The store is renamed Toys 'R' Us. Two years later, **Barbie** is born, destined to be the best-selling doll ever.

1966 Lazarus sells his four stores to Interstate Stores for $7.5 million and continues to run the toy operation.

1974 Interstate Stores, beset with problems in its discount stores, files for bankruptcy. It focuses on toys and appoints **Lazarus** CEO. Four years later, the company reemerges as Toys 'R' Us.

1983 The video-game craze, launched by Atari, peaks. A year later, Toys 'R' Us opens its first overseas stores. By 2000, there are 477 stores accounting for 27% of sales.

1990 Toys 'R' Us sales hit $4.8 billion, up from $480 million in 1980. They get a boost from another hot product: Nintendo's handheld **Game Boy.**

1994 Lazarus, 71, retires as CEO but remains chairman. A lucrative consulting package pays him $8 million in 1995 and more later. Michael Goldstein, an accountant by training, becomes CEO.

1996 Toby Lenk launches an online competitor, eToys.

1998 Wal-mart passes Toys 'R' Us as largest U.S. toy retailer. Goldstein steps down. Toys 'R' Us loses $132 million.

1999 Market turmoil is reflected in executive suite. Goldstein's replacement, **Robert Nakasone,** leaves after only 18 months. Most retailers have a good Christmas, but Toys 'R' Us struggles to stock store shelves and deliver goods through its toysrus.com Web site.

2000 John Eyler takes over as CEO, emphasizing proprietary toys and improved customer service. Toysrus.com and Amazon.com combine toy sites.

instead, linking up with Amazon.com Inc. last summer to create a joint Web site. "When I started, if you had good selection and good prices, that was the key," says Lazarus, now 77 and still a member of the board of directors. "There was only our price and a very high price, so customers were willing to withstand a lot. Today, our competition is very good, and we have to be better."

If customers do respond to Eyler's changes and the chain pulls off a respectable holiday season and a strong 2001, he will have gone a long way toward proving that he has figured out how to make a 1980s-style big-box retailer attractive to today's shopper. But he faces stiff headwinds. Retailers have already begun wringing their hands, worried about the gloomy shadow that a jittery stock market, higher gas prices, and a slowing economy might cast upon consumers. Normally consistent specialty merchants such as Gap Inc. and Home Depot Inc. have recently disappointed Wall Street.

With half of all of toy sales coming in the November-December-January quarter, toy retailers need a merry Christmas more than anyone. But this year, the lack of a must-have toy—Sony Corp.'s PlayStation 2 is trickling into the U.S. so slowly it's unlikely to have much impact until next year—could spell fewer trips to the toy store. Combine that with the Toys 'R' Us history of slow sales growth and disappointing earnings, and it becomes clear just what a steep wall Eyler is up against. The company's total stock returns have fallen 53% since Lazarus retired, compared with a 238% rise for the Standard & Poor's 500-stock index. "Toys 'R' Us has the incredibly unpleasant distinction of missing the fourth quarter in 14 out of the last 15 years, says Sanford C. Bernstein & Co. analyst Ursula H. Moran. "The big test for John Eyler is whether he can buck that trend this year."

Still, considering the recent troubles at Toys 'R' Us, many investors figure it can only improve. The stock resisted a general retail slide to rise 61% since Eyler's appointment, and it jumped $2 a share, to 18¼, on Nov. 13, when Eyler announced that third-quarter sales were down only 1% at stores open more than a year. That's considered good news—because the company was up against a very strong quarter last year, when Pokémon Game Boy cartridges sold like mad.

Giant Teddies

Eyler is betting that smart management of the chain's stronger assets-including Babies 'R' Us, and its international operations—plus an overhaul of its struggling U.S. stores, will spark what he calls "a second growth period." The company grew at a phenomenal 26% annual pace during its heyday in the 1980s. And Eyler's formula has worked before. As CEO at Schwarz, he made his name by greatly expanding things like in-store toy demonstrations and giant Schwarz-only stuffed animals.

But Eyler knew he was making a quantum leap in scale—and problems—when he came to Toys 'R' Us. The chain posted $11.9 billion in sales last year, 50 times as much as Schwarz, and operates 1,565 stores in 27 countries. And it had just blown 1999, the best toy-selling holiday of the decade. It was caught out of stock in many store items and struggled to deliver online orders. Although the company's sales last year rose 6%, they trailed the 10% increase for the toy industry.

The Toys 'R' Us board was looking for a long-term solution. Chairman Michael Goldstein says the company had been talking with Eyler on and off for more than a decade. In 1998, Goldstein's successor, Robert C. Nakasone, had tried to recruit him to be his No. 2, and even started negotiating to buy Schwarz to get Eyler on board. During a four-month search after Nakasone's departure, Eyler was always on top of the list of candidates. Goldstein relied heavily on the glowing reviews that Eyler got from key suppliers such as

Hasbro Inc. CEO Alan G. Hassenfeld and the now-departed Mattel Inc. Chief Exec Jill Barad. "Not one person said anything but 'Mike, get him,'" Goldstein recalls.

Eyler's route to becoming a retail rescuer wasn't obvious or direct. He grew up in Seattle with an engineer father who played an important role for Boeing Co. in the Apollo 11 space mission and the Minuteman Missile program. Eyler entered the University of Washington in the 1960s as a finance major, and got his MBA from Harvard University. His interest in retailing was sparked while writing a paper about eliminating middlemen from distribution. Eyler realized the nascent computer revolution would make it possible to measure the effectiveness of each link in the retail chain and could lead to consolidation. Figuring that would create opportunities for young executives, he took a management-trainee job at May Department Stores upon graduation.

Eyler was right about predicting a period of industry tumult, and he later found himself right in the thick of it. His major accomplishments include starting a chain of lower-priced shops for Federated Department Stores Inc. called MainStreet, which Eyler says was on an annual pace of $300 million in sales and on the brink of profitability when it was sold in 1988 to help reduce debt under the new owner, Robert Campeau. Next, Eyler ran the retail arm of upscale suitmaker Hartmarx Corp., only to see the stores eventually close down after the market shifted toward casual office wear. "Going through a failure helps you become a much more honest assessor of reality," Eyler says today.

Critics point out that Eyler has yet to pull off a turnaround anything like what he faces now. Even at Schwarz, whose sales, according to Eyler, grew from $60 million in 1991 to $225 million in 1999, profits were meager. "John has got a great reputation as a marketing and visual person," says one retail executive. "But it would be hard for anyone to say he's ever posted great numbers."

Eyler's first task upon joining Toys 'R' Us was to confront the mess of Christmas past. His analysis of the disastrous 1999 season showed that inventories had dropped to dangerously low levels, leaving the U.S. stores out of stock on 36% of items—including basics like Monopoly games. Even the strong third quarter that Toys 'R' Us thought it had enjoyed before Christmas turned out to be not nearly so good as it looked: Pokèmon fervor had masked deterioration in other areas. In fact, Toys 'R' Us had lurched from having too many toys in the previous years to too few. The glut had led to painful markdowns, a $698 million restructuring charge, and a sharp tightening of inventory controls.

Too tight, it turned out. By the summer of 1999, one former executive remembers, each store manager was limited to ordering 30 rolls of Scotch tape at a time, for instance. That severely restricted promotional opportunities during the holidays, when it is not unusual for the chain to sell 1 million rolls of tape a week—at 50% gross margins—the executive says. "Whole aisles collapsed" because of this merchandise paralysis, he says. Meanwhile, toymakers complained bitterly that in July, 1999, they still had received only partial Christmas orders from Toys 'R' Us. That was a key reason the board moved to oust Nakasone in August.

Huffy Customers

Eyler wanted to get his orders in early this year to steady the business and to begin mending fences with Hasbro, maker of Tonka trucks and Mattel, home of Barbie. His answer: more systematic stocking of the top 1,500 toys that make up two-thirds of the chain's sales. Toys 'R' Us, like every other retailer, knows it can't be sure it won't run out of the hot toys—the Pokémons and Tickle Me Elmos—the week before Christmas. But it can ensure that standbys such as Monopoly will be in stores 90% of the time. Eyler says that a one-season wonder might make $75 million in a year—sizable, but still only 1% of U.S. sales. "We can't make a consistently profitable business on the back of a hot toy," he insists.

So in February, when the toy industry descended on New York's 23rd Street for its annual Toy Fair, Eyler met with all the major suppliers to assure them that he would be ordering early this year. By late April, he had already placed 78% of his Christmas orders, up from less than 40% at that time the year before.

But if suppliers were quickly mollified, customers are going to take a lot longer to bring around. Their animosity goes much deeper than not finding enough of the right toys. A recent Sanford C. Bernstein study of U.S. shoppers' opinions of 15 big retailers found that Toys 'R' Us ranked near the bottom of the list on measures such as service—only Kmart Inc. ranked lower—and value for the dollar. Overall, shoppers ranked the chain 10th out of the 15 retailers. Indeed, when Bill Nygren bought Toys 'R' Us shares for his Oakmark Select mutual fund, he was shocked by a flood of shareholder complaints. "They'd write in saying, 'I was at a Toys 'R' Us store last year, and the store was dirty, the sales staff was unhelpful, they didn't have the merchandise I wanted. How could you be so stupid?'" Nygren marvels.

Just ask Kim J. McGinness, a 33-year-old mother of two who has been shopping in the Woodbridge (Ill.) Toys 'R' Us for years. Service at the store has improved of late, McGinness says. But she still gets angry recalling the time last year when she tried to buy an infant bathtub for her goddaughter's baby shower. After looking high and low for the item, she finally went to the customer-service booth to ask for help. The clerk replied that "if they had it, it was on the floor. If it wasn't on the floor, I was out of luck," she remembers. McGinness got her to check a computer and found five bathtubs were in stock. However, McGinness was told she would have to wait several hours until someone could take one down. She left without the bathtub. "I was ready to not go back there," she says. Only a call to the store manager got her an apology and a tub.

To make parents like McGinness a little happier, Eyler has launched a full-fledged remake of the stores that combines remodeling, new merchandise, and for the first time, a truly hard focus on customer service (Exhibit 2). At a cost of $200,000 to $800,000 a pop, depending on a store's condition, Eyler has remodeled 167 stores this year and will do a further 308 next year. In one test, 225 U.S. stores, including those that have been remodeled, increased their customer-service staff and upped their hours by 25% this year. Eyler

EXHIBIT 2 **Fixing the Store**

CEO Eyler has moved quickly to remake 167 of Toys 'R' Us's 707 U.S. stores in time for Christmas. The rest will be done by Christmas, 2002. Here is what he is focused on:

HELPING LONG-IGNORED CUSTOMERS To preach his message of improving store service Eyler conferred a dozen times face-to-face and by phone with senior field managers who run seven U.S. regions and met twice with every U.S. store manager. By Christmas, 225 Toys 'R' Us stores will have increased the number of people on the floor to help customers.

GETTING TOYS TO THE SHELVES Last year, Toys 'R' Us stores ran out of core merchandise. This year, it ordered early. Eyler is promising to be 90% in stock through Christmas, up from 64% last year. He's giving a big push to private-label toys, such as Animal Alley stuffed animals, and predicts they will go from 5% of sales last year to as much as 13% this year.

A NEW LOOK The new-store design does away with supermarket-style aisle displays, replacing them with toys clustered by interest in cul-de-sacs and X-shaped areas. The redo isn't cheap—it costs up to $800,000 per store. But sales are growing faster at the revamped stores. Next up: Eyler is building a lavish showplace store in New York's Times Square.

also has pushed staff training, including training managers on characteristics to look for in a good hire. He has increased wages as well.

Funny Hats

The new design, already in place at the Livingston (N.J.) store, does away with long aisles and instead bunches products together in cul-de-sacs and displays determined largely by gender and age: Boys' action figures are next to building sets. Baby dolls are near the displays of glittering nail polish and steps away from Barbie's corner. Up front are the customer-service and returns desks—now manned by as many as nine people during peak hours, up from one or two in the past. Spaces are set up for product demos, and staff wear bright red and the occasional funny hat, a big departure from the old denim shirts that made them indistinguishable from customers.

The feel is very unlike the grab-and-run atmosphere of the old Toys 'R' Us. Shopping in a new store in Selma, Tex., Eugene Perez and his wife, Elizabeth, went to look at a $225 Barbie jeep for daughters Sophia, 3, and Alexandra, 2, and were pleasantly surprised. "The old stores felt more like warehouses," he says. "This is really open, and it's a lot easier to find your way around." That should bring order to the chain's impressive but widely scattered selection of toys. Indeed, the one part of the Sanford Bernstein survey where Toys 'R' Us scored high was in having a wide assortment of products. That's what has kept Christine McCoy shopping for sons Justin, 4, and Doron, 2, at an unremodeled store in San Antonio. "No other store has this kind of selection," she says. "With Wal-Mart or Target, they may have it—or they may not."

Now Eyler just has to get the Toys 'R' Us team on board, too. Many managers and employees have emerged from the past four years with a sense of whiplash. A string of high-level executives departed, from CEO Nakasone to President Bruce Krysiak and U.S. merchandising chief Keith Van Beek. So Eyler these days attends national meetings to talk to store managers of Babies 'R' Us and clothing retailer Kids 'R' Us. He and his team have twice met with Toys 'R' Us store managers and have sat down with or talked with the seven U.S. field managers a dozen times in the past 10 months. At least once a month, Eyler e-mails employees with operations updates.

Upbeat

Outsiders have noticed a change. "Go back 12 months before John arrived, and there was really a very dispirited group of people at Toys 'R' Us," says Norman Walker, president of toymaker K'NEX Industries. "Now, they're much more up and positive. They feel they're going in the right direction."

In setting a tone, Eyler has borrowed heavily from his old employer. The year before he started at Schwarz in 1991, 25% of its sales came from proprietary products—that is, toys sold only at Schwarz. When he left, that had risen to 70%. At Toys 'R' Us, he has similarly upped exclusive goods from 5% of last year's assortment to 13% this year. He expects that to hit 20% in 2001.

At the top of Eyler's shopping list is stocking up on plush stuffed toys. Traditionally they haven't been a strong suit for Toys 'R' Us because they require a lot of display attention. Suppliers say clerks used to just throw them into bins and hard-to-reach shelves. As the slow sellers became shopworn, staff would keep jamming more of the stuffed animals onto the shelf, says Lee Schneider, president of Commonwealth Co., which makes plush stuffed animals for the new Toys 'R' Us label Animal Alley. "It was a mishmash," he says.

In the new stores, the Animal Alley line is displayed in cubby holes close to the entrance, making them more visible and, Schneider hopes, easier to fall in love with. Suppliers say margins on private-label plush toys reach as high as 60%—far above the 10% to 15% that a store might make on a highly promoted television-advertised toy. And stuffed lions, alligators, and other creatures can accomplish something else that would be novel for Toys 'R' Us—giving it a hit that discount competitors such as Wal-Mart can't touch.

But as Eyler expands beyond stuffed animals into other proprietary lines such as animatronic wild animals for its Animal Planet line, he runs the risk of competing with his own suppliers. In late October, he inked a deal to be the master licenser for the re-release of Steven Spielberg's film classic *E.T.* when it hits theaters in 2002. That means kids will be able get their *E.T.* gizmos only at Toys 'R' Us, but it also usurps a role that traditionally has gone to toymakers such as Hasbro and Mattel. So far, Eyler has avoided any conflict by using existing suppliers to make some of the Toys 'R' Us-exclusive goods. Hasbro chief Hassenfeld says he's fine as long as Toys 'R' Us does not compete directly with his Monopoly, G.I. Joe, and Tonka lines. "If they went in one of those areas, then I would not be the happiest of children."

Eyler must also manage relations carefully with his own board, which is dominated by two former CEOs, Lazarus and Goldstein (Exhibit 3). Goldstein stepped down as CEO in 1998 after a four-year term marked by erratic earnings, but he stayed on as chairman. Former insiders say he clashed with Nakasone and led the drive to oust him. Eyler, however, says he has had no problems working with the board. Goldstein did balk, though, when Eyler first suggested the lavish Times Square store. The company will not disclose its total cost, but New York real estate experts estimate that construction of the 105,000-square-foot site could easily hit $35 million. Annual rent is probably $9 million-plus a year. Goldstein considered it a sure money-loser—since many flagship stores have a way of not working out.

But Eyler eventually convinced Goldstein that there was a huge public relations benefit to the new store. It helped that his plan got rave reviews from other company executives and toy manufacturers. "If you wanted to set up an ad campaign [to reach the same number of people], you'd spend a fortune," Goldstein now concedes. An estimated 1.5 million people walk through Times Square each day, and Eyler predicts that his store will be profitable in its first year of operation.

Online Deal

Eyler has been astute enough to let Goldstein remain involved in the company. Says Goldstein: "If I think something's not a good idea, he thinks about it. He's not just doing it his way. He calls upon me." Eyler encouraged him to continue the spin-off of part of Toys 'R' Us Japan, for instance, which raised $315 million for the company in April and got the division's sizable debt off his balance sheet.

In August, Goldstein also helped negotiate one of the industry's boldest deals, a partnership between toysrus.com and Amazon.com, which should make the Toys 'R' Us site profitable more quickly than it would be on its own. Sanford Bernstein's Moran figures toysrus.com has cost the parent company $300 million in pretax expenses in the past two years. Amazon provides warehousing, order fulfillment, and site design. In exchange, it got warrants to purchase 5% of toysrus.com, as well as upfront cash payments—$34 million so far—and a share of the site's sales that analysts estimate at about 5%. Eyler thinks this is a fair price to pay, partly because he doesn't expect online toy sales to exceed 10% to 15% of the industry total in the long term, up from 2% to 2.5% today. Overall, retailers this year

EXHIBIT 3   Clubby Boardrooms 'R' Us

Last year, when then-CEO Robert Nakasone was shown the door, many investors became concerned that the primary problem at Toys 'R' Us Inc. might not have been operational woes but a personality conflict. At issue, say former executives and investors, was that Michael Goldstein, chairman of the board and Nakasone's predecessor, didn't like the way the new guy was shaking things up. Today, with John Eyler settled in the corner office, some observers still worry that the board may be too heavily influenced by Goldstein and company founder Charles Lazarus and that Eyler may not have the freedom to make much-needed changes.

Goldstein firmly denies that he exercises undue influence. He blames Nakasone's departure on a difference of opinion with the board and poor company performance. But Goldstein maintains that Eyler is in charge now. As proof, he points to his own plans to step down as chairman by June, with Eyler taking his place—a condition that Eyler set before accepting the CEO job. Eyler insists the board has been only helpful since he arrived.

DIVIDED LOYALTY. But the presence of two ex-CEOs on the board leaves some critics shaking their heads. John M. Nash, president of the Center for Board Leadership, says a CEO should step down from a board once he leaves day-to-day management to avoid divided loyalties among board members. The danger, says Nash, is "always having the old CEO second-guessing the new." And it doesn't help that there are no chief executives from other large companies on the Toys 'R' Us board to balance the company's former CEOs.

Compounding the question of who's running Toys 'R' Us are the hefty paychecks that both Lazarus and Goldstein have drawn from the company. Lazarus has received more than $35 million since stepping down as CEO in 1994 under a consulting deal outlined in the company's Securities & Exchange Commission filings. Goldstein is being paid $300,000 a year as a consultant to Toys 'R' Us, documents show, and for the five months last year when he was interim CEO, his salary rose to an annualized $900,000. "They're both being compensated at levels which suggest the company is looking to them for leadership," says James E. Heard, CEO of Proxy Monitor, an adviser to institutional investors on governance issues.

Lately, the board has made some progress toward establishing more independence. Howard W. Moore, who had been Lazarus' general merchandising manager in the 1980s and who runs a consulting firm whose clients have included major Toys 'R' Us suppliers, stepped down this year. Such close ties to a company can compromise a director's independence and are important to disclose in proxies, board experts say. But recently, Toys 'R' Us didn't disclose them. Also missing from filings until this year was the fact that long-term board member Robert A. Bernhard, who also recently stepped down, owns 25% of a company that has rented space to a Babies 'R' Us store in Tulsa for $334,000 a year since 1996.

Goldstein and Eyler are now searching for three new outside board members to add to the ranks—at least one of whom, Eyler says, is likely to be a CEO of another company. He says one of them could be named before the end of this year, the other two in early 2001. Maybe then the Toys 'R' Us board will look less like a private playhouse.

By Nanette Byrnes in New York

seem more sanguine about a shift to online sales. After several sites closed down, it now seems less likely that the Internet will be the threat to toy stores that it may be to music- and booksellers.

The Amazon deal also frees Eyler to concentrate on his stores. He has to show that his shakeup can produce more results than the chain's previous two efforts. Goldstein's 1997 renovation was meant to make the stores more attractive, but it wound up costing too much. Nakasone's version improved the merchandise mix at a lower cost per store. But in last year's Christmas rush shoppers couldn't find what they needed. That design boosted same-store sales by only 3%.

Eyler's early results have been encouraging: Sales at stores that have been redone for at least three months have risen 7 to 10 percentage points above the gains of unrenovated ones. But this Christmas is the first true test. And next year at this time, Eyler will finally be able to start advertising the new look, when stores in all of the top 23 media markets will be remodeled. He'll also have the Times Square store to generate excitement. Rival retailers are withholding judgment but say that Eyler has identified the right problems. "He seems to understand that what Toys 'R' Us should focus on is more service and creating a unique shopping environment says one competitor. "We're assuming he'll make Toys 'R' Us look as much like FAO Schwarz as he can. Time will tell whether it's smart or not."

With stiff competition from Wal-Mart, Target Corp., and others, there's little room for mistakes. "What Toys 'R' Us has lost is their uniqueness, and that they will not be able to recapture," says retail consultant Kurt Barnard. Eyler's out to prove the naysayers wrong. But with Christmas right around the corner, he has no time to play around.

With Ann Therese Palmer in Chicago and Lori Hawkins in San Antonio

Source: Nanette Byrnes, "Toys "R" Us," *Business Week,* December 4, 2000, 128–32, 134, 136, 140.

Case 6–3
Enterprise Rent-A-Car

On a bright January 1997 morning, Dean Pittman, Enterprise Rent-A-Car's area rental manager for Durham/Chapel Hill, North Carolina, got out of his car at Enterprise's new office on Hillsborough Road in Durham. He reached back in to retrieve his cellular phone and locked the new Dodge Intrepid, his latest company car. Then, leaning against the car, he admired the line of clean cars and the new office with its green and white Enterprise sign. To Dean, it seemed that dreams really did come true.

In the Fast Lane

A little over six years earlier, Dean had graduated with a degree in industrial relations from the University of North Carolina at Chapel Hill. In the job-search process, he had scheduled an interview with Enterprise Rent-A-Car, even though he'd known little about the firm. During the first part of the interview Dean had been skeptical. He wasn't certain that he liked the idea of renting cars for a living or of working at a retail job that included doing work such as washing cars. But he'd seen the potential to advance quickly, develop strong management skills, and learn about running a business. Enterprise had hired Dean and assigned him to Durham's University Drive office. He was promoted quickly to management assistant and then to branch manager at Enterprise's new office in Rocky Mount, North Carolina. Dean performed well, and a year ago the company made him an area manager, giving him responsibility for the Durham/Chapel Hill area. He now supervised three branch offices with 22 employees, 495 cars, and annual revenues of more than $3 million. Even though he worked for a big company, he felt as though he were running his own business. Enterprise gave its managers considerable autonomy and based their pay on a percentage of their branches' profits. Dean's starting salary was in line with those of his classmates, but within three years his pay had doubled, and now it had tripled. There couldn't be many other companies, Dean thought, where a person his age could have so much

This case was prepared by Dr. Lew Brown, Joseph M. Bryan School of Business and Economics, University of North Carolina at Greensboro; Dr. Gary Armstrong, Kenan-Flagler Business School, University of North Carolina at Chapel Hill; and Dr. Philip Kotler, Kellogg Graduate School of Management, Northwestern University. The authors wish to thank officials at Enterprise Rent-A-Car and Auto Rental News for their support in the development of this case. The case is for classroom discussion purposes only. Copyright © 1997 Lew Brown, Gary Armstrong, Philip Kotler. All rights reserved.

responsibility, so much fun, and such high earnings. He still had to work long hours and do his share of grunt work, but the rewards were there.

Dean's good fortune mirrored that of Enterprise itself. Starting its rental operation in 1962 with a single location and 17 cars in St. Louis, Missouri, Enterprise had grown dramatically to become the nation's largest rent-a-car company in terms of fleet size and number of rental locations. By 1997, the company had more than 3,000 locations, 325,000 cars, $3.1 billion in sales, $5 billion in assets, and 30,000 employees (Exhibit 1). In 1996, *Fortune* ranked Enterprise 37th on its list of the top 50 privately held U.S. firms. If it were public, Enterprise would have ranked about 390th among the Fortune 500.

The company's success resulted from its single-minded focus on one segment of the rent-a-car market. Instead of following Hertz, Avis, and other rent-a-car companies by setting up branches at airports to serve national travelers, Enterprise built an extensive network of neighborhood locations serving the "home-city" market—people who needed rental cars as replacements when their cars were wrecked or in the shop being repaired. Because these customers were often stranded at a body shop or repair garage and had no easy way to get to a rental office, Enterprise offered to pick them up. Enterprise's

EXHIBIT 1
Enterprise Rent-A-Car Growth in Units, Locations, and Employees

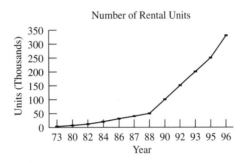

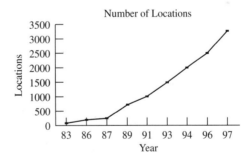

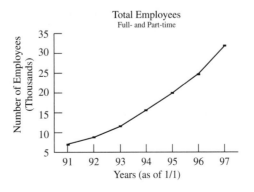

home-city strategy had been very successful—by 1997, the company had captured more than 50 percent of the replacement car segment. In recent years, Enterprise had consistently led the industry in growth and profitability.

A Surprise Guest

Out of the corner of his eye, Dean saw two men getting out of a nearby car. Dean recognized Dan Miller, Enterprise's regional vice president who was responsible for operations in eastern North and South Carolina, and Andy Taylor, Enterprise's president and chief executive officer. Andy had attended a management meeting in Raleigh the day before, and Dan had suggested that they visit the new Durham branch this morning before Andy's plane left for St. Louis, where Enterprise still had its international headquarters.

Dan knew that Andy liked to visit branches whenever he had the chance. As the son of Enterprise's founder, Jack Taylor, Andy started working for Enterprise at the age of 16 in his father's first office. Like Enterprise's other top executives who had started as entry-level branch employees, Andy still had branch operations in his blood. He and other executives visited branches regularly to stay in touch with employees and customers, learn about new ways to grow the market, and offer support to branch personnel. In fact, most Enterprise executives boasted that on occasion they still "got their ties caught in the vacuum cleaners" while cleaning cars and performing other chores to help out while visiting busy branches.

"Good morning!" Dean hailed across the parking lot.

"Hi, Dean," Andy responded as he threw up his hand. "Good-looking new office. That's a nice suit. Is it new, too?"

"Yes. I needed some new suits to go with the office. Glad you were able to stop by, Andy. I've scheduled an interview with a prospective employee this morning. Perhaps you'd like to sit in for a few minutes."

"That sounds great. Who's the candidate?"

"Her name is Rachael Van Doren. Based on her rèsumè and a preliminary interview by one of our recruiters, she seems to be bright, ambitious, and not afraid of hard work. More

important, she seems to be a real people person, someone who'd do well marketing to our referral sources and working with our customers. She also seems to be a team player with great management potential."

"I'd like to meet her," Andy responded. "Good people are the key to our business. As you know, we've got to hire a lot of new people this year if we are going to continue our rapid growth. In fact, recruitment may be the number one issue we face this year. We need to attract more employees with the right expectations and help them see that although it may not seem as glamorous as some other careers, working at Enterprise offers real opportunity."

As the three men entered the office, Dean spotted Rachael in the waiting area. "Good morning, Rachael, I'm Dean Pittman. I hope you didn't have trouble finding the office."

"No, your directions were very good."

"I appreciate your coming for an interview on such short notice. As it turns out, we're going to have a special guest in your interview. Rachael Van Doren, meet Andy Taylor, Enterprise's president and chief executive officer. And this is Dan Miller, our regional vice president."

"Hello, Mr. Taylor, Mr. Miller. It's a pleasure to meet you," Rachael responded as she shook hands.

"Please call us Andy and Dan—we aren't very formal at Enterprise," Andy responded. "I hope we're not overwhelming you. Whenever I have the chance, I like to visit our branch offices. Do you mind us sitting in?"

"Oh, no. That's fine," Rachael answered. "I guess I'm lucky to get to meet the president of the company."

"Well, Rachael, the branch office is the key to our company's success—it's where all the important action takes place. So it's always exciting when I get to spend time at a branch. We've grown more than 25 percent in each of the past 11 years. Needless to say, a key factor in continuing such growth is developing quality employees who want to run their own branches."

The Interview

As they walked through the office, Dean introduced the group to the other branch employees and showed off the new office. They stopped by a break room to pick up coffee, and Dean pointed out pictures on the bulletin board from the previous weekend's New Year's party. The Durham and Chapel Hill branches had held a contest in December to see which branch could grow its business the most that month. The Durham branch had won, and so the Chapel Hill group had arranged and paid for the party. "We're always competing like that," Dean noted. "It really adds excitement and challenge to our work."

The group moved to Dean's office, and he began the interview. "Rachael, we're interviewing you for a position in the Chapel Hill office. Normally, the branch manager, Sally Pinon, would be here, but she's on maternity leave now. Why don't you start by telling us a little about your background and how you came to apply at Enterprise?"

"I'm originally from Abington, Virginia," Rachael explained. "I graduated from the University of North Carolina at Greensboro last May with a degree in marketing. When I graduated, I wasn't sure what I wanted to do. I interviewed for a number of jobs but didn't find anything that really appealed to me. So for the last few months I've been working in a temporary administrative position at Duke University Medical Center while I continued looking for a permanent position.

"Last month, I went to a job fair in Raleigh and met one of your recruiters. I gave her my résumé, and she gave me some information on the company. Apparently, she sent my résumé to Hamilton Morales, your regional recruiter in Raleigh, and he called me for a preliminary interview last week."

"Did you know anything about Enterprise before you met our recruiter at the job fair, Rachael?" Andy asked.

"No, sir. I really didn't know much about the company. Once I looked at your materials, I did remember seeing some of your television ads with the wrapped car."

"After reading the brochures," Dan asked, "were you interested in the company?"

"To be honest, no," Rachael answered. "Enterprise seemed like a good company, but I had brochures from lots of companies at the job fair. I don't think I would've been interested if Hamilton hadn't called and invited me to the interview. My reaction was that a rent-a-car company didn't sound like a business that required someone with a college degree. I couldn't see myself renting cars like those uniformed people you see behind the counters at the airport."

"Did your interview with Hamilton change your opinion?" Dean asked.

"Yes. I could sense his excitement about working for Enterprise and his feeling that he had a real future with the company. I also met some of the other employees at the regional office, and I could tell they enjoyed their jobs. I learned that there's a lot more to this business than just working behind a counter."

Company Background

"I've also learned a lot about the company," Rachael continued, "but I'd be interested in your thoughts on why Enterprise has been so successful."

"Many factors have contributed, Rachael," Andy answered. "First, cars have become more important to people. People today just can't do without their cars, even for a day or two. And as more and more families have both adults working or are single-parent families, there is often no one else in the family who can pick you up when you have car problems. Tied in to this, the courts ruled in the 1970s that insurance companies have to offer coverage so that insured motorists can rent a replacement car if they lose the use of their car. As a result, those insurance companies began to offer rental replacement coverage in their policies.

"But perhaps the most important reason for our success is that we've adhered closely to my father's initial beliefs about how we should run the business. First and most important, we believe that we're here to serve the customer. That's why, from day 1, my father urged his employees to do whatever they had to do to make the customer happy. Sometimes it means waiving charges. Other times it means stopping everything and running out to pick up a stranded customer. Our employees know that they need to do whatever it takes to make customers happy.

"When my father first started this company, he also believed—and he still believes—that after customers come employees. If we're going to satisfy our customers, we need to have satisfied, challenged employees working as a team." Andy explained that all of Enterprise's branch employees, from assistant manager on up, earn a substantial portion of their pay based on branch profitability. In addition, the company has a profit-sharing plan for all employees. Enterprise hires primarily college graduates and promotes from within. Ninety-nine percent of its managers start as management trainees at the branch level. "As a result," Andy concluded, "they really know how our business works and understand our customer-centered culture."

Dean Pittman agreed. "That's really true. Jack Taylor believes that if you take care of the first two—customers and employees—profits will follow."

"A final piece of the puzzle," Andy continued, "is our conviction that Enterprise is a local-market business. We believe strongly that our branch employees know how best to respond to customer needs in their markets. We see our business not as a broad, national business but as a network of small, independent businesses—more than 3,000 of them now.

"We let our managers run their businesses, and we like to create friendly competition between branches. For example, employees at each branch see revenue and profit information for neighboring branches. As a result, all of these locally managed operations come up with many ideas about how to expand their businesses and serve their customers better. We weed out the ideas that don't work and share those that do with other Enterprise operating groups.

"Enterprise is a highly decentralized operation with a very small corporate staff," Andy explained. "The corporation provides capital to help branches fund their growth and a national marketing program. The only other centralized component of our business is our information system." As of 1997, the company had 23 IBM AS/400 computers in St. Louis, connected in real time via satellites to each branch worldwide. At peak times, the system processed some 834,000 transactions an hour. Enterprise knew the status of every car in its fleet at all times and was the only home-city rental company with that capability. The system also gathered all the information that corporate and branch managers needed to monitor each branch's performance. Another system allowed customers around the country to call just one telephone number and be connected to the nearest Enterprise office.

Marketing Strategy

"You mentioned that Enterprise began its rental business by targeting the home-city replacement market. Are you targeting other market segments?" Rachael asked.

"Yes, Rachael," Andy answered. "Although the majority of our business is in the replacement market, we're in two other markets as well. In the replacement market, of course, our end customers are the individuals who rent the cars. However, our initial customer is often the referral source—the insurance agent or auto body shop employee who recommends Enterprise to the stranded customer. Few of our customers get up in the morning thinking they'll need to rent a car—but then they're involved in a wreck. So referral sources are extremely important to us.

"The second segment of the home-city market is the 'discretionary' or 'leisure/vacation' segment. Friends or relatives may visit and need a car, or the family may decide to take a vacation and feel that the family car is not dependable. More and more people are renting for trips just to keep the extra miles off the family car. This is a rapidly growing segment for us as more people learn about Enterprise's nearby locations and low prices.

"Finally, we are seeing growth in our business from what we call the local corporate market. Many small businesses and some large ones have found that it's cheaper and easier for them to rent their fleets from Enterprise rather than trying to maintain their own fleets. For example, we do a lot of business with colleges and universities that have realized that it's cheaper to rent a 15-passenger van from us when the soccer team travels than to keep a van full-time for only occasional use."

"How big is the home-city market?" Rachael asked.

"That's a good question," Andy responded. "It's very hard to define accurately, but the trade publication *Auto Rental News* has made some estimates and sees the market growing at 10 to 15 percent per year (Exhibit 2). The entire rent-a-car market, including airport rentals—what we call the travel segment—is about $14.6 billion."

"I also read in several news articles that Enterprise's rental rates are about 30 percent lower than those of the rent-a-car companies that operate at airports. Is that true?" Rachael asked.

"Our local rates are much lower than those you typically find at the airport," Dean answered. "We tend to locate our offices where the rent is much lower than at the airport. We also keep our cars a little longer than the typical airport-rental company. These two factors, along with our efficient operations, help us keep our rates lower." Because home-city market car rentals peak during the workweek, Enterprise experiences excess capacity during weekends. Therefore, it also offers attractive weekend promotional prices in most markets, Dean explained.

"Who is your competition?" Rachael asked.

"We have a greater share of the total home-city market than any other single competitor," Andy answered. "A handful of major regional competitors, such as Spirit and Snappy, when combined, capture an equivalent share of the market. The airport-rental companies, such as Hertz, Avis, and Alamo, get only a small portion of the home-city business. In fact, Hertz is just now starting a small operation that focuses on the home-city replacement market. Local 'mom-and-pop' firms that often have just one office and a few cars serve the remainder of the market."

"As I noted earlier," Rachael began, "I'd never really heard of Enterprise. I'm very impressed with what I have learned, but I must admit that I wonder why so few people seem to know about the company. When I told my friends I was coming for an interview, few of them recognized the company name until I mentioned your ads with the car wrapped in paper and the 'Pick Enterprise. We'll pick you up' slogan."

"That's a problem," Dan agreed. "When our recruiters go to a university's career day, they often find that students sign up for interviews without knowing who we are. I'm sure even more would sign up if we were more widely known."

"We grew up as a very quiet company," Andy joined in. "We have always depended on word of mouth and our referral sources. It wasn't until 1989 that we did our first national advertising. At that time, marketing research showed that we had low awareness. If you showed people a list of company names and asked them to identify the rent-a-car companies, only about 20 percent picked us. We then started advertising nationally but still kept our ads low-key. Since then we have more than quadrupled our annual advertising and promotion spending.

EXHIBIT 2
The Replacement Car Rental Market:
Competitors, Revenue Estimates, and Other Market Data

Source: *Auto Rental News.*

I. Competitor	1996 U.S. Revenue	% Replacement[1]	Cars in Service (U.S.)
1. Enterprise Rent-A-Car	$2.61 billion[2]	78%	315,000
2. Ford and Chrysler Systems	$490 million	92	82,250
3. Snappy Car Rental	$100 million	100	15,500
4. U-Save Auto Rental	$115 million	60	13,500
5. Rent-A-Wreck	$85 million	35	10,942
6. Premier Car Rental	$66 million	100	9,500
7. Advantage Rent-A-Car	$76 million	33	9,000
8. Spirit Rent-A-Car	$50 million	100	7,500
9. Super Star Rent-A-Car	$43 million	100	5,250
10. Many independent companies	$750 million	53	
11. Airport-based companies: Hertz, Avis, Budget, Dollar, National, Thrifty, Alamo[3]	$360 million	100	—

II. Industry Average Pricing
Estimated industry average price per day for replacement rentals, not including additional insurance coverages or other rentals, such as cellular phones: Industry average daily rental is $23. Industry average rental period for replacement rentals is 12 days.

Additional insurance coverages produce about 5 percent of revenue, with other rental options producing about 2 percent of revenue. Per-day rental rates are often established through national contracts with insurance companies or automobile manufacturers' or dealers' warranty reimbursement programs.

There are approximately 150 major U.S. airport rental markets. Airport-based rental rates vary widely, depending on the competition. Airport rental companies also negotiate corporate rates with individual companies.

III. Overall Rent-a-Car Market
Overall 1996 U.S. market estimated at $14.62 billion broken down as follows: business rentals, 40 percent; leisure/discretionary rentals, 33 percent, replacement rentals, 27 percent.

IV. Advertising
Advertising Age estimated that U.S. car rental companies spent $384.4 million in measured advertising in 1994, about 2.8 percent of revenue. It estimated that Enterprise spent $22 million in 1994, up from $13 million in 1993. Enterprise's 1994 spending compared with $47 million spent by Hertz, $31 million by Alamo, and $24 million by Avis (Sept. 27, 1995).

Note: Estimates provided by *Auto Rental News*. Data are for case discussion purposes only. Use in case does not imply certification of estimates by Enterprise.
[1]Replacement market includes insurance replacement rentals, mechanical repair rentals, dealer loaner rentals, and warranty rentals.
[2]*Auto Rental News* estimate of U.S. rental revenue excluding leasing. Seven percent of revenue is from airport/traveler rentals, and 93 percent is from local market rentals. Local market includes replacement, business, and leisure rentals, with business and leisure about equal for Enterprise.
[3]Includes the portion of airport-based companies' revenue from local market operations that target the replacement market, including Hertz H.I.R.E. operations with 70 locations and Alamo with 115 locations. Hertz total fleet included 250,000 cars; Avis, 190,000; Alamo, 130,000; Budget, 126,000; National, 135,000; Dollar, 63,500; and Thrifty, 34,000.

"Our research shows that Enterprise's awareness is now up substantially. Still, only about one-third of those surveyed are aware of our pickup service, and only about one-third are aware that we have branches nearby. Further, few college-age people have direct experience with us even though we are one of the few companies that will rent to someone under 25 years of age. We realize that we still have a way to go in getting our name out."

The Management Trainee's Job

"I'd also like to know more about the management trainee position. Exactly what are the responsibilities of that position?" Rachael asked.

"When you come to work for Enterprise, your goal should be to learn all aspects of developing a business. First, you're assigned to a branch," Dean answered. "After initial training and orientation, we continue your on-the-job training by putting you on the front line to work alongside the other branch team members, dealing with customers who are renting or returning cars. Besides the work at the computer terminal, this involves picking up customers. Even though many of our branches have employees called 'car preps' who are assigned specifically to washing and preparing our cars for renting, all branch employees help prepare cars from time to time. They also check the repair status of customers' cars and inform insurance adjusters about how the repairs are coming along. In addition, they constantly monitor the branch's income statement and operating information to learn the logistics of running a business. This is exactly how Andy and our other senior managers started."

Dean went on to explain that aside from direct interaction with rental customers, the most important aspect of the trainee's job is managing relationships with referral sources. Each week, trainees spend time visiting the insurance agents, claims adjusters, and body shop and repair shop employees who generate much of the company's business by referring customers to Enterprise. "We visit these people every week, often taking donuts or pizzas, as a way of saying thank you for their business," Dean noted. In addition, trainees also make cold calls on referral sources and others who are not yet doing business with Enterprise. Building and maintaining these relationships is one of the most important parts of the job, he said.

"There is a lot of room for aggressiveness and creativity in this job, Rachael," Dean continued. "We need people who are willing to work hard for long hours (about 52 hours a week) while keeping a positive, friendly attitude toward customers and other employees. Our people must be dedicated to learning all aspects of branch operations, and they need to have good communication and interpersonal skills. They also need to be able to make decisions quickly, an important skill as they move up in management."

"What happens after the first few weeks?" Rachael asked.

"You spend several months learning how to run our business," Dan answered. "After six to nine months, your manager will give you what we call the Management Qualification Interview. Our employees call it 'the Grill.' The manager takes a couple of hours to ask you a full range of questions about every aspect of running a branch. If you pass this test, you get a raise and a promotion to management assistant, and you're on your way to becoming a manager." Dan explained that successful trainees move up quickly at Enterprise. Frequently within another six to nine months, they become the assistant manager of a branch. Then, within two to three years of joining the company, they are promoted to branch manager, assuming full responsibility for a branch with four to six employees and 100 to 150 cars. Within five to seven years, a successful employee could expect to become an area manager, with responsibility for two or more branches. Beyond that were positions as city managers, group rental managers, group managers, corporate vice presidents, and, of course, Andy Taylor's job as CEO.

"With advancement comes the opportunity for significant increases in income," Dan continued. "A management trainee starts at a competitive salary based on local market conditions, along with a full range of benefits and company profit sharing. Our typical branch manager is 27 years old and has doubled his or her initial salary. Managers continue to earn a percentage of the profits of the branches for which they are responsible as they move up in the organization."

"In my case," Dan noted, "I started with Enterprise 10 years ago in southern California. In about two years I became a branch manager with responsibility for satisfying customers, watching the bottom line, motivating employees, and managing more than $1 million in assets. Within seven years I was a group rental manager in Birmingham, Alabama. Two years ago I moved to Raleigh to become a regional vice president with responsibility for 30 offices and 4,000 cars, $60 million in assets, in eastern North and South Carolina. Our region grew 43 percent last year, creating lots of opportunities for advancement. One of my friends, Rob Hibbard, is now a corporate vice president after only 91/2 years, at the ripe old age of 33! In fact, you'd be amazed at how young our corporate officers are."

"That's impressive," Rachael responded, "but I'm not sure I'm very excited about starting out at a retail salary, working such long hours, and having to wash cars. As I mentioned earlier, I've been working at Duke University Medical Center in a temporary position. The center has offered me a permanent, full-time job with a higher starting salary and a more normal nine-to-five work schedule. I've also been interviewing with a large pharmaceutical firm that has outside sales positions starting at $30,000 with a company car. When I told my father that I was going to interview with you, he was a little skeptical. I'm not sure he sees working for a rent-a-car company as a good use of my college degree."

"We realize that people like you have lots of options," Dean answered. "That's why we think it's important that you understand our job and expectations so that you can decide if there's a good fit. The Duke job sounds like a good opportunity, but Enterprise employees typically prefer moving about and working with people rather than working behind a desk all day. Outside sales jobs like the one you mentioned often come with lots of travel, and some require you to relocate periodically. Perhaps more important, at Enterprise, unlike many other jobs, your pay increases significantly because it reflects your increasing value to the company. Further, although you can apply for open positions anywhere in our system, we don't force you to relocate. I guess it comes down to your deciding what is most important to you."

"Well, I've been thinking about those issues. I was a waitress while I was in college, and I know that I like being active and working with people. It's also important to me that I enjoy what I do. One thing I've noticed is that the Enterprise people I met in Raleigh and here this morning seem to be happy and to enjoy their work."

Role Playing

"It seems to me that you've been doing a better job interviewing us than we have of interviewing you," Andy joked. "Let me ask you a question like one you might get in the 'Grill' exam we mentioned. This question is based on an actual incident that Dan told me about this morning—something one of our employees faced last Friday at the Chapel Hill office. A management trainee went to pick up a young man at the university hospital's main entrance in order to bring him to the branch to get a rental car. The customer was a third-year medical student whose car had 'died' several weeks earlier. He wanted to rent one of our cars for the weekend at our special weekend rates. It was about 4:30 on a cold, rainy afternoon with lots of traffic congestion. With four employees on duty, our office was extremely busy. When our employee, who'd been on the job only about seven weeks, arrived at the hospital, the customer informed her that he'd just realized that his license had expired. Of course, we can't rent to someone with an expired license. The customer said he'd just called the Department of Motor Vehicles office, located about three miles away, and the DMV officer had indicated that if he came over, it would take only a few minutes to renew the license. The question is, If you were the employee, what would you do?"

"Rachael thought for a moment. "Well, you said the office was very busy, and if I did what the customer asked, I'd be away from the office longer than expected. So I guess I'd call the office to see if it was okay to take the customer to the DMV office," Rachael answered.

"Okay," Andy replied. "Let's assume you can't locate a phone quickly. What then?"

This time Rachael didn't hesitate. "You said earlier that customer satisfaction is number one. If I don't take the customer, he'll probably be without a car for the weekend. So I'd take him to the DMV office and try to call our office from there to let them know that I'd been delayed. Hopefully, it wouldn't take the customer long to renew the license, and I'd wait and take him back to our office to complete the rental."

"Well done, Rachael! Great answer," Andy exclaimed. "That's exactly what we'd expect from an Enterprise employee."

Back to the Airport

Dan broke in. "Excuse me, Rachael, but I've got to get Andy to the airport now. We'll leave you with Dean to complete your interview. Thanks for letting us sit in."

"I enjoyed the discussion, Dan," Rachael answered. "I learned a lot about your company. It was nice to meet you, Andy. I hope you have a good trip back to St. Louis."

*****

"Rachael seemed very sharp," Andy observed as he and Dan walked to the car.

"Yes, I wish we could find more prospective employees like her. But we have awareness and image problems. In this economy, with good college grads having so many choices, we've got to deal with those issues."

"How's your recruiting coming?" Andy asked.

"Pretty well. Hamilton Morales, my regional recruiter, has been on the job for three months now. I created that job and promoted him from one of our branch offices. This gives me someone who concentrates full-time on recruiting. We're doing all the normal recruiting activities, like going to college career days and advertising in the college newspapers. But we've got to find other sources and be creative if we are going to meet our hiring goals. We've got to hire about 75 college grads to meet our growth targets and cover normal turnover. I understand we need more than 5,000 recruits companywide.

"We learned last year," Dan continued, "how important it is to keep up the supply of good employees. Our demand skyrocketed. It's easy to add 40 to 50 cars to an office to meet demand, but we can't add people that fast.

"I've asked Hamilton to put together a recruiting plan for our region that outlines the general types of activities we should carry out. I've encouraged him to do some 'out-of-the-box' thinking. We've got to find new and more effective ways to recruit college grads if we're going to meet our growth goals."

Andy nodded. "I have just gotten some results from several recruitment studies that the corporate office commissioned. I think this information will be helpful to you (Exhibit 3). I was surprised by the results, especially the reasons candidates turned down our offers and why people chose to leave. It seems we aren't getting the word out about the future opportunities in terms of both pay and prestige."

"Andy, I think we've got to understand that recruiting is a marketing problem," Dan said. "We can use marketing techniques to attack this problem just as we use them to develop strategies to serve our customers. We're selling a dream."

"Yes," Andy replied. "And good recruiting will be essential if we want to keep growing at our current pace. We think we can double revenues again by the year 2001, but we're

---

EXHIBIT 3
Enterprise Rent-A-Car Recruiting Study Results

Source: Enterprise Rent-A-Car.

1. Top eight messages to communicate in recruitment advertising:[1]
   a. Fun and friendly work environment.
   b. Great earning potential.
   c. Earnings and responsibility are performance-based.
   d. Great place to start.
   e. Perfect place for well-rounded people.
   f. Promote from within.
   g. Not a desk job.
   h. Run a business in two years.
2. Top six messages to communicate to prospective employees:[1]
   a. Opportunity to advance.
   b. Promotion from within.
   c. Future earnings potential.
   d. People you work with.
   e. Learn a business.
   f. Team environment.
3. Backgrounds of successful managers:[2]
   a. Active in extracurricular activities.
   b. Worked their way through school.
   c. Officers in clubs/organizations.
   d. Come from full-time job.
   e. Active in athletics.
4. Top reasons our offers are turned down:[2]
   a. Compensation.
   b. Prestige.
   c. Hours versus pay.
   d. Don't see potential.
5. Why people leave[1]
   a. Long hours.
   b. Stress.
   c. Low pay.

[1]Based on a written questionnaire to 103 students and 53 graduates at 10 campuses.
[2]Based on a survey of 188 current Enterprise managers and 107 recruiters.

wrestling with a number of growth-related issues. What markets should we target? How should we position ourselves? Are there new services that we might offer? Do we need to be doing more to get the Enterprise story out to customers? How are we going to respond when Hertz and others decide to attack our home-city markets? And how can we keep up this rapid growth without losing our focus and the wonderful culture we've developed?

"All of our growth is driven not to create fame and wealth for Enterprise but to serve new customers and create opportunity for our employees. You're right, Dan. We do have a dream to sell—my father's dream. The Enterprise dream."

Case 6–4
Slendertone

Local auctioneer Eamonn McBride still remembers clearly the day in 1990 when Kevin McDonnell arrived in the truck in Bunbeg: "Kevin had asked me to organize accommodations for some employees of a new business he was setting up. I went to look for him on the industrial estate. I found him outside the factory in a big truck. He pointed to the equipment in the back of the truck and said, 'That's it there,' referring to his new business. I was totally stunned." McDonnell wanted to buy the remaining assets of a company called BMR, which had gone into liquidation. The deal included ownership of the company's brand names, NeuroTech and Slendertone. McDonnell had decided, against the advice of many, to reestablish the business in an old factory on the industrial estate outside Bunbeg. Bunbeg is a remote, windswept coastal village in the Gaeltacht (Irish-speaking) region of northwest Donegal. Within a few weeks McDonnell and five employees had begun production.

McDonnell says that he knew little about the business he was getting into when he loaded the truck in Shannon and drove north to Donegal. An accountant by training, he thought that on paper it seemed like a viable business. He now employs over 150 people in Ireland and another 70 in international subsidiaries of his company, BioMedical Research Ltd. Company revenue in 1998 was £22 million, £17 million of which was from sales of Slendertone, up nearly 60 percent from the previous year. The company has received a number of design, export, and enterprise awards, and McDonnell was voted Donegal Businessman of the Year in 1995. But McDonnell has little time or desire to reflect on his substantial achievements to date—not while he has still to attain one of his greatest goals: to develop Slendertone into a world-class brand.

McDonnell believes that Slendertone can be a £100 million a year business by the year 2002. He likes to relate how Slendertone now outsells popular brands such as Impulse and Diet Pepsi in the United Kingdom; or how Slendertone is now available in Selfridges, the prestigious department store in London. McDonnell is under no illusions about the arduous challenge that lies ahead. However, he believes he has the strategy to achieve his goal. He is confident that the recent marketing strategy devised by Brian O'Donohoe will enable Slendertone to achieve sales of over £100 million in two years and become a world-class brand. O'Donohoe, now managing director of Slendertone, joined the company as marketing director for Slendertone in April 1997.

This case was written by Michael J. Murphy, University College Cork. It is intended to be used as the basis for class discussion rather than to illustrate either effective or ineffective handling of a management situation. The case was made possible by the cooperation of BioMedical Research Ltd. Copyright 1999 by M. J. Murphy, University College Cork. Some of the figures, names, and other information in this case have been altered to protect company and customer confidentiality. However, all the data are representative of the actual position.

According to O'Donohoe, "BioMedical Research has gone from being a product-oriented company to a market-led one." In the process O'Donohoe has had to identify and deal with a number of critical issues. He believes that the foremost issue facing the Slendertone brand is credibility. He stresses the need to get away from the "gadget" image associated with Slendertone. O'Donohoe is confident that his strategy to reposition the brand will resolve this issue successfully. Product credibility is one of a number of important issues that have arisen since Slendertone's creation over 30 years ago. O'Donohoe knows that the future of Slendertone as a world-class brand depends on how well his strategy deals with these and other issues which have arisen more recently as a result of the company's dramatic growth.

Slendertone: The Early Years

Slendertone originally was developed by a company called BMR Ltd. in 1966. The company moved from England to the tax-free zone in Shannon in 1968. BMR manufactured a range of electronic muscle stimulation (EMS) devices under the Slendertone[1] and NeuroTech brands, serving the cosmetic and medical markets, respectively. By the end of the 1980s BMR's total annual sales were £1.5 million. Around 40 percent of revenue came from the sale of NeuroTech products, which were used by medical practitioners and physiotherapists to treat conditions such as muscle atrophy. The balance came from sales of Slendertone, which was used mostly for cosmetic purposes. Ninety-five percent of Slendertone sales were to the professional (beauty salon) market, with the remaining 5 percent coming from a limited range of home use products. The home use units were very basic and had few features. They retailed for between £250 and £400. Margins on all products were high. BMR claimed that Slendertone was available in over 40 countries by the late 1980s. All international sales were being handled by small local distributors or companies with diverse product interests (including an oil importer and a garden furniture dealer).

Kevin McDonnell was a creditor of BMR at the time of its liquidation; he had been supplying the company with printed circuit boards for four years. In that time he had learned something about the company's operations. When he heard BMR was going into liquidation, he immediately saw an opportunity. In an interview with *The Financial Times* in 1995 he stated: "I thought it was a bit odd that the company could go out of business, and yet, according to its business plan, it was capable of a 20 percent return on turnover." Few shared McDonnell's belief in the future of the Slendertone business. The managing director of BMR's German office felt that Slendertone was a fad which had little future.

McDonnell was not deterred. By the end of 1990 he had notched sales of £1.4 million, producing and selling much of the original BMR product range. With his focus initially on production, McDonnell continued to sell most of his products through distributors, many of which had previously worked with BMR. Over the next two years revenue grew gradually through increasing sales to distributors of the existing product range. McDonnell reinvested all his earnings in the business. Research into biomedical technology, with a view to developing new products, consumed much of his limited investment resources. The production facilities also were being upgraded: The company acquired a new and much larger factory in the Bunbeg industrial estate. McDonnell always believed that new product development was the key to future growth. By using distributors to develop export markets, he could focus his limited resources on developing better products.

[1]This case study focuses on the Slendertone division. Readers who are not familiar with EMS or Slendertone are advised to read the appendix before proceeding with the case.

The Gymbody 8

In late 1993 the Gymbody 8 was launched, the first "new" product produced by BioMedical Research Ltd. Designed primarily to meet the demands of a distributor in France, this "eight-pad stomach and bottom styler" was soon to outsell all the company's other products combined. Although it was much more stylish than anything else on the market at that time, initial sales of the Gymbody 8 were disappointing. Sales in general for home use products were very limited. Most sales of home use EMS-based consumer products were through mail order catalogs, small advertisements in the print media, and a very limited number of retail outlets, mainly pharmacies. After a few months of lackluster sales performance, the French distributor tried using an American-style direct response "infomercial" on the national home shopping channel, M6. This 30-minute "chat show," featuring interviews with a mixture of "ordinary" and celebrity users of the Gymbody 8, produced immediate results. Between interviews and demonstrations showing how the product worked, viewers were encouraged to order a Gymbody 8 by phone. By the end of 1994 Gymbody 8 sales (ex-factory) to the French distributor totaled £3.4 million. The French promotional strategy also involved the wide use of direct response (DR) advertisements in magazines and other print media. Over time retail distribution was extended to some pharmacies and a few sports stores. The soaring sales in France indicated a large untapped market for home use EMS products, a market larger than anyone in the company had anticipated.

Other Slendertone markets were slower to grow even after the introduction of the Gymbody 8. Those markets included mainland Europe, South America, Japan, and Australia. Sales in Ireland for the Gymbody 8 began to rise but were small relative to the sales in France. The Gymbody 8 was listed in a few English mail order catalogs, but sales were low. A distributor in Colombia was the only other customer of any significance for the Gymbody 8.

Distribution

With the exception of the home market, all sales of Slendertone were through distributors. By using distributors, the company believed it could develop new markets for Slendertone (or redevelop previous markets) more cost-effectively and quickly. The company's marketing resources were very limited because of the investments being made in research and production. Some of the distributors had handled Slendertone products previously for BMR, while others were newly recruited. Most of the distributors tended to be small operators, sometimes working from their homes. Most did not have the resources to invest in large-scale market development. Efforts to attract larger distributors already in the beauty market were proving unsuccessful in spite of the potential returns indicated by the ever-growing French market. Yet management was of the view that small distributors could also generate sales quickly by using direct marketing. Without the need to secure retail distribution and with an immediate return on all promotional spending, going direct would not require the levels of investment usually associated with introducing a new product to the market. The growing sales of Slendertone in Ireland from a range of direct marketing activities was proof of this.

Along with poorly resourced and inexperienced distributors, sluggish growth in most markets was blamed on legal restrictions on DR activity and cultural factors. In Germany, DR television was not allowed.[2] Combined with a very low use of credit cards, this did not augur well for a DR-oriented strategy in Germany. Other countries also had restrictions on DR activities. With regard to cultural factors, a number of BioMedical Research personnel

---

[2]Restrictions on DR activity in Germany, including TV broadcasts, have since been relaxed.

felt that the Germans were less likely to be interested in a product like Slendertone than were the Spanish, the French, and the South Americans. It was believed that the latter countries had a stronger "body culture" and that their people were not as conservative as those in Germany and Switzerland. Yet, it was argued, this couldn't explain the rapidly growing sales of Slendertone in Ireland, a relatively conservative country.

Direct Response Television

In the summer of 1995 a small cable television company in Ireland agreed to broadcast a locally produced infomercial. The infomercial featured local celebrities and studio guests and adopted the French "chat show" format. Broadcast periodically throughout the summer to a potential audience of fewer than 200,000 viewers, the infomercial resulted in direct sales of almost 1,000 Gymbody 8's. Sales of Gymbody 8's also increased in a handful of retail outlets within the cable company's broadcast area. There appeared to be an increase in demand for Slendertone beauty salon treatments in this area. The success of the Irish infomercial campaign, along with the French campaign, convinced management that DR television was the best way to sell Slendertone. It was believed that if infomercials worked well in both France and Ireland, it was likely that they would work in most other countries. The focus of the sales strategy switched from developing local distributors to securing more DR television opportunities. Intensive research was undertaken to identify infomerical opportunities around the globe, from South America to the Far East. A number of opportunities were identified, but the initial costs of producing infomercials for separate far-flung markets were a constraint. It was then decided to target "home shopping" companies. These companies buy TV time in many countries and then broadcast a range of direct response programming.

By the end of 1995 a deal had been signed with Direct Shop Ltd., which was broadcasting home shopping programming in over 30 countries at that time. The advantages of using Direct Shop were that it had access to TV space across a number of markets, would handle all negotiations with the TV companies, would buy product up-front, and could handle large numbers of multilingual sales calls. BioMedical Research produced a new Slendertone infomercial exclusively for Direct Shop, using the successful chat show format. Direct Shop ran the infomercial on satellite channels such as Eurosport and Superchannel, usually late at night or early in the morning, when broadcasting time was available. The Slendertone infomericals often were broadcast alongside presentations for car care products, kitchen gadgets, fitness products and "exercisers," and various other products. Direct Shop, like all TV home shopping companies, operated on high margins. This meant that BioMedical Research would get less than 25 percent of the £120 retail price for the Gymbody 8. The company was selling this product to other distributors for around £40. Direct Shop also had a liberal customer returns policy. This resulted in return rates of product from customers as high as 35 percent. Very often the outer packaging hadn't even been opened by the purchasers. Direct Shop also returned much unsold product when TV sales were lower than expected for some countries.

Sales to Direct Shop were not as high initially as management had expected. After a few months sales began to increase, reaching monthly sales of around 3,000 Gymbody 8's. The majority of these sales were to television viewers in England.

The Direct Model

Total sales of Slendertone continued to grow rapidly. Sales (from the factory) to the French distributor totaled £5.6 million in 1995. By early 1996 it appeared that annual sales to France for that year would be considerably higher than the budgeted £7.2 million. Irish sales for 1995 were £0.4 million and were well ahead of budget in early 1996. Sales to

Direct Shop were on the increase, though not by as much as management had budgeted. Sales on the order of £0.75 million were being made annually to the Colombian distributor. In early 1996 those four markets were accounting for over 90 percent of total Slendertone sales. Management continued to refine the direct model because of its success in those diverse markets.

One of the critical success factors of the direct approach was believed to be the way it allowed company representatives (either on the telephone directly to customers or through extended TV appearances) to explain clearly how the product worked. Management felt it would not be as easy to sell this product through regular retail channels. Retail sales, it was thought, required too much explanation by the sales staff, which might not be very knowledgeable about the products. Retail usually was limited to pharmacies and some sports stores. There was no definite strategy for developing retail channels. It was thought that there were some people who did not want to buy direct but who got their initial information from the infomercials, the company's telemarketing personnel, or other customers.

Going direct also allowed more targeted marketing efforts. While the target market for Slendertone was defined as "women between the ages of 25 and 55," a few niche segments also were targeted, including "prenuptials," "postnatals," and men. Postnatals were defined as women who had given birth recently and were now eager to regain their prepregnancy shape. Customer feedback had indicated that EMS was particularly effective in retoning the stomach muscles, which normally are "stretched" during pregnancy. This segment was reached by means of direct response advertisements in magazines aimed at new mothers and the "bounty bags" which are distributed in maternity wards. Bounty bags consist of free samples from manufacturers of baby-related products. The company would include a money-off voucher along with a specially designed brochure explaining how EMS can quickly and easily retone the stomach muscles. Prenuptials, those about to get married, were reached through wedding fairs and bridal magazines. EMS would allow the bride to be to quickly and easily tone up for the big day. It also was reported that increasing numbers of men were using the home use products. As an optional accessory the company supplied nonstick rubber pads which are attached to the body with a strap. These pads are suitable for men, for whom body hair can make adhesive pads uncomfortable.

Direct response enabled the company to gauge the effectiveness of all advertising and promotions directly. Advertisements were placed in a range of media, using different copy, graphics, and selling points to identify the most effective advertising methods. Direct response also meant that every advertisement produced immediate revenue or could be pulled quickly if it wasn't generating enough sales. This approach did not require the level of investment in brand development normally associated with introducing a new product to the market. In effect, all advertising became immediately self-financing.

Another important element of the direct strategy was to allow the company to develop an extensive customer database that could be used to market other products that the company would develop in the future. It had not yet been decided what those products would be other than that they would be sold under the Slendertone brand. The database also could be used to sell other products of interest to Slendertone customers and could be traded with other companies. The personal data from customers also proved useful for research purposes, helping the company identify its market.

Finally, for some customers, buying direct provided privacy when purchasing what some considered a personal product. One Irish pharmacist with a number of retail outlets reported that some customers would buy a Slendertone product at a pharmacy far from where they lived, presumably to avoid recognition by the staff or other customers. Some users of Slendertone products were reluctant to tell others they were using the company's products even when complimented on how well they were looking. The reasons given included, "No one says they are using these gimmicks" and "Because people would say to you, 'You don't need that.'" Some customers were reluctant to tell even a spouse that they had bought or were using Slendertone.

Customer Feedback

Attitudes regarding the sensitive nature of the purchase were revealed in a focus group of Irish customers conducted in 1995. A number of favorable comments about the Gymbody 8 were recorded, such as, "It's fabulous; I lost inches around the waist, and my sister got it and she looks fantastic." Some of the comments reflected an initial doubt about the efficacy of the product but subsequent satisfaction: "It's fabulous, I'm delighted, it's wonderful—it does actually work." One user was not so satisfied: "It's not very effective. I didn't see a visible difference; no one else did—no one commented."

The majority of the participants thought it was a very good value at £99. In determining "value" they tended to compare it to the cost of EMS treatment in a salon, joining a gym, taking fitness classes, or buying exercise equipment. The research also revealed generally low long-term use of the product. One issue raised related to uncertainty about using the unit, particularly how to place the pads on the body correctly. Another issue that arose was that using the products involved a certain amount of "hassle": attaching the pads to the unit, placing the pads on the body, and actually using the product for 40 minutes and then putting it all away again. All the focus group participants had bought their unit "off the TV," having seen the Irish infomercial. Most thought that the infomerical was very effective in explaining the product and that "it looked like a good product." Some found the TV presentation interesting and even entertaining (with some people watching it a number of times), while others thought it was "a bit over the top" or "false-looking."

The findings of this research supported anecdotal evidence and customer service feedback received by company personnel: initial doubt about the product's efficacy, a certain degree of surprise that it actually worked, mixed satisfaction (though mostly very high) with the results attained, and low long-term use. The low usage levels were confirmed by the low levels of replacement sales of the adhesive pads (which are used with the home use units to apply the current to the body and need to be replaced after 35 to 40 uses).

The Competition

Slendertone was the only product of its kind being marketed on television in 1995. A number of new EMS products entered the market during the mid-1990s, using a similar direct response approach in magazines, mail order catalogs, and other media. Other products had been available for many years, sold mostly through the mail order channel. With the exception of Ultratone, an English product, the competitor products in almost all markets tended to be of much poorer quality than Slendertone (though they were not necessarily much cheaper to buy). In this very fragmented market there were no international leaders. For instance, in Italy there were at least eight products on the market, none of which was sold outside the country. Other than the occasional mail order product, there did not appear to be any EMS units for sale in Germany. Ultratone was one of the biggest players in England but did not sell in France, which then was estimated to be the largest market for EMS products. In Spain a low-quality product called the Gymshape 8 was launched; it was priced lower than the Gymbody 8.

Management saw Slendertone as being at the "top end" of the market, based on its superior quality. Although the company had by then lost most of its mail order business to lower-priced (and lower-quality) competitors, management's attitude was that the biggest and most lucrative markets lay untapped. It was felt that the company had the products and the know-how to exploit those markets, as evidenced in France and Ireland. However, the increasing competition continued to put pressure on prices; most of the cost savings being achieved through more efficient production were being passed on to the distributors. From 1993 to the beginning of 1996 the retail price of the Gymbody 8 had fallen over £40 in France. To satisfy the French distributors' demand for cheaper products for certain channels, a "low-price" range under the Minibody and Intone brands was launched by BioMedical Research. Those products did not feature the Slendertone logo anywhere.

Given the fragmented nature of the market and a complete lack of secondary data for the EMS product class, it was hard to determine what market share different companies had. Lack of data also made it difficult to determine the size of the existing market for EMS products in each country. For planning purposes the company focused on the potential market for EMS, based on the belief that most countries had a large latent demand for EMS-based cosmetic products. Potential demand for each country was calculated on the basis of the size of the target market and the niche segments in that country. As revealed in the market research findings, the competition also had to be viewed in terms of the other means to improve body shape: the gym, fitness classes, exercise equipment, diets, diet foods, and the like.

The Professional Market

The salon business in Ireland experienced a big revival in the mid-1990s. The extensive marketing for the home use products helped create new or renewed awareness among salon users of EMS treatments and the Slendertone brand. Intensive media campaigns in Ireland were run to promote the salon products. In conjunction with salons, the company placed full-page "feature" advertisements in papers such as the *Sunday Independent.* A certain amount of tension arose between the company and the salon owners because the company was simultaneously marketing salon and home use units. For the price of 15 salon treatments one could buy a Gymbody 8.

The redevelopment of the salon market in the mid-1990s attracted a number of competitors to Ireland, including Ultratone, Eurowave, CACI, and Arysis. The increased competition led to greater promotional activity, which increased the demand for salon EMS treatments. Even though Slendertone had become a generic term for salon EMS treatment in Ireland, research in early 1996 indicated that some customers thought it represented "old" technology. Ultratone had positioned itself as the product with "newer" technology, one that was more effective and more comfortable and offered faster results in spite of using very similar, if not more basic, technology. In 1996 BioMedical Research promoted the fact that Slendertone had been in existence for 30 years. A special thirtieth-anniversary logo was featured on the promotional literature for the professional market. This was done to give buyers the assurance of long-term company marketing support and technical backup in the face of many new entrants into the market. Little effort was being made by the international distributors to develop the professional market in other countries in spite of very high margins on the larger professional units, which retailed at over £4,000. The French distributor was showing no interest in the professional market in France. It believed the size of the home use market offered much greater potential, and it did not require a sales team.

Product Development

After the success of the Gymbody 8, a number of other home use EMS products were developed by BioMedical Research before 1996, primarily to meet the requirements of the French distributor. Along with the low-cost Minibody and InTone brands, products developed under the Slendertone brand included the Bustyler (for lifting the breasts), the Face Up (a facial antiaging unit), and the Celluforme (to combat cellulite). Little market research was undertaken by the company while developing these products (the research that was done mostly consisted of prototype testing on a number of volunteers recruited locally in Galway, Ireland). The products would be developed, mostly in-house, according to criteria determined by the French distributor. The distributor also indicated the cost at which units would have to be supplied so that it could achieve certain retail price points in the targeted channels.

Rapid Growth

In March 1996 it appeared that annual Slendertone sales (from the factory) could break the £10 million barrier by year end. Sales for the Gymbody 8 represented over 70 percent of all Slendertone sales (including professional units). Over 75 percent of Gymbody 8 units being produced were for the French distributor. New employees were being recruited in a number of areas, including a large number of temporary workers in production. Many other workers chose to work overtime. There was a real sense of excitement throughout the company as orders continued to increase. The potential for Slendertone was enormous. If other countries achieved even a quarter of the per capita sales levels being attained in France or Ireland, the company would soon be a major Irish exporter. Plans were being drawn up to extend the factory and build a new headquarters in Galway. In spite of the impressive growth and the exciting potential, the board of the company was concerned about the growing dependence on one distributor.

The French distributor was becoming more demanding with regard to margins, product development, and pricing strategies. It continued to develop its own promotional material for the Slendertone range. The products were being sold as a form of "effortless exercise": "the equivalent of 240 sit-ups in just 40 minutes, while watching TV!" Some advertising featured topless models alongside sensational claims for the products' effectiveness: "the body you've always wanted in just three weeks." The distributor in France had arranged in 1996 for a well-known blond television celebrity to endorse the product. In the words of one of the Irish marketing staff, the distributor's approach was "very tacky." Still, few could argue with the ever-increasing sales. The distributor appeared to have found a large market that responded favorably to this type of promotion. Analysis of the French sales database, which was not computerized, indicated that sales were mostly to younger females; however, the distributor was very reluctant to share sales data with the company.

Developing the UK Market

A number of marketing meetings were held in April 1996 to develop a plan to reduce the company's growing dependence on this single customer. It was decided to develop the UK market directly, without any distributor involvement. This decision was made on the basis of a number of factors: the failure to attract good distributors in the past, the success of the company's direct campaign in Ireland, the reasonably successful sales to UK viewers by Direct Shop, and finally, geographic and cultural proximity to Ireland.

In May 1996 the board supported management's decision to develop the British market directly. This was going to require a substantial investment in terms of both money and management time. By the end of July an office had been established in London, with a general manager and two staff members. Direct response advertisements were soon being placed in a number of different print media, from *The Sunday Times Magazine* to the *News of the World*'s color supplement. Responses and sales were monitored closely to gauge the more likely market for the products. Sales were slow to grow; by the end of the first quarter the UK subsidiary was behind budget. The cost of maintaining an office in London also was affecting profitability. However, the Slendertone staff in both Ireland and England was optimistic about the longer-term prospects.

Slendertone in Turmoil

In late 1996 the size of the orders from the French distributor started to fall. Uncertainty about the reason for the sudden drop in French sales abounded, particularly as it was the buildup period to the normally busy Christmas season. The company quickly went from having a healthy cash surplus to being overdrawn. The banks were putting pressure on the company to address the situation. A decision was made to lay off all the temporary production workers. The situation continued to deteriorate. Over £1.5 million of raw material and stock, mostly for the French market, had accumulated in the factory. The staff was wondering whether the company could survive. McDonnell and his management team persevered with the plan to develop the UK market while addressing the serious situation developing in France.

After the slow start, sales in the United Kingdom were beginning to grow. Most sales were coming from direct response advertisements in magazines. Also, much public relations activity was being undertaken. Limited distribution had been secured in some nationwide retail chains, mostly on a trial basis in a few stores. Sales to Direct Shop (the television home-shopping company) were still disappointing, never rising above 4,000 Gymbody 8's a month. Sales in Ireland were up more than 30 percent over the previous year. Although sales to Ireland were now the highest per capita of any market, they still accounted for less than 10 percent of total sales. Sales to Colombia were about the same, while the sales of all the other distributors were down a little from the previous year.

The market in France deteriorated rapidly in early 1997. Subsequent analysis indicated that a number of factors were contributing to the dramatic loss of business there. The distributor had lost the television slot for the Gymbody 8 to a cheaper product. Other direct response channels seemed to have become "exhausted" or were being filled by cheaper products. To compound matters, a feature on EMS products in a consumer magazine gave poor ratings to many of the home-use products in the market. Although the Slendertone product range received the highest rating, this did not protect the company. A number of the low-quality competitors suddenly pulled out of the market, leaving a bad feeling in the "trade." The trade consisted of direct marketing companies that bought products from the distributors or manufacturers to sell to their existing customer base. It also included retailers: mostly pharmacies, sports shops, and a few department stores. The sudden fall in advertising for EMS products affected market demand and left many traders with unsold product. By the time BioMedical Research had received this information, it was too late to take any action. The company terminated its relationship with the French distributor later in the year, and all Slendertone sales in France soon came to an end.

At about the same time management ended its relationship with Direct Shop. The combination of lower than expected sales, low margins, and high return rates ensured that this was never going to be a profitable undertaking for the company. Furthermore, tension with existing distributors arose when Direct Shop began to broadcast across Europe, in many cases offering a price for the Gymbody 8 that was lower than what the distributors were charging for it locally. At least the company's own sales in the United Kingdom were growing. By selling direct to customers in the United Kingdom, BioMedical Research was earning a healthy margin (though the cost of the UK office and the increasing number of promotional campaigns had to be covered).

Restructuring

There had been a widespread belief throughout the company for many years that, in the words of one manager, "more marketing was needed." Efforts in 1995 and early 1996 to recruit a "marketing manager/marketing director designate," using advertisements in Irish and UK recruitment pages, were unsuccessful. It was suggested that the credibility issue concerning Slendertone might be having an effect on recruitment. With added urgency, the company succeeded in attracting O'Donohoe to the job of marketing director for Slendertone in April 1997. O'Donohoe had gained extensive marketing experience with Waterford Glass. He saw the opportunity to develop the Slendertone brand and welcomed the responsibility the job offered. But it was not easy at first: "When I joined in April, I had to go out to France, and everyone here in the office and factory would be waiting when I came back to see if I had gotten any new orders." Recognizing the opportunity presented by the trial placements for the Gymbody 8 in various UK stores, he immediately focused on developing the company's relationships in the retail channel.

While working on increasing retail sales, O'Donohoe initiated extensive research into the various markets for Slendertone. He started to build up a clearer picture of the markets for Slendertone and its brand positioning. His analysis of the French market identified the reasons for the drop in sales. It also revealed that Slendertone was not, or ever had been, the market leader in France. Based on the distributor's reports, the company had been under the impression that Slendertone had had some 70 percent of the home-use EMS market. O'Donohoe's findings revealed that Slendertone's market share had been only a fraction of that figure. His analysis also revealed that sales of replacement pads had always been extremely low, indicating low customer product usage; it previously had been assumed that the French distributor was using a different supplier for the replacement pads. Focus group research in a number of countries showed that Slendertone had a very confused positioning: It was variously associated with dieting, weight loss, health, fitness, exercise, toning, and body shaping. The focus groups also reinforced the credibility issue. Many people's first thought on seeing the product being advertised was, Does it work? Secondary data showed the size of the different markets for areas such as health, fitness, and cosmetics in different countries. O'Donohoe also gathered data on consumer behaviour and motivations relating to those different markets.

The Business Defined

The next stage for O'Donohoe was to decide exactly what business the company was in. "I've read about this business being described as everything from the 'EMS business,' whatever that is, to 'passive gymnastics.' Our consumer research showed that Slendertone had a very confused message. We're in the self-confidence business," he states emphatically. "Self-confidence through improved appearance." He now defines the Slendertone brand as "the most effective and convenient appearance solutions." The new slogan for Slendertone will be "living life and loving it." In terms of people's deeper motivations with regard to health and fitness activities, O'Donohoe stresses a core need to look good. He states that most people work out to look good rather than to be healthy. Likewise, "people diet not for the sake of losing weight but to improve their appearance through their weight loss." It is this core need to look good which O'Donohoe is targeting with Slendertone. In spite of the company's involvement in the health market with its NeuroTech range of products, O'Donohoe is clear that Slendertone is about appearance, not health. He sees it as misleading to talk in terms of health and beauty, a trade category into which many products are placed. He puts a value of $170 billion on the self-confidence market in Europe; this figure includes the combined markets for cosmetics and fashion.

Also included in this market are men. Originally recognized as only a niche segment, male users now represent an important and fast-growing market for EMS cosmetic products. In late 1997 BioMedical Research modified the Gymbody 8 by adding rubber pads and redesigning the packaging and launched the Gymbody for Men. This was very successful and opened up a new market segment for Slendertone.

The company has begun extensive consumer trials at a clinic in Galway to gain a better understanding of the exact physiological benefits of Slendertone and to identify new ways to measure those benefits. According to O'Donohoe, "We want to get away from the earlier measurements of effectiveness, such as 'inch loss.'" He is conscious of the added psychological benefits that these products might offer users. BioMedical's researchers also are using these trials to identify ways to improve product convenience and comfort.

Repositioning Slendertone

By early 1999 Slendertone products were being stocked in over 2,300 retail outlets, primarily in the United Kingdom. O'Donohoe states that the increasing emphasis on retail has to be seen in terms of a complete repositioning of the Slendertone brand. "Using Direct Shop [television home shopping] was the worst thing ever for this company. And look at these [French] magazine advertisements: lots of exclamation marks, sensational product claims, very cluttered, and the models used!" he remarks, reviewing the earlier marketing of Slendertone. O'Donohoe says it is these promotional tactics which have resulted in a "gadget" positioning for Slendertone, one he is working on changing. Furthermore, he says, by making excessive product claims the company was unlikely to meet customer expectations. This was jeopardizing the opportunity for repeat purchases of Slendertone products by existing customers. Gone, says O'Donohoe, are the promises of "effortless exercise": "We are telling customers they need to work with the products to get results. This is resulting in a different type of customer for Slendertone; we want to get away from the 'gadget-freaks.'" It is this different type of customer O'Donohoe hopes will also purchase other Slendertone-branded products in the future. The target market for Slendertone now is women and men age 20 to 60 years. The earlier niche segments, such as the "postnatals," no longer are being targeted separately. O'Donohoe believes it is important to keep the Slendertone message focused rather than having different messages for different segments of the market.

Central to O'Donohoe's strategy is the development of Slendertone into a brand in its own right. From now on O'Donohoe wants people to associate Slendertone with "effective and convenient appearance solutions" rather than EMS devices: "Slendertone will be a brand that just happens to have EMS products." The Slendertone range could in the future include many types of products. The company has just created the position of brand extensions manager to plan the development of the Slendertone range. O'Donohoe believes the company is now in a position to create an international brand: "People will tell you it takes hundreds of millions to create an international brand. We don't agree."

A priority for O'Donohoe in his goal to develop the Slendertone brand is an increased emphasis on the Slendertone name. In addition to a redesign of all the product packaging to reflect more "real" users in "real" situations (see Exhibits 1 and 2), all the product names have been changed. The original Gymbody 8 will now be marketed as the Slendertone Body, the Face Up is now the Slendertone Face, and the Celluforme has become the Slendertone Body Plus. The male products will be the Slendertone Body Profile and the

EXHIBIT 1
**The Cover of the
Gymbody 8 Case
(Used since 1994)**

EXHIBIT 2
**The Cover of the
'Slendertone Body'
Case (Introduced
in 1999)**

Slendertone Body Profile Sports, which has been adapted from the Total Body unit. Along with the Slendertone Total Body, these products constitute the full Slendertone home-use range, reduced from some 25 products three years earlier. A new professional unit, utilizing innovative touch-screen technology and "space-age" design, is about to be launched. O'Donohoe sees the professional market playing an important role in the development of Slendertone. He does not believe that the home-use and professional markets are competing; the company's experience has been that promotions for the home-use products raise awareness (and sales) for the professional market. The company currently has four staff members dedicated to developing the professional market in the United Kingdom.

Accessing the Market

O'Donohoe continues to put greater emphasis on developing retail channels, which, he says, "still represent over 95 percent of sales for all products sold worldwide in spite of the current hype about direct marketing." He believes he is able to secure retail space from important multiples because he is offering them unique access to the body-shape section of the appearance market. For these retailers Slendertone represents a new category of good, with higher than average revenues. On a shop-shelf "mock-up" in a small room at the back of the office, there is a display of the new Slendertone range, alongside massagers and shavers and other personal care products. O'Donohoe is conscious of the attention Slendertone has been attracting from the big players in the personal care market. In some cases they have been losing vital shelf space to this relatively unknown company from Ireland. He believes that BioMedical Research's expertise in the marketing of EMS products, a strong brand, and greater company flexibility (because of smaller size) will enable the company to defend itself against the multinational companies now looking at the EMS market.

The focus on retail does not mean an end to the use of direct marketing. Direct sales still account for around half of all UK sales. O'Donohoe sees direct marketing continuing to play an important role in developing the UK market and newer markets. The new direct response advertisements have been changed to reflect the move toward a stronger Slendertone brand identity and away from the "oversell" of earlier years.

The company will continue to use distributors for some markets. However O'Donohoe is determined to have greater company control over the brand than was the case in the past. By maintaining "control of the message" he believes the company can avoid a recurrence of what happened in the French market. Through a strong brand identity and a carefully controlled and differentiated image, he intends to protect the Slendertone name and market from the activities of other EMS companies. He does not plan to compete on price with the lower-quality producers; he believes that by investing in the Slendertone brand the company will be able to offer the customer greater total value at a higher price. The company will develop important markets such as Germany and France directly, as it has done successfully in the United Kingdom. Slendertone offices in Frankfurt and Paris have just been opened. O'Donohoe is conscious of the cost of establishing and maintaining international operations and the need to develop those markets successfully and promptly.

Slendertone: The Future

The company views the potential for Slendertone on two fronts: the existing potential for EMS-based products (including the existing Slendertone range and new, improved EMS products) and the potential for non-EMS Slendertone products. O'Donohoe believes he can restore Slendertone's fortunes in the French market: "The need is still there." He is conscious of bad feeling which may still exist within the trade, but other companies are operating again in this market (including BioMedical's former distributor, which now sells a lower-quality EMS product). There is still a lack of published secondary data for the EMS cosmetic market in any country. It is believed that the United Kingdom is now by far the largest EMS market. Company research indicates that the other markets with significant EMS sales are Spain and Italy. There is currently little EMS sales activity being observed by the company in Germany. In light of the level of sales being attained in Ireland (which has continued to grow every year since 1991) and the phenomenal recent growth in England, combined with a universal desire to look good, O'Donohoe envisages rapid growth for the existing Slendertone range in the short term. The potential for the extended Slendertone range in the longer term is much greater. Realizing this potential will depend on how effective the marketing strategy is in addressing all the issues and how well it is implemented.

For some the question might remain, Can Kevin McDonnell succeed in offering self-confidence to millions around the world from a factory in the wilds of Donegal? Certainly the locals in Bunbeg wouldn't doubt it.

Appendix
What Is Slendertone?

Beauty salons buy electronic muscle stimulation (EMS) units such as Slendertone so that they can provide their customers with a toning/body-shaping treatment. EMS devices work by delivering a series of electrical charges to the muscle through pads placed on the skin over the muscle area. Each tiny charge "fires" the motor points in the muscle. These charges are similar to the natural charges sent by the brain, through the nervous system, to activate particular muscles and thus cause movement. EMS therefore has the effect of exercising the muscle, but without the need to move the rest of the body. Customers use the EMS treatment over a period of weeks to help tone a particular area, primarily with the aim of improving body shape. This treatment also can improve circulation and the texture of the skin. EMS gives users improved body shape through improved muscle tone rather than through weight loss. Customers typically book a series of 10 or 15 one-hour treatments that are administered once or twice weekly. A qualified beautician who is trained in the use of EMS as part of the standard professional training for beauticians administers the treatment in the salon. A series of 10 salon treatments in Ireland costs in the range of £70. An alternative salon treatment to tone muscles is a manual "toning table," which works the muscles by moving different parts of the body attached to the table. Home use EMS units allow users to treat themselves in the comfort, privacy, and convenience of their own homes. A home use unit such as the Slendertone Body currently retails for £100 in Ireland. In terms of treatment, the home use unit should offer the user similar results to a salon treatment if used correctly and consistently.

Some customers prefer to go to a salon for EMS treatment, possibly enjoying the professional attention they get in a salon environment and the break it offers from everyday life. Booking and paying for a series of treatments in a salon also encourage customers to complete the treatment. Others prefer the convenience, privacy, and economy offered by the home use units. However, the home treatment requires a certain discipline to use the unit regularly. Home users sometimes report that they are uncertain if they are using the unit correctly; this mostly involves proper pad placement. EMS has been available in salons for over 30 years, but the home use market began to develop significantly only in the last 10 years.

Is EMS/Slendertone Safe?

EMS originally was developed for medical use. A common application of EMS is the rehabilitation of a muscle after an accident or a stroke. EMS frequently is used by physiotherapists for muscle rehabilitation after sports injuries and other injuries. Slendertone was developed to enable healthy users to "exercise" muscles without having to do any exercise. By remaining seated, lying down, or even doing minor chores, users could get the benefit of a vigorous workout. The effect of EMS is similar to that of regular exercise of a muscle. For many years the company compared the effect of using EMS (as applied to the abdominal muscles) to the effect gained from doing sit-ups. With the exception of well-stated contraindications (EMS should not be used by pregnant women, on or near open wounds, on or near ulcers, by diabetics, and on or near the throat area), EMS has proved to be perfectly safe for a variety of uses. Some people wonder what might happen when one stops using EMS. Again, the effect is like regular exercise: If one stops exercising, one may regain the shape one had before starting to exercise.

The U.S. Food and Drug Administration (FDA) has classified this type of EMS-based product as a Class II device. Class II devices must be prescribed by a "licensed practitioner" and only for very specified medical purposes. The FDA regulations governing the sale and use of EMS devices are based on proven efficacy and safety. According to the FDA, there is insufficient clinical evidence to support claims such as "body shaping," "weight loss," and "cellulite removal" for EMS treatments. The FDA's decision to impose stringent controls on the use of EMS was made after a number of home use EMS users suffered minor injuries. Users of a direct-current, home use EMS unit available in the United States in the 1970s suffered skin "burns" around the pad placement area. All Slendertone products, like the other cosmetic EMS products on the market today, only use alternating current, which will not cause burns.

Case 6–5

Intel Corp.

Intel Chief Executive Craig R. Barrett sounds nearly poetic when he describes why it has been so darn hard getting the giant chipmaker to charge into new businesses—and into the Internet Age, where the old rules of computerdom no longer hold. Not surprisingly, Barrett conjures up a Western metaphor. He does, after all, live in Arizona, commuting most weeks to Intel Corp.'s Silicon Valley headquarters. Barrett compares Intel's microprocessor business to the creosote bush, a tall desert plant that drips poisonous oil, killing off all vegetation that tries to grow anywhere near it. Microprocessors so dominated the company's strategy, he says, that other businesses could not sprout around it. Chips, he says, "are a dream business, with wonderful margins and a wonderful market position. How could anything else compete here for resources and profitability?"

How, indeed, unless you have a CEO who is kicking up a sandstorm to find a way. Nearly two years after Barrett took the reins at Intel, the chip giant is in the midst of a historic overhaul that is transforming its business and its culture—for a second time. The first, back in 1985, Intel fled the memory chip business and bet the farm on microprocessors, turning itself from a diversified maker of chips into one focused solely on producing the electronic brains of personal computers. It was a brilliant move that set up the company for a golden period of growth under legendary CEO Andrew S. Grove. But now, the days of Intel concentrating virtually all its energy and investment on PC chips are gone.

The Grove era is over. Instead, Barrett is reshaping Intel into a supplier of all sorts of semiconductors for networking gear, information appliances, and, of course, PCs. More startling, he's taking Intel into radically different terrain, such as e-commerce, consumer electronics, Internet servers, and wireless phones. "We're putting a new image on top of the big powerful chip monster that eats the world," Barrett says (Exhibit 1).

And how. Last September, Intel unveiled a new family of chips for the networking and communications gear that zips data traffic through the arteries of the Internet. That's a $7 billion opportunity—and it's growing 30% faster than PC processors. In the same month, Barrett launched an even wilder scheme: Internet services, a $3 billion business worldwide that is nearly doubling each year. Intel opened the first of a dozen gigantic computer centers that it's building around the world to run Web and e-commerce sites for other companies. Over the next two years, the chipmaker will spend $1 billion on this elaborate network of Internet data facilities.

Web War

Barrett's handiwork didn't stop there. In October, he paid $1.6 billion to buy DSP Communications Inc., a leading maker of digital wireless phone technology. Then, in January, Intel rolled out an ambitious plan to sell branded information appliances—screen phones, e-mail stations, TV set-top boxes—through phone companies and Internet service providers. And in February, the company barged into yet another new business, announcing a family of special-purpose network servers that manage Web traffic. The boxes will go head-to-head against gear from networking powerhouse Cisco Systems Inc. and a host of smaller rivals. "Craig stepped on the gas much more aggressively than I would have," concedes Grove, now Intel's chairman.

Each of these new schemes is ambitious in its own right. Taken together, they're a watershed. Within five years, Barrett intends all of Intel's new thrusts to be $1 billion-plus businesses and No. 1 or No. 2 in their markets. He's betting they will help Intel grow 15% to 20% a year, up from its paltry 8% compound growth over the past two years. So far, Wall Street is buying Barrett's vision, driving Intel shares up 40% since Jan. 1—easily the best growth among the 20 most widely held stocks in the U.S. By 2001, figures Merrill Lynch & Co. analyst Joseph A. Osha, products other than processors will make up a quarter of Intel's $38 billion in revenues and contribute nearly a third of its revenue growth. "Barrett is undertaking nothing less than a reinvention of Intel," says analyst Drew Peck of SG Cowen Securities Corp.

But no one is sure what he'll wind up with when he's done. Intel already is late to the Internet party. And the company is trying to break into new markets that already have scores of entrenched competitors. The result: Two years into Barrett's makeover, much of the payoff for Intel remains in the future. PC components are still the heart of its business, generating 90% of revenues and 100% of profits (Exhibit 2). "No organization its size can turn on a dime," says Peck. "This will be a slow, ponderous process, and meanwhile, expectations are very high."

Make that sky-high. Investors already are treating Barrett's plan as if success were a sure thing. That doesn't leave much margin for error. Barrett has to ensure that Intel's cash cow microprocessor business keeps throwing off beaucoup bucks to pay for the new gambits. In early March, for example, Intel will unveil the fastest PC chip ever sold, a Pentium III that runs at one gigahertz, or one billion cycles per second. But Intel's track record in its core business last year wasn't so good. The company had a rash of blunders in 1999—microprocessors and chipsets delivered months late, embarrassing design bugs, and supply

EXHIBIT 1   **Intel's Path Beyond the PC**

How the advent of the Internet and cheap PCs made Intel reboot

February 1997
Compaq unveils a $999 PC using a cheap Pentium clone chip. Intel execs downplay sub-$1,000 PCs as a fad, but the machines catch on, and Intel's share of the low end drops to 30%.

April 1997
Barrett wants the troops to break their old habits and diversify. He compares Intel's microprocessor business to a creosote bush, a plant that kills off nearby vegetation.

July 1997
Barrett is named president in May and, fearing the impact of low-cost chips, kicks off the first of eight seminars for Intel's top brass. The classes are aimed at getting them to dream up new businesses.

October 1997
Intel buys DEC's chip unit for $700 million. The deal contains a gem: Rights to the zippy StrongARM processor, which Intel adopts for some mobile and networking products.

December 1997
Intel ends the year with record sales of $25 billion and a blowout $6.9 billion in profits. But analysts worry about the potential financial impact of cheap PCs.

January 1998
Intel surveys 2,000 Internet service providers and discovers they want simple servers that do jobs such as encryption. So Intel develops server appliances that debut two years later.

February 1998
To kick-start a networking business, Intel hosts a press event in San Francisco and unveils dozens of products, including routers and switches.

March 1998
Barrett is named CEO. But lower chip prices in part prompt a warning of lower first-quarter results. To reclaim lost share, Intel launches the cheap Celeron chip. But it's poorly received.

July 1998
Barrett O.K.'s the launch of a new-business group to fund internal startups and asks manufacturing veteran Gerry Parker to head the new unit.

August 1998
The company forms a home-products group to develop Web appliances and Internet-enabled TVs and set-top boxes.

September 1998
Five managers, led by Renee James, study the Web-hosting business—but it's a risky leap from making chips. The board gives it the O.K. six weeks later.

November 1998
Intel completes a crash, 12-month program to set up Web-based order taking for its customers. In 1999, online revenues soar quickly to $1 billion per month.

February 1999
Intel unveils plans to codevelop a digital signal processor with Analog Devices. This could help it gain ground in markets such as cell phones and consumer electronics.

March 1999
Intel makes its largest acquisition, buying networking chipmaker Level One for $2.2 billion in stock. The company specializes in chips that connect network cards to wiring.

April 1999
Intel announces a home networking kit, the first product it will sell directly to consumers over the Web. The product sends data over phone wiring in homes.

June 1999
Straying far from its roots, Intel buys Dialogic, a maker of PC-based phone systems, for $780 million. Dialogic gives Intel technology for the convergence of voice and data networks.

September 1999
Intel unveils networking chips and opens its first Web-hosting center in Santa Clara. With a capacity for 10,000 servers, it could serve hundreds of e-commerce companies.

October 1999
Intel acquires DSP Communications, a leader in wireless phone technology, and IPivot, a maker of gear for speeding up secure e-commerce transactions.

January 2000
Barrett spells out a plan to sell info appliances through phone companies and ISPs later this year. The devices use Linux software—not Windows CE from its long-time partner Microsoft.

February 2000
Intel launches a line of seven server appliances, called the NetStructure family, that speed up and manage Web traffic. This puts Intel in competition with Cisco Systems and others.

EXHIBIT 2
**Computer
Processors**

Source: Robertson Stephens,
Semiconductor Industry Assn.

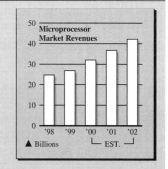

Still the heart of Intel's business, processors and companion chips for PCs and servers contributed 90% of revenues and 100% of profits in 1999. Analysts figure Intel's microprocessor business will account for less than 80% of total revenues in a couple of years.

THE BOSS Paul Otellini, 49, essentially No. 3 in the company, runs Intel's worldwide processor group. He's seen as a possible successor to Barrett.

PRODUCTS Pentium III and Celeron processors for desktop and mobile PCs; Xeon processors for servers and workstations. In the second half of this year, Intel will deliver its first 64-bit processor, called Itanium, which will help it grab more of the market for big corporate data systems. And it's about to introduce a gigabit chip, the fastest ever.

HOW INTEL STACKS UP Intel still has 84% market share in PC processors. But rival Advanced Micro Devices has hit big with its Athlon chip and Taiwan's Via also is coming on strong since buying the Cyrix processor from National Semiconductor.

ACQUISITION HELP Intel has made a few small acquisitions for its core business, such as graphics chipmaker Chips & Technologies and multiprocessing expert Corollary.

MARKET GROWTH The microprocessor sector just isn't the rocket ship it used to be.

shortages. Even loyal customers like Dell Computer Corp. and Gateway Inc. have taken the highly unusual step of publicly blaming the chip giant's gaffes for their recent earnings problems. Gateway was so incensed over supply problems that it's giving some orders to archrival Advanced Micro Devices Inc., which has caught up to Intel in chip performance.

That's prompting analysts to wonder if top management is prepared to handle the swirl of new initiatives. For starters, Intel is heading into territory unfamiliar to its executives—all of them veterans deeply rooted in chips. Analysts worry that the company's pell-mell rush into new businesses lacks focus. "They're throwing spaghetti against the wall to see what sticks," complains analyst Jonathan J. Joseph of Salomon Smith Barney. And rivals snort that Intel lacks key expertise in networking and data services—though they admit that its rich profits give it the means to buy into new markets. Barrett himself concedes that in its new endeavors, Intel will have to "compete, scratch, and claw for market share"—a bracing change from Intel's near-monopoly in PC processors (Exhibits 3–6).

PC Pothole

Barrett had little choice. After 10 years of 30%-plus compound annual growth, Intel hit a milewide pothole in 1998. Earlier attempts to expand into new businesses such as modems and video conferencing had gone nowhere. Then falling PC prices, computer industry consolidation, and increased competition piled on top of one another, causing Intel's revenue growth to slow to 5%, while earnings declined for the first time in a decade. The bad news drove Intel's stock down 30% and kept it off its peak for most of 1998.

The biggest culprit in Intel's slowdown was a changing PC landscape. For the first time since the IBM Personal Computer exploded onto the market in 1981, PCs were losing some of their luster. Instead of clamoring for more power to run fatter software programs, many

EXHIBIT 3
Networking Chips

Source: Merrill Lynch & Co., company reports.

Intel is "deadly serious" about being a player in the fast-growing networking industry, says CEO Barrett. In the past, networking was a sideline to sell more PCs. Now, Barrett is pouring billions into acquisitions, hiring, and marketing.

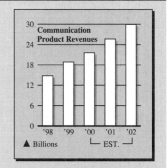

THE BOSS Mark Christensen, 40, is a rising star at Intel. With the company 18 years, he helped drive networking sales from zero to about $1 billion in the 1990s. Now he leads a 2,500-person group and reports directly to Barrett.

PRODUCTS The Network Communications Group sells chips used in modems, network interface cards, switches, and routers. Customers include Lucent, Nortel, Ericsson, and Nokia. A new family of 13 chips rolled out last September features a so-called network processor, a programmable chip that speeds and simplifies the design of new networking gear.

HOW INTEL STACKS UP Lucent Technologies Microelectronics Group is No. 1. Stalwarts like Motorola and Texas Instruments also play major roles, while newcomers Broadcom and Conexant Systems are favorites with investors. Intel is barely a blip on the radar screen in the market as a whole, but it's strong in some segments such as chips for broadband.

ACQUISITIONS Intel has spent big to get into this business. In 1999, it bought Level One Communications (for $2.2 billion), Softcom Microsystems ($149 million), NetBoost ($215 million), and the telecom chips group of Stanford Telecommunications (price not disclosed).

MARKET GROWTH Such chips are among the fastest-growing of all categories.

EXHIBIT 4
Communication Products

Source: Cahners In-Stat, company reports.

Nine years after launching its first networking gear, Intel has only a single-digit share of a $20 billion market. Now it's aiming for fast-growth segments: Home networking, broadband modems, PC-based telephony, and server appliances.

THE BOSS John Miner, 45, used to run the company's servers and workstations effort. Barrett tapped him last July to head a new 3,000-person Communications Products Group. Miner is gung ho: "Barrett says he'd rather come running after me and pull me back than have to push me out to the edge."

PRODUCTS Intel's lineup includes Ethernet hubs, small networking switches, and routers. It recently rolled out a line of specialized servers that manage Web traffic and speed up e-commerce. And it sells PC-based phone systems.

HOW INTEL STACKS UP Intel is up against 3Com, Nortel, and Cisco in home and small-business networking. As it pushes into broadband modems, it crosses Alcatel, Motorola, and others. And in specialty markets such as Web appliances and PC phones, it bumps into Alteon, Natural Microsystems, and others.

ACQUISITIONS Intel's most active area. In 1997, it bought Case Technology (for $72 million), a maker of low-end networking boxes. Since then, it has gobbled up the likes of iPivot ($500 million), which makes secure e-commerce servers; and Dialogic ($732 million), a leader in PC-based phone systems.

MARKET GROWTH Network gear is big business, but growth is slowing.

EXHIBIT 5
New Businesses

Source: International Data Corp., company reports.

Intel's New Business Group has pumped more than $50 million into 25 small projects. They vary from a secure medical ID system for doctors on the Net to terminals installed in the backs of seats at Madison Square Garden.

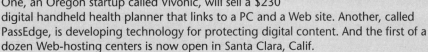

THE BOSS Gerry Parker, 56, is a widely respected 31-year Intel veteran who previously ran the company's manufacturing. Why an operations guy in business development? Because he makes things happen. "We're looking for as many ideas as possible," Parker says.

PRODUCTS Only a few projects have been revealed. One, an Oregon startup called Vivonic, will sell a $230 digital handheld health planner that links to a PC and a Web site. Another, called PassEdge, is developing technology for protecting digital content. And the first of a dozen Web-hosting centers is now open in Santa Clara, Calif.

HOW INTEL STACKS UP It's too early to say how Intel's startups will do. But Intel is not the first to spy the opportunity for Web hosting. The top players, including Exodus and IBM, have 30% of the market—with Intel nowhere in sight. Intel thinks it can break in by offering soup-to-nuts e-commerce services.

ACQUISITIONS In 1998, Intel bought Seattle-based iCat, a maker of easy-to-use e-commerce programs aimed at small to midsize businesses.

MARKET GROWTH Web hosting is one of the fastest-growing segments of the information technology business.

EXHIBIT 6
Information Appliances

Source: International Data Corp., company reports.

A few years ago, Intel was convinced that PCs were the ultimate information appliance. But the possibility that something simpler or cheaper could attract millions of non-PC households became too attractive to ignore.

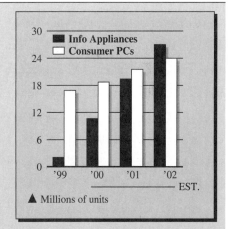

THE BOSS Claude Leglise, 44, who used to manage outside software developers, got a new mandate in August, 1998, "to move Intel into the home, somehow," he says. Just 18 months later, Intel rolled out services and prototype products that should appeal to consumers and Internet service providers.

PRODUCTS As yet undelivered, they'll use Celeron chips and Linux—not Microsoft Windows CE—software, and will be sold through phone companies and ISPs. Possible models include screen phones, e-mail terminals, and TV set-top boxes.

HOW INTEL STACKS UP There are zillions of rivals—from startups such as Network Appliance to giants like Motorola/General Instrument. Intel is behind since it hasn't shipped any products yet. Another promising avenue: Intel is moving aggressively into chips for wireless phones.

ACQUISITIONS DSP Communications ($1.6 billion).

MARKET GROWTH PC unit sales in the U.S. are expected to be eclipsed in 2002 by combined sales of e-mail terminals, Web pads, screen phones, Internet-enabled TVs, and other such high-tech gizmos.

customers just wanted cheap PCs to get online. Low-cost PCs meant low-cost chips, something rivals realized faster. Peering into the future, says Frank Gill, Intel's former top networking exec who retired in 1998, "Intel could see that the next 10 years wouldn't be as lucrative in processors." Adds Barrett: "It used to be that the PC was the center of the action, but now it's clearly the Internet."

There's no question that Intel is now a believer. Just look at the company's semiannual developers' conference on Feb. 15. As 3,200 digit heads crammed into a ballroom at the Palm Springs (Calif.) convention center, giant video screens flashed to life and the unmistakable riff of Steppenwolf's *Born To Be Wild* blared into the hall—only it had new lyrics: "Get your modem running, head out on the I-way. Looking for e-ventures, and whatever comes our way. Born to be wired." It was the warmup for a speech by Grove, the legendary chip warrior who barely sounded as though he were still in the semiconductor business, as he went on about e-commerce, gigabit networks, and facilities filled with servers. "For the first time in 15 years, we have found it necessary to change our corporate mission statement," said Grove. Now, instead of being just the leading purveyor of PC technology, Grove says, Intel aims to make the building blocks for the entire Net Economy.

To do that means undoing much of what Grove put in place. Within weeks of taking over in May, 1998, Barrett began dismantling Grove's rigidly centralized management structure, eventually breaking Intel into five groups whose managers report directly to him (Exhibits 2–6). He loosened Intel's conservative financial management to let more of its $12 billion cash hoard flow to acquisitions, equity investments, and internal startups. "We had to change the culture and the way we run our business," he says. Most of all, Barrett had to wean Intel from the defining strategy of the Grove era, when growth lay in stimulating demand for ever-more powerful PCs.

To flesh out his vision, Barrett has been on a spending spree. He's buying companies to beef up Intel's product line and help shed its notorious "not-invented-here" syndrome. In 1999 alone, the company spent $6 billion snapping up 12 companies—more, for the first time ever, than it spent on capital equipment, and nearly as much as the research-and-development and capital budgets combined. In a bid to mine fresh ideas within the company, the 60-year-old CEO has poured some $50 million into 25 homegrown startups that could someday become new product lines or be spun off as subsidiaries. And hundreds of other ideas are in the pipeline. Gerhard H. Parker, the Intel veteran who heads the company's New Business Group, says people are so excited about the opportunity that an employee recently chased him into the bathroom clutching a business plan. "It's wonderful to see that kind of enthusiasm," (Exhibit 5). Parker says. "It wouldn't have happened a few years ago."

Batting Average

Not without Barrett. While Grove is known for his fiery temper, Barrett is cool as ice. In his years before becoming CEO, he was known occasionally to bring a baseball bat to meetings to ensure—humorously—quick capitulation from intransigent colleagues. A native of the Bay Area, he studied metallurgy at Stanford University and went on to become an associate professor in the school's engineering department. After a sabbatical year working for Intel in 1973, he returned to Stanford for one day, then chucked it all and went back to Intel for good, rising through the ranks on the strength of his operational skills. He's credited with turning the company from an 80-pound weakling into an 800-pound gorilla in manufacturing, largely through inventing a technique called "Copy Exactly" in which every Intel plant is identical, down to the colors of paint. That made it easy for Intel to roll out new production techniques to all its factories—and dramatically boost quality and productivity.

So how did Mr. Manufacturing get Intel's troops jazzed about something besides their beloved microprocessor? He didn't need a baseball bat. When Compaq Computer Corp.'s $999 PC hit the market in February, 1997, carrying a chip from rival Cyrix Corp., Intel executives began to worry that cheap PCs could choke off its growth engine. Soon, inexpensive machines were flooding the market, and by mid-summer, Intel competitors AMD and Cyrix had grabbed 20% of the U.S. retail PC market, their highest share in half a decade.

That's when Barrett and then chief Grove decided to split Intel's Pentium line into distinct price and performance bands to target different markets. They devised the Celeron line for inexpensive PCs and the Xeon family for high-powered servers and workstations, while keeping the flagship Pentium III aimed at the middle tier of the market. Despite a cool reception at first, the Celeron has helped Intel climb back to 62% market share in sub-$1,000 PCs, up from 30% a year ago. And analysts now expect revenues from server-class chips to top $6.7 billion by 2001, up from $3.4 billion last year. The segmentation strategy has helped Intel maintain its juicy 60% gross margins by balancing high- and low-end sales.

But Barrett understood that segmentation alone wouldn't put Intel back on the growth curve investors had come to expect. Given Intel's size, growing at 20% per year required coming up with $5 billion or more in new revenues every year. And that meant Barrett had to think big. "He was looking to build Intel's next $25 billion business and knew he would have to significantly expand its charter," says David B. Yoffie, a professor at Harvard Business School and a member of Intel's board.

Thinking Green

The CEO-to-be knew the first place to start was inside Intel. In July, 1997, he arranged for three corporate strategy gurus to conduct a seminar series for Intel's top 400 managers. In eight groups of 50, executives retreated for a week to hotels near Intel's offices in Santa Clara, Calif., Phoenix, and Portland, Ore. "We had to figure out how to grow new businesses in the shadow of the creosote bush," Barrett says.

The first day was led by Robert A. Burgelman, a Stanford Business School professor who has studied Intel for years and co-teaches a course at the school with Grove. Burgelman specializes in helping companies develop and nurture an entrepreneurial spirit. He urged seminar attendees to divide Intel's businesses into "blue" products, its old bread-and-butter chips businesses, and "green" products—everything new. The goal was to get managers to jump faster on green ideas and escape the gravitational pull of the blue status quo. Executives at Intel now routinely use the blue vs. green descriptions when discussing strategies. "There's been a freeing up of thinking," says Paul S. Otellini, the head of Intel's processor unit.

On the second day, managers learned about the threat posed by so-called disruptive technologies. Clayton M. Christensen, a Harvard B-school professor and author of *The Innovator's Dilemma,* explained how makers of cheap steel reinforcing bars, known as rebar, once dismissed as insignificant by industry giants, had nibbled their way into the market for higher-value steel. The PC had done the same thing to mainframe computers, he said.

"Digital Rebar"

The third day of the seminar focused on business ecosystems. Led by James F. Moore, president of consultancy GeoPartners Research Inc. and author of *The Death of Competition,* the session taught Intel execs that to move beyond the familiar PC world, they would have to construct new webs of relationships and help seed emerging business ecologies. In the first few months of the seminar series, when Intel still believed that cheap PCs would be a short-lived craze, "there was a lot of denial of the message," Moore says. Then, with AMD's market share soaring, the mood turned to despair.

The big breakthrough came in September, 1997. At a dinner with Grove and other top execs following a seminar, the famously paranoid Grove latched on to the rebar story as an analogy for cheap PCs. "If we lose the low end today, we could lose the high end tomorrow," he exclaimed. From then on, Grove referred to cheap PCs as "digital rebar," and Intel became more aggressive in promoting the Celeron, even at the risk of cannibalizing sales of pricier chips.

Intel's execs also began to accept the idea of widening the company's mission. Their vehicle of choice was an investment fund Intel launched in 1991 to dribble money into PC industry startups whose products or technologies gobbled up PC power and, in the words of Grove, created "waves of excitement" among potential PC buyers. Now renamed Intel Capital, the fund has vastly expanded its outlays, from about $300 million in 1997 to $1.2 billion last year, and has stakes in more than 350 software and Internet companies.

Intel Capital has scored some notable hits, including eToys, Red Hat, and Inktomi. Its holdings are now valued at more than $8.2 billion, and it kicked $327 million in pretax income into Intel's fourth-quarter results—half of the company's 6¢ upside earnings surprise. But Intel Capital wasn't conceived primarily as a moneymaker. The investment in eToys, for example, was seen simply as a way to boost the growth of e-tailing—and the purchase of PCs. "My goal is to expose the company to every facet of the Internet economy," says Leslie L. Vadasz, manager of the fund. "It has already led to an opening of minds." The model worked so well that in 1999 Intel set up a separate $250 million fund to encourage software development for its new 64-bit Itanium processor and a similar $200 million fund to spur adoption of its new networking chips.

After the seminar series ended in 1998, the minds of Intel's managers were opened a bit more than the company could handle. At each session, attendees had broken into groups to dream up new business ideas. But "Barrett had gotten all these people excited with nowhere to go," says D. Craig Kinnie, director of Intel Architecture Labs, a research group in Oregon. The new CEO soon realized he needed more than just a cultural awakening: He had to change Intel's inflexible structure to allow new ideas to thrive.

Wad of Cash

That July, Barrett came up with a solution. He and chief financial officer Andy D. Bryant threw out Intel's rulebook for funding new programs and established the New Business Group. Rather than setting tight budgets and subjecting internal startups to rigorous reviews, they were treated like venture-capital-financed companies and given a wad of cash to spend until it ran out. Under this scheme, Parker's unit has launched about 20 seed projects, each with three or four employees and a budget of several hundred thousand dollars. Seven larger projects have received $5 million to $10 million in funding. The ideas range from a scheme to equip doctors with secure IDs to encourage online medicine, to installing 3,000 information terminals on the backs of seats at Madison Square Garden for hockey fans to look up information on their favorite players. Two potential spin-offs: An Intel business called Vivonic, based in Oregon, will sell handheld computers that help users monitor their diet and fitness starting this spring. Another Portland-based venture, called PassEdge, is set to be launched this April with technology for protecting online content, such as digital music and movies, against illegal copying.

By far, Intel's biggest gamble is its nascent Web-hosting business. The idea of running Net data centers had been floated in 1996 but was shot down because top execs didn't grasp the coming rise of Web services. Two years later, in September, 1998, Barrett directed Renee James, Grove's chief technical aide, to explore the idea again. She pulled in a team of five people and spent six weeks cobbling together a plan. "We pored over reams of data, but in the end we took a flyer," James says. Intel's board quickly approved the plan in November, and by January, 1999, it was launched. Just nine months later, Intel opened its first data center in Santa Clara. With a capacity for 10,000 servers, the center is now barely occupied. So far, only about a dozen companies—including Citigroup, an Excite@Home shopping service, and several customers from Intel's Pandesic joint venture with SAP Corp.—are using the service.

Web services couldn't be further from the chip industry. But Intel execs argue that being in the business will give the company insight into e-commerce trends. Plus, it's an insurance policy in case computing moves to a pay-for-service model and PCs are eclipsed by devices connected to Web servers. Besides, Intel executives point out, the company already does $1 billion in online business every month. "We run Intel.com 24 hours a day, 365 days a year," Barrett says. "We went from selling nothing online to more than $1 billion a month over our own infrastructure. We have expertise in this space."

Wireless Way

Still, analysts remain ambivalent about the likely success of the program. "I just don't get it," says Manoj Nadkarni, president of consultancy ChipInvestor.com, an investment research house based in Federal Way, Wash., that specializes in chip companies. Noting that the leading independent Web-hosting outfits, Exodus Communications Inc. and Verio Inc., are still losing money, Nadkarni and other analysts wonder what kinds of margins Intel can get from the business. Barrett won't comment on profits. Competitors, naturally, can't resist. "This is a mistake," says William L. Shrader, CEO of Internet service provider PSInet Inc., pointing out that Intel is going into business against its customers. "Intel looks like a joke. They'll retreat in less than two years as gracefully as possible." Adds Ellen Hancock, CEO of Web-service rival Exodus Communications: "It's a stretch for them to say they have some expertise here. We've taken years to set up our operations."

Barrett rejects such notions but admits that Intel Online Services isn't the centerpiece of his strategy (Exhibit 7). By comparison, networking and communications are "an order of magnitude" more important, he says, because the communications industry is larger than computing, yet Intel "doesn't play nearly as significant a role there." Intel, however, does stand a good chance of becoming a major supplier of wireless chip technology. The purchase of DSP Communications, combined with a joint venture with Analog Devices to develop a new digital signal processor chip, could give Intel a bigger piece of the explosive mobile-phone business. It's already the No. 1 supplier of memory chips used in cell phones. By packaging DSPC's software with Intel's energy-efficient StrongARM processor, Barrett figures he can parlay that position into selling the more profitable brains of wireless Internet-ready phones. It's a huge opportunity: Researcher International Data Corp. figures such devices could surge to 536 million units in 2003, up from 85 million in 2000. "Wireless access is the second coming of the Internet," says IDC researcher Iain Gillott.

But rivals aren't rolling over. The $7 billion communications chip sector is on fire, with projected 20% growth this year. Established players are beefing up their portfolios. Motorola, Conexant, and Lucent Technologies, for instance, all recently bought network processor startups, and IBM has a chip of its own. Competitors pooh-pooh Intel's

EXHIBIT 7   The Thrill of "Clawing for Market Share" Is Back

Craig R. Barrett, CEO of Intel Corp. since May, 1998, is as cool as his predecessor Andrew S. Grove was hot. But don't let Barrett's placid mien fool you: He's as tough as they come, with a biting wit. Trained as a metallurgist, Barrett quit his job as a Stanford University engineering professor to join Intel in 1974. He rose to the top on his operations talent—Barrett is credited with turning Intel into a nonpareil manufacturer—but in the past two years, he has been moving into the role of visionary-in-chief. Barrett spoke with Business Week *correspondent Andy Reinhardt in the CEO's unadorned conference room.*

Q: *How is Intel changing?*
A: We still are driving our core [microprocessor] business as hard as ever, and [it's] still doing pretty well. But we've supplemented it with new growth initiatives, which are very exciting and very different for us. We are acquiring companies, acquiring people, and putting a new image on top of the big, powerful chip monster that eats the world.

Whether it's networking or cellular communications, server appliances, or server farms, there's a lot more buzz and energy, which is causing the company to change the way it behaves. It's not just the big machine continuing to roll on. [We have] a bunch of smaller businesses starting up, which are forced to compete, scratch, and claw for market share.

Q: *You've started other businesses before. What's different this time?*
A: A lot of the initiatives we had in the past were not so much new business thrusts as something designed to augment and support the existing Job 1 business. But when you look at server farms [facilities with rows of computers] or cellular communications, these are pretty well removed from microprocessors. They're quite different, not just a pimple on our core business.

Q: *Why are you undertaking such a massive overhaul of your business?*
A: The PC was at the center of computing during the '90s, but if you look at the next decade, the Internet is clearly it. The PC is still very important in the Internet era. But if you want to be involved in this new era, you have to look for the new growth opportunities. That's exactly what we're trying to do.

Q: *Why are you doing so many acquisitions?*
A: We recognized one of the changes we had to make to continue to grow was to pump up the acquisitions. We really can't develop all this technology internally, so we had to go outside. This is generally accepted now as one of the ways people grow....Let's stop being squeamish; let's just go out and do it.

Q: *Your plan to host the Web operations of others baffles some people because it's so different from manufacturing chips. What expertise does Intel have to offer?*
A: If the argument were that we run big silicon factories so we can run big server farms, I would question it, too. But you have to look at it from the standpoint that we run Intel.com 24 hours a day, 365 days a year. We went from selling nothing online to more than $1 billion a month over our own infrastructure. We have expertise in this space. Forget about silicon factories.

Q: *What about your plan to sell information appliances? Couldn't they undermine sales of PCs?*
A: The Internet is too big, too powerful, too multifaceted not to have multiple points of entry. But the real question is, if you're going to send e-mail with photo attachments, how are you going to do that? I would argue that you're going to do that on a standard, fairly rich PC, not on a handheld device. As long as it works that way, the PC is still at the center of the action.

prospects, arguing it lacks expertise in custom chips and analog circuits—both crucial for networking. "Intel doesn't understand the communications market," snaps John T. Dickson, president of Lucent Microelectronics Group, the No. 1 supplier of communications chips. What's more, says Charles Boucher of Bear, Stearns & Co., after seeing how Intel sucked the profits out of the PC makers, networking companies "are suspicious of their intentions."

Adding talent through acquisitions could help, but Intel's track record in promoting outsiders is poor: Only three CEOs from the 20 companies Intel has bought in the last three years are now among its top 92 executives. Most others have stayed, but they toil deeper in the ranks. By contrast, Cisco's top tier is populated with former heads of acquired companies. Intel acknowledges, too, that while its overall turnover remains an enviable 4% per year, it has had trouble holding on to younger, midlevel managers who are defecting to dot-coms. Says one former Intel exec: "There aren't any whiz kids there."

Barrett is undaunted. He's driving Intel at a pace it has never known before, even during the heyday of "only-the-paranoid-survive" Grove. The new chief executive is bent on leaving a legacy every bit as large as Grove's, but he's managing a far more complex enterprise facing much greater challenges. If anything, the need to prove that Intel's success wasn't just a fluke has its managers fired up. "We felt like we had succeeded before the Net," says Sean Maloney, Intel's worldwide sales and marketing manager. "Now, we have to prove it all over again." And show the world that Intel is no creosote bush.

Source: Andy Reinhardt, "The New Intel," *Business Week*, March 13, 2000, 110–24.

Case 6–6
Pfizer, Inc., Animal Health Products (B)

Gail Oss, territory manager of the Pfizer, Inc., Animal Health Group in western Montana and southeastern Idaho, was driving back to her home office after a day of visiting cattle ranchers in her territory. The combination of the spring sunshine warming the air and the snowcapped peaks of the Bitterroot Mountains provided a stunningly beautiful backdrop for her drive, but the majestic beauty provided little relief for her troubled thoughts.

The North American Free Trade Agreement with Canada and Mexico had hit the local ranchers particularly hard. The influx of beef cattle into the U.S. market from those countries, as well as beef from other countries (e.g., Australia) that entered the United States as a result of more lenient import restrictions in Mexico, had wreaked havoc over the last year. Prices of beef had declined precipitously from the prior year. Ranchers in the past had retained sufficient reserves to come back from a bad year, but this year things were particularly bad. The prices being offered for the calves by the feedlot operators were in many cases lower than the costs of raising those calves. Ranchers' objectives had changed from making a modest income from their cattle operations to minimizing their losses.

In this environment, ranchers were actively seeking ways to cut costs. Gail sold high-quality animal health products, often at a premium price. One way in which ranchers could cut costs was to scrimp on animal health-care products such as vaccines and antibiotics or switch to a lower-cost alternative. The current environment posed a particularly severe threat not only to Gail's company but also to her livelihood. Gail had spent a substantial amount of time and effort cultivating long-term relationships with these ranchers, many of whom she had had to convince of her credibility, given her gender. Because of the time and effort she had spent cultivating these relationships, as well as the camaraderie she felt with her customers, she did not want to see the ranchers in her territory go under. Ranching was an important part of the history of Montana; many ranchers had ties to the land going back generations. They took pride in producing the food for many tables in the United States and other areas of the world. Gail felt that Pfizer could use its fairly significant resources to

This case was prepared by Jakki Mohr and Sara Streeter, University of Montana. Some of the information in this case has been modified to protect the proprietary nature of firms' marketing strategies. The case is intended to be used as a basis for class discussion rather than to illustrate either effective or ineffective marketing strategies. Support from The Institute for the Study of Business Markets, Pennsylvania State University, is greatly appreciated.

EXHIBIT 1
Supply Chain for Beef

| Cow/Calf Producers | → | Feedlot | → | Meatpacker | → | Customers (food service, retail, etc.) |

help these ranchers. Merely lowering the price of her products (if that was possible) would be merely a Band-Aid solution to the problem.

As part of Gail's weekly responsibilities, she communicated via an automated computer system to her sales manager, Tom Brooks (also in Montana), and to the marketing managers at headquarters (in Exton, Pennsylvania). She knew she needed to report the severity of the situation, but more important, she wanted to encourage headquarters to take the bull by the horns, so to speak. She was pondering the message she would write that evening from her kitchen table.

Industry Background

The supply chain (Exhibit 1) for beef begins with the cow/calf producer (the commercial rancher). Commercial ranchers are in the business of breeding and raising cattle for the purpose of selling them to feedlots. Ranchers keep a herd of cows that are bred yearly. The calves generally are born in the early spring, weaned in October, and shipped to feedlots in late October and early November. The ranchers' objectives are to minimize death loss in the herd and breed cows that give birth to low-birth-weight calves (for calving ease), produce beef that will grade low choice by having a good amount of marbling, and produce calves that gain weight quickly. Success measures include the conception rate of cows exposed to bulls, live birth rates, birth weights, weaning weights, loss from death, and profitability. By the time a rancher sells the calves to the feedlot, the name of the game is pounds. The rancher generally wants the biggest calves possible by that time.

Within a commodity market, basic laws of supply and demand are influenced by those in a position to control access to the markets. Four meatpackers controlled roughly 80 percent of the industry. Meatpackers have acted as an intermediary between the meat consumer and the meat producer. This situation has not facilitated a free flow of information throughout the supply chain, and therefore, the industry has not been strongly consumer-focused.

Exhibit 2 traces the market share for beef, pork, and poultry from 1970 through 1997 and projects changes in the market through 2003. The market share for beef has fallen from 44 percent in 1970 to 32 percent in 1997, a 27 percent drop.

EXHIBIT 2
Per Capita Meat Consumption, Percent Market Share (Retail Weight)

Source: USDA and NCBA.

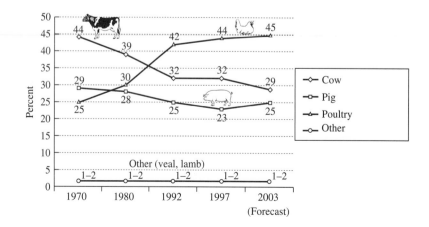

Some of the reasons for the decline were

- Changes in consumer lifestyles (less time spent preparing home-cooked meals). An interesting statistic is that two-thirds of all dinner decisions are made on the same day; among those people, three-fourths don't know what they're going to make at 4:30 P.M.

- Health/nutritional issues (dietary considerations involving cholesterol, fat content, food-borne diseases, etc.).

- Switching to alternative meat products.

In addition, the pork and poultry industries had done a better job of marketing their products. During 1997, the number of new poultry products (for example, stuffed chicken entrees, and gourmet home meal replacements) introduced to the market increased 13 percent from the prior year, compared to an increase of only 3.5 percent for new beef products. And retail pricing for beef remained stubbornly high (although this high price did not translate into higher prices for the calves on a per weight basis to the ranchers, as discussed below).

Based on the historical data shown in Exhibit 3, the beef production cycle spans a 12-year period in which production levels expand and contract. As the exhibit shows, the amount of beef produced (bars in the chart, millions of pounds on the left-hand scale) increased through the mid-1990s despite the declining beef consumption in the United States shown in Exhibit 2. This relationship between production and consumption is consistent with other commodity markets, where there is an inverse relationship between supply and demand.

Some of the reasons for increased beef production in the mid-1990s were

- Herd liquidation: Low cattle prices coupled with the high cost of feed drove some producers out of business.

- Improved genetics and animal health/nutrition increased production yields; indeed, although cow numbers had decreased by 10 percent since 1985 (as noted in Exhibit 4, on next page), productivity per cow increased by 29 percent.

- Exports of beef increased sevenfold since 1985 (to 2 billion pounds); key markets include Japan (54 percent of export volume), Canada (16 percent), Korea (11 percent), and Mexico (9 percent).

Exhibit 3 also shows that the price the ranchers received for their beef cattle varied inversely with production (right-hand scale). Although calf prices were expected to rise slightly through the late 1990s and early 2000s, the prices paid were still far below the

EXHIBIT 3
Beef Production and Price

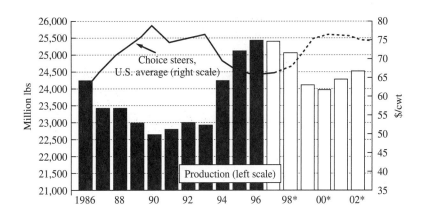

EXHIBIT 4
**Total U.S.
Inventory**

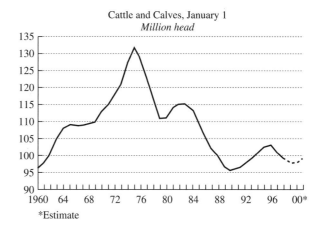

Cattle and Calves, January 1
Million head

*Estimate

relatively high prices consumers paid at retail. One of the reasons given for the relatively low prices paid to ranchers on a per pound basis for their calves was the high degree of concentration at the meatpacker level of the supply chain. As was noted previously, four packing houses controlled access to the market. Some ranchers believed that this gave the packing houses near-monopoly power in setting prices both for what they would pay feedlot operators for the calves and for the prices charged to their downstream customers (the grocery store chains). Although the U.S. government had investigated the possibility of collusion among packers, the evidence was not sufficient to draw any firm conclusions.

To further complicate matters, NAFTA, passed in 1989, had given open access to the U.S. markets to Mexican and Canadian ranchers. The lowering of trade barriers, coupled with weakness in the Canadian dollar and the Mexican peso, made imported livestock cheap compared to U.S.-grown animals. As a result, thousands of head of cattle came streaming across the borders. The flow was heaviest from Canada.

During the summer of 1998, ranchers had been quite vocal in drawing attention to the influx of cattle from Canada. Local governments were somewhat responsive to their concerns. Indeed, trucks carrying Canadian cattle had been turned back at the border for minor infractions, such as licensing. In addition, the trucks often were pulled over for inspections. A private coalition of ranchers calling itself the Ranchers-Cattlemen Action Legal Foundation (R-CALF) filed three separate petitions with the U.S. International Trade Commission (ITC) on October 1, 1998, two against Canada and one against Mexico, asking for U.S. government trade investigations. The group requested that antidumping duties be levied on meat or livestock imports from those two countries. The Montana Stockgrowers Association had been an early and steadfast supporter of R-CALF.

The ITC determined that there was evidence to support the charge that the Canadian cattle imports were causing material injury to U.S. domestic cattle producers. The Department of Commerce began to collect information on Canadian subsidies and the prices at which Canadian cattle were sold in Canada and in the United States. In the case against Mexico, the ITC determined that there was no indication that imports of live cattle from Mexico were causing "material injury" to the domestic industry in the United States. Dissatisfied with the response, R-CALF decided to appeal the case to the Court of International Trade.

Ranchers were doing whatever they could to minimize the impact of NAFTA on their livelihoods; however, some could not sustain their operations in light of the lower cattle prices. The number of cattle operations was declining. In many cases, smaller ranchers were selling out to their larger neighbors. This reality was reflected in the cattle inventory statistics shown in Exhibit 4.

The number of cattle kept by U.S. ranchers had declined from a high of approximately 132 million head in 1975 to just under 100 million head in 1998. As was noted previously, improvements in genetics and animal health and nutrition allowed ranchers to increase production yields even with fewer head.

Additional Industry Changes

Some of the changes that had occurred in the poultry and pork industries, including more ready-to-eat products and branded products, were expected to import into the cattle industry. Industry analysts believed that the beef industry would need to develop products that could be more easily prepared and develop branded products that consumers could recognize and rely on for quality and convenience. In addition, industry analysts believed that the beef industry would have to improve the quality of its products (in terms of more consistent taste and tenderness), as currently only 25 percent of the beef produced met quality targets.

The development of branded beef would require a tracking system from "birth to beef" in the supply chain. Such tracking would allow standardized health, quality, and management protocols as well as improved feedback through the entire production model. This change would also necessitate that the producers be more closely linked to the feedlots to improve the quality of the beef. Branded beef production would move the industry from a cost-based (production) model to a value-added model. Better coordination along the supply chain would ensure an increased flow of information from the consumer to the producer. Alliances between the cow/calf producer and the feedlots would allow ranchers to better track the success of their calves (based on health and weight gain). Such data could allow the ranchers to further improve the genetics of their herds by tracking which cow/bull combinations had delivered the higher-yield calves. As part of these trends, some degree of integration or vertical coordination will occur in the beef industry. Ranchers will have to participate to ensure market access for their product. Ranchers will have to think beyond the boundaries of their own ranches.

Pfizer Animal Health Group

Pfizer, Inc., is a research-based, diversified health-care company with global operations. Pfizer Animal Health is one of the corporation's three major business groups (the other two being the Consumer Health Care Group and U.S. Pharmaceuticals). The Animal Health Products Group accounted for roughly 12 percent of the company's revenues in 1998.

Pfizer Animal Health products are sold to veterinarians and animal health distributors in more than 140 countries around the world for use by livestock producers and horse and pet owners; the products are used in more than 30 animal species. Pfizer Animal Health is committed to providing high-quality, research-based health products for livestock and companion animals. The company continues to invest significant funds for research and development. As a result, Pfizer has many new animal health products in its research pipeline, a number of which have already been introduced in some international markets and will become available in the United States in the next several years.

As Exhibit 5 shows, the Animal Health Group is divided into a North American Region with a U.S. Livestock Division, a U.S. Companion Animal Division (cats, dogs, etc.), and Canada. The Cow/Calf division falls under the Cattle Business Unit within the Livestock Division. That division is organized further by product type.

The marketing managers for each cattle market segment work closely with product managers and sales managers to ensure that timely, accurate information is received from the

EXHIBIT 5
Pfizer Animal Health Organization

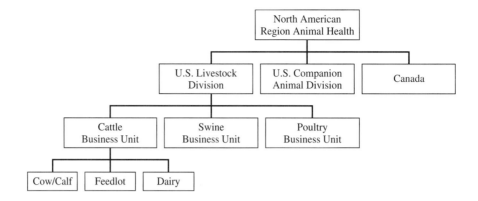

field. Territory managers responsible for all sales activities report to an area sales manager, who in turn reports to the national sales and marketing manager. Territory managers typically are compensated on a roughly 80 percent salary/20 percent commission basis. This percentage varies by salesperson by year: In a good year the commission might be a much higher percentage of overall earnings, while in a bad year the salary component might be a greater percentage of the salesperson's overall earnings.

Marketing Strategy

Pfizer's Cow/Calf Division offers a full range of products to cattle ranchers, including vaccines for both newborn calves and their mothers, medications (dewormers, antidiarrheals), and antibiotics (for pneumonia and other diseases). Pfizer's sophisticated research and development system has resulted in a number of new and useful products for the market. For example, Pfizer developed a long-lasting dewormer that was poured along the cow's back. This technology was a significant time-saver for the rancher, eliminating the need to administer an oral medication or an injection. Moreover, Pfizer had been the first company to come up with a modified live and killed virus vaccine, a significant technological breakthrough which provided safety in pregnant animals and the efficacy of a modified live virus.

Pfizer offered a diverse product line to cow/calf ranchers. Some of Pfizer's key product lines are compared to those of competitors in Exhibit 6.

Pfizer segmented ranchers in the cow/calf business on the basis of herd size, as shown in Exhibit 7.

Hobbyists in many cases are ranchers who run their cattle businesses as a sideline to another job. Traditionalists' main livelihood comes from their cattle operations. Business segment operations are large ranches owned by either a family or a corporation.

Pfizer's extensive network of field sales representatives visits the ranchers to inform them about new and existing products. Time spent with accounts typically was allocated on the basis of volume of product purchased.

Pfizer positioned its products on the combination of superior science (resulting from its significant R&D efforts) and high-quality production/quality control techniques. For example, although other companies in the market (particularly producers of generics) used similar formulations in their products, on occasion they did not have good quality control in the production line, resulting in batches of ineffective vaccines and recalls. Pfizer backed its products completely, using its Technical Services Department. If ranchers had any kind of health or nutritional problem with their herds, they could call on a team of Pfizer technical specialists who would work with the local veterinarian, utilizing blood and other diagnostics to identify the problem and suggest a solution.

EXHIBIT 6   **Comparison of Competitors' Product Lines**

Company	Pfizer	American Home Products (Fort Dodge)	Bayer
Sales and profitability	10-year average annual sales growth increase of 3.8%; average for global veterinary market is 6.9%. Profit rate in 1997 was 8.4%; market share in 1997 was 15.3%.	10-year average annual sales growth increase of 7.8%; average for global veterinary market is 6.9%. Profit rate in 1997 was 11.0%; market share was 9.0%.	10-year average annual sales growth increase of 10.2%; average for global veterinary market is 6.9%. Profit rate in 1997 was 16.8%; market share was 10.9%.
Bovine diseases covered by product range	IBR; P1-3; BVD; BRSV; leptospira; rotavirus; coronavirus; campylobacter; clostridia; *E. coli;* pasteurellosis; *Haemophilus*	Pasteurellosis; enterotoxaemia; chlamydia; salmonella; IBR; P1-3; brucellosis; rabies; *E. coli;* anaplasmosis; tetanus; BVD; BRSV; leptospirosis; trichomonas; campylobacter; papilloma; *Haemophilus*	IBR; FMD; IPV; P1-3; balanoposthitis; clostridia; *Haemophilus;* BRSV; BVD; leptospira; *E. coli;* rhinotracheitis; campylobacter
Significant products for cattle	Comprehensive product line; anti-infectives have formed basis of product line for many years; vaccine businesses also very important; also sells a performance enhancer, virginiamycin; parasiticides, led by Dectomax, starting to make significant impact on sales; Valbazen anthelmintic; broad range of general pharmaceuticals.	Predominantly a vaccine company; antibiotics centered on antimastitis products; anti-infectives based on penicillins, tetracyclines, sulphonamides, and quinolones; parasiticides led by Cydectin; main products in general pharmaceuticals are anabolic implants for muscle growth.	Product range biased toward parasiticides, particularly ectoparasiticides, and antibiotics; overall product range is diverse; some mastitis antimicrobials; wide range of pharmaceuticals, but sales value of each product is limited; focus is more on companion animal market.
Strengths	Strong manufacturing capabilities based on fermentation expertise and capacity; global marketing coverage supported by strategic local manufacture; strong range of new products in early commercialization; broad product range with strength in companion animals	Leading global vaccine business; good international exposure; comprehensive vaccine product range; potential for growth through Cydectin	Growing market in expanding companion animal sector; solid in-house manufacturing supported by global distribution capability; business focused on key market areas
Weaknesses	North America still dominates turnover; high proportion of sales due to off-patent products; heavily dependent on performance of livestock markets.	Business with disparate parts requiring strong central focus; except for vaccines, product range is dominated by commodity products; R&D likely to be reduced.	Underweight in United States; lack of critical mass in biologicals; no blockbuster product in North American market; narrow anti-infectives product portfolio; current R&D emphasis away from new product discovery.
Percent of R&D to sales*	5	3	3
Position on quality versus price†	5	3.5	3
Price support of distribution channel‡	2	4	3

Source: Wood MacKenzie Animal Health Market Review and Veterinary Company Profiles, both done on a worldwide basis.
*Specific ratios are considered proprietary. Hence, a general rating scale is used where 5 means a higher percentage of R&D/sales and 1 is a lower percentage.
†5 = focus on quality only; 1 = focus on low price only.
‡5 = strong emphasis on SPIFs (Special Promotional Incentive Funds) and price-related trade promotions; 1 = low emphasis.

EXHIBIT 7
Pfizer Market Segments, 1998

Segment	Number of Cattle	Number of Operations	Percent of National Cattle Inventory
Hobbyist	<100	808,000	50%
Traditionalist	100–499	69,000	36
Business	500+	5,900	14

Pfizer also was very deeply involved in the cattle industry. Each territory manager was given an annual budget that included discretionary funds to be spent in his or her territory to sponsor industry activities such as seminars on herd health, stock shows, and 4-H. Gail Oss, for example, chose to spend a significant portion of her discretionary funds to sponsor meetings and conferences for the Montana Stockgrower's Association which might include a veterinarian or a professor from the extension office of a state university speaking on issues pertinent to ranchers.

The majority of Pfizer's trade advertising was focused on specific products and appeared in cattle industry publications such as *Beef Magazine* and *Bovine Veterinarian.* One ad read, "More veterinarians are satisfied with [Pfizer's] Dectomax Pour-On" and went on to describe veterinarians' greater satisfaction with and likelihood of recommending Dectomax compared to a key competitor, Ivomec:

> Eighty-four percent of veterinarians who recommended Dectomax Pour-On said they were satisfied or very satisfied with its performance—compared to only 51% who were satisfied or very satisfied with Ivomec Eprinex Pour-On. . . . If choosing only between Dectomax and Ivomec, over three out of four veterinarians would choose to recommend Dectomax Pour-On.

Another ad read, "Calf Health Program Boosts Prices by Up to $21 More per Head." The data in the copy-intensive ad highlighted the fact that "cow-calf producers enrolled in value-added programs like Pfizer Select Vaccine programs are being rewarded for their efforts with top-of-the-market prices." Such programs are based on a consistent program of vaccinating animals with specific products and provide optimal disease protection. The programs result in cattle that perform more consistently and predictably in terms of weight gain and beef quality, resulting in higher prices at sale time.

Although the territory managers called on the ranchers (as well as the veterinarians, distributors, and dealers) in their territories, they sold no products directly to the ranchers. Ranchers could buy their animal health products from a local veterinarian or a distributor or dealer (such as a feed and seed store). The percentage of product flowing through vets or distributors and dealers varied significantly by region. In areas where feedlots (as opposed to cow/calf ranchers) were the predominant customers, 95 percent of the product might flow through distributors. In areas where ranchers were the predominant customers, vets might sell 50 percent of the product, depending on customer preferences.

Vets were particularly important in light of the fact that the overwhelming majority of ranchers said that the person they trusted the most when it came to managing the health of the herd was the veterinarian. Pfizer capitalizes on this trust in the vet in its marketing program. When the vet recommends a Pfizer product to a rancher, the vet gives the rancher a coded coupon which can be redeemed at either a vet clinic or a supply house. When the coupon is sent back to Pfizer for reimbursement, the vet is credited for servicing that product regardless of where the product is purchased.

Pfizer offers some trade promotions to vets and distributors, including volume rebate programs and price promotions on certain products during busy seasonal periods. However, Pfizer's competitors often gave much more significant discounts and SPIFs to distributors.

As a result, when a rancher went to a distributor to buy a product the vet had recommended, the distributor might switch the rancher to a similar product on which the distributor was making more of a profit. If it was a Pfizer product the vet had recommended, the distributor might switch the rancher to a competitor's product. Pfizer historically had avoided competing on the basis of such promotional tactics, feeling instead that redirecting such funds back into R&D resulted in better long-term benefits for its customers.

As Gail pondered these various facets of the company's market position and strategies, she decided to take a strong stance in her weekly memo. It was time to cut the bull.

Case 6–7
Capital

It is the end of July 1991 and most Parisians are preparing to leave on holiday. But not Dr. Andreas Wiele. He, as project and executive manager, and the other members of the Prisma Presse team developing a new business magazine called *Capital* have other things on their minds. The zero issue of *Capital* went down well with the focus group they have just been watching over closed-circuit TV. The problem is the market itself. The economic situation is bad—advertising in business magazines has dropped by about 20 percent since the beginning of the year and circulation is still stagnant. Should they go ahead with the planned launch in September or postpone until the economic situation improves? If they do launch, key marketing decisions still remain to be taken: the magazine's price, its distribution, and communication policies.

Prisma Presse: Gruner+Jahr's French Subsidiary

Prisma Presse, with offices in the center of Paris close to the Champs-Elysèes, was founded in 1978 by the then 41-year-old Axel Ganz as the French subsidiary of Gruner+Jahr (Exhibit 1), the German publishing company headquartered in Hamburg, itself a subsidiary of the multimedia Bertelsmann Group. Trained as a journalist, Axel Ganz had already held various senior positions with leading magazine publishing companies.

During its 13 years, Prisma Presse has launched six magazines and acquired two more, increasing the circulation of the latter by a factor of three since taking them over in 1989. All Prisma Presse magazines are among the leaders in their segments (Exhibit 2). This compares favorably with the industry average. Of a total 173 new consumer magazines launched between 1987 and 1990 in France, only 119 (69 percent) were still going at the end of 1990. This enviable track record has earned Axel Ganz such sobriquets as "magazine alchemist" and "man with the Midas touch."

With a 1990–91 turnover of F2 billion (Exhibit 3), Prisma Presse has become the second biggest magazine publisher in France. It concentrates effort on text and layout in its magazines, and outsources such activities as documentation, photography, printing, and distribution. Prisma Presse is structured around the individual magazine (Exhibit 4). Each is headed by a duo consisting of an executive editor and an editor-in-chief, jointly responsible for editorial policies, staffing, circulation, and revenues of the magazine. The executive editor, often working on two magazines, is specifically responsible for financial results, while

This case was written by Reinhard Angelmar, professor of marketing, INSEAD, with the assistance of Wolfgang Munk (MBA 1992) and Thierry Azalbert (MBA 1992). It is intended to be used as a basis for class discussion rather than to illustrate either effective or ineffective handling of an administrative situation. Copyright © 1994 INSEAD, Fontainebleau, France.

EXHIBIT 1
Gruner+Jahr Publications outside France

GERMANY

Magazines: *Art, Brigitte, Capital, Decoration, Elterns, Essen&Trinken, FF, Flora, Frau im Spiegel, Frau im Spiegel Rätsel, Geo, Geo Special, Geo Wissen, Häuser, Impulse, Marie-Claire,* Max,* Mein Kind und ich, Neues Wohnen, PM. Magazin, P.M. Logik Trainer, Schöner Wohnen, Prima, Saison, Sandra, Schöner Essen, Sonntagspost, Sports, Stern, Wochenpost, Yps.*

Newspapers: *Berliner Kurier, Berliner Zeitung, Dresdner Morgenpost, Chemnitzer Morgenpost, Hamburger Morgenpost, Mecklenburger Morgenpost, Leipziger Morgenpost, Sächsische Zeitung.*

SPAIN

Dunia, Geo, Mia, Mux Interessante, Natura, Ser Padres Hoy, Estar Viva, Cosmopolitan*.

UNITED KINGDOM

Best, Prima, Focus.

UNITED STATES

Parents, YM.

ITALY

Vera,* Focus*.

*Joint venture.

the editor-in-chief, usually assigned to one magazine only, is specifically responsible for execution of editorial policy. Each magazine has its own staff of journalists, art team, and advertising department. The advertising departments of the different magazines compete vigorously for business, sometimes against other Prisma Presse magazines. Coordination of advertising policy is one of the tasks of the corporate advertising business manager.

EXHIBIT 2   **Prisma Presses: Product Portfolio, 1991**

GEO
Travel/Discovery of the Beauty of
Nature and Civilization
upper middle class
Monthly circulation: 580,000
Nr. 1 travel magazine
Launch: 1979

ÇA M'INTÉRESSE
Scientific Popularization
adolescents/young adults
Monthly circulation: 350,000
Nr. 1 in segment
Launch: 1981

PRIMA
Women's Magazine
good housekeepers and wives
Monthly circulation: 1,220,000
Nr. 1 women's monthly
Launch: 1982

FEMME ACTUELLE
Women's Magazine
Weekly circulation: 1,800,000
Nr. 1 women's weekly
Launch: 1984

TÉLÉ LOISIRS
TV Magazine
Weekly circulation: 1,220,000
Nr. 4 TV Magazine
Launch: 1986

VOICI
The Celebrities' Private Lives
Weekly circulation: 600,000
Nr. 1 women's picture magazine
Launch: 1987

CUISINE ACTUELLE
Gourmet Magazine
Monthly circulation: 350,000
Nr. 1 food magazine
Acquired in 1989

GUIDE CUISINE
Family food magazine
Monthly circulation: 230,000
Nr. 2 food magazine
Acquired in 1989

CAPITAL
Monthly Business Magazine

Planned launch date:
September 1991

The staff of a successful magazine is regarded by management as a pool of talent from which inside members of future magazines are recruited. For example, *Prima* was the breeding ground for subsequent women's magazines. These insiders usually account for about half of the staff of a new magazine. They are used especially on the art team, because the visual concept across the range is basically the same. Outside recruitment brings in journalists with knowledge in content areas like economics, business, fashion, cooking, and travel.

EXHIBIT 3
**Key Data: Prisma
Presse,
Gruner+Jahr,
Bertelsmann**

	1987–88	1988–89	1989–90	1990–91
Prisma Presse (in Million FF)				
Total revenues	1,621	1,762	1,865	2,057
Growth		9%	6%	10%
Circulation revenues	1,253	1,335	1,433	1,606
Advertising revenues	347	401	405	424
Profits	83	104	119	159
% of revenues	5%	6%	6%	8%
Nr. of employees	414	448	481	527
Revenues/employee	4	4	4	4
Gruner1Jahr (in Million DM)				
Total revenues	2,773	2,987	3,099	3,284
Growth		8%	4%	6%
Profits	223	255	272	200
% of revenues	8%	9%	9%	6%
Nr. of employees	8,745	9,170	9,286	9,613
Bertelsmann Group (in Million DM)				
Total revenues	11,299	12,483	13,313	14,483
Growth		10%	7%	9%
Profits	362	402	510	540
% of revenues	3%	3%	4%	4%

Average 1991 exchange rates were: 3.3FF for 1DM, 5.6FF for 1$, 1.7DM for 1$. The financial year ends on June 30.

Market research, production and distribution management, and some other functions are taken care of by specialized departments covering all Prisma Presse magazines. Tight cost controls create a sense of leanness throughout the organization.

Editorial Principles at Prisma Presse

Axel Ganz has strong convictions regarding the basic editorial principles that he imprints on all Prisma Presse magazines, regardless of their content area.

Reader/Circulation Focus

Magazines derive revenue both from readers (circulation) and advertising. In contrast to some publishers who are more advertiser- than reader-oriented, Axel Ganz's priority is clearly the reader: "Circulation is where the business is. You can act on it—and we must do everything we can to maximize it—whereas advertising also depends on factors beyond our control, like the overall economic situation." A Prisma Presse executive confirms: "Ganz is obsessed with circulation; when a magazine's circulation starts declining, he sounds the alarm." Circulation determines the major part of bonus payments, which range from 60 percent of the annual salary for the managing duo to two months' additional salary for some of the regular staff. "When circulation objectives are not met, Axel Ganz puts on enormous pressure," comments one editor-in-chief. Managers who repeatedly fail to achieve objectives are asked to leave. "In this company, we get rid of teams that don't win," explains one executive.

EXHIBIT 4
Prisma Presse:
Simplified
Organization
Chart, 1991

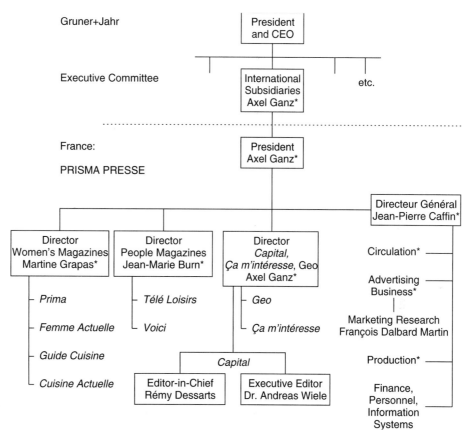

*Members of Prisma Presse's Executive Committee.

Because the bulk of Prisma Presse circulation comes from volatile newsstand sales rather than from more stable subscriptions, reader appeal shows up quickly in circulation figures. Days when circulation figures come out have everyone in a state of feverish excitement. Outstanding results are celebrated, whereas disappointing circulation calls for quick remedial action, which may escalate from minor changes to a major overhaul. For example, *Voici*'s circulation increased from 240,000 at launch to 600,000 three years later, thanks to a series of changes resulting in the complete repositioning of *Voici* from a family magazine to one concentrating on the "celebrities' private lives."

A constant stream of market research data provides each magazine with information about its readers, and many team members are usually present to watch the focus groups which are organized regularly throughout France. This close attention to the reader is rather unusual in the French press. According to one Prisma Presse executive, "Competitors are managed by Parisian journalists who only think of their egos and their connections, and who impose the dictate of their good taste. This is intellectual terrorism. As for us, we can put ourselves in the shoes of the reader from the Creuse [a backward rural area in France]." One observer put it like this: "Prisma is to the French press what Disney is to the French cinema."

A Clear Concept and Consistent Implementation

Each magazine must have a clear concept (for example, "to discover and show the beautiful things on earth, which need to be preserved," *Geo*) and every aspect of the magazine (topics, style of presentation, visuals, layout, cover, etc.) must be consistent with this concept. To Axel Ganz, a successful magazine is like any other successful brand that acquires a distinctive identity: "Why does a reader prefer one magazine to another, although often both cover the same subjects? Because each title projects a specific image and creates a special kind of relationship with the reader." The managing team must ensure that every issue fits the concept: "There may be doubts and discussions, but the managing team must identify enough with the concept of their magazine to sense immediately, nine times out of 10, whether a topic is right or not," Axel Ganz comments.

Precise, Well-Researched Information

Prisma Presse has a strict policy of not allowing advertisers to interfere in editorial content, unlike some other publishers, where advertisers sometimes influence articles that they judge detrimental to their own interests, or where journalists use company press releases as main sources for their articles.

Attractive Presentation

Presentation in all Prisma Presse magazines is geared for maximum readability: short articles ("right length for a ride in the Metro"), short words ("no more than three syllables"), short sentences, and comprehensible titles. "You have to understand the conditions in which people read—poor lighting, ill-fitting glasses, etc.—it's these kinds of details that make the difference," explains one executive. The marrying of text and visuals is vital. The editorial policy of most Prisma Presse magazines stipulates that "topics are chosen only if it is possible to produce a matching visual representation."

The art directors are the guardians of the Prisma Presse formula for attractive presentation. They train the journalists in the magic formula, follow each issue through until the final check, and are always on the lookout for changes that would enhance appeal. Together with the editors-in-chief they comprise the main bottleneck and constraint for the launch of new magazines by Prisma Presse.

Searching for a New Idea

To sustain Prisma Presse's growth, Axel Ganz has set as an objective the launching of a new magazine every 18 months. The new products should have high circulation potential, be innovative rather than imitative, and use primarily newsstand distribution, Prisma Presse's main channel. The only segments specifically excluded are newspapers and news magazines. "There are sensibilities that should not be hurt," Axel Ganz explains. "Newspapers and news magazines deal with politics, and even if we took an objective stand on an issue, we would probably be accused of taking a German view. The time isn't right. In two generations, possibly…"

Axel Ganz, together with Martine Grapas and Jean-Marie Burn, directors for the women's and people magazines respectively, are responsible formally for coming up with ideas for magazines. Ideas may float around for many years, and only a few ever make it into development. In his own search for new product ideas, Axel Ganz monitors market trends in all segments and different countries, until "one day, out of this observation emerges a hunch that a particular area might be promising." Axel Ganz may see promise where others see only desolation. For example, he launched *Prima* and *Femme Actuelle* in a segment that, despite being crowded with 15 magazines, had been declining for 10 years. He reasoned that the decline was due not to a lack of demand, but because the offering was unsatisfactory.

Axel Ganz had a hunch that the business magazine market in France might be promising. Business magazines provide readers with business and economic news and analyses across all industries. The leading title in France was *L'Expansion* (a biweekly), which created the market in 1967, followed in 1975 by *Le Nouvel Economiste* (a weekly). In 1984, the Mitterrand presidency's sudden shift from anti- to probusiness gave rise to an increased interest in business information and triggered a rash of product launches, not all of which survived.

Fortune France, the most recent business magazine launched in February 1988, was an intriguing case. The intention was clear: Take advantage of *Fortune*'s awareness and image among international advertisers and top executives, while overcoming the language barrier which resulted, for the English-language edition, in a circulation of a mere 5,000 in France. *Fortune France* was published by a 50–50 joint venture between *Fortune*'s U.S. publisher Time–Warner and its French partner Hachette, the leading publisher in France. They shared the launch investment of F40 million and expected to reach payback within three years. The circulation goal was 50,000 initially, rising to 80,000 after three to four years.

Fortune France's editorial team consisted of eight full-time French journalists plus a network of correspondents. Changes in content, layout, and paper quality resulted in a glamorous, lifestyle-oriented magazine which had little in common with its American counterpart. "This magazine does not appear to be willing to upset the business establishment. One finds in it neither the bite nor the impertinence which account for the appeal of the U.S. magazine," commented one observer. *Fortune France* cost F30, sold mainly through newsstands, and was launched with a F2.5 million advertising campaign on radio and in the national press as well as by a direct mail campaign. Advertising business took off briskly despite high rates, but circulation remained low. Paid circulation reached 37,000 when *Fortune France* was eventually discontinued in June 1990.

Axel Ganz felt that the French business magazines suffered from two weaknesses. First, the older magazines had not changed much and looked somewhat old-fashioned. Second, all titles appeared light on editorial quality, and most seemed to believe more in attracting subscribers through expensive direct mail campaigns than through a high-quality product.

Recruitment of a Management Team to Fill a Blank Sheet of Paper

In Fall 1989 Axel Ganz transformed his hunch into a formal development project code-named *Hermès,* due for launch in 1991. Funds for development were budgeted in the three-year 1990–93 plan approved by Gruner+Jahr.

Gruner+Jahr was already familiar with the business magazine market as the publisher of *Capital,* the leading business magazine in Germany. But Axel Ganz decided to start from a blank sheet of paper, without any *a priori* ideas about the concept or name. "I don't believe in a Euro-magazine which would be completely identical in all countries. You can't simply export and translate magazines, which are cultural products. You can transpose to another country a concept which has proven its worth elsewhere, but you have to reshape and modify it to adapt it to the local context. Up-market magazines like *Geo* can be internationalized more easily, because these consumers become more similar, whereas mass market magazines like *Prima* address a more popular audience, for which local peculiarities—eating and leisure habits, for example—are very important."

In Spring 1990, Axel Ganz set out to recruit the management team for the new magazine. He found a project and executive manager in 28-year-old Dr. Andreas Wiele, an assistant to the president and CEO of Gruner+Jahr in Hamburg, who had previously worked for one year as a journalist for a Hamburg newspaper after studying law. Dr. Wiele joined Prisma Presse in Paris in July 1990.

Finding an appropriate editor-in-chief took much longer, despite the large number of candidates attracted by Prisma Presse's reputation. Ganz was looking for somebody with experience in the French business press, not a star journalist, but someone willing to apply Prisma Presse's editorial principles to business magazines. The choice finally went to 36-year-old Rèmy Dessarts, a graduate of a Paris business school who had spent eight years at *L'Expansion* before becoming associate editor of the business magazine *A pour Affaires.* Rèmy Dessarts joined in September.

Forty-eight-year-old Thierry Rouxel, assigned as art director for *Hermès,* was the third key member of the team. An old hand with Prisma Presse, Thierry Rouxel brought with him the all-important Prisma Presse presentation know-how to the project.

Through the recruitment process, word got out about Prisma Presse's intentions. But competitors did not take the project seriously, doubting that a company publishing mainly for women could successfully enter the business magazine market.

Analyzing the Market for Business Magazines

Dr. Wiele's major task during the initial months consisted of gathering and analyzing information on business magazines and other relevant publications (Exhibit 5). He found that circulation stagnation was hitting not only business magazines (Exhibit 6), but all segments of the economic press, with the exception of personal finance magazines like *Le Revenu Français* (170,000 circulation) and *Mieux Vivre* (139,000 circulation), which had enjoyed a compound annual growth of 8 percent over the last 10 years. The number of advertising pages in business magazines had been declining since 1988, with advertising revenues dipping slightly for the first time during 1990 (Exhibit 7).

Dr. Wiele noticed some striking differences between the French and German business magazine markets:

- Total circulation was higher in France, yet supply was much more fragmented. France had many more titles, each with a relatively small circulation; e.g., *L'Expansion,* with 150,000 was the leading title in France, compared to 250,000 for *Capital,* the leader in Germany.

- French magazines invested less in editorial content. They employed fewer journalists, everyone of whom had to produce more editorial pages than their counterparts in Germany.

- Subscription discounts and sales were both much higher in France than in Germany; e.g., 84 percent of *L'Expansion*'s circulation came from subscriptions (Exhibit 8) compared to 59 percent for *Capital.*

- German business magazines featured many more "personal service" topics (e.g., how to reduce taxes, manage one's career, invest money) than French business magazines, which left these subjects to specialized magazines such as *Le Revenu Français* and *Mieux Vivre.*

To obtain a broader perspective on the topics that could be covered by *Hermès,* Dr. Wiele analyzed the leading business magazines in Europe and the U.S. This survey provided the basis for a detailed content analysis of the French business magazines (Exhibit 9).

The total reader potential for business magazines in France was estimated at 4.8 million, comprising 1.5 million senior and middle managers in business firms (*chefs d'entreprise et*

EXHIBIT 5   Main Economic Magazines in France, 1991

L'EXPANSION
general business magazine
twice a month
circulation: 149,000
Launch: 1967

LE NOUVEL ECONOMISTE
general business magazine
weekly
circulation: 89,000
Launch: 1975

SCIENCE & VIE ECONOMIE
general business magazine
monthly
circulation: 106,000
Launch: 1984

DYNASTEURS
general business magazine
monthly
circulation: 95,000
Launch: 1985

L'ENTREPRISE
business magazine for owners of
small businesses
monthly
circulation: 64,000
Launch: 1985

A POUR AFFAIRES
general business magazine
monthly
circulation: 42,000
Launch: 1985

CHALLENGES
general business magazine
monthly
circulation: 64,000
Launch: 1985

LE REVENU FRANÇAIS
personal finance magazine
monthly
circulation: 170,000
Launch: 1968

MIEUX VIVRE
personal finance magazine
monthly
circulation: 138,000
Launch: 1979

Note: All circulation figures refer to the average 1990 paid domestic circulation per issue.

cadres supèrieurs en entreprise), 1.2 million top nonbusiness professionals such as lawyers, doctors, and senior civil servants, and 2.1 million entry-level managers (*cadres moyens*). François Dalbard-Martin, Prisma Presse's market research specialist, pointed out that only 45 percent of the 4.8 million potential readers had actually read a business magazine during the preceding 12 months. The main reader target for *Hermès* would be the 1.5 million senior and middle managers in business firms. Only 59 percent of these were readers of business magazines.

EXHIBIT 6   Circulation of Main Business Magazines in France

| | Launch Year | Frequency | Paid Domestic Circulation per Issue (in thousand copies) | | | | Circulation Growth, 1987–90 | Share of Monthly Paid Circulation, 1990 | Gross Annual Circulation Revenue*** in million F (Estimate), 1990 | Share of Annual Gross Circulation Revenue (Estimate), 1990 |
			1987	1988	1989	1990				
L'Expansion	1967	Biweekly	160	175	159	150	−6%	29%	74	31%
Le Nouvel Economiste	1975	Weekly	93	80	84	90	−3	34	56	24
Science & Vie Economie	1984	Monthly	111	116	117	107	−4	10	25	10
Dynasteurs*	1985	Monthly	100	100	100	95	−5	9	31	13
L'Entreprise	1985	Monthly	61	62	65	65	7	6	20	8
Tertiel/A pour Affaires**	1985	Monthly	33	34	35	47	42	4	11	5
Challenges	1986	Monthly	45	67	73	74	64	7	22	9
Total monthly paid domestic circulation (thousand copies)			1,042	1,049	1,044	1,048	1	100		
Gross annual circulation revenue (millions of F)			217	233	240	239	10		239	100

*Circulation as indicated by publisher. Circulation data of all other magazines are audited.
**Tertiel relaunched as A pour Affaires in September 1989.
***Gross circulation revenue = Average price per copy (= Retail price − Subscription discount) × Total paid circulation (domestic and export).

EXHIBIT 7   **Advertising in Main Business Magazines in France**

	Number of Advertising Pages per Year				Growth in Net Rev., Adv. Pages 1987–90	Share of Adv. Pages, 1990	Gross Advertising Revenue,** 1990 (million F)	Share of Gross Adv. Revenue, 1990
	1987	1988	1989	1990				
L'Expansion	2,875	2,845	2,575	2,366	−18%	31%	274	42%
Le Nouvel Economiste	2,940	3,047	2,770	2,259	−23	30	184	28
Science & Vie Economie	242	231	225	224	−7	3	17	3
Dynasteurs	341	623	649	627	84	8	52	8
L'Entreprise	954	1,257	1,225	1,082	13	14	72	11
*Tertiel/A pour Affaires**	451	550	706	703	56	9	40	6
Challenges	222	223	352	343	55	5	19	3
Number of adv. pages per year	8,025	8,776	8,502	7,604	−5	100		
Gross advertising revenue per year (millions of F)	516	652	668	659	28		659	100

Tertiel relaunched as *A pour Affaires* in September 1989.
**Gross advertising revenue: List price per advertising page × number of advertising pages.
The net revenue amounts to approximately 60 percent of the gross revenue, with the difference including the commission for media wholesalers and the advertising agency.

Advertisers in French business magazines were also interested in reaching the top non-business professionals, in addition to senior and middle managers in business. The combined 2.7 million person advertising target group was called the executives (*affaires et cadres supèrieurs*). The price which a business magazine could charge for advertising space depended mainly on (1) its absolute number (or, equivalently, its penetration) of "executive" readers, (2) the share of "executives" among its readers, and (3) the total number of buyers (paid circulation). Exhibit 10 shows the readership profile of the main competitors and the desired profile of *Hermès* readers.

Two focus groups were held with members from the *Hermès* target group in Fall 1990 to understand their perceptions and attitudes toward existing magazines, as well as their expectations. Exhibit 11 summarizes the results.

The Decisive Weekend: A New Concept Is Conceived

At the end of October 1990, Axel Ganz, Dr. Andreas Wiele, Rèmy Dessarts, Thierry Rouxel, and François Dalbard-Martin met for a weekend to decide on the future course of the project. Most importantly, they decided to develop a prototype of *Hermès*. Prisma Presse develops products one at a time and, until now, every Prisma Presse project ever prototyped was subsequently launched.

The next major decision concerned the concept of the magazine. They decided that, compared to its competitors, the new magazine should be

- *Broader in scope.* In addition to the classic business coverage provided by French magazines, the new magazine should cover new trends, management techniques, and business philosophies (similar to the German *Manager Magazin*).

- *More entertaining.* The crucial role of individuals, with all their strengths and weaknesses, should be brought out more strongly; this required well-researched, thrilling

EXHIBIT 8 Marketing Mix and Revenue Structure of Business Magazines in France, 1990

	L'Expansion	Le Nouvel Economiste	Science & Vie Economie	Dynasteurs	L'Enterprise	A pour Affaires Economiques	Challenges
Marketing Mix: Circulation Market							
Product							
Avg. nr. pages/issue	189	112	107	140	190	162	109
Editorial/total nr. of pages	46%	60%	81%	59%	52%	57%	74%
Nr. issues/year	23	50	11	11	12	10	12
Total nr. of editorial pages/year	1,998	3,349	956	906	1,200	923	963
Avg. nr. of staff members	38	40	12	15	21	19	13
Nr. edit. pages/staff member/year	53	84	80	60	57	49	74
Price							
Newsstand price per copy	25F	15F	22F	30F	30F	27F	25F
Subscription discount*	48%	24%	18%	33%	41%	20%	23%
Distribution: newsstand unit sales							
% of total domestic paid circulation	16%	23%	34%	16%	32%	35%	22%
1990 media adv. (million F)	F8.8	F5.9	F2.8	N.A.	F2.5	F5.4	2.4
Per paid domestic copy (in F)	2.60F	1.30F	2.40F	N.A.	3.20F	11.40F	2.70F
% of gross newsstand revenue	68%	38%	31%	N.A.	33%	131%	55%
Marketing Mix: Advertising Market							
Price							
List price per 4-color page (in F)	117,600F	70,000F	65,000F	80,900F	61,900F	59,000F	59,500F
Cost per 1,000 paid domestic circul.	784F	778F	607F	852F	952F	1,255F	804F
Cost per 1,000 dom. exec. readers	162F	232F	230F	234F	141F	N.A.	342F
Advertising department (nr. persons)	7	8	4	4	7	4	5
Revenue Structure							
1990 gross revenue (estimate)							
Gross circulation revenue	74	56	25	31	20	11	22
Gross advertising revenue	274	184	17	52	72	40	19
Total gross revenue	348	240	42	83	92	51	41
Adv. rev. as a % of total gross rev.	79%	77%	40%	63%	79%	78%	47%
% of publisher's total revenue	35%	2%	N.A.	15%	9%	2.5%	10%
Name of publisher	L'Expansion	Hachette/Filipacchi	Excelsior	Pearson France	L'Expansion	C.E.P.	Le Nouvel Observateur

*In calculating the subscription discount, the retail price of special issues (e.g., travel guides) made available free of charge to subscribers is included.

EXHIBIT 9 Content Analysis of Business Magazines in France, 1990–91

	Mismanagement Stories	Success Stories	People	International File	Macroeconomic Data	Photos	Management Techniques	Career & Salary	Money & Investments	Lifestyle & Leisure	Business Travel
L'Expansion	2	2	3	4	3	3	2	2	2	2	
Science & Vie Economie	1	2	1	2	2		2		1	2	
Dynasteurs	1	3	3	2	3	1	3			3	
L'Entreprise				2			4				
A pour Affaires	3	3	2	2	1		4	2			
Challenges	2	3	3	2	2	2	2	2	3		

Coverage of this topic   1 2 3 4

625

EXHIBIT 10   **1991 Readership Profile of Business Magazines in France**

	L'Expansion	Le Nouvel Economiste	Science & Vie Economie
All Target Groups: Magazine Penetration (in %)			
a. Senior and middle managers in business firms	21%*	10%	6%
b. Highly educated professionals	8	4	5
c. Entry-level managers	12	7	4
Total (a+b+c)	14	7	5
Advertising Target Group: "Executives" (a+b)			
Magazine penetration (in %)	15	7	5
Share of "executives" among readers (in %)	62	56	60
Hermès Reader Target Group			
Number of readers: senior & middle mgrs. in bus. firms	300,068	136,466	79,535
Reader profile: senior & middle mgrs. in bus. firms			
Sex (in %)			
Male	80	89	85
Female	20	12	15
Region (in %)			
Paris metropolitan region	42	47	39
Rest of France	58	53	61
Age (in %)			
<35	23	20	29
35–45	34	37	41
>45	42	44	30
Annual Income (1,000 F) (in %)			
<180	15	11	16
180–240	23	19	24
240–360	37	37	32
>360	19	27	21
Firm size (nr. employed) (in %)			
<10	22	17	18
10–50	20	17	20
50–200	14	16	22
200–500	13	14	11
>500	31	37	29
Type of business (in %)			
Manufacturing	32	41	31
Trade	17	17	12
Services	51	42	57

Source: IPSOS Cadres Actifs 1991.

*Percentage of all French senior and middle managers in business firms who read the magazine during the week (*Nouvel Economiste*) or month (all other magazines) preceding the interview.

success and failure stories, the description of interesting personalities, including those working outside Paris, an understanding of how they operated, and a coverage of lifestyle/leisure trends relevant to managers (similar to what the U.S. magazine *Forbes* offered).

- *More useful.* More coverage of personal interest topics like career management, continuing education, salaries, insurance, personal investments, etc. (similar to what the German magazines *Capital* and *DM* as well as *Le Revenu Français* and *Mieux Vivre* covered).

- *More informative.* All articles should be well researched and objective.

Dynasteurs	L'Enterprise	A pour Affaires Economiques	Challenges	Total (in million)	Hermès Target Profile
14%	16%	7%	5%	1,5	
2	3	0	2	1,2	
6	9	2	3	2,1	
7	10	3	4	4,8	
8	10	4	4	2,7	
63	57	66	58		
202,546	231,562	96,924	73,080	1,5	
				(in %)	(in %)
83	77	69	79	82	80
17	23	31	21	18	20
50	39	42	46	45	40
50	61	58	54	55	60
21	22	23	24	24	35
38	39	40	42	38	45
41	39	37	34	38	20
7	10	15	12	16	17
17	20	12	20	23	22
38	38	44	35	34	39
31	25	23	27	20	22
18	18	21	18	21	15
16	26	27	20	18	15
20	17	18	11	18	20
10	11	8	13	8	20
36	29	27	37	35	30
36	45	41	40	41	40
21	14	12	10	14	15
44	42	47	50	45	45

- *More international.* International aspects should be covered systematically and be based on facts rather than national stereotypes.

- *More visual.* The layout should be more attractive, reading should be facilitated, and the photographic material should be original, rather than relying on easily available photos of a small number of business celebrities.

This concept was immediately translated into a "flat plan." Such a plan allocates pages to the various content areas, defines specific articles in each content area, and, finally, describes the order of appearance of the articles. Development of the flat plan drew on everybody's industry knowledge, and many features were inspired by other magazines, both

EXHIBIT 11
Perceptions, Attitudes, and Expectations Concerning Business Magazines

Source: Report on two focus groups with senior and middle managers. Eliane Mikowski, Paris, Fall 1990.

1. The Existing Magazines
- Repetitive in content and style, from one issue to another, between one magazine and the others.
- No title with a clear profile; no originality.
- The journalists are not credible. They are either too ideologically dogmatic or mere spokesmen for the firms, or they provide inaccurate information.
- The readers feel trapped:
    They are obliged to read this press to be informed.
    The magazines make no effort to seduce them; reading is a real chore.
- Readers notice a timid change, but this more concerns the presentation (more color, more illustrations) than the content and basic philosophy of the magazines.

2. Readers' Expectations
- Useful information, instead of nebulous and pedantic discourse.
- Articles should be credible:
    The author's point of view should be clear.
    The article should be rigorous, well written, and well summarized.
    The issues should be put in perspective (comparisons over time, etc.).
- More controversy:
    Stop bootlicking well-known business figures and companies.
    Present conflicting theories and points of view.
    Show some detachment through humor and irony.
    Put issues in historical and geopolitical context.
- A wider angle:
    Greater international perspective, less French-oriented.
    Coverage of cultural topics.
    One or two humorous pages.
- A more attractive presentation:
    Clear table of contents.
    Facilitate reading through titles, subtitles, a clear visual code.
    Many illustrations and schemas.
    The articles should be more "airy."
    One or two very incisive and conclusive articles on specific topics (a double-page maximum).

French and foreign. Two questions were asked throughout: (1) are the choices consistent with the product concept? and (2) do they lead to a clear competitive advantage?

The next immediate step was to produce a first prototype of the magazine by January 1991 and to test it with a group of potential readers. A second, revised prototype would be produced by April 1991 and a third by July 1991. The market launch was scheduled for September 1991.

Prototyping the New Concept

As Prisma Presse had no previous experience in the business market, five external journalists were recruited to work exclusively on the *Hermès* project. Some had extensive experience in the French business press, others were younger journalists. Just as for the editor-in-chief, it turned out to be difficult to find journalists having excellent business/economic knowledge, and willing to adapt to the editorial principles and culture of Prisma Presse. Recruitment remained a problem throughout, and several journalists were eventually asked to leave.

The team was given a separate, closed-off open-plan office in the Prisma Presse building. Access was highly restricted and, apart from the management duo, the art group, and Prisma Presse's senior management, the team had no contact with any other Prisma Presse staff, nor with other parts of the Gruner+Jahr organization, including the journalists working for Gruner+Jahr's *Capital* in Germany.

Organized around the main content areas of the magazine, the journalists immediately started to implement the flat plan. The important role of initiating them in the "Prisma Presse formula" fell to art director Thierry Rouxel, who discussed with each journalist at the outset the concept of the projected article, as well as the number and types of illustrations, and the layout on the page. Constant attention was paid to the integration of text, visuals, and layout as the articles progressed. At other magazines, the journalists' role was usually limited to writing articles, with editorial secretaries and visual staff adding their contributions afterwards. The tight schedule led to a very heavy workload, sometimes forcing journalists to work around the clock.

The first prototype was ready in January 1991. Kept under tight security control, the 50-page dummy had no cover page and no name. The articles chosen were deliberately sensational to find out how far one could go in the direction of entertainment and still be considered a serious business magazine. Many focused on power struggles (e.g., "1 seat for 3 pretenders," "The barons' conspiracy") or demolished well-known business figures (e.g., "Tapie doesn't have what it takes"). The dummy also included a psychological test ("Are you a real boss?"), an analysis of managers' difficulties with their children ("Daddy, I never see you!"), and a map of a fashionable Champs-Elysèes restaurant indicating celebrities' preferred tables.

The dummy was immediately tested with two focus groups composed of target group members. After a first quick flick through they expressed pleasant surprise with the numerous photos, the big headlines, and the clear layout, which made for easy reading. But as they read the articles in greater depth, their mood turned negative and even angry. The magazine was too sensational, too negative ("vitriolic"), and too superficial for them—it was only good "to be read at the hairdresser's."

Undaunted, the team proceeded to produce a second prototype. They made small modifications in layout, headlines, and subheadings of articles already tested (Exhibit 12), and concentrated on producing other articles that would demonstrate the seriousness of the magazine. A 16-page article on the battle between European and Japanese automobile manufacturers was the longest and most intensively researched article.

The second, 100-page prototype, still without cover page or name, was tested with two focus groups in April 1991. The magazine's presentation was again very well received. But this time, the content was also praised for its diversity, factual grounding, and good summarizing of important information. The managers liked the editorial style, which was "the opposite of the bland, insipid style" of the habitual business journalism and reflected a desire to "see things the way they really are." Most of them felt like buying the magazine, reading it from cover to cover, and keeping it for future reference.

As always, Axel Ganz was watching the focus groups over closed-circuit TV. Before the second group drew to an end, he fetched some champagne, popped the corks, and declared "we will launch this magazine!"

Up to this point, the project had cost about F6 million. Funding for further development including a test launch was available through the development budget already approved by Gruner+Jahr. A test launch would require some more recruitment, but the team of journalists would receive no guarantee of continuing beyond the test phase. A full-blown launch like the one Axel Ganz had in mind, however, involved a more massive and longer-term commitment and required the formal approval of Gruner+Jahr and Bertelsmann. Dr. Wiele prepared a 10-page (plus exhibits) report, which summarized the market situation,

EXHIBIT 12
The Evolution of
Capital

January '91

April '91

July '91

explained the product and marketing concept for *Hermès,* and specified the main assumptions underlying the eight-year projected income. If circulation after six months failed to exceed 50,000, the magazine would be discontinued. It was estimated that cumulative investment would have reached F60 million at this point. As expected, the Gruner+Jahr and Bertelsmann boards gave the green light in May and June, respectively.

The Zero Issue: *Hermès* Becomes *Capital*

The third prototype was the magazine's "zero" issue. Identical to a real magazine in presentation and editorial content, its main purposes were to test readers' response to the real product, to scale up and test the production process, and, last but not least, to draw advertising.

To produce the zero issue, the magazine's staff was increased to 32, mostly by hiring from the outside. Almost all articles were new. The main editorial response to April's market research results was yet another increase in the number of pages devoted to "service" topics (management techniques, career and salary, personal finance) to 26 out of 110 editorial pages in total (Exhibit 13). A separate macroeconomic section printed on pink paper (the same color as the *Financial Times* and the economic supplement of a leading French newspaper) was added in the center of the magazine, and a tongue-in-cheek page appeared at the end.

What should the magazine be called? Because it was originally thought that the name *Capital* had negative connotations in France, other names had been considered, including the once more available *Fortune,* which might open doors with advertisers and information sources. Negotiations failed, however, and in the end the name *Capital* was chosen, with the subtitle "The Essence of the Economy."

Capital was the first Prisma Presse magazine created with a completely integrated PC-based publishing system. This permitted several iterations before the final version was transmitted electronically to the Bertelsmann printing plant in Gütersloh, Germany.

Virtually everybody participated in the discussions of each version, including Axel Ganz. "He intervenes less in the content of articles than in the presentation, and occasionally shows a layouter how to solve a problem," commented Rèmy Dessarts. In the end, all remaining issues were solved by hierarchy and, as always, Axel Ganz gave the green light after having gone through the final version page by page, line by line.

EXHIBIT 13
Number of Editorial Pages per Content Category

Content Categories	Capital Flat Plan January 1991	Capital Zero Issue July 1991	L'Expansion July 4–17 1991
People	14	12	3
Business	16	16	14
Success stories			
Mismanagement stories			
International file and macroeconomy	21	22	21
The economy in pictures and special topics	21	18	18
Service topics	15	26	1
Management techniques			
Career & salary			
Money & investments			
Lifestyle, leisure, business travel	21	16	5
Total number of editorial pages	108	110	62

To Launch or Not to Launch…

Hot off the press, the zero issue of *Capital* was tested with two focus groups on July 23 and 24, with positive results (Exhibit 14). Normally, this would be a good basis for drawing advertising, for which Constance Benquè, former head of *L'Expansion*'s advertising department, has just been recruited.

But is this the right time to launch a new business magazine? Since the beginning of the year, advertising volume in business magazines has declined by about 20 percent, and there are no signs of recovery, despite the end of the Gulf war. The entire economic press is suffering. The L'Expansion group, all of whose titles are in the economic press, is rumored to be in the red and reducing staff. *A pour Affaires* merged with *L'Entreprise* in June. *Science & Vie Economie* cut short its relaunch advertising campaign prematurely. The Reader's Digest group has just withdrawn its new personal finance magazine *Budgets famille* only six months after launch.

Dr. Wiele is wondering whether he should recommend that the planned September launch of *Capital* be postponed. If they go ahead with the launch, they have to decide on its price, distribution, and communication policies. Dr. Wiele sees two main alternatives: a "subscription" strategy and a "newsstand" strategy.

The subscription strategy would be in line with the other business magazines: a high newsstand price (e.g., F25) combined with a high subscription discount and a massive direct mail investments, resulting in subscription sales mainly.

The newsstand strategy would be a new approach for the business magazine market: a F15 newsstand price, identical to that of the weekly news magazines, combined with a low subscription discount and high mass media advertising. If *Capital* were published on the same day as these news magazines (Thursday or Friday) and displayed prominently, a significant share of the 600,000 buyers of weekly news magazines at the newsstands might

EXHIBIT 14
Zero Number of
Capital:
Perceptions and
Attitudes

Source: Report on two focus groups with senior and middle managers. Eliane Mikowski, Paris, July 23–24, 1991.

The main attitude is one of surprise in front of an object that is new in the context of the economic press. This is backed up by the following perceptions:
- Great richness and variety:
  "This is life, this is the world."
- Great density and true information.
- Great ease of reading:
  "Freedom of reading, depending on the circumstances, how much time I have, and how I feel."
  "One can read over lightly, for entertainment, or go for a detailed reading."
- A style:
  "Sharp." "The journalists take position," "interrogative"
- Professional:
  "Well researched," "The journalists have good access," "The magazine is pleasant…good pictures…attractive colors."

Overall, *Capital* will create an event in the market. It has great competitive potential both in the business magazine market and in the news magazine market. But readers hesitate regarding the magazine's identity and personality:
- A business or a news magazine?
- A "people" or a business information magazine?
- Superficial or dense?
- Structured or muddled?
- Judicious advice or consumerism?
- Specialization or popularization?

pick up *Capital* once a month in addition to, or instead of, a news magazine. About 20 percent of news magazine readers fall into *Capital*'s reader target group.

Exhibits 15 and 16 summarize the key assumptions necessary to evaluate these alternative strategies. At Gruner+Jahr, magazines are expected to reach break-even within three to four years, pay back within five to eight years, and return 15 percent on investment in the long term.

EXHIBIT 15   **Key Economic Assumptions for Capital**

	1991–92	1998–99
Product		
Number of editorial pages/issue	110	120
Number of issues/year	10 (Oct.–July)	12 (August–July)
Editorial costs/editorial page	20,000 F	Increase: 3% p.a.
Mechanical costs/printed page	0.05 F	Increase: 3% p.a.
Department costs (management, advertising department)/year	6 F million	Increase: 5% p.a.
Newsstand Distribution		
Distribution margin (% of newsstand price)	55%	55%
% unsold rate (% of copies delivered to newsstands that are not sold)	50%	30%
Subscription Distribution		
Average cost of a new subscriber		
Via direct mail (mailing list purchase, direct mail)	300 F–1,000 F per subscription*	300 F–1,000 F per subscription*
Via self-promotion (subscription appeals included in *Capital*)	20 F per subscription	Increase: 3%
Self-promotion yield (share of newsstand copies for which subscription forms are sent)	1%	1%
Subscription renewal rate (%)	50–60%*	50–60%*
Average cost of renewing a subscription	20 F–80 F*	20 F–80 F*
Cost of serving a subscription (administration, postage, etc.)	4 F per copy	Increase: 3% p.a.
Advertising Market		
4-color ad page cost/1,000 circulation	755 F	Increase: 4% p.a.
Avg. net adv. revenue/adv. page	57%	57%
Advertising promotion/adv. page	3,200 F	Increase: 4% p.a.

*The greater the number of subscriptions, the higher the average cost of acquiring and renewing a subscription, and the lower the subscription renewal rate.

EXHIBIT 16   **Circulation Market Mix**

	"Subscription" Strategy			"Newsstand" Strategy		
Year	Newsstand Price (Subscr. Disct: 30%)	Media Adv. per Copy	Subscription Share (% of Total Circul.)	Newsstand Price (Subscr. Disct: 17.5%)	Media Adv. per Copy	Subscription Share (% of Total Circul.)
1991–92	25F	11F	70%	15F	21F	9%
1992–93	28F	5F	70	18F	10F	17
1993–94	30F	3F	70	20F	5F	24
1994–95	33F	3F	70	22F	5F	30
1995–96	35F	3F	70	22F	5F	34
1996–97	38F	3F	70	25F	5F	36
1997–98	40F	3F	70	25F	5F	37
1998–99	43F	3F	70	25F	5F	38

Case 6–8

Martha Stewart Living Omnimedia Inc.

It's a taping day at Martha Stewart's Westport (Conn.) studio, and the spotless halls are humming with activity. Helen Murphy, the new chief financial officer at Martha Stewart Living Omnimedia Inc., nervously gets ready to tape a presentation to investors. Crafts chief Hannah Milman fusses over terra-cotta-tinged roses for the new MarthasFlowers.com Web site, while Stewart's 85-year-old mother, Martha Kostyra, waits to make date squares with her daughter. The scene is festive, if slightly Orwellian. Permeating every part of the building is Stewart herself, chairman, CEO, and founder. Her husky voice rises from the speakers as dozens of screens show her juggling beanbags for her daily TV show.

It's a fitting image. Anyone who spends more than a few minutes with America's most famous homemaker learns that she is one heck of a juggler. On a recent day, Stewart, 58, rose at her usual 5:30 a.m. to work out in Westport before zipping into Manhattan to prepare Greek food with a guest chef, meet with her magazine staff, share dessert with restaurateur Warner LeRoy for the TV show, make a cookie tree on Letterman, and attend a party for her publisher—before jumping in her chauffeur-driven Chevy Suburban for the 90-minute drive back to Connecticut.

The dizzying routine seems to be working. Stewart's Web site racked up record Christmas sales, while her holiday TV special reached 7.8 million households. Recently, the former caterer pulled off her best party yet: a hot initial public offering on Oct. 19. Shares of Martha Stewart Living Omnimedia opened at $18 and quickly doubled, to about $36—as Stewart herself served brioches and freshly squeezed orange juice from a striped tent near the New York Stock Exchange. The stock price has since dropped to about $27, in part because of worries that the company relies too heavily on its driven founder. Even so, the offering made Stewart a billionaire on paper.

Blue Lights

Not bad, considering that Stewart's empire is still in its infancy. The domestic queen gained control of her crown jewel, *Martha Stewart Living* magazine, only in 1997. That's when she bought it for an estimated $75 million from Time Warner Inc., which launched it in 1991. Since then, Stewart has served up impressive gains on her modest base (Exhibit 1). In 1998, the company made $24 million, on revenues of $180 million—a 71% jump over 1997 net income. Sales for 1999 should exceed $225 million, and analysts expect her to near the $400 million mark by 2003. Last year, Kmart Corp. sold more than $1 billion worth of Martha Stewart Everyday products. Kmart's new BlueLight.com commerce venture with Yahoo! Inc., in which Stewart's company has a minority stake, could make those numbers grow.

EXHIBIT 1

MARTHA STEWART INC. . . .
PERCENT OF REVENUES*
MERCHANDISING—10%
TV—12%
INTERNET & CATALOG SALES—13%
PUBLISHING 65%
*THROUGH FIRST NINE MONTHS OF 1999

Data: Martha Stewart Living Omnimedia Inc.

...RAKES IN BIG SALES GAINS...
SALES
▲ MILLIONS └ EST.┘

Data: Bear, Stearns & Co.

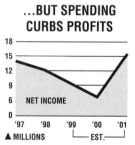

...BUT SPENDING CURBS PROFITS
NET INCOME
▲ MILLIONS └ EST.┘

But Stewart isn't ready to rest on her carefully cultivated laurels. The workaholic home-maker wants nothing less than to teach the masses how to create the good life, then sell them all the gear they'll need to do so. "Our market could be as big as everyone who has a house," Stewart asserts, knocking back a shot of vodka after taping a show at New York's Russian Tea Room.

While she is famed for esoteric tips such as how to make tinsel teardrops, Stewart's biggest lesson may be in how to build a true multimedia empire. Walk into any color-coordinated corner of Martha Inc., and it's clear that Stewart has turned the traditional business model on its head. She has created a brand that's equally at home—and equally recognizable—in a multitude of forms, from books to bedsheets. None of her rivals, from entrepreneur B. Smith to Meredith Corp.'s *Better Homes and Gardens,* has been able to match her reach.

So how has a woman who looks most at home wearing matching work gloves and galoshes pulled this off? For one thing, her view of her role is decidedly different from that of most media moguls. Stewart sees herself primarily as a purveyor of information rather than as a publisher or merchandiser. Her how-to advice, organized around a handful of core content areas, can show up as magazine articles, Web chat topics, or products on Kmart shelves—and preferably all three (Exhibit 2). Holding the enterprise together is a rising army of mini-Marthas, experts in their areas, who skate across different media and merchandising channels with the ease of their famous boss.

But now, Stewart is facing her toughest challenge since building her business. She must ensure that Martha Stewart the brand can outlive Martha Stewart the person. For a woman who has spent her life pursuing both fame and perfection, stepping back won't be easy. Stories of her obsession with details abound. At CBS, set builders still recall her wrath when she discovered that they failed to follow her specifications for cabinet hardware in her TV

EXHIBIT 2
Martha's World

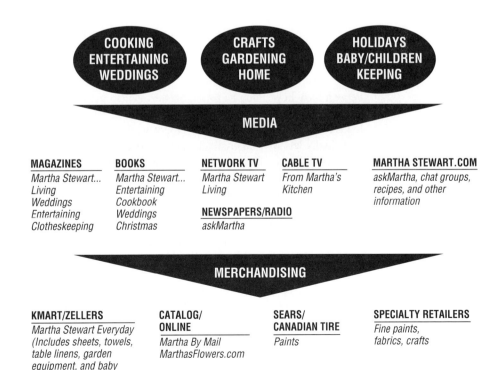

kitchen. But with the roaring growth of recent years, Stewart can no longer oversee every detail herself.

The problem goes beyond the usual management challenges of a maturing business. Stewart's smiling image dominates her TV show, magazine, and product packaging. If Martha Stewart Living is to outlast her, that has to change. While the company is now playing up other talent—and taking out massive insurance policies on its ubiquitous chief—Stewart remains the walking, talking personification of her brand. No wonder investors are worried about the fate of their stock if Stewart should, say, choke on a bad batch of buttercream. "That's a big risk," says Kevin R. Gruneich, an analyst at Bear Stearns & Co., who still likes the stock. Stewart herself is well aware of the problem and says the changes she's making will take her company to a new level. As she puts it: "We're just getting started."

Loyal Fans

But my, what a start. Not counting the weekly "ask-Martha" newspaper column, her media properties reach 88 million people a month. Thanks to good demographics and extraordinary fan loyalty, they also command premium rates, according to the Publishers Information Bureau. Books and magazines still bring home the bacon, generating 65% of the company's sales, while TV and radio account for 12%. But merchandising royalties have risen to 10% of revenue, up from almost nothing a few years ago. The three-year-old Martha Stewart Everyday line of bedding, bath, paint, and garden supplies is also exploding as new items are introduced. Then there are the other retail deals, the catalog business, and a new kitchen-and-tableware line.

What really has investors salivating, though, is Stewart's fledgling Web business. Organized around the core content areas, the site, with more than 1 million registered users, offers traditional how-to advice, chat rooms, and related merchandise. Internet and direct sales accounted for roughly 13% of revenues in 1999. This year, online sales should surpass catalog sales. Still, the Net remains a money-loser because of heavy investment in staff and site development. Also, critics say it's thin on fresh content. But even detractors admit that MarthaStewart.com is a hit with advertisers and consumers.

It's a recipe that appeals to fund manager Zack Shafran of Waddell & Reed Financial Inc. in Overland Park, Kan. He savors the "real dot.com flavor" of her business, although he won't say how much he owns. Stewart is also getting key support from Silicon Valley venture capitalists Kleiner, Perkins, Caufield & Byers, which invested $25 million and holds a 5% stake. Partner L. John Doerr, who sits on Stewart's board, argues that the Web will finally let "Martha create the perfect, personalized how-to experience in a direct way with her audience." Besides helping to lure fans to the Web, Doerr's company could be critical in finding West Coast talent—cyber-Stewarts who can translate her vision online.

Even those who scoff at Stewart's perfect-housewife image admit that she's a stunningly savvy entrepreneur. Her company, which raised $149 million in its IPO, posted record sales of $49.8 million in the third quarter, although the investment in e-commerce shrank profits to $1.9 million, down from $4.7 million a year earlier. Stewart controls 60% of the shares and 96% of the votes. Company President Sharon Patrick owns 5%, and a further 12% is in the hands of hundreds of employees or "founders" who have worked for the company at least a year. Rewarding staff was, Stewart says, a primary motive in going public.

Foremost among those founders is Patrick, who along with Stewart sets the strategy for the empire. The duo met while climbing Mt. Kilimanjaro in 1993 and quickly became inseparable, plotting Martha Inc. as they scaled the final peak. "I admired her ability to put everything down in a clear business plan," says Stewart. While Stewart may have seen a

EXHIBIT 3
Mini-Marthas

A handful of experts keeps the empire humming

GAEL TOWEY, creative director, 47: This former publishing executive joined Stewart when the magazine was launched in 1990. She oversees creative content in all its forms.

STEPHEN DRUCKER, editor-in-chief, 46: A veteran of *Travel & Leisure* and *The New York Times,* Drucker oversees editorial content and has edited *Martha Stewart Living* magazine since 1997.

SUSAN SPUNGEN, food editor, 40: A former restaurant and industry exec, this nine-year company veteran oversees all food and entertaining content.

MARGARET ROACH, garden editor, 45: Roach has been writing books and articles about gardening since 1985 and has worked full-time with Stewart since 1995. (For a profile, see the Jan. 17 issue online at www.businessweek.com.)

HANNAH MILMAN, crafts and holidays editor, 40: Before joining Stewart in 1991, Milman did style and product design for clients such as Donna Karan and Calvin Klein.

STEPHEN EARLE, style editor, 39: A former creative director at Polo Ralph Lauren, Earle oversees information on decorating and the care of everything from clothes to pets.

DARCY MILLER, weddings editor, 31: From her start as a Martha Stewart editorial assistant in 1992, Miller helped develop a Web site and new products, and she edits a quarterly magazine.

synergistic domestic-arts empire as her destiny from the start, outsiders credit Patrick with helping to package the vision for investors and execute it. "She complements Martha's strengths," says Don Logan, chairman and CEO of Time Warner's Time Inc., who dealt with Patrick in the protracted negotiations to sell Stewart majority ownership of her magazine. "What Sharon does is chase the details and do the deals." Not that she's a Martha clone. One merchandising executive calls her "a wild woman, this whirlwind who talks in sentence fragments and is hell-bent on getting product on the shelf."

But Patrick, a former McKinsey & Co. consultant and Cablevision Systems Corp. executive, does share Stewart's vision for creating original, high-quality content that can cascade through various media, retail outlets, and cyberspace. They believe the result will be shared costs, cross-promotions, and ultimately higher revenues and earnings. "If you're committed to content instead of the vehicle, you can do so much more," says Patrick, excitedly flipping through charts from the company's recent pre-IPO road show.

The trick is translating that rhetoric into an actual business. Each of the core content areas that make up the Martha Stewart brand is managed by its own team (Exhibit 3). Each leader must be equal parts writer, product designer, and—increasingly—TV personality. Margaret Roach, who joined as garden editor five years ago, points to a magazine article on Martha's rose garden. Roach used that as the basis for a TV segment, to help design garden tools for Kmart, and as how-to information on the Web. Like her boss, Roach thinks big, saying: "We want to change the way America gardens."

"Not About Attitude"

Team Stewart also relies on an army of marketers, designers, and other professionals who can carry their skills across the different media and merchandising outlets. "The culture is pervasive," says Lauren Rich Fine, a media analyst at Merrill Lynch & Co., who sees Stewart's depth of talent as a key to her long-term success. Indeed, staffers are inculcated with a sense of both the brand and the customer. Stephen Drucker, editor-in-chief of *Martha Stewart Living* magazine, visualizes the typical reader as a supremely confident 40-year-old woman with a part-time job, a nice house, and a family in the suburbs. "One of the things about Martha is self-reliance," says Drucker. He says that you'll never find articles in the magazine about getting a man, dieting, or fixing your hair. "[Martha Stewart] doesn't remind you that you're 10 pounds overweight." And like a starched schoolmarm, she has no time for urban sophistication or overly clever prose. "It's not about attitude," says Drucker. "It's about information."

Stewart believes the real key to capitalizing on that content, though, is to own it. She realized from the start that Martha Stewart could live up to its Omnimedia potential only if it controlled every piece of information passing through its universe. She had long produced and owned rights to her TV show, broadcast specials, books, syndicated column, and radio spots, but Time Warner controlled the flagship *Martha Stewart Living* magazine. As a mere editor—albeit a highly paid one—she couldn't mine the magazine for content to repackage or leverage for cross marketing deals. "They owned it, but they weren't interested in funding anything else," recalls Stewart, whose references to Time Warner seem tinged with "I told you so" bitterness. "Our whole business plan started with how to buy the magazine back."

Time insiders say that forays into merchandising and other areas simply weren't part of their plan for Martha Stewart. Logan says that the split was amicable and that he had long suspected Stewart might one day want control. "When we were originally discussing the idea, we assumed that could be one of the outcomes," says Logan, noting that Time Inc. now has a 5% stake in Stewart's company.

Flood of Magic

What gave Stewart the capital to buy her independence was a new arrangement with Kmart, which guaranteed millions in royalties. She had joined the discounter in 1987 as a consultant, but the deal spawned only a few sheet patterns and intense frustration. "They were very Midwest," says Stewart, cringing at the memory. "This was Kmart. This was maroon and black and dark green. It was bad." In 1995, just as Stewart was broaching the idea of a buyback with Time Warner, the retailer brought in Floyd Hall as chairman and CEO. Hall met with Stewart days after coming on board to try to forge a new relationship. "The word for Martha is 'coordinate,' and a lot of our shoppers are looking for assistance in that area," says Hall.

Kmart wanted to flood key corners of its store with Martha Stewart magic, and it was willing to give her control over her product to do it. Instead of consulting on a few floral sheet patterns, Stewart's people could produce thousands of different products and get astounding play with Kmart shoppers. About 60% of the chain's bed and bath section, for example, is now devoted to the brand, with other parts of the store being converted as product comes out, according to Steve Ryman, vice-president for merchandise. He says Stewart's attention to details such as stitching and fabric weight have pushed up overall quality, but he notes that the chain still has final say over what hits its shelves. The store rejected sage green for the three-month-old Baby Baby line, preferring to stick with the standard pink, yellow, and blue. "The typical American doesn't go to Kmart to find avant-garde baby colors," says Ryman.

Maybe not, but an awful lot of them go to find Martha Stewart-branded merchandise. On the strength of the Kmart deal, Stewart was able to buy control of her magazine—and to concentrate on expanding her empire's reach. To do so, she has had to give staff members, who number in excess of 400, more leeway to dream up and execute ideas on their own. After all, they quickly learn her color palette and style. The veterans know what Martha would say on most subjects, and how she would say it. Stewart splits her time between plotting strategy and keeping up her high-profile TV spots and guest appearances. She no longer reads every line of copy before it appears in the magazine, but she still keeps a close eye on her empire's operations through weekly staff meetings and doesn't hesitate to parachute in if necessary. "If there's something really bad, I'll step in to fix it," says Stewart. Recently, she nixed a "Peter Rabbit" cake that was set to appear in the magazine as "way too fancy" and asked staffers to come up with something simpler.

Think picky rather than perfectionist. While Stewart may revel in her image as the ultimate homemaker, she doesn't always look like a finishing-school ideal. Standing on the set of *The Early Show* on CBS, she'll take a spoonful of pumpkin bread pudding, pour on some rum sauce, and pop it straight into her mouth. If her assistant drops a fork while serving up barbecued turkey, she'll hand a guest the serving utensil to use instead of demanding new cutlery. She worries about her waistline and frets to her mother about eating several *pierogi* one night after work. She doesn't even have a place to stay in Manhattan because daughter Alexis Stewart and son-in-law John Cuti have crashed at her one-bedroom Fifth Avenue apartment for the past year while they renovate their own place—although Stewart could certainly afford a hotel room.

In many ways, the country-club image is undeserved. Stewart grew up one of six children in a Catholic family in New Jersey, modeling to pay her way through Barnard College before marrying, becoming a stockbroker at Monness, Williams & Sidel, and then a caterer. "What bothered Martha about the stock market was that there was an aspect she couldn't control, and that was stock prices," says former boss Andrew Monness. "She was a terrific businesswoman."

But the business of being Martha really began when Alan Mirken, former president of Crown Publishing Group, was so impressed by one of Stewart's catered parties in 1979 that he persuaded her to let his company publish her landmark *Entertaining* book three years later. The elaborate guide to good hostessing has since sold more than 500,000 copies and is now in its 30th printing. After attending her parties, Mirken is not surprised. "She created the most amazing ambience and food I'd ever seen," he says.

In 1989, he helped Stewart arrange a meeting with magazine titan S. I. Newhouse Jr., who helped her develop the prototype for an upscale how-to magazine but later abandoned the project because it didn't fit his group. Time Warner bought into the idea—but not without resistance. During one meeting, an executive leaned across the table to ask: "What if I find out on Page Six that you've run away with a rock star with a bone through his nose?" The curt response from Stewart, then fresh from a bitter divorce from book publisher Andy Stewart: "I don't have time for such silliness."

Family Affair

She has rarely had time or interest in anything but the company, and indeed it's hard to tell where the person ends and the brand begins. She stages photo shoots at her homes and claims actually to cut trees, repair deer fencing, and do the other heavy chores listed in her monthly calendar. Her idea of relaxing is to come home and tackle a project like taking the Chippendale legs off an antique stool to make a new base for her 18th century Japanese lacquer trays. On vacation in Egypt, she took time out to visit factories that made fabric for her line. Her only child, Alexis, 34, who has started helping out informally on the product side of MarthaStewart.com, admits to having been "vaguely irritated" when her mother devoted a *Martha Stewart Weddings* magazine column to her 1997 nuptials. Having grown up steeped in silk flowers and three-tiered *gâteaux à l'orange,* the younger Stewart kept the affair to a distinctly un-Martha-like five-person lunch. "I can't remember 10 seconds where Mom wasn't immersed in the business," says Alexis. Mom doesn't see the problem and has a look of wistful excitement when her daughter's name comes up. "I think she's getting warmer about coming to work with me full-time," says Stewart, who brushes off the notion that she's made any personal sacrifices for the sake of her business.

Stewart has already brought in plenty of other family members. Her mother cooks for the show, nephew Christopher sings on holiday specials, and sister Laura writes radio scripts. But outsiders form the heart of her enterprise. She wooed Marc Morrone to be her expert on pet-keeping after seeing him work with animals on late-night cable TV. She worked long and hard to bring in the widely admired Helen Murphy, who had helped build the Polygram label and then take it public, as her new CFO. "I expected to walk in, roll up my sleeves, and dig for figures and facts," says Murphy. But, in true Martha Stewart style, even the balance sheet was crisp and clean.

The next step is to give the company a life of its own. Stewart rarely appears on magazine covers anymore and is trying to groom some of her lieutenants as media personalities. She is even negotiating two TV shows this year that will not be hosted by her. But Stewart remains the lifeblood—the magic touch that forced Josefina Howard of New York's Rosa Mexicano restaurant to put marinated lamb shank in parchment paper on her menu because so many customers ordered it after seeing her prepare it on Stewart's show.

Despite her close identity with the brand, Stewart argues that her business can live on without her (Exhibit 4). "I have imbued this company with a tremendous amount of my spirit and my artistic philosophy," she says. "So much that emerges here now is a

EXHIBIT 4   **A Picture-Perfect Target**

Building an empire on gilded acorns and perfect pasta is bound to generate smirks. But few have smiled through as much sarcasm and sniping as Martha Stewart. She has been roasted as much as a field of free-range chickens. When not being skewered as a humorless, hard-driving tycoon, she's lampooned for her impossibly complex home crafts.

Her penchant for perfectionism makes Stewart an irresistible target for parody. A boggling array of books, sketches, and products play off the uptight homemaker image. Nash Co. in St. Paul, Minn., for example, sells a line of aprons and other products that carry messages like "Martha Stewart doesn't knead my dough." The Net contains such catty gems as the holiday calendar that had her bear a son and lay him in a potpourri-scented manger. Even talk-show host and fan David Letterman has lists like "10 ways to tell if Martha Stewart is stalking your dog" (No. 1: The dog droppings in your backyard have been sculpted into swans).

"SO SERIOUS." Many brands, of course, suffer backlashes, but most don't have as convenient a human target as Stewart. "She's so serious," says San Francisco branding consultant David Aaker, who thinks spoofs hurt the brand. Her name has become synonymous with a kind of unattainable—and slightly ridiculous—standard in the domestic arts, thanks to projects designed to take hours, if not days, to complete. Tyler Brule, founder of *wallpaper,* a London magazine, calls it "homemaker porn . . . projecting into a world you can't have."

Stewart takes the joking in stride. "It probably just makes me more human," she says. Stewart has even been known to take part in parodies of herself, like an American Express Co. commercial a few years back in which she tiled a pool with old credit cards. But she insists that she's selling useful how-to information and not an escapist fantasy for harried housewives. Tom Connor, co-author of three parody books, including *Is Martha Stewart Living?,* says elevating mundane chores to high art is a joke in itself. "The first time I opened her magazine, I started laughing because it was so over-the-top," says Connor, who featured Stewart making condoms from fresh-killed sheep. Stewart's laughing, too: all the way to the bank.

By Diane Brady in Westport, Conn.

combination of that and other people's creativity." Not everyone agrees. Clay S. Timon, chairman and CEO of brand consultancy Landor Associates, says that Martha Stewart Living has already become a truly mass-market brand. He describes it as "very middle-American, with a slight aspiration—not to reach Rodeo Drive, but to live life a little better." Can it survive without her? "Maybe," he says, "but not yet."

In any case, Stewart certainly has the means to start living life a little better herself. She earned about $5 million in pay and bonuses from her company in 1998 and is guaranteed at least $1.2 million this year. With stock that's now worth almost $1 billion, she can also afford a place in Manhattan that's big enough to house her cherished cats and dogs—and even her daughter, if need be. She'll still have five other houses: two in Westport, two in East Hampton, N.Y., and her favorite retreat—in Seal Harbor, Me. With all this activity in the home office, though, the windswept icon of country chic is planning to move to New York City full-time. Despite her massive net worth and a booming business, she'll no doubt arrive with her garnishing kit and glue gun in tow.

Source: Diane Brady, "martha inc.," *Business Week,* January 17, 2000, 63–66, 68, 70, 72.

Case 6–9

Avon Products Corp.

It's 8:30 on a Sunday evening in summer. Outside the Thomas & Mack Center in Las Vegas, where temperatures have hovered around 110°F all weekend, the desert heat is still oppressive. Inside is another matter. The air-conditioning has made for a chilly stage as Andrea Jung waits in the wings to address the biggest crowd she has ever faced. And Jung herself couldn't be more cool and composed. In her red floor-length ball gown with spaghetti straps and white shoes with sharp-pointed toes, Jung, at 41, looks more like a movie star than the CEO of a $5.3 billion company. As she strides onto the stage, she is met by an explosion of applause from some 13,000 mostly forty- and fifty-something Avon women reps who have traveled to Las Vegas from all across the U.S. to see Avon's new product lines, listen to Engelbert Humperdinck, applaud Suzanne Somers' keynote speech, and do aerobics with Richard Simmons to songs like *Breaking Up Is Hard to Do.* The contrast is striking: the svelte, fashionable, Ivy League-educated, New York fast-tracker preaching to the mostly Middle American moms and grandmas whose fashion tastes lean toward slacks for dressy occasions and sweat suits and sneakers for the rest of the convention.

Still, with a mike in her hand and giant TV screens in the background projecting her image, Jung has no problem firing up the crowd. "Avon is first and foremost about you," she proclaims. "I stand here before you and promise you that that will never change." She vows that Avon Products Inc. can be as big in the women's beauty business as Walt Disney Co. is in entertainment. She confides her proudest moment: Jung, the daughter of Chinese immigrants, traveled to China last year for the first time in her life to meet and speak to women in a Chinese factory. "We will change the future of women around the world!" she exclaims. And as the audience rises to a standing ovation, Jung wraps up with the most amazing declaration of all: "I love you all!"

To the uninitiated, it all sounds like a lot of hooey. But for Jung the stakes are huge: She desperately needs the support of the company's million sales reps worldwide to answer Avon's new calling: getting today's women to buy a brand that hit its peak when their mothers were first trying on lipstick. The pioneer of door-to-door selling, founded in 1886, Avon is at a critical turning point in its history (Exhibit 1). At the dawn of the Internet Age, when three-quarters of American women work, Avon's direct-sales model, dated for a generation,

EXHIBIT 1
From Ding-Dong to Dot.Com: 114 Years of Avon Ladies

Started in the 19th century, Avon has seen it all, from failed acquisitions and hostile takeover attempts to moves into retail and the Internet

1886 California Perfume Company founded in New York by salesman David Hall McConnell. Its first product: the Little Dot Perfume Set. First Avon lady, Mrs. P.F.E. Albee, launches direct-selling in Winchester, N.H.

1914 With nearly $1 million in sales, Avon opens its first international office in Montreal.

1928 First products sold under the "Avon" name, which founder McConnell adopted after visiting Shakespeare's birthplace in Stratford-upon-Avon.

1954 "Ding-Dong, Avon Calling" TV commercial debuts. Company begins selling in Latin America.

1960s Heavy advertising in magazines and television helps make the Avon Lady an American icon.

1970s Stock, which first traded publicly in 1946, is named to the "Nifty Fifty" by Morgan Guaranty Trust.

1979 Launches disastrous diversification binge, buying upscale jeweler Tiffany & Co. Later adds a chemical maker and a health-product company.

1988 Takes the second of two write-offs totaling $520 million for dismantling its health-care investment. Debt reaches $1.2 billion, and Avon stock hits a low of $5 per share after splits.

1989 Avon becomes target of the first of a series of hostile bids, including one from Amway Corp. with Minneapolis-based corporate raider Irwin L. Jacobs and another from Texas billionaire Robert M. Bass. Company successfully fends them off.

1997 Avon.com Web site launched, selling directly to customers for the first time and creating tension with many of Avon's 500,000 U.S. sales reps. Results have been uninspiring.

1998 Sets up mall kiosks around the country, its first U.S. retail stores, marking a major strategic shift.

1999 Andrea Jung named Avon's first female CEO.

2000 Relaunching Web site with emphasis on making Avon reps available online. Separately negotiating with big retailers for a new product line to be sold only in stores.

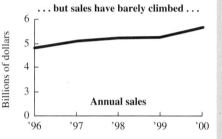

Avon profits are rebounding . . .

Annual net income

. . . but sales have barely climbed . . .

Annual sales

making investors wary

Monthly stock close

July '95   Sept. 5 '00

*Estimates, Bank of America Securities
Data: Bloomberg Financial Markets

now seems positively antiquated. As direct selling gets redefined by such Web players as Dell Computer Corp. and Amazon.com Inc., Avon ladies seem in danger of going the way of the horse and buggy. If it weren't for Avon's success in such markets as Latin America and Asia, the company would surely have faded long ago. Indeed, according to industry trackers Kline & Co., direct selling represented only 6.8% of the $27 billion of cosmetics and toiletries sold in the U.S. in 1999, down from 8% in 1995. Avon itself has seen sales growth—up only 5% a year over the past decade—slow even further, to a 1.5% increase in 1999. And though the company reversed a two-year decline in operating profits last year to post a 16% increase to $549 million, over the past 10 years profits are up only an anemic 4% a year. "We're in one of the greatest economies of all times, and Avon's still finding it hard to increase sales," says Allan Mottus, a consultant to beauty and retail companies.

The huge task of fixing Avon falls squarely on Jung's shoulders. Jung landed the top job last November in the wake of a fourth-quarter sales and earnings shock that sent Avon shares down 50%. Soon afterward, Jung's predecessor, Charles R. Perrin, resigned. Jung, with very little operating experience under her belt, was suddenly running a company with millions of independent sales reps and operations in 137 countries. Now, with the need to reconcile the intersection of the Internet's explosive growth with the company's Old Economy direct-sales business model, Jung is faced with what is shaping up to be one of Corporate America's toughest consumer-products turnarounds.

For a marketer who cut her teeth in high-end fashion at ritzy retailers like I. Magnin and Neiman Marcus, reinventing a dowdy megabrand like Avon would seem an unlikely career high. Precocious from the start, Jung was second-in-command at I. Magnin & Co. before she was 30 years old. At 32 she was in charge of all women's apparel for Neiman Marcus and regularly jetted to Europe for the runway shows. Two years later, in 1993, Jung married Bloomingdale's CEO, Michael Gould, 15 years her senior, left her job at Neiman Marcus in Dallas, and moved to Manhattan. Gould, whose previous job had been running the Giorgio Beverly Hills perfume business that Avon then owned, was already in the upper echelons of the New York retailing *glitterati.* In 1994, Jung joined Avon, making her mark by unifying Avon's many regional brands into one powerful global label.

Now, with her mission at Avon, Jung joins one of Corporate America's most elite groups: women, like Carly Fiorina of Hewlett-Packard Co., who are leading complex and problem-ridden corporations. "She's a young woman with a very big job," says executive headhunter Herbert Mines. "She has an opportunity to really demonstrate her abilities, and if she does well, others will undoubtedly reach for her." But if she fails, the business world will witness the collapse of one of the most-watched careers in American business. Another Jill Barad? It's possible. Even her supporters acknowledge that Jung has no easy task ahead. "Anytime you expand your business beyond your existing universe of operations, you have risk," says Larry D. Coats, portfolio manager at Oak Value Capital Management, which holds 1.7 million shares of Avon stock. "The key is in the execution—the careful, thoughtful, and deliberate execution."

Jung's vision for a new Avon is what she grandiosely calls the "ultimate relationship marketer of products and services for women." Her idea is to rebuild the organization from the ground up into a company that does much more than sell lipstick door-to-door. The Avon that Jung envisions will one day be the source for anything and everything a woman wants to buy. More than that, she wants to give busy women a choice in how they do their buying: through an Avon rep, in a store, or online. "Do you have an Avon rep? I don't," offers Avon board member Brenda C. Barnes. "People like us should be able to get the product."

The new Avon would be a radical departure from decades-old ways of doing business. For one thing, Jung is pushing into traditional retail, which Avon had always avoided for fear of competing against its reps. A trial run of 50 kiosks based in shopping malls is luring younger customers who had never before bought an Avon product. To squash any possible rep opposition, the kiosks are now being franchised to them. And this fall, in its boldest move yet, Avon will announce a deal to create a separate line of products for sale at a store-within-a-store at a major mass retailer such as Wal-Mart Stores Inc. or Kmart Corp.

It's the Web, however, that is Avon's best hope for the future, Jung says (Exhibit 2). Her biggest dilemma is figuring out just where all those Avon ladies fit in. One thing she's sure of: they will play a key role in Avon's reinvention. Jung knows independent sales reps have been the backbone of the company ever since one Mrs. Albee of Winchester, N.H., sold her neighbor a package of assorted perfumes in 1886. Today, reps still produce 98% of the company's revenue, though the top 20% of producers account for about 80% of sales. "If we don't include them in everything we do, then we're just another retail brand, just another Internet site, and I don't see the world needing more of those," says Jung.

EXHIBIT 2 **'I've Gone Through a Learning Curve That's Staggering'**

Len Edwards likes to think of himself as an entrepreneur. Since coming to Avon Products Inc., he has launched a bunch of new businesses. The most successful is a line of children's books and how-to videos for all ages that boasts more than $200 million in sales a year.

All that, however, might be small change compared to what Edwards is trying to pull off now. He is the man behind the Avon ladies' new Web site, which Avon says will have its official launch in late September. But even the most successful corporate entrepreneur has to learn a new set of rules when it comes to the Net. And Edwards is about to come face to face with just how tough it can be to attract online customers. He's facing a rash of new and fast-growing competitors with plenty of entrepreneurial energy of their own. "I've gone through a learning curve that is staggering," says Edwards, 52, who has worked at Avon for 17 years and, Net or no Net, still isn't averse to wearing a well-cut blue suit.

Looking for Action. That alone makes him a sharp contrast to the founders of the No. 1 beauty site, Eve.com. Eve's co-founders, Mariam Naficy, 29, and Varsha Rao, 30, are former roommates who have had more than their share of bumps along the way—such as having to buy the domain name Eve.com from a precocious 7-year-old in Virginia. With financial backing from Pasadena (Calif.)-based idealab! and a new management team from posh retailer Barneys New York, they're moving past just beauty products and into jewelry and accessories as well. "The chances of any venture succeeding are really slim," says Rao. "We wanted to do something where even if it wasn't a success, we'd have learned a lot and had a good time."

These days, everyone seems to want in on the good times. With online sales of health and beauty products at $756 million in the first six months of this year, it's no wonder major real-world beauty names like Avon, LVMH's Sephora stores, and Estée Lauder are all looking for a piece of the action. But as Avon and the rest of the pack come online, they have to face the fact that much of what they know about cosmetics in the real world just doesn't apply. For one thing, online customers are more affluent and better educated than the general population. Their purchasing behavior is different, too. Generally, makeup and skin care are thought of as "replacement" businesses—70% of what sells is someone's next tube of her favorite cream. But at Eve.com, Rao and Naficy have found that replenishment is only 40% of the Eve.com buying. The biggest share of sales are impulse buys, something a customer has never tried before. And the pair have also found that make-up brands with very little presence in the real world—like BeneFit and Nars—are among their most popular. "The Web is not similar to a physical store," says Naficy. "The shopping behavior is completely different."

Still, a real-world presence can have its advantages. Jim Kenny, chief executive officer of Sephora.com, says that by knowing what the hot products are in the stores, he can better stock his site. Avon's Edwards sees another plus: He says the $100 million Avon is spending on advertising this year has helped direct more motivated buyers to his site. The result is that 4% to 6% of people visiting his site actually buy something—compared with 1% to 2% for most sites.

Sites like Eve and Sephora offer a lot of choice, but's an eclectic mix and doesn't include some of the biggest names such as Estèe Lauder and Clinique. Those brands are teaming up with Chanel and Clarins to relaunch their gloss.com Web site next year. That powerful team may force a shakeout among the online beauty sites, says Forrester Research Inc. analyst Evie Black Dykema. Whatever happens, rest assured that by then, all the rules will have changed again.

Late Start

Can Jung really move Avon forward into an e-tailing future while keeping her reps happy? It's a long shot, but she has an ambitious plan. Jung is promising to offer them more business on the Net and ways for them to better manage the new reps that they recruit. She's earmarked $60 million to build a Web site focused around the reps and the Avon catalog. For $15 a month, any rep can become what Avon calls an "eRepresentative" who can sell online and earn commissions ranging from 20% to 25% for orders shipped direct or 30% to 50% for ones they do deliver. That's good money for very little work. And it's also good business for Avon. Today, most reps still fill out 40-page paper order forms in No. 2 pencil and send them in by mail or fax. The cost of processing that order is 90¢. On the Web, it's 30¢. Says Chief Operating Officer Susan Kropf: "Anything we can get off of paper has a significant cost advantage to us."

Unfortunately for Jung, Avon is getting a late start. Back in 1997, the company put up an early but basic Web site that offered only a small fraction of its products for sale. Management consciously downplayed the Net's role to avoid a backlash from reps. But as the importance of the Web became more obvious, it was clear that tack wouldn't work for long. But what would? The internal struggle over Net strategy dragged out over three long years and cost Avon its early online lead. Now, small upstarts like Eve.com are running away with the lion's share of the nearly $1 billion online beauty-products business.

While executives dawdled, reps, meanwhile, reacted with outrage last year when the company took the mild step of printing its Web address on catalogs. Many simply covered it with their own stickers and forced the company to quickly remove it. They also lambasted Avon for selling online while prohibiting reps from setting up their own sites. "It was like Avon was directly competing with the representatives that they claim to serve," says Jennifer Cobb, an Avon rep who quit nine months ago, in part out of frustration with Avon's Web policy.

Jung's response has been swift. To ensure the reps' concerns are considered, Avon has been polling them about the site, asking them what kind of technology could help them. Focus groups include both the Web-savvy and the technologically illiterate to create a site that everyone can use. The result: a Web-site design that gives customers an option to shop with Avon directly but first asks them if they'd like an eRepresentative in their Zip Code. "I don't believe [that] in the future, sitting alone in front of the Internet is how people are going to conduct their lives," says Jung. "What we do is about relationships, affiliations, being with other people. That is never going to go out." Already, 11,800 Avon reps have signed up to sell online. That's a small fraction of the total 500,000 U.S. reps, but Jung wants to get the 54% of them who aren't already online there by offering them Gateway Inc. PCs plus Internet hookups for $19.95 a month. At the Las Vegas conference, where Avon hyped the site heavily, "no one," says Len Edwards, head of Avon.com, "came up to me once and said, 'You're stealing my business.'"

If Jung's Web strategy prevails, she, for one, won't be surprised. Achievement has always been a given. Born in Canada, she grew up in Wellesley, Mass., the daughter of middle-class immigrant parents. There, she and her younger brother were raised in the demanding environment of a family determined to succeed. Her father, born in Hong Kong, received his master's degree in architecture from Massachusetts Institute of Technology. Her mother, born in Shanghai, was a chemical engineer before becoming an accomplished pianist. Jung excelled in school and studied Chinese and piano, which she still plays.

After graduating from Princeton University in 1979 with a *magna cum laude* degree in English literature, Jung surprised her family by entering the executive training program at

Bloomingdale's. As she rose through the ranks there, and later at I. Magnin and Neiman Marcus, she forged friendships with such successful fashion tastemakers as designer Donna Karan and Anne Sutherland Fuchs, then publisher of *Vogue*. Karan, on whose board of directors Jung once sat, today calls her a mentor. Later in New York, Jung and her husband were regulars on the party circuit, where her Armani gowns and good looks were chronicled on the society pages.

Making the Connection

Earlier in her career, some co-workers say they found Jung "aloof" and detached. But at Avon, she has lost some of that reserve, and that has helped her connect with Avon reps. "Four years ago, I saw an extremely private, incredibly brilliant person," says Brian C. Connolly, Avon's senior vice-president for U.S. sales and operations. "Now I see a leader who's willing to tell the story of her heritage, her grandmother, her daughter. She's more comfortable in herself."

From her start at Avon, Jung seemed to look at the company differently than management old-timers. Brought in to study whether it should be moving into retail, she came back with a quick "no," arguing that neither the products nor the sales reps were ready. Her no-nonsense views impressed then-CEO James E. Preston, who offered her a job as head of marketing. Once Jung was on board, Preston became her mentor and ally. He promoted her career, asking her to speak at board meetings. That put her on a par with executives who had been at Avon for decades. "We looked at the market through one set of glasses," says Preston, one of the old guard. "She had a fresh take on what Avon could be."

More than anything, Jung proved she was decisive. She would approve a detailed, million-dollar ad campaign in as little as 15 minutes. Early on, she sacked Avon's ad agency and ordered a complete packaging redesign. She killed Avon's hodgepodge of regional brands and replaced them with global brands like Avon Color, a line of cosmetics. That cut out 35% to 40% of Avon catalog items. "You don't sell anything to Andrea. She buys it or she doesn't," says Mary Lou Quinlan, the former CEO of N. W. Ayer & Partners, the agency that Jung brought in when she ran Avon's marketing.

Still, in 1997, when the board began a search for Preston's successor, Jung had two strikes against her: She had no operating experience and she had never worked overseas, where Avon now gets two-thirds of its revenue. In the end, the board picked outsider Perrin, a former chief of Duracell. Jung became chief operating officer and heir apparent.

Though passed over for CEO, Jung's promotion leapfrogged a number of candidates with far more time at Avon, including her then-boss Christina A. Gold, who soon left the company. Preston remembers a senior manager, with 25 years at Avon, who came to him in protest after Jung was promoted. "I think this is a mistake," he recalls the executive saying. "She's unknown, unproven. She won't be accepted outside the U.S." But six weeks later, Preston says, after Jung had made a two-day visit to Latin America, the executive had changed his tune. "He said, 'You were right. I was wrong. People loved her down here.' I thought, 'Bingo!'" Preston says.

Jung will need to deploy all her charisma as she begins to move Avon beyond cosmetics, jewelry, and clothing into an array of new products and services. Next year, Avon reps around the world will begin selling nutritional supplements and vitamins manufactured by pharmaceuticals manufacturer Roche Holding Ltd., a line that Avon says could reach $300 million in sales within 5 years. She's pushing Avon hard into multilevel marketing, where reps get a percentage of the sales of those they recruit. And she has just launched Beauty Advisor, which trains Avon reps as personal advisers to their customers on what products look and work best for them. It's an area where smaller competitors such as Addison (Tex.)-based Mary Kay Inc. have long dominated. But Jung is betting that she can marshal Avon's enormous sales force to capture plenty of it. The company's offerings could eventually expand to include in-store spa facials and massages. Down the road, Avon might even offer expert financial services and legal advice targeted toward women.

Too Much at Once?

It's a lot to do. But Jung insists that moving fast on several fronts is key. Until about five years ago, for example, sales in Taiwan were growing less than 5% a year. Then Avon's management in Taiwan introduced multilevel marketing and opened showrooms to sell Avon products directly to consumers. The payoff: Avon is now growing 20% a year in Taiwan.

Still, some wonder whether Jung isn't pushing too hard. In the late 1970s and 1980s, Avon went on an expansion tear, purchasing jewelry retailer Tiffany & Co., perfumer Giorgio Beverly Hills, and even a health-care company. Almost all lost the company money, and the result was $1.2 billion in debt and three hostile takeover bids in the early 1990s. "Their efforts at distribution and diversification," says Kline & Co. consultant Susan M. Babinsky, "don't have a real good track record." And though Avon cites a devalued Brazilian real and some weak holiday sales for its disastrous fourth quarter last year, others say the company was again trying to do too much at once: everything from exploiting technology to striving for double-digit increases in the beauty business, all while overhauling the Avon catalog in the U.S. To avoid a repeat of that kind of debacle, Jung is emphasizing open communication, including setting up a CEO advisory council of 10 top performers from every level of the company and from all around the globe.

That Jung, with her expensive designer suits and elegant jewelry, has found a way to bond with the average Avon rep may be her most surprising feat. As she walked the halls of the convention in the days leading up to her speech, Jung couldn't go more than a few steps without crowds asking her to pose for a group photo or sign an autograph. "I'm going to take a photo and have it blown up and put it on my wall for motivation," said Julie A. Mann, a 24-year-old rep from San Diego, who waited in line for 15 minutes.

Jung doesn't shrink from the idea that she's a role model, even though it's put her private life sharply in the public light. Ten years ago, she wouldn't have brought her daughter in to work. If she had a pediatrician's appointment, she would say she had an outside meeting. Today, she wants to set a different example, and her daughter, now 11, regularly visits the Avon offices and, for an occasional treat, Avon's Fifth Avenue spa. Not that Jung doesn't have her share of challenges at home. She's now separated from Gould, though they are both raising her daughter from a previous marriage and a 3-year-old adopted son. "She's the kind of woman that most women aspire to be," says Donna Karan. "But you're always asking, 'Oh my God. How does she do it all?'"

Just being home can be a challenge. Jung, who traveled to 20 countries last year and has plenty of long workdays in New York, admits to occasional doubts and guilt. Does her 11-year-old know that Jung is the boss? "Not really. But she did ask me one time what it means to be CEO," says Jung. "I try to make her feel like she's no different from anyone else's daughter."

With so many eyes on her, Jung is under intense pressure to perform. So far, few are betting against her. Since her first day as CEO, Avon's stock is up 23%, compared to an 11% gain for the Standard & Poor's 500-stock index. Excluding a special charge last year, sales and earnings for the first half of 2000 are up 9% and 40% respectively. "She bit off a lot.

The challenges are great," says investor Robert Hagstrom, senior vice-president of Legg Mason Fund Manager and director of Legg Mason's Focus Capital. But "at this point, it would be very hard to give her anything less than A's."

That's good for starters. Now Jung has to bring the same magic that she showed off in Las Vegas to the bottom line. Maybe then, Jung can turn Avon back into an "A" company.

Source: Nanette Bynes, "Avon: The New Calling," *Business Week,* September 18, 2000, 136–48.

Case 6–10

Konark Television India

On December 1, 1990, Mr. Ashok Bhalla began to prepare for a meeting scheduled for the next week with his boss, Mr. Atul Singh. The meeting would focus on distribution strategy for Konark Television Ltd., a medium-size manufacturer of television sets in India. At issue was the nature of immediate actions to be taken as well as long-range planning. Mr. Bhalla was the managing director of Konark, responsible for a variety of activities, including marketing. Mr. Singh was the president.

The Television Industry in India

The television industry in India started in late 1959 with the Indian government using a UNESCO grant to build a small transmitter in New Delhi. The station soon began to broadcast short programs promoting education, health, and family planning. Daily transmissions were limited to 20 minutes. In 1965 the station began broadcasting variety and entertainment programs and expanded its programming to one hour per day. Programming increased to three hours per day in 1970 and to four hours by 1976, when commercials were first permitted. The number of transmission centers in the country grew slowly but steadily during this period.

In July 1982 the Indian government announced a special expansion plan, providing 680 million rupees (Rs) to extend its television network to cover about 70 percent of India's population. By early 1988 the 245 TV transmitters in operation were estimated to have met this goal. The government then authorized the construction of 417 new transmitters, which would raise network coverage to over 80 percent of India's population. By late 1990 daily programming averaged almost 11 hours per day, making television the most popular medium of information, entertainment, and education in India. The network itself consisted of one channel except in large metropolitan areas, where a second channel was available. Both television channels were owned and operated by the government.

Despite the huge increase in network coverage, many in the TV industry still would describe the Indian government's attitude toward television as conservative. In fact, some would say that it was only the pressure of TV broadcasts from neighboring Sri Lanka and Pakistan that forced India's rapid expansion. Current policy was to view the industry as a luxury industry capable of bearing heavy taxes. Thus, the government charged Indian

This case was written by Fulbright Lecturer and Associate Professor James E. Nelson, University of Colorado at Boulder, and Dr. Piyush K. Sinha, associate professor, Xavier Institute of Management, Bhubaneswar, India. The authors thank Professor Roger A. Kerin, Southern Methodist University, for his helpful comments on this case. The case is intended for educational purposes rather than to illustrate either effective or ineffective decision making. Some data in the case are disguised. © 1991 by James E. Nelson.

EXHIBIT 1
**Production of TV
Sets in India
(00,000 omitted)**

| Year | Black and White | | Color | Total |
	36 cm*	51 cm*		
1980	—	3.1	—	3.1
1981	—	3.7	—	3.7
1982	—	4.4	—	4.4
1983	—	5.7	0.7	6.4
1984	1.8	6.6	2.8	11.2
1985	4.4	13.6	6.9	24.9
1986	8.2	13.3	9.0	30.5
1987	17.0	14.0	12.0	43.0
1988	28.0	16.0	13.0	57.0
1989	32.0†	18.0†	13.0†	63.0†

*Diagonal screen measurement.
†Estimated.

manufacturers high import duties on the foreign manufactured components that they purchased plus heavy excise duties on sets they assembled; in addition, state governments charged consumers sales taxes that ranged from 1 to 17 percent. The result was that duties and taxes accounted for almost one-half of the retail price of a color TV set and about one-third of the retail price of a black and white set. Retail prices of TV sets in India were estimated at almost double the prevalent world prices.

Such high prices limited demand. The number of sets in use in 1990 was estimated at about 25 million. This number provided coverage to about 15 percent of the country's population, assuming five viewers per set. To increase coverage to 80 percent of the population would require over 100 million additional TV sets, again assuming five viewers per set. This figure represented a huge latent demand, almost 16 years of production at 1989 levels (see Exhibit 1). Many in the industry expected that the production and sales of TV sets would grow rapidly if prices were reduced.

Indian Consumers

The population of India was estimated at approximately 850 million people. The majority lived in rural areas and small villages. The gross domestic product per capita was estimated at $450 for 1990.

In sharp contrast to the masses, however, the television market concentrated on the affluent middle and upper social classes, variously estimated at some 12 percent to 25 percent of the total population. Members of this segment exhibited a distinctly urban lifestyle. They owned videocassette recorders, portable radiocassette players, motor scooters, and compact cars. They earned MBA degrees, exercised in health spas, and traveled abroad. They lived in dual-income households, sent their children to private schools, and practiced family planning. In short, members of this segment exhibited tastes and purchase behaviors much like those of their middle-class, professional counterparts in the United States and Europe.

While there was no formal marketing research available, Mr. Bhalla thought he knew the consumer fairly well: "The typical purchase probably represents a joint decision by the husband and wife to buy. After all, they will be spending over one month's salary for our most popular color model." That model was now priced at retail at Rs 11,300, slightly less than the retail prices of many national brands. However, a majority in the target segment probably did not perceive a price advantage for Konark. Indeed, the segment seemed somewhat insensitive to differentials in the range of Rs 10,000 to Rs 14,000, considering their TV sets to be valued possessions that added to the furnishing of their drawing rooms. Rather than price, most consumers seemed more influenced by promotion and dealer activities.

TV Manufacturers in India

Approximately 140 different companies manufactured TV sets in India in 1989. However, many produced fewer than 1,000 sets per year and could not be considered major competitors. Further, Mr. Bhalla expected that many would not survive 1990; the trend definitely was toward a competition between 20 or 30 large firms. Most manufacturers sold in India only, although a few had begun to export sets (mostly black and white) to nearby countries.

Most competitors were private companies whose actions ultimately were evaluated by a board of directors and shareholders. Typical of this group was Videocon. The company was formed in 1983, yet it was thought to be India's largest producer of color sets. A recent trade journal article had attributed Videocon's success to a strategy that combined higher dealer margins (2 percent higher than industry norms), attractive dealer incentives (Singapore trips, etc.), a reasonably good dealer network (about 200 dealers in 18 of India's 25 states), an excellent price range (from Rs 7,000 to Rs 18,000), and an advertising campaign that featured Indian film star Sridevi dressed in a Japanese kimono. Onida, the other leader in color, took a different approach. Its margins were slightly below industry standards, its prices were higher (Rs 13,000 to Rs 15,000), and its advertising strategy was the most aggressive in the industry. Many consumers seemed sold on Onida before they ever visited a retailer.

The major competitors in the black and white market were considered by Mr. Bhalla to be Crown, Salora, Bush, and Dyanora. Those four companies distributed black and white sets to most major markets in the country. (Crown and Bush manufactured color sets as well.) The strengths of these competitors were considered to be high brand recognition and strong dealer networks. In addition, several Indian states had one or two brands, such as Konark and Uptron, whose local success depended greatly on tax shelters provided by state governments.

All TV sets produced by the different manufacturers could be classified into two basic sizes: 51 centimeters and 36 centimeters. The larger size was a console model, while the smaller was designed as a portable. Black and white sets differed little in styling. Differences in picture quality and chassis reliability were present; however, these differences tended to be difficult for most consumers to distinguish and evaluate. In contrast, differences in product features were more noticeable. Black and white sets came with and without handles, built-in voltage regulators, built-in antennas, electronic tuners, audio and video tape sockets, and on-screen displays. Warranties differed in terms of coverage and time periods. Retail prices for black and white sets across India ranged from about Rs 2,000 to Rs 3,500, with the average thought by Mr. Bhalla to be around Rs 2,600.

Differences between competing color sets seemed more pronounced. Styling was more distinctive, with manufacturers supplying a variety of cabinet designs, cabinet finishes, and control arrangements. Konark and a few other manufacturers recently had introduced a portable color set in hopes of stimulating demand. Quality and performance variations were again difficult for most consumers to recognize. Differences in features were substantial. Some color sets featured automatic contrast and brightness controls, on-screen displays of channel tuning and time, sockets for video recorders and external computers, remote control devices, high-fidelity speakers, cable TV capabilities, and flat-screen picture tubes.

Retail prices were estimated to range from about Rs 7,000 (for a small-screen portable) to Rs 19,000 (large-screen console), with an average around Rs 12,000.

Advertising practices varied considerably among manufacturers. Many smaller manufacturers used only newspaper advertisements that tended to be small. Larger manufacturers, including Konark, also advertised in newspapers but used quarter-page or larger advertisements. Larger manufacturers also spent substantial amounts on magazine, outdoor, and television advertising. Videocon, for example, was thought to have spent about Rs 25 million, or about 4 percent of its sales revenue, on advertising in 1989. Onida's percentage might be as much as twice that amount. Most advertisements for TV sets tended to stress product features and product quality, although a few were based primarily on whimsy and fantasy. Most ads would not mention price. Perhaps 10 percent of newspaper advertising appeared in the form of cooperative advertising, featuring the product prominently in the ad and listing local dealers. Manufacturers would design and place cooperative ads and pay upward of 80 percent of media costs.

Konark Television Ltd.

Konark Television Ltd. began operations in 1973 with the objective of manufacturing and marketing small black and white TV sets to the Orissa state market. Orissa is on the east coast of India, directly below the state of West Bengal and Calcutta. The early years of operation found production leveling at about 5,000 sets per year. However, in 1982 the company adopted a more aggressive strategy when it became clear that the national market for TV sets was going to grow rapidly. At the same time, the state government invested Rs 1.5 million in Konark in order to produce color sets. Konark also began expanding its dealer network to nearby Indian states and to more distant large metropolitan areas. Sales revenues in 1982 were approximately Rs 80 million.

The number of Konark models produced grew rapidly to 10, evenly divided between color and black and white sets. (Exhibit 2 shows a sales brochure describing Konark's top-of-the-line color model.) Sales revenues increased as well, to Rs 640 million for 1989, based on sales of 290,000 units. For 1990, sales revenues and unit volume were expected to increase by 25 percent and 15 percent, respectively, while gross margin was expected to remain at 20 percent of revenues. In early 1990 the state government added another Rs 2.5 million to strengthen Konark's equity base despite an expectation that the company would barely break even for 1990. Employment in late 1990 was almost 700 people. Company headquarters remained in Bhubaneswar, the state capital.

Manufacturing facilities also were in Bhubaneswar except for some assembly performed by three independent distributors. Assembly activity was done to save state sales taxes and lower the prices paid by consumers; that is, many Indian states charged two levels of sales taxes depending on whether the set was produced within the state. The state of Maharashtra (containing Bombay), for example, charged a sales tax of 4 percent for TV sets produced within the state and 16.5 percent for sets produced outside the state. Sales taxes for West Bengal (Calcutta) were 6 percent and 16.5 percent, while rates for Uttar Pradesh (New Delhi) were 0 percent and 12.5 percent. State governments were indifferent to whether assembly was performed by an independent distributor or by Konark as long as the activity took place inside the state borders. Current manufacturing capacity at Konark was around 400,000 units per year. Capacity easily could be expanded by 80 percent with the addition of a second shift.

The Konark line of TV sets was designed by engineers at Grundig, Gmbh., a German manufacturer known for quality electronic products. This technical collaboration saved

EXHIBIT 2   **Konark Sales Brochure**

Presenting the amazing new colour TV 'Galaxy Plus'

EXHIBIT 2   *(continued)*

The New Colour TV from Konark. 'Galaxy Plus'.
Incorporating all the sophisticated features likely to be introduced in the next few years.

Superior German technology. That's what sets the new 'Galaxy Plus' apart from all other colour TVS.

One of the latest models of GRUNDIG (W. Germany), world leaders in entertainment electronics. Brought to you by Konark Television Limited.

A symbol of German perfection

The Galaxy Plus combines the best of everything: World-famous German circuitry and components. The latest international TV technology. And the most demanding standards of picture and sound quality.

All of which make it more sophisticated. More dependable.

Features that are a connoisseur's delight.

The Galaxy Plus has several advanced features which offer you an extraordinary audio-visual experience, the like of which you will probably not feel with any other make.

What the Galaxy Plus offers you that other TVs don't

Never-before picture quality

Through the world's latest Colour Transient Improvement (CTI) technology. Which reduces picture distortion. And improves colour sharpness. Giving you a crystal-clear picture and more natural colours.

Programmes from all over the world

The Galaxy Plus is capable of bringing you the best of international TV networks. Thanks to satellite dish antenna, a unique 7-system versatility, and 99 channels with memory.

These features of the Galaxy Plus also help it play all types of Video Cassettes. Without any picture or sound distortion.

Simultaneous connection with external devices

An exclusive 20 pin Euro AV socket helps you connect the Galaxy Plus simultaneously with all external audio/video devices: Computers, VCRs, Video games. And cable TV.

While its automatic colour and brightness tuning save you the bother of frequent knob-fiddling.

Catch all your favourite programmes. Always.

You can preset the Galaxy Plus to switch itself on and off for your favourite programmes. Or, for worry-free operation by your children, in your absence.

Your own musical alarm clock

An on-screen time display reminds you of an important programme or appointment. While a built-in chimer wakes you up every day. Pleasantly.

Automatic pre-selection and operation

Select specific stations or external functions, code them in the 39+AV programme memory of the Galaxy Plus. And then, get them at the touch of a button. On the full-function Remote Control.

Handles wide voltage fluctuation

From a heart-stopping low of 140V. To a shocking high of 260V. The Galaxy Plus performs merrily through such a large range.

Richer, better TV sound

A higher audio output (8W) brings you all the beauty and power of full-bodied sound and clarity.

Saves power and money

Unlike other TVs, the Galaxy Plus uses only 60W. Besides, it also switches to the stand-by-mode automatically, when there is no TV signal for over 10 minutes.

Both features help you save precious electricity and money.

From Konark Television Limited

The futuristic Galaxy Plus is brought to you by Konark Television Limited. Through its nationwide network of over 500 sales outlets. Each of which also provide you prompt after-sales service. Should you ever need it.

The revolutionary new Galaxy Plus. See it in action at your nearest dealer. Compare it with every other make available in the local market.

And see how, feature by advanced feature, the Galaxy Plus is truly years ahead of its time. And the competition.

A marvel of German Technology

Konark Television Limited
(A Government of Orissa Enterprise)
Electronic Bhawan, Bhubaneswar 751 010. Phone: 53441 Telex: 0675-271

Konark a great deal of effort each year in designing and developing new products. And the resulting product line was considered by many in the industry to be of higher quality than the lines of many competitors. Circuitry was well designed, and production engineers at the factory paid close attention to quality control. In addition, each Konark set was operated for 24 hours as a test of reliability before being shipped. The entire line reflected Konark's strategy of attempting to provide the market with a quality product at prices below those of the competition. In retail stores in Orissa, the lowest-priced black and white model marketed by Konark sold to consumers for about Rs 2,200, while its most expensive color set sold for about Rs 15,000. Sales of the latter model had been disappointing to date. The premium market for color sets was quite small and seemed to be dominated by three national manufacturers.

Konark had a well-established network of more than 500 dealers located in 12 Indian states. In eight states Konark sold its products directly to dealers through branch offices (Exhibit 3) operated by a Konark area manager. Each branch office also contained two or three salesmen who were assigned specific sales territories. Together, branch offices were expected to account for about 30 percent of Konark's sales revenues and cost Konark about Rs 10 million in fixed and variable expenses for 1990. In three states Konark used instead the services of independent distributors to sell to dealers. The three distributors carried only Konark TV sets and earned a margin of 3 percent (based on cost) for all their activities, including assembly. All dealers and distributors were authorized to service Konark sets. The branch offices monitored all service activities.

In the state of Orissa, Konark used a large branch office to sell to approximately 250 dealers. In addition, Konark used company-owned showrooms as a second channel of distribution. Konark would lease space for showrooms at one or two locations in larger cities and display the complete line. The total cost of operating a showroom was estimated at about Rs 100,000 per year. Prospective customers often preferred to visit a showroom because they could easily compare different models and talk directly to a Konark employee. However, they seldom purchased—only about 5 percent of Orissa's unit sales came from the 10 showrooms in the state. Buyers preferred instead to purchase from dealers because dealers were known to bargain and sell at a discount from the list price. In contrast, Konark showrooms were under strict orders to sell all units at list price. About half of Konark's 1990 revenues would come from Orissa.

The appointment of dealers either by Konark or by its distributors was made under certain conditions (Exhibit 4). Essential among them was the dealer's possession of a suitable showroom for the display and sale of TV sets. Dealers also were expected to sell Konark TV sets to the best of their ability, at fixed prices, and in specified market areas. Dealers were not permitted to sell sets made by other manufacturers. Dealers earned a margin ranging from Rs 100 (small black and white model) to Rs 900 (large color model) for every TV set they sold. Mr. Bhalla estimated that the average margin for 1990 would be about Rs 320 per set.

The Crisis

The year 1990 seemed to represent a turning point in the Indian TV industry. Unit demand for TV sets was expected to grow only 10 percent, compared to almost 40 percent for 1989 and 1988. Industry experts attributed the slowing growth rate to a substantial hike in consumer prices. The blame was laid almost entirely on increases in import duties, excise taxes, and sales taxes, plus devaluation of the rupee—despite election year promises by government officials to offer TV sets at affordable prices! In addition, Konark

EXHIBIT 3 **Branch Offices and Distributors for Konark Television India**

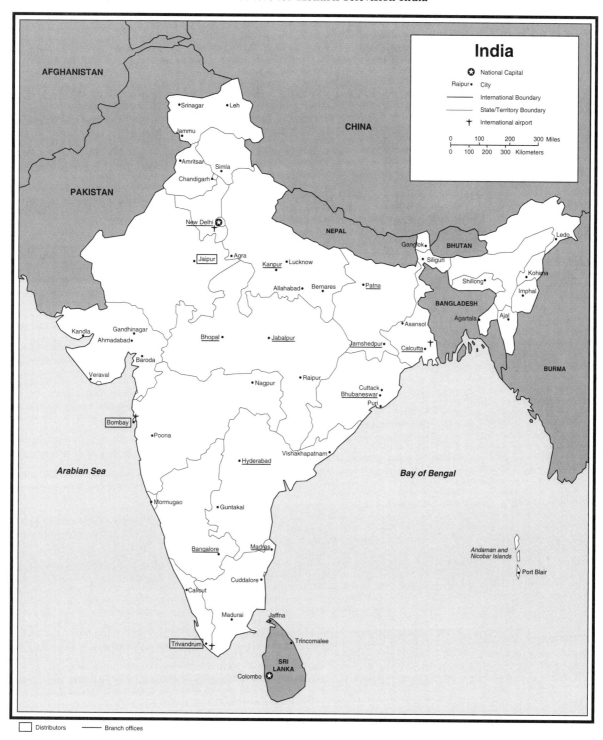

EXHIBIT 4
Terms and Conditions for Dealers of Konark TV Products

1. The Dealer shall canvass for, secure orders, and affect sales of Konark Televison sets to the best of his ability and experience and will guarantee sale of minimum of sets during a calendar month.
2. The Company shall arrange for proper advertisement in the said area and shall give publicity of their product through newspapers, magazines, cinema slides, or by any other media and shall indicate, wherever feasible, the Dealer's name as their Selling Agents. The cost of such advertisements may be shared by the Company and the Dealer as may be mutually agreed to.
3. The appointment shall be confirmed after 3 months and initially be in force for a period of one year and can be renewed every year by mutual consent.
4. The Company reserves the right to evaluate the performance of a Dealer.
5. This appointment may be terminated with a notice of one month on either side.
6. The Company shall deliver the Konark Television sets to the Dealer at the price agreed upon cash payment at the factory at Bhubaneswar. On such delivery, the title to the goods would pass on to the Dealer and it will be the responsibility of the Dealer for the transportation of the sets to their place at their cost and expenses.
7. The Company may, however, at their discretion allow a credit of 30 (thirty) days subject to furnishing a Bank Guarantee or letter of credit or security deposits toward the price of Konark Television sets to be lifted by the Dealer at any time.
8. The Company shall not be responsible for any damage or defect occurring to the sets after delivery of the same to the Dealer or during transit.
9. The Dealer shall undertake to sell the sets to customers at prices fixed by the Company for different models. Dealer margins will be added to wholesale prices while fixing the customer's price of the television sets.
10. The Dealer will not act and deal with similar products of any other company so long as his appointment with Konark Television continues.
11. The Dealer shall not encroach into areas allotted to any other Dealer.
12. Any dispute or difference arising from or related to the appointment of the Dealership shall be settled mutually and, failing amicable settlement, shall be settled by an Arbitrator to be appointed by the Chairman of the Company whose decision shall be final and binding upon the parties. The place of arbitration shall be within the State of Orissa and the Court in Bhubaneswar (Orissa) only shall have jurisdiction to entertain any application, suit, or claim arising out of the appointment. All disputes shall be deemed to have arisen within the jurisdiction of the Court of Bhubaneswar.
13. Essential requirements to be fulfilled before getting Dealership:
    a. The Dealer must have a good showroom for display and sale of Television sets.
    b. The Dealer should have sufficient experience in dealing with Electronics Products (Consumer Goods).

was about to be affected by the Orissa government's decision to revoke the company's sales tax exemption beginning on January 1, 1991. "Right now we are the clear choice, as Konark is the cheapest brand with a superior quality. But with the withdrawal of the exemption, we will be in the same price range as the 'big boys,' and it will be a real run for the money to sell our brand," remarked Mr. Bhalla.

Mr. Bhalla also was concerned about some dealer activities that he thought were damaging to Konark. He knew that many dealers would play with the assigned margin and offer the same Konark product at differing prices to different customers. Or, equally damaging, different dealers might quote different prices for the same product to a single customer. Some dealers recently had gone so far as to buy large quantities of TV sets from Konark and sell them to unauthorized dealers in Bhubaneswar or in neighboring districts. This problem was particularly vexing because the offending dealers—while few in number—often were quite large and important to Konark's overall performance. Perhaps as much as 40 percent of Konark's sales revenues came from "problem" dealers.

Early in 1990 Mr. Bhalla thought that an increase in the margins that Konark allowed its dealers was all that was needed to solve the problem. However, a modest change in dealer compensation had resulted in several national competitors raising their dealer margins even higher—without an increase in their retail prices. The result was that prices of Konark's models became even closer to those of national competitors, and Konark's decline in market share had actually steepened. By late 1990 Konark's unit share of the Orissa market had fallen from 80 percent to just over 60 percent. "Unless something is done soon," Mr. Bhalla thought, "we'll soon be below 50 percent."

The Decision

Some immediate actions were needed to improve dealer relations and stimulate greater sales activity. An example was Konark's quarterly "Incentive Scheme," which had begun in April 1989. The program was a rebate arrangement based on points earned for a dealer's purchases of Konark TV sets. Reaction was lukewarm when the program was first announced. However, a revision in August 1989 greatly increased participation. Other actions yet to be formulated could be announced at a dealers' conference Mr. Bhalla had scheduled for next month.

All such actions would have to be consistent with Konark's long-term distribution strategy. The problem was that this strategy had not yet been formulated. Mr. Bhalla saw this void as his most pressing responsibility as well as a topic of great interest to Mr. Singh. Mr. Bhalla hoped to have major aspects of a distribution strategy ready for discussion at the next week's meeting. Elements of the strategy would include recommendations on channel structure—branch offices or independent distributors, company showrooms or independent dealers—in existing markets as well as in markets identified for expansion. The latter markets included Bombay, Jaipur, and Trivandrum, areas that contained some 2 million consumers in the target segment. Most important, the strategy would have to address actions to combat the loss of the sales tax exemption in Orissa.

Case 6–11
Murphy Brewery Ireland, Limited

Patrick Conway, marketing director for Murphy's, picked up his issue of *The Financial Times* and read the following headline on May 13: "Grand Met, Guinness to Merge." He pondered the impact on his firm. Guinness was Murphy's most formidable competitor

This case was prepared by Patrick E. Murphy, professor of marketing, University of Notre Dame, Indiana, and former visiting professor of marketing, University College Cork in Ireland, and Don O'Sullivan, lecturer in marketing, Department of Management and Marketing, University College Cork. The case was distributed by the European Case Clearinghouse.

This case is intended to serve as a basis for a class discussion rather than to illustrate either effective or ineffective handling of a business situation. The authors would like to thank Patrick Conway, David Ford, and Dan Leahy of Murphy Brewery Ireland and Michael Foley of Heineken USA for their assistance in writing this case.

not only in Ireland but worldwide. Since a staff meeting was already scheduled for later Tuesday morning, he decided to examine the article closely and discuss it with his team. As he read on, the £22.3 billion merger between two of the four largest distillers (Seagram's headquartered in Canada and Allied Domecq, another British company, were the other two) appeared to have much synergy. The article pointed out that the geographic and brand fits were good between the two companies. The new firm, which will be called GMG, will be approximately equal in size to such major multinationals as Unilever, Procter & Gamble, and Philip Morris.[1]

During the 11 AM staff meeting, Patrick brought the merger to the attention of his colleagues. His company was in the middle of preparing its 1998 global marketing plan, and this news brought some urgency to the task ahead. Patrick stated that he felt a major assessment of Murphy's status in the worldwide market was needed. He called on David Ford, his export manager, to examine Murphy's position in the British and European markets. He said he would phone Michael Foley of Heineken USA (distributor of Murphy's in the states) to report on Murphy's progress there and asked Dan Leahy to look into Murphy's status in Ireland. He asked each man to report back to him within a week.

As part of his personal preparation, Patrick decided to dig into the files and reacquaint himself with the company history, since he had joined the firm only a few years previously. He also wanted to find out more about the merger. He rang the communications department to clip and route all articles from business publications on this topic to him. Patrick considered the impact these developments would have on Murphy's brands.

In 1997 Murphy's had become a truly international brand that maintained a unique identity in Ireland. The name Murphy, the most common surname in the entire country, is recognized internationally for its Irish heritage. Exhibit 1 shows that about 85 percent of Murphy's sales came from export business in 1996 and that the company now employs 385 people. He located a report from several years earlier that provided a historical perspective on the company.

Historical Background

James J. Murphy and Company Limited was founded in 1856 in Cork City, Ireland, by the four Murphy brothers—James, William, Jerome, and Francis. In 1890 they were described as follows: "These gentlemen applied themselves with energy and enterprise to the manufacture of an article, the reputation of which now extends far beyond the South of Ireland where the firm's stout and porter have been long and favorably known and where they command a very exclusive sale."[2]

James J. Murphy inherited the family business skills. His grandfather, also called James, had founded, with his brothers, the distillery James Murphy and Company in Midleton, County Cork (15 miles to the east of Cork City), in 1825. These Murphy brothers prospered as ship owners and tea importers and had been paid quite a large sum of money before founding their distillery. This company experienced significant growth and in 1867 amalgamated with four Cork distilleries to create Cork Distilleries Company Ltd. That firm enjoyed great success over the next century and in 1966 joined with the Dublin distillery John Jameson and Son and John Power and Son to create Irish Distillers Limited.

The Murphy Brewery is located at Lady's Well in Cork, whose name derives from a celebrated well on the hill opposite of the premises. It was dedicated to Our Lady and believed

---

[1]John Willman and Ross Tieman, "Grand Met, Guinness to Merge," *Financial Times,* Tuesday, May 13, 1997, p. 1.
[2]*Murphy Brewery Limited: A Profile,* undated.

EXHIBIT 1   **Export Sales versus Total Company Volumes**

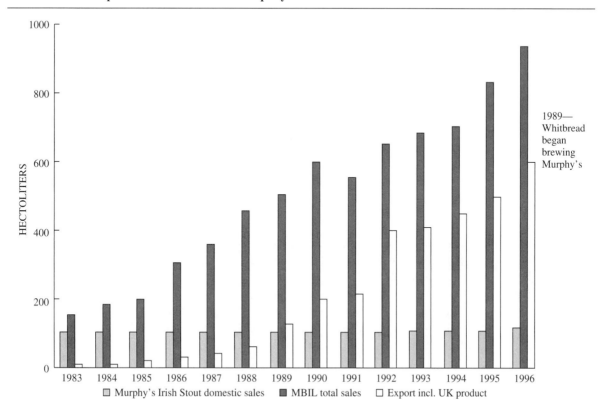

1989—
Whitbread
began
brewing
Murphy's

☐ Murphy's Irish Stout domestic sales   ■ MBIL total sales   ☐ Export incl. UK product

to possess miraculous properties. To the present day, pilgrimages take place to the shrine every year in the month of May. During the nineteenth century Lady's Well was one of Cork's largest breweries and was mentioned in the 1890 publication *Noted Breweries of Great Britain and Ireland,* which indicated that Murphy's Stout had become a formidable rival to Guinness in the south of Ireland.[3]

Initially, Murphy's brewed porter, but it switched exclusively to stout (the name *stout* denotes strong beers—see Exhibit 2 for a description of the product), and this remained its sole beer product until 1965. Over the years the brewery acquired a number of licensed products and developed a wholesale spirits and soft drinks bottling business.

Although Murphy's opened up trade in London, Manchester, South Wales, and other parts of England early in the twentieth century, the company began experiencing financial problems in the 1960s. There was considerable anxiety among the staff of 200 in Murphy's Brewery Cork concerning the continuity of their employment in the early 1970s. At that time they had an English partner (Watney and Mann), which wanted to dissolve the partnership. Colonel John J. Murphy, chairman of Murphy's, stated that "we are confident that we can satisfy" certain financial conditions to meet the demands of the creditors. The company at this time was well over 100 years old and had overcome difficult periods in the past.

In February 1975 Murphy's approached Heineken N.B. (the Amsterdam-based brewery which had been founded by Garard Adriann Heineken the same year the Murphy brothers opened their brewery in Ireland) with a proposal to begin a licensing operation for Heineken in Ireland. Heineken examined the possibilities of the Irish market and found

[3]Company sources.

EXHIBIT 2
What Is Stout, and How Was It Promoted?

Source: Partially adapted from Brendan O'Brien, *The Stout Book* (Dublin: Anna Livia Press, 1990).

Stout is a black beer with a thick white head. The black color is due mainly to the fact that it contains malted barley which is roasted in a similar way to coffee beans. The creamy white head is created from the "initiation" and "surging" of bubbles of nitrogen and carbon dioxide gas as the beer is poured. The gas enters the keg and forces the beer out. It is actually the nitrogen which causes the tight, creamy head.

The word *stout* has long been used to describe strong beers; it also meant stout, as in stout ale. The strength may have been in terms of taste or alcohol or both. Standard stout ranges in alcohol content from 4 percent to 5 percent. The word *stout* gradually made the transition from adjective to noun. The basic constituent of stout is barley, which consists mainly of starch. The barley becomes a malt and during this process is converted to sugar, which is fermentable. When the malt is roasted beyond the normal limits, this gives the stout its unusual dark hue. The highly roasted dark malt is 500 times darker than a pale malt and adds its distinctive color as well as flavor.

The resulting sugary liquid, called wort, is eventually formed. At this stage hops are added and boiled with wort to produce the liquid. When boiled for an hour or two, the hops release oils and resins which produce the characteristic bitterness and aroma. A comparison of the bitterness level among the leading brands of stout conducted by the European Brewery Convention found that Guinness rates 45 to 48 European units of bitterness, Beamish 40, and Murphy's 36 to 38.

Stout is synonymous with Ireland, and nowhere else is stout as popular or as intrinsically part of everyday life. The criterion by which a pub often is judged is likely to be whether it sells a good pint of stout. In the pub, pouring pints of stout is an activity full of tradition and custom. The pouring of the product is seen as having a major impact on product quality. Stout is poured in two stages. First the glass is filled to 75 percent capacity and allowed to "settle" so that the creamy head will separate from the dark body. To top off the pint, the tap is pushed forward slightly until the head rises just below the rim. This activity takes a minute or two and results in stout taking longer to pour. Interestingly, the product is poured in one go/pull outside Ireland.

Stout has its roots in colder climates in Ireland and Scandinavia, and traditionally it has been a winter brew. Comments such as "typically consumed in the dark winter months" and "a seasonal beer brewed only in the winter" are used regularly by stout breweries worldwide. Stout is thought to be a drink suited to quiet, reflective sipping. Both in Ireland and worldwide, it is now a year-round drink.

To return to the definition, stout is often considered a strong drink. Therefore, both Murphy's and Guinness have extensively used strength in their marketing and advertising. Murphy's utilized a circus strongman who was shown lifting a horse off the ground with the label "Murphy's Stout gives strength" for many years in the late 1800s and 1900s. Guinness has utilized posters throughout Ireland depicting superhuman strength achieved by drinking Guinness with the slogan "Guinness for strength."

them favorable, and a license agreement was signed. A marketing company, Heineken Ireland Limited, was set up as a fully owned subsidiary of Heineken N.B. Heineken was well known for its lager beer, which complemented the Murphy's Irish Stout offering.

Murphy's new policy of expanding as a broad-based competitor to the leading brands (e.g., Guinness and Beamish and Crawford) worked well at first. However, the company was hit by recessionary problems, and J.J. Murphy and Company Limited went into receivership in 1982. At that time the company employed 235 people. On July 14, 1982, the *Cork Examiner* confirmed a commitment from the Dutch brewing company Heineken to invest 1.6 million pounds in the brewery.

In 1983 Heineken International purchased the assets of James J. Murphy and Company Limited, which was then in receivership. Murphy Brewery Ireland Limited became a wholly owned subsidiary of Heineken International, a move which gave a new lease on life to Murphy's Brewery. This development preserved the long and respected tradition of brewing in the Cork area and the well-known brand name. Since then Murphy Brewery Ireland Limited has continued its brewing and marketing of Murphy's Irish Stout and Heineken. The adoption of Murphy's Irish Stout by Heineken International as one of its corporate brands meant that the brand became available to drinkers worldwide.

The Heineken Era

Heineken International is the world's second largest brewer (Exhibit 3) and a private company. Its flagship Heineken lager, the world's most exported beer, and the Amstel brand are also brewed under license by third parties. They are produced in over 100 plants and sold in 170 countries on all continents. The Heineken brand is sold in the same green bottle and promoted with the same brand imagery in the same price tier in China, Spain, the United States, and elsewhere. Heineken was the first beer to be imported into the United States after Prohibition was lifted in 1933. The United States is now its largest market.

Murphy's management during the Heineken years has been led by four managing directors. Currently, Marien Kakabeeke, a native of Holland, serves in that position. He assumed the post in August 1993. Heineken has demonstrated its commitment to Murphy's by opening a new office complex in the old Malthouse at the brewery. Murphy's became accredited in 1992 with the ISO 9002 mark for all aspects of operations—the first brewery in Europe to achieve that distinction.

Murphy's Brands and Packaging

Internationally, Murphy's Irish Stout (MIS) is now available in 63 countries worldwide, up from only 20 in 1992. Export sales of the brand grew by almost 200 percent during 1996. Growth markets include the United States, where MIS sales increased 163 percent, and Germany, France, Spain, Italy, and the Netherlands, where sales volumes grew 82 percent. MIS's output has grown by 700 percent in the last decade. Most of this increase was fueled by international consumption, with sales in Ireland increasing only 10 percent over that time (Exhibit 1).

This growth is reflected in an increased turnover for MBI from Ir £125 million to Ir £140 million. The total company volume now stands at almost 950,000 hectoliters.

EXHIBIT 3
World's Largest Brewers, 1994

Source: Havis Dawson, "Brand Brewing." *Beverage World,* October 1995, p. 52.
1994 is the latest year available.

Company	HQ	Prod./Vol.[1]	World Share	% of Sales in Exports
Anheuser-Busch	United States	105.1	9%	6%
Heineken	Netherlands	59.6	4.8	89
Miller	United States	50.1	3.9	5
Kirin	Japan	35.1	2.7	5
Foster's	Australia	34.7	2.7	73
Carlsberg	Denmark	30.4	2.3	82
Danone Group	France	27.7	2.4	65
Guinness	United Kingdom	24.2	2.1	84

[1]Production/volume is measured in hectoliters: 1 hectoliter = 26.4 gallons or .85 barrel.

For most of its first 135 years Murphy's Irish Stout was available only in draft form in pubs throughout Ireland. A packaging innovation (draughtflow cans) was launched in October 1992. A plastic device (called a widget) is fitted into the bottom of the can which nitrates the liquid after the can is opened, creating the famous creamy head and giving the product a publike taste. Consumer acceptance of the can is reflected in the distribution growth of the product, which makes it available in off-licenses/liquor stores. Within Europe a 330-milliliter cream-colored can is sold, while in the United States a 14.9-ounce can is marketed. One distinguishing feature of the can in Europe is the message "Chill for at least two hours. Pour contents into glass in one smooth action. Best before end—see base," which is reprinted in four languages on the cans.

Another packaging innovation for MIS was developed in 1995. A draughtflow bottle is now available in both the U.S. and European markets. The 500-milliliter (16.9-oz.) bottle has a long neck and is dark brown in color. It is used as a powerful unique differentiating point for the brand. The back labels acclaim the benefits of the draughtflow technology. Warning labels concerning alcoholic beverages are shown on the U.S. labels.

Murphy's Irish Amber, a traditional Irish ale, was launched in 1995 as Murphy's Irish Red Beer in Germany and France. It is brewed in Cork but is not available domestically in Ireland. In the United States Murphy's Irish Amber was introduced in both draft and a 12-ounce bottle in September 1996. The bottles are amber in color. The label's dark blue and red colors accented by gold signal a high-quality product. Compelled by the need for a stronger Murphy's portfolio due to increased interest in genuine red beers, the company believed this product would be successful. Thus far, Murphy's Irish Amber's success has far exceeded expectations.

Murphy's also offers Heineken's low-alcohol beer called Buckler. It contains 1/2 of 1 percent alcohol and about half the calorie content of normal beer. It sells in 330-milliliter bottles in bars, off-licenses, and supermarkets in the served markets.

The Competition

After returning from a business trip to the Continent a week later, Patrick Conway found on his desk a stack of articles sent to him from the communications department discussing the Guinness–Grand Met merger. Before turning his attention to them, he reflected on what he knew regarding the Guinness brand both in Ireland and elsewhere. Guinness Stout was the pioneer in this category and an even older firm than Murphy's. It was founded in 1759 by Arthur Guinness in Dublin. It was now the eighth largest brewer in the world in terms of volume, with over a 2 percent market share. Murphy's parent, Heineken, is in second place worldwide (Exhibit 3).

Guinness is brewed in almost 50 countries and sold in over 130.[4] In the stout category, it is the proverbial "500-pound gorilla" in that it commands a 70 to 90 percent share in almost all markets. When it moves, Murphy's and other competitors invariably pay close attention. The Guinness name defines the stout market in most countries and is the "gold standard" against which all other competing brands are measured. The company's marketing prowess is well known in that Guinness Stout is positioned as "hip in the United Kingdom," "traditional in Ireland," and a source of "virility" in Africa; a special microbrew is aimed at "creating a new generation of beer snobs" in the United States. Guinness plans to continue targeting continental Europe, the United States, and Asia in a bid to expand its markets and grow its business.

---

[4]Company fact sheet.

EXHIBIT 4
GMG Brands

Source: "GMG Brands: What the Two Sides Will Contribute," *Financial Times,* May 13, 1997, p. 27.

Division	Turnover (millions)	Pretax Profit (millions)
Guinness Brewing Worldwide: Guinness Stout, Harp, Cruzcampo (Spanish), Red Stripe	£2,262	£283
United Distillers & Vintners (Guinness Brands) Dewar's, Gordon's Gin, Bell's, Moet Hennessey, Johnnie Walker, Black and White, Asbach	£2,468	£791
(Grand Met Brands) Smirnoff, Stolichnaya, J&B (whisky), Gilbey's Gin, Jose Cuervo, Grand Marnier, Bailey's, Malibu, Absolut	£3,558	£502
Pillsbury Pillsbury, Green Giant, Old El Paso, Häagen-Dazs	£3,770	£447
Burger King	£859	£167

Note: Turnover and pretax profit numbers denote millions of pounds sterling.

Guinness has been very successful in building its stout brand around the world. The company is identified with its quirky advertising campaigns in Ireland and its high profile regarding other marketing and promotional endeavors. One significant effort involved the Irish national soccer team, which endorsed Guinness as its official beer for the 1994 World Cup. Sales of Guinness Stout rose dramatically in the United States during the World Cup finals. Another U.S.-based promotion program designed to appeal to the over 40 million Americans of Irish descent was the "Win Your Own Pub in Ireland" contest. This competition has been going on for several years and is featured in Guinness's Web page currently. Third, the huge development of the Irish pub concept around the world helped Guinness brands abroad and contributed to an increase in export sales of 10 percent in 1996. The company launched the Guinness pub concept in 1992, and there are now 1,250 "Guinness" Irish pubs in 36 countries. Four hundred more are expected to open in 1997.[5]

Patrick turned his attention to several articles about the Guinness and Grand Met merger. A rationale for the merger was that these firms could acquire new brands more easily than they may be able to find new consumers in the U.S. and European marketplace, where alcohol consumption is falling, the population is aging, and concerns about health are rising. The new firm will be a formidable force in the race to open up new markets in liquor and beer. The companies have complementary product lines and will be divided into four major divisions (Exhibit 4). The Guinness Brewery worldwide division will feature its signature stout, Harp (a lager), Kilkenny (a red ale), Cruzcampo (a Spanish beer), and Red Stripe.

The Economist noted that even though GMG will be the seventh largest company in the world, it faces major obstacles. One is that even though its brands are very well known, the combined company will lack focus. Grand Met has a long history of trying its hand at different businesses but has done so with mixed success. Guinness, however, has an even longer history of not doing much besides brewing beer, and its spirits business has been a struggle for the firm. *The Economist*'s conclusion gave Mr. Conway encouragement and reflected his own impression when the magazine stated: "Unless GMG manages to show very rapidly that they can mix these ingredients into something fairly tasty, then pressure will grow on it to simplify itself."[6]

[5]Barry O'Keeffe, "'Black Stuff' Underpins Profit Raise at Guinness," *The Irish Times,* March 21, 1997.
[6]"Master of the Bar," *The Economist,* May 17, 1997, p. 73.

Patrick recalled that Guinness is not the only competitor of Murphy's. Beamish & Crawford, also located in Cork, was founded in 1792 and currently employs about 200 people. In 1987 the company joined the Foster's Brewing Group. The primary brands offered by the company are Beamish (stout), Foster's (lager), and Carling Black Label (lager).

Beamish stout is available in most pubs throughout the southern part of Ireland. The brand is positioned on its Irishness, the heritage of Beamish Stout, and the fact that it is the only Irish stout exclusively brewed in Ireland. In the last three years Beamish has been marketed in Europe (Italy and Spain mostly) and North America (Canada and the United States). It is distributed through the Foster's Brewing Group in those markets.

The Irish Market

Dan Leahy sent Patrick the following report on the market for Murphy's in Ireland. His memo discussed both the importance of pub life in the country and the competitive situation. Patrick read with interest Dan's assessment of the Irish market:

> With a population of less than 4 million people, the Irish market is small in international terms. However, it is the market in which stout holds the largest share at nearly 50 percent of all beer sales. With one of the youngest populations in the developed world and one of the fastest-growing economies, it is an important and dynamic market for all stout producers. This is added to by the fact that the three competitors—Murphy's, Guinness, and Beamish— all use their Irishness as a key attribute in product positioning. A presence in the Irish market is viewed as being central to the authenticity of the Irishness claim.
>
> Pubs have long been a central part of Irish life, particularly in rural areas, where pubs are semi-social centers. Irish pubs are regularly run by owner-operators who buy products from different breweries. This is quite different from most international markets, where pubs tend to be run by or for the breweries. For example, in the Dutch market Heineken has 52 percent of the outlets. Partly as a result of this, Irish consumers are highly brand-loyal. Also, in the Irish market, breweries engage in higher levels of promotion.
>
> Irish pubs are perceived very positively in many parts of the world. They are seen as places which are accessible to all the family. Irish pubs are intimately linked with musical sessions and viewed as being open, friendly places to visit. This positive perception has resulted in a proliferation of Irish-themed pubs, particularly in the last decade. This development has been used extensively by Guinness and lately by Murphy's as a means of increasing distribution.
>
> Guinness dominates the Irish stout market with an 89 percent market share. Murphy's and Beamish have roughly equal shares of the rest of the market. Guinness's dominance of the market is reflected in the fact that the term *Guinness* is synonymous with stout. In many parts of the country it is ordered without reference to its name simply by asking for "a pint." Similarly, in Britain 1 million pints of Guinness are sold every day, with 10 million glasses a day sold worldwide.
>
> Guinness Ireland turned in a strong performance in 1996 with sales up 8 percent to 764 million pints.[7] The company began a 12-million-pound advertising campaign last year called "The Big Pint" and engaged in extensive billboard advertising emphasizing the size and strength of the brand.
>
> In Ireland, Beamish Stout is positioned as a value for money, Irish stout selling at 20 pence (10 percent) lower than the competitors. It is slightly ahead of Murphy's currently in the race for second place in Ireland. As with Murphy's, Beamish's traditional base has been in the Cork-area market. Today, 1 in every 4 pints of stout consumed in Cork is Beamish and 1 in every 14 pints in Ireland is Beamish.
>
> Within the lager market in Ireland, Heineken dominates with nearly 40 percent of the market, while Budweiser and Carlsberg (both distributed by Guinness) each have just over a

[7]O'Keeffe, "'Black Stuff' Underpins Profit Raise at Guinness."

20 percent market share. Harp, which once held an overwhelming 80 percent share, now accounts for only 8 percent.

Murphy's is priced on a par with Guinness in all markets in the country. The average price of a pint of stout in the market is Ir £2.00.

In parts of the market where demand for the brand is low, Murphy's has begun selling the product in an innovative 3/5-keg (a keg is a barrel containing 50 liters) size. This ensures that the product reaches the customer at the desired level of quality.

Murphy's has pursued market growth through the development of export markets and development of the take-home market. The development of these markets is driven by the fact that the domestic draught market is mature with static sales over the last number of years. In 1995 pub sales fell by almost 2.5 percent, while off-license sales grew by 37 percent. The growth in the off-license business is due in part to the impact of the new stronger drunk-driving legislation and in-home summer consumption.[8]

Both of these markets rely heavily on canned and bottled packaging for the product. Traditionally this has posed a difficulty for stout products as there is a perceived deterioration in quality compared to the draught version. Murphy's is selling its product in bottles and dedicating some advertising to the superior bottled taste and using it as a differentiating feature for all of Murphy's products and using the draught bottle as a brand icon for the firm.

Conway thought about the report on the Irish market and how difficult it was to compete against Guinness and the extreme brand loyalty of the Irish consumer to it. He thought about the new three-year 5-million-pound advertising campaign launched in 1996 and hoped that the unique approach would win new customers. One memorable TV ad featured a group of Japanese samurai warriors who arrive in a line at a bar, knock back bottles of Murphy's, and leave while a Guinness drinker drums his fingers on the counter waiting for his pint to settle. Conway believed that brand awareness was growing. One successful promotional endeavor is the company's sponsorship of the Murphy's Irish Open, which was part of the PGA European Golf Tour.

He knew that strides were being made in the distribution network outside its traditional stronghold of Cork City and County. One of the inducements the company was using was a lower trade price to the pubs so that they made more on each pint sold. The company followed this philosophy internationally as well in the effort to compete with Guinness.

He also recalled two *Irish Times* articles that gave his and Kakabeeke's views on the importance of the Irish market to the company. He asked his secretary to retrieve them from the files and routed them to the marketing group. Conway was quoted as saying, "Murphy's believes it has to have an advertising spend comparable to Guinness if it is ever to achieve a critical mass in Ireland. We have to differentiate ourselves, and there's no use doing it with a whisper. A better market share in Ireland would also provide Murphy's Irish Stout with a backbone from which to grow exports."[9] Mr. Kakebeeke said that "the brewery is not happy with the 5 percent position in the Irish market and with the level of domestic growth being achieved by Murphy's Irish Stout. I feel that sales can be improved in Ireland."[10]

The UK and Continental European Markets

The United Kingdom (England, Scotland, Wales, and Northern Ireland), Ireland's closest neighbor, represents the world's largest stout market in terms of consumption at 60 million hectoliters. The total population of the UK is approximately 60 million consumers. Murphy's market share stands at 15 percent, while Guinness (78 percent) and Beamish

[8]Paul O'Kane, "Murphy Boosts Exports," *The Irish Times,* March 7, 1996.
[9]Paul O'Kane, "Murphy's Aims to Double Its Sales in Three Years," *The Irish Times,* June 14, 1996.
[10]O'Kane, "Murphy Boosts Exports."

(6 percent) are the other two major competitors. MIS was launched in the UK in 1985 and has enjoyed continued growth in that market since then. Murphy's success in the UK may be attributed to several factors.

First, Heineken and Murphy's are distributed in the UK through the Whitbread Beer Company in Luton. Whitbread has an association with over 27,000 pubs in the country, which translates to an automatic distribution network for Murphy's products. Recently Whitbread has opened a series of themed bars under the banner "J. J. Murphy and Company" throughout the country. These outlets reflect the desired image for Murphy's and help raise the profile of the brand in the UK. As a point of comparison, Beamish is distributed in 10,000 outlets in Britain.

Second, Murphy's has also been successful with its advertising in the UK. Its continuing advertising theme "Like the Murphy's, I'm not bitter" campaign is a tongue-in-cheek poke at Guinness's taste. The campaign has received several awards and has resulted in a unique identity developed for the brand (see Exhibit 2 on stout). The firm has also sponsored the Murphy's English Open Golf Championship for five years.

Third, the brand has gained momentum since it was voted product of the year by the UK Vintners in 1990. Murphy's has a strong position in the minds of the British who prefer darker ales. The brand represents a viable option to those who do not like the taste of Guinness and/or seek an alternative to their favorite UK-based brands such as Thomas Hardy, Newcastle, Samuel Smith, Watney's, and Young's.

MIS is available in all Western European markets. It has excellent distribution in the Netherlands, where Heineken is headquartered. Guinness's recent Irish pub expansion program has also helped raise awareness for all entries in the Irish stout category. Murphy's experienced dramatic growth in volume and market share across Europe in 1996.

In Germany, the establishment of Murphy's Trading GmbH, a wholly owned subsidiary of Murphy Brewery Ireland, allows for greater focus and control of the Murphy's brands within this critical market. The year 1996 also saw Murphy's gain the exclusive beer rights to Paddy Murphy's, the largest chain of Irish theme pubs throughout Germany. Also, in Denmark MIS is distributed in the Paddy Go Easy chain in several Danish cities.

In 1996 new markets were developed in Eastern Europe, including Hungary and the Czech Republic. The potential of the emerging Russian market is also anticipated. With the introduction of the brand in Finland, Murphy's is now available in all the Nordic countries.

The American Market

As he reached for the phone to ring Michael Foley, current CEO of Heineken USA (Van Munching & Co. is the importer's name) and former managing director of Murphy Brewery Ireland from 1989 to 1993, Patrick thought about the United States. He knew that the United States, with its 270 million consumers and general high standard of living, represents the most lucrative beer market in the world. The $40 billion beer market in the United States is dominated by the "giants" Anheuser-Busch (10 brands and 45 percent market share), Miller (9/23 percent), and Coors (7/11 percent).[11]

Michael gave Patrick a status report on the Murphy's brand in the United States as of June 1997. Michael reiterated that the U.S. strategy is to "build slowly" and gain acceptance of Murphy's products by endorsement by customers rather than attempting to buy market share with mass advertising. The plan is to "keep off TV because it is too

---

[11]"Domestic Beer Shipments Drop 2.1% in '95 While Volume Dips 1.7%," *Beverage Industry,* January 1996, pp. 24–32.

expensive." Murphy's is seeking a premium brand positioning aimed at the specialty imported niche rather than the mass market.

Foley indicated that he was very optimistic about the Murphy growth possibilities in the United States. "Our 1996 sales were up 180 percent, and our target is 1 million cases by mid-1998," he said. Both Murphy's Irish Stout and Irish Amber are meeting the expectations set for them by Heineken USA.

Murphy's Irish Stout has been available in the United States since 1992 and has experienced steady growth since then. MIS has been on a gradual progression, from 100,000 gallons in 1992 to 400,000 gallons in 1994 and 600,000 gallons in 1995. It is now on tap at over 5,000 bars and pubs throughout the country. The distribution tends to be concentrated in the eastern corridor running from Boston through New York City (the largest market) to Washington, D.C. Another area of intense distribution is in south Florida. The "gold coast" area running from Miami to Fort Lauderdale is a stronghold for Murphy's, partially due to its attraction to British tourists who are already familiar with the brand. Other areas of focus for MIS are the major metropolitan areas of Chicago, Los Angeles, and San Francisco.

For the off-premises/carryout market, MIS has been available in cans since 1993. Their size is 14.9 ounces, and they are cream colored (like the "head" of the drink) and are priced relative to domestic U.S. beers at a premium level—$1.76 versus $1.99 for Guinness in the same size can. Foley stated that cans generally signify a "down market product" and the company would like to present more of a prestige image. Therefore, in September 1996 Murphy's introduced the draughtflow bottle in the United States. While Foley believes the glass package is "more premium," the company has experienced a problem with it in the United States. The serving size of 16.9 ounces is not correct for the market since most beer glasses hold only 12 ounces. The usual price is $1.99 per bottle. The size is not that important for in-home consumption, but in bars where MIS is sold by packages rather than on draft, this is a significant issue for the company. Another issue that has arisen is that the thick brown bottle takes substantially longer to cool than does a can.

Murphy's Irish Amber was introduced into the American market in late 1996. Its on-premise penetration has exceeded company expectations, and according to Foley, "the product is doing very, very well. It is the 'real deal' and replacing nonauthentic Irish products such as Killian's in many areas." The product is available in six-packs for off-site consumption. The rich-looking green and red package makes it attractive. The company has positioned it against Bass Ale and other premium-quality ales. Its price is in the $7.50 range, which is substantially higher than many of the specialty imports, which cost $4.00 to $6.00 per six-pack. Killian's sometimes is sale priced as low as $3.99, but its regular price is in the $5.50 to $6.00 range, and Sam Adams Red and Pete's Wicked Ale are priced at $5.49 and $5.99, respectively. Bass Ale, however, carries an even higher price ($7.79) than Murphy's.

Conway thanked Foley for his update on the status of the Murphy's brands in the United States and asked if Michael could spend a few minutes discussing trends in the beer market within the country. "I know import sales are increasing about 7 percent a year in the United States and that Heineken is the leading import brand," said Conway, "But where does Guinness fall?" Foley responded that they were in tenth place, while Bass Ale held down the eighth spot and beer imports from Ireland held the sixth position among all countries (Exhibits 5 and 6). Foley said that he recalled reading that the top 20 brands (out of a total of 400 import brands) account for 90 percent of U.S. import sales.

Patrick asked about trends in the U.S. beer market. "It has been flat the last several years," said Foley. "The most significant recent trend domestically is the growth in microbreweries." Michael said he remembered seeing on a Web site that microbreweries,

EXHIBIT 5   **Leading Imported Beer Brands in the United States (thousands of 2.25-gallon cases)**

Brand	Importer	Origin	1992[1]	1993	1994[2]	% Change 1993–1994
Heineken	Van Munching & Co.	Netherlands	26,700	29,200	31,200	6.8%
Corona Extra	Barton/Gambrinus	Mexico	13,000	14,000	16,000	14.3
Molson Ice	Molson USA	Canada	—	3,000	10,000	—
Beck's	Dribeck Importers	Germany	9,650	9,700	9,720	0.2
Molson Golden	Molson USA	Canada	8,500	8,600	8,700	1.2
Amstel Light	Van Munching & Co.	Netherlands	5,500	6,000	7,500	25.0
Labatt's Blue	Labatt's USA	Canada	5,900	6,200	6,500	4.8
Bass Ale	Guinness Import Co.	United Kingdom	2,850	3,390	4,160	22.7
Tecate	Labatt's USA	Mexico	2,900	3,400	4,000	17.6
Guinness Stout	Guinness Import Co.	Ireland	3,100	3,650	3,970	8.8
Foster's Lager[3]	Molson USA	Canada	3,500	3,700	3,800	2.7
Moosehead	Guinness Import Co.	Canada	3,400	3,350	3,340	−0.3
Molson Light	Molson USA	Canada	1,900	2,000	2,200	10.0
Dos Equis	Guinness Import Co.	Mexico	1,900	2,060	2,120	2.9
St. Pauli Girl	Barton Brands	Germany	2,200	2,000	2,000	0.0
Labatt's Ice	Labatt's USA	Canada	—	845	1,910	—
Molson Canadian	Molson USA	Canada	1,640	1,690	1,710	1.2
Labatt's Light	Labatt's USA	Canada	1,100	1,020	1,100	7.8
Corona Light	Barton/Gambrinus	Mexico	1,100	1,000	1,000	0.0

[1]Revised.
[2]Estimated.
[3]The gradual production switch from Australia to Canada began in April 1992.

EXHIBIT 6
Imported Beer Market
Market Share by Supplier, 1994 (Estimated)

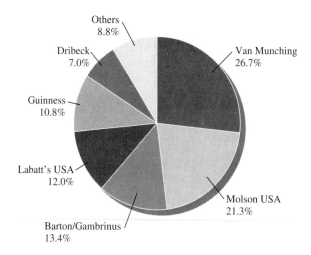

Others 8.8%
Dribeck 7.0%
Van Munching 26.7%
Guinness 10.8%
Labatt's USA 12.0%
Barton/Gambrinus 13.4%
Molson USA 21.3%

brewpubs, and regional specialty breweries totaled almost 1,300 in early 1997.[12] The microbrewery category has grown tenfold to 500 in 10 years. However, it still accounted for only a paltry 2 percent of the U.S. market in 1995.

Conway said good-bye and was just about to hang up when Foley said, "I almost forgot, but someone passed an article from *The Wall Street Journal* by me a few weeks ago that talked about Guinness and the microbrewery boom. I will send it to you with the other material" (Exhibit 7).

[12]"Craft-Brewing Industry Fact Sheet—February 1997," http://www.Beertown.org/craftbrew.html.

EXHIBIT 7
Buoyed by Boom in Microbrews, Guinness Pours Its Cash into TV

Source: Elizabeth Jensen, *The Wall Street Journal,* February 10, 1997, p. B2.

Guinness Import Co. poured about 33 percent more of its signature dark draft stout in the United States last year as the microbrew boom helped lift import sales by creating a new generation of beer snobs. Now Guinness hopes to keep the beer taps flowing with its first large-scale U.S. TV ad campaign for the Irish-brewed brand, breaking today.

At a time when sales of all beer in the United States rose just 1 percent last year, several of Guinness Import's major brands, including Harp lager and Bass ale, posted double-digit gains. Overall, sales of Guinness Import's brands (including Moosehead, whose distribution rights Guinness is shedding, effective at the end of March) grew 20 percent to about 17 million cases last year, according to Guinness.

The company's success is one of the factors that contributed to an estimated 10 percent rise in the sale of beers last year, according to Frank Walters, senior vice president of research at M. Shanken Communications, publisher of *Impact,* which tracks beer sales. Final numbers on sales of domestic beers are expected to be flat, although it's estimated that the tiny microbrewery and specialty segment jumped more than 20 percent. "It's a good economy, and people are indulging themselves more," says Mr. Walters of the sales of more-expensive imports.

Guinness stout's fast sales pace in bars and stores lifted it to the number 6 or 7 ranking among imports, up from ninth place in 1995, according to Mr. Walter's estimates. Guinness Import, a unit of Guinness PLC of London, attributes its success to changing consumer tastes in the wake of the microbrew explosion and a more intense distribution and marketing effort. "People are getting more into beers with taste," said Sheri Roder, marketing development director for Guinness Import, "and at the same time, we've gotten behind our brands more."

There have been eye-catching promotions, such as the annual "Win Your Own Pub in Ireland" contest, now in its fourth year. A "Great Guinness Toast," on February 28, hopes to get into the *Guinness Book of World Records* for the largest number of people making a toast. And the number of outlets selling the brand jumped by 20 percent in 1996.

Even more unusual, Guinness has been sending out a force of "draft specialists" armed with thermometers and training brochures to visit bars and make sure they're serving Guinness under the best possible conditions. Brewers can't own bars, so they can't control whether tavern owners serve the product in sparkling clean glasses or how often they flush out built-up yeast in the lines that carry the beer from the keg to the tap.

With distribution and the quality program in place, Guinness decided the time was right to launch the TV campaign. "There's no point in advertising a lot when people can't find you," says Ms. Roder. "There's a likelihood now that people will be able to find a pint of Guinness, poured well to our exacting standards. You don't want to get people too excited about something they can't find."

The TV ad campaign, with the tag line "Why Man Was Given Five Senses," will air through St. Patrick's Day, March 17, in 18 major markets, including New York, Los Angeles, and Atlanta. Guinness won't say what it is spending on the ad campaign, which will run in late prime-time and sports programs, but calls it a significant media buy. Chicago viewers of the Super Bowl saw the ad run twice; Guinness also has spots in NBC's high-rated Thursday prime-time lineup.

The quirky ad, which goes through the ritual of ordering a pint of Guinness, from the nod to the bartender to the long wait for the beer to settle, was created by Weiss, Stagliano of New York City. It got a five-week tryout in Chicago and Boston last fall with convincing results: Sales of Guinness in Boston were up 24 percent in December over a year earlier, compared with just an 11 percent gain for the rest of the Guinness portfolio, while in Chicago, sales are up 35 percent from a year ago, with distribution up 22 percent.

Murphy's World Market Positioning and Marketing

Dan Leahy stopped by Patrick Conway's office and handed him the information requested on Murphy's status in the world market. Patrick glanced at the statistics assembled by Dan and noticed that the specialty category (into which MIS and MIA both fell) had grown over the last few years (Exhibit 8). He was concerned that it was the second smallest of the five categories.

Dan left a revision of the Murphy's Positioning Statement on which Patrick and his colleagues had been working for several months. It read:

> Murphy's is a symbol of everything authentically "Irish." Its warm history takes time to discover but its taste is easy to appreciate.

Supporting this positioning was the image of Ireland that Murphy's planned to convey in its marketing strategy (Exhibit 9). While the words in the exhibit are a bit stereotypical, they describe the perception of both the country and its people. It is in this context that Irish products are viewed by consumers in other counties. The elements of the marketing mix were summarized by Dan in several accompanying pages.

The product consists of the two brands—Murphy's Irish Stout and Murphy's Irish Amber/Red Beer (MIA/RB). It is sourced in Ireland except for the UK and New Zealand markets. Ongoing new product development continues in line with positioning, umbrella branding, and premium packaging.

The distribution objective is one of controlled distribution growth. The focus is on quality Irish bars/pubs and specialty beer outlets. Package variants are available in low-volume outlets. Dual stocking of MIS and MIA/RB will occur wherever possible. Exclusivity is a goal but not a prerequisite for stocking. The existing Heineken distribution network will continue to be used wherever possible.

The pricing strategy is one of price parity with major specialty competitors. A reasonable margin is being offered to the trade. In fact, the company prices its products slightly below the competition to the trade as an enticement to carry the products.

The promotion and communications strategy is multipronged. The brands' Irish heritage and origin continue to be reinforced. The company engages in tactical advertising and

EXHIBIT 8
World Beer Market

Category	1994	1995	1996	Volume (Hectoliters)
Specialty	6.6%	7.4%	8.2%	103,000,000
Sophistication	11.9	12.4	12.9	162,000,000
Standard savings	63.5	62.7	61.0	763,000,000
Stay fit	15.9	15.5	15.8	189,000,000
Stay clear	2.1	2.0	2.1	24,000,000
Total	100	100	100	1,241,000,000

EXHIBIT 9
Image of Ireland

Perception of Country	Personality of People
Green	Relaxed
Environmentally friendly	Sociable
Natural	Friendly
Unspoiled	Different
Lost Arcadia	Humorous/witty
Underdeveloped	Pub atmosphere

promotion rather than larger-scale strategic campaigns. For example, St. Patrick's Day and Irish music nights are exploited. The communication focus is on both brands in most markets. The company plans to use still rather than electronic media to convey the authentic Irish image of the brands.

Murphy's Future Direction

Patrick Conway assembled the reports on the Irish, UK, European, and American markets as well as the world positioning and strategy. He circulated them to the members of his group with a memo calling a meeting in early June 1997. Conway indicated that he wanted to develop a long-term strategy for the Murphy's brand to take to Heineken management rather than develop a knee-jerk reaction to the Guinness–Grand Met merger.

He believed that Murphy's reputation was improving both in Ireland and throughout the world. He did not want to jeopardize the gains made in the last several years. However, he was concerned with the stagnant nature of the beer industry in Europe and North America. He called a meeting for June 10, 1997, to discuss the marketing strategy for Murphy's.

Before he met with the marketing department members, he stopped by Marien Kakebeeke's office. The managing director reminded him of the corporate goal for Murphy's, which is 20 percent of the world's stout market by the year 2000. "I know that is ambitious, Patrick, but I am confident you and your staff can achieve it."

"Do you realize that the Cork Brewery is almost at capacity now?" asked Patrick. "Even if we stimulate demand, how will we be able to meet it with production limits? Also, recall that we expanded the brewery in 1995."[13]

When Patrick, D. Ford, and Dan Leahy sat down that morning to discuss the future of Murphy's, they considered several questions:

How important is a strong showing in the Irish domestic market to Murphy's? Must it make a strong showing there to be successful worldwide?

Should Murphy's employ a global rather than local marketing strategy worldwide? The "I'm not bitter" campaign has been successful in the United Kingdom, so should several possible strategies be used, especially in the large markets of the United States and continental Europe?

Is Murphy's destined to be a "niche" product forever? Will these brands ever reach a place where they command a substantial market share?

Should the company continue to make the two brands only at the Cork brewery for the lucrative U.S. market, or should it consider making the product in that country? It worked for automobiles; why not beer?

Will Murphy's ever be able to achieve the status of other products that are famous for their Irish heritage, such as Guinness, Bailey's Irish Cream, Jameson Irish Whiskey, Waterford Crystal, and Belleek China?

[13]Paul O'Kane, "Murphy's Plans Major Expansion," *The Irish Times,* August 16, 1995.

Case 6-12
Apple Computer Inc.

It's 10 days before the July 19 (2000) Macworld trade show in New York, where Apple Computer Inc. Chief Executive Steven P. Jobs will once again try to wow the masses with his P. T. Barnum-style product introductions. I'm the reporter he has anointed to get an exclusive sneak peek at this year's lineup of new computers. Clad in shorts and a designer

T-shirt, he greets me like an old pal, warmly shaking my hand and ushering me into Apple's boardroom. Scattered around are a dozen or so objects, each hidden coyly beneath a black shroud.

High-tech's premier showman doesn't disappoint. First comes the small stuff: a see-through plastic keyboard and a sleek mouse. Then, off fly the covers from new versions of Apple's popular iMac computer—now in four rich new colors, including ruby and indigo. Then comes the climax: an 8-inch, cube-shaped Mac that packs Apple's most powerful technology into a clear plastic case about the size of a toaster. Laid out on a table with cute, baseball-shaped speakers and a flat-panel display, the cube's design is a showstopper. "Isn't that beautiful?" he gushes like a dad over his newborn. "It's the most beautiful thing we've ever done." I overcome my journalist's restraint and blurt, "Wow, it's great." But that doesn't satisfy Jobs. A day later, he wants to meet again. He's not convinced that I understand just how insanely great these products really are.

I'm in the Steve Jobs zone again, but this time it doesn't feel like his fabled reality-distortion field. The $1,799 Mac Cube has all the earmarks of a machine that might give Apple's strong growth another shove uphill. And every shove counts. Since returning three years ago to the company he founded, Jobs, 44, has worked the most unlikely comeback since the 1969 Amazin' Mets. Left for dead in 1997 with mounting losses and shriveling market share, Apple is back to making the most stylish products in computerdom. That has propelled its revenues up 17%, to $1.8 billion, in the quarter reported on July 18. That fell below analysts' expectations, driving the stock down 7% on July 19, to $53. The stock is up eight-fold since Jobs returned. And thanks to the products, analysts expect 25%-plus revenue growth in the year that ends Sept. 30, 2001.

For years, Apple seemed to define gravity. Now it's defying it. Credit Jobs's Midas touch with design and marketing (Exhibit 1). Both Dell and Compaq recently scrapped colorful iMac knockoffs just months after they were introduced, proving that only Apple knows how to make fashion count when it comes to a computer. And, thanks to the coolness factor, Apple gets away with charging up to 25% more than its competitors for a machine with similar capabilities. That helped give it a juicy gross profit margin of 29.8% in the most recent quarter, tops in the PC segment. But then, Apple has always been able to market circles around its rivals. Only this time, there's far more to Apple than curvy products and groovy ad campaigns. Get a load of this: The company known for its incorrigible, free-spirited, free-spending ways has become a master of operating efficiencies. Jobs has slashed expenses from $8.1 billion in 1997 to $5.7 billion in 1999 by outsourcing manufacturing,

EXHIBIT 1
What Apple Has Done Right

PRODUCT DESIGN Apple is tops at making eye-catching, easy-to-use computers. Having jumped from 3.8% to 6% share in its core markets, Apple hopes to add a point or two of share each year on new Macs like the Cube. If successful, the company could more than triple sales, to $20 billion in five years.

MARKETING While rivals spit out me-too PCs, Jobs turns Apple product debuts into front-page news. His ad campaigns are just as catchy: The three-year-old "Think different" campaign, featuring such creative geniuses as Pablo Picasso, puts rivals' ad efforts to shame. And the new iMovie ads are classic Apple—warm, fuzzy, and effective.

EFFICIENCY Once the industry's sloppiest operator, Apple now ends each quarter with less than a day of parts and work-in-progress inventory—vs. seven or so days for Dell. That's mostly because Jobs has trimmed Apple's product line from 15 to 5 models and pared back the number of suppliers.

STEVE JOBS With his keen artistic eye, Jobs has revolutionized product design with the iMac's exciting colors and contours. A virtuoso handler of the media, he keeps Apple on a par with far-larger rivals. And his fiery passion and attention to detail give Apple an inventiveness unmatched in the industry.

EXHIBIT 2
**The Challenges
Facing Apple**

INNOVATION The R&D cupboard may get bare. Jobs killed long-term research three years ago. Now, staffers focus on products due out within a year. If that doesn't change, especially when it comes to software that can take years to percolate, Apple may find itself falling behind rivals with far larger R&D kitties, such as Microsoft and Intel.

NEW MARKETS The PC has been the primary Net access device, but that could change fast as Web phones and other devices debut. Apple has shunned this market so far, but experts say it will have to follow suit. That will challenge the company to make money on cheaper, sub-$500 devices.

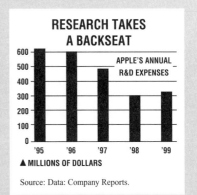

RESEARCH TAKES A BACKSEAT

APPLE'S ANNUAL R&D EXPENSES

▲ MILLIONS OF DOLLARS

Source: Data: Company Reports.

DISTRIBUTION Jobs cut back the number of Mac retailers to a handful in 1997 to match declining demand. Now, to gain share, Apple needs a bigger presence. Some analysts say it should emulate Gateway and establish its own stores. That would cost a lot, though, and could upend its newfound operating efficiency.

STEVE JOBS If the Good Steve has many strengths, the Bad Steve has many weaknesses. His mercurial, tyrannical management style burns out some employees. And his hardball tactics with suppliers could come back to bite him should Apple ever take another tumble.

trimming inventories, shifting 25% of sales to an online store, and slicing the number of distributors from the double digits to two. That, combined with the new products, has won back allies. On July 18, three years after dropping the Apple line, retailer Circuit City Stores Inc. said it will once again carry Mac gear. Says CEO W. Alan McCollough: "Much to Steve's credit, Apple has found its way again—and then some."

The question now: How far can Apple go? Jobs has restored Apple to health by retreating to its comfort zone: selling Macs to consumers, schools, and creative professionals who relish its style and ease of use. Now the Apple saga enters a chapter of greater opportunity and monumental challenges (Exhibit 2). To sustain its momentum, the company must go through the onerous task of upgrading its 16-year-old Mac software to the new, more reliable MacOS X program without rankling loyal fans. And to be an industry leader once again, Apple must extend its innovation lead on the desktop while moving beyond the Mac to make the appliance-like devices and handheld gadgets people will want in the Internet Age.

Indeed, so far Apple has taken only small steps toward regaining ground lost during the mid-1990s. It has eked out a 2-percentage-point share increase in the U.S. home market, to 7%. Yet its overall worldwide share is just 3.8%, down from its peak of almost 10% in 1993, according to market researcher Dataquest Inc. And to make what gains he has, Jobs has had to prop up short-term fortunes by slashing research and development from $604 million in 1996 to $314 million last year. That's just 5% of sales, a tad more than rival Compaq Computer Corp., which has the luxury of relying on Microsoft Corp. for its costly operating system.

Fashion Slave

All told, it's hard to see how Apple can hold its innovation lead. "The big thing that Apple is providing now is leadership in colors. It won't take us long to catch up with that," quipped Microsoft Chairman William H. Gates III last year. Even Jef Raskin, the ex-Apple manager who conceived the original Mac, isn't terribly optimistic about Apple returning to its glory. "I think they can remain what they are: a well-loved, influential bit player, the late Walter Matthau of the computer industry. But not the top star."

Jobs insists it isn't so. While he doesn't expect Apple to be the overall PC market-share champ any time soon, Jobs says the company can deliver years of sizzling growth and hefty profits. His goal: to make top-quality products for consumers, schools, and the artsy set—Apple's core buyers. Setting aside the corporate market, he aims to gain 1 to 2 percentage points of share a year; each share point is equal to $1.3 billion in additional revenue. Jobs says the company's product pipeline is bulging with goodies that will make this possible so there's no need for R&D costs to skyrocket now. "We may start looking at this next year, but we're not there yet," says Jobs. "There are so many exciting things in our headlights that will take us through the next two to three years. Only after that will we start to send people out into the darkness."

Now that Jobs has replaced Apple's dysfunctional culture with a speedy organization, he says the company is ready to rise to the next level. His plan: to take the personal computer where it has never gone before—and faster than rivals. Unlike other computer makers, Apple develops much of the underlying technology, both hardware and software. Jobs want to exploit this advantage to rush innovations to market quicker than rivals who must rely on software from Microsoft and chips from Intel Corp. While he won't give any details, Jobs says Apple is working on a handful of Internet appliances that could start appearing next year. And he intends to build new computers that are far easier to use and that help people make the most of what the Net has to offer—whether it's making home movies or making home pages.

Mad for Movies

Jobs' announcements on July 19 provide a peek into where Apple is headed. Along with the Cube, it upgraded its HomePage Web-site creation program, which Mac owners can use to easily set up shop online and share digital photos, résumès, or home movies with friends and family. Apple also launched an improved version of its iMovie software, which lets Spielberg wannabes add slick tricks like slo-mo and "fade to black and white" to their home flicks. "We think desktop movies will be bigger than desktop publishing," says Jobs of the market that put Apple on the map in the 1980s. "How many people want to make home movies compared to how many want to do newsletters?"

Apple is counting on such whizzy software to help drive sales of its Macs. The Cube, for example, is aimed at high-end consumers and creative professionals who want its power and its style but don't need to expand their Mac with lots of add-in cards (Exhibit 3). The entry-level iMac, formerly $999, will now start at $799—well within the booming sub-$1,000 market. At the high end, Apple pumped up its G4 line with two PowerPC processors and superfast networking. And the mouse has all-new insides. Based on optical technology, it can work on any surface and has no trackball to get gummed up over time.

All told, Apple execs figure this lineup will goose market share. The company already has jumped from a 3.8% share in 1997 to 6% in the combined markets of consumer, education, and artistic professionals (Exhibit 4). Now Apple execs figure they can hit 10% in five years—growing from $6.1 billion last year to $20 billion. "I see no reason why it can't get back towards 10% market share," says Donaldson, Lufkin & Jenrette Inc. analyst Kevin McDonald.

Other analysts aren't so sold. While Apple insiders believe first-year sales of the Cube could approach 800,000, analysts think that's overly optimistic. Many had hoped for the

EXHIBIT 3
The PowerMac G4 Cube

1 THE VENT ON TOP
When CEO Steve Jobs wanted a new Mac for his home office last year, he asked Apple's engineers to pack the power of Apple's high-end G4 machine in an 8-inch square box—but without a noisy fan. So engineers placed an air chimney through the center.

2 THE CD DRIVE
Forget skimpy-feeling CD trays: The Cube has a slick, slot-loading drive on top for CDs and DVDs. Works like a toaster.

3 THE PLASTIC
A clear plastic cover holds the Cube off the desktop. Apple built special injection molding tools to avoid imperfections. "Manufacturing hated us for this," says Jobs.

4 THE MOUSE
The clunky, round mouse that came with the iMac is history. This one is optical, so it works on all surfaces, and there's no trackball to get gummed up over time. Comes with all Macs.

5 THE SPEAKERS
Made with Harmon-Kardon, these baseball-size speakers complete the look.

EXHIBIT 4
Steve Jobs's Unfinished Business

Source: Dataquest Inc.

Apple has been winning back U.S. market share since 1997. Still, it's nowhere near its peak as a leader in home and education products.
(All based on U.S. unit sales)

HOME MARKET							
MAKER	**1984**	**MAKER**	**1997**	**MAKER**	**1999**
PACKARD BELL	32.4%	PACKARD BELL NEC	23.3%	COMPAQ	19.0%
APPLE	14.7	COMPAQ	18.8	H-P	16.1
COMPAQ	11.5	GATEWAY	11.1	GATEWAY	15.3
IBM	6.1	IBM	7.0	EMACHINES	11.0
GATEWAY	5.5	ACER	5.9	PACKARD BELL NEC	7.3
		APPLE	5.0	APPLE	7.1
OTHERS	29.8	OTHERS	28.9	OTHERS	24.2

BUSINESS MARKET							
MAKER	**1994**	**MAKER**	**1997**	**MAKER**	**1999**
COMPAQ	14.2%	COMPAQ	15.7%	DELL	22.4%
IBM	10.1	DELL	12.8	COMPAQ	15.0
APPLE	6.4	IBM	9.5	IBM	9.2
DELL	5.9	H-P	8.0	H-P	6.0
GATEWAY	5.3	TOSHIBA	5.6	TOSHIBA	4.7
		APPLE	1.4	APPLE	1.3
OTHERS	58.1	OTHERS	47.0	OTHERS	41.4

EDUCATION MARKET							
MAKER	**1994**	**MAKER**	**1997**	**MAKER**	**1999**
APPLE	47.0%	APPLE	27.2%	DELL	21.4%
IBM	8.5	COMPAQ	13.2	APPLE	16.5
DELL	4.3	DELL	10.7	GATEWAY	13.6
GATEWAY	3.3	GATEWAY	7.8	COMPAQ	9.2
COMPAQ	3.2	IBM	6.9	IBM	3.8
OTHERS	33.0	OTHERS	34.2	OTHERS	35.5

EXHIBIT 5
**Computer Design
According to Jobs**

1984 MACINTOSH Jobs drove the development of the Mac, which integrated the monitor, a mouse, and the graphical user interface, among other firsts, into a computer that actually was loveable.

1988 THE NEXT COMPUTER Three years after being kicked out of Apple, Jobs unveiled the computer he thought would be all that the Mac wasn't. It was a sleek black 12-inch cube with serious power. Alas, it was too pricey, at $6,500.

1998 iMac Jobs capped off his return to Apple with the iMac, a translucent blue showstopper with a futuristic, conehead-like shape. It was made for the Web, with built-in networking, no floppy drive, and just two cords to plug in.

1999 iBook It's the mod, mobile version of the iMac. The clear, clamshell case is a standout with a handle made for easy toting. While some 465,000 have been sold, analysts say it hasn't quite been the hit Apple had hoped for.

2000 POWERMAC CUBE After Apple came out with a slick 22-inch flat panel display in 1998, Jobs wanted a powerful G4 PC to go with it—but only if size and noise were reduced. He decided on a cube while engineers finagled keeping the machine cool without a noisy fan.

debut of a wireless device based on the popular Palm handheld that would attract new customers instead of another desktop computer that could replace older Macs. And some critics say Apple needs to crack the lucrative $80 billion corporate market, which account for nearly 40% of all PCs sold. That's something Jobs says he won't try because corporate buyers are more interested in low-cost PCs than in nifty features—Apple's forte. By selling to Mac loyalists, "it'll be a big year for them in market share," says Salomon Smith Barney analyst Richard E. Gardner. He looks for Apple unit sales to grow 34%, vs. 15% for the PC industry. "But from here on out, gaining share gets tougher."

Still, Apple can now go keyboard-to-keyboard with PC rivals when it comes to nuts-and-bolts management. It's a startling notion when you think back on Jobs's past (Exhibit 5). In the 1970s and '80s, he was Apple's twentysomething chairman—infamous for temper tantrums that earned him a reputation as the enfant terrible of the computer industry. He squirreled the Macintosh team away in a skunkworks that flew a pirate's flag while lavishing its staffers with massages and beer busts. After being booted from Apple, he spent an eye-popping $250 million of investors' money on his second startup, NeXT Computer Inc., but only sold about 50,000 computers. And Jobs sunk $60 million of his own fortune into Pixar Animation Studios before it hit the jackpot with the computer-animated films *Toy Story* and *A Bug's Life*.

Yet today, Jobs is a steady day-to-day manager who toes the bottom line. And what a cost-cutter. In his first few months back at the helm, Jobs slashed Apple's mind-boggling lineup of 15 product families back to just a handful that share common components. Even after adding the iMac, new Powerbook laptops, and the iBook sub-notebook, the company tries to use the same technology in all three. And Apple has just a few hundred people working on its MacOS X software. That compares with the thousands of Microsofties that developed Windows 98. The difference: Apple focuses on key features—say, video playback—rather than throwing in all the bells and whistles. "We have a true focus on shipping," says software Senior Vice-President Avie Tevanian. "Everyone here works on a deadline that's not too far off, usually within a year."

Daunting Task

The most striking change has been in operations. When Jobs took over, Apple ended each quarter with some 70 days' worth of finished products sloshing around its factories and warehouses, a $500 million-plus drag on profits that was the worst in the industry. Jobs quickly streamlined. He outsourced manufacturing of half of Apple's products to contractors who could do it far more efficiently, say analysts. That got inventory down to about a month by early 1998. Jobs still wasn't satisfied. He hired former Compaq procurement executive Timothy D. Cook to meet a higher goal: to get more efficient than Dell, the industry's best.

It was a daunting challenge. Cook recalls drawing a flowchart of Apple's operations, with all the linkages from suppliers to manufacturing to distributors, that "looked like a printed circuit board." And not a very fast one. Because many of the transactions between suppliers weren't processed in real time, it could take days for a parts order to be delivered to a factory. And Cook knew he would be facing an inventory management nightmare when Jobs unveiled five different colors of iMacs.

Cook wasted no time. In his first month on the job, he outsourced production of the printed circuit cards inside Macs, easing the complexity of the manufacturing job. He closed more than 10 warehouses for finished products, making do with nine regional sites. With fewer places for stuff to sit, the less stuff there would be, he reasoned. "If you have closets, you'll fill them up," says Cook.

Simplicity was the key. Cook trimmed Apple's list of key suppliers from more than 100 to just 24. That further eased the job of keeping track of all the parts used in Apple's products. And since it meant more business for each supplier, Apple wielded more influence with each—and better prices. Finally, his team scrapped an off-the-shelf software program for managing manufacturing and inventories that had been limping along. Instead, Apple devised its own build-to-order system for handling online purchases.

It has worked beautifully. Pundits snickered when Jobs predicted Dell-like online efficiency at a 1997 event. "We're coming after you, buddy," Jobs said, referring to founder Michael Dell. Today, Apple's online store is shipping 75% of orders on the day they're placed, up from 5% for the Apple of old. "That's as good or better than Dell or Gateway," says Salomon Smith Barney analyst Gardner.

But Cook's biggest claim to fame is getting the inventory of parts down to less than a day—obliterating the record in an industry where weeks or even months is the norm. One reason: Apple has persuaded key suppliers to set up shop close to Apple facilities, for just-in-time delivery. Another benefit of the new system: The entire production process has dropped from almost four months to just two, so Apple can more quickly move to the latest, fastest parts.

Supplier Hardball

It's not all logistical rocket science that has made this possible. Jobs's hardball business tactics have played a role, too. In 1998, for example, Jobs decided that Airborne Logistics Services, a division of Airborne Express that maintained a parts warehouse for Apple in Grove City, Ohio, wasn't delivering spare parts quickly enough. According to Jeff Cooke, who ran Apple's customer-service department at the time, Jobs ordered him to find a replacement for ALS. When Cooke resisted, citing concerns that ALS would sue for breach of contract, he says Jobs told him that "there won't be any lawsuit. Just tell them if they f—- with us, they'll never get another f—-ing dime from this company, ever," Cooke recalls. Jobs says he does not remember making the comment, but confirms that he was determined to drop ALS.

Sure enough, Apple became embroiled in a lawsuit with ALS, which was settled in mid-1999. Cooke resigned after just 100 days at Apple. "My stock options would be worth $10 million had I stayed, but I knew I couldn't have stood it—and he'd have fired me anyway," says Cooke. If some of Jobs's methods are distasteful, they do get results. After dumping ALS, Apple gave its spare-parts business to PC ServiceSource and demanded it slash the inventory by 75% in a matter of weeks, says former PC ServiceSource CEO Mark Hilz, now head of a Dallas real estate management company. "They got very, very results-oriented once Jobs got back there," says Hilz. "Under Steve Jobs, there's zero tolerance for not performing."

Can Apple really be that much better than its rivals? To be sure, it has an advantage. The company churned out only half as many machines as Dell did in their most recent quarters. What's more, some industry veterans wonder if Apple is creating the illusion of near-zero inventory by refusing to take delivery of parts at quarter's end and by pushing finished goods out to retailers on the other end. "They probably have a lot more than a day's worth of parts in the middle of the quarter and do some balance-sheet dressing at the end to make it look like that," says one Wall Street analyst. Cook denies this is even possible. And most analysts could care less, given how well Apple is operating.

Jobs now runs every aspect of the company with a quintet of trusted top executives—all of them handpicked by him except for Chief Financial Officer Fred D. Anderson, the lone survivor of the previous regime. Jobs quickly stripped out vestiges of bureaucracy, eliminating the chief administrative officer and chief technologist. Now, each exec is responsible for everything related to his specialty rather than a narrow product group or market segment. Hardware chief Jon Rubinstein, for example, can make sure every new Mac is built with parts that can be leveraged across as many models as possible.

This tight-knit management structure is crucial. Since almost all big decisions are made at Monday morning executive committee meetings, it's easy for various parts of the company to work closely together. And it lets Jobs easily impose his perfectionism on everything the company produces, from press releases to software to new PCs. Says hardware chief Rubinstein: "We don't sit around talking about how to drive up the stock or how to stick it to the competition. It's always about the products."

Apple's success in the consumer market is attracting renewed interest from computer-industry players. That's a big turnabout from just three years ago when companies, from PC game developers to retailers, had decided the Mac platform wasn't worth pursuing. Mouse-maker Logitech, which made almost no Mac products two years ago, now has Mac versions of almost every model, says CEO Guerrino DeLuca. Microsoft, which invested $150 million in Apple in 1997, confirmed its commitment on July 19 by announcing a new Mac version of its Office desktop productivity suite. It's similar with other software developers.

Oh sure, major obstacles remain. The biggest: making the transition to the new MacOS X. It's a necessary step—maybe the biggest upgrade of the Mac OS since it rocked the computer world in 1984 with its graphical user interface. Based on the NeXTStep program purchased when Apple bought Jobs's NeXT Computer Systems in 1997, MacOS X is designed to make Macs crash far less often and let them speedily do more than one thing at a time. Plus, MacOS X features a new user interface, dubbed Aqua, that's classic Jobs. Besides a delicious marine blue color, it's heavy on neato graphical tricks. Close a window in MacOS X, and it whooshes into a tiny icon on the bottom of the screen rather than simply disappearing and leaving the user wondering how to get it back.

Still, there are as many risks with the MacOS X as advantages. For starters, many observers doubt it will be ready by the January deadline Apple announced. Apple already has missed a summer target date. And while Apple has vowed that it will retain most of the feel so beloved by Mac loyalists, it adds a three-dimensional look that changes the way you navigate between programs—which could alienate the faithful. Even if successful, MacOS X won't reestablish the huge lead Apple used to have in ease of use. Indeed, Microsoft plans to upgrade its consumer version of Windows in September. "MacOS X just keeps Apple up with the status quo," says Raskin.

Another potential glitch for Apple: a paucity of retail outlets. It needs to expand distribution if it hopes to reach out beyond its loyal fans. Apple now has only 11,000 outlets, compared with 20,000 at its peak three years ago. And it has gone all-out to improve the buying experience at chains such as Sears and CompUSA, including sending out armies of Apple staffers to tidy up the aisles. Yet, market researcher Allison Boswell of *The Boswell Report* says that Mac sales at these major chains have flagged in recent quarters. Sales at Apple-only boutiques and at the online store have picked up the slack.

Poster Boys

Some analysts are calling on Jobs to imitate PC maker Gateway Inc. by opening its own stores. Apple has taken baby steps in that direction. At a CompUSA store in downtown San Francisco, Apple's business jumped from 15% to 35% of sales after Apple set up a special Mac section and a cybercafè outfitted with iMacs. Apple denies there are plans to build Apple-only stores of its own, but CFO Anderson does say that we're going to do what's necessary to improve the buying experience."

Jobs is determined to stick to the strategy that has brought Apple back this far—one that has his personal stamp on it. Rarely has a company been more the product of one man than Apple (Exhibit 6). His style permeates even the company's iMac factory in Singapore, where huge "Think different" posters featuring Jobs's personal heroes such as Einstein and Bob Dylan hang from the ceiling.

EXHIBIT 6 'If the PC Doesn't Change, It'll Go the Way of the Dodo'

Steven P. Jobs has done what many said was impossible: He has put the pizzazz back into Apple Computer Inc. With his flair for design and his marketing panache, Jobs has propelled Apple's revenue growth to 17% in the latest quarter—second only to Dell Computer Corp. And the Apple co-founder sees nothing but better times ahead. Is he right? Jobs lays out his thinking in an interview with Silicon Valley correspondent Peter Burrows.

Q: *You've been back at Apple for three years now, and the company is once again healthy. Now, you're expanding the product line and distribution. And you've said the company is looking into new product areas. Is Apple going for big-time growth again?*
A: This is about Apple hitting its stride. High-performance organizations take time to mature, but once you get there it's really great. I think Apple's entering a wonderful decade where it's going to make some major contributions again.

Q: *How much bigger can the company become?*
A: We have about 6% market share now [excluding the business market, where Apple doesn't compete]. If it's only 6% now, that means we only have to convince another 6% of PC buyers to buy from us and we can double the size of our company. That's exciting.

Q: *Apple's recovery has been about a return to its original strengths: product design and marketing. Is there anything the world doesn't get?*
A: I've seen Microsoft praised for the way they continuously improve their products—how even if they don't get it right the first time, they just keep coming. Well, I think we deserve some of that praise. There's just no relief around here, we just keep coming. To execute like we have been and bring out a major new product or initiative every nine months is just amazing to me.

Q: *You cut long-term research when you arrived. But some observers say that Apple is getting by on the strength of slick design and marketing, and that it's not sustainable.*
A: That's not a very insightful point of view. Making the iMac work without a noisy fan is not just fit-and-finish. It is hard-core engineering. If people think Apple's success is based on candy-colored iMacs that sell because of

(continued)

EXHIBIT 6 *(concluded)*

their colors, they're not seeing the whole story. Take the Cube. There is not another PC company in the world that could have designed the Cube. They don't have the engineering, nor do they have the design talent.

Q: *How can Apple stay ahead of the Wintel industry that includes Microsoft, Intel, and all those PC makers?*
A: What I observed early on in my career is what can be done if you have the right people. With most things in life, the difference between the best and the worst is maybe 30% to 50%. But when we created Apple, I realized that [co-founder] Steve Wozniak was at least 25 to 50 times better than the average. It's hard to put a number on it, because sometimes such people can do things that no amount of average people could do. And I think that's what we've built here.

Q: *Isn't a PC just a PC?*
A: Our industry has been in a coma for years—including us, until recently. But there's tremendous opportunity for innovation. We think the horizontal model for the PC industry [in which PC makers get software from Microsoft and chips from Intel rather than use their own] may have seen its better days. That works great when it's all about basically cranking out boxes. But we're the only company left that owns the whole widget. We can take responsibility for the whole user experience—and we're in a time when people want more from their PCs.

Q: *What about the talk that we're entering a post-PC era where people will use information appliances that do one thing well, rather than a PC?*
A: If the PC doesn't change, it'll go the way of the dodo bird and the dinosaur. But we have a very clear sense of what needs to be done. And while we agree that there will be planets around the sun, the PC will still be at that center.

Q: *There's a sense that if any company is a reflection of its CEO, it's Apple—from the marketing to the products. How much of what Apple does comes from your hunches?*
A: We are always having big drawn-out meetings about what is important and what is enduring. You can't believe the number of times we've talked about information appliances, for example, and whether that's a market we should get into. But so far, we've decided it's better to do a $799 iMac vs. a $499 iOpener that nobody's going to be happy with.

Q: *Dell and Compaq have recently announced that they will discontinue iMac-like PCs. Some analysts have taken that to mean that there's just not a big market for PCs with slick designs—Apple's specialty.*
A: Yeah, we've heard. I guess fashion is going out of fashion. But Apple really does believe design is important. It's hard to name another area of human purchase where it's not—in cars, in houses, even in spouses! It's not the only consideration, but it's a very important one....And everyone else is retreating because they've failed. We're the only one with the necessary engineering and the necessary design skills—and the courage—to pioneer new classes of computers. It looks easy, but it's not.

Q: *How would a breakup of Microsoft affect Apple?*
A: The amount of time we've spent talking about that is about a half-hour. I'm totally serious. We're not going to win or lose based on how they or any other competitor does. It'll be based on how we do.

Q: *Matt Drudge recently reported that Disney was thinking about buying Apple and Pixar, and that you would be groomed to replace CEO Michael D. Eisner. Any plans to leave?*
A: That again! All I can say is that if they're planning something, they haven't told me about it.

Jobs has even managed to impose his insistence on total secrecy at a company where leaks were once rampant. When a Web site called Mac OS Rumors got close to breaking news of the Cube, Apple threatened to sue. Indeed, only a few hundred of Apple's 10,000 staffers had heard of the machine when Jobs took the stage for his July 19 keynote. "We have cells, like a terrorist organization," laughs Rubinstein. "Everything is on a need-to-know basis."

But with so much of its future resting on the power—and instincts—of one person, Apple is vulnerable. What if Jobs gets distracted or falls off his game? While he has guessed right of late, he hasn't always been perfect. He was ousted from Apple in 1985 in part because his original Mac couldn't be expanded. His cube-shaped computer at NeXT was one of the great bombs in high-tech history. And now, his new Cube is as much a product of his personal taste as any he has done. "There have been two products that really brought a smile to Steve's face: the iMac and the Cube," says Anderson. If Jobs can keep clicking on all the keys, there will be plenty of reasons for Mac fans and investors to grin, as well.

With Jay Greene in Seattle

Source: Peter Burrows, "Apple," *Business Week,* July 31, 2000, 102–06, 108, 110, 112.

Case 6–13

International Business Machines

To prepare for his annual meeting with Wall Street last May (1999), IBM Chairman Louis V. Gerstner Jr. had an assistant pull the financial reports on 25 of the "real Internet standard bearers"—companies like Yahoo!, America Online, Amazon.com, eBay, and E*Trade. Last year, those companies generated combined revenues of about $5 billion—and lost $1 billion. Yet the market value of the Internet 25 together was 50% greater than that of IBM. "Go figure," Gerstner deadpanned when he delivered the news to analysts. "Now, I am not suggesting that you view us as an Internet company, but I think it is worth noting that IBM is already generating more [e-business] revenue and certainly more profit than all of the top Internet companies combined."

Get ready to adjust your thinking. The marquee names of the Internet Age may be dot.com companies, but the big dot in the New Economy these days is IBM. While Amazon's Jeffrey P. Bezos and Yahoo!'s Timothy Koogle get all the Internet kudos, Gerstner has been quietly zipping past competitors, large and small, to emerge as a leading arms supplier to the Information Age. Today, IBM is doing it all: helping merchants hang their shingles online, advising corporate chieftains on how to reshape their businesses top-to-bottom, even wiring local courthouses. "They get it," concedes Edward J. Zander, president of rival Sun Microsystems Inc. "Every day they're telling a better story."

No Choice

And its one that Zander and other rivals don't much enjoy hearing. Big Blue, despite its dinosaur image, is doing a boffo business from the Net. IBM estimates that 25% of its revenue—some $20 billion—is driven by e-business demand. That's nearly 50% more than Internet darling Sun, whose servers are de rigeur for most Web businesses. Even sweeter: About 75% of IBM's e-business revenue comes from sales of Net technology, software, and services—fast-growth, fat-margin businesses—and not the old mainframe computers for which IBM is so well known.

Just as surprising is how Gerstner is seizing the Internet inside IBM. The 57-year-old CEO, once jeered for his lack of computer industry experience, has done an extraordinary job of weaving the Web's vast reach into every corridor of the company—its products, its practices, its marketing. The results have been stunning: Online sales, mostly of PCs, are expected to top $12 billion for the year, skyrocketing nearly 400% from $3.3 billion last year. The productivity gains from using the Net have been just as profound. The company figures it will save $750 million by letting customers find answers to technical questions on its Web site. And by handling a portion of its internal training over the Net instead of in classrooms, IBM will save $120 million. All told, IBM will whack nearly $1 billion out of its costs this year by taking advantage of the Web.

Suddenly, International Business Machines is looking a lot more like Internet Business Machines (Exhibit 1). Surprised? Don't be. Gerstner doesn't have a choice. Every company from the tiniest dot.com startup to IBM's biggest rival is using the Net to skin costs to the bone and to reach new customers. And even though Gerstner has been hard at work doing just that, IBM's gargantuan size has made a wholesale Internet conversion tough. PC and

EXHIBIT 1   **IBM's e-Business Strategy**

E-IBM

The best way to learn is by doing. So IBM is becoming an e-business. By moving purchasing onto the Web, the company expects to save $240 million on the $11 billion in goods and services it will buy this year. Similar moves to put customer support online will save $750 million.

COMPETITIVE LANDSCAPE:

The field is split here. IBM is clearly ahead of rivals such as HP, Sun, and Compaq. Others such as Dell, Cisco, and Intel have been on Internet time longer than IBM.

E-SERVICES

IBM has 130,000 consultants and an e-service business expected to hit $3 billion this year. IBM has handled 18,000 jobs over the last three years—from Web-site design to hooking older corporate databases into new online systems—for companies such as DHL and Payless ShoeSource.

COMPETITIVE LANDSCAPE:

The giants are plunging ahead—Sun, HP, Intel, and EDS—along with upstarts Scient and Lante. Still, IBM has the advantage with corporate databases that need to be hooked into online systems.

E-ENGINEERING

This is where IBM sees e-business heading. Companies will use the Net to cut costs, turning for help on how to do it. United Technologies Corp. has already turned over procurement via the Web to IBM.

COMPETITIVE LANDSCAPE:

Not the usual crowd. Companies with specific skills such as Federal Express will get into logistics, while Andersen Consulting and other Big 4 consultants will help e-engineer business tasks.

PRODUCTS

IBM offers everything from laptop PCs to mainframes that plug easily into the Net. Its software, such as MQ Series, is becoming the glue that allows machines from different makers to pass messages over the Net. Other programs such as Net.Commerce handle huge amounts of e-commerce transactions.

COMPETITIVE LANDSCAPE:

IBM continues to stumble in PCs and servers, as pesky Dell Computer and Sun Microsystems roar ahead. In software, Microsoft looms, while upstarts such as BroadVision have been knocking Big Blue out of some key accounts, such as Ford and Sears.

RESEARCH

IBM pumps half of its $5 billion R&D budget into Internet-related areas. Gerstner isn't stopping there: He has created the Institute for Advanced Commerce, a think tank that includes outside consultants and academics as well as 50 IBM scientists—all working on electronic commerce. Initial focus: Auction software.

COMPETITIVE LANDSCAPE:

Growing your own takes time. Meanwhile, rivals Microsoft, Cisco, and Intel are using their sky-high stock valuations to buy what they need.

E-OUTSOURCING

Don't want to run your Web business? Let IBM host it for you at one of their mega data centers. IBM does the works. At Lego, for example, it runs everything, including contracting the Danish post office to handle shipping.

COMPETITIVE LANDSCAPE:

EDS is big, but it has been slow to move its business to the Net. New outsourcing players like Intel and Exodus are piling in. But IBM remains in the lead.

server sales, are going nowhere. While competitors Dell Computer Corp. and Sun rack up Internet-fueled sales growth of 25% and 40%, respectively, IBM's revenues have been stuck at an Old Economy rate of 7%. This year, analysts estimate, Big Blue will grow a tad faster—9%, bringing revenue to around $90 billion.

That's not nearly fast enough in the New Economy. But if Gerstner can hook more of IBM's revenue to the Net, he may be able to pull IBM out of the slow lane. With $15 billion of IBM's Net-driven revenues growing at more than 30%, the time may not be too far away when the company's slow-growth businesses such as mainframes and storage systems are no longer a drag.

This is Gerstner's chance for IBM to reclaim the mantle of leadership, and it may be his last. If IBM blows the Internet, which is becoming more pervasive with every mouse click, it blows its franchise—perhaps once and for all—as the leading high-tech supplier to Corporate America. In the Internet Age, it's not just Sun, Microsoft, Hewlett-Packard, or Compaq that Big Blue frets about. Every day, nimbler challengers, ranging from e-consultant Scient Corp. to Net software maker BroadVision Inc., keep chipping away at Big Blue's turf. Says IBM senior vice-president and longtime Gerstner confidant Lawrence R. Ricciardi: "We had to be ready to respond, or we would be dinosaur bones."

Y2K Freeze

In some markets, IBM is playing catch-up. The company has been slow to woo the dot.com crowd, for instance, leaving that to Sun, HP, and a slew of startups that sell PCs, servers, and software. The trouble is, Web companies will soon buy as much computer gear as traditional companies. "We've had to adapt our model to them," concedes Gerstner. "We were late."

The events of the past couple of months underscore IBM's urgency to focus on e-business. In early October, the company disclosed that it will yank its Aptiva home PC off retail shelves in North America, making them available only through its Web site. IBM also will lay off up to 10% of its PC workforce. The moves, IBM hopes, will stanch the flow of red ink in a unit that lost nearly $1 billion last year. Analysts expect IBM to lose approximately $400 million in PCs this year.

Then on Oct. 20, the company shocked Wall Street with news that sales of large computers—one of its slowest-growth areas, but among the most profitable—had dried up because customers were locking down their operations for the rest of the year to prepare for Y2K. The buying freeze, IBM told analysts, will hurt the company through the first quarter of next year. The news sent IBM's stock tumbling 15%, to 91 from 107. The company also announced another layoff of up to 6% of the workers in its computer server group.

And now IBM's accounting method has come under scrutiny. On Nov. 24 it was disclosed that Big Blue is being criticized for its policy of bundling one-time gains, such as the $4 billion earned from the sale of its Global Network business to AT&T, into operating income. That, critics claim, makes it difficult for the average investor to assess the company's performance because operating income is typically used as an indicator of pure sales success since it excludes taxes, interest and other items.

"Very Aggressive"

Nonsense, the company says, IBM maintains that it's following Securities & Exchange Commission guidelines and provides analysts with all the data they need to evaluate the company's efficiency. As for Y2K, IBM says, that's a temporary hit on big iron computers while customers sort out last-minute changes before the new millennium. But Gerstner says demand for e-services and software is strong. And analysts agree. They expect sales for online systems to gain momentum sometime after the first quarter, when companies will have finished wrestling with Y2K. "E-business is the next big thing on the road map for a lot of companies," says Gartner Group Inc. analyst Tom Bittman.

If Gerstner is right, after years of upheaval, Big Blue could once again be on solid terrain. Gerstner believes that the advent of the Internet will befuddle execs already struggling to take advantage of the new technologies. Companies around the globe will spend $600 billion a year by 2003 on e-business, according to market researcher International Data Corp. More importantly, some 62% of that amount will go to consultants and the like who can sort out how to use all the bedeviling technology. By contrast, just 29% will be spent on hardware and 9% on software. "The real leadership in the industry is moving away from the creation of the technology to the application of the technology," says Gerstner. "The explosive growth is in services."

That couldn't be better for IBM. Building powerful computers and software that don't fail, as well as providing tons of services—especially tons of service—is second nature to IBM. Its army of 130,000 consultants in its Global Services unit is unmatched in the industry and does three times more Net work than the $1.9 billion combined revenues of Andersen Consulting, Electronic Data Systems, and Computer Sciences, according to IT Services Advisory LLC, a research and advisory firm in Hillside, N.J. In the past three years, IBM has handled 18,000 Internet jobs for its customers, from shaping an Internet strategy to Web page design to hosting entire online storefronts.

Now IBM's e-business client roster is stoked with the biggest names in industry—from Ford Motor to Charles Schwab, and from Prudential Insurance to the New York Stock Exchange. In a Merrill Lynch Co. survey last month, 53 chief information officers at major corporations cited IBM as one of only two computer companies—the other was Sun—that are best positioned to handle their Internet projects. "They are very aggressive about building their expertise in the online world," says Rhonda Wells, director of e-commerce for Payless ShoeSource Inc., which chose IBM when it wanted to build a full-fledged e-commerce hub—in three months. "IBM has a strong knowledge of brick-and-mortar businesses, not just Internet businesses."

How did Big Blue catapult itself to such heights after such lows? Credit Gerstner. He recognized as early as 1994 that the killer app for the Internet was going to be transactions—not simply having the best browser or the coolest search engine. One of Gerstner's first moves was to shift 25% of IBM's research and development budget into Net projects. He declared that every IBM product must be Internet-friendly. And he began to push all software development toward the Java programming language. There was also a crash effort to tie Lotus Notes software tightly to the Web. "The Internet was a major change and opportunity for IBM. The first person who saw its value was Lou," says G. Richard Thoman, chief executive of Xerox Corp., who worked with Gerstner at IBM, RJR Nabisco, and American Express.

Mushrooming Services

To get the massive, 225,000-person organization focused, Gerstner shook things up. He set up the Internet Div. and appointed Irving Wladawsky-Berger, a respected IBM exec and computer scientist by training, to head it. Wladawsky-Berger made sure that every product in IBM would work with the Web. Then he sat down with his staff and figured out what IBM calls the "white spaces"—the empty spots where the company needs to develop products. Indeed, Gerstner looks back on his move as a "bet-the-company decision."

Gerstner's smartest move, though, may be e-business services. Today it seems like a no-brainer, but in 1995, the industry was obsessed with snazzy new products, from network computers to superfast search engines. Gerstner could have focused on trying to gain leadership in Web cruisers or browsers—after all, IBM had its own browser, which it wound scrapping. Instead, Gerstner decided to use services to distinguish IBM from the pack. "We concluded this [the Internet] was not an information superhighway," says Gerstner. "This was all about business, doing transactions, not looking up information."

Now service is paying huge dividends. The company's e-business services revenue is growing at a galloping 60% and is expected to hit $3 billion this year. And Gerstner says that number could easily double if you include (as he says competitors do) portions of IBM's huge outsourcing jobs that use the Net to deliver software and services. "They have an incredible pool of professional services," says Jeff F. Lucchesi, chief information officer for DHL Airways Inc. IBM helped create DHL Connect, an online shipment scheduling and tracking system that uses IBM software to connect a variety of computers so that customers can get estimated shipping charges immediately. When Lucchesi needed a special Java program, IBM had a team on the job within 24 hours. "That's something that tells me I'll use them again," says Lucchesi.

No wonder Gerstner is adding services as fast as he can. In the past year, IBM has launched 20 new Net-related services including privacy consulting and an online service designed for small to medium-sized business. For as little as $99 a month, IBM will provide all the hardware, software, and services that small businesses need to get online. Big Blue is even in the application service provider (ASP) market, delivering enterprise software from companies such as PeopleSoft, Great Plains Software, and ebank.com over the Net.

Still, the big money is in IBM's traditional customer base—the thousands of big companies that have yet to tap the Net and transform their businesses. IBM refers to such companies as below the e-line. Gerstner isn't just out to help them set up cybershops, he's zeroing in on Web-izing all of their business operations—their supply chains, customer service, logistics, procurement, and even training. "The Internet is ultimately about innovation and integration," says Gerstner. "But you don't get the innovation unless you integrate Web technology into the processes by which you run your business."

Above the e-line, IBM is a straggler. That's why in April, Gerstner created a swat team to focus exclusively on selling IBM products and services to Web companies (Exhibit 2). It's also trying a novel sales approach. Together with Conxion Corp., an Internet service provider, and the Silicon Valley Bank, IBM is offering up to $1 million in technology and services free of charge for six months to 24 Net startups. The idea is to help incubate

EXHIBIT 2   **How IBM Uses the Net**

e-Care	**e-Commerce**
Getting customers to use the Net to help themselves means big savings. For every service call handled through ibm.com, the company saves 70% to 90% of the cost of having a person take that call. This year, IBM expects to handle 35 million online service requests, saving an estimated $750 million in customer support costs.	Through the first three quarters of 1999, e-commerce revenue—from sales of everything from PCs to mainframe software—totaled $9.7 billion, up from $977 million during the same period last year. By yearend, e-commerce revenue is expected to be between $10 billion and $15 billion, vs. $3.3 billion in 1998.
e-Learning	**e-Procurement**
IBM estimates that for every 1,000 classroom days converted to electronic courses delivered via the Web, more than $400,000 can be saved. For the year, the company expects 30% of its internal training materials will be delivered online, with anticipated savings of more than $120 million.	In 1999, IBM expects to buy $11 billion in goods and services over the Web, saving at least $240 million. So far this year, IBM has plugged more than 6,700 suppliers into its online procurement system. Now, IBM can cut out rogue buying—employees who buy from suppliers that aren't pre-approved.

startups without them burning through all their funding. At the end of six months, the startup can buy or lease the equipment or simply take a hike.

For all these efforts, IBM's pole position in the Internet race isn't guaranteed. For one, Gerstner hasn't been able to solve his hardware problem. Sure, once companies get past Y2K they'll want more mainframe power to handle massive online businesses. But mainframe prices are falling faster than sales are rising. And in the white-hot Web server business, made up mostly of Unix computers, IBM has been a no-show. That's why its computer business looks anemic compared with Sun's 25% growth. For the year, IBM's sales of Unix systems are expected to reach $3.2 billion, up 7%, says Sanford C. Bernstein & Co. Says Sun Chairman Scott G. McNealy: "They're not nearly the systems provider they used to be."

"Uninspiring Competitor"

That has left IBM on the sidelines during one of the boom periods for Web servers. "We have been an uninspiring competitor against Sun and HP," admits Gerstner. "We're behind in that arena, and we have to take that share back."

Even so, hardware may be the least of Gerstner's worries. The e-biz field is no longer Big Blue's to romp in virtually uncontested. Sun and Microsoft are beefing up their focus on servicing e-biz customers. A revitalized HP is zeroing in too. Even chip giant Intel Corp. is steering its considerable might there, spending $1 billion to set up rooms of servers to host Web sites. And then there is the raft of hot startups that claim IBM and other big companies are just too bloated to work on Net time. "We have the look and feel of a speedboat," says Rudy Puryear, the former head of Andersen Consulting's e-business practice who now heads Chicago-based e-consultant Lante Corp. IBM, he says, is a "battleship."

Some rivals are even taking a page from IBM's playbook—and using it against them. Earlier this year, HP emulated IBM's hugely successful e-business marketing campaign with its own e-services campaign—even hiring a member of the team that launched the e-business campaign to do it. HP's e-services strategy could be a danger to IBM, if it works. That's because HP, which lacks IBM's consulting muscle, is trying to create do-it-yourself Net technologies. In HP's view companies should easily be able to add new features and services onto their Web sites, no big consulting contracts necessary. Says Nick Earle, chief marketing officer for HP's enterprise computing unit: "We always bristle when people say we copied IBM. We learned from the good things that they did, but that was over three years ago. In Internet time, that's a lifetime."

That's why Gerstner isn't letting up. He's pumping more than 50% of IBM's huge $5 billion R&D budget into Net projects, up from 25% in 1996. What's next? IBM wants to be the supplier of technology and services to link all manner of digital devices such as pagers, cell phones, and handheld computers. IBM will either license the technology to others or build the infrastructure and rent the capability.

Massage Chairs

To present this vision to customers—and within IBM—Gerstner is up to his old tricks. In Feb. of 1998, IBM set up the Pervasive Computing Div., headed by Mark F. Bregman, another former IBM research scientist. Much like Wladawsky-Berger did in the Internet Div., Bregman has spent the past 18 months analyzing the market and working with other areas of IBM to develop strategies centered on devices, software, and services that make the Net accessible anywhere, anytime.

The first offering: software that lets any type of digital device, say a cell phone or Palm handheld, fetch content off the Net. Sounds simple, but it isn't. Right now companies are struggling to deliver pages to screens of any size. Bregman's group has put together a service that companies can rent that will translate content from any Web site and deliver it to any screen. "The idea," says Bregman, "is to offer infrastructure as a service. It's more like a utility. You just pay the bill."

Already IBM is lining up customers. On Nov. 29, PlanetRx, an online pharmacy, will go live with a service that allows virtual shopping via Palm handheld devices. Telecom companies Nokia, Ericsson, and Sprint PCS have signed on, too. "Moving information from 17-inch screens on your desk to where it can be used on the Web from anywhere is an important trend," says John F. Yuzdepski, a vice-president at Sprint PCS. "IBM's technology allows a ubiquity of access to information."

The technology is one thing, but if Gerstner is going to build a new IBM, he has to create an Internet culture. That work began in Atlanta four years ago. When you walk in the door at IBM's Atlanta Web design office—dubbed the "Artz Cafe"—dogs are camped out alongside Web designers and an iguana. Four workers sit astride massage chairs getting worked over by masseuses. Ping-pong tables double as conference tables, and there's a billiard table upstairs where workers can go to clear their heads after long hours toiling at—gasp—Macintosh computers. "To attract the cool, younger people in the Internet business we had to break with the whole IBM culture" says Kerry Kenemer, a creative director who sports a goatee. "We're the only creative bone in the entire IBM body."

Now, IBM is trying to spread the culture throughout its organization. On Nov. 15, the company launched Project Springboard. After pouring $100 million into its four-year-old Atlanta Web design center, it's broadening that approach and opening e-business integration centers around the world. Instead of just design services, these centers will offer customers a place to tap IBM specialists and outside experts to set up next-generation e-business solutions.

The centers reflect a hipper IBM that the company hopes will be able attract Web-savvy employees. In some areas, IBM is angling to siphon off creative types by setting up shop in cool areas of the country. In Los Angeles, for example, the center will be near the MTV and Sony studios. The company is even lightening up on job titles. One worker in Chicago goes by the title "concept architect and paradoxiologist." (Translation: Someone who works on tough Internet strategies.)

That's not the only Silicon Valley-ish move the company is taking. Like Intel and Cisco, IBM has quietly invested $60 million in venture funds that focus on Web technologies. Of course the company wouldn't mind a big IPO payday, but it is mostly using these deals to provide "headlights" into cutting-edge technologies. IBM has hit pay dirt on at least one investment so far: In August, it invested $45 million in Internet Capital Group, a holding company that funds business-to-business Web companies. That was just before its public offering. Now IBM's investment is worth $619 million.

New Horizon

What's the next e-business frontier for Big Blue? It's getting companies to turn over entire business processes to IBM that are conducted over the Web. "The way we think of e-business is that it's really the opportunity to do the next level of transformation," says Richard B. Anderson, who has been given the task of taking IBM to the Web.

Consider what IBM is doing for United Technologies Corp. IBM uses the Net to handle $5.8 billion worth of general procurement for Carrier Corp., UTC's Farmington (Conn.) subsidiary. The company won't talk about the actual savings of the system, but says it has been a phenomenal success—increasing efficiency, cutting costs, and becoming a gold mine for collecting information about purchasing habits. Now UTC has the data that will allow the company to talk to suppliers and get better discounts. But UTC insists it's not about cutting costs. "This is all about turning data into information and turning that information into action," says Kent L. Brittan, vice-president for supply management for UTC.

That's the sort of phrase Gerstner might coin for his next analyst's meeting. Back in May, for just a few hours after Gerstner's Wall Street meeting, IBM was like a dot.com company: Its shares shot up 20 points, the kind of movement associated with Web giants eBay or Yahoo! But if Gerstner can continue to convince customers that he has truly remade IBM into Internet Business Machines, he may yet join the Internet 25 (Exhibit 3).

Contributing: Peter Burrows in Santa Clara, Calif., David Rocks in Atlanta, and Diane Brady in Greenwich, Conn.

Source: Ira Sager, "Inside IBM: Internet Business Machines," *Business Week E.Biz,* December 13, 1999, EB20–23, 26, 30, 40,.

EXHIBIT 3 Gerstner on IBM and the Internet

IBM Chairman Louis V. Gerstner Jr. may not be thought of as a tech visionary, but he was remarkably prescient about the Internet. In a conversation with BUSINESS WEEK'S Ira Sager, Gerstner shared his thoughts about IBM and e-business.

Q: *What shaped your early thinking about the Internet?*
A: I commissioned a task force [that] worked for a year on what it really meant to exploit network-centric computing. Their work came together in September of 1995. And we made a very important decision in October. It was the second bet-the-company [decision] that I made. The first was to keep the company together. We said, "If we really believe this, we're going to reprioritize all the budgets in the company." In a period of four weeks, we reallocated $300 million. We created the Internet division. It became the catalyst for change in the company.

Q: *You also made a decision that the Net was about business transactions. How did that come about?*
A: Our work concluded that this was all about business: doing transactions, not looking up information. That came about because every time I'd meet with the task force they would present all this wonderful technology to me, and I would say, "Well, what's a customer going to do with it?" That's where we really began to believe that every physical transaction in the world was going to be augmented or replaced by a digital transaction.

Q: *When you met with Wall Street in May you compared IBM's e-business to the top 25 Internet companies. Were you trying to get analysts to view IBM as an Internet company?*
A: If you define an Internet company as [one] that is totally committed to transforming its internal business, and in our case, to also have it [the Net] be the basis of our entire product offering, then I think there's no company that's as much an Internet company as we are. Now, if you say an Internet company is [one] that has rapidly growing revenue and no profits, then I don't want to be classified as an Internet company.

Q: *How can companies get the biggest payoff from using the Net?*
A: The Internet is ultimately about innovation and integration. Innovation is what your objective is—in cost structures, selling, marketing, sales, supply chain. But you don't get the innovation unless you integrate Web technology into the processes by which you run your business. And that's been the rude awakening for a lot of companies. The true revolution coming from the Web is when the Web can get integrated with business processes.

Q: *People talk about the Internet being a landscape-altering technology. Describe how the Net has changed the landscape within IBM.*
A: We discovered what every large company has: When you bring your company to the Web, you expose all the inefficiency that comes from decentralized organizations. Now, when a customer comes to you on the Web, they're expecting to be able to move across those departments. They're expecting to see a common look and feel.

Q: *But what will the Net do to traditional markets?*
A: All we have to do is watch television, see these guys raising their hands in these financial markets, and you say, "This is going to end." There has to be a more efficient way. And so we'll see the emergence of electronic marketplaces that will have powerful effects, real discontinuities, in the existing structure of markets. What we believe is going to be very important is the delivery of traditional software and services and hardware over the Net. That's a form of electronic marketplace.

Case 6–14
L'Oréal Nederland B.V.

Yolanda van der Zande, director of the Netherlands L'Oréal subsidiary, faced two tough decisions and was discussing them with Mike Rourke, her market manager for cosmetics and toiletries. "We have to decide whether to introduce the Synergie skin care line and Belle Couleur permanent hair colorants," she told him. Synergie had recently been introduced successfully in France, the home country for L'Oréal. Belle Couleur had been marketed successfully in France for two decades. Mr. Rourke responded:

> Yes, and if we decide to go ahead with an introduction, we'll also need to develop marketing programs for the product lines. Fortunately, we only need to think about marketing, since the products will still be manufactured in France.

Ms. van der Zande replied:

> Right, but remember that the marketing decisions on these lines are critical. Both of these lines are part of the Garnier family brand name. Currently Ambre Solaire (a sun screen) is the only product we distribute with the Garnier name in the Netherlands. But headquarters would like us to introduce more Garnier product lines into our market over the next few years, and it's critical that our first product launches in this line be successful.

Mr. Rourke interjected, "But we already sell other brands of L'Oréal products in our market. If we introduce Garnier, what will happen to them?" After some more discussion, Ms. van der Zande suggested:

> Why don't you review what we know about the Dutch market. We've already done extensive marketing research on consumer reactions to Synergie and Belle Couleur. Why don't you look at it and get back to me with your recommendations in two weeks.

Background

In 1992 the L'Oréal Group was the largest cosmetics manufacturer in the world. Headquartered in Paris, it had subsidiaries in over 100 countries. In 1992, its sales were $6.8 billion (a 12 percent increase over 1991) and net profits were $417 million (a 14 percent increase). France contributed 24 percent of total worldwide sales, Europe (both western and eastern countries, excluding France) provided 42 percent, and the United States and Canada together accounted for 20 percent; the rest of the world accounted for the remaining 14 percent. L'Oréal's European subsidiaries were in one of two groups: (1) major countries (England, France, Germany, and Italy) or (2) minor countries (the Netherlands and nine others).

The company believed that innovation was its critical success factor. It thus invested heavily in research and development and recovered its investment through global introductions of its new products. All research was centered in France. As finished products were developed, they were offered to subsidiaries around the world. Because brand life cycles for cosmetics could be very short, L'Oréal tried to introduce one or two new products per year

This case was prepared by Frederick W. Langrehr, Valparaiso University; Lee Dahringer, Butler University; and Anne Stöcker. This case was written with the cooperation of management solely for the purpose of stimulating student discussion. All events and individuals are real, but names have been disguised. We appreciate the help of J. B. Wilkinson and V. B. Langrehr on earlier drafts of this case. Copyright © 1994 by the *Case Research Journal* and the authors.

in each of its worldwide markets. International subsidiaries could make go/no go decisions on products, but they generally did not have direct input into the R&D process. In established markets such as the Netherlands, any new product line introduction had to be financed by the current operations in that country.

L'Oréal marketed products under its own name as well as under a number of other individual and family brand names. For example, it marketed Anaïs Anaïs perfume, the high-end Lancôme line of cosmetics, and L'Oréal brand hair care products. In the 1970s it acquired Laboratoires Garnier, and this group was one of L'Oréal's largest divisions. In France, with a population of about 60 million people, Garnier was a completely separate division, and its sales force competed against the L'Oréal division. In the Netherlands, however, the market was much smaller (about 15 million people), and Garnier and L'Oréal products would be marketed by the same sales force.

Dutch consumers had little, if any, awareness or knowledge of Garnier and had not formed a brand image. The Garnier sunscreen was a new product, and few Dutch women knew about the brand. It was therefore very important that any new Garnier products launched in the Netherlands have a strong concept and high market potential. To accomplish this, the products needed to offer unique, desired, and identifiable differential advantages to Dutch consumers. Products without such an edge were at a competitive disadvantage and would be likely not only to fail but to create a negative association with the Garnier name, causing potential problems for future Garnier product introductions.

The Dutch Market

In the late 1980s, 40 percent of the Dutch population (about the same percentage as in France) was under 25 years old. Consumers in this age group were the heaviest users of cosmetics and toiletries. But as in the rest of Europe, the Dutch population was aging and the fastest-growing population segments were the 25-or-older groups.

Other demographic trends included the increasing number of Dutch women working outside the home. The labor force participation rate of women in the Netherlands was 29 percent. That was much lower than the 50 percent or above in the United Kingdom or the United States, but the number of women working outside the home was increasing faster in the Netherlands than it was in those countries. Dutch women were also delaying childbirth. As a result of these trends, women in the Netherlands were exhibiting greater self-confidence and independence; women had more disposable income, and more of them were using it to buy cosmetics for use on a daily basis.

Despite their rising incomes, Dutch women still shopped for value, especially in cosmetics and toiletries. In the European Union (EU), the Netherlands ranked fourth in per capita income, but it was only sixth in per capita spending on cosmetics and toiletries. Thus, Dutch per capita spending on personal care products was only 60 percent of the amount spent per capita in France or Germany. As a result of both a small population (15 million Dutch to 350 million EU residents) and lower per capita consumption, the Dutch market accounted for only 4 percent of total EU sales of cosmetics and toiletries.

Synergie

Synergie was a line of facial skin care products that consisted of moisturizing cream, anti-aging day cream, antiwrinkle cream, cleansing milk, mask, and cleansing gel. It was made with natural ingredients, and its advertising slogan in France was "The alliance of science and nature to prolong the youth of your skin."

Skin Care Market

The skin care market was the second largest sector of the Dutch cosmetics and toiletries market. For the past five quarters unit volume had been growing at an annual rate of 12 percent, and dollar sales at a rate of 16 percent. This category consisted of hand creams, body lotions, all-purpose creams, and facial products. Products in this category were classified by price and product type. Skin care products produced by institutes such as Shisedo and Estée Lauder were targeted at the high end of the market. These lines were expensive and were sold through personal service perfumeries that specialized in custom sales of cosmetics and toiletries. At the other end of the price scale were mass-market products such as Ponds, which were sold in drugstores and supermarkets. In the last couple of years a number of companies, including L'Oréal, had begun to offer products in the midprice range. For example its Plénitude line was promoted as a high-quality, higher-priced—but still mass-market—product.

Skin care products also could be divided into care and cleansing products. Care products consisted of day and night creams; cleansing products were milks and tonics. The current trend in the industry was to stretch the lines by adding specific products targeted at skin types, such as sensitive, greasy, or dry. An especially fast-growing category consisted of antiaging and antiwrinkling creams. Complementing this trend was the emphasis on scientific development and natural ingredients.

Almost 50 percent of the 5 million Dutch women between the ages of 15 and 65 used traditional skin care products. The newer specialized products had a much lower penetration, as shown in Exhibit 1.

The sales breakdown by type of retailer for the middle- and lower-priced brands is shown in Exhibits 2 and 3.

EXHIBIT 1
Usage of Skin Care Products by Dutch Women

Product	Percentage of Women Using
Day cream	46%
Cleansers	40
Mask	30
Tonic	26
Antiaging cream	3

EXHIBIT 2
Sales Breakdown for Skin Care Products in Supermarkets and Drugstores

Type of Store	Unit Sales (%)	Dollar Sales (%)
Supermarkets	18%	11%
Drugstores	82	89
	100	100

EXHIBIT 3
Sales Breakdown for Skin Care Products by Type of Drugstore

Type of Drugstore	Unit Sales (%)	Dollar Sales (%)
Chains	57%	37%
Large independent	31	39
Small independent	12	24
	100	100

Competition

There were numerous competitors. Some product lines, such as Oil of Olaz (Oil of Olay in the United States) by Procter & Gamble and Plénitude by L'Oréal, were offered by large multinational companies; other brands, for example, Dr. vd Hoog and Rocher, were offered by regional companies. Some companies offered a complete line, while others, such as Oil of Olaz, offered one or two products. Exhibit 4 lists a few of the available lines along with the price ranges and positioning statements.

The Dutch market was especially competitive for new brands such as Oil of Olaz and Plénitude. The rule of thumb in the industry was that share of voice for a brand (the percentage of total industry advertising spent by the company) should be about the same as its market share. Thus, a company with a 10 percent market share should have had advertising expenditures around 10 percent of total industry advertising expenditures. But there were deviations from this rule. Ponds, an established and well-known company with loyal customers, had about 9 percent share of the market (units) but accounted for only about 2.5 percent of total industry ad expenditures. Alternatively, new brands such as Oil of Olaz (10 percent market share, 26 percent share of voice) and Plénitude (5 percent market share, 13 percent share of voice) spent much more. The higher ad spending for these brands was necessary to develop brand awareness and, ideally, brand preference.

Any innovative products or new product variations in a line could be quickly copied. Retailers could develop and introduce their own private labels in four months; manufacturers could develop a competing product and advertising campaign in six months. Manufacturers looked for new product ideas in other countries and then transferred the product concept or positioning strategy across national borders. They also monitored competitors' test markets. Since a test market typically lasted nine months, a competitor could introduce a product before a test market was completed.

Consumer Behavior

Consumers tended to be loyal to their current brands. This loyalty resulted from the possible allergic reaction to a new product. Also, facial care products were heavily advertised

EXHIBIT 4   **Competitive Product Lines of Cosmetics**

	Price Range (Guilders)*	Positioning
Lower End		
Nivea Visage[†]	9.50–11.50	Mild, modest price, complete line
Ponds	5.95–12.95	Antiwrinkle
Middle		
Dr. vd Hoog	10–11.95	Sober, nonglamorous, no illusions, but real help, natural, efficient, relatively inexpensive
Oil of Olaz (Procter & Gamble)	12 (day cream only)	Moisturizing, antiaging
Plénitude (L'Oréal)	10.95–19.95	Delay the signs of aging
Synergie	11.95–21.95	The alliance of science and nature to prolong the youth of your skin
Upper End		
Yvs Rocher	10–26.95	Different products for different skins, natural ingredients
Ellen Betrix (Estée Lauder)	12.95–43.50	Institute line with reasonable prices, luxury products at nonluxury prices

*One dollar = 1.8 guilders; one British pound = 2.8 guilders; 1 deutschmark = 1.1 guilders.
[†]Although Nivea Visage had a similar price range to Dr. vd Hoog, consumers perceived Nivea as a lower-end product.

and sold on the basis of brand image. Thus, users linked self-concept with a brand image, and this increased the resistance to switching. While all consumers had some loyalty, the strength of this attachment to a brand increased with the age of the user. Finally, establishing a new brand was especially difficult since Dutch women typically purchased facial creams only once or twice a year. Dutch women were showing an increasing interest in products with "natural" ingredients, but they were not as familiar as the French were with technical product descriptions and terms.

Market Research Information

Earlier, Mike Rourke had directed his internal research department to conduct some concept and use tests for the Synergie products. The researchers had sampled 200 women between the ages of 18 and 55 who used skin care products three or more times per week. They sampled 55 Plénitude users, 65 Dr. vd Hoog users, and 80 users of other brands.

The participants reacted positively to Synergie concept boards containing the positioning statement and the terminology associated with the total product line. On a seven-point scale with 7 being the most positive, the mean score for the Synergie line for all the women in the sample was 4.94. The evaluations of the women who used the competing brands, Plénitude and Dr. vd Hoog, were similar at 4.97 and 4.88, respectively.

The researchers then conducted an in-depth analysis of two major products in the line: antiaging day cream and moisturizing cream. Participants reported their buying intentions after they tried the Synergie product once and again after they used it for a week. Some participants were told the price, and others did not know the price. The results of this analysis are shown in Exhibit 5.

Belle Couleur

Belle Couleur was a line of permanent hair coloring products. It had been sold in France for about two decades and was the market leader. In France the line had 22 shades that were

EXHIBIT 5   **Buying Intentions for Synergie Products**

	All Participants	Plénitude Users	Dr. vd Hoog Users	Other Brand Users
Price Not Known				
Antiaging daycream				
After trial	5.37*	5.63	5.00	5.42
After use	5.26	5.55	5.08	5.17
Moisturizing cream				
After trial	5.34	5.60	5.38	5.11
After use	5.51	5.74	5.56	5.22
Price Known				
Antiaging daycream				
After trial	3.75	4.13	3.82	3.44
After use	3.60	3.76	3.54	3.54
Certainly buy†	24%	21%	23%	27%
Moisturizing cream				
After trial	4.08	4.36	4.17	3.77
After use	4.06	4.26	4.13	3.78
Certainly buy	39%	52%	38%	30%

*Seven-point scale with 7 being most likely to buy.
†Response to a separate question asking about certainty of buying with "certainly buy" as the highest choice.

mostly natural shades and a few strong red or very bright light shades. It was positioned as reliably providing natural colors with the advertising line "natural colors, covers all gray."

Hair Coloring Market

There were two types of hair coloring: semipermanent and permanent. Semipermanent colors washed out after five or six shampooings. Permanent colors disappeared only as the hair grew out from the roots. Nearly three-quarters (73 percent) of Dutch women who colored their hair used a permanent colorant. Over the past four years, however, the trend had been toward semipermanent colorants, with an increase from 12 percent to 27 percent of the market. Growth in unit volume during those years for both types of colorant had been about 15 percent per annum. The majority of unit sales in the category were in chain drugstores (57 percent), with 40 percent equally split between large and small independent drugstores. Food retailers accounted for the remaining 3 percent.

Competition

In the Netherlands 4 of 10 total brands accounted for 80 percent of the sales of permanent hair colorants, compared to 2 brands in France. Exhibit 6 gives the market share of the leading permanent color brands in the period 1987–1989. Interestingly, none of them had a clear advertising positioning statement describing customer benefits. By default, then, Belle Couleur could be positioned as "covering gray with natural colors."

Hair salons were indirect competitors in the hair coloring market. The percentage of women who had a hairstylist color their hair was not known, nor were the trends in the usage of this method known. It was projected that as more women worked outside the home, home coloring probably would increase because it was more convenient.

L'Oréal's current market entry (Recital) was the leading seller, although its share was declining. Guhl's and Andrelon's increases in shares between 1986 and 1989 reflected the general trend toward using warmer shades, and these two brands were perceived as giving quality red tones. In the late 1980s Guhl had changed its distribution strategy and started selling the brand through drug chains. In 1987 less than 1 percent of sales were through drug outlets; in the first quarter of 1990 drug-outlet sales had reached nearly 12 percent. Guhl also had become more aggressive in its marketing through large independents, with its share in those outlets climbing from 16 to 24 percent over the same period. Both the increasing shares of the smaller brands and the decreasing shares of the leaders sparked a 60 percent increase in advertising in 1989 for all brands of hair coloring.

Consumer Behavior

Consumers perceived permanent hair color as a technical product and believed its use was very risky. As a result, users had strong brand loyalty and avoided impulse purchasing.

EXHIBIT 6
Major Brands of Hair Colorant

Market Shares of	1987	1988	1989
Upper end (14.95 guilders)			
Recital (L'Oréal brand)	35%	34%	33%
Guhl	9	12	14
Belle Couleur (12.95 guilders)	—	—	—
Lower-priced (9.95 guilders)			
Andrelon	12	14	17
Poly Couleur	24	23	21
Others	20	17	15
Total	100	100	100

When considering a new brand, both first-time users and current users carefully read package information and asked store personnel for advice.

Traditionally, hair colorants had been used primarily to cover gray hair. Recently, however, coloring hair had become more of a fashion statement. This partially accounted for the increased popularity of semipermanent hair coloring. In one study the most frequently cited reason (33 percent) for coloring hair was to achieve warm/red tones; another 17 percent reported wanting to lighten their hair color, and covering gray was cited by 29 percent. It was likely that the trend toward using colorants more for fashion and less for covering gray reflected the increase in hair coloring by consumers less than 35 years old. In 1989, 46 percent of Dutch women (up from 27 percent in 1986) colored their hair with either semipermanent or permanent hair colorants. Exhibit 7 contains a breakdown of usage by age of user.

Hair coloring was purchased almost exclusively in drugstores; only 3 percent of sales were through supermarkets. The percentage of sales for drug outlets was chains, 58 percent; large independents, 22 percent; and small independents, 20 percent.

Market Research

As with Synergie, Mr. Rourke had the L'Oréal market researchers contact consumers about their reactions to Belle Couleur. Four hundred twelve Dutch women between the ages of 25 and 64 who had used hair colorant in the last four months were part of a concept test, and 265 of those women participated in a use test. A little over 25 percent of the participants colored their hair every six weeks or more often, while another 47 percent did it every two to three months. (The average French user colored her hair every three weeks.) Nearly 60 percent used hair color to cover gray, while the remainder did it for other reasons.

After being introduced to the concept and being shown some sample ads, participants were asked their buying intentions. The question was asked three times—before and after the price was given and after Belle Couleur was used. The results are shown in Exhibit 8.

In most product concept tests (as with the Synergie line) buying intentions declined once the price was revealed. For Belle Couleur, buying intentions increased after the price was given but decreased after actual use. As the exhibit shows, the percentage of

EXHIBIT 7
Hair Coloring by Age (%)

	1986	1989
Less than 25 years	35%	50%
25–34	24	54
35–49	32	55
50–64	24	33
65 and over	15	19

EXHIBIT 8
Buying Intentions

	Price-Unaware	Price-Aware	After Use
Certainly buy (5)	18%	26%	29%
Probably buy (4)	60	57	30
Don't know (3)	12	5	9
Probably not (2)	7	7	11
Certainly not (1)	3	6	21
Total	100%	100%	100%
Mean score	3.85	3.92	3.35

participants who would probably or certainly not buy the product after using it increased from 13 to 32 percent. In Exhibit 9 only participants who gave negative after-use evaluations of Belle Couleur are included, and they are grouped according to the brands they were using at the time.

To try to determine why some users didn't like the product, the dissatisfied women were asked to state why they disliked Belle Couleur. The results are shown in Exhibit 10.

Many of the women thought that their hair was too dark after using Belle Couleur and said it "didn't cover gray." Those who thought Belle Couleur was different from expected were primarily using the blond and chestnut brown shades of colorant. This was expected, since in France Belle Couleur was formulated to give a classical, conservative dark blond color without extra reflections or lightening effects and the product had not been modified for the Dutch test. The competing Dutch-manufactured hair colorant competitors, by contrast, were formulated to give stronger lightening effects. Thus, some of the negative evaluations of Belle Couleur were due to the fact that Dutch women tended toward naturally lighter hair colors, and the French toward darker shades.

EXHIBIT 9 **Purchase Intentions and Evaluation of Belle Couleur by Brand Currently Used**

	Brand Currently Used				
	Total Sample	Andrelon	Poly Couleur	Guhl	Recital (L'Oréal)
After-Use Purchase Intentions of Belle Couleur					
Probably not (2)	11%	12%	12%	14%	5%
Certainly not (1)	21	24	29	20	5
	32%	36%	41%	34%	10%
Overall mean score	3.35	3.4	3.1	3.4	3.95
Evaluation of Final Color of Belle Couleur					
Very good (1)	25%	24%	31%	22%	35%
Good (2)	43	40	31	44	49
Neither good or bad (3)	10	10	14	6	8
Bad (4)	12	14	5	18	8
Very bad (5)	9	12	19	10	. . .
Mean	2.37	2.5	2.5	2.5	1.89
Comparison to Expectations					
Much better (1)	11%	12%	14%	14%	14%
Better (2)	26	12	21	24	38
The same (3)	29	38	26	28	32
Worse (4)	19	24	19	18	11
Much worse (5)	15	14	19	16	5
Mean	3.0	3.17	3.07	2.98	2.57
Compared with Own Brand					
Much better (1)		17%	17%	24%	14%
Better (2)		21	19	24	32
The same (3)		21	31	14	30
Worse (4)		21	12	16	16
Much worse (5)		19	21	22	8
Mean		3.05	3.02	2.88	2.73

Note: Data for total sample not available.

EXHIBIT 10
Reasons for Negative Evaluations of Belle Couleur by Brand Currently Used

	Brand Currently Used				
	Total Sample	Andrelon	Poly Couleur	Guhl	Recital (L'Oréal)
Hair got dark/darker instead of lighter	13%	14%	17%	14%	5%
Irritates skin	8	10	7	2	11
Ammonia smell	5	7	—	2	—
Didn't cover gray	5	12	2	4	3
Color not beautiful	5	7	5	6	3
Color different from expected	5	5	10	4	3

Note: Some of the cell sizes are very small, and caution should be used when comparing entries of less than 10 percent.

Role of Distributors

Distributors' acceptance of the two product lines was critical for L'Oréal's successful launch of both Synergie and Belle Couleur. At one time, manufacturers had more control in the channel of distribution than did retailers. Retailers, however, had been gaining power as a result of the increasing size of retailers, the development of chains with their central buying offices, and the proliferation of new brands with little differentiation from brands currently on the market. Retailers had also increasingly been offering their own private-label products, since they earned a higher-percentage profit margin on their own brands.

Following are the criteria, listed in order of importance (3 being "most important"), that retailers used to evaluate new products:

1. Evidence of consumer acceptance   2.5

2. Manufacturer advertising and promotion   2.2

3. Introductory monetary allowances 2.0

4. Rationale for product development 1.9

5. Merchandising recommendations   1.8

L'Oréal's goal for developing new products was to introduce only products that had a differential advantage with evidence of consumer acceptance. It did not want to gain distribution with excessive reliance on trade deals or higher than normal retail gross margins. L'Oréal also wanted to have its Garnier product lines extensively distributed in as many different types of retailers and outlets as possible. This approach to new product introduction had been effective for L'Oréal, and it currently had a positive image with Dutch retailers. L'Oréal was perceived as offering high-quality, innovative products supported with good in-store merchandising.

For L'Oréal's current products, 35 percent of sales came from independent drugstores, 40 percent from drug chains, and 25 percent from food stores. For all manufacturers, drug chains and supermarkets were increasing in importance. These stores required a brand with high customer awareness and some brand preference. The brands needed to be presold since, unlike independent drugstores, there was no sales assistance.

Introducing a line of products rather than just a product or two resulted in a greater need for retail shelf space. Although the number of new products and brands competing for retail shelf space frequently appeared unlimited, the space itself was a limited resource. With

Belle Couleur, L'Oréal had already addressed this issue by reducing the number of Belle Couleur colorants it planned to offer in the Netherlands. Although 22 shades were available in France, L'Oréal had reduced the line to 15 variations for the Netherlands. As a result, 1.5 meters (about five linear feet) of retail shelf space was needed to display the 15 shades of Belle Couleur. Synergie required about half this shelf space.

Decision Time

After reviewing the information on the market research on the two product lines, Ms. van der Zande summarized the situation. L'Oréal Netherlands could leverage its advertising of the Garnier name by promoting two lines at once. Consumers would hear and see the Garnier name twice, not just once. As a result, Dutch consumers might see Garnier as a major supplier of cosmetics and toiletries. But she was concerned about the selling effort that would be needed to sell the L'Oréal brands that were already in the Dutch market and at the same time introduce not just one but two new brand name product *lines*. The Dutch L'Oréal sales force would have to handle both family brands, since the much lower market potential of the Netherlands market could not support a separate Garnier sales force, as in France. She was also concerned about retailer reaction to a sales pitch for two product lines.

   Ms. van der Zande reflected that she was facing three decision areas. First, she had to decide if she should introduce one or both product lines, and she had to make this decision knowing that L'Oréal would not reformulate the products just for the Dutch market. Second, if she decided to introduce either one or both of the product lines, she needed to develop a marketing program. This meant she had to make decisions on the promotion of the product line(s) to both retailers and consumers as well as the pricing and distribution of the line(s). Third, given that the Garnier product introductions might negatively affect the sales of her current product lines, she needed tactical marketing plans for those products.

Case 6–15
A.T. Kearney

Richard Ivey School of Business
The University of Western Ontario

IVEY

It was early Monday morning, September 22, 1996, and Brian Harrison, president of A. T. Kearney (Canada), was in his Chicago office preparing for an upcoming meeting. A. T. Kearney, headquartered in Chicago, Illinois, was one of the world's largest and most respected global management consulting firms. On Friday, Brian was to meet with the rest of the Toronto management team to review the activities of the firm since its acquisition by Electronic Data Systems (EDS) just over a year ago and to discuss the strategic direction of the firm moving forward. Of particular interest to the management team were the challenges A.T. Kearney faced in trying to take advantage of the new relationship it shared with EDS, a leader in the global Information Services industry.

   From a client perspective, many new opportunities were created by the acquisition. Clients could take advantage of a much broader range of services. In essence, the new EDS/A.T. Kearney organization was striving to become a "one-stop-shop," capable of servicing every client requirement. However, many consultants were concerned about the ability of these two very different organizations, with different skill sets and culture, to

Michael Carter prepared this case under the supervision of Professor Donald W. Barclay solely to provide material for class discussion. The authors do not intend to illustrate either effective or ineffective handling of a managerial situation. The authors may have disguised certain names and other identifying information to protect confidentiality. Copyright © 1998, Ivey Management Services.

work together in blending their services into a broad, seamless continuum. Senior consultants wondered about the implications it would have for the overall market strategy of the firm, and the changes that would have to be made for these two companies to benefit fully from the acquisition. Brian prepared himself for what he expected would be a rather lively discussion around this very issue.

Sipping his coffee, Brian smiled as he reviewed the results of a recent A. T. Kearney survey of information technology practices and perceptions at some of the world's largest corporations. Senior executives at Global 1000 companies were interviewed to explore their evolving attitudes toward the role of information technology in their core businesses. Information technology (IT) issues had indeed emerged on "the CEO Agenda." One particular excerpt caught Brian's attention:

> The results suggest a fundamental shift away from the days when information technology was viewed as one tactical item among others used to improve business productivity. No longer is IT just another tool the CEO might use to accomplish cost savings and operational ends. Today, information technology can help solve product problems, set new levels of service and create new distribution and communication channels. It has become sufficiently important to be included in the process of setting a company's strategic objectives.

The study reached the following main conclusions:

- Technology has been integrated into business strategy

- Technology investments will increase

- Corporations are embracing the philosophy of restructuring and reengineering

- Senior management is becoming technology-literate as, across all industries, major corporations increasingly view themselves as "technology-oriented companies"

- Senior management expresses satisfaction with return on technology investment, even in the absence of precise measurements.

These results were no surprise to Brian Harrison, who had played a key role in EDS's acquisition of A.T. Kearney and the subsequent merger of the firm into its new parent. The largest buy-out of a management consulting firm in history had been a bold strategic move for both organizations. The results of the survey highlighted the growing importance of technology as an area of concern and interest among senior management at the world's largest corporations, many of which were clients of A. T. Kearney.

Fred Steingraber, A. T. Kearney's CEO since 1983, suggested:

> The days are past when senior management could remain aloof from the adoption of new technology and still expect to increase quality, productivity, market share, and profits. Today, every enterprise is a high-technology business to the extent that technology, strategy and operational decisions must be made simultaneously to ensure a competitive advantage in the marketplace.

Industry

In 1994, general management consulting firms billed an estimated $40 billion of services to corporations around the globe. The world's top fifteen consulting companies, with over 91,000 consultants, accounted for $18 billion of this total.[1] In particular, services related to

---

[1] According to Consultants News—*Chicago Tribune*, "Consulting firms are no longer put on the shelf and forgotten," Wednesday, September 27, 1995.

information technology (i.e., IT planning, IT strategy, strategic procurement of hardware and software solutions) and process reengineering accounted for almost half of the total fees billed to clients. This segment was expected to grow faster than any other through the turn of the century at an annual rate of up to 15 per cent. Fred Steingraber suggested that total fees for the management consulting industry would double by the year 2000. So why all the growth in consulting?

Many suggested that it had to do with management's need for expert assistance as companies pushed further into the global marketplace and started to rethink strategy for the 21st century. Combined with increasing business uncertainty, senior executives would continue to look for guidance on the way their industries were headed, how to align business processes with strategy, how to empower employees, and how technology could be used to attain competitive advantage. For numerous reasons, it was often more effective for the agent of such changes to come from the outside. Heavy downsizing and cost cutting efforts by many companies in recent years also played a major role in the continued growth of the consulting industry, since corporations around the world had created their own shortage of capable staff.

Coupled with strong growth, the management consulting industry was also undergoing tremendous change. This transformation was being driven by significant trends in the marketplace, some of which included:

- The convergence of telecommunications, technology and information services, dramatically altering the structure of business and how companies competed in the global marketplace;

- The rapid pace of technology development and the movement of technology to the "front line" of operations and the desktop;

- The need to rapidly develop, customize and market new products and services world-wide.

Global clients, accompanied by global issues, were becoming the norm. There was a need to continuously demonstrate greater industry expertise, deep business knowledge and in-depth thought leadership to guide clients into the future and ensure flexibility in a rapidly changing environment. It was becoming a requirement that leading-edge information technology be incorporated into implementable solutions, as technology and convergence played an increasing role in driving strategy, and in restructuring industries.

Engagements were becoming longer with greater emphasis placed on achieving performance targets, and fees increasingly tied to tangible results. Consultants were evolving as "partners" in long-term business relationships. Fred Steingraber commented:

> For a long time, much of the industry's focus was on single-dimension projects. Now the leading consulting firms must possess multidisciplinary consulting capability to secure meaningful relationships with clients worldwide. The idea that consultants are just there for a single project has all but disappeared. Management consulting has new requirements and must develop enhanced capabilities to remain competitive and to be prepared to serve clients effectively in the 21st century.

Competition

The lines between strategy, operations and information systems consulting continued to blur. A broad range of service capabilities would be required for firms to achieve high impact, tangible results and the ability to position themselves in the high value-added end of management consulting. An integrated service continuum from strategy formulation to implementation was the direction in which many international players were heading.

(I) The "Big Six"—Classic IT Firms

The "Big Six" accounting firms (Price Waterhouse, Deloitte & Touche, KPMG, Coopers & Lybrand, Ernst and Young, and Andersen) were enjoying annual growth rates in excess of 15 percent. A large part of this growth was supported by their large share of the fast-growing IT/BPR (Business Process Reengineering) consulting market and a strong push into operations consulting as IT became increasingly strategic in nature and instrumental for reengineering.

(II) Operational and Strategic Firms

Traditional consulting firms like McKinsey, BCG, Bain, and Booz Allen & Hamilton, who were best known for their strategic expertise, were broadening their service offerings as they moved aggressively downstream into operations consulting. Both strategy and operational consultants were pushing information technology as clients demanded more implementation capabilities, and reengineering required information technology resources.

(III) Systems Integrators and System Vendors

Classical IT firms such as EDS, CSC (Computer Sciences Corporation), IBM, and Cap Gemini had moved into more traditional management consulting markets, recognizing that IT had become increasingly strategic in nature and critical for reengineering. With the exception of EDS, CSC, and Cap Gemini, these firms had built practices in the business and IT consulting area from the ground up.

(IV) New Information Technology Entrants

Some of the fastest-growing players were the new information technology entrants, such as AT&T and Oracle who, along with Andersen, had spotted the opportunity to consolidate client relationships by selling "upstream" consulting services on top of their core outsourcing and system integration skills. AT&T, for one, started AT&T Solutions in early 1995 to offer end-to-end solutions supplied through various units. They positioned themselves as the 'Technology Life Cycle Management' company who would increase their value to clients by tying computer and communications solutions to the customer's strategic business objectives. Many of these capital-strong, technology-oriented firms were establishing consulting practices through the acquisition of smaller generalists. Some industry analysts suggested that these IT giants would claim over 15 percent market share before the turn of the century.

Results to date suggested that full-service firms were performing better in terms of growth and profitability (Exhibit 1). Many were expanding and integrating their service portfolio, supporting the belief that technology and high value-added consulting went hand-in-hand. Industry observers had noted several competitors merging practices in convergent industries like telecommunications, media, entertainment, and consumer electronics. Many of the operational, generalist, and IT players continued to evaluate potential merger/ alliances to enhance their service portfolio (Exhibit 2).

A.T. Kearney

Founded in 1926, A.T. Kearney had evolved into one of the world's dominant management consulting practices. Its approach was to develop realistic solutions and help clients implement recommendations that generated tangible results and improved competitive advantage. The firm was well known for its ability to deliver value and results throughout the management process, from strategy development to business and market analysis to operations, process, and technology transformation. This mix of strategy and operations,

EXHIBIT 1 **Vertically Integrated Firms Perform Better**

Source: *Consultants News*, A. T. Kearney.

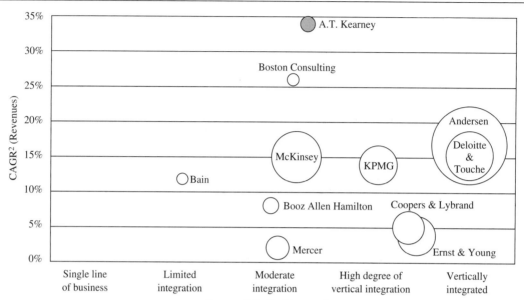

*Growth measured between 1990–1995.

combined with a focus on implementation, had differentiated A.T. Kearney from its competitors and driven the firm's outstanding results for over a decade. The leaders of the firm emphasized strong, lasting relationships (at the CEO level) with fewer, larger clients. To this end A. T. Kearney had been quite successful. Continuously challenging themselves to exceed their clients' expectations, more than 75 percent of their business volume was generated from clients who had used A.T. Kearney's services the previous year.

While striving to help global clients gain and sustain competitive advantage, A. T. Kearney pursued its own goals of globalization, growth and leadership. Before integrating with Management Consulting Services (MCS), EDS's management consulting arm, the firm had 40 offices in 22 countries. It was expected that over 65 percent of A. T. Kearney's revenues would be generated outside of the United States by 1997. This was quite remarkable considering that only 10 percent of revenues came from outside the United States as late as 1980. Accompanying its aggressive move towards globalization, A. T. Kearney had experienced tremendous growth over the last decade. From a staff of only 230 in 1984 to over 1,100 consultants in 1994, the firm had enjoyed double digit revenue growth for each of the last 13 years. A.T. Kearney had doubled its size every three years since 1983 and was recently listed in *Consultants News* as one of the five fastest-growing consulting firms in the world. Brent Snell, a Principal in the Toronto office, suggested that A. T. Kearney was, in fact, "growth-constrained only by having insufficient numbers of highly qualified new people at all levels of the organization."

Electronic Data Systems (EDS)

EDS started in 1962 with Ross Perot and a $1,000 investment. The fledgling company began by offering routine data processing services for Dallas-area companies on computers they didn't even own. In 1985, a year after Perot sold the information technology giant

EXHIBIT 2   Major Service Offerings of Leading Consulting and Information Technology Services Firm

Sources: A. T. Kearney, Gartner Group.

Management Consulting Capabilities	Andersen Consulting	AD Little	A.T. Kearney & EDS	Bain & Co.	Booz Allen & Hamilton	Boston Consulting Group	CSC & CSC Index	Coopers & Lybrand	Deloitte & Touche	Ernst & Young	Cap Gemini	IBM	KPMG	McKinsey	Mercer Management	Monitor
Strategic Consulting (enterprise)1																
Strategic Consulting (operations improvement)2																
Finance																
Marketing & Sales																
HR/benefits																
R&D																
Business Process Reengineering																
• Business Process																
• Organization (change management design)																
• IT Planning																
IT Strategy																

1 High level corporate or business unit strategy (i.e., deciding what business to participate in or to acquire).
2. Targeted business issue analysis (i.e., deciding how to improve customer service, or deciding on the most effective type of retail delivery system).

Legend: ■ Strong   ▨ Participating   ▢ New initiative or small practice   □ Not participating in this area

to General Motors for an estimated $2.5 billion, EDS reported revenues of $3.4 billion, a 264 percent improvement from the previous year. By 1995, as a subsidiary of the auto manufacturer, EDS was making most of its money running the computer networks of its clients more efficiently than they could. It helped customers use information and technology to recast their economics and to identify and seize new opportunities. This translated into 90,000 employees in 41 countries and revenues that were expected to exceed $12 billion. Considered by many to be the inventor of 'outsourcing', EDS had established itself as a world leader in information technology services (Exhibit 3).

EDS was very much a part of everyone's world. For soccer's World Cup of 1994, EDS developed the largest and most complex information system of its kind for the world's largest single sporting event (seen more than 31 billion times around the world). Instant information on each match, player biographies, and historical information for every World Cup ever played were available to some 15,000 journalists covering the matches in nine cities across the United States. In 1995 in the United States alone, EDS processed over 2.2 million Automated Banking Machine (ABM) transactions, 1.2 billion credit card authorizations and 500,000 airline reservations.

EDS defined its business as "shaping how information is created, distributed, shared, enjoyed, and applied for the benefit of businesses, governments, and individuals around the world." Its service offering included four different types of products:

EXHIBIT 3 **EDS and Its Major Competitors in the Computer Service Market**

Company	Location	Sales* (billions USD)	Net Income* (millions USD)	Major Customers
Electronic Data Services	Plano, Texas	$10.50	821.9	GM, Xerox, American Express Bank, Inland Revenue, Bethlehem Steel
Computer Sciences (CSC)	El Segundo, California	3.37	110.7	General Dynamics, Hughes Aircraft, Lucas Industries, Department of Defense
Andersen Consulting	Chicago, Illinois	3.45	N.A.	Bell Atlantic, LTV, British Petroleum, London Stock Exchange
Integrated Systems Solutions (a unit of IBM)	White Plains, New York	N.A.	N.A.	BankAmerica, McDonnell Douglas, Amtrak, Eastman Kodak

*Latest fiscal year for each company as of August 1995.
N.A. = Not available.
Sources: The companies, Disclosure Inc.—*The Wall Street Journal,* Tuesday, August 8, 1995.

1. *Systems Development*—EDS designed, developed, and implemented systems that supported and improved its clients' business processes and the way they served their customers.

2. *Systems Integration*—EDS became the single point of contact for a client, responsible for directing multiple vendors and ensuring that combinations of hardware, software, communications, and human resources worked together.

3. *Systems Management*—EDS assumed strategic management responsibility for a client's information technology resources.

4. *Process Management*—EDS provided comprehensive management of business processes, such as customer service, insurance claims processing, telemarketing, accounts payable, accounts receivable, and leadership and employee training programs.

By adding these types of information technology services to management consulting, the size of the global market ballooned to an estimated $280 billion. Growth in both industries was expected to be tremendous (Exhibit 4).

Under the leadership of Chief Executive Officer Les Alberthal since 1986, EDS had maintained its reputation as a hard-driving, results-oriented business. It had also lessened the firm's dependence on General Motors from 73 percent of revenues in 1986 to 39 percent in 1993. In 1995, the majority of EDS's revenue (over 75 percent) was generated from

EXHIBIT 4
Estimated Market Size and Growth (in $ billions)

Source: EDS Marketing Strategic Service Unit Market. Analysis, February 1995, Gartner Group.

Service Continuum	1994	CAGR	1999
Management Consulting	$40.0	14.20%	$80.0
Systems Development	50.8	6.10%	68.3
Systems Integration	56.2	11.90%	98.7
Systems Management	120.2	9.10%	185.8
Process Management	21.5	35.60%	98.3
Estimated Total Market	$288.7		$531

systems integration and systems management. A professional sales force focused on long-term contracts, generated over 70 percent of EDS's revenues from clients within the United States and almost 50 percent from corporations whose core business was manufacturing.

But for almost a decade, while EDS was making its fortune running other companies' mainframe computer operations, competition intensified, and margins began to deteriorate on these traditional lines of business. EDS started to look towards "higher value-added" services rather than data processing. This translated into business-process reengineering and client server technology, two trends that were reshaping the corporate landscape. EDS entered the management consulting industry as part of a strategy to offer business solutions rather than simply IT solutions to its customers.

EDS-Management Consulting Services (MCS)

EDS had been involved in management consulting since 1985 and formalized its efforts by creating MCS in 1993. By leveraging its tradition and strengths, MCS brought a new dimension to EDS. Over a short two-year period, EDS had built MCS into an organization of 1300 people, with 30 offices in 20 countries, generating an estimated $200 million in revenues. During its first year, MCS services were sold through the EDS sales force to give the firm a chance to get organized internally. During its second year, the consultants were selling on their own. The goals and objectives of the new Strategic Services Unit were simple:

- grow and be profitable while building a world-class management consulting organization;

- help grow EDS through leveraged downstream-influenced revenue; and

- act as a catalyst for EDS by bringing in new skills, particularly in relationship management and developing industry knowledge.

Despite the ability to combine expertise and intellectual capital with the delivery capability of EDS, MCS was having difficulties getting off the ground. In 1994 alone, the young organization lost an estimated $23 million. By approaching clients alongside EDS as an IT firm, MCS lacked a clear positioning in the marketplace as a formidable 'consulting' practice. One former MCS consultant suggested, "Any company would have had its difficulties turning a profit in such a short period of time, particularly considering the enormous growth rate of MCS." The majority of this growth came internally through a hiring frenzy while the growth in clients was not so quick. "It's hard to achieve profitability with half your staff not billing," commented the ex-MCS consultant. Rapid growth made it difficult for MCS to put in place some of the necessities for success in the global market. Lack of uniform business systems and processes, and inconsistent consulting methodologies, human resource practices, billing rates and quality measures all translated into an inconsistent positioning in the marketplace. Another struggle for MCS was in establishing its own culture. There were a tremendous number of highly talented people, but coming together so quickly from so many different places, made it impossible to establish a unified identity. The firm lacked a sense of cohesion among its broad base of consultants.

A. T. Kearney—Acquired by EDS and Merged with MCS (September 1995)

The acquisition of A. T. Kearney was the first significant move by an information technology firm into the upper echelon of the management consulting leagues. EDS had purchased seven management consulting firms over the last two years, but none of this magnitude. Gary Fernandez, EDS vice chairman and new chairman of A. T. Kearney, commented:

The addition of the A. T. Kearney team builds on the progress EDS has made to date in creating a world-class management consulting organization. Our enhanced management consulting capability coupled with EDS's traditional information technology and process management expertise represents a powerful combination of business insight, industry experience, and global delivery capability to help our clients successfully undertake enterprise-wide transformation initiatives.

EDS agreed to buy A. T. Kearney for $300 million in cash and contingency payments, plus a stock incentive provision of seven million shares to be earned at a rate of 10 percent a year by A. T. Kearney partners and 100 other key individuals. The total bill was estimated at just over $600 million. It was determined that the MCS practice would be integrated into the new A. T. Kearney, maintaining the brand name, procedures, policies, and standards that had made the Chicago-based firm one of the world's leading management consulting practices. Fred Steingraber would continue to function as the company's CEO. For the first time in EDS's long history, a fully independent subsidiary was created in order to assure the integrity and objectivity of a world-class management consulting firm. This subsidiary provided EDS with a credible, ready-made consulting practice that would have taken far too long for EDS to develop on its own.

This was an excellent match for both A. T. Kearney and MCS as consulting organizations because of the synergistic and complementary industry, functional, and geographic strengths. The operational and technology consulting strengths of MCS complemented the strategy and high value-added operational strengths of A. T. Kearney. The integration provided A. T. Kearney with an influx of new, talented consultants that were necessary for the firm to ramp up its capabilities and reach critical mass in many of its markets. Together, they brought an unparalleled spectrum of capabilities to clients. The combination of locations ensured that a broad and well-positioned global organization was in place to service clients worldwide. Industry coverage was also well matched and balanced; for example, A. T. Kearney was exceptionally strong in manufacturing, while MCS had particular strengths in the communications and electronics industries.

When EDS's information services and technology capabilities were added to the mix, the ability to have a near seamless link of strategy through implementation was created. One competitor suggested:

> The market is demanding integrated business and technology services. I think it will be tough for them, but it's the right move. It's very difficult to do process improvement as A. T. Kearney does and not leverage that into implementing systems.

The combined capabilities brought a range of skills and leading-edge solutions to clients of both A. T. Kearney and EDS. For clients involved in reengineering and transformation, process and functional issues could be addressed concurrently with the enabling technology and implementation issues. In addition, implementation expertise could be tapped into earlier in the development process. The relationship with EDS also helped ensure the availability of major investment resources for A. T. Kearney. It provided the infrastructure to support its rapid growth both from a geographic and practice development perspective. The relationship with A. T. Kearney gave the information technology giant the key high-level perspectives on business issues which helped it to sell its outsourcing and systems integration services.

A. T. Kearney was a key part of the EDS vision to become the new "Defining Entity." For A. T. Kearney, the partnership with EDS had placed it in a stronger position to pursue its goals of growth, globalization, and leadership. According to Fred Steingraber, A. T. Kearney viewed itself as "one of a new breed of management consultancies, rich in resources, global in reach, and integrated in solution delivery." Both companies felt the merger had provided them with a tremendous opportunity to take the lead in bringing the "next generation" of professional services capabilities to clients worldwide.

Risks, Challenges, and Obstacles

Despite all of the optimism of A. T. Kearney and EDS, skeptics were lining up to criticize the strategy. Many wondered whether vertically integrating services, so that a single consulting firm offered end-to-end consulting solutions, was an inevitable trend, and even if it was, integrating the existing MCS into A. T. Kearney would be no easy task. One such critic was James Kennedy, publisher of Consultants News:

> First you have entirely different cultures. What you are going to get is the propeller heads meeting the button downs. Kearney has been selling top management for decades, while EDS, which has only been in the consulting business since 1993, has been dealing mostly with the systems people. We're talking about two different levels here.

He went on to say:

> Consulting firms are very fragile entities. They cannot be transplanted easily. You have something equivalent to organ rejection when you try to mix and match consultants from one company with another. There are huge egos here.

Referring to the acquisition by the General Motors subsidiary, one A. T. Kearney consultant was quoted as saying, "We would go from being an independent, uninhibited place to being a small piece of the country's largest company. Talk about culture shock." Independence was a major issue for many A. T. Kearney consultants. It was felt that IBM Solutions was essentially created to sell IBM hardware solutions. The relationship between MCS and EDS was not much different. Many consultants feared that A. T. Kearney would be viewed as the front end for EDS. If so, this could have significant implications for A. T. Kearney's ability to both attract and retain good people—the main assets of any professional services firm. Some wondered whether there would be a mass exodus from the Kearney ranks. Clients had parallel concerns. Would A. T. Kearney still be able to maintain its objectivity in helping clients choose the right suppliers? Would clients continue to use A. T. Kearney services, particularly if they competed against EDS or General Motors?

One Year Later (September 1996)

No one would say that the first year had been easy. However, most would argue that it was successful. The integration of MCS into A. T. Kearney had gone smoothly. With 60 offices in over 30 countries, the consulting practice had grown to over 3,500 employees, 2,400 of whom were consultants. In 1995, revenues soared to $650 million which placed A. T. Kearney as the 11th largest consulting firm in the world (Exhibits 5 and 6) and the number two firm in the high value-added segment of the market. The marketplace had received the marriage between A. T. Kearney and EDS with open arms. In fact through June 1996, the two companies partnered on more than 20 successful initiatives resulting in $1.4 billion in new business for EDS and $140 million for A. T. Kearney. Perhaps the most exciting collaboration between the two companies was a 10-year engagement with Rolls-Royce worth over $900 million. Even more remarkable, its independence from EDS and its business systems and culture had been maintained. With almost no turnover of staff throughout the integration and absolutely no turnover of clients, A. T. Kearney had further established itself as a strong and successful player in the management consulting industry.

What Next?

Despite the consulting firm's success to date, Brian Harrison knew that the greatest potential from the merger had yet to be realized. The integration of MCS into A. T. Kearney was

EXHIBIT 5
**Top Consulting
Firms for 1995
(in $ 000s)**

Rank	Company	Revenues
1	Andersen	4,200
2	McKinsey & Company	1,800
3	Ernst & Young	1,500
4	KPMG	1,500
5	Deloitte & Touche	1,400
6	Coopers & Lybrand	1,200
7	Mercer Management	1,000
8	Price Waterhouse	1,000
9	Booz Allen & Hamilton	785
10	Towers Perrin[1]	767
11	A. T. Kearney	650
12	Boston Consulting Group	550
13	Cap Gemini	548
14	Arthur D. Little	514
15	Bain	375

[1]Estimate of 1994 revenues only.
Source: Worldlink, September/October 1996, p. 15–25.

EXHIBIT 6   **A. T. Kearney Growth & Performance Unparalleled in the Industry[1]**

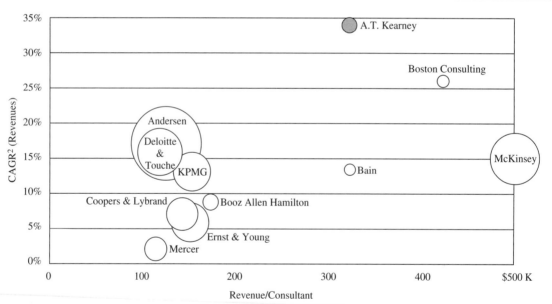

[1]Source: *Consultants News*.
[2]Growth measured between 1990–1995.

the first step. Now EDS and A. T. Kearney sought to take advantage of the synergy created from the merger by leveraging the capabilities of both organizations. While significant revenue had been generated to date from joint clients, most collaborative initiatives had been in response to client demand, or to competitive pressures created by a bidding process. In almost all cases, A. T. Kearney had reacted to opportunities, rather than having taken the initiative and proactively sought them out. One example of this was the Rolls Royce project. Competing with CSC for the engagement, EDS decided to include its consulting arm in the service mix since the services of CSC Index, CSC's consulting division, had been offered. The selling process was not initiated with both service offerings in mind. Most managers felt that a more proactive approach to similar situations was the ultimate objective of the firm. The question was how to make this happen. Leveraging and combining each others' strengths in the marketplace was a must.

Several courses of action were available to the two organizations in light of the merger. Substantial cross-marketing opportunities were created because of the minimal client overlap. EDS had significant positions in health care, insurance, communications and electronics, aerospace and defense industries, while A. T. Kearney's strengths resided in manufacturing, consumer products, transportation, and chemical/pharmaceuticals. They shared mutual strengths in industries such as automotive, financial services, energy and retail. Products and services that had made each company successful in the past could be offered to each others' clients.

Another opportunity was to offer the combined menu of these very same products to a whole new set of clients looking for a "one-stop-shop," where A. T. Kearney and EDS were not in a position to service these accounts effectively in the past. Most of the reactive collaborative initiatives to date had taken the form of one of these two approaches.

Brian, however, suggested this was not the primary purpose of the merger. Instead, there was an opportunity to draw on the strengths of both organizations and develop entirely new products. For example, these would be in the category of enterprise-wide transformation initiatives or in the development of technology-enabled strategies. Offered to either existing or new clients, these new products would significantly differentiate the new enterprise from its competition, and generate revenue streams that neither A. T. Kearney nor EDS could have enjoyed without this partnership. This was what Brian considered to be the most attractive opportunity. For example, A. T. Kearney and EDS had recently embarked on the development of a new service called CoSourcing. Once completed, this would be a collaborative initiative that integrated business process reengineering, information technology, outsourcing, and organizational transformation to deliver significant performance enhancements to prospective clients. However, before this or any other new initiative could possibly work, significant changes to both organizations had to occur, particularly with respect to sales and account management. The objective of these changes would be to create an environment where the two companies could remain apart, but at the same time, work together.

Brian sat back in his chair and remembered a comment Fred had made almost a year ago, when the merger was finalized:

> The offer has provided us with a catalyst in terms of looking at the next generation of success criteria that will be critical in this industry in the future. It has caused a lot of people to ponder the future of the consulting industry.

With this in mind, Brian began to prepare for his upcoming meeting on Friday.

Case 6–16
Camar Automotive Hoist

In September 2000 Mark Camar, president of Camar Automotive Hoist (CAH), had just finished reading a feasibility report on entering the European market in 2001. CAH manufactured surface automotive hoists, a product used by garages, service stations, and repair

This case was prepared by Gordon McDougall, Wilfrid Laurier University, as the basis for class discussion rather than to illustrate either effective or ineffective handling of an administrative situation. © Gordon McDougall 2001.

EXHIBIT 1
**Examples of
Automotive Hoists**

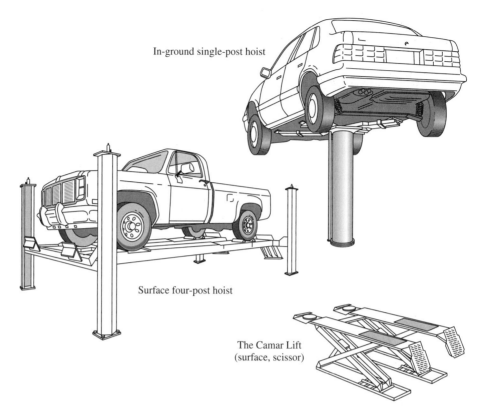

In-ground single-post hoist

Surface four-post hoist

The Camar Lift
(surface, scissor)

shops to lift cars for servicing (Exhibit 1). The report, which had been prepared by CAH's marketing manager, Pierre Gagnon, outlined the opportunities in the European Union and the available entry options.

Mr. Camar was not sure if CAH was ready for this move. While the company had been successful in expanding sales into the U.S. market, he wondered if this success could be repeated in Europe. He thought that with more effort, sales could be increased in the United States. However, there were some positive aspects to the European idea. He began reviewing the information in preparation for the meeting the following day with Mr. Gagnon.

Camar Automotive Hoist

Mr. Camar, a design engineer, had worked for eight years for the Canadian subsidiary of a U.S. automotive hoist manufacturer. During those years he had spent considerable time designing an aboveground, or surface, automotive hoist. Although Mr. Camar was very enthusiastic about the unique aspects of the hoist, including a scissor lift and wheel alignment pads, senior management expressed no interest in the idea. In 1990, Mr. Camar left the company to start his own business with the express purpose of designing and manufacturing the hoist. He left with the good wishes of his previous employer, who had no objections to his plans to start a new business.

Over the next three years Mr. Camar obtained financing from a venture capital firm; opened a plant in Lachine, Quebec; and began manufacturing and marketing the hoist, which was called the Camar Lift (see Exhibit 1).

From the beginning Mr. Camar had taken considerable pride in the development and marketing of the Camar Lift. The original design included a scissor lift and a safety locking mechanism which allowed the hoist to be raised to any level and locked in place. Also, the scissor lift offered easy access for the mechanic to work on the raised vehicle. Because the hoist was fully hydraulic and had no chains or pulleys, it required little maintenance. Another key feature was the alignment turn plates that were an integral part of the lift. The turn plates would allow mechanics to perform wheel alignment jobs accurately and easily. Because it was a surface lift, it could be installed in a garage in less than a day.

Mr. Camar continually made improvements to the product, including adding more safety features. In fact, the Camar Lift was considered a leader in automotive lift safety. Safety was an important factor in the automotive hoist market. Although hoists seldom malfunctioned, when they did, it often resulted in a serious accident.

The Camar Lift developed a reputation in the industry as the "Cadillac" of hoists; the unit was judged by many as superior to competitive offerings because of its design, the quality of the workmanship, the safety features, the ease of installation, and the five-year warranty. Mr. Camar held four patents on the Camar Lift, including the lifting mechanism on the scissor design and a safety locking mechanism. A number of versions of the product were designed that made the lift suitable (depending on the model) for a variety of tasks, including rustproofing, muffler repairs, and general mechanical repairs.

In 1991 CAH sold 23 hoists and had sales of $172,500. During the early years the majority of sales were to independent service stations and garages specializing in wheel alignment in the Quebec and Ontario market. Most of the units were sold by Mr. Gagnon, who was hired in 1992 to handle the marketing side of the operation. In 1994 Mr. Gagnon began using distributors to sell the hoist to a wider geographic market in Canada. In 1996 he signed an agreement with a large automotive wholesaler to represent CAH in the U.S. market. By 1999 the company had sold 1,054 hoists and had sales of $9,708,000 (Exhibit 2). In 1999 about 60 percent of sales were to the United States, with the remaining 40 percent going to the Canadian market.

Industry

Approximately 49,000 hoists were sold each year in North America. Hoists typically were purchased by any automotive outlet that serviced or repaired cars, including new car dealers, used car dealers, specialty shops (for example, mufflers, transmission, wheel alignment), chains (for example, Firestone, Goodyear, Canadian Tire), and independent garages. It was estimated that new car dealers purchased 30 percent of all the units sold in a given year. In general, the specialty shops focused on one type of repair, such as mufflers or rustproofing, while "nonspecialty" outlets handled a variety of repairs. While there was some crossover, in general CAH competed in the specialty shop segment and, in particular, shops

EXHIBIT 2
Camar Automotive Hoist, Selected Financial Statistics (1997–1999)

Source: Company records.

	1997	1998	1999
Sales	$6,218,000	$7,454,000	$9,708,000
Cost of sales	4,540,000	5,541,000	6,990,000
Contribution	1,678,000	1,913,000	2,718,000
Marketing expenses*	507,000	510,000	530,000
Administrative expenses	810,000	820,000	840,000
Earnings before tax	361,000	583,000	1,348,000
Units sold	723	847	1,054

*Marketing expenses in 1999 included advertising ($70,000), four salespeople ($240,000), the marketing manager, and three sales support personnel ($220,000).

that dealt with wheel alignment. This included chains such as Firestone and Canadian Tire as well as new car dealers (for example, Ford) which devoted a certain percentage of their lifts to the wheel alignment business and independent garages that specialized in wheel alignment.

The purpose of a hoist was to lift an automobile into a position where a mechanic or serviceperson could easily work on the car. Because different repairs required different positions, a wide variety of hoists had been developed to meet specific needs. For example, a muffler repair shop required a hoist where the mechanic could gain easy access to the underside of the car. Similarly, a wheel alignment job required a hoist that offered a level platform where the wheels could be adjusted and there was easy access for the mechanic. Mr. Gagnon estimated that 85 percent of CAH's sales were to the wheel alignment market to service centers such as Firestone, Goodyear, and Canadian Tire and to independent garages that specialized in wheel alignment. About 15 percent of sales were made to customers who used the hoist for general mechanical repairs.

Firms that purchased hoists were part of an industry called the automobile aftermarket. This industry was involved in supplying parts and service for new and used cars and was worth over $54 billion at retail in 1999 while servicing the approximately 14 million cars on the road in Canada. The industry was large and diverse; there were over 4,000 new car dealers in Canada, over 400 Canadian Tire stores, over 100 stores in each of the Firestone and Goodyear chains, and over 220 stores in the Rust Check chain.

The purchase of an automotive hoist was often an important decision for a service station owner or dealer. Because the price of hoists ranged from $3,000 to $15,000, this was a capital expense for most businesses.

For the owner-operator of a new service center or car dealership the decision involved determining what type of hoist was required and what brand would best suit the company. Most new service centers and car dealerships had multiple bays for servicing cars. In these cases the decision would involve what types of hoists were required (for example, in-ground, surface). Often more than one type of hoist was purchased, depending on the service center/dealership needs.

Experienced garage owners seeking a replacement hoist (the typical hoist had a useful life of 10 to 13 years) usually would determine what products were available and then make a decision. If the garage owners were also mechanics, they probably would be aware of two or three types of hoists but would not be very knowledgeable about the brands or products currently available. Garage owners and dealers who were not mechanics probably knew very little about hoists. The owners of car or service dealerships often bought the product that was recommended and/or approved by the parent company.

Competition

Sixteen companies competed in the automotive lift market in North America: 4 Canadian and 12 U.S. firms. With the advent of the North American Free Trade Agreement in 1989, the duties on hoists between the two countries were phased out over a 10-year period, and in 1999 exports and imports of hoists were duty-free. For Mr. Camar, the import duties had never played a part in any decisions; the fluctuating exchange rates between the two countries had a far greater impact on selling prices. In the last three years the Canadian dollar had fluctuated between $0.65 and $0.70 versus the U.S. dollar ($1.00 CDN bought $0.65 U.S.) and forecasted rates were expected to stay within that range.

A wide variety of hoists were manufactured in the industry. The two basic types of hoists were in-ground and surface. As the name implies, in-ground hoists required a pit to be dug

EXHIBIT 3
North American Automotive Lift Unit Sales by Type, 1997–1999

Source: Company records.

	1997	1998	1999
In-ground			
Single-post	5,885	5,772	5,518
Multiple-post	4,812	6,625	5,075
Surface			
Two-post	27,019	28,757	28,923
Four-post	3,862	3,162	3,745
Scissor	2,170	2,258	2,316
Other	4,486	3,613	3,695
Total	48,234	50,187	49,272

"in-ground" where the piston that raised the hoist was installed. In-ground hoists were either single-post or multiple-post, were permanent, and obviously could not be moved. In-ground lifts constituted approximately 21 percent of total lift sales in 1999 (Exhibit 3). Surface lifts were installed on a flat surface, usually concrete. Surface lifts came in two basic types: post lift hoists and scissor hoists. Compared to in-ground lifts, surface lifts were easy to install and could be moved if necessary. Surface lifts constituted 79 percent of total lift sales in 1999. Within each type of hoist (for example, post lift surface hoists) there were numerous variations in terms of size, shape, and lifting capacity.

The industry was dominated by two large U.S. firms, AHV Lifts and Berne Manufacturing, that together held approximately 60 percent of the market. AHV Lifts, the largest firm, with approximately 40 percent of the market and annual sales of about $60 million, offered a complete line of hoists (in-ground and surface) but focused primarily on the in-ground market and the two-post surface market. AHV Lifts was the only company that had its own direct sales force; all the other companies used only wholesalers or a combination of wholesalers and a company sales force. AHV Lifts offered standard hoists with few extra features and competed primarily on price. Berne Manufacturing, with a market share of approximately 20 percent, also competed in the in-ground and two-post surface markets. It used a combination of wholesalers and company salespeople and, like AHV Lifts, competed primarily on price.

Most of the remaining firms in the industry were companies that operated in a regional market (for example, California, British Columbia) and/or offered a limited product line (for example, four-post surface hoist).

Camar had two competitors that manufactured scissor lifts. AHV Lift marketed a scissor hoist that had a different lifting mechanism and did not include the safety locking features of the Camar Lift. On average, the AHV scissor lift was sold for about 20 percent less than the Camar Lift. The second competitor, Mete Lift, was a small regional company with sales in California and Oregon. It had a design that was very similar to that of the Camar Lift but lacked some of its safety features. The Mete Lift, which was regarded as a well-manufactured product, sold for about 5 percent less than the Camar Lift.

Marketing Strategy

As of early 2000, CAH had developed a reputation for a quality product backed by good service in the hoist lift market, primarily in the wheel alignment segment.

The distribution system employed by CAH reflected the need to engage in extensive personal selling. Three types of distributors were used: a company sales force, Canadian distributors, and a U.S. automotive wholesaler. The company sales force consisted of four salespeople and Mr. Gagnon. Their main task was to service large "direct" accounts. The initial step was to get the Camar Lift approved by large chains and manufacturers and then, having received the approval, sell to individual dealers or operators. For example, if General Motors approved the hoist, CAH could sell it to individual General Motors dealers. CAH sold directly to the individual dealers of a number of large accounts, including General Motors, Ford, Chrysler, Petro-Canada, Firestone, and Goodyear. CAH had been successful in obtaining manufacturer approval from the big three automobile manufacturers in both Canada and the United States. Also, CAH had received approval from service companies such as Canadian Tire and Goodyear. To date, CAH had not been rejected by any major account, but in some cases the approval process had taken over four years.

In total, the company sales force generated about 25 percent of the unit sales each year. Sales to the large "direct" accounts in the United States went through CAH's U.S. wholesaler.

The Canadian distributors sold, installed, and serviced units across Canada. Those distributors handled the Camar Lift and carried a line of noncompetitive automotive equipment products (for example, engine diagnostic equipment, wheel-balancing equipment) and noncompetitive lifts. They focused on the smaller chains and the independent service stations and garages.

The U.S. wholesaler sold a complete product line to service stations as well as manufacturing some equipment. The Camar Lift was one of five different types of lifts that the wholesaler sold. Although the wholesaler provided CAH with extensive distribution in the United States, the Camar Lift was a minor product within the wholesaler's total line. While Mr. Gagnon did not have actual figures, he thought that the Camar Lift probably accounted for less than 20 percent of the total lift sales of the U.S. wholesaler.

Both Mr. Camar and Mr. Gagnon felt that the U.S. market had unrealized potential. With a population of 264 million people and over 146 million registered vehicles, that market was almost 10 times the size of the Canadian market (population of over 30 million and approximately 14 million vehicles). Mr. Gagnon noted that the six New England states (population of over 13 million), the three largest mid-Atlantic states (population of over 38 million), and the three largest Mideastern states (population of over 32 million) were all within a day's drive of the factory in Lachine. Mr. Camar and Mr. Gagnon had considered setting up a sales office in New York to service those states, but they were concerned that the U.S. wholesaler would not be willing to relinquish any of its territory. They also had considered working more closely with the wholesaler to encourage it to "push" the Camar Lift. It appeared that the wholesaler's major objective was to sell a hoist, not necessarily the Camar Lift.

CAH distributed a catalog-type package with products, uses, prices, and other required information for both distributors and users. In addition, CAH advertised in trade publications (for example, *AutoInc.*), and Mr. Gagnon traveled to trade shows in Canada and the United States to promote the Camar Lift.

In 1999, Camar Lifts sold for an average retail price of $10,990 and CAH received on average $9,210 for each unit sold. This average reflected the mix of sales through the three distribution channels: (1) direct (where CAH received 100 percent of the selling price), (2) Canadian distributors (where CAH received 80 percent of the selling price) and (3) the U.S. wholesaler (where CAH received 78 percent of the selling price).

Both Mr. Camar and Mr. Gagnon felt that the company's success to date had been based on a strategy of offering a superior product that was targeted primarily at the needs of specific customers. The strategy stressed continual product improvements, quality workmanship, and service. Personal selling was a key aspect of the strategy; salespeople could show customers the advantages of the Camar Lift over competing products.

The European Market

Against this background, Mr. Camar had been thinking of ways to maintain the rapid growth of the company. One possibility that kept coming up was the promise and potential of the European market. The fact that Europe had become a single market in 1993 suggested that it was an opportunity that should at least be explored. With this in mind, Mr. Camar asked Mr. Gagnon to prepare a report on the possibility of CAH entering the European market. The highlights of Mr. Gagnon's report follow.

History of the European Union

The European Union (EU) had its basis in the 1957 Treaty of Rome, in which five countries decided it would be in their best interest to form an internal market. Those countries were France, Spain, Italy, West Germany, and Luxembourg. By 1990 the EU consisted of 15 countries (the additional 10 were Austria, Belgium, Denmark, Finland, Greece, Ireland, the Netherlands, Portugal, Sweden, and the United Kingdom) with a population of over 376 million people. Virtually all barriers (physical, technical, and fiscal) in the EU were scheduled to be removed for companies within the EU. This allowed the free movement of goods, persons, services, and capital.

In the last 15 years many North American and Japanese firms had established themselves in the EU. The reasoning for this was twofold. First, those companies regarded the community as an opportunity to increase global market share and profits. The market was attractive because of its size and lack of internal barriers. Second, there was continuing concern that companies not established within the EU would have difficulty exporting to the EU due to changing standards and tariffs. To date, this concern had not materialized.

Market Potential

The key indicator of the potential market for the Camar Lift hoist was the number of passenger cars and commercial vehicles in use in a particular country. Four countries in Europe had more than 20 million vehicles in use, with Germany having the largest domestic fleet, 44 million vehicles, followed in order by Italy, France, and the United Kingdom (Exhibit 4). The number of vehicles was an important indicator since the more vehicles there were in use, the greater the number of service and repair facilities which needed vehicle hoists and potentially the Camar Lift.

An indicator of the future vehicle repair and service market was the number of new vehicle registrations. The registration of new vehicles was important, as it maintained the number of vehicles in use by replacing cars that had been retired. Again, Germany had the most new cars registered in 1997 and was followed in order by France, the United Kingdom, and Italy.

EXHIBIT 4
Number of Vehicles (1997) and Population (2000 estimate)

	Vehicles in Use (thousands)			
Country	Passenger	Small Commercial	New Vehicle Registrations (thousands)	Population (thousands)
Germany	41,400	2,800	3,500	82,100
France	28,000	4,900	2,200	59,000
Italy	33,200	2,700	1,800	56,700
United Kingdom	23,500	4,000	2,200	59,100
Spain	15,300	2,800	1,000	39,200

Based primarily on the fact that a large domestic market was important for initial growth, the selection of a European country should be limited to the "Big Four" industrialized nations: Germany, France, the United Kingdom, and Italy. In an international survey companies from North America and Europe ranked European countries on a scale of 1 to 100 on market potential and investment site potential. The results showed that Germany was favored for both market potential and investment site opportunities, while France, the United Kingdom, and Spain placed second, third, and fourth, respectively. Italy did not place in the top four in either market or investment site potential. However, Italy had a large number of vehicles in use, had the fourth largest population in Europe, and was an acknowledged leader in car technology and production.

Little information was available on the competition within Europe. There was no dominant manufacturer as there was in North America. At that time there was one firm in Germany that manufactured a scissor-type lift. That firm sold most of its units within the German market. The only other available information was that 22 firms in Italy manufactured vehicle lifts.

Investment Options

Mr. Gagnon felt that CAH had three options for expansion into the European market: licensing, a joint venture, or direct investment. The licensing option was a real possibility, as a French firm had expressed an interest in manufacturing the Camar Lift.

In June 2000, Mr. Gagnon had attended a trade show in Detroit to promote the Camar Lift. At the show he met Phillipe Beaupre, the marketing manager for Bar Maisse, a French manufacturer of wheel alignment equipment. The firm, located in Chelles, France, sold a range of wheel alignment equipment throughout Europe. The best-selling product was an electronic modular aligner which enabled a mechanic to utilize a sophisticated computer system to align the wheels of a car. Mr. Beaupre was seeking a North American distributor for the modular aligner and other products manufactured by Bar Maisse.

At the show Mr. Gagnon and Mr. Beaupre had a casual conversation in which both explained what their respective companies manufactured, exchanged company brochures and business cards, and went on to other exhibits. The next day Mr. Beaupre sought out Mr. Gagnon and asked if he might be interested in having Bar Maisse manufacture and market the Camar Lift in Europe. Mr. Beaupre felt that the lift would complement Bar Maisse's product line and the licensing would be beneficial to both parties. They agreed to pursue the idea. Upon his return to Lachine, Mr. Gagnon told Mr. Camar about those discussions, and they agreed to explore the possibility.

Mr. Gagnon called a number of colleagues in the industry and asked them what they knew about Bar Maisse. About half had not heard of the company, but those who had commented favorably on the quality of its products. One colleague with European experience knew the company well and said that Bar Maisse's management had integrity and the firm would make a good partner. In July Mr. Gagnon sent a letter to Mr. Beaupre stating that CAH was interested in further discussions and enclosing various company brochures, including price lists and technical information on the Camar Lift. In late August Mr. Beaupre responded, stating that Bar Maisse would like to enter a three-year licensing agreement with CAH to manufacture the Camar Lift in Europe. In exchange for the manufacturing rights, Bar Maisse was prepared to pay a royalty rate of 5 percent of gross sales. Mr. Gagnon had not yet responded to this proposal.

A second possibility was a joint venture. Mr. Gagnon had wondered if it might not be better for CAH to offer a counterproposal to Bar Maisse for a joint venture. He had not worked out any details, but he felt that CAH would learn more about the European market and probably make more money if it was an active partner in Europe. Mr. Gagnon's idea was a 50-50 proposal in which the two parties shared the investment and the profits. He envisaged a situation where Bar Maisse would manufacture the Camar Lift in its plant with technical assistance from CAH. Mr. Gagnon also thought that CAH could get involved in the marketing of the lift through the Bar Maisse distribution system. Further, he thought that the Camar Lift, with proper marketing, could gain a reasonable share of the European market. If that happened, Mr. Gagnon felt that CAH was likely to earn greater returns with a joint venture.

The third option was direct investment, in which CAH would establish a manufacturing facility and set up a management group to market the lift. Mr. Gagnon had contacted a business acquaintance who recently had been involved in manufacturing fabricated steel sheds in Germany. On the basis of discussions with his acquaintance, Mr. Gagnon estimated the costs involved in setting up a plant in Europe at (1) $250,000 for capital equipment (welding machines, cranes, other equipment), (2) $200,000 in incremental costs to set up the plant, and (3) carrying costs to cover $1 million in inventory and accounts receivable. While the actual costs of renting a building for the factory would depend on the site location, he estimated that annual building rent, including heat, light, and insurance, would be about $80,000. Mr. Gagnon recognized that these estimates were guidelines but felt that the estimates were probably within 20 percent of the actual costs.

The Decision

As Mr. Camar considered the contents of the report, a number of thoughts crossed his mind. He began making notes concerning the European possibility and the future of the company:

- If CAH decided to enter Europe, Mr. Gagnon would be the obvious choice to head up the direct investment option or the joint venture option. Mr. Camar felt that Mr. Gagnon had been instrumental in the success of the company to date.

- While CAH had the financial resources to go ahead with the direct investment option, the joint venture would spread the risk (and the returns) over the two companies.

- CAH had built its reputation on designing and manufacturing a quality product. Regardless of the option, Mr. Camar wanted the firm's reputation to be maintained.

- Either the licensing agreement or the joint venture appeared to build on the two companies' strengths: Bar Maisse had knowledge of the market, and CAH had the product. What troubled Mr. Camar was whether this apparent synergy would work or whether Bar Maisse would seek to control the operation.

- It was difficult to estimate sales under any of the options. With the first two (licensing and a joint venture), it would depend on the effort and expertise of Bar Maisse; with the third, it would depend on Mr. Gagnon.

- CAH's sales in the U.S. market could be increased if the U.S. wholesaler would "push" the Camar Lift. Alternatively, the establishment of a sales office in New York to cover the Eastern states also could increase sales.

As Mr. Camar reflected on the situation, he knew he probably should get additional information, but it wasn't obvious exactly what information would help him make a yes or no decision. He knew one thing for sure: He was going to keep this company on a "fast growth" track, and at tomorrow's meeting he and Mr. Gagnon would decide how to do it.

Case 6–17

Stone & Lewis

Introduction

Tony Grant had just been appointed the new sales manager of the San Diego district in the Health Care Products Division of Stone & Lewis. He was leaving a job as a very successful section sales manager within the Phoenix, Arizona, district of the Personal Care Division of the company. The Personal Care Division produces consumer products, as is true for all of the other divisions of Stone & Lewis except for the new Health Care Products Division. Based on his past performance as a sales rep and section sales manager, he was among the select few who were expected to advance to upper-level management. He had interviewed for the job less than two weeks ago and was now in his second day at his new position. His predecessor, Ken Burns, had left the company suddenly, and Tony had been given very little information about the circumstances surrounding Ken's decision to leave. Tony had tried unsuccessfully to reach Ken to discuss the situation.

During the interview process, the Southern California regional sales manager of the division, Reed Taylor, had seemed reluctant to talk about the situation. He had emphasized what a great opportunity the new job would be for Tony to add to his experience by learning to deal with the problems of managing a sales force of approximately 25 people. He had seemed intent on selling Tony on the merits of the job and how it would be a necessary step in advancing his career. However, Tony had been unable to get a clear picture of exactly what types of problems he would be facing. The regional manager had seemed very eager to fill the district manager's position and had sidestepped any serious discussion of the job's negative aspects. Tony believed there were more problems than Reed Taylor was willing to discuss. However, after carefully considering what he knew of the situation, Tony decided to accept the job, thinking it would offer interesting challenges.

What little information Tony could gather in the short time before he accepted the job came from talking with the regional manager and through brief contacts with some of the other district sales managers in the Southern California region. He had found out that sales force turnover in the division was much higher than the average for the company as a whole. While the company had experienced a fairly steady annual turnover rate of 15 percent of the sales force over the past five years, the Health Care Products Division had annual turnover rates averaging 65 percent over the last three years. As if this was not bad enough, the San Diego district had experienced a nearly 225 percent turnover in the past 18 months, meaning that on the average a sales rep would be on the job only eight months before leaving. Tony learned that of all the employees in the district who had left their jobs in the past two years, only five had accepted new positions within the company. The rest had left the company.

After Tony accepted the new job, he talked with his three new section managers, each of whom supervised between six and eight sales and technical support employees. His impressions after these conversations reinforced his growing suspicions that he would be facing serious personnel problems. While it was obvious that turnover was a major problem, he sensed that his section managers were unwilling to admit to the seriousness of the situation. Each of them seemed preoccupied with presenting a picture of stability and convincing

This case was prepared by Neil M. Ford, University of Wisconsin at Madison. Christopher G. Gilmore and Christopher J. Pitts assisted in preparing this case. Copyright © 1996 Neil M. Ford.

Tony they had the situation under control. They were all quick to point out that for the latest year, which had ended four months ago, they had been fairly successful in meeting the sales volume quotas for their respective areas. Only the Los Angeles area had failed to reach its objective, but it had achieved 96 percent of its targeted sales volume. For the San Diego district as a whole, the sales objective had even been exceeded by 1 percent.

Tony had told the section managers that he was impressed with these results. However, he secretly wondered if the sales force was performing as well as it could. Last year's quotas had been set at volumes that were essentially the same as for the year before, but the previous district manager's files indicated he and the division sales management had extensively debated whether to increase quotas. It appeared the district manager had won his case by keeping quota increases to a minimum. This was surprising because the business in which the Health Care Products Division was operating was widely considered to be a growth industry. Aside from the fact that his section managers seemed a little too content with such apparently insignificant sales volume progress, Tony was disturbed by their lack of concern over the high level of turnover among the sales force. He decided he would need to take a much closer look to uncover possible causes of the problems facing his district.

Background Information

Stone & Lewis occupies a prominent position as a leading manufacturer and marketer of household consumer goods and personal care products. The majority of the company's products are sold in grocery stores and similar retail establishments. The company was founded over 75 years ago, and it has established a strong marketing tradition of advertising and promoting its products very heavily. Noted for its marketing-driven approach to sales, Stone & Lewis is also known for its conservative approach to innovation, which is usually the result of very extensive product testing and market research. The company has been criticized for being too slow to react to changing markets, with the result that it was being beaten by competitors in the introduction of new products.

Seven years ago Stone & Lewis diversified its line of products by moving into the growing and highly profitable area of health care products. The company acquired a pharmaceutical manufacturing firm that already produced some very successful nonprescription medicines. At the same time, the company began testing its own new product for adults with incontinence, or the inability to control bowel and bladder function. The new product, known as PRO-TEKS disposable briefs, is a revolutionary concept. It incorporates a patented plastic inner lining containing "mini-sorbs," which is extremely effective in drawing moisture away from the wearer's skin and trapping it in an absorbent fiber padding between the inner and outer linings.

The ability to keep skin drier for longer periods would mean healthier skin for incontinent patients in nursing homes and hospitals. Skin care is a major issue. With proper skin care, bedsores can be avoided. In some surgical cases, without proper skin care the patient may have to return for more surgery. At the same time, nursing staffs would be able to provide proper patient care with less effort and much greater convenience than afforded by other incontinence products, most of which were judged to be highly inferior to PRO-TEKS.

The basic PRO-TEKS brief is available in three sizes: small, medium, and large. The briefs have recently been improved by the addition of refastenable tapes, which allow a nurse to check a patient's condition without having to replace the brief each time. Both briefs and pads also have a pH strip that changes color when urine is present. The strips can be easily viewed by a nurse.

PRO-TEKS has now been on the market for three years and is currently the only product sold by the Health Care Products Division. Exhibit 1 shows the organization of the division. This organization is identical to other divisions of Stone & Lewis. Sales volume is generated primarily through nursing homes, retirement and health care centers, and rehabilitation centers. Hospitals, clinics, and medical supply stores provide a fair amount of additional sales. The product can be purchased directly from the company, but the majority of sales are made to independent wholesale distributors, which then sell to final customers. Exhibit 2 illustrates the distribution of PRO-TEKS.

PRO-TEKS is easily the most expensive product on the market, but the company and many health care professionals also believe it is the best product available. Exhibit 3 presents an evaluation of the available products prepared by an independent testing agency. PRO-TEKS currently holds a 24 percent market share. It has achieved its greatest success in Florida and the southwestern states where large numbers of relatively wealthy elderly persons reside.

The two strongest competitors are AmCo and Allied United, which are perceived by the market as having high-quality products. They have current market shares of 17 percent and 10 percent, respectively. Some 31 percent of the market have chosen reusable cloth diapers that require laundering. The remainder of the market uses lower quality disposable products of various types.

PRO-TEKS are sold by a sales force that includes regular Stone & Lewis sales representatives of the Health Care Products Division and nurses hired under contract from the HCR Corporation to provide technical selling assistance. The standard selling procedure includes a sales rep presentation to a prospective account. The presentation emphasizes

EXHIBIT 1   **Organization of Health Care Products Division: Stone & Lewis**

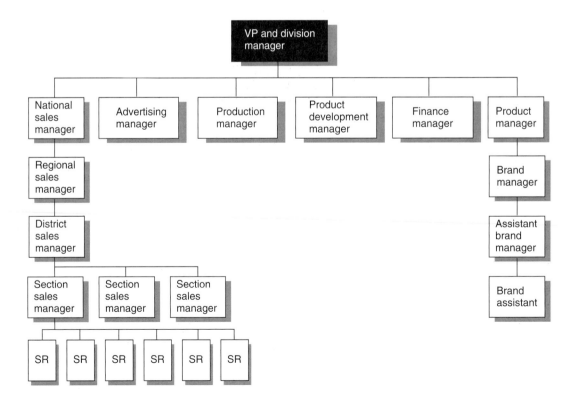

EXHIBIT 2
**Distribution of
PRO-TEKS**

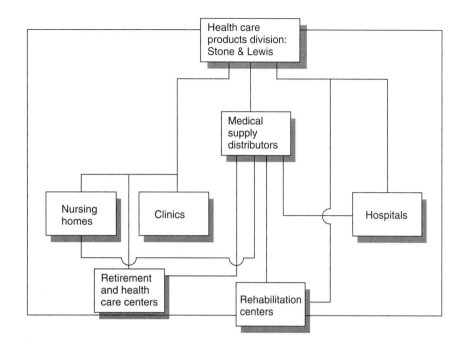

EXHIBIT 3
**Product
Comparison
Analysis**

Source: MED-TECH Testing
Laboratory Analysis.

Company/ Brand	Fit/ Wearability	Absorbency/ Leakage Protection	Comfort/ Breathability	Price/ Case	Quantity/ Case
Stone & Lewis				$39.17	60
PRO-TEKS	8	10	10	47.64	60
				42.32	40
AmCo				46.24	96
RE-LYS	7	7	6	58.50	96
				40.32	84
Allied United				51.60	120
COM-FORTS	10	8	7	66.48	120
				60.80	80
AmCo				36.82	300
Cloth diapers	2	4	8	31.12	200
				36.82	150

Note: All companies produce three sizes. Above prices are for small, medium, and large sizes. Rating scale information is based on a 10-point scale with 1 representing a weak product characteristic and 10 a strong product characteristic. According to MED-TECH, leakage protection and breathability are the most important product features.

the benefits of the product in keeping patients' skin in better condition, reducing laundry costs and labor, and improving the smell and condition of the living environment within the facility to make a favorable impression on the patients' families and other visitors to the facility.

The account can be further persuaded to try PRO-TEKS by receiving free products for three weeks for all of its incontinent patients. The support nurses are on hand to administer the trial and to instruct the facility's staff on the proper use of the product. At the end of the three-week evaluation period, the sales rep returns to summarize the results, which are expected to include improved patient skin care and actual or potential cost savings due to reduced laundry and labor. Cost savings at times have been substantial owing to a reduced demand for labor. In some cases, positions have been eliminated.

Much cooperation is required from the account and its staff to use the product correctly and to accumulate the necessary information to show cost savings. This type of product and the methods by which it is sold are substantially different from the traditional consumer package goods produced by other business units within Stone & Lewis (with their heavy emphasis on advertising and promotions) in which the company has been traditionally engaged and on which it has built its great strength.

One Week Later

Now that Tony had been on the new job for over a week, he had gathered more information from his sales reps and other district managers that would provide clues about the actions he would need to take to improve the operation of his district. The following is a summary of his findings.

1. The system of sales rep performance evaluation is based on a measure of the number of accounts that are sold, the number maintained as active customers, and the number of "theoretical" incontinent patients at each of these accounts. Theoretical users are determined by multiplying the number of beds in a facility by standard demographically based statistical percentages that indicate the expected number of incontinent patients for different types of facilities. Sales reps are given objectives of the number of theoretical users that are to be added within a given short-run time period, typically monthly or quarterly. Sales reps are then responsible for keeping their own records of which accounts are active buyers and therefore how many theoretical users they can take credit for. The results are reported by the sales reps to their section managers each month.

There is currently no other way for these numbers to be compiled, and the managers have no easy way of assessing their accuracy. The general feeling among the sales force seems to be that there is much cheating going on about how many accounts reported are actual buyers. This has created some bitter feelings because pay raises and promotions have been based to some extent on this measure of performance and because some of the more ambitious sales reps have apparently succeeded at reporting inflated results for the number of theoretical users.

The negative effects of this situation are compounded by the fact that the standard "theoretical" percentages used in calculating performance results usually bear little resemblance to the proportion of actual users in any given facility. Therefore, a sales rep may receive too much or too little credit for the actual contribution to the company from any given account.

2. Part of the reason for the inability of managers to check the accuracy of sales reps' reported results is the method by which the product is distributed. The company has traditionally used independent distributors to make its products available to end consumers, and this method has been carried over into the PRO-TEKS business. The company has tried to make the product as widely available as possible and therefore has recruited a large number of medical supply distributors. Sales reps perform a missionary sales function by persuading end-users to buy the product, but the company generally sells only to the distributors. Because the distributors are often unwilling to disclose who their customers are and how much they are buying, the company has no way of accumulating the information on which to base actual sales results to end-user accounts. This presents a much different situation from the retail store setting in which the company has traditionally done business and for which highly organized methods and services are available for auditing end-user buying.

3. Section sales managers are evaluated on the volume of sales to distributors within their territories. However, the end-users within a given section manager's territory cannot be required to buy from distributors within that territory. Distributors compete against each other on price and order servicing, and it is not unusual for a distributor in one territory to lower its price of PRO-TEKS to lure customers in another area manager's territory. Section managers compete with each other by trying to persuade distributors in their respective territories to adjust prices or service or by "requesting" that their sales reps persuade end-users to buy only from their own distributors. Pushing end-users to buy from a particular distributor, when that distributor consistently fails to match the price or service of a competitor in another territory, may damage the total PRO-TEKS business for the company. Aside from this, sales reps may feel caught in the middle between two battling section managers, with the result that their own performance suffers from lost accounts.

4. Sales reps report that they often lose sales because the expected cost savings fail to materialize. This is often due to uncooperativeness on the part of the facility staff in providing complete and accurate costs for a before- and after-PRO-TEKS comparison. In addition, the staffs often include a majority of low-paid and unmotivated aides who actually perform the tasks associated with the use of the product. In such a situation, it would be difficult for the sales force to provide the necessary level of training and supervision for using the product and for providing for a well-controlled evaluation.

5. Essentially all prospective accounts have been contacted since PRO-TEKS was introduced. When repeat calls are made to accounts that do not use the product, sales reps report they are often confronted by decision makers who tell them not to come back until they have something new to offer. The price of the product places it beyond the budget of many potential accounts, and they often have very strong preconceived negative impressions about the product. In some cases, this results from the use of plastic in the manufacture of PRO-TEKS, whereas many of the nurses on facility staffs have been trained on the merits of traditional cloth products. When refastenable tapes were introduced to PRO-TEKS, many accounts regarded this as insignificant and were therefore unimpressed by sales reps' claims that this was something new.

Sales reps are often told by accounts that they are simply hard-selling over and over again on the same worn-out themes, and in doing so they encounter great resistance from potential accounts. In many sales reps' opinions, the company is not responsive enough to the needs of the market and is not providing a sufficient product line to the sales reps. The reps believe the company is failing to meet the needs of customers with different financial constraints or different philosophies toward incontinent care.

6. The facilities in most accounts are headed by an administrator, who is concerned with overall management and financial considerations. However, there is also typically a director of nursing who is responsible for the facility's patient care operations. In the usual selling situation, the sales rep must persuade both persons to buy the product, although the administrator has the final authority. The two authorities often have conflicting goals: the director of nursing is interested in providing the best possible care and may be convinced of the product's merits, but the administrator sees only the short-run costs of buying an expensive product. Alternatively, the administrator may be convinced that PRO-TEKS will reduce overall costs of supplies and labor, but the nursing director and/or the rest of the staff may be opposed to using the product. The result is that the sales rep must often contend with selling to more than one decision maker, whose goals are in opposition.

As the size of the facility increases, the sales rep typically must call on more people. In addition to those already mentioned, other people include the director of gerontology, usually a doctor, and the social worker. Social workers are important contacts (influentials) since they are in a position to recommend services and products that patients will need on

EXHIBIT 4
Sample Daily Call Plan for Sales Reps

Name	Active Account	Number of Beds	Percent Occupancy	Percent Theoretically Incontinent	People to See*
Alvarado Hospital	Yes	214	58.2	10.0	PA GER DN SW
San Diego P&S Hospital	Yes	156	76.4	10.0	ADM DN
San Diego P&S Retirement Home	Yes	78	64.1	35.0	ADM
Mercy Hospital	No	457	70.3	10.0	PA GER DN SW
Sharp Memorial Hospital & Rehabilitative Center	Yes	415	76.1	10.0	PA DN SW GER ADM
St. Paul's Health Care Center	No	86	95.3	35.0	ADM DN

*ADM = Administrator
GER = Gerontologist
DN = Direct of Nursing
PA = Purchasing Agent
SW = Social Worker

discharge from the medical center. Exhibit 4 illustrates a daily call plan for one of Tony Grant's sales reps.

7. A final consideration is that while the product may be of the best quality available and would be chosen by the patient, the patient usually has no choice in the matter. Budget constraints in some cases render quality considerations unimportant. This is particularly true for the majority of patients in nursing homes who receive varying degrees of governmental assistance to pay for the care they receive. The current economic and fiscal climates have resulted in a reduction in government subsidies for health care of institutionalized patients.

After reviewing the information he had gathered, Tony thought he had some clues about where to find possible causes of his district's high turnover problems. His next task would be to decide what could be done to eliminate or reduce some of these problems. He would have to plan action for his own district and make recommendations to the regional and divisional sales managers to improve performance.

Case 6–18

Hewlett-Packard Co.

Since taking over as chief executive of Hewlett-Packard Co. 18 months ago, Carleton S. "Carly" Fiorina has pushed the company to the limit to recapture the form that made it a management icon for six decades. Last November, it looked like she might have pushed too hard. After weeks of promising that HP would meet its quarterly numbers, Fiorina got grim news from the finance department. While sales growth beat expectations, profits had fallen $230 million short. The culprit, in large part, was Fiorina's aggressive management makeover. With HP's 88,000 staffers adjusting to the biggest reorganization in the company's history, expenses had risen out of control. And since new computer systems to track the changes weren't yet in place, HP's bean counters didn't detect the problem until 10 days after the quarter was over. "It was frantic. The financial folk were running all around looking for more dollars," says one HP manager.

One might expect a CEO in this spot to dial down on such a massive overhaul. Not Fiorina. After crunching numbers in an all-day session on Saturday and offering apologies for missing the forecast to HP's board at an emergency meeting Sunday, Fiorina told analysts she was raising HP's sales growth target for fiscal 2001 from 15% to as much as 17%. "We hit a speed bump—a big speed bump—this quarter," she said in a speech broadcast to employees a few days later. "But does it mean, 'Gee, this is too hard?' No way. In blackjack, you double down when you have an increasing probability of winning. And we're going to double down."

The stakes couldn't be higher—both for Fiorina and for the Silicon Valley pioneer started in a Palo Alto garage in 1938. Just as founders Bill Hewlett and David Packard broke the mold back then by eliminating hierarchies and introducing innovations such as profit-sharing and cubicles, Fiorina is betting on an approach so radical that experts say it has never been tried before at a company of HP's size and complexity. What's more, management gurus haven't a clue as to whether it will work—though the early signs suggest it may be too much, too fast. Not content to tackle one problem at a time, Fiorina is out to transform all aspects of HP at once, current economic slowdown be damned. That means strategy, structure, culture, compensation—everything from how to spark innovation to how to streamline internal processes. Such sweeping change is tough anywhere, and doubly so at tradition-bound HP. The reorganization will be "hard to do—and there's not much DNA for it at HP," says Jay R. Galbraith, professor at the Institute for Management Development in Lausanne, Switzerland.

Fiorina believes she has little choice. Her goal is to mix up a powerful cocktail of changes that will lift HP from its slow-growth funk of recent years before the company suffers a near-death experience similar to the one IBM endured 10 years ago and that Xerox and others are going through now. The conundrum for these behemoths: how to put the full force of the company behind winning in today's fiercely competitive technology business when they must also cook up brand-new megamarkets? It's a riddle, says Fiorina, that she can solve only by sweeping action that will ready HP for the next stage of the technology revolution, when companies latch on to the Internet to transform their operations. "We looked in the mirror and saw a great company that was becoming a failure," Fiorina told employees. "This is the vision Bill and Dave would have had if they were sitting here today."

At its core lies a conviction that HP must become "ambidextrous." Like a constantly mutating organism, the new HP is supposed to strike a balance: It should excel at short-term execution while pursuing long-term visions that create new markets. It should increase sales and profits in harmony rather than sacrifice one to gain the other. And HP will emphasize it all—technology, software, and consulting in every corner of computing, combining the product excellence of a Sun Microsystems Inc. with IBM's services strength.

To achieve this, Fiorina has dismantled the decentralized approach honed throughout HP's 64-year history. Until last year, HP was a collection of independently run units, each focused on a product such as scanners or security software. Fiorina has collapsed those into four sprawling organizations (Exhibit 1). One so-called back-end unit develops and builds computers, and another focuses on printers and imaging equipment. The back-end divisions

EXHIBIT 1 **HP the Fiorina Way**

When Fiorina arrived at HP, the company was a confederation of 83 autonomous product units reporting through four groups. She radically revamped the structure into two "back-end" divisions—one developing printers, scanners, and the like, and the other computers. These report to "front-end" groups that market HP's wares. Here's how the overhaul stacks up:

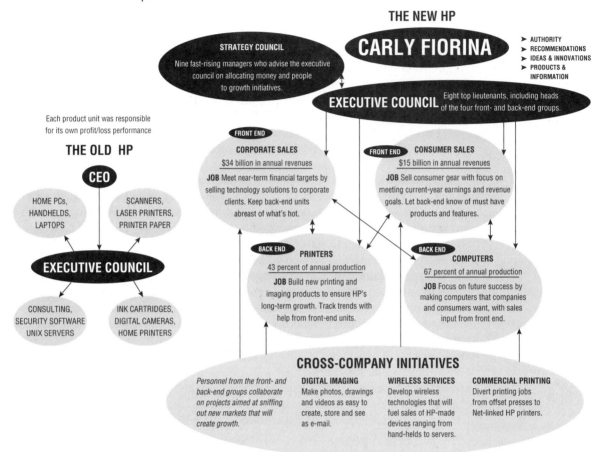

hand products off to two "front-end" sales and marketing groups that peddle the wares—one to consumers, the other to corporations. The theory: The new structure will boost collaboration, giving sales and marketing execs a direct pipeline to engineers so products are developed from the ground up to solve customer problems. This is the first time a company with thousands of product lines and scores of businesses has attempted a front-back approach, a strategy that requires laser focus and superb coordination.

Just as radical is Fiorina's plan for unleashing creativity. She calls it "inventing at the intersection." Until now, HP has made stand-alone products, from $20 ink cartridges to $3 million Internet servers. By tying them all together, HP hopes to sniff out new markets at the junctions where the products meet. The new HP, she says, will excel at dreaming up new e-services and then making the gear to deliver them. By yearend, for example, HP customers should be able to call up a photo stored on the Net using a handheld gizmo and then wirelessly zap it to a nearby printer. To create such opportunities, HP has launched three "cross-company initiatives"—wireless services, digital imaging, and commercial printing—that are the first formal effort to get all of HP's warring tribes working together.

Will her grand plan work? (Exhibit 2). It's still the petri-dish phase of the experiment, so it's too soon to say. But the initial results are troubling. While she had early success, the reorganization started to run aground nine months ago. Cushy commissions intended to light a fire under HP's sales force boosted sales, but mostly for low-margin products that did little for corporate profits. A more fundamental problem stems directly from the front-back structure: It doesn't clearly assign responsibility for profits and losses, meaning it's tough to diagnose and fix earnings screwups—especially since no individual manager will take the heat for missed numbers. And with staffers in 120 countries, redrawing the lines of communication and getting veterans of rival divisions to work together is proving nettlesome. "The people who deal with Carly directly feel very empowered, but everyone else is running around saying, 'What do we do now?'" says one HP manager. Another problem: Much of the burden of running HP lands squarely on Fiorina's shoulders. Some insiders and analysts say she needs a second-in-command to manage day-to-day operations. "She's playing CEO, visionary, and COO, and that's too hard to do," says Sanford C. Bernstein analyst Toni Sacconaghi.

Fiorina gets frosty at the notion that her restructuring is hitting snags. "This is a multi-year effort," she says. "I always would have characterized Year Two as harder than Year One because this is when the change really gets binding. I actually think our fourth-quarter miss and the current slowing economy are galvanizing us. When things are going well, you can convince yourself that change isn't as necessary as you thought." Fiorina also dismisses the need for a COO: "I'm running the business the way I think it ought to be run."

If Fiorina pulls this off, shell be tech's newest hero. The 46-year-old CEO already has earned top marks for zeroing in on HP's core problems—and for having the courage to tackle them head-on. And she did raise HP's growth to 15% in fiscal 2000 from 7% in

EXHIBIT 2 The Assessment	
Benefits
HAPPIER CUSTOMERS Clients should find HP easier to deal with, since they'll work with just one account team.
SALES BOOST HP should maximize its selling opportunities because account reps will sell all HP products, not just those from one division.
REAL SOLUTIONS HP can sell its products in combination as "solutions"—instead of just PCs or printers—to companies facing e-business problems.
FINANCIAL FLEXIBILITY With all corporate sales under one roof, HP can measure the total value of a customer, allowing reps to discount some products and still maximize profits on the overall contract.
Risks
OVERWHELMED WITH DUTIES With so many products being made and sold by just four units, HP execs have more on their plates and could miss the details that keep products competitive.
POORER EXECUTION When product managers oversaw everything from manufacturing to sales, they could respond quickly to changes. That will be harder with front- and back-end groups synching their plans only every few weeks.
LESS ACCOUNTABILITY Profit-and-loss responsibility is shared between the front- and back-end groups so no one person is on the hot seat. Finger-pointing and foot-dragging could replace HP's collegial cooperation.
FEWER SPENDING CONTROLS With powerful division chiefs keeping a tight rein on the purse strings, spending rarely got out of hand in the old HP. In the fourth quarter, expenses soared as those lines of command broke down.

1999. If she keeps it up, a reinvigorated HP could become a blueprint for others trying to transform technology dinosaurs into dynamos. "There isn't a major technology company in the world that has solved the problem she's trying to address, and we're all going to learn from her experience," says Stanford Business School professor Robert Burgelman.

Fiorina needs results—and fast. For all its internal changes, HP today is more dependent than ever on maturing markets. While PCs and printers contributed 69% of HP's sales and three-fourths of its earnings last year, those businesses are expected to slow to single-digit growth in coming years, with falling profitability. Last year, HP was tied with Compaq as the leading U.S. maker of home PCs and sold 60% of home printers, according to IDC. Those numbers make it hard to boost market share. In corporate computing—where the company is banking on huge growth—HP has made only minor strides toward capturing lucrative business such as consulting services, storage, and software. And the failure of Fiorina's $16 billion bid to buy the consulting arm of PricewaterhouseCoopers LLP leaves her without a strong services division to help transform HP from high tech's old reliable box-maker into a Net powerhouse, offering e-business solutions.

Careening

With the tech sector slowing, this may be the wrong time to make a miracle. In January, HP said its revenue and earnings would fall short of targets for the first quarter, and Fiorina cut her sales-growth estimates to about 5%—a far cry from the mid-teens she had been promising. In late January, the company announced it was laying off 1,700 marketing workers. HP's stock, which has dropped from a split-adjusted $67 in July to less than $40, is 19% below its level when Fiorina took the helm.

It's not just Fiorina's lofty goals that are so radical, but the way she's trying to achieve them. She's careening along at Net speed, ordering changes she hopes are right—but which may need adjustment later. That goes even for the front-back management structure. "When you sail, you don't get there in a straight line," Fiorina argues. "You adjust your course to fit the times and the current conditions." Insiders say that before the current slowdown, she expected HP to clock sales growth of 20% in 2002 and thereafter—a record clip for a $50 billion company. Fiorina won't confirm specific growth goals but says the downturn doesn't change her long-term plan.

Her overambitious targets have cost her credibility with Wall Street, too. While she earned kudos for increasing sales growth and meeting expectations early on, she has damaged her reputation by trying to put a positive spin on more troubled recent quarters. HP insiders say that while former CEO Lewis E. Platt spent a few hours reviewing the results at the end of each quarter, Fiorina holds marathon, multiday sessions to figure out how to cast financials in the best light. Not everyone is impressed. "I grew up with HP calculators, but they don't work right anymore," jokes Edward J. Zander, president of rival Sun Microsystems. "Everything they mention seems to be growing 50%, but the company as a whole only grows 10%." Fiorina says HP has accurately reported all segments of its business and that she makes no special effort to spin the results. "The calculators still work fine," she says.

Fiorina was well aware of the challenges when she joined HP, but she also saw the huge untapped potential. She had grown to admire the company while working as an HP intern during her years studying medieval history at Stanford University. Later, as president of the largest division of telecommunications equipment maker Lucent Technologies Inc., she learned the frustrations of buying products from highly decentralized HP. When HP's board asked her to take over, she jumped at the chance to show off her management chops. While she had spearheaded the company's spin-off from AT&T in 1996, then CEO Richard A. McGinn got all the credit.

"Perfectly Positioned"

Soon after signing on, Fiorina decided the front-back structure was the salve for HP's ills. With the help of consultants, she tailored the framework to HP's needs and developed a multiyear plan for rejuvenating the company. Step One would be to shake up complacent troops. Next, Fiorina set out to refine a strategy and "reinvent" HP from the ground up, a task she expected would take most of 2000. Only then—meaning about now—would HP be ready to unleash its potential as a top supplier of technology for companies revamping their businesses around the Web.

That's where the cross-company initiatives come in. So far, HP has identified three. There's the digital-imaging effort to make photos, drawings, and videos as easy to create, store, and send as e-mail. A commercial-printing thrust aims to capture business that now goes to offset presses. And a wireless services effort might, say, turn a wristwatch into a full-function Net device that tracks the wearer's heart rate and transmits that info to a hospital. "All the great technology companies got great by seeing trends and getting there first—and they're always misunderstood initially," says Fiorina. "We think we see where the market is going and that we're perfectly positioned."

The first chapters of Fiorina's plan came off as scripted. When she replaced 33-year HP veteran Platt on a balmy July day in 1999, Fiorina swept in with a rush of fresh thinking and made headway—for a time. She ordered unit chiefs to justify why HP should continue in that line of business. And she gave her marketers just six weeks to revamp advertising and relaunch the brand. After a few days on the job, she met with researchers who feared that Fiorina—a career salesperson—would move HP away from its engineering roots. She wowed them. In sharp contrast to the phlegmatic Platt, Fiorina moved through the crowd, microphone in hand, exhorting them to change the world. "There was a lot of skepticism about her," says Stan Williams, director of HP's quantum science research program. "But she was fantastic."

If she was a hit with engineers, it took a bit longer to win over HP's executive council. For years, these top execs had measured HP's performance against its ability to meet internal goals, but rarely compared its growth rates to those of rivals. In August, Fiorina rocked their cozy world when she shared details of her reorganization—and of her sky-high growth targets. She went to a whiteboard and compared HP with better-performing competitors: Dell Computer in PCs, Sun in servers, and IBM in services. She issued a challenge: If the executives could show her another way to hit her 20% growth target by 2002, she would postpone the restructuring, insiders say. Five weeks later, the best alternative was a plan for just 16% growth. The restructuring would start by yearend.

She dove into the details. While Platt ran HP like a holding company, Fiorina demanded weekly updates on key units and peppered midlevel managers with 3 a.m. voice mails on product details. She injected much needed discipline into HP's computer sales force, which had long gotten away with lowering quotas at the end of each quarter. To raise the stakes, she tied more sales compensation to performance and changed the bonus period from once a year to every six months to prevent salespeople from coasting until the fourth quarter. While some commissions were tied to the number of orders rather than the sales amount and contributed to the earnings miss, Fiorina has fixed the problem and accomplished her larger goal of kick-starting sales. "You can feel the stress her changes are causing," says Kevin P. McManus, a vice-president of Premier Systems Integrators, which installs HP equipment "These guys know they have to perform."

This play-to-win attitude has started to take root in other areas. Take HP Labs. In recent years, the once proud research and development center made too many incremental improvements to existing products, in part because engineers' bonuses were tied to the number, rather than the impact, of their inventions. Now, Fiorina is focusing HP's R&D

dollars on "big bang" projects. Consider Bob Rau's PICO software, which helps automate the design of chips used in electronic gear. Rau had worked for years on the project, but the technology languished. Last spring, Rau told Fiorina that the market for such systems was projected to grow to $300 billion as appliance makers built all sorts of Net-enabled gadgets. Within days, Fiorina created a separate division that operates alongside the two back-end groups and has grown to 250 people. Besides Rau's software, it will sell other HP technologies such as new disk drives to manufacturers. "It was like we'd been smothered for four years and someone was finally kind enough to lift the pillow off our face," says Rau.

Rough Edges

With Phase One of her transformation behind her, Fiorina launched a formal reinvention process last spring (Exhibit 3). First up: cutting expenses. Over nine days, a 12-person team came up with ways to slash $1 billion by fiscal 2002. HP could save $100 million by out-sourcing procurement. It could trim $10 million by letting employees log their hours online rather than on cardboard time cards. And the company could revamp its stodgy marketing

EXHIBIT 3
Carly to HP: Snap to It

Even before she took charge at HP in mid-1999, Fiorina had formulated a three-phase plan for returning the company to its former glory. Some highlights:

Phase I, 1999

Prepare the ground

SPREAD THE GOSPEL Held "Coffee with Carly" sessions in 20 countries to boost morale. Convinced top lieutenants that HP needs to match the growth of rivals.

ONE IMAGE Merged HP's fragmented ad effort under one all-encompassing "Invent" campaign.

SPARK INNOVATION Reoriented HP's R&D lab away from incremental product improvements and toward big-bang projects such as nanotechnology for making superpowerful chips.

Phase II, 2000

Improve growth and profits in core businesses

CONSOLIDATE Folded HP's 83 product divisions into four units: two product develop-ment units that work with two sales and marketing groups—one aimed at consumers, the other corporations.

SET STRATEGY Created a nine-person Strategy Council to allocate resources to the best opportunities rather than leaving strategy to product chieftains.

WHACK COSTS Lower expenses by $1 billion by revamping internal processes to tap the power of the Web.

Phase III, 2001 and Beyond

Build new markets

TRIGGER NEW PRODUCT CATEGORIES Establish cross-company initiatives to develop altogether new Net-related businesses.

WOO CUSTOMERS Offer soup-to-nuts solutions for customers by creating teams from across HP that sell to major accounts.

GOOD CORPORATE CITIZEN Use HP's resources to create subsidized or low-cost com-puter centers and services to make the Net available to everyone.

by consolidating advertising from 43 agencies into two. That would save money and, better yet, focus HP's campaigns on Fiorina's big Web plans rather than on its various stand-alone products.

But when the big changes really started to kick in, Fiorina's plan started to bog down. In the past, HP's product chieftains ran their operations, from design to sales and support. Today, they're folded into the two back-end units, leaving product chiefs with a far more limited role. They're still responsible for keeping HP competitive with rivals, hitting cost goals, and getting products to market on time. But they hand those products to the front-end organizations responsible for marketing and selling them.

The arrangement solves a number of long-standing HP problems. For one, it makes HP far easier to do business with. Rather than getting mobbed by salespeople from various divisions, now customers deal with one person. It lets HP's expert product designers focus on what they do best and gives the front-end marketers authority to make the deals that are most profitable for HP as a whole—say, to sell a server at a lower margin to customers who commit to long-term consulting services. "You couldn't miss how silly it was the old way if you were part of the wide-awake club," says Scott Stallard, a vice-president in HP's computing group. "A parade of HP salesmen in Tauruses would pull up and meet for the first time outside of the customer's building." These advantages, though, aren't enough to convince management experts or many HP veterans that a front-back approach will work at such a complex company. How do back-end product designers stay close enough to customers to know when a new feature becomes a must-have? Will executives, now saddled with thousands of HP products under their supervision, give sufficient attention to each of them to stay competitive? And with shared profit-and-loss responsibility between front and back ends, who has the final say when an engineer wants to take a flier on expensive research? "You just diffuse responsibility and authority," says Sara L. Beckman, a former HP manager who teaches at the Haas Business School at the University of California at Berkeley. "It makes it easier to say, 'Hey, that wasn't my problem.'"

Indeed, the front-back plan is showing some rough edges. While HP cited many reasons for its troubling fourth-quarter results, the reorganization is probably front and center. Freed from decades-old lines of command, employees spent as if they had already hit hyper-growth. In October alone, the company hired 1,200 people. Even dinner and postage expenses ran far over the norm. Such profligate spending was rare under the old structure where powerful division chiefs kept a tight rein on the purse strings. "They spent too much money on high-fives and setting themselves up to grow the following quarter," says Salomon Smith Barney analyst John B. Jones.

That situation could improve over time. Fiorina rushed the reorganization into place before the company's information systems were revamped to reflect the changes. Before Fiorina arrived, each product division had its own financial reporting system. It was only on Nov. 1 that HP rolled out a new *über*-system so staffers could work off the same books. Although it's too soon to say whether it's a winner, HP claims the system will let it watch earnings in powerful new ways. Rather than just see sales for a product line, managers will be able to track profits from a given customer companywide or by region. That way they can cut deals on some products to boost other sales and wind up with a more lucrative relationship.

Another restructuring red flag is the way Fiorina now sets strategy, a big departure from "The HP Way"—the principles laid out by the founders in 1957. Based on the belief that smart people will make the right choices if given the right tools and authority, "Bill and Dave" pushed strategy down to the managers most involved in each business. The approach worked. Not only did HP dominate most of its markets, but low-level employees unearthed new opportunities for the company. "HP was always the exact opposite of a command-and-control environment," says former CEO Platt. Although Platt wouldn't comment on Fiorina directly, he says, "Bill and Dave did not feel they had to make every decision." HP's $10 billion inkjet printer business, for example, got its start in a broom closet at HP's Corvallis (Ore.) campus, where its inventors had to set up because they had no budget.

Eyes on the Prizes

Fiorina isn't waiting for another broom-closet miracle. Since the halcyon mid-'90s, the old HP way hasn't worked quite as well. The last mega-breakthrough product HP introduced was the inkjet printer, in 1984. Growth had slowed to just 4% in the six months before Fiorina took over. To give HP better direction, Fiorina has created a nine-person Strategy Council that meets every month to allocate resources, set priorities, and advise her on acquisitions and partnerships. "This is a company that can do anything," Fiorina says. "But it can't do everything."

Again, the move makes sense on paper. By steering the entire company, the council can focus HP on a few big Internet prizes rather than myriad underfunded pet projects. But this top-down engine could backfire. Experts point out that except for visionaries like Apple Computer's Steve Jobs or IBM's Thomas J. Watson Jr., it's rare for the suits in the corner office to be able predict the future—especially in a market as fast-changing as the Net. "If we were to go too far toward top-down, it would not be right for this company," acknowledges Debra L. Dunn, HP's vice-president of strategy.

To be sure, Fiorina is quick to embrace ideas from below if she thinks they'll solve a problem. This spring, Sam Mancuso, HP's vice-president of corporate accounts, proposed a team-based plan that advances the front-back approach. Time was, PC salespeople weren't allowed to sell, say, printers. Mancuso has fixed that by pulling together 20-person teams to concentrate on the top 75 corporate customers. The teams create an "opportunity map" for each customer, tracking the total amount of business HP could possibly book. Then the team analyzes what deal would maximize earnings for HP. Mancuso says his operation has boosted sales to top customers by more than 30% since May. "We're taking the handcuffs off, so now we can be more aggressive," Mancuso says.

The shackles may be off, but HP still lags its competitors in many areas. For all HP's talk of becoming a Net power, in the fourth quarter, Sun held 39% of the market for Unix servers preferred by e-businesses, according to IDC. HP is in second place with 23% share, a slight improvement over the year before. But it faces growing competition from third-place IBM, which just introduced a product line that many analysts say handily outperforms HP's servers. "HP is just not making much headway," says Ellen M. Hancock, CEO of Exodus Communications Inc. Her company uses 62,000 servers in its Web hosting centers, virtually none of them from HP. And most of HP's Net schemes, such as Cartoga, a service that lets consumers post pictures on the Web, have failed to catch on.

Even fans of Fiorina acknowledge she has a ways to go. While wireless juggernaut Nokia Corp. just signed a deal to use HP software, Chairman Jorma Ollila questions how successful Fiorina's turnaround is likely to be. "Carly is very impressive," he says. "But the jury is still out on HP." Says Cisco Systems Inc. CEO John T. Chambers, who named Fiorina to his board on Jan. 10: "I'd bet that Carly will be one of the top 5 or 10 CEOs in the nation. But she has still got to get them running faster." Fiorina wouldn't disagree and says she plans to keep upping her bets. "The greatest risk is standing still," she says. She should hope she has picked the right cards, because she's gambling with Silicon Valley's proudest legacy.

Source: Peter Burrows, "The Radical," *Business Week,* February 19, 2001, 70–74, 76, 78, 80.

Case 6–19

Quaker Oats Company

In November 1994 Quaker Oats Co. negotiated a deal to acquire the iced tea and fruit drink marketer Snapple Beverage Corp. for $1.7 billion in cash, a move that took Quaker off the list of rumored takeover targets and greatly strengthened its position as a producer-marketer of beverage substitutes for soft drinks. Quaker's Gatorade brand commanded 85 percent of the sports drink segment in the United States, generated worldwide sales of almost $1.2 billion, and was Quaker's fastest-growing, most lucrative product. Snapple had 1993 sales of $516 million, up from $95 million in 1991, and was the clear-cut market leader in New Age or alternative beverages, with a national distribution capability and growing brand awareness among consumers. Quaker's acquisition of Snapple elevated it into a nonalcoholic beverage powerhouse with nearly $2 billion in sales, trailing only Coca-Cola and PepsiCo.

Quaker agreed to pay Snapple shareholders $14 a share for the 121,620,000 shares outstanding, a price roughly equal to the $13.75 to $14.25 trading range of Snapple stock in the few days before the agreement was announced. Shares of Snapple, which had traded in range of the $28 to $32 in late 1993 and early 1994, had fallen in recent months when sales growth during the first three quarters of 1994 slowed significantly, and ready-to-drink tea products carrying the Lipton and Nestea brands began to capture almost 50 percent of sales in supermarkets. The Lipton line was jointly produced and marketed by PepsiCo and Unilever's Thomas J. Lipton subsidiary; the Nestea line was the product of an alliance between Coca-Cola and Nestlé (Nestlé was the world's largest food products company and the producer of Nestea-brand teas).

Hours before the Quaker–Snapple agreement was announced, Snapple reported a third-quarter earnings drop of 74 percent, which analysts attributed to oversized inventories and intensifying competition. In NYSE trading on the following day, Quaker's stock fell nearly 10 percent, from $74.50 to $67.125. The drop in price was said to be a combination of Snapple's poor earnings report, the reduced likelihood that Quaker would be a takeover target, and the high acquisition price Quaker was paying for Snapple. Wall Street analysts regarded the outlook for Snapple's future sales and earnings as very uncertain. Whereas Snapple's management indicated in May 1994 that it was comfortable with a 1994 earnings per share projection of 86 cents a share, the confidential business plan Snapple gave Quaker during their negotiations contained a projection of only 55 cents a share; in a filing with the Securities and Exchange Commission in the week after the acquisition announcement, Snapple indicated that 1994 earnings of 40 cents a share appeared more reasonable.[1] The $14 acquisition price represented a multiple of 35 times Snapple's latest earnings projection of 40 cents per share and a multiple of nearly 20 times Snapple's estimated 1994 operating earnings (the latter multiple was well above the multiples of 10 and 11 that other recently acquired beverage companies had commanded).[2]

To finance the Snapple acquisition, Quaker borrowed $2.4 billion from NationsBank. Quaker planned to use the loan proceeds to (1) make cash payments of $1.7 billion to Snapple's shareholders for the outstanding 121,620,000 shares, (2) pay off $100 million in Snapple debt, (3) refinance $350 million in Quaker's debt, and (4) retain $250 million for working capital. Quaker management reportedly was seeking buyers for its European pet

This case was prepared by Arthur A. Thompson, Jr., the University of Alabama, and John E. Gamble, Auburn University of Montgomery. Copyright © 1995 by Arthur A. Thompson, Jr.
[1] Reported in *The Wall Street Journal,* November 7, 1994, p. A4.
[2] *The Wall Street Journal,* November 3, 1994, pp. A3, A4.

foods business and Mexican chocolate subsidiary (combined sales of $900 million) as part of an ongoing restructuring of its food products lineup and presumably to raise cash to pay down debt associated with the Snapple acquisition.

The Quaker Oats Company

In 1994 Quaker Oats was the twelfth largest food and beverage company in the United States, with worldwide sales of $6 billion (see Exhibit 1). The company operated 54 manufacturing plants in 16 states and 13 foreign countries and had distribution centers and sales offices in 21 states and 18 foreign countries. Nearly one-third of corporate revenues came from sales outside the United States. Quaker's worldwide grocery product portfolio included such well-known brands as Quaker Oats, Cap'n Crunch, Rice-A-Roni, Gatorade, Aunt Jemima, Ken-L Ration pet foods, and Van Camp's bean products; 81 percent of the company's sales came from brands holding the number one or number two position in their respective categories. Moreover, 82 percent of Quaker's worldwide sales came from brands positioned in categories where sales volumes were growing. Hot cereals were Quaker's oldest, best-known, and most profitable products. Of the top 25 cereal brands, Quaker had 4: Instant Quaker Oatmeal, Cap'n Crunch, Old Fashioned and Quick Quaker Oats, and Life Cereal.

Quaker's top management was committed to achieving real earnings growth of 7 percent and providing total shareholder returns (dividends plus share price appreciation) that exceeded the S&P 500 stock index over time. Management also believed it could enhance

EXHIBIT 1
The 25 Largest Food and Beverage Companies in the United States (ranked by 1993 food and beverage sales, in millions of dollars)

Source: The Food Institute.

Company	1992	1993
1. Philip Morris	$33,024	$34,526
2. ConAgra Inc.	16,201	16,499
3. PepsiCo	13,738	15,665
4. Coca-Cola	13,039	13,937
5. IBP Inc.	11,128	11,671
6. Anheuser-Busch	10,741	10,792
7. Sara Lee	6,622	7,206
8. H. J. Heinz	6,582	7,103
9. RJR Nabisco	6,707	7,025
10. Campbell Soup	6,263	6,586
11. Kellogg	6,191	6,295
12. Quaker Oats	5,576	5,731
13. CPC International	5,502	5,636
14. General Mills	5,234	5,397
15. Seagram Company	5,214	5,227
16. Tyson Foods	4,169	4,707
17. Ralston Purina	4,558	4,526
18. Borden Inc.	4,056	3,674
19. Hershey Foods	3,220	3,488
20. Procter & Gamble	3,709	3,271
21. Dole Foods	3,120	3,108
22. Hormel Foods	2,814	2,854
23. Chiquita Brands	2,723	2,522
24. Dean Foods	2,220	2,243
25. International Multifoods	2,281	2,224

shareholder value by prudently using leverage. Before the Snapple acquisition, Quaker issued $200 million in medium-term notes, increasing total debt to $1 billion. In fiscal 1994 Quaker used its debt proceeds and cash flow from operations to repurchase 3 million shares of common stock, make four small acquisitions, extend the company's record of consecutive dividend increases to 27 years, and make $175 million in capital investments to support growth and efficiency improvements. Exhibit 2 provides a 10-year financial summary of Quaker's corporate performance.

Quaker's Corporate Organization and Brand Portfolio

Quaker Oats' worldwide production and sales operations were structured around two broad geographic groups: U.S. and Canadian Grocery Products and International Grocery Products. The U.S. and Canadian Grocery group was subdivided into four product divisions: Breakfast Foods, Gatorade Worldwide, Diversified Grocery Products (pet foods and grain products), and Convenience Foods. The International Grocery Products group had three geographic operating divisions: Europe, Latin America, and Pacific. Exhibit 3 shows the financial performance of the two major product groups. Exhibit 4 shows the brands and sales of the divisional units.

The Gatorade Worldwide Division

Gatorade was developed in 1965 for the University of Florida Gators; it was sold to Stokely-Van Camp in 1967. Quaker acquired the Gatorade brand in 1983 when it bought Stokely-Van Camp. At that time Gatorade sales were about $100 million. Since the acquisition, sales of Gatorade had grown at an average annual compound rate of 22 percent, spurred by the addition of flavor and package-size variety as well as wider geographic distribution. Worldwide sales were just over $1.1 billion in 1994, up 21 percent over fiscal 1993. U.S. and Canadian volume increased 19 percent; international volume was up 31 percent. According to Quaker estimates, Gatorade held a 77 percent share of the $1.3 billion U.S. sports beverage category as of mid-1994 (down from 90 percent–plus in 1990–1991) and more than 40 percent of the global sports drink market. Quaker management believed that Gatorade's science-based rehydration ability to replace salts and fluids lost during exercise, strong identification with sports, and leading position domestically and globally made it an exceptionally profitable growth opportunity worldwide. Gatorade was Quaker's number one growth priority, and the stated mission of the Gatorade Worldwide division was "to quench hot and thirsty consumers in every corner of the world."

Gatorade's Market Scope

In 1994, Gatorade was marketed in 26 countries on five continents and had the leading market position in most of those locations. The brand's biggest markets in 1994 were the United States, Mexico, South Korea, Canada, Venezuela, Italy, Germany, and Taiwan. In 1994 sales of Gatorade totaled nearly $900 million in the United States and approximately $220 million in the other 25 countries where it was marketed. Management's objective was to increase sales in Latin America, Europe, and the Pacific to $1 billion by the year 2000.

In Latin America, Gatorade's sports drink share was in the range of 90 percent in all the countries where it was available. Mexico was Gatorade's second largest market after the United States. In 1994 sales in Brazil increased fourfold as Gatorade was relaunched successfully in the São Paulo region. Sales volumes continued to rise in Venezuela and the Caribbean, and Gatorade was introduced into Chile. To deal with the growing sales volume in Latin America, Quaker was investing in additional production facilities.

EXHIBIT 2 **Financial Summary for Quaker Oats Company, 1984–1994** (dollars in millions, except per-share data)

Year Ended June 30	5-Year CAGR[1]	10-Year CAGR[1]	1994	1993	1992
Operating Results[2, 3]					
Net sales	4.1%	7.7%	$5,955.0	$5,730.6	$5,576.4
Gross profit	6.3%	10.8%	3,028.8	2,860.6	2,745.3
Income from continuing operations before income taxes and cumulative effect of accounting changes	9.6%	6.0%	378.7	467.6	421.5
Provision for income taxes	10.3%	4.0%	147.2	180.8	173.9
Income from continuing operations before cumulative effect of account changes	9.2%	7.5%	231.5	286.8	247.6
Income (loss) from discontinued operations, net of tax			—	—	—
Income from the disposal of discontinued operations, net of tax			—	—	—
Cumulative effect of accounting changes, net of tax			—	(115.5)	—
Net income	2.7%	5.3%	$ 231.5	$ 171.3	$ 247.6
Per common share:					
Income from continuing operations for cumulative effect of accounting changes	12.3%	9.5%	$ 3.36	$ 3.93	$ 3.25
Income (loss) from discontinued operations			—	—	—
Income from the disposal of discontinued operations			—	—	—
Cumulative effect of accounting changes			—	(1.59)	—
Net income	5.6%	7.2%	$ 3.36	$ 2.34	$ 3.25
Dividends declared:					
Common stock	8.1%	12.2%	$ 140.6	$ 136.1	$ 128.6
Per common share	12.1%	14.4%	$ 2.12	$ 1.92	$ 1.72
Convertible preferred and redeemable preference stock			$ 4.0	$ 4.2	$ 4.2
Average number of common shares outstanding (in thousands)			67,618	71,974	74,881
Financial Statistics[4, 5]					
Current ratio			1.0	1.0	1.2
Working capital			$ (5.5)	$ (37.5)	$ 168.7
Property, plant, and equipment, net			$1,214.2	$1,228.2	$2,173.3
Depreciation expense			$ 133.3	$ 129.9	$ 129.7
Total assets			$3,043.3	$2,815.9	$3,039.9
Long-term debt			$ 759.5	$ 632.6	$ 688.7
Preferred stock (net of deferred compensation) and redeemable preference stock			$ 15.3	$ 11.4	$ 7.9
Common shareholders' equity			$ 445.8	$ 551.1	$ 842.1

Note: See footnotes at the end of this Exhibit on page 738.

Source: 1994 Annual Report.

1991	1990	1989	1988	1987	1986	1985	1984
$5,491.2	$5,030.6	$4,879.4	$4,508.0	$3,823.9	$2,968.6	$2,925.6	$2,830.9
2,652.7	2,350.3	2,229.0	2,114.6	1,750.7	1,298.7	1,174.7	1,085.7
411.5	382.4	239.1	314.6	295.9	255.8	238.8	211.3
175.7	153.5	90.2	118.1	141.3	113.4	110.3	99.0
235.8	228.9	148.9	196.5	154.6	142.4	128.5	112.3
(30.0)	(59.9)	54.1	59.2	33.5	37.2	28.1	26.4
—	—	—	—	55.8	—	—	—
—	—	—	—	—	—	—	—
$ 205.8	$ 169.0	$ 203.0	$ 255.7	$ 243.9	$ 179.6	$ 156.6	$ 138.7
$ 3.05	$ 2.93	$ 1.88	$ 2.46	$ 1.96	$ 1.77	$ 1.53	$ 1.35
(0.40)	(0.78)	0.68	0.74	0.43	0.47	0.35	0.32
—	—	—	—	0.71	—	—	—
—	—	—	—	—	—	—	—
$ 2.65	$ 2.15	$ 2.56	$ 3.20	$ 3.10	$ 2.24	$ 1.88	$ 1.67
$ 118.7	$ 106.9	$ 95.2	$ 79.9	$ 63.2	$ 55.3	$ 50.5	$ 44.4
$ 1.56	$ 1.40	$ 1.20	$1.00	$ 0.80	$ 0.70	$ 0.62	$ 0.55
$ 4.3	$ 3.6	—	—	—	$ 2.3	$ 3.6	$ 3.9
75,904	76,537	79,307	79,835	78,812	79,060	81,492	80,412
1.3	1.3	1.8	1.4	1.4	1.4	1.7	1.6
$ 317.8	$ 342.8	$ 695.8	$ 417.5	$ 507.9	$ 296.8	$ 400.7	$ 316.8
$1,232.7	$1,154.1	$ 959.6	$ 922.5	$ 898.6	$ 691.0	$ 616.5	$ 650.1
$ 125.2	$ 103.5	$ 94.2	$ 88.3	$ 81.6	$ 59.1	$ 56.3	$ 57.4
$3,060.5	$3,377.4	$3,125.9	$2,886.1	$3,136.5	$1,944.5	$1,760.3	$1,726.5
$ 701.2	$ 740.3	$ 766.8	$ 299.1	$ 527.7	$ 160.9	$ 168.2	$ 200.1
$ 4.8	$ 1.8	—	—	—	—	$ 37.9	$ 38.5
$ 901.0	$1,017.5	$1,137.1	$1,251.1	$1,087.5	$ 831.7	$ 786.9	$ 720.1

(continued)

EXHIBIT 2 *(concluded)*

Year Ended June 30	5-Year CAGR[1]	10-Year CAGR[1]	1994	1993	1992
Financial Statistics[4, 5] *(continued)*					
Net cash provided by operating activities			$ 450.8	$ 558.2	$ 581.3
Operating return on assets[6]			19.9%	21.1%	18.9%
Gross profit as a percentage of sales			50.9%	49.9%	49.2%
Advertising and merchandising as a percentage of sales			26.6%	25.7%	26.0%
Income from continuing operations before cumulative effect of accounting changes as a percentage of sales			3.9%	5.0%	4.4%
Total debt–total capitalization ratio[7]			68.8%	59.0%	48.7%
Common dividends as a percentage of income available for common shares (excluding cumulative effect of accounting changes)			63.1%	48.9%	52.9%
Number of common shareholders			28,197	33,154	33,580
Number of employees worldwide			20,000	20,200	21,100
Market price range of common stock—High			$ 82	$ 77	$ 75¼
—Low			$ 61⅞	$ 56⅛	$ 50¼

[1]CAGR = compound average growth rate.
[2]Fiscal 1994 results include a pretax restructuring charge of $118.4 million, or $1.09 per share, for work force reductions, plant consolidations, and product discontinuations and a pretax gain of $9.8 million, or $0.13 per share, for the sale of a business in Venezuela.
[3]Fiscal 1989 results include a pretax restructuring charge of $124.3 million, or $1.00 per share, for plant consolidations and overhead reductions and a pretax charge of $25.6 million, or $0.20 per share, for a change to the LIFO method of accounting for the majority of U.S. Grocery Products inventories.
[4]Income-related statistics exclude the results of business reported as discontinued operations. Balance sheet amounts and related statistics have not been restated for discontinued operations, other than Fisher-Price, due to materiality.
[5]Effective fiscal 1991, common shareholders' equity and number of employees worldwide were reduced as a result of the Fisher-Price spin-off.
[6]Operating income divided by average identifiable assets of U.S. and Canadian and International Grocery Products.
[7]Total debt divided by total debt plus total shareholders' equity including preferred stock (net of deferred compensation) and redeemable preference stock.

EXHIBIT 3 **Financial Performance of Quaker's Two Major Grocery Products Groups, 1989–1994** (dollars in millions)

Product Group	Fiscal Year Ended June 30					
	1989	1990	1991	1992	1993	1994
U.S. and Canadian Grocery Products						
Net sales	$3,630	$3,610	$3,860	$3,842	$3,930	$4,253
Operating income	256	373	429	435	447	431
Identifiable assets	2,055	2,150	2,229	1,998	1,877	1,999
Return on net sales	7.1%	10.3%	11.1%	11.3%	11.4%	10.1%
Return on assets	13.1%	17.7%	19.6%	20.6%	23.1%	22.2%
International Grocery Products						
Net sales	$1,250	$1,421	$1,631	$1,734	$1,800	$1,702
Operating income	93	172	104	105	128	106
Identifiable assets	482	638	656	842	745	786
Return on net sales	7.5%	12.1%	6.4%	6.1%	7.1%	6.2%
Return on assets	20.0%	30.7%	16.1%	14.0%	16.2%	13.9%

Source: 1994 Annual Report.

1991	1990	1989	1988	1987	1986	1985	1984
$543.2	$ 460.0	$ 408.3	$ 320.8	$ 375.1	$ 266.9	$ 295.5	$ 263.6
18.8%	20.4%	14.4%	18.3%	22.1%	25.8%	24.5%	24.4%
48.3%	46.7%	45.7%	46.9%	45.8%	43.7%	40.2%	38.4%
25.6%	23.8%	23.4%	24.9%	22.9%	21.7%	19.4%	18.4%
4.3%	4.6%	3.1%	4.4%	4.0%	4.8%	4.4%	4.0%
47.4%	52.3%	44.2%	33.8%	50.2%	35.7%	28.9%	35.4%
58.9%	65.1%	46.9%	31.3%	25.9%	31.2%	33.0%	32.9%
33,603	33,859	34,347	34,231	32,358	27,068	26,670	26,785
20,900	28,200	31,700	31,300	30,800	29,500	28,700	28,400
$ 64⅞	$ 68⅛	$ 66¼	$ 57⅛	$ 57⅝	$ 39¼	$ 26⅛	$ 16⅛
$ 41¾	$ 45⅛	$ 42⅝	$ 31	$ 32⅝	$ 23½	$ 14¼	$ 10¾

EXHIBIT 4   **Quaker Brands and Sales by Division, 1989–1994** (dollars in millions)

Division/Category	Brands/Products	Sales in Fiscal Year Ending June 30					
		1989	1990	1991	1992	1993	1994
Breakfast foods	Quaker Oatmeal, Cap'n Crunch, Life, Quaker rice cakes, Quaker Chewy granola bars, Quaker grits, Aunt Jemima cornmeal	$1,292	$1,280	$1,322	$1,313	$1,425	$1,573
Pet foods	Ken-L Ration, Gaines, Kibbles 'n Bits, Puss 'n Boots, Cycle	608	518	531	531	529	539
Golden Grain	Rice-A-Roni, Noodle Roni, Near East Golden Grain, Mission	283	275	297	309	269	305
Convenience foods	Aunt Jemima breakfast products, Celeste frozen pizza, Van Camp's canned beans, Wolf chili, Burry cookies, Maryland Club coffee, Proof & Bake frozen products, Petrofsky's bakery products	857	901	978	953	949	924
Gatorade (U.S. and Canada)	Gatorade	584	630	724	727	750	906
Europe	Quaker cereals, Gatorade, Felix cat food, Bonzo dog food, Cuore corn oil	969	1,085	1,326	1,355	1,336	1,164
Latin America and Pacific	Quaker cereals, Gatorade	281	336	305	380	465	538

Source: 1994 Annual Report.

Competition in the sports beverage market in Europe was fierce because in a number of important countries the market was already developed. When Gatorade was introduced in those country markets, it had to win sales and market share away from established brands. Quaker had pulled Gatorade out of the competitive British and French markets. Given the varying competitive intensity from country to country, Quaker's Gatorade division was focusing its marketing resources on the most promising European country markets. Sales were currently biggest in Germany and Italy. In 1994 Gatorade was introduced in Holland and Austria. Quaker management anticipated that Gatorade sales in Europe would evolve more slowly than they would in other global locations. In 1994 volume grew 9 percent in Europe, but sales revenue was lower because of weaker European currencies against the U.S. dollar.

Throughout most of the Pacific, Gatorade was sold primarily through licensing agreements. Quaker's most successful licensing agreement was with Cheil Foods in South Korea, where Gatorade was a strong second in the sports beverage segment. Gatorade volume in South Korea ranked third, behind the United States and Mexico. In fiscal 1994 Gatorade was introduced in Australia (where the brand was sold through an arrangement with Pepsi-Cola bottlers in Australia), Singapore, and Hong Kong. Although Gatorade was not the first sports drink marketed in Australia, the brand captured the leading share by mid-1994, less than 12 months after it was introduced.

The expense of underwriting Gatorade's entry into new country markets had pinched Gatorade's international profit margins. Quaker's profits from international sales of Gatorade were expected to remain subpar as the company pushed for expanded penetration of international markets. Quaker management believed that increased consumer interest in healthy foods and beverages, growing sports participation, expanded sports competition in the world arena, increasing acceptance of international brands, and a growing population in warm-climate countries and youthful age segments—especially in Latin America and the Asian Pacific region—all boded well for Gatorade's continued sales growth in international markets.

The U.S. Market Situation

The Gatorade brand was coming under increased competitive pressure in the U.S. market as a number of companies introduced their own sports beverage brands:

Brand	Marketer
Powerade	Coca-Cola Co.
All Sport	Pepsi-Cola Co.
10-K	Suntory (Japan)
Everlast	A&W Brands
Nautilus Plus	Dr Pepper/Seven Up
Snap-Up (renamed Snapple Sport in April 1994)	Snapple Beverage Co.

Soft-drink companies were looking for new market segments because the $47 billion retail soft-drink market had grown less than 3 percent annually since 1980. Both Coca-Cola and Pepsi were moving to market their brands directly against Gatorade's well-developed connections to sports teams, coaches, trainers, and celebrity athletes (Michael Jordan was Gatorade's athlete spokesman). Coca-Cola had maneuvered successfully to get Powerade named the official sports drink of the 1996 Olympic Games in Atlanta and was running Powerade ads to sponsor World Cup Soccer. Coca-Cola's Powerade ads on local television and radio carried the tag line "More power to ya." Coca-Cola had signed pro baseball–football star Deion Sanders to appear in Powerade ads. Pepsi-Cola's commercials for All Sport touted the theme "Fuel the fire" and showed gritty scenes of youths playing fast-action sports such as blacktop basketball. Pepsi also had enlisted pro basketball's Shaquille O'Neal to appear in its ads and was sponsoring telecasts of NCAA basketball games.

Snapple's ads for Snap-Up/Snapple Sport featured tennis celebrities Ivan Lendl and Jennifer Capriati. Suntory was seeking to attract preteens to its 10-K brand with ads featuring a 12-year-old boy who played five sports. Gatorade rivals were expected to spend $30 million to $40 million advertising their brands in 1994. Pepsi's All Sport and Coca-Cola's Powerade were considered particularly formidable brands because they were backed by nationwide networks of local soft-drink bottlers that delivered daily to major supermarkets (and at least weekly to other soft-drink retailers and vending machine outlets) and typically stocked the shelves of retailers and set up in-store aisle displays. With such distribution muscle both Powerade and All Sport could gain market exposure everywhere soft drinks were available.

To counter rivals' efforts to horn in on Gatorade's market share, Quaker doubled its 1994 ad budget to nearly $50 million and created ads that reduced Michael Jordan's role in favor of product-benefit claims. Quaker also expanded Gatorade's line to eight flavors, compared to four for Powerade and All Sport. Still, Gatorade's estimated market share was five percentage points lower in fall 1994 than it had been a year earlier.

In an attempt to develop a new beverage category, the Gatorade division was test-marketing a new product named SunBolt Energy Drink, designed for morning consumption or any time consumers wanted a "pick-me-up." SunBolt contained three carbohydrate sources, caffeine, and vitamin C equivalent to a whole orange; it was offered in four flavors. SunBolt was positioned in the juice aisles of grocery stores, where Gatorade was shelved.

Despite the entry of other sports beverages, Quaker management regarded water as Gatorade's biggest competitor as a "thirst quencher." Moreover, in many supermarkets Gatorade was located alongside fruit juices, whereas Powerade and All Sport often were located in the soft-drink section, something Gatorade executives believed was an advantage. Gatorade executives also believed that the entry of competing sports drink brands would help grow the category enough so that Gatorade sales would increase despite a declining market share. According to Quaker President Phil Marineau:[3]

> When you have a 90 percent share of a category and competitors like Coke and Pepsi moving in, you're not foolish enough to think you won't lose some market share. But we're going to keep our position as the dominant force among sports drinks. Greater availability is the key to the U.S. success of Gatorade.

Gatorade's Marketing and Distribution Strategies

Quaker executives concluded in early 1994 that U.S. sales of Gatorade were approaching the limits of its traditional grocery channel delivery system—Gatorade was shipped from plants to retailer warehouses, and stores ordered what they needed to keep shelves stocked. Sustaining Gatorade's sales growth in the United States meant stretching the distribution strategy for Gatorade to include other channels. Donald R. Uzzi, a Pepsi executive, was hired in March 1994 as president of Gatorade's U.S. and Canada geographic unit. Uzzi's top strategic priority was to develop additional sales outlets for Gatorade; the options included fountain service for restaurants and fast-food outlets, vending machines, direct deliveries to nongrocery retail outlets, and point of sweat locations such as sports gyms and golf courses. The customary way of accessing such outlets was by building a network of independent distributors who would market to and service such accounts. In 1994, Gatorade's strongest markets were in the South and the Southwest. In foreign markets, Gatorade relied on several strategies to establish its market presence:

- Shipping the product in, handling the marketing and advertising in-house, and partnering with a local distributor to sell retail accounts, gain shelf space, and make deliveries. This approach was being utilized in Greece with a food distribution company.

---

[3]As quoted in "Gatorade Growth Seen Outside U.S.," *Advertising Age,* November 15, 1993, p. 46.

- Handling the marketing and advertising in-house and having a local partner take care of manufacturing, sales, and distribution. This approach was being used in Australia.

- Contracting with a soft-drink bottler to handle production, packaging, and distribution, with Gatorade taking care of marketing functions and supervising the contractor. This strategy was used in Spain, where the contractor was a Pepsi-owned bottler.

- Handling all functions in-house: manufacturing, marketing, sales, and distribution. Such was the case in Venezuela, where Quaker had built facilities to produce Gatorade.

Snapple Beverage Corp.

Snapple Beverage Corp. originated as a subchapter S corporation in 1972. The company, operating as Mr. Natural, Inc., was the brainchild of three streetwise entrepreneurs: Leonard Marsh, Arnold Greenberg, and Hyman Golden. Marsh and Greenberg were life-long friends, having gone to grade school and high school together; Golden was Marsh's brother-in-law. Mr. Natural, headquartered in Brooklyn, marketed and distributed a line of specialty beverages for the New York City area; the company's products were supplied by contract manufacturers and bottlers. The company's sales and operating scope grew gradually. Its all-natural products sold well in health food stores; later, delicatessens and convenience stores began to carry the line. By 1988, the company had become a regional distributor and headquarters operations were moved to East Meadow on Long Island, New York. Exhibit 5 summarizes key events in the company's history.

Capitalizing on consumers' growing interest in natural and healthy beverage products, the three entrepreneurs launched an all-natural beverage line under the Snapple name in 1980. Over the years, more flavors and varieties were added; Snapple iced teas were introduced in 1987. The introduction of the iced tea line was supported with a creative and catchy advertising campaign stressing the message, "Try this, you'll love the taste, and it's good for you." Snapple's recipe for making a good-tasting iced tea involved making it hot and then bottling it; artificial preservatives and colors were avoided. Snapple's strategy was simple: make all-natural beverages that taste great and keep introducing new and exciting flavors. As sales grew (principally because devoted health-conscious consumers spread the word among friends and acquaintances), company principals Marsh, Greenberg, and Golden plowed their profits back into the Snapple brand. Wider geographic distribution was attained by signing new distributors and granting them exclusive rights to distribute the Snapple line across a defined territory.

By 1991 sales had reached $95 million. Revenues jumped to $205.5 million in 1992 and to $516.0 million in 1993 as distribution widened and more consumers tried the line. Snapple's sales in 1993 ranked it number 35 on the top 50 beverage companies list. Exhibits 6 and 7 present Snapple's financial statements. The company went public in December 1992 as Snapple Beverage Corp., with the three founders retaining 23.1 percent of the stock (7.7 percent each). After the initial public offering at a split-adjusted price of $5, the stock traded as high as $32.25 in late 1993 before trading as low as $11.50 in mid-1994. Responding to the concerns of investors and Wall Street analysts about whether the company's rapid growth was sustainable, Marsh said:

> For those of you who might have heard mumblings that we've grown too far, too fast, I suggest you consider Snapple in the proper context. The average American drank 500 soft drinks last year (1993) . . . and the average American drank only five Snapples last year. That's a 1 percent share of a $64 billion pie.[4]

[4]As quoted in Beverage World's *Periscope,* February 28, 1994, p. 21.

EXHIBIT 5   **Summary of Key Events in Snapple Beverage Corporation's History**

1972
Marsh, Golden, and Greenberg form a company in association with a California juice manufacturer to distribute 100% natural fruit juices in New York City, primarily through health food distributors.

1979
A production plant is purchased in upstate New York to produce a line of pure, natural fruit juices.

1980
The name *Snapple* makes its first appearance when Snapple Beverage Corporation became the first company to manufacture a complete line of all-natural beverages.

1982
Snapple introduces Natural Sodas and pioneers the natural soft drink category.

1986
All Natural Fruit Drinks join the Snapple family, including Lemonade, Orangeade, Grapeade, and more.

1987
Snapple launches its All Natural Real Brewed Ice Tea and revolutionizes the beverage industry with the first tea to be brewed hot instead of mixed from cold concentrate. Snapple's signature wide-mouth bottle also makes its first appearance.

1990
Snapple introduces Snapple Sport, the first isotonic sports drink with the great taste of Snapple.

1991
Snapple recruits its first international distributor in Norway.

1992
The Thomas H. Lee Investment Company buys Snapple and leads an effort to take the company public. The stock triples in the first three months and is listed among the hottest stocks in the country. The three cofounders retain 23.1% of Snapple's common stock, and Thomas H. Lee ends up owning 47.5% of Snapple's common shares.

1992–1993
Fruit Drink line expands to include such exotic flavors as Kiwi-Strawberry Cocktail, Mango Madness Cocktail, and Melonberry Cocktail.

1993
Snapple goes international, signing on distributors in the United Kingdom, Canada, Mexico, the Caribbean, Hong Kong, and elsewhere.

1994
Snapple introduces seven new products, including Guava Mania Cocktail, Mango Tea, Amazin Grape Soda, Kiwi Strawberry Soda, and Mango Madness Soda as well as new diet versions of some best-sellers—Diet Kiwi Strawberry Cocktail, Diet Mango Madness Cocktail, and Diet Pink Lemonade.

Source: Company promotional materials.

During the summer months of 1994 Snapple marketed 75 varieties and flavors in five categories (ready-to-drink iced teas, fruit drinks, natural sodas and seltzers, fruit juices, and sports drinks) and had distributors in all 50 states. Despite sales of more than $500 million, Snapple had fewer than 200 employees; production, bottling, packaging, and distribution were handled by contractors and independent distributors. Company activities focused on marketing, new product development (the company had expertise in flavor technology), and overall management of contractors and distributors. In May 1994, however, management initiated construction of the company's first production facility—a $25 million plant in Arizona, scheduled to begin operations in 1995 and to employ 100 people.

Snapple was widely credited with catalyzing a more pronounced consumer trend toward New Age beverages, spurring added sales growth in bottled waters, sports drinks, and

EXHIBIT 6
Snapple's Income Statement, 1992 and 1993

Source: Company annual report.

	1992	1993
Net sales	$205,465,595	$516,005,327
Cost of goods sold	127,098,086	298,724,646
Gross profit	78,367,509	217,280,681
Selling, general, and administrative expenses	45,455,818	105,693,741
Nonoperating expenses	10,626,742	9,116,664
Interest expense	19,086,213	2,459,297
Income before tax	3,198,736	100,010,070
Provisions for income taxes	1,262,919	32,387,498
Net income before extraordinary items	1,935,817	67,623,481
Extraordinary item	(2,632,904)	0
Net income	$ (697,087)	$ 67,623,481

EXHIBIT 7
Snapple Beverage Corporation Balance Sheet, 1992 and 1993

Source: Company annual report.

	1992	1993
Assets		
Cash	$ 97,486,632	$ 13,396,949
Receivables	17,428,379	53,010,325
Inventories	16,166,183	40,922,888
Other current assets	6,788,585	4,192,759
Total current assets	137,869,779	111,522,921
Net property, plant, and equipment	1,053,399	10,751,597
Deferred charges	3,705,001	18,552,625
Intangibles	82,770,827	97,819,997
Other assets	1,338,166	304,745
Total assets	$226,737,172	$238,951,885
Liabilities and Shareholders' Equity		
Accounts payable	$ 6,100,345	$ 7,326,411
Current long-term debt	150,469	8,949,665
Accrued expenses	16,999,258	17,573,454
Income taxes	446,892	6,034,860
Other current liabilities	90,000,000	3,860,844
Total current liabilities	113,696,964	43,745,234
Long-term debt	18,226,138	26,218,911
Other long-term liabilities	4,000,000	5,011,000
Total liabilities	135,923,102	74,975,145
Minority interest	0	1,499,717
Common stock net	1,213,766	1,216,096
Capital surplus	90,297,391	94,334,533
Retained earnings	(697,087)	66,926,394
Total shareholders' equity	90,814,070	162,477,023
Total liabilities and shareholders' equity	$226,737,172	$238,951,885

juices as well as its own line of flavored teas and fruit drinks. In 1993, New Age or "alternative" beverages constituted a $3 billion product category. Exhibit 8 shows trends in the per capita consumption of liquid beverages in the United States during the 1983–1994 period.

EXHIBIT 8   **Per Capita Consumption of Liquid Beverages in the United States, 1983–1994** (in gallons)

	1983	1984	1985	1986	1987	1988	1989	1990	1991	1992	1993E	1994P
Soft drinks	37.0	38.8	41.0	42.3	44.3	46.2	46.7	47.6	47.8	48.0	48.9	49.6
Coffee*	26.1	26.3	26.8	27.1	27.1	26.5	26.4	26.4	26.5	26.1	25.9	26.0
Beer	24.3	23.9	23.9	24.2	24.0	23.8	23.6	24.0	23.3	23.0	22.8	22.5
Milk	19.7	19.8	20.0	19.9	19.8	19.4	19.6	19.4	19.4	19.1	18.9	19.1
Tea*	7.2	7.2	7.3	7.3	7.3	7.4	7.2	7.0	6.7	6.8	6.9	7.0
Bottled water	3.4	4.0	5.2	5.8	6.4	7.3	8.1	9.2	9.6	9.9	10.5	11.2
Juices	8.2	7.0	7.9	7.8	8.3	7.7	8.0	7.1	7.6	7.1	7.0	7.0
Powdered drinks	6.5	6.4	6.3	5.2	4.9	5.3	5.4	5.7	5.9	6.1	6.0	5.9
Wine†	2.2	2.3	2.4	2.4	2.4	2.3	2.1	2.0	1.9	2.0	1.7	1.6
Distilled spirits	1.9	1.9	1.8	1.8	1.6	1.5	1.5	1.5	1.4	1.3	1.3	1.3
Subtotal	136.5	137.6	142.6	142.6	146.1	147.4	148.6	149.9	150.1	149.4	149.9	151.2
Imputed water consumption‡	46.0	44.9	39.9	39.9	36.4	35.1	33.9	32.6	32.4	33.1	32.6	31.3
Total	182.5	182.5	182.5	182.5	182.5	182.5	182.5	182.5	182.5	182.5	182.5	182.5

*Coffee and tea data are based on a three-year moving average to counterbalance inventory swings, thereby portraying consumption more realistically.
†Includes wine coolers beginning in 1984.
‡Includes all others.
E = estimated; P = projected.
Source: John C. Maxwell, "Annual Soft Drink Report," *Beverage Industry Supplement,* March 1994, p. 6.

Snapple's Marketing and Distribution Strategies

In Snapple's early days the product wasn't selling well; market research revealed that consumers thought the bottles were ugly and difficult to store. A packaging redesign followed, resulting in the use of clear wide-mouth 16-ounce glass bottles—a container that management said was "perfectly suited to the hot-brewed process we use to make Snapple beverages." The new bottles were affixed with redesigned labels. Sales perked up quickly, buoyed by an offbeat and catchy media campaign.

The company sparked demand for Snapple products with offbeat, witty ads and catchy themes. Snapple had gotten the greatest mileage out of an ad featuring a stereotypical receptionist, "Wendy the Snapple Lady" (who was actually employed in the company's marketing department), responding to customer inquiries. Snapple ads sometimes poked fun at things. Print ads compared Snapple sales to "hot cakes" and "greased lightning" with "more flavors than you can shake a stick at." Ivan Lendl and Rush Limbaugh appeared in Snapple television ads as celebrity endorsers. Most of Snapple's distributors were local soft-drink bottlers/distributors that had third-place or fourth-place market shares (usually behind Coca-Cola and Pepsi) and were eager to take on product lines where competition was less intense and profit margins were bigger. The average price per case for New Age beverages was around $9 to $11 versus $5 to $6 per case for soft drinks. On average, soft drinks offered bottlers and distributors a $1 margin per case compared with about $3 per case for New Age products. These distributors delivered Snapple directly to supermarkets, convenience stores, delicatessen outlets, and up-and-down-the-street retailers on trucks carrying an assortment of branded beverages (low-volume soft-drink brands, bottled waters, club soda, tonic water, ginger ale, and perhaps canned Gatorade). Snapple's distributors were responsible for everything—selling retail accounts, keeping shelves stocked, handling point of sale displays, and setting prices. Retail prices for a 16-ounce bottle were typically around 75 cents. Snapple's surging sales in 1992 and 1993—a boom that reportedly began in convenience stores and delicatessens, where trend-setting consumers bought Snapple from the cooler and drank it straight from the bottle—helped it recruit distributors willing to commit time and resources to the Snapple line. Snapple established a nationwide network of distributors in a matter of months, something few alternative beverage brands had been able to do. The attractive profit margins distributors earned on Snapple sales were a key factor in the company's ability to recruit distributors willing to invest time and resources in building the Snapple brand. Snapple's market research showed that half the U.S. population had tried Snapple by the end of October 1993. Snapple's sales were strongest in California and the Northeast; sales were weakest in the South and Southwest. By mid-1994 Snapple had begun introducing its brands in Europe. Launches in Britain, Ireland, and Norway came first, followed by Sweden and Denmark. Test marketing was under way in France and Spain. As of November 1994 only 1 percent of Snapple's sales were derived from overseas markets.

In April 1994 Snapple announced it had developed an exclusive glass-front vending machine capable of offering 54 different flavors simultaneously; the machine held 18 cases of the company's 16-ounce wide-mouth bottles. The company expected to place 10,000 units in service by year end to broaden its distribution beyond supermarkets, convenience stores, and delicatessens.

Competition in the Iced Tea/New Age Segment

Snapple's success in developing consumer interest in ready-to-drink iced teas and teas spiked with fruit juices attracted other competitors quickly. In 1993 Coca-Cola, Pepsi-Cola, Dr Pepper/Seven-Up, and Cadbury Schweppes/A&W Beverages all launched New Age offerings. Several regional products, most notably Arizona Iced Tea (packaged in distinctive tall cans with a Southwestern motif), also entered the market. As of 1994, the major players in the ready-to-drink iced tea segment were the following:

Brand	Marketer
Snapple	Snapple Beverage Corp.
Lipton	Pepsi-Cola and the Thomas J. Lipton division of Unilever
Nestea	Coca-Cola Nestlé Refreshments (a joint venture of the Coca-Cola Company and Nestlé)
Tetley	A&W Brands and Tetley Tea Co. partnership
Luzianne	Barq's Inc. and Wm. B. Reily partnership
All Seasons	Cadbury Beverages and Omni Industries
Celestial Seasonings	Perrier Group of America and Celestial Seasonings
Arizona	Ferolito, Vultaggio and Sons

Besides the major players, there were 5 to 10 niche brands of bottled teas. In addition, Pepsi-Cola had teamed with Ocean Spray Cranberries, Inc., to introduce a line of juices and lemonade. Minute Maid had announced a new line of juices, Very Fine and Tradewinds were planning lemonade entries, and Gatorade introduced its eighth flavor, Gatorade Iced Tea Cooler. An Information Resources survey of supermarket sales of canned and bottled iced teas during the 12 weeks ended April 17, 1994, showed the following:[5]

Brand	Case Volume (in millions)	Dollar Volume (in millions)
Snapple	2.5	$22.3
Lipton	2.3	14.9
Nestea	1.0	7.8
Arizona	0.5	5.0

[5]As reported in *The Wall Street Journal,* June 9, 1994, p. B6.

Snapple's market share (based on dollars) was 17 percentage points lower in this survey than in the comparable year-earlier period. The Arizona brand was gaining share and had edged out Snapple as the market leader in several markets in the West. However, Snapple's market share of convenience store sales was estimated to be in the range of 75 percent. Exhibit 9 presents estimated case sales of alternative beverage companies.

Industry analysts estimated that wholesale volume for iced tea flavors grew from $500 million in 1992 to more than $1 billion in 1993. Alternative beverage sales were breaking out into 40 percent take-home purchases and 60 percent single-service and on-premise consumption. Ready-to-drink teas and juice-based drinks were the fastest-growing products in the New Age category, while sales of "clear" products dropped to the range of 8 to 9 percent (down from 44 percent growth in 1992). Analysts were divided in their assessments about how long the booming growth in ready-to-drink teas and fruit beverages would last. Some analysts believed that teas and fruit drinks would experience continued growth because of their healthy, "all-natural" image with consumers and because the proliferation of brands and varieties would help develop greater buyer interest. Others were skeptical, observing that trendy products had comparatively short life cycles and that three or four

EXHIBIT 9
Estimated Case Sales of Alternative Beverage Companies, 1992–1993

Source: Compiled from "Annual Soft Drink Report," *Beverage Industry Supplement,* March 1994, pp. 22–23.

Company/Brand	Case Sales (in millions)	
	1992	1993
Snapple Beverage Company		
Snapple Iced Tea	28.33	52.63
Snapple drinks	19.73	45.41
Snapple sodas	1.52	3.10
Snapple Snap-Up/Sport	0.51	1.03
Snapple juices	0.51	1.03
Total	50.60	103.20
Coca-Cola Company		
Nestea	14.00	33.00
Powerade	1.20	10.00
Minute Maid Juices-to-Go	5.00	15.00
Total	20.20	58.00
PepsiCo		
Ocean Spray	6.50	16.00
Lipton	—	33.00
All Sport	2.00	3.00
H2 Oh!	0.50	0.63
Total	9.00	52.63
Perrier Group		
15-Brand totals	30.40	36.70
Cadbury beverages/A&W brands		
Tetley	2.90	4.30
Everlast	—	—
Others	17.30	17.30
Total	20.20	21.60
Ferolito, Vultaggio and Sons		
Arizona	—	2.00
All others	169.60	175.37
Segment totals	300.00	449.50

growth years were all many product categories ever experienced. While some cola bottlers had derisively referred to Snapple as a member of the "brand of the day" club, unconvinced of its power to sustain broad consumer interest, market research indicated that younger consumers (who had fueled the growth in New Age beverages) had gravitated to Snapple, Arizona, and unusual niche brands with distinctive packaging and a certain mystique. In fall 1994 industry observers saw bottled tea as becoming increasingly complex to market successfully because the market was overcrowded, the costs to support a brand were rising, shelf space was harder to obtain, and image was such a dominant factor in a brand's success or failure.

In late August 1994 Coca-Cola and Nestlé unexpectedly announced the dissolution of their iced tea alliance; Nestea sales had been disappointing, falling well behind supermarket sales of both Snapple and Lipton. It was not clear whether Nestlé would continue to market Nestea bottled teas on its own. Meanwhile, Pepsi-Lipton had begun running a series of radio ads attacking Snapple as being "mixed up from a tea powder." The announcer said, "Snapple. Isn't that a cute name. Kinda snappy. I bet they call it Snapple 'cause it's iced tea made in a snap." The spot went on to boast that Lipton Original varieties were "real brewed," a trait that Pepsi-Lipton believed was its best weapon against rivals.[6] Pepsi had also run Super Bowl ads for Lipton Original and promoted Lipton Original heavily in supermarkets, including a 99-cent value pack containing one bottle each of Lipton Original, All Sport, and Ocean Spray Lemonade.

Snapple management indicated its iced teas were made from "the finest tea leaves in India" but wouldn't specify how it was produced. Arnold Greenberg said:

> Pepsi would die to make tea taste so great. People don't care how it's made. They just care
> that it tastes good.[7]

Snapple management also pointed out that the less expensive Lipton Brisk varieties, sold in cans and 64-ounce bottles, were not "real brewed." Analysts estimated that during the first five months of 1994, about 60 percent of Pepsi's prepared iced teas were Lipton Brisk varieties. To counter the increased competition from rival teas, Snapple more than doubled its 1994 advertising budget and launched a new $65 million media campaign in April 1994.

[6]As quoted in *The Wall Street Journal,* June 9, 1994, p. B6.
[7]Ibid

Case 6–20

CUTCO International

It was CUTCO Cutlery's 1997 midyear companywide meeting in Olean, New York. Record sales and profits had been achieved for the first six months. CUTCO had seen record weekly shipments in June. Over 27,000 packages had gone out just the week before. Unlike some recent years, needed inventory was in place to meet seasonal demand. Further, record sales and profits were projected for the entire year. CUTCO employees could look forward

This case was prepared by William F. Crittenden at Northeastern University and Victoria L. Crittenden at Boston College as the basis for class discussion rather than to illustrate effective or ineffective handling of a managerial situation. The Direct Selling Education Foundation provided partial funding for the development of this case. Revised 2001.

to significant year-end profit-sharing bonuses.

The management team was proud of these achievements. However, Erick Laine (CEO/president, ALCAS Corporation), Fran Weinaug (president/CEO, CUTCO International), Bob Haig (president/COO, Vector Marketing Corporation), Mike Lancellot (president, Vector East), Don Muelrath (president, Vector West), and Jim Stitt (president/CEO, CUTCO Cutlery Corporation) were not satisfied. Growth was at record levels but not at plan.

According to Erick Laine, "Sales are up 11 percent over 1996, not the 20 to 25 percent we looked for. International sales in particular have been way off projections (15 percent growth versus the expected 75 percent). Although we've made some important adjustments, the second half of the year is unlikely to compensate."

He continued: "Other direct sales firms have had enormous success in the international arena. International markets are attractive to direct sellers. Direct selling allows market entry without fighting the battles of brand identity and entrenched distribution systems. With limited brick and mortar requirements, direct selling allows one to grow rapidly. We know it's [the market] there to be gotten."

CUTCO's corporate vision statement (Exhibit 1) to be the world's "largest, most respected and widely recognized" cutlery firm required substantial growth. Although product development and company acquisitions might be part of the strategic mix, management clearly viewed the international market as a critical element to growth. Yet decisions regard-

EXHIBIT 1

CORPORATE VISION

To become the largest, most respected and widely recognized cutlery company in the world while maintaining an equal commitment to these core values:

- Honesty, integrity and ethics in all aspects of business – founded on our respect for people.

- Recognizing and rewarding our people for dedication and high levels of achievement.

- Product pre-eminence, quality and reputation.

- First-class customer service and customer satisfaction.

- Strong consolidated corporate profitability and the strength and financial success of our field sales organization.

- Creating opportunities for our people to grow and share in the success of the enterprise.

ing which markets to enter, which approach to use, and the sequencing and timing of entry still needed to be made.

The ALCAS Corporation (the Parent)

In 1949 Alcoa and CASE Cutlery formed a joint venture, ALCAS Cutlery Corporation, to produce kitchen cutlery known as CUTCO. The product was exclusively marketed via in-home demonstrations by WearEver, Inc. (However, CUTCO and WearEver products were treated as separate entities and were not sold together.) In 1972, Alcoa bought out CASE and ALCAS became wholly owned by Alcoa. In 1982, the local management of ALCAS, headed by Erick Laine, a longtime Alcoa employee, purchased the company from Alcoa. Management converted ALCAS into a privately held corporation with headquarters in Olean, New York. Ownership remains closely held by five of the top managers. In 1996, the company acquired KA-BAR Knives, an established sporting knife company. Exhibit 2 outlines the corporate structure. Worldwide revenues from direct marketing and direct sales operations exceeded $100 million in 1996. (Sales just exceeded $20 million in 1987.) All corporations within ALCAS operate as profit centers.

CUTCO Cutlery covers a broad range of food preparation knives as well as scissors and hunting, fishing, and utility knives. (Exhibits 3 through 10 show examples of CUTCO products.) The product line is identified as "CUTCO—*The World's Finest Cutlery.*" Product pricing is consistent with this positioning at the high end of the spectrum. The product is sold as individual open stock, in wood block sets, or in a variety of gift boxed sets. According to Mark George (now international sales director and a former CUTCO sales representative), numerous features make CUTCO the world's finest cutlery: "the ergonomically designed handle, the thermo-resin handle material, the full tang triple rivet construction, the high-carbon, stain-resistant steel, and the exclusive Double-D® edge. All products are backed by the CUTCO 'Forever Guarantee.'"

EXHIBIT 2

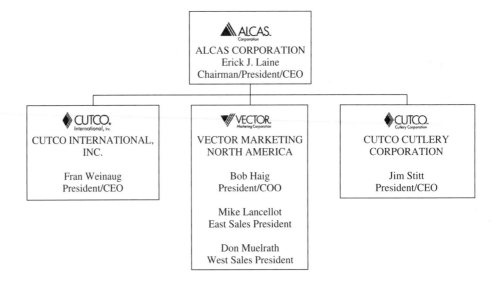

EXHIBIT 3

EXHIBIT 4

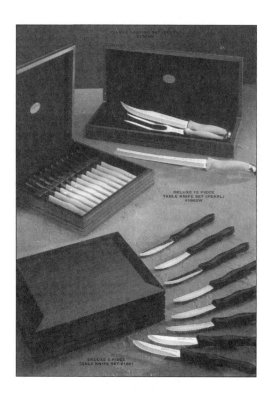

EXHIBIT 5

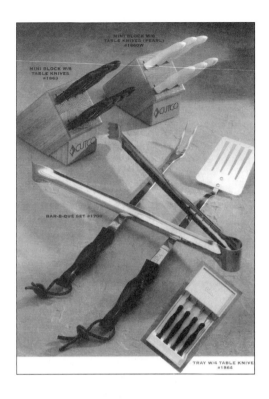

EXHIBIT 6

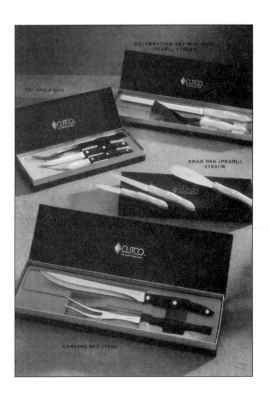

EXHIBIT 7

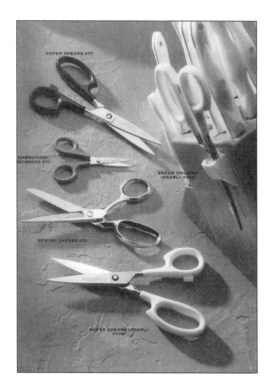

EXHIBIT 8

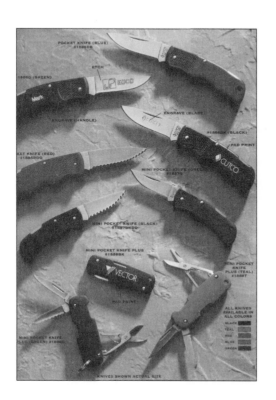

EXHIBIT 9

EXHIBIT 10
Fisherman's Solution

A total fillet knife system. Designed for lake, coastal or stream fishing.
The high-carbon, stain-resistant steel blade adjusts and locks from 6" to 9" to fillet any size fish. A patented Cam-Lock secures the blade tightly at any length. The Zytel® inner track system assures the blade's smooth adjustment. The sheath pivots open to become a gripper to help clean, skin and fillet or remove a hook. Notched line cutter and a built-in sharpening stone with a groove for fish hooks complete the sheath.

EXHIBIT 11		
Seasonal Sales	January–April	17%
	May–August	67
	September–December	16

Recognizing the importance of satisfied customers, CUTCO devoted considerable space in its Olean headquarters to its service department. The company has a goal of two to three days' turnaround on knives returned for free sharpening or guarantee issues.

CUTCO cutlery is marketed in North America by Vector Marketing Corporation. During peak selling periods, Vector Marketing operates around 400 offices in Canada and the United States. CUTCO is sold primarily by college students who are recruited to work during vacations as sales representatives. (Exhibit 11 shows the typical seasonal percentage of sales for CUTCO products.) Some students continue to sell during the school year. Recruiting, training, and ongoing management of the sales force are done utilizing over 200 district offices. Over 200 temporary branch offices are opened during the summer months and are staffed by college students with prior selling and management experience. All sales representatives are independent contractors. Sales training is completed over a three-day period. Vector has experimented with some catalog sales and has special policies in place that demonstrate sensitivity to its sales representatives. The typical CUTCO customer has household income of approximately $60,000, is well educated (with most holding a bachelor's degree and some with postgraduate degrees), is married with older children, holds a professional or managerial position, is approximately 40 to 54 years old, is a homeowner, and enjoys cooking, gardening, reading, and traveling.

CUTCO Cutlery Corporation manufactures CUTCO products in Olean, New York, and sells at wholesale to Vector and CUTCO International. Unlike many manufacturers, CUTCO has reduced outsourcing in recent years and has backward integrated into plastic molding (e.g., knife handles and cutting boards) and wood blocks. Jim Stitt, CUTCO Cutlery Corporation president and CEO, attributed the company's ability to stay competitive to its skilled work force and considerable investment in high-technology equipment. Additionally, the company processes its product very differently from competitors to provide a high level of product distinction (e.g., its unique recessed edge grind, freezing the blades, applying a mirror polish finish to the blades).

Cutlery

Cutlery is a term applied collectively to all types of cutting instruments. More specifically, in the United States it refers to knives employed in the preparation of food and for sporting and utility use. The first U.S. cutlery factory was established in Worchester, Massachusetts, in 1829. As American steel improved in quality and decreased in price, the industry developed steadily, particularly in the Northeastern states. (Exhibit 12 provides industry cutlery sales by retail outlet for 1996.)

Cutting instruments are clearly of worldwide importance—numerous international manufacturing sites have gained some renown. Sheffield in the United Kingdom and Soligen in Germany are especially well known for cutlery. However, substantial innovation at the high end and inexpensive imports at the other have hurt some of the sectors that are long known for expertise and quality. For example, the cutlery industry in Sheffield has been reduced from over 300 firms to around 12 in the past 35 years. Several cutlery manufacturers

EXHIBIT 12
Cutlery Sales by Retail Outlet, 1996

Mass merchants	33%
Department stores	20
Specialty stores	15
Warehouse clubs	13
Catalog showrooms	5
Other[1]	14

Note: Mass merchants, specialty stores, and warehouse clubs have gained in the past 10 years, with the "Other" category seeing the greatest decline as a percentage of the total.
[1]Includes hardware stores, home centers, supermarkets, drug stores, and direct mail.

recently have expanded into other product lines, including kitchen tools, pantryware, and garden implements.

While the number of successful cutlery firms was declining, cutlery sales increased throughout the 1990s. Sales were especially strong in specialty product segments (e.g., multitool, pizza cutters, potato peelers, nonstick cheese slicers, under-the-counter knife blocks), with new product innovations initially targeting upscale channels. In 1995 and 1996, U.S. consumers demonstrated renewed interest in known brands of cutlery rather than private-label goods and were buying more expensive brands.

In addition to specialty product segments, many cutlery vendors had begun focusing on niche markets such as bridal registries and Internet shopping. Regarding registries, Howard Ammerman, vice president of sales for J.A. Henckels (USA), stated, "Catching consumers early helps to avoid the looming issue of affordability. [Bridal] Registries are our opportunity to gain the next generation of Henckels' cutlery customers. They need to know why they're spending the money for high-end cutlery, and that it's a lifetime investment."[1]

By 1996, some knife manufacturers and retailers also were testing the Internet as a medium for promoting and selling cutlery products. According to Brice Hereford, national sales manager at Lamson & Goodnow, "We were most intrigued by the demographics. The demographics of an Internet browser—typically a college-educated person with above-average income—fits well with the profile of most consumers of high-end cutlery. This type of person is much more likely to buy an $80 chef's knife."[2]

Direct Selling

Direct selling is a method of marketing and retailing consumer goods directly to the consumer without reliance on direct mail, product advertising, or fixed retail outlets. Most direct selling employs independent salespeople to call on consumers, mainly in their homes, to show and demonstrate products and obtain orders. The goods are then supplied by the company either directly to the consumer or through the salesperson who obtained the order. The direct sales industry exceeds US$80 billion in annual worldwide sales. The United States represents less than 25 percent of total sales. Leading international direct sales firms include Avon, Tupperware, Shaklee, Stanhome, Amway, and Mary Kay Cosmetics. The Direct Selling Association, a worldwide trade association, represents most leading direct sales firms.

[1] *The Weekly Newspaper for the Home Furnishing Network,* April 14, 1997.
[2] *The Weekly Newspaper for the Home Furnishing Network,* February 26, 1996.

Generically, direct selling is a push marketing strategy. Direct selling is an especially effective strategy for products and services with a high personal selling elasticity, where procrastination in purchasing is easy, and when the product is a household item that benefits from demonstration in that environment. Push marketing strategies have been effectively realized by direct selling firms entering newly emerging economies where distribution systems, supporting infrastructure, and capital access are limited. Further, direct selling jobs are often attractive to citizens in such economies. Direct selling often is seen as the ultimate in equal-income-earning opportunity, with no artificial barriers based on age, race, sex, or education. Independent contractors have flexible hours and can pursue earnings full-time or while pursuing an education, raising a family, or holding down another job.

Two general forms of direct selling exist: party plan and one-on-one. With the party plan method, a salesperson presents and sells products to a group of customers attending a party in one of the customer's homes. The intention is to demonstrate the quality and value of a product to a group of people, many of whom then will purchase the product. The party, however, is more than just a sales presentation and often is viewed as a socializing opportunity for busy people. The party host/hostess is principally responsible for identifying, qualifying, and inviting attendees. Tupperware and Mary Kay Cosmetics principally utilize the party plan approach. The one-on-one approach is more personalized and requires the salesperson to focus on the needs and economic demand of each potential customer. This approach is especially useful when customers may require detailed instruction regarding product quality differences or appropriate use of the product.

CUTCO's Major Competitors

Henckels

J.A. Henckels Zwillingswerk Inc., a 266-year-old German manufacturer, is a dominant player in the upscale cutlery market and has a global presence in over 100 countries, with long-established subsidiaries in Canada, China, Denmark, Japan, the Netherlands, Spain, Switzerland, and the United States. Significant growth in sales over recent years has been attributable to increased accounts, the expansion of existing accounts, and a broadening of the company's customer base through the development of non-German sources for the production of moderately priced products for multiple channels under the Henckels International logo. Through non-German sources, Henckels has been able to offer additional price points: EverEdge, a never-needs-sharpening, Japanese-made brand has a suggested retail price of $29.99 for a seven-piece set; the Brazilian-made Classic and Traditional forged lines are considered a cost-efficient alternative at $149.99 to the German-made brands. The company offers over 10 brands in fine-edge and never-needs-sharpening cutlery, and its products are available in virtually every high-profile retail account worldwide.

Further stimulating demand for Henckels Cutlery has been the development of specialty gift sets, providing a prestigious presentation of commonly grouped individual items. Henckels also has taken a strong stance on advertising to build brand awareness, substantially increasing its television, co-op, and bridal advertising budget in recent years. Henckels also has attempted to be innovative through new packaging (e.g., clam sets) and in working with retailers to develop appropriate displays. (A clam set is one or more products in thermoformed packaging that allows a full view of product, shelf appeal, potential customer opportunity to grasp the handle, and blade protection. Clam sets can be pegged or self-supported on a shelf.) Numerous retailers and catalog firms have begun to advertise and sell their Henckels offerings through Internet Web sites. Henckels recently added new handles with an ergonomic "open-flow" design to comfortably accommodate each individual hand while maintaining safety.

In 1995, Henckels acquired German-based Wilkens tableware, moving the firm into the silverplate and stainless-steel flatware business. In 1996, the U.S. subsidiary doubled its available warehouse space to improve delivery performance. Recent estimates suggest that Henckels USA will have $70 million in 1997 trade sales. Karl Pfitzenreiter, president of J.A. Henckels, USA, explained, "We want to double our growth every five years, which we have so far been able to do by maintaining a 15 percent average annual growth rate in the U.S."[3]

Fiskars

Fiskars, founded in 1649, is the oldest industrial company in Finland and one of the oldest in the Western world. Over the years the company has solidified a reputation as a premier steel and ironworks company manufacturing a widening range of architectural, industrial, agricultural, and houseware-related products. Main market areas include North America and Europe, with 1997 estimated sales of US$550 million (of which over 90 percent was generated outside Finland). Headquartered in Helsinki, Fiskars has subsidiaries and/or manufacturing in Canada, the Czech Republic, Denmark, France, Germany, Hungary, India, Italy, Mexico, Norway, Poland, Russia, Sweden, the United Kingdom, and the United States. Markets targeted for further development or new expansion include Eastern Europe, Southeast Asia, Australia, and Latin America. The company is considered to be very strong financially and a major innovator in its many diverse product lines.

The Montana adjustable bread knife and the Raadvad cutter for bread, cabbage, and lettuce were examples of recent innovations. Fiskars cutlery features a full tang with synthetic handles, ergonomically designed and weighted and balanced to correspond to the blade length. Gift sets are housed in handcrafted solid walnut boxes lined with velveteen fabric and intended as heirlooms. Individual units may be purchased in clam shell packaging. Fiskars's worldwide sales of cutlery products are estimated to be US$70 million. Products in its homeware lines include scissors, knives, kitchen gadgets, and sharpeners. Trademarks include Alexander, Fiskars, Gerber, Montana, Raadvad, Knivman, Kitchen Devils, DuraSharp, and CutRite. The upscale Alexander line features such gift sets as a four-piece steak knife set retailing for US$197 and a two-piece carving set at US$260. Fiskars products are carried primarily in upscale channels, but the company continues to target mass merchants with select lines within its wide array of products. The Consumer Products Group generated 59 percent of its 1997 net sales in the United States. A 35 percent jump in U.S. sales was at least partly attributable to a strengthening U.S. dollar.

In late 1994, as part of its overall expansion strategy, Fiskars acquired Rolcut & Raadvad, a supplier of kitchen cutlery and garden tools. In July 1997 a greenfield startup, A/O Baltic Tool, began production of garden tools. In August 1997 Fiskars agreed to acquire the Italian knife manufacturer Kaimano S.p.A.

According to Stig Stendahl, the company president, "Our goal is to generate one-fourth of sales from new products which have been in the market for less than three years. Fiskars has gained a lot of positive publicity thanks to innovative product development and design."[4]

[3] *The Weekly Newspaper for the Home Furnishing Network,* October 7, 1996.
[4] President's Message on Fiskars Web page, 1997.

CUTCO International

In 1990, Vector Canada was established as the company's first international marketing entity. Patterned after the U.S. sales model of utilizing college students as salespeople, the international entry is considered to be quite successful. (Sales should approximate US$7.5 million in 1997.) Fueled by the rather immediate success in Canada, the company entered into the Korean marketplace in 1992 as Vector Korea.

CUTCO Korea

CUTCO entered into the Korean marketplace with the student salesperson model that had been successful in the United States and Canada. CUTCO's strategy for entering Korea was to utilize U.S.-trained, Korean-born managers to oversee administrative operations. CUTCO Korea operated in the student salesperson mode from May 1992 until early 1995. Sales were nowhere near company expectations during this 2½-year period. With the student program faltering, CUTCO Korea began entertaining, in early 1995, the group selling (party plan) approach to selling.

Tae S. Kim, former Korean manager in charge of administration and finance and current national administration manager for CUTCO Australia, identified two major reasons for the lack of success of CUTCO's original college program approach in Korea:

1. *Cultural.* Korean college students do not value earning income during their college days in the same manner as college students in the Western part of the world do. Money is not a motivating factor for Korean students since their parents continue to provide total financial support. Mr. Kim described Korean students as less aggressive and uncertain about going into sales.

2. *Distribution.* Korean students generally do not own automobiles. The vast majority utilize public transportation (subway or bus), which does not make it easy to make sales calls.

Once CUTCO Korea understood and accepted the fact that the student model could not work in Korea, a group selling approach, with a revised commission structure, was quickly implemented. This model started in March 1995 with five female-managed offices. At that point, Korean sales exploded. The typical Korean sales representative is now a married, middle-class female age 20 to 50. The student program was abolished completely by the end of 1995. There were 21 female-managed offices by February 1996, and 1996 sales hit US$8.2 million. Unfortunately, due to the loss of sales offices, the temporary relocation of a key employee to head up a Philippine pilot office, and a very weak Korean economy, 1997 sales were likely to fall significantly below 1996 levels.

CUTCO United Kingdom

In 1992, the company conducted a "college program" trial in the United Kingdom. An English-speaking country with a well-educated population exceeding 60 million, the United Kingdom seemed a promising market, with approximately US$1.4 billion in direct sales. Although sales were reasonably successful, high expenses (e.g., office and warehousing rent, recruiting ads) led the company to delay entry. Instead, in 1995, the company made a trial entry using a group sales (party plan) approach. This approach was not successful, and CUTCO's intention remains to re-enter with the college program in 1999.

Distributorships

The company has utilized one independent distributor in Mauritius. Sales there are small but growing. CUTCO has tried out two other distributorships, but neither succeeded. In the distributor agreement, CUTCO sells to the distributor on wholesale terms and the distributor organizes, develops, and manages its own sales force. Chris Panus (CUTCO international finance manager) indicated that the company spent a lot of time selecting, training, and developing these distributors and wondered if the effort—versus opening up its own operation—was worth it.

CUTCO Australia

In 1996, CUTCO entered Australia. The entry was modeled after Vector Marketing in the United States and Canada. Unlike the Korean entry, CUTCO Australia began with experienced CUTCO sales and administration people. Stephen McCarthy, national sales manager for CUTCO Australia, has been with CUTCO since 1986. Steve had a reputation as a top CUTCO sales manager. Tae Kim was transferred from Korea and appointed national administration manager for CUTCO Australia. In addition to Steve and Tae, CUTCO moved five American managers to Australia. Each of these five had been with CUTCO between 7 and 13 years, and each manages his own sales office in Australia. (Three offices are in Sydney, and two are in Melbourne.) Plans were to have a total of 21 sales offices by the end of 1998.

Australia appeared to offer a significant opportunity. According to Mark George, "Australia is a territory with 19 million English-speaking, qualified-income people and a university school break starting in November and ending in February. The culture is similar to that in the U.S."

With annual sales expected to be A\$3.0 million by the end of 1997, CUTCO Australia had definitely beat the odds of the typical international startup. CUTCO products were virtually unheard of in Australia in 1996. McCarthy reported, "The Australians thought our method of marketing knives was crazy. Our solicitors, our accountants, our consultants . . . all said, 'Students? You have got to be crazy!' They could not have been more wrong! Australian students like being entrepreneurial and goal-oriented. The student model is working wonderfully in Australia."

McCarthy's goal is to make Australia the CUTCO hub for the Asia–Pacific region. He envisions an all-Asian office to manage Singapore, Thailand, and Hong Kong as well as a proposed entry into New Zealand by 1999. As with Canada and other countries entered, he says that the long-term plan is to turn management of CUTCO Australia over to the Australians.

CUTCO Germany

In 1996 CUTCO began sales in Germany. Direct sales are extremely popular in Germany (almost US\$5 billion), and other U.S. direct sales firms had experienced great success there. However, Germany appeared to be another country where recruiting college students would be difficult. Therefore, based on its Korean experience, CUTCO pursued a party plan format in Germany. The profile of sales representatives was similar to that in Korea. Unfortunately, a sales director heading up the German expansion left the company and sales had not achieved the hoped-for level of success, with 1997 sales around US\$400,000 (approximately two-thirds of goal).

CUTCO Costa Rica

A launch in Costa Rica was made in June 1997. Two managers, from inside CUTCO, were available for transfer. One manager, a Spanish speaker with a Hispanic background, was from New York; the other was from Puerto Rico.

According to Mark George, "We picked Costa Rica because it was a small market with a nice middle- and upper-class structure. It is a safe place to do business, and although it's a small country, we believe we can develop Spanish-speaking managers who can help establish markets for CUTCO in the rest of Latin America. People are well educated, and the literacy rate is around 97 percent. We utilize the university student model, which helps us qualify the recruit to be able to get into the market that can afford our product."

International Market Expansion

CUTCO International was established in 1994 as a wholly owned subsidiary of ALCAS Corporation to manage the marketing and distribution of CUTCO products on an international basis. According to Fran Weinaug: "International operations are currently in the developmental stage." The management team had initially set a goal of wanting to open two countries each year for the foreseeable future.

Weinaug, George, and Panus all understood that a multitude of diverse issues could spring up in international markets. They had already experienced currency fluctuations, nontariff barriers, import duties, and language and gender considerations in recruiting sales representatives, plus variability in country laws for direct selling. Further, opening a market required a major outlay of capital. There are considerable cost-of-living considerations for expats (e.g., housing, cars, start-up funds). To facilitate market entry in places where language is a barrier, management has used an in-country sales manager and in-country financial officer. Selling a high-end set of cutlery isn't the same as selling plasticware or cosmetics, and using in-country managers requires a lengthy training process.

To ensure timely international delivery, CUTCO ships and warehouses product at each international site. Freight, warehousing, and insurance add approximately 10 percent to total costs. On a country-by-country basis, the company goal was to be at breakeven, covering annual costs, by its third year.

By mid-1997 international operations had yet to be profitable. Noting this lack of international profitability, Erick Laine commented, "Developing international markets is a very costly process, but we're convinced it's worth it for the long term—and we're grateful we have the financial resources to wait it out."

For the near term (in addition to a 1997 pilot test in the Philippines), Laine, Weinaug, and their management team are deciding among such diverse countries as Argentina, Austria, Brazil, Ireland, Italy, Japan, Mexico, Poland, Taiwan, and the United Kingdom. Longer-term markets under consideration include China, Hong Kong, India, and South Africa. (Exhibit 13 provides worldwide direct sales data.)

Weinaug, George, and Panus know that CUTCO management expects to move quickly into several of these new markets. During strategy meetings they have been fielding a laundry list of questions from the rest of the CUTCO management team. In developing a recommended sequence of countries for market entry (along with an overall entry timetable), the management team needs immediate answers to the following questions:

1. What criteria should CUTCO use to select countries for market entry?

2. Which countries offer the best market opportunities for CUTCO products?

3. What should be the composition of the new country's management team?

EXHIBIT 13
**Worldwide Direct
Sales Data**

Source: World Federation of
Direct Selling Associations.

	Year	Retail Sales (U.S.$)	Number of Salespeople
Argentina	1996	1.004 billion	410,000
Australia	1996	2.02 billion	615,000
Austria	1996	340 million	40,000
Belgium	1996	111 million	13,500
Brazil	1996	3.5 billion	887,000
Canada	1996	1.825 billion	875,000
Chile	1996	180 million	160,000
Colombia	1996	400 million	200,000
Czech Republic	1996	75 million	70,000
Denmark	1996	50 million	5,000
Finland	1995	120 million	20,000
France	1995	2.1 billion	300,000
Germany	1995	4.67 billion	191,000
Greece	1996	41 million	25,000
Hong Kong	1995	78 million	98,000
Hungary	1996	53 million	110,000
India	1995	70 million	12,000
Indonesia	1995	192 million	750,000
Ireland	1995	19 million	5,000
Israel	1996	80 million	14,000
Italy	1996	2.12 billion	375,000
Japan	1996	30.2 billion	2,500,000
Korea	1995	1.68 billion	475,988
Malaysia	1995	640 million	1,000,000
Mexico	1996	1.3 billion	1,060,000
Netherlands	1993	130 million	33,750
New Zealand	1996	126.5 million	76,000
Norway	1996	90 million	9,000
Peru	1996	295 million	177,000
Philippines	1996	320 million	630,000
Poland	1996	155 million	220,000
Portugal	1995	60 million	23,000
Russia	1995	300 million	250,000
Singapore	1996	96 million	34,500
Slovenia	1994	58 million	15,500
South Africa	1994	330 million	100,000
Spain	1995	652 million	123,656
Sweden	1996	90 million	50,000
Switzerland	1996	245 million	5,700
Taiwan	1995	1.92 billion	2,000,000
Thailand	1996	800 million	500,000
Turkey	1996	98 million	212,000
United Kingdom	1996	1.396 billion	400,000
United States	1995	19.50 billion	7,200,000
Uruguay	1995	42 million	19,500
Total		79.5715 billion	22,291,094

4. Should CUTCO continue to develop countries using both the party plan/hostess program approach and the college program approach?

Case 6–21
Longevity Healthcare Systems, Inc.

Kathryn Hamilton, president of Longevity Healthcare Systems, Inc., located in Grand Rapids, Michigan, was reviewing the 1993 annual statements. "We concluded another terrific year," she commented. "Our sales and earnings exceeded expectations, but I'm concerned about the next few years." Although Longevity was successful, it was beginning to experience competition and the uncertainty of health-care reform. In February 1994 a large hospital in Grand Rapids, Michigan, had converted an entire wing to a long-term care facility. The hospital also had initiated an aggressive sales and advertising campaign and was competing with Longevity for new nursing home residents.

Longevity's recent acquisition of seven nursing homes in Toledo, Ohio, was proving to be an unprofitable venture. Many of the residents were on Medicare and Medicaid, and those health insurance programs generally did not reimburse the full costs of care. Additionally, the families of the Toledo residents were becoming value-conscious and frequently commented about the quality and cost of nursing care. Kathryn realized that to improve the profitability, attention would have to be given to customer satisfaction and to attracting more profitable private-pay residents. Health-care reform was also a source of concern. It was her belief that reform of the health-care industry would be comprehensive, with increased emphasis on cost control, competitive pricing, and quality of care. She wondered what effect reform would have on Longevity and what the timetable for legislative action would be.

While increased competition and health-care reform seemed certain, the most profitable path for future growth was not clear because several marketing opportunities existed. An aging population had created a strong demand for long-term care in nursing homes. Alzheimer's disease was also becoming more common. Longevity recently had lost some nursing home residents to Alzheimer's treatment centers because the company did not offer a specialized facility. Kathryn had to decide whether offering Alzheimer's disease treatment would be desirable.

Opportunities to expand existing businesses were also an option. The Grand Rapids pharmacy acquired in 1992 had been successfully phased in Longevity, and Kathryn was wondering if a similar acquisition would work in Toledo. However, she was concerned about the impact of reform on the pricing of prescription drugs and medical supplies. To date, the pharmacy had been very profitable, but what would the future hold?

Geographic expansion of the firm's nursing and subacute care facilities also might be a profitable avenue for growth. Industry consolidation was making it possible to acquire nursing homes and unprofitable hospitals that could be converted to health-care facilities. However, Kathryn envisioned that a future industry trend might be toward vertical integration of health-care services. If so, it might make sense to further integrate Longevity's business in the Grand Rapids and Toledo markets before committing to additional geographic expansion.

Beyond decisions on the future direction of Longevity, Kathryn wondered if it was time to begin thinking about a more formal approach to marketing. "I really need to get some ideas about marketing in our different businesses down on paper so I can see how they fit with my views on an overall corporate marketing strategy," she remarked.

History of Longevity Healthcare Systems, Inc.

In 1972 Kathryn Hamilton, R.N., was searching for a nursing home for her mother in Grand Rapids, Michigan. Discouraged by a six-month wait for admission, she decided to move her into the home she occupied with her husband, Richard. Dr. Hamilton, M.D., had a medical practice in Grand Rapids specializing in care for older adults.

A Nursing Home Business

In 1974, Richard's mother and father joined the household and Kathryn and Richard continued to learn how to care for older adults. In 1976, the Hamiltons leased a small, outdated 40-bed hospital in a nearby suburb and converted it into a long-term care facility. After certification, the facility was opened in 1977 as the Longevity Nursing Home. In addition to their parents, 10 other adults over 65 entered the home during the year. All were "private-pay," meaning they paid directly for services with personal assets but without government assistance. By 1979 the nursing facility was fully occupied with private-pay residents. Longevity was incorporated, and Kathryn Hamilton became the president and director of nursing, while her husband provided medical services and continued his practice. The leased facility was purchased in 1979.

New Nursing Services

By 1980 Longevity found it necessary to add additional nursing services for aging residents. Two levels of care were added, and professional nurses were hired to provide the services. The new services were favorably received, and the referrals from residents and physicians kept the facility filled.

Expansion by Acquisition, 1980–1985

The demand for nursing care was strong in the early 1980s, and Longevity expanded. Eight unprofitable nursing homes with a total of 480 beds were acquired in Grand Rapids and nearby communities. All the homes were licensed, certified by Medicare and Medicaid, and occupied by residents requiring a variety of nursing services. Shortly after the acquisition, Dr. Hamilton left his medical practice to join Longevity full-time as its medical director. He added skilled nursing care for residents requiring 24-hour-a-day care, and rehabilitation services for those needing physical, speech, and occupational therapy.

Nursing Home Construction

From 1986 to 1988 Longevity expanded by constructing three 70-bed nursing homes in nearby communities. Each provided the full range of nursing and rehabilitation services and was licensed for Medicare and Medicaid patients.[1] The homes were quickly filled, and

[1] By 1988 all Longevity nursing homes were certified to receive Medicare and Medicaid patients. Medicare is a federally funded and administered health insurance program that reimburses health-care facilities for nursing and medical services. Medicaid is a state-administered reimbursement program that covers skilled and intermediate long-term care for the medically indigent. The benefits paid by Medicaid programs vary from state to state.

by the end of 1988 Longevity operated 12 nursing homes with a total of 730 beds. Employment had grown to 1,200 full-time and part-time employees.

New Business Opportunities

During a medical convention in 1990, Kathryn Hamilton noted a growing concern over the escalating costs of hospital care and the desire of insurance providers to shorten the hospitalization of patients requiring medical supervision but not the other services traditionally provided by hospitals. Sensing an opportunity, the Hamiltons converted a 30-bed wing of one of the Grand Rapids nursing homes to a subacute care facility for patients who did not need the full services of a licensed acute care hospital.[2] For patients moved from a hospital to the Longevity facility, the needed care was provided for about half the cost. The subacute care facility was licensed in 1991 and quickly filled with referrals from hospitals, physicians, and health-care insurers.

The growing recognition that treating patients requiring subacute care in low-overhead nursing facilities was a cost-effective alternative substantially increased the demand for Longevity's subacute care. In 1992, following marketing research, Longevity constructed a 50-bed subacute care facility near one of its nursing homes. It was completed in 1993 and within a few months operated at capacity with patients referred from insurance companies, physicians, and Longevity nursing homes.

As the demand for specialized nursing and medical care expanded, it became apparent that profitability could be improved by operating a pharmacy. In 1992 Longevity acquired a retail pharmacy in Grand Rapids from a retiring pharmacist. It was converted into an institutional pharmacy to provide prescriptions, medical equipment and supplies, and consulting services to Longevity facilities.

Geographic Expansion

Late in 1992 what appeared to be an exceptional business opportunity came to the attention of Kathryn and Richard Hamilton. A few hundred miles away, in Toledo, Ohio, a large health-care company was selling seven unprofitable nursing homes with a total of 280 beds for $12 million. The homes were occupied primarily by Medicare and Medicaid patients and operated at 70 percent of capacity. The Hamiltons decided to take a one-year option on the facilities while they raised the money to complete the purchase. Eventually, 40 percent of Longevity's common stock was sold to a large insurance company, and some of the proceeds were used to exercise the purchase option. Kathryn Hamilton hired an experienced administrator and assigned him the task of returning the nursing homes to profitability. To reflect the company's broadening scope in the health-care industry, the Hamiltons decided to change the company name to Longevity Healthcare Systems, Inc. As shown in Exhibits 1 and 2, Longevity ended 1993 with 12 nursing homes, two subacute care facilities, and a pharmacy in Michigan and seven nursing homes in Ohio. Exhibits 3 and 4 contain the financial statements for the year ending December 31, 1993. Exhibit 5 presents a five-year

---

[2]Medical services fall along a continuum of intensive care, acute care, subacute care, nursing care, and home health care. Hospitals offer intensive and acute care for patients with complex medical conditions. They have fully equipped operating and recovery rooms, radiology services, intensive and coronary care units, pharmacies, clinical laboratories, therapy services, and emergency services. Subacute care facilities owned by nursing homes serve the needs of patients who require nursing and medical care but not many of the specialized services and equipment provided by an acute care hospital.

EXHIBIT 1
**Longevity
Healthcare
Systems, Inc.,
Historical
Development,
1972–1993**

Date	Activity
1972–75	Nursing care for parents.
1976–77	Leased a 40-bed hospital and converted it to a nursing home.
1979	Business incorporated as Longevity Nursing Home.
1979	Corporation purchased leased nursing home.
1980–85	Acquired eight nursing homes in Grand Rapids area, 480 beds.
1986–88	Constructed three nursing homes in Grand Rapids area, 210 beds.
1990–91	Converted a 30-bed wing of Grand Rapids nursing home into subacute care.
1992–93	Constructed a 50-bed subacute care facility in Grand Rapids area.
1992	Acquired a retail pharmacy in Grand Rapids.
1992–93	Acquired seven nursing homes in Toledo area, 280 beds.
1993	Corporation name changed to Longevity Healthcare Systems, Inc.

EXHIBIT 2
**Longevity
Healthcare
Systems, Inc.,
Geographic
Location of
Facilities**

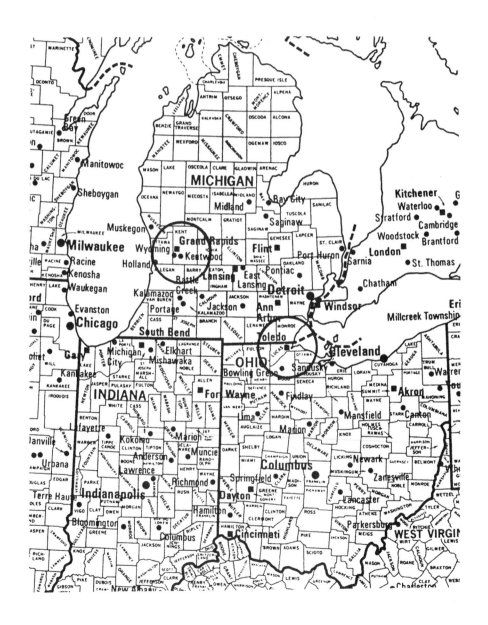

EXHIBIT 3
Longevity Healthcare Systems, Inc., Income Statement (Year Ending Dec. 31, 1993)

Net revenues	
Basic LTC services	$45,500,000
Subacute medical services	9,000,000
Pharmacy services	3,000,000
Total revenues	$57,500,000
Operating expenses	
Salaries, wages, and benefits	$20,125,000
Patient services	21,275,000
Administrative and general	3,450,000
Depreciation and amortization	575,000
Total costs and expenses	$45,425,000
Income from operations	$12,075,000
Interest expense	1,726,111
Earnings before taxes	$10,348,889
Income taxes	4,139,555
Net income	$ 6,209,334
Net income per share	$ 0.78

EXHIBIT 4
Longevity Healthcare Systems, Inc., Balance Sheet (Years Ending Dec. 31, 1993, and Dec. 31, 1992)

Assets	1993	1992
Current assets		
Cash and equivalents	$ 841,770	$ 501,120
Accounts receivable	3,265,584	2,702,552
Inventory	2,262,816	1,624,399
Property, plant, and equipment		
Land	9,959,051	7,690,249
Buildings and improvements	27,002,416	13,622,079
Equipment	2,917,136	2,179,842
Accumulated depreciation	(4,028,149)	(2,464,535)
Other assets		
Goodwill	791,794	655,278
Other long-term assets	5,163,275	4,063,190
Total assets	$48,175,693	$30,574,174
Liabilities and Shareholders' Equity		
Current liabilities		
Accounts payable	$ 1,250,201	$ 1,043,648
Accrued expenses	708,447	586,301
Accrued compensation	416,734	344,883
Current portion of long-term debt	2,041,995	2,700,120
Accrued interest	196,694	203,954
Long-term debt (net)	10,506,622	12,871,452
Shareholders' equity		
Common stock, $.01 par value	50,000	50,000
Additional paid-in capital	17,870,666	3,848,816
Retained earnings	15,134,334	8,925,000
Total liabilities and shareholders' equity	$48,175,693	$30,574,174

EXHIBIT 5
Longevity
Healthcare
Systems, Inc.,
Historical
Revenues and Net
Income

Year	Revenues	Net Income
1993	$57,500,000	$6,209,334
1992	46,575,000	5,029,560
1991	37,260,000	3,017,736
1990	26,715,420	2,987,692
1989	21,799,783	1,334,147

EXHIBIT 6
Longevity
Healthcare
Systems, Inc.,
Selected Pharmacy
Information (Year
Ending Dec. 31,
1993)

Income Statement	
Net revenue	$3,000,000
Operating expenses	2,430,000
Operating income	570,000
Net income	390,000
Financial Ratios	
Current ratio	1.94
Inventory turnover	4.20
Profit margin (percent)	13.00%
Return on assets (percent)	9.29%

sales and earnings history, while Exhibit 6 provides some financial information for the pharmacy.

Longevity Marketing

Marketing was used to promote high occupancy in Longevity facilities, expand the percentage of private-pay residents, and increase the profits of its institutional pharmacy. Operating information for the health-care facilities is shown in Exhibit 7, and the products and services marketed by Longevity are summarized in Exhibit 8.

Nursing care was marketed locally. The administrator and admissions director of each facility designed a marketing strategy to increase awareness of the nursing home and its services in the market it served. Personal selling using telemarketing and direct contact was targeted to referral sources such as physicians, hospital administrators, home health agencies, community organizations and churches, senior citizens groups, retirement communities, and the families of prospective residents. Longevity also distributed promotional literature discussing its philosophy of care, services, and quality standards. Frequently the literature was provided to prospective residents and their families when they inquired about nursing or toured the facilities.

Marketing for subacute care was directed by Kathryn Hamilton, who contacted insurance companies, managed care organizations such as HMOs, hospital administrators, and other third-party payers to promote Longevity's services.[3] Kathryn also attended professional meetings where she maintained contact with the various referral sources.

---

[3]Managed care organizations provide health-care products that integrate financing and management with the delivery of health-care services through a network of providers (such as nursing homes and hospitals) that share financial risk or have incentives to deliver cost-effective services. An HMO (health maintenance organization) provides prepaid health-care services to its members through physicians employed by the HMO at facilities owned by the HMO or through a network of independent physicians and facilities. HMOs actively manage patient care to maximize quality and cost-effectiveness.

EXHIBIT 7
Longevity Healthcare Systems, Inc., Operating Information for Facilities (Year Ending Dec. 31, 1993)

	Grand Rapids	Toledo	Total
Payer mix			
Private and other	69.7%	18.7%	44.2%
Medicare	8.4	17.8	13.1
Medicaid	21.9	63.5	42.7
Occupancy	96.4%	81.2%	88.8%
No. of beds	780	280	1,060

EXHIBIT 8
Longevity Healthcare Systems, Inc., Products and Services

Business	Products/Services
Nursing care	Custodial care
	Assisted living
	Intermediate nursing care
	Skilled nursing care
Subacute care for	Lung and heart disease
	Coma, pain, and wound care
	Spinal cord injuries
	Head injuries
	Intravenous therapy
	Joint replacements
Rehabilitation services	Occupational therapy
	Physical therapy
	Speech therapy
Institutional pharmacy	Prescription drugs
	Nonprescription drugs
	Medical supplies
	Medical equipment
	Consulting services

The products and services of the institutional pharmacy were marketed by the pharmacy manager and his assistant through direct contact with Longevity facilities, other nursing homes, hospitals, clinics, and home health agencies. In addition to drugs and medical supplies, management also provided consulting services to help ensure quality patient care. These services were especially valuable because they enabled the nursing homes to admit patients who required more complex and profitable medical services.

Nursing Home Services

Longevity nursing homes provided room and board, dietary services, recreation and social activities, housekeeping and laundry services, four levels of nursing care, and numerous specialized services. Custodial care was provided to residents who needed minimal care. Assisted living was used by persons needing some assistance with personal care such as bathing and eating. Intermediate care was provided to residents needing more nursing and attention but not continuous access to nurses. Finally, skilled nursing care was available to residents requiring the professional services of a nurse on a 24-hour-a-day basis. Rehabilitation therapy was also available for residents who had disabilities or were returning from hospitalization for surgery or illness. Rehabilitation was an important part of Longevity's care because it helped residents improve their quality of life.

Most of the residents in Longevity nursing homes were female and over 65. Although rates depended on accommodations and the services used, a typical nursing home bed

EXHIBIT 9
**Longevity
Healthcare
Systems, Inc.,
Example Resident
Statement for
Nursing Care (per
Month)***

Semiprivate room, $105.00 per day	$3,150.00
Basic telephone service	15.00
Rehabilitation therapy, 7.0 hours per month	840.00
Pharmacy and other specialized services	360.00
Miscellaneous personal expenses	50.00
Total	$4,415.00
Per day	147.17

*Based on private pay. Includes room and board, 24-hour professional nursing care, meals, house-keeping, and linen services. Social and recreational activity programs also are included.

generated monthly revenues of $4,415. It was common for residents to initially enter the nursing home needing only custodial care or assisted living and to progress to higher levels of nursing care as they aged. Exhibit 9 provides a typical schedule of monthly charges for a resident in a semiprivate room with seven hours of therapy.

All the Longevity nursing homes were licensed in their respective states. Generally, the licenses had to be renewed annually. For renewal, state health-care agencies considered the physical condition of the facility, the qualifications of the administrative and medical staff, the quality of care, and the facility's compliance with the applicable laws and regulations.

Subacute Care

Longevity marketed subacute care for patients with more complex medical needs that required constant medical supervision but not the expensive equipment and services of an acute care hospital. Subacute care generated higher profit margins than did nursing care, although patient stays in the facility were usually shorter.[4] Daily patient rates varied from $250 to $750, depending on the services and equipment required. Longevity's services included care for patients with lung and heart disease, spinal cord and head injuries, joint replacements, coma, pain and wound care, and intravenous therapy. Services at the subacute care facilities were not limited to the elderly. Younger patients discharged from hospitals were attractive because of their longer life expectancy and eventual need for nursing and rehabilitation. Based on an average rate of $1,000 per day charged by acute care hospitals, Longevity knew that its prices were substantially lower for comparable services. Like the nursing homes, the subacute care facilities were subject to licensing by the state health-care agencies and certification by Medicare. All Longevity subacute care facilities were licensed and certified.

Pharmacy Products and Services

Longevity provided pharmacy products and services to nursing homes, retirement communities, and other health-care organizations. The pharmacy's products were frequently customized with special packaging and dispensing systems and delivered daily. The pharmacy also consulted on medications and long-term care regulations and provided computerized tracking of medications, medical records processing, and 24-hour emergency services.

The Market for Long-Term Health Care

Long-term health care includes basic health care (such as that provided in nursing homes), rehabilitation therapy and Alzheimer's care, institutional pharmacy services, subacute care,

---

[4]Longevity profit margins for subacute care facilities were about 25 percent higher than those for nursing care facilities. The length of stay was usually 20 to 45 days versus eight months for private-pay nursing care and two years for Medicaid patients.

and home health care. In recent years spending for these and other health-care services has increased significantly. For example, in 1993, one out of every seven dollars that Americans spent went to purchase health care. Total expenditures are projected to increase from $585.3 billion in 1990 to $3,457.7 billion in 2010, an annual growth rate of over 9 percent.

Nursing homes are important providers of long-term health care. Expenditures for nursing home care are expected to increase at a comparable rate, from $53.1 billion in 1990 to $310.1 billion in 2010. This industry consists of about 16,000 licensed facilities with a total of 1,700,000 beds. It includes a large number of small, locally owned nursing homes and a growing number of regional and national companies. The industry is undergoing restructuring in response to stricter regulation, increasing complexity of medical services, and competitive pressures. Smaller, local operators that lack sophisticated management and financial resources are being acquired by larger, more established companies. At present, the 20 largest firms operate about 18 percent of the nursing facilities. Consolidation is expected to continue, but the long-term outlook is extremely positive for the businesses that survive. Nursing home revenues increased by about 12 percent in 1993 and are expected to experience similar gains in 1994. Several factors account for the optimistic outlook: favorable demographic trends, pressures to control costs, advances in medical technology, and a limited supply of nursing beds.

Favorable Demographic Trends

Demographic trends, namely, growth in the elderly segment of the population, are increasing the demand for health care and the services of nursing homes. Most of the market for nursing care consists of men and women 65 years of age and older. Their number was approximately 25 million in 1980 and is projected to increase to 35 million by 2000 and 40 million by 2010. The 65-and-over segment suffers from a greater incidence of chronic illnesses and disabilities and currently accounts for about two-thirds of the health-care expenditures in the United States.

Pressures to Control Costs

Government and private payers have adopted cost control measures to encourage reduced hospital stays. In addition, private insurers have begun to limit reimbursement to "reasonable" charges, while managed care organizations are limiting hospitalization costs by monitoring utilization and negotiating discounted rates. As a result, hospital stays have been shortened and many patients are discharged with a continuing need for care. Because nursing homes are able to provide services at lower prices, the cost pressures have increased the demand for nursing home services and subacute care after hospital discharge.

Advances in Medical Technology

Advances in technology leading to improved medications and surgical procedures have increased life expectancies. Adults over age 85 are now the fastest-growing segment of the population, and their numbers are expected to double over the next 20 years. Many require skilled care and the medical equipment traditionally available only in hospitals. Nursing homes are acquiring some of the specialty medical equipment and providing skilled nursing care to older adults through subacute care facilities.

Limited Supply of Nursing Beds

The supply of nursing home beds has been limited by the availability of financing and high construction and start-up expenses. Additionally, the supply has been constrained by legislation limiting licenses for new nursing beds in states that require a demonstration of need. The effect has been to create a barrier to market entry and conditions where the demand for nursing home services exceeds the available supply in many states.

National Health-Care Reform

The next decade will be a period of reform for the health-care system. Although it is not clear how comprehensive the reform will be and how it will be financed, the focus will be on controlling costs and providing universal access to quality health care. The most likely plan probably will reform the health insurance industry, build on the current employer-financed approach, and call for market incentives to control costs. To ensure universal access, insurance and managed care companies will be prohibited from dropping, rejecting, or pricing out of the market anyone with an expensive medical condition.

Reform will affect providers of long-term care such as nursing homes in several ways. It will regulate the insurance companies to make health insurance more price-competitive and affordable. This change will favorably affect long-term health-care providers by increasing the number of residents paying with insurance benefits. Reform also may extend Medicare coverage for home health care. A change such as this would encourage more older adults to receive health care at home instead of at a nursing facility, resulting in an unfavorable impact.

Employers also will have incentives to control costs and deliver quality care. Increasingly they will rely on managed care organizations, such as HMOs, that are likely to contract lower-cost providers, such as nursing homes, for subacute care and other cost-effective services. Companies capable of providing a variety of health-care services at attractive prices should see opportunities to expand demand.

Institutional pharmacies also will be affected by health-care reform. President Clinton's Health Security Act called for the addition of prescription drug coverage to the Medicare program. If adopted, this provision probably would decrease the prices of prescription drugs through regulation of pharmaceutical manufacturers. Price decreases, either legislated or achieved through managed care and the market system, may allow institutional pharmacies to earn higher profit margins while still providing medications at affordable prices to patients.

Regulation and Competition

Health-care providers are regulated at the state and federal levels. Regulation affects financial management and the quality and safety of care. Ensuring that health-care facilities are in compliance with regulatory standards is an important aspect of managing a health-care business. In addition, management increasingly is confronted with competition. Nursing homes and subacute care facilities compete for patients who are able to select from a variety of alternatives to meet their needs. Managed care and insurance organizations also negotiate aggressively with health-care providers to ensure quality care at attractive prices.

Financial Regulation

The Health Care Financing Administration (HCFA) is the federal regulatory agency for Medicare and Medicaid. Both programs are cost-based and use a per diem payment schedule that reimburses the provider for a portion of the costs of care. Each facility must apply to participate in the Medicare and Medicaid programs and then have its beds certified to provide skilled nursing, intermediate, or other levels of care. A nursing home may have a mix of beds at any time, but it must match patient services to each bed. A facility cannot place a Medicare patient requiring skilled nursing care in a bed certified for intermediate care without recertifying the bed for skilled care. Recertification often requires a month or more.

Quality and Safety of Care

Much of the current regulation facing nursing homes was developed in the Omnibus Budget Reconciliation Act of 1987 (OBRA 87). Facilities that participate in Medicare and Medicaid must be inspected regularly by state survey teams under contract with HCFA to ensure safety and quality of care. OBRA 87 also established a resident "bill of rights" that essentially converted nursing homes from merely custodial facilities into centers for rehabilitation. Nursing homes are now required to establish a care plan for patients and conduct assessments to ensure that the facility achieves the highest practical level of well-being for each resident.

Competition

Longevity competes with acute care and rehabilitation hospitals, other nursing and subacute care facilities, home health-care agencies, and institutional pharmacies. Some offer services and prices that are comparable to those offered by Longevity.

Nursing homes compete on the basis of their reputation in the community, the ability to meet particular needs, the location and appearance of the facility, and the price of services. When a nursing facility is being selected, members of a prospective resident's family usually participate by visiting and evaluating nursing homes over a period of several weeks.

Some of the competing nursing homes in Grand Rapids and Toledo are operated by nonprofit organizations (churches and fraternal organizations) that can finance capital expenditures on a tax-exempt basis or receive charitable contributions to subsidize their operations. They compete with Longevity on the basis of price for private-pay residents.

Longevity competes for subacute care patients with acute care and rehabilitation hospitals, nursing homes, and home health agencies. The competition is generally local or regional, and the competitive factors are similar to those for nursing care, although more emphasis is placed on support services such as third-party reimbursement, information management, and patient record keeping. Insurance and managed care organizations exert considerable influence on the decision and increase the competition by negotiating with several health-care providers.

The institutional pharmacy market has no dominant competitor in the markets served by Longevity. Twenty percent of the market is accounted for by the institutional pharmacies owned by nursing homes. Independent institutional pharmacies control about 35 percent of the market, and retail pharmacies supply the remainder. Retail pharmacies are steadily being acquired by nursing homes and independents to gain market share and achieve economies of scale in purchasing prescriptions and medical supplies. Institutional pharmacies compete on the basis of fast customer-oriented service, price, and the ability to provide consulting and information management services to customers.

Marketing Issues and Opportunities

Kathryn Hamilton believed that Longevity could improve its marketing. She was concerned about the efforts of individual nursing homes and the need to improve the marketing of subacute care to managed care providers. Finally, she believed that customer satisfaction would become an important competitive factor and that Longevity would need to assess the reactions of nursing home residents and their families to the quality of its services.

Continued growth was also on Kathryn's mind. Population demographics and health-care reform would create outstanding opportunities for businesses that could design and implement successful marketing strategies. For some time she had been thinking about expanding into Alzheimer's treatment because of the demographics and the growing need for facilities in the Grand Rapids area. Additionally, she saw an opportunity to further integrate Longevity by establishing a pharmacy in Toledo or acquiring nursing homes in a new market such as South Bend, Indiana. Each marketing opportunity seemed to make sense, and so the final choices would be difficult.

Local Marketing of Health-Care Services

Although local marketing had worked well, duplication of effort and overlapping market areas were becoming problems as the number of nursing homes in a market increased. Kathryn wondered what the marketing strategy for nursing home services should be and whether the marketing efforts of the Grand Rapids and Toledo nursing homes could be coordinated in each area to eliminate duplication and preserve local identity. One approach she was considering was to hire a marketing specialist to work with the nursing homes to attract more private-pay customers. Advertising was a related issue because it had not been used, and Kathryn questioned whether it should be part of the marketing strategy. Should an advertising campaign be created for all the nursing homes in a market, or should it be left to nursing home administrators to decide if advertising was appropriate in their strategy? If advertising was to be used, a decision would have to be made on the type of advertising, the creative strategy, and the appropriate media.

Marketing Subacute Care

Subacute care was viewed as an attractive marketing opportunity because of the profit margins. However, to further penetrate the market, a marketing strategy would have to be developed. Kathryn noted that managed care organizations and other referral sources were like organizational buyers as they made decisions on subacute care for the cases they managed. Instead of marketing the service to physicians and patient families, Longevity would negotiate directly with HMOs and insurance companies to determine services and a rate structure based on the patient's medical needs. Personal selling would be used to build a relationship with the case managers for both the insurance company and the hospital. The marketing objective was to convince the insurance companies that the subacute unit could achieve the same patient outcomes at a lower cost than a hospital. If a marketing strategy could be developed along with appropriate staffing, it might be desirable to expand this part of Longevity's business. Economics favored the conversion of a wing of an existing nursing home into a subacute care facility at a cost of $25,000 per bed. One possibility existed in Toledo, where an unprofitable 80-bed facility was operating at 60 percent of capacity. If part of the facility were upgraded to subacute care, she expected that within a short time, it would operate at capacity.

Customer Satisfaction

Occasional complaints from nursing home residents about the price and quality of care were of concern to management. Since Longevity depended on referrals, customer satisfaction was an important element of a successful marketing strategy. In thinking about the issue, Kathryn noted that the license renewal process generally assured the maintenance of high standards in each facility, but it focused heavily on the inputs necessary to provide quality nursing care, not on customer satisfaction. Kathryn needed to decide what should be done to monitor individual nursing homes to assure customer satisfaction with Longevity's services.

Acquisition of a Toledo Pharmacy

One marketing opportunity being considered was the acquisition of a Toledo pharmacy. From management's perspective, an acquisition was interesting because it further integrated the existing health-care operations and provided an incremental source of earnings from the Toledo market.

Management had identified an institutional pharmacy serving 15 nursing homes with 700 beds. It was offered at a cash price of $1,050,000 and generated annual revenues of approximately $1,450 per bed served. The pharmacy was quite profitable, with an average profit margin of 12.5 percent over the past five years. To consider the profitability of the acquisition, Kathryn believed it was reasonable to assume that the pharmacy would be able to serve the Longevity facilities in Toledo and retain 60 percent of the nursing home beds it currently served if it was staffed with appropriate marketing support.

One concern was the impact of health-care reform. Most of the nursing homes served by the pharmacy had a high percentage of Medicare and Medicaid patients. If the reimbursement rates for prescription drugs and medical supplies declined, what seemed to be an attractive opportunity could quickly change.

Alzheimer's Treatment

Alzheimer's treatment was being considered because the demand for care was not being met and the development of a cure or drug therapy for the disease was progressing slowly. Kathryn believed that the demand for Alzheimer's treatment would grow at least as fast as would the over-65 population. Projections from the U.S. Department of Health and Human Services indicated that by the year 2000, the Alzheimer's care market would increase by 50 percent from the base of 4,000,000 currently suffering from the disease.

Longevity was considering establishing an Alzheimer's wing in two of the Grand Rapids nursing homes that served areas near older community residents. Each unit would serve 30 patients and would be self-contained and secured to protect residents against their wandering habits. The furniture and fixtures would be renovated to meet the needs of the Alzheimer's patient, including softer colors, more subdued lighting, a separate nurses station, and a secured entrance. If an existing facility was converted, about six nursing rooms would have to be taken out of service to provide a separate activity and dining space. However, management reasoned that the revenue loss would be offset by average monthly revenues of $3,400 per patient and costs 15 percent lower than those for the average nursing home resident. Alzheimer's patients frequently required less costly care because of their younger age, better health, and a tendency to use fewer services. Longevity management had secured cost estimates that indicated that the conversion costs would be $2,000 to $3,000 per bed.

In thinking about the opportunity, Kathryn also recalled that Alzheimer's units typically had occupancy levels above 95 percent. Patients averaged a three-year length of stay and were almost always private-pay. The marketing for Alzheimer's units focused on Alzheimer's associations, Alzheimer support groups, and church groups. Kathryn would have to decide how to position and market the Alzheimer's units so that they would not appear to conflict with or be confused with the nursing home services. This would be a difficult but important marketing challenge because nursing homes that were known to operate Alzheimer's units tended to have better relationships with referral sources. Apparently they were perceived as providing an important community service.

Toward a Comprehensive Marketing Strategy

As Kathryn Hamilton completed her review of the financial statements, she was reminded of the need to make improvements in Longevity's marketing strategies. "I wish I could just write a one-paragraph statement of the corporate marketing strategy for this company. Then I could address each of the marketing issues and opportunities using my corporate strategy as a guide," she remarked.

Certainly one issue was improving existing marketing efforts. Marketing of nursing care, subacute care, and the institutional pharmacy had been reasonably successful, but Kathryn felt uneasy about going another year without making needed changes. Since most of Kathryn's time was now used to manage the business, additional marketing personnel would be necessary to develop and implement the marketing strategies for the various services. How many people would be needed and how the marketing effort would be organized also had to be decided.

Because Longevity was still evolving as a company with an uncertain marketing strategy, the most profitable direction for future growth was also important. Selecting attractive marketing opportunities was complicated because the choice depended on financial resources. Should Longevity expand the institutional pharmacy business or the subacute care business, or would resources be better utilized by offering Alzheimer's care? Each would bring Longevity closer to becoming an integrated health-care provider.

Just as Kathryn moved to turn her personal computer off for the day, she noticed an electronic mail message from the administrator of the Toledo nursing homes. It said that for the first quarter of 1994, the seven nursing homes were breaking even at 81 percent occupancy and 25 percent private-pay residents. When she arrived home that evening, she was greeted by her husband, who mentioned that she had received a telephone call from a commercial real estate broker in South Bend, Indiana. The broker had located five nursing homes with a total of 450 beds that were being sold in a bankruptcy proceeding for $5 million. During dinner that evening, Richard mentioned that they needed to discuss the South Bend opportunity because the homes were attractively priced in a desirable market. It was his belief that in the future, the most profitable health-care businesses would be vertically integrated and geographically diversified. Kathryn nodded in agreement as he handed her the summary information provided in Exhibit 10 and mentioned that a decision would have to be made in five days. She thought to herself, I wonder if it's financially possible?

EXHIBIT 10   **Longevity Healthcare Systems, Inc., Selected Demographic Information**

Category	Grand Rapids*		Toledo		South Bend†	
	Number	Percent of Adult Population by Category	Number	Percent of Adult Population by Category	Number	Percent of Adult Population by Category
Retired	235,513	18.9%	161,630	19.9%	119,401	20.0%
Age, household head						
55–64	77,383	12.4	54,421	13.2	40,661	13.4
65–74	71,142	11.4	52,772	12.8	39,448	13.0
75 and older	56,165	9.0	40,816	9.9	30,951	10.2
Median age	44.5		46.1		46.7	
Life cycle stage						
Married, 45–64	87,992	14.1	58,544	14.2	44,910	14.8
Married, 65+	61,157	9.8	42,053	10.2	34,289	11.3
Single, 45–64	44,932	7.2	31,746	7.7	23,365	7.7
Single, 65+	56,789	9.1	43,702	10.6	30,951	10.2
Median income	$32,928		$32,194		$31,264	
Adult population	1,246,101		812,212		597,003	
Nursing facilities‡	439		988		590	
Total nursing beds	49,927		92,518		64,263	

*Includes Kalamazoo and Battle Creek, Michigan.
†Includes Elkhart, Indiana.
‡Statewide statistics for certified Medicare and Medicaid facilities and beds.
Source: *The Lifestyle Market Analyst,* 1993. Health Care Financing Administration, 1991.

Case 6–22

SystemSoft Corporation

William O'Connell, senior vice president of strategic accounts and business development at SystemSoft Corporation, sat in his office and contemplated his company's future direction. SystemSoft had experienced tremendous growth since its founding in 1991 and was now the world's leading supplier of PC card software.[1] SystemSoft had gone public in August 1994, and now, just one year later, O'Connell faced a difficult decision regarding the company's growth strategy.

SystemSoft developed system-level software that allowed the operating system of a PC to interface with the hardware. The company had been highly successful in its core product lines of BIOS (basic input/output system), PC card, and power management software. SystemSoft operated in a highly competitive environment in which technological innovation was a key driver of success. O'Connell had to decide whether to proceed in developing a new "call avoidance" product category.[2] Call avoidance software had a significant market potential, and there was no comprehensive problem resolution software on the market.

O'Connell knew that SystemSoft had to continue to innovate and push into new categories and segments, but he was concerned that the call avoidance software was too different from the company's core product mix. While the rewards for pioneering a new product category could be tremendous, pursuing this opportunity could stretch SystemSoft's resources too far at a time when the company had to begin to understand and manage its growth. Pursuing growth through a strategy of product development would have far-reaching effects within SystemSoft. For example, O'Connell would have to decide whether the salespeople should be organized by product line or should be generalists, representing all of SystemSoft's products to an account. Some questioned whether SystemSoft should delve into this new category, given that it differed from its core product lines in many ways. O'Connell wondered, Was market penetration a safer route?

Company Overview

SystemSoft was cofounded in 1991 by four people from Phoenix Technologies as a developer of system-level software. SystemSoft's mission was to become the leading provider of connectivity and other system-level software for microprocessor-based devices. Its strategy was focused on technological leadership, strategic alliances, key customer relationships, further expansion into the desktop market, and finding additional markets for PC card software and power management technology. Exhibits 1 and 2 show SystemSoft's balance sheet and income statement for the past several years.

System-level software provides a layer of connectivity and ease of use for personal computers by allowing the operating system to recognize, configure, and communicate

---

[1]Formerly termed PCMCIA (Personal Computer Memory Card International Association). This is the industry standard for expansion slots on portable computers. PCMCIA slots accept a variety of PCMCIA cards from a variety of manufacturers. They can be used to add things such as memory, a modem, a fax, or LAN cards.

[2]Call avoidance software is intended to solve user problems on a PC, reducing the number of technical support calls to manufacturers.

This case was prepared by Lisa Robie Adam, graduate assistant, Boston College, under the supervision of Victoria L. Crittenden, associate professor of marketing, Boston College. This case was written to facilitate classroom discussion rather than to illustrate effective or ineffective corporate decision making.

EXHIBIT 1   **SystemSoft Corporation Consolidated Balance Sheet, January 31**

	1995	1994	1993
Assets			
Current assets:			
Cash and cash equivalents	$ 7,716,687	$ 2,758,318	$ 696,249
Restricted cash	—	—	125,000
Marketable securities	4,885,069	—	—
Accounts receivable, net of doubtful accounts	4,572,757	2,423,612	1,439,477
Receivable from related party	73,500	89,950	43,082
Prepaid and other current assets	481,626	298,142	62,761
Deferred income taxes	1,218,812	—	—
Total current assets	18,948,451	5,570,022	2,366,569
Property and equipment, net	1,060,048	521,437	447,595
Purchased software, net	—	—	575,293
Software development costs, net	1,088,926	1,302,990	429,148
Total assets	$21,097,425	$ 7,394,449	$ 3,818,605
Liabilities and Stockholders' Equity (Deficit)			
Current liabilities:			
Accounts payable	$ 614,501	$ 354,259	$ 1,032,226
Accrued expenses	302,392	284,229	208,927
Income taxes payable	391,143	7,000	—
Accrued commissions	734,715	339,752	318,846
Accrued compensation and benefits	622,470	563,502	205,797
Accrued royalties	237,707	122,263	318,591
Deferred revenue from related party	260,000	540,000	—
Notes payable, current portion	—	359,123	189,901
Total current liabilities	$ 3,162,928	$ 2,570,128	$ 2,274,288
Notes payable, net of current portion	—	60,045	183,943
Deferred income taxes	276,600	—	—
Commitments			
Redeemable convertible preferred stock	—	12,080,511	8,656,702
Warrant	—	500,000	—
Stockholders' equity (deficit)			
Common stock	98,611	29,393	28,997
Paid-in capital	22,453,812	—	—
Less treasury stock	(128,696)	(128,696)	(105,596)
Accumulated deficit	(4,765,830)	(7,716,932)	(7,219,729)
Total stockholders' equity (deficit)	17,657,897	(7,816,235)	(7,296,328)
Total liabilities and owners' equity	$21,097,425	$ 7,394,449	$ 3,818,605

with the system hardware, including the peripherals. Exhibit 3 describes system-level software. The end user typically is not familiar with system-level software because it operates between the computer chips and the operating system. In 1995, SystemSoft offered three categories of software products: PC card, power management, and BIOS. The company dominated the mobile computer market, but its share of the desktop computer market remained negligible.

EXHIBIT 2   **SystemSoft Corporation Consolidated Statement of Operations, January 31**

	1995	1994	1993	1992
Revenues				
Software license fees	$10,223,294	$6,281,190	$4,425,216	$2,188,881
Engineering services	2,532,588	1,279,630	1,153,129	481,575
Related party	2,419,298	1,077,408	711,488	260,251
Other	46,077	515,364	—	—
Total revenues	15,221,257	9,153,592	6,289,833	2,930,707
Cost of Revenues				
Software license fees	1,303,769	850,006	960,202	808,084
Engineering services	951,023	1,046,140	1,028,102	837,465
Related party	1,817,343	616,093	513,776	276,517
Other	40,181	455,977	—	—
Total cost of revenues	4,112,316	2,968,216	2,502,080	1,922,066
Gross profit	11,108,941	6,185,376	3,787,753	1,008,641
Operating Expenses				
R&D	2,252,491	1,506,891	1,076,379	709,301
Sales and marketing	5,073,194	2,685,619	2,250,633	1,750,793
General and administrative	1,900,779	1,579,877	1,782,670	1,593,646
Litigation settlement	—	—	1,019,225	—
Total operating expenses	9,226,464	5,772,387	6,128,907	4,053,740
Income (loss) from operations	1,882,477	412,989	(2,341,154)	(3,045,099)
Interest income	298,726	15,857	28,480	41,417
Interest expense	(10,005)	(38,164)	(37,092)	(12,432)
Income (loss) before income taxes	2,171,198	390,682	(2,349,766)	(3,016,114)
Provisions for income tax	125,798	160,340	242,495	157,185
Net income (loss)	2,045,400	230,342	(2,592,261)	(3,173,299)
Accretion of preferred stock	(412,640)	(759,378)	(497,986)	(144,246)
Net income (loss) available to comm. shareholders	$ 1,632,760	($529,036)	($3,090,247)	($3,317,545)
Net income (loss) per share	$ 0.22	($0.15)	($0.87)	($0.93)
Weighted average number of shares outstanding	7,342,619	3,559,074	3,554,381	3,568,687

Products and Competition

The advent of mobile computers had dramatically changed the way people worked and communicated by the mid-1990s. The rapid development of mobile devices created a need for additional technologies that addressed the limitations of mobile computers. For example, PC cards provided expanded memory and increased flexibility/functionality, while power management lengthened life between battery charges. Power management had also become more important on desktop PCs due to rising energy costs and the Environmental

EXHIBIT 3
**System-Level
Software**

SystemSoft is a supplier of PCMCIA and other system-level software to the rapidly growing market for mobile computers, which consist of laptops, notebooks, subnotebooks, and personal computing devices. PCMCIA is a published industry standard which enables PCs and electronic devices to automatically recognize, install, and configure peripherals (including, for example, modems, flash memory, and network cards) incorporated in credit card–size PCMCIA cards. System-level software provides both a connectivity layer, which facilitates the addition, configuration, and use of peripheral devices, and a hardware adaptation layer, which includes the communication link between a PC's operating system software and hardware. Each new version of hardware or operating system software generally requires new system-level software. PC manufacturers are able to offer enhanced functionality, flexibility, and ease of use by using the company's software in their products.

System-level software is one of the four basic technologies in the architecture of a PC: application software, operating system software, system-level software, and hardware.

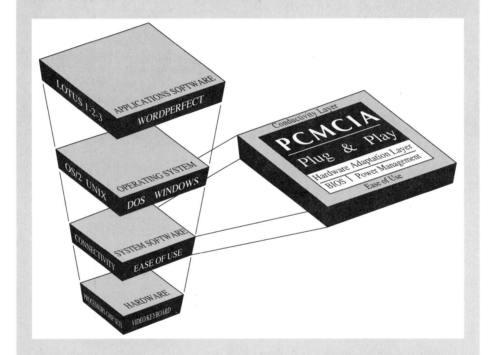

Application software is designed to perform end user tasks such as word processing and data analysis. WordPerfect and Lotus 1-2-3 are examples of widely used application programs. Operating system software allows PC hardware to control the sequencing and processing of applications and respond to a PC user's commands, such as storing data, displaying data, and running an application program. Microsoft's DOS and Windows are the dominant operating systems in the IBM-compatible PC market. System-level software is a necessary component in every PC, enabling the computer's operating system to recognize, configure, and communicate with the hardware, including peripherals. PC hardware consists of microprocessors, also known as central processing units (CPUs), CPU-support chipsets, memory, input–output devices (such as monitors and keyboards), and various other peripheral devices (such as printers, modems, and CD-ROM drives). Intel's *x*86 and Pentium chips are the leading CPUs in the PC market.

EXHIBIT 4
**Market Share by
Product Category,
1995**

Product	Market Share
BIOS and power management	
Notebook market	20% of available market,* 10% of overall market
Desktop market	Negligible
PC Card	64%

*The available market refers to personal computers that shipped with third-party BIOS and power management software. All OEMs used third-party manufacturers for PC card software.

Protection Agency's (EPA's) Energy Star Program.[3] The following list is a brief description of the functionality of SystemSoft's core product lines:

- *BIOS (basic input/output system)* software enables PC hardware components to accept commands from and deliver commands to the operating system software.

- *PC card* software gives users immediate access to the features contained in add-on peripheral cards. Users insert credit card–size cards into sockets built into PCs in a manner similar to the insertion of a floppy disk. PC card software enables a computer to identify the inserted card and reconfigure and allocate system resources without manual intervention by the user (such as setting jumper switches or configuring operating system software). PC cards incorporate a standard published by the Personal Computer Memory Card International Association.

- *Power management* software reduces the power consumption of PCs by slowing or stopping the operation of specific system components when a computer is not in use.

SystemSoft had different competitors in each type of software it developed. Phoenix Technologies was the only competitor that had developed software in all of SystemSoft's product categories. American Megatrends (AMI) was a leading competitor in the BIOS segment. Award competed with SystemSoft in the PC card segment.

SystemSoft's greatest success was its dominance of the PC card market. The company had approximately a 64 percent market share in 1995 and supplied 14 of the top 15 notebook vendors. Its BIOS and power management software were also highly successful, with approximately a 20 percent share of the available notebook market in 1995[4] (Exhibit 4). Phoenix was the leader in the notebook BIOS and power management market; AMI was second. SystemSoft's share of the desktop BIOS and power management market was small, but the company was looking to expand it.

Companies in the mobile computer industry operated in a highly competitive, rapidly changing technological environment. Innovation and the ability to change rapidly drive success. In addition to the leading direct competitors, there was always the competitive threat that operating system vendors would enter the market or incorporate enough features to decrease SystemSoft's revenues from original equipment manufacturers (OEMs).

Sales and Marketing

SystemSoft's sales and marketing efforts were focused on personal selling and attending trade shows. The company distributed data sheets on its products but did little advertising

[3]Energy Star is a voluntary program between the U.S. EPA and computer, monitor, and printer manufacturers that was developed in 1992 to conserve energy. To qualify for Energy Star, a computer must have a "sleep" feature that powers down the computer when it is not in use. This feature can cut power usage by up to 75 percent.
[4]The available market refers to notebooks that ship with a third-party BIOS. The available market is approximately 50 percent of 10 million units.

and promotion. Exhibit 5 shows a sample data sheet. SystemSoft's sales were driven by a direct sales force complemented by independent manufacturers' representatives for international sales. SystemSoft had a national sales office in California and international offices in Taiwan and Japan (the international headquarters). The software was licensed to OEMs, and SystemSoft received royalties on the systems shipped. There was no initial charge for the software unless SystemSoft customized or made adjustments to it for the customer.

Revenues from BIOS software ranged from US$0.10 to US$1.00 for every unit shipped. Power management software typically was sold along with BIOS software and added about 20 to 50 percent to the BIOS revenue. PC card software generated approximately US$1 to US$3 for each unit shipped, and the proposed call avoidance product was expected to generate US$3 to US$7 per unit.

EXHIBIT 5
Sample Data Sheet

EXHIBIT 5
(Continued)

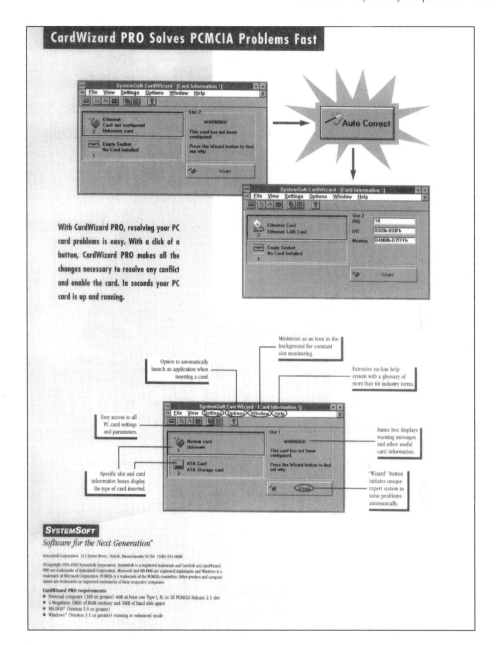

Customer Base

SystemSoft licensed its products to OEMs, including PC manufacturers, hardware component manufacturers, PC card manufacturers, and operating system software companies. The company had licensed its software to more than 100 PC manufacturers and more than 45 PC card manufacturers. Exhibit 6 lists a number of SystemSoft clients in various segments.

Much of SystemSoft's success was attributed to a number of key customer relationships and strategic alliances that it had developed over a few short years. In 1993, SystemSoft entered into a development and license agreement with Intel by which Intel licensed certain technologies to SystemSoft. SystemSoft in turn developed those technologies into products marketed under the SystemSoft name. The Intel agreement stipulated that the two

EXHIBIT 6
**Sample Customer
List by Segment**

Hardware Component Manufacturers
Intel
Advanced Micro Devices (AMD)

PC Manufacturers

Acer	Hewlett-Packard	NCR/AT&T
AST Research	Hitachi	NEC
Citizen	Hyundai	Seiko Epson
Clevo	IBM	Sotec
Compaq	ICL	Twinhead
Dell	Inventec	Wacom
Digital Equipment	LiteOn	
Gateway 2000	Mitsui	

Operating System Software Companies
Microsoft
Geoworks

PC Card Manufacturers

Adaptec	Megahertz
Advanced Micro Devices	Motorola
AMP	National Semiconductor
Epson America	New Media
Hayes	Qlogic
Integral Peripherals	Standard Microsystems
Kingston Technology	US Robotics

companies would meet quarterly to identify new product opportunities. In addition to this agreement, Intel had around 10 percent equity ownership in SystemSoft. The agreement with Intel was the most comprehensive agreement for SystemSoft. However, the company also worked with other companies, such as Microsoft, to codevelop software.

The Call Avoidance Marketplace

When an end user has trouble with her personal computer, she frequently calls the manufacturer's technical support line. This call involves an "interview" stage in which the technical support representative asks a series of questions to diagnose the problem. Many of these calls are for routine problems, yet the sheer volume of calls is quite costly to the manufacturer. SystemSoft's goal was to develop an expert system to diagnose and solve common PC problems. The proposed product was expected to solve many problems, including scanning for and repairing viruses as well as remedying general protection faults, resource conflict, and configuration problems. Automating this process would decrease the number of calls to technical support centers significantly, reducing both the cost to manufacturers and the number of unanswered technical support calls.

The idea for the new product was a result of SystemSoft's huge success with CardWizard, a product launched in early 1995 to solve problems with PC cards. CardWizard enabled mobile computer users to change PC cards without having to stop what they were doing, an ability called hotswapping. Before the release of CardWizard, users often had to restart Windows or even reboot the computer with a different configuration to change cards.

CardWizard simplified changing PC cards because it automatically solved configuration problems, allowing PC cards to be recognized upon insertion. SystemSoft assumed that if it could develop a successful product to solve problems on a specific part of the PC, it could expand the concept of CardWizard to the PC as a whole.

The market research firm Dataquest estimated that more than 200 million calls would be received at technical support centers nationwide in 1996, more than a 67 percent increase from 1992. Dataquest attributed this rise to the dramatic increase in the complexity of new hardware, operating system, and application software products. With the average cost per call exceeding $20, the PC industry would spend nearly $4 billion on "help desk" support in 1996. SystemSoft's proposed call avoidance software would help the PC industry handle its increasingly large number of customer support calls, significantly decreasing the enormous expense of technical support to PC manufacturers.

CyberMedia was the largest competitor in the call avoidance product category. Cyber-Media had a call avoidance software package, First Aid 95, in the retail channel, but the company did not have an OEM presence. First Aid 95 automatically caught problems with PCs and offered a variety of diagnostic programs that let the user pinpoint the cause of other problems, such as the wrong drivers for a sound card. While CyberMedia's product detected common problems, SystemSoft's new product entry would detect and remedy such problems on the spot. No company had developed such complete problem resolution software.

Issues with the New Product

The proposed new product raised both engineering and sales issues for SystemSoft. For the proposed call avoidance software to be successful, SystemSoft would have to enlist the help of many players in the PC industry. The company would need knowledge from software vendors, hardware vendors, and OEMs regarding what should be built into the software. While SystemSoft had established relationships and experience with OEMs, the company did not have experience with either hardware or software vendors. SystemSoft therefore approached Intel and Digital Equipment Corporation (DEC) to solicit feedback on the new product idea and request development assistance. Intel was excited about the possibilities of call avoidance software and provided SystemSoft with access to relevant patent portfolios to develop the product. DEC also was excited about the possibilities that call avoidance software offered. DEC's service arm, Multivendor Service Customer Support, expressed interest in helping SystemSoft determine product requirements and develop the product.

It was also clear that SystemSoft would need to hire additional engineers and create a separate engineering group for the new product. The company had two engineering groups: one dedicated to BIOS software and the other dedicated to PC card software. The two groups required similar skill sets and experience, and engineers could be transferred easily from one group to the other. However, the proposed product would run off servers and builders; therefore, it would require different engineering skills than did SystemSoft's line of system-level software.[5] SystemSoft would have to hire engineers with the appropriate skill sets and create a separate engineering group to maintain and enhance the call avoidance product.

---

[5]Servers are the hardware and software to which all machines on the network are connected. They run the network and store shared information. Builder software is a developmental tool for engineers that allows them to program new information into the knowledge base. It is used to enter information on new problems to keep the problem resolution software updated.

If O'Connell decided to pursue the new product, he had to recommend whether SystemSoft should market it to OEMs as it did its current products or launch it to the retail trade to compete directly against CyberMedia. While CyberMedia's call avoidance software was distributed through the retail channel, SystemSoft lacked a retail presence.[6] The retail channel was different from the OEM channel, particularly with regards to co-op funding and advertising. SystemSoft was an engineering-driven company, and large dollar outlays for such expenses did not fit with its core competencies or corporate strategy.

Selling the call avoidance product through the OEM channel required a very different sales process from that used for SystemSoft's other products. Basically, every PC needs BIOS software and all notebooks need PC card software. As a result, the decision for OEMs is simply a make-or-buy decision—they either purchase the software from another company or develop it themselves. Almost all OEMs purchase BIOS and PC card software as opposed to developing it on their own. Engineering departments typically decide which software to put into the PC; therefore, SystemSoft's sales force had experience in selling solutions directly to engineers.

Call avoidance software, by contrast, was not a necessary product. Thus, the sales force would have to convince companies of the benefits of this new product rather than simply persuading them to purchase SystemSoft software. Furthermore, the product was more complex than system-level software and the decision-making power did not rest with engineers. The technical support center would need a server with special software to run the call avoidance system, and the software would have to be included on each individual PC.

The complexity of the call avoidance system required that the product be sold to several people. SystemSoft's sales force would first have to convince the OEM call center that this product could significantly reduce the amount of calls it received and demonstrate the cost savings that would result from the product.[7] Second, the product manager for the PC line had profit-and-loss responsibility. Therefore, SystemSoft had to persuade the product manager to invest in the product to include it in the PCs. In effect, SystemSoft would have to sell both the call center and the product manager, a time-consuming process since the call center and headquarters of many OEMs are located in different areas of the country.

If O'Connell recommended pursuing the call avoidance market through the OEM channel, how should the sales force be structured? Selling the call avoidance product was more complex and required a different skills set than did selling system-level software. O'Connell could take the most successful salespeople from the PC card and BIOS software and have them sell the new product, but he was unsure how that would affect the current business. Furthermore, it would result in two SystemSoft salespeople calling on each account, which could confuse the customer.

The Decision

The call avoidance market represented a tremendous opportunity for SystemSoft to further its reputation as a technology leader. A successful new product could propel the company into new segments and help stimulate growth in the coming years. However, the risks were numerous. In addition to organizational issues surrounding engineering and sales, another factor complicated O'Connell's decision. The stockholders were pressuring SystemSoft to lower its rising software capitalization costs. Software companies are permitted to capitalize R&D expenses once a product reaches technological feasibility. O'Connell knew that

---

[6]SystemSoft launched its CardWizard PC card product into the retail channel in mid-1995, and while it received strong product reviews, retail was not a successful distribution channel for the company.
[7]An OEM call center is the facility at which technical support calls from customers are received.

pursuing this new product would boost the software capitalization even higher for up to two years. The capitalized costs threaten future earnings because they eventually have to be expensed through amortization. Would the stockholders accept that, or would many begin to sell shares, causing a decline in the valuation of the company?

Should O'Connell pursue this opportunity, or should he recommend that SystemSoft focus on pushing its core products into emerging technologies and further developing SystemSoft's presence in the desktop PC market?

CASE 6–23
LoJack Corporation*

It was February 15, 1994. Dan Michaels, vice president of sales for the LoJack Corporation of Dedham, Massachusetts, was reflecting on the future. One year ago, LoJack had reached an important milestone with the generation of positive earnings of $817,000 before interest, depreciation, and amortization. According to the firm's annual report, this was "the first such earnings in its history." Michaels looked forward to finishing the fiscal year in two more weeks on February 28, 1994. LoJack appeared to be on track toward a profitable year.

Michaels was assessing several strategic challenges faced by LoJack. As the automobile antitheft market continued to grow and the competitive environment became more intense, he needed to evaluate several issues and make recommendations to his boss, Sal Williams, chairman, president, and CEO of LoJack. Michaels needed to evaluate whether the present sales, distribution, and pricing strategies were adequate for future growth. He also had to make recommendations concerning the product line, which was currently limited to one product. Should LoJack diversify, expand within the product category, or find new applications for the product?

The Product

LoJack marketed the LoJack System, a proprietary method used to track and recover stolen automobiles. The LoJack System, LoJack Retrieve priced at $595, was a transmitter the size of a blackboard eraser, hidden by LoJack technicians in one of 30 locations in a vehicle. State police cruisers and municipal police cars in LoJack markets were equipped with scanning units that were used to track and recover stolen vehicles.

When a LoJack-equipped vehicle was stolen, the owner contacted the police. Law enforcement authorities then tracked the car's location, using scanning units in the police cruisers that communicated with the transmitter in the stolen vehicle. Each scanning unit/transceiver covered a distance of 12 to 15 square miles. Multiple cruisers equipped with LoJack equipment provided overlapping coverage and allowed a stolen vehicle, identified by its vehicle identification number, to be tracked within a metropolitan area.

Only 64 percent of stolen cars were recovered nationally. LoJack, however, claimed a 95 percent recovery rate, with most recoveries occurring within two hours of the reported theft. If a stolen vehicle was not recovered within 24 hours, LoJack refunded the cost of the system to the vehicle owner. Vehicles equipped with the LoJack System sustained average

---

*This case was written by Cathy Leach Waters under the supervision of Victoria L. Crittenden, associate professor of marketing at Boston College, as a basis for class discussion rather than to illustrate either effective or ineffective handling of an administrative situation. The material was taken from secondary sources. Pseudonyms are used throughout the case.

damages of $200 to $500, much lower than the national average of $5,000. LoJack's marketing emphasized that the system used only law enforcement personnel in its tracing mechanism, a reflection of the company's beginnings.

The Company

LoJack was formed in 1978 by Lewis McMahon, a former police commissioner in Medfield, Massachusetts. Without a working prototype, the firm was taken public in 1983 to raise funds for product development.

LoJack began marketing the LoJack System in its home state of Massachusetts in 1986. The company knew that before it could offer its antitheft device to the end-user (the car owner), it had to have the cooperation of the local police. The nature of the product rendered it useless unless the police had the monitors necessary to track stolen cars. LoJack donated 250 of these necessary tracking units (at a value of $1,750 each) to the Massachusetts State Police. In July 1986 the Massachusetts State Police began using and testing the LoJack System in conjunction with early sales of the product to car owners. The statistics established during this test were later used to promote the success of the product.

The same year, Sal Williams, an early investor in the firm and a LoJack director since 1981, became chairman after Lewis McMahon resigned when the board pressured him to bring in new management. At the time, the company's financial position was tenuous. Williams had run a sizable nursing home business which he subsequently sold after becoming chairman of LoJack.

In February 1994 LoJack operated in Massachusetts, parts of California, Florida, Michigan, Illinois, Georgia, Virginia, and New Jersey. The firm intended to establish an East Coast corridor by entering four new markets in 1994: Rhode Island, Connecticut, New York, and Washington, D.C. Exhibit 1 provides a map of LoJack's U.S. operations. Additionally, LoJack had signed licensing agreements in the Czech Republic, Slovakia, Greece, the United Kingdom, several Latin American countries, and Hong Kong in the fiscal year ending February 28, 1993, which were worth $2,162,000 in revenue.

At the end of fiscal year 1993, the firm employed 203 people and planned to add 70 during 1994. Exhibit 2 provides financial information on the company.

The Environment

Auto theft was the second fastest growing area of crime in the United States and the riskiest crime for law enforcement officers. In 1990, 1.6 million cars were stolen in the United States with an increase of 1.6 percent in 1991. After increasing for seven years, auto thefts decreased 3 percent in 1992. Reduction in theft stemmed from three main factors: increased public awareness prompting better habits, better coordinated law enforcement, and increased use of antitheft devices.

In Boston, Massachusetts, the "car theft capital of the world" in the mid-1980s, auto theft decreased more than 25 percent from 1987 to 1992, due in part to penalties and incentives offered by the insurance industry for the use of antitheft devices. Owners of selected high-priced cars were subjected to a surcharge of as much as 50 percent of their comprehensive (fire and theft) insurance coverage if they did not have an antitheft device. Furthermore, the insurers offered discounts of up to 35 percent off the annual comprehensive premium if a policyholder installed a recovery device and an alarm or ignition disabler.

Auto theft is not unique to the United States. Hungary had experienced an epidemic of auto theft, and auto theft was rampant in Kenya. Government officials in the United

EXHIBIT 1   LoJack Corporation Geographic Presence in the U.S.A.

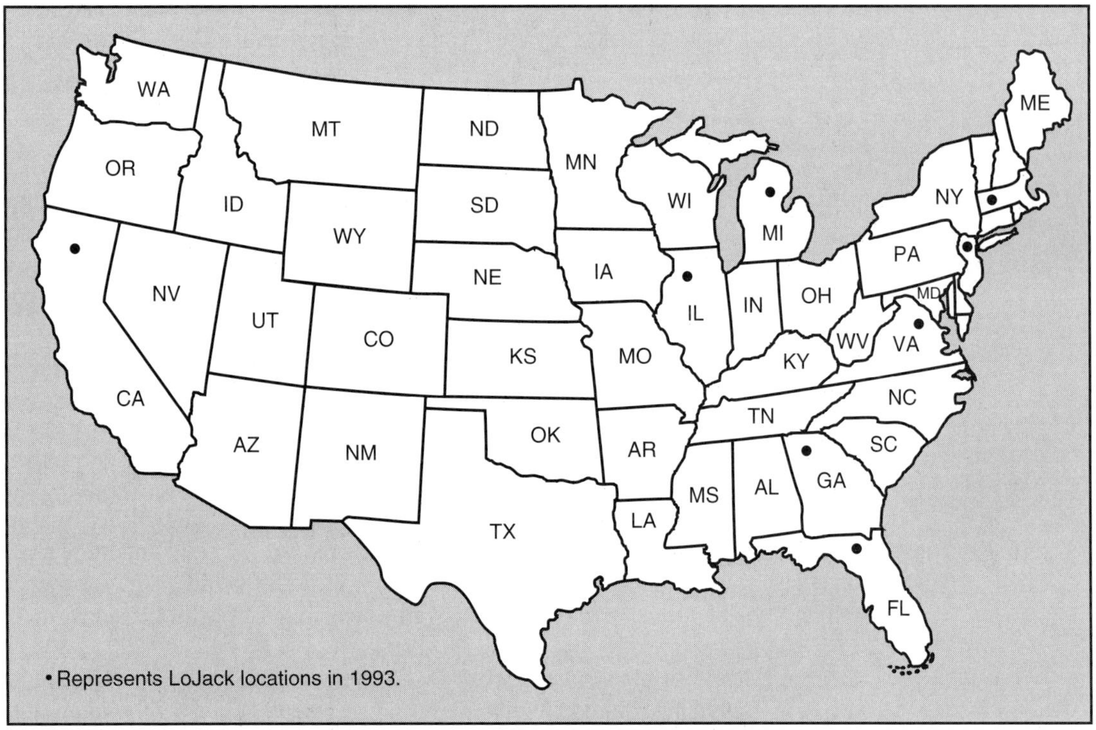

• Represents LoJack locations in 1993.

EXHIBIT 2
LoJack Corporation: Selected Financial Information

Year Ended February 28 ($000)			
	1993	1992	1991
Revenues	$23,346	$17,535	$14,056
Cost of goods sold	12,689	9,520	7,723
Gross margin	10,657	8,015	6,333
Costs and expenses:			
Marketing	5,748	5,202	6,261
Research and development	725	524	215
General & administrative	3,750	3,748	4,066
Depreciation & amortization	1,808	1,856	1,131
Total	12,031	11,330	11,673
Operating loss	(1,374)	(3,315)	(5,340)
Other income (expense):			
Interest expense	(381)	(1,425)	(1,368)
Interest income	14	101	448
Total	(367)	(1,324)	(920)
Net loss	$ (1,741)	$ (4,639)	$ (6,260)

Kingdom, reacting to the 575,000 cars stolen in 1991, had declared 1992 as Car Crime Prevention Year.

In addition to the theft of unattended cars, carjacking became a major concern in the early 1990s. Carjacking is the term used when a car thief confronts the driver of a vehicle and, by using force or threat, demands that the driver surrender the car. Several carjackings that resulted in the death of the driver received enormous media attention in the early 1990s. From 1991 to 1993, there were 40,000 carjackings in the United States, with a predicted 500 percent increase per year.

The Automobile Theft Deterrent Industry

Sales of antitheft devices were expected to grow by 9 percent a year through 1998. In 1992 Americans spent $500 million on antitheft devices for their automobiles. The automobile antitheft device industry included systems both for theft prevention and automobile tracking and recovery. Preventive devices included ignition disablers, steering wheel locks, audible alarms, and motion sensors, all of which were usually enough to deter joyriders. Joyriders are car thieves who steal a car not to dismantle it and sell the parts but for the thrill of the act. Tracking and recovery devices were more costly and aimed at professional thieves.

Preventive Devices

Preventive devices tended to fall into three categories: alarms, locks, and immobilizing devices. Using an alarm as a sole means of prevention was not advised because people walking or driving down the street tended to ignore them. However, alarms were still used as one "layer" in a strategy advocated by the New York City police, who recommended installing a visible preventative such as a sign or steering wheel lock, backed up by an alarm.

Steering wheel locks, a visible locking device, were considered to be the fastest-growing category within the automobile theft prevention segment. Of the $500 million spent on antitheft devices in 1992, 20 percent went toward steering wheel locks. Visible locking devices included The Club, by Winner International, which retailed for $59.95. The Club was a bar-type steering wheel lock that prevented the wheel from turning. The driver had to remember to lock such devices across the steering wheel before leaving the car. Thieves could outwit steering wheel locks by cutting the steering wheel. Winner International had been very successful at gaining a strong low-cost position in the antitheft device market. Over 10 million Clubs, according to Winner's promotional campaign, had been sold.

The Malvy Lock by Malvy Technology, priced at $600 to $800, disengaged the steering wheel from the steering column so it spun freely and no one could drive the car. It reengaged the wheel only after a special ignition key had been inserted. The company boasted that the key had 4 billion possible combinations and could not be duplicated. A similar product called The Blocker, costing $85 to $125, was an electric device that was wired into the ignition and required a proper ignition key to start the car.

Another technique used to prevent would-be thieves from moving a car was electric shock. Secure Products manufactured a device that gave a thief a 5,000-volt shock and shut off the car engine.

Many antitheft devices focused on making a vehicle difficult for a thief to operate after it was stolen. Over two dozen manufacturers marketed electronically operated antitheft devices that generally shut off the engine from afar. The Blackjack ($160) by Clifford Automotive, shut down the automobile engine when the car slowed to three or four miles per hour, if the system had not been deactivated with a private code. Frequently, thieves could duplicate private codes to bypass such systems; Clifford's was advertised as more complex and harder to duplicate. Beeping horns and flashing lights also accompanied the engine shutdown.

Other manufacturers sold similar systems that required the owner to punch a private code into a remote "key-ring" transmitter to disable the system before she could drive the car. Directed Electronics Inc. marketed the Viper 500 Plus system for $299, which included a shock sensor and electronic means of disabling the ignition. For an additional $59, the system could be equipped to prevent the car engine from starting after the owner had alerted the company's dispatch center. Directed Electronics reported sales of $47 million in 1992.

Tracking and Recovery Devices

Professional thieves, headed for a "chop-shop" where car parts were worth three times the market value of the car itself, required extra measures. Tracking and recovery systems appeared to be the best means of fighting the professional, who accounted for 80 percent of stolen vehicles.

Some systems required the owner of a stolen car to call a centralized dispatch center where the alarm company sent out a command to the car that stopped the vehicle. The Posse by Audiovox ($599) gave clients a 24-hour toll-free number to call after they discovered their car had been stolen. The dispatcher sent a signal anywhere in the United States by means of their Sky Tel satellite paging network that disabled the car after it had been turned off. A touted second-generation possibility of the Posse was the ability to locate vehicles using satellite-based global positioning.

Some remote shutdown devices were tied into cellular phones. When sensors determined that a vehicle had been stolen, the owner could dial a monitoring station that sent a stop command to the cellular phone in the stolen car. Code Alarm's Intercept, at $1,495 and monthly monitoring charges of $15, was one such system. It could also be used to track the car location anywhere cellular phone service was available. The tracking was done by the monitoring station and police were later alerted as to the car's whereabouts. Code Alarm made a variety of antitheft devices which were available on Chrysler, Ford, General Motors, and Mitsubishi automobiles. The company had a three-year, $21 million agreement with Ford to supply security devices and keyless entry systems. Code Alarm got about 40 percent of its revenue from sales through manufacturers. The firm's products were available through 10,000 domestic and foreign auto dealers.

In 1994 LoJack's chief competitor in vehicle recovery was International Teletrac of Inglewood, California. When a car equipped with a Teletrac transmitter was started without disarming the system, a signal was immediately sent to the Teletrac monitoring operation. The company tracked the vehicle location and notified police. The system cost $599 in addition to a $15 per month monitoring fee. The Federal Communications Commission (FCC) had approved licenses for Teletrac to operate in 140 of the largest United States metropolitan areas.[1] Teletrac quoted a 95 percent recovery rate of stolen vehicles and professed to be installed in over 8,000 cars. The system was sold mainly by accessory firms (retailers of automotive parts and supplies) who also installed the system. An alarm used to request roadside assistance could be purchased as an optional feature.

Teletrac had over 500 fleet customers and experience in fleet management. Teletrac's management system, installed in vehicles belonging to a fleet, such as a trucking company, was used to keep track of vehicle location for dispatching and routing purposes, among others. Teletrac also offered fleet drivers a remote panic button to ensure worker safety during long road trips and to thwart hijacking attempts. Teletrac used a land-based communications system to track vehicles.

Pinpoint Communications of Dallas, Texas hoped to begin offering low-cost vehicle location services through Value Added Remarketers in 1994.

---

[1]The FCC is an independent regulatory body that oversees domestic and foreign communications by radio, television, wire, and cable.

EXHIBIT 3 **LoJack Corporation Selected Competitive Data**

Company	1992 Revenue ($ millions)	Product	Category	Price
Winner International	$100*	The Club	Steering wheel lock	$60
Directed Electronics	$ 47	The Viper	Prevention, remote shutdown	$359
Audiovox	$344†	The Posse	Remote engine shutdown	$399
Code Alarm	$ 45.7	Intercept	Recovery system	$1,495 1 $14 monthly
International Teletrac	$ 31	Teletrac	Recovery system	$540 1 $15 monthly

*Winner International's 1991 Sales: $8 million.
†Includes business from cellular telephones, automotive sound equipment, automotive accessories, and consumer electronics.
Source: Revenue data from Infotrac; and Jennifer Reese, "How Crime Pays," Fortune, May 31, 1993, p. 15.

Exhibit 3 summarizes selective competitive data.

Technology

The technology used to communicate with vehicles was a key driving force in automobile tracking and recovery. There were four basic technologies used for vehicle tracking and recovery: radio communications, land-based positioning, satellite-based positioning, and cellular communications. Radio frequency communications, used by LoJack, was a mature, simple, and inexpensive technology that worked. The technology, as implemented by LoJack, was not as precise as the other three methods regarding vehicle tracking. LoJack's stolen vehicle network allowed a vehicle to be tracked to within one city block. Radio frequency systems, used by police departments for dispatching and communications for years, could support communication from a vehicle to a monitoring site for applications like roadside assistance. However, LoJack's system did not support such applications in 1994, and there were questions about how such services would be handled, given that LoJack's system was piggybacked on the law enforcement's Police Broadcasting Network.

Land-based systems (one version was used by Teletrac) and satellite-based systems allowed more precise tracking of vehicles, as the software that supported the systems allowed metropolitan maps and grids to be displayed at a monitoring station so dispatchers could literally "see" the route that a vehicle followed. Such systems could be temporarily defeated when vehicles were driven into underground parking garages. Both land and satellite-based systems could be used to provide additional applications besides tracking and recovery, such as roadside assistance and paging.

Most satellite-based systems used Global Positioning Systems (GPS), which sometimes encountered "interruptions" in urban environments where buildings could block communications signals. GPS was more expensive than land-based systems. One fleet-management firm, Qualcomm, charged $4,000 per truck, in addition to computer charges, to perform fleet management activities over their satellite-based communication system. Other satellite-based competitors were Motorola's Coverage PLUS fleet-management offering, and Orbcomm, which planned to offer stolen vehicle recovery service for under $500 early in 1994.

Data transmission over cellular networks (or CDPD—Cellular Digital Packet Data) was expected to become one of the predominant means of transmitting mobile data. McCaw Cellular planned to implement CDPD throughout its network by 1994. Along with providing cellular telephone communications and tracking and recovery over the cellular phone, CDPD also could provide applications such as emergency roadside assistance, data messaging services, fax capability, and paging facilities.

LoJack's Strategy

LoJack's market strategy was to expand the use of its technology into U.S. and international markets where the combination of population density, new car sales, and vehicle theft was high. Population growth statistics showed that Florida, where LoJack had operations, reflected the major growth in the United States during the 1970s and 1980s. Exhibit 4 lists the top 40 ranking of metropolitan statistical areas by population change from 1970 to 1990. Exhibit 5 shows a geographic breakdown of the U.S. resident population.

The world's 10 most populous nations included China, India, Russia, United States, Indonesia, Brazil, Japan, Nigeria, Bangladesh, and Pakistan. Fourteen European countries

EXHIBIT 4
Population Growth, 1970–1990: Metropolitan Statistical Areas

Source: American Business Climate and Economic Profiles.

1. Naples, FL
2. Fort Myers–Cape Coral, FL
3. Fort Pierce, FL
4. Ocala, Fl
5. Las Vegas, NV
6. West Palm Beach–Boca Raton–Delray Beach, FL
7. Orlando, FL
8. Sarasota, FL
9. Riverside–San Bernardino, CA
10. Daytona Beach, FL
11. Phoenix, AZ
12. Bradenton, FL
13. Austin, TX
14. McAllen—Edinburg–Mission, TX
15. Reno, NV
16. Bryan–College Station, TX
17. Olympia, WA
18. Fort Collins, Loveland, CO
19. Fort Lauderdale–Hollywood–Pompano Beach, FL
20. Las Cruces, NM
21. Provo–Orem, UT
22. Modesto, CA
23. Tucson, AZ
24. Santa Rosa–Petaluma, CA
25. Redding, CA
26. Tampa–St. Petersburg–Clearwater, FL
27. Bremerton, WA
28. Santa Cruz, CA
29. Vancouver, WA
30. Brownsville–Harlingen, TX
31. San Diego, CA
32. Boise City, ID
33. Laredo, TX
34. Vallejo–Fairfield–Napa, CA
35. Anchorage, AK
36. Chico, CA
37. Lakeland–Winter Haven, FL
38. Brazoria, TX
39. Oxnard–Ventura, CA
40. Sacramento, CA

EXHIBIT 5
U.S. Resident Population (thousands)

Source: U.S. Bureau of the Census, Statistical Abstract of the United States: 1993,113th ed. (Washington, D.C.: U.S. Government Printing Office, 1993).

	1990	1991	1992
Northeast			
Maine	1,228	1,234	1,235
New Hampshire	1,109	1,104	1,111
Vermont	563	567	570
Massachusetts	6,016	5,996	5,998
Rhode Island	1,003	1,005	1,005
Connecticut	3,287	3,289	3,281
New York	17,990	18,055	18,119
New Jersey	7,730	7,753	7,789
Pennsylvania	11,866	11,882	12,009
Midwest			
Ohio	10,847	10,941	11,016
Indiana	5,544	5,610	5,662
Illinois	11,431	11,541	11,631
Michigan	9,295	9,380	9,437
Wisconsin	4,892	4,956	5,007
Minnesota	4,375	4,432	4,480
Iowa	2,777	2,795	2,812
Missouri	5,117	5,157	5,193
North Dakota	639	635	636
South Dakota	696	704	711
Nebraska	1,578	1,593	1,606
Kansas	2,478	2,495	2,523
South			
Delaware	666	680	689
Maryland	4,781	4,859	4,908
Washington, D.C.	607	595	589
Virginia	6,187	6,280	6,377
West Virginia	1,793	1,803	1,812
North Carolina	6,629	6,736	6,843
South Carolina	3,487	3,560	3,603
Georgia	6,478	6,623	6,751
Florida	12,938	13,266	13,488
Kentucky	3,685	3,713	3,755
Tennessee	4,877	4,953	5,024
Alabama	4,041	4,091	4,136
Mississippi	2,573	2,593	2,614
Arkansas	2,351	2,373	2,399
Louisiana	4,220	4,254	4,287
Oklahoma	3,146	3,175	3,212
Texas	16,987	17,348	17,656
West			
Montana	799	809	824
Idaho	1,077	1,040	1,067
Wyoming	454	460	466
Colorado	3,294	3,378	3,470
New Mexico	1,515	1,549	1,581
Arizona	3,665	3,748	3,832
Utah	1,723	1,770	1,813
Nevada	1,202	1,283	1,327
Washington	4,867	5,012	5,136
Oregon	2,842	2,922	2,977
California	29,760	30,380	30,867
Alaska	550	570	587
Hawaii	1,108	1,137	1,160

EXHIBIT 6
Top Export Markets of The United States

1. Canada
2. Japan
3. Mexico
4. United Kingdom
5. Germany
6. Netherlands
7. France
8. Saudi Arabia
9. Benelux
10. Venezuela

were projected to have no increase in population through 2025: Austria, Belgium, Denmark, Finland, Germany, Greece, Ireland, Italy, the Netherlands, Norway, Portugal, Sweden, Switzerland, and the United Kingdom. However, some countries, such as Ethiopia, Kenya, Tanzania, Iraq, Libya, and Saudi Arabia, were expected to triple in population between 1987 and 2025. Exhibit 6 lists the top export markets for the United States.

U.S. new cars were running at an annual rate of 13 million in January 1994. This compared to slightly less than 12 million in January 1993. The three largest U.S. domestic brands were General Motors, Ford, and Chrysler. The largest noncaptive imports included Toyota (24 percent), Honda (17 percent), Nissan (16 percent), and Mazda (10 percent). (These percentages represent the company's portion of total noncaptive import new car sales in the United States.) The largest-selling luxury cars in the United States were represented by such European companies as Volvo, BMW, and Mercedes-Benz. As a whole, U.S. brands held the largest percentage (around 65 percent) of new car sales in the United States, with Japanese brands at about 30 percent of U.S. new cars sales, followed by European brands with 4 percent and Korean brands with 1 percent.

Within the United States, California represented about 10 percent of all new car sales. Rental companies purchased about 20 percent of the U.S. new car volume, with Florida rental agencies representing close to 5 percent of U.S. new car sales. The United States had approximately 25,000 car dealerships in the early 1990s.

Exhibit 7 lists the top 25 U.S. cities for motor vehicle theft when theft is adjusted for population.

New Market Entry

The first step in entering a market involved convincing the state police of LoJack's value as a tool in stolen automobile recovery. Concurrent to the process of convincing state police of LoJack's effectiveness, the firm also called on other groups who influenced law enforcement decisions. For example, LoJack government affairs personnel called on state insurance commissioners, other government and municipal officials, and insurance company executives to help influence the law enforcement decision-making process.

Once a state's police force agreed to use LoJack systems in their cruisers, an agreement was signed to use LoJack exclusively for auto recovery. The agreement was valid for anywhere from 5 to 10 years. LoJack donated the tracking systems, each worth $1,750, to the police. For example, LoJack donated 450 tracking units (valued at almost $1 million) to the Los Angeles police department, and also installed and serviced the units.

LoJack also had to interact with the Federal Communications Commission. In 1989, the FCC had allowed LoJack to use radio frequency 173.075 MHz nationwide to operate their tracking network. LoJack used existing police antennas to install the equipment needed to communicate over the radio-based Police Broadcasting Network.

EXHIBIT 7
Motor Vehicle Theft, 1991

Source: U.S. Federal Bureau of Investigation, *Crime in the United States.*

U.S. Cities	Offenses Known To Police per 100,000 Population
Newark, NJ	5,049
Fresno, CA	3,184
Fort Worth, TX	2,946
Detroit, MI	2,774
Atlanta, GA	2,732
Dallas, TX	2,439
Houston, TX	2,411
Boston, MA	2,350
Jersey City, NJ	2,350
Miami, FL	2,347
St. Louis, MO	2,313
Kansas City, MO	2,256
Memphis, TN	2,159
Milwaukee, WI	2,133
Tampa, FL	2,113
Cleveland, OH	2,085
Pittsburgh, PA	2,008
Sacramento, CA	2,004
New Orleans, LA	1,975
Los Angeles, CA	1,929
Oakland, CA	1,916
New York, NY	1,904
San Diego, CA	1,872
Stockton, CA	1,780
Chicago, IL	1,686

After appropriate law enforcement officials had agreed to use LoJack and after LoJack had trained police officers to operate the tracking system, the LoJack System was marketed to vehicle owners. It sometimes took up to four years to "sign up" a new market.

Ninety-five percent of LoJack's sales were through new car dealers. More than 3,000 dealers had been signed to sell the LoJack system. However, the firm was happy to install a LoJack system if a new car buyer requested it, regardless of whether the dealer was a designated LoJack dealer. Consumers could call LoJack directly on a toll-free telephone number to arrange for the installation of the LoJack System at their home, office, or dealership. LoJack installation technicians drove company vans to install the LoJack System wherever it was needed.

Licensing

In November 1993 the firm had agreed to license the LoJack recovery system to Clifford Electronics, a major competitor based in California. The nonexclusive license allowed Clifford to sell the LoJack System as "Intellisearch" through aftermarket automotive retailers. Intellisearch used LoJack's established tracking network for vehicle recovery. The agreement was viewed as a test of retail distribution for the product. Retail outlets, typically automotive shops that stocked parts and accessories, tended to sell many antitheft devices aimed at "DIYs" (Do It Yourselfers).

Pricing

LoJack's Prevent option provided an alarm and starter-disabler for $100, which could be purchasd on top of the basic $595 LoJack Retrieve system. To many customers, "their LoJack" was the remote starter-disabler attached to their keyring, the only visible part of the LoJack system. LoJack felt strongly about not charging monthly fees for tracking and recovery services since many customers never had to actually use their LoJack System. The company did not want a customer's only perception of LoJack to be a bill that had to be paid every month, like an insurance premium, for monitoring services. Furthermore, LoJack Corporation was not equipped to operate the billing and payment processing system needed to support monthly monitoring fees.

Advertising and Promotion

Radio advertising was the company's dominant form of communication with the marketplace. Ads featured true success stories and were a "play-by-play" format documenting what happened from the moment the owner of a LoJack-equipped car discovered his or her car had been stolen to the time the car was recovered by the police. The ads had an official tone to them, reminiscent of a news story or an official police bulletin. LoJack had experimented with limited television advertising outside the Massachusetts area. Approximately 25 cents out of every dollar of revenue was spent on advertising.

LoJack received a significant amount of publicity from news releases that documented successful vehicle recoveries that were attributable to the LoJack System. In addition, whenever a new market was opened, newspapers usually featured prominent local officials praising LoJack.

LoJack periodically motivated car dealers to sell LoJack Systems by offering discounts. Since dealers usually sold a variety of theft-prevention products, LoJack found that the dealers invariably sold whatever product was being discounted.

The Future

Dan Michaels was thankful to be involved with such an exciting product in a growing market. He could not help wondering if he should listen to comments made by LoJack customers and others about additional uses for the LoJack transmitter. Applications including child safety, furloughed prisoner and parolee tracking, and high-valued item protection were just a few of the ideas interested parties had brainstormed for LoJack. He needed to consider whether the firm was ready to take on the added complexity of new product applications in addition to addressing the issues already posed by the existing product. He picked up his telephone to schedule a meeting with Sal Williams to discuss the future marketing strategy for LoJack.

Sources

Alster, Norm. "A Car Thief's Nemesis." *Forbes* 149, no. 10 (May 11, 1992), pp. 124–25.

American Business Climate and Economic Profiles.

Beck, Ernest. "Budapest's Car-Alarm Entrepreneurs Capitalize on City's Easy-Street Image." *The Wall Street Journal*, October 25, 1993, p. A5A.

Blauth, John. "Ringing the Alarm on Soaring Car Crime." *Accountant's Magazine*, September 1992, p. 31.

Bohon, C. D. "Just How Bad Is It?" *Auto Age*, August 1993.

Candler, Julie. "Ways to Outsmart Vehicle Thieves." *Nation's Business*, July 1993, pp. 35–36.

Chappell, Lindsay. "Program Cars Turns Quagmire." *Advertising Age*, March 30, 1992, p. S51.

Coeyman, Marjorie. "Automotive Market Firms Up—But So Do Competitive Pressures." *Chemical Week*, March 2, 1994, p. 9.

Cohen, Jeffrey. "Making Car Theft More Difficult." *The New York Times*, October 28, 1993. p. C2.

Coxeter, Ruth. "Hey Car Thieves, Try to Drive This One Off." *Business Week*, November 8, 1993, p. 99.

"Directed Electronics Viper Line Adds Anti-Carjacking System." *HFD*, December 13, 1993, p. 105.

Driscoll, Clement. "Automated Vehicle Location Increases Productivity & Security." *Automotive Fleet*, September 1993, pp. 74–79.

Exportise: An International Trade Source Book for Small Company Executives (Boston: Small Business Foundation of America, 1987).

"Fall & Winter Selling Guide: Security Products." *Automotive Marketing*, July 1993, p. 67.

"FCC Allocates Spectrum . . ." *FCC News*, August 29, 1989.

Hass, Nancy. "Deal Them In." *Financial World*, September 3, 1991, pp. 20–22.

Hovelson, Jack. "High-Tech Systems Help Thwart Car Thieves." *USA Today*, October 1, 1993.

Kindleberger, Richard. "Top Stolen Cars to Be Costly." *Boston Globe*, August 1, 1990, pp. 55–56.

Kott, Douglas. "LoJack Puts Police on the Offensive to Recover Stolen Cars." *Road & Track*, November 1989, p. 133.

LoJack Annual Report—1993.

"LoJack License Pact with Clifford for Stolen Vehicle-Recovery System." *HFD*, November 29, 1993, p. 75.

Martin, Mary. "Reporting a Recovery." *Boston Globe*, February 6, 1994, pp. A4–A5.

Mwangi, Patrick. "Car Thefts Hit Kenyan Insurers." *African Business*, April 1993, p. 40.

Olenick, Doug. "Audiovox Corp. Shipping POSSE." *HFD*, November 15, 1993, p. 104.

———."Ford, GM Canada in Code Alarm Deal." *HFD*, September 13, 1993, p. 98.

Ryan, Ken. "Auto-Security Business Booms." *HFD*, April 12, 1993, p. 145.

Serafin, Raymond, and Cleveland Horton. "GM Claims the Inroads in California." *Advertising Age*, January 31, 1994, p. 36.

Sinanoglu, Elif. "Stop Carjackers in Their Tracks." *Money*, September 1993, p. 20.

Terpstra, Vern, and Ravi Sarathy. *International Marketing* (Chicago: Dryden Press, 1991).

Torcellini, Carolyn. "Beep, Beep." *Forbes*, December 25, 1989, p. 10.

———. "To Catch a Thief." *Forbes*, April 17, 1989, p. 202.

Ward's Automotive Yearbook—1993.

Woods, Bill. "Bad News for Crooks, Good News for You . . ." *Corvette World*, August 1990, p. 24.

Case 6–24

Powrtron Corporation

In mid-January 1998 senior management at Powrtron Corporation was grappling with an unprecedented problem of constrained capacity. Allyson Shelton (chief operating officer), Bryce Thomason (sales and marketing manager), and Jason Stewart (manufacturing manager) were meeting to discuss the capacity situation and its snowball effect on late deliveries and customer dissatisfaction.

Tension was high at the start of the meeting, and Shelton feared that the air would only become thicker when she delivered the message from Bradley Keith, the company's principal owner and CEO. Senior management had expected Keith to announce that the company would move to a larger location within the next year. However, on the previous day Keith had informed Shelton that such a move would definitely not take place within the next 12 months. Recognizing that some type of prioritizing would have to take place, he had advised Shelton to work out the capacity, delivery, and customer problems at her meeting with Thomason and Stewart the next day.

A bottom-line person, Shelton knew that Powrtron management quickly had to devise a way to determine the appropriate mix of product development, existing product management, customer prioritization, and customer service.

The Company

Located in Newton, Massachusetts, Powrtron was a private, predominantly family-held company with sales of around $8.4 million. Founded in 1965 by three brothers, the company still operated out of its original building (with some modest additions) on land owned by the founding families.[1] From its inception and into the late 1970s the company exclusively manufactured products in the analog integrated circuit business, using designs principally developed by the youngest of the brothers (then chief engineer), Bradley Keith.[2] Most Powrtron products were designed into customers' new applications. In the late 1970s Bradley Keith developed a unique, slim design for power converters which soon became a major part of the company's business. By the beginning of 1998 Powrtron was engaged in the manufacture and sale of electronic analog circuit modules, isolation amplifiers, and power converters.

Exhibit 1 shows the firm's organizational structure. Three of the functional managers, including the heads of manufacturing and sales and marketing, had been with the firm less than two and a half years. Top management viewed manufacturing as the strongest func-

---

[1] Increased real estate prices for industrial property in Newton (an immediate suburb of Boston) made the land worth many times its original cost. Estimated value exceeded $9 million.

[2] Unlike his older brothers, who were trained as financial economists at local Ivy League colleges, Bradley Keith received two math degrees from Boston College (BC). Then, over a seven-year span, while working on various defense-related projects at a local multinational electronics firm, Keith earned an engineering degree from Northeastern University (NU) in Boston. He had received four patents. He also had a number of other process and product inventions that probably were patentable if he took the time and effort to apply. Over the years Keith also completed various graduate business courses at BC and NU, but he had not completed a business degree program.

This case was prepared by Victoria L. Crittenden of Boston College and William F. Crittenden of Northeastern University as the basis for class discussion rather than to illustrate effective or ineffective handling of a managerial situation. Powrtron is a pseudonym, and some data have been disguised. All relevant relationships remain constant.

EXHIBIT 1
**Organization
Structure**

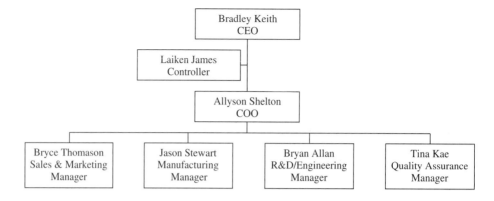

EXHIBIT 2
Income Statement

	1997	1996	1995
Sales	$8,415,393	$7,781,933	$7,548,474
Cost of sales	5,380,077	4,702,145	4,462,281
Gross margin	3,035,316	3,079,788	3,086,193
Operating costs			
Research and development	668,136	529,180	515,973
Sales and marketing	659,393	786,827	761,452
General and administration	1,067,474	1,062,321	1,028,858
OC subtotal	2,395,003	2,378,328	2,306,283
Operating income	640,313	701,460	779,910
Other income	0	0	38,900
Interest expenses			
Shareholders	264,000	264,000	264,000
Bank	118,397	121,878	128,843
Other expenses	218,837	274,584	298,821
Income before taxes	$ 39,079	$ 40,998	$ 127,146

tional area, with marketing seen as the weakest. The company's manufacturing capacity was physically constrained by the current location and a tight local labor market which made it difficult to find qualified new people at wages that would keep Powrtron's labor costs competitive. Exhibits 2 and 3 provide recent financial information.

Powrtron produced seven major products in-house. Its perceived competitive strength was providing customized, advanced-technology products to quality-conscious customers. Quality was designed into the product, and a rigorous quality assurance program kept returns at a level well below industry averages. A key accounts policy was viewed as the most effective way to take advantage of Powrtron's strengths, with a standard line of products being the means to generate accounts initially. Management believed that the key to implementing this strategy was to provide a balance of standard and custom products to its customers.

Products

Two analog business products—the pincushion integrated circuit module (PIN) and the isolation amplifier/analog multiplier (IAAM)—generally provided Powrtron with its best gross margins. The pincushion correction device corrected for geometric or focus distortion for CRT displays. Typical applications included airborne displays, air traffic control

EXHIBIT 3
Balance Sheet

	Dec 31, 1997	Dec 31, 1996	Dec 31, 1995
Current assets			
Cash	$ 123,812	$ 98,634	$ 93,523
Accounts receivables	803,732	784,991	787,524
Less: Allowance for bad debts	(31,000)	(31,000)	(31,000)
Inventory	318,453	321,964	326,047
Less: Allowance for obsolescence	(50,000)	(50,000)	(50,000)
Prepaid expenses	16,026	9,877	7,794
Total current assets	1,181,023	1,134,466	1,133,888
Fixed assets			
Machinery and equipment	1,457,023	1,457,023	1,457,023
Furniture and fixtures	253,685	253,685	253,685
Leasehold improvements	0	0	0
Automobile	38,979	38,979	38,979
Less: Accumulated depreciation	(1,529,223)	(1,502,623)	(1,476,023)
Net fixed assets	220,464	247,064	273,664
Total assets	1,401,487	1,381,530	1,407,552
Current liabilities			
Demand note payable	1,392,902	1,392,902	1,392,902
Current maturities of lease	0	0	0
Accounts payable	266,538	253,048	274,736
Payroll taxes payable	34,923	33,876	$35,023
Accrued payroll	235,039	243,024	293,024
Accrued interest	280,000	300,085	323,054
Other	103,726	111,234	109,067
Total current liabilities	2,313,128	2,334,169	2,427,806
Long-term liabilities			
Notes payable to shareholders	1,750,000	1,750,000	1,750,000
Shareholders' equity			
Common stock	920,000	920,000	920,000
Retained earnings	(3,581,641)	(3,622,639)	(3,690,254)
Total liabilities and equity	$1,401,487	$1,381,530	$1,407,552

systems, medical monitors, and CAD displays. Two distinct lines of the PIN product existed. Powrtron manufactured PIN100s, with PIN300s being a buy/resale product. Isolation amplifiers could be used in a variety of situations, including industrial process control, instrumentation (data acquisition), and medical (ECG, EEG, ENG, and other types of medical monitoring). Worldwide sales of analog circuit devices were estimated at around US$12 billion, with the consumer market (video and portable phones) accounting for approximately 40 percent of demand.

With the increased use of sophisticated analog and digital devices in many types of electronic systems, DC/DC power converters were necessary products for design engineers. The converter provided the electronic system with the regulated voltage required through local transformation of power supply voltages. Applications included telecommunications, robotics, remote systems, battery-operated systems, uninterruptable power systems, test instrumentation, and ground support equipment. Five products constituted Powrtron's major lines of DC/DC converters: DCD, DCT, DCJ, DCX, and DCZ. The depths of these product lines varied and depended on such issues as power range, input voltage, output voltage, and whether output was regulated. Problems had occurred in the DC/DC converter business, however, in that Powrtron had not been able to produce large quantities of low-cost standardized products successfully.

The worldwide power converter market was estimated at around US$10 billion. These sales experienced less volatility than did the sales of the more complex integrated circuits. However, there were industrywide concerns that this market had reached maturity, leading to long-term concern about the overall health of the marketplace. At the same time, there was surprise that the market had proved to be as resilient as it was to market encroachment by analog devices.

Stewart and Thomason provided numerous personal insights and concerns about each of Powrtron's seven products. The PIN and DCT offerings were thought to be good, stable products with continued market potential. Although the IAAM was an important contributor to company margins, each manager independently expressed some concern about whether Powrtron could compete in the long term with this product. Stewart had determined that the DCD market was not growing and had plans to phase out the line. However, Powrtron had experienced recent interest in the product. Thomason was attempting to determine if this was just a short-term blip on the screen or if the market was beginning to recover. The DCJ was a small-volume business and had extremely volatile margins. However, the firm continued to make the product and had seen sales increase in 1996 and again in 1997. Stewart viewed the DCX product line as the big loser in the firm. Thomason acknowledged that the DCX was in a decline but did not agree that it was a big loser. Both Stewart and Thomason agreed that the DCZ line of products was the future of power converters at Powrtron. However, although demand had jumped 600 percent, current sales were not meeting expectations and the company was having trouble perfecting the product for the marketplace.

Additionally, Powrtron made variations of the seven products ("specials") that did not fit solely within any of the product lines. Powrtron also would purchase products for resale if its customers needed products not available from Powrtron and did not want to shop around for the product themselves.

Customers

Powrtron had three tiers of accounts. The first tier consisted of three major customers for which Powrtron made unique, specialized products. Close business relationships existed between Powrtron and those three accounts. CEO Bradley Keith had himself made the original contact and sale with those long-time customers. Allyson Shelton, COO, now personally oversaw individual account sales of around $850,000 annually to each of those accounts. Powrtron management considered the first tier of accounts as a "separate business." The margins on business from those accounts approximated Powrtron's average, and those customers kept their promises and paid in a timely fashion.

Second-tier accounts consisted of 10 major customers and 7 minor customers, with total sales of around $4,000,000 annually. The 10 major second-tier accounts were labeled HF, TI, RO, GE, AT, GN, NA, AC, SA, and WC. Seven of the major accounts provided between $400,000 and $580,000 each in yearly sales. Thomason indicated that the remaining three major accounts had strong potential for growth. Nine of the 10 major accounts purchased Powrtron-manufactured products. Purchases from the tenth account (WC) consisted of the company's buy/resale product offering only. Shelton, Thomason, and Stewart agreed that the seven minor accounts were important to Powrtron because of their market potential or the combination of products purchased.

Powrtron attempted to develop second-tier accounts into key accounts (tier 1 accounts) through individual service provided by sales and marketing. However, actual purchases

EXHIBIT 4
Product/Account Purchases

Accounts	PIN	IAAM	DCD	DCT	DCJ	DCX	DCZ	Specials
HF				x		x		x
TI			x	x	x	x		
RO	x	x	x	x		x		x
GE	x	x						x
AT				x	x	x		x
GN	x						x	
NA			x				x	
AC								x
SA							x	

were made through the local sales representative and not directly to Powrtron. Sales representatives' commissions were 7 percent for sales made to three of the accounts (TI, NA, AC) and 6 percent for sales made to the remaining accounts. Exhibit 4 provides an overview of Powrtron-manufactured products purchased by the nine major accounts. Exhibit 5 shows total 1993–1997 second-tier account sales for each of the seven products manufactured by Powrtron.

The third tier of accounts consisted of around $1,900,000 in sales of Powrtron-manu-factured standard products to many different customers. Individual sales to each of those customers did not amount to a large enough dollar total to warrant separate consideration of each account. These customers did not receive special sales attention from a Powrtron manager and made purchases exclusively through the local manufacturer's representative organization. The rep organization's role was simply that of order taker.

Competition

Japanese manufacturers held the leading share (35 percent) in the $12 billion analog circuit business. This was followed by the United States (25 percent), Europe (20 percent), and then the rest of the world. Leading worldwide competitors and their estimated market shares included National Semiconductor (7 percent), Texas Instruments (6 percent), Philips/Signetics (5.7 percent), Toshiba (5.6 percent), Sanyo (5.5 percent), Matsushita (5.1 percent), SGS/Thomson (4.7 percent), Motorola Inc. (4.4 percent), NEC Corp. (4.3 percent), Hitachi (4.1 percent), and Mitsubishi (4.1 percent). These large firms had significant scale advantages throughout the value chain and tended to exclusively produce highly standardized products. The battle for market share among these firms was fiercely competitive, as even a fraction of a percentage point meant millions of dollars in sales. Midsize firms (those with less than 2 percent market share) tended to come under close competitive scrutiny whenever they appeared to encroach on the high-volume, standardized portion of this business. The most profitable midsize firms tended to be subsidiaries of much larger, vertically integrated firms. Smaller firms tended to be highly focused around a single core technology that was used as the basis for quickly producing a highly customized product.

Competition in the $10 billion power converter business was enormous, with thousands of worldwide competitors. The most successful competitors appeared to be able to blend high-margin customized production with high-volume, good-margin standardized manu-facturing. There were successful small firms that focused exclusively on customized pro-duction. However, those firms often incurred substantial problems in an economic

EXHIBIT 5
Product Sales and Average Price for Second-Tier Accounts

	Unit Volume	Total Sales	Average Price
PIN			
1993	309	$117,487	$380
1994	310	123,054	397
1995	341	141,731	416
1996	1,890	718,281	380
1997	2,701	1,059,091	392
IAAM			
1993	17	1,683	99
1994	158	13,866	88
1995	1,558	133,987	86
1996	5,039	428,355	85
1997	5,543	509,956	92
DCD			
1993	0	0	0
1994	66	10,248	155
1995	199	32,452	163
1996	66	11,838	179
1997	398	66,466	167
DCT			
1993	627	206,910	330
1994	1,739	554,741	319
1995	1,927	447,064	232
1996	1,884	465,348	247
1997	1,841	489,706	266
DCJ			
1993	1,254	109,098	87
1994	1,326	125,970	95
1995	838	71,896	86
1996	818	80,981	99
1997	917	80,696	88
DCX			
1993	1,686	153,246	91
1994	2,806	238,510	85
1995	123	14,637	119
1996	345	36,915	107
1997	80	9,280	116
DCZ			
1993	0	0	0
1994	0	0	0
1995	0	0	0
1996	2,085	223,095	107
1997	13,694	1,410,482	103

downturn. Companies operating in this industry included Vicor Corp., Theta-J, Unitech P.L.C., Rifa, Astec, and Lambda Electronics. Competitors seemed keenly aware whenever Powrtron captured significant business beyond its first-tier accounts. Thus, bids for repeat business, which would allow Powrtron to obtain some learning-curve advantages, were always highly competitive.

Operations at Powrtron

The manufacturing facility was located in the same building as management offices in Newton, Massachusetts. The manufacturing area totaled 14,500 square feet, the engineering area was 5,000 square feet, and the quality control area was 1,500 square feet. The engineering group (not including CEO Keith) had over 40 years of experience in the power design field. A computer-aided design (CAD) system was used for schematic design, layout, and documentation processes utilized by the engineering group. The CAD system had a direct parts-list link to the materials requirements planning (MRP II) system utilized by the manufacturing group. The MRP II system continuously monitored order status, inventory, and customer inquiries.

Although much of the manufacturing equipment was of an older vintage, every piece of equipment was kept in perfect operating condition. In addition, the shop floor was kept well organized and immaculate, and the equipment layout maximized the use of available space.

Powrtron employed 60 direct labor personnel and 10 indirect labor personnel in the manufacturing process. The manufacturing work force was unionized. Yet CEO Keith had a strong affinity with his production people, and labor issues were few and infrequent. Over 70 percent of the production work force had been with Powrtron for at least 20 years, and a number of workers had been with the company since its beginning. The company's location was near many long-time employees' homes and was convenient for those using mass transit systems. Keith knew all his employees and a fair amount about their families as well. During the recession of the late 1980s–early 1990s no one was ever laid off. Instead, workers were asked to take one day a month of unpaid time off.

Now that the economy was again strong and the firm was showing profitability, Stewart had suggested that a new office location/production facility be acquired to enhance the firm's capacity and production capabilities. With an order backlog of around 20 percent for tier 2 and tier 3 accounts (tier 1 account orders were prioritized and moved near the top of the queue) and sales projecting a 10 percent increase for 1998, Stewart looked toward moving to a larger facility with modern equipment and increased hiring to relieve capacity pressures.

While CEO Keith had established connections for offshore manufacturing capabilities in the Caribbean and the Far East, the company had never augmented its production volume through any of those sources. Engineering head Bryan Allan and quality assurance manager Tina Kae each expressed concerns regarding the sharing of proprietary information with firms in less developed countries (LDCs).

Every Powrtron product was subjected to a six-step quality inspection process as well as two electrical/functional tests. CEO Keith was proud that quality was designed into each of Powrtron's products and that the quality assurance program, although time-consuming, ensured that Powrtron maintained a lower failure rate than did most of its direct competitors.

Stewart allocated around 10,500 hours each quarter to producing the seven products for second- and third-tier accounts (approximately one-third of production time was allotted to servicing tier 1 accounts, and the remaining time was used for setup, maintenance and repair, and producing "specials" for second- and third-tier accounts). Overtime was very expensive, and most of the current work force preferred to not work extra hours. Stewart's expected allocated hourly product capacity utilization during 1998 for each product is shown in Exhibit 6. However, since the major factor was total production hour availability, Stewart used this only as a general guide to allocation. Exhibits 7 and 8 provide cost information (variable and setup) and production time for each of the major product lines.

EXHIBIT 6
Expected Allocation of Available Production Hours (Quarterly)

Product	Hours
PIN	1,300
IAAM	1,300
DCD	350
DCT	1,000
DCJ	400
DCX	350
DCZ	5,800

EXHIBIT 7
Variable Cost per Unit and Setup Cost per Run

Product	Variable Cost/Unit	Setup Cost/Run
PIN	$75.00	$5.20
IAAM	35.00	4.15
DCD	65.00	4.15
DCT	75.00	7.25
DCJ	65.00	4.15
DCX	45.00	6.25
DCZ	55.00	6.25

EXHIBIT 8
Production Time per Unit and Setup Time per Run

Product	Production Time/ Unit (hours)	Setup Time/ Run (hours)
PIN	1.00	0.25
IAAM	0.60	0.20
DCD	1.00	0.20
DCT	1.50	0.35
DCJ	1.00	0.20
DCX	1.05	0.30
DCZ	1.33	0.30

Although Powrtron's manufacturing group had not previously dealt with constrained capacity, Stewart and the production people were not at a loss for ideas on how to approach the problem. Some people believed they should fill orders relative to the desired amount. (Some thought this meant the largest orders should be filled first, while others believed it meant the accounts with smaller orders should be filled first.) Others thought the marketing group should be forced to rank orders by account priority. Some felt they should focus on producing the most standardized requests (those requiring the least customization of the core product), while others believed they should fill a certain minimum amount for each account. Other ideas generated throughout the organization included fill best prices first, fill orders by account profitability, and fill orders based on product profitability.

Current Problem

Basically, Shelton, Thomason, and Stewart were meeting to discuss how Powrtron could better balance supply and demand. But Shelton knew that the issue involved more than economics. Thomason and Stewart had literally been at each other's necks over the past couple of months. Not only did the company have irate customers due to slow or late deliveries, Powrtron's senior managers were barely speaking to each other.

Not wasting any time on social interaction at the start of the meeting, Bryce Thomason told Shelton that Stewart's group was responsible for the problems he was having with his second-tier accounts. Thomason said that Powrtron's competitors were promising (and delivering) in a maximum of six weeks from the sale. Therefore, he felt that he had to make the same commitment if Powrtron's second-tier accounts were to continue doing business with the company. Unfortunately, while Thomason indicated that Powrtron's competition was satisfying its delivery commitments, Shelton knew Powrtron had not delivered on time in the last four months. Thomason thought that Stewart was not dedicated to the firm's key account strategy. He felt that without this commitment, Powrtron might as well provide standard, off-the-shelf products and forget the key account focus.

Angrily, Jason Stewart told Thomason that sales and marketing was making unreasonable promises by pushing ahead its delivery date commitments. Stewart said that Thomason and his sales staff were being unrealistic by ignoring the firm's capacity limits, particularly with respect to backlog, run cycles, and downtime. With the current capacity situation, Stewart felt that the delivery cycle should be twice the time Thomason was telling customers. Stewart said that the only relief in sight was the upcoming move to a larger production facility. He said, "Powrtron will be able to expand its production capabilities once we are able to add equipment and laborers. Until then the company will not be able to make and deliver products any faster."

Things were heating up much more quickly than Shelton had anticipated. The meeting had not gotten off to a good start. Unfortunately, Shelton knew that her announcement about the delay in company relocation was going to make an already bad situation worse.

Case 6–25

Cima Mountaineering, Inc.

"What a great hike," exclaimed Anthony Simon as he tossed his Summit HX 350 hiking boots into his car. He had just finished hiking the challenging Cascade Canyon Trail in the Tetons north of Jackson, Wyoming. Anthony hiked often because it was a great way to test the hiking boots made by Cima Mountaineering, Inc., the business he inherited from his parents and owned with his sister, Margaret. As he drove back to Jackson, he began thinking about next week's meeting with Margaret, the president of Cima. During the past month they had been discussing marketing strategies for increasing the sales and profits of the company. No decisions had been made, but the preferences of each owner were becoming clear.

As illustrated in Exhibit 1, sales and profits had grown steadily for Cima, and by most measures the company was successful. However, growth was beginning to slow as a result of foreign competition and a changing market. Margaret observed that the market had shifted to a more casual, stylish hiking boot that appealed to hikers interested in a boot for a variety of uses. She favored a strategy of diversifying the company by marketing a new

Lawrence M. Lamont is professor of management at Washington and Lee University, and Eva Cid and Wade Drew Hammond are seniors in the class of 1995 at Washington and Lee, majoring in management and accounting, respectively. Case material was prepared as a basis for class discussion and not designed to present illustrations of either effective or ineffective handling of administrative problems. Some names, locations, and financial information have been disguised. Copyright © 1995, Washington and Lee University.

EXHIBIT 1
Cima
Mountaineering,
Inc., Revenues and
Net Income,
1990–95

Year	Revenues	Net Income	Profit Margin (%)
1995	$20,091,450	$857,134	4.27%
1994	18,738,529	809,505	4.32
1993	17,281,683	838,162	4.85
1992	15,614,803	776,056	4.97
1991	14,221,132	602,976	4.24
1990	13,034,562	522,606	4.01

EXHIBIT 2
Cima
Mountaineering,
Inc., Income
Statement, Years
Ended December
31, 1995, and
December 31, 1994

	1995	1994
Net sales	$20,091,450	$18,738,529
Cost of goods sold	14,381,460	13,426,156
Gross margin	5,709,990	5,312,373
Selling and admin. expenses	4,285,730	3,973,419
Operating income	1,424,260	1,338,954
Other income (expenses)		
Interest expense	(160,733)	(131,170)
Interest income	35,161	18,739
Total other income (net)	(125,572)	(112,431)
Earnings before income taxes	1,298,688	1,226,523
Income taxes	441,554	417,018
Net income	$ 857,134	$ 809,505

line of boots for the less experienced weekend hiker. Anthony also recognized that the market had changed, but he supported expanding the existing lines of boots for mountaineers and hikers. The company had been successful with those boots, and Anthony had some ideas about how to extend the lines and expand distribution. "This is a better way to grow," he thought. "I'm concerned about the risk in Margaret's recommendation. If we move to a more casual boot, then we have to resolve a new set of marketing and competitive issues and finance a new line. I'm not sure we can do it."

When he returned to Jackson that evening, Anthony stopped by his office to check his messages. The financial statements shown in Exhibits 2 and 3 were on his desk, along with a marketing study from a Denver consulting firm. Harris Fleming, vice president of marketing, had commissioned a study of the hiking boot market several months earlier to help the company plan for the future. As Anthony paged through the report, two figures caught his eye. One was a segmentation of the hiking boot market (Exhibit 4), and the other was a summary of market competition (Exhibit 5). "This is interesting," he mused. "I hope Margaret reads it before our meeting."

History of Cima Mountaineering

As children, Anthony and Margaret Simon had watched their parents make western boots at the Hoback Boot Company, a small business they owned in Jackson, Wyoming. They learned the craft as they grew up and joined the company after college.

**EXHIBIT 3
Cima
Mountaineering,
Inc., Balance Sheet,
Years Ending
December 31, 1995,
and December 31,
1994**

	1995	1994
Assets		
Current assets		
Cash and equivalents	$ 1,571,441	$ 1,228,296
Accounts receivable	4,696,260	3,976,608
Inventory	6,195,450	5,327,733
Other	270,938	276,367
Total	12,734,089	10,809,004
Fixed assets		
Property, plant, and equipment	3,899,568	2,961,667
Less: accumulated depreciation	(1,117,937)	(858,210)
Total fixed assets (net)	2,781,631	2,103,457
Other assets		
Intangibles	379,313	568,087
Other long-term assets	2,167,504	1,873,151
Total fixed assets (net)	$18,062,537	$15,353,699
Liabilities and shareholder equity		
Current liabilities		
Accounts payable	$ 4,280,821	$ 4,097,595
Notes payable	1,083,752	951,929
Current maturities of long-term debt	496,720	303,236
Accrued liabilities		
Expenses	2,754,537	2,360,631
Salaries and wages	1,408,878	1,259,003
Other	1,137,940	991,235
Total current liabilities	11,162,648	9,963,629
Long-term liabilities		
Long-term debt	3,070,631	2,303,055
Lease obligations	90,313	31,629
Total long-term liabilities	3,702,820	2,334,684
Other liabilities		
Deferred taxes	36,125	92,122
Other noncurrent liabilities	312,326	429,904
Total liabilities	14,672,043	12,820,339
Owner's equity		
Retained earnings	3,390,494	2,533,360
Total liabilities and owner's equity	$18,062,537	$15,353,699

In the late 1960s the demand for western boots began to decline, and the Hoback Boot Company struggled to survive. By 1975 the parents were close to retirement and seemed content to close the business, but Margaret and Anthony decided to try to salvage the company. Margaret, the older sibling, became the president, and Anthony became the executive vice president. By the end of 1976, sales had declined to $1.5 million and the company earned profits of only $45,000. It became clear that to survive, the business would have to refocus on products with a more promising future.

EXHIBIT 4   Segmentation of the Hiking Boot Market

	Mountaineers	Serious Hikers	Weekenders	Practical Users	Children	Fashion Seekers
Benefits	Durability/ruggedness Stability/support Dryness/warmth Grip/traction	Stability Durability Traction Comfort/protection	Lightweight Comfort Durability Versatility	Lightweight Durability Good value Versatility	Durability Protection Lightweight Traction	Fashion/style Appearance Lightweight Inexpensive
Demographics	Young Primarily male Shops in specialty stores and specialized catalogs	Young, middle-aged Male and female Shops in specialty stores and outdoor catalogs	Young, middle-aged Male and female Shops in shoe retailers, sporting goods stores, and mail order catalogs	Young, middle-aged Primarily male Shops in shoe retailers and department stores	Young marrieds Male and female Shops in department stores and outdoor catalogs	Young Male and female Shops in shoe retailers, department stores, and catalogs
Lifestyle	Adventuresome Independent Risk taker Enjoys challenges	Nature lover Outdoorsman Sportsman Backpacker	Recreational hiker Social, spends time with family and friends Enjoys the outdoors	Practical Sociable Outdoors for work and recreation	Enjoys family activities Enjoys outdoors and hiking Children are active and play outdoors Parents are value-conscious	Materialistic Trendy Socially conscious Nonhikers Brand name shoppers Price-conscious
Examples of brands	Asolo Cliff Raichle Mt. Blanc Salomon Adventure 9	Raichle Explorer Vasque Clarion Tecnica Pegasus Dry Hi-Tec Piramide	Reebok R-Evolution Timberland Topozoic Merrell Acadia Nike Air Mada, Zion Vasque Alpha	Merrell Eagle Nike Air Khyber Tecnica Volcano	Vasque Kids Klimber Nike Merrell Caribou	Nike Espirit Reebok Telos Hi-Tec Magnum
Estimated market share	5% Slow growth	17% Moderate growth	25% High growth	20% Stable growth	5% Slow growth	28% At peak of rapid growth cycle
Price range	$210–$450	$120–$215	$70–$125	$40–$80	Up to $40	$65–$100

EXHIBIT 5   **Summary of Competitors**

Company	Location	Mountaineering (Styles)	Hiking (Styles)	Men's	Women's	Children's	Price Range
Raichle	Switzerland	Yes (7)	Yes (16)	Yes	Yes	Yes	High
Salomon	France	Yes (1)	Yes (9)	Yes	Yes	No	Mid
Asolo	Italy	Yes (4)	Yes (26)	Yes	Yes	No	High
Tecnica	Italy	Yes (3)	Yes (9)	Yes	Yes	No	Mid/high
Hi-Tec	United Kingdom	Yes (2)	Yes (29)	Yes	Yes	Yes	Mid/low
Vasque	Minnesota	Yes (4)	Yes (18)	Yes	Yes	Yes	Mid/high
Merrell	Vermont	Yes (5)	Yes (31)	Yes	Yes	Yes	Mid
Timberland	New Hampshire	No	Yes (4)	Yes	No	No	Mid
Nike	Oregon	No	Yes (5)	Yes	Yes	Yes	Low
Reebok	Massachusetts	No	Yes (3)	Yes	Yes	Yes	Low
Cima	Wyoming	Yes (3)	Yes (5)	Yes	Yes	No	High

Source: Published literature and company product brochures, 1995.

Refocusing the Business

As a college student, Anthony attended a mountaineering school north of Jackson in Teton National Park. As he learned to climb and hike, he became aware of the growing popularity of the sport and the boots being used. Because of his experience with western boots, he also noticed their limitations. Although the boots had good traction, they were heavy and uncomfortable and had little resistance to the snow and water always present in the mountains. He convinced Margaret that Hoback should explore the possibility of developing boots for mountaineering and hiking.

In 1977 Anthony and Margaret began 12 months of marketing research. They investigated the market, the competition, and the extent to which Hoback's existing equipment could be used to produce the new boots. By the summer of 1978 Hoback had developed a mountaineering boot and a hiking boot that were ready for testing. Several instructors from the mountaineering school tested the boots and gave them excellent reviews.

The Transition

By 1981 Hoback was ready to enter the market with two styles of boots: one for the mountaineer who wanted a boot for all-weather climbing and the other for men and women who were advanced hikers. Both styles had water-repellent leather uppers and cleated soles for superior traction. Distribution was secured through mountaineering shops in Wyoming and Colorado.

Hoback continued to manufacture western boots for its loyal customers, but Margaret planned to phase them out as the hiking boot business developed. However, because they did not completely understand the needs of the market, they hired Harris Fleming, a mountaineering instructor, to help them with product design and marketing.

A New Company

During the 1980s Hoback prospered as the market expanded along with the popularity of outdoor recreation. The company slowly increased its product line and achieved success by focusing on classic boots that were relatively insensitive to fashion trends. By 1986 sales of Hoback Boots had reached $3.5 million.

Over the next several years distribution was steadily expanded. In 1987 Hoback employed independent sales representatives to handle the sales and service. Before long, Hoback boots were sold throughout Wyoming, Colorado, and Montana by retailers specializing in mountaineering and hiking equipment. Margaret decided to discontinue western boots to make room for the growing hiking boot business. To reflect the new direction of the company, the name was changed to Cima Mountaineering, Inc.

Cima Boots Take Off

The late 1980s was a period of exceptional growth. Demand for Cima boots grew quickly as consumers caught the trend toward healthy, active lifestyles. The company expanded its line for advanced hikers and improved the performance of its boots. By 1990, sales had reached $13 million and the company earned profits of $522,606. Margaret was satisfied with the growth but was concerned about low profitability as a result of foreign competition. She challenged the company to find new ways to design and manufacture boots at a lower cost.

Growth and Innovation

The next five years were marked by growth, innovation, and increasing foreign and domestic competition. Market growth continued as hiking boots became popular for casual wear in addition to hiking in mountains and on trails. Cima and its competitors began to make boots with molded footbeds and utilize materials that reduced weight.[1] Fashion also became a factor, and companies such as Nike and Reebok marketed lightweight boots in a variety of materials and colors to meet the demand for styling in addition to performance. Cima implemented a computer-aided design (CAD) system in 1993 to shorten product development and devote more attention to design. Late in 1994, Cima restructured its facilities and implemented a modular approach to manufacturing. The company switched from a production line to a system in which a work team applied multiple processes to each pair of boots. Significant cost savings were achieved as the new approach improved the profit and quality of the company's boots.

The Situation in 1995

As the company ended 1995, sales had grown to $20.0 million, up 7.2 percent from the previous year. Employment was at 425, and the facility was operating at 85 percent of capacity, producing several styles of mountaineering and hiking boots. Time-saving innovations and cost reduction also had worked, and profits reached an all-time high. Margaret, now 57, was still president, and Anthony remained executive vice president.

Cima Marketing Strategy

According to estimates, 1994 was a record year for sales of hiking and mountaineering boots in the United States. Retail sales exceeded $600 million, and about 15 million pairs of boots were sold. Consumers wore the boots for activities ranging from mountaineering to casual social events. In recent years, changes were beginning to occur in the market. Inexpensive, lightweight hiking boots were becoming increasingly popular for day hikes

---

[1]Two processes are used to attach the uppers to the soles of boots. In classic welt construction, the uppers and soles are stitched. In the more contemporary method, a molded polyurethane footbed (including a one-piece heel and sole) is cemented to the upper with a waterproof adhesive. Many mountaineering boots use classic welt construction because it provides outstanding stability, while the contemporary method often is used with hiking boots to achieve lightweight construction. Cima used the classic method of construction for mountaineering boots and the contemporary method for hiking boots.

and trail walking, and a new category of comfortable, light "trekking" shoes was being marketed by manufacturers of athletic shoes.

Only a part of the market was targeted by Cima. Most of its customers were serious outdoor enthusiasts. They included mountaineers who climbed in rugged terrain and advanced hikers who used the boots on challenging trails and extended backpacking trips. The demand for Cima boots was seasonal, and most of the purchases were made during the summer months, when the mountains and trails were most accessible.

Positioning

Cima boots were positioned as the best available for their intended purpose. Consumers saw them as durable and comfortable with exceptional performance. Retailers viewed the company as quick to adopt innovative construction techniques but conservative in styling. Cima intentionally used traditional styling to avoid fashion obsolescence and the need for frequent design changes. Some of the most popular styles had been in the market for several years without any significant modifications. The Glacier MX 350 shown in Exhibit 6 and the Summit HX 350 boot shown in Exhibit 7 are good examples. The MX 350, priced at $219.00, was positioned as a classic boot for men and had a unique tread design for beginning mountaineers. The Summit HX 350 was priced at $159.00 and was a boot for men and women hiking rough trails. Exhibit 8 describes the items in the mountaineering and hiking boot lines, and Exhibit 9 provides a sales history for Cima boots.

Product Lines

Corporate branding was used, and "Cima" was embossed on the leather on the side of the boot to enhance consumer recognition. Product lines were also branded, and alphabetic letters and numbers were used to differentiate items in the line. Each line had different styles and features to cover many of the important uses in the market. However, all the boots had features that the company believed were essential to positioning. Standard features included water-repellent leather uppers and high-traction soles and heels. The hardware for the boots was plated steel, and the laces were made of tough, durable nylon. Quality was emphasized throughout the product lines.

EXHIBIT 6
**The Glacier
MX 350
Mountaineering
Boot**

EXHIBIT 7
**The Summit HX
350 Hiking Boot**

EXHIBIT 8
**Cima
Mountaineering,
Inc.,
Mountaineering
and Hiking Boot
Lines**

Product Line	Description
Glacier	
MX 550	For expert mountaineers climbing challenging mountains. Made for use on rocks, ice, and snow. Features welt construction, superior stability and support, reinforced heel and toe, padded ankle and tongue, step-in crampon insert, thermal insulation, and waterproof inner liner. Retails for $299.
MX 450	For proficient mountaineers engaging in rigorous, high-altitude hiking. Offers long-term comfort and stability on rough terrain. Features welt construction, deep cleated soles and heels, reinforced heel and toe, padded ankle and tongue, step-in crampon insert, and waterproof inner liner. Retails for $249.
MX 350	For beginning mountaineers climbing in moderate terrain and temperate climates. Features welt construction, unique tread design for traction, padded ankle and tongue, good stability and support, and a quick-dry lining. Retails for $219.
Summit	
HX 550	For experienced hikers who require uncompromising performance. Features nylon shank for stability and rigidity, waterproof inner liner, cushioned midsole, high-traction outsole, and padded ankle and tongue. Retails for $197.
HX 450	For backpackers who carry heavy loads on extended trips. Features thermal insulation, cushioned midsole, waterproof inner liner, excellent foot protection, and high-traction outsole. Retails for $179.
HX 350	For hikers who travel rough trails and a variety of backcountry terrain. Features extra cushioning, good stability and support, waterproof inner liner, and high-traction outsole for good grip in muddy and sloping surfaces. Retails for $159.
HX 250	For hikers who hike developed trails. Made with only the necessary technical features, including cushioning, foot and ankle support, waterproof inner liner, and high-traction outsole. Retails for $139.
HX 150	For individuals taking more than day and weekend hikes. Versatile boot for all kinds of excursions. Features cushioning, good support, waterproof inner liner, and high-traction outsoles for use on a variety of surfaces. Retails for $129.

EXHIBIT 9
Cima Mountaineering, Inc., Product Line Sales

	Unit Sales (%)		Sales Revenue	
Year	Mountaineering	Hiking	Mountaineering	Hiking
1995	15.00%	85.00%	21.74%	78.26%
1994	15.90	84.10	22.93	77.07
1993	17.20	82.80	24.64	75.36
1992	18.00	82.00	25.68	74.32
1991	18.80	81.20	26.71	73.29
1990	19.70	80.30	27.86	72.14

Glacier Boots for Mountaineering

The Glacier line featured three boots for men. The MX 550 was designed for expert all-weather climbers looking for the ultimate in traction, protection, and warmth. The MX 450 was for experienced climbers taking extended excursions, while the MX 350 met the needs of less-skilled individuals beginning climbing in moderate terrain and climates.

Summit Boots for Hiking

The Summit line featured five styles for men and women. The HX 550 was preferred by experienced hikers who demanded the best possible performance. The boot featured water-repellent leather uppers, a waterproof inner liner, a cushioned midsole, a nylon shank for rigidity, and a sole designed for high traction. It was available in gray and brown with different types of leather.[2] The Summit HX 150 was the least expensive boot in the line, designed for individuals who were beginning to take more than the occasional "weekend hike." It was a versatile boot for all kinds of excursions and featured a water-repellent leather upper, a cushioned midsole, and excellent traction. The HX 150 was popular as an entry-level boot for outdoor enthusiasts.

Distribution

Cima boots were distributed in Arizona, California, Colorado, Idaho, Montana, Nevada, New Mexico, Oregon, Washington, Wyoming, and western Canada through specialty retailers selling mountaineering, backpacking, and hiking equipment. Occasionally, Cima was approached by mail order catalog companies and chain sporting goods stores offering to sell its boots. The company considered the proposals but had not used those channels.

Promotion

The Cima sales and marketing office was located in Jackson. It was managed by Harris Fleming and staffed with several marketing personnel. Promotion was an important aspect of the marketing strategy, and advertising, personal selling, and sales promotion were used

---

[2]Different types of leather are used to make hiking boots. *Full grain:* High-quality, durable, upper layer of the hide. It has a natural finish and is strong and breathable. *Split grain:* Underside of the hide after the full-grain leather has been removed from the top. Light weight and comfort are the primary characteristics. *Suede:* A very fine split-grain leather. *Nubuk:* Brushed full-grain leather. *Waxed:* A process in which leather is coated with wax to help shed water. Most Cima boots were available in two or more types of leather.

Mountaineering and hiking boots are made water-repellent by treating the uppers with wax or chemical coatings. To make the boots waterproof, a fabric inner liner is built into the boot to provide waterproof protection and breathability. All Cima boots were water-repellent, but only styles with an inner liner were waterproof.

to gain exposure for Cima branded boots. Promotion was directed toward consumers and to retailers that stocked Cima mountaineering and hiking boots.

Personal Selling

Cima used 10 independent sales representatives to sell its boots in the Western states and Canada. Representatives did not sell competing boots, but they sold complementary products such as outdoor apparel and equipment for mountaineering, hiking, and backpacking. They were paid a commission and handled customer service in addition to sales. Management also was involved in personal selling. Harris Fleming trained the independent sales representatives and often accompanied them on sales calls.

Advertising and Sales Promotion

Advertising and sales promotion also were important promotional methods. Print advertising was used to increase brand awareness and assist retailers with promotion. Advertising was placed in leading magazines such as *Summit, Outside,* and *Backpacker* to reach mountaineers and hikers with the message that Cima boots were functional and durable and had classic styling. In addition, cooperative advertising was offered to encourage retailers to advertise Cima boots and identify their locations.

Sales promotion was an important part of the promotion program. Along with the focus on brand name recognition, Cima provided product literature and point of sale display materials to assist retailers in promoting the boots. In addition, the company regularly exhibited at industry trade shows. The exhibits, staffed by marketing personnel and the company's independent sales representatives, were effective for maintaining relationships with retailers and presenting the company's products.

Pricing

Cima selling prices to retailers ranged from $64.50 to $149.50 a pair, depending on the style. Mountaineering boots were more expensive because of their construction and features, while hiking boots were priced lower. Retailers were encouraged to take a 50 percent margin on the retail selling price, and so the retail prices shown in Exhibit 8 should be divided by two to get the Cima selling price. Cima priced its boots higher than competitors did, supporting the positioning of the boots as the top-quality product at each price point. Payment terms were net 30 days (similar to competitors), and boots were shipped to retailers from a warehouse in Jackson, Wyoming.

Segmentation of the Hiking Boot Market

As Anthony reviewed the marketing study commissioned by Harris Fleming, his attention focused on the market segmentation shown in Exhibit 4. It was interesting, because management had never seriously thought about the segmentation in the market. Of course, Anthony was aware that not everyone was a potential customer for Cima boots, but he was surprised to see how well the product lines met the needs of mountaineers and serious hikers. As he reviewed the market segmentation, he read the descriptions for mountaineers, serious hikers, and weekenders carefully because Cima was trying to decide which of these segments to target for expansion.

Mountaineers

Mountain climbers and high-altitude hikers are in this segment. They are serious about climbing and enjoy risk and adventure. Because mountaineers' safety may depend on their boots, they need maximum stability and support, traction for a variety of climbing conditions, and protection from wet and cold weather.

Serious Hikers

Outdoorsmen, who love nature and have a strong interest in health and fitness, are the serious hikers. They hike rough trails and take extended backpacking or hiking excursions. Serious hikers are brand-conscious and look for durable, high-performance boots with good support, a comfortable fit, and good traction.

Weekenders

Consumers in this segment are recreational hikers who enjoy casual weekend and day hikes with family and friends. They are interested in light, comfortable boots that provide a good fit, protection, and traction on a variety of surfaces. Weekenders prefer versatile boots that can be worn for a variety of activities.

Foreign and Domestic Competition

The second part of the marketing study that caught Anthony's attention was the analysis of competition. Although Anthony and Margaret were aware that competition had increased, they had overlooked the extent to which foreign bootmakers had entered the market. Apparently, foreign competitors had noticed the market growth and were exporting their boots aggressively into the United States. They had established sales offices and independent sales agents to compete for the customers served by Cima. The leading foreign brands, such as Asolo, Hi-Tec, Salomon, and Raichle, were marketed on performance and reputation, usually to the mountaineering, serious hiker, and weekender segments of the market.

   The study also summarized the most important domestic competitors. Vasque and Merrell marketed boots that competed with Cima, but others were offering products for segments of the market where the prospects for growth were better. As Anthony examined Exhibit 5, he realized that the entry of Reebok and Nike into the hiking boot market was quite logical. They had entered the market as consumer preference shifted from wearing athletic shoes for casual outdoor activities to wearing a more rugged shoe. Each was marketing footwear that combined the appearance and durability of hiking boots with the lightness and fit of athletic shoes. The result was a line of fashionable hiking boots that appealed to brand- and style-conscious teens and young adults. Both firms were expanding their product lines and moving into segments of the market that demanded lower levels of performance.

Margaret and Anthony Discuss Marketing Strategy

A few days after hiking in Cascade Canyon, Anthony met with Margaret and Harris Fleming to discuss marketing strategy. Each had read the consultant's report and studied the market segmentation and competitive summary. As the meeting opened, the conversation went as follows:

Margaret: It looks like we will have another record year. The economy is growing, and consumers seem confident and eager to buy. Yet I'm concerned about the future. The foreign bootmakers are providing some stiff competition. Their boots have outstanding performance and attractive prices. The improvements we made in manufacturing helped control costs and maintain margins, but it looks like the competition and slow growth in our markets will make it difficult to improve profits. We need to be thinking about new opportunities.

Harris: I agree, Margaret. Just this past week we lost Rocky Mountain Sports in Boulder, Colorado. John Kline, the sales manager, decided to drop us and pick up Asolo. We were doing $70,000 a year with them, and they carried our entire line. We also lost Great Western Outfitters in Colorado Springs. They replaced us with Merrell. The sales manager said that the college students there had been asking for the lower-priced Merrell boots. They bought $60,000 last year.

Anthony: Rocky Mountain and Great Western were good customers. I guess I'm not surprised, though. Our Glacier line needs another boot, and the Summit line is just not deep enough to cover the price points. We need to have some styles at lower prices to compete with Merrell and Asolo. I'm in favor of extending our existing lines to broaden their market appeal. It seems to me that the best way to compete is to stick with what we do best, making boots for mountaineers and serious hikers.

Margaret: Not so fast, Anthony. The problem is that our markets are small and not growing fast enough to support the foreign competitors that have entered with excellent products. We can probably hold our own, but I doubt if we can do much better. I think the future of this company is to move with the market. Consumers are demanding more style, lower prices, and a lightweight hiking boot that can be worn for a variety of uses. Look at the segmentation again. The "Weekender" segment is large and growing. That's where we need to go with some stylish new boots that depart from our classic leather lines.

Anthony: Maybe so, but we don't have much experience working with the leather and nylon combinations that are being used in these lighter boots. Besides, I'm not sure we can finance the product development and marketing for a new market that already has plenty of competition. And I'm concerned about the brand image that we have worked so hard to establish over the past 20 years. A line of inexpensive, casual boots just doesn't seem to fit with the perception consumers have of our products.

Harris: I can see advantages to each strategy. I do know that we don't have the time and resources to do both, so we had better make a thoughtful choice. Also, I think we should reconsider selling to the mail order catalog companies that specialize in mountaineering and hiking equipment. Last week I received another call from REI requesting us to sell them some of the boots in our Summit line for the 1997 season. This might be a good source of revenue and a way to expand our geographic market.

Margaret: You're right, Harris. We need to rethink our position on the mail order companies. Most of them have good market penetration in the East, where we don't have distribution. I noticed that Gander Mountain is carrying some of the Timberland line and that L.L. Bean is carrying some Vasque styles along with its own line of branded boots.

Anthony: I agree. Why don't we each put together a proposal that summarizes our recommendations, and then we can get back together to continue the discussion.

Harris: Good idea. Eventually we will need a sales forecast and some cost data. Send me your proposals, and I'll call the consulting firm and have them prepare some forecasts. I think we already have some cost information. Give me a few days, and then we can get together again.

The Meeting to Review the Proposals

The following week, the discussion continued. Margaret presented her proposal, which is summarized in Exhibit 10. She proposed moving Cima into the "Weekender" segment by marketing two new hiking boots. Anthony countered with the proposal summarized in Exhibit 11. He favored extending the existing lines by adding a new mountaineering boot and two new Summit hiking boots at lower price points. Harris presented sales forecasts for each proposal, and after some discussion and modification, they were finalized as shown in Exhibit 12. Cost information was gathered by Harris from the vice president of manufacturing and is presented in Exhibit 13. After a lengthy discussion in which Margaret and Anthony were unable to agree on a course of action, Harris Fleming suggested that each proposal be explored further by conducting marketing research. He proposed the formation of teams from the Cima marketing staff to research each proposal and present it to Margaret and Anthony at a later date. Harris presented his directions to the teams in the memorandum shown in Exhibit 14. The discussion between Margaret and Anthony continued as follows:

Margaret: Once the marketing research is completed and we can read the reports and listen to the presentations, we should have a better idea of which strategy makes the best sense. Hopefully, a clear direction will emerge and we can move ahead with one of the proposals. In either case, I'm still intrigued with the possibility of moving into the mail order catalogs, since we really haven't developed these companies as customers. I just wish we knew how much business we could expect from them.

Anthony: We should seriously consider them, Margaret. Companies like L.L. Bean, Gander Mountain, and REI have been carrying a selection of hiking boots for several years. However, there may be a problem for us. Eventually the catalog companies expect their boot suppliers to make them a private brand. I'm not sure this is something we want to do, since we built the company on a strategy of marketing our own brands that are made in the U.S.A. Also, I'm concerned about the reaction of our retailers when they discover we are selling to the catalog companies. It could create some problems.

Harris: That is a strategy issue we will have to address. However, I'm not even sure what percentage of sales the typical footwear company makes through the mail order catalogs. If we were to solicit the catalog business, we would need an answer to this question to avoid exceeding our capacity. In the proposals I asked each of the teams to provide an estimate for us. I have to catch an early flight to Denver in the morning. It's 6:30; why don't we call it a day.

The meeting was adjourned at 6:35 PM. Soon thereafter, the marketing teams were formed, with a leader assigned to each team.

EXHIBIT 10   **Margaret's Marketing Proposal**

MEMORANDUM

TO: Anthony Simon, Executive Vice President
        Harris Fleming, Vice President of Marketing
FROM: Margaret Simon, President
RE: Marketing Proposal

I believe we have an excellent opportunity to expand the sales and profits of Cima by entering the "Week-ender" segment of the hiking boot market. The segment's estimated share of the market is 25 percent, and according to the consultant's report, it is growing quite rapidly. I propose that we begin immediately to develop two new products and prepare a marketing strategy as discussed below.

Target Market and Positioning
Male and female recreational hikers looking for a comfortable, lightweight boot that is attractively priced and acceptable for short hikes and casual wear. Weekenders enjoy the outdoors and a day or weekend hike with family and friends.

The new boots would be positioned with magazine advertising as hiking boots that deliver performance and style for the demands of light hiking and casual outdoor wear.

Product
Two boots in men's and women's sizes. The boots would be constructed of leather and nylon uppers with a molded rubber outsole. A new branded line would be created to meet the needs of the market segment. The boots (designated WX 550 and WX 450) would have the following features:

	WX 550	WX 450
Leather and nylon uppers	X	X
Molded rubber outsole	X	X
Cushioned midsole	X	X
Padded collar and tongue	X	X
Durable hardware and laces	X	X
Waterproof inner liner	X	

Uppers: To be designed. Options include brown full-grain, split-grain, or suede leather combined with durable nylon in two of the following colors: beige, black, blue, gray, green, and slate.
Boot design and brand name: To be decided.

Retail Outlets
Specialty shoe retailers carrying hiking boots and casual shoes and sporting goods stores. Eventually mail order catalogs carrying outdoor apparel and hiking, backpacking, and camping equipment.

Promotion

Independent sales representatives	Point of sale display materials
Magazine advertising	Product brochures
Co-op advertising	Trade shows

Suggested Retail Pricing
WX 550: $89.00
WX 450: $69.00

Competitors
Timberland, Hi-Tec, Vasque, Merrell, Asolo, Nike, and Reebok.

Product Development and Required Investment
We should allow about one year for the necessary product development and testing. I estimate these costs to be $350,000. Additionally, we will need to make a capital expenditure of $150,000 for new equipment.

EXHIBIT 11   **Anthony's Marketing Proposal**

MEMORANDUM

TO: Margaret Simon, President
         Harris Fleming, Vice President of Marketing
FROM: Anthony Simon, Executive Vice President
RE: Marketing Proposal

We have been successful with boots for mountaineers and serious hikers for years, and this is where our strengths seem to be. I recommend extending our Glacier and Summit lines instead of venturing into a new, unfamiliar market. My recommendations are summarized below:

Product Development
Introduce two new boots in the Summit line (designated HX 100 and HX 50) and market the Glacier MX 350 in a style for women with the same features as the boot for men. The new women's Glacier boot would have a suggested retail price of $219.00, while the suggested retail prices for the HX 100 and the HX 50 would be $119.00 and $89.00, respectively, to provide price points at the low end of the line. The new Summit boots for men and women would be the first in the line to have leather and nylon uppers as well as the following features:

	HX 100	HX 50
Leather and nylon uppers	X	X
Molded rubber outsole	X	X
Cushioned midsole	X	X
Padded collar and tongue	X	X
Quick-dry lining	X	X
Waterproof inner liner	X	

The leather used in the uppers will have to be determined. We should consider full-grain, suede, and nubuck since they are all popular with users in this segment. We need to select one for the initial introduction. The nylon fabric for the uppers should be available in two colors, selected from among the following: beige, brown, green, slate, maroon, and navy blue. Additional colors can be offered as sales develop and we gain a better understanding of consumer preferences.

Product Development and Required Investment
Product design and development costs of $400,000 for the MX 350, HX 100, and HX 50 styles and a capital investment of $150,000 to acquire equipment to cut and stitch the nylon/leather uppers. One year will be needed for product development and testing.

Positioning
The additions to the Summit line will be positioned as boots for serious hikers who want a quality hiking boot at a reasonable price. The boots will also be attractive to casual hikers who are looking to move up to a better boot as they gain experience in hiking and outdoor activity.

Retail Outlets
We can use our existing retail outlets. Additionally, the lower price points on the new styles will make these boots attractive to catalog shoppers. I recommend that we consider making the Summit boots available to consumers through mail order catalog companies.

Promotion
We will need to revise our product brochures and develop new advertising for the additions to the Summit line. The balance of the promotion program should remain as it is since it is working quite well. I believe the sales representatives and retailers selling our lines will welcome the new boots since they broaden the consumer appeal of our lines.

Suggested Retail Pricing

MX 350 for women:	$219.99
HX 100:	$119.00
HX 50:	$ 89.00

Competitors
Asolo, Hi-Tec, Merrell, Raichle, Salomon, Tecnica, and Vasque.

EXHIBIT 12
Cima
Mountaineering,
Inc., Sales
Forecasts for
Proposed New
Products (Pairs of
Boots)

| | Project 1 | | | Project 2 | | |
Year	WX 550	WX 450	MX 350	HX 100	HX 50
2001–02	16,420	24,590	2,249	15,420	12,897
2000–01	14,104	21,115	1,778	13,285	11,733
1999–2000	8,420	12,605	897	10,078	9,169
1998–99	5,590	8,430	538	5,470	5,049
1997–98	4,050	6,160	414	4,049	3,813

Note: Sales forecasts are expected values derived from minimum and maximum estimates.
Some cannibalization of existing boots will occur when the new styles are introduced. The sales forecasts provided above have taken into account the impact of sales losses on existing boots. No additional adjustments need to be made.
Forecasts for WX 550, WX 450, HX 100, and HX 50 include sales of both men's and women's boots.

EXHIBIT 13
Cima
Mountaineering,
Inc., Cost
Information for
Mountaineering
and Hiking Boots

	Inner Liner	No Inner Liner
Retail margin	50%	50%
Marketing and Manufacturing Costs		
Sales commissions	10	10
Advertising and sales promotion	5	5
Materials	42	35
Labor, overhead, and transportation	28	35

Cost information for 1997–98 only. Sales commissions, advertising and sales promotion, materials, labor, overhead, and transportation costs are based on Cima selling prices. After 1997–98, annual increases of 3.0 percent apply to marketing and manufacturing costs and increases of 4.0 percent apply to Cima selling prices.

EXHIBIT 14   **Harris Fleming's Memorandum to the Marketing Staff**

MEMORANDUM

TO: Marketing Staff
CC: Margaret Simon, President
           Anthony Simon, Executive Vice President
FROM: Harris Fleming, Vice President of Marketing
SUBJECT: Marketing Research Projects

Attached to this memorandum are two marketing proposals (see case Exhibits 10 and 11) under consideration by our company. Each proposal is a guide for additional marketing research. You have been selected to serve on a project team to investigate one of the proposals and report your conclusions and recommendations to management. At your earliest convenience, please complete the following.

Project Team 1: Proposal to enter the "Weekender" segment of the hiking boot market.
Review the market segmentation and summary of competition in Exhibits 4 and 5. Identify consumers who would match the profile described in the market segment and conduct field research using a focus group, a survey, or both. You may also visit retailers carrying hiking boots to examine displays and product brochures. Using the information in the proposal, supplemented with your research, prepare the following:

1. A design for the hiking boots (WX 550 and WX 450). Please prepare a sketch that shows the styling for the uppers. We propose to use the same design for each boot, the only difference being the waterproof inner liner on the WX 550 boot. On your design, list the features that your proposed boot would have, considering additions or deletions to those listed in the proposal.

2. Recommend a type of leather (from among those proposed) and two colors for the nylon to be used in the panels of the uppers. We plan to make two styles, one in each color for each boot.

3. Recommend a brand name for the product line. Include a rationale for your choice.

EXHIBIT 14   *(concluded)*

4. Verify the acceptability of the suggested retail pricing.

5. Prepare a magazine advertisement for the hiking boot. Provide a rationale for the advertisement in the report.

6. Convert the suggested retail prices *in the proposal* to the Cima selling price and use the sales forecasts and costs (shown in Exhibits 12 and 13) to prepare an estimate of before-tax profits for the new product line, covering a five-year period starting in 1997–98. Assume annual cost increases of 3.0 percent and price increases of 4.0 percent beginning in 1998–99. Discount the future profits to present value, using a cost of capital of 15.0 percent. Use 1996–97 as the base year for all discounting.

7. Determine the payback period for the proposal. Assume product development and investment occur in 1996–97.

8. Provide your conclusions on the attractiveness of these styles to mail order catalog companies and their customers. You may wish to review current mail order catalogs to observe the hiking boots featured. Assuming that Cima is successful selling to mail order catalog companies, estimate the percentage of our sales that could be expected from these customers.

9. Prepare a report that summarizes the recommendations of your project team, including the advantages and disadvantages of the proposal. Be prepared to present your product design, branding, pro forma projections, payback period, and recommendations to management shortly after completion of this assignment.

10. Summarize your research and list the sources of information used to prepare the report.

Project Team 2: Proposal to extend the existing lines of boots for mountaineers and hikers.
Review the market segmentation and summary of competition in Exhibits 4 and 5. Identify consumers who match the profile described in the market segment and conduct field research using a focus group, a survey, or both. You also may visit retailers carrying hiking boots to examine displays and product brochures. Using the information in the proposal, supplemented with your research, prepare the following.

1. Designs for the hiking boots (HX 100 and HX 50). Please prepare sketches showing the styling for the uppers. We propose to use a different design for each boot, so you should provide a sketch for each. On each sketch, list the features that your proposed boots would have, considering additions or deletions to those listed in the proposal. No sketch is necessary for the mountaineering boot, MX 350, since we will use the same design as the men's boot and build it on a women's last.

2. Recommend one type of leather (from among those proposed) and two colors for the nylon to be used in the panels of the uppers. We plan to make two styles, one in each color for each boot.

3. Verify the market acceptability of the suggested retail pricing.

4. Prepare a magazine advertisement for your hiking boots. Include a rationale for the advertisement in the report.

5. Using the suggested retail prices *in the proposal,* convert them to the Cima selling prices and use the sales forecasts and costs (shown in Exhibits 12 and 13) to prepare an estimate of before-tax profits for the new products covering a five-year period starting in 1997–98. Assume annual cost increases of 3.0 percent and price increases of 4.0 percent beginning in 1998–99. Discount the profits to present value using a cost of capital of 15.0 percent. Use 1996–97 as the base year for all discounting.

6. Determine the payback period for the proposal. Assume product development and investment occur in 1996–97.

7. Provide your conclusions on the attractiveness of these styles to mail order catalog companies and their customers. You may wish to review current mail order catalogs to observe the hiking boots featured. Assuming that Cima is successful selling to mail order catalog companies, estimate the percentage of our sales that could be expected from these customers.

8. Prepare a report that summarizes the recommendations of your project team, including the advantages and disadvantages of the proposal. Be prepared to present your product design, pro forma projections, payback period, and recommendations to management shortly after completion of this assignment.

9. Summarize your research and list the sources of information used to prepare the report.

Name Index

Subject Index